FROM PROTEST TO CHALLENGE

Volume 3

Volume 1: Protest and Hope, 1882-1934

Volume 2: Hope and Challenge, 1935-1952

Volume 3: Challenge and Violence, 1953-1964

Volume 4: Political Profiles, 1882-1964

From Protest to Challenge

A DOCUMENTARY HISTORY OF AFRICAN POLITICS IN SOUTH AFRICA
1882-1964

Edited by

Thomas Karis and Gwendolen M. Carter

Volume 3
Challenge and Violence
1953-1964

Thomas Karis and Gail M. Gerhart

HOOVER INSTITUTION PRESS

STANFORD UNIVERSITY • STANFORD, CALIFORNIA
1977

Hoover Institution Publications 123

© 1977 by the Board of Trustees of the
  Leland Stanford Junior University
All rights reserved
Printed in the United States of America
International Standard Book Number: 0-8179-6231-X
Library of Congress Catalog Card Number: 72-152423

To the African People of South Africa

For the role they have played "during the last 50 years to establish, peacefully, a society in which merit and not race would fix the position of the individual in the life of the nation."

Albert J. Lutuli
Nobel Peace Prize Address
December 11, 1961

Contents

Preface
The Authors

Part One

THE CONGRESS MOVEMENT, 1953–1956

Documents

The African National Congress Re-examines Its Tactics

The Congress of the People and the Freedom Charter

Unity and Disunity Before the Treason Arrests

Part Two

THE LAST STAGE OF NON-VIOLENCE
1957—MAY 1961

Documents

Multi-Racial Conference, December 1957

*The African National Congress While Its Leaders are on Trial,
1957–1959*

The Eve of Sharpeville and Afterwards, March-April 1960

*Does the ANC Advocate Violence? Treason Trial Testimony,
March-October 1960*

Part Three

THE TURN TO VIOLENCE
SINCE MAY 31, 1961

Documents

Preface

This volume and its companion volume of political profiles bring to a conclusion a project conceived in 1962. This third volume is the bulkiest of the three documentary volumes, and its introductory essays are book-length in themselves. The biographical appendix originally planned for inclusion in it is being published separately. Nevertheless, the project now seems but a stepping-stone for a new generation of scholars. It is being published at a time when still more original material is being located and made available in South Africa, Britain, and the United States (as indicated in the bibliographical note), and interest is growing in the analysis and reevaluation of South African history. Our awareness of research that is in the making underscores our recognition, expressed in the preface to Volume 2, of the incomplete nature of our own documentary holdings and the invaluable oral history that remains to be recorded. Our hope is that these volumes, together with the wider collection of primary material on which they are based, will contribute eventually to the writing of a definitive political history of modern South Africa. In particular, we look forward to historical studies written by Africans themselves.

A more extensive study would include the earlier period of African resistance to colonial settlement that preceded the eight decades of protest and challenge traced in these volumes. Other studies would examine post-1964 developments and their roots in the past. As M.T. Moerane observed in his review of Volume 1 in *New Nation* (May 1973), "how fascinating to see through these pages that the Black consciousness movement in vogue to-day has its antecedents in the 1880s in the same situation of political realities!"*

The aim of the introductory essays in this volume, as in Volume 2, is to provide a broad setting for the selected documents, to comment on their

---

*We have found stimulating or gratifying, or both, other reactions expressed privately or in printed reviews. For example, see *Sechaba: Official Organ of the African National Congress, South Africa* (Feb. 1973), *Azania News: Official Organ of the Pan Africanist Congress of Azania* (S.A.) (Nov. 1973), *The African Communist* (Fourth Quarter, 1973), *Reality: A Journal of Liberal and Radical Opinion* (Sept. 1973), and *The Times Literary Supplement* (Feb. 1, 1974).

significance, and to trace the main developments in African politics in South Africa. The volume also includes documents of political activities in which whites and Indians and Coloureds were closely involved with Africans, but omits documents that illustrate the independent efforts of Indians and Coloureds and of liberal and left-wing whites. One additional caveat: the space given to particular organizations and personalities is not necessarily a measure of our evaluation of their historical importance in South Africa. Although we have generally been guided by our view of such importance, we have also given substantial space to material that is illustrative of divergent trends of thought and thus would be of special interest to students of African political attitudes and ideas and, indirectly, to students of American race relations.

Thomas Karis, Professor of Political Science at the City College of the City University of New York, has written all except three of the introductory essays in this volume. "Origins of the Africanist Movement," "Formation of the Pan Africanist Congress, 1958–1959," and "The Eve of Sharpeville and Afterwards" were written by Gail M. Gerhart, whose 1974 doctoral dissertation at Columbia University analyzed recent black nationalist thought and politics in South Africa. In preparing final revisions of the essays, each writer benefited from extensive comments made by the other and by Gwendolen M. Carter. Dr. Carter, Director of the Program of African Studies at Northwestern University until recently, when she became Professor of Political Science at Indiana University, Bloomington, has also served throughout the preparation of Volume 3 as collaborator and coeditor.

We are again indebted to the many South Africans, inside their country and abroad, who granted us lengthy interviews in 1963 and 1964. Many people have helped us during the past decade through tape-recorded interviews or in lengthy conversations. Interviews on which we have particularly relied are cited in the footnotes in this volume, as are the unusually extensive interviews conducted in recent years by Dr. Gerhart. The notes do not include, however, the names of all those to whom we are indebted for insight as well as information.

We wish also to thank friends who have read and commented on sections of the introductory essays: Oliver Tambo, Fatima Meer, Peter Molotsi, Peter Raboroko, Duma Nokwe, Dennis Brutus, Helen Joseph, J. C. M. Mbata, Leo Marquard, David Welsh, Bishop Ambrose Reeves, Pearce Gqobose, Ernest Wentzel, and others who prefer not to be named. During January and February 1974, when we were denied visas to visit South Africa (at about the same time that the South African Minister of the Interior was visiting high officials in the United States), we were able, fortunately, to discuss sections of the manuscript with Benjamin Pogrund in Johannesburg, with A. P. Mda and Joe Molefi in Maseru, Lesotho, and with Frieda Matthews and Joseph Matthews in Gaberone, Botswana.

Without the Ford Foundation's support of our field trips to South Africa in 1963 and 1964 to study developments in the Transkei, we should not have had the concurrent opportunities, described in the preface to Volume 1, to collect or copy documentary materials and to interview older African leaders.

Dr. Peter Duignan, Director of the African Program at the Hoover Institution, provided the initial inspiration for the project in 1962, and his interest and advice have continued ever since. Over the years, we have deeply appreciated the Hoover Institution's support and its patience. At a time of rising publication costs, we have especially appreciated the fact that no suggestion has ever been made that we should abridge material beyond what we ourselves thought useful. It goes without saying that we have been completely uninhibited in our judgments regarding the scope and emphasis of these volumes. Our thanks go also to the staff of the Hoover Institution Press, in particular, Brien Benson, former Head of Publications, Christine E. Tapley, copy editor for Volumes 1 and 2, and Romayne Ponleithner, copy editor for Volume 3.

These books are dedicated to the African people of South Africa. We think with deep appreciation of those Africans who worked so hard, so long, and with so little return, to make South Africa the great nonracial country it could have become. To have had the opportunity to present evidence of their patient and courageous efforts through their own words is a source of enduring satisfaction to us. We are grateful also for the more personal reward that has accompanied our efforts: the warm friendship of South Africans of all races. Impersonal and apparently ineluctable though the fundamental forces at work in South Africa may be, it is our hope that they may be tempered in time by similar experiences of friendship between individual South Africans—black, white, and brown.

October 1974

Thomas Karis
Gwendolen M. Carter

Note: The introductory essays in Volume 2 used "nonwhite" as an inclusive term for Africans, Coloureds, and Indians because this term (like "non-European") was used by leaders of these groups themselves during the period covered by that volume. By the early 1970s, proponents of "black consciousness" had rejected "nonwhite" and "non-European" as negative and derogatory terms, coined by whites. We have generally avoided "nonwhite" in the introductory essays to this volume, but for the sake of clarity we have also avoided "black" as an inclusive term. When we have occasionally used "black," it refers to Africans. We recognize, however, that the "black consciousness" movement uses "black" to include all subjects of white domination.

Albert J. Lutuli's surname is often spelled "Luthuli," as it is in his autobiography, which was prepared for publication by friends. But Lutuli himself signed his name without an "h" and preferred this spelling; therefore it is followed in the introductory essays and headings in these volumes.

The Authors

Professor Thomas Karis, of City College, City University of New York, is responsible for most of Volume 2 and Volume 3. As a U.S. State Department officer, his research on South Africa began in 1951, and he first visited South Africa in 1955. He was a foreign service officer in the American Embassy in Pretoria in 1957–1959, traveled in southern Africa in 1963 and 1964, was Ford Professor of Political Science at the University of Zambia in 1968–1969, and visited Botswana, Lesotho, and Swaziland in early 1974. He is the author of "South Africa" in *Five African States: Responses to Diversity,* Gwendolen M. Carter (ed.), (Ithaca, N.Y.: Cornell University Press, 1963), *The Treason Trial in South Africa: A Guide to the Microfilm Record of the Trial* (Stanford, Calif.: Hoover Institution, 1965), and *South Africa: The End Is Not Yet* (New York: Foreign Policy Association, Headline Series, April 1966). He is also coauthor with Gwendolen M. Carter and Newell M. Stultz of *South Africa's Transkei: The Politics of Domestic Colonialism* (Evanston: Northwestern University Press, 1967).

Professor Gwendolen M. Carter, formerly director of the Program of African Studies at Northwestern University and now Professor of Political Science at Indiana University, Bloomington, has aided throughout as collaborator, critic, and editor. Her first visit to South Africa was in 1948–1949. She returned in 1952–1953 and has visited southern Africa frequently since then, including research trips (with Thomas Karis) in 1963 and 1964 and to Botswana, Lesotho, and Swaziland in early 1974. In 1974 and on earlier occasions, she and Thomas Karis have been denied South African visas. Her writings on South Africa include *The Politics of Inequality: South Africa since 1948* (rev. ed.; New York: Praeger, 1958, 1959), her share in preparing *South Africa's Transkei;* "African Nationalist Movements" in *Southern Africa in Transition,* edited by John A. Davis and James K. Baker (New York: Praeger, 1966); *African Concepts of Nationalism in South Africa* and *Black Initiatives for Change in Southern Africa* (Herskovits Memorial Lectures, University of Edinburgh, March 1965 and March 1973, respectively); and *Southern Africa: Prospects for Change* (New York: Foreign Policy Association, Headline Series, February 1974).

Dr. Gail M. Gerhart has assisted in the preparation of Volume 3 and is the author of the essays on "Origins of the Africanist Movement," "Formation of the Pan Africanist Congress, 1958–1959," and "The Eve of Sharpeville and Afterwards." She has also written the final draft of the political profiles in Volume 4. After graduating from Radcliffe College, she first visited South Africa in 1966. She lived in East Africa for five years and is now living in Botswana. She is an associate lecturer in Government and Administration at the University of Botswana and Swaziland and is now preparing "Black Nationalism as a Theme in African Political Thought in South Africa, 1943–1973," her Columbia doctoral dissertation, for publication by the University of California press.

Professor Sheridan W. Johns, of Duke University, is the author of Volume 1 and primarily responsible for Part I of Volume 2 in this series. He first visited South Africa in 1962–1963 while engaged in research for a Harvard University dissertation on the early history of the Communist Party of South Africa and returned in 1964. In 1968–1970 he taught at the University of Zambia and, as a Fulbright lecturer, again in 1974–1975. His writings on South Africa include "The Birth of Non-White Trade Unionism in South Africa," *Race,* no. 2, 1967; "Trade Union, Political Pressure Group, or Mass Movement? The Industrial and Commercial Workers' Union of Africa," in *Protest and Power in Black Africa,* edited by R. Rotberg and A. Mazrui (Oxford: Oxford University Press, 1971); and "Obstacles to Guerrilla Warfare—a South African Case Study," *Journal of Modern African Studies,* no. 2, 1973.

The Documents

In the documents, inconsistencies may occur in punctuation, format, spelling of certain words and proper names, and manner of speech. Because we believe that these variations enhance rather than detract from the value of the papers, we have made no attempt to edit beyond the correction of obvious typographical errors. Most of the documents are reproduced in their entirety. Deletions are indicated in the usual way.

PART ONE

The Congress Movement, 1953–1956

INTRODUCTION

After four decades of seeking change through petitions, deputations, and public meetings, the African National Congress in 1952 moved to challenge white supremacy in South Africa in a campaign of civil disobedience. The government's policy of retaliation during the next four years put the ANC and other groups in the African and radical opposition on the defensive. With increasing frequency and thoroughness, the special political branch of the police conducted raids in an effort to uncover evidence of subversion. These raids culminated in the early morning hours of December 5, 1956 with the arrest of 156 persons—the leaders of the ANC, its assorted allies, and other personalities as well—on a charge of high treason.

The charge of treason climaxed a long period of mounting conflict between whites and Africans. The ANC, established in 1912, two years after the formation of the Union of South Africa, was historically the leading political organization of Africans in South Africa. Some of its followers had taken part in spasmodic protests such as boycotts, strikes, and the burning of passes. Most of its leaders, however, did not employ militant tactics; they were educated, often professional, men of the African middle class. Their political values were liberal, and their political styles conciliatory. They sought to transcend tribal differences by building a common African self-consciousness, but in seeking to do so, they were not racially exclusive. The dominant strain in African political thinking during these decades sought the sharing of political power and the creation of a common South Africanism that would include Africans, whites, Coloureds, and Indians.

The trend of white policy had been steadily in the opposite direction. In contrast to the political nonracialism of the old Cape Colony constitution, the Act of Union had imposed a color bar on membership in Parliament. The year after the formation of the ANC, African rights to land were severely restricted by law. The steady succession of laws imposing segregation reached a political climax in 1936, when African voters in Cape Province were removed from the common voters' roll and given only token communal representation in Parliament (by whites). Meanwhile, the black proletariat was growing, as Africans in large numbers moved to the towns and into industry. Faint liberal hopes revived during World War II but were almost extinguished in 1948 when the exclusively Afrikaner Nationalist

Party of Dr. Daniel F. Malan came to power on a platform of apartheid. This party, which has won some English-speaking support, has been returned to power repeatedly, in large measure because of its success in coping with the challenge of African political aspirations.

During the forties, a younger generation of African nationalists—most of them well educated and professionally oriented like the older leaders—had risen to prominence in the ANC. They were impatient with traditional, moderate tactics and dissatisfied with the ANC's failure to develop into a mass movement. Their drive toward militancy led the ANC in 1949 to adopt the Programme of Action, which endorsed tactics of boycott, strike, and civil disobedience. The Defiance Campaign of 1952, in which some 8,500 Africans and their allies went to jail, marked the ANC's first major effort to implement the Programme of Action and to build a mass movement. With one exception, on March 21, 1960, it was also the last African effort at country-wide civil disobedience. The campaign was the first major joint action by Africans and Indians, a fact which contributed to a growing split among the younger men in the ANC over the question of whether the Programme of Action should be implemented by Africans exclusively.

The government's response to the Defiance Campaign was to enact a law in 1953 providing that anyone who committed any offense as a means of protest could be whipped as well as fined or imprisoned. In that same year the Nationalist government won a general election with an enlarged majority, thanks in part to its exploitation of white fears aroused by the campaign. Thereafter, as it proceeded with its legislative program of racial segregation, the government continued to use its arsenal of powers to immobilize and cripple the nonwhite and left-wing opposition, prohibiting meetings and restricting individuals through surveillance, harassment, banning, banishment, and imprisonment.

As South Africa moved in the direction of becoming a police state for all radical challengers of official policies, African political leaders were confronted with the need to reconsider their above-ground and nonviolent strategies. Nelson R. Mandela, president of the ANC in the Transvaal, wrote in September 1953 of the necessity for "new forms of political struggle." He viewed conditions in 1953, a year in which he himself was forbidden to attend gatherings, as "totally different" from the past (Document 2). Like Mandela, other leaders gave high priority to strengthening the organization and discipline of the ANC. But they were ambivalent regarding the aims of the new forms of organization. Should they act as if the ANC were—or were on the verge of becoming—illegal and subversive, facing the unavoidable though long-run eventuality of violent confrontation? Or should they reaffirm their commitment to nonviolence and redouble their efforts to exert extraconstitutional pressures on the white electorate through public demonstrations?

The principal aim of both the militant and moderate wings of the ANC was to mobilize and build a mass movement. Thus, as the old strategy of exerting extraconstitutional pressure was continued, the process of generating such pressure through popular campaigns took on new importance. Inspired by the vision of a general strike, the more militant leaders emphasized the importance of building a cell-based organization that was disciplined and centrally controlled. Mass action aimed at bringing down the government, however, seemed completely unrealistic in the near future. While struggling to operate under the shadow of overwhelming police power, the ANC also had to contend with chronic internal difficulties of restricted individual mobility, raising funds, and maintaining communication and morale. Thus, along with other extraparliamentary groups, it continued during 1953–1956 to act nonviolently, openly, and (with the shelving of tactics of civil disobedience) legally. Nevertheless, the government interpreted the demand for equality as an implicit call for violent revolution, and it was this interpretation that resulted in the arrests for treason in December 1956, a development which marked the beginning of a new phase in black political responses.

1953: INSIDE AND OUTSIDE THE POLITICAL ARENA

African political activity appeared subdued during 1953, as leaders once again re-examined their strength and tactics. The Defiance Campaign had died down, and the likelihood of its revival became dim when Parliament enacted new punitive legislation early in the year. Chief Albert J. Lutuli, who had been elected president-general of the ANC in December 1952, faced his first three-year term of office with little hope that the Nationalist government would ease its pressure on opposition political activity. In November he himself had been deposed as chief of a small Christian community when he refused to renounce the ANC. During the same month, the government had issued a proclamation providing that anyone who influenced an African to defy the law could be fined £300 or imprisoned for three years. Before the annual conference had met in December, both Walter Sisulu, who was to be re-elected as secretary-general, and Nelson Mandela were prohibited from attending gatherings and confined to Johannesburg.

New Legislation and the General Election

During the short parliamentary session preceding the general election of April 15, 1953, the first since Prime Minister Malan had come to power, the Nationalists introduced two bills designed to deal with "the black peril."

Not surprisingly, the United Party, the official opposition, felt politically unable to oppose them. Both measures were enacted speedily over the opposition of the small Labour Party and the three Natives' Representatives in the House of Assembly.

The Criminal Law Amendment Act posed an immediate threat if defiance were renewed. The act was justified by the government on the ground that no existing law provided means to deal with mass disobedience. The normal punishment for a minor statutory offense was a short jail sentence with the option of a fine. The new law provided that any person who committed any offense "by way of protest or in support of any campaign against any law" could be sentenced to a whipping of ten strokes, a £300 fine, three years in jail, or a combination of any two of these penalties. Upon a second conviction, whipping or imprisonment as well as a fine were obligatory. For the persons whose words or actions were calculated to cause another person to commit an offense as a means of protest, the maximum penalties above were increased by an additional £200 or two years.

The second act passed in 1953 was the Public Safety Act, which is one of the most far-reaching of all the government's statutory sources of authority. The Public Safety Act empowered the governor-general, that is, the cabinet, to declare a state of emergency if he thought public order was seriously threatened. (The act has been invoked only once, in 1960.) During this state of emergency persons can be summarily arrested and detained, and the government's only obligation is to submit their names to Parliament after thirty days. The emergency can last a year and is subject to renewal; while it is in effect, parliamentary and judicial functions can be suspended.

Early in 1953, Chief Lutuli and other ANC leaders addressed meetings protesting the two bills, but with each passing month bans prohibited more leaders from attending such gatherings. During the election campaign, African leaders were anxious not to supply the Nationalist Party with grist for its propaganda mill, although they denied that there was any substantial difference between the two contending white parties. Nevertheless, Dr. Yusuf Dadoo, president of the South African Indian Congress (SAIC), who had been a member of the Communist Party before its proscription in 1950, appealed to Coloured and Indian voters in Cape Province to vote for the United Party because the Nationalists were "the most vicious and dangerous group among the ruling class."[1] (Despite the pro-boycott position of the Non-European Unity Movement, which Dadoo attacked, Coloureds and Indians turned out in substantial numbers to vote for the United Party.)

The Nationalists made good use of Dadoo's statement and also of a judicial ruling on March 22, 1953 requiring "separate but equal" treatment in the case of an African defier who had entered a white waiting room in the

Cape Town railroad station.[2] Later in the year, the Reservation of Separate Amenities Act set aside any presumption of the common law that separate facilities must be equal, when it provided that they need not be "substantially similar to or of the same character, standard, extent or quality" as "those set aside for the other race."[3]

The general election of 1953 was the last election during the past two decades which the opposition to the Nationalist Party had a realistic chance to win, and the chance even then was a small one.[4] The Nationalists had the advantages of a redrawing of electoral district lines which favored them and of six pro-Nationalist South West African seats, which had been created after 1948. More important, the geographic distribution of white voters was to its advantage, particularly as Afrikaners continued to move townward into many marginal districts. Also, the pervasive issue of race underlay the Nationalist Party's propaganda regarding communism, parliamentary sovereignty (the Coloured vote issue, discussed below), white unity, and the indeterminate nature of the opposition's proposed solutions to the "Native question." On election day the Nationalists again won less than fifty percent of the votes cast but increased both their popular vote over the 1948 total and the size of their parliamentary majority. They were still short, however, of the two-thirds majority in the combined houses of Parliament necessary for any reduction of Coloured voting rights.

For the last time, the United Party conducted a campaign as the leader of a united front. This front included not only elements that were deeply conservative about white supremacy but also the liberally led War Veterans' Torch Commando and the Labour Party. The Torch Commando was an extraparty mass movement that came into being in 1951 during the constitutional crisis over the Coloured vote. The Labour Party was a small socialist party which had become more liberal in its attitude toward color after the War and had reformulated its racial policy in January 1953 to include a qualified franchise for all nonwhites.[5] Despite its leadership role, the United Party was weakened by defections from its ranks to the Nationalists, and by the failure of policies on nonwhite rights to appeal to the liberals. In his concluding broadcast of the campaign, J. G. N. Strauss, the United Party leader, criticized Indians and spoke of Native (i.e., African) "immaturity." Once the election was over, this attitude strengthened the disposition of many of the liberals in the United Party, few as they were, to split off and form a new organization.

Liberal and Other Reactions

South Africa's liberal tradition was old but feeble; 1953 was the hundredth anniversary of the Cape Colony's nonracial voting provisions.

Liberalism in South Africa in its most generous guise meant "equal rights for all civilised people and equal opportunities for all men and women to become civilised." These were key words in a statement issued in September 1952 during the Defiance Campaign by a distinguished group of twenty-two whites who recognized that the campaign was led by "acknowledged leaders."[6] These whites had worked within the United Party and hoped for its movement in a liberal direction. In 1952 and early 1953 they discussed race relations in liberal study groups and the Liberal Association. Young people who joined these groups introduced a new tone, a sense of urgency, and a desire to work closely with Africans.

Because of dissatisfaction with the United Party and pressure from young liberals in the Transvaal, older, well-known liberals in the Cape agreed to join in the formation of the Liberal Party on May 8–9, 1953. Mrs. Margaret Ballinger, one of the Natives' Representatives in the House of Assembly, became the leader. Others in the national leadership of the party were Leo Marquard, Oscar Wollheim, Donald Molteno, and Leslie Rubin—all of the Cape—and Alan Paton. All but Wollheim and Rubin had signed the September 1952 statement.[7]

In the aftermath of the United Party's defeat, a second minor party was formed in May 1953—the Union Federal Party. This party was concerned primarily with developing a federal system and, eventually, a United States of Southern Africa in which the province of Natal would have semi-autonomy. The Federal Party recognized "the increasing economic integration" of nonwhites and proposed "the long-term policy" of placing civilized nonwhites on the common roll of voters "over a considerable period of years."[8] Both the Federal Party and the Liberal Party attracted members from the Torch Commando, whose own support had declined rapidly although the constitutional crisis that had prompted its formation had not ended.

At its first national congress in July 1953, the Liberal Party adopted a policy of compulsory education for all South Africans and a nonracial franchise. Every new voter (including whites who were not yet on the voters' roll) was to have reached the age of 21 and completed Standard VI (the American eighth grade) or possess a modest income or property. A year later, in response to sharp criticism of these restrictions, the party accepted universal franchise as an ultimate aim.

African leaders during the Defiance Campaign had hoped to see the creation of a body that would prepare whites to accept nonracialism rather than serve merely as a white counterpart of the ANC. The Liberal Party did serve as a link between black and white and generally supported the ANC's aims. Liberals were disposed to cooperate with the ANC, and some ANC leaders welcomed such cooperation. ANC leaders were concerned, however, with potential competition, with the Liberal Party, which recruited African members, although the Liberals believed that an

African could belong to both organizations. The more radical nonwhites, on the other hand, greeted the Liberal Party with contempt, scorning its franchise policy and criticizing its adherence to constitutional methods of action (as contrasted with the Programme of Action). Nelson Mandela, writing a vitriolic article in a left-wing journal, asked, "Which side, gentlemen, are you on?"[9]

Like the Liberal Party, another white group—but one identifying itself fully with the ANC—emerged from the Defiance Campaign: the South African Congress of Democrats, which was formed in October 1953. It is described below, pages 12–13.

Africans in Mid-year

When Professor Z. K. Matthews, the pre-eminent African intellectual in South Africa and president of the ANC in Cape Province, returned from the United States on May 16, 1953, after being refused an extension of his passport, he found African political activity at a lull. Earlier in the year, ANC speakers had called for the organization of a one-day strike, an action that had been taken many times in the past. But no strike had been organized, although meetings were held in some major population centers on May Day.

Lutuli himself was banned at the end of May from attending public gatherings and prohibited from entering twenty-one cities and towns for one year.[10] Bans varied in their terms and statutory grounds. In a few cases, Africans were "banished" or deported to rural areas.[11] (Names of many of those who were restricted are noted in the documents.) Potentially more serious forms of harassment were raids by the Special Branch of the police on homes and offices in June to seize documents and other material that could be used as evidence of treason and sedition, as well as of violations of the Suppression of Communism Act, the Riotous Assemblies Act, and the Criminal Law Amendment Act.[12]

No strike or stay-at-home was organized for June 26, which had first been observed in 1950 as a "political strike" when all nonwhites were urged to stay home from work and keep their children from school. In 1952, demonstrations on June 26 had marked the start of the Defiance Campaign. By comparison, the program for June 26, 1953 was modest. Chief Lutuli issued a call to "all freedom-loving people, especially Non-European" to discuss in their homes "the struggle of the African people in particular and the Non-Europeans in general" and at 9 P.M. to "light a fire outside our homes or place a lighted candle or a lantern as a symbol of the spark of freedom which we are determined to keep alive . . . ."[13] ANC branches were required to report on the observance of June 26, but available records give no indication of the extent of these observances.

Lutuli also urged that churches observe Sunday, June 28, as "a day of commemoration and dedication." The day was more notable, however, as the beginning of the campaign against the removal of Africans from the Western Areas of Johannesburg. Some 1,200 delegates from the ANC, churches, and other groups in the area attended a private, legal meeting in Sophiatown's Odin Cinema, which they entered with a card of admission. Sisulu and Mandela, whose bans had expired and not been renewed, were among the speakers. Despite the peaceful nature of the gathering, heavily armed police surrounded the building, broke into the meeting, and came to the platform, where they forcibly arrested Yusuf Cachalia, joint secretary of the SAIC. (He was later released without charge.) The mood of the meeting was angry, but boos and hisses gave way to singing, and the crowd remained orderly.[14]

Constitutional Crisis over the Coloured Vote

On the first day of the new Parliament, July 3, political tension among whites rose again when Dr. Malan announced that a joint sitting would be held to validate the 1951 act that had removed some 50,000 Coloured (and Asian) voters in Cape Province from the common to a separate roll. The Appellate Division of the Supreme Court had unanimously held the 1951 act void, because it had been adopted by simple majorities rather than by the constitution's entrenched-clause procedure (used in 1936) requiring a two-thirds vote of all members of Parliament in joint session. The court had also, in 1952, held void an act providing that Parliament itself, acting as the "High Court of Parliament," could set aside judgments of the highest judicial court.

The issues of constitutional morality that the Nationalists had raised by ignoring the entrenched-clause procedure, which protected both nonwhite voting rights in the Cape and the equal status of English and Afrikaans, were to agitate white politics throughout the next four years. The highlights of these years may be briefly summarized here. In 1953 the government failed to win a two-thirds vote in a joint session. Once again it called a joint session, but with no more success.

In December 1954 the Nationalist Party's leadership shifted from the Cape to the more extreme Transvaal, when Johannes Strijdom, a blunt exponent of *baasskap* (boss-ship), became prime minister. He was readier than was Dr. Malan to use any means—that is, constitutionally correct means—to attain his political ends. In 1955 an act passed by simple majorities provided for the packing of the highest court, that is, for an enlarged court of eleven to hear constitutional cases. And in June (a few days before the meeting of the Congress of the People, discussed below), another act enlarged the Senate and changed the method of its election, with the result that the government acquired a sufficient majority in that body to gain a two-thirds majority in a joint session. In February 1956 a two-thirds majority re-enacted the 1951 act, removed the entrenchment of nonwhite voting rights in the Cape, and re-entrenched the equal status of the two official languages. In November 1956, the enlarged court upheld both the validated1951 act and the Senate act.

The Coloured Voters' Act of 1951 was one of the six measures whose repeal had been demanded during the Defiance Campaign of 1952. The act was an important step toward political apartheid, whose further implementation, the Nationalists had declared, was to include the removal of all representatives of Africans from Parliament. The act helped raise the political consciousness of the usually apathetic Coloureds, but the controversy it engendered was of relatively minor interest to Africans, who faced more immediate threats. In commenting on the constitutional crisis and the government's pursuance of doctrinaire goals, African leaders noted, however, that everyone in the opposition shared common interests.

One example of this attitude was the press release issued on May 26, 1955 by Oliver Tambo, acting secretary-general of the ANC, after the introduction of the Senate Bill. Tambo related the bill to earlier legislation also opposed by the ANC. "We appeal to the leaders of the United, Labour and Liberal Parties," the statement said, "to face the central reality of South African politics: that democracy is indivisible."

The United Party fought the bill all the way, and protest was voiced by some leading Afrikaner Nationalist intellectuals. But as was to be expected, this white opposition showed no interest in making common cause with the ANC. On the eve of the enactment of the Senate act, Professor Matthews recollected that "when Africans lost their franchise rights in 1936 many of the people who in 1955 are busy organising protest meetings about the entrenched clauses of the constitution were only too glad to give the government of the day the necessary two-thirds majority to deprive Africans of their rights" (Document 8).

New Approaches and Organizations

Shortly afterwards, Professor Matthews and Nelson Mandela each outlined a major approach to the strengthening of the ANC. In his presidential address to the Cape provincial conference on August 15, 1953, Professor Matthews suggested the organization of a multiracial "Congress of the People" campaign.[15] He noted that various groups were considering "the idea of a national convention at which all groups might be represented to consider our national problems on an all-inclusive basis" (Document 1). (Both the South African Institute of Race Relations and the Federal Missionary Council of the Dutch Reformed Church were interested at the time in organizing interracial meetings.) He went on to say:

> I wonder whether the time has not come for the African National
> Congress to consider the question of convening a National Con-
> vention, A CONGRESS OF THE PEOPLE, representing all the
> people of this country irrespective of race or colour to draw up a
> FREEDOM CHARTER for the DEMOCRATIC SOUTH
> AFRICA OF THE FUTURE.

The suggestion was adopted by the provincial conference and accepted in
principle by the national conference in December 1953.[16] The Congress of
the People was finally to meet on June 25–26, 1955.

Mandela's statement, presented to the Transvaal provincial conference
on September 21, 1953, in lieu of a presidential address because he was
under ban, urged implementation of a cell-based plan (the "M-Plan,"
named after Mandela) for mass organization (Document 2).[17] (See below,
page 35ff.) In suggesting a campaign that included a series of public
meetings, Professor Matthews was reverting to one of the "old methods"
criticized by Mandela. Like Mandela, however, Matthews was seeking
techniques that would produce steadfast members of the ANC. (Early in
1956, looking back over a period marked by several abortive campaigns,
Matthews observed, "Generally, I think people are too campaign-minded
and not enough organisation-minded.")[18]

Within two months of Professor Matthews' address, two national organizations had been formed: the South African Coloured People's Organization (SACPO) and the South African Congress of Democrats
(COD). Both were to participate in the Congress of the People campaign
and become members of the Congress alliance. SACPO was formed in
Cape Town on September 12, 1953, by liberals and trade-unionists, including Edgar Deane of the Cape Furniture Workers' Union, who was
elected chairman, Dr. Richard van der Ross, a school principal, S. Rahim,
Reginald September, and a left-wing Coloured, John Gomas, who had
been an organizer for the ANC. The founders of SACPO wanted to mount
a more determined opposition to the removal of Coloured voters from the
common roll than was being offered by the Coloured People's National
Union, led by George Golding, a school principal.[19] Although Golding
also opposed the change in the voters' roll, he was considered a collaborator with the Nationalists because of his participation in the government's Coloured Affairs Council and his readiness to compromise.
Unlike Golding, the SACPO leaders were prepared to cooperate closely
with Africans, in particular with the ANC.

Although membership in SACPO was open to any member of any race,
the organization was intended to be a mouthpiece for the Coloureds.
"Personally I deplore the fact that we always think in terms of racial

groups," said Dr. van der Ross, "but I believe that the Coloured person must first become aware of himself as a unit before he can effectively work together with other groups."[20]

The Congress of Democrats, formed in Johannesburg on October 10, 1953, was also open to all races, but it accepted the special role of appealing to whites. Although the aims of both new organizations were nonracial, that is, equal rights for every individual, they differed from the nonracial Liberal Party and the dissolved Communist Party in their acceptance of what amounted to a "national," or racial, form of organization comparable to that of the ANC and the SAIC.[21] Thus, the alliance of the four organizations was "multiracial"; and Africans, Indians, Coloureds, and whites were separately represented in the symbol of the Congress of the People: a wheel with four spokes (sometimes shown with an appropriate head in each corner).

The COD was the outgrowth of an effort by the ANC and the SAIC to attract wide sympathy among whites during the Defiance Campaign. The whites who attended a meeting sponsored by the two organizations in November 1952 represented many points of view. As it turned out, however, the initiative in forming a new organization was taken by former Communists and other left-wing whites, who organized the South African People's Congress. This group became the Johannesburg Congress of Democrats and then joined with the left-wing Springbok Legion (a war veterans' association with some ex-Communists among its leaders) and the Democratic League (formed in Cape Town in September 1953) to organize the South African Congress of Democrats. Eighty-eight delegates from the Transvaal, Natal, Cape Town, and Port Elizabeth elected Pieter Beyleveld, an Afrikaner, as president. Leonard Lee-Warden, one of the Natives' Representatives in Parliament, was elected vice-president, and Jack Hodgson, secretary. Hodgson and Lionel Bernstein, another of the organizers, had been members of the Communist Party; Beyleveld had not.[22]

The COD's policy was one of adherence to the Universal Declaration of Human Rights rather than to any Marxist program; "its emotive language," however, was "characteristically Communist."[23] The COD never had more than a few hundred active members and was, as one ANC leader described it, a "sect" or "ginger group" whose identification with the ANC was so complete that it proved unable to win the wide sympathy from whites that had been hoped for.

Two other nonracial organizations formed during this period became, in effect, adjuncts of the Congress alliance. The South African Peace Council was formed in Johannesburg on August 21, 1953, and the South African Congress of Trade Unions (SACTU) was formed in 1955. SACTU is discussed below, pages 53–56.

Although the sympathies of the South African Peace Council were with the Soviet Union in the cold war, it managed to attract a fairly wide cross-section of supporters from among the radical opponents of apartheid. The speakers at its inaugural conference included Nelson Mandela and representatives of the Labour Party, the Springbok Legion, and the Natal Indian Congress. The conference elected a white minister, the Rev. D. C. Thompson, as president. Chief Lutuli was elected, without his consent, as one of the six vice-presidents.[24] Another vice-president was Dan Tloome, an ANC leader who was also a former member of the Communist Party.

The United Nations and Apartheid

Apartheid had become an international issue during the Defiance Campaign. At that time, like the issues of South West Africa and the position of Indians in South Africa, it became a perennial concern of the United Nations. In 1953, with all the Western and a few Latin American countries abstaining on grounds of respect for domestic jurisdiction, a "United Nations Commission on the Racial Situation in South Africa" was established. The Commission was not allowed to enter South Africa, but it received a lengthy memorandum from the ANC and the SAIC, which the South African government's representative described as "Communist-dominated organizations," heard some witnesses (but no nonwhites from South Africa), and issued perceptive and substantial reports in 1953, 1954, and 1955.[25] Though severely critical of the situation in South Africa, the Commission looked for hope; its final report saw "gradualism and flexibility" and a slowing down of the pace at which apartheid was being implemented.[26] Professor Matthews disagreed with this observation "most emphatically" in December 1955, seeing "an ever-accelerating tempo" in "the policy of baasskap" (Document 13b).

The ANC's Annual Conference

As the ANC's annual December conference approached in 1953, there was a resurgence throughout the country of political meetings addressed by persons who had been banned under the Suppression of Communism Act. These addresses could be made because the Appellate Division of the Supreme Court had held in the case of Johnson Ngwevela that the minister of justice could not impose a ban without a hearing.[27] (The act was amended in 1954 to remove this restriction on governmental action.) The conference met on December 18–20 at Queenstown, one of the towns not included in Chief Lutuli's ban.[28] The terms of his ban, however, made it necessary to restrict the audience for his presidential address to ANC members at a closed session (Document 3a). Lutuli expressed "jubilation" at the Ngwevela decision and praised the courts. His address contained the kind of language that the Treason Trial prosecution was later to allege was violent in tendency; but in looking to the future, he spoke only in traditionally moderate generalities, urging that Africans should "exert pressure" to win from whites the extension of full partnership rights within the existing framework of the Union. Before the conference discussed and approved the proposal for a Congress of the People, Lutuli also spoke hopefully about the support for a national conference within the Dutch Reformed Churches and other religious and liberal circles.

(During the preceding month, the Federal Council of the Dutch Reformed Churches had invited English-speaking church leaders to a conference in Pretoria—an unusual but not unprecedented step—and had agreed to invite nonwhite clerics from outside the Dutch Reformed Church to a later conference. Such an interracial conference, with fifty-six nonwhites in attendance, met at the University of the Witwatersrand on December 7–10, 1954, to discuss "the extension of the Kingdom of God in multi-racial South Africa.")[29]

Early in the ANC conference, representatives of the SAIC, the COD, and the Liberal Party were on the platform. In greeting the 300 delegates, Patrick Duncan of the Liberal Party declared, "Everybody who likes to make Africa his home is an African."[30] Another feature of the conference was a report by Duma Nokwe of the Youth League on the trip he and Walter Sisulu had recently made abroad. Traveling without passports, they had spent five months on a tour that included, in addition to Britain, Holland, and Israel, a youth festival in Bucharest, a student congress in Warsaw, Czechoslovakia, the Soviet Union, and five weeks in China.[31] Other nonwhites were invited to attend Communist-sponsored conferences in Europe at about this time and to visit the Soviet Union or China, but no prominent African political leader visited the United States.[32]

Beginning on the second day of the conference, the delegates discussed a perennial question from 8:00 P.M. until 2:30 A.M.: whether or not to boycott the election of whites as Natives' Representatives in Parliament and the Cape Provincial Council, and the election of Africans to advisory boards. (No such controversy had agitated the pro-boycott All African Convention, whose forty-eight delegates had met in the same hall for three days immediately preceding the ANC conference.)[33] The Programme of Action of 1949 had accepted the boycotting of "all differential political institutions," but the ANC had never implemented its policy. The argument was to continue throughout the 1950s. Despite the 1949 boycott policy, ANC members, exhorted by both left-wing and liberal candidates, actively participated in electoral campaigns, ostensibly for tactical reasons. They also ran for seats on township advisory boards. The president of the ANC in the Transvaal, E. P. Moretsele, and P. Q. Vundla, a member of his executive, were themselves members of the Western Native Township Advisory Board.[34] The 1953 conference referred the question of boycott to the provinces.

In June 1954, the ANC in the Cape, where the election of three Natives' Representatives to the House of Assembly attracted much attention, resolved not to take an organized part in the November election but to allow each member to act according to his conscience.[35] The question of implementing or reconsidering the boycott policy, deferred in the national conferences of 1954 and of 1955, remained unsettled in the conference of 1956.[36]

There was little controversy, however, over the Programme of Action's endorsement of "immediate and active boycott" as an economic weapon. The first resolution adopted by the 1953 conference called for an economic boycott against selected business and governmental enterprises, with the aim of improving the conditions of African workers and the "treatment and service" accorded to African customers (Document 3b). Wide-scale action of this type was not actually launched, however, until some years later, when the ANC undertook a boycott of products made by Afrikaner Nationalist firms, and a boycott of potatoes, a commodity chosen to dramatize the wretched condition of African farm workers.

ORIGINS OF THE AFRICANIST MOVEMENT

The passage of the Suppression of Communism Act in 1950 had helped to lay the foundation of a new sense of defiance and solidarity among all elements of the nonwhite opposition. Nevertheless, there were many in the ANC, and in the Youth League in particular, who did not mourn the passing of the Communist Party as such, and who became, if anything, more antagonistic and suspicious of left-wing politicians after 1950 than they had been in the days of open Communist activity.

When cooperation and contact between African and Indian leaders began to increase during the planning stages of the Defiance Campaign, some Youth Leaguers found their hostility toward Indian leftists being eroded; others suspected that African interests were being subordinated for the sake of building an alliance with non-Africans. Some of these opponents of African-Indian cooperation defined "non-African" in ideological terms, stressing the danger that Communists would work to blunt the spirit of African nationalism if they were allowed to influence the formulation of ANC policies. Other Youth League critics of cooperation defined the danger more in racial terms, arguing that Indian economic interests were fundamentally in conflict with those of Africans, and that any cooperation between leaders of the two races on the political plane was bound to be manipulated by the Indians to safeguard their sectional interests.[37] In the senior Congress these concerns were echoed by R. V. Selope Thema and adherents of his "National-minded Bloc."

The Youth Leaguers who were skeptical about the role of non-Africans in planning the Defiance Campaign were not opposed in principle to the campaign itself (unlike the older and more conservative Thema).[38] Most of them chose to support the campaign on the condition that it was understood they were doing so "under the banner of African nationalism."[39] In describing the outlook of these members of the League, Peter 'Molotsi of the Orlando branch wrote in late 1951 that African nationalism meant "the noble urge to . . . arouse National Pride among the heterogeneous sections of the African people, . . . unleash the national sentiment against any form of foreign domination and to seize power in Africa."[40] In an effort to keep these goals paramount within the Youth League as the ANC entered the Defiance Campaign, a small group of young intellectuals in the eastern Cape began about January 1952 to issue pamphlets or bulletins purporting to represent the views of a "Bureau of African Nationalism." From these pamphlets it was evident that the Bureau regarded itself as a watchdog group formed to observe the work of the Joint Planning Council and to insure resistance to any attempt by non-Africans to reinterpret the goals and methods of the liberation struggle as set forth in the 1949 Programme of Action. The pamphlets, which contained unsigned pieces by A. P. Mda, T. T. Letlaka, Robert Sobukwe, C. J. Fazzie, J. N. Pokela, and others, were circulated to selected Youth Leaguers around the country. In some areas where African militants were in fact being wooed by Indian and white leftists, the Bureau's writings fell onto fertile ground.[41]

Among the recipients of the Bureau's bulletins in the Transvaal was a teacher named Potlako K. Leballo, an energetic and vocal member of the Orlando Youth League who had served in North Africa with an African unit of the South African Army during World War II. Leballo had returned to South Africa to become an enthusiastic adherent of the doctrine of "Africa for the Africans" then being preached by Anton Lembede. The leadership role taken by Indians and leftists in the Defiance Campaign stirred deep resentment in Leballo and other Youth Leaguers with a deep-seated "exclusivist" outlook. Rather than subsiding with the end of the campaign, this antagonism toward what were perceived as "non-African elements" intensified during 1953 when Nokwe, Sisulu, and others were invited to visit Eastern Europe, and the white Congress of Democrats was formed and welcomed into the expanding Congress alliance. By 1954 opposition to the ANC's increasingly closer ties with Indians and whites had crystallized in Orlando, the largest of the African residential areas southwest of Johannesburg, and in March 1954 Leballo was elected chairman of the Orlando Youth League. It was out of the circle of nationalist or "Africanist" Youth Leaguers around Leballo that the Pan Africanist Congress was to be formed five years later.

In November 1954 the Orlando Youth League began to issue a mimeographed journal called *The Africanist* under the editorship of Selby Ngendane, a law student who had previously studied at Fort Hare. Drawing on many of the authors who had contributed to the short-lived bulletin of the Bureau of African Nationalism, *The Africanist* defended the principles of "pure" nationalism and criticized both the government for its policies and the ANC for its alleged deviations.[42] Much prominence was given in its pages to projecting the Programme of Action as a prescription for the problems of the liberation movement, and to reviving the memory of Anton Lembede as a nationalist hero who had imparted to Africans the vision of a united and black-ruled continent.

These signs of mounting indiscipline were not left unchallenged by the top leaders of the Transvaal Youth League, Robert Resha, Duma Nokwe, and Henry Gordon Makgothi, all of whom favored a policy of multiracial alliances and rejected what they dubbed the "chauvinistic" and "racialistic" variety of nationalism preached first by Leballo and later by *The Africanist*. In May 1954 they expelled Leballo from the Youth League for his alleged attempts to "create disruption and strife in the liberatory movement."[43] Then, at the Youth League's annual national conference in late June, they succeeded in preventing the recognition of the Africanist delegates sent by the Orlando branch. These attempts to silence the Africanists and discredit their point of view did not prove altogether successful, however, partly because many Congress members shared to some degree the Africanists' dissatisfaction with the trend toward multiracialism in the ANC, partly because Leballo and his colleagues were unusually persistent in their attacks, and, not least of all, because the nonwhite press, in particular the popular *Bantu World,* shared many of the Africanists' opinions about the ANC and was quite willing to publicize the Africanists' statements and activities.

About the time the Orlando Youth League began to publish *The Africanist*, Robert Sobukwe, who had been teaching high school at Standerton in the eastern Transvaal since his graduation from Fort Hare in 1949, moved to Johannesburg to take up a prestigious post as a language instructor at the white University of the Witwatersrand. He gravitated quickly into local politics, becoming chairman of the ANC branch at Mofolo, one of the city's newer townships. His unassuming manner and relative isolation from the mainstream of ANC politics over the preceding five years combined to make Sobukwe appear an improbable champion of the Africanist cause, but his writings in the pamphlets of the Bureau of African Nationalism had revealed him to insiders in the Africanist faction as a fierce and articulate proponent of Lembedist principles—African self-reliance, self-assertion, and dedication to the building of an African-run nation-state. More by virtue of his intellect and deep commitment to nationalism than of any personal ambition, Sobukwe gradually assumed unofficial leadership of the Orlando Africanists, taking over the editorship of *The Africanist* and guiding the maturation of the group's ideas while Leballo remained its principal public spokesman and organizer.

1954: PLANNING THE 1955 CAMPAIGNS

During 1954 the ANC planned three campaigns, each of which came to a climax in 1955. The first campaign, and the most militant rhetoric of the period, was directed against the policy of moving some 58,000 Africans from the "Western Areas" of Johannesburg. The second campaign, based on boycott, was against the Bantu Education Act of 1953, a measure which potentially had a more profound and far-reaching impact than any other measure passed by the Nationalist government.[44] A third campaign, encompassing all issues, was the movement to hold a Congress of the People. One other particular concern was the old issue of the hated pass laws. These laws came to the fore again in 1956 as the object of protest, when the government attempted for the first time to issue passes to African women on a mass scale.

In planning the three campaigns, the four racially separate congresses— the ANC, SAIC, SACPO, and the COD, now known collectively as the Congress alliance—sought to develop a closely coordinated leadership. They also sought, but failed, to attract liberal whites as co-sponsors. Furthermore, as described above, chronic dissatisfaction in the ANC with the trend toward multiracial tactics erupted into open dissension within the ANC Youth League in the Transvaal, and some Africanist members were expelled.

The ANC, hoping to attract the widest possible sponsorship of the Congress of the People, invited some 200 organizations to send representatives to a planning conference at Tongaat, near Durban, on March 21, 1954. Invitations to the Nationalist Party and the United Party were formal gestures, but representatives came from the Liberal Party, the Labour Party, and some trade unions.[45] Only the four congresses became sponsoring organizations. Leaders of the Liberal Party continued to show interest and to discuss the evolving campaign with the ANC, but many Liberals were reluctant to become identified with a plan they had not helped to conceive and whose leadership already included left-wing personalities whom they did not trust.

The National Action Council set up at the Tongaat conference to run the campaign was composed of eight members from each of the four sponsoring organizations.[46] Its chairman was Chief Lutuli, and its secretariat consisted of Walter Sisulu (replaced by Oliver Tambo, who became acting secretary-general of the ANC in August 1954, when Sisulu's ban required him to resign from the position), Yusuf Cachalia of the SAIC, Lionel

Bernstein of the COD (replaced by Joe Slovo after the banning of Bernstein), and Stanley Lollan of SACPO.

The National Action Council had no policy-making powers, although sometimes it gave the impression that the Congress of the People was to be a stage in the process of creating a single national organization. Similar consultative groups at local and regional levels sometimes appeared to be assuming executive roles in their relations with local branches of the ANC.[47] National ANC leaders resisted any suggestion that the Congress of the People was an organization rather than a campaign. The National Executive Committee of the ANC retained its autonomy, usually meeting the day before the national executive committees of the four organizations met jointly. The meetings of the joint executives rather than those of the National Action Council served as a forum for coordinated policy-making.

The joint executives adopted a plan for the Congress of the People (Document 7c) ambitiously calling for the establishment by June 30, 1954, of provincial committees composed of equal numbers of representatives of each sponsoring organization. Congress of the People committees were to be organized also "on a town, suburb, factory or street basis." These committees were intended to mobilize support and to gather popular demands for incorporation in a Freedom Charter, not to serve as representative units that would send delegates to a national assembly. The suggestion of Professor Matthews that a voters' roll be prepared and electoral districts outlined had been rejected as unrealistic. No electoral units were defined. Instead, any group of people could elect, on a designated day, "by public vote" whenever possible, its delegates to attend the Congress of the People, which was to be "a mass assembly."

The ANC's National Executive Committee decided on April 17–18 that the Johannesburg Western Areas policy issue was too important in principle to be left to provincial or regional leadership and that the NEC itself should supervise the campaign (Document 7b). A few weeks later, on May 8 in Evaton, the joint executives, typically seeking to link a particular issue to overall policy, not only described the forthcoming June 26 as "Western Areas Day for Campaign and Solidarity" but also designated the Western Areas protest as part of a comprehensive campaign against all apartheid measures, to be known as the "Resist Apartheid Campaign." The Western Areas protest was described as the "pivot" of the "Resist Apartheid Campaign" (according to the ANC resolution of Dec. 1954, Document 7d). It was at the meeting on May 8 that Chief Lutuli read for the first time the newly composed "Call" to the Congress of the People. The "Call" was printed later in the year on two sides of a leaflet so that it could be publicly displayed (Document 9); explanatory material was included on the other two pages. Thousands of copies were issued in English, Zulu, Sotho, Xhosa, and Gujerati.[48]

On June 26–27, the ANC and its allies sponsored meetings in all provinces except the Orange Free State.[49] The largest and most enthusiastic meeting was held outdoors at Uitenhage, near Port Elizabeth, in conjunction with the annual provincial conference of the Cape ANC.[50] Chief Lutuli, whose one-year ban had expired, opened the Cape conference and called for 50,000 Freedom Volunteers to serve both the "Resist Apartheid Campaign" (in particular, the Western Areas campaign) and the Congress of the People.

These volunteers were sometimes confused by observers of the ANC with the volunteer defiers of 1952; their task, however, was to act as mobilizers, not defiers.[51] How many Freedom Volunteers were recruited by mid-1955 is not known. Toward the end of 1954, the NEC claimed some 10,000 (Document 7b).

The police attended the conference and were welcomed sardonically by Professor Matthews as "the main link between the Government and the African people" (Document 4). It was some satisfaction to Matthews that the delegates eluded the "swarming" Special Branch by meeting privately all night while the police observed a reception in the main hall.

The national conference of the ANC Youth League, meeting in Uitenhage at the same time as the Cape provincial conference, was faced with the problem of the rebellious Orlando branch. In his opening address Sisulu praised the Youth League's alliance with anti-colonial youth movements throughout the world and attacked the "isolationism" of "some elements" (the Africanists), which, he asserted, ran counter to the true intentions of Anton Lembede and A. P. Mda.[52]

Latent Africanist antagonism to left-wing, white, and Indian influence in the ANC had surfaced early in the year when Potlako Leballo, who attacked "Eastern functionaries" and nicknamed Sisulu "Mao Tse-tung," was elected chairman of the Orlando branch of the Youth League. Shortly before the national conference of the Youth League, Transvaal provincial officials expelled both Leballo and the chairman of the senior ANC Orlando branch, Macdonald Maseko. The senior Orlando branch, in turn, announced that it was expelling H. G. Makgothi, president of the Transvaal Youth League, and Leballo's branch reconfirmed him as chairman.[53] Leballo and three other men from the Orlando branch appeared at the national conference, but the conference, accepting Makgothi's judgment, excluded Leballo and allowed the others to attend as members, but not as delegates.[54] With the re-election of Joe Matthews (the son of Professor Matthews) as president-general and the election of Duma Nokwe as secretary-general, the existing orientation of the Youth League's national leadership was confirmed.

The police, who had been tricked at the Cape conference, were more alert when Lutuli flew to Johannnesburg on July 11 to speak at a Sophiatown rally on the Western Areas question. Upon his arrival, he was issued a banning order forbidding him to attend public gatherings for two years or to leave the magisterial district of his home in the village of Groutville, near Stanger, some fifty miles from Durban. His message was read to the rally, which had a claimed attendance of nearly 10,000 people. He called for "firm and decisive" action to oppose the Western Areas removal and "shake to repentance the hearts of white South Africa" (Document 5).

Lutuli returned to his home and to an isolation that was to pose new problems of communication for the ANC. The NEC held some of its meetings at Lutuli's home, however, and on August 15 the National Action Council met under his chairmanship.[55] On November 27, the NEC met at his home in one of the not-infrequent all-night sessions, from 11:20 P.M. until 8:30 A.M. At this meeting Professor Matthews was appointed deputy president-general.[56] And in December, two hundred delegates to the ANC's national conference traveled by bus to meet with Lutuli at his home.[57]

Early in the year, Sisulu had been unusually active, but he too was to be subjected to a new restriction. He had toured Cape Province in March and had made arrangements for a Transkei conference, which took place in Umtata on May 1, with both Lutuli and Dr. Conco, the acting treasurer-general, in attendance. (Lutuli, observing his earlier ban, stayed behind the scenes.) Delegates from the Transkei and Ciskei, some wearing traditional beadwork in ANC colors, attended the Cape conference of June 26–27.[58] Referring to Sisulu's activity in the Transkei, Professor Matthews said, . . . "They [the police] sought him here, they sought him there, they sought him everywhere, and when he had already returned to headquarters, they were still seeking. He will soon have to be known as Mr. Walter 'Scarlet Pimpernel' Sisulu, the ubiquitous General Secretary of the A.N.C." (Document 4). However, on July 23, the minister of justice placed a more stringent restriction on Sisulu than he had placed on Lutuli, ordering him to resign from the ANC and his position as secretary-general within thirty days and to stay away from gatherings for two years.[59] On the following day he was arrested; later he was sentenced to three months in prison because of his attendance at a gathering with five persons whose "common purpose" (according to the particulars of the charge) included having tea, discussing ANC matters, or having "social intercourse."[60]

In a statement made at the time of his resignation, Sisulu observed that almost the entire membership of the NEC had been removed from office, but that he himself would remain ready to answer any call from the ANC (Document 6). Leaders who were forced to resign continued to be regarded as leaders, to participate in policy-making behind the scenes, and—so long as they could elude the police—to attend meetings. Nevertheless, the ban undoubtedly had a "crippling effect," as Sisulu admitted in his statement; and as the imposition of bans continued, second-rank and third-rank leaders of limited experience arose to occupy positions of importance. At the same time, the ANC faced the problem of holding banned leaders responsible for their actions. The NEC recommended in December 1954 (Document 7b) that the exiled, arrested and banned leaders continue to be regarded as leaders, provided that at any conference a vote of confidence is passed on each and every one so that those whose activities are considered to be to the detriment of the organisation do not hide behind the bans and may in fact be expelled.

The annual conference voted "full confidence in the present leadership" (Document 7d).

Shortly before the 1954 national conference met, Johannes Strijdom became Prime Minister, succeeding Dr. Malan. He was termed a "fascist" by the ANC's working committee, over the signature of T. E. Tshunungwa; there was a difference, it said, in "the degrees of extremism" between Strijdom and Malan.[61] "Fascism" was a term used with increasing frequency during the 1950s. "After six years of Nationalist rule," according to the NEC, "fascism has arrived in South Africa" (Document 7b).

The annual conference was held at the Bantu Social Center of the YMCA in Durban with the permission of the City Council.[62] African-Indian cooperation was emphasized when Dr. G. M. Naicker, acting president of the SAIC, officially opened the conference, the first to be opened by an Indian leader.[63] Chief Lutuli, in his presidential address (read in his absence), described the United Party as "becoming indistinguishable from the Nationalist Party," despite the United Party's acceptance during the preceding month of racial integration in the economy as part of a reformulated native policy (Document 7a). The conference itself rejected the United Party's native policy "*in toto*" (Document 7d). Lutuli expressed gratitude to white liberals and the Liberal Party, as well as to the COD. The report of the NEC, on the other hand, reflecting the rivalry of the left wing and Liberals, dismissed the Liberals as persons who occasionally engaged in merely formal protest (Document 7b). Many Africans still distrusted the Liberal Party, although it had moved toward a more radical position during its first year of existence. Initially supporting a nonracial but qualified franchise, it had moved toward acceptance of a universal franchise as an ultimate aim at its national congress in July 1954.

The NEC gave prominent attention, with much left-wing rhetoric, to international developments, and expressed solidarity with opponents of Western imperialists, including the United States. "The ruling clique of America" was also singled out for condemnation in the conference's resolutions. Lutuli, on the other hand, briefly expressed gratitude for all "progressive opinion" and, in particular, for the support of Western churches.

Professor Matthews found at the conference "that it seemed as if the idea of the Congress of the People was going to suffer temporary eclipse" because the issues that mainly "agitated the minds of the African people" were Bantu education and the Western Areas removal.[64] The National

Action Council during the preceding month had set a series of deadlines, with the Congress of the People itself to be convened no later than June 1955. The annual conference again endorsed plans for the Congress of the People and the decision "to oppose and resist" the removals from the Western Areas. Tactics regarding Bantu education were stated in less general terms—children were to be withdrawn from primary schools—but no detailed plan of action was ready. Whereas the NEC recommended withdrawal of children for "at least one week," the conference recommended withdrawal "indefinitely as from April 1, 1955, until further directive from the National Executive Committee." Although not every eventuality could be anticipated, and publicity for detailed plans could not be expected, it was clear at the end of 1954, as events were to prove, that the ANC had not clearly or carefully completed its planning for the fateful campaigns of 1955.

WESTERN AREAS CAMPAIGN

Sophiatown, Martindale, and Newclare, the "Western Areas" of Johannesburg, had been established in 1905–1912 as townships in which Africans were permitted to own land in freehold. Land ownership by Africans symbolized their permanent residence in urban areas. Only a small number had been able to take advantage of the opportunity; most of the inhabitants were tenants living in crowded, slumlike conditions. On the other hand, the areas were free of many of the regulations typical of urban African locations. They had an atmosphere of vitality and some well-built homes, including that of Dr. A. B. Xuma, former president-general of the ANC. These were areas, said Dr. Xuma, "where there are nine registered schools, and old established missions, where our churches stand, where we have cinemas and shops and the only swimming bath for African children in the whole of Johannesburg."[65]

Slum clearance in the Western Areas was necessary, but other areas needed it even more. A more important reason for the removal of Africans from the Western Areas, in the government's view, was the fact that the areas had become "black spots," that is, African areas adjacent to or surrounded by the growing spread of white Johannesburg. Also of particular importance to the Nationalist government was the symbolic importance of eliminating African rights to the ownership of land.

White sentiment for removal of the Africans had been expressed since the eve of World War II. The United Party-dominated Johannesburg City Council, while endorsing removal, had been unable to move residents to outlying areas, however. In 1953 the national government bought a tract of land called Meadowlands some thirteen miles from the city for use in resettling the Africans in the Western Areas, and in 1954 bypassed the City

Council by means of the Natives Resettlement Act. The government prepared to start removals to Meadowlands early in 1955. At the same time, it endorsed two policies, both of them opposed by the Johannesburg City Council: to deprive Africans of freehold rights (although they could buy houses and lease land) and to group Africans in seven ethnic areas. These policies, which were in keeping with the philosophy of the Group Areas Act of 1950, had country-wide importance. One government directive in 1954 provided that municipalities should house Africans in "ethnic groups" within the townships or locations, and in 1955 another stated that Africans were eventually to be removed also from the western Cape Province.

Early in 1955, ANC propaganda proclaimed, "We shall not move." Most ANC leaders believed that this statement meant "we shall not move willingly or voluntarily," but they failed to make clear what form popular resistance could and should take. In the early hours of February 9, 1955, with more than 2,000 police and army reinforcements standing by during a local state of emergency, government lorries moved more than one hundred African families and their belongings from Sophiatown to Meadowlands. During the previous evening, Freedom Volunteers had helped some thirty to forty families to avoid their scheduled removal by moving them to other premises in Sophiatown. But many families moved willingly, a fact that was damaging to the ANC. During the next few years the mass removals of some 58,000 Africans did take place.

Although the ANC claimed success in some respects, the campaign not only failed to attain its objective of preventing the removals but also revealed major shortcomings of the ANC. Most remarkable, however, was the example the campaign offered of the difficulty of organizing effective political protest regarding even the most fundamental rights when Africans were divided over their immediate interests.

The basic issues at stake were African rights to the ownership of land, not only in the Western Areas but also in all of South Africa, and the right to be consulted and to influence a governmental process that could deprive individuals of existing property rights and human rights. In this situation, the government's determination to eliminate a "black spot" located near the center of Johannesburg led it to remove Africans from an area with a relatively free atmosphere, some well-constructed homes, and extensive community facilities to a new location with grim barracks-like housing and close control by officials and police. What undercut the strength of protest, however, was that for many tenants, in contrast to a small number of African homeowners and landlords, the move was from the squalor of a congested and expensive slum to less crowded and cleaner housing at modest rents, although with increased transportation costs.[66]

Originally the government had planned only a "site-and-service" scheme, but before execution the plan was altered substantially. ANC veteran leader J. B. Marks later claimed that these improvements were due to pressures by Africans and therefore constituted a "victory."[67] Because the government granted "major concessions in order to try to bribe the people," he wrote, Meadowlands "has brick houses, is one of the few African townships to have water-borne sewerage and individual water-taps to the houses, and boasts a fine new school." The government also had promised to relieve the overcrowding of transport to Meadowlands. The organizers of the African campaign failed to give adequate attention, said Marks, to the fact that the African population was not homogeneous and that tenants and landlords would respond differently to the threatened loss of freehold property.

> Insufficient importance was attached to the deep-seated need of many of the worse-off slum dwellers for a decent home; many saw in Meadowlands the only chance they would ever have to occupy their own home . . . .[68]

The "antagonism" between landlords and tenants was recognized also by the ANC's secretariat—the key members were Oliver Tambo and Robert Resha—in its evaluation of the campaign. The secretariat claimed that a survey (obviously biased) conducted by Freedom Volunteers had shown that a majority of the people in the affected area appreciated the principles involved and therefore did not want to move, but the secretariat admitted that "a substantial number . . . placed their need for a more adequate and comfortable accommodation above any other consideration." Furthermore, said the report, the government and its agents by their intimidation and propaganda and by "bribing" the people with better housing than was originally intended had increased the number of persons who were prepared to move or were undecided.

One conclusion that Marks drew from the experience was that political education for all Africans on the significance of the issues required more frequent mass meetings and occasional door-to-door and yard-to-yard canvassing. Not only should there have been more persistence in such canvassing, he said, but also propaganda should have been tailored to particular households and their differing interests. An even greater failure, as the secretariat saw it, was the ANC's inadequate appreciation of the importance of resistance by the landlords if there was to be unity with the tenants in a common struggle. In practice, there was only limited cooperation with the Anti-Expropriation Committee, led by Dr. Xuma, and the Rate Payers' Association.

The secretariat noted the chronic problems of organization, in particular the breakdown of communication and the failure to carry out directives. But "the major weakness," said the secretariat

> would seem to be the failure of the leadership to tell the people precisely what form of resistance was to be offered on the day of

removal. This information was requested time after time and at no stage was a clear and unequivocal answer given. The masses were given an impression, however, that Congress had the answer and would give it at the appropriate time.[69]

Inasmuch as there were many ways short of violence in which a tenant or homeowner could express his unwillingness to move, as the defense counsel in the Treason Trial later suggested, it was questionable whether the leadership in a political campaign should have prescribed precisely the way such unwillingness should be demonstrated. Tenants could have forced the authorities to move them bodily, for example, or could have refused to move until their belongings had been loaded on the lorries.

Outside Sophiatown, young African activists waited, without satisfaction, for more militant action. They hoped for directives that would bring large formations marching into Sophiatown to join in mass displays of resistance.[70] The dissident Africanists of the Orlando branch of the Youth League, on the other hand, could see no possibility of degrees of nonviolent resistance, according to one of their spokesmen writing in *The Africanist*:

> What is the use of calling on the people of Sophiatown to "resist" the removal "non-violently?" How is this possible? Is it not a contradiction in terms? One either "resists" violently or "submits" unwillingly. . . . A liberatory movement will stop at NOTHING to achieve its independence. And since white domination is maintained by force of arms it is only by superior force of arms that it can be overthrown.[71]

In retrospect, it was evident that the ANC's basic error in this abortive campaign was more one of commission, in particular of issuing propaganda vaguely promising effective challenge, than of omission or failing to give precise instructions. Many of the hundreds of speeches delivered at twice-weekly meetings held regularly on Sundays and on Wednesday nights for more than a year preceding the removals were characterized by flamboyant, fiery, and sometimes bloody rhetoric. The most widely circulated leaflet proclaimed. "We shall not move";[72] and Chief Lutuli himself was quoted as calling upon the people to make the campaign the "Waterloo of Apartheid."

Because of these effusions of rhetoric, the prosecution in the Treason Trial gave more attention to the Western Areas campaign than to any other in attempting to prove that the ANC's policy was one of violent intent. The prosecution dismissed as hypocritical camouflage the ANC's reaffirmations of its traditional policy of nonviolence. On February 8, 1955, the day before the removals began, the working committee, in a statement signed by Oliver Tambo, said that the people's "fight" would be "nonviolent."[73] The Treason Trial prosecution, however, after backing down from its original allegation that the ANC incited to violence at its public meetings, argued that in the total situation the ANC was willfully creating the conditions of a confrontation that would result in a bloodbath.

The minister of justice, in explaining his order of February 8 banning all public meetings in Johannesburg and Roodepoort for twenty days, not only cited the campaign's rhetoric but also stated that the police had "reliable information that the Natives in Sophiatown have in their possession a number of machine guns, revolvers, pistols, hand grenades, home-made rifles and home-made dynamite bombs."[74]

The ANC denied the allegations, and no evidence of any preparations for violence in the Western Areas campaign was submitted at the Treason Trial. For that matter, no violence of any kind, not even isolated stone-throwing at the police, occurred during the campaign. Apart from public meetings, canvassing, and the distribution of leaflets, the only active measure of opposition was the movement of some families by Freedom Volunteers—only about 300 Volunteers were at work in the Western Areas—the night before the police arrived. "The press and many people from the rank and file," Walter Sisulu wrote to Canon John Collins in London, "expected something dramatic to happen and were disappointed when nothing spectacular took place."

The campaign was essentially an occasion for local propaganda. Although no plan of action was waiting to be revealed at the appropriate time, a decision in principle had been taken to lead Africans in the country's major centers in "I.A.," that is, industrial action, meaning a stay-at-home from work on the day the first removals were due to take place. "I.A." was to be, in the usual language, "a means of lifting the struggle to a higher plane."[75] More concretely, the rationale for generating such widespread pressures was the belief that it would drain official manpower by diverting it to all major centers. The ANC hoped that if the government could be diverted from the Western Areas removals, it might abandon policies that could be implemented only by the use of force against a determined opposition that had white support and sympathy abroad. The ANC's plan was torpedoed when officials gave notice on February 8 that the first removals would be made the next morning. February 9 was three days in advance of the ANC's target for industrial action, and the government's decision to begin removals then threw "the arrangements into confusion," said the secretariat's report. The stay-at-home was called off at the last minute; in fact, few were ready to undertake it.

Other difficulties faced the ANC: continued bannings, opposition to the Transvaal and national leadership by Africanist factions, and the problem of sustaining public concern regarding a governmental relocation scheme whose implementation was piecemeal. Another difficulty was the fact that the ANC, while urging people not to move from an area where their dwellings were to be bulldozed, was unable to provide them with more than temporary accommodation. In these circumstances of difficulty and failure, the secretariat claimed that propaganda had aroused popular indignation throughout the country and that sympathetic mass meetings were held on February 9. But the main achievements to which it pointed were essentially negative, in particular, the claims that changes in the government's removal plan were a testimonial to the ANC's power and that the volunteers and the discipline of ANC supporters were responsible for the avoidance of violence.

It would not be surprising if individual members of the ANC had anticipated violence or hoped for the opportunity to exploit bloodshed. But violent resistance was not encouraged. Leaders of the ANC did not waver from their habitual disposition against violent tactics and their belief that such resistance was unrealistic. Although the tactic of a stay-at-home was held in abeyance, the Western Areas campaign did not revive. What happened in the period culminating on February 9 was "just the beginning of a hard and bitter fight," said the secretariat. Energies were shifting, however, to the campaign against Bantu education, which appeared to threaten the African future even more profoundly than did the forced termination of urban freehold rights.

BANTU EDUCATION CAMPAIGN

Africans deeply distrusted the Bantu Education Act of 1953, fearing that "Bantu education" would be of an inferior type, designed to condition Africans into accepting a position of subservience. Their fears had been fed by the official rationale for the legislation. The report of the Commission on Native Education, prepared during 1949–1951, urged reform that would "prepare Natives more effectively for their future occupations." It emphasized the importance of instruction through the medium of a student's mother tongue. A minimal knowledge of both official languages (not just one) would enable "the Bantu child . . . to follow oral or written instructions."[76] But the most widely quoted explanations were those of Dr. Hendrik F. Verwoerd, then minister of native affairs, who said:

> Education must train and teach people in accordance with their opportunities in life, according to the sphere in which they live . . . . education should have its roots entirely in the Native areas and in the Native environment and Native community . . . . The Bantu must be guided to serve his own community in all respects. There is no place for him in the European community above the level of certain forms of labor.

Vast disparities in the support of education for different racial groups also emphasized the low status of Africans. The average expenditure on education in 1951–1952 was £ 43.88 for each white student, £ 18.84. for Asian and Coloured students, and only £ 7.58 for each African student.[77] In March 1954, the government announced that henceforth its contribution to

Bantu education would be pegged at £ 6,500,000, with any additional sums to be raised from African sources only rather than from general revenue. Because education was not compulsory for Africans and was free only in the primary grades, only about 41 percent of African children of school age attended school in 1953. Enrollment doubled later, but only because short double sessions were introduced.

The Bantu Education Act dealt largely with administrative rather than substantive matters. Most African primary and secondary schools were operated by state-subsidized church and mission bodies. These bodies were given the choice of turning their schools over to the government or continuing them as private schools with gradually diminishing subsidies. The Catholics decided to assume the support of their schools; the Anglicans (Episcopalians) closed down several of theirs; but all other schools were turned over to the national government. In any case, all schools had to be registered by the government.[78]

The Bantu Education Act also provided for transferring control from the provinces to the national government and enlisting the participation of Africans in local school districts, reforms that in principle most Africans as well as whites considered long overdue. But control was vested in the much disliked Department of Native Affairs rather than in the Department of Education. Furthermore, some of the African members of newly established school committees and boards were to be appointed, and members elected by parents were to be subject to official approval. The organization of these bodies was also to be integrated into the developing structure of government-controlled tribal authorities under the Bantu Authorities Act of 1951.

In implementing this educational policy, the government proceeded slowly. Late in 1954 it issued a draft syllabus for the lower grades, allowing time for criticism to be expressed before the syllabus was to go into effect in 1956. Not until April 1, 1955—the day of transfer of control to the Department of Native Affairs—did the time seem suitable for mass protest. But even then, as we shall see, protests proved abortive.

Of all campaigns conducted by the ANC, the campaign against Bantu education was the most poorly planned, the most confused, and, for Africans generally, the most frustrating. Africans were virtually united in their opposition to control of African education by the Department of Native Affairs and they did share the fears noted earlier.[79] The stakes were seen to be of profound importance: the mental outlook of generations of children. But what could Africans do? They were divided over the perennial question of boycott, not only in regard to the government's school committees and boards, but also in regard to the poignant issue of withdrawing children from government schools. The ANC committed itself to the goal of their complete withdrawal. But determining what to do in the immediate situation was complicated by the necessity of calculating the long-run consequences of such action for the wider political struggle. If alternative education could not be provided for students withdrawn from school, and if parents who did not withdraw children came to acquiesce in the new status quo, how would these developments affect popular morale and confidence in African national leadership?

The ANC's strategy for opposing Bantu education appeared both vacillating and unclear during the year that followed the national conference of December 1954. The NEC recommended withdrawal of school children "at least for one week" (Document 7b) and reported that the Women's League and the Youth League would concentrate on the campaign under the supervision of the senior body.[80] The conference itself called for "total rejection" of the Bantu Education Act—the usual exaggeration of political rhetoric—and, more concretely, called on African parents to prepare "to withdraw their children from primary schools indefinitely as from April 1, 1955, until a further directive from the National Executive Committee" (Document 7d). The NEC, however, failed to work out a coherent program for alternative education or one that could be adapted to local circumstances. Nor was it able, in the months that followed, to maintain two-way communication with leaders at provincial and branch levels or to assert control over branches that ignored or defied national policy.[81]

In January 1955, the national secretariat issued detailed directives for a series of meetings looking toward the April 1 date when they expected the new syllabus to be introduced. It also called for the appointment of local action committees which were to submit regular reports. The Transvaal Youth League, at a large conference in Sophiatown early in the month, resolved to call for a thousand volunteer teachers.[82] Other conferences and mass meetings were held during January and February, 1955. Meanwhile, both Chief Lutuli and Professor Matthews, far removed from national headquarters and receiving only scanty reports, felt apprehensive about popular readiness for withdrawal on April 1.

Lutuli, in particular, felt out of touch. He had suffered a stroke in mid-January because of high blood pressure and was gravely ill. After permission was granted to leave the locale of his ban, Lutuli was admitted to a hospital in Durban, where he remained for two months. A letter written in his behalf on January 31 expressed his sense of being "haunted" by national affairs and his desire that the NEC meet immediately "to modify or endorse" the decisions of the December ANC conference regarding both Bantu education and the Western Areas.[83]

Professor Matthews wrote to Lutuli three weeks later, saying that it was "absolutely essential" for the NEC to meet.[84] He noted that he had suggested to the secretariat that the meeting take place not in Johannesburg, but in Durban, where Matthews might consult with Lutuli and also "for reasons which I need not go into at the present time," presumably Matthews' distrust of the influence and judgment of the Transvaal ANC leadership. Matthews recommended that the withdrawal of pupils from school be postponed. He was particularly concerned about the fact that many African parents were not members of the ANC. "Indeed," he wrote, "many of them are not sympathetic to the A.N.C. point of view" and could be won over only if more time were available. More time was necessary, also, because "the teachers have become so scared about how this step is likely to affect their positions that they are doing propaganda against the campaign & against the A.N.C."[85]

Matthews posed the question of "how the matter of a postponement can be presented to our followers without appearing as in the nature of a retreat from our resolution?" He suggested three grounds of justification. In the first place, April 1 was not a school day, as had been expected (schools did not open until April 12, after the Easter holidays). Moreover, although April 1 was the date on which the government hoped to have the machinery of school committees and boards in operation, the new syllabus would not become effective until January 1956. Third, many centers wanted more time, and the ANC also needed more time to consult with other organizations concerned with education.

The NEC, meeting in Durban on March 5, found that no reports on the progress of the campaign were available and that there was "no evidence that the country would be ready for withdrawal on the 1st April" (Document 13c).[86] The committee adopted Matthews' proposal to defer withdrawal until a date was fixed by the NEC.[87] (None ever was.) In the meantime, Africans were called upon not to participate in the election of school bodies nor to serve on them. The NEC noted Matthews' three reasons for deferment and added a fourth: "the expressed wish of . . . Lutuli, now lying seriously ill in Durban Hospital," that time be allowed for "further consultations with parents' organizations, church bodies and other associations . . . ." "Ultimate withdrawal" was reaffirmed as the ANC's objective. In preparation for that time, the NEC decided to set up a committee to plan for alternative educational and cultural activities.

Although the NEC saw the situation as one of general unpreparedness, some local leaders (Lutuli called them "enthusiasts")[88] had aroused popular expectations, particularly on the East Rand (the eastern Witwatersrand region of the Transvaal), and they were determined to carry on their campaign. Angry delegates to a special Transvaal conference held on March 13 openly defied the NEC. "Having fully considered the decision of the National Executive Committee," the conference reaffirmed the December conference resolution and decided to intensify preparations for an indefinite boycott of primary schools beginning on April 1.[89] Two weeks later, however, a second conference reversed this move and accepted the NEC's decision but requested the NEC to allow areas that were ready to boycott to do so.[90]

The caution urged by Lutuli and Matthews had prevailed within the NEC, many of whose members were widely scattered and lacking direct contact with centers where withdrawals were to take place.[91] But a more activist attitude marked the working committee, whose members resided in Johannesburg and its vicinity. Its cooperation was essential if NEC policy was to be implemented. Oliver Tambo, acting ANC secretary-general, disagreed with the NEC and identified himself with the policy of withdrawing children from school wherever it was possible to do so.[92] The NEC met again on April 9–10 in Port Elizabeth, during a conference sponsored by the ANC which brought together more than 700 delegates of organizations opposed to Bantu education.[93] The NEC then attempted to accommodate all points of view by endorsing both the aim of ultimate and complete withdrawal (set forth in the December resolution) and the deferment of a definite date (set forth in the March resolution). It also accepted, in principle, withdrawal of children from school, with the permission of the NEC, in any area where the people were ready and where alternative activities for school children had been arranged.[94]

Nevertheless, the scattered boycotts that began on April 12, when schools resumed, were "not inspired by the official leadership," according to a report of the secretariat to the NEC, "and became clearly a movement beyond their control."[95] Some of the boycotters believed they were implementing the decision of the ANC; others were "unruly and undisciplined elements" within the ANC, said the secretariat. The working committee considered whether or not to disclaim the local boycotts. Chief Lutuli had expressed his wish that parents who had made their protest should now send their children back to school. The working committee decided in a directive of April 23 to congratulate those who had withdrawn their children and, contrary to Lutuli's wishes, to make no recommendation to parents but to leave them to act as they wished in accordance with local circumstances. At the same time, addressing itself to the country generally, the working committee urged an intensification of the boycott beginning on April 25.[96] Dr. Verwoerd had warned that students absent on April 25 would be expelled. A writer in *New Age* praised the working committee's circular for doing much to clear up the confusion.[97]

The emphasis had now shifted from mass withdrawals on a designated day to "protest" withdrawals as "a prelude to the permanent withdrawal of children" (in the words of the working committee) and as part of a wider, evolving campaign against apartheid. Thus, *New Age* reported that at the beginning of the third week of the campaign, that is, April 25, the date of Dr. Verwoerd's ultimatum, "the boycott campaign in some areas like East Rand, having achieved its protest purpose and pioneered the boycott struggle, the children returned to school as planned."[98] But confusion continued during the year. Some withdrawals were prolonged; others began and ended sporadically. About 7,000 children dropped out of school, and the government dropped well over 100 teachers from their positions.

In reviewing the year, the NEC conceded that the campaign "may have appeared to be [composed of] sporadic, unrelated and ineffectual small incidents in various parts of the country" (Document 13c). Although the campaign had petered out and the government had been able to fill its school committees, much enthusiasm and pressure for withdrawal had been generated in a dozen centers in the Transvaal, notably Benoni, Germiston, Brakpan, Alexandra, Moroka, and Natalspruit. Beginning late in May there had been some active protest in Bethlehem in the Orange Free State and a flare-up of activity and school withdrawals in the area of Port Elizabeth in the eastern Cape Province. At the same time, local leaders and volunteers made hasty efforts to improvise "cultural clubs," nominally sponsored by the African Education Movement, both for students who had been expelled for participating in the boycott and for those who had been unable to find places in school.

Because operating an unregistered school was illegal, the clubs could not appear to be offering formal education. The police harassed the clubs with raids, and some "leaders" (rather than "teachers") were prosecuted, banned, or deported. Late in the year, Govan Mbeki, an ANC leader and representative of *New Age* in the eastern Cape, described the tense situation still existing in the Cape district of Peddie, where resistance to Bantu education had been accompanied by arson, arrests, police patrolling, and raids.[99]

Meanwhile, the clubs were faced with even more formidable shortages of money, equipment, premises, qualified leaders, and discipline. One meeting of leaders discussed "unpunctuality, irresponsibility, and truancy . . . to say nothing of fighting and flirting!"[100] Strenuous efforts were made to maintain the clubs. But a report in September or October 1956, which listed seven clubs with 1,517 children and 22 leaders, described "general deterioration" and listed the consequences of insufficient money to pay the leaders as "rifts, disputes, frictions and antagonisms."[101] Perhaps most galling to those who persevered with the boycott was the complaint that the children of "leading Congressites" were attending government schools.

Bitterness and recrimination arose both within and without the ANC. Militants accused unnamed but "very prominent and high-ranking Congress officials" of "choking and strangling" the spirit of resistance.[102] Joe Matthews wrote to Walter Sisulu, complaining bitterly of "passivity" and stating that he was "really fed up with the whole leadership."[103] Youth League dissidents of Orlando, writing in *The Africanist*, decried "irresponsible excitement."[104] The Society of Young Africa (SOYA), which was sponsored by the pro-boycott Unity Movement, issued a leaflet condemning the boycotters as cowards who "shift the burden of the struggle on to the backs of our children."[105]

The heaviest press publicity, however, was accorded to the older and more conservative personalities who had once been active in the ANC and who believed, with Dr. Xuma, that younger leaders had acted "for propaganda reasons" and "aroused vain hopes" (Document 13d). They advised making the best of the education that was available and working for African interests within the system, an outlook that the Liberal Party shared.[106] Among the critics were the *Bantu World,* R. V. Selope Thema (who became chairman of the board of education for Orlando and Meadowlands on the eve of his death in 1955), Paul Mosaka, Dr. William Nkomo, and the leaders of the Transvaal Interdenominational African Ministers' Federation. P. Q. Vundla, a member of the NEC who apparently believed he was acting in accordance with ANC policy, joined Mosaka and Nkomo in a deputation that sought the readmission of expelled children to school. Afterwards, Vundla was physically assaulted by ANC loyalists and later expelled from the ANC.

Somewhere in the center was Professor Matthews, whose attitudes were a complex blend of cautious realism, commitment to the ANC's goals, and an historic sense that included both a keen appreciation of organizational needs and difficulties and confidence in the future. Unlike more militant members of the ANC who condemned school board members as "stooges, reactionaries, escapists, and traitors,"[107] Matthews did not condemn fellow Africans whose tactics for opposing Bantu education differed from those of the ANC (Document 8).

At the same time, because of his convictions about the importance of education, Matthews could feel that his friends who went as part of a deputation to secure the readmission of children to school would "come to realize that education for ignorance and for inferiority in Verwoerd's schools is worse than no education at all." Even so, he expressed confidence that the majority of African teachers would side with their people and do their best in "educating the African child for a free society." Meanwhile, he said, the ANC had to organize and establish "alternative cultural, recreational and social activities" for children; it had to follow the road of persuading African parents to withdraw their children from government schools, and maintain confidence that after a long and non-violent struggle Bantu education would finally be defeated.[108]

PROBLEMS OF ORGANIZATION AND THE "M-PLAN"

On January 7, 1953, Joe Matthews wrote to his father, then a visiting professor at Union Theological Seminary in New York, about a "secret meeting . . . of the top leaders of both the S.A.I.C. & A.N.C., half of whom were banned." They had planned the future with "cold-blooded realism," he wrote. He promised a later "confidential letter" but went on to say:

Broadly speaking the idea is to strengthen the organisation tremendously. To prepare for the continuation of the organisation under

> conditions of illegality by organising on the basis of the cell system.
> The continuation of the [Defiance] Campaign and its widening into
> the mass campaign and Industrial Action.[109]

But the Defiance Campaign, as we have seen, was neither widened nor
even continued. Young Matthews confidently predicted "that we will
make a big advance this year," but, if he was referring to significant
organizational improvements, they were not to be achieved.

Later in the year Nelson Mandela, president of the Transvaal ANC,
prepared a detailed statement that set forth much of what Matthews had in
mind. As noted earlier, it was presented to the Transvaal provincial
conference on September 21, 1953 in lieu of a presidential address because
Mandela was under ban (Document 2). Mandela's statement was to be a
major exhibit in the Treason Trial, where the prosecution was to allege that
it advocated violence in accordance with the aims of international communism. Mandela did foresee "a clash" and used language as bitter as any
used during this period: the people, he wrote, would "resist to the death the
stinking policies of the gangsters that rule our country." Furthermore, his
identification with "the people of Korea and Kenya" was linked with
condemnation of "imperialist America and her satellites." However,
Mandela's analysis was concerned primarily with the problems immediately facing the ANC: the spate of bannings and the extreme danger
and difficulty involved in attempting to use "the old methods of bringing
about mass action through public mass meetings, press statements and
leaflets." What had to be implemented immediately in his view was the
"M-Plan," which had been adopted by the NEC after consultation with
the National Action Committee of the ANC and the SAIC. The plan was
named after Mandela. The idea of a cell-based organization was not new,
however; A. P. Mda, an early Youth League leader, had advocated it in
the 1940s.

The "M-Plan" acquired some false notoriety outside the ANC, and
even within it, which stamped it as a secret plan designed to enable the
ANC to operate underground. But in fact there was no effort to keep its
features and purpose secret. Mandela himself said the "M-Plan" was
"popularly known" by this name. Although the plan was aimed at
strengthening the ANC in case it was forced underground, its immediate
purpose was to build a mass membership and to organize it through a
hierarchy of accepted leaders who could transmit policy and decisions from
the national level to the grass roots.[110] Tying every member into a tightly
knit organization would enable the ANC to function without calling public
meetings or issuing public statements. The emphasis of the plan was on
efficient and effective organization requiring detailed and duplicated
membership cards, financial records, and records of activities (fund-raising
bazaars and teaparties were suggested), as well as weekly meetings of
cell-stewards, chief-stewards, and prime-stewards within each branch.

Cell-stewards were to be in charge of a street, i.e., a cell which was divided into blocks of about seven houses, with each block under a unit-steward. Chief-stewards were in charge of a zone of about seven streets, and each zone was to have a lecturer to conduct discussions on politics and the ANC's policy. Prime-stewards were placed in charge of a ward of about four zones; together with the branch secretary, the prime-stewards constituted the branch secretariat. Authority flowed downward from the branch. After an elaborate nomination procedure, the officers of the branch were to be elected at cell meetings in which voting was by a show of hands.

In practice, with few exceptions, branches were unable to implement the "M-Plan," a failure that was only one of many shortcomings and weaknesses described in the reports of national and provincial organs of the ANC during 1953-1956. Included in the reports were complaints that the "M-Plan" itself had not been adequately explained, that money was not available for paid organizers, and that morale was often low. The reports of the NEC of 1954 and 1955 and the executive report to the ANC (Transvaal) (Documents 7b, 13c, and 17b) contained typical descriptions of organizational weaknesses and the failures of provincial and branch units to report to, or even to acknowledge communications from, higher authorities. "Dissension, stagnation and suspicion" were said to exist; sometimes they were blamed on personal rivalries or on whispering campaigns allegedly started by the Government.[111] A further explanation of the disarray was the reluctance of many Africans who worked long hours to devote much time to organizing small groups at the local level or to involve their wives and children in dangerous activity. Also of some importance was the fact that those who were politically minded tended to be attracted to public activity at the branch level, which still appeared to be possible.

In aiming to strengthen "the ties between Congress and the people" (and, presumably, in strengthening the ANC to operate if necessary under conditions of illegality), the "M-Plan" also sought to centraiize the ANC's leadership and to create more direct national control over local branches. A draft constitution to this effect, intended to supplant the existing, so-called Xuma constitution of 1943, was presented to the ANC's national conference of December 1952. The draft came to be identified with Oliver Tambo, the convenor of the constitution committee. It circulated in many versions among the provinces and branches, but final action on the draft was repeatedly deferred. Not until December 1957 was a new constitution finally adopted (Document 27). It is discussed below, p. 279.

Younger leaders in the Transvaal—Mandela, Sisulu, Tambo, Resha— and some in the eastern Cape, notably Joe Matthews, hoped that a new constitution could (in Matthews' words) "tighten up the organization and give the national executive the power to enforce the policies of the organization throughout the country."[112] But older leaders in the Cape and Chief Lutuli quietly resisted any change that would eliminate provincial authority and unduly centralize control in Johannesburg. Just as tensions between the Cape and the Transvaal often marked Afrikaner politics, so did African leaders from outside the Transvaal often harbor a mistrust of what were seen to be the more extreme approaches of Transvaal leaders. In a "confidential" letter to T. E. Tshunungwa on February 6, 1956, Professor Matthews wrote:

> The danger in this new constitution proposed by the Eastern Cape [one of the amended versions of the draft constitution] is the abolition of Provincial conferences. There will be too much centralization and I am sure it will kill the whole organization in a few months' (not years') time. It would take one too long to argue this adequately in a letter. This is another Transvaal move intended to hide their deficiencies. They think that in this way they will be able to get hold of the Cape branches with their better financial organisation. They are supported in this by some of our Cape leaders who do not see what is behind this move. But only experience will teach them.[113]

Shortly before the ANC's special conference at the end of March 1956, Chief Lutuli took an extraordinary step (for him) when he warned privately that "I may have to seriously consider whether or not I can honourably continue to act as President-General." In a letter of March 22 to Dr. Arthur Letele, treasurer-general, he said that he felt strongly about "Abolishing in any new Constitution the Provincial level in our organisational structure. I do not like overcentralization. Power must be shared or else you create dictators."[114]

Neither Professor Matthews nor Mandela was ambivalent about the necessity to act openly and within the law. Their activities—both the Congress of the People and the "M-Plan"—were defensive, undertaken largely in response to the government's initiatives, or concerned with the chronic problem of "the instilling of political consciousness" (in Matthews's words) in a people who were economically impoverished and dominated by a network of controls. Both Matthews and Lutuli as president-general explicitly affirmed the ANC's commitment to nonviolence. Mandela's rhetoric, on the other hand, was open to inferences that violence was ultimately unavoidable; but clearly, all ANC leaders were anxious to avoid any violence that might provoke brutal reaction by police. Ambivalence was most evident in the differing attitudes of leaders regarding the seriousness of threats to the ANC's existence and the necessity of adopting internal security practices appropriate to a movement that was already partly underground.

Long accustomed to traditional types of open political activity, ANC leaders had difficulty in adopting more surreptitious practices. Late in 1954, Joe Matthews wrote a letter to Tshunungwa, the ANC national organizer, in which he warned him, "You must adopt security measures regarding documents, letters, etc. Do not keep a letter and memorise addresses and phone numbers. Only keep records of official documents that are published openly. Things you wish to keep for historical or other interests put in inaccessible places. Fascism has arrived, these chances that we take are dangerous now."[115]

Because Tshunungwa, like many others in the ANC, did not take such warnings seriously, the letter was seized in a police raid, and became one of some 9,000 documents available to the prosecution at the Treason Trial.

A year later, at the ANC's national conference of December 1955, the minutes of the 1954 conference could not be read because they had been seized in the country-wide raid of September 27, 1955. A delegate pointed out (according to the minutes of the 1955 conference) that "past experience should have taught the Secretary not to keep important documents in accessible places [and] severely criticized the Secretary, Mr. [Alfred] Hutchinson, for negligence. . . ." Two leaders came to his defense, one saying, "the C.I.D. [Criminal Investigation Department] were unpredictable." The discussion was concluded by the Rev. James A. Calata, the ANC's leader in the Cape during the 1930s and 1940s, who was serving as the speaker of the conference. According to the minutes,

> Mr. Speaker [Calata], advocating a more lenient and sympathetic attitude toward Mr. Hutchinson's unfortunate experience, reminded Congress that he (Mr. Speaker) was accustomed to raids, having already had 4 in his experience. People should not laugh at other people's misfortunes.[116]

The eventual prospect of a final confrontation, of operating underground, of violence, was not far below the surface of private discussion. In a worried and thoughtful letter in May 1955, Tambo, after noting the leadership's uncertainty and confusion on the question of withdrawing children from schools as a protest against Bantu education, wrote to Dr. Wilson Z. Conco, the deputy president-general:

> It seems to me that the A.N.C. is irretrievably committed to a bitter struggle—and maybe a long and eventful struggle, in which there will be many losses and gains of varying magnitude and effect, before the approach—rather the dawn of the day of freedom. For the leadership at least, if not for the general masses, clarity is indispensable; an honest, objective and fearless "looking of the facts in the face" is called for. If any venture proves ill-advised at any given time the necessary readjustments in our tactics must be made. On the other hand the mere fact that a particular line of campaign turns out to be beset with numerous difficulties is no reason, by itself, to justify a retreat, for, in the final analysis, the situation in South Africa today is such that alternative modes of struggle have been reduced and are being daily reduced to the barest minimum, and we shall not wait long

for the day when only one method will be left to the oppressed people of this country—precisely what that method will be is impossible to say, but it will certainly be the only method, and when that has been employed and followed up to its logical or historic conclusion, there will be no more struggle—because the one or the other of the present conflicting forces—democracy and fascism will have been crushed and vanquished.[117]

MEMBERS, MONEY, AND THE AFRICAN PRESS

Any evaluation of the potentialities of the ANC to create change must take account of the members and funds available to support its efforts. The ANC's claim to be the mouthpiece for the Africans of South Africa, and the grandiose scale of its plans, seemed to many onlookers to be ludicrously contradicted by its actual membership. The estimated paid-up membership at the time of the 1953 conference, for example, was 28,900, divided among the provinces as follows: Cape, 16,000; Transvaal, 11,000; Natal, 1,300; and Orange Free State, 600. How many "adherents even beyond the ranks of our paid-up membership" (as Professor Matthews put it) did the ANC have? (Document 8). This question was an old and chronically difficult one, impossible to answer accurately.

The discussion that follows, like the preceding discussion of problems of organization, may be read as a catalogue of weakness and failure. The evidence of African self-criticism contributes to this impression, but the impression is misleading unless one bears in mind the pressing burdens and often-exhausting difficulties that Africans had to surmount in order to carry on political activity. Except for a small number in the professions and business, ANC members typically worked long hours at low wages, were poorly housed, and felt the pull of obligations to their families. For leaders who had to travel long distances, travel and accommodation were expensive and often difficult to arrange. They also found it difficult and expensive to maintain communication among themselves in the provinces and throughout the country. Communicating with a potential following among whom illiteracy was widespread and who spoke diverse vernaculars was an even greater problem. When one adds to these difficulties and constraints the pervasive restrictions and threats to movement and association imposed by the government, the record of political activity is far from negative.

Membership

The contrast between what the ANC proclaimed it would do and the fluctuating size of its small paid-up membership was striking indeed. One

American diplomat in South Africa some years later soberly dismissed the ANC by stating that its actual membership amounted only to one-half of one percent of the African population. Many African leaders would have been happy to settle for this number of active and reliable members, that is, about 55,000.[118] Fundamentally, however, the ANC's significance was not as a party but as a national movement having "omnibus" appeal. Although the number of its adherents could not be measured reliably, there could be no doubt that the ANC was the pre-eminent African political organ in southern Africa and that its annual conferences were a kind of African parliament, certainly far more representative of African interests and aspirations than was the white Parliament in Cape Town. Furthermore, the ANC was able repeatedly to hold mass rallies that attracted many thousands of people.

Membership usually referred to paid-up membership, those who made the annual payment of two shillings and sixpence laid down in the constitution. Officials at conferences continually attempted to enforce the rules limiting representation to paid-up members. Many persons who were in arrears but took active part in demonstrations thought of themselves, and were thought of, as members, however. In this sense, African leaders were disposed to claim a more realistic, and larger, "membership" than was officially represented at conferences. They spoke of a rise to 100,000 members during the Defiance Campaign.[119] In August 1953, an ANC memorandum submitted to the United Nations stated that membership was 106,000.[120]

What the government described as truly representative of Africans was S. S. Bhengu's Bantu National Congress, which was created early in 1952. This pro-apartheid organization, which was supported financially by Afrikaner nationalists, was unable to generate any popular interest except among some tribal chiefs. Largely by adding up the populations headed by these chiefs, the organization and its sponsors could make membership claims ranging between 400,000 and 2,000,000. Bhengu himself, an herbalist who was ridiculed by political activists as a witch doctor, was publicly discredited when he was convicted in April 1954 of theft and fraud and sentenced to prison for five years and nine months.[121]

The great increase in the ANC's membership in 1952 was not seen as an unmixed blessing. According to Nelson Mandela, local branches failed to examine the "past history and political characteristics" of new members carefully (Document 2).

As a result of this, there were many shady characters ranging from political clowns, place seekers, splitters, saboteurs, agents-provocateurs to informers and even policemen, who infiltrated into the ranks of Congress.

Yet the ANC's aim was a mass membership, although it was one organized (after 1952) in accordance with the "M-Plan." In 1954, the ANC again aimed at a membership of 100,000.

More realistically, the NEC reported in December 1954 that "the alarming fluctuation in the membership" presented the ANC with problems of organization that were "much deeper and more fundamental" than ever before (Document 7b).

> How are we to explain the great reduction in our membership during the two years [1953 and 1954]? Are the Africans no longer interested in the cause for which the Congress stands, in the fight for freedom and equality, or are they now afraid?

In reply, the report professed to find that Africans were "still as militant and courageous as ever" but then outlined eight causes for the decline in membership, mainly failures of leadership and organization that resulted in feelings "of impotence and helplessness."

The report also pointed out the danger of becoming "urban-based and urban-orientated." The ANC faced formidable problems in its recurring effort to provide political education and win support in the rural areas, particularly in the Transkei, and among farm laborers. Three months after the Congress of the People campaign culminated in June 1955, the Natal provincial executive of the ANC submitted an annual report which described apathy, complacency, and defeatism on the part of the Zulu people, "once renowned for their courage." ". . . we are working among an extremely conservative people, the Zulus," it observed, "who sometimes show too docile respect for the whites in South Africa."[122]

In a letter written from the rural area to which he had been banished, M. B. Yengwa, the Natal provincial secretary, wrote of the difficulties of making rural people "conscious of their oppression."[123] Therefore, he was raising "local issues" and organizing a Peasants Association, planning a farmers' cooperative, and applying for membership in the Mapumulo Traders Association.

Money

Another perennial and formidable problem was finances. The NEC estimated in December 1953 that the subscriptions of 30,000 members plus special levies and donations would yield £2,000 a year, and that the ANC could manage to get along on that amount. The annual subscription of two shillings and sixpence per year specified in the 1943 constitution had remained at that level despite the rising cost of living.[124] Each branch was obligated to pay two-thirds of each subscription, or twenty pence, to the provincial executive committee, which was then to pay half this amount, or ten pence, to the national working committee. Occasionally anonymous well-wishers donated money, as for example when £ 100 was received in early 1956, earmarked for use as the president-general thought fit.[125]

Extraordinary expenses, however, such as those involved in legal appeals and relief for persons victimized by the government could not be covered by income from subscriptions and occasional donations. The more enterprising branches held fund-raising events—concerts, dances, and other social affairs—and sold ANC souvenirs such as brooches. In December 1954, in order to raise money nationally, the national conference imposed a special levy of two shillings a month on each member for "the Banned and Deported Leaders' Fund."[126] Branches were often negligent in collecting this levy, however, and little money was passed on to the national treasurer. Extraordinary expenses were more likely than not to be met by the provinces most directly involved. In 1954, Cape Province acted alone in raising £ 224 for a judicial appeal in the cases of A. S. Gwentshe and J. M. Lengisi, who had been deported to distant rural areas.[127]

The national conference of 1954 established a new full-time post of administrative secretary in the national office in Johannesburg and stated that he was to be paid "about £20" a month,[128] a substantial increase in the approximately £35 monthly expenditure of the national office.[129] Alfred Hutchinson, a graduate of Fort Hare who had been dismissed from his teaching position when he was jailed during the Defiance Campaign, was appointed to the position.[130] But the national office could not pay him regularly, so Hutchinson felt forced to accept a temporary teaching position in an Indian school. In May 1955, Tambo wrote to Dr. Conco, who was acting as treasurer-general in place of Dr. Silas Molema, to complain of the lack of funds and to warn of "the collapse of administration."[131] Dr. Conco replied:

> You may perhaps be surprised to learn that ever since Conference last year, there have been no monies coming into this office at all. The bank balance in the national office is—NIL. Shortly after Conference in January, I sent directives re all Congress funds & subscriptions to all the Provinces & I have had no response.
>
> Conference had resolved that all subscriptions of Congress together with levies & donations must be sent to the National Head-Office quarterly. This office, I regret to say, has been completely drained of funds. Re—the administrative secretary's allowance, for which appeals were made, nothing has been forthcoming.[132]

The overall financial condition of the ANC was more complex and uncertain, however, than any report of the treasurer-general could indicate. The sums reported by various units varied from nil to thousands of pounds. In the absence of careful accounting and independent certification, which had on occasion been undertaken during Dr. Xuma's presidency, rumors were certain to crop up. Thus, one Africanist opponent of the ANC's leadership is reported to have alleged that "huge sums of money from India and China" were coming into the country.[133] That Indians contributed to the joint campaigns was suggested by the report of the National Action Committee of the ANC and SAIC in April 1953. It stated that neither the ANC nor the SAIC had directly contributed to the NAC fund for the Defiance Campaign, although such contributions were part of the original plan; but it had received £3,500 in donations for the campaign, legal fees, compensation for organizers, etc.[134] At the other end of the organizational scale was New Brighton branch in Port Elizabeth, which also dealt with relatively substantial sums. Claiming 1,618 members, it balanced its detailed financial sheet in August 1955 at £761.16.8.[135]

Branches and provinces were irregular in forwarding money, but they also provided services for national headquarters that were sometimes reported and sometimes not. Moretsele, the Transvaal president, told the NEC in November 1955 that the Transvaal paid most of the accounts of the NEC, for example, those for rent and telephone.[136] Apparently these contributions were not reported to the treasurer-general.[137] Professor Matthews at about the same time asked that the contribution of the Cape Province to the national headquarters should take into account the Cape's payment of an allowance to the national organizer and payment for his telephone calls in addition to traveling expenses for Cape members of the NEC.[138]

Despite the difficulty of maintaining a full-time administrative secretary at national headquarters, ANC leaders continued to envisage the appointment of a number of full-time organizers. During 1954 and 1955, the national organizer for both the ANC and the Congress of the People, T. E. Tshunungwa, served also as provincial secretary in the Cape. To visit branches in the western Cape, he found it necessary to "instruct" each branch to send him £4.[139] In any event, his task in a country the size of South Africa was an impossible one. Early in 1956, when charged by the national conference with the immediate task of raising £15,000, the NEC decided to employ full-time organizers at the national, provincial, and regional levels.[140] More ambitious was the plan of the Transvaal executive committee in November 1956 to appoint "as a beginning" a full-time organizer for every 800 houses in a location or 800 persons in town. He was to retain £15 of the money he collected each month. But none of these ambitious plans was realized.

The Press

A more fundamental weakness, and an even greater disappointment, was the ANC's failure for financial reasons to establish a national newspaper. Abortive campaigns, confusion, disunity, dissension could all, with some justification, be blamed upon the absence of an official national organ published in the several vernaculars as well as in English. Such an organ could have provided authoritative and timely communication from national headquarters to all levels and could have helped to build national consciousness and cohesion. The ANC had once had an official, national organ, *Abantu-Batho*. This newspaper had begun publication in 1912 but had declined and died by 1935. In the years that followed, the ANC passed frequent resolutions about the importance of re-establishing a newspaper. But it proved unable to amass the initial capital needed, to tap adequate African business experience, or to attain the assurance of a securely situated printing plant, distribution facilities, and steady income from readers and advertisers, not to mention an editorial staff unrestricted by the government. Widespread illiteracy and the necessity of publishing in several major vernaculars were further problems.

During 1954, the NEC once again formed a committee to review the matter and also considered registering the mimeographed Cape newsletter, *Inyaniso*, as a national newspaper.[141] But the plans were never implemented,[142] although *Inyaniso* was once described in 1955 as a national bulletin.[143] In 1956, a representative of Chief Lutuli visited George Houser of the American Committee on Africa in New York City and discussed financial aid and the establishment of a newspaper, but by the time of the treason arrests at the end of the year, no arrangements had yet been made.[144]

Instead of one national organ, Africans published more than a dozen different newsletters, bulletins, and journals during this period. These publications were usually mimeographed, and sometimes crudely produced; at other times, they were well edited and had printed cover sheets.[145] Some of these publications were ephemeral, issued irregularly or only a few times; in at least one case, *Modisa Umalusi*, the sponsorship and date cannot be clearly determined. *Congress Voice*, which was referred to as the official ANC bulletin, was one of the more important in 1955–1956, though apparently it was issued only a few times.

The Transvaal ANC issued *Sechaba*, devoted largely to organizational matters and notices of meetings; and the Natal ANC issued *Afrika* (probably short-lived) and *Mayibuye I-Afrika*, which began to appear in mid-1955. The Natal ANC also sponsored *Flash* jointly with the Natal Indian Congress. The activities of both organizations were publicized by *Call*, an "independent progressive monthly," which began publication in February 1955. Another pro-ANC independent journal, *Isizwe*, issued in 1955–1956 in Port Elizabeth, contained articles in Xhosa. The African Education Movement, which was concerned with the cultural clubs set up to take the place of government schools in 1955 and 1956, published a specialized journal, *African Education Movement News*. The Youth League, which had been given a special responsibility in the campaign against Bantu education, also issued a *Bantu Education Boycott Bulletin*.

The most prolific writers, and those much concerned with ideological matters, were members of the Youth League. The League's national executive committee published *Afrika,* a "journal of uncompromising African youth." The Youth League in the Transvaal issued *African Lodestar* during 1950–1956 as its official organ and also, for a short time, *Youth League Bulletin.* The left-wing orientation of *Lodestar* was attacked by *The Africanist,* the journal of the Youth League in Orlando, Johannesburg (see Document 12). Another publication of a Youth League branch was *Pioneer,* issued in Jabavu outside Johannesburg. The variety of these publications illustrated the diversity of opinion within the ANC. Both political and trade-union news was circulated nationally after April 1955 in *Workers' Unity,* published by SACTU in Zulu, Sesotho, Shangaan, Xhosa, Afrikaans, and English.[146]

News of African political activity appeared in those white-owned newspapers which had African staffs and were aimed at nonwhite readers: the *Bantu World* (as of January 1, 1956, *The World*), published by the white-financed and controlled Bantu Press twice a week in Johannesburg under the editorship first of R. V. Selope Thema and then of J. Nhlapo; *Golden City Post* (later, *Post*), a popular weekly; and *Imvo Zabantsundu* and *Ilanga lase Natal,* two African-founded newspapers that were taken over by the Bantu Press. (*Inkundla ya Bantu* was the only African-owned paper when it ceased publication for financial reasons in 1951. Its last editor was Jordan Ngubane.) *Drum*, a monthly magazine with a white editor and some African staff members, also reported on African politics.

Although they sometimes agreed with the ANC's policy, these publications were often critical of the ANC's campaigns. An especially influential critic was the *Bantu World,* which had a national circulation and regularly attacked left-wing influence in the ANC after the Defiance Campaign. Ngubane, who was a member of the Liberal Party, expressed similar criticism in his "African Viewpoint" page in *Indian Opinion.* Its editor until 1956 was Manilal Gandhi.

The vacuum caused by the lack of an official national organ for the ANC was partly filled by a left-wing weekly newspaper which appeared without a break under a succession of names: *Guardian,* which was published from 1937 until it was banned in 1952 under the Suppression of Communism Act; *Clarion,* the *People's World,* and *Advance* (the last-named summarily banned in October 1954 without any grounds being given or charge being brought); and *New Age,* which was not finally banned until November 30, 1962.[147] At the time *Advance* was banned, its directors were Sam Kahn and Fred Carneson, and its editor, Brian Bunting; all were white and all had been members of the Communist Party before it was dissolved. The head office of the paper was in Cape Town; branch offices were in Johannesburg, Durban, and Port Elizabeth. According to its publisher, *New Age* was financed partly from sales and advertising but mainly from donations, with very little financial assistance "from any of the mass organisations themselves." In 1955, its circulation fluctuated between 20,000 and 29,000 copies a week, with an average of about 25,000. Bulk distribution was through the South African Railways and the General Post Office.

New Age and its predecessors publicized the policies of the ANC and its allies but remained independent of their control. It also emphasized support for the Soviet bloc. Its detailed coverage of African campaigns was of great value to the ANC, but its white, left-wing sponsorship and apparent presumption to speak for the Congress movement disturbed some older Congress leaders and became a source of dissension within the ANC. Nevertheless, ANC leaders in the Transvaal and younger leaders in the Cape, in particular, urged members to read *New Age*. A typical exhortation appeared in a circular "to all Cape A.N.C. branches, officers and members" early in 1955: "Branches must encourage their members to read, sell and support the people's paper '*NEW AGE*', which is the only newspaper in South Africa today that supports the Congress and its decisions without reservations."[148]

Many less widely circulated left-wing publications supported the ANC, including *Liberation, Fighting Talk, Workers' Unity* (a SACTU bulletin), *Peace Council Bulletin* (an organ of the South African Peace Council), and *Counter-Attack,* the bulletin of the Congress of Democrats. Older ANC leaders like Lutuli indicated in their testimony at the Treason Trial that they did not see these publications often, were not very interested in them, and had little knowledge of their editors or sponsors. Among younger ANC activists, however, some of these publications found a wider audience.

Liberation: A Journal of Democratic Discussion was a theoretical journal that began publication in February 1953 with Dan Tloome, an African former member of the Communist Party, listed as publisher. Appearing ten or fewer times a year, *Liberation* included Mandela, Sisulu, and Duma Nokwe, as well as Tloome, among its periodic contributors. *Fighting Talk* was for many years the organ of the radical Springbok Legion of ex-servicemen. After the Legion expired about 1953, an independent committee produced *Fighting Talk,* under the editorship of first Lionel Bernstein and then, beginning in April 1955, Ruth First. It became a livelier, more popular publication than *Liberation,* emphasizing news commentary more than theoretical discussion. It too had African contributors, but most of its writers were whites.

CIVIL RIGHTS AND LIBERTIES

In discussing "general civil rights," the 1954 report of the government's Tomlinson Commission for the Socio-Economic Development of the Bantu Areas presented "the following facts":

. . . nobody . . . is exposed to arbitrary arrest, detention or banishment . . . . the Bantu, like other population groups, have the full right to form either amongst themselves or together with members of other population groups . . . organisations of a political nature (for example the A.N.C., the Liberal Party, etc.) . . . .[149]

This statement was misleading in two respects: in overstating the extent of the rights held by all South Africans and in suggesting that Africans had no special civil and political disabilities.

Long-standing policies designed to prevent any radical disruption of the status quo in race relations affected the freedoms of all South Africans. Freedom of speech, assembly, press, and movement had long been subject to controls under legislation enacted before the Nationalists came to power in 1948; amendments and new legislation enacted during the following decade not only tightened the web of control over Africans but also increasingly restricted the rights of whites and other non-Africans. Administrative discretion was further enlarged and the role of the courts in protecting civil liberties was steadily diminished. The most notable of the legislative acts that could be used to curtail the rights of all radical opponents of white supremacy were the Riotous Assemblies Act of 1930 as amended in 1956 and the Suppression of Communism Act of 1950.

Meanwhile, Africans were subjected to severe restrictions not imposed on Coloureds and Indians. Moreover, legislation and regulations that limited the rule of law for Africans and controlled their movement were made more repressive during the 1953–1956 period. Africans alone were directly affected by the Urban Areas Act of 1923 and its amendments, particularly that of 1956, by legislation in 1953 regarding labor grievances and strikes, and by the withdrawal of injunctive relief and the ending of the special status (described below) of Africans in Cape Province.

The enactments noted above were only a few in the arsenal of overlapping laws. A review of legislation and executive powers can be misleading because the statute book sometimes looked worse than practice revealed. On the other hand, legislation did not adequately indicate the subtle changes in the political atmosphere in the mid–1950s resulting from overt surveillance, harassment, and intimidation by the Special Branch, that is, the "political police." Their attentions in 1953–1956 were directed primarily at the ANC and its white and Indian allies. But in 1958, two white authorities on civil liberties, Edgar H. Brookes and J. B. Macaulay, saw their still wider impact and concluded: "The battle for the rights of white South Africans has largely been lost in advance by the lack of care for the rights of black South Africans."[150] Restrictions on African rights of movement, speech, assembly, press, and due process had become formidable indeed by the late 1950s.

Movement

"Influx control" had long restricted African freedom of movement. Africans lived (and continue to live today) under detailed regulations that govern entry into and residence within urban areas and require that they register at a labor bureau and report to it. For example, no African in the mid–1950s could or can today legally remain in an urban area for more than 72 hours without official permission or unless he met certain conditions of continuous residence, employment, or relationship to a qualified African. An African who was considered to be "idle and disorderly" could be ordered to leave an urban area or be committed to a farm or work colony. Before 1956, such action could be taken only after complaint, notice, and due inquiry before a judicial officer and could be appealed to the Supreme Court. These procedures were omitted from legislation in 1956 that empowered an urban local authority to banish an African if it believed his presence was "detrimental to the maintenance of peace and good order" in the area. This grant of power was justified by the minister of native affairs as necessary to enable local authorities to cope with "agitators."[151]

The central government had authority under the Native Administration Act of 1927 to banish a tribe or an individual African from one place to another if it was deemed expedient in the general public interest. A 1952 amendment provided that if the tribe or individual refused to move, the banishment could be effected summarily, without a trial. The chairman and the secretary of the East London branch of the ANC, A.S. Gwentshe and J. M. Lengisi, were deported under this law in 1954 to a farm in the eastern Transvaal (Document 8).[152] A 1956 amendment eliminated the necessity of giving notice or a grace period before deportation. The minister of justice was required to furnish reasons for the action but only to the degree that the information he provided was not deemed detrimental to the public interest.[153]

The most commonly used statutory authorities for banning individuals of any race from a defined area were the Suppression of Communism Act of 1950 and the Riotous Assemblies Act of 1956. Both acts enabled the minister of justice to act arbitrarily, inasmuch as there was virtually no judicial appeal against his judgment. Although the minister could be challenged if it were proven that he had acted in bad faith (a 1954 amendment to the former act obliged the minister to supply the reasons for his orders), such a challenge could hardly be effective in practice because, in banning cases as well as in deportation cases, he was allowed to withhold information on which he based his judgment if he deemed its release detrimental to the public interest. Various appeals to the courts probed for statutory interpretations that would limit administrative discretion but these efforts either proved fruitless or exposed loopholes that were soon closed by amendment.

Under the Suppression of Communism Act, the minister of justice could act when he was satisfied that a person was encouraging or likely to encourage "the achievement of any of the objects of communism." "Communism" in the act included any doctrine "which aims at bringing about any political, industrial, social or economic change within the Union by the promotion of disturbance or disorder, by unlawful acts or omission or by the threat of such acts or omissions." The Riotous Assemblies Act, enacted in its first form in 1930, authorized the minister to act whenever he was satisfied that a person was promoting feelings of hostility between whites and nonwhites.

Control of movement by South Africans was extended in 1955 to travel outside South Africa (except to Basutoland, Bechuanaland, and Swaziland). The Departure from the Union Regulation Act required the possession of a passport or, for holders of British passports, a permit in order to travel. The law gave the minister complete discretion and provided no redress if an application were refused. Although professedly an anti-Communist measure, the act was not limited to persons "named" under the Suppression of Communism Act; in fact, genuinely anti-Communist critics of the government have been refused passports.[154]

Speech, Assembly, and the Press

Freedom of speech was limited by the Native Administration Act of 1927 in cases in which words were used "with intent to promote . . . hostility between Natives and Europeans." The Criminal Law Amendment Act of 1953, enacted after the Defiance Campaign, provided severe punishment for anyone who used words calculated to cause someone to commit any offense as a means of protest. Incitement to civil disobedience was also punishable under the Suppression of Communism Act or the Riotous Assemblies Act. The latter act penalized anyone who used words whose probable consequence would be public violence. It also was applicable to strike situations when there was "intimidation or annoyance of persons, their relatives or dependants in relation to their employment."[155]

Restrictions on freedom of assembly also served to restrict speech. The government officially prohibited public meetings of more than ten Africans, unless they were granted a permit or were in an exempt category, in the reserves in 1928 and in African urban areas in September 1953.[156] The exempt category included various social and recreational meetings and those concerned with African representation in Parliament or the Cape Provincial Council. Permits, which limited meetings to the announced agenda, were often not applied for, and the prohibition on meetings often was not enforced.[157] In 1956 amended regulations prohibited meetings of more than ten Africans, unless exempted or permitted, in all of Port Elizabeth and Humansdorp. Similar prohibitions were imposed in the same year by the Native Resettlement Board in locations to which Africans had moved from the Western Areas of Johannesburg.[158]

Under the Urban Areas Act of 1945 urban local authorities were empowered to regulate African assemblies, in private as well as public places. Professor Z. K. Matthews advised the National Executive Committee of the ANC on November 27, 1954 that local authorities could regulate but not prohibit meetings; therefore, he urged the sponsors of meetings, after supplying the agenda, to make repeated applications if there were repeated refusals and then the matter could be taken to court.[159]

More comprehensive, because they were not limited to Africans, were the restrictions on assembly imposed under the Suppression of Communism Act and the Riotous Assemblies legislation. Under the initial Riotous Assemblies Act of 1914, a magistrate with ministerial approval could prohibit a meeting that he believed posed a serious danger to the public peace. The act of 1930 set forth as a criterion the engendering of hostility between whites and nonwhites, as noted earlier, and authorized the prohibition of a person's attendance at "any public gathering in any public place" within any area for a specified time.[160] This legislation was the authority for a ministerial ban of twenty days on gatherings in Johannesburg and Roodepoort issued on February 8, 1955, the eve of the first removal of Africans from Sophiatown. Unless permitted by the police, *all* gatherings of more than twelve persons of any race were banned, including gatherings for purposes of religion, entertainment, or sport, whether held indoors or outdoors.[161]

Such wholesale bans were never applied under the Suppression of Communism Act, but this act too could be used both for prohibiting a gathering and prohibiting a person from attending a particular gathering or all gatherings. Furthermore, a person who was deemed a Communist by the minister could be ordered to resign from his office and membership in any specified organization and to resign from any legislative body.

Freedom of the press could be curtailed in the reserves under the 1927 act or, if the government considered that a publication was calculated to engender hostility, under the Riotous Assemblies Act of 1930. In the latter case, a court could set aside a ban if the probability of hostility was disproved. After 1952, however, the courts could not lift a ban imposed under the authority of the Suppression of Communism Act. The left-wing *Guardian* was banned under this act in May 1952, and *Advance,* its successor, was banned on October 22, 1954 (to be succeeded by *New Age,* which was banned in April 1960 under the Public Safety Act). Publications could also, of course, be banned during any emergency called under the Public Safety Act.[162]

Prior restraint on publication, i.e., censorship, was not (and still is not) authorized, but long-standing law on the importation of goods, consolidated and tightened in the Customs Act of 1955, provided for prohibiting the importation of "objectional" publications. In practice, this meant political censorship of material deemed fundamentally subversive of white supremacy.[163]

Due Process

Many of the statutes noted above provided wide discretion for search and seizure by the police; the Criminal Procedure Act of 1955 further widened and consolidated authority for the police in this regard. Formerly, police entry to a home or other premises was permitted only with a search warrant issued with the concurrence of a judicial authority that reasonable grounds existed for suspecting that there were objects upon a person or premises that were directly related to an offense or planned offense. The warrant authorized a search only for such objects. Search without a warrant was permissible only if a police officer of the rank of sergeant or above had reasonable grounds for believing that delay would defeat the object of the search.[164] Under the new criminal code introduced in 1955, any policeman could make this judgment. More important, search and seizure were now permitted without warrant if any policeman believed that internal security was "likely to be endangered by or in consequence of any meeting." No longer was inquiry tied to an offense that was likely to be committed or was being prepared, nor was seizure similarly limited. Thus, the statutes could be invoked "simply to allow the police to be present at a private meeting in order to listen or put a stop to discussion lawful in itself but deemed likely to endanger the internal security of the Union."

Special note should be made at this point of a 1956 amendment to the Native Administration Act, extending the Natal Native Code to Cape Province. The origin of the Code lay in an 1849 proclamation in Natal by which the lieutenant-governor had assumed the powers of "Supreme Chief" over all Africans, presumably those of the despotic chiefs Tshaka and Dingaan. But such powers were not typical of "the Bantu tradition" which, as Brookes and Macaulay point out, was "not one of despotism." In their words: "It is as though a liberal-minded Asian conqueror of Europe had proclaimed himself 'Fuehrer' on the supposition that Hitler was the normal type of European ruler." The conception of "supreme chief" was extended to the Transvaal before Union and to the Orange Free State some time after Union, but it had not previously been considered applicable to Cape Province where thousands of Africans were enfranchised, tribalism had been actively discouraged since late in the nineteenth century, and Africans were educationally the most advanced in the country.

Extension of the Code to Cape Province in 1956 meant that without permitting any recourse to habeas corpus, the governor-general could authorize the summary arrest and detention of an African for up to three months if he was considered dangerous to the public peace, or an African could be summarily fined or imprisoned if he disobeyed an administrative order. The 1956 amendment was not of importance in controlling political radicals; in practice it was applied to Africans in the reserves. But it had a symbolic importance in indicating the increasingly authoritarian direction of governmental policy.

Another step excluding Africans from the rule of law was legislation in 1956 that prohibited Africans from obtaining an interdict, or injunction, which could suspend a removal order until the order was judicially reviewed. This revision was needed, said the minister of native affairs, to prevent abuse of legal procedure "as a demonstration."[165]

TRADE-UNION RIGHTS AND
THE SOUTH AFRICAN CONGRESS OF TRADE UNIONS

This review of legislative policy affecting Africans during 1953–1956 requires a brief description of another complex and vital area: the rights of Africans as workers. For decades Africans had been the victims of white trade-union pressures, apprenticeship regulations, and varied customary and legislative color bars. African trade unions could not register under the law and therefore could not make use of the official machinery of industrial conciliation to arrive at enforceable agreements on labor standards. Although these unions were not illegal, they led a precarious existence. Many were informally recognized by employers and, before 1948, by government departments. At the same time, Africans had long been subject to criminal penalties for breaking labor contracts. In 1942, War Measure 145 defined existing restrictions in detail and made "all strikes of all African workers in all circumstances illegal," to use the words of Margaret Ballinger.[166]

Remarkable efforts to organize African unions in the face of almost crippling restrictions were made in the late 1930s and during the war, efforts in which white and African Communists played a leading role. Meanwhile, right-wing Nationalists were attempting to split racially mixed unions (that is, unions with Coloured and Indian members) and to create separate all-white unions led by Afrikaner Nationalists. After 1948, Nationalists sought to achieve these aims through legislation. In 1953 the Native Labour (Settlement of Disputes) Act superseded the 1942 War Measure and again prohibited African strikes under still harsher penalties; the act also imposed stiff penalties on anyone who incited, expressed sympathy with, or supported a strike by Africans. The act established cumbersome, white-dominated—and, in practice, ineffectual—machinery for dealing with African labor grievances.

Earlier, a Nationalist-appointed commission had recommended that African unions be recognized and that their right to strike not be completely excluded. But African unions should be treated separately, it said, and should not be allowed to act politically. The commission expressed itself as "satisfied that a sufficient number of native workers in commerce and secondary industry know enough about trade unionism to make the recognition of native trade unions a practical proposition, provided suitable measures for the guidance and control of those unions are introduced."[167] Nevertheless, Ben Schoeman, the minister of labour, declared,

> I think the hon. members must realize that if we give that incentive to natives to organize—and we must bear in mind that they are primitive and illiterate natives who have not the faintest conception of the responsibilities of trade unionism, that they are people who cannot even read the constitution of a trade union, who know nothing about negotiation or the industrial set-up of South Africa—if we give them that incentive to organize and they should become well organised—and again bearing in mind that there are almost 1,000,000 native workers in industry and commerce today—that they can use their trade unions as a political weapon and they can create chaos in South Africa at any given time. I think that we should probably be committing race suicide if we gave them that incentive.[168]

The new law did not make African unions illegal, but Schoeman expected that all "would probably die a natural death."[169] A year later he urged that employers "must on no account discuss or negotiate with native political organizations such as the African National Congress."[170]

Not until 1956 did Parliament complete passage of an extensively amended Industrial Conciliation Act. The act prohibited the future registration of racially mixed unions and facilitated the splitting of existing unions along racial lines and, for those unions which did not split, insisted on racially separate branches and all-white executive committees. The act also empowered the minister to reserve jobs by race, without any effective judicial appeal.

Racial job reservation was a by-product of white fears that some working-class whites might fall below working-class Africans in the economic scale. White interests were not so obviously served, however, by the new policies regarding trade unions. The combined working-class strength of whites and nonwhites was diluted as a result of racial fragmentation and by the divisiveness introduced by Afrikaner Nationalists whose primary loyalty was to Afrikanerdom rather than to shared interests with fellow workers. Regarding the rights of white trade unionists, the conclusion of Brookes and Macaulay quoted earlier is equally applicable: "The battle for the rights of white South Africans has largely been lost in advance by the lack of care for the rights of black South Africans."

One consequence of the racial splitting of the South African trade union movement was the formation of the South African Congress of Trade Unions in Johannesburg on March 5–6, 1955. SACTU was not formed at the instigation of leaders of the Congress alliance, nor was it intended to be primarily a political organ. To understand its formation, it is necessary to review the relations of African unions with other unions during the preceding decade.[171]

Before the 1950s most unions were affiliated with the Trades and Labour Council (TLC). Among these unions were unions for whites only, racially mixed unions of whites, Coloureds, and Indians, and unions composed of both Coloureds and Indians. Unions of whites, Coloureds, and Indians were registered and had the many advantages provided by South Africa's system of industrial conciliation. African men, although not legally "employees," sometimes became members of racially mixed, registered unions. According to official statistics, 6,232 African men were members of such unions in 1953. Because it was technically illegal, such membership declined to 696 by 1956 and thereafter came to an end. The TLC also accepted the affiliation of African unions, which could not be registered, although probably not more than seven (in 1945) became affiliated. Other African unions were sometimes assisted informally by officers of the newer industrial unions, which were less racially prejudiced than the older craft unions of miners and artisans. Beginning in 1947, however, unions withdrew on several occasions from the TLC and formed new coordinating bodies which excluded racially mixed or African unions.

At about this time, most of the African workers who were organized belonged to unions that were affiliated with the Council of Non-European Trade Unions. In 1945, this Council claimed 119 unions representing 158,000 members, mostly Africans but including some Coloureds. African union leaders and their white allies, handicapped by organizational and financial difficulties, were unable to maintain this level of membership, and membership declined after 1945. The Nationalist government raised new obstacles. It fanned the fears of rank-and-file white workers and described as Communist-inspired those who urged equality of treatment for all workers. In 1953, acting under the Suppression of Communism Act, the government ordered some fifty of the most experienced union leaders, including leaders who had not been Communists, to resign from their positions and to stay away from gatherings.

In 1954 the Industrial Conciliation Bill (not enacted until 1956) provided for the racial splitting of trade unions. Hoping, but failing, to regain its old strength in order to oppose the bill, the TLC dissolved itself in 1954 and was succeeded by a new coordinating body, the South African Trade Union

Council, which excluded African unions and racially mixed unions with African members. The few African unions affiliated with the TLC and some of the racially mixed unions that had been affiliated with the TLC but opposed the new policy then joined with the Transvaal Council of Non-European Trade Unions to form SACTU, in which all unions would be equal members.

The founding unions included eight African unions, three Coloured or racially mixed unions, and a small union of white laundry workers. Other African unions—existing, revived, or newly formed—soon joined, as did additional Coloured unions. Accurate membership figures are difficult to determine. An Institute of Race Relations report estimated that SACTU represented about 30,000 workers at the end of 1955. *New Age* reported that delegates from 34 unions with 42,000 members attended the inaugural conference. Five all-African unions which did not join SACTU were led by Africans who distrusted the leadership of the new nonracial body and left the Council of Non-European Trade Unions when it became part of SACTU.[172] These unions were to become affiliated with FOFATUSA (the Federation of Free African Trade Unions of South Africa) in 1959, under leaders who joined the Pan Africanist Congress (see below, pages 323–324.).

SACTU's officers were Pieter Beyleveld, who was also the first head of COD, as president; Leslie Massina, formerly the secretary of the Transvaal Council, as general secretary; two Africans as vice-presidents; and a white treasurer, Leon Levy.[173] In the troubled years that followed, SACTU unions—some of them registered and therefore having access to employers through legal channels, others dealing unofficially with employers when they could—managed despite chronic obstacles to pursue unionist goals with a high level of proficiency.[174] But unlike most unions, which traditionally maintain that they should avoid politics, SACTU accepted political involvement as inescapable. At its inaugural conference, it welcomed the Congress of the People and endorsed the submission of workers' demands for inclusion in the Freedom Charter.

THE CONGRESS OF THE PEOPLE AND THE FREEDOM CHARTER

In mid-1953, in the small town of Alice in the eastern Cape, Professor Z. K. Matthews led a discussion on campaigns that would "capture the imagination" of the people. The meeting at his home included Frieda Matthews, his sons, Dr. James Njongwe, until recently the acting president of the provincial ANC, and Robert Matji, Cape secretary. As Professor Matthews has recalled, the group was intrigued at first by the idea of organizing Africans for a mass "going-away-from-the-towns." That is,

Africans would go to work one morning but leave at mid-day and walk from the towns to the reserves, thus symbolically carrying out what was presumably white policy. But this notion was impractical, and the group then agreed to aim for a series of public meetings to which everyone, even Afrikaner Nationalists, would be invited. These meetings were to culminate in a national convention and the adoption of a manifesto. Thus originated the idea of a Congress of the People and a Freedom Charter.[175] In August 1953, as noted earlier, Professor Matthews suggested the organization of such a campaign in an address to the Cape provincial conference. The conference adopted the proposal, as did the ANC's national conference in December 1953.

The calling of a new national convention that would be more representative than the convention of 1908–1909, which led to the formation of the Union of South Africa, had been suggested from time to time both by Africans and by sympathetic whites. As conceived by Professor Matthews, the convention would be nonracial, although attendance by whites might be in only token numbers, and therefore more representative than were the "all-in" African conventions of 1935–1937. And unlike the ANC's "Africans' Claims" of 1943, a document formulated by intellectuals and leaders at the invitation of Dr. Xuma, then president-general, the Freedom Charter was to reflect the demands, or visions, of a future society, filtered upwards from the mass of common men and women. The underlying aim of the Congress of the People, as Professor Matthews said later, was "the instilling of political consciousness into the people and the encouraging of political activity."[176]

The prosecution in the Treason Trial was to maintain, in contrast, that the campaign had a subversive aim: the establishment of alternative organs of government. This interpretation was based on a memorandum of Professor Matthews proposing that the sponsoring organizations prepare a common voters' roll of everyone over twenty-one, that the country be divided into electoral districts, and that a general election for representatives to the Congress of the People be held on a certain date.[177]

In explaining the idea of the Congress, Sisulu and other speakers did, indeed, intimate that alternative organs of government were being created. Joe Matthews, writing to his father on January 13, 1954, referred to one such "dangerous statement" by Sisulu in Port Elizabeth and warned, "Now quite clearly no government can tolerate that sort of thing. A brochure must be prepared . . . which will pin down the authorities to the written document. . . . I'm scared of these references to our government and our parliament." When the prosecution read this passage in the Treason Trial, Professor Matthews saw nothing incriminating in it but found it an "entirely salutary warning."[178] Because of the danger of misunderstanding and the practical impossibility of organizing and conducting elections, the scheme was dropped at the meeting of sponsoring organizations held on March 21, 1954. What took its place was a loose form of representation that, in effect, allowed any group or unit of any size to elect or designate one or more delegates.

The Treason Trial prosecution found subversion also in some of the language in Professor Matthews' memorandum for the March 1954 meeting, particularly his reference to "freedom for all in our lifetime" (which was said to imply advocacy of violence because only violence could reasonably be expected to achieve this end), and his conception of the Freedom Charter as an instrument that would "galvanize the people of South Africa into action and make them go over on the offensive against the reactionary forces. . . ."[179] Later, reflecting on the weight placed by the prosecution on words such as these, Professor Matthews wrote:

> The only explanation I can find for this alarm over such innocent metaphorical expression is that owing to our bilingualism in South Africa, we are becoming less and less able to follow idiomatic English.[180]

The government, searching for evidence of treason and apparently giving rope to the Congress leaders, did not ban the holding of the Congress of the People on June 25–26, 1955, or the many local and provincial meetings preparatory to it. On the other hand, it did impede the planning through intimidation, harassment, and the banning of individuals. To these obstacles were added the ANC's chronic difficulties of organization, money, and publicity. In early 1955, ANC leaders were preoccupied with the Western Areas and Bantu education campaigns but sought to link them to the campaign for the Congress of the People. Among other difficulties, they encountered suspicion that a new organization was being formed and that non-Africans were leading it. T. E. Tshunungwa, the ANC's national organizer, reported after his visit in January 1955 to the western Cape that "extreme . . . confusion" about cooperation with the ANC's allies was caused when Africans found "the C.O.D. men taking a lead in the A.N.C. meetings. . . . A politically raw African who has been so much oppressed, exploited, and victimized by the European sees red whenever a white face appears."[181]

The COD and the SAIC initially had little enthusiasm for Professor Matthew's proposal, but once they became committed to it, they expended much energy and skill in promoting the campaign. Meanwhile, Tshunungwa expressed a familiar complaint to the ANC's National Executive Committee on May 21, 1955: he had no money, he had been ordered out of Queenstown, and he had been unable to organize for the Congress of the People since his visit to the western Cape.[182] The National Action Council, however, which was composed of eight members from each of the four sponsoring organizations, had been distributing large quantities of circulars and the printed "Call" to the Congress, which was issued in many languages (Document 9). The Council also widely distributed crudely Marxist "lectures" on South Africa without clearance by senior leaders of the ANC or the SAIC. These lectures were given prominent attention by the prosecution in the Treason Trial.[183] As June approached, local ANC branches, regional committees of the National Action Council, and *New Age* all joined in publicizing the forthcoming rally.

In looking back upon the Congress of the People, Chief Lutuli later claimed that "nothing in the history of the liberatory movement in South Africa quite caught the popular imagination as this did, not even the Defiance Campaign."[184] The unsystematic process of calling meetings and electing (or soliciting or designating) delegates began in mid-April. The ANC's national secretariat appealed for the widest possible representation of all rural and urban centers, including areas having no branch of the ANC and each of the twenty-six districts of the Transkei. "Areas which are not able to send delegates," Tambo advised in a circular of March 31 to provincial secretaries, "should elect people who are near to the place where the Congress is to be held."

The most distinctive tactic in preparation for June 25–26 was the effort to collect grievances, demands, and wishes as a basis for drafting the Freedom Charter (Document 11). In calling for expression from the grass roots, the leadership had various aims in mind, which may have accounted later for the Charter's mixture of both detailed and poetic provisions. The leaders sought to link the Congress with immediate and concrete grievances and then to link these grievances to what Professor Matthews (anticipating Martin Luther King) called a "dream" of the future (Document 8). A press release of the National Action Council on April 1, 1955, signed by Tambo, stated that the Freedom Charter was "being compiled from thousands of written statements . . . gathered at thousands of small meetings." On the eve of the Congress, *New Age* stated that "for months now the demands have been flooding in to C.O.P. headquarters, on sheets torn from school exercise books, on little dog-eared scraps of paper, on slips torn from C.O.P. leaflets."[185]

A number of ANC leaders, in reminiscing about the period, have described their experiences in soliciting grievances and demands at street meetings, often receiving unexpected replies, and their surprise at the number of written suggestions that were submitted, especially from the eastern Cape and Natal.[186] Talk of written demands "flooding" headquarters may be somewhat exaggerated, however, since the apparently common practice was to have one person record the suggestions made at a meeting or to collect written suggestions locally and summarize them in a memorandum for transmittal to a regional committee of the National Action Council. In any event, because no statistics were kept on the number of participants or demands, it is impossible to make any quantitative assessment of the process.

In the hurried preparation for the meeting of the Congress of the People, the Freedom Charter itself was drafted by a small committee of the National Action Council and reviewed by the ANC's National Executive Committee on the eve of the Congress. The resulting document was thus not the end-product of a protracted process of discussion at all levels of the ANC like that which resulted in adoption of the Programme of Action in 1949. The drafting committee apparently acted after subcommittees had dealt with the various categories of subjects into which suggestions fell. One published description of the Charter as "a vague, haphazard document assembled from all kinds of contradictory suggestions from Congress branches" is similar to the observation of an ANC leader who found the Charter, which he supported, a "hodge-podge," obviously the work of a number of persons.[187]

On June 22, the ANC's working committee met to discuss the Charter.[188] Sisulu, Mandela, and Joe Matthews were among the banned members who saw the draft in the days before the Congress met. Some of the draft's formulations were questioned, but time was short and, in any event, thousands of copies of the Charter had already been reproduced. On June 25, the following members of the ANC's National Executive Committee reviewed the draft: Dr. Wilson Z. Conco (who had just arrived as Lutuli's representative at the Congress), Dr. Arthur Letele, Robert Resha, P. Q. Vundla, Leslie Massina, T. E. Tshunungwa, and E. P. Moretsele; Caleb Mayekiso attended as an observer. The committee resolved to "work harder for the achievements of the demands as contained in the Freedom Charter. . . ."[189]

Even though Lutuli's recovery from his illness was slow and his ban made communication difficult and attendance at the Congress impossible, it is noteworthy that he did not see the charter in draft form.[190] Nor did Professor Matthews see the draft, although one non-African member of the National Action Council has claimed otherwise. Matthews too was absent from the Congress, because he was busily engaged in the process of readmitting students expelled from Fort Hare following a controversial series of events at the college.[191]

The Congress itself was remarkable for its size, the preparations made for housing and feeding delegates, and the discipline of those present in the face of police intimidation. Many delegates traveled long distances, usually by bus or truck. In some cases they were stopped en route for a check of their papers or a check of the vehicles, and about two hundred were prevented from reaching Johannesburg.[192] Figures are not available on the numbers who traveled from various centers or on the groups they represented. At the Congress itself, it was announced that 2,884 delegates were present, including 320 Indians, 230 Coloureds, and 112 whites (Document 10). "Freedom volunteers," wearing armbands with the ANC's black, green, and yellow colors, met delegates, arranged for their accommodation, and served as ushers and aides at the meeting.

The Congress was a colorful and spirited two-day mass meeting in clear weather on a private athletic field at Kliptown, some fifteen miles from Johannesburg. "Perhaps it was the first really representative gathering in the Union's history," Lutuli has written.[193] Although it was not constituted by any electoral process that would have made it formally representative of the broad scope of South African society, the Congress reflected great diversity.

As described by a British journalist, those present included:

large African grandmothers, wearing Congress skirts, Congress blouses or Congress doeks on their heads, traipsing around with bagging suitcases; young Indian wives, with glistening saris and shawls embroidered with Congress colours; grey old African men, with walking sticks and Congress arm-bands; young city workers from Johannesburg, with broad hats, bright American ties and narrow trousers; smooth Indian lawyers and businessmen, moving confidently among the crowd in well-cut suits; and a backcloth of anonymous African faces, listening impassively to the hours of speeches that are the staple of every Congress meeting.[194]

Whites from the COD, Indians and Coloureds prominent in staging the Congress were in key positions on the platform, behind which stood a large replica of a four-spoked wheel representing the four racial groups in the Congress movement or alliance. Representatives of the Liberal Party and the Labour Party attended as observers. The decision of the Liberal Party not to join in sponsoring the Congress was to damage its reputation among some members of the ANC who concluded that Liberals were reluctant to accept African leadership.[195] The Liberals, however, believed they saw signs of Communist predominance in the role of the COD, the presence of a "Peace Pavilion," left-wing banners and leaflets, and messages from Chou en-Lai and other Communist leaders. Yet, as Fatima Meer, the Indian sociologist and political activist, has observed, a multiplicity of political influences—not only Communist slogans and trappings—were in evidence. Also present at the fringes, though not as delegates, were Potlako Leballo and other Africanists selling a special edition of *The Africanist.*[196]

White and African police and the plainclothesmen of the Special Branch were present from the beginning, photographing all white persons who entered the wired enclosure and taking notes on everything that was said (Document 10).[197] Once the opening messages and announcements had been made and an award presented to Father Trevor Huddleston, the outspoken Anglican priest of Sophiatown, and (in absentia) Chief Lutuli and Dr. Dadoo, each section of the Freedom Charter was read and discussed by various speakers. The crowd adopted each section by acclamation, with a show of hands and shouts of "Afrika!" Then, with two sections remaining to be approved, in mid-afternoon of the second day, the meeting was dramatically interrupted. According to *New Age:*

> The conference was in its final stages this afternoon when at about 3:30 p.m. a large force of police was suddenly rushed to the area in trucks, and then stormed the delegates' enclosure.
>
> The first warning the crowd had of this was an announcement from the platform by Mr. P. Beyleveld: "Armed police are approaching. We don't know what they want. Please keep your seats." Then he asked the crowd to rise and sing the anthem "Inkosi Sikaleli."
>
> As the voices rose, about 15 Special Branch detectives, escorted by a group of police armed with sten guns, mounted the platform. Every document in sight was removed, cameras and rolls of films confiscated, and all those on the platform were searched. It was announced that treason was suspected, and the names and addresses of every delegate were to be taken.
>
> Mounted police sealed off the area backed by the railway line, and constables armed with rifles, which they held at fixed position as they moved through the crowd, threw a double cordon round the conference square, taking up position a few feet apart from one another to prevent anyone entering or leaving the conference site.
>
> The police came well prepared. Hurricane lamps were standing by so Special Staff men could continue laboriously to record names and addresses as darkness fell; and separate tables were set up for Europeans and Non-Europeans. As each delegate left the conference site, he was interrogated at the police table and searched. Documents found on him were retained and sealed in an envelope with his name. Every single European delegate was photographed by a flash camera. . . . The questioning and search went on until about 8 p.m.
>
> The police also confiscated all monies lying on tables collected from literature sales, and carted away huge quantities of literature.[198]

The crowd has been described as laughing and singing, and "teetering on the very edge of violence," but the meeting continued and ended without violence.[199] Manilal Gandhi has described the police, who were standing with Sten guns below the platform while persons above were being searched, as having "a wild look on their faces. Some jeered at the delegates and while the delegates were shouting 'Africa' with their thumbs up some of the police were responding with their thumbs down."[200]

THE FREEDOM CHARTER AND THE ANC

Although it had been adopted by the Congress of the People, the Freedom Charter could become official ANC policy only after adoption by an ANC national conference. The Charter was finally adopted without any revision at a special ANC conference on March 31–April 1, 1956. Before reviewing the events of the intervening nine months, we shall first consider the Charter itself.

The Charter, Reactions, and Dissension

The Freedom Charter was essentially a restatement of long-standing aims. It was consistent with the 1943 Bill of Rights, which was part of "Africans' Claims," with one exception: if the ANC accepted the Charter, it would for the first time in its history be endorsing a nationalization plank. The Charter stated that "the mineral wealth beneath the soil, the banks and monopoly industry shall be transferred to the ownership of the people as a whole . . . ." (Some ANC leaders have maintained that the principle of nationalization had been implied by the call in the Bill of Rights for "a fair redistribution of the land.") Adoption by an ANC conference of the nationalization plank alone at that time would have been doubtful. Potentially more disruptive, however, was the preamble's statement "that South Africa belongs to all who live in it, black and white . . . ." For the Africanists, this phrase epitomized the ANC's formal commitment to a policy of multiracialism rather than "pure" African nationalism, a policy Africanists were to continue to oppose with mounting vehemence.

The Charter envisaged a bourgeois democracy based on natural rights liberalism, and formal equality of opportunity for individuals. It also had points of similarity with the People's Charter of the English Chartist movement of the 1830s and 1840s. That the formulations of the Freedom Charter were not Marxist was convincingly demonstrated some time later by H. J. Simons of the University of Cape Town, a Marxist scholar and former member of the central committee of the South African Communist Party. In a lengthy analysis of the Charter prepared for defense counsel in the Treason Trial, he pointed out the omission of any reference to the abolition of classes and the establishment of public ownership of the means of production. The nationalization that was proposed was, in the context of the Charter, characteristic of state capitalism; for a Marxist, he said, the failure to specify terms of transfer was inexcusable. Furthermore, although a liberal capitalist democracy could be a stepping-stone to a classless and socialist society, the Charter contained no suggestion to this effect. Nevertheless, in the conditions of South African autocracy, Marxists could be expected to work for a bourgeois democracy. In his analysis of other elements of the Charter, Simons used words like vague, reactionary, meaningless, muddle-headed, and addled.

In another analysis prepared for defense counsel, Thomas Hodgkin, the British scholar of African nationalism, described the language of the Charter as essentially that of "Rousseauian democratic nationalism—an ideology which Communists regard as petty bourgeois, romantic, utopian." The Charter, he said, advocated reforms "such as a late 19th century British Fabian could approve." It was, therefore, "clearly not a revolutionary document," although Hodgkin recognized that the simultaneous application of all its reforms would have a revolutionary effect in South Africa. The function of manifestos like the Freedom Charter, he pointed out, was to outline broad goals. The main purpose of his analysis, however, was to compare the language of the Charter with that used in African nationalist literature in other parts of the continent. He found "a close resemblance—as regards both language and ideas—to the texts of comparable charters" issued during the period of colonial rule. But there were differences: the Freedom Charter was "more moderate in tone," emphasized liberties rather than independence, and took for granted "the continuance of a multi-national rather than an essentially Negro-African state."

The Freedom Charter was to be the key document in the Treason Trial because the prosecution considered the Charter's aims—the abolition of all racial discrimination and the granting of equal rights to all—unrealizable in South Africa without violence. Without conceding such an inference, Nelson Mandela described the Charter as "a revolutionary document precisely because the changes it envisages cannot be won without breaking up the economic and political set-up of present South Africa" (Document 14). He pointed out, however, that the Charter was "by no means a blue-print for a socialist state." It visualized the transfer of power, he said, and opened the way to the development of a nonwhite bourgeoisie, whose members would be able to own mills and factories.

Liberals found in the socialist elements of the Charter additional grounds for disapproval of the Congress alliance. Their anti-communism found its most extreme exponent in Jordan Ngubane, the African journalist who was to break with Lutuli and the ANC in late 1955 and to become a leading member of the Liberal Party. He did not claim that the Freedom Charter was a Communist document, but saw Communist motives behind it. Communists supported a deliberately vague document, he charged, in order to accustom Africans to the idea of nationalization and to commit them to an all-inclusive organization that would be controlled by a small Communist core. The Charter's ultimate aim, he claimed, was "to condition the African people for the purpose of accepting communism via the back door."[201]

The group most opposed to the Charter's "multiracial" premises was the Africanists. Because they termed themselves African socialists (a claim scoffed at by left-wing members of the ANC), it was not the nationalization plank that inspired their opposition. To them, the sticking point was the Charter's declaration "that South Africa belongs to all who live in it, black and white"—a phrase by which they claimed the ANC had summarily forfeited the Africans' inalienable right to full "ownership" of South Africa. To refer to blacks and whites as "brothers," as did the Charter (the "Kliptown Charter," as the Africanists preferred to call it), was to fail to recognize that Africans were still "slaves" in their own land, that other sections ultimately had a right to remain in South Africa only if they recognized their position as "guests" of the African nation and accepted rule by an African majority. In rejecting the Charter's guarantee of "equal status . . . for all national groups and races," the Africanists described the Charter as "multiplied racialism" and proclaimed themselves "nonracialists" (who recognized people as individuals, not as members of racial groups) rather than "multiracialists."[202] Building on these premises, the Africanists professed to accept individuals of all colors as future citizens.

Chief Lutuli also disliked the term "multiracial" and preferred "nonracial."[203] ("Multiracial" did not appear in the Charter.) Both he and Professor Matthews were critical of some aspects of the Charter and wary of the possible influence of groups or individuals whose aim might be to redefine the political goals of the ANC. Their main concern, however, was to maintain momentum and to avoid appearances of disunity. In Lutuli's words, the ANC, while defining "all inclusive African nationalism" to include persons of all races, "should not dissipate its energies by indulging in internal ideological feuds" (Document 13a). During the months preceding the special conference at which the ANC formally adopted the Charter, and at the conference itself, this concern on the part of Lutuli and Matthews prevailed over their disquiet and reservations.

Lutuli, who had socialist sympathies, felt no difficulty in accepting the limited nationalization plank of the Charter. He generally agreed with the program of the British Labour Party, although it favored nationalization of the "means of production, distribution, and exchange," whereas, Lutuli pointed out, the ANC did not favor abolition of private ownership of the means of production. And although the ANC favored redistribution of the land, it also envisaged widespread individual ownership.[204]

Lutuli and his colleagues in Natal prepared detailed reactions to the Charter and suggestions for revision, which appeared in resolutions adopted by the Natal provincial conference, when it met in October 1955.[205] The criticisms were not fundamental. The conference expressed "loyalty" to the four allied organizations, congratulated them on the

Congress of the People, and expressed its "concurrence" with the principles of the Charter, "an admirable document under the circumstances." While "not averse to . . . the general socialistic base of the state envisaged," it strongly urged "critical scrutiny" and full discussion before final ratification. The conference criticized the section on equal rights for "national groups" for tending to overemphasize racial distinctiveness and suggested a substitution that would emphasize the building of "one united nation." It criticized some provisions as possibly "good propaganda but . . . not appropriate in a factual document." The Charter was intended to be "an all-time document," it said, and therefore should not be "padded" with unnecessary detail, for example, specifying a forty-hour week and the kinds of assistance to be given to farmers. Finally, in order to achieve "clarity," a number of questions were raised. It was suggested, for example, that the courts be impartial and not necessarily "representative" of all racial groups, that lazy persons could expect to go hungry, and that making "unused housing space" available should not require two or more families to live under one roof.

Despite both sympathetic and hostile criticism from within the ANC, the ANC's working committee and Indian and white allies centered in Johannesburg proceeded to deal with the Charter as if its acceptance by the ANC's forthcoming national conference in December 1955 were a foregone conclusion.[206] Since June 26, the ANC had faced a practical problem: how could it deal with pressures for publicizing and winning support for the Charter and at the same time allow for normal discussion within the ANC and possible revision of the Charter? Once the Congress of the People had adopted the Charter, in whose preparation many ANC leaders had been involved, protracted deliberation at all levels was hardly to be expected. Yet there was no doubt that only the national conference had authority to adopt a new policy statement and no doubt that some ANC leaders, while supporting the Charter in general, believed it should be amended.

On July 6, Tambo directed the provinces to win unanimous endorsement for the Charter and to promote its display in every home.[207] Local ANC meetings were held during July to endorse the Charter. On the other hand, the ANC's National Executive Committee, meeting at Lutuli's home on July 30, with Professor Matthews present, discussed amendments to the Charter and agreed that endorsement required action by the national conference.[208]

On the following day, the executive committees of the four congresses met and agreed to recommend adoption of the Charter to their respective conferences. The executive committees also accepted the ANC's proposal to conduct a joint campaign to collect a million signatures by June 26, 1956, in support of the Charter and to replace the National Action Council, an ad hoc body concerned with the Congress of the People, with a permanent national consultative committee whose immediate task would be the signature campaign.[209] The new committee, established in 1956, was never officially an executive body; but because it gave equal representation to the constituent elements of the Congress alliance, it was subject to the same criticism that had been directed at the earlier council.

On the same day that the executive committees of the four congresses met, July 31, the Africanist-led Youth League branch in Orlando sponsored an event that contrasted sharply with the Congress of the People and was aimed in part at reaffirming the pre-eminence of the Programme of Action: a "Lembede Memorial Service." In a quasi-religious program, the Africanists marked the eighth anniversary of Lembede's death and paid tribute to "national heroes"—African chiefs and leaders of the nineteenth century who had resisted the European conquest.[210] A. P. Mda, although not identified publicly as an opponent of the ANC's leadership, submitted an address to be read at the service, the text of which appeared in the July-August issue of *The Africanist*.[211]

Some four months later, on November 19–20, 1955, in another meeting at Lutuli's home, the National Executive Committee discussed the significance of individual signatures endorsing the Charter prior to its formal acceptance by the national conference.[212] Professor Matthews rather testily commented that he would not sign prior to such acceptance and that the conference would not be intimidated by individuals. Yet he expected adoption. In an atmosphere of some confusion and tension between older and younger leaders regarding issuance of directives to branches, both Chief Lutuli and Professor Matthews warned that only the ANC and not any consultative body could issue directives to ANC branches. Robert Resha, while criticizing the ANC for acting slowly, denied that anyone had gone over its head.

Meanwhile, little progress had been made in the signature campaign. Many of the forms to be used in the campaign had been confiscated in police raids during September and October, and few volunteers persevered in collecting signatures. The attention of ANC members was again being distracted by other activities, particularly by the developing campaign against the government's policy of imposing pass requirements on African women (to begin in 1956 but to be implemented slowly because of the administrative task of issuing new "reference books," i.e., passbooks).

During the two years following the Defiance Campaign of 1952, the Special Branch of the police had intensified its surveillance and conducted raids from time to time on suspected organizations and persons. Of special importance in preparing for the future Treason Trial was the raid on the Congress of the People. Most important of all, however, was the raid that began in the early morning hours of September 27, 1955, the largest nationwide raid ever undertaken in South Africa's history. In a vacuum-cleaner operation, armed with search warrants authorizing the seizure of practically anything that might be evidence of high treason, sedition, or violation of the Suppression of Communism Act or the Riotous Assemblies Act, some 1,000 or more police searched about 500 persons in their homes and offices, including *New Age* offices in Johannesburg and Cape Town. A list of forty-eight "organizations" to be investigated included designations such as "Defiance Campaign" and "Liberatory Movement," as well as a number of defunct bodies.

According to *New Age,* Special Branch officials claimed "to be following a trail they picked up as far back as 1935."[213] Among those raided were Dr. Moroka, Father Huddleston, and Professor Matthews. Matthews lost material on the ANC, which he had been collecting for a documentary history, and his typewriter during a search of both his home and office that lasted nearly four hours.[214] Afterwards, Liberal and Labour Party spokesmen and the Anglican Bishop of Johannesburg, Ambrose Reeves, joined leaders of the Congress alliance and of nonwhite trade unions in meetings called to protest the raids.

In addition to the raids and the spate of new banning orders that followed, internal dissension arising from the Africanist challenge became more intense, particularly in the Transvaal. When the Transvaal provincial conference met in Orlando on October 8–10, Potlako Leballo was allowed to make a fiery speech attacking "foreign ideologies" and calling for a return to the policy of "Africa for the Africans."[215] E. P. Moretsele, the provincial president, who was not strongly ideological, attacked those who were "trying to bring about a split in Congress between 'Right' and 'Left' " and who did "Mr. Swart's dirty work by hunting for so-called Communists." He went on to say:

> We know that there are men and women in the ANC who were in the Communist Party before it was dissolved. Most of them are hardworking, sincere members who abide loyally by the Constitution and the aims of the African National Congress. As long as they continue to do so they are welcome and they have every right to be with us.[216]

Because of wrangling over credentials, the conference did not complete its agenda. Neither of two competing delegations from Alexandra township in Johannesburg—one led by Josias Madzunya, a dissident allied with the Africanists, and the other by J. A. Mavuso and Alfred Nzo—was seated at first. But afterwards the provincial executive recognized the Mavuso-Nzo delegation.[217] When the provincial conference was resumed on November 6, it resolved "to intensify" the signature campaign for the Freedom Charter.

On the eve of the December 1955 national conference, *The Africanist,* then a year old, recapitulated the Africanist outlook in an editorial (Document 12) by Peter 'Molotsi. The goals of the Charter, 'Molotsi asserted, would never be achieved unless the ANC returned to the ideology of African nationalism underlying the 1949 Programme of Action; for, he wrote, "there can be no question . . . as to the correctness and dynamism of African Nationalism as an outlook for giving the African people the self-confidence and subjective liberation, without which no national oppression can be effectively challenged."

Annual Conference and Special Conference

The national conference reflected the increased difficulties and internal divisions confronting the ANC, with the result that a decision on adopting the Freedom Charter was postponed until a special conference three months later. Preparations for the December conference had been poor. Neither the proposed draft constitution nor the report of the National Executive Committee had been circulated to the branches, and advance publication of extracts of the report in *New Age,* contrary to a directive of the preceding year, produced some acrimonious discussion. Even the minutes of the 1954 conference, seized in a raid, were missing. The first-rank leaders, both national and provincial, were prevented by bans from attending. The number of delegates was unusually large—307 representing 81 branches, according to the minutes—but they were prevented by the Bloemfontein City Council from convening on the traditional meeting day of December 16, Dingaan's Day (as the Africans preferred to call it) officially celebrated as the Day of the Covenant. Following a short Saturday morning session of the Women's League, the conference met in a marathon session that lasted all night and, following elections, came to an end on Sunday evening some time after Transvaal delegates had to leave in a rush to catch their trains. Despite the shortness of the conference there was lengthy discussion on the question of expelling the reporter of the *Bantu World,* because of its "hostile attitude." In accordance with a resolution adopted by the Transvaal provincial conference in October, the reporter was expelled.[218] In protest against the expulsion, other representatives of the press walked out.

Lutuli, in a special message (Document 13a), envisaged "an all inclusive African nationalism which . . . embraced all people . . . regardless of their racial and geographical origin who resided in Africa and paid their undivided loyalty and allegiance [to Africa]"—a formulation similar to later formulations by Sobukwe. In his peroration, Lutuli invoked the "inspiration" to be drawn from the Freedom Charter. The Charter and the signature campaign were praised in the report of the National Executive Committee (Document 13c), though it said that "not enough energy, drive and direction has been shown" in the campaign; and the report recommended the establishment of "a permanent coordinating machinery" of the

ANC and its allies "subject to supervision by the National Executive only." A resolution to this effect was referred by the conference to the provinces, and, as noted earlier, the national consultative committee was established later in 1956; it included the South African Congress of Trade Unions.[219] Professor Matthews, addressing the conference, spoke with characteristic propriety and caution regarding the Charter. He had become acting principal of Fort Hare on December 1 and only attended the conference on Sunday to represent Lutuli.[220] In his address (Document 13b), he noted the importance of the Charter's adoption by the Congress of the People, expressed appreciation for the ANC's allies, and reminded the conference of its authority to decide whether or not to adopt the Charter.

The statement that produced the most controversy was an open letter to the conference from Dr. A. B. Xuma, expressing alarm and distress "over certain tendencies" (Document 13d). Xuma, who had been president-general of the ANC throughout the 1940s, bitterly accused the ANC's leadership of turning against the "Nation-building Programme of the 1940's" and of merging with other racial groups, which were able to avoid "making sacrifices themselves." The Rev. James Calata, the ANC veteran who was acting as speaker, opposed a reading of the full letter as contrary to the interests of the ANC; and Dr. Arthur Letele, the acting president, ruled that only extracts should be read. The Africanists, who were in possession of the full text, threatened to disrupt the conference unless it was read. Although the letter was not read in full then, it was eventually printed in full in *The World* (known as the *Bantu World* until after the conference).[221]

The heated and confused debate was marked by controversy about the accreditation of delegates and the exclusion of nondelegates from the hall following a short adjournment. Nevertheless, Africanist speakers, shouting "Africa for the Africans," made themselves heard and accused the ANC of failing to boycott advisory boards and communal elections in accordance with the Programme of Action. A number of resolutions were adopted, although one calling for the disciplining of members who took part in advisory board elections was referred to the provinces. Before the conference ended, it re-elected Lutuli as president-general for a second three-year term. "Chief Luthuli was to have accepted nomination," Jordan Ngubane asserted later, ". . . on condition the head office came to Natal, near him."[222] No change was made, however; indeed, the new National Executive Committee was heavily dominated by Transvaal members, one of whom was the first elected woman member, Lilian Ngoyi. Tambo was elected secretary-general, and Dr. Letele, treasurer-general.[223]

The Freedom Charter was finally adopted by the ANC in a special conference in Orlando on the Easter weekend of March 31–April 1, 1956, in the midst of disruption and scuffling between ANC loyalists and Africanists. (Leballo and a number of Africanists, despite their expulsion from the Youth League, had remained members of the ANC, entitled to attend conferences of the senior body.) A major aim of the conference was to discuss tactics in the campaign against passes for women. The Africanists claimed that the December conference had deferred discussion of the Freedom Charter until the next annual conference. Afterwards they charged that the meeting had been packed and that the Charter had been railroaded through by the acclamation of nondelegates. *New Age* reported that only sixteen Africanists were present among 224 delegates, whereas Leballo claimed that he had the support of nearly half the delegates.[224] In any event, the reservations and proposed amendments of Natal were not seriously considered. "Unfortunately," in the judgment of Lutuli, there was no adequate discussion of the economic clauses of the Charter; "the ranks were closed against what was regarded as the obstructionism" of the Leballo group.[225]

Left-wing Influence

Shortly before the conference, Lutuli had written to Letele expressing the hope that Letele could attend because Lutuli, referring to Transvaal or left-wing elements, was "very uneasy about certain new trends or cliques in Congress." He would seriously consider resigning the presidency, he said, if, for example, a new constitution provided for "over-centralization" or if the ANC were to "tie ourselves so fast to the Congress of Democrats" that groups disagreeing with some aspect of the Freedom Charter were excluded from cooperation with the ANC.[226] A few months earlier in *Drum,* Jordan Ngubane had referred to an alleged public statement by Lutuli to the effect "that he would sooner resign from the Congress presidency than see this body turn in the Communist direction."[227] Responding to Ngubane's persistent criticism, Lutuli entered into an open controversy with him in *Indian Opinion.* Despite his "uneasiness," Lutuli expressed confidence that the ANC was not under "communist influence or control." Nor did he and his Natal followers believe, Lutuli later wrote, that the inadequacy of discussion of the Charter or the adoption of the economic clauses were sufficiently important to bring about a split in the ANC.[228]

Mary Benson, a sympathetic historian of the ANC, has observed regarding the Congress of the People and the Freedom Charter that "the left-wing" won a notable victory by bringing socialism into the ANC's program for the first time.[229] Some observers have gone much further and seen the circumstances of the Charter's adoption as evidence of Communist manipulation, in spite of the fact that the final document was essentially a restatement of long-standing aims. Believing that Communists had dominated the planning and staging of the Congress of the People, one young Liberal later described it as "a farce from beginning to end."[230] The Congress was "a classical Communist frame-up . . . a classical Leninist object lesson," another observer has claimed; the Communists succeeded in cutting off the masses from the leaders by confronting these leaders with a mass rally where discussion was impossible. Having been caught in a cleft stick, it was suggested, the leaders had to choose between accepting certain demands or appearing reactionary.[231]

The nature of the campaign for the Freedom Charter no doubt contributed to these impressions of left-wing influence. Unlike the campaigns against Bantu education or the Western Areas removal, the campaign to publicize the demands of the Charter was an undertaking in which non-Africans as well as Africans could wholeheartedly involve themselves. The upsurge of activity among the ANC's non-African allies, both before and after the meeting of the Congress of the People, was therefore not an unnatural development. Because so many of the ANC's most vocal and energetic non-African supporters were themselves radical leftists, an impression of a significant leftward tendency in the Congress movement was created, particularly when, in promoting the Freedom Charter, *New Age* and even individual members of the COD often used language that suggested they were speaking on behalf of the ANC. It was difficult for first-string ANC leaders to counteract such impressions because many were under ban and many were committed to the ANC's policy of multiracial cooperation. To some experienced leaders like Lutuli and Matthews, standing in the center between the left and right wings of the ANC, the issue of left-wing influence must often have seemed rather a red herring, given what appeared, to them and to many others, to be the far more important issues of unity and action against white oppression. Meanwhile, however, the Africanists, in trying to muster popular support for their more extreme form of black nationalism, were finding anti-Communist sentiments a useful weapon to employ in their attacks on the ANC's non-African allies. These attacks, publicized by *The World*, attracted increasing attention, including the favorable attention of whites and foreign observers.

The special conference of March 31–April 1, 1956, looked forward to effective and united action on the newly pressing issue of passes for women. Directions were diffuse, however, as the following extract from the resolutions adopted at the special conference indicates:

We call upon the Africans, in towns, locations, villages, farms and reserves to organize every man and woman into the campaign against the pass laws and to embark upon any effective political action commensurate with the state of organization and not to relax until the pass system has been abolished.[232]

Before another national conference could be held, the government was to make its half-expected and radically new attack on the extraparliamentary opposition: its mass arrests (of Africanists as well as "Charterists") for treason.

BEFORE THE TREASON ARRESTS

After the mass raids of September 27, 1955, African leaders waited apprehensively for mass arrests and prosecution for high treason. On April 30, 1956, Charles Swart, the minister of justice, told Parliament, "Everything still has to be correlated, but it is expected that about 200 people will be charged" with treason and other offenses.[233] Meanwhile, the extraparliamentary opposition continued to engage in traditional tactics, illustrated most strikingly by three happenings in which the ANC was active behind the scenes. The first demonstrated once again the unwillingness of the government to listen to appeals: five men on a pro-ANC deputation from the officially sponsored joint advisory boards of Johannesburg traveled to Cape Town early in May; but Dr. Hendrik Verwoerd, the minister of native affairs, refused to grant them an interview.[234] The second (the background is described below) was a spectacular mass demonstration against passes by some 20,000 women who converged on the Union Buildings in Pretoria; the prime minister refused to see its leaders. The third (concerned with the Tomlinson Commission report on Bantu homelands and described below) was the most widely representative African conference since the mid-1930s; the Afrikaner Nationalist press dismissed it as an unrepresentative and white-instigated gathering.[235] In the early hours of December 5, mass arrests were made at last, making it clear that, so far as the government was concerned, dialogue with African leaders and their allies was irrelevant.

Demonstrations by Women Against Passes

The extension of the hated pass system to African women was the subject of more impassioned and widespread protests during 1956 than any other source of grievance. African women in the Orange Free State had resisted the issuance of passes to them as early as 1913, and soon afterwards the provincial requirements ceased to be enforced. In 1952, the Natives (Abolition of Passes and Coordination of Documents) Act nominally abolished passes but provided for "reference books" that were to be carried by African youths over sixteen and African women.[236]

The act applied also to Africans who had formerly been exempt because of their profession, e.g., teachers or clerics, although they were to carry reference books of a different color.[237] Government spokesmen argued that the books were protective in nature and essentially the same as the identity cards required of everyone under the Population Registration Act. The reference book, however, contained work contracts, tax receipts, and other documents essential to the enforcement of "influx controls," curfews, and other restrictions. Africans who had formerly been exempt continued to be exempt from curfew regulations but became subject to influx control. If an African failed to produce the reference book on demand, he or she was subject to criminal penalties. He was liable to a fine of £10 or one month's imprisonment, which might mean serving under harsh and degrading conditions as a farm laborer. By 1956, when the government began systematically to issue reference books to all African women, opposition leaders had no difficulty in convincing them that passes were badges of subordinate status, symbols of humiliation and harrassment, and instruments for the control and supply of cheap labor.

Much of the initiative in organizing demonstrations by women was taken by the Federation of South African Women, a nonracial organization which became an adjunct of the Congress alliance. Among its founders in April 1954 were Helen Joseph, a leading member of the Congress of Democrats, Ray Alexander, a trade-union leader and former Communist who became the Federation's first national secretary; Ida Mntwana, the first national president; and Fatima Meer, who had been a leader in Indian passive resistance.[238] Although individuals could join, the Federation was composed mainly of affiliated bodies of the various racial groups, nonwhite trade unions, and small women's groups. The ANC's Women's League worked closely with it but was not formally affiliated with it.[239] Lilian Ngoyi, one of the first vice-presidents of the Federation, was elected national president at its conference of August 11–12, 1956, when she was also national president of the ANC Women's League. The year before, she had traveled in Europe and China and attended the World Congress of Mothers in Lausanne. This Congress had been convened by the left-wing Women's International Democratic Federation, with which the South African Federation maintained contact though not formal affiliation.

Late in 1955 and during 1956, the ANC Women's League and the Federation stimulated a remarkable series of spirited demonstrations by African women, usually outside the offices of Native Commissioners throughout the country. Lutuli, paying tribute to the strength of women in the anti-apartheid movement, said in August 1956, "When the women begin to take an active part in the struggle as they are doing now, no power on earth can stop us from achieving Freedom in our Lifetime."[240] An early instance of illegal protest by women occurred on April 9, 1956, in the small town of Winburg in the Orange Free State, where the government had chosen to begin issuing reference books. Several hundred women who had accepted books claimed that they had been "tricked," returned to the site of the magistrate's court, and burned their books.[241] A series of arrests and prosecutions followed.

The most widely publicized demonstrations were multiracial processions through the streets of Pretoria and the gardens of the Union Buildings. The first took place on October 27, 1955, when petitions were left at the door of the minister of native affairs, and the second on August 9, 1956, when petitions were left for the prime minister. The women's leaders also left a statement (Document 15) describing passes for African women as an "insult to all women." The first demonstration attracted an estimated 1,000 to 2,000 women from the Transvaal. The second attracted a vast and colorful crowd of up to 20,000 women, including about 200 from other provinces, notably Mrs. Lutuli and a group from Stanger, Natal.[242] Some women members of the Liberal Party joined the demonstration; the women of the Black Sash, originally organized to protest the packing of the Senate, expressed sympathy but explained that their constitution forbade joining with other bodies. On both occasions, authorities sought to impede the mobilization with tactics similar to those that preceded the Congress of the People; the women also found it necessary to circumvent bans on walking in procession and holding a meeting.

As 1956 was coming to a close, the government was still moving slowly, issuing reference books only in small, out-of-the-way centers. "The present struggle against passes for women," said a report of the national consultative committee late in the year, "can well prove to be the decisive turning point of the whole long drawn out war" (Document 20). On December 2, 1956, a regional conference of the Federation in the Transvaal resolved "to organize a final mass protest to the Union Buildings in the event of legislation being introduced to prohibit such demonstrations."[243] Three days later, leading members of the ANC's Women's League and the Federation were among the nineteen women arrested in the treason raids. Because reference books were issued slowly, it was not until December 1960 that all African women were expected to possess a reference book and liable to arrest if they did not.[244]

Reactions to the Tomlinson Commission Report

While protests were being made against the immediate threat to African women, white and African leaders were discussing—in most cases, separately—the long-range implications of the report of the government's Tomlinson Commission for the Socio-Economic Development of the Bantu Areas. This important commission had submitted its 3,755-page report to the cabinet in October 1954. In 1955 a one-volume summary was published, and in May 1956 a "white paper" stated the government's position. The Commission laid the groundwork for advancing beyond the establishment of Bantu authorities (defined in the Bantu Authorities Act of 1951) toward the creation of Bantu homelands. Its report differed sharply from that of the Fagan Commission in 1948, which had accepted as irreversible the fact of "a settled, permanent Native population" in the urban areas.[245] The Tomlinson Commission disagreed and posed a clear-cut choice between "either the path of ultimate integration . . . or that of ultimate, complete separation between Europeans and Bantu."[246] It urged vigorous and costly action to promote industrialization within the reserves and consolidation of the 264 scattered pieces of land reserved for African occupancy around seven Bantu "heartlands," where separate political development toward some form of modern autonomy could take place.

The Tomlinson report set off a great debate in South Africa. Late in 1954 the United Party reaffirmed its acceptance of the middle course endorsed by the Fagan Commission, that is, to continue the policy of segregation while recognizing that "a large and permanently detribalized Native urban population" had become "an integral part of the South African economy."[247] The government's white paper rejected some basic recommendations of the Tomlinson report; in particular, it opposed private white capital investment in the reserves and rejected measures such as private ownership of land that would weaken the effort to bolster tribalism.[248] But it accepted, of course, the main principles of the report.

In July 1956, an Afrikaner *volkskongres,* organized by the Dutch Reformed Churches and other Afrikaner organizations including the South African Bureau of Racial Affairs (a body of Afrikaans-speaking intellectuals), met for three days to discuss the report. The *volkskongres* resolved to support territorial separation on the ground that "there is no possibility of the peaceful evolutionary development of White and Black in South Africa into an integrated society."[249]

An African religious organization, the Interdenominational African Ministers' Federation, took the initiative in organizing a response to the opinions of the Afrikaner *volkskongres* and the white Parliament. IDAMF, as it was known, was organized about 1945 as a national federation of four existing provincial associations of African ministers. It had a general concern with promoting the temporal well-being of Africans, published a quarterly organ, held annual conferences, and attempted to raise money for scholarships. Its leaders, who belonged mainly to the established denominations, sought to discourage secession from churches, to encourage separatist churches to come together in larger groupings, and to uphold the aim of building one united African church. The political side of this aim was evident in the fact that IDAMF's first two presidents were both elder statesmen of the ANC, the Rev. James Calata and the Rev. Z. R. Mahabane (who held the post in 1956).[250] Responding to the "grave national anxiety of the African people," IDAMF issued a press statement in mid-1956 to announce the holding of a conference that it hoped would represent "all shades of African opinion: religious, cultural, educational, political, industrial and sports organizations."[251]

The "all-in" conference that followed, on October 4–6, 1956, in Bloemfontein, was another example of the capacity of African leaders to come together at critical times to discuss fundamental national issues. In keeping with the respectability of the conference's sponsorship and past practice, IDAMF invited the mayor of Bloemfontein to open the conference. He had welcomed the *volkskongres* earlier as a body concerned with "life and death" for the Afrikaner, but he declined the IDAMF invitation. [252] According to A. L. Mncube, general secretary of IDAMF, more than 394 accredited delegates (representatives of organizations and independent individuals) attended and almost the same number of observers. The shades of opinion at the conference covered an extraordinarily wide spectrum, although there were no delegates from the AAC, the only one of twenty-one invited organizations, according to Mncube, that was not represented. Only two chiefs attended. Observers included members of foreign embassies, but no one came from the Department of Native Affairs or the South African Bureau of Racial Affairs. "A platoon of the Special Branch men attended," wrote Mncube later, but how, he went on, could SABRA, "composed mostly of 'enlightened' professors," have failed to use "this glorious opportunity for research? Who can in future take the deliberations of SABRA as genuine?"[253]

The most notable features of the conference were that all its participants were African and that they included most of the best-known intellectual and political leaders, many of whom had taken part in the "all-in" conferences of the mid-1930s. In contrast, of eight speakers on the agenda of another conference on the Tomlinson report, called by the Natal ANC in Durban a week earlier, all but Chief Lutuli had been white. At the IDAMF conference, after an opening address by the Rev. Mahabane, prepared papers were read by Dr. Xuma, the Rev. Calata, Professor Matthews, R. H. Godlo (president of the Location Advisory Boards' Congress), Selby Ngcobo, Dr. Don G. S. Mtimkulu, the Rev. B. Zulu and, among younger delegates, Oliver Tambo, G. M. Pitje, and Duma Nokwe. Paul Mosaka was present and, most dramatically, Chief Lutuli. Lutuli's ban had expired recently and he had come from speaking at the Durban meeting. After the conference divided into committees for discussion, Lutuli, Dr. Xuma, and Professor Matthews served on an elected fourteen-man committee which prepared a final statement (Document 16). What emerged, said *The World*, was "the fruit of all shades of thought."[254]

The conference received extraordinary praise both in *The World* and *New Age* for its seriousness and objectivity. Because of the thoroughness of the papers, said *The World*, comments from the floor were "remarkably short and to the point."[255] There was some disagreement with Xuma's suggestion that demands for fair implementation of separate development might be successful in embarrassing the government and with Mtimkulu's suggestion that Africans might use Bantu school committees to their advantage.[256] The conference heard some praise of members of the Commission and commended proposals for development of the reserves.[257] But "total rejection" of the Tomlinson report, that is, of territorial apartheid, was unanimous. The conference denied that "cooperation and interdependence between the various races" would threaten the survival of the white man and rejected "the concept of separate national homes" because that policy was coupled with the relinquishing of all African rights in the rest of the country.

The ANC embraced the IDAMF conference from the outset and endorsed its report. Joined by its allies, the ANC promoted the call of the conference for a broader "united front." Lutuli and others also called for the holding of a multiracial conference, a proposal that was "almost unopposed," *New Age* reported.[258] Lutuli had feared earlier that proponents of the Freedom Charter might insist on adherence to it as the price of cooperation, but Moses Kotane now declared that restricting the united front to those who accepted the Charter would be "utterly wrong."[259] Alan Paton, national chairman of the Liberal Party, endorsed the conference's "noble document," and both he and the Labour Party, as well as some English-language newspapers, expressed support for a multiracial conference.[260] More than a year later, a broadly representative multiracial conference was held (Document 21), but in circumstances even more restricted than those prevailing in 1956.

Other Activities in 1956

Although the IDAMF conference and the women's demonstrations were carefully planned major events in which the ANC was involved, the ANC's leadership itself did not mount any coordinated national initiatives during 1956. The year was marked by sporadic local protest demonstrations and occasional boycotts. New legislation and restrictions, increases in rent, pass raids and arrests, banishment of individual leaders, removal of people (particularly Indians) as the policies of the Group Areas Act were implemented, and clashes with the police in which Africans were killed or wounded—all these occurrences were grist for *New Age* and occasions for pamphleteering and protest.[261] At the Transvaal conference of the ANC in November, the provincial president and executive committee reviewed the government's actions and popular response (Documents 17a and 17b). Two examples of local flyers vividly detailing the brutality and humiliation of police raids are in Document 18.

The recent campaigns of the ANC, notably the Defiance Campaign and the Congress of the People, were commemorated on June 24, the Sunday preceding the anniversary date of June 26. Locally organized meetings were held around the country, and a multiracial football game was played at Kliptown. Once again, as in 1953, Lutuli called for the symbolic lighting of lamps and bonfires at 9 P.M. on Tuesday, June 26.[262]

The ANC's leadership was not responsible, however, for the most sustained mass effort of the year: the bus boycott in Evaton, a township of some 58,000 residents about twenty-eight miles from Johannesburg.[263] The boycott was led by local Africanists; leaders of the PAC later claimed that it was far more successful than the Defiance Campaign in enlisting mass support.[264] The boycott was punctuated by violence, arrests, and finally by attacks on the boycotters by African gangs. After more than a year it ended successfully in August 1956 with a return to the original fares and provision for bus shelters, a new timetable, and the employment of Evaton Africans by the company.

Toward the end of October two international crises began to develop which were to compel attention among both whites and Africans and to cause some ideological strain within the ANC. On October 29, Israel invaded Egyptian territory. Four days later, Britain and France, acting in collusion wtih Israel, joined the invasion; but after warnings from both the United States and the Soviet Union, the war ended on the tenth day. Meanwhile, revolutionary forces in Hungary, promising withdrawal of Soviet forces and free elections, triumphed on October 30. Two days later, Soviet units went into action; the revolt was crushed soon afterwards and a new regime installed. Within twelve hours of news of the invasion of Egypt, the ANC (presumably the working committee) issued a statement condemning the aggression.[265] Reactions to the Hungarian developments were more complex. Lutuli, expressing the views also of Tambo and Conco, condemned the Soviet Union's "ruthless intervention."[266] But Moses Kotane, writing in the November 29 issue of *New Age,* deplored any distraction of attention from the Egyptian situation and argued for delay and fuller information about "the regrettable events" in Hungary before making judgment. The argument was also made, on Prime Minister Nehru's authority, that the Egyptian and Hungarian situations were not comparable.[267]

The reluctance of some persons to pass judgment on the situation in Hungary was in part a reaction to the street demonstrations by Afrikaans-speaking students in behalf of anti-Soviet Hungarians and the government's grant of £ 25,000 for assistance to refugees. Others like the Rev. W. S. Gawe, writing to a Queenstown newspaper in criticism of its attention to Hungary, criticized white insensitivity to "the feelings of the Africans whose territory has been violently attacked . . ." by countries one of which (Britain) was "at the moment killing the unarmed liberators of Kenya."[268]

Within the ANC's National Executive Committee, there was "a sharp division," according to Lutuli. "I and some others thought that there had been an aggression which must be condemned as such. Others wished to explain events in Hungary in a way to justify Russia. Eventually the secretarial report contented itself with deploring the bloodshed that had taken place but otherwise not committing itself to a definite view."[269] The annual conference, meeting in Queenstown during December 15–17, following the treason arrests, resolved to condemn the invasion of Egypt but passed no resolution on Hungary.[270] Reports circulated during November that because of the Hungarian issue, some supporters of the Soviet Union, for example, Lionel Forman, were drifting away from the Soviet position. After the treason arrests, however, all such points of internal disagreement within the Congress movement became subordinated to the need for unity.

The treason arrests were foreshadowed by governmental actions and threats going back a decade. Following the 1946 African miners' strike, the entire national executive committee of the Communist Party had been tried, inconclusively, for sedition. In 1948, Johannes Strijdom had described opposition to apartheid as treason, a loose equation that was to be used in many speeches. During the debate on the Suppression of Communism Bill in 1950, the minister of justice had warned (without evidence) of secret plans by Africans to poison water supplies and to murder their enemies, while the leaders of the parliamentary opposition had suggested that Communist activities be regarded as high treason. And prior to the Defiance Campaign in 1952, the prime minister had warned the ANC against "inciting subversive activities of any nature whatsoever." The raids made after 1952 prepared the way for the arrests of 1956.

During the year, the Special Branch of the police was busy collating thousands of documents seized in raids and stenographic and taped records of meetings, filled with inflammatory rhetoric. On November 22, the police acquired their most sensational example and prize exhibit. Listening to a microphone hidden in the ceiling at a closed meeting in Johannesburg, they heard Robert Resha, chief Freedom Volunteer in the Transvaal, saying to ANC branch leaders: "When you are disciplined and you are told by your organisation not to be violent, you must not be violent; if you are a true volunteer and you are called upon to be violent, you must be absolutely violent, you must murder! Murder! That is all."[271] The audience responded with applause.

The Arrests for Treason

Thirteen days later, on December 5, 1956, the long-awaited swoop took place. Beginning at four and five o'clock in the morning, police knocked on doors in all parts of South Africa and arrested about 140 persons on charges of high treason and other offenses. They were to be accused of being members of "a country-wide conspiracy," inspired by international communism, to overthrow the state by violence. With aircraft waiting to fly the accused to Johannesburg, the carefully planned and coordinated action had the appearance of a military operation designed to meet a clear and present danger. Even Communists seem to have been surprised by the show of power, despite the warning in the latest issue of *New Age* that a "Reichstag trial" was imminent.[272]

The net dropped by the government came up with a catch that was, as one might expect, racially mixed, ideologically diverse, and anomalous in its inclusion of small fry and opponents of ANC leadership and its exclusion of some major personalities. Later arrests brought the total to 156: two-thirds, or 104, were Africans, 44 were whites and Indians (nearly the same number of each), and 8 were Coloureds. Among the accused were the main officers of the ANC and its allied organizations. Africans ranged in outlook from Moses Kotane to Chief Lutuli and a few Africanists. Among the Africanists were Joseph Molefi and Vus Make, leaders of the Evaton bus boycott, A. B. Ngcobo and Elliot Mfaxa, who were to be leaders of the PAC, and T. E. Tshunungwa, the former national organizer who had become secretary to Chief Kaiser Matanzima and been expelled from the ANC. The older and younger generations were represented also by Professor Matthews and his radical son, Joe. Even Dr. Xuma (though not Dr. Moroka) was listed among the eighty-six alleged co-conspirators when the indictment was issued later. Others so listed were P. Q. Vundla, who had been expelled from the ANC in late 1955 and become politically emasculated by joining the Moral Re-Armament movement, and an assortment of minor figures.

Most of the whites, for example, Joe Slovo, Ruth First, and Lionel Bernstein, and some of the Indians, had been members of the Communist Party. But J. B. Marks was listed only as a co-conspirator, and Yusuf Dadoo, David Bopape, Michael Harmel, and Sam Kahn were neither arrested nor listed in the indictment. Apparently their long-standing bans had removed them from incriminating activity during the indictment period, which began in October 1952. Other whites and Indians either had an outlook indistinguishable from those who had been Communist Party members, had been attracted to the Communist-led world peace movement, or had identified themselves with the humanitarian cause of African advancement. Some of the Indians were followers of Gandhi. The anomalies in the list of the accused and co-conspirators were explained partly by legal considerations of evidence and partly by white ignorance, or imprecise knowledge, regarding the leadership of the extraparliamentary opposition.

The government's conception of the scope of the conspiracy was matched by its perception of the danger to white South Africa toward the end of 1956. By this time, according to the prosecution in the trial, "the accused had deliberately created an explosive situation." Quoting the words of Alex LaGuma, one of the Coloured accused, it presented the following as "an accurate description" of conditions prevailing in South Africa:

South Africa is littered all over with dry firewood which will soon be kindled into a conflagration. We need only to look at the development of the militancy of the people, the Defiance Campaign, the strikes of the non-European workers, the Congress of the People, to see that it will not take long for these sparks to become a 'prairie fire.'

Despite this assessment, which was far too pessimistic as an estimate of the immediate future—or too optimistic from the standpoint of the Congress movement—a Supreme Court judge fixed low bail; whites paid £250, Indians and Coloureds, £100, and Africans, £50. All but one (who was serving a jail sentence) were released in time for Christmas. This lenient treatment of men and women accused of a conspiracy to overthrow the state by violence did not mask the fact that the arrests marked the end of a historic period. The depth of the conflict that had developed since Union between Africans and whites was commensurate with the majestic charge of high treason.

NOTES

Note: Interviews recorded in notes or in transcripts of tape recordings were conducted by Gwendolen M. Carter, Thomas Karis, Sheridan Johns, and Gail M. Gerhart. Many provided background; some are cited below. Unless reference is made to the interviewer, the notes refer to interviews conducted jointly by Carter and Karis.

1. *Advance,* March 26, 1953.

2. The court held that a governmental agency could not provide unequal facilities if it lacked legislative authorization to do so. Leo Kuper, *Passive Resistance in South Africa* (New Haven: Yale University Press, 1957; Yale paperbound, 1960), p. 59.

3. Quoted in Edgar H. Brookes and J. B. Macaulay, *Civil Liberty in South Africa* (Cape Town: Oxford University Press, 1958), p. 47.

4. On the election, see Gwendolen M. Carter, *The Politics of Inequality: South Africa Since 1948* (New York: Praeger, 1958), chapters 5–7.

5. For extracts from the program of the Labour Party, see United Nations, *Second Report of the United Nations Commission on the Racial Situation in the Union of South Africa* (United Nations General Assembly, Official Records: Ninth Session, Supplement No. 16 [A/2719]), p. 64. Extracts from the Liberal Party's constitution and decisions on the franchise adopted in July 1953 are on pages 63–64.

6. For the full text of the statement and a list of the signatories, see Volume II, pages 437–438.

7. On the background of the Liberal Party, conversations with Mrs. Margaret Ballinger (Jan. 18, 1964) and Julius Lewin (Feb. 15, 1964) have been useful. See also Margaret Ballinger, *From Union to Apartheid: A Trek to Isolation* (Folkestone, England: Bailey Brothers & Swinfen, Ltd., 1969), and Janet Robertson, *Liberalism in South Africa: 1948–1963* (Oxford: Clarendon Press, 1971).

8. The program of the Federal Party is in D. W. Kruger (ed.), *South African Parties and Policies, 1910–1960: A Select Source Book* (Cape Town: Human & Rousseau, 1960), pp. 101–103.

9. Nelson Mandela, "Searchlight on the Liberal Party," *Liberation,* June 1953, pp. 7–8. In "The Liberal Party Replies," in *Liberation,* Sept. 1953, pp. 10–13, Professor T. W. Price returned the vitriol in a manner that was not characteristic of most Liberal leaders. He dismissed as unrealistic Mandela's "Old, heart-warming clap trap about 'mass struggles' and 'people's fights' " and concluded that Mandela favored "the complete victory by force of the blacks over the whites." Ruth First, a former member of the Communist Party, defended Mandela in a milder article, "The 'Constitutional' Fallacy," in *Liberation,* Nov. 1953, pp. 10–14.

10. He was banned under the Riotous Assemblies Act and the Criminal Law Amendment Act. *Advance,* June 4, 1953.

11. By the end of 1954, the ANC could list in an annexure to its annual report (Document 7b, but the annexure is not reproduced in this volume) the names of 95 members of the ANC or allied organizations who were under some kind of ban: 36 Africans, 19 Indians, 38 whites, and 3 Coloureds. In addition, four Africans, including two who were listed as banned, were listed as banished.

12. Possible violations of all these statutes and the law of treason and sedition were cited by warrants held by the police when, for example, they raided the offices of the ANC (Transvaal) and the Transvaal Indian Congress in June. *Advance,* June 18, 1953.

13. Albert J. Lutuli, "A Message to the African People and Their Allies in the Struggle for Freedom in the Union of South Africa," June 15, 1953. This call was reproduced in various formats and, in slightly altered form, also appeared under the name of Professor Matthews.

14. *Advance,* July 2, 1953; Mary Benson, *The African Patriots: The Story of the African National Congress of South Africa* (London: Faber & Faber, 1963), p. 203; "The Report of the Secretariat on the Western Areas," n.d.; and Father Trevor Huddleston, *Naught for Your Comfort* (London: Collins, 1957). Father Huddleston, an Anglican priest in Sophiatown and superintendent of St. Peter's Secondary School, was one of the speakers at the meeting.

15. In an unpublished memoir, Frieda Matthews has written, "In 1955—one dark, winter morning [September 27]—we were roused at 5 A.M. by detectives. . . . The detectives were excited to find copies of the speech he [Professor Matthews] had given to the African National Congress on the proposed Congress of the People, although it had been fully reported in the Press at the time!"

16. The text of the resolution adopted by the national conference was as follows: "Conference instructs the National Executive Committee to make immediate preparations for the organization of a 'Congress of the People of South Africa,' whose task shall be to work out a 'Freedom Charter' for all peoples and groups in this country. To this end, Conference urges the African National Congress National Executive to call a meeting of the National Executives of the South African Indian Congress, the Coloured People's Organization, the South African Congress of Democrats, and any other democratic organization for the purpose of placing before them the plan of Congress and obtaining their cooperation in creating a truly representative 'Convention of the People of South Africa.' " Quoted in "Draft Memorandum of the Congress of the People" by Z. K. Matthews, n.d. (prepared for the ANC's National Executive Committee meeting of March 21, 1954).

17. In an introduction to a reproduction of the statement, Robert N. Resha, president of the Youth League in the Transvaal, noted that it was important for the future "that we compile our literature." Mandela's "historic address," he wrote, was "the best ever."

18. "Confidential" letter from Z. K. Matthews to T. E. Tshunungwa, Feb. 6, 1956.

19. The inaugural meeting was preceded by a "People's Convention" on August 15–16, attended by delegates from thirty-three organizations. Golding was jeered at, and he walked out. *Advance*, Aug. 13 and 20, 1953. See also the issue of Sept. 17, 1953.

20. *Advance*, Aug. 13, 1953.

21. On the COD, see *Advance*, Sept. 17, 24, Oct. 8 and 15, 1953.

22. Beyleveld testified later in court that he joined the underground Communist Party in 1956. See Edward Feit, *Urban Revolt in South Africa, 1960–1964: A Case Study* (Evanston: Northwestern University Press, 1971), p. 294.

23. Carter, *The Politics of Inequality*, p. 378. A COD policy statement appears on pp. 489–490.

24. Lutuli, declining an invitation to attend a peace congress in Europe, described himself as "not yet a member of the South African Peace Council although I am in sympathy with the work of the Peace Council" in a letter of Nov. 9, 1954. He explained, "It could be used to disastrous effects among our less politically educated Africans by our reactionary enemies, especially the Government."

25. For a review of the work of the Commission, see Carter, *The Politics of Inequality*, pp. 402–406; and "Memorandum on the Nature and Effects of Racial Discrimination in South Africa Submitted jointly by the African National Congress and the South African Indian Congress . . . , August 10, 1953" (46 pp.).

26. United Nations, *Third Report of the United Nations Commission on the Racial Situation in the Union of South Africa* (General Assembly, Tenth Session, Supplement No. 14 [A/2953], 1955), p. 94.

27. The Appellate Division held (in the words of a historian), "that nothing in those [Suppression of Communism] Acts deprived of his right to be heard any person who was liable to be affected by the Minister's acts thereunder, that the vital words in these Acts, 'in the opinion of the Minister,' implied that the said Minister had taken reasonable steps to form that opinion, and that the mere presence of the name of a person on the list of members of an unlawful organisation by no means entitled the Minister to issue an order against him or her, because that person might have severed all connection with it before ever either Act had come into force." Eric A. Walker, *A History of Southern Africa* (London: Longmans, Green, 1957), pp. 849–850.

28. "Report of the 41st Annual Conference of the A.N.C. Held at the Mallet Hall, Queenstown, from the 18th to 20th, December, 1953." The report noted that 265 delegates were present on the afternoon of the first day: 139 from the Cape, 113 from the Transvaal, 12 from Natal, and 1 from the Orange Free State. About 300 delegates and 200 ordinary ANC members and observers attended, according to Robert Resha. *Fighting Talk*, Feb. 1954, p. 10.

29. *God's Kingdom in Multi-racial South Africa: A Report on the Inter-Racial Conference of Church Leaders, Johannesburg, 7 to 10 December, 1954.* Papers were read by the Rev. Seth Mokitimi, an African minister of the Methodist Church in the Transkei, and the Rev. S. S. Tema, an African minister of the Dutch Reformed Church in Pretoria and a member of the ANC. The conference set up a committee to arrange for inter-church consultation and to convene a general conference every three years. Just three years later, the secular Multi-Racial Conference was to meet in the same place. Carter, *The Politics of Inequality*, pp. 276–279; Walker, *History of Southern Africa*, pp. 855–856, 908–909.

30. "Report of the 41st Annual Conference," cited above.

31. *Advance*, Dec. 10 and 31, 1953; Walter Sisulu, "I Saw China," *Liberation*,

Feb. 1954, pp. 5–9. *Advance,* Sept. 10, 1953, reported that Sisulu wrote from London to the UN Commission while it was in session in Geneva, asking it to provide him with the equivalent of a passport so that he might come to Geneva to testify. His request was not granted.

Among others who traveled to Communist countries were Alfred Hutchinson, a member of the ANC's National Executive Committee, and Greenwood Ngotyana, who attended the Bucharest festival of 1953 (*New Age,* Oct. 6, 1955; Benson, *The African Patriots,* p. 199), and Paul Joseph, an Indian, who represented the Transvaal Council of Non-European Trade Unions in Vienna in October 1953, and then visited Moscow at the same time as Sisulu and Nokwe did. Ruth First (ed.), *South Africans in the Soviet Union* (printed booklet, n.d.); Paul Joseph, "The Vienna World Trade Union Conference," *Fighting Talk,* Feb. 1954, p. 5.

32. Dr. Richard van der Ross, a founder of the South African Coloured People's Organization, was one of several nonwhites who visited the United States during this period. In mid-1954, Professor Matthews was invited to attend an international conference on race relations at the University of Hawaii, but he was refused a passport. On this conference, see United Nations, *Third Report,* cited above, pp. 88–90.

33. "Minutes of All African Convention Conference Held at the Mallet Hall, Queenstown on 15th, 16th, 17th December, 1953."

34. *Drum,* April 1954.

35. *Advance,* July 1, 1954.

36. "Minutes of A.N.C. Conference held at Bloemfontein, 17th December, 1955" (handwritten); *New Age,* Dec. 20, 1956.

37. It was sometimes alleged in the 1950s, for example, that the ANC was being restrained from organizing economic boycotts because such action would adversely affect Indian shopkeepers. See the *Bantu World,* May 1, 1954, and "Minutes of the Meeting of the Executive Committee of the African National Congress (Natal)," June 6, 1954.

38. For expressions of Thema's opinions about the Defiance Campaign, see the editorial "Wise Decision," *Bantu World,* March 29, 1952, and "African National Organizations," *South African Outlook,* May 1, 1952, p. 72.

39. Interviews of Gerhart with Peter Raboroko and Matthew Nkoana.

40. "African Nationalism and the African National Congress Youth League—II," *African Lodestar,* Oct. 1951.

41. Information on the Bureau of African Nationalism is from interviews of Gerhart with A. P. Mda, T. T. Letlaka, Elliot Mfaxa, and P. K. Leballo. Also see Volume II, pages 413–414.

42. The majority of contributors to *The Africanist* were government-employed teachers who wrote their articles under pseudonyms to avoid losing their jobs.

43. "Resolutions of the 10th Annual Conference of the African National Congress Youth League (Transvaal)," May 23, 1954, Johannesburg.

44. Both the Western Areas removal campaign and the Bantu education campaign have been analyzed by Edward Feit, *African Opposition in South Africa: The Failure of Passive Resistance* (Stanford: Hoover Institution Press, 1967), chapters 4 and 5.

45. Conversations with Z. K. Matthews and Joseph Matthews.

46. "Report of Working Committee of the ANC," n.d. Five members of each group of eight representatives from the four sponsoring organizations were to be residents of the Transvaal. The National Action Council itself was scheduled to meet each fortnight.

47. Conversation with Peter Hjul, Jan. 26, 1964.

48. The text of the "Call" appeared in *Fighting Talk,* June 1954. *Advance,* Sept. 2, 1954, stated that the "Call" had been published. See also the *Treason Trial Record* (the mimeographed record of the Treason Trial of 1956–1961, *Regina vs. F. Adams and Others*), pp. 6,493–6,494.

86

49. In Johannesburg, the police entered the Trades Hall, claiming to be investigating a case of treason, and took the names of the thousand persons attending the meeting. *Drum* (date not known).

50. Z. K. Matthews, unpublished manuscript. "Enthusiasm was an eye opener" to those who did not know what was happening to the ANC.

51. Lutuli, in his "Pre-Conference Presidential Call" of Nov. 12, 1954, noted that there was "some confusion among people," who thought the task of the Freedom Volunteers was to defy the laws. He explained that "Freedom Volunteers are 'Field-Workers' mobilizing the people for a great Congress of the People."

52. "Address of the Secretary-General of the African National Congress, Mr. W. M. Sisulu, to the National Conference of the A.N.C. Youth League at Uitenhage, on the 26th, 27th June 1954."

53. Conversation of Gerhart with Charles Lakaje, and unpublished autobiographical manuscript by Lakaje.

54. "Transvaal Delegation Report on [Youth League] National Conference [of June 26–27, 1954]," n.d.

55. "Supplementary Report of ANC Secretariat," n.d.

56. "[Minutes of] National Executive Meeting of the African National Congress, 27th November, 1954."

57. *New Age*, Dec. 23, 1954.

58. Benson, *The African Patriots*, p. 205.

59. *Advance*, July 29, 1954.

60. The text of the particulars to the charge is in *Fighting Talk*, Oct. 1954, p. 5. See also *Advance*, Aug. 5, 1954.

61. "The New Prime Minister of South Africa," n.d.

62. "[Minutes of] National Executive Meeting of the African National Congress, 27th Nov. 1954."

63. *New Age*, Dec. 23, 1954.

64. Z. K. Matthews' handwritten notes for the Treason Trial defense.

65. Dr. A. B. Xuma, "African Reactions," in *The Western Areas Removal Scheme: Facts and Viewpoints* (Johannesburg: South African Institute of Race Relations, 1953), p. 27. Dr. Xuma headed the African Anti-Expropriation Ratepayers' Association and Proper Housing Movement.

66. A report of the Non-European Affairs Department of the Johannesburg City Council in 1950 estimated that 523 African families owned houses in Sophiatown and Martindale and 46 in Newclare. Many properties listed under white names, it noted, might be partly owned by Africans, with whites acting only as bondholders. Dr. Xuma claimed that his organization alone included the names of more than 600 African owners in the Western Areas. "African Reactions," cited above, pp. 8 and 26.

67. *Fighting Talk*, April 1955, pp. 3 and 11.

68. *Ibid.*

69. "The Report of the Secretariat on the Western Areas," n.d.

70. Conversation with Tennyson Makiwane regarding Alexandra township. Resha testified in the Treason Trial that the secretariat had discarded the idea of assembling the volunteers to block the approach to the houses in order to prevent people from loading their property on the lorries or getting on the lorries themselves.

71. Article by "Nzana," *The Africanist*, Vol. I. No. III (May 1955), p. 6.

72. The leaflet said that anyone who moved willingly was helping the government to enslave the African people. Such a person was a traitor who brought shame to Africa. The call to action was as follows: "Don't fill in the forms, don't

get into the lorry to go to Meadowlands, be ready to obey Congress' call, join the A.N.C., enroll as a volunteer, resist apartheid, we are not going to move." Treason Trial defense memorandum on the Western Areas campaign.

73. The struggle in the Western Areas "like all others, will be conducted in a disciplined and peaceful manner and the people are called upon to remain calm in the face of all provocation."

74. *House of Assembly Debates*, Feb. 9, 1955, col. 867.

75. "The Report of the Secretariat on the Western Areas," n.d.

76. The report and the statement by Dr. Verwoerd that follows in the text are quoted by David Welsh in Monica Wilson and Leonard Thompson (eds.), *The Oxford History of South Africa* (London: Oxford University Press, 1971), Vol. II, p. 225.

77. For the data in this paragraph, see Carter, *The Politics of Inequality*, pp. 101 and 106. Also see Muriel Horrell, *Bantu Education to 1968* (Johannesburg: South African Institute of Race Relations, 1968).

78. In 1956, the Bantu Education Amendment Act gave virtually complete power over registration to the Minister.

79. H. G. Makgothi, president of the Youth League in the Transvaal, said on Jan. 9, 1955, "Verwoerd, in his Bantu Education, says that Africans must first be taught religion and, of course, a smattering of English and Afrikaans in order to understand the commands of their bosses. But why must the syllabus be made so narrow? Why must children learn Afrikaans and no History or Geography? Why a three hours time-table?" (By decreasing school hours to three a day, government schools were able to provide for more students in double sessions. Students were also expected to help in maintaining the school premises.) "Anti-Bantu Education Action Committee Conference Held at Mathabe Hall, Sophiatown on Sunday the 9th January, 1955."

Late in 1956, Father Martin Jarrett-Kerr, Trevor Huddleston's successor, reviewed Dr. Verwoerd's methods of control. "First, he has made sure that any rivals are removed from the field. Hence the casualties, one after another, among private schools: first, Christ the King, Sophiatown; then Adams College, Natal . . . ; then the Itereleng Private School, Germiston . . . not to mention the refusal of registration to others that had applied; nor such schools as St. Peter's, Rosettenville, that voluntarily died rather than be ignominiously closed. Then the control over what was left. . . . Hence the widespread sacking of teachers on purely political, not professional, grounds. Then of course, the syllabus; the School Boards which, nominally 'Bantu', are in fact mere mouthpieces of the Minister. . . . Then the ethnic grouping and the vernacular medium, in order to lessen the possible dangers of contact with a wider world." *A. E. M. News, Official Organ of the African Education Movement*, Vol. I, No. 4, Nov. 1956.

80. Tambo wrote to the national secretary of the Youth League on Aug. 30, 1955: "Although the National Executive has requested the Youth League to specialise on the Anti-Bantu Education Campaign, this office has received no reports."

81. In a circular on the Bantu education campaign "To All Provincial Secretaries," Tambo, the acting secretary-general, wrote: "Our problem in the head office has always been and still remains to be the complete lack of information as to the state of affairs in the different provinces or regions. . . . Unless this situation is attended to, we shall be faced with a chaotic position within the organisation."

82. "Anti-Bantu Education Action Committee Conference . . . 9th January, 1955."

83. P. H. Simelane to the Secretariat, Jan. 31, 1955.

84. Z. K. Matthews to Lutuli, Feb. 21, 1955.

85. *New Age*, May 5, 1955, reported the publication of additional regulations in the *Government Gazette*, listing thirteen types of "misconduct," including

88

action judged by the Secretary of Native Affairs to be deleterious to one's position as a teacher.

86. In notes prepared later for the Treason Trial defense, Professor Matthews wrote, "The reports from the various provinces placed before the Executive indicated that insufficient preparations had been made by the branches. . . ."

87. "Resolution Adopted by the National Executive Committee of the African National Congress on Bantu Education," March 5, 1955.

88. Conversation of Karis with Lutuli, June 21, 1955.

89. "Resolutions Passed at the Special Conference of the African National Congress Held at Sophiatown, on the 13th March, 1955."

90. "Minutes of the National Executive Meeting Held in Durban on the 21st, May, 1955."

91. Not all the minutes of NEC meetings in 1955 were available to the authors in the preparation of this volume, but it can be determined from those that were (for May 21, June 25, July 30, and Nov. 19–20) that the following members were present at (at least) three of these four meetings: Lutuli, Dr. Wilson Conco, and P. H. Simelane, from Natal; Z. K. Matthews, T. E. Tshunungwa, and Dr. Arthur Letele, from the Cape; and E. P. Moretsele, Robert Resha, Alfred Hutchinson, and Leslie Masina from the Transvaal.

92. The minutes of the NEC meeting of May 21, referred to above, noted that Tambo (on a date not specified) had informed Matthews, the deputy president-general, of his "identification" with "the beginning of the boycott" (presumably that it was going to begin on April 12 or that it had begun). Matthews, according to the minutes, had replied that "he did not believe in supporting acts of defiance of National Executive decisions" and had advised Tambo to consult with Lutuli. Tambo then read a statement over the telephone to Lutuli, who said he could not endorse it because it was a matter for the NEC.

93. *Counter Attack*, March–May, 1955. Most of the delegates represented ANC branches and local "vigilance committees." The COD sent two delegates from Johannesburg, and the Liberal Party sent three from Cape Town.
   One of the Liberal Party delegates was Peter Hjul, whose recollections (on Jan. 26, 1964) of the meeting of April 9–10, 1955, included the following: "I'll never forget one of the most impressive ANC meetings I went to . . . as we got up to the meeting, there was a line of young Africans, all wearing khaki longs, khaki bush jackets, and a black beret with each of them having a little fish shell, a mussel shell, with the yellow and green colors of the ANC painted with the thumb up in the middle. . . . Everyone wore one. And all the women wore these green, yellow, and black colored skirts. . . . It was perfectly organized. There were all these young uniformed men around the sides. They saw that everyone was seated properly. And then, of course, they always had the singsongs. *Mayibuye* . . . *Nkosi Sikelel'*. They had several other songs . . . But this time it was a serious meeting. And Matthews got up and said, 'We are cutting this proceeding short. Now I want a careful assessment of a very difficult situation.' And he told them how difficult it was. He spoke frankly. And then Jimmy Gibson [of the Liberal Party] was asked as the senior lawyer present to give a legal explanation of what the position was about the Bantu Education Act. And he had prepared a long talk, which he gave. The COD was there. They got up and started to talk emotionally again. And Helen Joseph was the one who was rapped over the knuckles. . . . She talked about the suffering of the people, and Matthews cut her short. He said, 'Mrs. Joseph, we are here to discuss tactics, policy. We know that there's suffering. We know that this is wrong. Please confine yourself to the subject.'"
   Speaking generally of the ANC meetings he had attended, Hjul said, "There was always a lot of laughter and a lot of spontaneous sort of singing in it. Many of its members had a wonderful political flair."

94. Since no record of the NEC's decision is available, the text is based upon notes prepared by Professor Matthews for the Treason Trial defense, "Minutes of the National Executive Meeting Held in Durban on the 21st, May, 1955," and a circular from Tambo, "To All Provincial Secretaries," April 19, 1955. A later

report by the NEC on the Bantu education campaign, which is not available, is described in *New Age*, June 2, 1955.

95. "The Secretarial Report to the National Executive of the African National Congress," n.d. (before May 23, 1955).

96. *Ibid.* See also *New Age*, April 28, 1955, p. 7; "NEC Minutes of May 21, 1955"; Tambo to Conco, May 15, 1955.

97. "Titshala," *New Age*, April 28, 1955, p. 7.

98. *Ibid.*, p. 1.

99. *New Age*, Nov. 10, 1955, p. 5.

100. *A.E.M. News, Official Organ of the African Education Movement*, Vol. I, No. 4, Nov. 1956.

101. "Our Cultural Clubs," no author, no date, but issued in September or October 1956.

102. *Loc. cit.*

103. J. Matthews to Sisulu, Oct. 25, 1955.

104. *The Africanist*, Feb. 1956.

105. Quoted in *New Age*, May 12, 1955.

106. A letter by J. T. R. Gibson to *New Age*, April 21, 1955, expressed the Liberal Party's belief that boycott was impractical, and alternative education "almost impossible to supply" both for practical and legal reasons. See also *New Age*, Sept. 8, 1955, p. 1.

107. *Congress Voice* (n.d., but before Oct. 30, 1955).

108. More than a year after Matthews' speech, Lutuli suggested to the NEC the appointment of an "African National Congress Committee of Inquiry" into Bantu education. The committee was set up with Matthews as chairman and the following members, several of whom were former teachers: from the Transvaal, Duma Nokwe, G. M. Pitje, and Ezekiel Mphahlele; from Natal, P. V. Mbatha, P. O. Sikakane, and Dr. Don Mtimkulu; from Cape Province, A. P. Mda and T. T. Letlaka; and from the Orange Free State, L. K. Ntlabathi and two others to be appointed. Tambo to Matthews, July 2, 1956.

In a letter to Tambo dated July 13, 1956, Matthews accepted the assignment, saying, "The more I think about the system of education under review, the more I am satisfied that the underlying philosophy and the administration of it are even more important than the content of the syllabuses etc."

The committee was to communicate through correspondence, with individual members consulting with teachers and taking care to avoid the "victimisation" of those who cooperated. Matthews hoped to have a progress report ready for the December 1956 conference. What was accomplished before the arrests for treason on December 5 is not known.

109. J. Matthews to Z. K. Matthews, Jan. 7, 1953.

110. This paragraph and the one following are based on "Essentials of 'M-Plan' Organization" (5 typewritten pages, n.d.).

111. "Secretarial Report to the Provincial Conference, ANC (Cape), held at Cradock on the 15th/16th August 1953" (13 typewritten pages),p. 10.

112. J. Matthews to Sisulu, Oct. 25, 1955. On the first draft, see Robert Resha, "A.N.C. Conference at Queenstown," *Fighting Talk*, Feb. 1954, p. 10. Also conversation with Tambo, Sept. 1964.

113. In the same letter, Professor Matthews expressed his regret that a special national conference was to be held March 31–April 1, 1956 in Johannesburg. ". . . the Conference will be dominated by Transvaal delegates who come from [a] Province without branches or members," he wrote with obvious exaggeration. "They will force on the country as a whole things which they themselves will not be able to do."

On Nov. 23, 1956, the Rev. W. S. Gawe sent Professor Matthews "a memorandum of amendments to the draft constitution which were sent to Head Office by our Cape Eastern Region." He commented: "While my Provincial

90

Secretary claimed that they were the ones we drew up at our executive meeting, I spotted that they were still bent on killing the Provincial arrangement. Fortunately they were not able to find support from any quarter.''

114. Another matter, in particular, that Lutuli felt strongly about was his opposition to "making the Freedom Charter the [essential] basis [in every detail] for co-operation with any group in the future." See below, p. 71.

115. J. Matthews to T. E. Tshunungwa, Nov. 9, 1954.

116. Minutes of A.N.C. Conference held at Bloemfontein, (handwritten), Dec. 17, 1955, p. 9.

117. Tambo to W. Z. Conco, May 15, 1955.

118. ANC leaders characteristically spoke with more realism and humor about the number of their active and reliable members than did the leaders of the Pan Africanist Congress, which was formed in 1959. Professor Z. K. Matthews, Frieda Matthews, and Robert Resha in 1964 laughed at the assessment of the American diplomat noted in the text. Resha referred to a claim by Patrick Duncan that 57 percent of the Africans favored the PAC and 35 percent, the ANC; he remarked, "If only we had 35 percent," and Professor Matthews added, "Or 5 percent." Conversation of Karis with Professor and Mrs. Matthews and Resha, June 18, 1964.

119. Kuper, *Passive Resistance in South Africa*, p. 146, refers to a press report of a statement by Lutuli that the 100,000 members were paid up.

120. "Memorandum on the Nature and Effects of Racial Discrimination in South Africa, submitted jointly by the African National Congress and the South African Indian Congress to the United Nations Commission on Racial Discrimination in South Africa" (mimeographed, Aug. 1953). The memorandum also claimed that the SAIC had 45,000 members, grouped as follows: Natal Indian Congress, 32,000; Transvaal Indian Congress, 12,000; and Cape Indian Assembly, 1,000. Indians were not permitted to live in the Orange Free State.

121. Kuper, *Passive Resistance in South Africa*, pp. 150–151; *Advance*, April 22, 1954.

122. ANC (Natal), "Report of the Provincial Executive for the Year Commencing November 1, 1954 and ending September 30th, 1955."

123. M. B. Yengwa to Dr. W. Z. Conco, June 17, 1955.

124. ". . . the idea of the annual subscription derives from the old concept of the annual conference as the main Congress activity, and ignores the regular branch meeting." Alan Doyle, "The Special Conference of the A.N.C.," *Liberation*, Feb. 1956, p. 15.

125. Lutuli to Dr. A. E. Letele, March 3, 1956.

126. Tambo circular, Jan. 1, 1955.

127. Z. K. Matthews to Conco, Nov. 28, 1955. Professor Matthews noted in a postscript that his letter was handwritten because the police had failed to return his typewriter, seized in a raid. "Isn't it a nuisance?" he asked.

128. Attachment to letter from Office of Treasurer-General to the Provincial Secretary-Treasurer, Jan. 27, 1955. In mid-1954, the ANC (Cape) opened an office in New Brighton, Port Elizabeth, and hired a full-time clerk at the basic salary of £5 a month. ANC (Cape), "Minutes of the Last Executive Meeting Held at Cradock on the 11th September, 1954."

129. "Minutes of the Executive Held on the 18th April, 1954 at the Clermont Township, Pinetown, Natal."

130. "National Executive Meeting, March 5, 1955."

131. Tambo to Conco, May 6, 1955. Dr. Conco was banned after presiding at the Congress of the People in June 1955. Dr. Arthur Letele became acting treasurer-general and then was elected to the post in December 1955. He found Conco's accounts in good shape but Molema's "in a terrible state." Conversation with Letele, March 1964.

132. Conco to Tambo, May 10, 1955.

133. Potlako Leballo was said to be the author of "this malicious allegation." He also charged that Congress funds "were wasted in sending certain people overseas" and described Walter Sisulu and others who had traveled to Moscow and Peking as "Eastern functionaires." Quoted in memorandum on *Lodestar*, the official organ of the ANC (Transvaal) Youth League, prepared for the Treason Trial defense.

134. "Report of the National Action Committee," Dec. 5, 1953.

135. Its statement, presumably an annual report, noted that only £43 was disbursed to the province from subscriptions. Income included £184.19.2 earned in concerts, £100 in refunded bail, and £52 for the sale of brooches.

136. "Meeting of the National Executive of the African National Congress Held on the 19th & 20th November, 1955, at Groutville."

137. "Owing to the proximity of Tvl. Province and N. E. office, the Headquarters drew money directly from the Transvaal Treasury. Such transactions should be recorded and reported to Treasurer-General's Office." "Minutes of the A.N.C. Conference held at Bloemfontein, 17th December 1955."

138. Z. K. Matthews to Conco, Nov. 28, 1955.

139. Circular "to all branches of the Western Cape," from T. E. Tshunungwa, June 29, 1955.

140. Circular from Tambo, Feb. 29, 1956.

141. "Minutes of the Executive Held on the 18th April, 1954 at the Clermont Township, Pinetown, Natal" note the decision to form a committee. Professor Matthews was appointed the convenor. On *Inyaniso*, see "National Executive Meeting of the African National Congress" (handwritten), n.d.

142. Statement by Professor Matthews, *Treason Trial Record*, p. 18,199.

143. An undated questionnaire of the ANC (Transvaal) to all branches asked in 1955: "How many copies of the national bulletin, 'INYANISO', have you received?"

144. Lutuli to George Houser, June 8, 1956. Lutuli noted that the use of the printing facilities of *Indian Opinion* would be a great help. In a "confidential" letter to Tambo on the same day, Lutuli noted that Houser had raised "even in this early stage the question of the Editor." Lutuli then commented, "I suppose he wants to make sure that their money does not help leftist ascendancy in the African National Congress. Whatever we may do internally by way of editing the paper, could we not for their purpose say that you or I were Editors? This would dispel American fears and suspicions."

145. Much of the following discussion is based on a memorandum prepared by the defense in the Treason Trial.

146. Brian Bunting, *The Story Behind the Non-White Press*, a reprint of articles in *New Age* of Nov. 20, 27, and Dec. 4, 1958. Also see this pamphlet and Carter, *The Politics of Inequality*, pp. 43–47, for the following paragraph in the text.

147. Thomas Karis, "South Africa," in G. M. Carter (ed.), *Five African States: Responses to Diversity* (Ithaca, N. Y.: Cornell University Press, 1963), p. 553; memorandum, "The Real Printing & Publishing Co., (Pty.) Ltd., Publishers of 'New Age.'" The memorandum is the source for data on circulation, finance, and distribution.

148. "Circular No. 1, 1955," n.d.

149. *Summary of the Report of the Commission for the Socio-Economic Development of the Bantu Areas within the Union of South Africa* (Pretoria: The Government Printer, U.G. 61/1055), pp. 32–33.

150. Brookes and Macaulay, *Civil Liberty in South Africa*, p. 166.

151. See Elizabeth S. Landis, "South African Apartheid Legislation I: Fundamental Structure," and "South African Apartheid Legislation II: Extension, Enforcement and Perpetuation," *Yale Law Journal*, Nov. 1961, pp. 1–52, and Jan.

1962, pp. 437–500; Brookes and Macaulay, *Civil Liberty in South Africa*, pp. 65–66; H. R. Hahlo and Ellison Kahn, *The Union of South Africa: The Development of Its Laws and Constitution* (London: Stevens & Sons Ltd., 1960), p. 810.

152. Also see ANC (Cape) Executive Report for Oct. 30–31, 1954 meeting, p. 3.

153. On the Native Laws Amendment Act, 1952, as amended, see Brookes and Macaulay, *Civil Liberty in South Africa*, pp. 63–65.

154. *Ibid.*, pp. 69–71.

155. *Ibid.*, p. 81, and Hahlo and Kahn, *The Union of South Africa*, p. 788.

156. Brookes and Macaulay, *Civil Liberty in South Africa*, pp. 160–161.

157. Regarding "the submission of the agenda of all meetings called by the people's organisations for approval of the magistrates," W. M. Tsotsi, president of the AAC, gave the following example in his presidential address on Dec. 15, 1953: "An example of how this power is being used comes from the Glen Grey District where the local Parents' Association was not allowed by the magistrate to include on the agenda of its meeting a discussion on the Bantu Education Bill because this discussion is political!"

158. Brookes and Macaulay, *Civil Liberty in South Africa*, pp. 84–85.

159. "Minutes of ANC National Executive Committee, Nov. 27, 1954."

160. Hahlo and Kahn, *The Union of South Africa*, p. 143.

161. *House of Assembly Debates*, Feb. 9, 1955, cols. 859 ff. See also *New Age*, Feb. 17, 1955.

162. See Hahlo and Kahn, *The Union of South Africa*, p. 141.

163. *Ibid.*, pp. 141–142; Brookes and Macaulay, *Civil Liberty in South Africa*, p. 74.

164. This and the following paragraph are based on Brookes and Macaulay, *Civil Liberty in South Africa*, pp. 6–8, 31, 38, 67, 154–158.

165. Quoted in Landis, *South African Apartheid Legislation*, Part II, p. 463.

166. See Volume II, pp. 76–77.

167. Quoted in Brian Bunting, *The Rise of the South African Reich* (Harmondsworth, Middlesex, England: Penguin Books, 1964), p. 266.

168. Quoted in Bunting, cited above, pp. 265–266.

169. Carter, *The Politics of Inequality*, p. 115. See also p. 113.

170. Quoted in Bunting, *Rise of the South African Reich*, p. 267.

171. For the following discussion of the trade-union movement, see Muriel Horrell, *South African Trade Unionism* (Johannesburg: South African Institute of Race Relations, 1961), pp. 22–23, 25, 70–79, 137–138; *New Age*, March 10, 1955; Alex Hepple, "Labour and Labour Laws in South Africa," *Africa South*, Oct.–Dec. 1956, pp. 24–32; Bunting, *Rise of the South African Reich*, pp. 274–275, 277–278; Peter Beyeleveld, "The Thorny Road to Unity," *Fighting Talk*, June 1954, p. 7; Michael Harmel, "Trade Unions Face the Future," *Liberation*, No. 10, 1954; Mike Muller, "Trade Union Tasks," *Fighting Talk*, April 1955; and Carter, *The Politics of Inequality*, p. 72.

172. Conversation of Johns with Jacob Nyaose, 1964.

173. The vice-presidents were C. Sibande and Lucy Mvubelo. *New Age*, March 10, 1955.

174. Conversation of Carter and Johns with Alex Hepple, Feb. 28, 1964, and of Karis with Hepple, Feb. 14, 1964.

175. The discussion of the origin of the idea of the Congress of the People is based on a conversation with Z. K. Matthews, March 19, 1964.

The prosecution in the Treason Trial suggested that Professor Matthews got the idea of the Congress of the People from Paul Robeson, the radical American Negro leader, while he was in the United States, a suggestion Professor Matthews firmly denied.

176. "The Concept of the Congress of the People," a memorandum by Z. K. Matthews prepared for the defense in the Treason Trial.

177. "Draft Memorandum of the Congress of the People," by Z. K. Matthews, n.d. The memorandum, requested by Lutuli in a letter of Feb. 9, 1954, was the basis of discussion at a meeting on March 21, 1954 of the National Executive Committee with a large number of organizations (including the Nationalist Party and the United Party) which had been invited to join in the sponsorship of the Congress of the People.

178. *Treason Trial Record*, pp. 18,046–18,047. In his memorandum for the defense in the trial, Professor Matthews wrote, "I, myself, was being metaphorical when, in my presidential address to the Cape Congress in June 1955 [Document 8], I said, 'We . . . wish the Congress of the People the success their efforts deserve. Unlike the exclusively white Parliament . . . , the Parliament of the People will, we have no doubt, send a message of hope to every home in South Africa.'. . . When the Native Representative Council was in existence, it was frequently referred to by the Africans as 'Parliament bantu', which meant 'Parliament of the people', but they did not by that imply that it constituted an alternative government to the existing government."

179. "Draft Memorandum on the Congress of the People," by Z. K. Matthews, n.d. Matthews's address in August 1953 suggesting a Congress of the People (Document 1) did not use the slogan "freedom for all in our lifetime." Lutuli in his presidential address in December 1953 (Document 3a) stated that the ANC "unequivocally demands full democratic rights now, during our lifetime. . . ."

180. Z. K. Matthews, unpublished manuscript.

181. T. E. Tshunungwa. "Report on my visit to the Cape-Western Region—A.N.C. Branches," Jan. 1955.

182. "Minutes of the National Executive Meeting Held in Durban on the 21st, May, 1955."

183. The printed "lectures" were probably prepared by members of the COD.

184. Albert Luthuli, *Let My People Go: An Autobiography* (London: Collins, 1962; New York: McGraw-Hill, 1962), p. 159. Lutuli overestimated the extent of press coverage when he wrote, "The noisy opposition in most of the white Press advertised the Congress and the Charter more effectively than our unaided efforts would have done."

185. *New Age*, June 23, 1955.

186. Dr. Arthur Letele, for example, has said that messengers to tribal locations and workers' compounds near Kimberley naturally asked leading questions, such as, "What is your idea of being free?" One reply was: "ten wives." One of the non-African members of the National Action Council has stated that a committee of the Council received "thousands of little pieces of paper, many of them with specific demands, for example, 'The district commissioner [magistrate?] is not fair to us; we want him removed.' "

187. Available historical sources do not provide an adequate record of the drafting of the Charter. The published description is by Anthony Sampson, *The Treason Cage: The Opposition on Trial in South Africa* (London: Heinemann, 1958), p. 108. The ANC leader referred to has said that the distinctive style of the Freedom Charter and the "Call" (Document 9) was most likely the contribution of Lionel Bernstein. This possibility has little relationship, however, to the unrealistic and undocumented charge of Jordan Ngubane that "the bosses of the underground Communist Party" were "the real originator of policy" in the Congress alliance. See his *An African Explains Apartheid* (New York: Praeger, 1963), p. 164.

188. A circular, "To Members of the Working Committee of the A.N.C.," was issued on June 21, 1955, calling "an urgent meeting" for the following day to discuss the Freedom Charter and other matters. Minutes of the meeting itself are not available.

94

189. "Meeting of the National Executive Committee, 25th June 1955" (handwritten, 2 pp.). Dr. Conco did not see the draft until after he arrived in Johannesburg. Conversation of Carter with Jordan Ngubane, and Ngubane, *An African Explains Apartheid*, p. 164.

190. "Statement Taken from Chief Albert J. Luthuli" for the defense in the Treason Trial (typed, 21 pp.).

191. United Nations, *Third Report*, cited above, pp. 54–56. Some African critics of the Congress of the People have claimed that Matthews deliberately stayed away in order to avoid public association with the rally's left-wing organizers. Persons who knew Matthews well, however, scoffed at this assertion.

192. The estimate of two hundred is from an article by Manilal Gandhi, *Indian Opinion*, July 1, 1955, quoted in United Nations, *Third Report*, cited above, pp. 81–82. Gandhi also stated that more than 3,000 observers were present in addition to the delegates. Presumably he was referring to observers outside the wired enclosure for delegates.

193. Luthuli, *Let My People Go*, p. 158.

194. Sampson, *The Treason Cage*, p. 106.

195. Robertson, *Liberalism in South Africa*, p. 164.

196. Conversation of Carter, Karis, and Johns with the PAC Presidential Council, March 9, 1964. Leballo on another occasion recalled that he had become involved in a "physical fight" at Kliptown.

197. Benson, *The African Patriots*, p. 214.

198. *New Age*, June 30, 1955.

199. Benson, *The African Patriots*, p. 216. An American State Department official visiting South Africa at the time was discouraged by the American consul-general in Johannesburg from attending the Congress, because the consul-general had been told by the police that the danger of violence was great.

200. Quoted in United Nations, *Third Report*, cited above, p. 84.

201. Conversation with Ngubane, 1964; unpublished manuscript. See also Ngubane, *An African Explains Apartheid*, pp. 99–100.

202. Conversations with the PAC Presidential Council, March 9, 1964, A. B. Ngcobo, and Peter 'Molotsi, Aug. 10, 1963. Bloke Modisane, *Blame Me on History* (London: Thames and Hudson, 1963), pp. 236–240, described the Freedom Charter as "racialist," citing, for example, its provision that "all national groups shall be protected by law against insults to their race and national pride."

203. One contribution of the NEUM, according to Frieda Matthews, was the constant harping on the term "nonracial" in preference to "multiracial." In the judgment of Joseph Matthews, however, the issue was semantic because the two words meant the same. Conversation, Feb. 3, 1974.

204. "Statement Taken from Chief Albert J. Luthuli" for the defense in the Treason Trial.

205. "Conference Resolutions: Annual Provincial Conference, African National Congress, Natal Province, Held in Durban, October 8–10, 1955."

206. After the Congress of the People, it was evident that the fears of some ANC members had been groundless: fears that the Congress might do more than adopt a Charter and, indeed, might be transformed into a new organization. The minutes of the National Executive Committee of May 21, 1955, had stated that "Chief Luthuli felt that any attempts to make the C.O.P. an organisation were to be strenuously opposed." At the Congress, a resolution was adopted dealing with future work on behalf of the Charter. As drafted, the resolution "mandated" the ANC and its allied organizations "to work together and campaign for the achievement of the demands of the Charter." When this resolution was presented to the ANC's National Executive Committee on June 25, the committee deleted the words "mandate" and "together and campaign." The form of the resolution as presented to the Congress of the People is not known; the original form was reported by *New Age* on June 30 as having been adopted.

207. O. R. Tambo, "Circular Letter to Provinces," July 6, 1955. Recognizing that there had been failures in the campaign, he asked also for "frank and honest criticism."

208. "Minutes of the Meeting of the National Executive Committee of the African National Congress Held in Durban [*sic*] on the 30th July, 1955." Disagreement on whether or not the committee should recommend adoption is suggested by the typewritten minutes. These report such a recommendation, but it is crossed out in pencil, and it is recommended instead that the Charter be placed before the conference "for its consideration."

209. O. R. Tambo to "The Province Secretary," Aug. 20, 1955.

210. Conversation with the PAC Presidential Council, March 9, 1964.

211. Mda also wrote for *The Africanist* under various pseudonyms, including "UmAfrika," "Sandile," and "Ilya." *The Africanist* of July–August, 1955, has an article on the event by Peter 'Molotsi.

After reading the *Bantu World*, Joe Matthews wrote from Port Elizabeth to Tambo in Johannesburg on Aug. 26, 1955, asking for information and "the real attitude of the leadership" toward a memorial for Lembede. Dr. Letele had just been in Port Elizabeth and told him that he had sent a message to the memorial service "in all innocence" (in Matthews' words). "I find it difficult," Matthews wrote, "to believe that A. P. could join an attempt by renegades like Leballo to question the bona fides of the present leadership of Congress in so far as the cause of African liberation is concerned."

212. "Meeting of the National Executive of the African National Congress Held on the 19th & 20th November, 1955, at Groutville."

213. *New Age*, Oct. 6, 1955.

214. Z. K. Matthews, unpublished manuscript.

215. *New Age*, Oct. 20, 1955.

216. "Presidential Address Delivered to the Transvaal African National Congress Held at Orlando from the 8th to the 10th October, 1955."

217. "Report of the Continuation Conference held at Communal Hall, Orlando on 6/11/55" (handwritten).

218. Letter to *New Age*, Feb. 16, 1956.

219. Article by Govan Mbeki, *New Age*, Dec. 29, 1955.

220. Z. K. Matthews to Lutuli, Dec. 9, 1955.

221. *The World*, Jan. 28, 1956, which also reports on the attitudes of Calata and Letele.

222. *Indian Opinion*, Feb. 17, 1956.

223. One effect of organizational strains in the ANC by the late 1950s was an increased tendency to follow irregular procedures. During January 1956, the Natal provincial executive committee, meeting under the chairmanship of Lutuli, "recorded its alarm on hearing [from S. Dlamini] of the election of Congress Officials by mass vote instead of accredited delegates." The committee also expressed concern about the Transvaal's representation at the December conference "in the absence of proof of its membership." "Minutes of the Meeting of the Provincial Executive Committee of the African National Congress (Natal Branch) held at Groutville on the 21st and 22nd of January, 1956." The new National Executive Committee co-opted P. H. Simelane and G. S. D. Nyembe of Natal as members "under Emergency Regulations," *loc cit.*, and "Minutes of the Meeting of the Provincial Executive Committee of the African National Congress, Natal Branch, held at Groutville, on the 12th of May, 1956."

224. *New Age*, April 5, 1956; conversation with the PAC Presidential Council, March 9, 1964, and 'Molotsi, Aug. 10, 1963.

225. "Statement Taken from Chief Albert J. Luthuli" for the defense in the Treason Trial.

226. Lutuli to Letele, March 22, 1956.

227. *Drum*, Dec. 1955, p. 63.

228. "Statement Taken from Chief Albert J. Luthuli" for the defense in the Treason Trial.

229. Benson, *The African Patriots*, pp. 226–227.

230. Neville Rubin, quoted by Robertson, *Liberalism in South Africa*, p. 165.

231. This observer prefers to remain anonymous.

232. "Resolutions Passed at the Special National Conference of the African National Congress Held in Orlando Communal Hall, 31st March–1st April, 1956."

233. *House of Assembly Debates*, April 30, 1956, col. 4594.

234. Members of the deputation said, at a press conference in Cape Town, that the minister had refused to meet representatives of the advisory boards on previous occasions. On this occasion they were unable to make an appointment through the Native Commissioner in Johannesburg and the Natives' Representatives in Parliament in order to request the withdrawal of the Native Administration Amendment Bill, the Urban Areas Amendment Bill, and the Natives (Prohibition of Interdicts) Bill. (See above, pages 51ff.) The deputation had visited the Senate, where a Nationalist senator pointed to "those Natives sitting up there" as supporters of apartheid and to the Natives' Representatives as "instigators." W. S. Pela, chairman of the deputation, expressed shock at the suggestion that the minister believed they could not act independently. *New Age*, May 10, 1956, pp. 1 and 4.

235. *Die Transvaler*, quoted by W. B. Ngakane in *New Age*, Nov. 1, 1956, p. 2.

236. On pass requirements, see Brookes and Macaulay, *Civil Liberty in South Africa*, pp. 55–60, and Landis, "South African Apartheid Legislation II," pp. 457–462.

237. In 1947, 51,134 Africans were exempt: chiefs and headmen, teachers, professors, lecturers, ministers of religion who were marriage officers, advocates, attorneys, medical practitioners, dentists, and holders of exemptions under the Native Administration Act, in particular, registered African voters and land owners. Landis, "South African Apartheid Legislation I, II," pp. 43 and 459.

238. The history of the Federation is reviewed in a 14-page memorandum, "The Federation of South African Women," prepared for the Treason Trial defense.

239. Duma Nokwe, assistant secretary-general of the ANC, wrote to the national secretary of the Women's League on Oct. 1, 1956, regarding a question she had raised about the League's relationship to the Federation. The working committee and National Executive Committee recommended affiliation, he said, although the decision was the League's to make.

240. Quoted in *New Age*, Aug. 16, 1956.

241. *Ibid.*, April 19, 1956.

242. Pictures of the second demonstration are in a printed booklet, *"Strijdom . . . You have struck a rock"* (Federation of South African Women) n.d.

243. "The Federation of South African Women," memorandum prepared for the Treason Trial defense.

244. Wilson and Thompson, *Oxford History of South Africa*, p. 199.

245. Department of Native Affairs, *Report of the Native Laws Commission, 1946–48* (U.G. No. 28–1948), p. 19.

246. *Summary of the Report of the Commission for the Socio-Economic Development of the Bantu Areas within the Union of South Africa* (Pretoria: The Government Printer, U.G. 61/1055), p. 106.

247. Quoted in Carter, *The Politics of Inequality*, p. 284.

248. In the meantime, the government had won what appeared to be a breakthrough for official policy: the unanimous vote in April 1955 of the members of the Bunga (the United Transkeian Territories General Council) to accept the Bantu authorities system in principle. The Bunga, a large majority of whose members were chiefs or headmen, had responded to the government's powers of persuasion,

its promise of enhanced authority, and hard evidence that opposition was fruitless. Just what this decision meant, in fact, to the individual members of the Bunga is difficult to determine. The night before the vote, most of the Bunga's members had given a unanimous vote of confidence to two of the parliamentary Natives' Representatives at a meeting in which the latter advocated restoring Africans to the common voters' roll. During the Bunga's discussions the following day one prominent member coupled his support for Bantu authorities with his hope for eventual "direct representation in Parliament." But the prevailing hope at that time was for wider authority within the Transkei. This note is taken from Gwendolen M. Carter, Thomas Karis, and Newell M. Stultz, *South Africa's Transkei: The Politics of Domestic Colonialism* (Evanston: Northwestern University Press, 1967),pp. 18–19.

249. *Ibid.,* p. 18. Also see Document 21.

250. The third president, holding office in the early 1960s, was the Rev. S. S. Tema, a Dutch Reformed Church minister who had been a member of the ANC from the late 1930s until he associated himself with Selope Thema's National-minded bloc in the early 1950s. The discussion of IDAMF is based on a conversation with Tema, April 4, 1964.

251. *Sechaba: Bulletin of the Transvaal African National Congress,* No. 2, Aug. 1956, p. 2.

252. The quotation is in *New Age,* Oct. 18, 1956. In describing the forthcoming conference as the most important in twenty years, *The World* (Oct. 6, 1956) also used the words "life and death." IDAMF's invitation to a minister of the Dutch Reformed Church was also declined. The conference was opened by the Anglican Archdeacon of Bloemfontein. *New Age,* Sept. 27 and Oct. 18, 1956; Sampson, *Treason Cage,* p. 113.

253. Statements by Mncube in *New Age,* Oct. 25 and Dec. 20, 1956.

254. *The World,* Oct. 20, 1956.

255. *Loc. cit.*

256. Article by Govan Mbeki, *New Age,* Oct. 18, 1956.

257. *The World,* Oct. 20, 1956.

258. *New Age,* Oct. 25, 1956.

259. *Ibid.,* Nov. 29, 1956.

260. *Ibid.,* Nov. 8, 1956.

261. In its issue of April 19, 1956, *New Age* itemized "eight bloody clashes between Africans and the police during the last seven weeks."

262. *Ibid.,* June 21 and 28, 1956; *Counter Attack,* June 1956; and "A Presidential Message and Call on the Eve of the 1956 Anniversary of 'June 26,' by Albert J. Lutuli." For 1953, see above, p. 9.

263. See *New Age,* particularly the issues of July 5, Aug. 9 and 30, 1956.

264. Conversation of Gerhart with T. T. Letlake, Z. B. Molete, A. B. Ngcobo, and Peter Raboroko, Sept. 9, 1968. See also Socialist League of Africa, "10 Years of the Stay-at-Home," n.d., 19 typed pages.

265. "Report of the National Executive Committee of the African National Congress to the Annual Conference Held in Queenstown, December, 1956," n.d.

266. Benson, *The African Patriots,* p. 230.

267. "Report of the National Executive Committee . . . December, 1956."

268. The Rev. W. S. Gawe to The Editor, *The Daily Reporter,* Queenstown, n.d.

269. "Statement Taken from Chief Albert J. Luthuli" for the defense in the Treason Trial. The National Executive Committee's report stated: "We must point out that unlike the situation in Egypt rational judgment at present of the Hungarian situation is made difficult by the undoubted hysterical whipping up of anti-Soviet feelings by the Western powers, as shown by the anti-Russian demonstrations in some of our Universities in the Union and by the manner in which the

Union Government which proclaimed its neutrality in the Egyptian crisis caused by Great Britain, France and Israel had been quick to offer financial aid to Hungarian refugees, when it did nothing and is still doing nothing about alleviating the suffering of the people of Egypt brought about by the wanton attack on the people of Egypt by Great Britain. Under the circumstances, we reserve final judgment on the situation in Hungary until the air is cleared of obvious partisan charges and counter charges."

The report was seized by the Special Branch at the annual conference. In a copy of the report available at the Treason Trial, the paragraph quoted above appeared near the end of the report, and a similar paragraph, near the beginning of the report, was crossed out. One of the deleted sentences suggested that public attention was being diverted from Egypt. The following sentence was added: "The African National Congress feels a sense of disappointment and regret at the bloodshed in Hungary and sincerely hopes that peace will be restored without delay in this country."

270. *New Age*, Dec. 20, 1956; *The World*, Dec. 29, 1956.

271. *Treason Trial Record*, p. 8,152. For the discussion of the Treason Trial of 1956–1961, see Thomas Karis, "The South African Treason Trial," *Political Science Quarterly*, June 1961, pp. 217–240, and *The Treason Trial in South Africa: A Guide to the Microfilm Record of the Trial* (Stanford: Hoover Institution, 1965).

272. *New Age*, Dec. 6, 1956.

Documents

THE AFRICAN NATIONAL CONGRESS
RE-EXAMINES ITS TACTICS

Document 1. Presidential Address by Professor Z. K. Matthews, ANC (Cape), August 15, 1953

Sons and Daughters of Africa,

It is my pleasant duty, first of all, to say a word of welcome to all the delegates who have come from different parts of the Cape Province to attend this Conference. Our area of operation covers a considerable proportion of the Union of South Africa. Our branches are scattered all over this vast area, and therefore it is by no means easy for a conference of this kind to be assembled, more particularly if this is done more than once a year. As you know the normal practice is for us to hold our Provincial Conference during the month of June. In 1952 we were compelled by circumstances to depart from this custom. During that year, you will remember that we held a Special Conference at Port Elizabeth on April the 12th, in response to a directive from our National head-quarters in connection with preparations for the Campaign for the Defiance of Unjust Laws.

At that Conference it was decided to convert the special conference into our annual conference so as to obviate the holding of a further meeting in June 1952. It was hoped, then, that it might be possible to hold another meeting later in the year, but as all the world knows, the second half of the year 1952 was taken up with the historic Defiance Campaign in which the Cape Province played such an important role, so that it was not feasible for the Provincial Conference to be held until February, 1953. When I returned from the United States in May, 1953, I realised that it would probably be impossible to resume immediately our normal practice of holding our Conference in June 1953. Our Provincial Executive, which met at Port Elizabeth in June, decided, however, that the Provincial Conference should be held as soon as arrangements for it could be made in view of important developments, not only in the Province but in the country as a whole. August 15th, 1953, at Cradock was therefore decided upon. It is hoped, however, that in future we shall be able to resume our normal practice and so hold our next annual conference in June, 1954.

In the second place, may I, on behalf of the Province, say a word of thanks to the Cradock branch of the African National Congress (Cape) for the readiness with which they consented to assume the responsibility of acting as hosts for this Conference. Normally when a branch is called upon to receive the Provincial Conference, it is given a whole year's notice, so as to give it a reasonable period within which to make the necessary arrangements. In this case Cradock was given a little more than a month's notice but they did not hesitate to undertake this heavy responsibility. The last occasion on which we met here was in June, 1951, and many of us still have happy memories of the excellent treatment accorded to us then, and so we have come here full of pleasant expectations which we know will not be disappointed.

A word of thanks is also due to the Town Council of Cradock which has once more permitted us to meet within its area of jurisdiction. The Town Council of Cradock has not yet joined those local authorites which mistakenly suppose that peace and harmony between white and black can only be maintained by denying the black man the expression of his legitimate aspirations. For the denial of a group of people of the freedom to express their views on matters affecting their welfare does not mean that they either cease to have those views or cease to believe in the justice of their cause. On the contrary, the enforced quiet or silence gives those in authority a false sense of security which is rudely shaken when the superficial calm is disturbed, as it inevitably must be, by the irrepressible urge to freedom for which all people yearn, without distinction of race or colour or creed.

We can only express the hope that Cradock, which is one of the principal centres of the Cape Midlands, essentially a farming area, will continue to maintain the open door, and will not succumb to the blandishments of those who are trying to propagate the dangerous doctrine that the interests of the different sections of our population are diametrically opposed to one another or who see some menace to their position whenever two or three Africans are gathered together in some place.

In the African National Congress we believe that the interests of white and black in South Africa are so inextricably interwoven that no policy which either overtly or covertly seeks to employ the machinery of the State to secure advantages for one section of the population at the expense or to the detriment of other sections of the population will, in the long run benefit, even the so-called privileged section, to say nothing of the rest. When the day comes for which all true South Africans are working, when we shall have achieved a united South African nation, honour will go to those who throughout South African history have not allowed their temporary or fortuitous positions of advantage to cloud their vision of a South African state based upon justice, fair play and equal opportunity for all.

PRESENT SITUATION.

We are meeting at a time which is very critical in the history of the country. Those of you who have eyes to see and ears to hear will agree that the present state of affairs in South Africa shows signs of an ever deepening crisis in the relations between the various groups represented here. The present government has just been returned to power with a majority which in the view of some of its supporters entitles it to put into effect a policy of "white South Africa" first, second and last, whatever the consequences to the country as a whole. The size of the government's majority becomes even greater when it is borne in mind that the opposition parties are in the main but pale reflections of the government party as far as their colour policies are concerned. But we are satisfied that no amount of "Coffee-Drinking" over it, will result in the production of a state of affairs in South Africa in which the interests of non-whites can safely be ignored.

The removal of African voters from the common roll did not bring about the white millenium which was hoped for in 1936. Similarly the removal of the Coloured voters from the common roll in 1953 with or without a two-thirds majority, with or without consultation of the Coloured people, will not make that millenium any less of a pipe-dream. The same applies to much of the ideological legislation which is now before the Special Session of Parliament in which Ministers are vieing with each other in putting various apartheid measures on the Statute Book. The Minister of Labour has discovered a method by which he hopes successfully to prevent nearly a million African workers in industry from having an effective say in matters affecting their welfare, their terms and conditions of employment. The voteless workers concerned, being totally unrepresented in the white Parliament, will not be able to prevent him from putting his 'Native Settlement of Disputes' Bill on the Statute Book. The advice of government commissions on which the workers were not represented, the past experience of the Departments of Native Affairs and Labour which had already recognised the existence of African Trade Unions though they could not register them in terms of the law, the unqualified opposition of organised labour both white and non-white, developments in other parts of the African continent . . . [sic] all these have been brushed aside. But the mere fact that a law has been placed on the Statute book will not of itself make it workable, and whether the legislation concerned will achieve its objective will not depend on the machinery created under the Act alone. The African workers will, in due course, give their reply to this measure.

The Minister of Native Affairs is proceeding with his plan to transfer African education to the Department of Native Affairs. Once again, it is believed that once this transfer is effected, the aims, content and financing of African education will be streamlined to fit into the apartheid mould. The voteless African will not be able to prevent this step from being taken. But no amount of departmental jugglery will indefinitely prevent the African from achieving his destiny in matters educational. The process may be delayed by artificial obstacles of various kinds but the African people who are determined not to be fobbed off with any inferior brands of education will give their emphatic reply in deeds, not words, as they have done from time to time in connection with other schemes which purported to be intended for their benefit but were shot through with implications with which the African people were in fundamental disagreement.

Another Minister is busy putting on the Statute Book a law to entrench the principle of separate and unequal public amenities and to make sure that this principle of which white South Africa is so proud shall not be interpreted by the Courts in favour of justice and fair play for all. Naturally this law will not make provision for separate and unequal charges for separate and unequal amenities. That would be unfair discrimination against the whites!

The South African idea that wrong can be made into right by the use, or the abuse, of the sovereignty of a Parliament in which only one section of the population is adequately represented is bound, if not abandoned, to have disastrous consequences not only on the relations between white and non-white but also on the relations between white and white. The exercise of power or force can never be adequate criterion for the settlement of questions of human relations from which moral considerations can by no means be ruled out. But although we are convinced that in the long run these attempts to solve national problems on a unilateral basis are doomed to fail, we must remember that a great deal of misunderstanding and perhaps, much hardship will probably be brought about before their futility is recognised.

The people we represent are the ones who are most likely to suffer as a result of ill-conceived schemes. It is because the African National Congress cannot look on and fold its arms or pass by on the other side that we must continue to work for the removal of the disabilities under which our people labour, in spite of the fact that we may be misunderstood in official quarters and elsewhere. We are aware that attempts are being made in some quarters to represent the African National Congress as either an anti-white or a subversive organisation which is out to overthrow the government of the country and to substitute for it some kind of anarchic regime. In some quarters it is alleged that the African National Congress is under some kind of non-African domination. The trouble is that there are so many people in this country who are themselves accustomed to pushing the African from pillar to post that because the African is no longer at their beck and call, he must be subject to the influence of someone else. They are not willing to give the African credit for ever being able to do anything on his own initiative. These are the people who refuse to recognise the new spirit of self-direction and self-determination which is abroad in the new Africa. But we need not be deterred from our primary goal by the misrepresentation of our motives. We need make no apology for rejecting all policies or schemes which are inspired by principles with which we disagree. The African people, like any other group, claim the right to do all in their power to safeguard their interests and to make sure that they are not regarded by any group, however powerful, as mere means to the ends of others. In making these claims we are not inspired by any ill-will towards any group, white or non-white. On the contrary the African National Congress is prepared to work with any group for the achievement of a more united South Africa, provided only that this cooperation is based on the principle of equal rights for all. To demand equal rights for all is, we know, regarded as the greatest heresy in certain South African circles.

All the parties, which are busily engaged in searching for a political structure that will best serve to ensure a stable and harmonious multi-racial society in South Africa, proceed on the assumption that if there is one thing which is to be avoided at all costs it is equal rights for all. Directly or indirectly all of them from the extreme right wing of the Nationalists to the Liberals are anxious to preserve a position of privilege for one section of the population; whether they describe it as "white" or as "civilised" makes no difference.

The African National Congress and its allies on the other hand take the view that harmony, stability and peace can only be achieved through the establishment of a truly democratic South Africa, i.e. one based on the principle of equal rights for all regardless of race or colour. Peace, harmony and prosperity can only exist, we believe, where the principle is accepted, and acted upon, that all peoples in the country have a full share in/and responsibility for the decisions affecting their welfare, unfettered by artificial restrictions or man-made laws which they had no share in making.

As far back as 1945, when the African National Congress drew up a "Bill of Rights" which embodied our principal demands, included among them was the following:

"THE ABOLITION OF POLITICAL DISCRIMINATION BASED ON RACE . . . AND THE EXTENSION TO ALL ADULTS, REGARDLESS OF RACE, OF THE RIGHT TO VOTE AND BE ELECTED TO PARLIAMENT, PROVINCIAL COUNCILS AND OTHER REPRESENTATIVE INSTITUTIONS."

The African National Congress has not yet been given by any body any convincing grounds to justify a change of front in this regard. Those who are unable to contemplate a state of affairs in which they might have to share their cherished rights and privileges with others cannot blame us for working for a state of affairs which holds no terror for us.

But we must be on our guard against minimising the gravity of the problems with which we are confronted. I recall that one of the last words I addressed to the members of the African National Congress (Cape) before my departure overseas was that they should remember that the struggle on which we are engaged is not a picnic. It is a grim affair. The events of 1952 served to remind us all of this. If we are going to be able to discharge our duty and to fulfill our mission we shall have to build up our organisation into an even better force that it has proved thus far. It will be your duty during this Conference, as you listen to and consider the reports which come from our branches in different parts of the country, to give serious attention to the question of strengthening our organisational machinery. This aspect of our work is not spectacular, but unless it is done we shall not be able to carry on successfully the struggle which lies ahead.

The African National Congress (Cape) has an important part to play in our National struggle. On December 17th, 1951 when the African National Congress, assembled at Bloemfontein, took the now historical decision to launch the momentous campaign for the Defiance of Unjust Laws, participating in that debate on behalf of the Province I represented, I expressed the view that when the hour of decision and action struck, the Cape Province would not be found wanting. It was with a great deal of satisfaction, as I followed the Campaign from a distance, that I noted the honourable role which the Cape played. You can all be proud of the excellent contribution you made to every aspect of the struggle. . . . [sic] The number of Volunteers, the increased membership of our organisation, the personal sacrifices made by leaders and followers, the attention paid to the integration of the rural and urban aspects of the struggle, the attention paid to the welfare of the dependants of the volunteers, the maintenance of the code of discipline and self-control associated with a non-violent struggle, the adherence to sound principles and the increased solidarity in our ranks which made it impossible for informers, agents-provocateurs and other enemies of the people to have any influence on the movement.

I should like to congratulate you one and all on the excellent reply you gave to those who previously had no respect for the African's determination and ability to stand up and fight for his rights in the land of his birth. But we cannot afford to rest on our laurels. One phase of the struggle has come and gone, but contrary to popular belief in some quarters, the struggle is by no means at an end. Depending upon surrounding circumstances, the struggle may assume one form at one period and another at a different period, but as long as our main objectives have not been fully achieved, how can there be an end to the struggle? Our National Executive has the matter in hand and it is for us to intensify our organisation and to be prepared, with a strong senior Congress, a sound women's section and a vigorous Youth League. As the President-General has reminded us,

"REMEMBERING THE PAST AND BEARING IN MIND OUR DUTY FOR THE FUTURE WE MUST DEDICATE OURSELVES AFRESH FOR THE OBJECTIVES FOR WHICH OUR ORGANISATION STANDS."

Various groups in the country as you know are considering the idea of a national convention at which all groups might be represented to consider our national problems on an all-inclusive basis. The sponsors of these conventions are hoping to invite various groups to send delegates to such meetings. I wonder whether the time has not come for the African National Congress to consider the question of convening a National Convention, A CONGRESS OF THE PEOPLE, representing all the people of this country irrespective of race or colour to draw up a FREEDOM CHARTER for the DEMOCRATIC SOUTH AFRICA OF THE FUTURE. Once the principle of the establishment of such a CONGRESS OF THE PEOPLE was accepted, the details of its implementation could be worked out either by the National Executive or by an ad hoc committee with that special duty.

In conclusion, I would like to say a word of thanks to the office-bearers of all the branches and to my colleagues in the Provincial Executive for the manner in which they have discharged their duties, especially during my absence overseas. As I said in the message I sent to the branches recently: "I make no apology for making special mention of the distinguished work done by Dr. J. L. Z. Njongwe of Port Elizabeth, who took over the duties of Acting-President, at such short notice and during such an eventful period in the history of our struggle. His fearless and inspired leadership, his untiring efforts and his selfless devotion to the cause of Africa were in no small measure responsible for the remarkable achievements of the African National Congress (Cape) in the campaign which made such an indelible impression upon South Africa. In this work he was ably supported by the Provincial Secretary, Mr. Matji and other members of the Provincial Executive and by our branch officials throughout the province. All of them, one and all, acquitted themselves like true sons and daughters of Africa. This was due, among other things, to the admirable and loyal support which they received from the rank and file of our members. When our principal office-bearers were compelled to relinquish their duties owing to various bans imposed upon them, other members stepped into the breach. In this connection, I want to express my personal thanks and the thanks of the organisation to the Rev. W. B. Tshume, who succeeded Dr. Njongwe as Acting-President and the Rev. A. A. Tsekeletsa who temporarily took over the duties of Provincial Secretary after the Conference held in February 1953.

I trust that in all our deliberations we shall be inspired by a sense of the gravity of the issues which will be placed before us and the responsibility we owe to those we represent here.

AFRIKA'S CAUSE MUST TRIUMPH!

A F R I K A.

Document 2. "No Easy Walk to Freedom." Presidential Address by Nelson R. Mandela, ANC (Transvaal), September 21, 1953

Since 1912 and year after year thereafter, in their homes and local areas, in provincial and national gatherings, on trains and buses, in the factories and on the farms, in cities, villages, shanty towns, schools and prisons, the African people have discussed the shameful misdeeds of those who rule the country. Year after year, they have raised their voices in condemnation of the grinding poverty of the people, the low wages, the acute shortage of land, the inhuman exploitation and the whole policy of white domination. But instead of more freedom repression began to grow in volume and intensity and it seemed that all their sacrifices would end up in smoke and dust. Today the entire country knows that their labours were not in vain for a new spirit and new ideas have gripped our people. Today the people speak the language of action: there is a mighty awakening among the men and women of our country and the year 1952 stands out as the year of this upsurge of national consciousness.

In June, 1952, the AFRICAN NATIONAL CONGRESS and the SOUTH AFRICAN INDIAN CONGRESS, bearing in mind their responsibility as the representatives of the downtrodden and oppressed people of South Africa, took the plunge and launched the Campaign for the Defiance of the Unjust Laws. Starting off in Port Elizabeth in the early hours of June 26 and with only thirty-three defiers in action and then in Johannesburg in the afternoon of the same day with one hundred and six defiers, it spread throughout the country like wild fire. Factory and office workers, doctors, lawyers, teachers, students and the clergy; Africans, Coloureds, Indians and Europeans, old and young, all rallied to the national call and defied the pass laws and the curfew and the railway apartheid regulations. At the end of the year, more than 8,000 people of all races had defied. The Campaign called for immediate and heavy sacrifices. Workers lost their jobs, chiefs and teachers were expelled from the service, doctors, lawyers and businessmen gave up their practices and businesses and elected to go to jail. Defiance was a step of great political significance. It released strong social forces which affected thousands of our countrymen. It was an effective way of getting the masses to function politically; a powerful method of voicing our indignation against the reactionary policies of the Government. It was one of the best ways of exerting pressure on the Government and extremely dangerous to the stability and security of the State. It inspired and aroused our people from a conquered and servile community of yesmen to a militant and uncompromising band of comrades-in-arms. The entire country was transformed into battle zones where the forces of liberation were locked up in immortal conflict against those of reaction and evil. Our flag flew in every battlefield and thousands of our countrymen rallied around it. We held the initiative and the forces of freedom were advancing on all fronts. It was against this background and at the height of this Campaign that we held our last annual provincial Conference in Pretoria from the 10th to the 12th of October last year. In a way, that Conference was a welcome reception for those who had returned from the battlefields and a farewell to those who were still going to action. The spirit of defiance and action dominated the entire conference.

Today we meet under totally different conditions. By the end of July last year, the Campaign had reached a stage where it had to be suppressed by the Government or it would impose its own policies on the country.

The government launched its reactionary offensive and struck at us. Between July last year and August this year forty-seven leading members from both Congresses in Johannesburg, Port Elizabeth and Kimberley were arrested, tried and convicted for launching the Defiance Campaign and given suspended sentences ranging from three months to two years on condition that they did not again participate in the defiance of the unjust laws. In November last year, a proclamation was passed which prohibited meetings of more than ten Africans and made it an offence for any person to call upon an African to defy. Contravention of this proclamation carried a penalty of three years or of a fine of three hundred pounds. In March this year the Government passed the so-called Public Safety Act which empowered it to declare a state of emergency and to create conditions which would permit of the most ruthless and pitiless methods of suppressing our movement. Almost simultaneously, the Criminal Laws Amendment Act was passed which provided heavy penalties for those convicted of Defiance offences. This Act also made provision for the whipping of defiers including women. It was under this Act that Mr. Arthur Matlala who was the local [leader] of the Central Branch during the Defiance Campaign, was convicted and sentenced to twelve months with hard labour plus eight strokes by the Magistrate of Villa Nora. The Government also made extensive use of the Suppression of Communism Act. You will remember that in May last year the Government ordered Moses Kotane, Yusuf Dadoo, J. B. Marks, David Bopape and Johnson Ngwevela to resign from the Congresses and many other organisations and were also prohibited from attending political gatherings. In consequence of these bans, Moses Kotane, J. B. Marks, and David Bopape did not attend our last provincial Conference. In December last year, the Secretary-General, Mr. W. M. Sisulu, and I were banned from attending gatherings and confined to Johannesburg for six months. Early this year, the President-General, Chief Luthuli, whilst in the midst of a national tour which he was prosecuting with remarkable energy and devotion, was prohibited for a period of twelve months from attending public gatherings and from visiting Durban, Johannesburg, Cape Town, Port Elizabeth and many other centres. A few days before the President-General was banned, the President of the S.A.I.C., Dr. G. M. Naicker, had been served with a similar notice. Many other active workers both from the African and Indian Congresses and from trade union organisations were also banned.

The Congresses realised that these measures created a new situation which did not prevail when the Campaign was launched in June 1952. The tide of defiance was bound to recede and we were forced to pause and to take stock of the new situation. We had to analyse the dangers that faced us, formulate plans to overcome them and evolve new plans of political struggle. A political movement must keep in touch with reality and the prevailing conditions. Long speeches, the shaking of fists, the banging of tables and strongly worded resolutions out of touch with the objective conditions do not bring about mass action and can do a great deal of harm to the organisation and the struggle we serve. The masses had to be prepared and made ready for new forms of political struggle. We had to recuperate our strength and muster our forces for another and more powerful offensive against the enemy. To have gone ahead blindly as if nothing had happened would have been suicidal and stupid. The conditions under which we meet today are, therefore, vastly different. The Defiance Campaign together with its thrills and adventures has receded. The old methods of bringing about mass action through public mass meetings, press statements and leaflets calling upon the people to go to action have become extremely dangerous and difficult to use effectively. The authorities will not easily permit a meeting called under the auspices of the A.N.C., few newspapers will publish statements openly criticising the policies of the Government and there is hardly a single printing press which will agree to print leaflets calling upon workers to embark on industrial action for fear of prosecution under the Suppression of Communism Act and similar measures. These developments require the evolution of new forms of political struggle which will make it reasonable for us to strive for action on a higher level than the Defiance Campaign. The Government, alarmed at the indomitable up-surge of national consciousness, is doing everything in its power to crush our movement by removing the genuine representatives of the people from the organisations. According to a statement made by Swart in Parliament on the 18th September, 1953, there are thirty-three trade union officials and eighty-nine other people who have been served with notices in terms of the Suppression of Communism Act. This does not include that formidable array of freedom fighters who have been named and blacklisted under the Suppression of Communism Act and those who have been banned under the Riotous Assemblies Act.

Meanwhile the living conditions of the people, already extremely difficult, are steadily worsening and becoming unbearable. The purchasing power of the masses is progressively declining and the cost of living is rocketing. Bread is now dearer than it was two months ago. The cost of milk, meat and vegetables is beyond the pockets of the average family and many of our people cannot afford them. The people are too poor to have enough food to feed their families and children. They cannot afford sufficient clothing, housing and medical care. They are denied the right to security in the event of unemployment, sickness, disability, old age and where these exist, they are of an extremely inferior and useless nature. Because of lack of proper medical amenities our people are ravaged by such dreaded diseases as tuberculosis, venereal disease, leprosy, pelagra, and infantile mortality is very high. The recent state budget made provision for the increase of the cost-of-living allowances for Europeans and not a word was said about the poorest and most hard-hit section of the population—the African people. The insane policies of the Government which have brought about an explosive situation in the country have definitely scared away foreign capital from South Africa and the financial crisis through which the country is now passing is forcing many industrial and business concerns to close down, to retrench their staffs and unemployment is growing every day. The farm labourers are in a particularly dire plight. You will perhaps recall the investigations and exposures of the semi-slave conditions on the Bethal farms made in 1948 by the Reverend Michael Scott and a *Guardian* Correspondent; by the *Drum* last year and the *Advance* in April this year. You will recall how human beings, wearing only sacks with holes for their heads and arms, never given enough food to eat, slept on cement floors on cold nights with only their sacks to cover their shivering bodies. You will remember how they are woken up as early as 4 a.m. and taken to work on the fields with the indunas sjamboking those who tried to straighten their backs, who felt weak and dropped down because of hunger and sheer exhaustion. You will also recall the story of human beings toiling pathetically from the early hours of the morning till sunset, fed only on mealie meal served on filthy sacks spread on the ground and eating with their dirty hands. People falling ill and never once being given medical attention. You will also recall the revolting story of a farmer who was convicted for tying a labourer by his feet from a tree and had him flogged to death, pouring boiling water into his mouth whenever he cried for water. These things which have long vanished from many parts of the world still flourish in S. A. today. None will deny that they constitute a serious challenge to Congress and we are in duty bound to find an effective remedy for these obnoxious practices.

The Government has introduced in Parliament the Native Labour (Settlement of Disputes) Bill and the Bantu Education Bill. Speaking on the Labour Bill, the Minister of Labour, Ben Schoeman, openly stated that the aim of this wicked measure is to bleed African trade unions to death. By forbidding strikes and lockouts it deprives Africans of the one weapon the workers have to improve their position. The aim of the measure is to destroy the present African trade unions which are controlled by the workers themselves and which fight for the improvement of their working conditions in return for a Central Native Labour Board controlled by the Government and which will be used to frustrate the legitimate aspirations of the African worker. The Minister of Native Affairs, Verwoerd, has also been brutally clear in explaining the objects of the Bantu Education Bill. According to him the aim of this law is to teach our children that Africans are inferior to Europeans. African education would be taken out of the hands of people who taught equality between black and white. When this Bill becomes law, it will not be the parents but the Department of Native Affairs which will decide whether an African child should receive higher or other education. It might well be that the children of those who criticise the Government and who fight its policies will almost certainly be taught how to drill rocks in the mines and how to plough potatoes on the farms of Bethal. High education might well be the privilege of those children whose families have a tradition of collaboration with the ruling circles.

The attitude of the Congress on these bills is very clear and unequivocal. Congress totally rejects both bills without reservation. The last provincial Conference strongly condemned the then proposed Labour Bill as a measure designed to rob the African workers of the universal right of free trade unionism and to undermine and destroy the existing African trade unions. Conference further called upon the African workers to boycott and defy the application of this sinister scheme which was calculated to further the exploitation of the African worker. To accept a measure of this nature even in a qualified manner would be a betrayal of the toiling masses. At a time when every genuine Congressite should fight unreservedly for the recognition of African trade unions and the realisation of the principle that everyone has the right to form and to join trade unions for the protection of his interests, we declare our firm belief in the principles enunciated in the Universal Declaration of Human Rights that everyone has the right to education; that education shall be directed to the full development of human personality and to the strengthening of respect for human rights and fundamental freedoms. It shall promote understanding, tolerance and friendship among the nations, racial or religious groups and shall further the activities of the United Nations for the maintenance of peace. That parents have the right to choose the kind of education that shall be given to their children.

The cumulative effect of all these measures is to prop up and perpetuate the artificial and decaying policy of the supremacy of the white men. The attitude of the government to us is that: "Let's beat them down with guns and batons and trample them under our feet. We must be ready to drown the whole country in blood if only there is the slightest chance of preserving white supremacy."

But there is nothing inherently superior about the herrenvolk idea of the supremacy of the whites. In China, India, Indonesia and Korea, American, British, Dutch and French Imperialism, based on the concept of the supremacy of Europeans over Asians, has been completely and perfectly exploded. In Malaya and Indo-China British and French imperialisms are being shaken to their foundations by powerful and revolutionary national liberation movements. In Africa, there are approximately 190,000,000 Africans as against 4,000,000 Europeans. The entire continent is seething with discontent and already there are powerful revolutionary eruptions in the Gold Coast, Nigeria, Tunisia, Kenya, the Rhodesias and South Africa. The oppressed people and the oppressors are at loggerheads. *The day of reckoning* between the forces of freedom and those of reaction is not very far off. I have not the slightest doubt that when that day comes truth and justice will prevail.

The intensification of repressions and the extensive use of the bans is designed to immobilise every active worker and to check the national liberation movement. But gone forever are the days when harsh and wicked laws provided the oppressors with years of peace and quiet. The racial policies of the Government have pricked the conscience of all men of good will and have aroused their deepest indignation. The feelings of the oppressed people have never been more bitter. If the ruling circles seek to maintain their position by such inhuman methods then a clash between the forces of freedom and those of reaction is certain. The grave plight of the people compels them to resist to the death the stinking policies of the gangsters that rule our country.

But in spite of all the difficulties outlined above, we have won important victories. The general political level of the people has been considerably raised and they are now more conscious of their strength. Action has become the language of the day. The ties between the working people and the Congress have been greatly strengthened. This is a development of the highest importance because in a country such as ours a political organisation that does not receive the support of the workers is in fact paralysed on the very ground on which it has chosen to wage battle. Leaders of trade union organisations are at the same time important officials of the provincial and local branches of the A.N.C. In the past we talked of the African, Indian and Coloured struggles. Though certain individuals raised the question of a united front of all the oppressed groups, the various non-European organisations stood miles apart from one another and the efforts of those for co-ordination and unity were like a voice crying in the wilderness and it seemed that the day would never dawn when the oppressed people would stand and fight together shoulder to shoulder against a common enemy. Today we talk of the struggle of the oppressed people which, though it is waged through their respective autonomous organisations, is gravitating towards one central command.

Our immediate task is to consolidate these victories, to preserve our organisations and to muster our forces for the resumption of the offensive. To achieve this important task the National Executive of the A.N.C. in consultation with the National Action Committee of the A.N.C. and the S.A.I.C. formulated a plan of action popularly known as the "M" Plan and the highest importance is [given] to it by the National Executives. Instructions were given to all provinces to implement the "M" Plan without delay.

The underlying principle of this plan is the understanding that it is no longer possible to wage our struggle mainly on the old methods of public meetings and printed circulars. The aim is:

(1) to consolidate the Congress machinery;

(2) to enable the transmission of important decisions taken on a national level to every member of the organisation without calling public meetings, issuing press statements and printing circulars;

(3) to build up in the local branches themselves local Congresses which will effectively represent the strength and will of the people;

(4) to extend and strengthen the ties between Congress and the people and to consolidate Congress leadership.

This plan is being implemented in many branches not only in the Transvaal but also in the other provinces and is producing excellent results. The Regional Conferences held in Sophiatown, Germiston, Kliptown and Benoni on the 28th June, 23rd and 30th August and on the 6th September, 1953, which were attended by large crowds, are a striking demonstration of the effectiveness of this plan, and the National Executives must be complimented for it. I appeal to all members of the Congress to redouble their efforts and play their part truly and well in its implementation. The hard, dirty and strenuous task of recruiting members and strengthening our organisation through a house to house campaign in every locality must be done by you all. From now on the activity of Congressites must not be confined to speeches and resolutions. Their activities must find expression in wide scale work among the masses, work which will enable them to make the greatest possible contact with the working people. You must protect and defend your trade unions. If you are not allowed to have your meetings publicly, then you must hold them over your machines in the factories, on the trains and buses as you travel home. You must have them in your villages and shantytowns. You must make every home, every shack and every mud structure where our people live, a branch of the trade union movement and *never surrender*.

You must defend the right of African parents to decide the kind of education that shall be given to their children. Teach the children that Africans are not one iota inferior to Europeans. Establish your own community schools where the right kind of education will be given to our children. If it becomes dangerous or impossible to have these alternative schools, then again you must make every home, every shack or rickety structure a centre of learning for our children. Never surrender to the inhuman and barbaric theories of Verwoerd.

The decision to defy the unjust laws enabled Congress to develop considerably wider contacts between itself and the masses and the urge to join Congress grew day by day. But due to the fact that the local branches did not exercise proper control and supervision, the admission of new members was not carried out satisfactorily. No careful examination was made of their past history and political characteristics. As a result of this, there were many shady characters ranging from political clowns, place-seekers, splitters, saboteurs, agents-provocateurs to informers and even policemen, who infiltrated into the ranks of Congress. One need only refer to the Johannesburg trial of Dr. Moroka and nineteen others, where a member of Congress who actually worked at the National Headquarters, turned out to be a detective-sergeant on special duty. Remember the case of Leballo of Brakpan who wormed himself into that Branch by producing faked naming letters from the Liquidator, De Villiers Louw, who had instructions to spy on us. There are many other similar instances that emerged during the Johannesburg, Port Elizabeth and Kimberley trials. Whilst some of these men were discovered there are many who have not been found out. In Congress there are still many shady characters, political clowns, place-seekers, saboteurs, provocateurs, informers and policemen who masquerade as progressives but who are in fact the bitterest enemies of our organisation. Outside appearances are highly deceptive and we cannot classify these men by looking at their faces or by listening to their sweet tongues or their vehement speeches demanding immediate action. The friends of the people are distinguishable by the ready and disciplined manner in which they rally behind their organisation and their readiness to sacrifice when the preservation of the organisation has become a matter of life and death. Similarly, enemies and shady characters are detected by the extent to which they consistently attempt to wreck the organisation by creating fratricidal strife, disseminating confusion and undermining and even opposing important plans of action to vitalise the organisation. In this respect it is interesting to note that almost all the people who oppose the ''M'' Plan are people who have consistently refused to respond when sacrifices were called for, and whose political background leaves much to be desired. These shady characters by means of flattery, bribes and corruption, win the support of the weak-willed and politically backward individuals, detach them from Congress and use them in their own interests. The presence of such elements in Congress constitutes a serious threat to the struggle, for the capacity for political action of an organisation which is ravaged by such disruptive and splitting elements is considerably undermined. Here in South Africa, as in many parts of the world, a revolution is maturing: it is the profound desire, the determination and the urge of the overwhelming majority of the country to destroy for ever the shackles of oppression that condemn them to servitude and slavery. To overthrow oppression has been sanctioned by humanity and is the highest aspiration of every free man. If elements in our organisation seek to impede the realisation of this lofty purpose then these people have placed themselves outside the organisation and must be put out of action before they do more harm. To do otherwise would be a crime and a serious neglect of duty. We must rid ourselves of such elements and give our organisation the striking power of a real militant mass organisation.

Kotane, Marks, Bopape, Tloome and I have been banned from attending gatherings and we cannot join and counsel with you on the serious problems that are facing our country. We have been banned because we champion the freedom of the oppressed people of our country and because we have consistently fought against the policy of racial discrimination in favour of a policy which accords fundamental human rights to all, irrespective of race, colour, sex or language. We are exiled from our own people for we have uncompromisingly resisted the efforts of imperialist America and her satellites to drag the world into the rule of violence and brutal force, into the rule of the napalm, hydrogen and the cobalt bombs where millions of people will be wiped out to satisfy the criminal and greedy appetites of the imperial powers. We have been gagged because we have emphatically and openly condemned the criminal attacks by the imperialists against the people of Malaya, Vietnam, Indonesia, Tunisia and Tanganyika and called upon our people to identify themselves unreservedly with the cause of world peace and to fight against the war policies of America and her satellites. We are being shadowed, hounded and trailed because we fearlessly voiced our horror and indignation at the slaughter of the people of Korea and Kenya. The massacre of the Kenya people by Britain has aroused world-wide indignation and protest. Children are being burnt alive, women are raped, tortured, whipped and boiling water poured on their breasts to force confessions from them that Jomo Kenyatta had administered the Mau Mau oath to them. Men are being castrated and shot dead. In the Kikuyu country there are some villages in which the population has been completely wiped out. We are prisoners in our own country because we dared to raise our voices against these horrible atrocities and because we expressed our solidarity with the cause of the Kenya people.

You can see that "there is no easy walk to freedom anywhere, and many of us will have to pass through the valley of the shadow (of death) again and again before we reach the mountain tops of our desires.

"Dangers and difficulties have not deterred us in the past, they will not frighten us now. But we must be prepared for them like men in business who do not waste energy in vain talk and idle action. The way of preparation (for action) lies in our rooting out all impurity and indiscipline from our organisation and making it the bright and shining instrument that will cleave its way to (Africa's) freedom."*

Documents 3a-3b. ANC Annual Conference of December 18–20, 1953

Document 3a. Presidential Address by Chief A. J. Lutuli

SONS AND DAUGHTERS OF AFRIKA,

AFRIKA! AFRIKA! MAYIBUYE!
INKULULEKO NGESIKATHI SETHU! FREEDOM IN OUR LIFETIME!

My first pleasant task is to join Mr. Speaker in welcoming you all, delegates and visitors to this Conference of the African National Congress. It is most encouraging to me, as your President-General, to know that, at a great sacrifice of your time and money, you have travelled, many of you, long distances to come to this conference impelled by nothing other than a high sense of duty and loyalty to the cause of liberating our country, the Union of South Africa, from the exclusive domineering and selfish rule by whites to a true democracy where all people domiciled in the land will have full civic rights and obligations.

This annual getting-together of ours may be a most unwelcomed event among those whites who mistakenly believe that denying us opportunities for free association and free speech will stop us from fighting for our rights and so ensure white domination over us. They forget that the urge and yearning for freedom springs from a sense of *DIVINE DISCONTENT* and so, having a divine origin, can never be permanently humanly gagged and that, human effort to artificially gag it by means of harsh discriminatory laws and by threats must result in suspicions, strains, and tensions among

---

*The last four sentences are quoted with some minor changes from Jawaharlal Nehru, *The Unity of India: Collected Writings 1937–1940* (New York: John Day Co., 1942), pages 131–132. The reference to this source is provided by Ruth First (ed.), *No Easy Walk to Freedom: Articles, Speeches, and Trial Addresses of Nelson Mandela* (London: Heinemann, 1965), page 31.

individuals or groups in a nation, as, unfortunately, is the state of things in our country, the Union of South Africa.

On the other hand, our annual meeting is an event always most welcomed and eagerly awaited for, by all freedom loving people in our land and, in other countries, who truly desire the realisation of PEACE in the world and know that no true peace and progress can be secured and maintained in any country so long as there are others in that country denied full democratic rights and duties.

I am happy, at this point, to express, on behalf of the African National Congress, the sincerest and deepest appreciation and thankfulness to the local authority of Queenstown for consenting to our meeting in their area of jurisdiction. When the African National Congress is non persona grata in many quarters among whites, it is most reassuring to find a White civic authority that does not indulge in the dangerous and undemocratic action of attempting to muzzle people from voicing their legitimate aspirations and feelings and so becoming guilty of doing a disservice to one's country, helping to create and increase discord, suspicion, tensions and strains in human relationships in the country.

Another pleasant task of mine which I am happy to perform now, is that of thanking most sincerely, on behalf of the African National Congress, the Congress authorities and people in the Cape province, at both the provincial and local levels for consenting at very short notice to undertake, most willingly, the heavy responsibility of acting as hosts to this Conference. In this connection, a special word of thanks is due to the local Congress branch and the people of Queenstown, who, in the circumstances, must bear the brunt of providing us all hospitality.

Last year, the annual Conference of the African National Congress honoured me greatly and placed on my shoulders the heavy responsibility of leading Congress, at one of the most difficult and critical periods in her history and that of the Union of South Africa. Very significant moves and changes are evident in the Union and in the world. I may refer to some of those more specially later.

I am glad to say that despite the ban imposed on some leaders of the people by the Government with the specific object of crippling the *Liberatory movement of the people,* we are able to carry on the work of our Congress fairly effectively. We maintained the policy of working with other National organisations accepting our objectives and programme. In this connection I must specially mention the most active and effective co-operation between us and the South African Indian Congress.

My deepest appreciation and thanks go to my colleagues for their helpful and loyal support.

I must now pass on from the very necessary and pleasant duty of expressing appreciation and thanks, and, address myself to some aspects of Congress activities, views and observations.

SOME SIGNIFICANT TRENDS IN
OUR SOUTH AFRICAN SITUATION.

We, who are vitally concerned with the emancipation of Africans in their land, should keep a keenly observant eye on events and trends in our homeland that manifest themselves from time to time in our country since prudence demands that our programme of action should take account of these trends and events. Within the compass of one address and having regard for the need for brevity, I can do no more than briefly touch upon a few illustrative instances.

DETERIORATION IN HEALTHY HUMAN RELATIONS

Since Union, legislation discriminating most disastrously against non-whites, especially Africans, has increased in volume and severity. This has been due, mainly, to the ascendency of conservative and reactionary forces among whites. These forces, at whose vanguard must be placed the Nationalist party of Dr. Malan, became more aggressive and virulent with the coming into power of the Nationalist party in 1948.

Since this year we have witnessed an accelerated crescendo in the singing and acting of the apartheid song. All this has brought about suspicion, severe strains and tensions within and between the white groups themselves, but, even more so, between black and white. With apartheid as the dominant note in the Union of South Africa, how could it be otherwise? From the utterances of the Nationalist leaders themselves, apartheid is intended to maintain white supremacy, which, conversely, means the permanent subjugation and domination of non-whites by whites.

Apartheid laws are being enacted in great haste and impatience and are being implemented in the same tempo and ruthlessness with studied utter disregard for human feelings and sufferings of the people affected; who happen to be voteless and, therefore, voiceless and defenceless non-whites. It is precisely because the vote is the key to the security of an individual in a state, that the African National Congress *unequivocally demands* full democratic rights *NOW; during our lifetime and not in infinity.*

THE GROUP AREAS ACT.

The basic wickedness of this Act is that it unashamedly robs people without compensation by the state for their property, often acquired at much sacrifice of hard-earned savings or by instalment, which is, in fact, a form of mortgaging one's future for that property.

We are told that the act is meant to create better and healthier relations between the races. Even if this were true, which is not the case, what a price to pay! But the tragedy is that this argument is based on a fallacy that "IN SEPARATION OF RACES IS AUTOMATIC EVIDENCE OF CONTENTEDNESS". History and general human experience have many examples that prove the contrary to be more in accordance with facts. How could non-Europeans in the Western Areas of Johannesburg, Charlestown in Natal and other areas affected by the Act be expected to be happy?

INDUSTRIAL LAWS.

The influx control laws deny the Africans the fundamental human right to sell one's labour in the most remunerative market, according to his ability and tastes. Taken together with other industrial laws of the country, these laws, with their colour-bar practice, create conditions most inimical to the interests of the African workers and make a mockery of the Union in the civilised world.

It becomes difficult to see how a country claiming to be civilised and to be Christian, could allow such discrimination to go on and, how it could give white farmers permission to build private gaols to ensure cheap labour.

THE SEPARATE AMENITIES ACT.

This Act removes from apartheid measures any sugar-coating which may have deceived some people to accept apartheid as a fair policy. The Act merely legalises the evil that was being practiced. It removed the fig-leaf which concealed the nakedness of the unjust policy of apartheid and has showed up, most convincingly, the Nationalist conception of separation or apartheid. It revealed it as basically "separate and unequal" and not, "separate but equal". In the African National Congress we stand for equality; hence we find ourselves so violently opposed to apartheid.

It is for that reason, basically, that we shall continue to oppose, by all legitimate means, apartheid acts like the Bantu Education Act. To add insult to injury to embrace without protest all apartheid laws because it is alleged that they are made for our protection and convenience. [sic] In the African National Congress, we shall continue to protest most vehemently against discrimination.

THE UNION OF SOUTH AFRICA
BECOMING A FASCIST STATE.

The non-violent Defiance Campaign against unjust laws has helped to show up most convincingly that the Union of South Africa under the

Nationalist regime is fast becoming a dictatorship. The Nationalist government of Dr. Malan will go down in history, not only as a government that has made the most tyrannical laws with sweeping dictatorial powers such as we find in the Suppression of Communism Act, the Public Safety Act and the Criminal Laws Amendment Act, but also as a most ruthless government in dealing with opposition to it. In and out of parliament it has shown the tendency to crush anyone opposing it. On the pretext of fighting Communism and the non-violent Defiance Campaign it has banned many leaders of political and Trade Union organisations. It has deposed chiefs who have tried to oppose government measures. On behalf of the African National Congress I would like to express our sympathy to all who in any way have become victims of the ruthlessness of the Malan government in suppressing free speech, free association, due to a guilty conscience of the public wrongs it has committed against those who have sought the welfare of the Union of South Africa in ways different from their own. As President-General of the largest political organisation in the Union, I call upon all freedom loving people to regard no sacrifice too great in opposing the fascist government of Dr. Malan's before it is too late.

RISE TO POWER OF THE AFRIKANER UNDER THE LEADERSHIP OF THE NATIONALIST PARTY.

Some of us are violently opposed to the Nationalist party led by Dr. Malan. Our opposition arises from the fact that we regard as undemocratic and un-South African, most of the political theories and practices, such as their master-race theory, their idea of regarding civilisation as the white-man's prerogative or exclusive possession, their claim to exclusive white supremacy etc; but we must not be blinded by our opposition to them, to admire them for the way they worked hard and sacrificed much to attain the position they are in.

Their success was due, inter alia, to some of these qualities, if my observation is correct: Loyalty to an idea or ideal and a singleness of purpose in working for the realisation of that idea or ideal. The ideal was: THE FOUNDING OF AN AFRIKANER NATION, and so, *AFRIKANER NATIONALISM BECAME THEIR FOCAL POINT OF RALLYING THEIR PEOPLE.*

We are now in a position in Union politics when we have two main opposing forces: *AFRIKANER NATIONALISM and AFRICAN NATIONALISM.* Some of us hope and believe that African Nationalism shall remain broader, democratic and progressive, in keeping with the declared policy of the African National Congress of seeking to establish in the Union of South Africa a democracy which shall provide for a partnership in the Government of the Union of S.A. within the present framework of the Union.

THE GROWTH OF THE LIBERATORY
MOVEMENT AMONG NON-WHITES.

It is well for us to note that the African National Congress and the South African Indian Congress, whilst retaining their full identity as National Organisations in their own communities respectively are no longer isolated organisations but, [are] together with other national liberatory movements whose object is to waken the political consciousness of the non-white and white masses and to get the present rulers in the Union to accept the non-white on *the basis of equality AND no other* and extend to them full democratic rights so as to enable them to share in the government of the country.

Further, we must regard our liberatory movement in the Union as part of the liberatory movement in the whole of Africa. In this connection, I am happy to say that the African National Congress is already interesting itself in the proposition of a Pan-African Conference.

We welcome the interest taken in this matter by the Prime-Minister of the Gold Coast, Mr. Nkrumah; The President of Egypt, General Naguib and the Prime Minister of India, Mr. Nehru.

The African National Congress has played a noble role in setting into motion the liberatory movement. It can well regard itself as being the vanguard of the movement in the Union. Contrary to the criticisms of some of our critics, it was the African National Congress that took the initiative in inviting other national organisations in the Union to discuss the matter OF JOINTLY PROSECUTING A MILITANT PROGRAMME AGAINST THE OPPRESSIVE MEASURES BY THE PRESENT RULERS OF THE UNION.

It was in 1949 that this militant programme took shape and received the approval of the Annual Conference of the African National Congress. It is well to point out that, in this programme of action, many forms of carrying on the militant programme of action were agreed upon in principle. Non-violent Passive Defiance Campaign of great fame was only one of the forms of militancy.

SOME SIGNIFICANT EVENTS IN
THE UNION OF SOUTH AFRICA.

THE NON-VIOLENT CAMPAIGN FOR
THE DEFIANCE OF UNJUST LAWS.

The non-violent campaign for the defiance of unjust laws organised and jointly launched in 1952 by the leading political organisations among the non-whites: The African National Congress, The South African Indian

Congress and the Franchise Action Council, will rank as one of the most outstanding events in the political history of the Union of South Africa. Whether it is admitted or not, its effects have been profound and far-reaching. Many events have followed precipitously in its train. It accounts for the notorious short session of parliament which produced the twin anti-defiance Acts: The Public Safety Act and the Criminal Laws Amendment Act. It brought about the hurried formation of the Liberal party of South Africa.

In Church circles and Liberal circles it has brought about talks on the need to hold a Nation-wide National Conference to discuss Non-European affairs, with the Dutch-Reformed Church seeming to take a lead in the matter. The Christian Council of S.A. and the Institute of Race Relations have spoken about the matter too.

The Campaign has so sharpened the political issues in the Country as to leave no room for middle-of-the-road individuals or groups. Hence the dissension in the great Smuts' party, the United Party, and also the Labour Party of S.A. Hence also the silence of some leading people in our own communities. One has to accept the justice of the claim of the Non-whites for freedom and work unreservedly and openly for its realisation or, be guilty of directly or indirectly assisting the Nationalist party in its relentless and unmitigated oppression and suppression of the Non-White peoples in their claim for free democratic rights.

In a word, the non-violent campaign has caused much heart searching among some people and much ire and violent reaction with others in all communities. Much to the discomfort of the present rulers of the Union, the search-light of the world has been focussed on the Union of S.A. more than ever before by the Campaign. Racial discrimination has become an international issue and no amount of talk about domestic jurisdiction will deceive the world regarding its true nature and effect.

WHAT ABOUT ITS EFFECT ON
THE NON-WHITES AS A WHOLE?

It is no exaggeration to say that the effect of the Campaign on the non-white peoples as a whole, especially those who took an active part in it, has been profound and beneficial. It accelerated greatly the political consciousness of the people. It gave them a new feeling of courage and confidence in themselves as a people. But, even more profound, it forcefully brought them a new awareness of the potency of *UNITED AND CO-OPERATIVE ACTION* among all oppressed people irrespective of colour or class. The co-operation of the Non-White groups in the political sphere has come to stay whatever lying propaganda may be made against it. Prudence on our part demands its continuation.

I must, at this point, on behalf of the African National Congress, express the deepest appreciation and thankfulness of the African people to those who, directly or indirectly assisted to make the Campaign the success it became. I must mention in particular in this regard, the nine thousand men and women who, by the indelible ink of their sacrifice and sweat in gaols all over the Union of South Africa, wrote, in the history book of humanity the protest and opposition of ten million non-whites in the Union against studied oppression by the present rulers of the land since they came into our country three hundred and one years ago.

WHAT NEXT?

A perfectly legitimate question is being asked by well-wishers and opponents alike, but, naturally, with differing motives.

The reply is that the Defiance Campaign, being one of the several forms in our Programme of Action is kept in abeyance at our pleasure. But, the struggle in some form will be carried on until we do reach our goal. What is important and that to which I direct my PRESIDENTIAL CALL IS THAT:

"WE MUST KEEP UP THE SPIRIT OF DEFIANCE AND THUS KEEP OURSELVES IN READINESS FOR ANY CALL TO SERVICE IN THE INTEREST OF OUR LIBERATORY MOVEMENT."

We can assure the world that it is our intention to keep on the non-violent plane. We would earnestly request the powers that be to make it possible for us to keep our people in this mood.

We call upon our people and all other freedom loving peoples to join our ranks in large numbers in order to give a death blow to the discriminatory laws in the Union of South Africa designed to hinder our progress and injure our human dignity.

RELATION TO OTHER POLITICAL ORGANISATIONS.

I have already indicated that the year 1952–53 saw the formation of new political parties initiated by the whites. They are the Federal Party, the Liberal Party of S.A.; and also the Congress of Democrats. Our general stand is that we are prepared to co-operate fully on the basis of equality with any National political party or organisation provided we share common objectives and common methods of achieving our ends. The co-operation would always be ON THE BASIS OF EQUALITY AND MUTUAL RESPECT FOR THE INDIVIDUAL IDENTITY OF OUR ORGANISATIONS.

I should state further that on this basis of equality and mutual respect for the identity of our respective organisations we may co-operate on specific issues with any group if we feel that it is entirely in the interests of our *LIBERATORY MOVEMENT to do so*. It is appropriate to state here that the Liberal Party, then still an Association, wrote us and sought understanding and co-operation on agreed specific issues. We must be on guard against members of the A.N.C. becoming members of political Parties whose objectives are different from our own. Divided allegiance would be difficult for the individual concerned. In general, we should not give respite to the Government and those who support it, by indulging in a dog-fight with other groups, provided of course, those groups by word and deed do not stand on our way; but in frankness, I must say that any African desiring an unqualified emancipation of the non-whites, must join the Liberatory movement through the African National Congress.

NOTABLE VICTORIES.

I have already referred to the success of the Defiance Campaign. I must here put on record other victories won by the democratic front.

I must record with appreciation the fact that our policy of co-operating with other groups for our emancipation has withstood the onslaught of malicious propaganda by the government and other enemies of the people. The government has been frantic in its effort not only to enact and implement new apartheid laws, but, to deprive people of the rights they already enjoyed. We are glad that so far the government has failed to legally enact the "Separate Voters' Act"; I make an appeal to the Coloured community to join our liberatory movement and not be delayed by useless offers by the Government of what are merely apartheid palliatives.

In its hurry to enact and implement its unjust laws, the government has not only been morally and politically wrong, but, quite often legally wrong. As a result it has lost ignominiously, many legal battles in its efforts to crush opposition to its undemocratic policy and practices. We note, with much jubilation the invalidation of the ban illegally imposed on some of our leaders; I refer to the recent decision of the Appellate Division of the Supreme Court, on the Ngwevela appeal. Whether won or lost we applaud the fight behind these appeals; by this judgement the higher organs of the judiciary of the Union have once more proved themselves to be bulwarks of legal justice and guardians of the rule of law.

IN THE REST OF AFRICA AND THE WORLD.

Our interest in freedom is not confined to ourselves only. We are interested in the liberation of all oppressed people in the whole of Africa and in the world as a whole. This accounts for our taking an active part in the Pan African Conference movement. Our active interest in the extension of freedom to all people denied it makes us ally ourselves with FREEDOM FORCES IN THE WORLD. It is a matter of great concern to us that most territories in Africa are still under the grip of Imperialistic powers of Europe who maintain colonialism that keeps the inhabitants of these territories in subjection and poverty.

There are encouraging signs that the people in some of these territories are becoming politically conscious. We condemn most strongly the imperalistic powers controlling these territories for meeting the progressive move of the people by tyrannical suppression. I would cite here the indiscriminate shooting and bombing of the African people in Kenya, on the pretext of restoring law and order when, in fact, it is to maintain their imperialistic hold on Africa. The revolt is no doubt prompted by the legitimate aspirations of the African people; and so, the extension of freedom to the people of Kenya should be the reply of the British government and not bombing and shooting. We also condemn most strongly the action of the British government in banishing the Kabaka of Uganda for supporting his people in their demand for self-government. In this condemnation we also include the continued deposition and banishment of Seretse Khama, and the high-handed manner in which the British Colonial Office deposed a constitutionally elected government of the people of British Guiana and placed the territory under the autocratic rule of the governor.

I would like here to reiterate our stand on the protectorate question namely, that we are most strongly opposed to the incorporation of the High Commission territories by the Union government. We are entirely opposed to the increase in number of people subject to the racial and discriminatory policies of the Union of S.A.; the incorporation would result in the increase when we are fighting for the liberation of Africans and other peoples in the Union.

Let me state unequivocally that we regard as an unfriendly action towards Africa, the allowing of the United States of America to establish air-bases in Africa, nor do we welcome the making of Central Africa by the British government, a war arsenal since the forced withdrawal from India and its precarious hold and maintenance of influence in the East and Middle East.

AFRICA LIKES TO ENJOY PEACE, PROSPERITY AND FREEDOM AND WOULD LIKE TO ALLY ITSELF WITH THOSE FORCES OF PEACE AND FREEDOM AND SO, DOES NOT LIKE TO BE MADE A WAR ZONE IN ANY WAR THAT WAR-MONGERS MAY PLUNGE THE WORLD IN.

In this matter of working for the liberation of colonial peoples we applaud progressive elements in Great Britain and other colonial powers that fight against the oppressive policies of their governments and champion the cause of freedom for colonial peoples.

In the world scene I must express our gratitude for the continued interest taken by the United Nations in fighting against racial discrimination practised by some of its member-nations. We note with deep appreciation the initiative taken in this matter by countries like India, under the leadership of its Prime-Minister, Mr. Nehru.

CONCLUSION.

You will agree that the masses of the African people live in abject poverty in both rural and urban areas and so many Africans find themselves landless and homeless; they find themselves suffering from hunger, malnutrition and disease. You must agree that the basic cause of this deplorable state of affairs is due, inter alia, to:—

(1) The inadequacy and crowdedness of the land allowed them, being only about 12% (twelve percent) of the land surface of the Union, for eight million Africans as against, practically, the rest for the 2½ million whites.

(2) The uneconomic wages they receive.

(3) The economic and political restrictions placed on them to make it impossible for them to exploit, each according to his ability, the resources of their God-given land.

HOW WILL THESE DISABILITIES BE REMOVED?

Certainly not as some fondly and foolishly believe that it will be by the voluntary benevolence of the white-man! These disabilities will only be removed as has happened with other people in other lands, all through the ages to our day, by the united struggle of the oppressed people themselves, to exert pressure on the rulers to grant them freedom. AND SO, I CALL UPON ALL AFRICANS WHO TRULY DESIRE TO SEE THESE DISABILITIES REMOVED, TO JOIN THE AFRICAN NA- TIONAL CONGRESS, TO FIGHT IN THE COMRADESHIP OF OTHER OPPRESSED PEOPLE FOR THE ATTAINMENT OF FREEDOM WHICH IS THE MAIN KEY TO THE REMOVAL OF MAN-IMPOSED DISABILITIES.

AFRIKA! MAYIBUYE!!
INKULULEKO NGESIKATHI SETHU!!!

Yours in the National Service;
A. J. LUTHULI:
PRESIDENT-GENERAL: A.N.C.

Document 3b. Resolutions

— 1 —

That this Conference urges branches, Regional Committees, Provincial Executives and the National Executive Committee to make plans for and embark upon an immediate campaign of economic boycott directed against selected individual firms, business undertakings and government enterprises for the purpose of forcing them to:—

(a) Make available skilled training and employment opportunities for Africans.

(b) Accord proper treatment and service to African customers.

(c) Compel them to pay living wages to African employees.

(d) Generally recognise their dependence on African purchasing power.

— 2 —

Conference instructs the National Executive Committee to make immediate preparations for the organisation of a "CONGRESS OF THE PEOPLE OF S.A." whose task shall be to work out a "FREEDOM CHARTER" for all peoples and groups in the country. To this end, Conference urges the A.N.C. National Executive Committee to call a meeting of the National Executives of the South African Indian Congress, the Coloured People's organisation and the South African Congress of Democrats or any other democratic organisation for the purpose of placing before them the plan of Congress and obtain their co-operation in creating a truly representative "CONVENTION" of the peoples of South Africa.

— 3 —

That the National Executive Committee is hereby directed to go into the question of preserving and expanding an effective and well directed National Volunteer Corps for freedom and that Volunteers must be given thorough political training and instruction. Conference further instructs the National Executive Committee to hasten the compilation of a roll of honour of all Volunteers who participated in the Defiance Campaign and that they must be presented with certificates of merit for their services in the cause of African freedom.

— 4 —

That the A.N.C. warns the government not to proceed with the plan to remove Africans from their homes in the Western Areas of Johannesburg, such a step can only lead to a further worsening of race relations.

— 5 —

That the A.N.C. condemns the crushing burden of taxes such as, dipping fees, hut-taxes, dog-taxes, stock-rates etc, which are imposed on the peasants with the sole purpose of forcing them to leave their homes to seek work on the farms and the mines. The taxes, coupled with the unimaginative and fraudulent rehabilitation scheme, are creating an explosive situation for which the government must bear full responsibility. The A.N.C. demands that the government revise radically its policy towards the African people in the reserves.

— 6 —

This Conference instructs the National Executive Committee to appoint a Committee to go thoroughly into the question of the Africans labouring on European farms, with a view not only to analysing the terrible conditions under which the people live and work on these farms, but also to devise practical plans that will enable the farm labourer group to be firmly a part of the National Liberatory movement. Conference is convinced that a tremendous revolutionary potential lies untapped in the white farming areas.

— 7 —

Conference is totally opposed to the so-called Bantu Education Act and calls upon the African people to do everything possible to compel the government to repeal this Act.

— 8 —

Conference is opposed to the terms of the Native Labour ('Settlement of Disputes') Act and urges the A.N.C. to support the Non-European Council of Trade Unions with its plan to fight this Act.

— 9 —

Conference confirms its solidarity with other colonial peoples in their struggle against imperialism, for self-determination and independence.

Document 4. Presidential Address by Professor Z. K. Matthews, ANC (Cape), June 26, 1954

My first duty is to welcome the delegates who have come from different parts of the Cape Province to attend this annual conference. Owing to the size of the area for which we are catering and the meagre resources at the disposal of our clientele, attendance at conferences of this kind is a major undertaking for our people, involving a great deal of sacrifice in both time and money. The number of delegates present here bears eloquent testimony to the determination of our people and their devotion to the cause for which the A.N.C. stands—the total liberation of the African people from every form of oppression, both overt and covert. During your stay here I have every confidence that you will make your contribution to our deliberation and will receive the inspiration which comes from association with those of like mind to yourselves and will return to your different stations refreshed in mind and in spirit and with a renewed determination to work for the achievement of freedom in our lifetime.

My second duty is to welcome to our midst the distinguished visitors who have come to us from beyond our Province, first place in this regard goes to our honoured President Chief A. J. Luthuli. In us he will never cease to be Chief Luthuli, because his claim to that title does not rest upon recognition by the Governor-General, but upon that place which he occupies in the hearts of our people. We are glad that because of his temporary freedom, it has been possible for him to visit us and feel honoured that ours should have been the first Provincial Conference for him to visit since his temporary liberation. We do not know how long he will retain his freedom of movement, [this] does not rest in his hands, but while he is free, I am sure that he will make good use of that freedom. We welcome you, Sir, and grant you the freedom of our Conference and pledge you the loyalty of every corner of the Cape Province.

As for the General Secretary, it is hardly necessary for me to welcome him here. He is a son of the Cape Province and he was with us quite recently. During his recent Cape tour he was instrumental in taking the A.N.C. right into the heart of the Transkei, that area which is supposed to be surrounded with an Iron Curtain. During his brief sojourn there, they sought him here, they sought him there, they sought him everywhere, and when he had already returned to headquarters, they were still seeking. He will soon have to be known as Mr. Walter "Scarlet Pimpernel" Sisulu, the ubiquitous General Secretary of the A.N.C.

I must say a word of welcome too, to the representatives of the law who have been detailed to attend our meetings. It will be recalled that we obtained permission to hold our meetings in Uitenhage on condition that we agreed not only to allow the police to attend our meetings, but also to permit them to take notes. I suppose these conditions were [not] really intended to be accepted. It was probably fully anticipated that we would reject them. We accepted them. Firstly because we will not allow ourselves to be intimidated by the presence of the police. The stand we take on the policies of this country is well known to all, police or non-police alike. We are neither an illegal or a subversive organisation; our constitution is a public document and all our activities are public. The only information which we would keep from the police is that which we keep from all non-members of our organisation. All organisations have their legitimate private affairs which they do not disclose and I need hardly say that as far as such matters are concerned, we shall not disclose them to non-members of our organisation, whatever their official positions may be. The fact that Africans cannot forgather today without having to be surrounded by police and detectives is a sad commentary on the relations that exist between the government and the African people in this country. That means that for all practical purposes the policeman and the constable constitute the main link between the Government and the African people. The Government must go to the police to get the views of the African people on matters affecting their welfare. I am aware that there is another new substitute for direct contact between the Government and the African people and that is the so-called Information Officers of the Department. Those who have seen these officers at work will admit that they are a very poor substitute for direct representation. Anyway seeing that the police have now become the channel through which our views may be brought to the attention [sic] we can only express the hope that they will give a truthful and accurate account of what they hear and see. We would like the Government to know what we think and how we feel about what is happening to our people and we are prepared to use the only channel that is open to us to transmit our views to the powers that be.

It is usual on occasions for us to be told that we are passing through critical times. As far as the Africans are concerned there can be no other times for us except critical times until we achieve our liberation. It is therefore unnecessary for me to repeat that threadbare expression. You know as well as anybody else that everywhere in this country the African people are in a state of insecurity. It is not only in the Western Areas of Johannesburg that the African people are confronted by the problem of removal. Both in the urban areas and in the rural areas there is no place where the African can say to himself "this is my own, my native land", "here I intend to remain", "here I will invest all my hard-earned savings knowing that I will not overnight be faced with a total loss of my earnings because someone would like to displace me". I say there is no place where the African can lay his head in safety from arbitrary interference. This applies not only in the matter of residence. In the field of employment, unlike other sections of the population the African cannot freely choose the type of employment in which he is going to engage in accordance with his natural aptitude. All over the country we can see able-bodied and able-minded Africans compelled to waste their talents on unskilled jobs while the country is suffering from a serious shortage of skilled labourers. The industrial development of the whole country is held [up] because ideological considerations prevent us from tapping the human resources available in the country to the full. In the field of education we are confronted with the Verwoerd resolution which purports to be designed to streamline African education to make it serve the needs of white South Africa. In the political sphere the socalled Bantu Authorities are expected to exercise authority on behalf of their white masters and the system of separate representation is to keep the non-whites scrambling for the crumbs of office while the white political machine goes on grinding out its wonted output of discriminatory legislation.

The question that arises from all this is what is to be the reaction of the African people to this situation? There are several attitudes which may be adopted. One is the attitude of resignation, that of accepting the situation. That is of course what our enemies would like to see us do, but that attitude is not deserving of a moment's consideration. We have not been created to serve or to surrender or to worship ordinary mortals like ourselves. No tin gods for us, only the Almighty God whose sovereignty we acknowledge. Therefore no resignation and no surrender is our minimum policy.

Another line that may be taken is that of blind aggressiveness, a kind of wild hitting out at any and everybody in the hope of finding a target somewhere. That kind of emotional outburst may give temporary relief to [the] sense of frustration, but it gets those who indulge in it nowhere. On the contrary such outbursts are apt to be followed by deeper fits of depression and despair. You cannot beat a well organised foe with that kind of unorganised and unco-ordinated reaction.

There is a third attitude which many adopt and that is the search for scape goats within our own ranks, people who may be blamed for the situation in which we find ourselves. The people who indulge in this witch hunting generally adopt a kind of self-righteous attitude. They themselves have never done anything either right or wrong, but they are very skillful in picking out the contributors to our downfall. The African Chiefs, the missionaries, the liberals, the members of the Native Representative Council, the members of the Advisory Boards—these are the people on whom all blame must be laid for the disabilities under which we labour. The result is that instead of getting on with the struggle against our main foe, our time is taken up with dog fights among ourselves. All of which is not only entertaining but very helpful to our enemies. The situation was very well summed up by members of the C.I.D. who were asked by a member of Congress why they seemed to pay no attention to the activities of a certain organisation, but concentrated all their attention on the A.N.C. Their reply was that there was no need for them to direct any attention to that organisation because it is fighting the A.N.C. It is clearly recognised by the police that any organisation or individual fighting the A.N.C. is part of the arm of the police.

This brought me to what I consider to be the right attitude for us, namely the building up of a well organised fighting force. That fighting force is the A.N.C. The A.N.C. as an organisation stands for the political independence of the African people. The Programme of Action which was adopted by the A.N.C. in 1949 states this quite clearly: "The fundamental principles of the programme of action of the African National Congress are inspired by the desire to achieve national freedom. By national freedom we mean freedom from white domination and the attainment of political independence. This implies the rejection of the conception of segregation, apartheid, trusteeship or white leadership which are all in one way or another motivated by the idea of white domination or domination of the whites over the blacks. Like all other people, the African people claim the right of self-determination."

There we have our goal set out for us. Nothing that is done to us should make us deviate from that goal. The passing of laws or the drawing up of schemes by the government which are designed to defeat our objectives must and will be regarded by us as merely temporary setbacks, which will be overcome by one thing and one thing only—the building up of a mighty A.N.C. The spirit of the A.N.C. must be instilled into every man, woman and child, whether they are members of the A.N.C. or not. This means that we must put all our energies not into parrying temporary blows directed at us, but into building for the future which we know to be ours. It means that we must not become panicky and jittery. We must not lose our heads. . . . [sic] It means that we must face the future without fear and with our plans to counteract the schemes that are intended to thwart our struggle. We must pick up the gauntlet and meet the challenge of our day and generation.

It is in that spirit that we must enter into our deliberations at this conference. Our conference must be devoted not to discussing the latest laws passed by a Parliament in which we are not represented, but to considering how we can make the A.N.C. our parliament—into a more effective instrument for mobilising the forces of liberation in this country.

The forces of liberation in this country are not as weak as is generally supposed. [In] all sections of our population—Europeans, Coloureds, Indians and Africans—there are people who believe in equal citizenship rights for all. But their principal weakness lies in the fact that they are not only unorganised but are frequently disorganised by a tendency to go off on tangents.

Document 5. Message to "Resist Apartheid" Campaign, by Chief A. J. Lutuli, July 11, 1954

Note: Reproduced in *Treason Trial Record*, pages 11,522–11,525.

Sons and Daughters of Africa!

MAYIBUYE! INKULULEKO NGESI KHATI SETHU!

On account of the ban re-imposed on me last night immediately after my landing at the Airport, I cannot be with you in the flesh, but I am with you in the spirit, and the spirit is a greater human force than the flesh. I am glad to bring to you not just the greetings and best wishes of your fellow-countrymen I have the honour to lead through the African National Congress, but to bring you also their messages of determination and assurance to be with you in your hour of trial, when forces of reaction, as represented by the Government of Dr. Malan seek to uproot you from your sacred shrines and castles—your homes—acquired through hard-earned savings. The fact that it is legalised robbery does not make the action less a sin.

Your invitation has given me an opportunity to reiterate my call for RESIST APARTHEID CAMPAIGN. We have met here today primarily to unitedly demonstrate in unmistakable terms our solidarity in supporting this Congress Call for RESIST APARTHEID CAMPAIGN, and for THE CONGRESS OF THE PEOPLE ASSEMBLY, whereat people from all walks of life in our multiracial nation will have the opportunity to write into this great Charter of Freedom their aspirations on freedom.

The Western Areas Removal Plan of the Government represents their major implementation of their apartheid policy and, no doubt, is a fore-runner to what will be done in other centres; and so our RESIST APARTHEID CAMPAIGN in connection with this scheme must be firm and decisive. The fate of Africans in the cities of the Union rests on the stand we take against this tyrannical action of the Government. As leaders we shall do all in our power to consolidate the country to oppose the carrying out of this outrageous tyrannical scheme. I must here publicly acknowledge with the deepest appreciation the support already given us by individuals and groups from other communities, especially *our allies in the freedom struggle*; the S.A.I.C., the S.A.C.O.D., the S.A.C.P.O.

We are met here to express our utter resentment at the claim made by South Africa through its governments and parliaments since Union to determine and shape our destiny without ourselves, and arrogantly assign us a position of permanent inferiority in our land. Contrary to the plan and purpose of God our Creator, who "created all men equal," and to us too, not to whites only, He breathed the divine spirit of human dignity. And so we have all the human and moral rights to resist laws and policies which create a climate inimical to the full development of our human personalities as individuals, and our development as a people. The laws and policies of White South Africa are no doubt inimical to this development. And so I call upon our people in all walks of life—Ministers of the Gospel of Christ who died to save human dignity, teachers, professional men, business men, farmers and workers to rally round Congress at this hour to make our voice heard. We may be voteless, but we are not necessarily voiceless; it is our determination more than ever before in the life of our Congress, to have our voice not only heard but heeded too. Through gatherings like this in all centres, large and small, we mean to mobilise our people to speak with this

one voice and say to white South Africa: WE HAVE NO DESIGNS TO
ELBOW OUT OF SOUTH AFRICA ANYONE, BUT EQUALLY
WE HAVE NO INTENTION WHATSOEVER OF ABANDONING
OUR DIVINE RIGHT, OF OURSELVES DETERMINING OUR
DESTINY ACCORDING TO THE HOLY AND PERFECT PLAN
OF OUR CREATOR: APARTHEID CAN NEVER BE SUCH A
PLAN.

Friends, let us make no mistake, the road to Freedom is always full of
difficulties. Before we reach the summit of freedom, many will have fallen
by the wayside as a result of enemy action; and others through personal
despondency may abandon the fight. But I call upon you as true sons of
South Africa to be true to Africa, and count no sacrifice too great for her
redemption. Now and here, I call upon all men and women present to
pledge themselves and come forward to enlist themselves as Volunteers in
this noble cause of freedom under the rallying cry of RESIST
APARTHEID CAMPAIGN. I am confident that this my call will, as in
the past, provoke the greatest response which will shake to repentance the
hearts of white South Africa. MAYIBUYE!

**Document 6. Statement by W. M. Sisulu, after being ordered to resign from
the ANC and from his position as Secretary-General, August 20, 1954**

I have been ordered by the Minister of Justice, Mr. C. R. Swart to resign
from the African National Congress and from my position as Secretary-
General. I was elected to this position by you in 1949, since when I have
endeavoured to the utmost of my ability to serve my people and to be
worthy of the confidence you placed in me.

Now I am forced to resign from the Congress but I wish to assure you
that I shall be entirely at your disposal and will not hesitate to answer any
call which may be made by the African National Congress. In my message
to the members of the African National Congress and to all oppressed
people I wish firstly to remind you about the statement of the A.N.C. and
its allies in 1950 on the Suppression of Communism Act, in which we
showed that the primary aim of the Act was to silence all opposition to the
tyranny of the Malan Government, especially from the Non-European
organisations. The truth of this assertion will not be denied today, even by
those who did not believe us at the time. The wisdom of the leaders of the
Liberatory Movement was shown by their swift action when for the first
time they called a nation-wide political strike and created unity among all
democrats as an answer to what they correctly believed to be a major step
in the establishment of a police state.

The ruthlessness of the Government in the use of this Fascist measure
has affected even those who feared to participate in a positive struggle

against the Nationalist onslaught. Whilst we cannot deny the effects of these bans on the National liberation and Workers movements, we are nevertheless confident, placing our faith in the invincible spirit of broad masses of the people, that they cannot succeed in their oft-proclaimed intention to crush the People's movement. The crippling effect of these bans on the leading most energetic and unwavering champions of Freedom in South Africa must not be minimised. The People's leaders have been forbidden to attend any gatherings whatsoever, they have been forced to leave their place of employment, some have been exiled. Almost the entire National Executive of the African National Congress has been removed from office. Some of the provinces and branches have also been affected, and it is clear from what has already taken place that our organisations are going to be affected in all provinces and all the branches. Yet despite all this [our] movement is growing in strength, gaining new adherents and reaching new levels of effectiveness and determination.

Let me remind you once more that these bans have affected gallant and beloved leaders of the people with outstanding records in the liberatory struggle, such as Moses Kotane, J. B. Marks, Mandela, Tloome, Njongwe, Mji, Molema, Bopape, Matji, Tshume, Matthews, Ngwevela, Mhlaba, Motshabi; the exiled leaders Ngwentshe and Lengisi and many others of the African National Congress. Also Dr. Dadoo, Cachalia, and Nana Sita of the Indian Congress; Fischer, Williams, Kahn, Bernstein, Watts, Bunting and Hodgson of the Congress of Democrats; James Phillips of the Coloured People's Organisation and Ray Alexander, Kunene, Reddy, Du Toit, Moumakoe and Weinberg of the Trade Union movement. These and all the other banned leaders still belong to you. They will remain your leaders because they still believe in our liberation struggle and still find some way to make their contribution. They have not been rejected by us but forcibly thrown out by our enemies.

What should be our answer to this? The only way whereby the oppressed masses of this country can express their implicit trust and confidence in their elected leaders and prevent the effectiveness of these bans is:

* to carry out unreservedly the policies of the national organisations as enunciated from time to time.

* to carry on more effectively the work they have been engaged on.

* to be loyal to the principles and ideals for which the leaders have pledged themselves.

* to prevent opportunism, sabotage and careerism, and to expose relentlessly the reactionary tendency and reactionary leadership.

* to fight vigorously the penetration of spies and government stooges planted in our organisations.

You are called upon to intensify your campaign in the fight for freedom and to build the most powerful organisation and to produce even more efficient leadership, even more Illustrious Sons of the Soil than those I have already mentioned. You are called upon to recruit our fine youth and women for the struggle in a manner never before achieved. You are called upon to resist Apartheid—to defeat the Western Areas Removal Scheme, the Bantu Education Act, the Group Areas Act, the Schoeman anti-trade union measures and many others. You are called upon to make the greatest sacrifice in the preparation of the Great Congress of the People in the building of a United S. A. by which means you can crush finally and for all times the reactionary rulers of the present day.

This is how you can make easy the tasks of those who still remain; the tasks of Chief A. J. Luthuli, beloved president of the people, the task of Dr. Naicker, Dr. Van Der Ross, Beyleveld and Massina, and all those who work and stand with them. In this you must be guided by the rich literature our organisations have produced, especially since the first nation-wide political strike of 1950 up to the present day of the Congress of the People.

This can only be useful and appreciated when you use it as a guide in your practical work so that your understanding is clear at all times. Honesty, selflessness, vigour, initiative, determination and faith are some of the qualities you require. The government has already been shaken, the time has passed when they could rule the country as if we, the people, did not exist. Time is against them, the world is against them! We on the other hand are encourged by the great spirit of the people of S.A., by the growth of the national liberatory movement, by the unprecedented political conscious-ness of the people, and by the fact that the truth is with us. We enjoy the confidence of the entire world in this noble and just task for which we are pledged to fight until the dawn of Freedom.

Documents 7a–7d. ANC Annual Conference of December 16–19, 1954

Document 7a. Presidential Address by Chief A. J. Lutuli

Sons and daughters of Africa,

      Afrika!   Afrika!   Mayibuye!   Mayibuye!

I greet you all on behalf of myself and thousands of others within and without Congress who share with you our hope for the attainment of freedom for all in our land in the not-distant future.

I ask you to receive special greetings and best wishes for a successful conference from your banned and banished leaders who are with you in spirit. Thank God that Divine Providence has not endowed Minister Swart with the power to ban Congress out of the people's hearts.

I ask that your loving remembrance of our own banned and banished leaders should embrace the banned and the banished of our allies in the Liberatory Movement.

As an act of remembrance and re-dedication of ourselves to the cause of freedom in our land, I would ask the Conference, at this point, to stand and perform the acts which I have proposed to Mr. Speaker.

The wholesale banning of our leaders should challenge us all—banned and unbanned—to devote ourselves unreservedly to the cause of freedom.

I am glad to report that despite the bannings, Congress work at both National and Provincial levels has been carried on at a high level of efficiency but this was possible only at great personal sacrifice on the part of those Congress officials who are still free of the notorious bans.

On your behalf, I am sure you would want me to thank all those who in any way have helped to keep the machinery going. I have much pleasure in publicly thanking them.

The treasury will submit to conference a formal appeal for funds to enable us to meet special obligations Congress has to our banned and banished leaders and also to help us to meet our increased administration costs. I feel confident that our leaders at all levels—national, provincial and branch—will do all they can to get the masses to contribute generously to this special appeal for funds. Let me close my introductory remarks by thanking most sincerely the authorities of the City of Durban for allowing us to hold our Annual Conference in their area of jurisdiction.

Our warmest and sincerest thanks go to the authorities of the Beatrice Street Y.M.C.A., Durban, for making available to us the excellent facilities of their great establishment to enable us to carry on under comfortable conditions the various activities of our Conference.

Last, but not least, we express our deepest appreciation to the Natal Provincial Division of the African National Congress for voluntarily inviting the Annual National Conference of the African National Congress to come to Natal and for sparing no effort to secure facilities necessary for the convenience and comforts of delegates. In our warm thanks to the Natal Provincial authorities of the African National Congress we gladly associate the local Congress organs and officials in the Durban District who must have borne the brunt of the burden of Natal playing host to the Annual Conference of her mother body, the African National Congress.

I must now bring to an end the felicitous aspect of my address and in conformity with traditional practice touch very briefly upon some activities and events in the political scene in our country, in particular, and the world in general, especially those events and activities that have a direct bearing on the noble task of emancipating mankind in Africa.

I. *NOTABLE VICTORIES:*

We find ourselves so busily engaged in the terrific political battle in our country that we miss to note the gains we make here and there, no matter how small.

In my opinion, despite the ruthless intensification of the Apartheid policy, we have on the credit side a few notable victories.

a. *The success of the Congress of the People Campaign.*

We have still much to do to rally all sections of our country to the Congress of the People Campaign, but it is making no extravagant claim when I say it grips the imagination of the common man wherever the campaign had reached. The frantic way in which the government is seeking to cripple the Campaign is evidence of its political potency.

Let us intensify our call for 50,000 Freedom Volunteers.

I can see through the Congress of the People thousands and thousands of South Africans from all sections of our multi-racial nation marching together to freedom as a direct result of this campaign. In any case the campaign has already enlarged and consolidated our united FREEDOM FRONT considerably.

b. *The Christian Churches and Apartheid.*

There is no doubt that speaking generally the Church has made no noticeable impact on the political thinking of the Ministry in general and in the laity, both black and white. There have been lonely voices here and there that have condemned the South African Native Policy on Christian grounds.

There is a tendency, especially in the African section of the Church to dismiss politics as other worldly matters. We do not expect the Church to back up any political party or theory but we do expect it to arm its adherents with Christian principles that will enable them to pass intelligent judgment in terms of Christian principles on any political programme or theory.

Whilst, with the exception of the Dutch Reformed Church and, maybe, a few Lutheran Churches that support the Bantu Education Act, of 1953, there is no unanimity among church leaders as to what to do with schools in terms of the Bantu Education Act; it has come to us as a refreshing breeze to hear them give a unanimous categorical rejection of the Act on grounds of incompatibility with Christian principles of the Apartheid principles and practices inherent in the Act.

In the African National Congress we support the uncompromising rejection of the Act by the Roman Catholic Church and the Authorities of the Diocese of Johannesburg under the Rt. Rev. Ambrose Reeves. This year will be remembered for the unequivocal public condemnation of the policy of Apartheid by a good number of churches in the Union and overseas, especially the Church of England in Great Britain. It was heartening to hear the condemnation of Apartheid coming from such a world-important body as the Assembly of the World Council of Churches which recently met in Evanston, Illinois, U.S.A.

We shall not forget the visit to our country of that great Christian Crusader, Canon Collins. We thank God for men like Canon Collins who live the words of the Christian hymn which say "Let courage rise with danger."

c. *The rise of Spirit of Resistance among Workers.*

This year, especially in Durban, we witnessed with joy the rising tide of opposition by African employees to unsatisfactory conditions of service. We single out for mention the Dock Workers, the United Tobacco Company workers and workers in some Pine Town factory.

Congress at both National and Provincial levels should establish closer cooperation between itself and Trade Union leaders and organisations.

We regret the sell-out of labour interests made by the recent so-called Unity Conference [of October 1954, resulting in the formation of the South African Trade Union Council] which ended up as a Disunity Conference in support of the Apartheid policy of the Minister of Labour, Mr. Schoeman; it refused to recognise African Unions or mixed Unions with African membership.

II. *THE STORY OF OUR SUFFERING:*

I feel called upon to remind the African people of the grim fundamental facts of our situation which are painful reminders of our enslavement by White South Africans. While it is true that the propaganda of the Nationalist Government through the information section of the Native Affairs Department tries to cleverly conceal the evils of Apartheid by promises which are nothing but deceptive palliatives, yet on the other hand, we should be grateful to the Nationalist Party Government for unambiguously making it plain that in the interest of perpetuating white domination they will stop at nothing in their determination to realise their goal of keep non-Whites in a state of permanent servitude. What is surprising is that in the face of this frankness you should find some Africans in positions of influence counselling the African people to submit to the status quo.

These false persons generally support the betrayal of the African people by false reasons such as these: "Half a loaf is better than no loaf"; "the African people are not yet ready for freedom"; "convert the white man first by being moderate in your demands." Indulging in wishful thinking they ideally say that without exerting ourselves God in his own time will give us freedom. They forget that God has long been waiting for African Freedom Volunteers whom He could harness to the noble cause of bringing freedom to all people in Africa. These false leaders would have the African accept the shadow for the substance, thus rendering himself guilty before God of having a perverted sense of values which exalts expediency above principles and a mere mess of pottage—crumbs of apartheid—above freedom, our basic God-given heritage.

WHAT ARE SOME OF THESE GRIM FACTS OF OUR SITUATION?

In order to convince you of the seriousness of our situation let me remind you of some of the grim facts of our situation.

a. *Decline of Liberalism in the Union of South Africa:*

It is a sad commentary on the attitude of white South Africa that in the Union of South Africa liberalism should be held to such extreme and malicious scorn that any white person showing any leanings towards liberalism is regarded as a renegade and so shunned if not completely ostracised. It is a measure of the littleness of our little Union of South Africa that such great South Africans as the late J. H. Hofmeyr should have been abused even by members of their own party. White South Africa should know that Africans applaud and honour those Europeans who work for the liberation of Africans on the basis of making the Union of South Africa a true Democracy for all people regardless of their colour, class or creed. Hence we are grateful to the formation of the Congress of Democrats with which the African National Congress is in alliance in the Liberatory Movement, especially in the campaign of the Congress of the People. We are grateful also for the existence of the Liberal Party between whom and ourselves there exists a warm sympathetic understanding and friendly cooperation on specific issues where our policies agree.

Let me here most emphatically state that while the African National Congress must naturally work for its own growth, yet it is equally committed to the policy of forming a multiracial united Democratic front to challenge the forces of reaction in this country.

b. *The Ascendency of the Forces of Reaction.*

We must not be blind to the fact that the baasskap spirit of the Boer Republics is in the ascendency in the Union. This accounts for the fact that every day the United Party is becoming indistinguishable from the Nationalist Party. The long-waited-for new Native Policy of the United Party can be described as being a mark time order from Drill Master, Mr. Strauss, with an occasional "March backward" order, as in the case of their decision not to give recognition to African trade unions whereas the Party at one time seriously considered giving recognition to African trade unions.

After all both the United Party and the Nationalist Party vie for the position of being Guardians of the traditional Native Policy of South Africa and the essence of this policy is the baasskap spirit of the Boer Republics where each white farmer was a supreme lord over his African servants.

c. *The Economic Advance of the African is deliberately curbed by legislation which is reinforced by a hostile public opinion.*

This curb of our economic advancement became marked after Union when in 1913 Africans were deprived of the right of buying land in freehold title. The grim story of our being robbed of opportunities for economic advancement is too long to narrate in a Presidential address.

d. *Deliberate Efforts to Suppress and Dwarf our human personality.*

Leaders of white public opinion take every opportunity to present us in the world as sub-human beings incapable of assimilating civilisation. This vilification has been going on since the whites first met us. This matter of dwarfing our personality and trying to make us believe we are nobodies is the worst sin the whiteman has committed against Africans.

In the Bantu Education Act of Dr. Verwoerd, an effort is being made to use the school as an instrument of dwarfing our human personalities. The African child is to be made to feel that he is the inferior of the white child.

III. *WORLD SCENE.*

We are grateful as we always have been to progressive opinion in the world that has not hesitated to champion our cause in the Union of South Africa. We watch with interest the developments towards full democracy in Western African territories under British rule.

The British Government must not allow its policy to be dictated by white settlers who selfishly try to grab as much wealth as they can from Africa, otherwise she will find herself confronted with man-made situations as in East Africa, or extremely strained relations as in Uganda and Bechuanaland, where people rightly resent the banishment of their hereditary heads.

IV. *WHAT MUST WE DO TO MEET THIS CHALLENGE OF BEING SPIRITUALLY IF NOT PHYSICALLY DESTROYED AS A PEOPLE?*

Let me conclude my address by asking you this question! What must we do to meet this challenge of a people spiritually, if not physically, destroying us as a people?

a. We must join our national organisation, the African National Congress, where the true significance, purpose and probable disastrous outcome of Government policy would be explained to us by our own people who work for our liberation.

After all, the whiteman has told you that he wants to make you his servant forever and so what good thing can there be for you in his policy? Do not listen to propaganda of the Information Section of the Native Affairs Department.

b. Develop in you the spirit of resisting anything that curbs or limits the development of your talents to their fullest capacity.

c. Cultivate a sense of service and sacrifice without which Africans can never gain freedom. Freedom comes only to people who are prepared to pay dearly for it.

AFRIKA !   AFRIKA !   MAYIBUYE !   MAYIBUYE !

Document 7b. Report of the National Executive Committee

PART ONE

A. *PREFACE*

Our National Organisation is facing a serious crisis. Its existence as the leader and spokesman of the African people is gravely threatened by the actions of the Nationalist Government. Among other things, therefore, this Report deals with the very vital and urgent question of organisation, the question that must in the end determine whether the African National Congress shall survive the attacks of the Government and continue actively and fearlessly to fight for the rights and the dignity of the African people in their fatherland.

It is the duty of every delegate to this Conference, of every Congressman and every lover of and believer in the cause of African freedom, therefore, to do all in his power to prevent the calamity and ensure that the Congress shall emerge triumphantly from this crisis.

We shall win if we follow and diligently carry out the instructions and directives of the Conference and the National Executive Committee of our Congress.

B. *POLITICAL REVIEW*

The March to Fascism:

After six years of Nationalist rule, fascism has arrived in South Africa. The first five of these six years were occupied with the building of the legal framework for the naked police state. After sweeping to power on a wave of intensified racialist propaganda, the Nationalist machine set to work. The reactionary anti-people legislation inherited from former South African regimes was made more efficient. What had been mere practices before were transformed into rules of law, and measures previously scattered in different acts of Parliament were consolidated into single comprehensive pieces of legislation. These laws were comprehensive not because they detailed and defined laws but because they left all powers of making laws to individual ministers. Into this category came the Group Areas Act, the Bantu Authorities Act, the Natives (Abolition of Passes and Coordination of Documents) Act, the Native Laws Amendment Act, the Population Registration Act, the Natives Resettlement Act and the Suppression of Communism Act. In the last Act the Nationalist Government, following the Hitler pattern, prepared the legal machinery for crushing the most militant opponents of their rule, the working class and national liberatory organisations.

Fascism does not arise until conditions call for it. It arises when the ruling class can no longer look forward to unlimited profits and to acquiescent people willing to be exploited. As the political consciousness of the people grows and their organisations become mature and effective in their struggles for economic and political rights, the ruling classes drop the methods of peaceful flattery, diplomacy and bribery, and employ force as the ordinary means of enforcing their rule. It is true that force is always there, but before the rise of fascism force was resorted to in times of "crisis". Under fascism the crisis becomes a permanent feature of life, and force and intimidation become the ordinary everyday methods of rule.

Here in South Africa the methods of the Nationalist Party Government are those which the ruling class must continue to use increasingly in its fight against the people. As the Acts passed in the first five years of Nationalist rule were not achieving their purpose and the Non-European liberation organisations were stemming the tide of Nationalist onslaught, more acts of Parliament and administrative orders and regulations became necessary. More amendments to the Urban Areas Act, the Suppression of Communism Act, the Land and Trust Act, Urban Bantu Authorities Act and others. Finally the Criminal Laws Amendment Act and the Public Safety Act were passed to meet the situation created by the historic Campaign for Defiance of Unjust Laws. The Nationalists have acted in complete disregard and contempt of the rule of law and the rights of Parliament. In the Public Safety Act they made provision for the Executive, when it deems it necessary, to declare a state of emergency, suspend all laws and assume dictatorial powers.

Today there are more reactionary laws: the Schoeman Anti-Labour laws, the Verwoerd notorious Bantu Education Act and streamlined Trust regulations. Meetings are totally banned in rural areas and virtually banned in urban areas. Foremost leaders of the National Liberation Organisations and leaders of Trade Unions have been banned from political activity; persons have been exiled and deported without trial and without regard to the welfare of their families; newspapers have been banned; fighters for freedom have been convicted for protesting against unjust laws; armed police intimidate people at meetings and homes; raids and searches are now commonplace; and to crown it all, our Secretary-General has been sentenced to three months imprisonment with compulsory labour for a crime unique in history, namely:

"Attending a gathering in order to partake of, or be present whilst others partake of refreshment (in the nature of tea and/or edibles and/or a meal)."

Yes, fascism has indeed arrived in South Africa. What has been the reaction of the people to it? On the Parliamentary front there has been no opposition to the Nationalists at all. There has not even been an attempt at a formal protest on the part of the United Party in particular. This is understandable. As the representative of an important segment of the ruling class this party could not very well oppose the anti-popular legislation. The groups represented by the United Party in their short-sightedness acquiesced in the reactionary policies of the Nationalists, crude as they were. The policy of the official opposition in Parliament has therefore been one of surrender all along the line. The same may be said of the liberals and reformist trade unions. Although they did now and again give expressions of formal protest against isolated acts of Nationalist tyranny they have made no attempt to actually resist the onslaught of the fascists outside Parliament. Not only did the Liberals and those of their kind encourage the illusion of social change through Parliament among themselves, but they spread the illusion even among those who have no parliamentary rights at all!

The one major force which has fought the Government consistently and organised the people against fascism has been the African National Congress and its allies. No action of the Government, no matter against which group it was directed, has not evoked condemnation and resistance from the forces allied to and under the leadership of the African National Congress. In this connection we recall the freedom strike in the Transvaal on the 1st May, 1950; the first Nation-wide political strike on 26th June, 1950; the Cape Coloured Protest Strike on 7th May, 1951; the Witzieshoek Clash in November, 1950 where 13 Africans were killed, 9 committed to terms of imprisonment ranging from 6 months to 5 years; the Demonstration of 100,000 people on 6th April, 1952 against 300 years of white domination; the most historic Defiance Campaign which began on the 26th June, 1952, a day which has truly become a National Day for all South Africa and a day on which we remember all those who have laid down their lives in the struggle for a Free South Africa—a day of re-dedication and pledge.

The Defiance Campaign in particular is not only the most important event of this period but was the highest form of struggle ever undertaken in South Africa. It produced a solid and strong democratic front between Africans and other oppressed groups. It indeed changed the political situation in the country. In these political struggles, two other important things happened:

(i) The African National Congress became recognised and accepted by all democratic and progressive organisations and individuals in this country as the true voice and leader of the struggle for freedom, equality and justice;

(ii) June 26th was set aside as the National Day, a day on which fighters for freedom remember all those heroes who laid down their lives in the struggle for a Free South Africa—a day of re-dedication and pledge.

TWO WRONG VIEWS

All fighters for freedom are warned against the danger of under-estimating and minimising the fascist beast, and of falling victim to the propaganda of the enemy and enemy agents. The enemy and his agents are not only brutal and ruthless but also cunning, deceitful and brazen. They do not hesitate to exploit the basest and meanest prejudice or racial or sectional difference and fear. No lie is too big or too terrible for them; they will use any dirty and nasty thing in order to achieve their purpose of dividing, confusing and rendering their opponents impotent. He who repeats to Congressmen the ideas and propaganda of the enemy is undermining the cause for which the Congress stands. The African National Congress stands for freedom, equality and justice for all, irrespective of race, colour or religion.

Having described the six years of Nationalist rule as a period of determined effort to destroy everything democratic and progressive in the political, economic and social life of South Africa, and having cited a long list of obnoxious and iniquitous laws which, added to existing oppressive and discriminatory laws, form a massive wall of dark reaction and cruelty, we should also show the reverse side of the picture, the credit side, as it were. Apart from the wealth of experience—the mirror—that we now possess, our cause has now gained an army of some 10,000 volunteers, men and women upon whom the cause of African freedom has been indelibly imprinted. Furthermore, these six years of struggle have created a general political consciousness among the masses of our people. They have given us a "LUTHULI".

The year 1954 was the year for the preparation for a new period—a period for the changing of tactics, a period for an advanced form of organisation to prepare for advanced forms of struggle.

The Congress of the People and the Resist Apartheid Campaigns are the two Campaigns on which we are going to base our future struggle. The

Resist Apartheid Campaign is an issue on which we mobilise our forces in defence of our rights and our organisations.

On the other hand, the Congress of the People Campaign will open a new page, another turning point in the history of our country, when, for the first time a Peoples' Charter shall be drawn up by the masses from all walks of life and from all racial groups in the country—a Charter of a new South Africa. We are striving to bring the masses of our country the vision of a new South Africa—a South Africa wherein there shall be no starvation, and in which racial antagonism will be eliminated and all alike will share in the natural resources and prosperity of the country.

While it is dangerous to underestimate fascism and the power of the ruling class generally, it is equally dangerous to over-estimate the power and popularity of these reactionary and barbaric hordes. No force is more powerful than the power and will of the people. If the people are organised and united their power is invincible. The organised power and united actions of the people will defeat the fascist demons in South Africa. We must therefore organise the people properly, politicise and activise them and lead them against the forces of fascism and reaction.

WIDEN THE ANTI-FASCIST FRONT

We know that in every country where the fascists came to power they did so because the masses of the people did not wage determined struggles against those fascists, and in some instances, as in Germany and Italy, because the masses of the people supported them. Here in South Africa too, the fascists came to power because the mass of those who have political rights, those who decide governments and administrators, supported our local fascists. Fascism came to South Africa as a result of an electoral majority in an election in which Non-Europeans have no say.

From the point of view of the ballot box, therefore, the Non-Europeans can do nothing to their overlords and tyrants. Yet all concerned can successfully resist and defeat these oppressors. They must be fought outside Parliament, in the towns, on the farms—in the economic, political and industrial spheres; they must be fought everywhere! The policy of the African National Congress in this connection is inter-racial cooperation on the basis of mutual respect and equality. This policy the African National Congress proclaims boldly to all interested groups and organisations and to the world at large.

Our policy of co-operating with other racial groups through their national organisations has made great strides and constitutes a very real threat to the present regime which is anchored on the idea of racial exclusiveness and domination. In the fight against fascism we must see to it that more and more of the other groups are part and parcel of the struggle. The Africans as the leading element in this alliance must do all they can to see that the Coloureds are really part of the fight, similarly with the Europeans. The Indian people led by the South African Indian Congress and inspired by that tried and tested leader, Dr. Y. M. Dadoo, are old and trusted allies. We hope that the vigorous and active, though small, Congress of Democrats, and the South African Coloured Peoples' Organisation will grow strong and swing more representative groups among their respective people to our side.

THE CONGRESS AND RURAL AREAS

As far as the Africans are concerned, the creation of an anti-fascist front means broadening the social basis of the National movement. There is a danger of the African National Congress becoming an urban-based and urban-oriented organisation. It may tend to forget and ignore the vast potential represented by the peasants and farm labourers. During the Defiance Campaign a great deal of contact was made with people in the reserves and farming areas especially in the Eastern Cape where there are many Congress branches in the country areas. This contact has not however, been sufficiently strengthened by concretely and actively taking up the demands of the people in those areas and by incorporating into the programme of the Congress the immediate demands of the peasants and the farm labourers. As a National movement the Congress cannot afford to ignore the demands and interests of large sections of the African population. Congress must voice and interpret the demands, feelings and aspirations of all sections of the nation. And, let us not forget that our nation consists of these sections:

The urban workers; the peasants; the farm labourers; the domestic servants; the businessmen; the intellectuals and professional men; the women and the young people—the youth.

It is the business of Congress to draw up programmes designed to reflect the vital interests of all these groups, and to see that the programmes drawn up should reach the people for whom they are drawn up.

The same applies to the question of our Women and Youth sections. It is essential that they too should see to it that the demands of their respective sections are taken up seriously and that in both their short-term and long-term programmes and activities they set themselves out to attract the mass of women and youth and get them to participate in the nation-building tasks in which the principal body, the African National Congress, is engaged. Congressmen must understand that the people will not readily respond to mere appeals to them to fight for freedom in the abstract. They must be able to see what freedom would mean to them in terms of things they clearly see in their own lives as a result of oppression and lack of opportunities.

THE NEED FOR A CONGRESS PRESS

The press is an important factor in the life of a nation and of a political organisation. A newspaper which expresses the correct point of view can mean everything for an enterprise. A Congress newspaper can serve as the political educator and leader, the organiser, the propagandist and agitator, the supplier of information, and the medium of cultural advancement and the trainer of future journalists and writers. But can Congress afford a newspaper or even just a quarterly journal?

It is impossible to start and maintain a newspaper without sufficient capital or a great deal of financial support from the general public. It is quite obvious that with its present meagre resources Congress is not in a position to run any decent publication at all. If we want to start publishing anything on a national scale, we shall first have to accumulate the funds necessary for the production of such publication. Accumulation of funds is a subject that has been discussed at many Congress conferences, and some of our provinces have at one time or another collected moneys towards the establishment of a Congress newspaper.

The pertinent question is: do we really want a Congress newspaper? The answer to this question is that we are not yet serious about the matter. It is true that a large sum of money would be required to finance such a newspaper, yet, it is equally true that if the African National Congress seriously intended to raise the necessary capital, there could be no possible difficulty in doing so. All members of the Congress are ready to make sacrifices whenever the cause of African freedom demands that sacrifices should be made. Now, assuming that the Congress has a membership of 100,000; if each member is asked to contribute the sum of £1 towards a Congress press, an amount of £100,000 could be realised in no time. 10/- a member would bring in an amount of £50,000! We can do it, but only if we really want to do it.

PART TWO

INTERNATIONAL SITUATION

The African National Congress as a leading Political Organisation in the country and a representative of the people of South Africa, has a foreign policy opposed to that of the Government who represent less than 20% of the country's population. The White rulers in South Africa support the war aims, imperialism, and white domination. During the 2nd World War, the President-General of the African National Congress appointed a special committee in 1943 to examine the place of an African in the post-war period and in the light of the Atlantic Charter. The Document drawn up by this Committee covered the international and national policy of the African National Congress, which was unanimously adopted at the National Conference in December, 1945, and finally published in a booklet entitled "African Claims in South Africa." [The findings of the Atlantic Charter Committee were adopted by the annual conference of December 1943. See volume II, page 122.]

This policy has been enforced by the successive Presidents of the African National Congress and was sharply raised by Lutuli's Presidential Address last year.

The cardinal points of our foreign policy are, opposition to war and an uncompromising stand for world peace, and opposition to colonialism and white domination.

Africa, the second-largest continent with its 200 million people and richly endowed by natural resources, is ruled over by no less than 6 colonial powers. These powers are counted amongst the greatest powers in the world. Therefore the struggle to free South Africa and indeed all Africa is a serious problem that will mean a struggle against six major imperialist nations [see below] and their satellites such as Malan, Roy Welensky, Blundell and others. This is a formidable prospect. And yet the dynamics of history say that the imperialists are doomed to ignominious defeat at the hands of the oppressed Africans. Already the whole continent is awakened and is tramping the road to freedom. The nature of our programme, the forces ranged against us, mean that the freedom of Africa can never be a local problem—an internal or domestic affair. However we look at it, the freedom of Africa is an international question. It is true, the struggle will only be fought by the Africans themselves under their own independent leadership but they will have to keep a very clear eye open for international developments detrimental or advantageous to us. We must look for allies and without going any further we must ask ourselves the following regarding any prospective ally:—

(i) Is this country or group in the imperialist camp or in the anti-imperialist camp?

(ii) Is this country or group for equality or for racial discrimination?

(iii) Is this country or group pro-African or anti-African Freedom?

(iv) Is this country or group anti-colonialism?

On the answer to all these questions we will base our attitude to any country.

As you all know, the Defiance Campaign of 1952 sharply focussed the attention of the United Nations on the problem of racial discrimination in South Africa. We once more wish to record our highest appreciation to the United Nations Organisation for the continuous support it has given us, particularly do we want to do so to the United Nations Commission on racial discrimination in South Africa and those countries who have supported our cause despite strong opposition from the imperialist countries, who are in league with South Africa.

We are aware of the reasons for this attitude on the part of the imperialist countries. The liberation of the colonial and semi-colonial people will bring an end to the huge profits they are making through the cruel exploitation of subject peoples.

The expulsion of colonial powers in the great land of Asia is a source of inspiration to the African people. The emergence of the two great powers in this continent, China and India, both enemies of war and imperialism have shattered the hopes of the imperialist powers and made their rule impossible even under the military might of the United States of America, Great Britain and France.

We have year in and year out expressed our great concern over imperialist wars in Indo-China and Malaya. We now not only enthusiastically salute the victorious struggle of the Viet Minhs against the powerful imperialists of France and America, but have every reason to celebrate this victory and the end of the war in this part of South-East Asia. Yet, friends, the brutal wars are still being waged in Malaya, Kenya, Algeria, Tunisia and Morocco—all of which are in the continent of Africa except Malaya.

We express our solidarity and sympathy with these countries in bitter and bloody struggles, not excluding the people of British Guiana and other oppressed peoples in other parts of the world.

We call upon the British and French Governments to withdraw their armed forces and to release the gaoled leaders and thus pave the way for permanent peace in the world.

We appeal to the civilised world, to all democracies and peace-loving peoples to call for an immediate peace in Kenya and other affected places, to save innocent and defenceless people from the horrors of war.

AFRICA AND WORLD PEACE

The rise of the National Liberation movements in Asia and the Pacific regions and the loss of those vast countries as war bases and centres for investment has forced the imperial powers to turn their eyes on Africa. Here the imperial powers of Britain, Belgium, France, Holland, Portugal and Spain have either their chief or their only colonial dependencies. The rivalries amongst these colonial powers contain the seed of an extremely dangerous situation to peace and security in Africa.

To protect their markets and investments, to crush the national liberation movements and to forestall the rise of revolutionary democracy in Africa and to ensure an abundant cheap labour supply, America and her satellites have established military bases all over the continent. America has land, sea and air bases in Morocco, Libya and Saudi Arabia. There are British military bases in Egypt, East Africa, Somaliland and the Sudan. The Supreme Allied Commander in the Mediterranean in 1944 writing in "Optima" of June, 1953, a quarterly review published by the Anglo-American Corporation, put the matter very clearly:

"The spread of Communism to China and the uncertain political situation in other countries in the Far East are bound to have the effect of contracting the sources of supply of certain raw materials necessary for the manufacture of armaments, which will result in the intensification of prospecting and development in Africa."

According to him, the role of the two Rhodesias and Kenya, should be to protect and develop sea communications, to be ready to send forces overseas and to develop its industries to maximum capacity for war needs. To do this, he says, it would be necessary for the three colonies to come under one Central Command. In 1946 the "Rand Daily Mail" made the position equally clear:

"The British decision to quit Palestine, Burma's secession from the Commonwealth, the weakening of the ties with India and the uncertainty of Britain's tenure in Egypt have hastened the adoption of plans for a new Commonwealth defence system . . . Kenya is the new centre of Commonwealth defence and South Africa its arsenal."

It will thus be seen that the struggle for national liberation is inextricably linked up with the fight for peace and against imperialism. It will also be seen that the people of South Africa and of this continent will be the first victims of a future war. Their industries will produce armaments, their raw materials will be used not to develop their own economies but to destroy those of others. It is precisely because of this fact that the question of war and peace has become of immediate concern to us all. It is also because of this fact that we welcome the participation of our leaders in the Peace Movement. It is because of this dangerous situation to peace and security in Africa that we urge the widest sections of our people to take up the cause of peace and to uphold it until the scourge of imperialism is vanquished from the face of the earth.

PART THREE

GENERAL ACTIVITIES FOR THE YEAR 1954

CONGRESS OF THE PEOPLE

The most important resolution of the 1953 Conference of the African National Congress was on the Congress of the People, which read:

"Conference instructs the National Executive Committee to make immediate preparations for the organisation of the Congress of the People of South Africa, whose task shall be to work out a Freedom Charter for all the true people and groups of the country. To this end the Conference urges the African National Congress Executive Committee to invite the National Executives of the South African Indian Congress, the South African Congress of Democrats, the South African Coloured Peoples' Organisation or any other democratic organisation, for the purpose of placing before them the plan of the Congress and obtaining their co-operative support in creating a truly representative CONVENTION OF THE PEOPLES OF SOUTH AFRICA."

In terms of this resolution a Conference was called on the 21st March, 1954, at Tongati, Natal. In this Conference a sub-committee was appointed to draw up plans which subsequently were adopted, according to which a National Action Council for the Congress of the People was set up consisting of 8 members from each sponsoring organisation. (See Annexure "A") [Document 7c]

The National Action Council on the recommendation of the African National Congress appointed Mr. T. E. Tshunungwa as National Organiser. He was also appointed National Organiser for the African National Congress. The full report of the activities of the Congress of the People which forms part of this report, is herewith attached and shall be read to Conference by Mr. T. E. Tshunungwa.

THE WESTERN AREAS ANTI-REMOVAL AND RESIST APARTHEID CAMPAIGN

At the meeting of the National Executive on the 17th–18th April, 1954, in Cleremont Township, Natal, the National Executive carefully considered after a full report by the Working Committee, the gravity of the situation created by the decision of the Nationalist Government to forcibly remove the Non-European people from the Western Areas of Johannesburg. It came to the conclusion that the matter had assumed dimensions of National importance and that the responsibilities of the Anti-Removal Campaign must be under the supervision of the National Executive itself working through its agencies.

It made an appeal to all sections of South Africa, Black and White, to unite and oppose by all means possible the cruel scheme of Dr. Verwoerd. On the 8th May 1954, the National Executive of the A.N.C., the S.A.I.C., the S.A.C.O.D. and the S.A.C.P.O. approved a plan of Campaign now known as the "RESIST APARTHEID CAMPAIGN" in terms of which was fixed the 26th–27th June as the WESTERN AREAS DAY FOR CAMPAIGN AND SOLIDARITY throughout the country. On these days, meetings and conferences were called in Natal, Transvaal and the Cape Province. The President-General, Chief A. J. Luthuli, made a clarion call to the nation for 50,000 "FREEDOM VOLUNTEERS" both for the Western Areas as well as for the Congress of the People.

The response of the people and their very high spirit shocked the Government and showed a clear demonstration of the Peoples' solidarity. The significance of the Western Areas Day was marked by the reaction of the entire ruling class press and comments of the people in the areas where meetings were held. The RESIST APARTHEID CAMPAIGN embodies all Apartheid measures, in particular:

1. BANTU EDUCATION ACT.
2. NATIVE RESETTLEMENT ACT.
3. PASS LAWS.
4. GROUP AREAS ACT.
5. SUPPRESSION OF COMMUNISM ACT.
6. ANTI-TRADE UNION MEASURES.

BANTU EDUCATION

The Bantu Education question has been handed over to the women and youth sections of the African National Congress working together with other organisations whose purpose is to fight against this Devil's piece of legislation. This means that they work under the supervision of the senior body, but specialise on this campaign.

The plans have been drawn up which recommend a withdrawal of children at least for one week. A speaker on the subject will enlighten you more as to precisely what should be done.

Another important measure on the RESIST APARTHEID CAMPAIGN is that of the ANTI-TRADE UNION MEASURES which have already led to the splitting of the Trade Union Movement into two camps.

We fully support the decision of the Non-European Council with fourteen other Trade Unions who have refused to be parties to the Apartheid measures of Schoeman. We acclaim their decision to form a National Council representing the workers of South Africa.

ECONOMIC BOYCOTT

The application of the economic boycott by the Cape Province was successfully carried out and carefully handled in such a manner that it can serve as a model in the use of this weapon by other provinces. The active centre of operation was the Eastern Cape where a number of firms were forced to negotiate with the African National Congress branches.

In giving directives to the provinces, the National Executives emphasise the need for a great care in the use of the boycott weapon. It also considered the special conditions and difficulties prevailing in different parts of the country and decided that where conditions are considered unfavourable at any particular centre, that centre need not embark on the boycott campaign. The branches were also instructed to obtain the sanction of the provincial office before undertaking any boycott except under special circumstances.

There is now a boycott campaign on throughout the country of the United Tobacco Company products arising from the dismissal of 364 African tobacco workers in Durban.

The boycott is not only carried on by the African National Congress, but a decision of the other three National Organisations and a number of Trade Unions including the Non-European Council was taken.

ACTIVITIES OF NATIONAL OFFICIALS

It was significant that the Transkei should have been visited by the four leading officials of the African National Congress. This vast territory is the largest single unit occupied by the African peasants and has not been properly tackled by the African National Congress in the past. As a result of arrangements made by Mr. Sisulu during his tour of the Cape Province, a Conference was held on the 1st of May. Both Chief Luthuli, President-General and Dr. Conco, acting Treasurer-General visited Umtata, the capital of the Transkei, to attend this Conference. Due to the ban imposed on Chief Luthuli not to attend public gatherings, Dr. Conco opened the conference and a message from Chief Luthuli was read to the conference. Later the National Organiser visited that area.

The tour of the Secretary-General was particularly successful in the Eastern Cape. A series of meetings were arranged for him culminating in a big regional meeting at Veeplaats on Sunday, 28th March at which meeting close on £ 100 was collected apart from a sum of £ 22 collected by the Women's Section. The Korsten Branch donated to the head office a new typewriter. The National Executive wishes to express its appreciation to the Eastern Cape Region, Korsten Branch, Women's Section, and not forgetting Grahamstown, Cradock as well as Queenstown.

The Provincial Conference of the Cape Province held at Uitenhage in June was opened by the President-General, whereat he made a call for 50,000 Freedom Volunteers. The Secretary-General opened the National Conference of the African National Congress Youth League at Uitenhage at the same time.

By far the most important visit of the year was that of the President-General to the Western Areas of Johannesburg, which is threatened with forcible removal by Dr. Verwoerd. On his arrival on the 10th July, at Jan Smuts Airport he was served with a banning order, one of which prohibited him from attending public gatherings as from the time he received the order. Nevertheless, close to 10,000 people assembled at Sophiatown on the 11th July to meet a People's Leader. On the advice of the working committee, he did not personally address the gathering but his message was enthusiastically received, in which he said that the removal of the Western Areas was a testing ground in the implementation of the outrageous tyrannical apartheid policy of the Nationalist Government. He called on all South Africans to consider no sacrifice too great in opposition to this scheme.

Other activities of the officials were Dr. Conco's visit to the Transvaal; the Transvaal President, Mr. Moretsele's visit to Natal; the Acting-President, Dr. Njongwe to the Western Areas; and the visit of the National Organiser, to the Transvaal and Natal. Apart from the visit of the National officials, it is recommended that the inter-change of Provincial officials be encouraged.

BANS

We have already referred to the banning and deportation orders but we must mention a number of leading officials who have been affected by these laws during the year. (For list of banned people, see Annexure "B" [not reproduced here].)

Congress officials, Chief A. J. Luthuli, President-General; W. M. Sisulu, Secretary-General; Dr. J. L. Z. Njongwe, Acting-President, Cape Province; O. R. Thambo, Acting Secretary-General; R. M. Matji, Provincial Secretary, Cape; J. Motshabi, Provincial Secretary, Transvaal; M. B. Yengwa, Provincial Secretary, Natal; and J. Matthews, President of the African National Congress Youth League; have been banned during the last year.

The new method which the Government is using is that of deporting Congress leaders to some obscure corner of the country. This began with the deportation of Mr. Sibande from Bethal; the deportation of the Ficksburg Branch Secretary to Basutoland; during this year Mr. A. S. Gwentshe and Mr. J. M. Lengisi have been deported from East London to the Transvaal; Mr. Yengwa from Durban to Mapumolo.

The National Executive recommends that the exiled, arrested and banned leaders continue to be regarded as leaders, provided that at any conference a vote of confidence is passed on each and every one so that those whose activities are considered to be to the detriment of the organisation do not hide behind the bans and may in fact be expelled.

SUMMARY OF PROVINCIAL REPORTS

The Cape Province has once more been very active during the period under review. This is shown by the economic boycott campaign which has resulted in many commercial companies negotiating on favourable terms with the African National Congress. This is particularly the case in the Eastern Province.

The Transvaal is the only Province which called a Parent-Teachers Conference on Bantu Education as directed by the Conference. Its Youth and Women's Sections have also called special conferences on this issue. The progress on Bantu Education has been very slow in all the Provinces.

All the provinces observed the 26th June as directed. The Conferences of the Congress of the People have been held in all provinces, either on a regional or provincial basis, except the Orange Free State where plans misfired.

ECONOMIC RENTS

The Government issued a proclamation authorising the local municipalities to raise rent by charging an economic rental on all those who earn more than £15. This increase will result in more than 100% increase in some areas and more than 30% in those who earn less than £15.

The fight against economic rental in the municipal townships has been taken up by Natal, the Cape and the Transvaal.

We are happy to report that the proclamation has been set aside or declared null and void by the Transvaal Provincial Division [of the Supreme Court], in an action brought about by Orlando Residents' Protection Tenants Association and by the Johannesburg Co-ordinating Committee. We do however want to add that the fight is not ended, that we should now mobilise for the second phase, that is mass action, as we expect that the authorities will re-impose the Economic Rentals.

PART FOUR

ORGANISATIONAL PROBLEMS

The key-note of the report to this Conference and of the discussion is the finding of a solution to our organisational problems. Because of the crippling attacks of the Government on the Congress, the state of unpreparedness of our people in the face of these attacks, and because of the alarming fluctuation in the membership and the failure to carry out some of our important decisions, it has been necessary and imperative that we should place before this Conference the question of our organisational problems as the most urgent issue for consideration.

The report of the Executive deals with the achievements and failures of the organisation and the difficulties facing it between conferences. The report therefore affords an opportunity of examining ourselves and rectifying our past mistakes, whereby we shall be able to forge new methods and new spirit in the execution of whatever Conference decisions are taken. The Presidential address deals with matters of policy. It also affords an opportunity to discuss in full the policies of our organisation with a view to confirming them or amending whatever is considered to be no longer in keeping with the progress of the organisation.

We wish to emphasise that the report of the Executive and the Presidential address are the two basic documents which will provide the central theme for Conference deliberations and decisions.

Your attention is directed to two important questions that emerge from this report:

(i) The growing oppression since the coming into power of the Nationalists in 1948.

(ii) The position of the African National Congress in such a situation. In other words, the re-organisation and the functioning of the African National Congress under conditions of a fully-fledged police state in which we live.

From year to year we have complained about the inefficiency of our machinery; the lack of proper co-ordination between the branches and the provincial committees on the one hand and the provincial committees and the National Executive Committee on the other hand. Instructions are not properly carried out; most of the correspondence is not attended to, and as a result people are not properly informed about Congress affairs.

We have warned the branches about the bannings and deportations which are now taking place; we have warned them of the danger of planted spies and disruptive elements within the organisation; we have warned them of the difficulties of holding meetings and have worked out the form of organisation which would meet the difficulties, the "M" Plan. But in spite of this our machinery has not improved. We have shamefully failed to implement the "M" Plan.

The branches have been directed to hold discussions on the re-organisation of our machinery, and to discuss the problems of organisation with a view to recommending effective methods and combatting the serious weakness in our national organisation.

But the problems of the Congress organisation seem to us much deeper and more fundamental today than they have been before. How are we to explain the great reduction in our membership during the two years? Are the Africans no longer interested in the cause for which the Congress stands, in the fight for freedom and equality, or are they now afraid?

The Africans are still very much interested in the struggle for freedom and equality, and they are still as militant and courageous as ever. That this is so, no-one will deny. But if this is the case, what then is wrong? The reason for the drop may be found in a variety of causes. Some of these being:

(a) Lack of proper supervision and direction by the Provincial Committees.

(b) No properly defined conditions of membership.

(c) Lack of political education and training for members.

(d) Huge and unwieldy branch membership.

(e) The fact that members are only financially valuable once a year.

(f) Lack of unit life, activities and responsibility.

(g) Lack of interest in each individual member and his disregard as an asset by the Congress governing and responsible units.

(h) A feeling in members of impotence and helplessness engendered by inactivity and non-participation in the strivings and undertakings of the organisation.

Some of our provincial committees show bad supervision and administration. This is largely due to lack of organisational experience and political under-development. Members of provincial committees sometimes do not work as a team and have failed to direct and regularly check up the work and activities of branches under the area of their jurisdiction.

When they join Congress members are not given any defined or specific duties which may be regarded as conditions of membership. Apart from paying 2/6 a year as membership subscriptions, therefore, they feel no further obligation to the organisation. Members should be given political education and made to understand that *they* are the Congress; that *they* have to fight for their freedom and emancipation; that they are responsible for the success, failure and growth of the Congress; and that they have to finance its every activity and to obey and carry out the instructions and directives of their governing bodies.

Branch committees cannot be expected to look properly after a large membership of between 500 and 1,000. It is obvious that branches have no apparatus to cope with such big numbers of individuals. This difficulty is further complicated by the fact that members are only financially valuable once a year. Consequently there is an incessant urge for more and more new members who also get forgotten as soon as they have paid their 2/6 subscriptions. Branch membership should be limited in size to something like 40 to 50, or better still to the Constitutional position of 20 to 25 members. With low political development officials of these unwieldy branches tend to become conceited and to regard themselves as chiefs and bosses and not as servants which they are. There is some virtue in numerous small branches which are united under some regional controlling committee. They stimulate a spirit of competition which is healthy and necessary for development and growth.

To stop the decline and fluctuation in membership then, we must remove the conditions that are responsible for the decline and fluctuation. Conference must be bold enough and take the necessary and appropriate measures.

With regard to the two points raised earlier, namely:

(a) the growing oppression since the coming into power of the Nationalists in 1948, and

(b) the position of the African National Congress under conditions of fully-fledged police state in which we live,

it is quite clear that Congress cannot survive unless it changes its present organisational structure. If it is not yet clear it should be made abundantly clear to all concerned that the Nationalists are determined and mean to deprive us of and deny us the elementary human rights of freedom of speech, freedom of assembly, freedom of organisation and freedom of movement. Their aim is to divide the Africans further and to prevent us from ever uniting. Their aim is to scatter the whole African population and keep and treat the Africans as unattached individuals.

With that aim in view they are busy destroying our national organisation and our trade unions by banning and deporting leaders of these organisations and by prohibiting public meetings and intimidating and terrorising both the speakers and the audience. In all matters affecting Africans today the police have a final say and the power to veto. No local authority and no location superintendent would dare to hire out a public place without the consent of the police.

To be able to meet these stringent and hostile conditions, therefore, the Congress must be placed on an entirely new organisational footing. Congress leaders and activists must recognise and accept this basic fact. The organisation should be highly centralised on the national and provincial planes, but highly decentralised on the branch and membership levels. It must be re-organised along the lines laid down in the "M" Plan.

THE SCHEME ENVISAGED

(a) It should be based on small manageable units.

(b) Several of these units should be united under and controlled by a sub-committee consisting of leaders of each unit.

(c) Units sub-committees to be responsible to branch committees.

(d) All units and units sub-committees to be equipped with the knowledge necessary to enable them to carry out their duties and functions.

(e) Branch committees to be responsible for seeing to it that all units and units sub-committees are activised and efficient.

(f) Greater use to be made of the printed word, but where and when this becomes impossible to make use of the word of mouth.

(g) Provincial committees to be more alive and to exercise their supervisory and administrative control strictly and conscientiously.

(h) Each member of a provincial committee to be personally responsible to the provincial committee for the proper and efficient functioning of a given branch and units and units sub-committees under the control of such branch.

(i) Each member of the National Executive to take an active and leading part in the work of the provincial committee in his province.

(j) For the purposes of proper and efficient administration each member of the National Executive to be given some aspect of our national life to study and periodically report on to the Executive. The National Executive to pay special attention to the work and activities of the provinces.

Now, how are we going to begin, how are we going to start remedying the weakness mentioned above? The answer to this question lies in the hands of the delegates to this Conference. However, whilst recognising that the remedy lies with this Conference, your Executive offers the following recommendations:

(1) The Conference should adopt the re-organisation scheme suggested above and instruct the provinces to act upon it early in the new year.

(2) (a) That every secretary of the African National Congress from the highest to the lowest must undertake a compulsory course of training for at least three months.

    (b) That every member of the Executive must undertake a course of theoretical, political and organisational training for at least two months.

    (c) That every Freedom Volunteer must undertake a course of political and organisational training for at least one month.

    (d) That before elections are conducted members must be informed of these conditions.

(3) (a) That every branch must have a copy of:

      i. the constitution of the Congress;
      ii. the booklet entitled "African Claims" (for policy); and
      iii. this report.

    (b) That every member of the Congress be required to know fully the policy and programme of the African National Congress.

    (c) That all instructions must be read in the Executive meetings and then to the general members meetings.

    (d) That reports are compulsory, at least a monthly report in the case of a branch and a quarterly report in the case of a province. This also applies to the Working Committee reporting to the National Executive Committee.

    (e) That all Congress Secretaries and officials shall promptly attend to all correspondence received by them.

(4) That anybody who deliberately distorts or undermines the policy and decisions of the Congress should be dealt with immediately.

(5) That it be the accepted duty of all branches to build up a powerful mass youth organisation which must be subordinate to the branch and also the women's section.

Lectures for courses mentioned above [are] already available, and provinces are asked to place their orders.

In conclusion, Sons and Daughters of Africa, we are placing this Report before you for your most careful attention and consideration. We have implicit faith in this assembly of delegates who have come from all corners of South Africa, and we are fully confident that from their deliberations there will emerge concrete and far-reaching decisions which will raise the organisational efficiency, and with it the political effectiveness, of the African National Congress, and thus place the Liberatory Movement and the progressive forces on the path to inevitable victory.

Friends, you are all aware that Mr. Strijdom, the fanatic of the Nationalist regime, has replaced Dr. Malan and displaced Mr. Havenga. Thus, the predictions of your leaders have once again proved true—as we have warned you before, we are heading for a fully-fledged fascist state not unlike the Hitlerite regime in Germany.

The Strijdom-Verwoerd-Swart combination is possibly the greatest political misfortune that has ever befallen this unhappy land. We can now promise you nothing but greater hardships, more forced labour, bannings and deportations on an unprecedented scale, concentration camps, a suspension of the rule of law and other manifestations of the principle of "government by brutal force," which will apply as much to the Non-European people as to the non-Nationalist European people of this country.

There can be no doubt that the salvation of the people of South Africa today lies with the mighty strength of the African National Congress and its allies and in the knowledge that history and the world are on our side, and provided we are determined to resist fascism and increase the pace of our march, we must see victory and freedom within our life-time.

LONG LIVE OUR BANNED LEADERS!
LONG LIVE THE LIBERATORY MOVEMENT!
INKULULEKO KA NAKO EA RONA!
MAYIBUYE I AFRIKA!

Document 7c. "The Congress of the People." Annexure A to the Report of the National Executive Committee

As a result of the historical call made by the African National Congress at its Conference in Queenstown, the National Executives of the African National Congress, South African Indian Congress, Congress of Democrats and the South African Coloured Peoples Organisation have decided to call on the people of South Africa to come together in a great assembly—THE CONGRESS OF THE PEOPLE.

The South African peoples' movement can be proud of its long record of unbroken struggle for rights and liberty, but never before have the mass of South African citizens been summoned together to proclaim their desire and aspirations in a single declaration—A CHARTER OF FREEDOM.

The drawing up and adopting of such a charter of freedom is the purpose for which the Congress of the People has been called. Never in South African history have the ordinary people of this country been enabled to take part in deciding their own fate and future. Elections have been restricted to a small minority of the population; franchise rights, particularly in recent times have been threatened and curtailed. There is a need to hear the voice of the ordinary citizen of this land, proclaiming to the world his demand for freedom.

WHAT IS THE CONGRESS OF THE PEOPLE?

The Congress of the People will not be just another meeting or another conference. It will be a mass assembly of delegates elected by the people of all races in every town, village, farm, factory, mine and kraal. It will be the biggest single gathering of spokesmen ever known in this country. The representatives of the people who come to the Congress will consider the detailed demands of the people, which have been sent in for incorporation in the Freedom Charter, and will embody them into a declaration. This Freedom Charter will be the South African peoples' declaration of human rights, which every civilised South African will work to uphold and carry into practice.

By decision of the joint National Executive Committee of the sponsoring bodies, the Congress of the People must be held as soon as possible, and in any case, not later than June 1955. In view of the tremendous number of delegates who will be gathering at the Congress of the People, a centrally situated place for holding the Congress is being considered. The exact date and venue of the Congress will be announced in good time. The Congress of the People will be made the occasion for a great cultural festival of the national and folk arts of all sections of our population.

HOW WILL THE CONGRESS OF THE PEOPLE BE ORGANISED?

The first task will be to make the whole country conscious of the Congress of the People, and to imbue them with a feeling of the tremendous importance of such a gathering. This can only be done through the greatest possible campaign of printed propaganda material side by side with a string of hundreds of meetings, house to house canvasses and group discussions. The central aim of all these activities will be to get citizens of the country to speak for themselves, and to state what changes must be made in their way of life, if they are to enjoy freedom.

Every demand made by the people at these gatherings, however small the matter, must be recorded and collected for consideration by the Congress of the People for inclusion in the Freedom Charter. In this way, it will become the Charter of the people, the content of which has its source in their own homes, factories, mines and reserves. It has been decided that all these demands must be formulated by October 30th, 1954.

CAN WE SUCCEED ON SUCH A SCALE?

The main burden of such a campaign of national awakening as this will fall on those politically conscious and active people who make up the membership of the national liberation organisations. If the campaign is to succeed, the message of the Congress of the People and the news of the Freedom Charter must be carried to every corner of the country. It is unthinkable that the funds can be found by the organising committee to hire the large teams of full-time organisers needed for this work.

But if there is sufficient understanding of the radical changes that such a campaign can make in the South African situation, then the same spirit of self-sacrifice and discipline, which was the hall-mark of the Defiance Campaign, will be created. With such a spirit, people will once again come forward, volunteering to give up their holidays, weekends and spare time without pay in order to carry the campaign into those parts of the country where there are no existing organised political groups. We must expect from the advanced people in all the Congresses, those sacrifices made by 8500 volunteers during the Defiance Campaign who sacrificed their liberty and their jobs in the cause of freedom.

We will create a corps of Freedom Volunteers, who will be the core of the campaign, and make themselves available to the organisers of the campaign for whatever work in whatever place they are required.

HOW TO SET ABOUT IT

To carry through the campaign, the four Congresses have set up "THE NATIONAL ACTION COUNCIL FOR THE CONGRESS OF THE PEOPLE" composed of equal numbers of representatives of each body, which will act throughout the campaign, subject to the guidance and supervision of the sponsoring bodies.

A CALL TO THE CONGRESS OF THE PEOPLE has been adopted. Every Union-wide organisation, without exception, is being asked to support and endorse this call. Those organisations who do so will be asked to appoint representatives to the National Action Council.

The aim is to establish CONGRESS OF THE PEOPLE COMMIT-TEES on a provincial basis, and on a town, suburb, factory or street basis. At all these levels, attempts will be made to draw in the participation of every local organisation and group.

The immediate task is the establishment of Provincial Committees by the 30th June. These committees will be composed of equal numbers of representatives of each of the original sponsors. Their first duty will be to convene a Provincial Conference, to which every organisation possible will be invited, and which will elect additional members to the Provincial Committee.

Whenever possible, this procedure must be repeated on a town or district basis. Only through setting up such active committees on the widest possible scale, drawing in thousands of active workers to assist them, can the campaign succeed on its greatest scale. Through these committees, the demands of the people everywhere will be gathered, the people be canvassed and local delegations to the Congress of the People be organized.

Above all it must be remembered that the creation of a network of local committees in every corner of South Africa will in itself be a major political achievement, which will be of tremendous value in every struggle of the future to achieve the demands set out in the Freedom Charter.

HOW TO MOBILISE FOR THE CONGRESS OF THE PEOPLE.

The message of the coming Congress of the People cannot inspire people unless everywhere it is linked in people's minds with their own burning problems, and with the vital issues of the day. When speaking to farm squatters the Congress of the People must be linked in their minds with their own struggle against ejectment from their homes; to town workers, with the fight for trade union rights and better wages; to the people on the trust farms, with the culling of cattle. Every vital issue, whether it be the eviction of people from the Western Areas, the introduction of apartheid at the Universities, the expropriation of property under the Group Areas Act, or the removal of voting rights under the Separate Representation of Voters' Act must be linked with all the propaganda for the Congress of the People.

WHO WILL VOTE?

Because of the long history of indirect and sham representation from which the Non-European people have suffered, it has been decided that the basis of election to the Congress of the People should be direct. That means that representatives elected by the people in any area or unit will go direct to the Congress of the People.

Every person over the age of eighteen, without distinction of race, colour or sex, will be entitled to vote for his representative.

Since the aim of the Congress of the People is to hear the desires of every group in South Africa, it is obvious that each voting unit will not be composed of the same number of people. If a European farm, employing fifteen African labourers decides to send a delegate, that is all to the good. On the other hand, large urban townships cannot be expected to send one representative for every fifteen inhabitants.

At this stage of the campaign, it is not possible to define precisely what will make up an electoral unit. It is only after the preparatory work has been successfully carried out that a more definite demarcation can be made, based on the number of local committees. In the last resort, local committees will have to decide what units in their locality will have to be represented, based on a target set by the National Action Council.

HOW WILL PEOPLE VOTE?

Election Day should be made the occasion for great political demonstrations and rallies in every part of the land.

Wherever possible, election of delegates should be held by public vote at a meeting of the electors. There may be cases however, such as on a mine or farm, where the holding of a meeting may not be possible. In such cases a canvass of the electorates by the local committees may prove to be the only practical method. It must be stressed that delegates to the Congress of the People are not delegates from local committees, but from the people in the areas where the local committee organises the work.

HOW WILL THEY GET THERE?

Thousands of delegates converging on the central venue for the Congress of the People must take place in an atmosphere of great political demonstrations. Where a large number of delegates are travelling together, Freedom Processions to greet them in every town they pass through, must be organised. Where possible, Freedom trains should be arranged to carry delegates, but where funds are not available for this, delegates should band together on a Freedom March, even though it may take some days for them to reach the Congress.

It is obvious that the National Action Council will not be able to meet the bill for the expense of delegates. We are confident that if we have created sufficient enthusiasm for the Freedom Charter and the Congress, the electors themselves will be prepared to make the sacrifices necessary to see that their chosen representatives reach the Congress.

WHO WILL PAY THE BILL?

In spite of this, the National Action Council will require tremendous sums of money to see that a copy of the "Call" to the Congress of the People gets into every home in the land, and to see that delegates are provided for at the Congress. It is therefore most important that every unit taking part in organising the Congress of the People should seize every opportunity to collect funds from the people for the campaign.

Not only must every supporter be asked to pledge regular sums of money to the campaign, but in the countryside particularly, people must be asked to make pledges of cattle and other foodstuffs to feed the delegates at the Congress.

The campaign for the Congress of the People is not a campaign for members of the Congresses alone. All those who wish to hear the voice of the people must be encouraged to join in. There can be no neutrals.

Those people and those organisations who refuse to take part, will stand exposed as fearing the democratically expressed opinions of the majority of South African citizens, and will lose the support and allegations [allegiance?] of all decent freedom-loving citizens.

In such a campaign as this, thousands of new active workers will rally to the support of those who have initiated and carried through the main burden of the campaign. New strength and new enthusiasm will grow in our ranks making it possible for us to lead our people forward to the winning of the Freedoms set out in the Charter which our people will write and adopt.

Document 7d. Resolutions

1. This Conference declares its unqualified support for the great Congress of the People sponsored by the National Organisations of this country. In this connection Conference enjoins all National Organisations, Church movements and associations to support, join in and participate in the great Campaign for the calling of the mighty Congress of the People having as its aim the drawing up of a Freedom Charter embodying the aspirations of the people of South Africa for a future free, united, multi-national, democratic community in which oppression and exploitation will be a thing of the past. The organisation of the Congress of the People is a common task in which all democrats can participate. Therefore, Conference pledges its support for the Call for 50,000 Freedom Volunteers issued by the Peoples' President, Chief A. J. Luthuli, to gather the demands of the people and to ensure that the Congress will be the most representative assembly in the history of our country.

2. That Conference expresses its full confidence in the present leadership of the African National Congress which has led the movement and the people in their struggles during the past five years and which continues to point the way forward to freedom. That the National Conference of the African National Congress pledges itself to adhere strictly to the forward-looking, democratic and dynamic policy of freedom for which our leadership and organisation are being persecuted, banned and exiled.

Conference calls upon the National Executive to make use of the Extraordinary Powers granted to it at the National Conference of 1952 so as to preserve our present leadership and ensure that we continue to be led and guided by the political leadership of our own choice whatever eventuality may arise. In this respect, Conference views with very serious concern the unwarranted acts of the Minister of Justice, Mr. C. R. Swart, in depriving the liberatory movements of their democratically-elected leaders and the deportation powers which have recently been used against some of our leaders.

3. This Conference rejects *in toto* the Native Policy of the United Party because it views it as indistinguishable from the heinous Apartheid Policy of the Government and other Native policies that have been propounded and even practiced in the past.

4. This Conference salutes the people of the Western Areas of Johannesburg for their solidarity in the fight to defend their homes and properties and calls upon all Africans and indeed all people of South Africa to centralise our national effort against the Natives Resettlement Act in the Resist Apartheid Campaign which shall have as its pivot the Western Areas of Johannesburg. Therefore Conference re-affirms the decision of the African National Congress to oppose and resist this act of legalized robbery.

5. Conference realises that the problems of Kenya cannot be solved by intimidation and violence perpetrated upon peaceful peasant populations. Consequently, the British Government must be urged in the long-term interests of all the people in Kenya to end the emergency in Kenya and produce a healthy atmosphere and to this end to:

(a) Release Jomo Kenyatta and all other persons charged with political offences and held in concentration camps all over Kenya,

(b) Remove the ban on the Kenya African Union as a prelude to the return of normal political life in the country,

(c) Stop all military measures against the peaceful population of Kenya and withdraw unnecessary troops from the territory,

(d) Arrange a round-table conference of all parties and groups in Kenya to decide the early transfer of power to a democratic government in which the mass of the people in Kenya genuinely have confidence.

6. This Conference of the African National Congress meeting at a time when there is no major conflict in the world after the Geneva Conference and the Indo-China Armistice, salutes the struggle of the World Peace Movement and asserts its faith in the peaceful co-existence of the peoples with their varying political systems through the principle of negotiation. Therefore, Conference condemns the plans of the ruling clique of America to precipitate a Third World War through the creation of war pacts such as N.A.T.O. and S.E.A.T.O., and whole plan to rearm German Nazis. This Conference considers that the modern weapons praised by

war-mongers are inhuman and maintains that the energy in atomic and hydrogen bombs should be diverted to the peaceful reconstruction of the world.

7. This Conference in acceptance of, and in response to, our President's Address as well as the report of the National Executive, resolves to widen its co-operation with the trade union movement and hereby calls upon the National Executive Committee to form a sub-committee for the purpose of co-ordination of activities and better organisational efficiency with the trade unions and furthermore to allot a portion of the funds in its treasury to the trade union movement as a positive contribution towards the strengthening of trade unionism among Africans. In this connection, Conference calls upon the National Executive to instruct all provincial organs to contribute to the treasury of the co-ordinating committee.

8. Conference insists that the correct policy to be observed towards Bantu Education is one of fighting an uncompromising consistent battle against the implementation of the Bantu Education Act and therefore resolves upon total rejection of Verwoerd's evil Act as the moral and spiritual enslavement of our children. To defeat this Act it calls upon African parents to make preparations to withdraw their children from primary schools indefinitely as from April 1, 1955, until further directive from the National Executive Committee. Furthermore, Conference calls upon the National Executive Committee to keep a vigilant eye on the situation and issue directives from time to time that will give a disciplined lead to our opposition as well as to approach individual sympathetic societies for their support.

9. As the people in the rural areas are constantly threatened with the imposition of oppressive regulations under the Native Trust and Land Amendment Act against their will, Conference resolves that the Resist Apartheid Campaign should be extended to these areas and an intensified campaign of resistance be launched immediately as some districts in the so-called Native Reserves have already been affected.

10. Whilst we realise the invalidity of the proclamation of the increased rentals that was imposed upon us by the Government, Conference feels that the economic rentals will be re-imposed in one form or another and calls upon the National Executive Committee to prepare plans for mass action in opposition to such an eventuality.

Document 8. Presidential Address by Professor Z. K. Matthews, ANC (Cape), June 18-19, 1955

Sons and Daughters of Africa,

Once more this time has come round for me to speak to you in my capacity as President of the African National Congress in the Cape. The preparation of an address of this kind is a matter which engages the attention of the President from the moment one annual conference is concluded until the next one begins. During the year, while individual members of our organisation are primarily concerned with the work of Congress in their respective areas, it is the duty of the President to endeavour to see the work of Congess in the province as a whole as well as to keep in touch with developments in other parts of the country as far as the liberation movement is concerned. The organisation to which we have the honour to belong is Union-wide in its ramifications and our responsibility for its welfare and its success must always be broadly conceived. Any action we take either as individuals or as groups may have, indeed is bound to have, repercussions far beyond the area for which it is intended, and may either promote or hinder the work in which we are engaged, namely, to weld into a mighty, disciplined and irresistible force for freedom and independence, the African people who have been subjected for so long to so much oppression and humiliation in the land of their birth. I say it is not always easy for us as individuals to see our work in its proper perspective in our day to day activities, but I conceive it to be one of our duties, at least once a year, to focus our attention on the need for us all to see things from a broader point of view, to look beyond our local needs and local problems, to take stock of the road we have travelled since last we met, to record our successes and to note our failures and so learn from our experiences how best to prosecute the struggle in which we are engaged.

BANS AND DEPORTATIONS.

You will recall that soon after that memorable conference which we had at Uitenhage, the government of this country through its appropriate ministers took against some of our most prominent members, certain steps designed to cripple the work of our organisation. In the first place two of our most trusted leaders, namely Dr. J. L. Z. Njongwe—our Vice-President—and Mr. R. M. Matji, our Provincial Secretary, were banned and were called upon to resign from the A. N. C. and a number of other organisations apparently chosen at random by the powers that be. It is not necessary for me to remind you about the valuable services which these Sons of Africa had rendered to our organisation in the Cape. One day when the story of the freedom movement in South Africa is fully told, as it must and will be, their names will rank high among those who by their selfless devotion and their undoubted gift for leadership advanced our cause by an appreciable amount. No tribute that we can pay them can be too high. It is of course impossible for any Minister to ban anybody from the A.N.C. in any real sense. As far as the A.N.C. is concerned these Sons of Africa are still members of our organisation with their names written indelibly not on bits of paper which can be confiscated but in the hearts of their people where they are beyond the reach of governmental interference. Their enforced inactivity speaks louder to the members of the A.N.C. than any actions of their own. The banning of these Sons of Africa was followed by the deportation from East London of Mr. A. S. Gwentshe and Mr. S. M. Lengisi. Without bringing any charge founded or unfounded against them the Governor-General exercising the powers granted to him under that notorious law—the Native Administration Act 38 of 1927—"to remove any Native from any place to any other place," decided to remove them to different parts of the Northern Transvaal, there to live among people among whom they would presumably be unable to exercise any influence in favour of the principles for which A.N.C. stands. Deportation is one of the severest penalties which can be imposed on an individual because he is separated from the members of his family and is deprived of his normal means of livelihood. It is a form of punishment which is designed to break the spirit of the individual concerned and to convert him into a sort of spineless individual. But African heroes who have had this treatment meted out to them have not reacted as they were expected to. They have proved themselves true Sons of Africa able to adapt themselves to any area to which they have been sent and to preach the gospel of freedom wherever they have gone. Set down among people whose languages and customs were strange to them, they have found that the language of freedom is intelligible to oppressed peoples everywhere. The result is that our colleague A. S. Gwentshe has had to be removed from the area to which he was originally sent to another where it is hoped his message will be less effective. There can be no doubt as to what will happen there. While I am on this subject I want to remind you about the duty we owe to those members. As you know efforts are being made by the A.N.C. to secure the rescission by the Supreme Court of these deportation orders which we believe to be of doubtful legality. The response of our branches to our appeal for contributions towards the cost of these applications has been very gratifying but we must not lose sight of the fact that provision must also be made for the maintenance and support of our deported friends and any donations specially earmarked for this purpose will be appreciated and will be forwarded to them without delay. Finally on the subject of bans and deportations I want to refer to the confinement of our President-General, Chief A. J. Luthuli, to the district of Lower Tugela and to the ban imposed on our Secretary-General W. M. Sisulu. It has been said that it is the tallest trees that have to bear the force of the strongest blasts of the winds. In the wilderness which comprises the South Africa in which we live today the A.N.C. has had more than its fair share of tall trees which have had to bear the blasts of this stormy period in our history.

But not only has the hand of the government of the Whites rested heavily upon the leaders to whom I have referred and upon others to whom I could refer—our hats go off to all of them—but the ordinary common people have also felt the slings and arrows of the outrageous fortune which is theirs in the land of their birth. Need I remind you about what has happened in the Western Areas of Johannesburg—the City of Gold which would have been nothing but a mudheap but for the blood, sweat and toil of thousands upon thousands of Africans. For generations the flower of African youth have gone down into the bowels of the earth there to run the gauntlet of industrial diseases, mutilating accidents and cruel masters in order to bring to the surface the wealth which has made Johannesburg the richest City on the African continent. There in that City for which thousands of them have made the supreme sacrifice, the Africans found themselves both wanted and unwanted, with no place in which they can have a secure and a permanent home. From the Western Areas in which they have lived under indescribable conditions of filth and squalor for reasons beyond their control they are now being bundled out at the point of the gun to Meadow-lands with no greater prospect of security. As sure as the sun rises in the East in a few years time some new pretext will be conjured up for removing them from Meadowlands to some other area. Not even in the sky is the African safe from the designs of those who will not rest as long as there is some African who has some place in which he can lay his head. Africans who had no more respectable place in which they could be housed than the roofs of flats have become guilty of the offense of creating "locations in the sky" and they are to be bundled out of those roofs into the "site and service" nigger-heavens which are being created in different parts of the country.

Not only in the Western Areas of Johannesburg but everywhere where Africans have settled down, aquired properties at great cost to themselves and built themselves such homes as their meagre resources permitted, they are confronted with the spectre of compulsory removal. Latterly it is not only the Africans who are being subjected to this sense of insecurity.

We in the A.N.C. have always maintained that the type of treatment meted out to Africans constitutes the yardstick for the rights of other sections of the population. In the past other sections of the population enjoyed better rights than the Africans and some of them were inclined to adopt an air of superiority towards Africans. They appeared to believe that what happened to Africans could never happen to them. Instead of helping Africans to protect and defend their meagre rights as they were systematic-ally whittled down by legislation year after year, they left them to their own devices and acquiesced in the gradual diminution of their rights. When Africans lost their franchise rights in 1936 many of the people who in 1955 are busy organising protest meetings about the entrenched clauses of the constitution were only too glad to give the government of the day the necessary two-thirds majority to deprive Africans of their rights. After all only African rights were involved. It never occurred to them then that the entrenched clauses represented a pledge of honour to defenseless and voiceless people. Depriving mere "kaffirs" of their rights was not such a bad thing after all and some of their so-called friends spared no efforts in an attempt to persuade Africans then that the system of separate representation introduced in 1936 was better than the franchise on the Common Roll which they had enjoyed before. In 1955 it is not only the Coloureds who are faced with the prospect of being given "something better" than they had had hitherto. Other sections of the population will be given a taste of "something better". The Appellate Division Quorum Bill and the Senate Bill and others still to come constitute a "writing on the wall" which needs no Daniel to interpret. The mills of Justice like those of God grind slowly but they grind exceedingly fine. The white people in the Transkei who for generations have lived in perfect safety among millions of Africans and have been treated like princes on every hand—did they ever speak when their African friends were being deprived of one right after another? No, every deprivation which the Africans suffered only served to widen the gulf between them and the Africans until the Transkei became as apartheid-ridden as any other part of our so-called sovereign state. Today for them also the writing is on the wall. For their comfort they have been assured that for them there will be no compulsory removal, but a gradual diminution or elimination of white interests in the Transkei.

There will no doubt be some Africans who will be taken in by this move to the extent of believing that it represents some sort of gain for the Africans; there will be a few extra trading licenses here and there, a post here or a post there for some African, but on balance this action will do nothing more than pile one wrong upon another. The A.N.C. representing a people who have had more than their fair share of wrongs in this country has no hesitation in saying that a few doubtful "rights" in the Transkei can never make up for what Africans have lost and are losing in the country as a whole. Our claim is not for a few miserable privileges in a corner of South Africa but for full citizenship rights in South Africa as a whole. Our opposition to the Transkei proposal is not based on any doubt regarding the ability of the African to govern himself, on the contrary it is because we believe that the Africans together with freedom loving persons from other groups can and should govern the whole country, that we are not prepared to accept this geographical circumscription of his right to share in the government of the country.

Other disabilities which hitherto seemed reserved for Africans but which are gradually being extended to other sections of the population include the pass system, euphemistically called population registration in the case of non-Africans; the regulation of departure from the Union; the grant to the police of the right of entry to all, not only African, public meetings; the banning from attendance at gatherings and from membership of certain organisations; the denial to teachers of the right to take part in public affairs; the surveillance of the activities of certain individuals by members of the Special Branch of the C.I.D. including tampering with correspondence and the tapping of telephone conversations. These are everyday occurrences to which the Africans have become, in a sense, accustomed, and whether these are evidences of a Police State or not they are certainly the marks of what someone has called the prison house which was once our country.

But easily the biggest thing that has happened to the Africans since last we met has been the transfer of African schools to the control of the Bantu Education Division of the Native Affairs Department since April 1, 1955. It is common knowledge that the object of this transfer is to make Bantu Education the handmaiden of the policy of white supremacy. We have been reminded ad nauseam that permanent white *baasskap* is to be the keynote of Union Native policy. That policy cannot of course become permanent unless it is accepted by the people on whom it is imposed. Some method must therefore be devised of conditioning the African to make *baasskap* acceptable to him. On the principle that the child is father to the man the apostles of *baasskap* believe that if they can condition the African child through a special system of education prepared for him, if they can give him the right environmental and other studies, he will grow up into a man who will willingly accept the status accorded to him by his white masters. Now a systematic process of conditioning to control the minds of people in such a way as to make them react the way they are expected to is quite a possible thing. A process of conditioning combined with a systematic control of the mass media of communication such as the Press, the wireless, literature, the cinema, etc. plus the rigid stamping out of all those who deviate from the official policy can produce the necessary servility in the population for which it is intended. It has been done before with highly civilized and educated nations. It was done in Nazi Germany. It was done in Fascist Italy and Fascist Spain. Even in the so-called free countries, it is common knowledge that the mass media of communication and propaganda are widely used to destroy freedom of opinion, speech and action. Independent thinking has always been regarded by rulers as a dangerous thing to encourage among the common people.

In other words looked at from the point of view of the believers in *baasskap* it is logical for them to take the African schools from the voluntary agencies such as churches and other organisations which are not necessarily amenable to the dictates of the *baasskap* school of thought and to place them in the care of handpicked Africans who are prepared to play ball with their masters. The officers of the government have been at pains to explain that "Bantu" education will in no way be inferior to the education previously given to Africans. In fact they go so far as to say that no system of education could be worse than the system that has hitherto existed in African schools. Be that as it may. What no officer has dared to contradict is that the new system is intended to do better what the previous system had not been able to do well enough for the liking of the apostles of apartheid, namely to produce a race of docile Africans willing to accept the status accorded to them by the laws of the white man.

Now the African National Congress does not and never will accept the concept of white supremacy. The white man can go on believing that he is a superior being if he is content to subscribe to illusions which fly in the face of reality. But when he wants the Africans themselves to accept these illusions, it is necessary for us to remind him, that we have lived long enough with him in this country to know that he is just an ordinary mortal no better and no worse than the ordinary run of men. The African National Congress is opposed to the system of Bantu Education because of the principles and policies underlying it. It is not going to be misled by the elaborate facade of so-called "history making" Bantu School Boards, School Committees, Secretaries, sub-inspectorships, etc. Nor is it impressed by the flowing reports regarding the ready co-operation of Africans of all grades in the new system of education. Every scheme designed to deprive Africans of their rights has always been accompanied by similar fanfares of trumpets, but with the passage of time its real nature has come to light and the propaganda has turned out to be sound and fury signifying nothing but misery. The South Africa Act, the Natives Land Act of 1913, the Native Affairs Act 1920, the Natives Urban Areas Act 1923, the Native Taxation and Development Act of 1925, the Native Representation Act of 1936, the Natives Land and Trust Act, 1936, the Bantu Authorities Act of 1951—one and all were supposed to usher in the millenium, but the Africans who have to live under these laws alone know what they have meant and have done to African society.

The African National Congress is quite unrepentant in its attitude towards all these laws and will continue to fight against them. The same applies to the Bantu Education Act. But in our campaign against these laws we must remember that we are engaged in a long struggle. Any idea that victory will be obtained overnight is wishful thinking of the worst type. We are dealing with a well organized powerful and relentless group which will stop at nothing to achieve its aims. We have deliberately chosen non-violence as the basis of our method of struggle, a method which requires a high degree of discipline and a highly developed sense of responsibility.

Various methods have been suggested for dealing with the situation created by the Bantu Education Act.

In the first place Africans throughout the country whether they belong to the A.N.C. or not are unanimous in condemning the principles and the policies underlying "Bantu" Education. There are no Africans who believe in the idea that their children should be sent to school in order that they should become better servants of the white man. For them as for all parents their object in sending their children to school is to enable them to prepare themselves for a wider not a narrower sphere of life, for an enhanced not a lower status, for greater freedom and not for more subservience. How then are Africans going to prevent their children from suffering the fate that is prescribed for them?

There are those who say that Bantu Education should be fought against from within. In other words what is suggested here is that African parents, teachers and children should, while appearing to accept Bantu Education, engage in a widespread campaign of sabotage of the system. The members of the school committees and school boards should discharge their duties in such a way as to make the system unworkable. The teachers should expose every untruth contained in the syllabus they are supposed to follow and imbue the children they teach with the spirit of freedom and opposition to the conception of white supremacy. In this way it is believed the whole superstructure of Bantu Education would eventually crumble like the walls of Jericho. To those who intend to fight Bantu Education in this way we can only say that we do not envy them the chamelion-like role which they have chosen to play. We can only wait and see how they will preserve their will to fight from within.

Then we have the cynical school of thought which consists of individuals who intend to make the most of any benefits, material or otherwise, that happen to be associated with the new system of Bantu Education. For them it does not really matter what the content of Bantu Education is. They are concerned with making the most of it while they can be feathering their own nests and clearing out as soon as they have to. Such individuals, of course, make no pretence of fighting against Bantu Education, but want to exploit it to the full for their personal benefit. Any African who can gain any advantage out of the white man is welcome to it, but when he does so at the expense of his fellow Africans, he must remember that the sufferings of his people will be on his head. So members of school committees and school boards, make the most of such opportunities as are to be had. Teachers and supervisors, take the promotions which are available under the new system but remember that man does not live by bread alone and beware of selling the birthright of your children for a mess of apartheid pottage.

Then there are others who look upon the new system of education as providing the African people with an opportunity of capturing the whole school system by getting into all the key positions in school committees, boards, staffs etc., and once having done that turning the whole system into a powerful arm of the liberation movement. This will I suppose call for the creation of a kind of *Broederbond* to direct this necessarily underground movement.

The African National Congress has adopted the total withdrawal of African children from Bantu Schools as a method of fighting against the Bantu Education Act. The A.N.C. has, as usual, not indulged in any condemnation of those who have decided on the different ways of fighting

Bantu Education mentioned above, but has rather put forward its own programme. This is to embark on a campaign of persuading African parents to withdraw their children from schools under the control of Dr. Verwoerd and the establishment of alternative cultural, recreational and social activities for such children. In doing this the A.N.C. has as usual chosen the hard road. That this road is not an easy one has been realised by those who, understandably impatient to be rid of Bantu Education as soon as possible, decided to embark upon spontaneous local campaigns. The experiences gained from the campaigns conducted in Benoni and other areas have made it plain that a mighty organisational effort is required if the A.N.C. is to achieve success in this campaign. We shall have to close our ranks, get rid of mutual recriminations among ourselves, beware of the activities of agents-provocateurs whose aim is to produce division and confusion, and to intensify our propaganda efforts and follow the directives of our National Executive. It will be for this conference to consider ways and means of making this campaign the effective blow for freedom which it ought to be. For its success this campaign will naturally depend upon the co-operation óf African parents. If we fail to persuade them that withdrawal is the right road to take, we shall have to consider alternative methods of defeating the Bantu Education Act, but defeat it we must.

It is hardly necessary for me to point out that the A.N.C. stands for full educational opportunities for African children. The A.N.C. has always been in the forefront of the battle for better educational facilities for African children, better terms and conditions of service for African teachers and a greater share of responsibility for African parents as far as management and control of schools for their children is concerned. The A.N.C. stands for free, compulsory education and the assumption of financial responsibility by the state for the education of African children in the same way as is done in the case of children of other sections of the population. Under the Bantu Education as you know, the Union government has not accepted responsibility for the financing of the education of African children but has limited its responsibility to an amount of six and a half million pounds. The government has given itself the right of 100% control of African schools. Nobody will be allowed to run a school as defined in the Act for African children unless he has the permission of the Minister of Native Affairs to do so. The right of any group of parents to establish a school for their children and to raise funds for this purpose has been taken away from them. Many an African child has begun his education in a private school of this type. With a population such as ours where the majority of children of school-going age (60%) have no school facilities, the right of people to be free to add to the meagre facilities for their children is of great importance.

The status of the teachers under the Bantu Education Act is worse than that of any group of unskilled workers. From being a respectable profession, teaching in African schools has become almost menial. Teachers have been converted into yes-men to all and sundry, who must look over their shoulders everytime they wish to express an opinion on public affairs. These men and women who by their devotion to duty and self-sacrificing service are largely responsible for the progress which has to date been made in African education are in the future to be treated as if they constitute a potentially "subversive" element. We have full confidence that the majority of African teachers will ignore the ridiculous regulations framed for them under the Bantu Education Act and get on with the business of educating the African child for a free society and not for a slave society as contemplated by the Act. Although they will have to keep their mouths shut, nobody except themselves can keep their hearts closed as far as concerns the welfare of their people, who will not be unaware of which teachers are with them and which against them.

Dr. Verwoerd, who has confidence in his own word, has threatened that every African child withdrawn from school as a result of boycott opposition to the Bantu Education will be refused all further educational opportunities or rather will be denied such opportunities as he has to offer.

As you know in the Transvaal over 7,000 children in the East Rand have been placed in this position and in spite of tearful pleas by deputations of so-called "leaders" who pride themselves on having lost the will to fight for their rights which they say they once had, Dr. Verwoerd has turned a deaf ear to all their appeals and advised them to go to the A.N.C. and ask the A.N.C. to withdraw its boycott resolution which is hanging like a sword of Damocles over African schools. These emissaries of Dr. Verwoerd have not yet approached the A.N.C. but they had better be prepared for the reception they will receive. The A.N.C. is not in the habit of allowing its policy to be dictated by ministerial threats. The withdrawal resolution was adopted by the National Conference of the A.N.C., our supreme legislative body, and only that body can decide whether or not to abandon that resolution, and my suspicion is that the activities and threats of the Minister of Native Affairs will strengthen rather than weaken the determination of the A.N.C. to go on with its campaign. 60% of the African children of school-going age are without educational facilities of any sort, and we are not impressed by Dr. Verwoerd's decision to deny a further 7,000 children all further educational opportunity. As the years pass under the new dispensation even our deputation friends will come to realise that education for ignorance and for inferiority in Verwoerd's schools is worse than no education at all. It is the future of the African child, not the present, which must be safeguarded. The African fight for the education of the children has been a long and painful one. That fight has been concerned not only with the erection of school buildings which have largely been provided out of the meagre resources of the people. For many years African parents had to provide the money for the payment of teachers' salaries and for the provision of equipment by means of school fees and contributions to concerts and other fund-raising efforts organised by the teachers. It is only recently that Africans have been relieved of the burden of paying school-fees and other charges. African parents have also had to fight to see that their children are not fobbed off with an inferior system of education. They have had to be vigilant and to examine every new scheme introduced into the African educational system to satisfy themselves whether it was a forward or backward step. Every move which they have regarded as a backward move has in the long run been defeated by the people. Attempts have been made in the past to give medical aides instead of medical doctors; agricultural demonstrators instead of agricultural officers; school farms instead of schools; native teachers certificates instead of teachers certificates. Some of these specially adapted courses have been success-fully imposed on the African, others have had to be abandoned. But in every case the African has had to put up a fight for his education. The position which has been created by the Bantu Education Act is nothing new. It is simply a more comprehensive and more ruthless attack on the African educational system which will set the clock back for many years but which will not deter us from our main purpose, namely to fight for the placing of the education of the African child on a sound basis. That basis will be determined by the African people themselves who will co-operate with schemes which are for their benefit but will withhold their co-operation from schemes which are designed to make them into tools for the ends of others. Some people are of course overwhelmed by the fact that the government possesses the funds necessary to enable it to carry out their schemes and the people themselves have not got the money to enable them to fight back. But money is not everything. People in different parts of the world, not excluding South Africa, have shown before now that financial resources and the instruments of force are not sufficient to overcome a people's will to resist what they believe is not in their interest. For that reason we are not afraid of the Bantu Education Act; we know that in the long run it will be defeated by the will of the people to resist the evil doctrine of white supremacy.

The African National Congress stands for a free South Africa for a free people who enjoy equal rights whatever their colour, race or creed. It is for that reason that we are opposed to the narrow nationalism which would seek to create a caste society in South Africa with an apex of a minority of so-called national-minded whites with various grades of underlings ranging from so-called un-national minded whites through Coloureds, Indians and down to Africans below them. That kind of South Africa has no future in the modern world. Slowly but surely the people of South Africa will come to realise that they have been led up a blind alley far too long and that they must make a right-about-turn and march out of this separationist blind alley into the larger freedom which is the destiny of man. The mighty Congress of the People to be held in Johannesburg this month is a step in that direction. There a vast concourse of peoples drawn from every racial group and from every part of the country will gather and will speak freely to South Africa and to the world about the kind of South Africa they would like to see established in this country. The Freedom Charter which they will draw up will sound a dream to the reactionary elements which have been in the ascendancy for too long in this country, but the vision which the Congress of the People will set before the people of South Africa will with the passage of time become clearer and clearer and will set before all, goals for which to strive in the years that lie ahead. We congratulate all those who have worked hard to bring this campaign to a successful culmination and wish the Congress of the People the success their efforts deserve. Unlike the exclusively white Parliament which is just about to conclude a session in which it has as usual broadcast dragons teeth from which this unhappy land will reap an ever more doleful crop, this Parliament of the People will, we have no doubt, send a message of hope to every home in South Africa.

The present session of parliament has been remarkable for the manner in which the ruling party has exposed the nakedness of the policies of the opposition parties and especially that of the United Party, which has not yet learnt the lesson that they will never return to power by trying to out-Nationalist the Nationalists. Only a party with a policy diametrically opposed to that of the Nationalists' party will ever remove them from office. No such party has yet emerged from among the people who enjoy the franchise in South Africa. Such a party when it eventually does emerge will probably be in the wilderness for some time, but it will be the only party with a future in S.A. and will constitute a genuine alternative government to that of the Nationalist Party. It is such a party and such a party alone which will be able to preserve South Africa not for white civilisation, but for civilisation as such.

In conclusion I should like to say a word of thanks to the members and officials of all branches of the African National Congress as well as to the members of the Provincial Executive for the manner in which they have performed their duties throughout the year. They have laboured under great difficulties. In many centres public authorities have done all they could to hamper the work of the organisation through the prohibition of public meetings, through police interference with our meetings, by removing our members and officials through bannings and deportations and by involving our members in litigation over trivial offenses, all of which actions might have intimidated a less determined people. But our organisation has gone from strength to strength. Our membership con-tinues to increase and the message of freedom which we preach continues to win adherents even beyond the ranks of our paid-up membership. We know that those who are not against us are for us but we are out to save even those who are against us, from the bondage in which they would like to keep all of us—the bondage of mutual fear and insecurity in the land of our birth. I would be failing in my duty if I did not conclude with a personal word of thanks for the loyalty and confidence which you have reposed in me during my terms of office and my colleagues in the provincial executive will agree with me when I say that as we lay down our offices we hope you will show the same loyalty to the new executive which is to be elected at this Conference and thus maintain the proud record of the A.N.C. (Cape Province) in the fight for the liberation of South Africa. This does not mean that we can afford to rest on our laurels. There are many things which require to be put right in our organisation so as to make it a more effective fighting force. We must examine and re-examine our machinery with a view to removing from it all the things that clog the wheels of progress. You have shown in the past that this can be done and we appeal to you for greater efforts in the future. Mayibuye.

THE CONGRESS OF THE PEOPLE
AND THE FREEDOM CHARTER

Document 9. "Call to the Congress of the People." Leaflet issued by the National Action Council of the Congress of the People, [n.d.]

WE CALL THE PEOPLE OF SOUTH AFRICA BLACK AND WHITE— LET US SPEAK TOGETHER OF FREEDOM!

WE CALL THE FARMERS OF THE RESERVES AND TRUST LANDS.
Let us speak of the wide land, and the narrow strips on which we toil.
Let us speak of brothers without land, and of children without schooling.
Let us speak of taxes and of cattle, and of famine.
LET US SPEAK OF FREEDOM.

WE CALL THE MINERS OF COAL, GOLD AND DIAMONDS.
Let us speak of the dark shafts, and the cold compounds far from our families.
Let us speak of heavy labour and long hours, and of men sent home to die.
Let us speak of rich masters and poor wages.
LET US SPEAK OF FREEDOM.

WE CALL THE WORKERS OF FARMS AND FORESTS.
Let us speak of the rich foods we grow, and the laws that keep us poor.
Let us speak of harsh treatment and of children and women forced
to work.
Let us speak of private prisons, and beatings and of passes.
LET US SPEAK OF FREEDOM.

WE CALL THE WORKERS OF FACTORIES AND SHOPS.
Let us speak of the good things we make, and the bad conditions of our
work.
Let us speak of the many passes and the few jobs.
Let us speak of foremen and of transport and of trade unions;
of holidays and of houses.
LET US SPEAK OF FREEDOM.

WE CALL THE TEACHERS, STUDENTS AND THE PREACHERS.
Let us speak of the light that comes with learning, and the ways we are
kept in darkness.
Let us speak of great services we can render, and of the narrow
ways that are open to us.
Let us speak of laws, and government, and rights.
LET US SPEAK OF FREEDOM.

WE CALL THE HOUSEWIVES AND THE MOTHERS.
Let us speak of the fine children that we bear, and of their stunted
lives.
Let us speak of the many illnesses and deaths, and of the few
clinics and schools.
Let us speak of high prices and of shanty towns.
LET US SPEAK OF FREEDOM.

LET US SPEAK TOGETHER
ALL OF US TOGETHER — African and European, Indian and
Coloured. Voter and voteless. Privileged and rightless. The happy
and the homeless. All the people of South Africa; of the towns and of
the countryside.
LET US SPEAK TOGETHER OF FREEDOM. And of the
happiness that can come to men and women if they live in a land
that is free.
*LET US SPEAK TOGETHER OF FREEDOM. And of
how to get it for ourselves, and for our children.*
LET THE VOICE OF ALL THE PEOPLE BE HEARD. AND LET
THE DEMANDS OF ALL THE PEOPLE FOR THE THINGS
THAT WILL MAKE US FREE BE RECORDED. LET THE DE-
MANDS BE GATHERED TOGETHER IN A GREAT **CHARTER
OF FREEDOM.**

WE CALL ON ALL GOOD MEN AND TRUE, to speak now of freedom, and to write their own demands into the Charter of Freedom.

WE CALL ALL WHO LOVE LIBERTY to pledge their lives from here on to win the Freedoms set out in the Charter.

WE CALL ALL THE PEOPLE OF SOUTH AFRICA TO PREPARE FOR:

THE CONGRESS OF THE PEOPLE—Where representatives of the people, everywhere in the land, will meet together in a great assembly, to discuss and adopt the Charter of Freedom.

Let us organise together for the Congress of the People.
Let us speak together of Freedom.
Let us work together for the Freedom Charter.
LET US GO FORWARD TOGETHER TO FREEDOM!

This Call to the
CONGRESS of the PEOPLE
is addressed to all South Africans, European and Non-European.

It is made by four bodies, speaking for the four sections of the people of South Africa:—by the African National Congress, the South African Indian Congress, the Congress of Democrats, and the South African Coloured People's Organisation.

It calls you all to prepare to send your chosen spokesmen to:

THE CONGRESS OF THE PEOPLE,
a meeting of elected representatives of all races, coming together from every town and village, every farm and factory, every mine and kraal, every street and suburb, in the whole land. Here all will speak together, freely, as equals. They will speak together of the things their people need to make them free. They will speak together of changes that must be made in our lives, our laws, our customs and our outlooks. They will speak together of freedom. And they will write their demands into

THE FREEDOM CHARTER.
This Charter will express all the demands of all the people for the good life that they seek for themselves and their children. The Freedom Charter will be our guide to those "singing tomorrows" when all South Africans will live and work together, without racial bitterness and fear of misery, in peace and harmony.

THIS IS A CALL for an awakening of all men and women, to campaign together in the greatest movement of all our history.

Our call is to you—the People of South Africa. We invite all Union-wide Organisations to join as sponsors of the CONGRESS OF THE

PEOPLE, and to take part in its direction. Those who are not afraid to hear the voice of the people will join us. We will welcome them, and work together with them as equals.

We invite all local and provincial societies, clubs, churches, trade unions, sporting bodies and other organisations to join as partners in the CONGRESS OF THE PEOPLE Committee, and to share the work. Those who are not afraid to speak of freedom will join us. We will welcome them, and work together with them as equals.

We invite all South African men and women of every race and creed to take part as organisers of the CONGRESS OF THE PEOPLE and awaken others to its message. Those who are prepared to work together for freedom and the Freedom Charter will join us. We will welcome them, and go forward together with them to freedom.

OUR CALL IS TO YOU!

- **Give your time to spread the message of the CONGRESS OF THE PEOPLE.**
- **Become a Volunteer to organise for freedom.**
- **Tell your neighbours and workmates of the nation-wide elections that are coming.**
- **Rouse the people to discuss what they want of freedom.**
  LET US WORK TOGETHER FOR FREEDOM!

THE CONGRESS OF THE PEOPLE
will take place

- when all the people's demands for inclusion in the Freedom Charter have been gathered in;
- when the whole country has been awakened to speak of freedom, and the call for elections has been made;
- not later than June, 1955—at a date and place still to be announced.

THE CONGRESS OF THE PEOPLE
will be organised

- by 50,000 Volunteers, who will give their time to carrying through the campaign as directed;
- by a network of committees in every village, town and factory, representing and uniting all sections and all races.
- by the National Action Council, composed of all national bodies that agree to act as sponsors.

DO THESE THREE THINGS–NOW!

ONE: SEND IN YOUR NAME AND ADDRESS TO A PROVINCIAL COMMITTEE OF THE CONGRESS OF THE PEOPLE, stating that you are interested and would like to assist.

Transvaal Committee, Box 11045, Johannesburg.
Natal Committee, Box 2299, Durban.
Western Cape Committee, Box 4552, Cape Town.
Eastern Cape Committee, Box 1294, Port Elizabeth.
O.F.S. Committee, 3397 Masito Street, Bloemfontein.

TWO: FORM COMMITTEES to campaign for the Congress of the People.

THREE: GATHER GROUPS to send in their demands for the Freedom Charter.

●

DO NOT THROW THIS LEAFLET AWAY! PASS IT ON TO A FRIEND. DISCUSS IT WITH OTHERS. SEE THAT IT IS READ BY MANY PEOPLE.

Issued by the National Action Council of the Congress of the People, Box 11045, Johannesburg.

Document 10. Police record of the Congress of the People, Kliptown, Johannesburg, June 25–26, 1955 [Extracts]

Note: Only punctuation marks and capitalization have been changed in this police record as it appears in the *Treason Trial Record*, pages 6,486–6,526.

(The meeting [on Saturday, June 25] commenced with the singing of the National Anthem—Nkosi Sekelele Afrika.)

CHAIRMAN: (Dr. Conco.) "Well, the time has come that we will commence our conferences, and I ask you all to be seated. We have got a very long agenda and will have to start now if we want to get through our agenda before tomorrow.
   "Our next item will be a short prayer by Rev. (   ). There will be no interpretation."
   Prayer by Rev. (   ).

CHAIRMAN: "Friends, you will have a welcome by Mr. Moretsele, who is the President of the Transvaal African National Congress."

MORETSELE: "Mr. Chairman, honourable members, delegates to this Congress of the People, we welcome you. Delegates and friends, I welcome you all to this gathering here this afternoon. This gathering is open to all, people of all classes, people of all races, people of all languages, and with these short words, I welcome you all."

CHAIRMAN: "Friends, after the welcome, our agenda here shows that we have the opening address by our President General, Chief A. J. Luthuli. We are just getting that ready and we will skip that item and go on to the fourth—the explanation of the agenda. The agenda is very long, and I ask you all to assist us so that we can finish in good time.

"We have got the first session, which should take us up to about half past four. I hope we will get through. The second session starts immediately and ends at six o'clock. It starts with the reading of the Charter. The third session starts tomorrow at 9 o'clock, and I would be pleased if we all come here on time—the time is 9 o'clock. The last session—we will have a lunch hour break and that will take us one hour and we will have our last session from 1.20 to 5.15. I want you all to appreciate that the time is against us."

(Explanation of Agenda in Native.)

"Friends, we have got a lot of messages here before us from people who felt that they should convey messages to this great gathering, the Congress of the People, and I will now ask Dr. Press to read the messages that we have here."

DR. PRESS: "It is interesting to know, by the world-wide nature of these messages, that we have friends all over the world. I have a message here from Mr. Chou-En-Lai and it reads as follows:—"

(Reading of messages.)

CHAIRMAN: "Friends, our next item is coming before we get the Chief's message read to you. That is getting ready and you will have it shortly after this ceremonial that will be held now. This is a new feature in the liberatory struggle of the people of South Africa. It is Isitwalandwe. There will be here presentations made to individuals who have distinguished themselves in the struggle of the people of South Africa.

"These individuals are, our national leader of the African National Congress, Chief A. J. Luthuli, Father Huddleston and Dr. Y. M. Dadoo, who will get the presentations today. I might as well, friends, make an explanation of what Isitwalandwe is. This is an honour which was given in African society to a great man in our society who has distinguished himself either on the national service or in war—in war time. Isitwalandwe is a man and he used to lead the impis, the warriors to success in any battle, and therefore every man who was given this honour got the highest distinction in African society.

"Friends, the first presentation will be made by Mr. Beyleveld to Chief Luthuli's daughter, who is here amongst us."

P. BEYLEVELD: "We of the African National Congress, South African Indian Congress, South African Congress of Democrats, South African Coloured Peoples' Organisation, have the great honour to present this honour to Chief Luthuli for his great services that he has rendered to the people of South Africa, for his wonderful and selfless services which he has given, and the amount of esteem [and] affection in which he is held amongst the Africans, Indians and Coloureds alike. He stands for democracy and equality.

"The African National Congress, the South African Indian Congress, the South African Congress of Democrats and the South African Coloured Peoples' Organisation confer upon Chief Luthuli the title of Isitwalandwe, the highest honour that the people can award.

"Chief Luthuli has sacrificed his position himself for the cause of leading our people on the road of liberation. . . ."

SPEAKER: "On behalf of Chief Luthuli, Mr. Chairman, I take this occasion of being highly honoured to take the presentation to a great man, a great leader of the African people, of the people of South Africa. . . . Despite that Chief Luthuli has been handicapped at this time and cannot be present, the spirit of the man lives as that of a great leader of his people, which he wants to see liberated in our lifetime. Mr. Chairman, I thank you on behalf of Chief Luthuli. It is Chief Luthuli's wish that after this we sing one verse of Mayibuye Afrika."

(Singing.)

SPEAKER: "Friends, I have the pleasure of presenting this great honour of Isitwalandwe which is the highest distinction of the liberatory struggle of the African people, to the Rev. Father Huddleston, who is here on my left—on my right, in recognition of his many years of honourable and selfless service in the cause of the nation, and as a man of experience and affection in which he is held by both men and women, African, Indian, Coloured and Whites, who seeks to build a better life for our country on the basis of equality.

"The African National Congress, South African Indian Congress, South African Coloured Peoples' Organisation, South African Congress of Democrats confer upon Father Huddleston the title of Isitwalandwe.

"Friends, the title of Isitwalandwe which is the highest honour that the people can award, I am now going to present on behalf of the people of all colours to this man because he has given us without fear, his courage and services. He has refused to compromise whether in the field of education or freedom of speech."

FATHER HUDDLESTON: "Mr. Chairman and friends, I find it very difficult to express my gratitude for the honour which I was awarded this afternoon. It is a great pleasure to receive the title of Isitwalandwe on an occasion like this. I cannot help feeling sad that of the three people to whom this honour is given, I am the only one who is present to receive it, and I don't know whether it is to be blamed on the part of our friends, the police, or not, but the fact is I am here.

"I would just like to give you one personal message, but I will wait for the South African Railways to finish their work first. I have never known the South African Railways to be so efficient as they are this afternoon, and I am quite sure it is a demonstration to this Congress by the Minister of Transport.

"The Minister of Justice is very well represented here in the background and I hope they have a happy afternoon to see if they can spot some of their friends in this large gathering. I dare say in this Congress there is a lot of people.

"Here in Kliptown this afternoon we have only one answer to the Government in this country. The Government in this country wants to deprive people of their rights, the Government in this country uses unconstitutional methods, methods which are used to deprive majorities of their rights. Here this afternoon . . . we meet openly. We want to discuss freedom. We meet to plan a Charter which will be the basis of action for the coming years. Those are the principles we hold so dear, of justice and of peace in our time, and so I thank you from my heart and I wish this Congress of the People every blessing in the years to come. Thank you very much."

CHAIRMAN: "Friends, our next presentation of Isitwalandwe is to Dr. Dadoo, President of the South African Indian Congress, a man who has given all his time to the liberation of the people of South Africa. Dr. Dadoo cannot be amongst us, and we have the honour of having Dr. Dadoo's mother with us to receive the presentation.

"This is a presentation to Dr. Dadoo in recognition of his many years of honourable and selfless service in the cause of human dignity and liberty and as a mark of his human affection in which he is held by countless good men and women, Africans, Indians, Whites and Coloureds, who seeks to build a better life in our country for equality.

"This presentation is made by the African National Congress, South African Indian Congress, South African Coloured Peoples' Organisation, South African Congress of Democrats, who confer upon Yusuf Mohamed Dadoo the tital of Isitwalandwe. . . .''

DADOO'S MOTHER: "Mr. Chairman and fellow delegates, I am pleased to come here this afternoon to receive this honour on behalf of Dr. Dadoo. It is well known that he cannot be here today in person because he has been stopped from attending gatherings and from participating in the activities of Congress and other organisations—democratic organisations—of our people by those banning orders of Swart.

"He has been taking an active part in politics since his student days. I remember too, in school days, oh! how he used to come home after having scraps with school children who used to insult non-European children by calling them Koelies, Kaffirs and Hotnots. And in those early days Yusuf's political activities and anxiety gradually took form, that freedom does not fall from Heaven, but that the people have to struggle. . . . Today I see delegates around me who have gathered from the four corners of the Union to draw a Freedom Charter as a mighty weapon for uniting all the democratic forces in the country in the noble struggle to defeat the evil forces of racialism and oppression, and for the betterment of all the peoples of South Africa—ensuring peace, freedom and human life, better and higher living conditions and unbounded social activities for all the people, both white and non-white. I wish every success to your deliberations. Afrika!''

CHAIRMAN: ''Friends, we are through this occasion of the presentations, which I hope the liberating struggle of the organisations, through the Congress of the People, might see to it that the spirit of service that has been shown by individuals, and also by those who might not be present, might be carried on and we hope this will be a feature which will be carried on in our fight for freedom.

''Our next item which we will have is the opening message to this conference by Chief A. J. Luthuli, President of the African National Congress, who is not amongst us. This message will be read by Dr. Letele to you and will be summarised in Zulu and also in Sutho—this message from Chief Luthuli.''

DR. LETELE: (Reading message of Chief Luthuli.)

CHAIRMAN: ''Friends, there are just a few announcements to make. Will the volunteers who are responsible for the catering report at the kitchen straight away. Mr. Kunene of Newclare, kindly report with your delegation at the entrance. Mr. Kunene, of Newclare please report at the entrance.

''Friends, I ask you again to control yourselves, and I ask you people to sit down and we will have now the report of the Action Council of the Congress of the People, and due to the time it will not be discussed. It will be read as it is presented. Mr. Patel will present the report of the Action Council of the Congress of the People, and please sit down it will not be very long.''

PATEL: ''Mr. Chairman and fellow delegates, it gives me great pleasure to present to this great assembly the report on behalf of the National Action Council. This great peoples' Congress is the termination of long months of freedom campaigning by our peoples' united ideas and harmony. . . .

''In this campaign we spent two to three hundred pounds, money collected by the people. Over a quarter million leaflets have been distributed, organisers sent out to the remotest corners of our land, and . . . the Congress has been brought close to the people.

"The campaign was launched in several stages, popularising the Congress of the People, formulating and sending in freedom demands and finally election of delegates. Our delegates assembled here are not only from the organisations and groups. They have been elected from the factories, from the streets and blocks, in the locations and townships, by small groups of housewives, by farm squatters, by miners in the compounds, by people gathering in large numbers and small. Our delegates assembled here speak with the voice of the people everywhere who have been taking part in the direct democratic election and have spoken of their demands from their hearts. The authorities tried from the outset to crush this campaign. Leaders were banned, conferences invaded by the police, individuals intimidated and things like that, to people planning freedom, and the campaign for the Freedom Charter gathered strength. We have been planning freedom as fast as ever with the spirit of determination in all of you in the face of intimidation and police terror and no Government intervention has succeeded in culling us. No intimidation or terror will succeed. From here we will go on to even bigger achievements in the campaign for our future in freedom.

"In conclusion I wish to thank the delegates who have come from far and near on behalf of the National Action Council and on behalf of the four sponsoring organisations. I only hope and trust that when you return to your places where you come from you must see that it is your duty that the Freedom Charter becomes a reality and a document and a Charter of the people of South Africa. I thank you."

CHAIRMAN: "Friends, we have come to the conclusion of the session, of this of which I was the Chairman, and I will now call upon Mr. Hurbans, who is the Chairman of the second session, which we are going into now."

CHAIRMAN: (Hurbans.) "Ladies and gentlemen, we are far behind our scheduled time, and it is not my intention to make a speech. However, I appreciate the recognition given me by the South African Indian Congress in that they have asked me as one of the nominees of the Congress to preside over this session. . . .

"You have, ladies and gentlemen, the Freedom Charter circulated amongst the people. There is no doubt that ultimately success must come to our movement. I want to explain one or two things about the agenda and about what is to be done under my presidency, so that you have the knowledge of the items, and with your co-operation it might be possible that we take a shorter time than it might otherwise take.

"The . . . paragraph comprises five items. The first is the reading of the whole Charter in three different languages. Then it is the call for the names of those who desire to speak. The third is the discussion of the Preamble of the Charter. The fourth, the first item is given as 'The People Shall Govern', and the fifth, which is headed 'All National Groups Shall Have Equal Rights'.

"Now ladies and gentlemen, we have these five things to go over and after that we will adjourn until tomorrow. I would like to call for the names of those who desire to speak under the different headings [of the entire draft charter] . . . .

"Now friends, in sending in the names, please write down your names and indicate the section [of the draft charter] under which you would like to speak and also indicate from where the speakers come, and it will be quite in order if you merely put them down numerically.

"Now, the first item is the reading of the whole charter by Mr. Benghu in Zulu. Mr. Benghu! Will Mr. Benghu please come forward to read the Charter in Zulu? Is Mr. (   )? here to read it in English? Mr. Peter Beyleveld will read it in English."

(Benghu reading Draft Freedom Charter in Zulu.)

CHAIRMAN: "Ladies and gentleman, we have decided that the Charter be read in Sutho and in English and thereafter we adjourn until tomorrow morning 9 o'clock."

(Announcements made about accommodation—not heard.)

(Reading of Draft Freedom Charter in English by P. Beyleveld.)

SUNDAY 26TH JUNE, 1955.

10 A. M.

CHAIRMAN: "Friends, please be seated. We will now resume with our next session. Delegates, please be seated. We will now resume!

"We are calling Mr. A. S. Hutchinson. Will Mr. Hutchinson please come to the platform. Mr. Matla! Will Dr. Letele please come to the platform immediately. Please be seated so that we can start.

"Ladies and gentlemen, please be seated. We will now begin with our morning session. First of all I want to point out the Draft Freedom Charter comprises eleven paragraphs. Please write your name on a piece of paper, also state where you come from and also indicate the subject—number your draft charter and indicate under what you will speak.

"The first item this morning is the reading of the Preamble. There is none who wishes to speak on the Preamble."

P. BEYLEVELD: "Mr. Chairman and friends, (Reading Preamble of Draft Freedom Charter.)

CHAIRMAN: "Fellow delegates, you have heard the Preamble read by Mr. Peter Beyleveld, and he is going to discuss it now."

P. BEYLEVELD: "I am honored to be called upon to speak on the Preamble of the the Freedom Charter of this Congress of the People, which is of great significance not only to the people of South Africa, but to the people of the world—to those people all this charter is of significance. . . . This charter has been drafted, not by a few people sitting in an office, but it is written from the demands, the expressions of all the people of all walks of life.

"Yesterday you saw a board here with thousands of letters. These people told us how they wanted this charter to be drawn up and that is what we say in this Preamble. I was very glad to see yesterday that the world press was so well represented here. What the people demand from the country in which they live and in which they work, the world should know . . . and we pledge ourselves to strive together to achieve this. . . .

"Let me say this in conclusion, what we demand here is freedom, the creator of apartheid is the creator of oppression, freedom will eventually be ours. Thank you Mr. Chairman."

CHAIRMAN: "Are there any other speakers on the Preamble? Ladies and gentlemen, if there are no other speakers and if we are satisfied that the Preamble should be adopted I will formally ask you to accept the Preamble by raising up your hands. Thank you very much.

"The next item on the agenda is the first subject of the Freedom Charter titled 'The people shall govern'. Mr. N. T. Naicker will lead the discussions on this matter."

N. T. NAICKER: "Afrika! Mr. Chairman and fellow delegates, it is my special pleasure this morning to move the first resolution of the Freedom Charter of the Congress of the People. 'The people shall govern'. . . .

"Mr. Chairman and delegates, this is an historic conference. . . . Those people who have political rights in South Africa and are now going to have those rights snatched away from them will have to choose between the forces of democracy and the forces which are heading towards a dictatorship. . . .

"Over the last fifty years people who are voteless look forward to that right, but we have seen in the last fifteen years the reverse process being the case. There has been a consistent denial of these rights. The first time such liberties of the people have been taken away from them was even before the Act of Union. By 1924 municipal franchise was taken away from them. The African people who were in it were removed from that roll, and after that we had the passing of the Native Representation Act, which is greatly responsible for the tyranny and oppression which was to follow. In 1951 we saw the next attempt. The Nationalist Government did not stop; they came with the Separate Voters Act. The Nationalist Government have come up now with the Senate Act. . . . we condemn the Senate Act.

"Mr. Chairman and friends, from the resolution you will notice that our demand is very very clear, it is not on racial lines, it is the demand we want for all the people of South Africa, and as such I call upon you fellow delegates to support the resolution in complete unanimity."

CHAIRMAN: "The Charter will be read to you in Sutho now. I would like Mr. J. Mtini of Cape Western to come to the platform as he has indicated that he would like to speak under this subject, and will he please come to the platform in the meantime. Will Mr. T. Msuli from Newclare please come to the platform. T. Msuli, he desires to speak under this section."

T. MSULI: "Mr. Chairman and fellow delegates, we are gathered here today in this conference to draw up a Freedom Charter. . . .

"Now, the people shall govern. Now these people—we in South Africa—are governed by a minority which are people with different minds, people with a different attitude towards other people. They differ . . . from everybody in the world. They think that they are the only people created by GOD to come and rule the people of South Africa. It is not like that. But it is now time that the people should take over, the people who are not allowed to bring out their own views on the Government of South Africa.

"Today we have come here to tell the people, that the Nationalist Government will have to step aside. Conference will give the people a chance to go and sit in Parliament. They have tried by all means to stop us to come to this conference, but this will not bar us to draw up our Freedom Charter, and after it is drawn up we shall see that it is carried out. Each and everyone will help, each and every individual who is here will try and see to that, and there will be no oppression, no apartheid, no discrimination irrespective of colour or creed. With these words, Mr. Chairman and fellow delegates, I thank you all very much and say Afrika!"

CHAIRMAN: "Are there any other speakers? There are no other speakers and therefore I will put to you this second paragraph of the first subject of the Freedom Charter for approval. Will you please signify your acceptance by raising your hands. The next item on the agenda is, 'All National groups shall have equal rights'. Dr. Letele."

DR. LETELE: "Sons and daughters of Africa, I am going to speak on the topic which I think is the most important, because the basis of our struggle is to secure equal rights for all national groups. Before coming to it I will just read the Draft Charter referring to this section. . . . I wish to tell you that apartheid is not really a new thing that has come with the present Nationalist Government. We have had apartheid from all the Governments in this country. The only thing is that it is turning up in a different way. Apartheid, baasskap, white supremacy, those names all aim at the same thing. The thing I am referring to is to keep the one race from having the right to develop. Apartheid is supposed to aim at separate development, but I wish to point out that South Africa is a country, a multi-racial country.

"The only way to get happiness in this country is to do away with racial discrimination by having moral respect and fellowship in this country. One racial group has been given an inferior kind of education that brings problems which we will never get over. It stops us to rise to the highest possible levels. These rights must be protected. Different racial groups can however exist peacefully together on a basis of racial respect.

". . . We claim the right to rise to any level. We do not say that everybody must do the same kind of job, but we want the right to rise to any level that the human being is capable to.

"Anyway ladies and gentlemen, I will not keep you here for a long time, because this subject can take all day. All National groups shall have equal rights. Afrika!"

CHAIRMAN: "The following speakers will speak on this section. Will they please come to the platform? Martinia of Cape Western, Leslie of Bloemfontein, Madula of Benoni. I have a request here that Mr. Archie Kunene from Natal Midlands please report at the. . . ."

MARTINIA: (Cape Western) (Speaking in Native.)

CHAIRMAN: "Mr. Leslie of Bloemfontein will speak to you in Sutho."

LESLIE: (Bloemfontein.) (Speaking in Native.)

CHAIRMAN: "Mr. Isaac Madula!"

ISAAC MDULA: "Mayibuye! Mayibuye! Afrika! Mr. Chairman and fellow delegates, the preaching and practice of Nationalist race and colour discrimination are punishable crimes. Mr. Chairman, for the last three hundred years we have been governed by a Government which is prepared only to oppress the people of South Africa. . . . Why, why should I not be allowed because of my education, to vote freely in South Africa? Why should I not be given a chance to represent my people in South Africa? Why, why should a clique of people be created by God, why should they take it upon themselves of saying that we are discriminating because it is God that wants these things?

"Mr. Chairman I would like to touch Bantu Education because here in our Freedom Charter we are demanding free education. Why should a clique of men take it upon themselves to draw up education for us? Why today we have got Bantu Education, which is poisoning us, which is put there to poison the minds of the African children. . . . Mr. Chairman, we do not want Bantu Education, I would like that this mass gathering should go back to their organisations and intensify the boycott against this Bantu Education."

CHAIRMAN: "Ladies and gentleman, there are not other speakers under this section, the section 'All National groups shall have equal rights!' I would like you therefore to approve this Charter by raising up your hands. Will you please signify by raising up your hands. Thank you.

"At this stage ladies and gentlemen, I have great pleasure in introducing to you Mr. George Peake of the Coloured Peoples' Organisation. While he is coming up we will have a song 'Tina Sizwe' led by Miss Ida Mntwana."
(Singing 'Tina Sizwe' led by Ida Mntwana.)

CHAIRMAN: (George Peake). "Afrika! Mayibuye! Comrades, I greet all freedom forces on behalf of the South African Coloured Peoples' Organization. Delegates from the Cape, I much regret, some of our delegates are in gaol at Beaufort West. I am justly proud of the honour placed upon me. It is a momentous occasion. We now move forward to the new age, new age of intensified struggle and determination to win, a South Africa free of hatred. They brought vicious measures against us. We will only win when we cast aside oppression. We are going forward to a day of liberation, comrades. Comrades, we stand fully on the demand of freedom, let us not be intimidated. There is only one road to freedom. Forward to freedom, forward to the mutual idea.

"I now have great pleasure to call upon Mr. B. Turok to move, 'The people shall share in the country's wealth'.

B. TUROK: "Mr. Chairman and friends, it is right that the Congress of the People are being held here in Johannesburg. It is right because Johannesburg has seen the beginning of a rotten South Africa. Friends, you know that here in Johannesburg the greatest contrast exists, a contrast between the rich and a contrast between the poor. . . .

"Friends when you enter Johannesburg you are met by those ugly things, the Gold Mines. They are not only ugly to the eye but they are ugly to the minds. They are ugly for many reasons, but the most important reasons are that there in Johannesburg you find the most oppressed worker in South Africa. In these Gold Mines you will find cheap labour. Let me tell you just how cheap this labour is. . . .

"Friends, the system of the Gold Mines is a curse, not a benefit for South Africa. Friends, with the Gold Mines have also come the colour oppression of South Africa, because how else can you get cheap labour if not by a colour bar? How can you keep this cheap labour if not by oppressing people and by calling them Kaffirs and other things? All the Governments of this country, all the gold miners have used the colour bar to make you do the cheap labour. Friends, we say that the Gold Mines mean the robbery of the people of this country. It is nothing else but the thieving of the labour of the people, and we say this must come to an end. This low wage of the Gold Mines is a curse.

"Friends, we are often told that the African is lazy, we often are told that the African people do not work hard. I say to Mr. Strydom, if you think the African mine worker does not work hard, then you go down yourself. Let us see Mr. Strydom, let us see the Ministers of the Cabinet, let us see the police at the back, let us see them sweating down in the Gold Mines. And I must say I will not be very sorry if they contract a few diseases down there.

"Mr. Chairman and friends, it is not only the Gold Mines that are a curse to South Africa, it is also the monopoly industry, it is also the big factories throughout the country, it is also the factories that you find outside Johannesburg, inside Johannesburg, in Cape Town, in Port Elizabeth and in every big town. Wherever you find big factories you find many workers, and where you find many workers you find low wages, and where you find low wages you find a fat boss, a rich boss, a boss who oppresses you.

"Friends, you know that the owners of the big factories take an active part in South Africa. They will not have these lovely big Buicks that they drive around in. The whole system of the big factories and the Gold Mines in this country are the enemies of the people. Let us only look at a time when the workers are demanding higher wages. We see when they go on strike the police are called in, how the pickets are pushed around from pillar to post. Friends, let us see an end to the big factories and an end to the big great mines which give profits to the rich only.

"Mr. Chairman, we have just dealt with two aspects of South Africa's economy, and people everywhere are asking how we can right this. This is a great wrong and it is obvious to everyone. Every man sitting in front of me here knows very well how wrong it is, and our Freedom Charter says this. It says ownership of the mines will be transferred to the ownership of the people. It says wherever there is a Gold Mine there will no longer be a compound boss. There will be a committee of the workers to run the Gold Mines. Friends, we also say that wherever there is a factory and where there are workers who are exploited, we say that the workers will take over and run the factories. In other words, the ownership of the factories will come into the hands of the people.

"Friends, there is one more other thing that worries me a little bit. When you walk down one of the streets in Johannesburg, you see a very impressive looking building, and outside there you see various banks, and when you go inside you will find plenty of money. That money, friends, does not come back to you. It goes to our friends living in Lower Houghton. Let the banks come back to the people, let us have a people's committee to run the banks. . . . We say to all of you, stand behind the Charter which we are going to adopt today. We say let us have a move forward to freedom. Long live unity! Long live the Congress of the People! Long live the people of South Africa."

CHAIRMAN: "Friends at this stage three speakers have indicated their intention to speak. We are calling Mr. Billy Meer [Nair]. Mr. Mulundi!"

MULUNDI: (Speaking in Native.)

CHAIRMAN: "Will Mr. Billy Meer please come to the platform."

BILLY MEER: "Afrika! Afrika! Mayibuye! Comrade Chair and comrades, I fully support this demand of the people's Charter on behalf of the trade unions of Natal of which I am President. Now comrades, the biggest difficulty we are facing in South Africa is that one of capitalism in all its oppressive measures versus the ordinary people—the ordinary workers in the country. We find in this country, as the mover of the resolution pointed out, the means of production. The factories, the lands, the industries and everything possible is owned by a small group of people who are the capitalists in this country. They skin the people, they live on the fat of the workers and make them work, as a matter of fact in exploitation. They oppress in order to keep them as slaves in the land of their births.

"Now friends, this is a very important demand in the Freedom Charter. Now we would like to see a South Africa where the industries, the lands, the big businesses and the mines, and everything that is owned by a small group of people in this country, must be owned by all the people in this country. That is what we demand, that is what we fight for and until we have achieved that we must not rest. I appeal to you all to fight and struggle towards this until we have achieved it. Now comrades, I have been asked to be short and brief, I will conclude now by saying Afrika! Afrika! Mayibuye!"

PETER SELEPE: "My fellow comrades, I am here to speak to the delegates of this conference, particularly my people, the African people, who are subjected to oppressive laws in this country. The African people are the only nation which the Government in this country fears. In this case, friends, I want to tell you that the freedom of the black man lies within his reach, but we have to struggle to drive the enemy away from us. I will speak from this platform, friends, without fear. I know the police are here but that is not important to me. . . .

"I do not see my African leader here, I do not see Dr. Dadoo, I do not see J. B. Marks. . . . If the white man is not prepared to cooperate with the Africans, let them go back. I must tell you friends without fear that a white man came to this country to rob us, to rob us. I have received a letter from my father who is about 670 miles away from here. This man is having a difficult time. They have no way to plough. The government say they cannot have more than six cattle. How are they going to live? I would like you to ask yourself. However, I understand time is very short here and I cannot say much.

"Now friends I must say that under the African National Congress we must see that the Nationalist Party is moved from their chair. When they call my father a boy, they do that because we have no political franchise. I want to see an African in that Parliament representing our people. I do not want to see my child a slave, otherwise I am not a father. I hope you friends will understand from here that the education of our children should be an education of the people and not Bantu Education."

MARTHA MKWANE: (Bloemfontein.) (Speaking in Native.)

CHAIRMAN: "We still have two speakers under this section and we are short of time. These people should be as brief as possible. Will Isaac Mashana of Randfontein please come to the platform. Please be short."

ISAAC MASHANA: (Randfontein.) (Speaking in Native.)

CHAIRMAN: "Friends, I am very sorry there are still two speakers under this section. I will appeal to those speakers to send in notes to speak on some other section. We now move to number fourteen on our agenda. I call upon Mr. Tshunungwa to move this section. I will ask the people to show by their right hands their acceptance of the previous section."

TSHUNUNGWA: (Speaking in Native.)

CHAIRMAN: "Friends, before I call upon speakers to speak under this section, I have two announcements to make." (Announcements not heard.)

SPEAKER: (Speaking in Native.)

ARCHIE SEBEKO: (Speaking in Native.)

CHAIRMAN: "I wish every speaker will keep to the point. John Nkosi and Samson Masheko!"

SAMSON MASHEKO: (Speaking in Native.)

CHAIRMAN: "Samson Masheko, thank you, John Nkosi."

JOHN NKOSI: (Speaking in Native.)

CHAIRMAN: "Mr. Luthenye—Orlando."

LUTHENYE: (Orlando.) (Speaking in Native.)

CHAIRMAN: "The next speaker on this item is Mr. Mzume and he has promised to speak only for two minutes."

MZUME: (Speaking in Native.)

CHAIRMAN: "I will now ask delegates by the show of their right hands the acceptance of this section. We now have number fifteen moved by Dr. Sader."

DR. SADER: "Mr. Chairman, and fellow delegates, my presence on this platform I regard as a great honour. I shall now read this section, 'All shall be equal before the law'. . . .

"Where people have come from all corners of our land is of great significance . . . . today we want to free South Africa from racial discrimination, tyranny and racial oppression, laws which have kept the people in subjugation. The entire construction of this Government is based on racial lines. This is not only unjust but absolutely wrong. Laws that govern the people of this land have brought about untold misery . . . . History has proved time and again that oppression has its unnatural end. The Suppression of Communism Act and the Anti-Defiance measures all aim at converting the country into a police state. Yes, look at the representatives of the Minister of Justice. How long can they stand? The gathering here this morning is proof of this. The days of oppression are numbered. The united stand of all sections of the people of South Africa can and must and will stun the tide of reaction. It can and it must. In it there is a great idea of freedom and this is right and there is no force strong enough to stop this. History has awakened us and it is moving forward. Freedom, freedom in our lifetime. Afrika! Afrika!''

SALOOJE: (Indian to English.) ''Mr. Chairman and delegates, . . . There are about 70 laws which affect the Indian people in South Africa, the African people are subjected to more than 70 laws in this country. The ways of this Government is the same as that of the Governments in Europe. Therefore we will try to see that all laws apply equally to all the people in this country.''

SPEAKER: (Speaking in Afrikaans.)

WOMAN SPEAKER: (From New Brighton.) ''Mr. Chairman and friends, here it is true that everything depends upon woman. I am standing here with the full right as a mother to condemn the Bantu Education. Dr. Verwoerd claims that we are foolish, but we do not want Bantu Education for our children. I want to give you a clear picture of the commencement of the boycott . . . women are the downfall of a nation. You are the downfall of a nation, and you only can pick up a nation. Take out your children from the schools. We must only do what our leaders are telling us today.''

CHAIRMAN: ''Stanley Kaba.''

S. KABA: ''Mr. Chairman, I ask you this question, shall we be ruled by foreigners? Anybody who is a foreigner has the right to rule this country. Any such country will never be progressive.''

CHAIRMAN: ''Friends, I regret to make an announcement, the family of Madiba, report immediately at . . . . the father was involved in a fatal accident this morning. I will ask the conference to rise a minute.''

S. KABA: ''My fellow delegates, . . . We condemn the Government of South Africa.''

CHAIRMAN: ''Maduba from Benoni.''

MADUBA: (Benoni.) (Speaking In Native.)

CHAIRMAN: ''Molasi—Sophiatown.''

MOLASI: (Sophiatown.) "Mr. Chairman and fellow delegates, . . . If we want equality we should struggle to get our demands. Our tasks, ladies and gentlemen, shall be to struggle."

CHAIRMAN: "Friends, we arrive at the end of our speakers, and I will ask the people to raise their hands in acceptance of this section. We move now to number sixteen on our agenda, 'All shall enjoy equal human rights' moved by Sonia Bunting from Cape Town."

SONIA BUNTING: "Mr. Chairman and fellow delegates, together with the other forty delegates, we are only two from Cape Western. The others were held up. We all travelled a thousand miles to attend this large gathering, and I am sure that I can speak on behalf of all of them. We would have travelled ten thousand miles in order to be here today. To see everybody here today is an inspiration to everybody who has the privilege to be present.

"We have gathered here to talk of freedom, and we cannot have freedom unless we have fundamental human rights, and this is the section which I have the privilege of introducing to this gathering today. The whole history of mankind is full of struggle for his freedom . . . . Each turn of history has extended the rights of the people to more and more sections of the population. (Train—not heard.) . . . .

"We know that the Nationalist Government will try to stop our rights. How many leaders are not here because they have been banned, because they are not allowed to be here? But for everyone that is banned there must be a hundred, a thousand voices to take their place. For every leader that is exiled there must be a thousand leaders more, for we comrades, we are the people, we are the majority of people living in South Africa. No force on earth, let alone the forces of Africa shall prevent us from winning our freedom. We shall take the one course that is open to us, to fight and to organise for freedom and human liberty to become a reality for every man, for every woman, for every child in South Africa, in our lifetime. I have much pleasure in moving this section: . . . .

CHAIRMAN: "Mrs. ?—from Orlando—will she please come to the platform. Mrs. Katie White."

SPEAKER: (Not heard—train.)

MRS. MOOSA: "First of all, Mr. Chairman and comrades, I am delighted to be here this morning to address you. I have always dreamt that one day I will address such a gathering, and today my dream has come true. I am speaking on behalf of the women . . . . Comrades, as a mother and as a woman I speak to you, that we demand equal rights for our children. They have not got the same opportunities as the Europeans. I say, friends, we see today that we have not got schools, houses, no playgrounds for our children. We must organise and see that we get these demands that we ask for today. Since this Government came into power they introduced all sorts of laws. They cannot do without our black people. We see today that in the white homes, African people must see to their children, to their food and to everything. Where is apartheid? . . . . Friends, I appeal to you to step in for our children for a better life, for a better future in this country."

CHAIRMAN: (Calling upon speaker—name not heard.)

SPEAKER: ". . . because the present Government restricts us from all things, the present Government at present is trying to make us a kind of animal. We as Africans are really counted as people who know nothing. Now today we here struggle hard to receive our human rights. These rights were given to man by God. It should be given to all people. We are supposed to have freedom of movement as human beings, but we cannot go freely through these Pass Laws."

CHAIRMAN: "Is Mr. Seki ready to speak?"

SEKI: "Mr. Chairman and fellow delegates, today I wish to speak on human rights. . . . In all the other countries of the world the progress is going forward whereas in South Africa it is going backwards. In South Africa we have pass laws for the Africans and other regulations for the Indians. These laws and many others must be the aim of this assembly to have repealed as soon as possible. The laws should be equal for everybody. The police raids at any time of the night must be stopped, and everyone must have equal rights."

WOMAN SPEAKER: (Margaret Castle.) "Comrade Chair and comrades, you all know that the policy of the Nationalist Government is condemned by democratic people all over the world. The Government is going ahead with their policy. We must put a stop to it. . . . My appeal to this conference is that we must not be intimidated."

WOMAN SPEAKER: (Not heard.)

ISOP JESSOP: "People of South Africa, we the youth of South Africa are interested in the Freedom Charter because we are fighting for the things that are inside the Freedom Charter, because we are confident to see that we get it. We are the people who are going to inherit this country. All people irrespective of colour and creed should be given a chance for equality. We should all be given a chance. We, the youth, demand that there should be no segregation in universities. Everybody should be given the opportunity to proceed to higher education. We are going to see freedom and we are preparing for that, friends. We believe that we shall enjoy the freedom which our great grandfathers had. That is freedom in our lifetime. . . ."

CHAIRMAN: "I will now ask you to raise your hands in acceptance of the Charter. The next item shall be moved by Mr. L. Masina."

L. MASINA: "Comrade Chair and delegates, . . . On behalf of the South African Congress of Trade Unions, I wish to thank the congress for calling this mass conference of all the people in South Africa to discuss this Freedom Charter.

"We are denied the right to protect trade unions, but we shall fight side by side until we have won . . . . Comrades, we shall fight together until we have won. No longer shall our children die within seconds of their birth. We shall oppose child labour. We shall become skilled and useful in our country. Let us not spare ourselves in our opposition. Let us unite. Let us take courage and let us speak together of freedom. Long live the Freedom Charter."

SPEAKER: "Mr. Chairman, comrades and fellow delegates, I first of all would like to bring a message from my president who will not be present here today in view of the fact that they have not been given permits to come to Johannesburg. We will fight to the end to see that liberation should come to sunny South Africa.

"We are the people that control the economy of the country. Let me tell you that although we are cheap labour, we will see that our labour will not be cheap any longer but as expensive as the work we put out.

"Friends, I would like to say that under the Industrial Conciliation Bill the Minister said there shall be apartheid in labour. I say, friends, if we unite our forces there will be no apartheid. We the people that work in the mines, in the factories, let us look to the end of nationalising all the industry in this country."

SPEAKER: (Speaking in Native.)

SPEAKER: (Speaking in Afrikaans.)

CHAIRMAN: (Making announcements.)

SPEAKER: (Speaking in Native.)

CHAIRMAN: "The last speaker under this section is . . . from Kimberley."

NATIVE WOMAN: (Speaking in Native.)

SPEAKER: (From Kimberley—not heard.)

CHAIRMAN: "Friends, all those people in the kitchen please come this way. I will now ask the delegates to accept this by the show of their hands."

PETER BEYLEVELD. (Chairman.) (Making announcements about lunch.)

CHAIRMAN: "We will now start our last session of conference. The fourth session starts with section eighteen on our agenda, the doors of learning and culture shall be open. I will call upon Mr. E. Mphahlele."

E. MPHAHLELE: "Mr. Chairman and friends, Afrika! Afrika! It is my duty this afternoon to open this discussion on culture and education. When we talk of culture we include education, sports and music, books they read and books they write. When I talk of culture I am going to say that you are going to get all the nonsense of Bantu culture. Bantu culture is an animal that is formed in Parliament by Dr. Verwoerd, the dirtiest thing that you can think of. You are here today to reject Bantu education, Bantu culture and everything that is Bantu. Friends, I speak here firstly as a human being with feelings to express like everyone of you.

"I speak here as one of three men who have condemned Bantu Education when it was still the Eiselen report. Today, friends, the three of us cannot teach anywhere in South Africa. Why, it is because of this today, let me say for quite a few years now, your children have been taught a type of history—your children are being taught that Chaka was a murderer. And now I say to you, my friends, that I refuse to tell them what I am told to tell them . . . . I refuse to tell my children that they are inferior to the white man.

"Friends, when we are talking of culture we must realise that we are here to talk of human feelings. The Nationalist Government believes in the theory of human dignity and human feeling. Therefore, I say this, friends, that from here today our Indian friends must go and tell their Indian friends. I say here that they can also tell their friends who own the Majestic Theatre to go and open this cultural organisation for the black man, for the coloured people, to open it for other non-European friends. I say here to you, my African friends, that you all must teach your children to respect the coloured man, to respect the Indian man,

"Friends, thereby we shall be able to build a culture which is a culture that does not leave room for nationalism in the nationalist sense. Here we shall have a nationalism in a democratic form.

"Friends, when I was a small boy born and bred in the slums of Marabastad near Pretoria, I mixed very well with Indians. I lived with them, and we called one another by pet names. We loved one another, and now that I am grown up I am told that I must live in group areas. I refuse to deteriorate into that state of mind.

"Friends, we here say that we want equal rights with the white man. We want equal opportunities, equal chances. But I do not want to be equal with the white man. I want to be better than the white man. I want to be better than the white man because the white man has made a terrible mess of everything. The white man has made a mess of his Government. The white man has made a mess in the cultural field, a mess of education, and here we are being told that we should accept Bantu Education, which we detest so much. The white man has given us a religion, a religion he himself does not respect. The white man has given you the Bible to cheat you; whilst you are reading the Bible on your knees he wants to rob you of your country . . . .

"Gentlemen, mothers, fathers, sons and daughters of Afrika, I want to tell you a little tale. A snake went up a tree and found the nest of a dove. The dove had its little ones in the nest. The snake swallowed the little ones of the dove, and the dove flew away. The mother dove began to cry, and when she was crying a musician was walking by. The musician realising, hearing the cry of the dove for the loss of its chickens, started to compose a song to the time of the weeping of the dove, and he did this in such a way that his music so moved and stirred all the other animals in the world that they came together and joined forces. They drove the snake out and killed it. That is the tiny tale, that is the tiny story.

"Today here we see in our country that music and dancing and many other things can be the cause of justice. Those animals wanted justice and killed the snake. I am not asking you to kill the snake. I am saying this, that if we all join together we will make the snake so afraid that he will hide in his hole and die there of hunger.

". . . . I am looking forward to a day when our culture will so much unify us, we shall no more talk of the Congress of the People as an organisation of Coloureds, Indians and Africans and Europeans. We shall have one movement. We shall have absolutely no distinction, and we will stand together for a united cause. Our culture—this culture is now growing up. It will not be a culture of Indians, of the Africans. It will be a culture of the people of South Africa, and it is this culture that is going to grow up now.

"I want to say this in conclusion, I am looking forward to a day when every year we can have our own festival."

CHAIRMAN: "The first speaker on this section is Miss Doreen Motsabi."

DOREEN MOTSABI: (Speaking in Native.)

CHAIRMAN: "Our next speaker is Mr. Mervin Dennon. He is a representative of the South African students."

MERVIN DENNON: "Mr. Chairman I want to make it clear that I am not speaking on behalf of any particular students' organisation. Friends, our students' delegation over here consists of—we have students over here, students who are law students, students helped to draw up the Charter. As we fight we are going to learn from you. Our numbers are very small but I am glad to tell you that every week more and more join us.

Friends, education belongs to everyone. Education of a certain section is not education at all. The day will come when you will do the teaching . . . ."

(Entering of police.)

[See above, page 62, for a description. Then, according to *New Age,* June 30, 1955, "The chairman asked the meeting if it wished to proceed and when the crowd roared its assent, Mrs. Helen Joseph rose to introduce the section of the Charter demanding houses, security and comfort for the people."]

LEON LEVY: "Friends, I greet you in the name of peace today. Yes, my friends, we shall have friendship and peace for all. In the capital of Finland the people are gathering just as we are today to talk about peace, to talk about the Hydrogen bomb. We in South Africa, friends, we are doing the same. . . . We warmly greet you and wish you every success. Let us go forward to peace, let us go forward to freedom. There is no freedom without peace, and there is no peace without freedom."

CHAIRMAN: "The next item on our agenda is the Credential Committee's report. It will be brought to you by Mr. Resha."

RESHA: "Mr. Chairman, sons and daughters of South Africa, we have had here to decide the future and the destiny of South Africa. This ground on which we are standing here today is holy, friends. This shall be the monument of the people of South Africa. Friends, let it be clear to us that this great assembly of the people of South Africa is an assembly whereby the people will from today march on to freedom."

(Singing of Mayibuye Afrika.)

"There are 2,884 [*sic*] delegates representing . . . people. We will give you some idea of the places from which the delegates have come. There are delegates representing the reserves. There are delegates from Natal, from Sekukuniland, Zululand, Transkei, Ciskei, delegates from the farms and the trust lands, from the mines and the factories. Almost every place in the Transvaal is represented here. From Cape Town, from Durban, East London, Port Elizabeth and every town in the Union. Even Meadowlands is represented here. Every Native section of the population is represented here. We have 2,186 African delegates, 320 Indian delegates, 230 Coloured delegates, 112 European delegates, 721 women. Some were voiceless by the actions of the police. They were prevented from coming to the conference. Their demands are here before us. Even though they are not here, their voices will be heard. The Charter will have a greater support than any other document that has ever been drawn up."

Document 11. "Freedom Charter," adopted by the Congress of the People, June 26, 1955.

PREAMBLE

We, the people of South Africa, declare for all our country and the world to know:—
That South Africa belongs to all who live in it, black and white, and that no government can justly claim authority unless it is based on the will of the people;
That our people have been robbed of their birthright to land, liberty and peace by a form of government founded on injustice and inequality;
That our country will never be prosperous or free until all our people live in brotherhood, enjoying equal rights and opportunities;
That only a democratic state, based on the will of the people can secure to all their birthright without distinction of colour, race, sex or belief;
And therefore, we, the people of South Africa, black and white, together—equals, countrymen and brothers—adopt this FREEDOM CHARTER. And we pledge ourselves to strive together, sparing nothing of our strength and courage, until the democratic changes here set out have been won.

THE PEOPLE SHALL GOVERN!

Every man and woman shall have the right to vote for and stand as a candidate for all bodies which make laws.
All the people shall be entitled to take part in the administration of the country.
The rights of the people shall be the same regardless of race, colour or sex.
All bodies of minority rule, advisory boards, councils and authorities shall be replaced by democratic organs of self-government.

ALL NATIONAL GROUPS SHALL HAVE EQUAL RIGHTS!

There shall be equal status in the bodies of state, in the courts and in the schools for all national groups and races;
All national groups shall be protected by law against insults to their race and national pride;
All people shall have equal rights to use their own language and to develop their own folk culture and customs;
The preaching and practice of national, race or colour discrimination and contempt shall be a punishable crime;
All apartheid laws and practices shall be set aside.

THE PEOPLE SHALL SHARE IN THE COUNTRY'S WEALTH!

The national wealth of our country, the heritage of all South Africans, shall be restored to the people;
The mineral wealth beneath the soil, the banks and monopoly industry shall be transferred to the ownership of the people as a whole;
All other industries and trade shall be controlled to assist the well-being of the people;
All people shall have equal rights to trade where they choose, to manufacture and to enter all trades, crafts and professions.

THE LAND SHALL BE SHARED AMONG THOSE WHO WORK IT!

Restriction of land ownership on a racial basis shall be ended, and all the land re-divided amongst those who work it, to banish famine and land hunger;
The state shall help the peasants with implements, seed, tractors and dams to save the soil and assist the tillers;
Freedom of movement shall be guaranteed to all who work on the land;
All shall have the right to occupy land wherever they choose;
People shall not be robbed of their cattle, and forced labour and farm prisons shall be abolished.

ALL SHALL BE EQUAL BEFORE THE LAW!

No one shall be imprisoned, deported or restricted without a fair trial;
No one shall be condemned by the order of any Government official;
The courts shall be representative of all the people;
Imprisonment shall be only for serious crimes against the people, and shall aim at re-education, not vengeance;
The police force and army shall be open to all on an equal basis and shall be the helpers and protectors of the people;
All laws which discriminate on grounds of race, colour or belief shall be repealed.

ALL SHALL ENJOY EQUAL HUMAN RIGHTS!

The law shall guarantee to all their right to speak, to organise, to meet together, to publish, to preach, to worship and to educate their children;
The privacy of the house from police raids shall be protected by law;
All shall be free to travel without restriction from countryside to town, from province to province, and from South Africa abroad;

Pass laws, permits and all other laws restricting these freedoms shall be abolished.

THERE SHALL BE WORK AND SECURITY!

All who work shall be free to form trade unions, to elect their officers and to make wage agreements with their employers;

The state shall recognise the right and duty of all to work, and to draw full unemployment benefits;

Men and women of all races shall receive equal pay for equal work;

There shall be a forty-hour working week, a national minimum wage, paid annual leave, and sick leave for all workers, and maternity leave on full pay for all working mothers;

Miners, domestic workers, farm workers and civil servants shall have the same rights as all others who work;

Child labour, compound labour, the tot system and contract labour shall be abolished.

THE DOORS OF LEARNING AND OF CULTURE SHALL BE OPENED!

The government shall discover, develop and encourage national talent for the enhancement of our cultural life;

All the cultural treasures of mankind shall be open to all, by free exchange of books, ideas and contact with other lands;

The aim of education shall be to teach the youth to love their people and their culture, to honour human brotherhood, liberty and peace;

Education shall be free, compulsory, universal and equal for all children;

Higher education and technical training shall be opened to all by means of state allowances and scholarships awarded on the basis of merit;

Adult illiteracy shall be ended by a mass state education plan;

Teachers shall have all the rights of other citizens;

The colour bar in cultural life, in sport and in education shall be abolished.

THERE SHALL BE HOUSES, SECURITY AND COMFORT!

All people shall have the right to live where they choose, to be decently housed, and to bring up their families in comfort and security;

Unused housing space to be made available to the people;

Rent and prices shall be lowered, food plentiful and no one shall go hungry;

A preventive health scheme shall be run by the state;

Free medical care and hospitalisation shall be provided for all, with special care for mothers and young children;

Slums shall be demolished, and new suburbs built where all have transport, roads, lighting, playing fields, crêches and social centres;

The aged, the orphans, the disabled and the sick shall be cared for by the state;

Rest, leisure and recreation shall be the right of all;

Fenced locations and ghettoes shall be abolished, and laws which break up families shall be repealed.

THERE SHALL BE PEACE AND FRIENDSHIP!

South Africa shall be a fully independent state, which respects the rights and sovereignty of all nations;

South Africa shall strive to maintain world peace and the settlement of all international disputes by negotiation—not war;

Peace and friendship amongst all our people shall be secured by upholding the equal rights, opportunities and status of all;

The people of the protectorates—Basutoland, Bechuanaland and Swaziland—shall be free to decide for themselves their own future;

The right of all the peoples of Africa to independence and self-government shall be recognised, and shall be the basis of close cooperation.

****

Let all who love their people and their country now say, as we say here: "THESE FREEDOMS WE WILL FIGHT FOR, SIDE BY SIDE, THROUGHOUT OUR LIVES, UNTIL WE HAVE WON OUR LIBERTY."*

****

UNITY AND DISUNITY BEFORE THE TREASON ARRESTS

Document 12. "The Editor Speaks: We Shall Live." Editorial in *The Africanist*, December 1955

To-day we are a year old. It is fitting for us to pause and make a retrospective view of our short history; to study objectively our successes

---

*A few very minor variations from this text appear in the text of the Freedom Charter printed in *New Age*, June 30, 1955. The *New Age* text also appears as an appendix in Helen Joseph, *If This Be Treason* (London: Andre Deutsch, 1963).

and failures. We have seen the ups and downs of African politics. In the affairs of the African National Congress we found a dangerous vacuum which was readily being filled by unacceptable chaff. We addressed ourselves to the African people on vital matters of national struggle and national leadership. Consequently the response was tremendously overwhelming and heartening.

We made a debut at a time when the need for an independent, wholly African mouthpiece was too great to be ignored. The people were clamouring for a journal that would fearlessly portray to the White oppressors the true aspirations of our people. The entire population was groaning under the grinding mill of colour discrimination, economic exploitation and national strangulation when, against odds, we took the front line on behalf of our people.

From our inception we saw the burning need for educating our people politically. We emerged at a time when confusion, worst confounded, reigned supreme in A.N.C. ranks. Without fear or favour we have energetically laboured to clear the stinking mess left to us as a legacy by the opportunistic leadership that served, loyally, interests other than those of Africa. We have relentlessly waged a struggle to restore and maintain the independence of the African National Congress, whose potential has been reduced by a superfluous multiplicity of pacts with insignificant organisations. We boldly championed the course of those A.N.C. men and women whose opinion, particularly in the Transvaal, was being deliberately stifled to placate the lackeys, flunkeys and functionaries of non-African minorities. We have not hesitated in exposing the stooges and careerists who callously sought to turn the African National Congress into their private family property.

From our inception we saw the burning need of ridding the A.N.C. of foreign domination. We expressly and vigorously propounded African Nationalism as the sole ideological basis for the salvation of our people. Unlike our sheepish opponents, we sternly refused to be reduced to the level of doormats and instruments of selfish White capitalist liberals and the Indian merchant class. We restored self-confidence to our people who were being mischievously led by schizophrenic elements to believing that they were incapable of winning freedom for themselves and by themselves.

From our inception we have put the necessary emphasis on principles as opposed to foolish practices. We have unequivocally opposed sporadic, frantic and irresponsible actions by certain Congressites. We wanted nothing short of proper organisation in all campaigns. We have consistently condemned collaborators who postpone our day of liberation by supporting dummy institutions—Advisory Boards, Bungas, Verwoerd School Boards, and etc.

Our major task has been to put the 1949 Programme of Action in its proper perspective. Even the "Freedom Charter" can never be realised

210

unless the Programme of Action is implemented. Or what other route is there to achieving the goal as set by the Kliptown Charter? There can be no question on the ideological plane as to the correctness and dynamism of African Nationalism as an outlook for giving the African people the self-confidence and subjective liberation, without which no national oppression can be effectively challenged.

And from our inception we have stood for the return to the orthodox LEMBEDE stand. In our opinion the situation has not changed to warrant a compromise or somersault on principles. We have found it absolutely impossible to tolerate deviationists and pacifists. NO WHITE MAN HAS EVER IMPRESSED US, liberal democrat or democratic liberal. Both are hypocrites, for they cannot accept clear cut African Nationalism. Despite fierce and hostile opposition, we have grown by leaps and bounds, and we shall live till freedom comes.

Documents 13a–13d. ANC Annual Conference of December 17–18, 1955

Document 13a. "Special Presidential Message" by Chief A. J. Lutuli.

1. *INTRODUCTORY REMARKS:*

It is proper and fitting that my friend and close colleague in Congress, Professor Z. K. Matthews, having acted for me the whole of this year as President-General on account of my illness throughout this year, should speak to Congress and to the world, through the medium of the Presidential Address.

I embraced with great joy and eagerness the privilege extended to me by the National Executive to speak to conference through a special Presidential Message, if I felt that my health permitted my doing so. I am indeed very happy to be able to do so.

I would be untrue to the deepest human feelings if I did not, on behalf of my family and myself, commence my message by expressing our deepest thanks to the Almighty for bringing about my miraculous recovery. I would like to closely associate in these thanks to the Almighty the staff of McCord Zulu Hospital who were willing and devoted instruments in God's hands in bringing about this recovery. Our feelings—my family and myself—would not be adequately expressed if I did not say that we were deeply touched by the concern and sympathy in my ill-health and the welfare of my family shown by many, many people in our land and abroad during those difficult times. It was this concern and sympathy which helped my family, especially my wife, to bear with such great fortitude the burden of my illness.

II. MY MESSAGE: THE AFRICAN NATIONAL CONGRESS IN RECENT YEARS: ESPECIALLY THE LAST SEVEN YEARS.

The chief burden of my message is to make a brief appraisal—not flinching from even an agonising critical appraisal—of the reaction of the African people in general and the African National Congress in particular to the political situation in the Union of South Africa, as it has affected Africans in recent years.

It is a matter of common consent that the African National Congress has been unusually active in recent years: WHAT IS THE BACKGROUND TO THIS ACTIVITY? Any appraisal of Congress activity and the general reaction of the African people to this activity must be preceded by a brief, if only cursory reply, to this question—"What is the background to our present Congress activity?"

III. THE SIGNIFICANCE OF AND BACKGROUND TO PRESENT-DAY CONGRESS ACTIVITY.

In my judgement this period in the national history of the African people will go down as one of the most outstanding periods in the all-round political awakening of the African people, despite the almost insurmountable obstacles put in their way by the White rulers of South Africa, who have selfishly created barriers to African progress and advancement in South Africa in order to promote their own selfish interests.

One of the most significant features in the development of our struggle is that the African National Congress in recent years, after much internal questioning and discussion, adopted a militant Programme of Action in 1949. This Programme was a direct outcome of a conviction that had been growing among the people that the White people in South Africa had no intention of extending democratic rights to the Non-Whites. The discriminatory laws that disgrace the statute books of successive White governments from colonial days to the present day are proof enough of the White man's hostility to the progress of Africans and the Non-White people in general. The Act of Union itself put the Non-Whites outside the orbit of enjoying citizenship rights in a supposedly democratic, civilised and Christian country. Time and space will not permit the enumeration of such diabolic discriminatory laws. But can anyone even with only a cursory knowledge of the position of things as affecting the African truly blame them under such circumstances for having lost confidence in the declared, but as yet unexecuted, good intentions of the White governments that have in succession ruled South Africa? It is under numerous bitter experiences and disappointments with White rule that Africans under the leadership of the African National Congress, came to realise after their further betrayal in 1936 that the only correct course to take was no longer merely to struggle for the amelioration of economic and social disabilities here and there, under which they suffered, but to attack the whole citadel of White supremacy and domination, protected by a network of discriminatory laws designed to keep the African people and the non-Europeans in general in a state of perpetual servitude.

Congress, in alliance with her allies in the liberatory movement: the South African Indian Congress, the South African Coloured Peoples' Organisation and latterly the South African Congress of Democrats, has consistently directed her resources and energies in resisting tyranny and oppression. On June 26, 1950 Congress together with her allies called upon the people of South Africa to observe this as a day of Mourning and Prayer, as a protest against injustice by White Governments to non-Europeans. In June 26, 1952, the great Defiance of Unjust Laws Campaign which was to have a great impact on the world and South African politics was launched. Since then all along the line Congress has sought to develop in the hearts of the people a spirit of defiance of anything that degrades human dignity and arbitrarily sets limits to the development of any person's mental, physical and spiritual faculties to their utmost. Still on that historic day, June 26, 1955, in response to a clarion call issued by our Congress movement to the people of South Africa, black and white, the Congress of the People, met at Kliptown and unanimously adopted the Freedom Charter as the basis for our struggle now and in the future. The Charter is now placed before you for consideration and ratification.

One is happy to record that during this period the African National Congress has emerged as the universally accepted leader of the liberatory movement in South Africa. In co-operation with other progressive groups, it is building slowly but surely a solid united front against oppression. No one can deny that in the last seven years Congress has played no mean part in mobilising all progressive forces regardless of race or class, into a growing, formidable army, which in due course will cleanse South Africa of all traces of domination, racialism, and exploitation. The initial success which has attended the efforts of Congress in building up a solid opposition to apartheid has driven terror into the selfish hearts of the White rulers of South Africa, hence the shameful ruthlessness of the Nationalist Party Government in its attempts to stem the rising tide of freedom forces about to engulf and destroy this evil thing "Baasskap Apartheid."

IV. *SOME URGENT PROBLEMS IN THE PRESENT SITUATION OF CONGRESS.*

We would be less than human if we would not have made grievous mistakes in our Congress under the Militant Programme of Action which was adopted in 1949. As intelligent people we should take cognisance of our failures and shortcomings—and God knows they are legion—and try to make them "stepping stones to success."

What are some of these problems and shortcomings? Here again time and space can only allow a fleeting mention of only a few.

1. We have been busily engaged in a laudable effort to establish a spirit of defiance of unjust laws and treatment along non-violent lines and in getting Africans to see that no one is really worthy of Freedom until he is prepared to pay the supreme sacrifice for its attainment and defence. We have, unquestionably, met with a measure of success in both our objectives since we can truthfully claim that Congress followers have shown marvellous restraint in the face of police provocation. We can also claim that we have established an inner core of bitter-enders in fighting oppression—"the faithful few" of whom we can say, as said Sir Winston Churchill to defenders of Britain in the Battle of Britain during the World War II: "Never have so many owed so much to so few." But for all this we cannot claim to have prosecuted our campaigns with anything bearing semblance to military efficiency and technique. We cannot say that the Africans are accepting fast enough the gospel of "SERVICE AND SACRIFICE FOR THE GENERAL AND LARGE GOOD WITHOUT EXPECT-ING A PERSONAL (AND AT THAT IMMEDIATE) REWARD"; they have not accepted fully the basic truth enshrined in the saying "NO CROSS, NO CROWN."

It is time we took stock of methods of planning and prosecuting our campaigns. I would suggest that the incoming National Executive should be charged with the task of making a study of general organisational machinery with special reference to its fitness for our present situation.

2. CLARITY IN THE IDEOLOGICAL FIELD.

Faced as we are with the battle for FREEDOM it seems a wise stand to say that the African National Congress should not dissipate its energies by indulging in internal ideological feuds—a fight on "isms". It is not practical and logical, however, to expect Congress to be colourless ideologically. She must in some way define or re-define her stand and outlook as regards, for example, her interpretation of AFRICAN NATIONALISM which she made the philosophic basis of our struggle for Freedom. Fighters for Freedom in Africa, it is fair to infer, were to be mobilised under its banner. It is also fair to infer that the African National Congress, having accepted the fact of the multiracial nature of the country, envisaged an ALL IN-CLUSIVE AFRICAN NATIONALISM which, resting on the principle of "FREEDOM FOR ALL" in a country, UNITY OF ALL in a country, embraced all people under African Nationalism regardless of their racial and geographical origin who resided in Africa and paid their undivided loyalty and allegiance. Congress should not be ashamed to tell the African people that it is opposed to TRIBALISM but for obvious practical considerations it must gradually lead Africans from these narrow tribal loyalties to the wider loyalty of the BROTHERHOOD OF MAN throughout the world.

3. *STRENGTHENING OF DISCIPLINARY CONTROL.*

There does seem to be laxity in the machinery of Congress, resulting in lack of sound disciplinary behaviour in some Congress levels. Manifestations of such behaviour at any Congress level anywhere must create confusion and uncertainty in the ranks of Congress, especially among the masses and to say nothing about its most disastrous effect in lowering the dignity of Congress in the eyes of the world. This observation leads me to close this aspect of my "agonising re-appraisal" of Congress activity by repeating what I suggested earlier, namely, that it might pay Congress handsome dividends in efficiency and dignity if from time to time it took stock of its workings and its machinery.

V. *WHAT OF THE FUTURE.*

Let me close my message by drawing you away from our failures and disappointments to a vision of a GLORIOUS FUTURE that awaits us: A SOUTH AFRICA WHERE ALL PEOPLE SHALL BE TRULY FREE. OUR CAUSE IS JUST and we have the DIVINE assurance that right must triumph over wrong—and apartheid is an evil policy and the methods by which the Nationalist Government seeks to get a following among the people are base and false. They are based on submission through coercion and not through acceptance by love—the only sure basis for any lasting acceptance. They are based on acceptance of apartheid by an appeal to the baser instincts of man: selfishness and greed: personal aggrandisement.

Let us march together to FREEDOM saying: "The road to Freedom may be long and thorny but because our Cause is just, the glorious end—Freedom—is ours."

Let us truly pledge to work together in love of Freedom for all in our lifetime—not just freedom for "EUROPEANS ONLY"—and as we march pledge to struggle together for FREEDOM. Let us draw inspiration from the Freedom Charter—THE PEOPLE SHALL GOVERN.

A F R I K A ! M A Y I B U Y E !
INKULULEKO NGESIKHATHI SETHU!

Yours in the cause of Freedom.

Document 13b. Address by Professor Z. K. Matthews

Introduction:

1. Owing to his personal inability to undertake this responsibility which rightly belongs to him, the President-General, our Chief A. J. Luthuli, has asked me to deliver the Presidential Address at this Conference on his behalf. I naturally feel honoured in being called upon to substitute for this worthy son of Africa. As I am fully aware that it will not be possible for me to do what he would have done, for your consolation I am glad to be able to report that apart from this address there will be read to you a message from the President-General.

2. As you know there are two main reasons why the President-General is not able to be with us today. The first is the ban which the Minister of Justice has thought fit to impose upon him which confines him to the district of Lower Tugela. It is apparently not appreciated in some quarters that it is impossible to place geographical limitations upon the indomitable spirit of Chief Luthuli. Not only has this ban not been able to reduce the quality of his leadership, but it has converted what was otherwise an insignificant district—the district of Lower Tugela—into an important centre visited by all those who want to become aquainted with the principles underlying the liberation movement among Africans in the Union. Chief Luthuli has become the most important symbol of the liberation movement, and from his place of confinement he continues to inspire, to guide and direct the African National Congress and all those interested in seeing South Africa become a truly united country. Another reason why our President-General is not with us is because of the state of his health. As you know during the early part of this year Chief Luthuli was very seriously ill, and it is only because there are more things wrought by prayer than this world dreams on that he has made the recovery that he has made. I am sure you will all wish me to place on record our deep indebtedness to the Superintendent and the staff of the McCord Hospital, Durban for the skill and devotion with which they cared for him. But in spite of his large measure of recovery, the President-General's health does not yet permit [him] to resume his normal activities, and I am sure that before its conclusion this Conference will resolve to send him its best wishes for a more complete restoration of his health.

Crisis After Crisis

3. It is becoming such a hardy annual for our Presidential address to draw attention to the fact that we are meeting at a critical time in the history of our people that some of us may be tempted to treat this statement as a

purely formal statement without much meaning. Would that we never yield to that temptation! The life of the African in South Africa is without doubt made up of one crisis after another. Just when our people are beginning to say to themselves that surely the situation could not get worse than this, some fresh injustice is added to their already heavy burden, and therefore it is not necessary for us to apologise to anyone for reiterating the disabilities under which they labour and for discussing ways and means of overcoming them. The reports which will be placed before you from different parts of the country will remind us once more about what our people have to put up with day after day. The policy of baasskap shows no signs of abating. For that reason we disagree most emphatically with the latest report of the U.N. Commission on the Racial Situation in the Union of South Africa which claims to have found a certain measure of "gradualism and flexibility" in the implementation of the policy of apartheid. On the contrary, our experience is one of an ever-accelerating tempo and a relentless pursuit of declared objectives with a complete disregard of the consequences of the policy of separation to its victims.

Ten years ago who would have thought that the missions would be treated as they have been over the transfer of African schools to the Government? Who would have thought that one day in a country in which there was no compulsory education for African children it would become a crime for parents to give their children, at no cost to the state, the kind of education they would like them to have? Who would have thought that teachers of long standing would be dismissed from their posts on the mere ipse dixit of some official without any specific charge being levelled against them, to say nothing of such a charge being established. Who would have thought that in the twentieth century people could by a stroke of the pen be deprived of property rights which they had acquired legally, without offer of adequate compensation and be removed to some place in which they are not granted rights similar to those of which they have been deprived. We are living in a country in which freedom of speech is a privilege reserved for those who are prepared to indulge in fulsome praise of government representatives or government schemes whose implications they do not understand. However naive or blasphemous their utterances, they are committed to print in "Bantu-Bantoe" [a government publication] and given the widest publicity as representing the voice of the "Bantu." On the other hand, anyone who dares to express any doubt about the infallibility of government officials or the wisdom of government proposals or schemes runs the risk of being banned or deported or fired from his job. The freedom of Africans to meet and discuss matters affecting their welfare has been so severely curtailed that only at religious services, weddings or funerals are Africans expected to talk freely to one another, and even on such occasions they can never be sure that members of the Special Branch in some disguise are not present.

The Year 1955

The period under review—1955—will go down as one of the blackest years in the political history of South Africa. To give an account of outstanding political events in the year now drawing to its close is to give a sorry catalogue of assaults upon the rights of the people, and especially upon the voteless and defenceless non-white groups: the forcible removal by soldiers and police armed to the teeth of the people of the Western Areas of Johannesburg to the much vaunted Meadowlands; the threat, now being implemented in certain areas, to remove the entire African population from the Western Province of the Cape; the virtual compulsory transfer of African schools from unwilling churches and missions to the Native Affairs Department and the introduction into African schools of curricula designed to condition the African child to acquiesce in a status of permanent inferiority in his homeland; the conversion of the status of African teachers from that of members of an honourable profession to that of cringing sycophants on pain of dismissal on the pretext of being "unsuitable" or "undesirable"; the introduction of ethnic grouping into urban locations which will promote tribal antagonism and internecine disputes, thus undermining the growing spirit of unity among them for which the A.N.C. stands; the enforcement of the anachronistic Bantu Authorities Act for the same reasons; the creation of future slums under the so called site and service schemes imposed upon local authorities; the continuation of the system of banning and/or deporting from their homes of African leaders and the constant raids by Special (political) Branch officers of the C.I.D. on public meetings, private homes, private offices of any individuals thought to exercise some influence in their communities; continuation of the pass system and the threat of its extension to African women in 1956—all these are measures which can by no stretch of the imagination be described as conducive to the promotion of a peaceful state of mind among those who are subject to them.

But the Africans are not the only people whose fundamental rights and freedoms have recently been adversely affected by governmental policy. The implementation of the Population Registration Act has given other sections of the population some idea of the meaning of bureaucratic regimentation; with the application of the Group Areas Act the spectre of complete ruination faces many an Indian community. The enforcement of the Senate Act and the passing of the Quorum Act has removed the scales from the eyes of many who clung to the belief that certain things just could not happen here.

The result of the relentless pursuit of its policies by the present government is that South Africa is a land that is becoming more and more divided against itself. Co-operation between different sections of the population in the political sphere becomes more and more difficult. The

218

government is becoming more and more resentful of criticism. Honest differences of opinion on matters of policy are regarded as evidence of subversive activities. But even those who do not express any opinions at all are not safe from being looked upon as being behind the failure of the government to get anything other than either downright opposition or lukewarm support for its schemes.

The Brighter Side

But the picture of 1955 is not entirely without its brighter side. Every cloud has a silver lining. If this is the year which saw the further whittling down of the civil rights of the people, it is also the year during which the Congress of the People was held. There were several wonderful things about the Congress of the People. The first is the fact that it was held at all. Here for the first time was a Congress which brought together people drawn from all sections of the population to consider and give expression to their vision of the South Africa of the future. The sponsoring organisations issue a challenge to any other group of organisations including the Nationalist Party to convene a similar conference and see whether they could evoke an equal or a better response from the people of South Africa. A most important aspect of the Congress was the adoption of the Freedom Charter. That document is going to be placed before this Conference in the course of your deliberations. I shall therefore not say anything about it at this stage except to remind you that the Freedom Charter was drawn up, not by the African National Congress but by the Congress of the People and it is therefore necessary for you to ratify the Freedom Charter and to make it part, if you so desire, of the policy of the African National Congress. But to my mind the most significant thing about the Congress of the People was the dignified behaviour of the people in the face of what any less disciplined people might have regarded as extreme provocation. What undiscerning [persons] thought was just a rabble which could easily be roused to acts of indiscretion proved to be a group of people embued with a singleness of purpose and a devotion to a cause from which they could not be diverted by intimidation. That was the people's finest hour.

No, this year has had its compensations. Not only among those attending the Congress of the People, but even among those who were not in a position to participate in that august assembly, it is abundantly clear that the people remain undaunted by the trend of events in South Africa. This is particularly so among the women who have been galvanised into action by the government's threat to subject them to the humiliations of the pass system. This is probably the most dangerous scheme that the government has ever embarked upon, and there can be no doubt as to where responsibility belongs for whatever may happen. Again and again the leaders of the people have warned the government against subjecting African women to the indignities and the abuses associated with the pass system. But this warning has fallen on deaf ears. African men have in the past, rightly or wrongly, done their best to keep African women out of political agitation, but it seems that the government is determined to drag African women into this fight. One need not be termed an alarmist for taking a gloomy view of what is likely to come out of this development.

Another bright spot has been the magnificent response of the people of South Africa to the appeal of the Catholic Bishops for funds to enable that church to retain control of its primary schools for Africans. The success of that appeal is proof, if proof were needed, that it is a mistake for the government to think that the people of South Africa are solidly behind them in their educational policy for Africans. The African people are deeply indebted to the Catholic Church for the effort it is making to maintain the place of voluntary agencies in the African educational system, thus preventing the system from degenerating into the dead level of uniformity which is going to be the curse of Verwoerd's Schools already groaning under the burden of proclamations and regulations which are destructive of all initiative and character.

The cultural clubs which have been started in certain centres and the family centres which the diocese of Johannesburg, under the able leadership of the Bishop of Johannesburg, is establishing will help to broaden the outlook of the African child and lead him to an appreciation of the fact that being a servant of the white man does not represent the sum-total of his destiny in South Africa. The conception of the fundamental aim of education which runs through the syllabuses that have been drawn up for African schools is that the individual exists for the group. This totalitarian idea of treating people in the mass rather than as individuals who count in and for themselves is a doctrine to which we do not subscribe. The regimentation of people which it implies can never be condemned enough, especially in the modern world which tends to worship size and quantity rather than individuality and quality.

4. What does the Government hope to achieve by these methods? Are we wrong in suspecting that the object is the conversion of the African people into a docile population of yesmen and yeswomen who are continually singing the praises of their fairy godfather—the government—who will say "thank you baas," whatever is done to them? Is that the kind of people we are expected to become?

The Task of ANC

5. It is not necessary for me to remind you that we have not inherited such attitudes from our forefathers. Our forebears in this land fought back

every inch of the way in defence of their homeland and of their freedom, and although they lost many a battle no one can say that they did so because of lack of courage or poverty of spirit. Why should a kind of supine submission to everything be expected from their descendants?

6. The African National Congress was founded specifically for the purpose of fostering among the African people that love of freedom and determination to be inferior to none in the land for which their forefathers gave their lives on many a battle field. The African National Congress has since its inception been in the forefront of the battle for equal rights for all in this country. As an organisation with such objectives it has never been popular among those who believe in the permanent subjugation of the African people. All kinds of attempts have been made to discredit the organisation. This happened in the past just as much as it is happening today. The leaders of the A.N.C. have at various times been described as agitators or as anti-white or as extremists or as communists—whatever the popular political swear-word of the time. It has been suggested at various times that the A.N.C. is dominated by one or other group of non-Africans—sometimes it is Europeans, at other times it is Indians that are held responsible for doing what is called stirring up or "inciting the Native". But all these ideas are wide of the mark. Those of us who know something of the inner history of the A.N.C. know that our strength does not come from sources outside of ourselves. In fact it can be said without fear of contradiction that the most constructive work in the building up of the A.N.C. has always been done by the Africans themselves. Naturally we have had our friends and supporters among other racial groups represented in South Africa, for among them also are to be found outstanding examples of individuals who are devoted to the cause of freedom for all. God forbid that it should be otherwise. But our best friends have always insisted, like our leaders, that it is the efforts of the African people themselves which will bring about their liberation, and that it is lack of effort on the part of the African people themselves which will be responsible for retarding their march to freedom. No, it is a great mistake to [place] today the blame for what happens among the African people upon the wrong shoulders. If there is anything that should be blamed for the Africans' determination to be satisfied with nothing less than first-class citizenship, it is that urge to freedom and self-determination which has been planted in every people. Nobody ought to appreciate that better than the Afrikaner people whose history as a small nation is a proof of the irrepressibility of that urge. What the Afrikaner has achieved for himself he cannot possibly deny to the African people except at the cost of the embitterment of the relations of black and white, to his detriment no less than to that of the African.

7. The only reply which the African can give to the official racial discrimination to which he is subjected in this country is the strengthening of the African National Congress. In spite of all the onslaughts that have

been directed against it by the government and by the puppet organisations or individuals that sometimes masquerade as spokesmen for the African people, the A.N.C. remains the vanguard of our struggle for liberation. It has been and is being chastened and purified by the attacks to which it is subjected and therefore becomes more and more precious to us. It therefore behooves every member of the African National Congress to work for its success and for the spread of its spirit into every household. Now that we are confronted with the almost Union-wide prohibition of meetings, our slogan must be "Every Home a Branch and Every Branch a School." Wherever two or three are gathered together, there the gospel of the A.N.C. must be preached, until the principles for which it stands become part of our very nature.

8. But the A.N.C. must not only become a powerful mass movement, it must become a movement distinguished for the sense of responsibility and the high ideals by which its members and its leaders are inspired. The A.N.C. is no place for individuals who do not know what they are about. The task which confronts the A.N.C. is a serious one affecting the lives of millions of people. There is therefore no room in this movement for place-seekers and people who regard public affairs as a kind of parlour game in which the people are merely pawns. There are organisations which can be joined by those who are interested in the theoretical study of the problems affecting the African people. We have no quarrel with people who are interested in knowledge for its own sake. But the A.N.C. is an action group, not a study circle. This does not mean that members of the A.N.C. must not make a close study of the questions with which it is confronted. Action, if it is to be sound, must be based upon prior analysis and careful study of the facts of the situation. But the process of study and analysis must be followed by a programme of action which the members must seek to carry out to the best of their ability. The Programme of Action of the A.N.C. was adopted in 1949 after protracted deliberation not only in the Annual Conference, but in the Provincial Conferences and in our branches thoughout the country. I know that it is felt in some quarters that the Programme of Action is in need of review in the light of developments that have taken place in the liberatory movement in South Africa since 1949. But although there may be amendments in points of detail here and there, I am of the opinion that the fundamental principles on which it was based have stood the test of time, namely, African nationalism, the claim of the right to self-determination and co-operation with other sections of the population strictly on the basis of equality. The nationalism which we express is not the narrow nationalism which seeks to exclude others from South African nationhood as we are excluded today but a broad nationalism which is all-inclusive, with no position of special privilege for any group such as we find is the case in this country today. The right of self-determination which we claim is not a right to set up some sort of Bantustan in some undefined and undefinable place, but a right to equal

opportunity in all spheres of life in South Africa as a whole, as we know it. The co-operation which we seek with others is not one in which others shall determine what our destiny shall be and expect us merely to acquiesce like sheep led to slaughter. Our motives may be questioned, the practicability of the objectives which we have set ourselves may be doubted, the length of time which must elapse before our aims are realised may be unascertainable, but our faith in ourselves and in our destiny need not be shaken on that account. We need not be deterred from our goal by lack of immediate results in the practical sphere. We can have immediate results in the spiritual sphere by freeing our minds and spirits from the bondage of those who believe that they have no power in themselves to help themselves. It is only to the extent that we achieve this spiritual freedom—the freedom of men created in the image of God—that we shall be able to work for the improvement of the physical conditions under which we live. The implementation of a programme of action requires careful organisation and sustained effort. In the carrying out of a programme of action the worst enemies of a movement are those who are interested in sensations and excitement and have no time for the routine work which must both precede and accompany the implementation of any programme if it is to achieve success.

In the course of the Conference you will be called to discuss and make preparations for various campaigns which form part of our programme of action. You will be asked to give careful consideration to the adoption of the new Constitution and to the improvement of our organisational machinery. In dealing with these matters we must be on our guard against the temptation to indulge in cheap sensationalism and in facile optimism regarding the difficulties which confront us. The odds against us are great enough in all conscience. Let us not add to them by our failure to face up to them and to assess them realistically. In the decisions and resolutions which we adopt let us be faithful to the trust reposed in us by those who have sent us here and who look to us for sound leadership in the perilous days that lie ahead.

In the course of this Conference, after you have adopted the new Constitution you will be called to elect a new National Executive to guide and direct the affairs of the A.N.C. for the next three years. On behalf of the President-General and, if I may say, of myself as Deputy President-General during the past year, I should like to express my appreciation for the loyal support and co-operation we have received from members of the outgoing Executive. That Executive was elected in 1952 and since then one by one the members of our National Executive have been muzzled in one way or another by the government in its attempt to stifle the voice of Africa. In spite of handicaps and difficulties which I need not detail here, the Executive has carried on its work to the best of its ability. Our thanks also go out to the Secretarial Staff, which has throughout carried a very heavy burden. As long as we can get such devoted service from our members, the idea of Freedom in our Life Time will be realised. Finally a word of appreciation must be said about our friends and allies in the S.A.I.C., the S.A.C.P.O., the C.O.D. and other organisations and individuals who in spite of the interpretations and abuse to which they are constantly subjected by those who fear the unity of all the people of South Africa have co-operated with us in all our endeavours.

Document 13c. Report of the National Executive Committee

Sons and Daughters of Afrika!

We of the African National Congress meet once again to review South African and world events; our Congress policy of rights and progress for all the people of our country; our desire for world peace and friendship among the peoples of the world.

THE PEOPLE FIGHT TO BE FREE.

Apartheid is enslaving the people of South Africa today but in the great world outside race discrimination and colonialism are being replaced by human brotherhood and the independence of nations. Countries which less than one decade ago were the subjects of colonial powers have thrown off their bonds and asserted their right to take part in international affairs as complete equals. In the last ten years the maps have had to be re-drawn, the face of the world has changed, the people of great parts of Asia have risen to their feet, and now the freedom struggle is spreading to our own continent, Africa. Centuries of colonial oppression have been ended for many millions and for millions more the struggle for liberation is reaching new heights. *We do not doubt that within our lifetimes the millions still oppressed throughout the world will govern themselves freely.*

The road to freedom is no easy one. Savage wars have been unleashed against the peoples of Kenya, Malaya and Vietnam, savage campaigns of annihilation against the peoples of French Africa, by those seeking to stamp out the peoples' freedom movements. The colonialists strive to prevent the floodlight of world enquiry being focussed on what happens in their colonies; they seek to deny the United Nations the right to discuss their policies and to actively safeguard those liberties enshrined in the U.N. Charter and the Declaration of Human Rights.

The deprivation of human liberties; policies of genocide or mass extermination against a subject people; the denial of rights to a people

224

because of their colour; these evils are not the domestic concern of ruling nations: they are the affair of all peoples. Even from those colonies in Africa where the people have been kept in the most dire subjection, denied rights of assembly and organisation and cut off from contact with the outside world, the demands for self-government, for independence and for freedom are ringing out.

Colonialism will be overthrown. It will take longer in some countries than others. Nowhere will freedom come about independently of the peoples' struggles, and everywhere the colonial and master powers will fight bitterly to retain their possessions. But everywhere the peoples' movements are growing, developing, maturing; new militant forms of struggle are being adopted; a new determination is growing among the people; a brotherhood and a confidence for freedom are being forged and the day to liberation draws nearer.

BANDUNG MARKED A NEW ERA.

This was the great significance of the Bandung Conference held in Indonesia in April of this year. The conference of 29 Asian and African powers represented the new era of colonial liberation and was therefore one of the most important events of our time. *There entered into the world arena a great new force for freedom and for peace.* The resurgent peoples of Asia and Africa who for centuries experienced the bitterness of colonial oppression will not rest until all are liberated from this evil. So the conference at Bandung pledged to fight until the last remains of colonialism have been wiped from the face of the earth. The conference deplored the policies of racial segregation and discrimination which form the basis of government and human relations in large regions of the still exploited world—including our own country, South Africa. It proposed economic and cultural co-operation between the Asian and African people, and demanded increased representation for the people of these two continents in the United Nations.

With the greatest enthusiasm, we greet the achievements of the Bandung Conference which will inspire colonial people everywhere to redouble their efforts for freedom.

We greet with enthusiasm the decision to convene yet another Afro-Asian conference next year in Cairo.

FOR PEACE.

The coming together of the Asian and African powers is a great force in the world not only for freedom but also for peace, and none should feel the need for peace more deeply than the colonial people who have seen so many wars fought against them in their own lands to rob them of their country's natural wealth and of their liberty. *National rights and independence are not secure in a world at war;* and *peace is needed for the people to advance and prosper.* All mankind needs the ending of the cold war that divides the world into two hostile armed camps and prevents the development of trade, of economic and cultural exchange.

The pessimism of those who once used to say that war is inevitable has been confounded by the great victories for peace won recently by the peace-loving people of the world. Concrete steps towards peace and the easing of world tension were taken at top level meetings of the Big Powers. The pressure of the people brought to a stop the colonial wars in Korea and Vietnam.

The people see the choice clearly as one of *co-existence*: all nations, governments and systems learning to live together in one world—or of *no existence:* a war of atomic horror weapons which threatens to wipe out mankind. The people made their pressure felt and forced their governments to negotiate around the conference table. Great steps have been taken to preserve the peace but the dangers of war can only be averted while the people remain vigilant and organise and fight for peace. War is an opportunity and the means to colonial powers to invade new territories, to swell their profits from the armaments industry and the pillage of subject countries.

The colonial peoples need liberation, freedom, independence. But *we who fight for freedom fight also for peace that our children may grow up in a world of prosperity and international friendship.*

At Bandung where Africa and Asia took their stand so firmly for world peace and freedom were present Moses Kotane and Maulvi Cachalia. In the great Bandung Assembly our voice was heard, and Kotane spoke there for the real aspirations of the South African people, as he had done for many years at home.

SOUTH AFRICAN RACIALISM DENOUNCED BY THE WORLD.

At the United Nations, by contrast, the South African government representatives have withdrawn from this session of UNO rather than face the criticism and denunciation of the world. But running away from criticism does not defeat the critics and serves only to condemn the South African government and isolate it from world opinion. South Africa cannot evade the judgement of the world: the judgement is against apartheid and discrimination and for equality and human rights.

Apartheid Disaster.

The suggestion in the latest United Nations Report on South Africa, while still condemning the apartheid practices of our government, is that the application of apartheid is "slowing down", that the operation of this policy is characterised by "gradualism" and "flexibility". The events of the past year alone do not bear out this theory, nor do the experiences of those who are the chief victims of the apartheid policy: the Non-White people.

Above all, this approach misses so sadly the real purpose of the apartheid policy of the Nationalists. Under cover of the airy talk of complete territorial apartheid, of the endless discussions by the Dutch Reformed Church Ministers and the SABRA professors, one bout after another of oppressive, discriminatory legislation is being inflicted on the people. While its longterm aims are theorised about in the press and the debating chambers, the people are already experiencing the disasters of apartheid. The repression of the state has never been so severe, both the attacks on the political movements and on the rights of the individual and the family; and these attacks have never been directed against such large numbers of the people as they are today. What are these if not the results of apartheid? The talk may be of "separate homes for the Africans in the Reserves", of "their own cities", rights in "their own areas" and "separate development"; but these plans are an apartheid pipe dream, an illusion, and the *actuality of apartheid today is the denial of all rights to those millions living and working in the towns and poverty-stricken rural areas.*

This is exactly the purpose of the apartheid theory: to inflict discriminatory laws on the Non-White people under the guise of letting them develop one day in their own areas. It may well be recognised that the facts of history work against this illusion of apartheid and that it is a political and economic impossibility, but meanwhile none should fail to see that the Nationalists are *today* whittling away our rights, sacrificing us on the altar of apartheid, and reducing the people to a state of semi-slavery.

If ever there was a year when apartheid played havoc with the rights of the people, it is the period under review.

The forcible removal by army and police of the people of Johannesburg's Western Areas to Meadowlands; the plans of the Minister of Native Affairs, Dr. Verwoerd, to move the entire African population of the Western Cape Province; the enforcement of the Bantu Education System; the packing of the Senate by Nats. in preparation for the removal of the Coloured voters from the common roll; the implementation of the Population Registration Act; the re-classification of Coloureds; the alteration of the judiciary to suit the interests of the Nats.; the enforcement of the Bantu Authorities Act; the continuation of exiles and bannings of leaders; the ruthless raids on people's meetings, private offices and private homes and even religious institutions; the introduction of ethnic grouping; and the creation of slums under the site-and-service scheme; the application of the Group Areas Act with the sole purpose of economically ruining the non-Europeans—the Indians in particular; the shameless pass and beer raids, persecution of people under the pass laws and finally the threat of the extension of pass laws to women by January next year.

Here in South Africa none can be in doubt as to the growing ruthlessness of the Nationalists and their determination, to use the words of the Prime Minister, to pursue their policies "relentlessly".

THE REAL OPPOSITION.

The relentless pursuance of Nationalist policies, instead of serving to stiffen the Opposition of the United Party has helped to dismember it. Instead of presenting to the electorate an alternative to Nationalist Party policies, the United Party offers a copy of these policies, a slightly milder version. "To get into power again the United Party must get more votes, and these votes can only come from the moderate Afrikaners," said Sir De Villiers Graaff, chairman of the Cape United Party, in November. "The moderate Nationalists must be made to feel that there is a place for them in the United Party." Here is a simple telling admission of the policies of capitulation followed by the United Party, policies which have led many former United Party supporters to abandon the fainthearted policies of the Official Opposition and to seek more principled opposition to the Nationalists in such protest movements as the Covenant Movement and the campaigns of the Black Sash women. The will to fight the Senate Act and other dictatorial measures is stirring many European voters who have turned to mass protest movements in an attempt to revive and revitalise the opposition. *But so long as it is not recognised that the only real bulwark, the only firm defence against dictatorship and fascism is the will of the Non-White people for democracy, all opposition politics of White voters alone will continue to be shadow play, unreal and ineffective.*

More votes, yes, that is the issue. Not winning Nationalist votes to the side of the United Party, but extending the vote to all the people.

"No government can justly claim authority unless it is based on the will of all the people," says the Freedom Charter.

"The People Shall Govern.

Every man and woman shall have the right to vote for and to stand as candidate for all bodies which make laws.

All people shall be entitled to take part in the administration of the country.''

This is the only way to defeat the police state, this is the only way forward.

FORWARD WITH THE FREEDOM CHARTER.

The great road forward is lit by the Freedom Charter, adopted at the Congress of the People at Kliptown on June 25 and 26.

Which of us who heard the idea of the Congress of the People first proposed at our Queenstown Conference by Professor Matthews foresaw that it would be such a brilliant success? History was made at Kliptown in June of this year. The Freedom Charter was not just another political document, the Congress of the People just another conference. *The Freedom Charter is the sum total of our aspirations, but more: it is the road to the new life.* It is the uniting creed of all the people struggling for democracy and for their rights; the mirror of the future South Africa. The defeat of the Nationalists and the course of the Congress movement depends on every fighter for freedom grasping fully the meaning and significance, and the purpose of the Freedom Charter.

The Charter is no patchwork collection of demands, no jumble of reforms. The ten clauses of the Charter cover all aspects of the lives of the people. The Charter exposes the fraud of racialism and of minority government. It demands equal rights before the law, work and security for all, the opening of the doors of learning and culture for all. It demands that our brothers in the Protectorates shall be free to decide for themselves their own future; it proclaims the oneness of our aims for peace and friendship with our brothers in Africa and elsewhere in the world.

This is the pattern of the new South Africa which must make a complete break with the present unjust system.

The Freedom Charter has opened up a new chapter in the struggle of our people. Hitherto we have struggled sometimes together, sometimes separately against pass laws, and Group Areas, against low wages, against Bantu Education and removal schemes. With the adoption of the Charter all struggles become part of one: the struggle for the aims of the Charter.

THE CHARTER: OUR GUIDE AND ORGANISER.

It is not enough to have adopted the Freedom Charter. It must not become a document framed and hanging on the wall. *The Charter can and must be the inspiration of the people in their freedom fight: it must be their organiser.*

Every signature won to the Charter is an adherent to our cause and a fighter for the Congress movement. Every local battle fought around some local grievance but related to the overall demands of the Charter is another battle won in the peoples' understanding of how political campaigns will win the new South Africa and help to bring final victory against the Nationalists nearer.

One million signatures for the Freedom Charter: 450,000 in the Transvaal; 350,000 in the Cape; 150,000 in Natal; and 50,000 in the Free State. If we take the Freedom Charter among the people to organise and teach and activise them, this can be the training of a mighty Congress force that will replace what is old, rotten and unjust with the new, the vital, the just.

The Nationalists seek to return us to the days of tribalism, to make the chiefs the "bossboys", the "indunas" the policemen of apartheid; to divide the tribes from one another; to teach our children not only to believe in the natural inferiority of the African people but also that the children of the different tribes should not play with one another. The Africans who ride to the Verwoerd indabas in black cars are the agitators, said the Minister of Native Affairs, and for mortal fear of the so-called agitators who preach the unity of the African people, who demand not Bungas and Bantu Authorities but full and equal franchise, who organise in trade unions and strike for higher wages, the Native Affairs Department has organised a vast army of civil servants at work in every corner of the countryside trying to wean the Africans from their political organisation into hostile tribal units under the N.A.D.

This is a diabolical scheme to confine us to the kraal and the eroded soil. Bantu Authorities and Bantu Education are presented as the salvation of the African people, but we know them to be our doom. Yet in many areas where Congress is not strong organisationally and where the N.A.D. stuffs the ears of the people with fairytales of so-called positive apartheid the Verwoerd propaganda is gaining some ground. To deny this is to close our eyes to the truth of what is happening in some areas.

How answer the lies of the apartheid propagandists? How fight the apartheid theories? By telling them the truth of the government's intentions, giving the people the alternative and taking the Freedom Charter to them. We have an unassailable case; it has only to be put to the people and hundreds of thousands in the Reserves and on the Trust Farms will reject apartheid, and fling it from them, and will take the Freedom Charter into their homes and their daily lives.

We are confident in the justice of our cause, but we must not let this confidence blunt the edge of our energy and persistence in carrying the work of Congress among the people.

Often Congress lets burning grievances of the people and local issues go by without offering the positive lead of our organisation. We must face the fact that in the Freedom Charter campaign for the collection of one million signatures not enough energy, drive and direction has been shown. The campaign has been too slow in getting under way. No campaign is merely a routine task, least of all the collection of signatures for the Freedom Charter. The people will not sign with enthusiasm if they think signing consists merely in making a mark on a piece of paper. But if we present the Charter to them as we understand it: the organiser and inspiration of the people in a united political struggle, the signatures will flow in. *The Charter* cannot be explained just by words. *It must be related to struggle, it must be illustrated by life itself.* In every campaign we undertake against passes for women, against Bantu Education, against the classification of the Coloured people, against ethnic grouping and the Bantu Authorities, against site-and-service and bad transport, the overall demands of the Freedom Charter must be related to the peoples' needs.

The Congress who gave birth to the Freedom Charter must not merely meet together from time to time in a joint meeting. To give the Charter the drive and inspiration it needs, the Congresses must forge a *mighty alliance in action* for the Freedom Charter and there common plans must be hammered out, all the events in our political life discussed and related to the Charter so that it takes on its real meaning for the people as the road forward.

STRUGGLE AGAINST PASSES.

The pass laws are one of the most burning grievances of the people. The Africans know the passes as their badge of slavery. The passing of the Population Registration Act means the extension of pass laws to other sections of our community and to the African women in particular. The Abolition of Passes and Co-ordination of Documents Act is just part of this. Under this law all Africans irrespective of sex over the age of 16 are obliged to carry the composite pass known as the Reference Book. It is under this law that the Minister intends forcing our women to carry Reference Books from January, 1956. The African National Congress has time and again rejected the passes by whatever name they are called. We reject the pass system under the Population Registration Act as well as under the Abolition of Passes and Co-ordination of Documents Act.

We who know the suffering the pass laws have brought to us over the decades will not tolerate the extension of this hated system to our womenfolk. We warn the government: making women carry passes will be like tramping on the tail of a puff adder.

The pass laws humiliate and terrorise us at every turn. Influx control keeps man and wife apart; endorsement out of the urban areas breaks up our families and make our children orphans. Our young boys grow up in terror of the sight of the roving pick-up van and the shouts for passes. The labour bureaus force us to accept work on the farms; our youth are denied a future.

Must our women also be herded into the police cells, detained in a lockup because they have forgotten a piece of paper while their children are motherless at home? Must our wives too work out 14 and 21 days of hard labour because some detail had not been entered in their identification books?

This is what the pass laws will bring to our women.

We must fight the extension of these laws to African women with every breath in our bodies.

Yet we must show that passes for African women are just another aspect of apartheid, and therefore our struggle against passes is part of the total fight against apartheid. It is a burning issue, yet not an issue that stands alone. We must join the battle against passes with all the other freedom battles we wage.

We accordingly suggest that the National Consultative Committee working under the directives and supervision of the National Executive Committee of the Congress movement jointly or individually should be given authority to launch a planned campaign in order to mobilise all sections of the people against the Population Registration Act and the Abolition of Passes and Co-ordination of Documents Act in whatever shape or form. We are confident that they will find the legitimate form of resistance.

THE CAMPAIGN AGAINST BANTU EDUCATION.

The campaign against Bantu Education has many lessons for Congress work in all spheres.

The 42nd Annual Conference of the A.N.C. held in Durban last year decided as a means of fighting and opposing Bantu Education, that African children should be withdrawn from Bantu Schools for an indefinite period as from the 1st April, 1955, and further called for a boycott of Bantu Education school committees and boards.

In January, 1955, instructions were issued by the National Secretariat, giving directives to Provinces for the holding of a series of meetings and assemblies, the appointment of various local committees and the submission of regular reports on the progress of the campaign which was planned to culminate in the mass withdrawal of children on the 1st April, 1955.

When the National Executive met in Durban in March, 1955, to consider reports on the progress of the campaign in the various centres, no such reports were available and there was no evidence that the country would be ready for the withdrawal on the 1st April. In the circumstances your Executive decided to postpone the withdrawal to a date which would be announced later. The resolution of the National Executive adopted at this meeting also called for the formation of a National Council of Education, consisting of representatives of all organisations opposed to Bantu Education.

In pursuance of the decision of the Executive, the Secretariat convened a conference of various organisations at Port Elizabeth in April, 1955, at which conference the principle of establishing an educational council was approved. Such a council was duly established and is known as the African Education Movement, with its headquarters in Johannesburg.

On the 1st April, 1955, some areas, which were ready for withdrawal on that date, staged protest withdrawals and the children stayed away from Bantu Education schools in spite of Dr. Verwoerd's threats to exclude such children permanently from his schools.

Since the decision of the Annual Conference of December, 1954, the campaign against Bantu Education has been conducted with varying degrees of intensity in different centres. On the Reef and in the Eastern Cape, these areas where mass withdrawals have taken place, children withdrawn have in the main been absorbed into cultural clubs established for the purpose by the African Education Movement. Your Executive wishes to pay special tribute to the magnificent service being rendered by the organisers of the cultural clubs, who are working under what are in some cases extremely difficult conditions and in the face of persistent police interference.

There can be no doubt that the struggle against Bantu Education was one of the most important campaigns embarked upon during the period under review. Nor can there be any doubt that its enforcement revealed the united hostility of the vast majority of the people against this tyrannical measure. Persons and organisations of varying shades of opinion joined together in their vehement condemnation of Bantu Education. The few disgruntled, self-seeking vultures who are conducting campaigns to popularise Bantu Education have exposed themselves as traitors to the people.

Whilst on the one hand the fight against Bantu Education has served to expose the treacherous intentions of the authors of this inhuman scheme, it has on the other hand revealed difficulties and mistakes which must be examined and considered by this conference if ultimate victory is to be the reward for our present struggle.

Firstly, education is essentially a slow process whose mass effects may take generations to become noticeable. An evil system of education therefore cannot be effectively attacked by means of sensational, dramatic campaigns of short duration, except where such campaigns flow systematically from, and are part of a steady, deep-rooted and enduring campaign, planned and conducted on the clear understanding that it involves a long and bitter struggle.

For a sustained campaign of this kind an efficient organisational machinery is absolutely essential; and if, because of organisational weaknesses the fight against Bantu Education has fallen short of our expectations, the reason is that Provincial and local branches paid little, if any, attention to the Executive Report adopted by the last Annual Conference. It is impossible to over-emphasise the fact that where there is no organisational machinery, any struggle must ultimately perish.

Secondly, it appears that undue emphasis was laid on the provision of alternative education as a condition precedent to children being withdrawn from Bantu Education schools. This emphasis lent considerable weight to the argument advanced as an apology for retreating from the struggle, namely, that "Bantu Education is better than no education." In the absence of adequate literature and propaganda material through which the people could be made to develop the proper approach to the struggle against Bantu Education, it has not been easy to neutralise and destroy the pro-Bantu Education propaganda disseminated from Pretoria and broadcast through the agency of paid employees of the Native Affairs Department. These difficulties point unmistakably to the urgent need for a Congress bulletin or newspaper, to reinforce, and widen the field at present covered by such newspapers and bulletins as "New Age", "Fighting Talk", and "Liberation."

Thirdly, your Executive was embarrassed in this campaign, as it was in other respects, by the fact that membership subscriptions and special levies due to the Head Office were not forwarded to the appropriate treasury, except in very isolated instances. In the result your Executive was unable to do all that was necessary to guide, direct and control the development of the campaign in all its phases, and so prevent it from breaking up into what may have appeared to be sporadic, unrelated and ineffectual small incidents in various parts of the country. The chronic lack of adequate funds to enable the Head Office to perform its proper functions is a question of organisation which we have mentioned earlier in this report.

Fourthly, there seems to have been failure on the part of our organisers to realise that Bantu Education is intended and calculated to undermine the entire liberatory struggle and is therefore an open target and should be the object of persistent attack in any meeting or assembly of freedom-loving people. To this extent the campaign against Bantu Education should not be handled in isolation from other campaigns as if it were something which has its own beginning and its own end.

We must learn that it is one thing to wish to see a complete national withdrawal of all children from Bantu Education schools. It is another thing to achieve this; organisational preparedness does not happen over-night. It is the result of steady, even slow, patient, persistent work and we must face the fact that Congress branches everywhere had not and still have not put in this necessary spade-work.

There is no doubt about the long-term aim which is to prevent the functioning of Bantu Education by a boycott. But talk of permanent boycott in the isolated areas where the people are carrying out this slogan will eventually end in the disillusionment and dropping of morale if the campaign remains isolated and localised. We must beware of creating the false impression that by isolated local boycotts the Bantu Education Act can be defeated. The struggle is a long one and the people must see this campaign as all others, as a stage on the road to victory. Impatience will not bring victory nearer of its own. If the people do not all follow us, we must educate them to the point when they will. The total boycott will not be "proclaimed" by a certain date chosen on the calendar, but it will develop from local actions that spread, that join up and grow nationally. At the same time we must not deceive ourselves or the people into believing that in the immediate future we can, with our own resources, substitute a national education system. We have no state budget behind us. The average parent who follows our local call in the belief that his child will be given adequate alternative education will become disillusioned with the Congress if such education is not provided. He must act therefore out of political conviction, and he must be made aware of the sacrifice this campaign, as well as others for freedom, will entail.

Whatever difficulties have been revealed, in this campaign, however, the people have shown their rejection of Bantu Education, their readiness to fight it, and the correctness of the resolution of the last Annual Conference is beyond challenge. The fight against Bantu Education must go on. We must build steadily, carrying the people with us, exposing the wickedness of the new Bantu Education syllabus and the way the children are to be indoctrinated, achieving the boycott of the school boards and committees, adapting the form of protest to the state of preparedness in the area and the local conditions there.

WESTERN AREAS REMOVAL SCHEME.

In the field of resistance to apartheid we were faced with the removal of the Western Areas in Johannesburg from the very beginning of the year when the government was forced to change its tactics in the face of strong opposition to their plans. Early in the morning of the 9th February, the military trucks and more than 2000 police with military force standing by, were used in the forcible removal of the people. A state of emergency was declared for twenty days in Johannesburg and Roodepoort and a great indignation was aroused amongst the residents of the area. Thanks to the guidance of the A.N.C. leadership, a blood-bath was avoided which the government had intended to bring about by its provocative action. Despite the forces, out of 150 families, 40 families refused to go to Meadowlands. Great credit is due to the Sophiatown people and our beloved volunteers who remained calm whilst struggling against the evil forces at the same time. Isitwalandwe Trevor Huddleston right through the day was amongst the people and participating in the "resistance".

Although certain concessions were extracted and the government's task made difficult, we must admit that there were, however, mistakes committed and a great confusion created, the failure to indicate what type of action was to be taken and the creation of an impression in the propaganda campaign that the removal could have been stopped even in the face of military operation, in other words, the failure to indicate clearly that by not moving was meant that the people would not on their own free will move and also the failure to recognise that the appeal to landlords could not be exactly the same as the one to the tenants. The tenants were in need of better houses, especially those who lived under bad conditions, and the minimum unity between the two groups was not achieved. To call the campaign a failure, whilst recognising mistakes made, would be going to the other extreme.

ORGANISING THE PEASANTS.

The peasants and farm labourers in the countryside are amongst the most oppressed of our people. Hungry for land, denied security, harassed by the squatter's act and cast adrift with their families when ejected from land they have tilled and reaped but cannot call their own, these people cry out for organisation and a lead on the issues which beset them.

The Congress of the People showed clearly that the great gap in our organisation is on the farms and in the Reserves.

We pass resolutions on the need to organise the peasantry, but fail to follow them up. The question of organising the peasants must be tackled with resolve and energy.

We greet the formation of the new peasants' movement, the Sebata Kgomo. Congress pledges all aid in the organising of the peasants and the people of the countryside and in the coming year must devote detailed attention to this task.

Strengthening the Trade Unions.

In South Africa the racial divisions of our society are reflected in the state of the trade union movement. Whilst in most countries the working people, irrespective of race or colour, unite in trade unions against the exploitation of the employing class, in South Africa the working class has been divided on colour lines. The fundamental principle of the unity of all workers against their common enemy—economic misery—has been diverted by the colour and race divisions of our country.

This is the factor chiefly responsible for the unhealthy development of South Africa's trade union movement. These divisions have been the obstacle to the growth of a united front of all workers against the inroads being made on their rights. The division of the workers' organisations into watertight racial compartments has left them in a state of relative helplessness.

It is for these reasons that we welcome warmly the formation of the South African Congress of Trade Unions, a federal trade union body which will coordinate the activities of all workers, without consideration of their race or colour. This bold step ushers in a new era in the development of our trade union movement.

This new movement depends for its growth on the A.N.C. building it in the residential areas, speaking about it in all our meetings and getting our members to be its organisers in the factories, on the farms, in the gold mine compounds, in the men's and women's hostels, in the vineyards and in the sugar plantations of Natal. We are called not only to assist the existing unions, as Chief Luthuli said last year, but also to assist in the establishment of new trade unions. It was the A.N.C. which brought into existence the once militant Mine Workers' Union. This must come to life again. Farm labourers unions must be established to attend to the labourers' grievances and many other unions need the assistance from the African National Congress. Two [years] ago we made a demand of a minimum wage of one pound a day but that only remained on the paper. Something more positive is now required. We must see to it that the government does not freely play about with the workers' rights.

A strong trade union movement will mean a strong Congress movement, and the message of both the trade unions and the factories must be carried into every factory and workshop in the land.

THE WOMEN'S LEAGUE OF THE CONGRESS.

The women of the liberation movement have played an increasingly active and inspired role in the struggles of the past year.

This conference salutes the courageous and historic protest of the 1600 women who took their demands to the Union Buildings in Pretoria in October.

The women have been active on those major issues that most keenly affect them: Bantu Education, the threat of passes for women, the home, the children, the family.

They have administered to us all a lesson on how the peoples' daily needs can become the kernel of a united protest campaign so that even those not previously active in political affairs, feel compelled to join in.

The realities of apartheid under the Nationalists are being brought home to the women daily and their bitterness against site-and-service, Bantu Education, lack of schools and social services, is today rapidly reaching boiling point.

The Women's League has grown rapidly. Our women are proving themselves brave and undaunted politicians. Yet the women need special attention and training to assist them to become leaders of the people. The Women's League is not just an auxiliary to the African National Congress, and we know that we cannot win liberation or build a strong movement without the participation of the women.

We must therefore make it possible for women to play their part in the liberation movement by regarding them as equals, and helping to emancipate them in the home, even relieving them of their many family and household burdens so that women may be given an opportunity of being politically active. The men in the Congress movement must fight constantly in every possible way those outmoded customs which make women inferior and by personal example must demonstrate their belief in the equality of all human beings, of both sexes.

Through the Federation of South African Women, the Women's Section of the Congress has taken part in militant actions with women of all races. This co-operation should be furthered and both the A.N.C. Women's League and the Federation strengthened by affiliation of the Women's League to the Federation.

YOUTH.

The Youth everywhere has always been in the vanguard in every struggle of a people. This was realised by the A.N.C. when it resolved in 1943 to create an African Youth movement for the purpose of attending to the youth problems and a recruiting ground for the Liberation movement from which will arise the future leaders.

The African National Congress Youth League was thus formed as an auxiliary body to the African National Congress to undertake the above tasks. But although it has had its influence in the struggle yet it has not become a mass movement embracing all sections of our youth, workers, peasants, and intellectuals, in spite of the fact that it has been in existence now for ten years. Its relation with the A.N.C. is far from satisfactory. This conference must give this matter its consideration. The youth must be directed to pay attention not only to the political, but more especially to the cultural, social and educational needs of our youth. Our youth must be

238

properly guided and given necessary assistance. We highly appreciate the efforts of the A.N.C.Y.L. in the fight against Bantu Education, which was their special task during the period under review.

CHIEF LUTHULI.

During the past year the Executive and the country were shocked by the sudden and severe illness of our President-General, Chief Luthuli. Thanks to the skill and care of the staff of McCord's Zulu Hospital, the President-General regained his health though he is still not completely recovered. The thoughts of the African people were with Chief Luthuli all through his illness and it is with joy that we welcome him back among us again, where he continues to inspire and guide our organisation with his wisdom and foresight. Chief Luthuli is not just the President of the African National Congress but is a symbol of unity whose leadership and ability is recognised and accepted by all sections—a man who cannot basically be replaced. Professor Z. K. Matthews, Deputy President-General, acted for Chief Luthuli during his illness.

ISITWALANDWE AWARD.

The Executive considered and approved the suggestion for the National Action Council to establish a title and award in our movement. "Isitwalandwe" is accepted as the highest award in our movement. It was further agreed that this award be bestowed on Chief Luthuli, the President-General of the African National Congress, Dr. Y. M. Dadoo, former President of the South African Indian Congress, and Father Huddleston, an Anglican Missionary whose unqualified association with the Congress movement and selfless devotion to the struggle earned him a high position in the South African society among all sections. These are the first three men to receive this highest award. It will also be given to the deserving cases in the near future. Your Executive recommends that people who received this title should also be accepted into position of Congress leadership [as] honorary members of the President-General's Special Council.

EXECUTIVE MEETINGS AND COMPOSITION.

Your Executive during the period under review held five Executive meetings, three Joint Executive meetings and eight Working Committee meetings. This list of Executive members elected in 1952 and those who have been co-opted due to banning orders and failure of some others, is marked Annexure C. Mr. Maseko's and Mr. Vundla's names were removed from the members list on grounds of expulsion.

DEPORTATIONS AND BANS.

Among the peoples' leaders exiled from their homes during the year were Korea Monare, now confined in Vryburg, and Mrs. Silinga, deported from the Western Cape Province to the Transkei.

A number of Congress leaders have been banned from gatherings and prohibited from taking part in the work of the Congress.

CONGRESS BULLETIN.

The Bulletin has at last been created as the most indispensable method of bringing about co-ordination and consolidation of our organisation. This Bulletin is also introduced as a prelude to the coming into being of a Newspaper.

CO-ORDINATING MACHINERY WITHIN THE CONGRESS.

Since the Defiance Campaign which was conducted by the A.N.C. and the S.A.I.C., a unity of all democrats has grown and the scope of alliance has now embraced the four main sections of our community. This has been clearly demonstrated in the campaign for the great Congress of the People from which has come the Freedom Charter which must serve as a basis for unity—an acid test of our alliance.

As a result of which your Executive considered the advisability of the establishment of a permanent co-ordinating machinery of the African National Congress and its allies in view of the growing unity amongst all the people who are struggling against the oppression and white domination. As this involves the change of policy from that based on *ad hoc* committees of the past, your Executive now recommends that this principle be accepted and that all joint activities be conducted through this machinery subject to supervision by the National Executive only.

PROBLEMS AND TASKS OF ORGANISATION.

During the year your Executive examined the organisational machinery of Congress and it was felt that in order to end the present lack of co-ordination and co-operation between the National and Provincial offices on the one hand and between the Branches on the other, the suggested scheme of centralisation be implemented by taking practical steps to bring about close and direct contact between the National head office and its branches—provincial, regional and local branches. This could be done without in any way usurping the provincial rights to guide, supervise, and co-ordinate the work of its branches just as the provinces guide and supervise the branches without taking away the right of the region of co-ordinating the work of the branches. Any constitution of the A.N.C. must of necessity take this into account.

It is clear that we have not been successful in getting both the *provincial* organisations and the branches to make a serious effort to remedy the weaknesses in the organisation. Efforts to raise the political and ideological level and to stimulate an interest in theory have not yet made any appreciable headway in our organisation. We can do no more here than refer the conference to our last year's organisational plan: . . . . [see Document 7b]

It was further decided to recommend for consideration the principle of full-time Congress workers—the employment of officials and organisers in the national and provincial levels at present.

The National Executive Committee is to all intents and purposes isolated from the general stream of activities of the Congress as a result of not being kept in touch with day-to-day activities (developments) in the provinces.

The failure of the provinces in submitting reports and in implementing directives gives cause for perturbation. Can it be due to the weakness of organisation or are there other potent factors responsible for this?

Until we are sufficiently alive to our great task of raising our political propaganda and the organisational level of our members, until we have more than just mere sentiment and emotion for our cause, we will find it difficult to make headway. The weaknesses continue to exist because the people are politically backward. It must be appreciated that political and organisational problems are interwoven and are due to lack of unified theory, ideology. We should end this vicious circle by getting our people to discuss these problems from the lowest organs of the organisation to the highest; we must discourage all unprincipled discussions and unpolitical tendencies; we must teach ourselves to practice self-criticism and destroy individualism and conceit; we must tackle all the small issues affecting the people and pay attention to individual grievances of our members. We must study the literature which is now becoming abundant in the liberatory movement.

The national liberation movement has not yet succeeded in the organisational field in moving out of the domain of mass meetings and this type of public agitation. Mass gatherings and large public activities of

Congress are important, but so is house-to-house work, the building of small local branches, the close contact with members and supporters, and their continual education in the aims and policies of the Congress movement. This is the true art of leadership; to have the branch and the local unit of Congress who issues directives, who acts on his own, who gives commands and does not consult and work within Congress democratic machinery, is a hindrance not an aid to our progress.

Congress branches and members have shown lack of discipline on some occasions.

In the Congress of the People campaign, although the African National Congress was responsible for the creation of the Congress of the People, many of its leaders and many of its branches showed a complete lack of activity as if some of them regretted the birth of this great and noble idea.

Congress propaganda has also been found wanting in the past year. If Congress material had reached the Transkei and the Ciskei as it should have done, the Bungas there would never have been taken in by the Bantu Authorities Act. Congress policy must be heard on every issue of concern to the people. The people are hungry to read, and in the coming year Congress must produce small booklets and leaflets, must use what bulletins and publications it can to carry its policy on the hundred and one vital problems confronting the people.

FINANCE.

The problem of finance requires the immediate attention of the organisation. An organisation like the A.N.C. cannot hope to execute the tasks that face it without sound financial resources. A machinery for the efficient raising and management of funds must be immediately set up. Owing to shortage of money, head office has experienced great set-backs in carrying out the work of administration. The problem of finance is inextricably bound up with that of organisation.

The in-coming Executive should set itself the task of raising an amount of £ 15,000 during its term in office. This can be done.

PROVINCIAL.

The information from the Provinces has either been not adequate or has not reached this office, or has reached it late—although efforts have been made to communicate with the Provinces in time. As a result of this regrettable state of affairs the Provincial secretaries have been requested to submit supplementary reports dealing in particular with regional and branch activities and reflecting especially the following:

1. Organisational problems in the branches.
2. Numbers of branches and membership—total—Provinces.
3. Financial position of the Provinces.
4. Local and Provincial issues tackled.

We would, however, be failing in our duty if we did not express our high appreciation of the efforts made in the carrying out of our major campaigns during this period.

In the Anti-Removal campaign, in the Western Areas, the Anti-Bantu Education campaign, the campaign for the Congress of the People, there are regions and branches which distinguished themselves as a result of which they have emerged strong.

In conclusion, friends, we thank all those who made it their duty to put personal business aside in order to serve the nation during the period under review. We further call upon them in the coming year and upon all true patriots, all democrats, all lovers of freedom to resolve once more that South Africa shall become a free land, free from Nationalist tyranny and become a happy place for all to live in, during our lifetime.

Mayibuye Afrika!

O. R. Tambo

ANNEXURES.   Acting Secretary-General
AFRICAN NATIONAL CONGRESS

Document 13d. Letter on "certain tendencies," from Dr. A. B. Xuma to the ANC Annual Conference, in *The World*, January 28, 1956

The President-General and Delegates to the Annual Conference of the African National Congress.

Fellow Africans,

I send you, one and all, heartiest greetings. My apologies and regrets for inability to attend this important Annual Conference.

In following up the affairs of the African National Congress one is alarmed as well as distressed over certain tendencies which have developed in Congress in recent years.

These tendencies are undermining and weakening the Congress as a National Liberation Movement and mouthpiece of the African people. To mention but a few I would say:

(a) The African National Congress has lost its identity as a National Liberation Movement with a policy of its own and distinct African Leadership. One hears or reads of statements by the "Congresses" and one hardly ever gets the standpoint of the African National Congress.

As such, many Africans are confused and wonder who are their leaders and whom must they follow as a consequence.

(b) The National Movement is disintegrating into splinters of disaffected groups, such as the A.N.C. (National-Minded Block) and the Bantu National Congress, besides the African National Congress. This causes much confusion in the loyalty of the Africans.

We cannot ignore these divisions whatever their respective strength. Their very existence weakens and undermines and brings mockery to our National struggle as a National aspiration of our people.

Then I remind you that when I took over leadership of the Congress in 1940 the Transvaal was divided into seven sections, Natal into two and the Cape Province into two and the Orange Free State could only claim Bloemfontein for the Congress.

Now you can see why my heart bleeds when I see the emergence of these splits, cracks, antagonisms and struggle for office for personal reasons and control of the Organisation which we had healed and buried after I took over the leadership. There were none in 1949.

(c) The National Congress seems to fear to face criticisms—constructive and otherwise from its following and others. People who voice their reasonable and considered views on Congress policy and/or no policy and on actions in the name of the African National Congress are referred to as "sellers-out" or "agents" or "friends of the Government" instead of being shown where they are wrong.

Many who dare to criticise the hierarchy have been expelled or "liquidated" individually or en masse without a democratic hearing.

This attitude is foreign to Congress as a democratic movement and smacks of totalitarianism or authoritarianism which a movement like Congress cannot countenance and still claim to be fighting for freedom from domination and suppression.

(d) The Congress leadership seems to have turned their backs against the African National Congress Nation-building Programme of the 1940's and have even forgotten the Congress Charter of Human Rights "The Africans' Claims" in South Africa of December 16, 1945, which can only be superseded by the Charter of Human Rights of the United Nations instead of other vague, inconclusive so-called charters, which merely defer and confuse the Africans' just and immediate claims.

Congress agreed in 1946 to co-operate with other non-European fellow-nationals on all points of common interest but insisted that the respective national organisations must maintain their identity as integrated regiments in the struggle for common citizenship.

This was intended to make each organisation play its full part in the struggle and bear the necessary sacrifices. It was to avoid the danger of sections using others without making sacrifices themselves.

Many of the delegates are new in Congress. To them I say: Ask the old stalwarts with whom I have struggled in the forties where we stood then.

Above all, ask my "Kindergarten Boys" of the African National Congress Youth League whose foundation representatives met with me in my library at home and were baptised and established by me and the late Mr. R. V. Selope Thema at the B.M.S.C. in Johannesburg as the African National Congress Youth League, what they stood for. To them I say remember the 1940's, Remember Africa!

(e) By acting on the principle "of action for action's sake and for propaganda reasons" instead of aiming at achieving results, Congress, through the Defiance Campaign, the Western Areas Removal Scheme and the School Boycott, the Congress aroused vain hopes in the breasts of the struggling Africans and made promises of "secret weapons" and "provision of services" for which no preparations were made.

It will be wise for Congress not to embark on revolutionary tactics unless the leaders with the rank are prepared to pay the price.

If leaders arouse the masses and the leaders then fail the masses in the testing hour the loyalty and faith of the masses is shaken in the leadership, and what is worse, in the Organisation itself.

Such actions, under the circumstances, tended to set the clock of our progress back many years.

I appeal to the Annual Conference to rescind its resolution of School Boycott.

With no effective alternative system of education, the boycott of schools with its interference with children and teachers, is bound to be worse for African progress than Bantu Education; in fact, it is not only negative but harmful in that in the long run, it will cause the African people to turn against the A.N.C.

I must appeal to all delegates to make this Conference one of the most constructive conferences, for examination and re-assessment of our methods, policies and attitudes.

One and all must realise no one else will ever free the Africans but the Africans themselves.

Their genuine friends can help them, but the Africans themselves must rely on themselves.

We must learn to do things for ourselves in order to grow, to plan our programme and campaigns and rely upon our own leadership.

Until we can do that, have faith in ourselves as well as self-reliance, depend upon our inner strength, we do not deserve freedom and could not maintain it if it were offered us on a platter.

Let us re-organise our people, re-integrate the African National Congress as the mouthpiece of the African people.

We must organise ourselves not against other nationals, or to gain anything at anyone else's expense, but only that we must gain strength in our unity because "charity begins at home" and there can be no internationalism without nationalism.

Leadership means service for and not domination over others.

True and genuine leaders serve the cause of the people and do not expect the cause to serve them or become a source of profit and honour for them.

Africa expects all her sons and daughters to serve the cause of the people loyally, sincerely and honestly.

Let us close ranks, fellow-Africans and do our duty.

I wish your deliberations every success.

"Right not might, freedom not serfdom."

Yours for the cause,

A. B. Xuma

Document 14. "In Our Lifetime." Article by Nelson R. Mandela, in *Liberation*, **June 1956**

The adoption of the Freedom Charter by the Congress of the People at Kliptown in June of last year was widely recognised both at home and abroad as an event of major political significance in the life of this country. In his message to the C.O.P. Chief A. J. Luthuli, the banned National President of the African National Congress, declared:

"Why will this assembly be significant and unique? Its size, I hope, will make it unique. But above all its multi-racial nature and its noble objectives will make it unique, because it will be the first time in the history of our multi-racial nation that its people from all walks of life will meet as equals, irrespective of race, colour and creed, to formulate a Freedom Charter for all people in the country."

The editorial of *New Age* of June 30, 1955, characterised the C.O.P. as the most spectacular and moving demonstration this country had ever seen; and that through it the people had given proof that they had the ability and the power to triumph over every obstacle and win the future of their dreams. *Fighting Talk* of July, 1955, saw several signs at the C.O.P. that the liberation movement in South Africa had come of age and in the same issue Alfred Hutchinson, reporting on the C.O.P., coined for his article the magnificent title "A New World Unfolds . . ." which accurately summarised the political significance of that historic gathering.

The same theme was taken up by *Liberation* of September last year when, in its editorial comment, it predicted that the text books of the future would treat the Kliptown meeting as one of the most important landmarks in our history. John Hatch, the Public Relations Officer of the British Labour Party, in an article published in the *New Statesman and Nation* of January 28, 1956, under the title "The Real South African Opposition," conceded that some degree of success was achieved by the Congress Movement when it approved the Charter. Finally, in his May Day Message published in *New Age* of April 26 this year Moses Kotane reviewed the political achievements of 1955 and came to the conclusion that the most outstanding one was the C.O.P. which produced the world-renowned document—the Freedom Charter, which serves as a beacon to the Congress Movement and an inspiration to the people of South Africa.

WORLD-WIDE ATTENTION

Few people will deny, therefore, that the adoption of the Charter is an event of major political significance in the life of this country. The intensive and nation-wide political campaigning that preceded it, the 2,844 elected delegates of the people that attended, the attention it attracted far and wide and the favourable comment it continues to receive at home and abroad from people of divers political opinions and beliefs long after its adoption, are evidence of this fact.

Never before has any document or conference been so widely acclaimed and discussed by the democratic movement in South Africa. Never before has any document or conference constituted such a serious and formidable challenge to the racial and anti-popular policies of the country. For the first time in the history of our country the democratic forces irrespective of race, ideological conviction, party affiliation or religious belief have renounced and discarded racialism in all its ramifications, clearly defined their aims and objects and united in a common programme of action.

The Charter is more than a mere list of demands for democratic reforms. It is a revolutionary document precisely because the changes it envisages cannot be won without breaking up the economic and political set-up of present South Africa. To win the demands calls for the organisation, launching and development of mass struggles on the widest scale. They will be won and consolidated only in the course and as the result of a nation-wide campaign of agitation; through stubborn and determined mass struggles to defeat the economic and political policies of the Nationalist Government; by repulsing their onslaughts on the living standards and liberties of the people.

The most vital task facing the democratic movement in this country is to unleash such struggles and to develop them on the basis of the concrete and immediate demands of the people from area to area. Only in this way can we build a powerful mass movement which is the only guarantee of ultimate victory in the struggle for democratic reforms. Only in this way will the democratic movement become a vital instrument for the winning of the democratic changes set out in the Charter.

FOR ALL CLASSES

Whilst the Charter proclaims democratic changes of a far-reaching nature it is by no means a blueprint for a socialist state but a programme for the unification of various classes and groupings amongst the people on a democratic basis. Under socialism the workers hold state power. They and the peasants own the means of production, the land, the factories and the mills. All production is for use and not for profit. The Charter does not contemplate such profound economic and political changes. Its declaration "The People Shall Govern!" visualises the transfer of power not to any single social class but to all the people of this country be they workers, peasants, professional men or petty-bourgeoisie.

It is true that in demanding the nationalisation of the banks, the gold mines and the land the Charter strikes a fatal blow at the financial and gold-mining monopolies and farming interests that have for centuries plundered the country and condemned its people to servitude. But such a step is absolutely imperative and necessary because the realisation of the Charter is inconceivable, in fact impossible, unless and until these monopolies are first smashed up and the national wealth of the country turned over to the people. The breaking up and democratisation of these monopolies will open up fresh fields for the development of a prosperous Non-European bourgeois class. For the first time in the history of this country the Non-European bourgeoisie will have the opportunity to own in their own name and right mills and factories, and trade and private enterprise will boom and flourish as never before. To destroy these monopolies means the termination of the exploitation of vast sections of the populace by mining kings and land barons and there will be a general rise in the living standards of the people. It is precisely because the Charter offers immense opportunities for an over-all improvement in the material conditions of all classes and groups that it attracts such wide support.

CAN IT COME ABOUT?

But a mere appraisal of a document however dynamic its provisions or content might be is academic and valueless unless we consciously and conscientiously create the conditions necessary for its realisation. To be fruitful such appraisal must be closely linked up with the vital question of whether we have in South African society the requisite social forces that are capable of fighting for the realisation of the Charter and whether in fact these forces are being mobilised and conditioned for this principal task.

The democratic struggle in South Africa is conducted by an alliance of various classes and political groupings amongst the Non-European people supported by white democrats. African, Coloured and Indian workers and peasants, traders and merchants, students and teachers, doctors and lawyers, and various other classes and groupings: all participate in the struggle against racial inequality and for full democratic rights. It was this alliance which launched the National Day of Protest on June 26, 1950. It was this alliance which unleashed and waged the campaign for the defiance of unjust laws on June 26, 1952. It is this same alliance that produced the epoch-making document—the Freedom Charter. In this alliance the democratic movement has the rudiments of a dynamic and militant mass movement and, provided the movement exploits the initial advantages on its side at the present moment, immense opportunities exist for the winning of the demands in the Charter within our life-time.

THE FORCES WE NEED

The striking feature about the population of our country and its occupational distribution is the numerical preponderance of the Non-Europeans over Europeans and the economic importance of the former group in the key industries. According to the 1951 Population Census the population of the country consists of 2,643,000 Europeans as against 10,005,000 Non-Europeans, a numerical disparity which is bound to have a decisive bearing on the final outcome of the present struggle to smash the colour bar. According to the *Official Year Book of the Union of South Africa (No. 27—1952–53)* there were 46,700 Europeans employed by the gold mines and collieries at the end of 1952. The number of Africans and Coloureds employed on the mines for the same period was 452,702, a proportion of 1 European employee to nearly 8 Non-European employees. The racial composition of industrial employees in establishments with over 10 employees during the period 1948–49 was as follows: Europeans 33 per cent; African 51.5 per cent; Asiatics 3 per cent and Coloureds 12.5 per cent. According to the same Year Book, during 1952 there were 297,476 Europeans employed on farms occupied by Europeans and 2,188,712 Africans and 636,065 other Non-Europeans.

These figures reveal the preponderant importance of the Non-European people in the economic life of the country and the key task of the movement is to stimulate and draw these forces into the struggle for democratic reforms. A significant step was taken in Johannesburg on March 3, 1955, when a new trade union centre—The South African Congress of Trade Unions—was formed with delegates from 34 unions with a total membership of close on 42,000 and when for the first time in the history of trade unionism in South Africa, African, Coloured, European and Indian workers united for a fighting policy on the basis of absolute equality. Peter Beyleveld, who was elected the first president of the Congress, emphasised in his opening address that trade unions would be neglecting their members if they failed to struggle on all matters affecting them. The trade unions, he pointed out, should be active in the political field as in the economic sphere for these two hung together and could not be isolated from one another. With 42,000 organised workers on our side and fighting under the flag of a trade union centre that has completely renounced racialism and committed itself to a militant and uncompromising policy, it only remains for us to redouble our efforts and carry our message to every factory and mill throughout the country. The message of the new centre is bound to attract the support of the majority of the workers for they have no interest whatsoever in the country's policy of racial discrimination.

OUR ALLIES

The workers are the principal force upon which the democratic movement should rely, but to repel the savage onslaughts of the Nationalist Government and to develop the fight for democratic rights it is necessary that the other classes and groupings be joined. Support and assistance must be sought and secured from the 452,702 African and Coloured mine workers, from the 2,834,777 Non-European labourers employed on European farms and from the millions of peasants that occupy the so-called Native Reserves of the Union. The cruel and inhuman manner with which they are treated, their dreadful poverty and economic misery, make them potential allies of the democratic movement.

The Non-European traders and businessmen are also potential allies, for in hardly any other country in the world has the ruling class made conditions so extremely difficult for the rise of a Non-European middle class as in South Africa. The law of the country prohibits Non-Europeans from owning or possessing minerals. Their right to own and occupy land is very much restricted and circumscribed and it is virtually impossible for them to own factories and mills. Therefore, they are vitally interested in the liberation of the Non-European people for it is only by destroying white supremacy and through the emancipation of the Non-Europeans that they can prosper and develop as a class. To each of these classes and groups the struggle for democratic rights offers definite advantages. To every one of them the realisation of the demands embodied in the Charter would open a new career and vast opportunities for development and prosperity. These are the social forces whose alliance and unity will enable the democratic movement to vanquish the forces of reaction and win the democratic changes envisaged in the Charter.

UNITY BRINGS STRENGTH

In the present political situation in South Africa when the Nationalist Government has gone all out to smash the people's political organisations and the trade union movement through the Suppression of Communism Act and its anti-trade union legislation, it becomes important to call upon and to stimulate every class to wage its own battles. It becomes even more important that all democratic forces be united and the opportunities for such united front are growing every day. On March 3, 1955 a non-colour-bar trade union centre is formed. On June 26 the same year "in the most spectacular and moving demonstration this country has ever seen" 2,844 delegates of the people adopt the Charter and 4 months thereafter more than 1,000 women of all races stage a protest march to Pretoria to put their demands to the Government—all this in the course of one year. In fact, the rise of the Congress Movement and the powerful impact it exerts on the political scene in the country is due precisely to the fact that it has consistently followed and acted on the vital policy of democratic unity. It is precisely because of the same reason that the Congress Movement is rapidly becoming the real voice of South Africa. If this united front is strengthened and developed the Freedom Charter will be transformed into a dynamic and living instrument and we shall vanquish all opposition and win the South Africa of our dreams during our lifetime.

Document 15. "The Demand of the Women of South Africa for the Withdrawal of Passes for Women and the Repeal of the Pass Laws," Petition presented to the Prime Minister [sponsors not shown], August 9, 1956

We, the women of South Africa, have come here today. We represent and we speak on behalf of hundreds of thousands of women who could not be with us. But all over the country, at this moment, women are watching and thinking of us. Their hearts are with us.

We are women from every part of South Africa. We are women of every race, we come from the cities and the towns, from the reserves and the villages. We come as women united in our purpose to save the African women from the degradation of passes.

For hundreds of years the African people have suffered under the most bitter law of all—the pass law which has brought untold suffering to every African family.

Raids, arrests, loss of pay, long hours at the pass office, weeks in the cells awaiting trial, forced farm labour—this is what the pass laws have brought to African men. Punishment and misery—not for a crime, but for the lack of a pass.

We African women know too well the effect of this law upon our homes, our children. We, who are not African women, know how our sisters suffer.

Your Government proclaims aloud at home and abroad that the pass laws have been abolished, but *we women know this is not true,* for our husbands, our brothers, our sons are still being arrested, thousands every day, under these very pass laws. It is only the name that has changed. The "reference book" and the pass are one.

In March 1952, your Minister of Native Affairs denied in Parliament that a law would be introduced which would force African women to carry passes. But in 1956 your Government *is* attempting to force passes upon the African women, and we are here today to protest against this insult to all women. For to us an insult to African women is an insult to all women.

We want to tell you what the pass would mean to an African woman, and we want you to know that whether you call it a reference book, an identity book, or by any other disguising name, to us it is a PASS. And it means just this:—

- That homes will be broken up when women are arrested under pass laws
- That children will be left uncared for, helpless, and mothers will be torn from their babies for failure to produce a pass
- That women and young girls will be exposed to humiliation and degradation at the hands of pass-searching policemen
- That women will lose their right to move freely from one place to another.

In the name of women of South Africa, we say to you, each one of us, African, European, Indian, Coloured, that we are opposed to the pass system.

We voters and voteless, call upon your Government not to issue passes to African women.

We shall not rest until ALL pass laws and all forms of permits restricting our freedom have been abolished.

We shall not rest until we have won for our children their fundamental rights of freedom, justice, and security.

Document 16. Statement, by the All-in African Conference called by the Interdenominational African Ministers' Federation, October 4–6, 1956

The African people of the Union of South Africa, at the invitation of the Interdenominational African Ministers' Federation, assembled in conference held in Bloemfontein from the 4th–6th October 1956, to consider the Tomlinson Report.

The representative character of the conference was indicated by the fact that over 394 delegates drawn from all parts of the country, both rural and urban, and representing all shades of African political and other opinion, were in attendance.

Careful consideration was given to all aspects of the report, the discussion being preceded by papers prepared by leaders of African thought who are acknowledged authorities in their field with which they dealt.

After detailed examination of the principles and policies enunciated in the report, the conference desires to place on record its total rejection of the report as a comprehensive plan for the implementation of Apartheid in South Africa, for the following reasons:—

(1) The Tomlinson Report concedes at chapter 25 par. 22 "that a solution of this problem will only have been achieved, when a satisfactory arrangement in regard to the political aspect is arrived at."

This conference can find nothing in the report remotely resembling a satisfactory arrangement in regard to the political aspect. An arrangement on their own premises could logically only mean sovereign independence for the so-called Bantu Areas.

(2) The report states the choice before South Africa in the following terms, chapter 25 par. 42, "The commission believes that it is possible so to regulate our race relations in this country, as to ensure to both groups a maximum degree of satisfaction. It is evident that one group should not seek to further its interests and future position at the cost of the other. Satisfaction can only be obtained on the basis of an ethical formula, which meets all the requirements of justice and equity. This can be stated as follows:—

"That as the Bantu come to share our Christian principles and our civilisation, and their sense of duty and of responsibility develops, all rights and privileges, as well as duties and responsibilities will have to be accorded them either (a) together with the Europeans (i.e. as part and parcel of the European community); or (b) together as Bantu (i.e. in their own communities). There can be no middle course in the future. Indeed, the present so-called middle way leads, as already pointed out, inescapably towards integration. The only alternatives available are, therefore, either the path of ultimate complete integration (i.e. of fusion with the Europeans), or that of ultimate *complete* separation between Europeans and Bantu."

This conference does not subscribe to the view that the choice before South Africa consists only of two cast-iron alternatives—viz. "ultimate complete integration" or "ultimate complete separation between Europeans and Bantu." Conference maintains that a proper reading of the South African situation calls for co-operation and interdependence between the various races comprising the South African nation and denies that this arrangement would constitute a threat to the survival of the white man in South Africa.

(3) The conference finds that the net result of the implementation of the Tomlinson report will be a continuation of the status quo and indeed an

aggravation of the worst evils of the present system including their extension to the protectorates. Under the present conditions the policy and practice of Apartheid denies the African inalienable and basic human rights on the pretext that the African is a threat to white survival and denies him:—

(a) A share in the Government of the country.

(b) Inviolability of the home.

(c) Economic rights, the rights to collective bargaining and to sell labour on the best market.

(d) The right to free assembly and freedom of travel, movement and association.

(e) Inviolability of person.

(f) Civil rights.

ECONOMIC

This conference has examined the detailed plans for the economic development of the Reserves put forward by the Commission but can find no justification for the view that this development should be linked with the application of the policy of Apartheid. The Conference maintains that any programme of rehabilitation and development of these distressed areas of the Union based upon this ideological approach will not command the desired support and co-operation of the African People.

The general economic development of the resources of all parts of the country in which the skills and abilities of all its peoples are utilised is sound policy. But a separate plan of development of the Native areas based on the policy of Apartheid and the concept of separate national homes for the Africans coupled with deprivation of basic and economic opportunities and rights in the rest of the country is something totally unacceptable to this conference.

Furthermore, this conference notes that the Government itself in its white paper on the report has rejected some of the principal and most significant recommendations of the Commission and has thus undermined the goals which it sets out to achieve. Thus the claim that the Government is moving in the direction of these goals emerges as a hollow political bluff.

CIVIL RIGHTS

In dealing with the question of civil liberties, the Tomlinson Report is at pains to prove that in regard to their "wider civil rights" the Africans are "substantially in no worse position than other sections of the population."

This conference rejects this false picture of the South African situation which seeks to gloss over the glaring inequalities and disabilities from which the Africans suffer under the mounting discriminatory legislation of a Parliament in which they have no effective representation.

The continuation of this policy has already created a grave situation in which orderly government and the foundations of South Africa as a viable state are seriously threatened. Police raids, banishment orders, dismissals for political non-conformity, extension of the pass system to women, detention camps, farm prisons, convict labour, the slave markets, euphemistically called the labour bureaux and all the other trappings of a police state constitute an insufferable burden to the African people.

The conference reiterates the demand of the African people for the abolition of discriminatory laws and the extension of full citizenship rights to all which alone will guarantee peaceful and harmonious relations between black and white in South Africa.

EDUCATION

The recommendations of the Tomlinson Report on Education are unrealistic as they propose to prepare pupils for a life in a society which is non-existent—a mythical Bantustan. Economic and world forces tend to channel African development in the opposite direction of co-operation and interdependence.

One of the tests of a good educational system is whether it is able to throw up leaders of ability and character. In spite of the promise of full development opportunities in the future separate sphere, it seems that the training of leaders does not occupy a very high place in the priorities of the new system. Thoroughness, breadth of vision and individual excellence are being played down as against superficial education of the mass of the people.

Further the compulsory use of the African languages as media of instruction throughout the educational system will tend to reduce horizons and make true university education impossible by diminishing the opportunities of inter-communication between the African groups themselves and the wider world in general of which they form a part.

The contemplated establishment of a Bantu University of South Africa with constituent colleges organised on an ethnic basis would be a further threat to academic freedom. The colleges established under such a scheme of differentiation would not only be starved of adequate financial support but would also suffer from isolation from the other university institutions of the country and deterioration in academic standards, equipment, staff and personnel.

CHURCHES

The Commission looks upon the Church or Churches as something to be controlled and used by the government to further its own schemes. The conference disagrees with the Commission on the grounds that the Churches are the instruments of God for the establishment of His Kingdom on earth. And therefore answerable to God with a right to intervene in moral issues affecting the nation as a whole.

SEPARATE AREAS AND NATIONAL HOMES

Conference rejects the theory that there can be in South Africa so-called European Areas and Bantu Areas. Africans and other Non-Europeans claim that there is not an inch of South African soil to which they are not entitled on an equal basis with Europeans. Conference therefore asserts that Africans and other Non-Europeans are entitled to all rights, privileges and immunities enjoyed by Europeans wherever they live and work. Conference therefore condemns the mass removals of Non-Europeans and their dispossession of freehold rights under the Native Resettlement Act of 1952, the Group Areas Act of 1950 as amended and similar legislation.

Conference rejects the concept of National homes for Africans in certain arbitrarily defined areas for the following reasons:—

a. Africans are the indigenous inhabitants of the country with an indisputable claim to the whole of South Africa as their home.

b. They reject the concept on the futher ground that there is no part of the country to whose development they have not made their full contribution.

c. They reject the concept finally because it facilitates the exploitation and economic strangulation of the Africans and perpetuates white domination.

TAXATION

The Tomlinson Report has suggested a revision of the direct taxation paid by the Africans, "With a view to an increase in such taxation commensurate with their high earning capacity and the low monetary value of the pound."

In the opinion of this conference it is difficult to appreciate the Commission's suggestion and reasoning because for precisely the same reason of low monetary value of the pound the earning capacity and the ability to pay direct taxation of the African are affected. It must be noted, further, that the Commission seems to have taken no account of the increase in recent years of the number of Africans who pay Income Tax on the same basis as Europeans. The Commission has also not considered the inequality of the present system of direct taxation of the Africans upon which it has based its recommendations, nor can direct taxation alone be a true index of the full contribution of the African People to the total revenue of the country without taking into account their contribution in indirect taxation.

The belief so widely held by white South Africans that it is so-called white monies that are financing African services and welfare is in total disregard of the fact that the very profits and incomes made by Europeans are the result of the use of Africans as an essential factor in production and low wages paid to them. In other words it is the Africans who are subsidising Europeans and not vice versa.

CONCLUSION

This conference is convinced that the present policy of Apartheid constitutes a serious threat to race relations in the country. Therefore in the interests of all the people and the future of our country this conference calls upon all National organisations to mobilise all people irrespective of race, colour or creed to form a united front against apartheid.

This conference welcomes the initiative of Idamf [Interdenominational African Ministers' Federation], in bringing together African leaders to consider the Tomlinson Report and its implications for South Africa and appeals to the Christian Churches in South Africa to take a clear and unequivocal stand in the defence of Christian and human values now being trampled underfoot in the name of Apartheid.

Conference appeals to that strong and powerful body for which the Dutch Reformed Church speaks with recognised authority to re-examine its approach to the race question. Conference calls upon all South Africans who realise the dangers and effects of Apartheid to take positive steps to break down the colour bar in group relations. We urge them furthermore to ensure that democratic and Christian opinion expresses itself on discriminatory legislation in ways most likely to impress on the mind of the people of South Africa the urgent need for a positive alternative to Apartheid or separate development.

> Signed on behalf of Conference
> (Rev.) Z. R. Mahabane
>   Chairman of National Conference
> (Rev.) A. L. Mncube
>   Secretary of National Conference

Documents 17a–17b. ANC (Transvaal) Annual Conference of November 3–4, 1956

Document 17a. Presidential Address by E. P. Moretsele

Mr. Speaker, ladies and gentlemen, the Nationalist Government continues to launch savage attacks on the democratic movement in South Africa. The amended section of the Natives' Urban Areas Act, which gives power to the Government and the local authorities to refuse the entry of Africans into proclaimed and urban areas is increasingly being used to attack and frighten all Africans who oppose the repressive policies of the Government. Anna Silinga and Greenwood Ngotyana, two leading Congressites in Cape Town, were arrested, prosecuted and expelled from the peninsula under this vicious section. Moses Kotane, a well known leader, Simon Tyiki, Chairman of the Sophiatown branch of the African National Congress, and scores of others in different parts of the country, became the victims of this notorious measure. It is also being used to effect the removal of thousands of Africans from the urban areas and to compel them to work on European farms.

Fresh assaults on the movement were made during the last session of Parliament when the Government introduced two Bills to amend the Native's Urban Areas Act and a third one known as the Native's (Prohibition of Interdicts) Bill, all of which are now law. The first amendment gives power to local authorities to banish any African within the jurisdiction of a local authority if, in the opinion of such authority, the presence of any African in such area is detrimental to the maintenance of peace and order. The case of Viola Hashe, a prominent trade unionist, and that of the four Natalspruit leaders who are being banished from Germiston by the City Council of that town, reveal that this measure is intended to be used against those who oppose the reactionary policies of the Nationalist Government.

The second amendment empowers the Government to banish any African from one area to another without prior notice and has already been used in two instances to secure the removal of two chiefs from their tribes. Chief Msutu of Peddie in the Cape and Chief Ramadiba Mokgatla of Zeerust were recently exiled without previous notice and without being given an opportunity to defend themselves. The Native's (Prohibition of Interdicts) Act deprives an African of the right to seek redress in a court of law against his banishment. Thousands of freedom fighters, known and unknown, have been persecuted under section 10 and unless the Congress adopts effective measures to stop and deter the Nationalists, thousands of other fighters and democrats will fall victim to even more brutal onslaughts from the Nationalists.

The government's decision to extend passes to African women is being opposed and fought by the Congress movement throughout the country. A nation-wide campaign of agitation was launched last year, culminating in a demonstration to Pretoria in October of the same year, by 10,000 women of all races. Since then the campaign has been developed and intensified and successful demonstrations by women to local authorities and Native Commissioners were held in almost every important city in the country. In August this year, 20,000 African, Indian, Coloured, and European women staged a historic march to Pretoria to voice the nation's militant opposition to and uncompromising rejection of the extension of passes to African women. Hardly any other issue has ever stung the women of South Africa into action as this decision of the Government. Hardly any other issue has ever united the women of our country as this one.

But in spite of the remarkable and far-reaching success of the campaign so far, serious organisational weaknesses still exist and a lot of work requires to be done. In a population of 12½ million, 20,000 is still a small number. More women must be drawn into the movement so that the issue might be fought in an organised and disciplined fashion. Opposition is not as yet strong and powerful enough to compel the Government to withdraw its decision and the movement has not penetrated deeply into the country dorps and rural villages.

Because of these weaknesses, and in defiance of the well-expressed wishes of the people primarily affected, the Government has not been deterred and plans are afoot to introduce Reference Books on the farms and country dorps. The plan of the Government is perfectly clear. Alarmed by the resistance it is encountering in the cities and being aware of the weaknesses in the countryside, they have decided to isolate and encircle the areas where resistance is most effective. At present the passes are being introduced to women in the countryside and thereafter the cities will be attacked with all the viciousness and brutality for which the Nationalists are famous.

In rejecting the Group Areas Act the Congress has repeatedly pointed out that the whole purpose of the act is to uproot the Non-European people from their homes and business premises and to protect Europeans from economic competition. Subsequent events have fully justified our standpoint. In almost every sitting of the Board set up in terms of the Act the question at issue has invariably been that of removal of Non-Europeans from some area. In no case has it been used against Europeans. In terms of the recent Group Areas Proclamation in Johannesburg, Indian shopkeepers in Newclare and Newlands which serve approximately 13,000 Africans have been ordered to close their shops by not later than the 3rd August, 1958. At a Conference of the people of the Western Areas of Johannesburg held in Sophiatown on the 14th of last month and organised by the Western Areas Anti-removal Committee, a resolution was passed to fight the removals under the Proclamation. It was also decided to place the whole question of the operation of the Group Areas Act before the United Nations and the Afro-Asian group of nations. The recent conference of the South African Indian Congress held in Johannesburg during last month also resolved to fight the removals to the bitter end. As the vanguard of the liberation movement in South Africa it is our sacred duty to arouse the people of South Africa to stand up and fight against the removal of people from their homes and business premises.

The General Election for the Union Parliament will be held in 1958, and in their desire to entrench themselves in power for many years to come the Nationalists are groping desperately for vote-catching issues which will guarantee their victory in the forthcoming elections. The Republican issue is no longer the favourite theme it used to be, for even the extremists in the Nationalist party apparently have realised that the time is not opportune for the pressing of the matter and that to do so might damage their own interests.

Two important steps have been taken by the Nationalists in this direction. Firstly, about six months ago [April 30, 1956], the Minister of Justice, Mr. C. R. Swart, announced in Parliament that the police were investigating a case of high treason and that in due course about 200 people would be arrested and prosecuted for this offence. Pressed for more particulars regarding the matter, the Minister became evasive, vague and ridiculous in the extreme. It could not have been otherwise for he very well knew, even as he made his announcement, that the whole question of the so-called high treason was a political stunt and a deliberate falsehood calculated to frighten the Whites into believing that the oppressed people of South Africa were plotting an uprising against the State. A European public stirred into panic by deceitful stories of insurrections and rebellion by the Blacks might connive at the persecution of the opponents of apartheid and the suppression of the Congress movement.

Six months have elapsed since the Minister made his announcement and still no action whatsoever has been taken to punish those who are alleged to be guilty of this crime in spite of the fact that, according to the Minister, the very existence of the state is in serious danger. Why, the Minister knows only too well that no high treason has been committed, that the security of the state has not been in any way threatened, and that the whole affair is an election stunt to win them votes. In all probability the Nationalists will carry out their threat, but they are in no hurry to do so for the election takes place two years from now. An arrest and prosecution at the present moment might lead to an acquittal long before the elections are held with serious political repercussions to themselves. The plan therefore, is to time the arrest in such a way that the final decision of the courts might not be known until after the elections. This is a fraud which the Congress movement must immediately bring to the notice of the country. The whole country must be told without delay that the Nationalist Government, like all fascists, have learnt the trick of framing up those who do not want to submit to their reactionary policies.

The Congress does not conceal its violent hatred of the racial policies of the Government and has vowed to fight repression to the bitter end. As your President, I call upon you to dedicate yourselves unconditionally to the greatest cause for which we fight—the cause of freedom. I call upon you to participate fully and without reservation in this great task and to reckon with death and disaster without flinching from the task. Only by doing this can we save the people of South Africa from the ravages of Nationalist rule.

In spite of all the efforts of the Government to suppress democracy in South Africa, the Congress movement is growing in strength and influence and is rapidly becoming the real voice of the people of South Africa. In June, 1955, harassed and intimidated by the police and overcoming numerous difficulties, more than 2,000 elected delegates of the people attended the historic Congress of the People in Kliptown and unanimously adopted the Freedom Charter. In October, last year, 10,000 women marched to Pretoria, and this number was doubled this year when the women of South Africa again staged a protest march to the capital. All over the country the people are astir, vital battles against exploitation are being fought and important victories won. In this connection, I think it proper to refer to the well-known and famous Evaton Bus Boycott where the people have successfully carried on a stubborn and militant struggle for more than a year. This event has extremely significant lessons for us for it shows that important victories will be won by the movement once the people are united and determined. On your behalf, I wish to congratulate the people of Evaton and to wish them even more success in their future struggles against injustice.

Our struggle for a democratic South Africa is being resisted by the Supreme Council, the Bantu Congress of Bhengu, and National-Minded Bloc, the Africanists, *Bantu World* and by some unimportant individuals and cliques. The first three organisations have completely disappeared from the political scene and the Africanists are a mere clique of confused intellectuals and their views have no impact whatsoever on the thinking of the people. The *Bantu World* has for a long period consistently conducted a ruthless and malicious campaign of lies and slander against the African National Congress. It openly supported the policy of the National-Minded Bloc and practically became its mouthpiece. It opposed our policy of democratic unity and accused us of being dominated by foreign groups and ideologies. In September this year it published a front page report, wherein it alleged that the Transvaal Executive had called a secret conference of Congress branches that supported the Freedom Charter and left out those branches that are opposed to the Charter. In the same article it deliberately lied and said that there was a move to replace me from the Presidency. In an effort to create disharmony and strife at the Bloemfontein Conference called by the Interdenominational African Ministers' Federation, it suggested that Congress had secretly planned to disorganise the Conference. These instances clearly show that the *Bantu World* is, in spite of its name, not working for the true and best interests of the African people.

I have been a member of Congress for more than thirty years, and I have seen it fighting many battles and winning important victories. I am confident that on the basis of the Freedom Charter the democratic forces [will defeat the forces] of reaction. Neither the brutality of the Nationalist Government, nor the lies of the *Bantu World* can divert us from our sacred goal—namely FREEDOM IN OUR LIFETIME!

Document 17b. Executive Report [Extracts]

As a matter of policy and programme the Transvaal Executive in realising the immensity of organisational problems set itself the task of drawing up the plan to alleviate its organisational problems and difficulties. The plan reads as follows: . . . .

In regard to organisation . . . each and every branch of the Congress has regular annual elections as failure to have these elections will create quarrels and endless disputes. At least once a month there must be a members' meeting to discuss the report of the branch committee, relating to the progress of the branch regarding recruiting, local issues, finance and propaganda, etc. The methods of raising funds, organisation, recruiting of more members into the organisation, local day-to-day issues affecting the people, progaganda and correspondence from the senior A.N.C. organs, in particular, and other bodies in general, and educating of members and special training necessary to equip leaders, with knowledge to run the affairs of Congress [must be discussed].

Failure on the part of the branch committee to perform its duties as indicated above, must be regarded as serious by the provincial executive committee, which must meet at least once a week to discuss reports of the various sub-committees, as outlined above, in addition to other incidental matters connected with the movement. Regular mass propaganda meetings must be organised by every branch at least once a month.

(4) *ORGANISATION OF BRANCHES:*

The whole success of a Provincial Executive Committee depends on its ability to organise the most important units of the Congress, i.e., the branches. It is the primary duty of the Province to assist the Branch

Committees in the art of Organisation. Different methods are required for different branches according to the local conditions. For example, the methods of organisation in regard to the central branch of Johannesburg and Orlando are different to some extent and differ greatly from rural branches. The central branch must be organised on the factory and hostel system. There must be a Congress steward for every factory, and every hostel must be sub-divided into groups of two hundred persons under the leadership of a steward. There must be a meeting of all factory and hostel stewards at least once a month to discuss finance, organisation, propaganda and linking up of local issues and the Freedom Charter.

Location areas must be organised on the basis of the M-Plan. The branch committee must nominate stewards for every hundred houses in the street. These houses must be visited regularly and Congress propaganda propounded. The first task of an organiser or steward is to propagate the programme of the A.N.C. in such a way that can be understood. Do not start with asking people to join. Start with finding first the interest of the family or person concerned and then connect the interest of that family with the principles of the A.N.C. and the Charter. When you have successfully convinced these people, then you ask them to join the A.N.C. Do not bully people into joining Congress in a parrot or fanatic fashion. Conviction must be the most important principle.

(5) The method of appointing full-time functionaries for the Congress has been considered seriously by this Provincial Executive. As a beginning there should be appointed a full-time organiser for every 800 houses in a location or 800 persons in town. The duty of such an organiser would be to get at least 500 persons to become members of Congress and collect 2/6 per member and the monthly 1/- levy. The salary to be £15 per month. . . .

(6) To achieve the above objectives the organiser to be appointed must receive at least three months training in Congress policy and politics. The provincial committee, the branch committee, full-time organisers and part-time stewards must also receive special training provided by the province in regard to political theory, political education of the masses, propaganda, and organisations. In all aspects of organisation, special attention must be given to the Freedom Charter and passes in general and their extension to African women. The implementation of the plan necessitated the inclusion of all the Congress Organs, viz., the women and youth leagues. . . .

EFFICIENCY CAMPAIGN.

The Executive committee has taken a survey and discussed the state of the branches and their style of work. The Executive is convinced that in some branches there is no awareness of the need to be alert and vigilant in branch activities. There is a great deal of sluggishness and inefficiency in our style of work. Some branch officials are aware of the abnormal times in which the struggle is being conducted today, and as a result the efficiency of our work has suffered tremendously. . . .

In a mass multiracial demonstration against unjust laws, 20,000 women descended on Pretoria to present their protest to the Prime Minister. Pretoria has never seen anything like this. It was yet another warning to the Nationalist Government that African women do not want passes. The 9th August 1956 will be recorded in our history. Women from the four Provinces demonstrated their solidarity against the pass—no matter what it was called.

Prior to the historic march, local protests, demonstrations were staged in many parts of the Transvaal and beyond our borders. Native Commissioners and local location Superintendents and their officials were besieged by thousands of women who demonstrated their opposition to the extension of passes to African women. Women also resented very strongly the open and callous raping of the education of the African child. The fight goes on. After these demonstrations at some centres women were arrested and charged for staging an illegal procession in Ermelo. Mrs. V. Hashe was issued with a banishment order in Roodepoort, Messers Rampai, Mofokeng, Ngwenya and Mkwanazi in Natalspruit are also issued with banishments.

In Klerksdorp women, men and children and old women were clubbed by the municipal police. This was the result of the attitude of the municipality of Klerksdorp. This council is noted for its notoriety in oppressing the Africans.

We note the cruel and the inhuman banishment of Mr. Duma, a member of the organisation, by the same Klerksdorp Council. Then followed Mrs. Sophi Moremi and many others have been threatened. Members will note that it is the same council which was quoted when Parliament was busy crucifying the African with its Prohibition of Interdicts Bill—now an Act. The organisation now, more than ever, must intensify its campaign by contacting every other African, by implementing the M plan. Every house, factory, farm and reserve must be mobilised. It is the duty of every Congress member to go out to the people.

EVATON.

Another centre of sharp activities was Evaton. We have on record a boycott of Buses by the residents against the increase of fares. This was one of the longest in the history of any bus boycott. This boycott was won by the consistent sustained solidarity of the residents. We regret also to note the loss of eight lives. It was tragic. After a year when a settlement is reached, what do we see? The members of the police attacked the leaders of the boycotters by framing charges of murder against them. However, their case continues. . . .

MASS REMOVALS.

Going far into the country we still note with regret the open day-light robbery of people's lands by the Nationalist Government—the following areas were pounced upon: e.g., Mamahlola tribe and Mametja tribe, Tzaneen, many others are taking place; others are threatened.

Places where Africans own titled properties, the Nationalists have made it their business to grab these places, because, it has always been the policy of the white Governments of this land to disown Africans of land, as such. The African is landless, moneyless, hungry, naked and in fact slaves in their land of birth. Today, the people of Sophiatown, New Clare, Lady Selborne and Evaton are the victims of this gangsterism, old people will be driven into farms and our sons and daughters will be deprived of all things that are good and essential in life.

The appeal to members is to organise and organise until every force in this land replaces the present Government with a Government of the people.

In Brakpan there is also a bus boycott, in spite of all the foul methods applied to foil the boycott. The people of Brakpan have proved by their solid stand that a united people can always achieve their needs. Here again the Council has brought in the Native Urban Areas Amendment Act to banish the people's leaders. Hence, some are already the victims of this Act, namely Mr. Ncala who has been ejected and Mr. Thauthau who is also awaiting his fate. These banishments have gone on almost in most of the Urban and Rural Areas. The victims have been the chiefs and Congress members.

Places like Venterspost, Albertynsville, Hamanskraal, Rustenburg, Bushbuckridge etc. etc. have received their fatal blow.

One could go on indefinitely, for also, mention must be made of the new attack made on places where Africans enjoyed the Freedom of movement. The introduction of the permit system is one mean Act the Government has introduced in places like the Western Areas, Alexandra and very recently Evaton. Leaders like Mr. Tyiki of Sophiatown and other Congress members and also Mr. Moses Kotane of Alexandra were made targets of this vicious and barbarous system. In any event, we can be certain that the progressive world is on our side for a new world is unfolding before us.

MAYIBUYE! I–AFRIKA!
FREEDOM DURING OUR LIFETIME!

Document 18. "Why are we treated like animals?" "Police brutalities in Newclare!!!" Two flyers issued by the ANC, calling meetings on December 1 and 2, 1956

WHY ARE WE TREATED LIKE ANIMALS?

IN OUR HOMES IN THE WESTERN AREAS,
WE ARE TREATED WORSE THAN ANIMALS!

ARMED POLICE INVADE OUR HOMES, DRAG US, OUR MOTHERS OUT OF THEIR BEDS ALMOST NAKED, BEAT THEM UP, THROW THEM IN THE TROOP CARRIERS AND FINALLY CHARGE THEM FOR NOT HAVING PERMITS!

WE MUST PROTEST!!

EVERY MAN, WOMAN AND CHILD IN SOPHIATOWN . . .
MARTINDALE . . . NEWCLARE AND WESTERN
NATIVE TOWNSHIP MUST JOIN THE
MASS DEPUTATION
to NEWLANDS POLICE STATION

TO PROTEST TO THE DISTRICT COMMANDANT OF THE POLICE AGAINST THESE DAILY POLICE RAIDS AND BRUTALITY!

PROTEST DAY
SATURDAY 1st DEC. 1956
at 9:30 AM

POLICE BRUTALITIES IN NEW CLARE

POLICE ARMED WITH RIFLES, REVOLVERS, AND STICKS ARE TERRORISING MEN AND CHILDREN IN NEW CLARE. HUNDREDS HAVE BEEN ARRESTED. FROM 3.0'CLOCK IN THE MORNING ON MONDAY, SCORES OF EUROPEAN AND NON-EUROPEAN POLICE INVADED THE HOUSES OF PEOPLE IN *NEW CLARE.*

THEY DRAGGED MEN AND WOMEN OUT OF THEIR BEDS AND DEMANDED FOR PASSES, AND PERMITS, MEN AND WOMEN WERE BEATEN UP AND CHILDREN TERRORISED.

266

TO SUBJECT DEFENCELESS OPPRESSED PEOPLE TO SUCH
INHUMAN TREATMENT SHOULD MAKE THE CONSCIENCE
OF ALL DECENT PEOPLE REVOLT.

The African National Congress calls upon the Authorities to put an immediate stop to the iniquitous raids.

AN INJURY TO ONE IS AN INJURY TO
ALL!!

Therefore the African National Congress appeals to all Freedom loving people to rally in their thousands to a mass meeting of protest, to be held in "No. 1 SQUARE, NEW CLARE" on Sunday 2nd Dec. 1956, *at 9.30 A.M.*

DOWN WITH ALL POLICE RAIDS!!!
Issued by the A.N.C.

Document 19. Telegram of December 6, 1956 from the Secretaries of the ANC (Natal) and the Natal Indian Congress to the Minister of Justice and Statement to the press regarding the arrests for treason on December 5

TELEGRAM:
African National Congress (*Natal*) and Indian Congress, behalf vast majority of people in Province strongly condemns your action causing arrest of officials and members of our congresses. We advise you that such action will not intimidate our people but will spur them on to greater efforts to resist Nationalist tyranny and fight for and win Freedom and Democracy for all South Africa, irrespective race, colour or creed.

* * * * *

STATEMENT:
The African National Congress and the Natal Indian Congress strongly condemn the action taken by the Nationalist Government in the arrest yesterday of over 140 leaders of the National Liberation Movement in our country. This action is an outrageous frameup by the Nationalist Government to remove from the mass of the people all those democratic leaders who stood firmly against the vicious and offensive policies and practices of the Government.

In Natal those arrested include the President-General of the A.N.C., Chief Albert J. Luthuli and the President of the S.A.I.C., Dr. G. M.

Naicker, the provincial secretaries of the African National Congress and the Natal Indian Congress and members of the Executive Committees of the Congress.

The Government alleges that these popular leaders have committed high treason. The people of South Africa now know too well how the Nationalists have, unashamedly, branded as a "communist" every democratic person who has had the courage boldly to oppose their misdeeds and evil intentions. Having failed to deceive the vast majority of the people into withdrawing their support from the Congresses, Mr. Swart and his colleagues are now resorting to the nauseating tactics of trying to stampede the country by dramatic arrests on charges which have been unknown in peacetime in the history of South Africa.

These arrests and charges follow the familiar fascist pattern set by Hitlerite Germany. It is significant that they have taken place on the eve of the opening of Parliament in January next year and the General Elections in 1958. For a long time now Mr. Swart and other Cabinet Ministers have been telling the electorate that the Police were raiding the homes and offices of many persons with the object of unearthing treason and that soon hundreds of people would be arrested. The Government has kept the country, particularly the electorate, in suspense and at a carefully planned time have staged the "coup d'etat". It is no mere coincidence that the arrests have taken place in December, 1956.

We warn white South Africa, including Nationalist supporters, that they will be sealing their own fate if they allow themselves to be deceived by the present moves of the government. There is no doubt that during the next session of Parliament the Government will seek even more ruthless dictatorial powers under the pretext that they are necessary to deal with the "enemies of the state."

In the midst of these alarming and despotic attacks it is the duty of all South Africans to stand steadfast in their struggle for freedom and democracy in South Africa and to oppose with all their might any attack on their fundamental rights of freedom of speech, organisation and assembly.

We call upon all South Africans black and white who value freedom to struggle unitedly against the dictatorship of the Nationalists of whom it may be said in classical terms that those whom the Gods wish to destroy they make mad first. The Congresses will not be intimidated or subdued by these arrests and new leaders will rise to take the place of those removed. We will not rest until our leaders are freed and our country firmly marches on the road to full democracy for all irrespective of race, colour or creed.

We are also confident that democratic world opinion will be on our side in this struggle and we call upon the nations of the world big and small to condemn in no uncertain manner the Fascist actions of the Nationalist Government in South Africa.

Document 20. "The Struggle Against Passes." Report of the National Consultative Committee to the Joint Executives of the ANC, SAIC, SACPO, SACOD, and SACTU, December 1956

"The Struggle Against Passes."

1. *Is this a new struggle?*

The struggle against passes has gone on, sometimes fiercer, sometimes quieter for many years. The new round of struggle, which is opening as a result of the threat to extend the passes to African women, does not mark the beginning of the struggle but only a new phase. It opens up the possibility of widening and making changes in the whole struggle against passes and of rousing great sections of the people for the struggle.

2. *Can Victory be won in a single battle?*

In such a long drawn out war as the war against the pass laws it would be foolish to expect that victory can be won by a single action of the people. The pass system is the foundation of the whole cheap labour system in South Africa; the ruling class will not easily be forced to give it up. It follows, that victory in the struggle against pass laws must not be looked for in every minor skirmish against the enemy. In a long drawn out battle, there will be many minor victories, minor defeats, many advances, many retreats. But final victory for the people means the end of the cheap labour system of South Africa. It can only be achieved finally by the overthrow of the ruling class, and by the winning of the Freedom Charter as the ruling policy of South Africa.

3. *Is the present struggle item of any importance?*

The present struggle against passes for women can well prove to be the decisive turning point of the whole long drawn out war. There is no aspect of the pass sytem which will cause such bitter opposition as this; and the present situation therefore enables us to bring thousands of new militant fighters into the struggle, to rouse those who have become accustomed to and tolerant of the pass laws for a new effort and to awaken the conscience and the resistance of those sections of the people, white, coloured, Indian, who do not themselves directly suffer under these laws.

4. *Is this a struggle of the women alone?*

Clearly the women are in the front rank of the battles now opening. They are the victims the government has singled out for its latest attack. But the struggle is not one for women alone. It is one in which women and men must join together, each helping, assisting and encouraging the other as circumstances demand. By themselves, the women can perhaps resist the latest attacks. But their resistance would be stronger and lead more surely to victory if the menfolk fight with them. But even a temporary victorious resistance of the women to the present attack will not end the struggle against the pass laws. Alone, it will only postpone the day of the attack till the government can muster greater force. It will only be a breathing space before a new attack in a new direction. This must be a joint campaign of men and women, whose aim is to end the pass system and the government which upholds it.

5. *Is the slogan 'Women shall not carry passes' correct?*

It is argued by some, that the present battles will be decided, won or lost on the question of whether the womenfolk take the new passes. Therefore, it is argued, the political line of the campaign must be to encourage women under no circumstances to accept the passes. From this line of policy, it is clear, develops the concept that the pass laws can be fought and beaten only by acts of passive resistance—individual or collective—by acts of standfast refusal on the part of the women to accept the new passes. No one can deny that such acts would be of tremendous significance, advancing the struggle of the people and giving new morale and enthusiasm to the whole campaign. Nothing should therefore be said or done which would discourage such acts of defiance, passive resistance.

But this is not the only way to fight, nor even the best way. Even widespread acts of passive resistance alone cannot, in the long run, deter the government from its course, if it is determined to use all its force, authority and power to enforce its will. This was one of the lessons taught us by the Western Areas Removal Campaign, which we cannot forget. We must not let our enthusiasm blind us to the prospects of overwhelming government force—mass deportations, sackings from jobs, evictions from homes, etc.—which can be unleashed against passive resisters, to break their resistance. Passive Resistance is good, effective, valuable at the right time, in the right circumstances. But it is not the only way. . . .

6. *What other slogans can be advanced?*

There are other ways of struggle against the pass laws, each of which has its place. Pass laws can be fought by demonstrations and strikes, by petitions and meetings, by boycott and resistance and disobedience, by active struggle as well as passive. Which of these ways is the best? This can only be conceived in the precise circumstances in which we find ourselves in each area at any one time. Sometimes one and sometimes another, we must learn from the errors of the Bantu Education and Western Areas Campaigns not to be rigid, formal, tied by preconceived ideas about the only possible way to forms of action which do not fit the circumstances. We must be ready to use any and every means of struggle which are appropriate and possible at any time and which advance us to our goal.

The campaign against the new passes for women must not therefore be allowed to stand or fall by the success or failure of passive resistance by the women. The campaign must be conducted—as befits a longdrawn out war—with flexibility and skill, now using one weapon, now another, now passive now active. The slogan to be instilled into the minds of the masses is not therefore 'the women shall not carry passes', but rather 'We shall struggle every inch of the way, against passes', 'down with passes'.

7. *How do we decide what precise action to take?*

We must rely on the good sense, responsibility and flexibility of our leaders. They must weigh up at every stage of the campaign what the state of organisation preparedness is. What are the people ready to do? What action will meet with the united support of the people and carry forward the struggle? There must be no reckless 'militant sounding' calls to action which are not attuned to the reactions and state of militancy of the people. We must beware of calls to action which do not lead all the people into action but serve only to cut the militant vanguard off from the masses. But we must be active, organising, explaining, agitating the people, preparing them for struggle. And we must be bold when the time for action comes. Mass work, mass agitation, leading to struggle. This is the A.B.C. of Congress policy of the pass laws.

PART TWO

The Last Stage of Non-violence
1957—May 1961

OVERVIEW OF 1957-1959: PRE-SHARPEVILLE

As the Nationalist government continued to shower legislative and judicial blows on the ANC in 1957, and cabinet ministers openly threatened to ban the organization, Congress faced again the troubling prospect that it might have to go underground to survive.[1] Yet just when the need for Congress members to pull together had never seemed greater, dissension in the organization appeared to be spreading. Torn between the traditions of democratic procedure and the pressing demands of unity, ANC leaders sometimes found themselves in the uncomfortable position of having to steamroller decisions and stifle criticism arising from the general membership. In the Transvaal, communication between leaders and ordinary members was further impaired by the high-handed methods sometimes employed by less able or experienced cadre who were filling leadership positions left vacant through bannings and the enforced presence of most top Congress officials at the Treason Trial.

The treason arrests in late 1956 had provoked a defiant response in Congress, which was summed up in the slogan "We Stand By Our Leaders." In the Transvaal Congress, however, the spirit of unity expressed in the slogan proved to be short-lived. At a provincial conference in October 1957 the incumbent Transvaal executive (many of whom were on trial) invoked the call to "stand by our leaders" and prevailed upon the assembled delegates to return them to office *en bloc* as a show of unity and loyalty. Nevertheless, by the time the national conference met in December, it was clear that there was serious dissatisfaction with the running of Transvaal affairs. A group of "petitioning" branches filed complaints alleging that the provincial election had been unconstitutional, and that outlying branches had not been invited to the provincial conference. The financial statement presented to the conference was attacked as unsatisfactory.[2] The African press chided the Transvaal leadership for treating ordinary Congress members like "babies" and mere "voting cattle."[3] Similar disputes plagued areas of the Cape. Instead of uniting under the pressure of government harassment and restrictions, the ANC appeared to be slipping into a morass of squabbles and petty rivalries. The Africanists, convinced that the ANC's leadership was out of touch with mass sentiment, mounted new attacks on the leadership. Eventually, the Africanists' failure to prevail within the ANC was to lead them, in November 1958, to a complete break, a development that will be described more fully later.

During the late 1950s, when the gulf between Africans and the white government was becoming wider, Afrikaner Nationalist intellectuals joined other whites in reaching out to engage African leaders in dialogue. These moves will also be described more fully later.

Treason Trial

The Treason Trial, which was to attract international attention as one of the largest-scale political trials ever held, began after the arrest of 156 persons in December 1956. It was to go on for more than four years, until March 29, 1961, when the accused were finally judged not guilty. The trial immobilized or preoccupied many leaders of the ANC, boosted their prestige, strengthened solidarity with non-African allies, and blurred the distinction between long-standing African aspirations and Communist aims. Because of the trial, younger and less experienced leaders, both loyalist and Africanist, rose to prominence. Meanwhile, the trial helped to foster unity between the Congress alliance and white liberals. Sympathetic whites accepted the heavy burden of obligation to provide for the defense and care of the accused and, to some extent, the care of their families. But while liberals sought closer relations with Africans, left-wing whites and Indians sat day after day in the unsegregated dock of a segregated courtroom, closely identified as fellow accused with the African opposition.

Demonstrative crowds of Africans gathered in the Johannesburg streets when the trial's preparatory examination began on December 19, 1956. On the following day, the police, acting "with evident glee," according to a foreign observer, used clubs and shot above the crowd; they were publicly rebuked by their officers.[4] The preparatory examination and the trial itself soon settled into a tedious, complex, and protracted affair. Meanwhile, the accused were on bail, free to meet privately with outsiders (within the terms of individual banning orders) when the court was not in session. In December 1957, charges were withdrawn against sixty-one persons, including Lutuli and the second-ranking official of the ANC, Oliver Tambo. Their dismissal seemed inexplicable when later it became clear that the allegedly violent policy of the ANC itself was the central issue of the trial. When proceedings finally began again under a revised indictment in January 1959, the number of accused was reduced to a first string of thirty. Only a few were ANC leaders of importance; many but not all of the thirty were distinguished from others who had earlier been among the accused by the more violent tone of the rhetoric they had used. Nevertheless, Lutuli, Professor Matthews, and other leaders who were not on trial but testified for the defense were, in effect, as much on trial as were the thirty.

The government's control of the extraparliamentary opposition and its restrictions on the leaders were so pervasive and its unused statutory

powers so extensive that invocation of the law of treason seemed superfluous unless the intention was to hang the accused. Speaking privately in
January 1959, however, Oswald Pirow, the chief prosecutor, provided a
different view of government intentions. When the accused were convicted, he said, he would recommend that the "stooges" among them be
given suspended sentences as a "warning" and that the "worst Natives,"
for example, Robert Resha, be imprisoned for five years.[5] On the other
hand, he said, he would support the discharge of Professor Matthews if
Matthews took the witness stand and disavowed the incendiary documents
found in his possession, thus showing that he had learned a lesson.
(Matthews was discharged at an early stage but testified later for the
defense.) More important to Pirow than five-year jail terms, however, was
the desirable effect of the trial itself, which he considered to be largely
responsible for a rapid decline in agitation after December 1956 and a
generally quiet period during 1957–1958. The trial also had bought the
government valuable time, during which the police could become more
efficient in dealing with the small number of "agitators," according to
Pirow, who played upon a "hysterical" Native population. The government now had time to go ahead with plans for separate development that
appealed to the Natives, 90 percent of whom were "good." However,
Pirow noted bluntly, if any serious threat to white rule were to arise, the
shooting of 5,000 Natives by machine guns would provide quiet for a long
time to come.

Johannesburg Bus Boycott

In focusing on the decline of agitation (as he saw it) following the arrests
for treason, Pirow overlooked an extraordinary demonstration of the
capacity of urban Africans, acting on their own initiative, to unite in
another prolonged protest on a bread-and-butter issue: because of a penny
increase in fares, more than 50,000 Africans in Johannesburg began a
boycott of their overcrowded and uncomfortable buses on January 7, 1957.
For three months, they walked to work, some persons walking up to twenty
miles a day.[6] Their boycott followed a similar year-long effort by blacks in
Montgomery, Alabama, which had ended successfully in December 1956.
The precedent for the Johannesburg boycott was the Evaton bus boycott of
1955–56. Economic grievances rather than political aims inspired the
boycott, although leaders of the ANC saw it as an opportunity for
politicization. So did some of the other leaders of the boycott who were
active in the broad coalition of local groups that voiced the spontaneous
sentiments of affected Africans. The boycott was remarkably free of
violence, although the government charged that the bus riders were intimidated, and boycott leaders accused the bus company of hiring thugs to

beat up some of the leaders. The boycott also was an example of African success in winning satisfaction on an economic grievance and recognition from both employers and government of the necessity of subsidizing transport so long as wages were depressed.

Inevitably, the boycott, beginning just one month after the treason arrests, took on political significance. B. J. Schoeman, the minister of transport, accused the ANC of attempting to "test its strength" as a "subversive organization." "If we are to give in now," he declared, "I do not know what the future has in store for us."[7] But ANC leaders were only a part of the coalition that coordinated the boycott as it spread rapidly from Alexandra, eight miles from the center of Johannesburg, to other townships in the vicinity and to Pretoria.

ANC leaders who were on trial but lived in Alexandra while on bail were involved in organizing the rallies that initiated the boycott. Senior leaders of the ANC sitting in the preparatory examination of the trial in the large Johannesburg Drill Hall frequently discussed the boycott and consulted with representatives from the townships, who visited freely with the accused during the tea and lunch breaks.[8]

Local initiative was of major importance, however, and the boycott took on an impetus of its own. In Alexandra, for example, the People's Transport Committee coordinated a number of groups, among whom Africanists and Trotskyites were prominent. According to *The World,* these groups included "the Standholders and Tenants' Association; the Movement for a Democracy of Contact; Tenants' Association; Workers' League; the local branch of the A.N.C.; A.N.C. (Madzunya group); the A.N.C. (National Minded)."[9] *The World* reported that these groups were led by the Alexandra Vigilance Association and described Josias Madzunya (see below) as "the soul of the . . . bus boycott movement."[10] But no single person could be credited as the leader. Other important figures (who were not on trial) included the ANC activists Thomas Nkobi and Alfred Nzo.[11]

As the boycott wore on, sympathetic protests and boycotts began elsewhere on the Rand and in Port Elizabeth, East London, Uitenhage, and other centers. White drivers sometimes showed sympathy by giving lifts to African walkers despite police intimidation. Employers, concerned about the fatigue of their employees and the potentialities of the boycott, sought contact with African leaders. One of the remarkable features of the bus boycott was the fact that representatives both of the government and of employers finally found it necessary to consult with popular leaders, not merely with individual African personalities who were reputedly "moderate."[12]

In a number of private meetings beginning in February, representatives of chambers of commerce and industry, the Johannesburg City Council, and the Native Affairs Department and Department of Transport talked with leaders of an older generation: Dr. Xuma, Dr. William Nkomo, Paul Mosaka, P. Q. Vundla, D. Xorile, and others. (Nkomo and Vundla were active in the international Moral Re-Armament Movement and were thus prominent "moderates.") Writing in *The World*, Dr. Xuma referred to himself as "an outsider," however, and insisted that he, unlike Mosaka and Xorile, had disavowed the status of leader and had attended in order to urge consultation with persons actively leading the boycott.[13] Private talks between these leaders, including ANC treason trialists, and businessmen were finally arranged. A key intermediary in making these arrangements was Ambrose Reeves, the Anglican bishop of Johannesburg.

Mass meetings voiced disapproval of one plan proposed by white businessman: to refund one penny at the end of each bus ride (thus requiring another queue) while efforts were made during a three-month period to raise wages. By early April, general agreement was reached on a plan whose formation had involved some of the treason trialists: the Chamber of Commerce would sell four-penny vouchers that could be exchanged for five-penny tickets. Negotiations proceeded despite continued threats against the boycotters by the minister, disunity among the leaders, and a good deal of popular confusion and clamor for continuance of the boycott. Opposition to the plan was expressed in a leaflet headed "Azikwelwa!" ["Don't ride—don't get on!"] (Document 22), which described ANC leaders as "purely loud-mouthed self advertisers" who would "sell-out" the struggle.

The boycott came to a halting end in Johannesburg in mid-April. A settlement was delayed in the Pretoria boycott and the boycott was resumed there. The extent of the boycotters' success became evident in June, when the government quickly put through a bill (the Native Services Levy Act of 1957) requiring employers to make a monthly payment for each African employed in commerce and industry as a subsidy for transport. The government also contributed to the subsidy. "It was the first act of parliament in the forty-seven years of the Union to have been passed as a direct result of African pressure." wrote Anthony Sampson.[14] In July, fares reverted to the pre-boycott level.

The bus boycott gave rise to a new campaign slogan—"Asinamali! ["We have no money!"] We want £1 a Day!"—and a renewed interest in the efficacy of boycott. In February 1957 a SACTU conference called for a £1-a-Day campaign.[15] Later in the month the ANC in Cape Province, suspending its sympathetic boycott of buses, declared that it would campaign for £1 a day and the boycott of Nationalist-produced commodities and Nationalist-controlled finance houses.[16] Africans were to carry out a number of economic boycotts against local targets, especially in eastern Cape Province, during the late 1950s. The tactics expressed the confidence of Africans in their potential economic power and a growing sense of political destiny for Africans everywhere on the continent. This sense of destiny was strengthened by news of Ghanaian independence in March 1957.

Despite the treason arrests, local and provincial organizations continued to hold conferences. The secretarial report of the ANC Youth League in the Transvaal on June 15–16, 1957, listed eighteen members among the accused in the Drill Hall (Document 25). Demonstrations also continued to take place. On June 13, 1957, for example, African and other women demonstrated outside Parliament (Document 24). In preparing for the annual commemoration of June 26, the national consultative committee of the Congress alliance, inspired by the bus boycott, warned of the importance of local "initiative" and "imaginative planning" in accordance with local circumstances.[17] It suggested a timetable of religious services on June 26, combined with sporting and cultural activities, and torchlight processions. A printed flyer (Document 26, which the committee hoped would be adopted by local groups and reproduced) suggested other activities: family gatherings to read the Freedom Charter, "mass gatherings," and prayers at 11 A.M.

Anticipating the possibility of a stay-at-home on June 26, 1957, both employers and the police undertook to stifle activity and warned that absenteeism for political purposes would be dealt with severely. The police once again raided offices and seized leaflets. Meanwhile, the president of the Transvaal Chamber of Industries publicly described the £1-a-day demand as "reckless and completely irresponsible."[18] Writing to all members of the Chamber in a "confidential" and "urgent" memorandum of June 24, he warned that June 26 was "a 'test of strength' feeler which must be faced by Industry with resolute solidarity. . . ."[19] Members were urged to advise "Native employees" that they would have police protection in coming to work and that absentees would be summarily dismissed and, if "guilty of misconduct," banished from urban areas.

When June 26 arrived, the treason accused stood in silent prayer in the courtroom, while in Johannesburg, according to one foreign observer, "more than half the workers stayed at home. . . . the most effective protest that Congress had yet achieved."[20] In most large factories, especially in the industrial areas to the west of Johannesburg, The Star reported that "the strike was 70 to 80 percent effective."[21] Stay-at-homes in the eastern Cape and mass meetings and torchlight demonstrations elsewhere were reported by New Age. No future observances of June 26 were to compare in effectiveness with that of 1957.

Because "the vast majority" in the townships was believed to be law-abiding, according to the Chamber of Industries memorandum, the absenteeism that did occur could be interpreted by employers as the consequence of intimidation; apparently few workers were dismissed. In some cases of public employment, however, there were mass dismissals of absentee Africans, most of whom were re-employed, except for a small number of "ringleaders."

New ANC Constitution

During 1957 and 1958, Africanist dissension embroiled many conferences of the ANC. The annual conference of mid-December 1957, however, finally adopted a new constitution (Document 27) that sought to meet some of the organizational problems presented by the Africanists and, more importantly, a long-felt need for more centralized direction as well as local initiative. There was support also for a constitution more detailed than the so-called Xuma constitution of 1943 (Volume II, Document 29a), a brief document which had replaced the original, exceedingly detailed constitution of 1919 (Volume I, Document 23). Discussion of possible changes in the constitution had begun in 1952, and after the appointment of a committee headed by Tambo in 1953, various drafts were made and circulated.[22] One was identified with the Cape; another, providing for a major shift in power from the provinces to national headquarters in Johannesburg, was identified with the Transvaal.[23] The document finally adopted is sometimes spoken of as the Tambo constitution.

The new constitution did not realize the fears of Lutuli and Professor Matthews that the provincial organizations would be eliminated or reduced to facades, nor did it incorporate any pronounced leftist bias. Nevertheless, a shift toward more centralized direction, de-emphasis of the unwieldy provincial organizations, and encouragement of local or regional initiative were evident in the following changes: (1) branch treasurers were obligated to pay one-third of membership dues directly to the national treasurer, whereas formerly provincial executive committees were expected to transmit this amount, but in practice, sometimes failed to do so; (2) although the old membership dues of two shillings and sixpence annually were retained, the National Executive Committee was authorized to impose a national levy on all members; (3) higher organs were given disciplinary power over lower organs (for "conduct detrimental to the interests of the Congress or the African people"), whereas formerly they had had disciplinary power only over individuals; (4) the National Executive Committee was reduced in size from 18 members to 12 (if one excludes the participation of provincial officers); and (5) several provisions specified the authority of national organs and the obligation of individuals and subordinate units to comply with national policy. The constitution also provided that three or more branches within a province could organize a regional committee and that this committee was obligated to implement the instructions of the National Executive Committee as well as of provincial units.

Although some leaders looked upon the new constitution as one that would prepare members for the possibility that the government might outlaw the ANC, its provisions were typically bureaucratic in their detailed concern with defining hierarchical relations, official positions, and obligations for reporting. The new office of deputy president-general was created, but no provision was made for the succession in the event of the death of the president-general. (Upon Lutuli's death in 1969, Tambo, who had been elected deputy president-general in 1958, became acting president-general.) The Women's League and the Youth League were given constitutional recognition in the hope that they would be encouraged to act independently in building "auxiliary" mass movements. Finally, the new constitution not only retained the principle of nonracialism in its qualifications for membership but also incorporated the Freedom Charter, explicitly endorsed the aim of "universal adult suffrage," and expressed support for "national liberation . . . in Africa and the rest of the world."[24]

1957–58: New Policies and Protests

As 1957 came to an end, the ANC looked back upon still another year of added restrictions in the implementation of apartheid and toward another general election and the possibility of still more restrictions. The most vehement criticism by white opponents of the government during 1957 had concerned the enactment of the Native Laws Amendment Act, which granted the government new powers to forbid contact between Africans and whites. The act also sought to curb the growing numbers of urban Africans by narrowing the qualifications for residence in urban areas.[25] English-speaking church leaders threatened disobedience if Africans were prohibited from attending churches in white areas, and even the Dutch Reformed Church expressed concern about church autonomy. The act dealt with more than churches, however, providing in broad terms that the minister of native affairs could ban multiracial meetings. (This provision was supplemented by a 1957 amendment to the Group Areas Act imposing a racial limitation on attendance at a public cinema or place of refreshment in an area designated for residence by a particular race.) A typical consequence of the new legislation was the action of the multiracial International Club in Pietermaritzburg in June 1957; anticipating a ministerial order and anxious to prevent victimization of its members, the club announced it was going to close down.

Speaking later at a Nationalist Party conference, Dr. Verwoerd foresaw the end within five or ten years of a system that produced Africans who sought inclusion within the ranks of the whites. "We will use an iron hand," he said, "with regard to mixed gatherings aimed at undermining the Government's apartheid policy."[26] In the same month, the Department of Native Affairs declared that, beginning in 1958, whites would not be allowed in African locations for any purpose without special permission.

Striking at a particularly important area of contact—the racially "open" English-speaking universities and Fort Hare (which Africans of all tribal backgrounds, Coloureds, and Indians were eligible to attend)—the government in 1957 proposed to extend apartheid and tribal separation to higher education. Opposition to the bill spurred local demonstrations and international condemnation, especially among academics. In May 1957, in an unprecedented demonstration, more than 3,000 faculty and students, many in academic gowns, were led by the principal of the University of the Witwatersrand in a march through downtown Johannesburg to protest the bill. A similar march of more than 300 students and staff members, led by Ambrose Makiwane, president of the Fort Hare Students' Representative Council, was held in the small town of Alice. Nonetheless, in June 1959, the bill was enacted as the Extension of University Education Act (discussed below).

Apartheid was also intensified in 1957 by legislation that removed nonwhite nurses, despite their protest, from the governing bodies of the profession and provided for separate registers of white, African, and Coloured nurses. Another bill opposed by African organizations, which became law in 1958, taxed African women for the first time and increased the taxes paid by every African male over eighteen.

ANC-sponsored demonstrations in opposition to these and other apartheid policies were nonviolent, in accordance with long-standing ANC policy. (Whether or not ANC policy was nonviolent was currently at issue in the Treason Trial.) In the rural areas, however, although opposition was usually quiet, there had been sporadic eruptions of violent hostility against stock culling and soil conservation schemes, especially in the years after 1945 when the Smuts government introduced its Rehabilitation Scheme.

Rural opposition, sometimes fanned by local ANC leaders, was also directed at passes for women (in 1958, official teams entered some reserves to begin issuing passes), at increased taxation, and at the influx controls imposed on tribesmen looking for work in towns. The government's migratory labor system kept high the number of townsmen who returned periodically to the reserves, and urban grievances during the late 1950s became linked with tribal grievances. Discontent focused upon the establishment of the ''Bantu authorities'' scheme, which brought still more government controls into the system of indirect rule. In seeking to strengthen the chiefs, the government in 1957 shifted some powers, such as the power to allocate land, from the headmen to the chiefs. Some chiefs were disliked because they were autocratic and occasionally (like some of the headmen) corrupt. Local rivalries and grievances also raised tensions in rural areas during the late 1950s.[27]

Despite official warnings that tribal groups would lose financial and social services if they did not accept the Bantu authorities system, smoldering resistance and violence burst into open revolt in the Sekhukhuneland and Zeerust areas of the northern Transvaal, and disorder and rioting flared up in eastern Pondoland in the Transkei. Although the extent of the ANC's involvement is difficult to determine, the government on March 17, 1958, acting under the Native Administration Act of 1927, declared the

ANC to be "an unlawful organization" in certain areas because it was "detrimental to the peace, order, and good government" of Africans falling under the jurisdiction of the minister of native affairs. The minister banned the ANC from Sekhukhuneland, the Zeerust area, and two other rural areas of the Transvaal. It appeared that a piecemeal banning of the ANC in rural areas was under way.[28] ". . . Even in the Areas where it has not yet been banned," the National Executive Committee said in its report to the December 1958 conference (Document 31), "the fact that meetings cannot be held without the consent of a Chief and the Native Commissioner places the organisation in a position of illegality." In the circumstances, the report recommended the creation of "a core in every reserve" and "a peasants organisation" rather than mass membership in the ANC.

Despite the partial banning of the ANC, rural tensions continued to increase. During 1957–1960 in the Transvaal and the Transkei there were incidents of hut burnings, murders of Africans considered to be collaborators, and scenes of mass hostility: meetings of tribesmen, burning of women's passes, refusals to pay taxes, and bloody clashes with the police. Tribal leaders were deposed and deported, mass arrests were made and mass trials held, and large areas sealed off. Referring both to rural and urban demonstrations, including women's demonstrations against beer halls in the towns and in support of home brewing, the ANC's National Executive Committee observed in 1959 that "political struggles . . . are very often untidy, tempestuous and destructive." The executive agreed with Lutuli, however, on the necessity for planning and coordination.[29] Earlier, Lutuli had praised "the dynamic local struggle—interest and leadership" in the Transvaal, Cape, and Natal but criticized the failure to recognize the "need for a more coordinated plan with specific objectives for each stage."[30]

The ANC and the General Election of April 1958

The approach of another white general election on April 16, 1958, the tenth year in power of the Nationalist government, posed a test for the extraparliamentary opposition. Did an election in which only whites could vote make any difference? Africans in Cape Province elected three whites to the House of Assembly, but the government's policy was to remove even this token representation. Should Africans attempt to influence the election? Or was the election merely another occasion for African propaganda?

In an interview published in *New Age* on November 7, 1957, Lutuli discussed the forthcoming election. It did matter, he said, and he was explicit about "our desire for a United Party victory." Although "the

United Party tries to poison you slowly" while "the Nationalists murder you most ruthlessly," he said "a United Party government would provide a "respite" and also "opportunities" for whites and nonwhites "to come together," whereas continued Nationalist rule "will almost certainly strain already dangerously tense conflicts past breaking point, and bring about a national disaster." He urged the formation of a united front among all anti-Nationalists, including the United Party, an approach much favored by the ANC's allied organizations, which endorsed Lutuli's position.[31] Later, in an undated printed "Message to every voter from the African National Congress" (Document 28), Lutuli declared that the ANC supported neither the Nationalist Party nor the United Party; nevertheless, his desire for a United Party victory was clear enough. Voters were voting for the disenfranchised as well as for themselves, he said, and "we shall all of us live to regret" the consequences "if it [the Nationalist Party] is allowed to continue."

Lutuli suggested in his November 1957 interview that "election day could very well be a day of mass prayer and dedication to the freedom cause." A more ambitious demonstration was to be attempted, however. On March 16, 1958, a "National Workers' Conference" resolved to organize a week-long stay-at-home throughout the country, to begin two days before the election.[32] The conference itself was an outdoor weekend meeting (the first day was rained out) in Newclare, Johannesburg. The South African Congress of Trade Unions and the other organizations in the Congress alliance sponsored the conference, which was organized loosely, as the Congress of the People had been. According to *New Age*, 1,673 delegates were present, and about 3,000 observers.[33] Later, in order "not to be unrealistic," the Congress leaders decided that the stay-at-home should be only three days long, including election day, and should be undertaken only "where possible."[34]

The futility of any African effort to intervene in a white election soon became apparent. United Party spokesmen and supporting newspapers charged that the ANC really intended to stampede voters into voting for the Nationalists. "Stupid propaganda," said Tambo; the stay-at-home was "not designed to help either the United Party or the Nationalists."[35] Chief Lutuli expressed a similar reaction to a Nationalist Party charge that the ANC and the United Party had an electoral agreement. Africans did not intend to assist any particular party, he said; their intention was to make themselves heard.[36] The English-language press continued to claim that any stay-at-home would play into the hands of the Nationalists; and *The World* accused the ANC's leadership of having "lost touch with the masses," who opposed the stay-at-home and found the issues "unintelligible, confused, and wild."[37] Many persons had the impression that the stay-at-home was a SACTU, not an ANC, affair (Document 31). Further confusion resulted from criticisms by moderates like Dr. William Nkomo and continuing attacks by the Africanists, the latter suggesting that "the real sponsors of the show" had "ulterior motives."[38]

Once again, officials and employers reminded workers that they would be protected by the police and warned them of the severe consequences of absenteeism. Thousands of heavily armed police were mobilized, and the defense force alerted. On April 12, four days before the election, gatherings of more than ten Africans in all major urban centers were banned. (The ban, which had been in effect in some magisterial districts since 1954, was removed in piecemeal fashion over a period of nearly five months.)

The emerging policy of the ANC appeared confusing to urban Africans, and the stay-at-home proved a fiasco. At both national and branch levels, the reputation of the ANC's leadership suffered severe damage. On April 14 "the overwhelming majority" of the people in the Johannesburg areas of Sophiatown, Western Native Township, and Newclare and "thousands of workers all over the country" had stayed at home, according to a statement signed by Duma Nokwe, assistant secretary-general; yet "the overall picture was one of failure . . . bitterly disappointing, humiliating and exceedingly depressing" although "certainly not a fiasco."[39] That evening, the steering committee in charge of the campaign called off the stay-at-home. Some critics had argued for picketing on the morning of the second day to prevent people from going to work. In its wide-ranging post-mortem, the leadership criticized the proposed methods of picketing as a "very ugly" reliance on force—"you picket a minority—and *not* the majority." The ANC "must educate and convince people," its statement said, and work hard to implement the "M-Plan" with its emphasis on "slow and tedious house-to-house work" and word of mouth whereas at present ". . . we prefer the easy way, the way of streetcorner meetings, mass meetings and mass conferences, and large cumbersome units consisting of persons from [a] wide area."[40]

On April 16, 1958, whites went to the polls in the second general election since 1948. Both in 1948 and in 1953, the Nationalists had won parliamentary majorities with a minority of the popular vote. (In 1948 they had had the help of a minor party.) During the decade after 1948, there had been not only two redrawings of electoral district lines favorable to the Nationalists but also a steady migration of Afrikaners to cities and towns, especially on the Witwatersrand, which strengthened the Nationalists in a number of marginal districts. The United Party's professional organizers had no illusions about the possibility of defeating the Nationalists in 1958. In the election, the latter's estimated popular vote rose to roughly 50 percent—up from 40 percent in 1948—taking into account uncontested seats. (Not until the 1960 republican referendum were the Nationalists to win a clear majority of the popular vote; in the general election of 1961 they were to do even better.) Despite the evenness of the popular vote, the Nationalist majority in the House of Assembly rose to 66 percent of the seats elected by whites, a sharp contrast to the slim parliamentary majority of 1948. The Labour Party, which had appealed to the economic interests of white labor, failed to withstand the counter-appeals of nationalism and racism. Its five seats in Parliament were lost, and the party soon became defunct. The Liberal Party also took part in the election, with no expectation of winning a seat in a white district, but it broke new ground by using an African speaker in behalf of a white candidate.

In reviewing the year, the National Executive Committee (Document 31) reported that the election had "shattered" the "illusion" of change through the electoral system and that African intervention had shattered the myth that elections were a whites-only affair. The return of the Nationalists to power was not unexpected, Lutuli said, "but not the near land-slide that it was." White South Africa had fully endorsed the Nationalists' "*baasskaap* apartheid."[41] Nevertheless, both Lutuli and the National Executive Committee saw an encouraging growth in the number of "white freedom lovers."

The First Coloured Election

The new House of Assembly included four whites who had been elected by Coloured voters on April 3, 1958, the first communal election for Coloureds since their removal from the common roll in 1956. This election too was a disappointment to the Congress alliance. The South African Coloured People's Organisation had decided to participate and sponsored two white candidates: Pieter Beyleveld, president of the Congress of Democrats and a defendant in the Treason Trial, and Piet Vogel, a leader of the COD in Port Elizabeth. Long-standing arguments for and against boycott were canvassed once again. Six members of SACPO's Transvaal Committee, including Lionel Morrison and Adam Daniels, resigned in protest; and their support of the boycott was criticized by James LaGuma, the national president, as "negative, shortsighted and politically unscientific at this stage."[42]

Some 130,000 Coloured males were probably qualified to vote in Cape Province, but the number who were registered declined markedly (from about 48,000 in 1953 to some 24,000 in 1959). Because of the usual political apathy among Coloureds and support for boycott, only 14,451 Coloureds voted.[43] Most who voted were older members of the Coloured electorate who traditionally supported the United Party. They elected four pro-United Party candidates and gave only 813 votes to Beyleveld and 96 votes to Vogel.

New Hopes and Fears

Once again, during the months following the general election and the show of force and intimidation, there was a period of apparent inactivity by Africans. Because of the continued ban on African meetings (other than meetings for purposes of religion, sport, or entertainment or to hear members of Parliament or the provincial council), the ANC did not call a mass rally until Sunday, October 5, in Sophiatown (Document 29). Another mass rally held later in the month in Benoni was part of the fifteenth annual conference of the Transvaal Youth League (Documents 30a and 30b). In the meantime, in recognizing the June 26 anniversary, Congress leaders called for solidarity with the people of Zeerust and Sekhukhuneland and for collections of money to aid in their legal defense. Indians also chose that day for a mass meeting to protest new Group Areas proclamations for Durban, which would require 81,000 Africans, 65,000 Indians, and 7,000 Coloureds, but only 3,000 whites, to move. Despite the absence of Africans and (because June 26 was a weekday) of Indian workers, *New Age* estimated that about 20,000 people participated in the most impressive rally since the passive resistance campaign of 1946–1947.[44]

The death of Prime Minister Johannes Strijdom on August 24, 1958 appeared to Africans to mark the beginning of a new and ominous period because he was succeeded by Dr. Hendrik F. Verwoerd. As minister of native affairs, Verwoerd had become the foremost ideologist of positive apartheid or separate development, a man of "ruthless mind" and "the most ardent and relentless apostle of Apartheid," said Lutuli.[45]

While African leaders waited apprehensively for the forthcoming parliamentary session, they saw signs of growing support abroad. Opponents of apartheid in the United Nations had made perennial, impassioned attacks on South Africa's policy since 1946, but in October 1958 a change in U.S. policy occurred that disturbed Afrikaner Nationalist leaders more than all preceding actions of the United Nations. Under the presidency of Dwight Eisenhower, the United States ended its practice of abstaining on resolutions critical of apartheid and, out of step with the United Kingdom, voted for a relatively mild resolution expressing "regret and concern" that South Africa had not modified its racial policy.

Two months later, the All-African People's Conference in Accra, Ghana, helped increase the sense of identity felt by Africans in South Africa with movements on the continent for African independence and an end to racial domination.[46] (See below, page 322.) The conference called for economic sanctions and boycott of South African goods. Earlier in the year the first Conference of Independent African States, meeting in Accra on April 15, had condemned apartheid. (April 15 was celebrated a number of times thereafter in South Africa as Africa Freedom Day.) Meanwhile, during the second week in December, 1958, South Africans themselves were delegates to a nongovernmental conference in Accra that was widely representative of political parties and trade unions throughout Africa. Three delegates from the Liberal Party came from South Africa: Jordan Ngubane and, as the only white delegates from Africa south of the Sahara, Patrick and Cynthia Duncan. Ezekiel Mphahlele, having left South Africa for Nigeria, headed a delegation that represented the Congress alliance and, according to Ngubane, maintained a united front with the Liberals despite reports of antagonism.[47]

The events in Accra were greated enthusiastically at the ANC's annual conference in Durban on December 13–14, 1958. At the conference, the first to be held after the Africanist breakaway (described below), much stress was laid on the re-establishment of unity. A banner above the platform proclaimed "Free Our Leaders and Unite Behind Congress."[48] The Treason Trial, in recess after a withdrawal of the indictment, was to be resumed in January under a new indictment against only 30 of the 156 originally accused. Although there were some grounds for satisfaction with developments in the trial, the burden of numerous prosecutions and mass trials was much in the minds of delegates. "The theatre of political conflict is shifting to the law courts," the National Executive Committee said (Document 31) as it referred to:

The scores of Treason accused, the numberless crowds who have been prosecuted following the government's attempt to impose passes on Zeerust women, the hundreds who are facing mass murder trials in Sekhukhuniland, . . . the dozens who have been charged with incitement following the stay-at-home of April 14th, the trials involving thousands of women who took part in anti-pass demonstrations. . . .

The conference displayed "an astonishing upsurge of confidence," Mary Benson has written; the ANC had emerged (according to the liberal journal *Contact*) "more tightly knit and more powerful."[49] Chief Lutuli was elected to his third three-year term as president-general without opposition; Tambo was elected to the new post of deputy president-general; he was succeeded as secretary-general by Duma Nokwe, the young Transvaal advocate. Resolutions adopted by the conference foresaw "a long and bitter struggle" against passes and called upon the incoming National Executive Committee to appoint an anti-pass Planning Council and a council to plan national economic boycotts.[50]

Chronic problems remained, however; "on the propaganda side," for example, the National Executive Committee reported that "the main problem of publishing a regular official bulletin and a newspaper" had not yet been "tackled." The ANC also faced a new challenge from the Africanist group, which was planning its inaugural conference.

AAC and Anti-CAD

Like the ANC, the AAC had been wracked by severe strains, not so much internally as in its relations with the Coloured leaders of the National Anti-CAD, with which it was affiliated in the Non-European Unity Movement (NEUM). These strains came to a head at the AAC's annual conference of December 14–16, 1958, at Edenvale, Natal, the first annual conference since 1956. The AAC leaders debarred from the conference the delegates of the Society of Young Africa (SOYA, the AAC's youth organization) and the Cape New Era Fellowships, apparently because their leaders were considered to be revisionists. The latter groups were small discussion clubs composed mainly of Coloureds. Fraternal delegates from the Anti-CAD walked out in protest.[51] In his presidential address (Document 34), W. M. Tsotsi condemned revisionists who saw only class oppression and who denied "the reality of colour oppression." Such persons, he said, gave "a leftist interpretation" to the NEUM's 10-Point Programme, thus subjecting the movement to the danger of prosecution under the Suppression of Communism Act. Tsotsi also deplored their failure to recognize that "emergent African nationalism" was a progressive political force "in so far as it is genuinely anti-imperialism and anti-colonialism."

Some observers detected a parallel between the Africanist-loyalist split within the ANC and the split between the AAC and the Anti-CAD.[52] The analogy could be misleading because the latter split was a far more arcane mixture of dialectical dispute and personal rivalry. Nevertheless, the AAC–Anti-CAD dispute, like the Africanist-loyalist split, had racial overtones because of the long-standing effort of Coloured intellectuals in the Cape Town area to constitute themselves a vanguard of leadership for Africans in the AAC.

The treason arrests had provided an occasion for the expression of NEUM sympathy with the Congress movement, but SACPO participation in the Coloured election of 1958 had revived the pro-boycott passions that had both distinguished the NEUM and served to unify it. At the same time, showing signs of impatience with boycott, the AAC had begun to organize resistance to the Bantu Authorities Act. Tsotsi in his presidential address saw the act as an effort "to crush the rising African professional and business class which demands a share in the economic power based on capitalist democratic rights"; the Coloured leaders, however, described the AAC's concern as anti-working class, anti-peasant, and really an effort at "sharing the spoils with Imperialism at the expense of the people."[53]

The controversy was elaborated during 1959 in lengthy and vitriolic pamphlets issued by each side.[54]

1959: New Policies and Protests

In January 1959, at the beginning of the new parliamentary session, Prime Minister Verwoerd announced that the time was ripe to take the next step "towards placing the Natives on the road to self-government in their own areas."[55] These areas, to become known popularly as Bantustans, were provided for in the Promotion of Bantu Self-Government Act of 1959. The government obviously hoped that this development would decrease external pressures on South Africa. Eric Louw, the minister of external affairs, quoted the liberally inclined *Rand Daily Mail* as saying that the government, rather than the opposition, was seeking to adapt itself to "the post-Accra situation in Africa."[56] The bill passed its second reading in the House of Assembly on May 26, the day before a new ban was placed on Lutuli. It recognized eight Bantu "national units," that is, ethnic units rather than geographical areas. Tribal representatives (commonly described as ambassadors) were to serve as links between a national unit and its members who were working in the urban areas.

The act not only signaled a new development but also, by providing for the removal of the representatives of Africans in Parliament, marked the culmination of the long process of deterioration of African political rights. In 1910, Africans had been excluded from eligibility for membership in Parliament; in 1936, they had been removed from the Cape Province common voting roll; in 1951, the Natives' Representative Council, a national if ineffective mouthpiece, was abolished; and now Parliament was eliminating (as of 1960) a provision of the 1936 "settlement": the election of three whites to the House of Assembly by registered African male voters in Cape Province (some 18,000 in 1959) and the indirect election of four whites to the Senate by Africans in the four provinces.

Sir de Villiers Graaff saw the act as eliminating "the vital link" that "symbolized" the democratic system for millions of Africans. In August 1959, the United Party Congress reaffirmed its support for the representation of Africans in the House of Assembly and endorsed an expansion of such representation to all the provinces, not just the Cape, but maintained its policy of a whites-only Parliament and said the number of Natives' Representatives should be limited to eight.

The Promotion of Bantu Self-Government Act, growing out of the Bantu Authorities Act of 1951, furthered "*groot*" (great) apartheid. Similarly, the Extension of University Education Act of 1959 extended the principles of the Bantu Education Act of 1953 to university education, an action that was widely condemned in South Africa and in academic circles abroad as a violation of the universality implicit in higher education. The act provided for additional facilities for Africans, Coloureds, and Indians, but closed to them the doors of the racially "open" (though socially segregated) University of Cape Town and University of the Witwatersrand, except in the case of students who were already enrolled or had special ministerial permission to attend. (In June 1958, 73 Africans and 180 Coloureds and Indians were enrolled in mixed classes with whites at Witwatersrand and 37 Africans and 515 Coloureds and Indians at Cape Town. Nonwhites also attended the University of Natal but in separate classrooms.) Official policy proposed establishing separate Coloured and Indian colleges and three separate "ethnic" or tribal colleges for Africans. The University College of Fort Hare was to become a college for Xhosa and Fingo students.

For forty-three years, Fort Hare had had a racially mixed staff enjoying equal conditions of employment. Its student body, drawn from all African ethnic groups and (before 1953) from outside the Union, included Coloureds, Indians and, from time to time, a few whites.[57] Fort Hare had served as an example of racial harmony although the government viewed student protest there as a "smouldering and undesirable ideological development."[58] Its graduates, in the eyes of the government, were "black Englishmen" (Document 33). Academically, Fort Hare compared favorably with other South African universities. Its graduates, of whom Professor Matthews was the first—and its expellees—were among the leading African professional men and leaders both inside and outside South Africa.

On January 1, 1960, the minister of Bantu education was scheduled to take over control of Fort Hare, and its autonomy and academic freedom were to come to an end. Governing bodies and conditions of employment were to be racially defined. Because Fort Hare's faculty were to become civil servants, subject to official codes of discipline, Matthews saw them as "automatons hardly able to breathe or pass on to their students the spirit of free inquiry usually associated with universities."[59] Late in 1959 he was offered a contract on condition that he resign from the ANC and accept the new conditions.[60] He resigned from Fort Hare instead, thus giving up substantial pension rights at the age of 57, with three of his five children still in school. Other faculty members also resigned or had their services terminated before the end of the year.

Neither *groot* nor university apartheid had any immediate effect on the ordinary African. His grievances continued to be the pass system and its extension to women, arbitrary controls on movement and residential rights, police harassment, and the actions taken by chiefs and headmen in implementing unpopular official policies. Underlying these grievances were low wages, unemployment, and increasing taxes—poverty and the "ever-widening gap between earnings and essential family expenditure."[61] In impoverished rural areas where cattle culling was needed to reduce overstocking, the purpose of the scheme was not only misunderstood but also deeply resented because of the traditional importance of cattle and the historic shortage of land. Women also resented a new policy in some areas of demanding, rather than paying for, their services in the community dipping of cattle (to remove parasites). In urban areas they objected to prohibitions on the traditional home brewing of beer, which was a source of income for many families, and demonstrated to force the closing of municipal beer halls, which drained their husbands' incomes.

Although the incidence of protest is difficult to measure, there were a remarkable number of spontaneous and undisciplined demonstrations involving African women during 1959, particularly in rural areas. Much attention was focused on Natal, where there was sporadic turmoil both in urban "locations," notably in the Cato Manor slum of Durban, and the adjacent rural reserves for several months beginning in June. Despite restrictions on African meetings, women came together in mass gatherings, which were sometimes broken up brutally by white and African police, charging with batons.[62] There were scenes of rioting and bloody casualties, the destruction of government property, and mass arrests. About 2,000 women were arrested in Natal, according to the ANC (Document 33). In South Africa during the year, "close on 4,000, mostly women" were arrested and convicted, on trial, or under restriction, said Lutuli in December.[63] Minor protests included local bus boycotts, a hunger strike by nurses, and wildcat strikes. In Durban early in the year, some 1,500 African stevedores struck for higher pay and closed the harbor for twenty-four hours. The strikers were fired and denied the right to be in Durban, and outside labor was brought in.[64]

After a tour of Natal, Dr. W. W. M. Eiselen, secretary for Bantu administration and development, concluded that ANC agitators were responsible for the destruction (Document 32). On the other hand, Peter Brown, national chairman of the Liberal Party, observed from Pietermaritzburg that "the new militancy of the African women seems to have taken everyone by surprise, not least their own menfolk." He commented, "I have yet to meet a member of the ANC who knows how the demonstrations started, or who is anything but astounded by their extent." Demonstrations had been "more contagious than organized," he said, and had taken place "in areas where there has never previously been any sign of organised opposition to authority."[65] During the demonstrations, ANC leaders reaffirmed the policy of nonviolence, and volunteers sought to provide guidance and to win support for the ANC. They succeeded in bringing nearly 400 delegates from 45 rural areas to join more than 600 other delegates, according to New Age, in a Natal People's Conference in Durban on September 6.[66] Women delegates from rural Natal were also prominent, along with delegates from the Transkei, at the ANC's last annual conference in December 1959.[67]

In contrast to the disorganized protest in Natal were the ANC's attempts during 1959 to pursue its anti-pass campaign by organizing selective economic boycotts throughout the country, which they hoped would be reinforced by an international boycott of South African goods. Local initiative had begun boycotts during the preceding several years, especially in the eastern Cape Province. In Uitenhage in February 1959, the ANC circulated pamphlets directed at shopkeepers who sold cigarettes produced by the pro-Nationalist Rembrandt company of Anton Rupert. (The apprehensiveness of businessmen about the potentiality of boycotts was clearly evident in 1957 when the Rembrandt company sought and won a temporary injunction, later withdrawn at its request, against ANC boycott efforts.)[68] Meanwhile, the National Anti-Pass Planning Council, provided for by the ANC's 1958 annual conference, was considering the effectiveness of the recurring call for a bonfire of passes. It concluded that the use of economic power—"Industrial action in its various forms, strikes and go slow strikes"—was more effective. In particular, the Council pointed out, "by withdrawing our purchasing power [approximately £ 400,000,000 per annum, said the report] from certain institutions we can, as Chief Lutuli said, 'punch them in the stomach.' " Thus, passes and, ultimately, the system of oppression could be uprooted "despite the fact that almost all the forms of our struggle are now illegal."[69]

The report of the Council was read at the ANC's "mass national conference" of May 30–31, 1959, in Johannesburg. At the conclusion of the conference, Robert Resha called for a boycott of potatoes to begin at midnight as a new protest against bestial treatment of African farm laborers. The forced and illegal recruitment of these laborers and their abject conditions of life had recently been exposed once again, largely through habeas corpus petitions initiated by Joel Carlson, a Johannesburg attorney.[70] The boycott proved to be surprisingly successful during the following months until its official end on August 31, and probably contributed to a suspension of the farm labor system until a 1959 amendment to the Prisons Act provided that convicts could be sentenced to farm labor. On June 26, a wider boycott of the products of Nationalist-controlled firms was begun, with the intention of intensifying it from time to time. Africans were also called upon to observe that date as "a day of self denial," according to the Planning Council's report.

"Afrika!" became a common call, or shout, during 1959. The sense of identification with the continent that it expressed was dramatized on Africa Day, April 15, the first anniversary of the first Accra Conference of Independent African States. Celebrations were organized during the week of April 12–19. In Johannesburg on April 15 a float symbolizing Africa moved through the central part of the city and the African areas, and "Freedom" placards were displayed on the City Hall steps. The largest gathering, which was on Sunday, the 19th—estimated in size from several to seventeen thousand—met in Alexandra, Johannesburg. Many ANC speakers, like many in the crowd, appeared uncharacteristically in traditional dress. By wearing the dress of groups other than their own, the speakers demonstrated their respect for the ethnic heritage of all Africans. Meanwhile, the Pan Africanist Congress (PAC), which had been formally established earlier in the month, issued a press statement calling for "a three-minute period of silence and rededication" at 9 P.M. on the 15th.[71]

Chief Lutuli addressed a mass meeting in Durban on Africa Day and was scheduled to appear before the Johannesburg mass meeting on May 31. In 1952 he had been restricted to his home village, Groutville, not far from Durban, for two years; and in 1954 he had been banned from all gatherings for two years. Although arrested for treason in December 1956, he had been dismissed as one of the accused a year later. By 1959 he had made dozens of public and private appearances before groups that included many moderate whites, who acclaimed him in the English-language press.[72] Late in May, while he was at his home, the government banned him from attending all gatherings for five years and, as of June 3, confined him to the Lower Tugela district of Natal for five years. The English-language press prominently reported and deplored the government's action, whereas on the two previous occasions of Lutuli's restriction, it had shown little reaction. In order to protest the ban, the Liberal Party called public multiracial meetings during June in the city halls of Pietermaritzburg and Johannesburg, each attended by more than 2,000 people of all races.

Because of the timing of the official order, Lutuli was able to travel to Johannesburg and back before the terms of his confinement went into effect. His receptions en route took on the appearance of a triumphal tour, although he was prohibited from attending the planned meetings in Johannesburg. In confused circumstances, last-minute bans caused a cancellation of the outdoor rally. The two-day conference was held in a packed hall instead. The hall was only briefly raided. Once back in his home, under constant surveillance, Lutuli attracted many visitors, although they were permitted to speak with him only one at a time. In September 1959, the American ambassador, Philip Crowe, was among those who visited Lutuli. But the ANC's operations had been damaged not only by the ban on Lutuli but also by similar bans on movement and attendance at gatherings imposed during June and July on Tambo, Nokwe, Resha, and the provincial presidents in the Transvaal and the Cape—Gert Sibande (also banished to a remote area) and Oscar Mpetha. At about the same time, eighty Saracen armored personnel carriers were delivered to South Africa from Britain.

Formation of the Progressive Party

Another of Lutuli's visitors was Dr. Jan Steytler, an Afrikaans-speaking member of Parliament. Following the August 1959 United Party

Congress, he and eleven other members—some of the younger and abler members of Parliament—resigned from the United Party but retained their seats. They had become increasingly impatient with the party's growing conservatism and had finally resigned over a relatively minor issue, albeit one of principle: the party's opposition to the purchase of additional land for African reserves. The group also reflected the small but growing white sentiment for consultation with African leaders.

In November 1959, eleven of the twelve who had resigned participated in the formation of the Progressive Party. Its platform was essentially the same as that of the Liberal Party in 1953, that is, support of high but nonracial qualifications for the franchise, and rigid constitutional safeguards of individual rights. The party's emergence demonstrated that political liberalism had won important allies and grown in respectability during the past six years. The party's leader was Steytler; its chairman, Harry Lawrence, a veteran parliamentarian and former minister of justice; its most prominent member was Harry Oppenheimer, South Africa's wealthiest mining magnate. Although there were Afrikaners among its leaders, most members were well-to-do English-speaking urban voters. A number of English-language newspapers, notably the *Rand Daily Mail,* extended their support. Africans, Coloureds, and Indians who met the party's proposed franchise qualifications were invited to become members; in time, a small number did.

The ANC welcomed the Progressives, although it criticized their franchise policy, and expressed the hope that their activities would not be limited "to purely Parliamentary methods of struggle" (Document 33). The PAC, on the other hand, dismissed the Progressives as another diversionary effort by white liberals, whose promises "might have taken in the African people twenty years ago."[73]

On the Eve of 1960

As 1959 neared its end, the radical opposition saw differing trends. In the October provincial council elections, for example, Liberal Party candidates in three districts in the Transvaal and the Cape were encouraged when they won 4,562 votes against 17,415 for United Party and Nationalist candidates. (In a fourth, Natal district, the Liberal Party candidate lost his deposit.) Meanwhile, however, the Nationalists increased their provincial strength.[74] On the international front, the ANC's advocacy of a boycott of South African goods, endorsed by the Liberal Party, was adopted as official policy by several countries in the West Indies and won the support of some leading members of the British Labour Party and of other groups in Africa and abroad.[75] But "the most important event for years," said the Johannesburg *Sunday Times* in mid-December, was the formation of the

South Africa Foundation, richly financed by South African, American, and British businessmen. The aim of the Foundation was to mount a propaganda counter-offensive "to present the real South Africa to the world" and to counter "increasing economic pressure on South Africa through boycotts and sanctions . . . [which might] eventually lead to military action . . ."[76] The association of Oppenheimer with the founders of this organization dismayed some of his admirers.

Meanwhile, at a time when unrest and scattered violence in the Native Reserves were attracting attention abroad, trouble of truly international significance occurred on the night of December 10–11, 1959, in Windhoek, South West Africa, the mandated territory whose "international character" South Africa recognized. After nearly a week's boycott of African facilities, conducted to protest the intended removal of residents from an old residential quarter to a new site some distance from town, about a thousand Africans rioted. In response to attacks by stone throwers and their own fear of being overwhelmed, the police fired, killing eleven Africans and wounding forty-four others.[77] Reactions in the United Nations foreshadowed those that were to follow the Sharpeville shootings some three months later.

Although high officials diligently sought to avoid the embarrassment of such incidents, there was no question of the government's readiness to act decisively whenever necessary to maintain its control. Indeed, in discussing the reorganization of the South African defense force. F. C. Erasmus, the minister of defense, caused a stir by referring to the example of the French forces in Algeria. Late in December 1959, Patrick Duncan, the editor of *Contact,* the liberal fortnightly, reported a talk by Erasmus at a meeting of army officers, " 'You must not think,' he told them, 'that we are arming against an external enemy. We are not. We are arming in order to shoot down the black masses.' " Duncan added the near-incendiary comment that Erasmus "rolled the words 'om die swart massas neer te skiet' round his mouth with enjoyment."[78]

The political year 1959 ended for the ANC and the PAC with a sense that 1960 would be a historic time. An unprecedented number of black African states were to become independent; April 15, therefore, was to be an extraordinary Africa Day. May 31 was to be a time for counter-demonstrations because white South Africa was to celebrate the fiftieth anniversary of Union on that day. For months there had been talk of a boycott of the white "festival." The Rev. James Calata, for example, had proposed at a conference of the Interdenominational African Ministers' Federation that a day of mourning and prayer meetings be planned.[79]

But there was also a sense that popular impatience was pushing African leadership faster than it was prepared to go. The ANC's last conference in South Africa was an enthusiastic rally that clamored for action. The conference began with an outdoor mass rally in Durban, estimated at from

5,000 to 8,000 people; it was followed by an indoor conference for 386 official delegates. An additional commemorative day was endorsed: March 31, 1960 was to be celebrated for the first time as the anniversary of the anti-pass demonstration on that day in 1919.[80] But in his message to the annual conference of December 12–13, Chief Lutuli spoke of the need for more popular training in nonviolent action and warned against "reckless haste and impatience which would be suicidal and might be playing into the hands of the Government."[81]

A week later, the Pan Africanist Congress, which had been born out of the Africanist movement in April 1959, held its first and last annual conference. It too planned an anti-pass campaign, one that would take the initiative away from the ANC. R. M. Sobukwe, the PAC national president, was to set the fateful starting date.

NEW MOVES TOWARD INTERRACIAL DIALOGUE

The events of 1960 appear tragic because of their seeming inevitability. By the late 1950s, the Nationalist government was moving to decimate and outlaw the extraparliamentary opposition, whose political demands it considered diametrically opposed to official policy. The treason arrests of 1956 had stigmatized the main leaders of the radical opposition as persons beyond the pale of political dialogue, and the five-year bans on Lutuli and others in mid-1959 increased the difficulties of consultations across the color line. African leaders, on the other hand, already deeply committed to goals of equality and universal suffrage, were responding to mounting pressures for militant action and becoming emboldened by pan-Africanist developments in Africa to the north.

Meanwhile, other developments in the late 1950s make 1960 appear doubly tragic. Optimistic moves were being made toward interracial dialogue. In particular, Afrikaans-speaking intellectuals, after years of soul-searching and long-range analysis, were making private and extensive contact with African leaders. The time for these overtures had not appeared ripe until after the Nationalists' resounding victory in the election of 1958. But then there was too little time left for the slow process of consultation to divert the drift toward confrontation.

Interracial Contact and a National Convention

Over many decades, interracial contact between white and black leaders had occurred on a variety of occasions and in various forums. Political contact between white politicians and educated Africans had taken place during the long period of a nonracial franchise in Cape Province and also while Africans were on a separate roll after 1936. Another form of white-African contact was provided by the Joint Councils of Europeans and Bantu, which were organized in the major South African cities in the 1920s and 1930s. These councils had sponsored National European-Bantu Conferences and in 1929 had participated in founding the South African Institute of Race Relations, which has sponsored multiracial meetings ever since.[82] By the late 1950s, however, the Joint Councils had become largely inactive. Multiracial meetings were also held by church groups, including the Dutch Reformed Church, especially after World War I. (Proceedings of some of the conferences referred to above are in Volume I.) Among the Africans who took part in such meetings were DRC ministers, for example, the Rev. S. S. Tema, who belonged also to the ANC.[83]

Left-wing organizations also were active in sponsoring multiracial meetings. Writing in *New Age,* Lionel Forman described "South Africa's first multi-racial conference": a meeting called by the white International Socialist League on August 5, 1917 and attended by representatives of the ANC—R. V. Selope Thema was one of the speakers—and of an Indian trade union.[84] Beginning in 1927, on the initiative of the most prominent Coloured leader, Dr. Abdul Abdurahman, a series of "Non-European" conferences were held. There were many left-wing-sponsored multiracial meetings in the 1930s and 1940s. With the organization of the Congress movement and the Liberal Party, and the broadening of a common ground of opposition to Nationalist government policies during the 1950s, multiracial meetings were frequently organized. At the same time, the government was moving systematically to restrict multiracial contact, not only politically but also socially and in religious gatherings.

What was missing in the efforts of whites and blacks to come together was discussion between senior leaders of the ANC and conservative whites of national stature. In May 1953, B. A. Tindall, a former judge of the Appellate Division of the Supreme Court who was acting at the request of the South African Institute of Race Relations, sent invitations to eight Africans and eight whites.[85] His letters, marked "strictly private and confidential," invited attendance at an expense-paid, off-the-record, six-day meeting in August at Adams College in Natal. There was "an urgent need," he wrote, "for discussions between Africans and Europeans on the question of how Africans can be more fully associated with the government and development of the country." Inasmuch as the discussions were to be "in no way regarded as negotiations," no officials or current members of Parliament were invited. And although the aim was "to bring together people who are, in a broad sense, representative of various trends of thought," the persons invited had been "selected on grounds of their individual worth and not because they represent any particular organisation."

The eight Africans invited were Chief Lutuli, the president-general of the ANC, and two former presidents, Dr. Xuma and Dr. Moroka; two other important leaders of the ANC, Dr. Molema and Dr. Njongwe; Paul Mosaka, the leading African businessman; and D. G. S. M'timkulu, a prominent educator. In addition to Dr. A. W. Hoernlé and Leo Marquard of the Institute of Race Relations, the whites invited were the venerable Professor B. B. Keet, professor of theology at Stellenbosch University; Dr. H. J. van Eck, the leading expert on South Africa's industrial development; W. van Heerden of *Dagbreek* and a leading proponent of separate development; Dominee J. Reyneke, Dr. B. F. T. Schönland, and B. A. Ettlinger, Q. C. When the meeting took place, as Leo Marquard recalled twenty years later, Professor Matthews and Jordan Ngubane attended in place of Moroka and Molema; the whites in attendance, in addition to himself, were Tindall, Reyneke, Schönland, and the following: A. H. Broeksma and Graeme Duncan (both of them "Queen's Counsels" or advocates), Dr. Simon Biesheuvel, Mrs. Winifred Hoernle, and Quintin Whyte.

During the meeting, one of the whites informed the Africans that Dr. Malan and other high officials were interested in meeting African leaders if they could do so without embarrassment.[86] Both sides at the conference "evinced a very strong desire to grapple with the realities," according to Ngubane, but "the majority on the white side wanted us to pursue a course so moderate our people would promptly lynch all of us." Because of "the very wide gulf which sealed off the whites from the Blacks," there was a failure to establish "real communication," Ngubane concluded. But everyone agreed that further meetings would be useful.

By the late 1950s, many bridges of interracial contact had been weakened or broken down. "The existing forms of consultation, such as do exist," said Lutuli in a letter to Prime Minister Strijdom on May 28, 1957 (Document 23), "are, in my opinion, not only inadequate, but undemocratic: the quarterly meetings of African chiefs, the Bantu Authorities (where these exist) and the Advisory Boards in urban areas; [and] . . the so-called Native Representatives in the Senate and in the House of Assembly . . . "[87] Arguing that the lack of contact and consultation was "at the root of the growing deterioration in race relations," Lutuli asked Strijdom to make "contact with the leadership of organisations and bodies, among them the African National Congress, representative of organised African opinion" and "to consider the advisability and possibility of calling a multi-racial convention to seek a solution to our pressing national problems." Later in conversation, Lutuli pointed out that he had made no demands of Strijdom but had asked only for discussion between Africans and the government, after which he would have asked for a multiracial conference.[88] He received only a brief acknowledgment of his letter.

In appearing to use "conference" and "convention" interchangeably, Lutuli was blurring the distinction between a meeting called to discuss certain matters and a constituent body (like the South African National

Convention of 1908–1909) summoned to write a constitution. The call for a multiracial conference was sometimes a political rallying cry—the flyer announcing the June 26 day of protest in 1957 concluded with the slogan: "Forward to a Multi-racial Conference!" (Document 26). Such a conference was sometimes regarded as a stepping-stone to a new national convention. Occasional calls for such a constituent meeting were made over the years. On February 8, 1957, Alex Hepple, leader of the Labour Party, introduced a motion in the House of Assembly calling for a national convention "of all sections of the community . . . to consider . . . the establishment and maintenance of a democratic society . . ."[89] Liberal Party members supported the motion. But the United Party said that "the ideal of a National Convention is now impracticable," and Dr. Verwoerd described it as "positively dangerous" (Document 21).

Discussions of a multiracial conference or a national convention began with certain basic questions. Who was to sponsor the meeting? Who were to be invited and how were they to be chosen? And to what end? But the fundamental question was whether or not there was sufficient common ground to attract persons representative of the full spectrum of South African opinion. *The World* expressed one set of assumptions in an editorial on January 26, 1957. In order to avoid "national disaster," it said, representatives of all groups should "sink our differences" and come to a multiracial conference "with an open mind" in order "to find a workable solution acceptable to all the people irrespective of colour." Presumably in accordance with such assumptions, invitations to the multiracial conference of December 1957, discussed below, were sent both to the Nationalist Party and to the United Party and to leaders of the Dutch Reformed Churches.

To what extent did the various individuals and groups calling for the conference genuinely hope for fruitful discussion and seriously expect to influence opinion? The question is almost impossible to answer. For many leaders of the ANC, a multiracial conference appears to have been an expedient for political education and building a united front. Some leaders of the South African Bureau of Racial Affairs (SABRA), discussed below, apparently had similar motives—or, at any rate, expected to influence opinion—when, in 1959, they privately looked forward to the convening of a multiracial conference that would meet publicly and include representatives of the ANC, if not the Pan Africanist Congress, then in the process of forming. On the other hand, Duma Nokwe, secretary of the ANC's working committee, was less optimistic than these SABRA leaders. Writing in anticipation of the 1957 multiracial conference he welcomed diversity of opinion but pointed out that it was "quite unrealistic to expect the upholders of racial supremacy—call it baasskap or leadership or trusteeship—to attend or to play any useful and constructive part at such a conference."[90] Dr. Verwoerd undoubtedly agreed. Nevertheless, it did not follow that contact and consultation would not be useful.

300

Multiracial Conference, December 1957

On December 3–5, 1957, a multiracial conference of some 350 active participants and 300 observers met in the "Great Hall" of the University of the Witwatersrand in Johannesburg. It was the outgrowth of the "all-in" African conference called by the Interdenominational African Ministers' Federation in October 1956 to discuss the Tomlinson Commission report. Afterwards, representatives of IDAMF had met with white sympathizers, and in mid-1957 invited a number of prominent men to become sponsors of the conference. The invitation was signed by Lutuli, Ambrose Reeves, Anglican archbishop of Johannesburg, whom Lutuli later called "the architect of the multi-racial conference,"[91] Dr. Yusuf Dadoo, Leo Marquard (a prominent liberal member of the South African Institute of Race Relations), and the leaders of the Black Sash and the Labour and Liberal parties. By September, 63 sponsors, including Dr. Xuma, Mr. Justice F. A. W. Lucas, and leading churchmen, were listed. Invitations were sent later to some 1,000 persons, who were asked to participate in the conference as individuals rather than as delegates of organizations.[92]

During 1957, organizers of the multiracial conference sought the active cooperation of leading members of the Dutch Reformed Church and SABRA. (The final statement of the 1956 IDAMF conference had concluded with an appeal to the Dutch Reformed Churches and all other Christian churches.) DRC leaders, according to Walter Sisulu, suggested to IDAMF the organization of a conference that would not attack apartheid or the government. (In his opening address to the multiracial conference, the Rev. Z. R. Mahabane, president of IDAMF, was to say, "This is not an anti-apartheid conference, and it is not an anti-Government conference, but a conference to find ways and means of living together in a multi-racial society.")[93] Another cautionary note was sounded by the Institute of Race Relations, which urged delay until SABRA and the DRC could be persuaded to join.[94]

The appeal for sponsors was worded so as to avoid exacting prior commitments. It quoted a resolution of the IDAMF conference demanding "the abolition of discriminatory laws" but, instead of reiterating this demand, it proposed that the multiracial conference "consider whether it should be adopted, amended or replaced by another resolution" (Document 21). When the sponsors met to plan the agenda, they adopted a similarly noncommittal resolution: that the conference "discuss and explore the steps which can bring about friendly and effective cooperation among the different racial groups in our country." They agreed also that inasmuch as the conference was to be "exploratory," it should adopt no resolutions and should include minority views in the "findings" of the small discussion groups into which the conference was to be divided.

Despite these cautious approaches, no prominent members of SABRA or the DRC participated in the conference, although some members attended as unofficial observers, as did members of the Nationalist Party and the United Party. After the conference was over, W. E. Barker, a Roman Catholic Afrikaner Nationalist member of the conservative wing of SABRA and its Transvaal secretary, wrote a critique in which he recognized that an attempt had been made to persuade Afrikaners to join in sponsoring the conference. The "emissaries," however, were men who had "hardly endeared themselves to the Afrikaner people." Barker also quoted with approbation *The World's* observation: "We also blame the DRC and SABRA for having been too slow to respond to the advances of the IDAMF and in this way driving them into the enticing hands of the [Congress of] Democrats and the Liberals whose philosophy is not the solution to the worries of this land . . ."[95]

The conference did not bring together as diverse a group of prominent Africans as did IDAMF's "all-in" conference in 1956, and it incurred the hostility of *The World*. But as a multiracial conference, though one attended mainly by whites, its participants and observers made it the most diverse national conference in South Africa's history. Standing by in the wings under constant observation by the Special Branch were Lutuli and others whose current bans prohibited attendance at gatherings. To foreign observers, the atmosphere was one of good will and intense interest, both in plenary sessions and in discussion groups, and in the multiracial mingling at tea breaks and lunch.[96] For some whites, the conference was undoubtedly a memorable and provocative experience. For example, Philip Pistorius, a University of Pretoria professor who had been active in the Nationalist Party and later became prominent in the Progressive Party, met Lutuli for the first time when they had tea together in the university's dining hall.

Twelve papers were presented to the conference after being circulated in advance. Five of them were by Africans, including a paper on "political arrangements" by Professor Matthews, and one was by the South African-born Catholic archbishop of Durban, Denis E. Hurley. Among Africans who spoke from the floor in plenary sesssions were Josias Madzunya, a well-known ally of the Africanists (although Africanists generally avoided the conference), Jordan Ngubane, Alfred Nzo, and Oscar Mpetha.[97] Barker of SABRA later criticized "the scramble by White and Indian speakers to catch the chairman's eye" and commented that "many people have yet to learn the art of holding discussions with the Bantu and adapting their impatient Western ways to the calmer temperament of the Bantu."[98]

Although the conference did not adopt any resolutions, it accepted without written dissent the findings of the separate commissions or discussion groups (Document 21). The conference also approved a proposal that the planning committee serve as a continuation committee. The findings, couched in general terms for the most part, unequivocally condemned apartheid. The fundamental aim of the "findings" (a misleading word for choices among policies) was "the creation in South Africa of a common society" having as one political "goal" the achievement of "universal adult suffrage on a common roll." (Professor Pistorius issued a statement describing the political aims as "unrealistic and extremist."[99]) Basic freedoms, said another finding, "should be entrenched in a written constitution" which "would require the assent of a new National Convention, representative of all races in South Africa." Bishop Reeves delivered the final address; the end came after a moment's pause when a resounding voice from the rear of the auditorium began the African anthem, "Nkosi Sikelel' I-Africa," and, as the song was taken up, participants and observers rose to their feet.

SABRA Initiatives

During the period of preparation for the multiracial conference, Professor B. B. Keet of Stellenbosch University described as a "supreme tragedy" the absence of the "slightest notice . . . in responsible quarters" of the goodwill expressed at the IDAMF conference of October 1956.[100] A small number of Afrikaans-speaking intellectuals, however, were privately discussing at that time the usefulness of a multiracial conference.[101] Although none of them attended the IDAMF conference, an Afrikaner *volkskongres,* an "all-in" Afrikaner counterpart to the IDAMF conference, meeting a few months earlier had recognized the need for better understanding between Afrikaner and African. The report of the December 1957 multiracial conference noted that the *volkskongres's* continuation committee, including members of SABRA, was "suggesting the holding of a conference with Non-White leaders." The initiative was to be taken by SABRA itself.

SABRA had been established by prominent Afrikaans-speaking intellectuals, high government officials, and churchmen four months after the Nationalist Party came to power in 1948. (Colonel Charles Stallard of the Dominion Party was also one of SABRA's founders.) SABRA was formed to engage in research and to lead the way toward, and prepare public opinion for, the fullest possible territorial separation of the races. Most of its strength was in the Cape. By the late 1950s, it had 2,000 to 3,000 members, nearly all of them Afrikaans-speaking; affiliated with it were about 100 Dutch Reformed congregations, 70 municipalities, and more than 60 cultural organizations.[102]

Differences in tone and policy between SABRA's relatively progressive and conservative elements were often identified with the difference between the tolerant racial outlook of the Cape and the more rigid attitudes of the Transvaal. The range of attitudes on racial policy held by intellectual supporters of the Nationalist Party was more complex, however, than the Cape-Transvaal dichotomy suggests. The degrees of inflexibility and doubt were many, and racial attitudes were evolving, even among some men who were in middle age or older. SABRA itself appeared solidly committed to separate development, yet Afrikaners who had changed their orientation regarding race served as reminders that such changes in racial attitudes were possible.

The Cape leaders at Stellenbosch University, in particular, impressed outsiders as forward-looking men, diligently engaged in the long-run task of reconciling white identity with Christianity and racial justice. Some SABRA leaders quietly criticized legislative proposals that, within the broad apartheid framework, appeared unfair, for example, racially separate faculty and governing councils within the separate universities for Africans, Indians, and Coloureds. Significant differences of opinion also existed regarding the status of the Coloureds. Yet dissenters always felt constrained lest they jeopardize the government's hold on power.

The SABRA intellectuals rejected the liberalism of individual rights in a common society, but they endorsed equal rights within racially separated areas. A few of them foresaw nonracial rights in a racially mixed area in which whites were in a majority. Indeed, men like Professor Tomlinson and Christian Prinsloo, the chief information officer of the Department of Native Affairs in the 1950s and early 1960s, professed to embrace liberalism as a potential alternative if separate development failed. In conversations with outsiders, Tomlinson stated in 1955 that he would have to join the Liberal Party if certain essential policies of his commission's report were not adopted within a certain period of time. Tomlinson never did join the Liberals. Prinsloo maintained that if separate development failed, the resulting common society would have a larger number of trained Bantu than it would otherwise have had.

More challenging to orthodox thinking at the time were the independent views of a very small number of Afrikaners. For example, Professor L. J. du Plessis of Potchefstroom University, a founder of the Broederbond, attacked Dr. Verwoerd for his opposition to informal contact between the races (for example, at the formerly open International Club of Durban) and to consultation with the "real nonwhite leaders" rather than "government stooges."[103] At the University of Pretoria, Professor Ben Marais, the theologian, was the guiding light of a very small minority of critics of racial thinking within the Dutch Reformed Church. Professor Pistorius, as noted above, was in the process of moving from the Nationalist Party to the Progressive Party. Probably the most widely respected theologian was Professor Keet of Stellenbosch, who described territorial apartheid as "a fantastic dream, one impossible of fulfillment" and did not blink even at the possibility of interracial marriage.[104]

Among prominent Afrikaners, however, the most dramatic story of altered views was that of the prominent lawyer Abram Fischer. The son of a distinguished Nationalist Afrikaner family in the Orange Free State, Fischer had been a segregationist during his college days. His experience as a leader of the Bloemfontein Joint Council of Europeans and Bantu in the late 1920s was the beginning of a process that ultimately resulted in his joining the Communist Party, the only legal party at the time that was unqualified in its support for racial equality. Before being sentenced to life imprisonment in 1966 for conspiracy against the state, Fischer told the court that his conduct had been

> directed toward maintaining contact and understanding between the races of this country . . .[to] help to establish a bridge across which white leaders and the real leaders of the non-whites can meet to settle the destinies of all of us by negotiation and not by force of arms . . .[105]

In an effort to build bridges, a small policy committee of SABRA was formed in November 1957 (a month before the multiracial conference at the University of the Witwatersrand) to look into the question of a multiracial conference. Once the Nationalist Party had entrenched itself further in political power in the general election of April 1958, the way seemed clear. At its congress of April 29–May 2, 1958, SABRA delegates enthusiastically supported a resolution to sponsor a multiracial conference later in the year.[106] The political sensitivities touched by this proposal were aggravated when Verwoerd, whose resignation from SABRA had been announced at the congress, became prime minister in September 1958. He opposed contact between whites and Africans outside official channels.

Nevertheless, in an extraordinary series of meetings held between December 1958 and February 1959, small groups of SABRA professors, totaling about fifteen, met privately with some 200 Africans, including ANC and Africanist leaders, mainly in Johannesburg, Durban, Port Elizabeth and East London. What Abram Fischer had been experiencing for decades was for the Afrikaner intellectuals who participated in these meetings a new and epochal experience, the most important event since 1652, said one. Many of them were talking on a man-to-man basis with educated and politically sophisticated Africans for the first time in their lives. For many of the Africans also, the conversations with SABRA intellectuals were a new experience.

The Afrikaner participants included Professors N. J. J. Olivier, J. L. Sadie, S. P. Cilliers, and van der Walt of Stellenbosch; L. J. du Plessis, D. W. Kruger, J. H. Coetzee, van Wyk, and Keet (not B. B. Keet) of Potchefstroom; J. J. Ross, van Heerden, and Van Rooyen of the Orange Free State University; and, for one day, Dr. F. R. Tomlinson. The Institute of Race Relations assisted in making arrangements. An extraordinary and largely unbroken silence was maintained by the press during much of the period of the meetings. The African participants, like the whites, pledged themselves not to publicize the talks. The Afrikaners met Lutuli in Durban at an almost day-long session; Xuma at his home in Sophiatown; Mosaka, Tambo, Mandela, and Nokwe (the last two among the accused at that time in the Treason Trial). On January 9, 1959 they met with six Africanists in the offices of the United States Information Services in Johannesburg—Robert Sobukwe, Potlako Leballo, Peter Raboroko, Zachius Molete, Nana Mahomo, and Zephania Mothopeng. They also met Africanists in Durban. Among the Africans with whom they talked were members of advisory and school boards, businessmen, and church leaders.

Professor Olivier had said at the 1958 SABRA congress that "The Bantu must be given an opportunity of testing us and our sincerity."[107] The Afrikaner participants in the interracial meetings appear to have been impressive in demonstrating their sincerity and believed that they had had a "fantastic" effect on many of the Africans, observing that some Africans were "almost in tears" because of the realization that Afrikaners, like themselves, believed in human dignity. The Africanists, however, were considered by the Afrikaners to be anti-white. The Africans generally were willing to meet again, although relatively conservative Africans, as well as Xuma and others, said that so long as SABRA supported apartheid, there could be no basis for future discussion. Nevertheless, the ANC's National Executive Committee in its 1959 report commented that SABRA members had displayed "doubts . . . although . . . not on fundamental issues" and that "even among Nationalists the thaw was setting in" (Document 33). More than three years later, Chief Lutuli recalled that he had been quite shocked at Professor Olivier's response when Lutuli said that he would initially accept a very limited franchise. Olivier had replied that the government could not agree to even the most limited franchise. Even if it were to do so with the support of a majority of the voters, he had said, there would be civil war in South Africa.[108]

After the meetings, a SABRA deputation (excluding Olivier) visited an angry Verwoerd in February 1959 to discuss what had been going on. The deputation issued a statement later, saying that participants in the talks had taken part as individuals rather than as SABRA representatives. Nevertheless, at SABRA's congress of March 31–April 3 the mandate for a multiracial conference was reaffirmed. Dr. A. L. Geyer, a former editor of *Die Burger*, forecast in his presidential address a series of meeting "with Bantu," no restrictions being noted, during 1959 and 1960 in preparation for a major conference. In order to counter speculation about disunity, Olivier, the prime mover of the earlier meetings with Africans, offered a resolution praising Verwoerd that was carried unanimously. Speaking privately, he looked forward with confidence to the holding in 1960 of a public conference that would include ANC leaders and other opponents of separate development and would be planned so as to avoid open antagonism.

Other Moves Toward Interracial Dialogue

SABRA's meetings and its humane concern about the humiliations and pinpricks of apartheid were encouraging to white liberals.[109] (Democrats were "inclined to clutch at any sign of goodwill," said Dr. H. J. Simons, a Marxist scholar at the University of Cape Town; ". . . independent, critical thought on colour policies is so rare among Nationalists that its occurrence causes a minor sensation.")[110] Also encouraging was the growing interest among white moderates in Lutuli's advocacy at many private and public meetings of genuine multiracialism. One ugly incident occurred in Pretoria in August 1958, however, when some Afrikaners temporarily broke up a public meeting sponsored by a study group composed mainly of Afrikaner intellectuals and assaulted Lutuli on the stage. Lutuli continued nevertheless to accept invitations from whites. In April 1959 he was greeted with enthusiasm in Cape Town at a series of press conferences and meetings and outside Parliament.[111] Document 32, a tape-recorded address delivered before some 300 whites at a meeting in Johannesburg sponsored by the Congress of Democrats, is typical of his addresses at this time. In discussing white fears and African aspirations, he recognized that democracy had developed in homogeneous societies but expressed his belief that a segmented South Africa could become homogeneous "on the basis not of colour but of human values."

In Durban in another packed public meeting the possible shape of meetings to come was suggested when Lutuli shared the platform with a prominent local Nationalist, Dr. C. J. Jooste. The meeting was of a so-called "brains trust" organized by the Black Sash shortly before the 1959 SABRA conference. Others on the platform were Alan Paton, Fatima Meer, and the leader of the Federal Party.[112] But with the banning of Lutuli and other ANC leaders from gatherings for five years, beginning late in May, the government placed additional limits on interracial dialogue.

In April 1959, in an effort to broaden the basis for consultation among anti-government groups that were not prepared to join a united political front but might cooperate for specific purposes, Bishop Reeves became chairman of a multiracial "consultative committee," sometimes known as the "Bishop's Committee." Representatives of fourteen organizations agreed to hold day-long meetings at his home, without publicity, every three months. They included the Black Sash and the Liberal Party in addition to the Congress bodies. The PAC, which attacked the committee, was absent.[113] Several meetings were held, attended by some twenty-five to forty people who were carefully screened at the door by representatives of the Bishop. The meetings were unstructured, without agenda or minutes. No resolutions were adopted, nor decisions taken, but the group arrived at what Bishop Reeves has called "a common mind."

No comparable effort was made in Cape Town. However, the Anglican archbishop, Dr. Joost de Blank, with the cooperation of ANC representatives, convened a multiracial conference in August. The conference's continuation committee, which included Albert Centlivres, the retired chief judge of South Africa's highest court, was mandated to consider how the Union's fiftieth anniversary in 1960 could be appropriately—that is, critically—observed and how a national convention might be called to reform the constitution.[114]

Toward the latter part of 1959 another series of interracial meetings behind the scenes occurred. Members of Parliament and their business allies, who had left the United Party and were planning to form the Progressive Party, said that consultation with "moderate" African leaders—with "responsible Natives"—was essential, if there was to be racial cooperation.[115] Dr. Jan Steytler, an Afrikaner who became the new party's leader, met with Lutuli; and before the party was formed in November 1959, members of the progressive group had met with more than a hundred Africans, Indians and Coloureds.

But the rise of the Progressives came too late to sustain the hopes of African leaders for a progressive share in political power, although Progressives themselves hoped they had time to convince the white electorate to accept a nonracial policy—even one theoretically leading to rule by an African majority. After the shootings at Sharpeville and the outlawing of the ANC and the PAC, leading whites, including supporters of the government and representatives of commerce and industry, made the most urgent appeals ever heard in South Africa for consultation with Africans. South Africa had undergone a political convulsion, however, and opportunities for consultation were becoming increasingly rare.

FORMATION OF THE PAN AFRICANIST CONGRESS, 1958–1959

Africanist Breakaway

The Orlando Africanists, swept by the general mood of anti-government solidarity in the opening months of the Treason Trial, at first refrained from pressing their attack on the Transvaal Congress.[116] But as 1957 wore on, and dissension and impatience spread among the rank and file, Leballo and his group began to step up their criticism of the Congress alliance in the hope that popular dissatisfaction could be molded into a movement to oust the "multiracialists." "We have witnessed during 1957 a desire for unity and solidarity among the masses and a tendency towards crippling and contemptuous bureaucracy on the part of our leaders," declared an editorial in the December *Africanist* (Document 35). It was a new form of the same charge made a decade before by Youth League militants: the people were ready for action, but the leaders were holding back. The perseverance of Evaton and Alexandra residents in carrying on the bus boycotts begun in 1955 and 1957 lent weight to the claim that the masses were prepared to be militant, even without guidance from politicians.

The Africanists' attempt to call for a vote of no confidence in the Transvaal executive failed to carry at the national conference of December 1957, but the so-called petitioning branches, which were dissatisfied with the conduct of the Transvaal provincial elections, were assured that a new conference would soon be convened to consider their grievances. When this special one-day conference met in the Orlando Communal Hall on February 23, 1958, a showdown appeared inevitable. The Africanists, few in number but adept at manipulating their less ideological fellow dissidents, had by this time closed ranks with the "petitioners" led by Steven Segale of the Sophiatown ANC. Their combined strength posed a credible threat to the provincial office-bearers and their unpopular stand-ins. Wrangling and fist-fighting broke out as "volunteers" loyal to the executive attempted to screen out hostile would-be "delegates." Most of the afternoon had elapsed before substantive discussions got under way. Tambo's suggestion that some points might be conceded to the dissidents was rejected by the acting provincial president, A. Mthembu, who insisted on reading out a long statement defending the provincial executive committee. There were shouts from the floor of "vote them out *en bloc*." Riding on the mood of the meeting, Leballo moved that new elections be held immediately. Enthusiastic applause welcomed the motion. But just as it seemed that the dissidents would prevail, the chairman declared the meeting closed because time had expired for use of the hall. Loyal delegates rose and broke into strains of "Nkosi Sikelela," but newspaper reporters estimated that most of those assembled remained seated in confusion and protest.[117] The Transvaal had reached a new organizational low, bordering on complete collapse. After more haggling behind the scenes, the disputed executive was eventually persuaded to resign, and the National Executive Committee assumed emergency powers to direct the affairs of the Transvaal.

The failure of the election-day stay-at-home in April 1958 drove the stocks of Transvaal leadership still lower, and the Africanists, who had opposed the calling of the strike, did not hesitate to exploit this new evidence that the ANC was out of touch with mass sentiment. Hoping to isolate the Africanists and offset this criticism—and perhaps also hoping to turn the Africanist "disrupters" into scapegoats for the failure of the stay-at-home—a top-level Congress caucus (consisting mostly of banned leaders) decided in May to expel Leballo from the ANC. Josias Madzunya of Alexandra was also expelled.

Madzunya, a street peddler with a flamboyant personality and an elementary school education, had been portrayed by *The World* and *Golden City Post* as a leading Africanist, but he was in fact only on the periphery of the Africanist movement. A brief association with the Communist Party had made Madzunya a strong critic of the South African left, and like the Africanists, he was opposed to any cooperation between the ANC and the Congress of Democrats. His distinctive appearance (he was heavily bearded and always appeared in a black overcoat) and his knack for calling a spade a spade from the public platform made him good copy for journalists seeking sensational news. The Africanists were not particularly concerned at this stage with publicly projecting the subtler points of their evolving ideology, and they felt they could use Madzunya's popularity to augment their own limited support, without suffering unduly from being identified with his crude "anti-white" style. The more the press built Madzunya up as a spokesman of African opinion, the more convenient it became for the Orlando Africanists to use him as a stalking horse to publicize their case against the Congress alliance. Madzunya on his part played the role of fire-eating nationalist with gusto, largely unaware that his Africanist colleagues considered him a politically dispensable decoy.[118]

A few days before the general election in April 1958 the government placed a ban on all political meetings of more than ten Africans in all major urban centers.[119] When this restriction was lifted about five months later, disputes which had been simmering behind the scenes began to come into the open. A new Transvaal provincial conference was called for October, but postponed until the first weekend in November. The issue of incompetence and irregularities in the provincial administration had died down somewhat with the resignation of the old executive and the takeover of provincial affairs by the National Executive Committee. When the clash between loyalists and Africanists surfaced again, the ground had shifted back to ideology and strategy, with the Africanists reasserting their attack on the alliance with new fervor. It is impossible to gauge with any accuracy the extent to which Africanist hostility to the multiracial front actually reflected the sentiments of Africans either inside or outside the ranks of the ANC. The Africanists were convinced that they were closer to the mood of the masses than were the Congress leaders. In any case, the latter took the position that the ANC, rather than pandering to popular resentment against non-Africans, had to lead and educate the masses to accept the more enlightened concept of struggle that the alliance represented.

Within the ANC, the Africanists could call on the support of some of the former petitioning branches, factions of varying sizes within other Transvaal branches, Madzunya's followers from Alexandra, and a small bloc of nationalist intellectuals in Congress who opposed the alliance on the grounds that it was divisive and harmful to the ANC's popular image. Under the direction of Peter Raboroko, an early Youth Leaguer and member of the Africanist "inner circle," an ad hoc grouping called the Anti-Charterist Council was formed to coordinate these forces as the November provincial conference approached. To test the strength of anti-alliance sentiment in the ANC, the Council proposed to run its own candidate for Transvaal president: Josias Madzunya. Madzunya, who was contesting his expulsion and hoped to have it overruled at the conference, agreed to run and to publish an Africanist election manifesto ghost-written by Raboroko.[120]

The two-day conference opened the afternoon of November 1, 1958, with an address by Lutuli denouncing the Nationalist Party and blaming the government for injecting "the virus of prejudice and sectionalism" into the African community.[121] White "panderings to racialism," he said, were causing some Africans to try to "emulate the Nationalists in claiming exclusive control of South Africa. . . . We have seen developing—even though it is in its embryonic stage—a dangerously narrow African nationalism, which itself tends to encourage us to go back to a tribalism mentality."[122] In the fierce debate that followed the address, Africanist spokesmen held forth on their theory that Africans would have to fight alone if they were to achieve maximum strength in the struggle. A crowd of tough Africanist camp-followers clustered at the back of the hall heckled the speakers who rose to support Lutuli, and expressed their support for Africanist speakers by stamping their feet and shouting "Afrika!"

As tensions rose and the test of voting strength approached, the inevitable dispute over credentials ensued. Africanist branches and branch factions had sent representatives, but their credentials were challenged by loyalist representatives from the same areas. The Africanists refused to recognize the credentials committee on the grounds that it was biased, a charge they had raised at earlier Transvaal conferences. Tambo, who was attempting to chair the meeting, remained calm, but the hall seemed ready to explode into violence at any moment. When the first day's session closed, it was ruled that the conference would be open the next day only to accredited delegates.

The next morning it became clear that the loyalists were prepared to back up their "delegates only" ruling with force if necessary. A crowd of ANC "volunteers" assembled behind the conference hall, armed with sticks and lengths of iron. A crowd of Africanist supporters, some similarly armed, gathered in front. Each group numbered at least a hundred men. The loyalists were posted at the doors of the conference hall, and the screening of delegates began. Police and Special Branch detectives watched from a safe distance, anticipating an explosion if the Africanists tried to enter the conference.

But no explosion came. Realizing that they had been outmaneuvered, the Africanists held a quick caucus outside the hall. Some argued for an attempt to enter the conference, but in the end a majority were persuaded that the time had come for a parting of the ways. A letter declaring an Africanist breakaway was drawn up and delivered to the door of the conference hall as elections were proceeding inside among the loyalists. The Africanists, declared the letter (Document 37), were not a "paramilitary clique" and were not prepared to settle their quarrel with the ANC by violence; nor were they prepared any longer to remain tied to an organization that had adopted the "Kliptown Charter" in defiance (in their view) of the principles of African nationalism embodied in the earlier Programme of Action of 1949. They were therefore launching out, they said, "as the custodians of the ANC policy as it was formulated in 1912"—a reference to the original all-African character of the ANC—"and pursued up to the time of the Congress Alliances."

The break was neither wholly spontaneous nor wholly premeditated. A few individuals in the Africanist "inner circle" had been pressing for an independent organization for several years. The majority of influential Africanists, however, including Sobukwe, had clung to the hope that Congress would eventually adopt or, in their view, readopt, their ideological views. A. P. Mda, whose opinions on ideology and strategy had strongly influenced nearly every member of the Africanist leadership, had always opposed the establishment of any rival organization aimed at competing with the ANC. His consistent advice to the Africanists had been to work within Congress, building support for "unadulterated" African nationalism, so that the organization might eventually be brought back to the doctrines of the early Youth League. Whatever its failures or successes, its weakness or wisdom, the ANC was unquestionably an African tradition, an institution enshrined in the hearts of the people, as even its bitterest critics were compelled to admit. The ICU, the AAC, the African Democratic Party, and the National-minded Bloc had all come and gone while the ANC remained, surviving every political storm. It was therefore with some trepidation that the Africanists began to launch out on an independent course, for they too had a strong faith in the durability of the ANC.

Predictions varied widely as to how strong the new movement might become. From the perspective of the ANC's national leadership, the Africanists appeared to constitute just one more ephemeral "mushroom" grouping, closest in form and motivation to the short-lived National-minded Bloc of the early 1950s. In interpreting the conflict to their less sophisticated rank-and-file followers, Congress leaders could easily dismiss the Africanist walk-out as the action of a clique of disappointed position-seekers. It was clear to any unbiased observer that both the

African and white press had consistently exaggerated the actual strength of Leballo and Madzunya. As a result, when newspapers referred to a "Big-Scale ANC Split" at the November conference,[123] many ANC leaders and loyalists reacted with scorn and dismissed such journalistic pronouncements as mere sensationalism or malicious anti-ANC propaganda. Among ANC partisans who were sincerely apprehensive about the growth of an aggressive black nationalism, there was a tendency to take the Africanist threat more seriously, but at the same time to feel a sense of relief that the Congress had at last shed its extremist or "racialistic" wing. Caught between the Africanists and the ANC multiracialists were those Congressites who were opposed both to the disruptive tactics of the Africanists and to the basic trend of ANC policies regarding cooperation with non-Africans. This element, sometimes referred to as the "nationalists," was not a cohesive group but remained for the most part within the ANC, awaiting further developments.

The inclination of journalists to overrate the actual strength of the Africanists was no doubt derived in part from an uneasy sense that any movement in South Africa that was, in their words, "anti-white" could probably command enormous support from Africans if it were allowed to develop unchecked. In the minds and imaginations of frightened whites, the distinction between potential and actual support for such a movement could easily become blurred. ANC politicians, drawing on long years of experience in trying to raise the level of African mass political consciousness, were in a position to make a much more realistic, and less exaggerated, assessment of the Africanists' potential strength; yet even they were unable to predict with any certainty what the popular response to the new movement might be.

At the time of the breakaway, the Africanists themselves realized that their numbers were few. Those who consciously thought of themselves as orthodox Lembedist nationalists had never numbered more than a few dozen at the most. Of these, only Leballo had any wide reputation outside the Transvaal. What influence the Africanist movement had enjoyed inside the ANC before November 1958 had, on the whole, been derived less from the strength of nationalist thinking per se within the Congress than from the ability of Africanist spokesmen to identify themselves with the more generalized sense of grievance and impatience among ordinary members and lower-ranking cadre. No one could foresee how far the Africanists might be able or inclined to go, once they were outside the ANC and its traditions of moderation. Anyone could see that frustration and impatience were widespread, especially among the young, but how could this discontent be harnessed to achieve a political end? No African organization in South Africa's history had yet found a satisfactory answer to this question.

At the time of their breakaway from the ANC, the Africanists had only the rudiments of an internal organization of their own, consisting mainly of an informal network of contacts between Leballo's circle in Johannesburg and small groups of like-minded Congress members in other centers. During the Treason Trial, some opportunity was afforded for direct contact between the Transvaal Africanists and Africanists from Natal and the Cape who were defendants in the trial. Communication was otherwise confined to occasional letters and visits. But in spite of the rather unsystematic nature of their organization, the Africanists were acutely conscious of their identity as a distinct group within the ANC, and rather grandiosely referred to the Africanist "Cencom" or central committee of the movement's top leaders. Leballo and Selby Ngendane were openly referred to in *The Africanist* as the chairman and secretary of the Africanist movement; behind the scenes, the key figures included Robert Sobukwe, Zephania Mothopeng, Peter 'Molotsi, Peter Raboroko, and Dr. Peter Tsele.

Africanists outside the Transvaal were taken by surprise by the events of November 2, 1958, and a number of weeks passed before formal secessions took place in Natal and the Cape. (In the Free State, always the most politically lethargic province, there was little Africanist activity until after March 21, 1960.) Neither in Natal nor in the Cape had the divisions within the ANC become quite so severe and near-violent as they had in the Transvaal; but once the Transvaal Africanists had broken off, their sympathizers elsewhere, confronted with a *fait accompli,* had little choice but to follow suit. In Natal, the secession was announced without fanfare at the annual conference in Durban in mid-December by A. B. Ngcobo, a Natal Youth League leader and former treason trialist. Africanist sentiment was not widespread in Natal, in part because of Lutuli's popularity among his fellow Zulu. In the Cape, where many nationalist-minded Africans had long resented attempts by whites to use the ANC in their campaigns for election to Parliament as Natives' Representatives, two rival provincial executives, one loyalist and one Africanist, had coexisted throughout most of 1958. In spite of efforts by the national executive to bring about a reconciliation, the split deepened and in the early months of 1959 branches and branch factions began to defect from the ANC to the Africanist side.[124]

Apart from the recruitment of followers, the most imposing challenge facing the Africanists after the breakaway was the task of reshaping their public image and projecting a more positive formulation of their ideology. Press statements by prominent Africanists after the break revealed a concerted attempt to disassociate the movement from the extremist cry of "Drive the white man into the sea," a slogan many people had come to associate with the Africanists on account of wide press coverage given to Leballo's and Madzunya's bellicose speeches. In an effort to convey the depth of their opposition to the Congress alliance before November 1958, Africanists had frequently referred to whites and Indians as "alien" and

314

"foreign" minorities, and the use of such terms had reinforced the faulty impression that they stood ideologically for the expulsion of these groups from South Africa. As long as the Africanists had remained within the ANC and had continued to view the Congress of Democrats and the Indian Congress as the major obstacles to the adoption of a strategy based on nationalism, most of their energies had inevitably been spent in making negative attacks on these "enemies." It was only after they had completely separated themselves from the ANC that they were able to concentrate on a more positive presentation of their political philosophy, reshaping the arguments for exclusive nationalism in an effort to attract wider support.

Inaugural Convention of the PAC

The Africanist movement formally transformed itself into the Pan Africanist Congress at a three-day conference held at the Orlando Communal Hall in Johannesburg over the Van Riebeeck Day holiday weekend in April 1959. Among the three to four hundred people who attended, Transvaal representation was the heaviest, but delegates were also present from Natal and the Cape, along with a small number from the Orange Free State. Placards carrying nationalist and pan-Africanist slogans lined the walls of the hall: "Africa for Africans, Cape to Cairo, Morocco to Madagascar," "Imperialists Quit Africa," "Forward to the United States of Africa," and "Izwe Lethu iAfrika" ("Africa, Our Land"). In accordance with African political tradition, the conference opened with prayers and sermons by prominent clergymen, but in keeping with the particular inclinations of the Africanists, the principal clergyman invited to speak was the Rev. Walter M. Dimba, leader of what was then the country's largest federation of African independent churches.[125] Cabled greetings from Kwame Nkrumah of Ghana and Sekou Toure of Guinea were triumphantly read out, further underscoring the Africanists' determination to identify their cause with the continent-wide progress of anti-colonial struggles. "Today, 307 years ago," proclaimed the conference agenda for April 6, Van Riebeeck Day, "began the act of Aggression against the Sons and Daughters of Afrika, by which the African people were dispossessed of their land, and subjected to white domination. As it was here, and on this day that it began, it is imperative that it should be here, and on this day that it should be buried."[126]

Newsmen covering the conference reported being impressed with the serious and orderly atmosphere prevailing among the Africanists, in contrast to their disruptive and frustrated conduct over the preceding years.[127] A further surprise for the press was Madzunya's failure to win so much as a seat on the national executive committee of the new organization, in spite of the fact that some papers had suggested that he might be elected president. Instead, the movement's leading backroom intellectual, Robert Sobukwe, emerged as president in a unanimous vote. Leballo was chosen national secretary, and A. B. Ngcobo became national treasurer. Among the fifteen men elected to the national executive, eight were teachers or former teachers, three were university students, three were small businessmen, and one was a trade unionist. Five were studying law, but none had yet qualified. Six of the fourteen were in their early or mid-thirties, and another four were still in their twenties. Ethnically, six were Sotho-speaking, four were Zulu-speaking, and five, including Sobukwe, were Xhosas from the Cape. In terms of education, occupation, and ethnicity, they did not present a startling contrast to the leadership of the ANC, but in age they were significantly younger. Not since the earliest years of the ANC, when prominent roles were played by young intellectuals like Seme, Mangena, Thema, and Plaatje, had such young men so openly asserted a claim to national leadership in disregard of the strong African tradition of gerontocracy.[128]

The PAC inaugural convention was presented with a series of documents for discussion and approval, including a Manifesto, Constitution, Disciplinary Code, and Oath of Allegiance (Documents 39b–39e). These documents, together with Sobukwe's opening address (Document 39a), set forth the new movement's views on organization, ideology, and broad strategy, leaving the question of specific tactical action in abeyance until such time as the organization had become better established. Organizationally, the PAC chose to zone the country into six regions rather than recognize the "white" provincial divisions. In other respects the PAC modeled its structure quite closely on the ANC's, following a pattern of local branch and regional executives, answerable through a hierarchical chain of command to a national executive committee whose decisions, along with those of a smaller national working committee, were to be reviewed by an annual national conference. As it turned out, the lifespan of the PAC as a semi-legal organization in South Africa was too short for the structure of regional executives to take full shape outside the Transvaal and the western Cape, and only one annual conference, that of December 1959, was actually ever held.

It was in relation to ideology and broad strategy rather than organization that the PAC struck out on a new course distinct from that of the older Congress. Both movements envisaged the same ultimate goal for African political action: the creation of a democratic society in which individual merit and not race would determine status and advancement. In more specific terms than these, however, the difference in outlook between the leadership of the two organizations was fundamental and apparently irreconcilable.

The Africanists claimed that they were returning to the principles of 1912; yet they consciously drew their ideology from a much more recent source—the philosophy of Anton Lembede as he had preached it in the Youth League in the mid-1940s. Lembede had drawn heavily on European political thinkers of the eighteenth and nineteenth centuries, and in collaboration with his close friend, A. P. Mda, had formulated the most detailed doctrine of African nationalism set forth in South Africa, up to his time.[129] The essential feature of this nationalism was the vision of an African nation-state, at the least encompassing South Africa, and at its most grandiose stretching across the entire continent from "Cape to Cairo" and obliterating the boundaries drawn by European colonial powers. Lembede had preached this dream of an "Africa for Africans" with emotion and eloquence, and some of those in the fledgling Youth League who had been exposed to his philosophy were convinced that Lembede's ideas were correct and that Africa's destiny was indeed as he had envisioned it.

The senior Congress, however, in spite of its tolerant attitude toward Lembede and his Youth League disciples, had never embraced the view that South Africa should be a nation politically dominated by Africans. Although most older Congress members eventually endorsed the wording of the 1949 Programme of Action, which pledged the ANC to a struggle on the basis of African nationalism, the great majority never understood this endorsement to imply an acceptance of Lembedist principles. Most Congressmen, or those who attempted to sort out in their own minds what the goals of African liberation ought to be, interpreted nationalism in a broader way than Lembede, not as aimed at the creation of an African "nation," but rather as the achievement by Africans of an equal place in the more heterogeneous South African "nation." The ANC in the 1950s, in keeping with its traditional adherence to Christian principles and moderate modes of action, continued to work and hope for a reconciliation between the races of South Africa. The PAC, returning to the outlook of Lembede, and carried on a wave of impatience and frustration characteristic of the younger generation of urban Africans, chose instead to turn its back on all hopes of reconciliation and compromise, and to strike out toward a new and more radical goal: the complete replacement of minority rule with African government.

Sensitivity to racial tensions and white fears had always exerted a restraining influence on the ANC and had caused it throughout much of its history to project African aims in such a way as to minimize the possibility of white backlash. In their anxiety never to be guilty of practicing racialism in any form, Congress leaders had many times found themselves constrained by the tendency of whites to label any suggestion of an African takeover of power as "black racialism" or "apartheid in reverse." By the 1950s, the ANC was clearly on record in support of universal franchise, a policy that would unavoidably place dominant political power in the hands of Africans, who would comprise roughly 70 percent of the electorate. Yet

ANC leaders in their speeches and writings still tended to stress the goal of Africans sharing rather than ruling South Africa, lest any suggestion of support for "African domination" arouse shocked and violent reactions from whites.

To the young PAC militants, no such political taboos or considerations of white opinion seemed relevant to the African struggle. Unlike the leaders of the ANC, the PAC's new executive took no pains to avoid the question of how they wanted political power distributed after freedom: Africans would rule. Questions of ultimate justice and ideological principle took precedence in their thinking over matters of immediate political reality. Africans, they said, were entitled to rule, not just because they were the majority, but also because as the indigenous people they were the rightful "owners" of South Africa (see Document 36). Whites had stolen the country by military conquest and time had not erased the injustice of this historic "theft," according to Africanist thinking. Once the country was returned to its rightful owners, people who were of foreign extraction would be permitted to stay only if they acknowledged the right of Africans to govern every inch of Africa. If they acknowledged this right and showed respect for Africa's indigenous peoples, they could qualify as assimilated "Africans" and could become citizens of South Africa, entitled to full citizenship rights. There was no reason why in a future nonracial society Africans should not elect a white to represent them in Parliament, Sobukwe told a reporter from the Johannesburg *Star* the day after the PAC inaugural convention; but the PAC could guarantee no "minority rights," said Sobukwe, because in a free nonracial South Africa there would be no minority groups.[130] All would be Africans, and all would be guaranteed human rights as individuals.

The verbal battle that had raged between the ANC and the Africanists in the mid-1950s did not die down with the founding of the PAC. Each side accused the other of utopian thinking. The PAC was indulging in dangerous fantasy if it thought the rights of minorities would not have to be protected after freedom, wrote Joe Matthews in the July 1959 issue of *Liberation;* in heterogeneous countries like South Africa, he declared, it was an essential condition of democracy that minority groups be allowed to "develop their languages, culture and customs without let or hindrance" (Document 40). Other ANC leaders accused the PAC of being unrealistic in its belief that Africans could fight under the banner of exclusive nationalism and then establish a political order in which members of other races could be accepted without bitterness as "Africans."

The PAC countered with the accusation that the ANC itself was being utopian and unrealistic in its approach to the struggle. Underlying the fundamental perspective of the PAC was a belief that the real problem facing Africans was one not of ends but of means. In the Freedom Charter the ANC held out the utopian vision of a free South Africa, but offered the people no realistic means of achieving that utopia. Moreover, claimed the PAC, just at the time when Africans were striving to find themselves as a people, the ANC was trying to hold out the wholly inappropriate model of a struggle organized on multiracial lines. Multiracialism, charged the PAC, would never inspire the masses because it was anti-democratic—a mere cloak, Sobukwe alleged, for an elitist concept of social and political change. "It must be confessed," he wrote in an angry retort to Matthews' article, "that the Africanist view of democracy must be startling and upsetting to all those who have been bred and fed on the liberal idea of an African elite being gradually trained, brain-washed, fathered and absorbed into a so-called South African Multi-racial Nationhood, whilst the vast masses of Africans are being exploited and denied democratic rights on the grounds of their unreadiness, backwardness and illiteracy."[131]

The ANC's approach, the PAC argued, could only confuse the masses and "de-fuse" their latent nationalist sentiments. Both organizations agreed that liberation could be achieved only by using the numerical strength of the African masses to create irresistible pressure for change; the problem was how to mobilize support for African demands on a scale massive enough to overcome white resistance. In the PAC's view, an ideology based on multiracialism and "compromise" goals lacked sufficient emotional appeal to mobilize African support on the scale necessary for success. Only a doctrine of exclusive nationalism could be dynamic enough to inspire Africans to the heights of sacrifice they would need to reach in the course of the revolutionary confrontation PAC envisaged. Africans possessed the numerical strength to bring South Africa to a halt through strikes and civil disobedience; all that stood between the masses and a realization of this potential, Sobukwe believed, was a mental transformation among Africans themselves. Yet the ANC had chosen a path that could never effect this transformation.

Sobukwe and his colleagues, following the approach taken by Lembede, based their thinking on the premise that the African's most fundamental weakness was a psychological one. Whites were able to dominate South Africa, Lembede had maintained, because they indoctrinated Africans with a belief in the innate superiority of whites and an acceptance of their own inferior status. Before any African could wholeheartedly work for African liberation, he had to abandon his slave mentality and begin to believe instead in the inherent worth of his own people. Shame and the habit of dependence had to be replaced in his mind by pride and self-confidence. Only then would he be prepared to make an uncompromising and unstinting demand for his rights as a citizen and a human being. African nationalism had been the antidote prescribed by Lembede for the defeatist mentality plaguing the masses, and Lembede's diagnosis still appeared valid to his PAC disciples. It followed that the fundamental task of African leadership was to strive to achieve such a mental transformation among the masses through the preaching of African nationalism—the "building of a nation." This, said the PAC, had been the message of 1912 and the underlying strategy of the "nation-building" Programme of 1949, a strategy the ANC had repudiated by its entrance into a multiracial alliance.

Only an exclusive nationalism, propounded by Africans alone and geared to their material and spiritual interests as a group, could galvanize the illiterate and semi-literate masses into a united and determined force, Sobukwe told the inaugural convention. Only in an all-African organization could they be free to "formulate policies and programmes and decide on the methods of struggle without interference from either so-called left-wing or right-wing groups of the minorities who arrogantly appropriate to themselves the right to plan and think for the Africans" (Document 39a).

In the PAC's view, the mere presence of whites and Indians in the leadership circles of the liberation struggle was enough to undermine the ordinary African's sense of self-reliance, because most Africans had been conditioned to think of these groups as superior. An educated middle-class African might value the symbolism of multiracial leadership and might not feel that the ANC was being "dominated" by the white and Indian Congresses; the average African, however, in Sobukwe's view, had yet to be convinced of the wisdom of his own leaders, and the mere existence of the alliance served to reinforce his doubts about the worth and ability of his own people. As long as such doubts lingered in the minds of Africans, they would continue to be mental slaves, unable to press their demands on South Africa's ruling class.

The ANC, in turn, persistently denied that its leaders were in any way subordinate within the alliance, and scornfully accused PAC leaders of having an inferiority complex if they assumed that in any multiracial grouping it was always the whites and Indians who took the lead. In any case, said the ANC, the African people had to be taught that the struggle was based on principles, not on a simplistic and "racialistic" confrontation between blacks and whites. The people looked to their leaders for guidance, and it was irresponsible and harmful to the African cause to preach to the people that all whites and Indians were enemies, when in fact many were sympathetic and made themselves useful in the struggle. The PAC's approach, they maintained, catered to the worst popular instincts and eventually could lead only to undisciplined violence and more government repression. Politicization of the masses was the ANC's goal, but it was unwilling to strive for this goal by building on the foundation of racial hatred; should Africans build on such a foundation, the ANC held, they would be no better than the white racialists they were fighting against.

The PAC, while trying to lay positive stress on its goal of a nonracial future, argued that in the pre-liberation phase of the struggle it was illogical to equate the anti-black prejudices of whites with the justifiable anti-white sentiments of Africans; whites were the oppressors and Africans were the oppressed. The material interests of all whites lay in the perpetuation of a racially stratified society; all blacks stood to gain by the leveling of society and the installation of an African government. Thus the conflict was unavoidably one of Africans versus whites, the dispossessed versus the dispossessers. To tell the African masses that there were some "good" whites could only confuse them about the nature of the conflict and make them incapable of decisive action in an ultimate black-white confrontation.

Given that the conflict was one between dispossessed and dispossessors, dominated and dominators, said the PAC, it was clear that the masses could reach the necessary peak of revolutionary fervor only if motivated by the unadulterated pursuit of their own material and spiritual interests as the dispossessed and dominated. These interests could be expressed only in the doctrine of exclusive African nationalism, and they could be realized only through the creation of a new political order in which Africans would hold the reins of power. The PAC stood without qualification for the philosophy of nationalism, and for that reason, Sobukwe noted, *all* whites had stigmatized it as "anti-white, extremist, poisonous and irresponsible. . . . That to me," he said, "is sufficient proof . . . that PAC is the embodiment of the aspirations of the African people whose interests stand in pointed contradiction to the interest of the ruling group as a whole."[132]

In this light the ANC's decision to work in cooperation with members of the privileged groups (among which the PAC officially included the Indian "merchant class" as well as all whites, but not the Coloureds)[133] could be seen as a sell-out of the Africans, because it compelled the ANC to accommodate itself to the political views of these allies (see Document 38). This was fatal, declared the PAC Manifesto, because all members of these privileged groups were "tooth and nail against the Africans gaining the effective control of their own country," and were bound by their material interests and domination-oriented values to oppose every manifestation of nationalism among the African masses.

Pan-Africanism and the PAC

At the very time the Africanist movement was transforming itself into a new and ambitious political organization in South Africa, a vast political transfer of power was under way across the entire face of Africa. Earlier predictions by the imperial powers that Africans would require decades or even centuries to prepare themselves for self-rule fell rapidly out of fashion as nationalist leaders persisted in invoking the right of Africans, in Nkrumah's words, to "manage or mismanage" every inch of Africa. In a political environment where the hopes of generations seemed to be coming true nearly overnight, the imaginations of optimists naturally turned anew to the old vision of W. E. B. DuBois, George Padmore, Nkrumah, and other ideological fathers of pan-Africanism, who had spent years dreaming of a time when Africans would come together to form an independent "United States of Africa."

South Africans looked on from the sidelines, reading their own hopes and fears into events in the rest of the continent as European governments retreated and international prestige and legitimacy were bestowed on the black leaders of new African states. For whites, the expansion of African power and the world's recognition of the principle of African self-determination seemed a grim harbinger of future discord within South Africa's own system of internal colonialism. For many politically conscious and idealistic Africans, on the other hand, independent Africa took on the quality of a New Jerusalem and its leaders the appearance of infallible prophets of freedom. To the Africanists, it seemed that Lembede's predictions about the destiny of Africa might at last be coming true.

Older ANC leaders were unaccustomed to thinking of South Africa in the context of Africa as a whole, and when they did refer to African countries to the north it was often to draw distinctions between them and South Africa. "South Africa," wrote Professor Matthews in late 1957, for example, "differs from other territories in Africa such as Ghana or Nigeria . . . where the black man outnumbers the white man to such an extent that it is ridiculous to talk about the country being anything other than black man's country. In South Africa, in addition to the Africans we have settled here significant numbers of other groups . . . and therefore the country must frankly be recognized as a multiracial country with all that that implies."[134] Thus South Africa's large population of non-Africans made it an exception, in the view of Matthews and others in the ANC, to the pattern of politics taking shape in the rest of Africa. While Africans in South Africa might draw pride and inspiration from the political progress of Africans elsewhere, it was inappropriate in South Africa, and inconsistent with the policies of the ANC, to give to the terms "self-determination" or "independence" the meanings that were attributed to them in the rest of the continent.

From their side, PAC leaders, whose thinking was shaped by quite a different set of assumptions about South Africa's past and future, perceived developments in the rest of Africa in a radically different light. In keeping with the tendency to ignore practical obstacles and moral complexities and to reduce the terms of the struggle to a set of ideological absolutes, Africanist leaders put heavy emphasis on what they conceived to be the identity of interests of Africans in South Africa and Africans in the rest of the continent. As the number of independent African states continued to multiply, Sobukwe, with a ring of drama and triumph, began to make the claim that the Africanists were marching in step with the continent—toward the goal of African nationhood and an "Africa for the Africans." "The Africanists do not at all subscribe to the fashionable doctrine of South African exceptionalism," Sobukwe told the PAC inaugural convention. "Our contention is that South Africa is an integral part of the indivisible whole that is Africa. . . . We take our stand on the principle that Africa is one and desires to be one and nobody . . . has the right to balkanize our land.''

Lembedist traditions, sincere conviction, and a large measure of political expediency all combined to lead the Africanists into an espousal of pan-Africanism. Lembede had preached a pan-Africanist doctrine, looking forward to a time when Africa would emerge and take its place as one united country among the nations of the world. The appeal of Lembede's concept had been revived among the Africanists by George Padmore's book, *Pan-Africanism or Communism?*, published in 1956, which outlined a scheme for the creation of regional federations which would later merge into a single United States of Africa. In November 1958, just at the time the Africanists were launching out on their independent course, Ghana was announcing its ''union'' with Guinea, and it could have appeared to African optimists that a United States of Africa was already in the making. In December 1958, the historic All-African Peoples Conference, meeting in Accra, brought together the continent's most prestigious leaders in a highly impressive show of pan-African unity and purposefulness. No part of Africa could consider itself truly free, the conference proclaimed, until every part of the continent had been liberated. The year 1963 was set as the projected deadline for total liberation. The Africanists, always pan-Africanists at heart but now swept by the intense enthusiasm generated at Accra, decided to adopt the doctrines of the All-African Peoples Conference *in toto*. By the time the Africanist inaugural convention had met in April 1959, pan-Africanism had been incorporated into the name of the new movement, and virtually every tenet of pan-Africanist doctrine had been incorporated into PAC ideology as an article of faith.

''The African people of South Africa,'' declared the PAC Manifesto, ''recognize themselves as part of one African nation, stretching from Cape to Cairo, Madagascar to Morocco, and pledge themselves to strive and work ceaselessly to find organizational expression for this nation in a merger of free independent African states into a United States of Africa.'' The PAC, said its Constitution, pledged itself to promote the concept of a Federation of Southern Africa. ''Positive neutrality'' as endorsed by Nkrumah would be PAC's position in foreign relations, and the PAC would strive to project the ''African Personality'' as a social and cultural goal. The PAC's flag, the inaugural convention decided, would show a green field with a black map of Africa and a gold star in the northwest of Africa, beaming its light southward from Ghana.

The formulations of Accra came as an inspiration to the PAC's leaders just when they were seeking ways to reinforce and justify their own version of nationalist ideology.[135] If other African nations were freeing themselves without the assistance of ''foreigners,'' why could not Africans in South Africa do the same? If African nationalist heroes like Nkrumah and Mboya were warning against the ''imperialism of the East,'' was PAC not also justified in taking a stand against Communists in South Africa? If other African nations were committing themselves to the goal of a united Africa, why should not Africans in South Africa do the same? Expediency and idealism complemented one another in the adoption of this pan-Africanist perspective.

If all of Africa could be viewed as a single nation, it became far easier to dismiss South Africa's few million whites as an insignificant minority within the larger population. "In a United States of Africa . . . with freedom of movement from Cape to Cairo . . . the concentration of so-called minority groups will disappear," Sobukwe wrote in an article for *Drum* magazine in late 1959 (Document 46).[136] "The crucial issue today," wrote Raboroko several months later, "is whether the interests of the five million Europeans throughout Africa must continue to dominate over those of the two hundred eighty-million Africans, or whether the reverse process should obtain."[137] Such a perspective, by denying the uniqueness of South Africa's race problem, made it possible to deny that South Africa deserved any unique political solution; if "Independence" and "Africa for the Africans" were the correct nationalist line elsewhere, they could also be the correct line for South Africa.

The ANC's efforts had consistently failed to bring Africans in South Africa any closer to the goal of freedom, yet to the north other Africans were achieving startling and rapid political successes under the banner of African nationalism. The PAC, by dissociating itself from the ANC and identifying instead with the independence movements of tropical Africa, hoped to shed the image of past failure and surround its efforts with the aura of success. In adopting slogans like "Independence in 1963" and "Forward to the United States of Africa," both of which were widely used in the anti-pass campaign of March 1960, PAC leaders were assuming that the example of emerging states to the north would have a significant ego-boosting appeal to rank-and-file Africans, building their sense of confidence and resolve, and leading them to place their trust in African leadership that was "in step with the continent."

Federation of Free African Trade Unions of South Africa

When SACTU was formed as a multiracial trade union coordinating body to succeed the Trades and Labour Council upon its dissolution in 1954 (see p. 55 above), five African unions that had been members of the TLC refused to join it on the grounds that it was too closely tied to the left-leaning Congress alliance. Another union, the large Garment Workers Union of African women, joined SACTU but later disaffiliated from it and joined the dissenting unions, which had formed a loose grouping called the Action Committee. Throughout the mid-1950s these unions maintained an unofficial liaison with the Trade Union Council of South Africa (TUCSA), the major coordinating body representing registered unions (i.e., unions for white, Indian, and Coloured workers). TUCSA in turn was associated with the pro-Western International Confederation of Free Trade Unions (ICFTU) headquartered in Belgium.

The prime movers in the founding of the PAC recognized the need to forge links with organized African labor, and in looking for labor support they naturally turned to trade unionists who were not affiliated with SACTU. They found a willing ally in Jacob D. Nyaose, the general secretary of the African Bakers and Confectioners Union, and the leading figure in the anti-SACTU Action Committee. Nyaose was persuaded to take the post of secretary of labor in the PAC national executive commit-tee, and he in turn made his union's office in Mylur House in downtown Johannesburg available to the PAC as a headquarters.

In June 1959, two months after the PAC's inaugural convention, Nyaose and leaders of the Garment Workers Union convened a conference of nine anti-SACTU unions and proposed that a new coordinating body be es-tablished to represent African workers on an all-African basis in an or-ganization free from leftist "infiltration."[138] Nyaose charged that SACTU had lost its autonomy as a trade-union movement and had become the political tool of the Congress alliance "multiracialists." Contrary to the best interests of workers, he said, SACTU had backed the ANC's futile call for a stay-at-home to protest the white general election and "defeat the Nats" in 1958; African workers, wisely refusing to be made pawns in white politics, had ignored SACTU's call. Attacking Nyaose and his supporters, SACTU and ANC spokesmen denounced what they called the attempt to introduce racial exclusiveness or "apartheid" into trade unionism; they also rejected the assertion that politics and trade unionism could be sepa-rate spheres in South Africa, and pointed to Nyaose's connection with the PAC as proof that his own claim to autonomy was hollow.

In early October 1959, Nyaose's efforts bore fruit; nine unions, claiming to represent 17,000 African workers, came together to form the Federation of Free African Trade Unions of South Africa (FOFATUSA), with Nyaose as president, and Lucy Mvubelo and Sarah Chitja, both of the Garment Workers Union, as vice-president and secretary-general, re-spectively.[139] In the hope that financial support would be forthcoming, the new federation maintained contact with the ICFTU, and in December 1959 Mvubelo represented FOFATUSA at an ICFTU conference in Geneva.

But FOFATUSA soon proved just as ineffective as most other efforts to organize African workers into strong trade unions in South Africa. As a result, it failed to attract the international support for which it had hoped.[140] Though its following looked quite substantial on paper, its ability to trans-late numerical membership into effective action was negligible. Thus the PAC, while continuing to hope that FOFATUSA would prove a political asset, was compelled to direct its appeal to African workers more as individuals than as organized groups.[141]

THE EVE OF SHARPEVILLE AND AFTERWARDS

The leaders of PAC, convinced of the mass appeal of an exclusive nationalist creed, confidently set themselves a high target for membership. Three months before the PAC inaugural convention in April 1959, an editorial in *The Africanist* predicted that the movement would report a paid-up enrollment of 100,000 by July, a number equal to the peak membership of the ANC at the time of the Defiance Campaign.[142] At a Johannesburg meeting marking the PAC's "National Heroes' Day" on August 2, the national executive committee announced that membership had reached 24,664—a figure far short of the target, but nevertheless a substantial showing for a newly formed organization. The breakdown of figures subsequently reported put the provincial membership at:[143]

Transvaal	47 branches	13,324 members
Cape	34	7,427
Natal	15	3,612
O.F.S.	5	301
	101	24,664

The movement's failure to reach its target, Leballo explained, was due to inexperience in methods of organization and to lack of funds; but in spite of these setbacks, the PAC could still say "Sikifile!" ("We have arrived!")[144]

Membership figures did not tell the whole story of either the PAC's or the ANC's support, as any political organizer knew. Both organizations could expect support, and even active participation, from many people who were reluctant to become formal members, either because of the financial strain of paying dues or because of the risk involved in having their names listed in branch records. Government-employed teachers, many of whom became adherents of the PAC, accounted for a large number of politically minded people in this latter category.[145] Nevertheless, paid enrollment does serve as an indicator of an organization's popularity, and there was no denying that the PAC had overestimated its own drawing power.

The overconfidence which was so apparent in the PAC's membership drive, and which was later to mark the launching of its ambitious anti-pass campaign of March 1960, was an important clue to the thinking of Sobukwe and his colleagues. Like politicians in the ANC, they had a strong underlying faith in the ultimate triumph of the African cause. But among the Africanists this faith was buttressed by more than a general emotional belief that justice or history were on the African side; it was also based on a genuine intellectual conviction that exclusive nationalism as the objective "truth" was the cure for South Africa's ills. They sincerely believed—perhaps projecting some of their personal hopes and ambitions onto Africans generally—that the masses were yearning for self-realization and nationhood. The popularity of the ANC itself, throughout all its years of failure, they argued, was testimony to this striving, for the ANC had always stood as a symbol of Africans' "unity as a people, an expression, in organizational form, of their deep-seated urge to nationhood."[146] The ANC's undoing, according to the PAC's analysis, had been its failure to acknowledge and build on this true foundation of its own appeal. Consequently, the ANC had failed to imbue the people with a sense of direction in the form of a clear ideology which would feed their deepest aspirations and mold them into an effective fighting force.

Ultimate power in South Africa rested with Africans, the PAC believed, because their total noncollaboration could bring the country's economy to a standstill; all that Africans needed in order to come into their own was a mental transformation arising from the clarity of a correct ideology. This the ANC had failed to provide, in the Africanists' view. But now the PAC had arisen to fill the ideological void, or so its leaders felt. An organization of the people was now prepared to preach a creed that would show the way to the self-realization the masses so much desired. Surely, the PAC could optimistically conclude on the basis of these *a priori* premises, success could now be only a matter of time.

As the immediate and sobering problems of day-to-day organization began to impress themselves on the Africanists, this mood of buoyant optimism gave way gradually to a more realistic appraisal of the difficulties involved in mobilizing mass support. Experience proved that there was more to attracting a large following than merely preaching a political "true religion." The PAC's success, it became clear, would also depend on its ability to deliver some proof of its efficacy as an organization. As long as the Africanists had remained an opposition faction within the ANC, it had made little sense to criticize them for not taking independent action; their role, as they and their sympathizers saw it, had been simply to press for new directions within the ANC. Once outside the ANC, however, the Africanists were free to take new initiatives. Popular dissatisfaction with the ANC's cautious policies was running high, especially among younger Africans, and expectations grew that the tough-talking new leaders of the PAC would be men of action.

Specific plans for action, however, had always assumed a secondary place to the Africanists' preoccupation with theory and ideology. Mental revolution was the key to liberation, and once it was achieved, PAC leaders felt assured, specific action to effect emancipation would be dictated by the circumstances at hand. In the meantime, they said, mere "stunts" of the type staged by the ANC, because they were not geared into an ideology or a systematic or "programmatic" strategy for transforming the African's outlook and self-image, would only dissipate the people's energies. The 1949 Programme of Action (Volume II, Document 60) had embodied such a "nation-building" ideology and strategy, in the Africanists' view, but the ANC had abandoned the Programme out of fear that a blossoming of African nationalism would wreck middle-class African dreams of a multiracial society. The ANC's general membership had continued to support the principles of the Programme, the PAC maintained, but the leadership had quietly tried to overlook the decisions of 1949 and redirect popular loyalties toward the multiracialist Freedom Charter.

ANC spokesmen scoffed at the frequent assertion that the Programme of Action had been abandoned. The Programme, they said, had set forth no new ideology; it had merely committed the ANC to more militant forms of action.[147] Sobukwe, who had played a major role in writing the Fort Hare draft proposal for the Programme in 1949, had always seen it in a different light. In his view, the Programme of Action had been more than a mere set of activities designed to make the ANC more militant. He believed it had embodied a long-term strategy aimed at conditioning the African masses to shake off their mentality of defeat and to embrace the principle of non-collaboration, thus moving toward the goal of "independence" and the creation of an African nation-state. The Programme had, in other words, committed the ANC to the principles of Lembedist nationalism.

The wording of the Programme adopted by the 1949 conference had in fact been so general that both militant nationalists like Sobukwe and more conservative older Congressites had been able to endorse it without feeling compromised in matters of principle. That the Youth League nationalists could believe they were successfully selling Congress their ideology as well as their tactics was merely an indication of their enthusiasm and innocence in 1949. Whatever the realities of that time may have been, however, the conviction lived on in Africanist circles that the ANC—or its followers if not its leaders—had actually endorsed Lembedist nationalism. Ten years later, for anyone who wanted to know the PAC's plans for action, the answer was a clear one that had been reiterated time after time in the pages of *The Africanist*: the PAC was going back to implement the neglected Programme of 1949, if not in all its particulars, at least in its basic "nation-building" principles.

The idea of a long-range building and conditioning process, geared to the needs of an African population struggling against the psychological legacy of oppression, was a grand conception of the type that appealed to Sobukwe's intellect and idealism, and after years of thinking along such lines it was not easy for him to accept that the idea had some practical disadvantages. Most important, any plan of action directed primarily at arousing the most demoralized and politically apathetic members of African society was, almost by definition, a plan that bypassed the group from which in practice most of the PAC's followers were attracted, namely the ranks of relatively politicized and impatient urban working-class youth. No African organization could hope to put a country-wide program of political education into effect without a large number of devoted party cadre, but the activists who came forward to join the PAC from the time of its founding were almost all attracted by the prospect of militant action; the notion of merely spreading propaganda among the apathetic and unawakened masses did not hold much appeal for them. With time and the development of a strong organization, the PAC hoped to train its followers politically and prepare them to wage a protracted struggle. In practice, in the short time the PAC was free to operate legally, the fulfillment of this hope proved to be beyond the capability of its fragile organization.

In the earliest stages of plotting its course of action, however, the PAC did adhere to its principle of "nation-building," resisting the pressures from its youthful followers who were impatient for tougher forms of action. In "The State of the Nation" (Document 41), an address to a PAC conference in Johannesburg on August 2, 1959, Sobukwe announced the organization's intention to embark on a "status campaign" directed at exorcising the African slave mentality and teaching the people to assert their "African personality." The immediate target for the first stage of this unfolding campaign was to be shops and businesses that failed to give courteous service to African customers or persisted in addressing Africans as "native," "kaffir," "boy," "girl," "Jane," or "John." Such businesses would be picketed and boycotted, Sobukwe warned, unless their differential treatment of Africans was stopped forthwith.[148] "It must be clearly understood," he said, "that we are not begging the foreign minorities to treat our people courteously. We are calling on our people to assert their personality," and to be mindful "that acceptance of any indignity, any insult, any humiliation is acceptance of inferiority."[149]

The idea of the "status campaign" was not a new one. Sobukwe had urged the adoption of economic boycotts of this type as early as 1957 (Document 35).[150] But explaining the principle behind such a campaign was not the same thing as mobilizing PAC cadre for its implementation, and it was an inescapable fact that patient, disciplined, and relatively "safe" action of the boycott type was not the kind of defiant political activity the movement's militant young recruits were seeking. As a result, although general plans for launching the campaign were not abandoned after Sobukwe's August 1959 announcement, their implementation was postponed to the indefinite future. Eventually, in early 1960, the PAC executive sent out letters to a large number of firms threatening pickets and boycotts.[151] There were ripples of reaction, but no wide-scale response or

329

mass action to back the threats, in part because the energies of party members were by this time being directed into a new channel—the organization of a campaign against the pass laws.

Anti-Pass Campaign

In the latter part of 1959, PAC membership was still below expectations, and it became clear to the leadership that the movement would have to produce some concrete results if it wanted to hold and increase its following. When the national executive committee convened in Bloemfontein in September, it decided to propose an anti-pass campaign for ratification by the organization's first annual conference in December.

The conference met in an atmosphere of anticipation. PAC headquarters had announced that plans for "positive action" would be drawn up, and the *Golden City Post* had mooted that the PAC was preparing to unveil a master plan for liberation. The executive committee's report (Document 42) betrayed a certain pessimism about the movement's organizational efforts, but echoing Leballo's characteristic optimism, it assured the delegates that they had come together with "one aim in view—to take positive steps to crush, once and for all, White colonialism and imperialism in our Fatherland." When delegates complained that the organization had been taking too soft a position on action, Sobukwe called for the conference to give the executive a mandate to launch an anti-pass campaign. The response, as PAC leaders had anticipated, was unanimously favorable. The movement, declared Sobukwe, was about to "cross its historical Rubicon."[152]

Sensing that there was a "do or die" spirit among many of its youthful followers, and that the mood of the country might be favorable, the PAC by early 1960 was asserting, first, that many people had taken its message of nationalism to heart and, second, that many more were ready to follow any clear, determined initiative taken by a bold leadership. This second assertion was a significant one, for it indicated the importance the concept of heroic leadership had assumed in the PAC's outlook. As we have seen, the Africanists, and the early Youth League before them, believed that the African rank and file were politically more advanced than their leaders. The history of the ANC, the PAC alleged, was studded with evidence that leaders hung back at times when the masses were prepared to forge ahead and make sacrifices. If the people had become disillusioned with the ANC by the late 1950s, the PAC claimed, it was because they had seen time and again how the people, at the urging of their leaders, had borne the brunt of government action and suffered imprisonment while their leaders hired lawyers, paid fines, and went free on bail. Dr. Moroka's embarrassing attempts to obtain clemency for himself after his arrest in the Defiance

Campaign were frequently recalled as the most egregious example of this "betrayal" by African leadership, but the PAC alleged that there was a pattern of such avoidance of suffering among the ANC's leaders generally.[153] "No bail, no defence, no fine" would be the slogan under which the PAC's leaders would launch their campaign, Sobukwe told a PAC conference in May 1959.[154] Leaders would inspire the masses with their heroic example of self-sacrifice (Documents 43, 45, and 47). Given such a courageous lead and spirit of martyrdom, the PAC was confident, the masses too would be imbued with a willingness to suffer and sacrifice for the cause of liberation.

Africanist leaders recognized that they were launching a gamble, but sensed that time might be running out for Africans in their race against a government whose unconcealed intention was to perfect counter-revolutionary controls. They felt that there was at least a chance that the time was ripe for confrontation, and that determined action by the vanguard of politically conscious Africans might snowball and draw the masses into an unfolding campaign of widespread noncooperation. The pass laws and the whole exploitive and humiliating system of labor control which these laws facilitated were universally resented, and this resentment seemed to be intensifying.

In addition, a series of events early in 1960 appeared to shake the government, in some respects, and put it on the defensive. Momentum had begun to gather internationally for a boycott of South African goods. The British prime minister, Harold Macmillan, in a speech before Parliament in Cape Town on February 3, 1960, goaded the Nationalist Party by criticizing apartheid and proclaiming that "winds of change" were sweeping through Africa.[155] The week before Macmillan's speech, African women at Cato Manor in Durban, protesting against police raids for illegal liquor, had sparked a riot in which nine policemen had been murdered by an angry mob. And in Pondoland in the eastern Transkei, resentment against the imposition of Bantu Authorities touched off a series of fierce reprisals by Africans against government collaborators in early 1960.[156] Even within the ranks of the ANC it seemed as though pressure for action was mounting, for at its December 1959 conference delegates had called for bolder action and had chided the ANC executive for its cautious leadership.[157]

In February 1960, Sobukwe, Leballo, and Howard Ngcobo, a PAC executive committee member from Durban, drove to Cape Province to assess the state of the PAC's organization there and to lay plans for the anti-pass campaign. Ngendane joined the group in Cape Town, and Elliot Mfaxa, the party's national organizer, accompanied them as they touched centers of PAC activity in the eastern Cape. In Port Elizabeth and other urban areas where support for the ANC was traditionally strong, popular interest in the touring Africanist delegation was meager. In Cape Town, however, where the ANC was relatively weak and had made little effort in the 1950s to address itself to the grievances of the city's many migrant and semi-urbanized workers, the PAC leaders were enthusiastically received. A crowd of about 2,000 assembled to hear Sobukwe speak at Langa township on February 14 (Document 44).[158] The PAC was guiding Africans toward the creation of a New Africa, Sobukwe told his audience. The first targets in its unfolding program were abolition of the pass laws and the achievement of a guaranteed minimum wage of £35 ($98) a month for all Africans. African men were to prepare themselves, he said, to receive the call from national headquarters. When the call came, all were to leave their passes at home and surrender for arrest at their local police stations; no one was to resort to violence or to let himself be provoked by police or *agents provocateurs*.

The final aims of the campaign were left somewhat ambiguous. On the one hand, passes and low wages were singled out as the chief grievances of Africans. On the other hand, there was a strong suggestion in all PAC pronouncements that the campaign would not ultimately confine itself to these issues alone; rather, it would be the first step in a rapid march to total freedom. The PAC opposed every piece of the government's apartheid legislation, Sobukwe often told his audiences, but when a man's house was flooding, the solution was not to try to throw the water outside; instead, the PAC aimed at "closing the tap from which all this vile legislation flows,"[159] and it would not rest until all white rule was overthrown.

The problems the PAC might face once it had been decapitated by arrests were the cause of some concern to the organization's leaders, but they did not allow this concern to dissuade them from the course they had set for themselves. With some degree of foresight, they formulated a plan according to which subordinate "layers" of leadership within each region would be chosen and trained so that another set of leaders could come forward when top men were jailed. In practice, however, implementation of this plan had not progressed very far at the time of the March 1960 launching.

Over the doubts of some of the PAC's most influential supporters, including Jordan Ngubane and A. P. Mda, Sobukwe and Leballo pressed forward with plans to launch the campaign in early 1960.[160] The ANC at its December 1959 conference had resolved to launch an anti-pass campaign of its own with March 31 as the date for its initial action. Its campaign was to begin with the sending of deputations to local authorities and Bantu Affairs commissioners throughout the country to demand abolition of the pass laws.[161] The PAC, its national working committee felt, would have to launch its campaign before the 31st if it hoped to seize the initiative and set the tone of resolute action. The choice of an exact starting date was left to Sobukwe.

On March 4, Sobukwe sent his final instructions for the campaign to all branches and regional executives of the PAC. (Document 50 quotes this letter almost in full.) The people were to be instructed to observe the rules of strict nonviolence; no one was to resort to violence and emotionalism in the belief that the PAC was trying to engage in "revolutionary warfare." In a somewhat different vein, a party flyer issued at about the same time declared that the pass laws had to be "blown to oblivion this year, now and for ever" (Document 45).

On Wednesday, March 16, Sobukwe wrote to Major-General Rademeyer, Commissioner of Police, to inform him that the PAC would begin "a sustained, disciplined, nonviolent campaign" and its members would surrender themselves for arrest on Monday, March 21 (Document 48). Warning of "trigger-happy, African-hating" police officers, he assured Rademeyer that the people would disperse if the police gave them clear orders and adequate time to do so.

On Friday, March 18, Sobukwe announced at a press conference in Johannesburg that the campaign would begin on the following Monday (Document 49). PAC circulars announcing the launching date were already in the streets (Document 47). "I have appealed to the African people," Sobukwe told the press, "to make sure that this campaign is conducted in a spirit of absolute nonviolence, and I am quite certain they will heed my call. . . . If the other side so desires," he went on, sounding a prophetic note, "we will provide them with an opportunity to demonstrate to the world how brutal they can be. We are ready to die for our cause. . . ."

On Saturday, March 19, a conference of FOFATUSA delegates met in Johannesburg and resolved unanimously to strike in support of the PAC campaign.[162] On the following day the *Sunday Times* reported the response of the ANC to an invitation from the PAC to join the campaign on March 21. A letter from Duma Nokwe stated that the ANC was unwilling to support action which had "not been properly prepared for, and which has no reasonable prospects of success"; it would carry on instead with its own program of action against passes.[163] Unmoved by this rebuff, PAC leaders geared themselves for Monday morning. On Sunday, March 20, on instructions from Sobukwe, two members of the movement's national executive committee, Nana Mahomo and Peter 'Molotsi, slipped across the Bechuanaland border to carry abroad the case for the PAC's action.

Sharpeville

If police had not shot into the crowd of demonstrators that gathered at Sharpeville location outside Vereeniging on March 21, 1960, the day might have marked just one more abortive campaign in the history of African protest. Contrary to the expectations of the PAC's leaders, response to the PAC's call was almost negligible in Johannesburg. Publicity for the campaign had been inadequate, opposition from the ANC had been appreciable, Madzunya had decided to oppose the campaign in Alexandra township, and the relatively materialistic and sophisticated Africans of the southwestern townships showed themselves to be little disposed toward risky political protest. When Sobukwe, Leballo, and other members of the PAC executive presented themselves for arrest at the Orlando police station, they were followed only by some 150 volunteers. In Durban, Port Elizabeth, and East London, no demonstrations took place.

Thirty-five miles south of Johannesburg, however, in the industrial complex around Vereeniging, PAC militants had organized well with little or no competition from the ANC, which had never been strong in that area.[164] The long bus boycott at Evaton (between Vereeniging and Johannesburg) in 1955–1956 had impressed political organizers with the strategic importance of the transport systems carrying Africans to their jobs in the white cities of Vereeniging, Vanderbijlpark, Meyerton, and Johannesburg. Local activists were adept at coercing and cajoling African bus drivers into cooperation, and in the hours before dawn on March 21, they brought transport out of Sharpeville to a near standstill. At Evaton, a predominantly African town, thousands of people gathered and were addressed by PAC organizers.[165] Several hundred men presented themselves for arrest without passes, but police refused to imprison them on the grounds that jail facilities were inadequate. Military aircraft were sent to swoop low over the assembled crowds in the morning; by nightfall no violent incidents had occurred. At Vanderbijlpark, a large industrial town about 12 miles from Evaton, several thousand protesters who were gathered at the police station refused to disperse either when the aircraft dived at them or when police threw tear gas. Police fired at protesters who were throwing stones, and two men were killed. A police baton charge eventually scattered the crowd, and by mid-day police reinforcements began shifting from Vanderbijlpark to Sharpeville a few miles away, where the demonstration appeared to be getting out of control.

Eyewitness accounts of the "Sharpeville massacre" vary considerably in their assessment of the mood of the large crowd that surrounded the location police station there on March 21. Witnesses sympathetic toward the demonstrators testified, both at the official commission of inquiry and at the trial of the Sharpeville PAC leaders, that the crowd was unarmed, amiable, well-mannered, and unaggressive. They estimated that at the time the shooting occurred in the early afternoon, the size of the crowd was between 3,000 and 10,000. Police witnesses testified that the number of people was much larger (official reports placed it at 20,000), that many were armed with sticks and other weapons, and that the crowd's mood was hostile, aggressive, and volatile. Tear gas had failed to halt demonstrators marching through the town earlier in the day, and some witnesses estimated that diving aircraft had only attracted more people to the site of the demonstration. Moreover, apparently unknown to the police, a rumor had spread in the township that a high-ranking official was coming to address the crowd at the police station.

The size of the crowd, the insults and threats (including cries of "Cato Manor") shouted by individuals in the throng, combined with the natural anxiety of white men surrounded and outnumbered by people whom they regarded as the "enemy," brought police nerves after several hours to the snapping point. No order was given to shoot, and no warning shots were fired to frighten the crowd back from the fence surrounding the station. In a moment of panic, a line of white police opened fire on the crowd and continued to fire (for from 10 to 30 seconds, according to the findings of the commission of inquiry) as the demonstrators fled.[166] Sixty-seven Africans were shot dead, the great majority hit in the back as they ran; 186 others were wounded, including 40 women and 8 children.[167] White press reporters on the scene recorded the carnage in a series of grisly photographs that were to appear in newspapers all over the world in the days that followed.

In the principal African locations of Cape Town—Langa and Nyanga—large crowds also gathered the morning of the 21st, and many workers did not report to their jobs in the city. PAC organizers had done their work efficiently, and by Monday morning several thousand men were prepared to offer themselves for arrest. At a series of large meetings on Sunday, March 20, PAC speakers had exhorted Africans to avoid violence of any kind, and at two meetings, one in Langa and one in Nyanga, Philip Kgosana, the PAC regional secretary for the western Cape, had delivered a "launching address" (Document 50) quoting Sobukwe's final instructions for the campaign.

At dawn on Monday morning, a large throng marched from Nyanga to Philippi police station, and about 1,500 men gave themselves up for arrest. After their names were taken, they were told to go home and appear in court on a later date.[168] At Langa large crowds which had gathered in the early morning were ordered by police to disperse. PAC organizers told people to assemble again in the late afternoon, and despite a government order banning further meetings, a crowd estimated at about 10,000 people had gathered at Langa by 5:30 P.M. As at Sharpeville, rumors had spread at Langa that a high official would make an announcement, and the crowd became confused and angry when police arrived in force and, instead of making the anticipated announcement, launched a baton charge. When some people resisted this attempt to disperse the crowd, the police used firearms and two demonstrators were killed. As the people scattered, full-scale rioting erupted, lasting several hours. Whites on the scene were attacked, public buildings were set afire, African policemen were stoned and assaulted, and a Coloured driver employed by the *Cape Times* was killed.[169] By late evening the rioting had subsided, but for the city of Cape Town it was only the beginning of three tense weeks of violence and confrontation.

The PAC's national leadership had taken to heart the experience of the 1952 Defiance Campaign when eruptions of violence had provided government authorities with an opportunity to "restore law and order" by means of force. It was on this practical consideration and not on any philosophical commitment to passive resistance as such that the PAC based its call for nonviolence in 1960. Sobukwe had realized, as his terse letter to the South African Commissioner of Police on the eve of the campaign indicated, that there was considerable potential for violence in the situation the PAC was trying to create; but if police acted in such a way as to provoke violence from Africans, Sobukwe's letter implied, it would not be the responsibility of the PAC, because the organization was issuing "strict instructions," not just to its own members "but also to the African people in general," that they should be nonviolent.

PAC leaders optimistically hoped that the campaign would unfold into widespread disciplined acts of civil disobedience; realistically, however, they had scant grounds for supposing that the campaign would actually develop in this way. The number of people who felt bound by PAC instructions was relatively small, and even within the organization's membership there were some, like Madzunya, who did not consider orders from national headquarters to be binding. In contrast to this small number of Africans prepared to respond in a disciplined way to the PAC's initial call for action stood a much larger number of unruly action-oriented youths—the *tsotsi* or petty-gangster element so prevalent in large cities— itching to strike out at symbols of white authority in any possible way and on any pretext. Predictably, once a crisis situation had evolved, this violence-prone element rapidly became uncontrollable, most notably in Johannesburg where a *tsotsi* orgy of destruction convulsed the southwestern townships on March 28. Had police still needed an excuse to use counterviolence to restore order, they would not have had far to look; by this time, however, they had already begun to take the offensive throughout the country, citing the alleged need to protect law-abiding Africans from "terrorist intimidation" by the PAC and ANC.

State of Emergency and Banning of the ANC and the PAC

The widely publicized shooting at Sharpeville confronted the South African government with a political crisis of unprecedented magnitude. All efforts by Verwoerd and other Nationalist Party leaders to make light of the incident proved futile as the waves of reaction mounted in South Africa and abroad.[170] In Cape Town and the Transvaal gun shops sold out their stocks within days to panicky whites, and inquiries about emigration inundated the offices of Canadian and Australian diplomatic representatives.[171] International condemnation and isolation, merely a worrisome threat to whites before March 1960, now seemed an imminent reality as protests against South Africa's policies poured in from every corner of the world. In a surprising move on March 22, the American State Department released a statement directly rebuking South Africa for the deaths on March 21 and expressing the hope that Africans in the future would "be able to obtain redress for legitimate grievances by peaceful means."[172] On April 1 the United Nations Security Council intervened in the South African situation for the first time. The United States voted for a resolution (9–0, with the United Kingdom and France abstaining) that blamed the South African government for the shootings and called upon it "to initiate measures aimed at bringing about racial harmony based on equality."[173] To many whites it looked as though South Africa had reached a point where change might be unavoidable.

Political uncertainty brought immediate economic repercussions. Massive selling plagued the Johannesburg Stock Exchange, and speculation grew that the crisis would retard or halt the flow of foreign investment so vital to white South Africa's prosperity. In Cape Town, where Parliament was in session, the African stay-at-home, which had begun on the 21st, spread in the days that followed until, by the end of the week, it was virtually total, crippling the city's docks and industries. In the Vereeniging area absenteeism among African workers was also high throughout the week. When Lutuli called for Monday the 28th to be observed with a nationwide stay-at-home as a day of mourning for the Sharpeville and Langa victims, the prospect of a general strike by Africans momentarily loomed large.

Pleas from the United Party, liberals, and businessmen calling for the government to restore stability by making concessions to Africans, met with refusal from Verwoerd, who took the characteristic Nationalist Party view that concessions would only cause Africans to make further and bolder demands. Nevertheless, in an effort to bring the situation under control, government orders went out on March 26 that pass arrests should temporarily be suspended. That evening in Pretoria, where he was appearing as a witness in the Treason Trial, Lutuli ceremoniously burned his passbook and urged all Africans to follow suit.

The government's moratorium on pass arrests was a purely tactical move to deflate the African spirit of rebellion. Accompanying the move were strong measures to counter the African challenge and to suppress all threats to white control. Armored vehicles moved in to patrol location trouble spots around the clock; all police leaves were cancelled; and white citizen reserve units were called up to supplement police and military forces. Meetings were outlawed in main centers throughout the Union, while raids and arrests systematically battered anti-government organizations.

Although the specter of violence and disorder hung over the African residential areas of Johannesburg and the Reef as the crisis entered its second week, it was in Cape Town that the security of whites appeared to be most directly threatened by African rebelliousness. After police had agreed to jail about 100 anti-pass volunteers surrendering at Caledon Square police headquarters in downtown Cape Town on March 24, a crowd of 2,000 men from Langa location gathered at the same place the next day to court arrest. Police refused to jail them, and they marched without incident back to the township, but not before many whites had become thoroughly alarmed at the sight of the large crowd massed in the city center. By this time the African stay-at-home that had begun on the 21st was virtually complete, and businesses and industries that relied on African labor found themselves at a near-total standstill.

On Monday, March 28, the day designated by the PAC for the funerals of the Langa riot dead, a crowd estimated at 50,000 (a figure nearly equal to the entire adult African population of Cape Town) jammed the township and heard PAC funeral orators call for the strike to go on until African demands were met. These demands, repeatedly stated since March 21, were for the abolition of passes, a £ 35-a-month minimum wage, and no victimization of strikers. Never had an African urban population been so solidly united in its determination to defy white authority.[174]

On the same day, serious rioting erupted in Johannesburg, and several hundred thousand Africans across the country observed Lutuli's stay-at-home call. In Parliament, the government introduced a bill calling for emergency powers to ban the ANC and the PAC and to increase the legal punishments for political acts of defiance.

On Wednesday, March 30, the government declared a state of emergency and assumed broad powers to act against all forms of alleged subversion, including the power to arrest and detain indefinitely any person suspected of anti-government activity. Early that morning police had begun conducting nationwide swoops to arrest leaders and supporters of the campaign. In Cape Town they entered Langa and Nyanga, beat up striking workers, and began a systematic roundup of known PAC leaders. As word of the arrests and beatings spread, people began to congregate. By mid-morning a broad column of Africans began to move out of Langa along the ten-mile route toward the city. A white journalist who witnessed the march expressed the tension of Cape Town's whites:

> There were about 5,000 when the march began. By the time I saw them, coming along the curved dual carriage-way that leads around the side of the mountain to the heart of Cape Town, there must have been at least 15,000. They were marching about twelve abreast, dressed in their workingmen's shirts, trousers and coats, and looking exactly like some sentimental Leftist painting, 'The Peasants' Revolt.' But this was real.[175]

Philip Kgosana was at the head of the marching column as it entered the city. He intended to lead the crowd to the Houses of Parliament and to demand an interview with the minister of justice, but was persuaded by police to divert the march into Caledon Square. As Saracen armored cars and troops barricaded the approaches to Parliament and an Air Force helicopter circled overhead, Africans poured into Caledon Square and the surrounding streets. Press reporters estimated the crowd then to be about 30,000 strong.[176]

The spontaneous massing of such a large crowd of Africans in the center of a "white" city was unprecedented, and neither the marchers nor the police were prepared with any plan of action. The marchers were unarmed, but had they become violent, perhaps in response to a police show of force, the toll in lives and property could have been immense. The outcome rested in the hands of Kgosana, a 23-year-old Cape Town University student with a flair for leadership, who had dropped his studies a few months earlier to devote himself full time to politics. Negotiating on behalf of the demonstrators, Kgosana asked for the release of the arrested leaders, an interview with the minister of justice, and an assurance that police would stop using force to break the African stay-at-home. After consultations among high-ranking police, Kgosana was informed that his last two demands would be met if he would request the crowd to disperse. The gullible Kgosana, not realizing that his only bargaining power lay in his ability to keep the crowd behind him, took a police microphone and directed the people to return to Langa, telling them that the police had agreed to make concessions. The marchers returned home. That evening when Kgosana and several colleagues returned to the city for their promised "interview," they were arrested and jailed under the terms of the new emergency regulations. A decisive historical moment had come and passed by, leaving whites shaken but still firmly in control.

From March 31 onwards, police throughout the country spared no efforts in crushing all manifestations of rebellion and pre-emptively silencing prospective troublemakers. Severe new penalties for any publications deemed guilty of incitement or subversion curtailed freedom of the press. Thousands of Africans were arrested and charged with minor infractions.[177] The Treason Trial defendants were rearrested and jailed, and nearly 2,000 other political activists, including many prominent non-Africans, were detained under emergency regulations which waived the right of *habeas corpus*.[178] For the first time leaders of the Liberal Party were among those detained and jailed.

On April 1 in downtown Durban police opened fire at thousands of African demonstrators, killing three. Outbreaks of violence and pass-burning in Port Elizabeth, Bloemfontein, and other scattered centers met with swift police retaliation. In Cape Town, residents of Langa and Nyanga awoke the morning after their massive march to find the townships cordoned off by police and units of the Army and Navy. During the week that followed, strike-breakers were permitted to pass out through the cordon in the early morning hours. Then police staged house-to-house raids, seizing anything resembling a weapon and indiscriminately assaulting workers with clubs and whips. By the second week of April, the strike broken and their mopping-up operations complete, the police ended their blitzkrieg in the sullen Cape Town locations. Enforcement of the pass laws was resumed throughout the country, and on April 8 the government announced in Parliament the banning of the ANC and the PAC under the terms of the newly passed Unlawful Organizations Act.

The parliamentary debate on the Unlawful Organizations bill afforded white politicians an opportunity to set forth their views on the proper limits and functions of political activity among Africans. The debate also revealed the paucity of parliamentary knowledge and understanding of African political history, personalities, and opinion. In support of the banning of the ANC and the PAC, Nationalist Party spokesmen took essentially the same position as the prosecution line of argument in the Treason Trial, then stretching into its fourth year in Pretoria: these organizations had far exceeded the limits of legality because their fundamental aim was violent overthrow of the government. Their actions bordered on revolution, the minister of justice, Francois Erasmus, told Parliament during the second reading of the bill on March 29. "Their aim is to bring to its knees any White Government in South Africa which stands for White supremacy and for White leadership . . . [They] do not want peace and order; what they want is not £ 1 a day for all the Bantu in South Africa; what they want is our country!"[179] Furthermore, maintained de Wet Nel, the minister of Bantu administration and development, the force being employed by these organizations to intimidate peace-loving Africans revealed their violent intentions. "Luthuli and these agitators," he said,

are playing the diabolical role of inciting these people to revolt and then they issue pious statements in which they say that they are not in favor of violence, but behind the scenes the "spoilers" [hoodlums] and similar people are encouraged to commit violence. The tragic part of it all is that there are actually people who believe that Luthuli and his associates are honest when they say that they do not want bloodshed and violence . . . Having inspired such mass psychology, particularly on the part of the Bantu who has not yet reached the standard of civilization of the White man, it is then very easy [for agitators] to strike the match, in which case the law-abiding Bantu become the victims of what is happening in the country today.[180]

Armed with legislation to increase tenfold the penalties for acts of intimidation, argued Erasmus, the government would be able to protect innocent Africans and call a halt to the ANC-PAC "reign of terror." "The combined membership of these two organizations," he hastened to point out to Parliament, was "only about 70,000 . . . . These two organizations are not at all representative of the Bantu in South Africa. They represent less than 1 percent of the Bantu population . . . . They are just a small coterie of terrorists."[181] Given that the ANC and the PAC were extremist fringe groups with openly subversive aims, what could possibly be achieved by consultations or negotiations with them? What justification was there for even allowing them to exist?

In criticizing the government's position, opposition members from the United and Progressive Parties argued that although the ANC and PAC had undesirable aims, their organizations did not pose a serious threat to the existing system. Far more serious, the Progressives argued, was the possibility that leadership among Africans would pass into even more extreme hands if the more moderate legal organizations were driven underground. This pattern had already become apparent when the PAC had emerged after more moderate leaders in the ANC had been silenced by bans. Stability could be insured, both opposition parties maintained, only if urban Africans were allowed some channels for expressing their views. Their political organizations, particularly the ANC with its preponderance of leaders from the middle class, were just such a safety valve and therefore served a positive function in spite of the unconscionable nature of their stated goals.

The current crisis had arisen in part, said the leader of the United Party, Sir de Villiers Graaff, because of the government's failure to

> recognize the emergent class of Native in our urban areas, a responsible class, a middle class . . . which could be a stabilizing influence and which could co-operate in the maintenance of law and order . . . a class entitled to own their own property in their own areas set aside for them, who have an interest, a stake . . . and who will accept with us the responsibility of maintaining Western standards in our South African community.[182]

The pass laws, Graaff said, could have a part to play in this process of encouraging a buffer class of "responsible" African leaders; if returned to power, the United Party would restore pass exemption certificates for middle-class Africans, a provision of the pass laws the Nationalist Party had done away with after 1948.[183]

But faced with the most threatening challenge to their dominance in the history of modern South Africa, most whites were not prepared to reject the strong-arm tactics of the Nationalists in favor of the more subtle strategy of the United Party. Sensing strong white public opinion in support of the government, the United Party in the end defied the logic of its own arguments and voted in favor of the banning bill, leaving only the Progressives and the three Natives' Representatives voting "no."[184] In spite of the distinctions between the ANC and the PAC which were pointed out by a few better-informed members of Parliament, there was no sentiment to support banning the PAC while permitting the less extreme ANC to remain legal.[185] No mention was made of the ineffectual All African Convention or of the Non-European Unity Movement, both of which were spared when, on April 8, the government declared both the ANC and the PAC to be unlawful organizations.[186]

Even before bans officially terminated the semi-legal existence of the two Congresses, their operations had been drastically curtailed by arrests and police raids. The arrest of Sobukwe, Leballo, and other top Africanists in Johannesburg on March 21 left the PAC virtually leaderless overnight. ANC leaders who were still defendants in the Treason Trial were jailed when the emergency was declared, and others who were not on trial went into hiding in an attempt to avoid arrest. A few, like Tambo, who crossed the border into Bechuanaland the night of March 26, sought asylum in the neighboring British High Commission Territories.[187] Hundreds more were to follow them into exile in the 1960s.

In the weeks that followed Sharpeville the weakness of the ANC and the PAC and the imbalance between their power and the might of the government became manifestly clear. Although leaders of both parties had foreseen a stepping up of government pressure, and the ANC had specifically formulated its "M-plan" in anticipation of being forced underground, neither Congress was adequately prepared for the massive crackdown launched by the government during the early days of the emergency. In a statement issued on April 1, the ANC boldly declared that it would not submit to a ban and would continue to "give leadership and organization" to the people until freedom had been won (Document 51). Realistically, however, action other than the issuing of occasional clandestine bulletins (Document 52, for example) had already become more than the ANC could effect; mere survival in the face of the police onslaught had become as much as either Congress could hope for.

The PAC was even less prepared for illegality. In areas where it had been sufficiently well organized to appoint men to understudy the top office-bearers, police swoops netted activists down to the third and fourth layers of contingency leadership. PAC headquarters in Johannesburg was left in the hands of William Jolobe, a student who had previously been the organization's office manager. The "no bail, no defence, no fine" slogan, effective as it may have been in building an image of the PAC as a resolute movement whose leaders were prepared for sacrifice and suffering, became a handicap once the campaign against passes had collapsed and the PAC was forced to struggle for its very survival. With Sobukwe jailed for three years on a charge of incitement, and other top Pan Africanists in the Transvaal also removed from the scene for long periods, the PAC rapidly fell into a state of total disarray from which it was never fully to recover.[188]

Writing in the London *Observer* of April 3, 1960, Colin Legum, a veteran political analyst, posed a question uppermost in the minds of many South

342

Africans when he asked, "Is this the revolution which people have been expecting in South Africa?" It was not *the* revolution, he concluded, but a forerunner of greater conflict probably to come, perhaps like the abortive Russian revolution of 1905.

Was 1960 an attempted revolution? Judging from the frightened reactions of whites during the crisis, from the use of massive force to suppress African resistance, and from the intensive efforts of the South African government from 1960 onwards to build up counter-revolutionary defenses on both the military and propaganda fronts, it seems clear that whites did regard the African threat in March 1960 as a potentially revolutionary one, to be opposed by every means possible. At the same time, the proclamation of a national emergency and the making of mass arrests were reactions more of panic than of logic. By exaggerating the capacity of the PAC and the ANC to sustain action, the government revealed its own incomprehension of the weakness of these organizations. The arrest of some 200 whites, Indians, and Coloureds, including persons who had not been politically active in years, also revealed the government's inability to conceive of an independent African leadership.

Sobukwe and his colleagues also regarded their March 21 initiatives as a revolutionary action, though they did not use the word "revolution," and though they sometimes hoped in their naive overconfidence that the overthrow of white rule might be achieved without full-fledged violence. What neither side was initially capable of gauging accurately was the extent to which ordinary urban Africans were prepared to plunge themselves into a daring confrontation with white authority, for it was on the mood of the masses that the outcome of any revolutionary initiative ultimately depended.

The thin popular response to the PAC's call for action on March 21 not only revealed the inadequacies of the party's organization and propaganda machinery, but also reflected the deep-seated and pragmatic conservatism of most urban Africans, very few of whom were prepared in 1960 to take odds on the African side in any test of strength between the South African government and African political organizations. Many Africans who knew about plans for the campaign, and many adherents of the PAC as well, chose to take no action on March 21 or the following days in spite of all the party's exhortations to self-sacrifice. The challenge being thrown out by the Pan Africanists was phrased in all-or-nothing terms, and the goal of the campaign was often openly defined as black rule; Africans with any degree of sophistication easily could and did construe this goal as an invitation to pit themselves against the full might of the government. Most declined the invitation, not because they were indifferent to the grievances against which the campaign was launched, nor because they necessarily rejected the political goals of the PAC, though many probably did. For most Africans the essential consideration must have been a practical one: did the campaign have any prospect of success? Given the long history of unsuccessful efforts to move the government by means of similar campaigns, there was no reason for the average African to suppose that the results of this campaign would be any different. Only extraordinary, widespread confidence in the new and untested Pan Africanist leadership could have provided a basis for fresh optimism, but in March 1960 the organization and following of the PAC were still spread very thinly.

Had the ANC been able to rally much wider support than it did at the height of the crisis, Lutuli might have been able to call successfully for a prolonged general strike instead of a one-day stay-at-home. The threat to white rule might then have been more credible, with consequences that could not be foreseen. But the ANC, almost as much as the PAC, lacked the strength to support its verbal threats with action or to inspire the masses with a belief in the possibility of their own victory. In the end, neither African leaders nor followers proved able to match the strength and determination of white South Africa.

In reaction to the shock of the Sharpeville shooting and the deepening crisis of the emergency, African political attitudes readjusted somewhat to take new realities into account.[189] Whatever disappointments the crisis period eventually held in store for Africans, there was nevertheless a feeling that white defenses had at least temporarily been breached. African action had forced a brief suspension of the pass laws and had threatened for a short time to paralyze the nation's industries. Many Africans had at least glimpsed the potential power of civil disobedience and economic disruption, and they had begun to sense the important new influence of international opinion. The reality of fear and moral uncertainty had temporarily broken through white South Africa's veneer of smug self-confidence.

An English-speaking Transvaal farmer, apparently deranged by the crisis, narrowly failed in an attempt to assassinate Verwoerd on April 9. Ten days later Paul O. Sauer, minister of lands and senior member of the Cabinet, delivered a speech in which he said that the "old book" of South African history had closed at Sharpeville and that there was a need for the country "in earnest and honestly" to reconsider its whole approach to race relations.[190] Some employers raised the wages of their African workers.

All these developments were cause for measured optimism among Africans. On the negative side, however, stood the obvious determination of the whites to maintain their position by any means at their disposal, including open violence and the suppression of all expressions of African dissent. By mid-April when workers began to queue at government offices to get replacements for their burned passes, it was evident that African demoralization was nationwide. A well-publicized call from the underground ANC for Africans to stage a week-long stay-at-home beginning on April 19 received no popular support.

344

The methods of organization that had been tested and employed by Africans over decades of political activity became obsolete once the two Congresses were declared illegal. Although the rousing of African political consciousness and the mobilization of mass action remained the prime objectives of both the ANC and the PAC, they could no longer pursue these goals through the convening of public meetings, rallies, and conferences. Leaders could not be elected publicly or hold office openly. Divisive internal disputes, declared the underground ANC *Congress Voice* in May 1960, could no longer be tolerated as in the past; in accordance with the imperative need for absolute secrecy, members would have to learn iron discipline, asking—and answering—no questions about the activities of the Congress. Government informers, a nuisance but not a significant problem in the days of semi-legal politics, now became a critical threat endangering the success of all underground activity and the security of the movement's secret leaders and followers. In both Congresses the word went out for large branches to disband and reconstitute themselves into small cells of a few trusted members each.[191]

Just as the crises of 1935–36 and 1948–49 had brought to prominence new African leaders disillusioned with old strategies and bent on greater militancy, the watershed events of the Sharpeville emergency initiated a new and tougher political generation. For many younger Africans receiving their political baptism in 1960, the principal lesson of the crisis was negative, discouraging to all but the most stout-hearted: past methods had proved unequal to the task of liberation, and new methods, more extreme and probably violent, would be necessary if Africans were ever to prevail in the struggle against white supremacy.

THE TREASON TRIAL:
DOES THE ANC ADVOCATE VIOLENCE?

The Treason Trial took on a new importance in 1960. The government, maintaining that a Communist-inspired conspiracy was behind the Sharpeville demonstrations, looked upon the trial as a partial substitute for the judicial inquiry demanded unsuccessfully by the parliamentary opposition.[192] On May 20, 1960, the last day of Parliament, Prime Minister Verwoerd said that no major commission of inquiry would be appointed before the trial was concluded "as this trial itself has in part the character of an inquiry into the causes of disturbances."[193]

The trial had proceeded during 1959 under a revised and narrower indictment against only thirty defendants. Not all the Africans in this group were ANC leaders of importance. The accused generally were distinguished from others against whom charges had been withdrawn by the more violent or bloody tone of their rhetoric. The prosecution's case was not limited to proving the intention of the accused to act violently. The crux, however, according to the particulars to the indictment, was more specific: whether or not violence was the policy of the ANC and its allied organizations. Thus, Chief Lutuli, Professor Matthews, and M. B. Yengwa, who were no longer among the accused, were, in effect, as much on trial as were Dr. Wilson Zami Conco, Nelson Mandela, Robert Resha, and Gert Sibande, who were. The testimony of these seven men is excerpted in Document 53.

Lutuli and Matthews were elder statesmen. Mandela was a founding member of the Youth League and volunteer-in-chief in the Defiance Campaign in 1952, the year he became president of the ANC in the Transvaal. Since then, while in legal practice with Oliver Tambo, he had been banned from public activity but was active behind the scenes, especially in promoting the "M-Plan" for cell-level organization. Both Conco and Yengwa were devoted followers of Lutuli. Conco had been second-in-command to Lutuli in Natal and his chief deputy at the Congress of the People. Yengwa, who was studying for admission to the bar, had been secretary of the ANC in Natal since 1952. Sibande was nearly sixty years old, a long-time activist who had sought to organize farm workers and to expose the abject conditions of their life. He was a self-educated man with no formal schooling and no fluency either in English or Afrikaans. In the late 1950s he had been elected president of the ANC in the Transvaal. Resha, forty years of age, had only eight years of formal education, but after working in the mines had become a free-lance journalist. After participating in the Defiance Campaign, he had become one of the ANC's most aggressive leaders in the Transvaal and served as volunteer-in-chief in the Western Areas campaign, on which the Treason Trial prosecution focused much attention (see above, pp. 24–29).

Early in March 1960, the prosecution concluded its examination of some 150 witnesses and 4,000 (initially nearly 10,000) documents, and the defense opened its case. Conco was the first witness. On March 21, the day of Sharpeville, Lutuli took the stand. The trial then entered a new phase. Lutuli continued to testify, but on March 30 he and many of the accused (who had been free, without bail) were among nearly 2,000 political activists detained in early-morning raids. The three-man special criminal court adjourned and did not meet again until late in April. In the meantime, the government outlawed both the ANC and the PAC. With the ending of the emergency on August 31 and the release of the accused from jail, the proceedings were almost back to normal.

The prosecution's argument, reflected in the cross-examination in Document 53, had a simplicity so grand that one can understand the exasperation with the defense occasionally shown earlier by Oswald Pirow, the chief prosecutor (who died in October 1959). "The essence of the crime" of high treason, said Pirow, was "hostile intent." Such intent was evident in the demands of the accused for full equality. They knew, as alleged by the revised indictment, that to achieve the demands of the Freedom Charter (the prosecution's key document) "in their lifetime" would "necessarily involve the overthrow of the State by violence." Or, "in any case the accused must have known," said Pirow, "that the course of action pursued by them would inevitably result in a violent collision with the State resulting in its subversion."

"The essence of the case," in the view of the prosecution, was the fact that the liberatory movement was part of an international communist-inspired effort "pledged to overthrow by violence all governments in non-communist countries where sections of the population did not have equal political and economic rights." The importance of communism in the trial, said Pirow, was that it illuminated the nature of the conspiracy and the conspirators' intent. Pirow also referred to motivations that had deeper and wider roots than ideological communism; the accused were "inspired by communist fanaticism, Bantu nationalism, and racial hatred in various degrees."

Pirow admitted that the prosecution's case included "voluminous particulars"—all kinds of evidence of spoken and written words, attendance at meetings, possession of documents, and so on—much of which appeared innocent. But there was no doubt about the existence of a treasonable conspiracy, he said, if one looked at each fact in the light of all the facts. "Insistence upon violence runs through the case in an unbroken thread." For illumination of intent, the prosecution looked also at the circumstances in which words were uttered. Intent "or what could reasonably have been intended," said Pirow, could partly be determined by "gauging the probable reaction of the people who formed, for example, the bulk of the audience at meetings of the ANC." The prosecution declared that it had evidence (but the evidence was not introduced) to demonstrate that "the bulk of the country's non-European population is likely to respond more quickly, more irresponsibly, and more violently to illegal agitation than would be the case with a group whose general standard of civilization is higher." The prosecution also looked at intent in the penumbra of circumstances of clear and present danger. Adducing such circumstances was not necessary to the legal argument, but the gravity of the charge appears to have required the justification of imminent revolt. Thus Pirow argued that the situation at the time of the arrests in 1956 was "explosive." Nevertheless, intent remained of the essence.

Subtle but sharp differences distinguished the approach of the prosecution from the approach of the defense to the facts in the case. The defense saw the ANC as a loosely organized movement encompassing many points of view but held together by common grievances and aspirations and officially committed to nonviolence. For the prosecution, African grievances had been exploited by agitators. If one were realistic, according to the prosecution, the primary significance of African aspirations lay in the means their fulfillment implied in the circumstances of South Africa. For the defense, the grievances were to be expected in the circumstances of South Africa, and it was realistic to accept the fact that moderate and responsible African leaders saw in the Freedom Charter, as in the Universal Declaration of Human Rights, a vision of the future. Where the prosecution stressed the power of the accused to start a conflagration, the defense stressed the belief of the accused in the possibility of peaceful change in response to nonviolent pressure. For the prosecutor, the secretly recorded "murder! murder!" speech by Robert Resha was a revelation of intent made by a leader in circumstances in which the usual camouflage of nonviolent affirmation was unnecessary. For the defense, the speech was an example of irresponsible and rather incoherent demagoguery by a flamboyant individual, for whose words no accused could be held responsible in the absence of convincing evidence of endorsement. For the prosecution, sophistication about Communist-inspired conspiracy meant that one proved an individual's complicity by relating his activity to a complex pattern of seemingly innocent facts. The defense view of the prosecution's attitude from the outset was, according to I. A. Maisels: "Let's throw in everything the police have been able to find and see what comes out at the end." In place of vague allegations, said Maisels, each individual among the accused was entitled to particulars that informed him precisely about the nature and extent of his adherence to the alleged conspiracy.

In short, the defense denied that the ANC was a conspiracy motivated by hostile intent. It denied the prosecution's contention that no middle ground existed between the ballot box and treason. The activities of the accused, it maintained, were characteristic of extraparliamentary and nonviolent movements in countries that excluded a large section of the population from the political process. Such movements tended to be amorphous and undisciplined. Their leaders, more than the leaders of Western political parties, could not be held accountable for everything said by their followers. The prosecution had selected for its case only a tiny proportion of all the speeches made. Furthermore, the grab-bag nature of the arrests, the discharge later of major leaders, and the presence of minor personalities among the thirty accused demonstrated, the defense suggested, that no conspiracy existed.

Professor Matthews was the concluding witness for the defense in October 1960. The prosecution's closing argument, interrupted by several adjournments, extended into March 1961. On March 29, when the defense was in the fourth week of its final argument, with many weeks still to go, Justice Rumpff interrupted to announce a unanimous verdict of not guilty. There was no necessity for the defense to continue, he said. The ANC's alleged policy of violence was "the cornerstone of the case," and the prosecution's failure to prove this policy "inevitably meant a collapse of the whole case."

On all the evidence presented to this Court and on our findings of fact, it is impossible for this Court to come to the conclusion that the African National Congress had acquired or adopted a policy to overthrow the State by violence, i.e. in the sense that the masses had to be prepared or conditioned to commit direct acts of violence against the State.

Nor, went on Justice Rumpff, had the prosecution succeeded in proving "a case of contingent retaliation," that is, "that the African National Congress had adopted a plan which revealed a general expectation of violence by the State and an intention to use the masses in retaliation."

The court did make certain findings of fact: the ANC and its allies were working "to replace the present form of State with a radically and fundamentally different form of State"; the Programme of Action "envisaged the use of illegal means" and illegal means were used during the Defiance Campaign; some ANC leaders "made themselves guilty of sporadic speeches of violence which in our opinion amounted to an incitement to violence"; "a strong left-wing tendency manifested itself" in the ANC during the indictment period; and the ANC frequently revealed "anti-imperialist, anti-West and pro-Soviet" attitudes.

In the court's view, in opinions issued later, communism was relevant only to the issue of violence, and all three judges agreed that the prosecution had not proved that the ANC as a national organization was Communist or that the Freedom Charter pictured a Communist state. One indication that the ANC had not adopted communism, they pointed out, was that in 1956 Nelson Mandela, for example, "foresaw a non-European bourgeois advance under the Freedom Charter." Nor had the prosecution proved, said the court, that members of the Communist Party after its banning had infiltrated the ranks of the ANC and become executive leaders. The ANC allowed both Communists and anti-Communists freely to become members if they subscribed to the ANC's policy. The evidence showed that when the Communist Party dissolved itself, "a small number of executive leaders" of the ANC were already members of the party.

The ANC's demands were "far-reaching," said Justice Bekker, and could not be reconciled with "a 'mild' form of socialism." But the Court was "not convinced," said Rumpff, "that the African National Congress had acquired a policy which caused it to cross the dividing line between non-communism and communism in the spectrum of socialist belief."

Finally, with regard to the Freedom Volunteers, to whom Resha had made his much-quoted speech, the prosecution had proved the existence of such an organization, said Rumpff, but not that the ANC's policy was to use it for violent action. However, he issued a gentle reminder to the ANC on the last page of his opinion: "Of course, a political organization with members who are supposed to wear a type of uniform and who are liable to strict discipline and to the carrying out of orders without question, and who intend to bring the Government to its knees and to establish a new form of state through mass action, must not be surprised if it is regarded with suspicion by the State."

The judges' skepticism about Communist inspiration had been widely shared by observers of the trial. Despite the prosecution's effort to stress Communist influence, hardly any foreign observers or editorial commentators accepted the trial as a justifiably anti-Communist proceeding. It failed to promote acceptance abroad of Verwoerd's claim that South Africa was the West's "best friend and most faithful ally on the African continent." Foreign comment mainly impugned the government's motives and sympathized with the tribulations of the accused. No one, however, made the charge that the trial was staged or rigged. The regularity of the trial's procedure was highly praised although it sometimes meant little to the individuals accused. In any event, the prevailing judgment abroad was that, in the words of the *Manchester Guardian* (November 15, 1958), the trial was "a political trial, pursued with pitiless pertinacity."[194]

"ALL-IN" EFFORTS, 1960–1961

During the period of national emergency that followed the banning of the ANC and the PAC in April 1960, African leaders who were in detention talked often about the apparent unavoidability of violent methods. The talk was speculative, however; once the emergency was over, they moved to restore morale by taking advantage of the opportunities for political activity that remained open. In December 1960, prominent Africans who were not under ban moved to fill the vacuum in leadership and came together as individuals to take stock of the political situation. For many of them, the meeting was a last opportunity to plan the building of a united front for pressure on, and negotiation with, white authority. Once again Africans from nearly all points on the political spectrum demonstrated their extraordinary capacity to unite momentarily in expressing their common grievances and fundamental aims. Once again, however, long-standing suspicions and differences were to undermine that unity. Nevertheless, a last abortive major effort at organizing nonviolent political protest was made, culminating on May 31, 1961, the date on which South Africa became a republic. The government's response was to mount the most formidable array of official intimidation and force ever mustered to quell African protest.

Changes During and After the Emergency

African plans to boycott the festivities of the Union jubilee on May 31, 1960, proved to be unnecessary; because of the emergency, festival events for Africans were canceled. Many Indians and Coloureds took no part in the celebration either. The conclusion of the celebration, held in Bloemfontein stadium, attracted few English-speaking spectators. and no Africans attended because the city council had refused to allot a block of seats for them. In Natal, a small number of Africans, whites, and Indians marked the day with fasting and prayer. And in Cape Town, about 8,000 people of all races, led by the Anglican archbishop, the former chief judge of the Appellate Division of the Supreme Court, and prominent Africans and Coloureds, testified to the ideal of nonracial South Africanism by marching in a solemn procession through the downtown streets.

In May the government lifted the state of emergency in some areas and at the end of June a large number of those who had been detained without charge were released. But not until August 31 was the emergency finally ended and the most important detainees released. Meanwhile, a few African leaders were active outside the country. Before Sharpeville, the ANC had sent Tambo, its deputy president-general, out of the country to represent it in Africa and abroad, and the PAC had sent 'Molotsi and Mahomo. These men were joined later by a few activists who left South Africa for Basutoland, Swaziland, and Bechuanaland during the emergency. Most leaders of both the ANC and the PAC, however, remained in South Africa.

Meanwhile, during the months following Sharpeville, prominent whites made the most urgent appeals ever heard in South Africa for consultation with Africans. Those calling for a fresh inquiry into the causes of racial tension included leaders of SABRA, *Die Burger* in Cape Town, United Party leaders, and spokesmen for commerce and industry, as well as religious and liberal groups. The conditions of the emergency, however, made the problem of identifying representative spokesmen of African opinion and consulting with them far more difficult that it had been before.

With the ending of the emergency and of detention without habeas corpus, South African political life began to resume its familiar form. The ANC's allied organizations in the Congress movement renewed their activity, and *New Age* and *Torch*, which had been temporarily banned, resumed publication. The government now concentrated on harassing individuals, prosecuting them for incitement or other offenses or subjecting them to various restrictions. New elements in the scene were the appearance of occasional ANC leaflets and the painting of slogans on walls (for example, the word "Uhuru," Swahili for "freedom," an East African slogan), evidence that a rudimentary underground had come into existence.

Another underground organization also began making itself known: the "South African Communist Party." After the "Communist Party of South Africa" had dissolved itself in 1950, its members had moved underground, organizing the new party in 1953 while working above ground in the Congress movement; during the 1960 emergency, the party began the illegal distribution of leaflets, proclaiming its existence.[195] The leaflets called on Communists to move toward "the first stage" of democratic rights by working within the Congress Alliance and for the Freedom Charter.[196]

Taking advantage of the vacuum above ground, the Liberal Party held multiracial meetings and recruited African members. Some of its founding white members who had always favored a qualified franchise left the organization in this period. With the departure from Parliament of white liberals elected by Africans, the party gradually became (in the words of a Cape leader) "a more militant body, heavily engaged in extra-parliamentary activity."[197]

When leaders of the banned ANC and PAC were released from detention and faced once again the split between their organizations, they learned of the creation abroad of the South African United Front, composed of representatives of the ANC, PAC, SAIC, and the South West African National Union (SWANU).[198] ANC leaders welcomed its creation; PAC leaders were less enthusiastic but nevertheless agreed to join. Tambo, 'Molotsi, and Mahomo had all been in Accra in April. Also present were Tennyson Makiwane of the ANC Youth League, who had been abroad since 1959, and Dr. Dadoo of the SAIC. Cut off from South Africa, anxious to present a united front, and encouraged by Kwame Nkrumah and other African leaders, they agreed in principle to work together but rejected suggestions for the formation of a government-in-exile. A formal agreement was made in Addis Ababa in June 1960, at the time of the Second Conference of Independent African States. SWANU, represented by Jariretundu Kozonguizi, joined the United Front later. (The South West African People's Organization was affiliated during only part of 1961.) With a few additional members of the ANC and PAC, the United Front had established offices, each staffed by an ANC and a PAC member, in London, Accra, Cairo, and Dar es Salaam by the end of 1960 and sent two-man or three-man delegations to the United Nations and to African and Asian countries.

During the first year of the Front's existence, its members, working together with a minimum of personal dissension and suspicion, found unity to be a great advantage in making international representations. The United Front was strengthened by the evidence of a brief unity at home and won acclaim, especially for its campaign for the exclusion of South Africa from the Commonwealth. But during the first half of 1961 it found itself more and more in the anomalous position of seeking to present to outsiders a front of unity that had not been achieved within South Africa itself.

On October 5, 1960, 90.8 percent of the white electorate—and only whites—voted on the referendum question that Verwoerd had promised in January: should South Africa become a republic? Before the vote, Verwoerd declared that a republican South Africa would apply for

352

continued membership in the commonwealth. The Nationalist Party's popular vote had increased steadily in general elections since 1938 but not until 1960 did the Nationalist position win a clear majority of the vote—52.04 percent. South African voters were still fairly evenly divided along party lines, although the majority probably included a small number of English-speaking persons. With the historic and contentious republican issue eliminated, white progressives and liberals now hoped that attention could focus realistically on the racial issue.

The ending of the national emergency had been an important step for the government in its effort to restore the domestic and international image of an orderly and harmonious South Africa. But on November 30, 1960, the government felt compelled to impose a state of emergency in eastern Pondoland and other rural districts of the Transkei.[199] Since February 1960, there had been sporadic, violent protests in these areas in opposition to unpopular chiefs and headmen, increased taxation, enforced soil conservation, and other policies. Protests took the form of mass meetings of tribesmen, refusals to pay taxes, rioting, the burning of huts and kraals, and occasional stoning of white motorists. Some Africans, detested as collaborators, were murdered. (Twenty-five Africans, including two chiefs, had been murdered in Pondoland, according to a ministerial statement in January 1961.) Emergency regulations (still in effect in 1976) provided for detention without right of *habeas corpus* and a ban on all meetings of ten persons or more unless an official permit was obtained.

Large areas were sealed off from newsmen and other observers, and thousands of specially trained riot police and heavily armed troops with helicopter support moved into the Transkei. The police made mass arrests, followed by mass trials, for tax and pass violations, possession of dangerous weapons, and for more serious offenses. Some of the opponents of pro-government chiefs hid in the mountains, where they appear to have organized a cell-based movement known as the "Congo" (or Congress), with a hierarchy of leaders called "the Hill." To some extent they maintained contact with and sought financial aid from Pondos living in urban areas. *New Age* and *Contact* gave prominent coverage to Pondoland developments, and Rowley Arenstein, a white Durban lawyer, gave valuable legal assistance to individual Pondos. Though the direct participation of whites seems to have been of negligible importance, government officials charged that they had instigated the disturbances by exploiting intratribal feuds. Accordingly, toward the end of 1960, the government granted senior chiefs in the Transkei power to apprehend and hand over to the police persons described by the minister of Bantu administration and development as "White Communist agitators."

In January 1961, the minister of justice disclosed that 4,769 Africans had been taken into custody in Pondoland, and that 2,067 had already been brought to trial. On April 20, he explained that 524 Africans were still in detention; 114 were to be charged with murder, 121 with arson, and 288 "for multifarious breaches of the law." By this time, government control had been restored in Pondoland, and by the end of May 1961, most of the troops had been withdrawn.

Consultative Conference, December 1960

The troubles in Pondoland, the dangers of spontaneous and violent eruptions by an embittered African population, apprehension about republican changes in the constitution, the talk among liberal and progressive whites of the desirability of a national convention—all contributed to the need felt by leading Africans for consultation and stock-taking among themselves.[200] J. Congress Mbata, a staff member of the Institute of Race Relations who had been a founder of the ANC Youth League, proposed a small meeting in letters written during the emergency to elder statesmen, such as Selby Msimang in Pietermaritzburg and R. H. Godlo in Uitenhage, and to Liberals such as Jordan Ngubane, the party's vice-president, and Hyacinth (Bill) Bhengu in Natal. Shortly after the emergency, the Interdenominational African Ministers' Federation, which had sponsored the "all-in" African conference of 1956 on the Tomlinson report, called for the convening of another "all-in" conference. ANC leaders asked IDAMF to convene a meeting, but IDAMF declined because it was involved at that time in church conferences and negotiations with the government on church matters. In order to avoid further delay, invitations to a consultative conference of African leaders were sent out by Chief Lutuli, Professor Matthews, Duma Nokwe, W. B. Ngakane (who had been on the staff of the Institute of Race Relations), and the Rev. N. B. Tantsi, all formerly associated with the banned ANC and now acting as individuals.

Responding to the invitations, some thirty-six Africans met in the Donaldson Orlando Community Centre in Johannesburg on December 16 and 17, 1960. Three of the convenors could not attend—Lutuli and Nokwe, because they were under ban, and Professor Matthews. Other absentees were ANC and PAC men who were in prison or under restriction and several AAC leaders who had been invited but were detained in the Transkei under emergency regulations. Nevertheless, Dr. Njongwe, Dr. Conco, G. M. Pitje, and Govan Mbeki of the ANC sat alongside Joe Molefi, Z. B. Molete, and Francis Mbelu of the PAC. Many other participants had not recently been active either in the ANC or the PAC or were uncommitted. Ngubane, who was present with other members of the Liberal Party, had not been on the original invitation list, but he had agreed to come after meeting with Lutuli at the latter's home. The two old friends had not met for years, following Ngubane's public charge that Lutuli had become a Communist tool, but Lutuli had apologized for the lateness of the invitation and urged him to attend. Among others present were ministers, other professional men, businessmen, and leaders of cultural and sporting groups, for example, the Rev. Z. R. Mahabane, president of IDAMF, the Rev. Benjamin Rajuili, the first African member of the Progressive Party, Paul Mosaka, president of the Johannesburg African Chamber of Commerce, and Mbata.

The beginning of the conference was delayed by an incident in which the PAC insisted that the conference be limited, as planned, to Africans, and the ANC supported such a limitation. ("ANC" and "PAC" are to be understood as banned organizations throughout this discussion, and their members as "former members.") A white member and a Coloured member of the Liberal Party (Timothy Holmes and K. Hendrickse), who had driven from Cape Town with Mbelu and an African Liberal, Joseph Nkatlo, were admitted by Tantsi, who had been elected chairman. There was some support for Tantsi's decision, but when Molefi and Molete threatened to leave, Mbeki and Ngakane asked the white and Coloured Liberals to leave so that the conference could proceed.

Dr. Arthur Letele's paper, read in his absence by Dr. Conco, described the PAC as a body representing "a definite point of view in African political thinking" and suffering "the same fate as that of the ANC."[201] Participants concentrated on bases of agreement and adopted resolutions without dissent (but with no recorded vote) testifying to "the urgent need for African Unity" and the need for "effective use of non-violent pressures against apartheid" and for "a non-racial democracy." "An all-in conference representative of African People" was called for in order to "demand the calling of a National Convention representing all the people of South Africa" (Document 54). After a police raid and the confiscation of all papers toward the end of the conference, the resolutions had to be reconstructed by persons still in attendance.[202]

Continuation Committee

The thirteen-man continuation committee elected by the conference from the floor was, on its face, remarkably diverse. Ngubane became chairman although, living in Natal, he was not in the best position to promote close cooperation. Another Liberal became chairman of the action committee composed of members living in the Johannesburg area: Julius Malie, a journalist who had worked for the YMCA and the Institute of Race Relations and had never been politically active before joining the Liberals and becoming their Transvaal organizer. A third Liberal, Bhengu, was also a member of the continuation committee, as were several relatively cautious personalities: Mosaka, Mbata, Rajuili, Ngakane, and the 70-year-old Tantsi. Other members were Mark Shope of the African

Laundry Workers' Union, three ANC activists—Nokwe, Mbeki, and Alfred Nzo—and only one member of the PAC, Joe Molefi.

The mandate of the continuation committee was to organize an "all-in" African conference based upon the unity manifested by the consultative conference. The projected conference took place in Pietermaritzburg on March 25–26, 1961, but unity had already been shattered and the conference was predominantly an ANC affair. Assessing blame for the breakdown in unity is a difficult and tentative matter. The consultative conference itself met primarily under ANC auspices; and although discussion was frank and affirmative, both PAC and Liberal Party members were apprehensive from the outset about the possibility that the ANC and its allies would act to exert control behind a facade of unity. During the two months following the conference, PAC and Liberal Party members concluded that their fears were confirmed. Some members were not informed of early meetings of the continuation committee. In mid-February, a printed leaflet announcing the Pietermaritzburg conference was distributed with the label: "issued by the Continuation Committee of African Leaders" (Document 55) without discussion or approval either by the full committee or by the action committee. The leaflet was criticized by some members for pro-ANC bias.

More troublesome than specific examples of uncoordinated action, however, was a growing sense of uneasiness among some members who felt that both committees were being manipulated by behind-the-scenes forces. According to Ngubane and Mbata, money seemed to be coming to certain members of the committee from sources that were never identified. Ngubane has written that he saw "an invisible hand" of communism, that he believed money had come directly from Moscow via Basutoland, to be handled by Indian rather than African Communists in Johannesburg.[203] There is some irony in these charges by Ngubane, a member of the Liberal Party, since a reliable source who cannot be named has said that money was being channeled at this time to the organizers of the "all-in" conference from non-Communist sources, including African governments and members of the Liberal Party.

PAC members were concerned because they suspected that plans were afoot to build up Mandela as a hero in opposition to Sobukwe. The PAC participants do not seem at any time to have been committed to the "all-in" effort; and it is doubtful that in the closing session of the consultative conference, which was interrupted by a police raid, they expressly endorsed the national convention called for by the conference resolutions. Molefi was not active in the work of the continuation committee. Early in February, when talk of the forthcoming conference and *New Age* publicity were accentuating the ANC role, *Contact* quoted Molete as opposed to the holding of a multiracial national convention and "a little doubtful that the African Nationalists" would support the Pietermaritzburg conference.[204]

The PAC had clearly withdrawn by early March, when Molefi, Molete, and other PAC leaders, writing as "African Nationalists," stated that the Pietermaritzburg conference had shifted its aim from African unification to preparations for a multiracial convention. "Africans alone," they said, "can solve the problems besetting South Africa. . . . We therefore cannot be party to any conference based on preparation for a futile barren indaba [conference or palaver]."[205]

When members of the continuation committee who belonged to the Liberal Party or were unaffiliated asked for a withdrawal of the "call" and the preparation of new and approved leaflets, ANC members apologized fervently for their "mistakes" but argued that it was too late to undo what had been done. The critics proposed that the conference be postponed to allow time for rebuilding unity. Agreement was reached that there should be consultation on the question with elder statesmen and others on the committee who lived outside the Johannesburg area: Lutuli, Matthews, Mahabane, Mbeki, and Tantsi. The consultation was delegated to Ngubane and Nokwe, who was banned from meetings but could travel. (A third person was unable to take part.) Advice was solicited by telegram, and the answer was unequivocal: planning for the conference should proceed as scheduled.[206] Because of the lack of unity resulting from the absence of PAC support, however, Ngubane, Bhengu, and Mbata resigned on March 4. Mosaka, who was in poor health, had resigned during the preceding week for personal reasons. Malie succeeded Ngubane as chairman and, after consultation with Liberal Party colleagues, remained in order to observe events from the inside and to insure that control did not fall into ANC hands.

Although the ANC activists attempted from time to time to repair the damage to unity, they developed no close working relationship among all elements of the continuation committee. Some of the lapses in communication were no doubt due to inefficiency and clashes of personality. Nokwe and those with whom he was accustomed to working, both inside and outside the ANC, apparently found it difficult to take the younger and less experienced PAC men seriously or to appreciate their sensitivity, and that of the independent members, to rhetoric and allies taken for granted by the ANC.

ANC men had dominated the "all-in" effort from the beginning. Nevertheless, it is difficult to understand their failure to anticipate the need for maintaining both the appearance and the reality of good faith in relations with men like Ngubane, Malie, and Mbata, as well as with the PAC. Nor was there any cultivation of moderate personalities like Mosaka, who attended none of the continuation committee meetings, or Rajuili, who attended few if any. Furthermore, secrecy about money poisoned relations within the committee, whether or not the money came from Communist sources (undoubtedly some did) or from non-Communist sources (there is ample evidence of money from white liberals). In any event, the question remains as to whether or not antagonism and suspicions were not already too strong in 1961 to be overcome.

On March 20, 1961, five days before the Pietermaritzburg conference and nine days before the end of the Treason Trial, the government took action that had the extraordinary effect of reuniting all members of the continuation committee. In the early morning hours, Special Branch police served warrants at the homes of Nokwe and Molefi, who were still among the accused at the Treason Trial but not confined, and arrested ten other members of the committee. Nzo was arrested later, and, after the Treason Trial ended, so were Nokwe and Molefi, bringing to thirteen the number of persons arrested. The wholesale arrest of this conglomerate group was ironic—especially at the time that it occurred—to any observer of African politics and still another indication of the government's simplistic understanding of such politics. All thirteen were charged with publishing documents calling for the Pietermaritzburg conference, acts said to be "calculated" to further the aims of the ANC.

Many of the accused might have disassociated themselves from the charge. Instead, no one testified, and the defense rested on a vitally important legal issue: were the accused guilty of furthering the aims of the ANC if the prosecution demonstrated a similarity or coincidence between the aims of the continuation committee and those of the ANC as expressed in the Freedom Charter and other documents? Or should there be proof of the intention of each accused to further the aims of the ANC? The magistrate found "such a marked degree of similarity established that coincidence can be disregarded entirely."[207] On October 12, all the accused except Molefi, who had fled to Basutoland, were found guilty and sentenced to a year in prison but freed on bail pending appeal. In April 1962, two judges of the Supreme Court upheld the appeal; in seeking to promote the conference, they said, the accused conceivably could act in a manner that did not endanger the public safety or order.[208] Six months later, the government announced that it was withdrawing its own appeal.

"All-in" Conference, March 1961

Despite the arrest of some of its key organizers, the Pietermaritzburg conference took place as scheduled. Unlike the "all-in" conferences of 1935–1936 and 1956, which had been composed of prominent Africans of widely diverse orientations, the 1961 gathering was dominated by ANC speakers, songs, and slogans. Instead of being a small conference allowing fruitful discussion, it was a mass meeting of some 1,400 rank-and-file representatives of groups in all parts of the country and large numbers of participants from both rural and urban areas of Natal. Organizers claimed that delegates had been elected by 145 organizations. The credentials committee report listing the names and addresses of delegates and organizations is not available, but Nelson Mandela later gave the following examples of organizations that sent delegates: IDAMF (apparently delegates from local units), the Southern Transvaal Football Association, the Apostolic Church in Zion, and the Liberal Party.[209] A handful of African Liberals and PAC members were present, and white, Indian, and Coloured observers were welcomed and in attendance. Because of its national reach and the enthusiasm and determination of its participants, the conference was impressive, inasmuch as all of its participants could reasonably have expected arrest. It was to be the last large conference organized publicly on a national scale by African political leaders in South Africa for many years.

Preparations for the conference had been accompanied by the usual harassments, culminating in the discovery that the Special Branch had installed recording equipment in the public hall in Edendale outside Pietermaritzburg, where the conference was to take place. Participants then walked two miles in a drizzling rain to an Indian hall, where the meeting continued until dawn. The dramatic highlight of the conference was the appearance of Nelson Mandela, the expiration of whose ban eleven days earlier had been overlooked by the government. Restricted by successive bans, he had not spoken on a public platform since 1952. He now emerged as a charismatic personality of commanding presence and national stature. An attorney and the son of a Tembu chief, he had been one of the founders of the Youth League and was a former president of the ANC in the Transvaal. In his opening speech, he called on Africans "to refuse to cooperate" with the republic if the government refused to call a national convention; and he promised "militant campaigns," aided by external pressures that would be generated by the South African United Front abroad.[210]

The call for a national convention with "sovereign powers" was made by the conference as an ultimatum, to be met by May 31, 1961, the day South Africa was to become a republic (Document 56). If the call was ignored by the government, the conference resolved "to stage country-wide demonstrations on the eve of the proclamation of the Republic" and (in typical ANC style) called for the support of Indians, Coloureds, "and all democratic Europeans." Mandela became the secretary of a National Action Council (NAC). The identity of the other members was kept secret, and Mandela himself disappeared after the conference. A warrant was issued for his arrest. Excerpts of the resolutions appeared in the major newspapers. On May 8, the minister of justice said that "it is just as well that we know what they resolved" and read the full text to the House of Assembly.[211]

Renewed Hopes and "Walls of Granite"

Although no one expected that the ultimatum demanding a national convention would be met, sentiment in favor of interracial dialogue and either a multiracial conference or movement toward a new national convention had spread widely by 1961 among opponents of the government. In an article published in March 1961, Professor Matthews insisted that the call for such a convention—"a genuine, representative, all-in Convention"—was "not a cheap political debating point" but an appeal that was winning wide support. The question remained, he said, "whether the Whites of South Africa can rise to the occasion and refrain from spurning the hand of friendship while it remains outstretched."[212]

An example of the kind of gathering Matthews hoped for was the "Natal Convention," a well-organized multiracial conference that had been in the making since late 1960. Its moving spirit was Peter Brown, a Liberal Party leader. The conference met on April 17–19, 1961, at the University of Natal in Pietermaritzburg.[213] Its 210 listed participants and 67 participating or observing organizations represented an unusually wide range of opinion within each racial group, although the most conservative white opinion in this conservative province was not represented. The conference took positions that were surprisingly radical to many observers. For example, although splitting sharply on the question of a universal franchise, it agreed that the franchise should be nonracial on a common roll. For African participants like Yengwa, the nonracial orientation of the conference, the frank discussion, and the sense of meeting "at a moment of grave and urgent crisis," according to the final report, was gratifying. Especially so was the conclusion that the time was "ripe" to press for "an all-South African Convention."

Looking back at early 1961 from the vantage point of the 1970s, it is difficult to appreciate the extent to which African leaders and other radical opponents of the government felt that the trend of events was in their favor. Historically, South African blacks have felt optimistic about achieving full rights, an optimism that contrasts with the pessimism sometimes found among American blacks. As South Africa entered the 1960s, morale was boosted by the emergence of black independent states on the continent and the gradual mounting of pressures against South Africa. A world-wide economic boycott appeared to be in the making, and sanctions by governments against South Africa were being seriously discussed. In November 1960, the World Court case on South West Africa (to decide whether South Africa had violated its League of Nations obligations to develop that territory in the interests of its inhabitants) began in response to applications filed by Liberia and Ethiopia on behalf of the African group in the United Nations. The proceeding was one in which a legally binding judgment was possible, rather than an advisory opinion, as in the past. In January 1961, Dag Hammarskjold, secretary-general of the United Nations, visited South Africa in pursuance of the Security Council resolution that called on South Africa after Sharpeville "to abandon its policies of apartheid." The Africans he saw were selected by the government, but he was told by Dr. Xuma, Dr. Nkomo, and K. T. Masemola, a member of a Pretoria advisory board, that men like Lutuli and Sobukwe were regarded as (in Nkomo's words) "the real leadership."[214]

Because of harsh criticism of apartheid at the Commonwealth Prime Ministers' Conference, where he stood alone, Verwoerd withdrew his request on March 15, 1961, that South Africa be allowed to continue its membership in the Commonwealth after becoming a republic. Lutuli had spoken out in favor of South Africa's expulsion, for which the South African United Front abroad had campaigned, and hailed the outcome.[215] The outflow of capital from the country, which had begun after Sharpeville, was now renewed, and the apprehensiveness of investors was aggravated. In April, the United Kingdom and Australia, which previously had abstained or voted against UN resolutions critical of South Africa, voted alongside the United States for a resolution calling on all states to consider taking such action as was open to them to bring about the abandonment of apartheid. A few days later, Verwoerd stated frankly that "in the light of the pressure being exerted on South Africa," the government would gradually have to introduce the elective system into the Bantu Authorities system and allow the development of separate Bantu states, possibly even to the point of full independence.[216]

The place of the Coloureds within the Nationalist scheme was also a subject of dispute within South Africa. The political consequence of this dispute and of Nationalist policy generally was an upsurge of Coloured interest in a Coloured front and common cause with Africans. During 1960, however, some Afrikaner intellectuals urgently advocated closer association of Coloureds with whites. Among Coloureds, for example, the small membership of George Golding's Coloured People's National Union, there still existed the traditional aspirations for privileged treatment as whites. Such hopes were rekindled when Nationalists expressed gratitude for the "loyalty" of the Coloured population during the disturbances after Sharpeville and urged a more rapid enhancement of their status. Some SABRA members went farther and suggested that Coloureds elect Coloureds to Parliament; and a few Afrikaner voices, seeking to enlarge the white camp, spoke in support of total integration of Coloureds and whites. These visions were summarily deflated by Verwoerd. In a political speech on November 30, he declared that the government would be "as unyielding as walls of granite" in applying apartheid and under no circumstances would allow Coloureds into Parliament.[217]

The "granite wall" speech gave new impetus to a growing movement among moderate and unaffiliated Coloureds to join in a broad anti-government front, which became known as the Coloured "convention" movement. A newly formed committee of this movement was represented among the speakers at the Liberal Party's Africa Day rally in Cape Town on April 16, 1961, which attracted some 10,000 people. The left-wing South African Coloured People's Congress (prior to December 1959 named the South African Coloured People's Organization), which itself had probably only a few hundred active members, was only one of many Coloured groups to endorse the end-of-May demonstrations and the meeting of a Coloured National Convention in July.

Protest and Response as South Africa Becomes a Republic

Dozens of multiracial rallies were held throughout South Africa during April and early May. Typical of their militant tone was an "Africa Day" message by Lutuli, who said that "defiance" should be "even more granite-like" than the posture of Verwoerd.[218] The reaction of *Die Burger* was to warn that enemies of South Africa were precipitating "altogether the most serious crisis in South African history . . . not in the undefined future but in the next couple of months."[219] In mid-April, 1961, the National Action Council wrote to the Prime Minister informing him of the Pietermaritzburg resolutions; and on May 23, Mandela wrote to Sir de Villiers Graaff, leader of the United Party, asking where the United Party stood on the question of a national convention. The alternatives were "stated bluntly" by Mandela's letter to Graaff: "talk it out, or shoot it out" (Document 58). Neither letter was acknowledged, although when asked in the House of Assembly, Verwoerd said that Mandela's "arrogant" letter with its "threats" had been received.[220]

Tens of thousands of flyers and leaflets were distributed throughout the country, and statements from Mandela were mailed from the underground to the press. One among several flyers that were directed to special groups was "An Appeal to Students and Scholars," which called on all students to participate in "the forthcoming demonstrations" and to boycott the republican celebrations (Document 57).[221] Not until nearly mid-May did the NAC declare that protest would take the form of a three-day stay-at-home on Monday, Tuesday, and Wednesday, May 29–31. Flyers (for example, Document 60) called on everyone to stay quietly at home, but other NAC statements made it clear that what was hoped for from whites was not a stay-at-home but a selective boycott of the republican festivities or, at least, neutrality.

On May 4, the liberal periodical *Contact*, which had criticized the

Pietermaritzburg conference for not being representative, praised Mandela's council for taking the initiative and expressed its belief that the campaign would be nonviolent and would not seek to further "any particular ideology." Therefore, *Contact* endorsed the demonstrations and urged everyone to stay at home at the end of May. On May 18, *Contact* observed that "the desire to demonstrate has spread even beyond the bounds of influence of the Action Council." In particular, it said, "the mass" of Coloureds in Cape Town had adopted the campaign. Predictably, however, the members of the Anti-CAD considered it a "stunt." Toward the end of May, both the Liberal Party and moderate whites who had participated in the Natal Convention called on employers not to dismiss workers who were absent.[222] There may have been a growing tacit support for the campaign among groups and persons who were usually not influenced by the Congress leadership. Indeed, *New Age* claimed on May 11 that many former PAC members were joining the campaign and pointed out later that no PAC leader had spoken openly against the strike. Nevertheless, PAC leaders in jail looked upon the stay-at-home as an opportunistic diversion, a futile protest against a white event—the proclamation of a republic—comparable to the futility of the ANC's effort to involve itself in the 1958 election.

These PAC views were discussed in prison and set forth in a printed pamphlet, *Mafube (The Dawn of Freedom)*, edited and produced in Johannesburg by Matthew Nkoana (with financial help from liberal whites) after his release from prison.[223] An anonymous statement in the first issue of this publication (Document 62) was written by A.P. Mda. During the last weekend of May, a mimeographed flyer (Document 61) issued in Port Elizabeth was distributed under the name of the PAC urging the people to go to work. The flyer was headed "Poqo. Poqo. Poqo.," the Xhosa vernacular equivalent (literally, "independent" or "standing alone") of PAC. *New Age* reported later that many people believed such leaflets were fakes produced by the police. In response to a questionable flyer by "African Nationalists," 25,000 copies of which were said to be distributed in Johannesburg, the ANC, under its own name (Document 59), denounced PAC members for acting as "police agents" in calling for the disclosure of the names of members of the National Action Council. Although many of the preparations for the stay-at-home had the familiar appearance of similar tactics in the past, the underground origins of the propaganda and the secrecy of the NAC were signs of how precarious African protest had become.

The government's response to the planned demonstrations also had a familiar appearance: the show of police strength, the banning of virtually all gatherings, beginning on May 19 and extending to the commemorative day of June 26, raids and arrests, preparations to maintain essential services, public and private warnings of dismissal, and efforts to convince Africans that they would be protected while traveling to work. But with the experience of Sharpeville and the days afterwards in mind, the government was obviously ready to take unprecedented steps in order to maintain total control and to do so without incurring the embarrassment—and further loss of foreign capital—that would be caused by the proclamation of an emergency. It avoided such a proclamation but took legislative and police action that amounted to placing the country in a state of temporary emergency. The unparalleled intimidation of would-be demonstrators implied that the threat was, indeed, grave. Control was maintained, but a pall was cast over the birth of the republic.

Detailed new legislation provided for closer coordination between military forces and the police in "the prevention or suppression of internal disorder." Other legislation empowered the Attorney General to prohibit a court for twelve days (instead of forty-eight hours) from releasing an arrested person on bail. Late in May, police conducted large-scale raids and arrested not only suspected leaders (though failing to find Mandela, who continued to issue statements) but also up to 10,000 Africans. The latter, who were arrested for minor or technical offenses, were suspected as persons who might intimidate Africans wanting to go to work. (Some of the persons arrested were released on bail after twelve days; in many other cases, charges were withdrawn without explanation.) Members of the Liberal Party were also arrested, and the Liberal Party and the Black Sash were among the organizations denied permission to hold meetings. Military and civilian forces were strengthened and brought to a state of readiness. Police loudspeakers and vernacular leaflets attacked African leaders, charging that many had absconded. Helicopters with searchlights flew low over African townships looking for gatherings, and Saracen armoured cars patroled the streets. White tensions rose, amidst rumours of violence and sensational press stories, and whites were reported to be buying guns and hoarding food. As the end of the month neared, many public and private employers renewed their warnings of dismissal and expulsion from town.

Verwoerd himself issued stern warnings not only to "agitators" but also to "members of the ordinary public," including "some intellectuals and some only pseudo-intellectuals as well as some newspapers," who were "busy playing with fire" by advocating a multiracial national convention. This proposal was made by Communists, he said, and "everyone who lends support to this proposition will, whatever his personal aims may be, become jointly responsible for what is their [the Communists'] aims."[224]

On Monday, May 29, the Associated Press reported to American readers that in some of the Johannesburg townships "buses normally jammed at 6 A.M. were going into the city about 90 percent empty." But beginning at 7 A.M., the South African government radio was reporting "total" failure.[225] The New York Times correspondent, on the other hand, reported that about half of the city's African labor force had stayed away from work. It appears that the stay-at-home was only partially successful in a few centers. New Age, however, concluded that it was "the biggest national strike on a political issue ever staged in South African history."[226] South Africa's daily press reported that dozens of industries and factories were crippled to some degree, but pronounced the campaign a failure. Agreeing with a mixed verdict, Mandela described the first day of the stay-at-home as "not the national success I had hoped for"; on the second day, he called off the campaign.[227]

Africans appeared to have stayed at home in large numbers only in Johannesburg on May 29 and in Port Elizabeth on May 30 and 31. In Port Elizabeth there was scattered violence, and some African bus drivers were stoned and refused to drive. Only a few Africans struck in Cape Town and Durban, but larger numbers of Coloureds and Malays in Cape Town and Indians and Coloureds in Durban stayed away. Elsewhere there was little activity, and absentee workers (except in Port Elizabeth) soon began to return to work. Nevertheless, the total number of persons who had responded to the call ran into many thousands. Many schools were closed down because of poor attendance, and the entire student body of Fort Hare was sent home.

In retrospect, it is extraordinary that the stay-at-home was as extensive as it was and that the government thought that the full range of its counter-measures was necessary. Pickets were absent. Leaders were not visible. Organization was skimpy, and communication had broken down. Confusion and uncertainty were made worse by anti-strike propaganda and by PAC opposition. The call for a national convention was "too academic" a goal for serious risks to be run by poor people, as *Contact* observed, especially when lack of unity meant that protestors suffered victimization.[228] Finally, the question had to be asked: could public protest be organized on a mass and nonviolent scale if it were countered by the full force of state power? For the government, the stakes required such an exercise of power. South Africa was resisting "the grabbing hand of communism," Verwoerd said on May 29, and seeking to preserve itself as a "pillar of Christian Western civilization in Africa."[229] On the same day, Nelson Mandela said, "As long as the grievances remain, there will be protest actions of this kind or another. If peaceful protests like these are to be put down by the mobilisation of the army and the police, then the people might be forced to use other methods of struggle."[230]

NOTES

1. Oliver Tambo, in "Annual Report of the National Executive Committee to the 45th Annual Conference of the African National Congress," Dec. 1957, p. 12, refers to "Ministerial declarations and rantings regarding the Government's intention and determination to smash the African National Congress, and the threat of the Cabinet to ban the organisation."

2. *Contact,* March 8, 1958, p. 3.

3. *The World,* Dec. 7, 1957; *Golden City Post,* March 2, 1958.

4. "No detached onlooker who saw it happen can believe that the clubbing and shooting were ever necessary." Cyril Dunn, a reporter for the London *Observer,* quoted in *New Age,* Jan. 10, 1957; also see *New Age,* Dec. 27, 1956.

5. Conversation of Karis with Oswald Pirow, Jan. 20, 1959. Pirow was a colorful figure in South Africa's political history, a brilliantly pugnacious barrister who entered Hertzog's cabinet as minister of justice in 1929, opposed South Africa's entrance into World War II, and founded the New Order, an authoritarian group opposed to parliamentary democracy. He came out of semi-retirement to head the prosecution toward the end of the preparatory examination in January 1958 and died in October 1959.

6. See Anthony Sampson, *The Treason Cage: The Opposition on Trial in South Africa* (London: Heinemann, 1958) pp. 207–214.

7. Quoted in *New Age,* March 7, Jan. 31, 1957. The pro-boycott Society of Young Africa, the youth arm of the AAC, praised the boycott as a political showdown and attacked the Liberal Party for regarding it as motivated solely by economic reasons. *The World* (referring to SOYA as "Sons of Young Africa"), Feb. 23, 1957.

8. Conversations with Joseph Matthews and Tennyson Makiwane.

9. *The World,* Feb. 16, 1957.

10. *Ibid.,* Oct. 4, 1958.

11. Conversation with Makiwane.

12. Mrs. Ballinger urged the minister to "establish contact with what he himself obviously regards as moderate African opinion . . . so that we can win the support of the moderate people." Quoted in *New Age,* Feb. 28, 1957.

13. In a long letter to *The World,* March 9, 1957, Xuma described the boycott as "economic and critical" and referred to four private meetings he had attended, the last three with the "blessing and full knowledge" of the boycott leaders. Mosaka and Xorile, he said, were "leaders of nobody."

14. Sampson, *The Treason Cage,* p. 214.

15. *New Age,* Feb. 7 and 14, 1957.

16. *Ibid.,* Feb. 28, 1957.

17. "June 26th," a statement issued by the National Consultative Committee, n.d.

18. Quoted in *New Age,* July 4, 1957.

19. *TCI Bulletin,* from L. Lulofs, President, "To All Members," 24th June, 1957.

20. Sampson, *The Treason Cage,* p. 220.

21. Quoted in *New Age,* July 4, 1957.

22. Discussion of the new constitution is based on conversations with Tambo on November 15, 1963 and later.

23. Some in the ANC, who did not fully trust the Transvaal leadership and were concerned about the role of Lutuli, favored transferring headquarters to Durban. The constitution, however, left the location of headquarters to the National Executive Committee. The Xuma constitution had provided that the national conference designate the national headquarters.

24. According to *New Age,* Dec. 26, 1957, the conference approved a memorandum of the National Executive Committee that concluded that the Programme of Action and the Freedom Charter were "complementary." Only 5 of the 305 delegates supported the Africanist assertion that the documents were in conflict.

25. Unless he had been born in an urban area or had been in continuous employment there for ten years, an African had to be a "continuous" resident, instead of a nominally "permanent" resident, for fifteen years in order to remain.

366

26. Quoted in *New Age*, Sept. 19, 1957.

27. On rural opposition, see Gwendolen M. Carter, Thomas Karis, and Newell M. Stultz, *South Africa's Transkei: The Politics of Domestic Colonialism* (Evanston: Northwestern University Press, 1967), pp. 20–21; Govan Mbeki, *South Africa: The Peasants' Revolt* (Harmondsworth, Middlesex, England: Penguin Books Ltd., 1964); and Charles Hooper, *Brief Authority* (London: Collins, 1960). Hooper deals with events in Zeerust between March 1957 and March 1958.

28. Proclamation No. 67, 1958, and Government Notice No. 400, March 17, 1957.

29. "Executive Report Submitted to the African National Congress Annual National Conference, December 1959, Held at Durban."

30. Presidential Address by Albert J. Lutuli, Dec. 13–14, 1958.

31. *New Age*, Dec. 5, 1957. The tactic of maintaining unity against the Nationalists was followed by members of the Liberal Party as well as the Congress of Democrats in the October 30, 1957 elections to the Johannesburg city council. Seven Liberal Party candidates and one COD candidate ran, but not in any ward in which there was a United Party candidate. *New Age*, Oct. 30, Nov. 8, 1957.

32. The full text of the resolution appears in *New Age*, March 20, 1958.

33. *Ibid.*

34. "Statement to A.N.C. Branches on Protest Week, for Circulation and Discussion," signed by Duma Nokwe, Assistant Secretary-General, April 28, 1958.

35. *New Age*, April 3, 1958.

36. *Ibid.* April 10, 1958.

37. *The World*, April 26, 1958.

38. Statement by S. T. Ngendane and Potlako Leballo in *New Age*, May 8, 1958.

39. "Statement to A.N.C. Branches . . . , April 28, 1958."

40. *Ibid.*

41. Presidential Address by Albert J. Lutuli, Dec. 13–14, 1958.

42. *New Age*, Jan. 23, 1958. A response by the six, reaffirming their belief in the Freedom Charter, was printed in *New Age*, Feb. 6, 1958.

43. For the election results and a review of the election by Reginald September, general secretary of SACPO, see *New Age*, April 17, 1958.

44. *New Age*, July 3, 1958.

45. Presidential Address by Albert J. Lutuli, Dec. 13–14, 1958.

46. Articles by Homer Jack and Patrick Duncan, *Contact*, Jan. 10 and 24, 1959, and *Lekhotla La Basabetsi*, no. 1 [April 1959], mimeo.

47. Jordan Ngubane, unpublished manuscript.

48. *The World*, Dec. 20, 1958.

49. Mary Benson, *The African Patriots: The Story of the African National Congress of South Africa* (London, Faber & Faber, 1963), p. 253.

50. "Resolutions Adopted at the 46th Annual Conference Held in Durban on the 13th–16th December, 1958."

51. The rival groups were led by I. B. Tabata and W. M. Tsotsi of the AAC and Ben Kies and Hosea Jaffe of the Anti-CAD. The rivalry was evident late in 1956 when the Tabata group suspended Sastri Mda, the secretary of SOYA, on the grounds that, according to *New Age*, Dec. 5, 1957, "he was writing in Marxist terms and thus rendering SOYA liable to attack under the Suppression [of Communism] Law." Mda and his uncle, C. M. Kobus, said *New Age*, were among the few Africans associated with the Kies-Jaffe group. Another conflict occurred at the June 1958 conference of the Teachers' League of South Africa, a Coloured group long dominated by Kies. His candidate for general secretary was defeated by Allie

Fataar, a Coloured who associated himself with the Tabata group, *New Age,* Dec. 5, 1957; see also *New Age,* July 3, 1958; *Contact,* April 4, 1959.

52. *Contact,* April 4, 1959. Kies and his associates accused the AAC leaders of "a glorification of nationalism" and compared them to the Africanist, who was "an inverted Verwoerd . . . [who dreams of the ascendency of a historically ordained 'African personality.']" "What Has Happened in the Non-European Unity Movement?" a ten-page printed pamphlet issued by R. E. Viljoen, S. A. Jayiya, C. M. Kobus, and B. M. Kies, identified as "Foundation members of the Non-European Unity Movement and members of the Head Unity Committee," Feb. 1959.

53. "What Has Happened in the Non-European Unity Movement?", p. 8. Thus, the AAC leaders were said to be inclined toward "the sordid fraud of Ghana" and made much of the December 1958 Accra conference, which was "for the greater part . . . nothing but a contrived orgy of drum-beating and ballyhoo."

54. *Ibid.,* and "The Wreckers of Unity at Work: Who Is the National Anti-C.A.D. Committee?" an eight-page printed pamphlet issued by the Secretary, All-African Convention Committee (W.P.), June 23, 1959. The pamphlets were, respectively, about 8,000 and 5,000 words long. Anti-CAD views were regularly expressed by *Torch,* published weekly in Cape Town; the AAC published occasional leaflets and *Ikhwezi Lomso.*

55. Quoted in Carter, Karis, and Stultz, *South Africa's Transkei,* p. 39. See pages 51–67 for the debate on the Promotion of Bantu Self-Government Bill, following Dr. Verwoerd's announcement.

56. *Ibid.,* p. 59.

57. *A Short Pictorial History of the University College of Fort Hare, 1916–1959* [no author] (Lovedale, Cape Province: The Lovedale Press, 1961).

58. *Ibid.,* p. 42.

59. Z. K. Matthews, "The Nationalists and the Universities," unpublished manuscript.

60. *Contact,* Nov. 14, 1958, p. 5; Nov. 28, 1958, p. 5.

61. According to Hansi Pollak of the Institute of Race Relations, quoted in *Contact,* July 11, 1959, p. 2.

62. In describing the dispersal of a crowd of women in Lady Selborne, Pretoria, *Die Vaderland,* according to *Contact,* March 21, 1959, p. 4, pointed out that African police struck the women harder than did white police.

63. Presidential address dated Dec. 3, 1959 and read at the ANC annual conference, Dec. 12–13, 1959.

64. *Contact,* March 7, 1959, p. 9; May 30, 1959, p. 4.

65. *Contact,* Sept. 19, 1959, p. 7. Later, in retrospect, the ANC in exile claimed that ". . . the Natal demonstrations in 1958–59 which involved the destruction of dipping tanks and other Government installations, were all inspired by the A.N.C. and were concrete manifestations of its militant line." The African National Congress (External Mission), *The African National Congress of South Africa,* Dar es Salaam [1962], p. 17.

66. *New Age,* Sept. 10, 1959.

67. Joe Gqabi wrote of the conference in *New Age,* Dec. 7, 1959, that "the age-old custom of the Zulus prohibiting women from speaking publicly has been broken."

68. *Contact,* Feb. 21, 1959, p. 2.

69. "Report of the National Anti-Pass Council. Signed by Duma Nokwe, Secretary-General of the ANC, Submitted to the 'Mass National Conference' of May 30, 1959." This document is listed as Document 32 in the table of contents of Volume III that appears in Volume I. In the preparation of Volume III, however, another document was substituted for it.

70. Joel Carlson, *No Neutral Ground* (New York: Thomas Y. Crowell, 1973), chapters V–VII. See also Ruth First, *The Farm Labour Scandal . . . An Exposure* (*New Age* pamphlet, 1959).

71. *The Africanist*, May/June, 1959, pp. 14–15.

72. *Contact*, June 27, 1959, p. 7; Oct. 17, 1959, p. 3.

73. *Contact*, Nov. 28, 1959, p. 3.

74. *Contact*, Oct. 31, 1959, pp. 2 and 7.

75. Peter Brown, national chairman of the Liberal Party, issued a statement in July 1959 saying that Walter Stanford, a Liberal Party member of Parliament, was not expressing party policy when he wrote to the London *Times* in opposition to a boycott of South African goods. "The Liberal Party," said Brown, "recognizes the dangers and shortcomings of boycott as a political weapon. Nevertheless it is one of the few remaining peaceful means of making those who support racial discrimination in South Africa aware of the great weight of opposition to their policies. In responsible hands it is a legitimate means of exerting political pressures on those who deny the use of all normal constitutional channels to their opponents." *New Age*, July 23, 1959. Later in the year, Eric Louw, the minister of external affairs, said, with reference to the Liberal Party and the National Union of South African Students, "South Africa is the only country in the world in which its own citizens act in so disloyal a manner." *Contact*, Dec. 26, 1959, p. 7.

76. The first quotation is from Sir Francis de Guingand's speech at the Foundation's inaugural meeting, quoted in *Contact*, Dec. 26, 1959, p. 6. The second is from *The Foundation Reports . . .*, an undated brochure published by the South African Foundation about 1962.

77. *Report of the Commission of Enquiry into the Occurrences in the Location on the Night of the 10th to the 11th December, 1959, and into the Direct Causes Which Led to Those Occurrences* (U.G. 23/1960).

78. *Contact*, Dec. 26, 1959, p. 7.

79. *Contact*, July 11, 1959, p. 6.

80. *New Age*, Dec. 17, 1959; *Contact*, Dec. 26, 1959, p. 2; "Report on the A.N.C. Conference Held in Durban on the 12th and 13th December, 1959," by the Field Officer, South African Institute of Race Relations, mimeographed, RR 11/60, Jan. 6, 1960.

SACPO (the South Africa Coloured People's Organization) changed its name to the South African Coloured People's Congress (SACPC) at its conference on December 27, *New Age*, Dec. 31, 1959.

81. "The Presidential Address by Albert J. Luthuli . . . December 12th and 13th, 1959."

82. Jeffrey W. Horton, "South Africa's Joint Councils: Black-White Cooperation between Two World Wars," *South African Historical Journal*, Nov. 1972, No. 4.

83. During Lutuli's detention in 1960, Dominee Reyneke, a retired minister of the Dutch Reformed Church who had known Lutuli on the Christian Council, visited him twice in the prison hospital. Luthuli, *Let My People Go*, p. 225.

84. *New Age*, Aug. 15, 1957.

85. B. A. Tindall to Z. K. Matthews, May 12, 1953.

86. Jordan Ngubane, unpublished manuscript: "One of the delegates who had been very close to Dr. Malan, the Prime Minister, revealed that the Nationalist leader had, at about the time of the resistance movement [i.e., the Defiance Campaign], expressed a strong desire to meet Dr. Moroka, the President-General of the ANC, to talk on a man-to-man basis on the laws against which the Africans had demonstrated. This person was convinced that right up in the government there were men who, if approached in ways that would not embarrass them, were keen to meet African leaders and see if African Nationalism and its Afrikaans opposite could not start exploring the possibilities of some form of agreement on ultimate objectives. Steps had been taken to establish contact between Dr. Moroka and Dr.

Malan. Somewhere along the line a bottleneck had been encountered and Dr. Moroka had not received the Prime Minister's message—possibly not in time to react to it one way or the other." The source was Dominee Reyneke.

87. On the eve of the December 1957 multiracial conference, Lutuli wrote, "There is a complete breakdown in contact between the Government and the non-whites and hardly any friendly contact between whites and blacks on a personal level." *New Age*, Nov. 28. 1957.

88. Conversation of Carter and Johns with Lutuli, March 28, 1964.

89. Document 21. In February 1959, Margaret Ballinger introduced a resolution requiring the government "to convene a conference of freely elected representatives of all racial groups throughout the country on the basis of the franchises now in operation in the Cape Province." Muriel Horrell, *A Survey of Race Relations in South Africa, 1958–1959* (Johannesburg: South African Institute of Race Relations, 1960), p. 8.

90. *New Age*, Oct. 3, 1957.

91. Foreword to Ambrose Reeves, *Shooting at Sharpeville: The Agony of South Africa* (London: Victor Gollancz, Ltd., 1960), p. 14.

92. An incomplete list of sponsors appeared in *New Age*, Oct. 3, 1957.

93. *New Age*, Dec. 12, 1957.

94. Walter Sisulu, "A Review of the Multi-Racial Conference," *Liberation*, Feb. 1958, p. 24.

95. W. E. Barker, "The Multi-racial Conference—A Liberalist Failure," *Journal of Racial Affairs*, April 1958, pp. 117–122.

96. The writer was an observer at the conference.

97. *New Age*, Dec. 12, 1957.

98. Barker, "The Multi-racial Conference," p. 117.

99. *New Age*, Dec. 12, 1957.

100. B. B. Keet, "The Ethics of Apartheid," Hoernle Memorial Lecture delivered on July 3, 1957 (Johannesburg: South African Institute of Race Relations, 1957), p. 18. See also Professor B. B. Keet, "The Bell has Already Tolled," in *Delayed Action! (An Ecumenical Witness from the Afrikaans-speaking Church)* by A. S. Geyser, B. J. Marais, H. du Plessis, B. B. Keet, A. van Selms, and others (Pretoria: The authors, [about 1961]), pp. 5–12.

101. The discussion of Afrikaner and SABRA activities in this section is based to a large extent on conversations and notes taken by the writer in South Africa during 1957–1959.

102. H. J. Simons, "Nothing New from Sabra," *Fighting Talk*, Aug. 1958, p. 6 ff. Simons credits Edwin Munger for some of the facts in his article. See also Zach de Beer, "The Nice, Kind Nats of SABRA," *The Forum*, May 1959, pp. 9–10.

103. Quoted by Edwin S. Munger in "The 1959 Paradox in Afrikaner Nationalism," American Universities Field Staff Report, March 27, 1959, p. 10.

104. *Ibid.* In a conversation with Karis in 1955, Professor Keet said that if "making friends" resulted in interracial marriage, he was prepared to accept that.

105. Quoted in Nadine Gordimer, "Why Did Bram Fischer Choose Jail?" *The New York Times Magazine*, Aug. 14, 1966, p. 30. For a reference by Dr. A. B. Xuma to Fischer's work with the Bloemfontein Joint Council and a private night school for Africans, see Volume 1, p. 226.

106. Edwin S. Munger, "Self-confidence and Self-criticism in South Africa," *Foreign Affairs*, July 1958, p. 667.

107. *Ibid.*, p. 667.

108. J. C. B., "An Interview with ex-Chief Luthuli," Institute of Current World Affairs letter, June 29, 1962. Ngubane has observed that in the talks "Professor Olivier, for example, advanced the thesis that it would make things very much

370

easier for people like him if the Africans had their first loyalty to South Africa and did not look to the rest of Africa for help in solving the race problem." Unpublished manuscript.

109. See *Contact*, March 21, 1959, p. 2.

110. Simons, "Nothing New from Sabra," p. 6.

111. "Ex-Chief Luthuli's Influence on White Opinion," *The Forum*, July 1959, pp. 12–13; Peter Brown, "The Long View," *Contact*, June 27, 1959, p. 7.

112. *Contact*, April 4, 1959, p. 4. The SABRA congress was, of course, all white, but at its public opening a small group of Africans and Indians sat in the audience without incident. *Daily News* (Durban), April 2, 1959.

113. Ambrose Reeves, *South Africa—Yesterday and Tomorrow: A Challenge to Christians* (London: Victor Gollancz, Ltd., 1962), *passim;* and Ambrose Reeves, "New Moves for Multi-Racial Discussions," *The Forum*, June 1959, pp. 4–5. Conversation of Karis with Bishop Reeves, April 30, 1974.

The Africanist, May–June 1959, p. 16, reported the following news item: "A so-called United Anti-Nationalist Government Front has recently been formed. The *Front* consists of the reactionary White United Party, the liberal Liberal Party, the defunct Labour Party, the fifty-member strong Congress of Democrats, the ideologically-bankrupt African National Congress, the merchant-class Indian Congress, the lilly-livered White Black Sashers, and some lost Afrikaner *Sabra* professors. Bishop Reeves is reported to be their leader! SHAME. WE SAY NON-COLLABORATION WITH THE ENEMY IN AFRIKA." The United Party and SABRA were not, in fact, represented on the committee.

114. *New Age*, Aug. 6, 1959.

115. "Responsible Natives" are Dr. Jan Steytler's words. Horrell,*A Survey of Race Relations in South Africa, 1958–1959*, p. 7.

116. Information on the Africanist movement and the PAC has been obtained in part from interviews of Gerhart with Charles Lakaje, P. K. Leballo, T. T. Letlaka, Elliot Magwentshu, Nana Mahomo, Joseph Matthews, A. P. Mda, Elliot Mfaxa, Ellen Molapo, Joseph Molefi, Z. B. Molete, Peter 'Molotsi, A. B. Ngcobo, Matthew Nkoana, Duma Nokwe, J. D. Nyaose, Benjamin Pogrund, and Peter Raboroko, and from interviews of Carter and Karis with Peter Hjul and Joseph Matthews, Karis with 'Molotsi, and Carter with Ngubane.

117. Descriptions of this conference appear in *The World*, March 1 and 8, 1958; *New Age*, Feb. 27, 1958;*Rand Daily Mail*, Feb. 25, 1958;*Golden City Post*, March 2, 1958; and *Contact*, March 8, 1958.

118. Information on Madzunya is drawn from interviews of Gerhart between 1968 and 1970 with Leballo, Mahomo, 'Molotsi, Molete, and Raboroko. For an example of the notoriety given Madzunya by the press, see*Sunday Express*, March 9, 1958, which claims that Madzunya has "dramatically seized control" of the entire ANC.

119. Muriel Horrell, *A Survey of Race Relations in South Africa, 1957–58* (Johannesburg: South African Institute of Race Relations, 1958,), pp. 24–25.

120. *The World*, Sept. 27, Oct. 4, 1958; *Contact*, Nov. 1, 1958. Interviews of Gerhart with Raboroko and Molete, 1969.

121. Descriptions of this conference appear in *The World*, Nov. 1 and 8, 1958; *Rand Daily Mail*, Nov. 3, 1958;*Cape Times*, Nov. 3, 1958; and*Drum*, Dec. 1958.

122. Quoted in *Contact*, Nov. 15, 1958.

123. Headline in *Rand Daily Mail*, Nov. 3, 1958. *Golden City Post*, Nov. 9, 1958, proclaimed: "Now There Are Two ANCs."

124. "Report on Cape Dispute," Annual Report of the National Executive Committee of the 46th Annual General Conference of the African National Congress, Dec. 1958. *The World*, Sept. 6, 20; Oct. 25, 1958;*Rand Daily Mail*, Feb. 10, 1959. Interviews with Hjul and (by Gerhart) with Magwentshu.

125. For references to Dimba and background on African religious separatism in South Africa, see the definitive work by Bengt Sundkler, *Bantu Prophets in South Africa* (London: Oxford University Press, 1961, second ed.), especially p. 306. According to Benjamin Pogrund, Madzunya was applauded at the PAC inaugural convention for advocating the founding of an African national church, a long-cherished dream among some politically minded Africans.

126. Agenda for the Africanist Inaugural Convention. The conference, after sitting late into the night on April 5, ended with a vote by delegates to establish the name of the new organization. Among the other names considered were the Africanist Liberation Congress, the All African National Congress, the Africanist Congress, and the Africanist Revolutionary Party. It was felt by the conference that the word "Congress" should be retained for sentimental reasons and that the word "Africanist" should be carried over with a new and more positive connotation. It was 3 A.M. on April 6 when the name was chosen, and Selby Ngendane rose to close the proceedings by relating the story of the landing of the "thief," Van Riebeeck, on April 6, 1952. Interviews of Gerhart with 'Molotsi and Ngcobo. Descriptions of the PAC inaugural convention appear in *The World*, April 11, 1959; *The Star*, April 4, 1959; *The Times* (London), April 7, 1959; *Contact*, April 18, 1959; *Drum*, May 1959; and *New Age*, during April 1959.

127. Differences between PAC and ANC organizational styles noted by Pogrund at this and later conferences included the PAC's greater attention to punctuality, its lower tolerance for long-winded speeches and resolutions, and its greater use of African languages in place of English.

128. The National Executive Committee of the PAC between April 1959 and March 1960 was comprised of:

President: Robert M. Sobukwe
National Secretary: Potlako K. Leballo
Treasurer General: Abednego B. Ngcobo
National Organizer: Elliot Mfaxa
Secretary for Pan African Affairs: Peter 'Molotsi
Secretary for Foreign Affairs: Selby Ngendane
Secretary for Publicity and Information: Z. B. Molete
Secretary for Education: Peter Raboroko
Secretary for Culture: Nana Mahomo
Secretary for Labor: Jacob D. Nyaose
Secretary for Finance and Economic Development: Hughes Hlatswayo
Other members: Zephania Mothopeng
              Howard S. Ngcobo
              C. J. Fazzie
              M. G. Maboza

129. See Volume 2, pp. 98 ff. and Documents 48, 51, 52, and 53. Other writings by or about Lembede can be found in the *Bantu World*, April 22, July 15, Aug. 5, and Sept. 9, 1944; April 7, Sept. 8, and Nov. 3, 1945; *Inkundla ya Bantu*, Sept. 17 and October second fortnight, 1945, August second fortnight 1946, Feb. 27, June 26, and July 31, 1947; *African Advocate*, Aug./Sept. 1947; *The Africanist*, Dec. 1954, July/Aug. 1955, July/Aug. 1959, and March 1969; *Azania News*, Aug. 25, 1966; *Contact*, July 16, 1960; and *Drum*, Jan. 1954. Also see Ngubane's unpublished manuscript.

130. *The Star*, April 7, 1959.

131. *The Africanist*, Dec. 1959.

132. Speech by Sobukwe to the Witwatersrand regional conference of the PAC, May 31, 1959, reproduced in *South Africa: a Collection of Political Documents* (Hoover Institution microfilm).

133. It was official PAC policy to regard Coloureds as Africans, on the grounds that Africa was their place of geographical origin and that they had shared the black man's experience of dispossession and degradation. This policy was never fully

adhered to by PAC branches in the western Cape, however, where South Africa's Coloured population is concentrated and antagonism between Coloureds and Africans is strong. Sobukwe personally favored the acceptance of poorer Indians into the PAC, but this suggestion met with overwhelming objections, especially from Natal Africanists. Interviews of Gerhart with Magwentshu, Molete, and 'Molotsi.

134. Z. K. Matthews, "Non-White Political Organizations," *Africa Today*, Nov./Dec., 1957, p. 21.

135. See M. Nkoana, "S. A. Africanist Movement Plans for Convention," *Contact*, Jan. 24, 1959.

136. R. M. Sobukwe, "My Idea of Africa in 1973," *Drum*, Nov. 1959, pp. 48–49. A slightly amended version of this article was issued in mimeographed form in March 1960 under the title of "One Central Government in Africa" (Document 46).

137. P. N. Raboroko, "Congress and the Africanists, (1) The Africanist Case," *Africa South*, April/June 1960, p. 25.

138. *The World*, June 20, 1959.

139. Ellen Molapo, another member of the Garment Workers Union, was the only woman ever to be prominent in the PAC. She was an influential Africanist in Newclare, Johannesburg. Her prominence was derived in part from her membership in one of the leading chiefly families of Basutoland.

140. After Sharpeville, FOFATUSA apparently did receive some direct support from the ICFTU, according to Alex Hepple. In 1962 it reported a membership of twenty affiliated unions with some 36,000 individual members. Later it began to decline and in late 1965 it dissolved. See M. Horrell, *South Africa's Workers*, (Johannesburg: South African Institute of Race Relations, 1969), p. 28.

141. This section is based in part on the interviews with Hepple and on interviews of Gerhart with Nyaose, Molapo, and Molefi.

142. *The Africanist*, Jan. 1959.

143. *Ibid.*, Oct./Nov. 1959.

144. *Ibid.*

145. Many African high school students joined or identified with the PAC, partly as a result of the influence of these teachers.

146. *The Africanist*, Dec. 1959.

147. Duma Nokwe was quoted in *Contact*, Nov. 1, 1958, as saying: "One of the chief arguments of the Africanists is that the ANC has not adhered to the 1949 Programme of Action. But this programme is merely a set of activities. It lays down no policy whatever. . . . The programme does not define the content of African nationalism. It does not say that the brand of African nationalism to be followed is narrow, racialistic and chauvinistic."

The same point of view was expressed by Joseph Matthews in an interview with Gerhart in 1970: "The Programme of Action was exactly what the title denotes. It was a plan for specific types of action. . . . It wasn't a creed. It wasn't a statement of beliefs. The Freedom Charter was. The Charter wasn't a program of action. So one can't say that one was scrapped in favor of the other, because they simply weren't comparable. I never saw the Programme of Action as anything more than what we saw it at the time, that is a way of mobilizing the ANC to replace the older policy of *hamba kahle* ['go slowly']."

148. PAC letter, "To All Public and Private Institutions, Commercial and Industrial Enterprises," Jan. 25, 1960, reproduced on Hoover Institution microfilm.

149. "The State of the Nation" (Document 41).

150. Sobukwe had also put forward the idea of a status campaign in early 1957 in a speech to the Basutoland Congress Party, "Facing Fearful Odds," reproduced in *The Commentator* (Maseru), Aug. 1968.

151. *Golden City Post*, Jan. 17, Feb. 7, 1960; *The World*, Feb. 6, 1960.

152. Address by Sobukwe to the PAC conference of December 19–20, 1959. For detailed treatment of the pass laws, see M. Horrell, *The "Pass Laws"* (Johannesburg: South African Institute of Race Relations, 1960).

153. Moroka disassociated himself from the other arrested ANC leaders, hired separate counsel and gave evidence in his own defense. See Volume II, page 421.

154. Address by Sobukwe to the conference of the Witwatersrand Region of the PAC, May 31, 1959.

155. The full text of Macmillan's speech appears in Peter Calvocoressi, *South Africa and World Opinion* (London: Oxford University Press, 1961), pp. 45 ff.

156. For a summary of events in the period December 1959–May, 1960, see Muriel Horrell, *Days of Crisis in South Africa* (Johannesburg: South African Institute of Race Relations, 1960).

157. *Contact*, Dec. 26, 1959.

158. *The World*, Feb. 27, 1960.

159. Address by Sobukwe to the PAC conference of December 19–20, 1959. This metaphor is repeated in the Cape Town speeches of Sobukwe and Ngendane (Document 44).

160. Evidence does not support the claim made by Ngubane in his own account of March 1960 that Sobukwe was pressured into launching the campaign by his more impetuous colleagues. See Jordan Ngubane, *An African Explains Apartheid* (New York: Praeger, 1963), pp. 104–105.

161. Muriel Horrell, *A Survey of Race Relations in South Africa, 1959–60* (Johannesburg: South African Institute of Race Relations, n.d.), p. 54.

162. "Extracts from Presidential Speech" and "Resolutions" of the FOFATUSA Special Conference, 19 March, 1960, reproduced on Hoover Institution microfilm.

163. Letter from D. Nokwe, quoted by *Sunday Times* (Johannesburg), March 20, 1960.

164. Vereeniging is about 35 miles south of Johannesburg, 12 miles southeast of Evaton, and 6 miles east of Vanderbijlpark. Vereeniging in 1960 had a population of 24,564 whites and 52,424 Africans (*South African Statistics, 1968*, Pretoria, 1968, p.A–25).
The population of Sharpeville location consisted of approximately 8,655 men, 6,843 women, and 20,863 children. See *Summary of the Report of the Commission Appointed to Enquire into and to Report on the Events which Occurred in the Districts and Vereeniging and Van Der Bijl Park on the 21st Day of March, 1960*, p. 2.
Evaton, like Alexandra township in Johannesburg, was an area where Africans had freehold rights in 1960. Its population consisted of 2,000 whites and about 50,000 Africans. Vanderbijlpark had a population of 21,916 whites and 19,232 Africans (*South African Statistics*, p. A–25).

165. *The World*, March 16, 1960. *Cape Times*, March 22, 1960, and *Rand Daily Mail*, March 22, 1960, estimated the Evaton crowd at 10,000. *Cape Argus*, March 21, 1960, put the figure at 2,000, and the judge who conducted the official inquiry estimated the Evaton crowd at between 15,000 and 20,000 (*Summary of the Report. . . . 1960*, p. 7).

166. *Summary of the Report. . . . 1960*, p. 25.

167. Horrell, *Days of Crisis in South Africa*, p. 10. For an account of the Sharpeville incident strongly sympathetic to the African side but hostile to the PAC, see Ambrose Reeves, *Shooting at Sharpeville: The Agony of South Africa* (London: Victor Gollancz, Ltd., 1960). The record of the Sharpeville Commission of Inquiry is on microfilm (6 reels) in the CAMP collection under the title *Commission of inquiry into the occurrences at Sharpeville (and other places) on the 21st of March 1960*.

168. *Cape Argus,* March 21, 1960.

169. *Report of the Langa Commission of Enquiry,* July 14, 1960, p. 61.

170. A good indication of white reactions and interpretations of the crisis can be found in the debates in the House of Assembly from March 21, 1960 onwards.

171. *Cape Times,* March 24, 25 and 31, 1960.

172. *Cape Times,* March 23, 1960. The statement was a major subject of discussion in Parliament on March 23. See also Vernon McKay, *Africa in World Politics* (New York: Harper & Row, 1963), pp. 299–300, which includes the text of the statement.

173. For the text of the Security Council statement, see Calvocoressi, *South Africa and World Opinion,* pp. 58–59.

174. In comparison with most South African cities in 1960, Cape Town was atypical. In a total population of 807,211, Africans numbered only 75,200, or approximately 9 percent. Whites numbered 305,155 and Coloureds, the largest group, 417,881 (*South African Statistics,* p. A–25). Monica Wilson and Archie Mafeje, in *Langa: A Study of Social Groups in an African Township* (Cape Town: Oxford University Press, 1963), p. 2, quote different census figures, but the percentage of Africans in the total population is also cited as 9 percent in 1960. A high proportion of Cape Town Africans were migrant Xhosa laborers from the Transkei, living in "bachelor" barracks in Langa and Nyanga. In 1960, out of the approximately 25,000 inhabitants of Langa, 19,549 were men, 17,920 of whom were housed under bachelor conditions, 1,870 were women, and 3,685 were children. (*Report of the Langa Commission of Enquiry,* p. 14) Ethnically, this population was highly homogeneous; Kgosana, a Sotho-speaker from the Northern Transvaal, was an outsider.

Ronald Segal, a Cape Town journalist, noting the relatively small number of Africans in the city, commented, "Here they could not see, as they saw so starkly everywhere in Johannesburg and its satellite cities, the promise of survival and ultimate victory in the sheer pressure of their numbers. Even their right to live in Cape Town at all was disputed, and the government had already announced . . . its intention to remove them altogether from the Western Cape, which could then be turned into an ethnic labour monopoly of the Coloured. I had always measured Africanism as a manifestation of despair, and the city's Africans, threatened with expulsion . . . to the slow starvation of the Reserves, had cause enough for their despair." *Into Exile* (London: Jonathan Cape, 1963), p. 273.

The ANC had a long-established tradition in Cape Town, but only among the very small, more permanently urbanized African population, which had left the field open to the PAC when it formed in 1959.

175. Kenneth Mackenzie, *The Spectator* (London), April 8, 1960, quoted by Myrna Blumberg, *White Madam* (London: Victor Gollancz, Ltd., 1962), p. 27.

176. For newspaper accounts of the Cape Town march, see *Cape Argus* and *The Star,* March 30, 1960; *Cape Times* and *Rand Daily Mail,* March 31, 1960; and *Contact,* April 16, 1960. Other accounts appear in Blumberg, *White Madam,* and in Kgosana's unpublished autobiography. Two fictionalized accounts of the crisis period in Cape Town are Richard Rive, *Emergency* (London: Collier-Macmillan, 1970), with an introduction by Ezekiel Mphahlele, and Anna M. Louw, *20 days That Autumn* (Cape Town: Tafelberg-Uitgewers, 1963). Also see Segal, *Into Exile,* pp. 272 ff.

177. The minister of justice told Parliament on May 6 that 18,011 arrests had been made since the beginning of the emergency, not counting political suspects. Horrell, *A Survey of Race Relations in South Africa, 1959–60,* p. 84.

178. For details of the Treason Trial during the emergency period, see Horrell, *A Survey of Race Relations, 1959–60,* pp. 38–39, and Thomas Karis, *The Treason Trial in South Africa: A Guide to the Microfilm Record of the Trial,* pp. 37 ff. For a detailed account of all major events of the emergency period, see Horrell, *Days of Crisis in South Africa.*

179. *House of Assembly Debates,* March 29, 1960, col. 4302–3.

180. *Ibid.,* col. 4328.

181. *Ibid.,* col. 4302. One member of Parliament, G. F. Fronemen, expressed the prevailing opinion in the Nationalist Party when he stated in the debate on March 30 that "The Government has responsible, sound bridges with the Bantu by way of the tribal authorities. As a matter of fact the Government has sound and firm links with 99 percent of the Bantu. It is only the 1 percent, which is represented by the PAC and the ANC with which it has no links, and with which it does not want to have links, because they are irresponsible criminals, who commit murder and arson. . . . 99 percent of the Bantu people support the apartheid policy of the Government." *Ibid.,* col. 4368.

182. *Ibid.,* March 29, 1960, col. 4317 and 4321.

183. *Ibid.,* col. 4322. All African men 16 years of age or older were required to carry the same type of pass or "reference book" after passage of the Natives (Abolition of Passes and Co-Ordination of Documents) Act of 1952. See Horrell, *The "Pass Laws",* p. 2.

In defense of United Party policy, one member of Parliament, D. E. Mitchell, said, "The experience of the past has shown that this exemption certificate has been kept by the Native as something so precious that I believe the number who ever forfeited them through misdemeanour was negligible through the years. Here was a way to get past the pin-pricks . . . and it was a way that carried with it the approval of the Bantu themselves. By this means we built up a class of folk that we knew were going to be with us. . . . That was worth a lot. Can we not return to it?"*House of Assembly Debate,* March 31, 1960, col. 4510–11.

Kgosana in his "launching address" (Document 50) attacked Nokwe for his hostility to the PAC and added the barb, "Perhaps Duma Nokwe is not carrying a pass," a reference to the fact that under the old system Nokwe, a highly educated professional, would have been an "exempted" African.

184. After the formation of the Progressive Party in November 1959 there were 12 Progressive members of Parliament. In the general election of October 1961, all but one, Mrs. Helen Suzman, were defeated. The Natives' Representatives were eliminated in 1959, but the incumbents remained in Parliament until the 1961 election.

185. One MP, Len Lee-Warden, the Natives' Representative for the Cape, did indirectly propose this on March 30 when he said, "If ever there was a need, it exists today for the Government to realize that it has in the ANC a friend and not an enemy, because these two organizations that we are asked to ban are so diametrically opposed that the Government should seize the opportunity of appealing to the ANC to assist it to restore peace and order in South Africa." *Ibid.,* col. 4385.

186. For details of the Unlawful Organizations Act and its passage see Horrell, *A Survey of Race Relations in South Africa, 1959–60,* pp. 69–72. Besides empowering the government to ban the ANC, PAC, and any other organizations attempting to further their aims, the Act provided that persons found guilty of intimidating others to stay away from work or to commit any offense by way of protest against a law, would be liable to a maximum penalty of a £500 fine, or five years imprisonment, or 10 strokes, or a combination of any two of these. The previous penalties for such offenses were a £50 fine or six months imprisonment or both, under the Criminal Law Amendment Act of 1953. The Unlawful Organizations Act contained the provision that bannings, unless extended by Proclamation, were to be reviewed by Parliament at the end of every twelve months. This provision was dropped under the terms of the General Law Amendment Act of 1962. See Muriel Horrell, *A Survey of Race Relations in South Africa, 1962* (Johannesburg: South African Institute of Race Relations, 1963), p. 32. For a review of these acts and related legislation, see Thomas Karis, "South Africa," in G. M. Carter (ed.) *Five African States: Responses to Diversity* (Ithaca, N.Y.: Cornell University Press, 1963), pp. 549–551.

187. Segal, *Into Exile,* pp. 277 ff. has an account of Tambo's departure.

188. A microfilm of the trial record in the case of Regina vs. Robert Sobukwe and others in the magistrate's court for the regional division of Johannesburg was obtained by Benjamin Pogrund and is available from the Cooperative Africana Microform Project of the Center for Research Libraries. Not all the documents presented in evidence are included on the microfilm.

On April 25, 1960, according to the trial record, Sobukwe began to address the court; he concluded his address on April 29. On May 4, just before sentencing, he addressed the court "in mitigation," according to the record. These addresses are not reproduced in the record but are recorded on tape. Legally permissible efforts by a lawyer in Johannesburg to obtain a transcript of the tape recording of the first address proved fruitless. It is possible that the tapes have been damaged or destroyed.

A transcript of Sobukwe's statement of May 4, 1960, was obtained, however. The full text follows (from Belt 70 of Case No. L.173/60, The State vs. Robert Sobukwe and 22 Others): "It will be remembered by this court that when this case started the accused refused to plead and the reason they gave was that they felt no moral obligation whatsoever to obey the laws made exclusively by a white minority.

"It will also be remembered, Your Worship, that at the beginning of this case I said that we did not intend at all to impugn your personal honour and integrity and we still say so, even now. But I would like to quote what was quoted by somebody before—'that an unjust law cannot be justly applied' and that is our contention even now.

"We have said in this court that we believe in one race only, the human race and that we belong to that race too. The history of that race, Your Worship, is a history of struggle, struggle for the removal of restrictions, mental, physical and spiritual and we would have failed the human race if we had not made our contribution for the removal of restrictions and we are satisfied that we have made our contribution.

"We as individuals, Your Worship, do not count. We are the tools—tools made in this particular case to use. I think we must continue to make another move, at an appropriate time, to be used as other tools as well. (?) [*sic*] We are not afraid to face the consequences of our actions, Your Worship, and it is not our intention to plead for mercy.

"That is all, thank you, Your Worship."

An abridged and not fully accurate version of this statement, reported in *The Star,* is in Bernard Sachs, *The Road to Sharpeville* (Johannesburg: The Dial Press, 1961), p. 61.

Sobukwe was sentenced to three years, and then, in a series of annual enactments, was imprisoned for a further six years after the General Law Amendment Act of 1963 had given the government special powers to keep him in detention. See Muriel Horrell, *A Survey of Race Relations in South Africa, 1963* (Johannesburg: South African Institute of Race Relations, 1964), pp. 44–45.

189. For an assessment of the mood of Johannesburg Africans during the crisis, see two articles by Anthony Sampson: "The Bantu Listens to a Louder Drum," *New York Times Magazine,* April 24, 1960, and " 'A Cop Even Called Me Mister!' " in *The Observer,* April 3, 1960.

190. *Cape Times,* April 20, 1960.

191. *Congress Voice,* vol. 2, no. 2, May 1960, and a one-page flyer, "A Call to PAC Leaders!" (n.d.) issued in the early days of the emergency.

192. This section consists mainly of excerpts from Karis, *The Treason Trial in South Africa,* cited above. This guide includes a detailed, topical chronology with page references to the *Treason Trial Record.* The writer was particularly indebted to Michael Parkington, who instructed the defense team, Sydney Kentridge, and I. A. Maisels, defense advocates, Gustav Hoexter, an advocate for the prosecution, Oswald Pirow, the chief prosecutor, and Dean Erwin Griswold of Harvard Law School.

193. *House of Assembly Debates*, May 20, 1960, col. 8343.

194. *Manchester Guardian*, Nov. 15, 1958.

195. A. Lerumo [pseud.], *Fifty Fighting Years: The Communist Party of South Africa, 1921–1971* (London: Inkululeko Publications, 1971, pp. 97 and 105). In October 1959, the first issue of the party's journal, *The African Communist*, appeared in Johannesburg.

196. "An Anonymous Correspondent," *Africa South*, Jan.–March 1961, p. 17; *Contact*, July 30, 1960, p. 2, and Aug. 27, 1960, p. 4. See the *Africa South* article, pp. 17 and 21–22, regarding two Marxist groups organized during the emergency in opposition to the Communist Party and the Congress movement: the Socialist League in Johannesburg and the Workers' Democratic League in Cape Town.

197. Peter Hjul, *Contact*, Sept. 24, 1960, p. 5.

198. Discussion of the United Front is based on conversations with Tambo, Makiwane, 'Molotsi, and the PAC Presidential Council, and chapter 13, "The South African United Front," of an unpublished manuscript by Philip Kgosana. The constitution of the United Front is appended to the Kgosana manuscript.

199. The discussion that follows is taken from Carter, Karis and Stultz, *South Africa's Transkei* pp. 25–26.

200. The discussion of the consultative conference and continuation committee that follows is based largely on conversations with J. C. M. Mbata, Duma Nokwe, Benjamin Rajuili, Julius Malie, Tambo, and an unpublished manuscript by Ngubane.

201. *New Age*, Dec. 22, 1960.

202. The resolutions were printed in *New Age*, with many minor differences in wording from Document 54 but no substantial differences.

203. See Ngubane, *An African Explains Apartheid*, pp. 169–171, and Ngubane's unpublished manuscript.

204. *Contact*, Feb. 11, 1961, p. 3.

205. *New Age*, March 9, 1961.

206. Ngubane has complained that Nokwe went alone to see Lutuli, contrary to the understanding. Nokwe saw Lutuli from time to time but, in accordance with the agreement, relied on replies by telegram.

207. See D. A. Leonard, "Proscribed Ideals (The State v. Duma Nokwe and 11 others)," in Marion Friedmann (ed.), *I Will Still Be Moved: Reports from South Africa* (London: Arthur Barker, Ltd., 1963), pp. 100–110.

208. *Race Relations News*, Oct. 1962, pp. 7–8.

209. *Contact*, May 4, 1961, p. 3. According to Mbata, IDAMF as a national body did not participate officially.

210. *Contact*, April 6, 1961, p. 5. *Contact's* anonymous correspondent was Benjamin Pogrund, the well-known white reporter who was critical of Communist influence and convinced that the left-wing was deliberately embellishing Mandela's image in later descriptions of his appearance at the conference. Although he himself wrote that Mandela, "bearded in the new nationalist fashion," was "the star of the show," he did not report that he found both Mandela's delivery and the proceedings uninspired. Conversation of Karis with Pogrund, March 1975. On the other hand, *New Age*, March 30, 1961, reported that during Mandela's "inspiring" address "every sentence was either cheered or greeted with cries of 'shame.'"

211. *House of Assembly Debates*, May 8, 1961, cols. 6064–6065.

212. Professor Matthews' article appeared in the left-wing monthly, *Fighting Talk*, March 1961, pp. 2–3, rather than in a newspaper or publication that circulated widely among whites.

213. *Proceedings of the Natal Convention held in the University of Natal, Pietermaritzburg on 17th to 19th April, 1961* (booklet published by the Natal Convention Committee, n.d.). See also *Contact*, May 4, 1961, pp. 2, 4–5.

214. Quoted in Edward Callan, *Albert John Luthuli and the South African Race Conflict* (Kalamazoo: Western Michigan Press, 1962, a booklet), p. 47; *New Age*, Jan. 19, 1961.

215. Callan, *Albert John Luthuli*, pp. 47–48.

216. Quoted in Carter, Karis, and Stultz, *South Africa's Transkei*, pp. 26–27.

217. Quoted in *New Age*, Jan. 5, 1961. See Margaret Ballinger, *From Union to Apartheid: A Trek to Isolation* (Folkestone, England: Bailey Brothers & Swinfen, Ltd., 1969), pp. 453–457.

218. *New Age*. April 13, 1961.

219. *Ibid.*, April 20, 1961.

220. *House of Assembly Debates*, May 5, 1961, col. 5971.

221. The appeal was originally drafted by Thami Mhlambiso, secretary of the Students' Representative Council at Fort Hare at the time he was expelled in March 1961. He had then entered the non-European section of the University of Natal and soon became vice-president of the National Union of South Africa Students. NUSAS, the organization of representative councils of students at English-speaking universities, moved toward a sympathetic association with African radicals during the period from 1960 to 1964.

222. *New Age*, May 25, 1961.

223. Conversations of Gerhart with Ngcobo, 'Molotsi, Molefi, and Nyaose.

224. *House of Assembly Debates*, May 23, 1961, col. 6947.

225. *New Age*, June 1, 1961.

226. *Ibid.*, June 8, 1961. Evaluation of the stay-at-home is based in part on conversation with Mbata. For another review, see South African Congress of Trade Unions, "Special Newsletter, Stay at Home—May 29th, 30, 31st 1961," 4 mimeographed pages, June 16, 1961.

227. *New Age*, June 1, 1964; Mary Benson, *The African Patriots: The Story of the African National Congress of South Africa* (London: Faber & Faber, 1963), pp. 288–289.

228. *Contact*, June 1, 1961, p. 4.

229. *New York Times*, May 30, 1961.

230. *New Age*, June 1, 1961. Mandela wrote a detailed analysis of the stay-at-home that was issued in June 1961 and is reprinted in Ruth First (ed.), *No Easy Walk to Freedom: Articles, Speeches, and Trial Addresses of Nelson Mandela* (London: Heinemann, 1965), pp. 94–106.

Documents

MULTI-RACIAL CONFERENCE, DECEMBER 1957

Document 21. Reports

I.
The Need for Inter-Racial Talks

In December 1957, a conference of South Africans of all races was held in Johannesburg. This multi-racial conference was important, not so much because of the matters it discussed, but in that it was held at a time when the Nationalist Government was systematically eliminating all points of contact between the races. It took place in the midst of a tragic situation, where the South African nation was being hurtled towards a head-on collision between the forces of White domination and the rapidly advancing non-White majority.

Claiming that its policy of baasskap apartheid was the only sure means of avoiding such a clash, the Government had speeded up its programme for the enforcement of racial separation in the social, economic, religious and education fields. One after another, laws were being enacted to compel the people of South Africa to obey the policy of *baasskap apartheid*, as decreed by the Nationalist Party.

Socially, the main instrument, the Group Areas Act, was being wielded with relentless vigour. Non-White communities were receiving orders to get out of their homes and businesses and move to racially reserved areas.

Economically, the trade unions and Non-White workers were under pressure because of the extension of compulsory apartheid to employment and to workers' organisations. In terms of the amended Industrial Conciliation Act of 1956, unions were ordered to separate their members into White and Non-White sections, and eliminate racial intermingling at all levels.

This law also provided for the reservation of jobs on a racial basis, enabling the Minister of Labour to decree that certain industries, trades or occupations be reserved for workers of a specific race.

The churches, too, had been enmeshed in the web of compulsory apartheid. The Bantu Education Act confronted them with the unhappy choice of surrendering their mission schools to the Government, or struggling to survive without the Government subsidies, upon which they had come to depend. For some churches this was a crippling blow to mission work amongst the Africans.

Religious activity in the urban areas was further challenged by an amendment to the Native (Urban Areas) Act, approved by Parliament during its 1957 Session. This amendment extended the application of a prohibition against Africans attending church services in urban areas (i.e. areas reserved for White occupation).

This amendment also gave the Minister of Native Affairs the power to prohibit the holding of any meeting or gathering in an urban area, if it were attended by Africans.*

These and many other things created a restricted atmosphere for effectual talks across the colour line. Furthermore, the official attitude towards such talks was sufficiently hostile to be powerfully dissuasive.

The arrest of 156 South Africans of all races in December 1956 on charges of high treason, added to the fears and anxieties of those who publicly opposed and attacked Government policies.

The crisis in human relations in South Africa demanded inter-racial talks before it was too late, but the unhappy situation made it difficult for a satisfactory meeting to be arranged.

Those who agreed that the ideology of White supremacy would lead to disaster, had differences on the best means to break from it. Those who sought the establishment of a non-racial democracy in South Africa, were not all in the same religious, social or political camps.

The tragic lack of organised communication between White and non-White leaders made it impossible to have satisfactory consultation between the various races on matters which affected them all.

The Government refused to meet the chosen leaders of the Non-White people, preferring to rule these subjects in its own authoritarian way.

Yet somehow, somewhere, the people had to be brought together, to examine and discuss the common problems of the Nation, to determine the tasks and responsibilities in which all should share.

In the end, it was the Africans who initiated the calling of a Conference of South Africans of all races.

---

*The Minister of Native Affairs had the power under this law (and others) to prohibit the Multi-Racial Conference, but did not do so.

The Multi-Racial Conference, held in Johannesburg in December, 1957, was inspired by a Conference of African leaders at Bloemfontein more than a year earlier, called by the Inter-denominational African Ministers' Federation, to discuss the Tomlinson Report.

The IDAMF Conference

The gathering at Bloemfontein, which took place on the 3rd., 4th. and 5th. October 1956, in the Bochabella Location, was attended by some 400 African delegates, drawn from a wide cross-section of cultural, religious, occupational and political organisations. In addition to the delegates, there were about 400 observers present.

This Conference (which has become known as the IDAMF Conference) has been described variously as "the most momentous meeting of Africans since the coming of the White man", "the most vital African effort of its kind since the Nationalists came to power in 1948", "the most important of its kind for 20 years."

The delegates took a serious interest in the proceedings. African experts read papers on the various sections of the Tomlinson Report and in the discussions which followed, the delegates showed themselves to be both familiar with the Report and well-informed on the subjects.

At the end of the discussions, the Conference unanimously agreed upon a long resolution which read in part as follows:— [see Document 16].

Included in the Resolution was an appeal "to that strong and powerful body, for which the Dutch Reformed Church speaks with recognised authority, to re-examine its approach to the race question."

The "Volkskongres"

It so happened that the three Dutch Reformed Churches had themselves taken part in a conference to discuss the Tomlinson Report, three months earlier, in July, 1956. That Conference was also held in Bloemfontein, but in the University Hall, to which Non-Whites are not admitted. It was an all-White Conference ("Volkskongres") convened by SABRA, the F.A.K. and three Dutch Reformed Churches. It was attended by 800 delegates representing 544 groups and organisations. The Rev. W. A. Landman, Chairman of SABRA, hailed this gathering as *"The most important and decisive moment in the history of the people, overshadowing even Blood River."*

The mood of the "Volkskongres" was also one of serious concern for the future of race relations and more than one speaker mourned the loss "of the link between the Afrikaner and the Bantu." But the delegates remained firmly to the belief that apartheid could and must be made to work and that the Tomlinson Report contained a positive hope of peacefully keeping the races apart.

The "Volkskongres" formed a continuation Committee drawn from the three sponsoring groups and this Committee is now suggesting the holding of a conference with Non-White leaders.

The IDAMF Conference, seeking just the opposite in race relations, warmly applauded the hope expressed by Chief A. J. Luthuli, that it might lead to the holding of "a multi-racial Conference, one truly representative of South Africa." In pursuance of this objective, the Interdenominational African Ministers' Federation, under the Chairmanship of Rev. Z. R. Mahabane, was given a mandate to work towards the calling of a Multi-Racial Conference.

II.
Steps Towards A Multi-Racial Conference

Soon after the IDAMF Conference, an announcement was made, proposing the calling of a multi-racial conference. This was welcomed by the Labour Party, the Liberal Party, the Methodist Conference and a large number of individuals from all walks of life.

The possibility of such a gathering was soon thereafter tested in Parliament, when the Leader of the Labour Party, Mr. Alex Hepple, on the 8th February, 1957, introduced a motion, proposing the calling of

". . . a National Convention, representative of all sections of the community, White and Non-White, to consider —

(a) ways and means of fulfilling the common desire of all South Africans for inter-racial harmony and co-operation

(b) . . . . the establishment and maintenance of a democratic society in South Africa. . . .

(c) . . . . plans . . . for the implementation of the report of the Tomlinson Commission."

Both the Government and the major opposition, the United Party, opposed the proposal. Speaking for the Government, Dr. H. F. Verwoerd, Minister of Native Affairs (and now Prime Minister) described the suggestion as "positively dangerous," saying, "such a Convention has only one object. It is to create a set of circumstances as the result of which apartheid, segregation will be destroyed forever . . . . What is aimed at in this sort of consultation is . . . something dangerous. . . . The Government rejects it in toto. . . ."

The United Party, through its spokesman Mr. S. F. Waterson, moved an amendment rejecting the proposition on the grounds that, *"in view of the steadily increasing rigidity of the ideological policies of the Government, the ideal of a National Convention is now impracticable."*

Parliament's refusal to take the lead in bringing together representatives of the various sections of the South African people, threw the onus back upon those outside Parliament.

The initiative was thereupon taken by a number of representatives of the Bloemfontein Conference, who met a group of sympathetic Europeans and discussed the feasibility of staging a broad conference of South Africans of all races.

To explore the matter further, a Committee of individuals belonging to various organisations was set up.

This Committee decided that a multi-racial Conference was both desirable and practicable and should be designed to attract people representing all shades of opinion. It was agreed that the Conference should provide the opportunity for discussion of a broad agenda dealing with relationships in a multi-racial society.

To give the Conference status, the first step was to invite responsible people to sponsor it. To this end, the following appeal was issued on the 7th July, 1957:—

South Africans of all races are face to face with grave problems. Our daily lives are beset by them; our future, if they remain unsolved, is an ominous question-mark.

We, the undersigned, therefore, welcomed the Conference at Bloemfontein, called by the Interdenominational Federation of African Ministers. We welcomed it because we felt that it was an attempt to discuss some of these problems and seek a solution. We believe that another conference should now be called to take up where that Conference left off and we believe that the second conference should be a multi-racial one, bringing together people of all races who are concerned to find a way of life acceptable to all South Africans.

The Bloemfontein Conference passed the following resolution:

"The Conference reiterates the demand of the African people for the abolition of discriminatory laws and the extension of full citizenship rights to all, which alone will guarantee peaceful and harmonious relations between Black and White in South Africa."

The conference we are proposing to call would discuss this resolution and consider whether it should be adopted, amended or replaced by another resolution.

The Conference would further discuss the practical implication of this or other similar resolution.

We believe that you will readily see the desirability of the calling of a multi-racial conference of this nature and we earnestly ask you, therefore, to assist us by agreeing to act as a "sponsor" of such a conference.

It is our intention to call together the sponsors of the conference for the purposes of discussing the agenda.

SIGNED: Inter-denominational African Ministers' Federation.

A. L. Mncube.

†Ambrose, Johannesburg
Leo Marquard
A. J. Luthuli
Ruth Foley
Y. M. Dadoo
Alex. Hepple
Alan Paton

The response was immediate and copious. The number of persons offering to act as sponsors encouraged the Committee to proceed at once with further plans for the holding of the Conference.

The sponsors were called to a meeting in Johannesburg on the 2nd September 1957, at which the following resolution was adopted:—

"That an inter-racial Conference be held to discuss and explore the steps which can bring about friendly and effective co-operation among the different racial groups in our country."

This meeting also agreed upon the Agenda for the Conference and decided that it should be held in Johannesburg in December 1957.

In view of the exploratory nature of the proposed conference, it was felt that no attempt should be made to pass resolutions but that the gathering should have as its objective the establishment of a common endeavour amongst the widest possible section of South Africans in evolving methods of ensuring peaceful existence for all races in South Africa.

Accordingly, it was resolved that papers on six subjects would be read by authorities in each field, to be followed by general discussion, which would be summarised in the form of findings, including minority views, and submitted to plenary sessions of the Conference.

On the question of representation, the Sponsors decided that the most satisfactory results would emerge from a conference of individuals, rather than from one of delegates representing organisations. It was generally agreed that individuals would be able to express their views freely if they were not tied to the policies of the organisations to which they belonged.

It was also felt that a Conference of mandated delegates would not provide a forum for the full and free exchange of views, which was what everyone desired.

Through the good offices of Prof. I. D. MacCrone, the Planning

Committee was granted permission to hold the Conference at the University of the Witwatersrand, from the 3rd to 5th December 1957.

III.
The Conference

"Perhaps never before in the chequered history of this land of many colours, varying cultures and civilisations, divergent social conditions, varying stages of advancement and cluster of languages and tongues has such a glorious and priceless opportunity presented itself for representatives of the racial groups on both sides of the colour line to come together, reason and think together, exchange views in the grim quest for the solution of the impasse. A three-centuries quest for a suitable formula has met with no success. The problem persists and calls for a new approach . . ."

> The Rev. Z. R. Mahabane—President of the Multi-Racial Conference, in his address opening the Conference.

———————————

Invitations to the Conference were sent to some 1,000 people prominently active in all spheres. Leading members of all churches, including the Dutch Reformed Churches, all political parties, including the Nationalist Party and the United Party, employers' and workers' organisations, teacher and student bodies, and the press were invited to participate or attend as observers.

The acceptances were gratifying, although members of the Dutch Reformed Church, the Nationalist Party and the United Party generally ignored the invitation. A few individuals from these organisations did attend as observers, however.

Chambers of Commerce and Industry and White trade unions were poorly represented, while few, if any, delegates or observers came from the Afrikaans universities and student bodies.

All other bodies gave strong support, particularly the churches. The English-speaking Universities' staff and students, the Congress movements, the Labour and Liberal parties, the Black Sash, the Institute of Race Relations all had members participating or watching as observers. In addition, there were many individuals not connected with any of these groups.

Among the observers were several consular representatives of foreign countries, and local and overseas pressmen attended throughout and reported the Conference fully.

When the Conference opened, there were about 350 participants and almost as many observers present.

The procedure of the Conference was designed to provide all participants with abundant opportunities for the exchange of views.

During the first two days, papers were read on six subjects, after which members divided into a large number of small commissions for further discussion and the preparation of suitable findings.

The Papers read were:—

"HUMAN RELATIONS IN A MULTI-RACIAL SOCIETY"
The Rev. Z. R. Mahabane
Prof. I. D. MacCrone

"THE RESPONSIBILITIES OF RELIGIOUS COMMUNITIES IN A MULTI-RACIAL SOCIETY"
The Most Rev. Denis E. Hurley, O.M.I., D.D.

"EDUCATIONAL POLICIES IN A MULTI-RACIAL SOCIETY"
Mr. G. M. Pitje
Dr. R. E. Van der Ross
Dr. S. Cooppan

"ECONOMIC RIGHTS AND DUTIES IN A MULTI-RACIAL SOCIETY"
Dr. S. T. Van der Horst
Mr. G. A. Mbeki

"CIVIL RIGHTS AND DUTIES IN A MULTI-RACIAL SOCIETY"
Mr. W. B. Ngakane
Mr. Alan Paton

"POLITICAL ARRANGEMENTS IN A MULTI-RACIAL SOCIETY"
Prof. Z. K. Matthews
Prof. G. H. Le May

The various Commissions brought together Africans, Whites, Coloureds and Indians in small groups where discussion was more intimate and exhaustive than would have been possible in the Conference hall itself.

Educationists, sociologists, professors, churchmen, trade unionists, politicians and others shared in the discussions in a wider circle than they had previously known. Anglicans, Roman Catholics, Methodists and other Christians met in discussions on the various topics with Jews, Moslems and Hindus. Members of the four Congresses were thrown together with Liberal, Labour and other party stalwarts.

Often the discussions in the Commissions were lively. Several of the participants declared afterwards that the debates in the Commissions had been a new and profound experience.

The Conference arrangements provided other opportunities for the exchange of views. Some of the most earnest discussions took place on informal occasions, when the participants gathered outside or in the tea room. Lunches were prepared by members of the Black Sash and supplied at a nominal charge. Arguments begun in the Commissions were often pursued in the tea room during the lunch hour, and South Africans of all races could be seen engaged in animated, friendly discussion.

The recommendations of the various Commissions were collated by sub-committees and embodied in single findings on each subject. These findings were then submitted to the Plenary session for approval.

The findings were unanimously accepted by the Conference and are reproduced in the next chapter.

The only event that marred the proceedings was the constant surveillance of the police. Throughout the Conference members of the Special Branch kept watch in the foyer and outside the University buildings.

The Conference unanimously agreed that further action should be taken to foster closer relations and better understanding between South Africans of all races. To this end, it was resolved that the Planning Committee should be instructed to act as a Continuation Committee, to publish the findings of Conference and investigate ways and means of their implementation.

The Continuation Committee was empowered to co-opt additional members.

The Conference was closed by the Rt. Rev. Ambrose Reeves, who said in his speech:—

> "This Conference may well go down in history as the turning of the tide in South Africa. Those few people who responded to the call of the 1956 Bloemfontein Conference of the Interdenominational African Ministers, never envisaged that this brief conference would be an end in itself or would produce a blue-print for a multi-racial society in South Africa. It is rather a beginning—the next stage in the process begun by the African Ministers' Conference at Bloemfontein. . . . Here we have demonstrated that it is still possible in South Africa for those of various ethnic groups and holding widely divergent views to speak reasonably with one another. This is an achievement of which we may be justly proud."

IV.
The Findings

Report on the Findings of the Commission on Human Relations in a Multi-Racial Society

The danger facing South Africa is that of a headlong collision between the forces of white domination and those of counter-domination. The Conference believes that such a collision would be disastrous for the country, but it is equally convinced that a turning-point has been reached, where South Africa must choose between the concept of a common society, or a bitter conflict between these two wills to dominate, which can only result in collision.

The supporters of Apartheid do not hesitate to voice their fear that the desire of the black man is to drive the white man into the sea. This fear is as old as their first encounter. But the presence of 400 people in the Great Hall of the University is a proof that this is not the inevitable end. These 400 people are the representatives of millions of South Africans who do not desire such an end. But many of them testified that their respective groups stand at the crossroads, where the choice is between co-operation and irreconcilability.

Apartheid offers no solution to this threatening impasse. It offers security to nobody. It condemns white South Africa to live out its historical span behind the walls of a fortress, and it condemns non-white South Africa to an unrelenting struggle to breach these walls. For both, ordinary life is becoming more and more impossible, and each is condemned to an unnatural life of increasing vigilance, anxiety and fear.

Conference believes that the days of white supremacy are past, and that it is completely outlawed by an overwhelming world opinion. South Africa must accept a political and economic structure that will eliminate these bitter conflicts. Conference believes that White South Africa has no adequate conception of the repugnance felt by non-white citizens towards the doctrines of apartheid, and that it has no conception of the sufferings and deprivations inflicted on its non-white fellows by apartheid legislation, of the ways in which they are harried by laws and officials during every moment of their lives. Those white people who tried to understand it were often rejected and made to suffer by their own community and many white people who were convinced of the injustices of apartheid laws, failed to oppose them because of the fear of ostracism and victimisation.

The point was made that the whole Nationalist philosophy is based on racial difference. But Conference regards such differences as only incidental to a basic common humanity, on which foundation, and on that alone, just and peaceful policies can be based. This indeed is the teaching of the Christian religion, and non-white people were disillusioned when white people denied the values of the religion that they had taught to their fellows. Most white South Africans had a double standard; they responded to the teachings of Christ so long as they thought these did not contradict apartheid, white supremacy, white leadership or the many new forms of racial discrimination. Non-white South Africa rejected this double standard; nor did it wish to return to the status quo ante 1948 to which many white South Africans hoped to return when the extreme policies of apartheid had been rejected.

The Conference recognises the depth of White fear of granting rights to non-white people, but notes that policies based on fear offer no real security to white people. On the contrary they heightened such fear, and drove white South Africa into more and more dangerous policies. Politicians played on these fears to seize political power. Conference wishes to reassure white South Africa that it recognises the interdependence of white and non-white, and wishes only to guarantee basic human rights of all people. Conference affirms its allegiance to the aspirations of the Universal Declaration of Human Rights, and suggests December 10, the anniversary of the Declaration, be observed as a new Day of Covenant offering security and hope to every inhabitant of multi-racial South Africa.

Report on the Findings of the Commission on Religion

The following considerations emerged from the discussion on the responsibilities of religious communities in a multi-racial society:—

Religion brings human life to a real and practical communion with God the Eternal, and all religious faiths in a greater or lesser degree look upon human life as a direct creation of God, the Father of all mankind. From this universal standpoint follows immediately the conviction that all men are made in the image of God for a divine purpose, endowed with reason and free will, possessed therefore of an inviolable personal dignity, irrespective of race, colour or culture, and entrusted with duties and rights that have their source in God.

Religion is therefore vitally concerned with the essential equality of all men before God. Inequalities in development, even when they are based on the historical growth of human societies are not ordained by the Divine Will as permanent features; rather they provide situations that are a challenge to the good will of men.

Religious communities confess the failure of their members to teach and implement fully in practice the brotherhood of man. They acknowledge the tendency to compromising and giving way to collective egoisms. If human life is directed to another and higher life, as most religions assert, the greatest and most important reality is the person and all historical or present obstacles raised in the way of the individual in striving for the goal of his higher life, must be changed into opportunities towards that end, even through the acceptance of personal suffering.

When in a multi-racial society misunderstandings and prejudice tend to obscure fundamental truths, religious communities have a grave obligation to emphasise them and to train the moral judgment of their members in regard to duties of justice and charity. In the Divine command, "Render unto Caesar the things that are Caesar's and to God the things that are God's," we have no statement of fully equal allegiance. Our first bond of obedience is to God, and our loyalty to the state is limited in its scope by the prior claims of this duty.

Conference recommends that religious communities make use of all available means to achieve the ends of moral education in social and racial matters, namely, the pulpit, the religious press, religious schools, classes and meetings; that reference be made to specific and concrete issues; that the situation of those depressed and frustrated by social injustice be brought home forcibly to the more fortunate; and that practical applications of inter-racial collaboration be fostered in worship, discussion, social exchanges and in charitable and cultural undertakings.

Conference believes that in this way religious communities will contribute their share to bringing about a change of heart and a change of social structure by peaceful methods, thus helping to embody what has been enunciated as fundamental truths in the life of South African society.

Report on the Findings of the Commission on Education

The Commission expressed its belief that education must seek to provide for the intellectual, emotional, spiritual and physical growth of every human being, without distinction of race. It must create such conditions that the native abilities of all people can thrive and come to fulfilment.

The Commission therefore endorses Articles 26 and 27(1) of the Universal Declaration of Human Rights, viz:—

Article 26:
1. Everyone has the right to education. Education shall be free, at least in the elementary and fundamental stages. Elementary education shall be compulsory. Technical and professional education shall be made generally available and higher education shall be equally accessible to all on the basis of merit.

2. Education shall be directed to the full development of the human personality and to the strengthening of respect for human rights and fundamental freedoms. It shall promote understanding, tolerance and friendship among all nations, racial and religious groups, and shall further the activities of the United Nations for the maintenance of peace.

3. Parents have a prior right to choose the kind of education that shall be given to their children.

Article 27(1):
Everyone has the right freely to participate in the cultural life of the community, to enjoy the arts and to share in scientific advancement and its benefits.

With specific reference to South Africa's present and future the Commission rejects current educational policies which seek to perpetuate white domination, accentuate ethnic differences and resuscitate tribal nationalism. The Commission further rejects uniracial formulation of educational policy. The Commission deplores the use of mother tongue education for political ends. It rejects the Bantu Education Act, the Separate Universities Bill, the Nursing Amendment Act, the proposals of the Cape Commission for separate Coloured Education and finally, the narrow sectionalism of certain parts of the Christian National Education programme.

Further, the Commission affirms its faith in the common destiny of the various racial elements which comprise the South African nation and believes that the fundamental social aim of our education should be to promote a common patriotism, common citizenship and the welding of the various elements in South Africa of a peaceful multi-racial society. We believe that it will be necessary to encourage the multi-racial classroom and to end compulsory segregation in schools. As a start in this direction, we feel that private schools should be permitted to admit children of all races, if they so desire.

We earnestly recommend to the Conference that a Continuing Committee on Education be set up which shall investigate *inter alia*:

a) how rapidly education can be made compulsory for all children;

b) how most effectively and speedily adult illiteracy can be ended and the general education of adults extended;

c) how the present inequalities of educational opportunities can most speedily be reduced.

Report on the Findings of the Commission on Economic Rights and Duties in a Multi-Racial Society

This Commission assumes that economic advance is important, that poverty is an evil and tends to breed evil, and that therefore it is the duty of the state to take the necessary measures to put an end to poverty. This cannot be done by way of doles and subsidies, but only by securing to every member of the community equal justice and an equal right to live and work. Everyone shall have the right to earn his living in any legitimate way, according to his skill and ability. He should also have the right to acquire and hold full and secure possession of land. This would require a more equitable distribution of land. In time this would make possible the eventual disappearance of the reserve system, with its implication of territorial separation of the races.

A just economic policy must be based on the right of each member of the community, without discrimination or limitation, to develop to the full, and use in any legitimate way, his capacity and abilities. This implies that all colour bars in industry should be abolished and all workmen should be entitled to a living wage according to civilised standards. The belief that there is only a limited pool of jobs makes white workers think that the colour bar is necessary for their protection. It is felt that the entry of new competitors into that labour pool would mean a loss of their jobs and a reduction in their standard of living. This is an unfounded fear. If our land, with its natural resources, were made available for full use by all our peoples, our economy would expand with full opportunity for everyone in town and country, in agriculture and industry, to employ himself or to be employed to his full capacity. The colour bar denies to those excluded by it their inherent natural right to be able to use their talents fully. Such a denial is unjust and cannot be defended on any moral or economic ground.

It is an essential in a growing community that the economy of the country should be an expanding one. At present in the Union, such expansion is gravely hampered by the colour bar and by restrictive legislation, such as the Group Areas Act, the Pass Laws and influx control, and generally the interference with the mobility of workers.

Any legal obstacles in the way of the worker's freedom to choose his own calling should be abolished, particularly those which interfere with:—

a) his right to be trained for any occupation or calling;

b) his right to combine with others in trade unions for the protection of his interests, including the right to strike.

The system of using migrant labour is unsocial and uneconomic, and dangerous to the welfare of the country. Every effort should be made to provide for a stable family life for the worker near his place of work.

Provision for social welfare should be available for all without racial discrimination.

To sum up. Apartheid imposes a crippling cost on the economy of the country. The aim should be to remove all discriminatory restrictions based on the colour of the worker and all other obstacles in the way of production as soon as possible, and that the state should encourage the expansion of the economy by all means in its power.

Report on the Findings of the Commission on Civil Rights and Duties in a Multi-Racial Society

1. We believe that any good society must guarantee civil rights to its citizens, and that these civil rights are fundamental to human freedom.

2. Such rights, as upheld in democratic societies, and affirmed in the United Nations Declaration of Human Rights, include: freedom of speech and association; the right to publish opinions; the right to own

and occupy property; freedom of worship and conscience; freedom from arbitrary arrest and banishment; freedom of movement—including travel and passport rights; freedom to choose a marriage partner and to found a family; the privacy of the home and of correspondence; the right to equal protection of the laws and freedom to participate in the government of the country. We recognise that these rights must be exercised with regard to the rights of others, and in the interests of the whole community.

3. To deny these rights to any group in the nation is to prevent men from living a free and dignified life, in harmony with society. The result is resentment and frustration; and a sense of oppression which if not remedied, can lead to rebellion.

4. To withhold civil rights, for reasons of race or colour or creed, is a violation of moral principles and civilised standards. To try to limit such rights to one racial group, in a multi-racial society must lead ultimately to the limitation of the rights of all.

5. The effect on the dominant group is the destruction of the values of their society, with a tacit reliance on force to maintain their dominance. The effect on the subordinate groups may be to encourage resistance or the will to counter-domination, or slavish submission to the state.

6. These general statements have detailed and practical application to our South African society. Since the Act of Union, a variety of restrictive laws have been passed, which limit or withhold civil rights, and which have reached a crescendo in the apartheid laws. Some of these laws have curtailed the personal freedom [of] the governing group. Their essential purpose has been, however, to apply restraints, prohibitions and racial discriminations to the non-white groups. If these laws are maintained and extended, the moral, material and intellectual decay of our total society will inevitably result. In the subordinate group, arrests for technical offences—which under full civil rights would not be offences at all—are so numerous that imprisonment has tended to lose its stigma. The effect of this is to diminish respect for the law, which is often seen as the instrument of racial domination; and a resultant instability and insecurity in our society as a whole.

7. The remedy is the repeal of all laws denying or restricting civil rights. In addition, the basic freedoms, to which every individual in a democratic society is entitled, should be entrenched in a written constitution, through a bill of rights. Such a constitution would require the assent of a new National Convention, representative of all races in South Africa.

8. The ultimate entrenchment of civil rights is not, however, dependent only upon law. It requires the vigilance of all citizens, and their

knowledge and determination that if they allow any breach in civil rights, at the expense of one group, they endanger the rights of all.

The Commission, as a practical recommendation, advises:
That a standing committee be elected by the conference:

a) to publicise the pernicious effects of the denial of civil rights involved in the pass and other discriminatory laws, and the effect of these laws upon all sections of the people:

b) to encourage united opposition to laws withholding civil rights, in order to bring about the repeal of these laws.

Report on the Findings of the Political Arrangements Commissions

1. This Conference accepts as its fundamental aim the creation in South Africa of a common society.

2. Conference is convinced that only universal adult suffrage on a common roll can meet the needs and aspirations of the people of this country. It appreciates, however, that there is disagreement as to the ways and means of achieving the transition from white supremacy to a non-racial democracy in which these franchise rights may be exercised.

   Conference believes that it should start working immediately towards the achievement of the goal of universal adult suffrage.

3. Conference is of the opinion that the basic human rights of individuals should be safeguarded by means of a Bill of Rights which should be an integral part of the Constitution.

4. Conference suggests that a committee be appointed to consider certain topics relating to political arrangements, raised by various delegates.

THE AFRICAN NATIONAL CONGRESS WHILE ITS LEADERS ARE ON TRIAL, 1957-1959

Document 22. "Azikwelwa!" Leaflet on the bus boycott issued by the Alexandra Peoples Transport Action Committee, [n.d.]

The bus boycott has been treated as a major event in Africa by Press and Parliament. IT IS! The attempt to increase the fare by a penny is a final economic burden that can only aggravate the present abject standard of living. For that and for no other reason we resist—in Alexandra, Orlando, Moroka, Jabavu, Sophiatown, Western Native Township and Pretoria.

We oppose the official voice, coarse and stupid, of mis-Minister Schoeman by a unity in struggle that has alarmed the white minority Government and PUTCO—a private company which calls itself public. We have walked in the interest of all of us for close on 14 weeks, losing our shoe leather, our time, energy and in many cases wages and we are absolutely determined NOT TO GIVE UP.

Many swindle attempts have been made by so-called authorities to "settle" the miseries of the people (how sympathetic can these sympathetic exploiters be?) ALL of which have been rejected as swindle by mass public meetings in all affected areas. This last hopeless attempt to induce the people to ride is just ANOTHER SWINDLE. Some people have allowed themselves to be cheated—but are gradually realising their mistake. Many people who board the buses along the route without a 4d. voucher are required to pay 5d. WHAT MUST BE CLEARLY UNDERSTOOD IS THAT IT IS ONLY A TEMPORARY "SETTLEMENT" FOR THREE MONTHS. When the £ 25,000 from the Chamber of Commerce runs out—what then? WE CANNOT SELL OUR 14 WEEKS STRUGGLE FOR A 12 WEEKS "SETTLEMENT" (according to the A.N.C.) The Government has PROMISED to step in when the boycott is smashed and the Chamber is bankrupt to bring about their permanent settlement. Why drive the Chamber to bankruptcy, why drive the people to distraction? An authority which behaves in this way is highly suspect. We refuse to settle our economic affairs on the basis of PROMISES—from the enemy. Since when must we have confidence in a White Government who are the source of our ruin?

We reject the scheme out of hand and insist on A 4d. FARE FOR A 4d. TICKET ON A LONG-TERM BASIS. The investigation into our economic misery for higher wages is rubbish—our misery has already been known for three hundred years—and the promise of higher wages is—a PROMISE—as noisy and as empty as an old tin can. We are not donkeys even though we are short of carrots. Our voice, not coarse, not stupid, says simply—AZIKWELWA! FOR A 4d. FARE, FOR A 4d. TICKET ON A LONG-TERM BASIS.

Some groups on the Boycott Committees must be immediately exposed. The A.N.C. (purely loud-mouthed self advertisers), the Vigilance Association and the Standholders Association have tried to sell-out many times:—witness their recommendation to collect 1d. back at a kiosk—AFTER HAVING PAID 5d.—a proposal that was publicly burnt by those leaders who are struggling in the interests of their people. The A.N.C. leaders are from time to time the main anti-boycott spokesmen. A struggle properly conducted—a struggle in which the interests of the people are placed FIRST—above the individual leader—above self-importance—above organizations—such a struggle will always expose the quislings in our midst. We must take note. A man in the police uniform is easy to spot, but a man dressed in strong talk and weak actions—has to be DIS-COVERED through his actions. This is the case with the A.N.C., the Vigilance Association and the Standholders Association in our present struggle.

Let us get this quite clear. We are not to be taken in by swindles and swindlers. AZIKWELWA! ON WITH THE BOYCOTT FOR A REAL SETTLEMENT! Should PUTCO and their government agent Mr. Schoeman continue to behave in their hitherto stubborn stupidity WE have other weapons of struggle to use in our own time. Why should we exhaust ourselves walking to white cities for white profit and black poverty? We have struggled for 14 weeks against THEIR opposition. Let us now oppose our tiredness and determination to their face-saving stupidity.

The Boycott is by no means over.

———

Note: "Azikwelwa" means "Don't ride–don't get on," according to *New Age*, July 5, 1956.

Document 23. Letter on the current situation and suggesting a multi-racial convention, from Chief A. J. Lutuli to Prime Minister Strijdom, May 28, 1957

28th May 1957.

The Honourable the Prime Minister,
Union of SouthAfrica,
House of Assembly
CAPE TOWN

Honourable Sir,

At a time when in many respects our country is passing through some of the most difficult times in its history, I consider it my duty as leader of the African National Congress, a Union-wide premier political organisation among the African people in the Union of South Africa, to address this letter direct to you as head of the government to apprise you personally of the very grave fears and concern of my people, the Africans, at the situation now existing in the Union, especially anent matters affecting them.

I shall venture to place before you respectfully what I consider to be some of the disturbing features of our situation and suggest steps that could be taken by the Government to meet the position.

I have addressed this letter to you, Sir, and not to any Department for two reasons.

Firstly, because the gravity of our situation requires your direct personal attention and, secondly, because what I shall say fundamentally affects the welfare of the Union of South Africa as a whole since both basically and in practice, the so-called "Native Affairs" are, not only inextricably interwoven with the true interests of other racial groups, but are a key to a proper understanding and appraisal of South African Affairs and problems for indeed "ALL SOUTH AFRICAN POLITICS ARE NATIVE AFFAIRS."

One of the tragic aspects of the political situation in our country today is the increasing deterioration in race relations, especially in Black-White relations. There can be no two viewpoints on this question. Never has there been such an extremely delicate relationship as now exists between the Government of Whites only, of which you are head, and the vast masses of non-European people in general, and the African people in particular. This unfortunate state of affairs has resulted from a number of factors, the basic one being the policy of segregation, especially its more aggressive form, White baasskap and apartheid.

It is in the economic sphere that this disastrous policy of discrimination has affected Africans hardest and most cruelly. It has brought on them an economic plight that has shown itself in the dire poverty of the people both in the urban and in the rural areas. This fact has long been attested to from time to time by economic experts and by findings of Government Commissions. Recently, as a result of the Rand and Pretoria Bus Boycott, the extreme poverty of Africans in urban areas has been acknowledged by even commerce and industry. It is not necessary for one to describe the generally admitted horrifying state of degradation this poverty has brought upon the African people or to refer in any detail to the tragic social consequences such as disease, malnutrition, bad housing, broken families and delinquency among children and youth.

The denial to the African people of the democratic channels of expression and participation in the government of the country has accentuated the stresses and strains to which they are subject. My people have come to view with alarm every new session of Parliament because it has meant the passing of more oppressive discriminatory legislation there. As a result of this annual influx of new legislation there are already in the Statute Books of the Union of South Africa a large number of laws which cause my people tremendous hardship and suffering. The African people view these laws as further weapons of attack on their very existence as a people. For the sake of brevity I shall refer to only a few of such laws in support of my charge. Here are the categories of some of such laws. I cite:

1.   *THE LAND LAWS* which to all intents and purposes deny the African people the right to own land in both the rural and the urban areas. In rural areas Africans are tenants in State rural reserves or in privately-owned land. In urban areas they are tenants in municipal lands.

The land allocated to Africans in rural areas is most inadequate. It will only be 13% of the entire land surface of the Union when all the land promised them in the Natives' Land and Trust Act of 1936 shall have been acquired. On account of this inadequacy of land the African people live under extremely congested conditions in rural areas and in the urban areas and find it difficult to make a living above subsistence level from the land. These land laws are in many respects reminiscent of the worst features of the feudal laws of mediaeval days.

2.   *THE PASS LAWS*, which not only deny the African people freedom of movement, but are enforced in ways that cause the people much unnecessary suffering and humiliation.

They are definitely an affront to human personality and it is not surprising that their extension to our womenfolk has resulted in Union-wide protests and in the expression of deep indignation by the entire African population. These protests and demonstrations are indicative of a state of unrest and intense tension among the African people.

Section 10 of the Natives (Urban Areas) Consolidation Act of 1945, as substituted by Section 27 of Act 54 of 1952, places serious and far-reaching restrictions on the right of my people to enter into and remain within an urban area in order to compel them to seek employment on European farms where working conditions are extremely shocking. Acting under this provision local authorities and members of the police force have forcibly removed from their homes and families thousands upon thousands of my people in the interest of the European farming industry.

3.   *THE MASTER AND SERVANT ACTS*, which are designed effectively to limit to unskilled categories the participation of the African people in industry and commerce. This relegates the bulk of African workers to low uneconomic wages. My people note with grave concern the efforts of your Government to destroy the African Trade Union Movement.

The current session of Parliament affords the country no respite from Apartheid legislation. It has before it a large number of measures of far-reaching consequences for the country in general, and the African people in particular. There is the Native Laws Amendment Bill, which is seen by the African people as another measure attacking the civil and religious liberties of the people and aimed at preventing contact on a basis of human dignity and equality between the African people and the rest of our multi-racial population.

The African people are similarly disturbed by other measures now before Parliament such as the bill on Apartheid in University Education, the Apartheid Nursing Bill, the measure to increase indirect taxation of the African people despite their poverty, and a bill intended to prevent the operation of alternative bus services where the boycott weapon has been effectively used by a people who have no other means of seeking redress against an economic injustice.

We are greatly concerned at the policy of Apartheid and the administrative action flowing from it because we honestly believe that these are against the true interest of democracy and freedom. I would like to point out here that the enforcement of the discriminatory apartheid laws brings the African people into unnecessary contact with the police. Unfortunately, the impatient and domineering manner in which the police often do their work among Africans results in unfortunate clashes between the people and the police. The net result is that Africans tend to lose respect for the law and come to look upon the Union of South Africa as a Police State.

What does my Congress stand for?

My Congress is deeply wedded to the ideals of democracy and has at all times emphasised its firm and unshakable belief in the need for the creation of a society in South Africa based on the upholding of democratic values: values which are today cherished the world over by all civilised peoples.

We believe in a society in which the White and the non-White peoples of the Union will work and live in harmony for the common good of our fatherland and share equally in the good things of life which our country offers in abundance. We believe in the brotherhood of man and in the upholding of human respect and dignity. Never has my Congress preached hatred against any racial group in the Union. On the contrary, it has stretched out its hand of friendship to all South Africans of all races, emphasising that there is sufficient room for all in this beautiful country of ours in which we can and must live in peace and friendship. Unfortunately, there are people, among them Ministers of the Crown—Mr. Louw, Mr. Schoeman, Dr. Verwoerd, to mention some—who, according to Press reports, believe that the aims and objects of the African National Congress are to drive the White man out of Southern Africa and to set up a "Native State". These people charge that the African National Congress is highly subversive and fosters a communistic-tainted African Nationalism or a rabid tyrannical and narrow African Nationalism and intend, in either case, to deprive the White minority in South Africa of their share in the Government of the country.

This is not—and never has been—the policy of my Congress. On the contrary, Congress believes in a common society and holds that citizens of a country, regardless of their race or colour, have the right to full participation in the government and in the control of their future. Anyone who has taken the slightest trouble to study the policy of my Congress and followed its activities should know how baseless and unfounded these fears about Congress are.

Why do we believe in a common society?

Firstly, we believe in a common society because we honestly hold that anything to the contrary unduly works against normal human behaviour, for the gregarious nature of man enables him to flourish to his best in association with others who cherish lofty ideals. "Not for good or for worse", but for "good and better things" the African has accepted the higher moral and spiritual values inherent in the fundamental concepts of what, for lack of better terminology, is called 'Western Civilisation'. Apartheid, so far, has revealed itself as an attempt by White South Africa to shunt the African off the tried civilised road by getting him to glorify unduly his tribal past.

Secondly, we believe that the close spiritual and normal contact facilitated by a common society structure in one nation makes it easier to develop friendship and mutual respect and understanding among various groups in a nation; this is especially valuable in a multi-racial nation like ours and these qualities—friendship, mutual respect and understanding, and a common loyalty—are a sine qua non to the building of a truly united nation from a heterogeneous society. In our view, it will not be easy to develop a common loyalty to South Africa when its people by law are kept strictly apart spiritually and socially. Such a state of affairs is likely to give rise to unjustified fears and suspicions which often lead to deadly hatreds among the people and, more often than not, end in disastrous antagonisms within the nation.

Lastly, we hold the view that the concept of a common society conforms more than does apartheid to the early traditional closer Black/White contact. This, undoubtedly, accounts for the relatively rapid way in which Africans, from the days of these early contacts, to their advantage and that of South Africa as a whole, took to and absorbed fairly rapidly Christian teachings and the education that accompanied it.

Strongly holding as we do the views I have just stated, you will appreciate, Sir, with what heartfelt concern, alarm and disappointment we learnt recently from Press reports that the Government intends banning the African National Congress and arresting 2,000 more of its members. I humbly submit that such an action would serve to increase the dangerous gulf that exists between the Government and the African people and, in particular, those African leaders who have knowledge of social and economic forces at work in the modern South Africa of today and the world in general. No loyal South African, White or non-White, should view with equanimity such a situation. It is this loyalty and deep concern for the welfare of the Union that makes me say most emphatically that your Government has no justification whatsoever in banning the African National Congress and making further arrests of its members. I would support my plea by emphasising with all the strength at my command that such actions would be against the true interests of South Africa.

I make no undue claim when I say that my Congress represents the true and fundamental aspirations and views of practically all the African people in the Union, and these aspirations and views are not alien to the best interests of our common country. Rather, it will be found that they conform to the United Nations Charter and the international Declaration of Human Rights.

If it should appear that my Congress pleads strongly and uncompromisingly for the advancement of the African people only, it would not be because it is actuated by a partisan spirit, but rather because the African people are at the lowest rung of the ladder. I am sure that with the same zeal, vigour and devotion it would espouse—and in fact does espouse—the uplift of other under-privileged peoples regardless of their colour or race.

My people crave for an opportunity to work for a great United South Africa in which they can develop their personalities and capabilities to the fullest with the rest of the country's population in the interest of the country as a whole. No country can prosper when antagonisms divide its people and when, as we Africans see it, Government policy is directly opposed to the legitimate wishes and interests of a great majority of the population.

I might here point out that the African National Congress has always sought to achieve its objectives by using non-violent methods. In its most militant activities it has never used nor attempted to use physical force. It has used non-violent means and ways recognised as legitimate in the civilised world, especially in the case of a people, such as we are, who find themselves denied all effective constitutional means of voicing themselves in the sovereign forum of the country.

I would, for emphasis, reiterate that it is our ardent desire in Congress to see human conduct and relations motivated by an over-riding passion for peace and friendship in South Africa and in the world in general and so we would as strongly be opposed to Black domination, or any other kind of domination from whatever source, as we are uncompromisingly opposed to White domination. We regard domination, exploitation and racialism as arch enemies of mankind.

What should be the Government's reply to the views and aspirations of my organisation which I have tried faithfully to present?

In my opinion, the only real answer the Government could give to the stand of my Congress and its inevitable agitation, is for it to make an earnest effort to meet the progressive aspirations of the African people and not to attempt to silence Congress and its leadership by bannings and arrests, for it is the African National Congress and its leadership that is the authentic and responsible voice of the people.

Rather than outlaw the African National Congress or persecute its members and supporters, the Government, in a statesmanlike manner, should reconsider its "Native policy" with a view to bringing it in conformity with democratic and moral values inherent in any way of life meriting to be described as civilised.

It is the considered view of my Congress that the lack of effective contact and responsible consultation between the Government and the non-European people is at the root of the growing deterioration in race relations and in the relation between the African people and the Government.

Unless healthy contact and purposeful consultation take place at the highest level between the Government and the accredited leaders of the people, misunderstanding and strained relations must grow.

Persistently to ignore the legitimate wishes and interests of the African people and permanently to close the door to consultation with representative organisations enjoying the loyalty of the people, is not the path of statesmanship and can lead only to even more dangerous tensions and chaos in the country.

The Government should earnestly address itself to seeking means and ways of establishing some permanent democratic machinery to enable all citizens to participate intelligently and effectively in the government of the country as is done in all truly democratic states. The existing forms of consultation, such as do exist, are, in my opinion, not only inadequate, but undemocratic: the quarterly meetings of African chiefs, the Bantu Authorities (where these exist) and the Advisory Boards in urban areas; even the so-called Native Representatives in the Senate and in the House of Assembly can be no substitute for truly democratic representation and consultation.

My Congress is convinced that it is today urgently necessary for the Government to devise *new ways* to meet the challenging problems before South Africa. It is eminently in the interest of the country as a whole that this present impasse be broken and the danger to future tensions recognised and averted before it is too late.

It should not be beyond the capacity of statesmen in South Africa—and I would not like to believe that South Africa is bankrupt of statesmanship—to take in faith steps which could inaugurate a new era in interracial co-operation and harmony in our country.

As I have stressed directly and indirectly throughout this letter, no time should be lost in making contact with the leadership of organisations and bodies, among them the African National Congress, representative of organised African opinion, with a view not only to discuss the problems and issues such as I have drawn attention to in this letter, but to consider the advisability and possibility of calling a multi-racial convention to seek a solution to our pressing national problems.

In the name of the African National Congress, I am happy to make this approach to you in the hope that our country's future and happiness will triumph over established conventions, procedures and party considerations.

I need hardly mention that in the event of your Government not acceding to this request, my organisation must continue to fight for the rights of my people.

> I am,
>> Honourable Sir,
>> Yours respectfully,
>>> A. J. Luthuli.
>>> *PRESIDENT-GENERAL.*
>>> AFRICAN NATIONAL CONGRESS

Document 24. "Repeal the Pass Laws . . . A Great Demonstration to Parliament." Flyer issued by the Federation of South African Women and the ANC Women's League (Cape Western), June 13, 1957

Repeal the Pass Laws

Who knows better than any African woman what it means to have a husband who must carry a pass? The women know that:

- **PASSES MEAN PRISON;**
- **PASSES MEAN BROKEN HOMES;**
- **PASSES MEAN SUFFERING AND MISERY FOR EVERY AFRICAN FAMILY IN OUR COUNTRY;**
- **PASSES ARE JUST ANOTHER WAY IN WHICH THE GOVERNMENT MAKES SLAVES OF THE AFRICANS;**
- **PASSES MEAN HUNGER AND UNEMPLOYMENT;**
- **PASSES ARE AN INSULT.**

And the Government is trying to force our WOMEN to carry passes too

No woman is fooled by the "Reference Book." We know that this is the same as a pass. If a woman is found without this book or if all the papers inside are not in order, she will be pushed into the Kwela-Kwela and taken to gaol.

Her children will be left motherless.

TO PAY 3/6 FOR THIS "REFERENCE BOOK" IS TO BUY SLAVERY.

Why should women carry passes?

The Government has tried to make women carry passes for many years and each time the women have given their answer. By standing united, protesting with one voice and organising all areas around this wicked law, the women are trying to achieve the abolition of the pass law system with its vicious attack on their liberty.

AS IN THE BUS BOYCOTT, THE GOVERNMENT MUST FAIL THIS TIME TOO.

Women of South Africa will always oppose the carrying of passes. With all our strength we must fight against this attack on ourselves, our mothers, sisters, children and families.

EVERY WOMAN MUST SIGN A PLEDGE, STATING HER FIRM OPPOSITION TO THE PASS SYSTEM.

- Let us pledge ourselves to end the whole pass system—for men as well as for women.
- Let us have the biggest demonstration of women ever held.
- Let us show Verwoerd that we will never bow down to his brutality.
- DOWN WITH THE PASS SYSTEM!
- Passes are passports to prisons.
- LET US GIVE THE GOVERNMENT THE ANSWER BY HOLDING

A GREAT DEMONSTRATION TO PARLIAMENT

on THURSDAY, 13th JUNE, 1957, at 2 p.m.

Meeting Place at Medical Centre, Dock Road (Bottom of St. George's Street), Cape Town

Issued by Federation of S.A. Women and ANC Women's League (Cape Western), P.O. Box 2706, Cape Town. Printed by Pioneer Press (Pty.) Ltd., Forgate Street, Woodstock, Cape.

Document 25. Secretarial Report of the ANC Youth League (Transvaal), June 15–16, 1957

Dr. M. Chuene, Mr. Speaker, Sons and Daughters of Africa,

When we review the international situation today, we discover that profound transformations have taken place in the world in which the Youth find themselves today. In these developments the Youth has played an active role. They have made an important contribution in declaring for peace and friendship and understanding between nations and peoples; above all they have made an important contribution for the relaxation of international tension and world peace. Today the Youth are preparing for the . . . Congress of WFDY [World Federation of Democratic Youth] and the 14th World Festival of Youth and Students to be held at Bucharest and Moscow (Russia) respectfully [sic]. This will be another important stage on the road to understanding and co-operation.

Recently new dangers have arisen with which the Youth are directly concerned. When Egypt nationalized the Suez Canal as a Sovereign and National Independent State, colonial aggression by the Imperialist forces of Israel, Britain, France and U.S.A., was perpetrated against the Egyptian people, thus endangering peace in the whole world. This is clear indication, friends, that Imperialism is collective, one and indivisible. We of the ANC Youth League also joined forces and have expressed, on more than one occasion, our solidarity with the struggle against colonialism and for national independence. We held demonstrations and rallies in support of the Egyptian people in their just struggle to safeguard their national sovereignty. We also witnessed with deep sorrow the pitiable events which here struck the Hungarian people and Youth. We hope that a new spirit will arise and bring once more solidarity of the Hungarian people. We are witnessing with deep sorrow the subtle diplomacy and trickery of the American Imperialism in the Middle East—and serious deliberate threat of the extensions of the conflicts in the Middle East. We join in the world-wide support to the people of Algeria, Cyprus, Kenya, Nigeria etc. fighting for National independence and self determination. We greet our brothers and sisters of the African territories who have gained national independence.

The attainment of National Independence by Ghana on March 6th, 1957, under the Premiership of Dr. Kwame Nkrumah, not only goes down in the annals of Gold Coast History as the greatest event of the year, but also as a landmark in the history of Africa. This is a clear indication that "A new rejuvenated and a dynamic mother Africa will be born." Ghana has opened the gate; therefore, it means that the rest of Colonial Africa has to march with greater measure of optimism on the road to freedom. "Be sure that the night of Colonialism is ending, and that the sun of National freedom is about to rise! The struggle for National Independence has provided for all of us a rallying point and a fire of inspiration." (Dr. Sukarno, President of the Republic of Indonesia, when opening Asian African Students Conference June 7th, 1957.)

SOUTH AFRICA:

Here at home during our term of Office, we have witnessed the implementations of poisonous and most humiliating and degrading Acts passed by Parliament. The meeting of the 14th Annual Conference of the Youth League is very timely. It meets at a time when the Nationalist Government have increased tremendously their repressive and restrictive measures on the people; at a time when the Nationalist Government are bent on imposing on the majority an Afrikaner tribal rule.

When we review the recent current political developments in the country, we come to only one conclusion, that a situation exists more than ever before for the building of a mighty militant Youth Organisation which will be capable of withstanding and resisting the Nationalist onslaught on the people. The entire Province of the Transvaal is focussing its attention on the Conference. We should, therefore, amalgamate our common interest into a single united front, above all let us declare to canalise our isolated ideas into a common democratic front so that all should strive for peace, justice and security in our mother land.

The implementation of the Group Areas Act in the Western Areas is sheer robbery and blunder "in the name of the Law." This will mean the displacement of tens and thousands of non-whites and the elimination of about 750 Indian traders. We call upon the Youth to send protests to the press, municipalities, Government and to organise meetings and protests. We have noticed how under this Act and its sister Act, the Native Urban Areas Amendment Act, Advocate Duma Nokwe has been finally notified by the Native Affairs Department he cannot take up chambers in His Majesty's Buildings. This will make it virtually impossible for Mr. Duma Nokwe to carry on his practice. We would like to express solidarity and appreciation to the majority of the Johannesburg Bar Council Members who have stood by Mr. Nokwe and are still fighting the issue.

We have witnessed how under the Native Urban Areas Act a number of Africans, chiefs etc., were banished, deposed and deported.

THE ARREST OF OUR LEADERS:

On the dawn of December 5th, 1956, 156 progressive South Africans were arrested on allegations of High Treason. It would not be wisdom on our part to comment on the arrests lest it become *sub-judice*. But this much we can say: that we know who these 156 accused are! that we know what they stand for. And if what they stood for is a crime, then we submit that all progressives—freedom fighters—are guilty of the crime.

Whisperings coming from different parts of the country and abroad indicate that all sections of the population have been deeply scared by these happenings. People of diverse political and religious beliefs; those who have never shown any interest in the peoples' struggles for democratic and just changes, and those who have even been openly hostile to the liberatory movements, are now stepping forward with pledges of solidarity and support.

But it is unfortunate that we as a Youth League organisation have played a very insignificant role as regards these arrests. But the Youth as members of the liberatory movements have played an important role either individually or collectively. We earnestly appeal to the Youth that wherever they are, they must of necessity focus the attention of the people on the Treason Trials. The Youth must assist to raise money to augment the Bishop's Fund.

Because of these arrests our Organisation has suffered serious devastations and dislocations. Among the 156, 18 of them are Youth from the Transvaal—included in this list are our own Executive Members. Mr. H. G. Makgothi (President Youth League TVL), Mr. P. Molaoa (Treasurer Youth League TVL), Miss B. Mashaba (Assistant Secretary Youth League TVL), Mr. P. Ntithe and Mr. Radebe (O.P.O. TVL), Mr. T. X. Makiwane (Executive Member). Other Youth arrested are Messrs.: R. Resha, J. Matlou, J. Modise, H. Tshabalala, C. Ntsibande, T. Musi, A. Bokala, J. Masemola, J. Molefe, V. Make, D. Nokwe and Mpho. We were therefore, compelled to co-opt members into the Executive so as to continue with the struggle to emancipate the African Youth and African people in general.

THE NEW APARTHEID MEASURES:

The announcement from the Throne by Dr. Jansen—Governor-General on Friday 12th January, 1957—during the opening of the Union Parliament—is clear manifestation and must be placed on record that the action taken by the Nationalist Government is a deliberate attempt to sabotage the political and economic and social aspirations of the African Youth in this country.

(i) *THE SEPARATE UNIVERSITIES EDUCATION BILL 1957:*

The separate Universities Education Bill gives Dr. Verwoerd power of life or death over African University Colleges. Professors and Scientists are to become direct employees of the State Department—such as Native Affairs Department or Education, Arts and Sciences. This is a negation of University traditions and standards and in keeping with the policy of indoctrination, (Prof. Z. K. Matthews—interview with *New Age*—28/3/57).

We as Youth protested vigorously to the press and on political platforms to the introduction of such legislation. The protests staged by the professors, lecturers and students throughout the country show how the government has angered the people. We saluted these professors, lecturers and students who upheld the principle of non-segregation. We would recommend that a National Conference of all students must be convened to protest against such legislation; and out of such a conference should develop the creation of a Federal Non-European Students Organization.

(ii) *THE NURSING AMENDMENT BILL 1957.*

The Nursing Amendment Bill before Parliament makes such discrimination between White and Non-white nursing as completely to destroy the Non-Europeans' last stronghold of faith in the European Society. The Bill proclaims to the Non-Whites of this country that even in the profession of medicine the white man is not to be trusted. . . . a Non-White practitioner is to be considered always as inferior (R.D.M. Edition Friday 14th June, 1957.) We salute the hundreds of nurses for having rejected Apartheid in the Nursing Profession. We call upon the Youth to intensify the campaign against the Bill—form processions and protest marches to show their solidarity.

(iii) *NATIVE LAWS AMENDMENT BILL 1957.*

The aim of this Bill is that Verwoerd wants power to end all Black-White contact. These must meet only on Master-Servant relationships. . . . There are quite a number of Hitlerite provisions contained in Dr. Verwoerd's new Native Laws Amendment Bill. In all Union Towns and Cities all meetings attended by Africans, meetings of Committees, Trade Union Branches etc., private Social gatherings may be banned if the Minister of Native Affairs and the Local Town Council feel that they will constitute a nuisance and are undesirable. Other poisonous features in the Bill is the threat to the Churches founded since 1938 admitting Africans.

This Bill, we maintain, encroaches on all individuals whether political, religious, social or not and it will require a mobilization of all our forces of Youth to kill it before it is too late.

THE BUS-BOYCOTT:

On January 7th 1957, PUTCO decided to increase the Bus fares by one penny (ld) on its main routes. As a result of this action the people replied by saying "AZIKHWELA." AZIKHWELA (we shall not ride) became a household word of every boycotter. Within a few days most of the Reef towns came out in sympathy with the Boy-cotters. But this did not end there because other Provinces too came out in sympathy with the Boy-cotters in the Rand and Pretoria. In spite of intimidation from the Police; in spite of threats from the Minister of Transport (Mr. B. Schoeman), the People's reply was walk, cycle, motor rather than pay a farthing ¼d extra. The Bus-Boy-cotter has clearly demonstrated that the African People are living below the bread-line level. What was more impressive was that throughout the Boy-cott our Youth were in the forefront and formed the cream—particularly in Pretoria, Sophiatown and Randfontein. We salute those untiring workers for freedom in our Land. Many gallant sons and daughters of Africa have demonstrated their selfless courage in the struggle for better wages and living conditions. We regret to announce that because of the ruthless and barbaric uncalled for action of the Police, some of our Youth were brutally murdered. To quote one such example—Joel Ramosodi of Pretoria who was shot by the Police. The people are back to the Buses but have won a great victorious battle!!!

OTHER ACTIVITIES:

From time to time our organization has been busy organizing protests, meetings, functions, film-shows to raise funds. We have organised parties at Germiston and Sophiatown. A Colonial Youth rally organised jointly with T.I.Y.C., COD YOUTH, SACPO YOUTH. We have also rendered assistance to the Peace Convention Conference;

The Women's demonstrations at Pretoria, the Inter-Denominational African Ministers' Conference which rejected the Tomlinson Report.

ORGANISATIONAL:

To do justice to the Report we must reflect some characteristic of the Youth of failing in their duties. As far as Organization is concerned our

Youth is still in a backward state of Organization. For instance, with one or two exceptions Youth League Branches have not carried their duties of submitting their monthly reports, of acknowledging correspondence. Some branches have not even submitted their reports to the Provincial Conference. Purely for administrative purposes the Provincial Executive decided to have its own Youth League membership cards, but at the time of drawing the Report the Treasurer of the Youth League has not received all the monies from the Branches. At certain Branches the Youth League is confined to a small clique which has no contact with the Masses of Youth that they are supposed to lead. This is the sorry level to which our Youth League has shrunk.

It is quite true that new Youth sprung up and took up the tasks that had been left, new determined Youth came to fill up the places of the fallen leaders and refused to allow the foundations of the Organisation to distintegrate. But still there is lacking complete unity of action.

A CALL TO YOUTH:

Mr. Speaker, the A.N.C. Youth League as a Youth Organisation still has to strengthen and perfect its work tremendously; and as far as the African Nation is concerned the African Youth must emerge from the twilight more vigorously than ever before, and must establish contact with non-Youth League members, e.g. Students, Nurses, etc. and guide them. Go out to the whole Nation—go and serve the masses—lead the masses, and draw all those who hesitated into playing an active part into this determined struggle—because "STRUGGLE MUST GO ON". Let there be no spectators in the struggle! Apartheid, Oppression and Exploitation are cancers eating us up while we watch. But time alone will tell when White Domination will tumble like the last days of Pompeii because the volcano is surely to erupt one day.

"Youth of the Transvaal and South Africa, know Ye that freedom is a habit and just like any other habit if we are deprived of it for long we tend to forget it. You are therefore charged with the noble task of rebuilding your Nation at all costs. In this task you must be armed with love for your people, patience, perseverence and sacrifice! Rest not until the goal is reached."

LONG LIVE THE WORLD FEDERATION OF DEMOCRATIC YOUTH!!
LONG LIVE THE A.N.C. AND ITS ALLIES!!

FORWARD TO THE 14TH WORLD FESTIVAL OF YOUTH
AND STUDENTS!!
FORWARD TO JUNE 26TH—NATIONAL DAY!!!
LONG LIVE THE AFRICAN NATIONAL CONGRESS YOUTH
LEAGUE!!

MAYIBUYE I AFRIKA!!

Document 26. "June 26th Day of Protest, Prayer and Dedication."
Two-page flyer issued by the National Consultative Committee of the ANC,
SAIC, SACOD, SACPO, and SACTU [1957]

JUNE 26TH
DAY OF
PROTEST, PRAYER
AND DEDICATION

Since the great protest day of 1950, June 26th has become an important
historical day in the struggle of the South African people, both White and
Non-White, for the defeat of Apartheid tyranny and for freedom.

On this day we honour the memories of all those brave patriots who have
fallen in the struggle. We reaffirm our vow to make every effort and offer
every sacrifice for the realisation of the noble principles enshrined in the
Freedom Charter.

STOP THE NATIONALISTS!

The Nationalist Government is continuing its fierce and furious
onslaught on the people. The arrest of the 156 national leaders of the people
on a charge of High Treason, mass police raids, deportations of chiefs and
leaders, passes for women, the application of the Group Areas Act,
University Apartheid, Nursing Apartheid, the Native Laws Amendment
Bill, and the proposal to increase taxation are causing deep resentment and
anger among all sections of the people.

The mad career of the Nationalist Government must be halted!

On June 26th we must demonstrate on a countrywide and effective basis our protest against Apartheid tyranny and show our desire for a united front of all those who are opposed to the Nationalist Government.

WHAT MUST WE DO ON THE 26th JUNE?

As an individual: Take a solemn vow to carry on the sacred struggles for freedom.

As a family: Gather all members, young and old together, and read and discuss the Freedom Charter.

As a community: Assemble in mass gatherings in appropriate places in all areas, both urban and rural, to protest against oppression.

At the hour of 11 a.m. at all these mass gatherings and in homes and places of work, offer prayers for the deliverance of South Africa from the scourge of a Police State.

- STAND BY OUR LEADERS!
- ASINAMALI! WE WANT £1 A DAY!
- ASINAMALI! NO INCREASE IN TAXATION!
- NO PASSES FOR WOMEN!
- STOP POLICE RAIDS!!
- AWAY WITH GROUP AREAS!
- NO BANTU EDUCATION!
- WITHDRAW THE NATIVE LAWS AMENDMENT BILL!
- NO INTERFERENCE WITH FREEDOM OF WORSHIP!
- STOP DEPORTATIONS, BANNINGS, CENSORSHIP!
- OPEN UNIVERSITIES FOR ALL!
- NO APARTHEID IN NURSING!
- VERWOERD MUST GO!
- DOWN WITH APARTHEID!

FORWARD TO A MULTI-RACIAL CONFERENCE!

Issued by the National Consultative Committee of the African National Congress, S. A. Indian Congress, S. A. Congress of Democrats, S. A. Coloured People's Organisations, S. A. Congress of Trade Unions.

Document 27. Revised Constitution, adopted by the ANC Annual Conference, December 1957

1. *NAME:*

The name of the organisation shall be the African National Congress, hereinafter referred to as the "Congress".

2. *AIMS AND OBJECTS:*

The aims and objects of the Congress shall be:—

(a) To unite the African people in a powerful and effective instrument to secure their own complete liberation from all forms of discrimination and national oppression.

(b) To promote and protect the interests of the African people in all matters affecting them.

(c) To strive for the attainment of universal adult suffrage and the creation of a united democratic South Africa on the principles outlined in the Freedom Charter.

(d) To support the cause of national liberation and the right to independence of nations in Africa and the rest of the world.

3. *MEMBERSHIP:*

(a) Membership of the Congress shall be open to any person above the age of 18, who accepts its principles, policy and programme and is prepared to abide by its constitution and rules.

(b) Any person desiring to be a member of the Congress shall apply to the secretary of the nearest branch or to any member of the Congress authorised to receive applications for membership. Such secretary or member shall immediately submit the application for consideration by the local branch committee, or in the absence of a branch committee such application shall be made to the provincial secretary who shall refer it to the provincial executive committee within whose jurisdiction the applicant resides.

(c) The branch committee or provincial executive committee, as the case may be, shall have power to accept or refuse any application for membership submitted to it, provided that the acceptance or refusal of any application by any organ of the Congress shall be subject to review by the next higher organ.

(d) Upon any application for membership being granted by a branch committee or provincial executive committee, a membership card, signed by the Treasurer-General, and endorsed by the secretary of such branch or provincial secretary, as the case may be, shall, on payment of the prescribed subscription, and subject to the results of any review instituted in terms of sub-clause (c) above, be issued to the applicant.

4. *ORGANISATIONAL STRUCTURE:*

The Congress shall consist of the following organs:—

(a) The National Conference, which elects the National Executive Committees.

(b) The Provincial Conferences, which elect the provincial executive Committee.

(c) The Regional Conferences which elect regional committees.

(d) The branch meetings, which elect a branch committee.

5. *DECISIONS:*

Subject to the rules and regulations of Congress:—

(a) Decisions of the National Conference and those of the National Executive Committee shall be binding on all members and lower organs of Congress;

(b) Decisions of a provincial conference and those of the provincial executive committee shall be binding on all members and lower organs of the Congress in the particular province concerned;

(c) Decisions of a regional committee shall be binding on those members and lower organs of the Congress whose branches are constituent parts of that regional committee;

(d) Decisions of a branch meeting and of a branch committee shall be binding on all members and generally,

(e) Decisions of the majority shall be binding on all members and those of higher organs shall be binding on lower organs.

6. *RIGHTS AND DUTIES OF MEMBERS:*

(a) *RIGHTS:* A member shall have the right:—

(i) To take part in the discussion and formulation of the policy of the Congress;

(ii) To criticise any official or decision of the Congress; such criticism shall be made to members of Congress or at a properly convened meeting of the members of the Congress;

(iii) To take part in the elections and to be elected to any committee, commission or delegation of the Congress; and

(iv) To submit proposals or statements to his branch and to his provincial executive committee.

(b) *DUTIES:* A member shall have a duty—

   (i)   To take an active part in the work of his branch;

   (ii)   To understand thoroughly and to carry out the policy, aims and programme of Congress;

   (iii) To raise the level of his understanding of the political, economic and social problems of South Africa;

   (iv) To explain the policy and programme of the Congress to the people;

   (v)   To combat any propaganda which is detrimental to the interests of the Congress;

   (vi) To observe discipline and to submit loyally to the decisions of the majority or to decisions of the higher committee; and

   (vii) To inform his branch committee before leaving his area, and to report to branch secretary of the area to which he has moved.

7. *AUXILIARY BODIES:*

1. *Women's League.*

Women who are members shall enjoy equality of status in the Congress and shall be entitled to join ordinary branches and take part in elections for and be elected to any position or office in the Congress. However, in order to arouse the interest and assist the widespread organisation of women, there shall be established an auxiliary organisation to be known as the African National Congress Women's League. The League shall:—

(a) Be under the political direction and control of the Congress and shall follow the policy and programme of the Congress;

(b) Recruit and organise the African women into a strong organisation which shall act as an auxiliary force to the Congress in the struggle for national liberation;

(c) Take up special problems and issues affecting women;

(d) Carry on propaganda against apartheid and discriminatory laws among African women;

(e) Be entitled to have its own rules and regulations provided that these shall not be in conflict with the policy of Congress.

2. *Organisation for Youths:*

For the purpose of drawing the youths into the struggle and preparing them for leadership, the Congress shall organise the African youths into an organisation for youths to be known as the African National Congress Youth League, which shall be open to any person whose age does not exceed 30 years provided that such person shall upon reaching the qualification for Congress membership become a registered member of Congress subject to all the privileges and obligations of Congress membership in addition to such special privileges and duties of a member of the Youth League. The League shall:—

(a) Mobilise the African youths and mould their political and social outlook in accordance with the Congress principles;

(b) Promote social and cultural activities among the young people;

(c) Popularise the policy, programme and decisions of the Congress among the youth; and

(d) The provisions of Clause 7(1)(e) shall mutatis mutandis apply to the Youth League.

8. NATIONAL CONFERENCE:

The National Conference shall be the Supreme ruling and controlling body in Congress. It shall:—

(a) Consist of delegates from the branches of the Congress, elected by branch general meetings on the basis of one delegate for every twenty members; provided that the number of delegates from any one branch shall not exceed ten; Provided further that members of the National Executive Committee may attend ex officio and shall have the right to speak and vote.

(b) Be held once a year: Provided that Special National Conferences may be convened by the National Executive Committee at its own instance at such times as it may deem fit, and shall be convened upon requisitions addressed to it by not less than two provincial conferences.

9. DUTIES AND POWERS OF THE ANNUAL NATIONAL CONFERENCE:

The National Conference shall:—

(a) Decide and determine the policy and programme of the Congress;

(b) Receive and discuss the reports of the National Executive which shall include the Presidential Address and the Treasurer-General's Report, the Provincial Executive Committees, the African National Congress Women's League, and the African National Congress Youth League;

(c) Lay down the basic principles and policy, examine and where necessary, revise the programme and constitution of the Congress;

(d) Have the right and power to review, ratify, alter or veto any decision taken by any of its constituent bodies or units of the Congress;

(e) Elect the President-General; the Deputy President, the Secretary-General, the Treasurer-General and eight other National Executive Committee members. Members of the National Executive Committee shall hold office for three years and shall be eligible for re-election. Nomination shall be by delegates at the Conference, and elections of all officials and members of the National Executive Committee shall be by ballot;

(f) Have the power to elect or appoint any Commission or Committee and assign specific tasks and duties to such commission or committee.

10. *NATIONAL EXECUTIVE COMMITTEE:*

The National Executive Committee, which is elected by the National Conference once every three years, shall:—

(a) Consist of the President-General, the Deputy President-General, the Secretary-General, the Treasurer-General, eight other members, the provincial presidents and secretaries of the Congress or their respective deputies, and the national presidents or national secretaries of the African National Congress Women's League and the African National Congress Youth League who shall be *ex-officio* members of the National Executive Committee.

(b) Meet on the day of its election to appoint the National Headquarters, the National Speaker, the Deputy National Speaker, the National Chaplain and shall thereafter meet at least twice a year. The National Speaker, the Deputy National Speaker, the National Chaplain need not be appointed from among the members of the National Executive Committee;

(c) Appoint the National Organising Secretary;

(d) Appoint from amongst its members the National Working Committee of not less than seven persons residing within a radius of fifty (50) miles of the National Headquarters;

(e) Carry out the decisions and instructions of the National Conference;

(f) Issue and send directives and instructions to and demand and receive reports from the provincial committees, regional committees and the branches;

(g) Supervise, direct and control the work of the Congress generally;

(h) Be responsible for ensuring that provincial committees and other committees of the Congress discharge their duties and functions properly and efficiently;

(i) Supervise the work of the auxiliary bodies;

(j) Manage and control all national property and funds of the Congress;

(k) Submit annual reports to the National Conference;

(l) Do all things necessary in furtherance of the policy and programme of the Congress.

11. *NATIONAL WORKING COMMITTEE:*

The National Working Committee is a sub-committee of the National Executive Committee. It shall:—

(a) Meet as provided for in the rules and regulations;

(b) Carry out decisions and instructions of the National Conference and the National Executive Committee;

(c) Conduct the current work of the Congress and ensure that the provinces, regions and branches carry out decisions and instructions of the Congress;

(d) Issue propaganda and educational material to the provinces and

(e) Submit a report to every National Executive Committee meeting.

12. *DUTIES AND FUNCTIONS OF OFFICIALS.*

(1) *President-General:*

The President-General is the head and chief directing officer of the Congress and the leader of the house in a National Conference. He shall:—

(a) Present to the Annual Conference a comprehensive statement of the state of the nation and the political situation generally;

(b) Make pronouncements for and on behalf of the National Executive Committee outlining and explaining the policy or attitude of the Congress on any question;

(c) Preside over meetings of the National Executive Committee and conduct the business in conformity with the Constitution, by-laws and rules of procedure adopted by the National Executive Committee;

(d) Be an ex officio member of the National Working Committee

(e) Have a casting vote only.

(2) *Deputy President-General.*

The Deputy President shall assist the President-General and deputise for him whenever necessary.

(3) *Secretary-General.*

The Secretary-General is the chief administrative officer of the Congress. He shall:—

(a) Keep the Minutes of the National Conference, the National Executive Committee and the National Working Committee, as well as other records of the Congress;

(b) Conduct the correspondence of the National Executive Committee and the National Working Committee and send out notices of all conferences, National Executive and National Working Committee Meetings;

(c) Convey the decisions and instructions of the National Conference, the National Executive Committee and the National Working Committee to the Provincial Committees, regional committees and branches of the Congress, and shall see to it that all units of the Congress carry out their duties properly;

(d) Prepare yearly reports on the work of the National Executive Committee and the National Working Committee, and such other documents as may from time to time be required by the National Executive Committee and the National Working Committee.

(4) *Treasurer-General:*

The Treasurer-General is the chief custodian of the funds and property of the Congress. He shall:—

(a) Receive and bank all monies on behalf of the National Executive Committee, and shall, together with any two (2) National Executive members, operate a banking account;

(b) Keep such books of account as may be necessary to record clearly the financial position of the Congress;

(c) Submit annually to the National Conference a report showing the Income and Expenditure Account and the Balance Sheet of the Congress for the past year, and shall submit periodical reports to the N.E.C. and the N.W.C.;

(d) Be responsible, together with the President-General and the Secretary-General, for working out plans and schemes for raising funds for the Congress, and shall direct and take an active part in a campaign for raising funds.

(5) *National Speaker:*

The National Speaker shall preside over and sign Minutes of all National Conferences. In his absence the Deputy Speaker shall preside at such Conferences.

(6) *National Chaplain:*

The National Chaplain shall lead the delegates in prayer at National Conferences and shall conduct the National Service or otherwise provide spiritual leadership for the organisation.

(7) *National Organising Secretary:*

It shall be the duty of the National Organising Secretary acting in consultation with and under the direction of the Secretary-General, to organise the Congress nationally and to strengthen the organisational machinery throughout.

13. *PROVINCES.*

For organisational purposes the country shall be divided into provinces. A province shall be determined and defined by the Congress.

14. *PROVINCIAL CONFERENCE:*

The Provincial Conference shall:—

(a) Be the highest organ subject to Clauses 8 and 10 of the Congress in each Province;

(b) Be held annually in each province. Special provincial conferences may be convened at such other times as the provincial committee may deem fit, and shall be convened upon the requisition addressed to the Provincial Executive Committee by at least one-third of branches or one regional committee;

(c) Consist of:

    (i) Delegates from local branches of the Congress in the province who shall be elected by local branch meetings on the basis of one delegate for each twenty (20) members; provided that no branch shall be represented by more than 10 delegates;

    (ii) Members of the Provincial Executive Committee and National Executive Committee who shall attend *ex officio* and shall have the right to speak and vote;

(d) Carry out the decisions and instructions of the National Conference, the National Executive Committee or the National Working Committee;

(e) Receive and consider reports submitted by the Provincial Executive Committee;

(f) Elect the Provincial President, Secretary, Treasurer and eight other members of the Provincial Executive Committee;

(g) Carry out the policy and programme of the Congress in the province.

15. *PROVINCIAL EXECUTIVE COMMITTEE:*

The Provincial Executive Committee which is elected annually by the Provincial conference shall be the administrative body of the Provincial Conference. It shall:—

(a) Consist of the Provincial President, the Provincial Vice-President, the Provincial Secretary, the Provincial Treasurer, the Provincial Presidents or Secretaries of the African National Congress Women's League and the African National Congress Youth League and eight other members of the Provincial Committee;

(b) Meet on the day of its election to elect the Provincial Working Committee, and shall thereafter meet at least once every three months;

(c) Appoint the Provincial Organiser, the Provincial Speaker and the Provincial Chaplain, all of whom need not be members of the Provincial Executive Committee;

(d) Carry out the decisions and instructions of:—

   (i) The Provincial Conference, and

   (ii) The National Executive Committee or the National Working Committee;

(e) Manage and control the property and funds of the Congress in the Province;

(f) Submit reports to the National Executive as often as required on the state of organisation, the financial position of the province and such other matters as may be specified;

(g) Organise and establish Branches and Regions in the Province;

(h) Enforce the Constitution of the Congress in the province;

(i) Give members of the Congress in the Province political education;

(j) Carry out the policy and programme of the Congress, and do all things necessary to further the interests, aims and objects of the Congress.

16. *PROVINCIAL WORKING COMMITTEE:*

The Provincial Working Committee is the sub-committee of the Provincial Executive Committee. It shall consist of not less than seven members who reside within a radius of 100 miles of the Provincial Headquarters, and shall:—

(a) Perform the duties and functions of the Provincial Executive Committee;

(b) Submit a report to the Provincial Executive Committee.

17. *DUTIES AND FUNCTIONS OF PROVINCIAL OFFICALS:*

With the exception of clause (8), the provisions of Section (12) shall, with necessary alteration of details, apply to duties and functions of provincial officials of the Congress.

18. *REGION:*

Any three or more branches in a given area may, for the purpose of co-ordination of activities and better organisational efficiency, be formed into a region at the instance of the Provincial Executive Committee or on application to the Provincial Executive Committee by at least two branches within an area of a proposed region.

19. *REGIONAL COMMITTEE:*

Whenever a region has been established the branch executives of such region shall at a properly convened meeting elect a regional committee which shall consist of a chairman, secretary, treasurer, two members, and a member from each branch within the region.

(a) Meet as provided for in the rules and regulations.

(b) Co-ordinate the work and activities of the Constituent branches and submit reports to the Provincial Executive Committee;

(c) See to the implementation of the instructions of the N.E.C., Provincial Executive Committee or the Provincial Working Committee.

20. *BRANCHES:*

(a) The basic unit of organisation in the Congress shall be the branch;

(b) The branch shall consist of a minimum of twenty members; provided that the N.E.C., Provincial Executive may establish a provisional committee as provided by rules and regulations;

(c) Every new branch shall apply to the Provincial Executive Committee for registration;

(d) The branch shall:—

    (i)   Meet as provided for in the rules and regulations;

    (ii)   Elect at an annual branch general meeting, a branch chairman, secretary, treasurer and six other branch committee members.

21. *BRANCH COMMITTEE:*

The branch committee shall:—

(a) Meet on the day of its election to elect the branch sub-committee, and thereafter shall meet as provided for in the rules and regulations;

(b) Carry out propaganda and organisational work among the people in its area in pursuance of the policy, programme and decisions of the Congress;

(c) Build and increase the numerical and political strength of the Congress within its area;

(d) Submit reports on its work to the branch committee, regional committee periodically as provided in the rules and regulations and to the Provincial Executive Committee every quarter;

(e) Carry out such instructions as may from time to time be issued by the Provincial Executive Committee or the Provincial Working Committee.

22. *CONGRESS FUNDS:*

(a) The basic membership subscription for Congress shall be 2/6d.

(b) All subscriptions shall be payable in advance.

(c) The National Executive Committee may impose a national levy on all members of the Congress. All monies derived from a national levy shall be paid into the national treasury.

(d) The Provincial Executive Committee may with the prior approval of, and subject to such conditions as may be laid down by the National Executive Committee, impose levies on all members of the Congress in their respective provinces. All monies from Provincial levies shall be paid into the provincial treasuries.

(e) All levies, national and provincial, shall be [for] stated periods and specified amounts.

(f) The branch treasurer shall pay to the provincial treasurer and National Treasurer respectively one-third of the subscriptions.

(g) The Provincial Executive Committee shall pay to the National Executive Committee an agreed proportion of all monies received by them through donations, collections, concerts, functions, etc.

(h) Proper records shall be kept of all monies received and expended by branch committees, regional committees, provincial executive and national executive committee.

23. *DISCIPLINE:*

(a) A branch committee, Regional, provincial and National Executive Committee shall have power to reprimand, suspend, expel, or take any other disciplinary action against a member for breach of the Constitution or conduct detrimental to the interests of the Congress or the African people.

(b) Any higher organ of the Congress shall have power to investigate, reprimand, re-organise, suspend, dissolve, dismiss or take any other appropriate disciplinary action against any lower organ under its jurisdiction for breach of the Constitution or conduct detrimental to the interests of the Congress or the African people.

(c) Before any disciplinary action is taken against any member or organ in terms of clauses (a) and/or (b) of this section, such member or organ shall, in the absence of extra-ordinary circumstances justifying the contrary, be given an opportunity to appear before the relevant tribunal and there admit, deny or otherwise account for the conduct complained of.

(d) Any member or body of members against whom disciplinary action has been taken by any organ of the Congress shall have a right to appeal to the next higher organ. The National Conference shall be the final court of appeal.

(e) When a member is suspended, the committee suspending him shall state the period and conditions of such suspension.

(f) A member who fails to pay his subscription for a period of six months and who does not pay his subscription after he has been personally spoken to about the matter by a representative of his branch committee shall be lapsed from membership.

(g) All cases of suspension, dismissal, expulsion or dissolution by way of disciplinary action shall be fully reported to the Provincial Executive Committee and the National Executive Committee.

(h) No case of expulsion by a branch or region shall be published in the press without the consent of the Provincial Executive Committee.

24. *QUORUM:*

(a) A third of the members shall form a quorum for all [*sic*]

(b) Fifteen members or 50% (fifty percent) of the branch membership, whichever is the lesser, shall form a quorum of all meetings of a local branch,

(c) Delegates from 40% (forty percent) of the total number of branches in a province shall form a quorum for all provincial conferences,

(d) In the case of National Conference, delegates from two provinces, representing at least 33⅓% (thirty-three and one-third percent) of the total membership of the Congress, shall constitute a quorum.

25. *VACANCIES:*

(a) The office of any member of a committee of the Congress shall be vacated by resignation, suspension, expulsion or absence from meetings for a period prescribed in the rules and regulations.

26. *RULES:*

(a) The National Executive shall have power to frame rules and regulations relating to the control and administration of the affairs of the Congress generally.

(b) Each Provincial Executive Committee may frame rules and regulations for the conduct and management of the affairs of Congress organisation within its jurisdiction, provided that any rules and regulations so framed shall not become operative until they have been approved by the National Executive Committee.

(c) Rules and regulations framed in terms of "a" and "b" of this section shall not be inconsistent with the provisions of this Constitution.

27. *AMENDMENT OF CONSTITUTION:*

This Constitution may be amended by resolution passed by a two-thirds majority of the delegates present and voting at a National Conference. Notice of such a resolution shall be submitted in writing to the Secretary-General not later than six months before the date of the National Conference. The National Executive Committee shall circulate all proposed amendments to the Constitution to Provincial Executive Committees, and all branches of the Congress at least two months before the National Conference.

28. *GENERAL:*

The Congress shall have perpetual succession and the power, apart from its individual members, to acquire, hold and alienate property, enter into agreements and do all things necessary to carry out its aims and objects.

(Sgd.) A. J. LUTULI
PRESIDENT-GENERAL.

O. R. TAMBO
SECRETARY-GENERAL.

Document 28. "A Message to Every Voter from the African National Congress." Flyer signed by Chief A. J. Lutuli, issued before General Election of April 16, 1958 [n.d.]

Sir or Madam,

You may be surprised to receive this message from the African National Congress: surprised because this is something unusual and because you have no connection with the African National Congress. The African National Congress is the oldest and the biggest and most representative organisation of Africans. For many years we have addressed protests, petitions, memoranda, deputations and other memoranda to the Government. These appeals have fallen upon deaf ears. Today we are addressing ourselves directly to you, the voters, who in the last resort are responsible for the Government.

On April 16 you are going to exercise your right to vote for your representative in Parliament. You may perhaps ask what this has to do with us, who have no votes. It has a great deal to do with us. Parliament makes laws which govern non-Whites as well as White. We have to obey those laws—which always bear more severely upon us than upon anyone else—though we have never been consulted about them, or given any say in choosing those who make them.

Frankly, we are by no means satisfied with this state of affairs. We consider it neither fair nor just, and we shall never rest content until the democratic principle which is conceded for Europeans is extended to include the entire population.

But so long as this unfair position continues, and our people are excluded from the franchise, have we not at least the right to state our views? And have not you, the voter, a solemn duty to consider those views carefully and without prejudice? We are sure that we have that right, and that you have that duty: a duty to remember that you vote not only for yourself but also on behalf of many fellow-South Africans who are denied the franchise.

Neither the Nationalist Party nor the United Party represent or are supported by the African National Congress. They both stand for a narrow policy of racialism and racial domination. We who stand for a broad and true South Africanism extending to all in our country, irrespective of race or colour, can never accept or support the policy of either party.

But we must say that never since Union have our people suffered such hardships, humiliations and sheer brutality as we have had to undergo during the past ten years of Government by the Nationalist Party. Both in the towns and in the rural areas we have known no peace; people have been removed in their thousands and in their tens of thousands, their homes and their families broken up. While prices have gone up, our wages have been pegged down, and our poverty has become desperate.

Every door through which we might have sought advancement, culture and a higher civilisation has been slammed in our faces. Our schools are being turned into schools for ignorance, tribalism and servitude. The universities are being closed to us. Any sphere of employment other than ill-paid unskilled labour is being closed to us. Every means of legitimate national expression and protest is being closed to us. Our leaders and spokesmen are arrested, banned, deported and silenced.

Where can this road lead our country, South Africa? We see the crime rate rising day by day. Savage punishments, whippings and floggings will not stop it rising—for the crime has its roots in the slums and the poverty, the hopelessness and the frustration in which the people are living.

We see unrest and disturbances occurring more and more widely and frequently. It is not the African National Congress or the "agitators" which are responsible for these things, nor will more repressions, bannings and police terror prevent them. They are signs of deep discontent, of something profoundly wrong in the way in which our people are treated.

You may have been led to believe that our Congress is anti-White, that it is a reckless organisation out to stir up racialism. Nothing could be further from the truth. We are a serious and responsible minded body of men and women, and our aim, as we have stated many times, is neither White supremacy nor Black supremacy, but a common South African multi-racial society, based upon friendship, equality of rights and mutual respect.

The Nationalist Party, with its policy of blatant oppression and racialism, is, however, creating a legacy of bitterness and hatred which, if it is allowed to continue, we shall all of us live to regret. And it is not only as Africans, but also as fellow-South Africans, deeply concerned with the future of our country and all who live in it, that we speak to you on the eve of this crucial election. We trust most earnestly that you will heed our message.

Yours, in the service of South Africa,

ALBERT J. LUTHULI, President-General
AFRICAN NATIONAL CONGRESS
P.O. Box 9207, Johannesburg.

428

Document 29. "Mass Congress Rally . . . 5th October, 1958." Flyer issued by the ANC, [n.d.]

M A S S
CONGRESS RALLY

against

Increase in Poll Tax
Passes For Women
The Vicious Permit System
The Group Areas Act

FREEDOM   SQUARE,   SOPHIATOWN

on

Sunday, 5th October, 1958
at 9:30 a.m.

Every man, woman, and youth must attend
in their thousands.

DEMAND £ A DAY LEGISLATION

Rally in your thousands and raise your voices
in protest against all Apartheid Laws

Prominent and top level Congress leaders
will address you

Issued by African National Congress, 31, Bezuidenhout St., Ferreirastown

Documents 30a–30b. ANC Youth League (Transvaal) Annual Conference of October 25–26, 1958

Document 30a. Report of S. S. Ditira, Provincial Secretary

Mr. Speaker, Sons and Daughters of Africa, I wish to apologise very greatly that this executive has delayed so much before convening this conference, but as you are all aware of what the position has been as regards our meetings, I am sure you will give us your sympathy.

On revising the Executive Report presented to our last Conference, I find that the report dealt at length with the international situation and the part played by youth in the struggles in the different parts of the world. He further emphasised that we of the A.N.C. Youth League also joined forces and have expressed on more than one occasion, our solidarity with the struggle against colonialism and for national independence. I would not like to deal further with this point because the position was greatly clarified in the last executive report; all I would say is that we express great sympathy with the Negro people in Little Rock and those of Nottingham Hill, as we know better the persecution that they are suffering and we urge them to keep up the struggle as their success is not only theirs, but of all the oppressed people in the world.

In the political situation in South Africa, we know that 1958 was a year of importance, since it was a year for the General Parliamentary Election. We all know what the results of the election were; shocking! yet not surprising. Not only a majority for the Nationalist party, but an increase in the number of votes over the number they had in the last election. This point illustrates that the white man in South Africa has come to realise that the African is fighting tooth and nail for his freedom, and therefore to stamp him down they are prepared to go to any level, even joining the Nationalist Party because this party will fight the African with "ungloved hands" as one of their Cabinet Ministers put it, even though they, themselves, are not convinced that the Nationalist Party will lead them anywhere.

We have witnessed this year the inhuman and tyrannical attitude of the Nationalist Party, especially Dr. Verwoerd—who, by the way is our Prime Minister today, not that he has not been in practice at least—in torturing the people of Linokana, because these people did not want what the "lord" Verwoerd in his wisdom thought it was right for them. These people have had to leave their homes and lands. Where they used to live happily, ploughing the lands and irrigating them with the waters of the many small streams that pass through the country, the many streams from which the place got its name. Today those people are homeless. They are wandering all over the country seeking shelter wherever they can find it because they fear the persecution of Dr. Verwoerd. Again we find an almost similar situation in Sekhukhuniland. Where the chief was solid behind the people in the peoples' struggle, that appreciated the conditions under which the people would live if they accepted the Bantu Authorities Act, that were not prepared to sell out their people to Dr. Verwoerd being deposed, deported and persecuted. We know as we are sitting here today that 200 people in Sekhukhuniland are facing a murder charge. As we cast our eyes to the near past we shudder because we see not so long ago 22 Africans being hanged as sequel to the Bergville disturbances, we shudder, because nothing can stop these Nationalist nazis from massacring 200 people.

Sons and daughters of Africa, as I write about these happenings I seem to be transcribing from a history book, because it was some centuries ago that

430

the human race had tyrants that could do whatever they could to other people without even giving it a second thought. It is in history books where we learn of the mass massacre of people, the torturing and all the sufferings that human beings could suffer and we in the 20th century call ourselves more advanced. I would like to know how, because what is the difference between Charles I of England and Verwoerd except that the former wore cloaks and skirts whereas the latter wears pants and jackets. Yet, Sons and daughters of Africa, it is the same history books that we learn that Charles I was beheaded, that all the tyrants were overthrown, that no matter what degree the oppression could assume, the oppressed always came out the victors at last, but poor Dr. Verwoerd, like a criminal who reads a story of a former colleague always thinks that he will not make the mistake that Charles I or Hitler made; quite true he may not but he will make his own mistake.

In encouraging the struggle of the oppressed people, I think this executive could be failing if it did not point out the great victory we achieved against the Nats. I am sure that everybody in South Africa, irrespective of colour, creed or nation has been following the proceedings of the trial, and I am sure that everybody will agree with me, be he nationalist party or not, that so far we are ahead on points. We know how step by step the defence has been crushing the Crown until it culminated in the Crown's withdrawal of the indictment. What the next step by the Crown will be I do not know, but if there is a step at all it will be a wobbly one.

I must say that I am disappointed as regards our struggle on passes. The struggle is rather haphazard as far as I can see it and slowly the number of women carrying passes is increasing. I will not here point out why it is bad for women to carry passes. I think we have passed that stage. The point at issue at the present moment is to see that they do not and I would appeal to the A.N.C. to set out a definite pattern of how our purpose would be achieved. But that does not mean that the youth should sit and wait. They should always try as best they can to fight these evils wherever they are.

In reviewing the activities undertaken by the African National Congress over the past year, and the part played by the African National Congress in particular, I am rather disappointed. I have found that though many campaigns were undertaken, they were in most cases haphazard and there was no [sic] at all. Take the example I have quoted above, the fighting against the passes for women. I find that the difficulty in this campaign is the lack of contact between the leadership and the masses in all organs of Congress. This lack of contact is mainly due to the fact that the leadership isolates itself from their respective branches. For an example, I as secretary of the provincial executive committee issued out a directive to the branches, but what do I do when I come to my branch to see to it that they carry out the directive? I seem to feel that my job is done now that I have sent a directive to the branch. This and other difficulties as pointed out by one of the papers that will be presented today will illustrate the loose ends in the movement that will need some tightening up.

I would like to point out to this Conference that many of our leaders have been arrested on an incitement charge, including even our vice-president. The only way to assist these arrested leaders is to show the Nationalist government that whatever we do in the struggle is not through incitement by an individual but because we are convinced that what we are doing will bring us freedom; therefore the struggle must be so intensified that there is no more place in the prisons for criminals but every space is occupied by incitors.

Administration: I have deliberately left this topic to last because I think that its importance is always underestimated and therefore I would like to emphasise that the movement depends on good administration as a living being on water. Our administration is very very poor.

The very first point I would like to emphasise to branches is that they think it unnecessary to acknowledge directives. This may seem a minor point, but if viewed closely one can see that it is a very important point indeed. Since without acknowledgment this office does not know whether the branch received the directive or not.

The second point is the failure of branches to report to the office constantly whatever campaigns they would like to embark on and whatever difficulties they meet. This also leaves the head office groping in the dark. I will not deal with this matter at length as it was dealt with at the joint meeting of branch executives meeting held on 27th September 1958 and hence the resolution concerning the formation of regions and the elections.

Lastly I would like to thank all the branches that helped this executive committee to send a mighty delegation to the National Conference held at Queenstown last year and hope that in future our delegation to National Conference will yet be stronger.

I wish all the best to the in-coming executive committee and hope that all branches will do their utmost best to co-operate.

S. S. Ditira
Provincial Secretary

Document 30b. "Politics in Our Country and the Role of the Youth." Address by P. P. Nthite

Sons and daughters of Africa, let us rise and salute the 15th anniversary of the African National Congress Youth League.

Africa! Africa! Long live the Youth League!

When the African National Congress Youth League was formed 15 years ago, its formation was received with mixed feelings by the leadership of the African National Congress, for among other reasons (which I shall deal with later), the task of the Youth League was to bring pressure to bear on the leadership of the African National Congress and force it to change its policy of hamba-kahle and hat-in hand to one of militant struggle for democracy and onwards to freedom in our time.

Today, because of our contributions, the African National Congress has become a mass movement expressing the aspirations and desires of the mass of the African people.

The continued strength and militant struggle of the African National Congress lies at the doorstep of the Youth League. Upon us depends the development of the African National Congress and our co-operation is essential if we are to obtain freedom in our time, and victory over the brutal oppressive policy of the present Nationalist Government.

It must be obvious, then, that our immediate task is to mobilize all our forces in a country-wide campaign to get the Youth organized within our ranks to ensure victory after victory in our honourable struggle against our oppressors.

Our struggle against Bantu Education and the removal of the people from the Western Areas, besides the struggle for the protest day, have proved that while many of us as individuals have learned lessons from these struggles, on the whole, the campaigns were a dismal failure due to the fact that there was not sufficient mass support for them. Therefore, the bitter lesson we must learn from our failure to succeed in our struggle is the fact that our efforts were so hopeless because the youth were not mobilized and organised as the spear-head of these campaigns; and for this we must be criticised.

Friends, let us examine the position of the African Youth in our society to-day; let us select a few special features of our life to enable us to see that time and the necessary conditions are on your side in our task of organising a mass movement of youth.

The vast majority of the African Youth are workers, in fact unskilled labourers, subjected to miserable low wages and working conditions; still worse is the fact that youth under the age of 18 years are paid still lower wages than those over the age of 18 years.

The reservation of skilled work for whites, and the new further "Job Reservation" by Minister de Klerk throws our youth into further depths of despair and frustration. The pass-office unemployment section is the busiest office in South Africa; abuse, indignity and finally the horror of being "endorsed out" of the urban areas is the unenviable lot of our youth, imposed upon them by the government servants of the pass office. All this is being constantly done to our youth to develop the attitude in them of a timid and inferior human being—a yes Baas to the "Herrenvolk".

Continued terror is used against our youth in a continuation of this policy of trying to make the African feel inferior. The policy of the police to hand-cuff African Youth together and force them to stand on street corners while they collect their other victims is a further indication of the whole policy of the Nationalist Government, to force the African into a position of being terrorized into accepting their policy and inferior position in our country.

It is a recognised fact in modern society to-day that the freedom of a worker (male or female) to seek employment where they choose, and for the best wages they can command is their democratic right, and the attitude of the government—now adopted by the Johannesburg City Council—to force the African Youth to work where they like is nothing more or less than a calculated move to prevent the African from earning a living wage and make their labour power economically impotent and so weaken their whole strength in their struggle for freedom, and to become an economic force in the country.

The excuse that the African lacks the necessary qualifications for skilled or semi-skilled work is exposed by the shameful degeneration of Bantu Education, which has been placed on our statute books to keep the African Youth in constant subjection. The same attitude applies to our struggle for Technical Education and vocational schools; all these acts are calculated to throw our youth on the scrap heap of unemployment at an early age, and so ensure a continuation of their cheap labour policy.

The pass system is designed to label and number the African as a slave, deprives our youth of a fundamental human right, to roam the streets and foot-paths of their country in search of suitable employment. It again gives the government (by the high-handed use of their police, and local authorities) the satanic power to maintain a constant labour force in the rural areas.

When the Africans in these areas have begun to learn how to organise and propagate [sic] against such government actions, they are immediately deported, deposed and isolated from their people, their friends and relatives, they are condemned to homelessness and loneliness, servitude and starvation.

The problems of the Urban and Rural youth are our problems. Their sufferings, frustrations and reactions to the Nationalist Government are the same as our struggles and frustrations and must result in the development and organisation of the African National Congress Youth League.

One of the most unfortunate features of the "Location Life" of our youth to-day is the so-called tsotsi element. Most of these youths are basically decent people, they are entirely different from the ordinary gangsters, they simply have a grudge against life and society, which has forced them into an anti-social attitude. They are potential good Youth League members and sincere fighters for freedom in our time. They have been forced into thuggery against their own people by unemployment, pass raids and hunger. They seek revenge against society by using terror against both black and white.

We in the Youth League cannot condone organised or individual thuggery, but at the same time our attitude to the tsotsis must be a positive one. It is our task to redirect and divert their energies to the correct channels, i.e. in our joint struggle against Nationalist oppression.

We must learn to take up the day to day demands of the Youth, in our respective areas. We must apply ourselves without reserve to the daily needs of the youth. Fight police mass raids, demand dignified handling of prisoners, demand employment for the unemployed, social and cultural facilities for all youth. No injustice perpetrated against the youth must be too small for us to fight against, and each small victory won leads us closer to the day of freedom in our time.

Such a struggle will certainly bring us to a strong militant mass youth movement.

Reviewing the composition and character of the Youth League since its formation, we must acknowledge that it has remained at the tail end of the youth instead of at its head, and this fault is sure because the youth league does not conduct its own campaigns for specific rights of the youth, and their day to day struggles, but is always duplicating the lead of the African National Congress and its campaigns.

Before we can hope to launch mass support for the African National Congress campaigns successfully, our call to the youth must be for a struggle against their disabilities and to rally them around the struggle of their own problems. Our resolutions, once adopted, must be carried out to the last letter. The sacrifice will be high, but cannot be avoided in our struggle to win the Youth to a mass organisation.

The pass-system and its far reaching repercussions must be our rallying point. Already Congress is fighting the extension of passes to African women. We must throw all our resources into this campaign, and along with our anti-pass campaign must go a new struggle organised by us against the present system of sending convict labour to the farmers.

The brutal beating of the youth hired out to the farmers, and sometimes even resulting in their death must be stopped immediately. The Youth League must lead in this struggle and must carry it out to a victorious conclusion, irrespective of the consequences.

This departure from the usual attitude of the Youth League will facilitate a militant change in our Congress movement.

Document 31. Report of the National Executive Committee of the ANC, submitted to the Annual Conference, December 13-14, 1958

PREFACE.

1. Delegates from the African National Congress Branches in many parts of South Africa are once more assembled in Durban to review the events of the past year in this country and in the rest of the World. Our purpose is to examine the progress made, the setbacks suffered, and to plan afresh in the light of new experiences gained during the period under review.

2. It is our duty to mention at the outset that every statement in this report is not just made in order to fill pages but is made in order that it should receive your serious attention and careful study and deliberation. As a people we are to-day facing a grim future, we are confronted with many grave problems which threaten our political, economic and social progress.

3. It is therefore the desire and earnest request of the National Executive Committee that delegates should discharge their responsibilities in a manner befitting responsible men and women charged with the affairs of a people whose life is beset with serious dangers and difficulties. We are confident that delegates, subduing their feelings and emotions, will rise to the need of the hour!

4. The main issues which face us to-day and which conference is called upon to consider are roughly these: unity, discipline, alertness and loyalty in the African National Congress; the strengthening and development of the Congress alliance; the Government threat to ban the Congress; state of organisational preparedness and new methods of political work in the light of the changed conditions; the ruthless Government attacks on our people in the towns, in the countryside and in the reserves; mass arrests and mass trials; the creation of a leadership personnel, and the financing of the work and activities of our National organisation. These then are some of the most important and pressing problems before our 46th Annual National Conference.

FOREIGN AFFAIRS.

5. Great strides have been made in scientific discoveries and developments. Not satisfied with putting artificial satellites on the earth's orbit and

with sending dangerous missiles round the earth, men of science are to-day talking about conquering the moon. There can be no doubt that recent discoveries and inventions in the field of science open up vast possibilities for the progress of mankind. It is equally certain, however, that science has developed and perfected the most deadly weapons of destruction imaginable, and unless the nations and peoples of the world are vigilant in the preservation of peace, science will annihilate mankind.

6. Yet there are still some strange forces in this world which regard this great scientific progress as a means by which to promote their predatory interests. In the destructive nuclear weapons they see their chance to world domination. During the year we narrowly escaped the outbreak of war over the Middle East and Far East situations. But popular forces of peace succeeded in staying the hands of the villains and thus in averting a world conflagration. It is a matter of regret and great concern to all peace loving people of the world that the great powers—the United States, Great Britain and the Soviet Union—have not found an answer to the question of disarmament and prohibition of the use of nuclear weapons.

7. As an oppressed people we are very much interested in the freedom of all other oppressed people regardless of their colour, racial origin or religious beliefs. We are therefore pleased to note the increase in the area of freedom and national independence since our last Annual National Conference. And, the further consolidation of Asian and African solidarity.

8. The peoples of French Guinea and Madagascar have now attained some measure of political independence and those of Nigeria, Sierra Leone, Tanganyika, Uganda and even that of Kenya are in varying degrees and tempo moving towards National freedom and independence. Nearer home, in the Central African Federation, the African people of Nyasaland, Northern and Southern Rhodesia are in the throes of the struggle for freedom, equality and justice, and our small mountainous island, Basutoland, has also started preparations towards that cherished end. They have been granted legislative power. We congratulate them for this achievement.

9. In spite of bitter and slanderous propaganda and economic sabotage by representatives of imperialist and colonial powers, as well as all those who are ill-disposed towards them, the young independent states of Asia and Africa have steadily consolidated their political power and developed their economies. Thus we have seen the emergence of the United Arab Republic, the idea of a West African Federation or Union, and the new political re-orientation in a number of these countries. In connection with the question of developing their economies, some have benefited from the

concept and policy of Soviet Russia regarding economic and technical assistance.

10. Having so far only emphasised the struggles of those countries and peoples who have emerged from national oppression and attained freedom and independence, let us now say a few words about the peoples of Africa who are still languishing under the strain of national oppression and racial discrimination. The whole of the African continent is awakening and beginning to find itself, its various peoples are captivated by the spirit of the time, the spirit of freedom, human dignity, self-respect and self-determination. Their march to freedom may at times be retarded but can never be stopped.

11. Savage atrocities have been committed against the peoples of Africa in the name of "Western Civilisation".

We have in mind here some of the harrowing deeds of the Portuguese, Belgian, French and British Governments. Each of these powers has at one time or another committed acts which are at variance with its declared policies and professed aims. But these brutal attacks and repressive measures have not succeeded in totally silencing or suppressing the people's struggle for freedom and justice, in the given territories. Doubting Thomases are invited to look beyond their borders and see what is happening there. Even areas which seemingly appear peaceful and politically tranquil are in reality simmering with discontent below the surface and suffer periodic political eruptions.

PAN-AFRICAN CONFERENCE.

12. Africa is to-day both important and valuable. It is important for its sons and daughters because of its political awakening and achievements, as well as its developments. It is valuable to Great Powers and colonial powers who see in it a field of investment and battleground for their ideological struggles. They are therefore antagonistic to the people's struggles for freedom and liberation. These facts have increased the ever-existing need for the coming together of the peoples of the various countries and regions of Africa, and the formation of some sort of political co-operation among them.

13. With this object in view and with a view to checking the intentions of the colonialists, a most historic all-Africa conference has just ended in Accra, Ghana. The conference started on the 8th and ended on the 12th December, 1958. The Conference has struck fear into the hearts of racialists and imperialists. It is hoped that the Conference will have succeeded in establishing a machinery to step up the process of liberation

and to bring about an effective co-operation. No one in the continent of Africa could be happier about this step than the A.N.C. and the progressive forces in South Africa. South Africa was represented by delegates including the President of the Basutoland Congress and Mr. Z. Mphahlele and [Alfred] Hutchinson. Our foreign policy flows from the Bandung Declarations on which decisions of the Pan-African Conference should be based.

THE APARTHEID POLICY IN SOUTH AFRICA.

14. The apartheid policy of the Nationalist Government has again been attacked at the United Nations. The delegates from various countries expressed concern that the Union Government continues to turn a deaf ear and has ignored numerous appeals from the world body to revise its racial apartheid policy. More and more delegates are joining in the attack as shown during the last session.

15. During last year's General Assembly, the Nationalist Government decided to boycott U.N.O. debates on the racial policy of the Government. This year the Government was forced to abandon its unwise boycott. It is also significant that the Government allowed a U.N.O. Commission to enter South Africa for the purpose of investigating the position of South West Africa.

16. The commission recommended the division of South West Africa into two sections, one to be annexed by the Union and the other to be administered by the international organisation. The recommendation was consistent with the apartheid policy. It was correctly rejected by the people of South West Africa and the General Assembly. It was obviously an attempt by the Union Government to evade the real issue, the demand that South West Africa should be administered by U.N., which would prepare the people for self-government instead of apartheid.

17. Whilst we do not imagine for a moment that our liberation will come through the United Nations, we are naturally pleased to know that the world is with us in its condemnation of the racial policies of the Nationalist Government and in recognising the fact that racial discrimination is an international issue fraught with serious dangers to world peace. The policy of reaction has no place in the progressive world of today.

RETURN OF THE NATIONALISTS.

18. The white electorate gave strength and power to the most reactionary force in the country. More votes and more seats went to the Nationalists.

The official opposition, the United Party, has been further weakened. The more progressive party, the South Africa Labour Party, was for the first time in 45 years completely eliminated as a parliamentary party. To many who did not understand the S.A. situation this reaction was completely puzzling and shocking. But to us it was a mere confirmation of what we have been warning the country about since 1910.

19. South Africa is to-day governed by the most reactionary elements within the Nationalist Party itself. The European electorate did not only place the most reactionary party in power by giving more votes and more seats to the Nationalists in parliament but also elevated the most hated ruthless arrogant and stubborn fascist dictator as the Prime Minister of our country.

20. The illusion of changing the South African situation through the present electoral system has been shattered for all times. The correctness of the people's view that there can be no democracy whilst the majority of the people are voteless has been confirmed. We have repeatedly warned that instead of progress there will be more and more reaction in our country. Dictatorship has been installed; the Nationalists can be got out of power not by the voters but by the voteless masses, by extra-parliamentary means. When we told the country this last year that the change in the S.A. situation depends not so much on the United Party as on the voteless masses we were misunderstood. We had no illusions then about the colourless United Party. But some people still believed that the United Party had chances of winning the elections and that our demonstrations would have the effect of driving the voters into the hands of the Nationalists. As a result of this outlook we failed to achieve unity among the Anti-Nationalists and to get the necessary support for the mass action.

21. The return of the Nationalists brought disillusionment and desperation especially amongst Europeans. In almost all the areas under United Party control a general capitulation has taken place. This was particularly the case in Johannesburg where the City Council has surrendered the rights of citizens to the police and the N.A.D. This is not quite the case among the non-Europeans. They have faith in the future and are determined to work for a better South Africa. It is encouraging to see the growth in the number of Europeans who are joining the struggle against Nationalist tyranny.

FORWARD MARCH.

22. The People have decided to challenge the Nationalist Party and the very cornerstone of the conception of white domination. During the election week the Congress movement decided to intervene by demonstrations and by putting forward the people's demands. No one can doubt the

effectiveness and the impact this decision had on the whole country. Indeed it is the most historic, and marks a turning point in our politics. We can no longer fold our arms and allow the minority to elect without our intervention.

STAY-AT-HOME.

23. Although the stay-at-home was not as successful as we might have liked it to be, and was in fact a disappointment, it would be naive to underestimate the action. As Chief Luthuli puts it: "At this time when white South Africa was electing a government it was necessary for non-white people to make their demands known. The electing period was obviously the most opportune moment for doing so. After all if there is a time when policies and demands are given expression to, it is election time. In such a situation we would not as responsible leaders of the National Liberatory Movement remain silent. In making our views known we, of course, had to employ the only weapon available to us. Furthermore we did want our people to cease to regard the general elections as 'White man's Affair.' This has been the attitude in the past. In spite of this, leaders of white political parties have exploited us as bogey, in every election. There have been elections in which 'Black Manifestos' and anti-black propaganda have featured with us as passive on-lookers. This time we decided to intervene actively as an independent force to shatter the myth of elections as white man's affair for good. The campaign intended to demonstrate the vital interest we have in the elections. We saw the entire state machinery, cabinet, army, police, and officials mobilised in a massive demonstration to crush all opposition. Our intervention became a matter of serious concern to leaders of white political parties which reacted by making all manner of extravagant statements. I do not recall any elections in which a political organisation was discussed as much as the African National Congress [was] in this [election]. Our demands, particularly for legislation for a minimum wage of one pound a day, were recognised by all, including leaders of Commerce, Industry and Civic Affairs. A great political revival centering around our demands went through the country and the results of this will be felt and seen more and more in the future."

24. The critics and enemies of the A.N.C. were very jubilant over what they had considered to be the downfall of the A.N.C. They made positive statements that the A.N.C. had not only lost initiative but had ceased to be a force in the country. We in the A.N.C. fear nothing. We admit mistakes and failures but we shall never relax or allow enemies of the organisation to make wild statements for the sole purpose of destroying the organisation.

25. In regard to what took place in the three days the working committee issued a well considered statement for discussion by the branches. The branches were invited to discuss frankly and send their views to the National Congress. Few branches responded. The majority of branches may or may not have discussed the statement; we do not know. As this was a joint campaign, a Conference of joint Executives took place on the 1st May and the whole campaign was analysed in a statement annexed herein. [The statement of April 28, 1958 is referred to in the introductory essay.]

26. A summary of the points of the events of that week which emerged from the discussions is as follows:—

(i) that campaign was not a failure in the sense that the intervention shook the country and that in spite of the powerful propaganda and the whole state machinery used against the people the strike did take place. In some factories and in some areas, e.g. the Western areas, the strike was successful. The Country took note of the demands.

(ii) the calling-off, although the manner in which it was done is subject to criticism, on the whole it left the initiative of the campaign in the hands of the Congress movement, and prevented a division which might have followed.

(iii) failure was due to inadequate preparation—the lack of neat organisational machinery; the confusion as to the place of the A.N.C. in the whole campaign—in other words many people regarded it as a mere SACTU Affair.

(iv) As against the disunity within the A.N.C. and the Anti-Nationalist camp, the whole propaganda machinery of the state and the Africanists and other reactionary elements united and geared their forces against the campaign.

27. There can be no doubt that the whole liberation movement took the shortcomings and criticisms seriously, as a result of which the period after the stay-at-home has been used to re-organise and to re-unite the people and we can happily and proudly report that the unity within the A.N.C. has been achieved and sealed. The unity within the Congress movement, the alliance which had shown signs of weakening, has once more been firmly established.

28. We have reached a position to-day whereby the progressive forces, even outside the Congress movement, are closing up their ranks—the initiative once more is in the hands of the people's movement.

442

UNITED FRONT.

29. There is to-day wide realisation among the people of South Africa, that the future of their country lies in their unity. The fighting spirit exists in varying degrees among the anti-Nationalist forces. The United Party itself is under fire from its rank and file and from some of its leaders for its vacillating policy of wanting to out-nat the Nationalists, and its double faced attitude on the question of race relations. The Black Sash and Liberal Party took a firm stand on the question of increase in poll-tax, banning meetings, opposition to pass-laws and the sell-out policy of the City Councillors controlled by the United Party. On the question of high wages too they have shown great interest. The Trade Union Council has also made a clear statement in regard to the increase of wages. Unfortunately the Liberation movement has not found an appropriate method to bring about the necessary co-operation of all these forces. We must particularly confess our failures in our participation in the multi-racial Committee which showed such great possibilities when it held a Conference on the 5th December in Johannesburg, in that the continuation committee does not receive sufficient attention from the A.N.C. The incoming Executive should be directed to include, among many tasks, the task of carrying out this good work.

30. A clear demand of unity has been put forward by the editor of the "Rand Daily Mail" [L.O.V. Gandar] writing under the name of Owen Vine, with clarity and foresight. This call for unity unfortunately embarrassed some of those organisations who have claimed to stand for a free and united democratic society. It has not yet been possible for them to sink their petty differences.

31. The A.N.C. welcomes the call and will unhesitatingly work for such unity. It is our belief that there is a great task which faces progressive people in this country; that task is to educate the European public, the millions who have been fed on false and poisonous racialistic propaganda. The unity of the potential progressive forces is the key to the overthrow of the Nationalist regime.

A REPUBLIC.

32. The Nationalists' last act to seal their aim of a fascist dictatorship will be the establishment of a fascist republic in the next few years. We are certainly opposed to the type of a republic contemplated by the Nationalists.

MASS TRIALS.

33. It seems clear that the Nationalist Government has committed South Africa to a future of mass trials as a mode of dealing with the demands of the people, and in an effort to crush the popular movement against the enactment and enforcement of the undemocratic and anti-democratic laws. The scores of Treason accused, the numberless crowds who have been prosecuted following the government's attempt to impose passes on Zeerust women, the hundreds who are facing mass murder trials in Sekhukhuniland, arising from ill-advised and ill-timed meddling by the people of the Native Affairs Department, the dozens who have been charged with incitement following the stay-at-home of April 14th, the trials involving thousands of women who took part in anti-pass demonstrations—all these combine to produce a picture in which the theatre of political conflict is shifting to the law courts, in as much as every effective mass demand or mass resistance to tyranny and fascism leads, almost inevitably, to mass arrests and prosecution on some charge or other.

34. It is obvious that the policy of the Government is to arrest [and] whenever possible to exhaust all resources of the liberation movement. More and more arrests are still going to take place; the problem of defence, bail and fines is mounting by the day. These are problems facing this conference; they should be properly examined and the discussions must be objective if we are to find a way out. It is easy of course for some one to stand up and say, "No defence, no bail, no fine," and by that the house may be under the impression that it has solved the problem. It is also easy to stand up and say we must defend every case, find money for bail and fines in all cases; the position is not so simple.

The problem is much deeper than that. Some people use the fact that in the treason case defence and bail was found and that in every case the principle must apply.

The question to be considered is the advantage to be gained by the movement of any step we take and the concrete conditions prevailing at any given time. On the question of the women's demonstrations some people simply said, "no bail, no fines"; this approach did not take into account the actual conditions. A large number of women went to jail not in the same way as people did in the Defiance campaign, i.e. having prepared themselves to serve. Many women did not expect arrest; this created a problem because whether you liked it or not relatives were ready to bail them out and pay fines, particularly when the cases appeared to be prolonged. It therefore became necessary for the leaders to act, in order to prevent confusion and chaos which might have followed.

35. When a spontaneous movement takes place, the duty of the leadership is not just to follow spontaneously, but to give it a proper direction. We hesitated to do this in the women's demonstration and the results were not of the best. These lessons are useful in preparing ourselves for what is to be done from now on, in the light of the Government policy to arrest and in the light of the defence and money problems. Even when we decide that people must be prepared to stay in gaol without bail and fines, there may be cases which will require defence, bail, fine. This brings us to one important political problem, that is, new methods of struggle must emerge; they must be found. We can no longer rely only on the old forms; we must discard what is not useful and use what we think is suitable.

THE ECONOMIC POSITION IN SOUTH AFRICA.

36. The Government tries by all means to hide the fact that the country is faced with some sort of a crisis; there is recession in the country. After all, South Africa is part of the Western economy which is affected by the economic upheavals.

37. Secondary Industry plays an important part to-day in our economic affairs. It would be foolish to deny that the leading branches within the secondary industry are faced with tremendous difficulty; some of the factories are closing down. Unemployment is growing, and some people are employed part time. How can this not affect the economic situation in the country?

38. The economic position of South Africa cannot be expected to improve. It will deteriorate, because its human resources are wasted and ignored. Yet our country has vast resources both human and material, most of which are as yet not tapped; the country is rich and wide. If its wealth and its manpower, black and white, are properly used and given an opportunity to contribute in production, then the evils of starvation and un-employment could be banished for good. That means removing artificial colour barriers, segregation, apartheid, baasskap and racial discrimination, pass laws, group areas, all of which are in one form or another an obstacle to the progress of the country.

39. Racial disease affects every sphere of South African life. No real development can take place as long as this position remains. Europeans in this country and to some extent even overseas try to look for solution only within the framework of the present-made South African system, as if the system is permanent. They miss the point that no country can afford to suppress two-thirds of its population and still hope to make progress.

40. It is obvious that in our struggle we should wage a relentless struggle on the economic front as well. The investors in this country and elsewhere must be taught to look at the situation realistically and to adjust themselves or face the consequences of the situation. We must study the role of various business organisations such as Sake Kamer, Chambers of Commerce and Industries, mining and farming organisations. Their role during election time and stay-at-home, as disclosed in the memorandum published in *New Age* from the Chamber of Industries, reveals a lot for us.

ECONOMIC BOYCOTT.

41. The economic boycott is going to be one of the major political weapons in the country; our organisation must prepare itself for this major struggle. It is to be regretted that our handling of the boycott campaign has not been of the best in the past.

42. For this gigantic task we need a permanent commission to look into all economic aspects and to recommend from time to time necessary and effective actions.

£ 1 A DAY CAMPAIGN.

43. Although we succeeded to focus the attention of the whole country on the question of higher wages and the demand for £1 a day we did not consistently follow up as the A.N.C. The farm and mine workers have not been aroused on this question of higher wages, yet this is the most exploited group. As a result of the campaign for the increase of wages, the employers are now talking of raising wages. The impression might be created that the increase in wages is due to the sudden change of heart among the employers. The role of the organisation in bringing about these proposals is obscured. This is due to lack of propaganda on our part. We must now correct this attitude and make the people realize the true reason for the proposed increases by employers.

INCREASE OF TAX.

44. In spite of the outcry in the country against the miserable wages paid to African workers, the government has taken an outrageous action when the Minister of Finance introduced a Bill which is now law raising the Poll Tax of the African Males over the ages 18 by 75% and in the same measure is contained a clause raising the Tax in a sliding scale and also forcing the African women to pay Tax. In 1960 Taxes will go up again.

Every man earning up to £ 15 a month or £180 a year will have to pay £ 1.15.0d. poll tax, but if you earn more than that, you will also have to pay more.

A sliding scale will be introduced which will increase taxes still further on all incomes over £180 a year.

Men earning between £ 180—£240 a year will pay £2.
Men earning between £ 240—£300 a year will pay £2.15.
Men earning between £ 300—£360 a year will pay £3.10.
Men earning between £ 360—£420 a year will pay £4.5.
Incomes over £420 will be taxed £ 4.5.0d. plus £ 1 for every £60 over that.

In addition to the fundamental objections of no taxation without representation, we maintain that tax must be based on the ability of a man to pay, not on race. There is no other country except S.A. where the burden of tax is on the shoulders of the people who do not only have no say in the government of the country but form the poorest section. Further, Africans who earn £ 15 a month are liable to various other taxes, e.g. they have to pay economic rent in some cases up to 200% notwithstanding the fact that in 1957 the people in the Rand categorically said they could not pay 5/– increase in bus fares per month; the cost of living in raising any direct taxation must of necessity affect the lower income groups.

GROUP AREAS.

45. In some of the main cities of the Union Group areas have been proclaimed resulting in economic ruin for a large number of people. Although the main victims of this drastic measure are Indians, it is a mistake to consider that no other section of the community will be affected. Already Lady Selbourne, Sophiatown and other areas owned by Africans have been proclaimed. This is one of the most unhuman and scandalous measures in our country and the issue must be brought sharply to the United Nations Organisation.

STRUGGLE AGAINST PASSES.

46. The broad policy statement issued 2 years ago is still applicable in the present situation. In reviewing the anti-pass campaign launched in 1955 we find that the role played by the African women is most inspiring. In many parts of the country protests, demonstrations, burning of passes, deputations, boycotts and strikes have taken place. The resistance of the

people to this notorious Pass system is mounting. Its development takes place in accordance with our statement of policy, namely, that it is a prolonged struggle now taking one form and now another. To hope that by striking one blow we would defeat the system would result in disillusionment. On the other hand, we cannot sit until everybody is ready to enter the battle field; others may follow to-day or the day after or even months afterwards. The campaign must systematically widen, taking different forms at different times in different places. The truth is that the struggle for the repeal of Pass-laws has begun; there is no going back but "forward ever".

47. We proudly salute the women freedom volunteers from Winberg, Lichtenberg, Zeerust, Sekhukhuniland, Uitenhage, Standerton, Durban, Pietermaritzburg and two-thousand Johannesburg women. Men must prepare themselves "Amadoda Makazi lungiselele kuba engayazi imini neyure". [Men must prepare themselves because they do not know the day and hour.]

TRADE UNION.

48. In recent years we have said quite a lot about the A.N.C. playing an important role in assisting to organise workers into Trade Unions. It is true that we speak about this assistance nearly in all our meetings. This is far from being satisfactory; our resolutions require that we should do something more than this, the actual creation of Trade Unions and also seeing to it that A.N.C. members join the Trade Unions and organise branches. We should take advantage of this and educate our people about industrial organisations. A large number of Non-Europeans are unemployed. The government is not satisfied with this ugly position; to aggravate the position people are prohibited from certain jobs purely on the grounds of race under the job reservation measure.

THE RURAL PROBLEMS.

49. The conditions are even worse in the countryside. The Reserves are overcrowded and unproductive. The migratory labour system just makes the position worse; the workers only work for train fare. It is in the field of economics where apartheid proves more unrealistic.

The proposed finance co-operation is of no value to most of the population; its purpose is just to create some sort of traitor class. This does not mean that we say it must be boycotted or that everyone who participates in it is a traitor. We are only warning the people to be vigilant about it.

50. The most hard-pressed section of our community is to be found in the the European farms. There are two groups of farm workers, the labour tenants and the ordinary farm labourers. We have received complaints of rotten cheating of the labour tenants by farm owners who take advantage of the fact that these people have nowhere else to go. They cannot go to the Urban Areas because of influx control, and there is no place in the Reserves. There is a general complaint among labour tenants who have no protection against farmers who blackmail them and do not pay them for their products.

51. The other group consists of labourers who are locked up in the compounds with no contact with the outside world. They are ill treated . . . . [sic] and earn a starving wage. They dare not complain nor leave the farm for fear of arrest.

THE RESERVES.

52. The country people continue to struggle in spite of the difficulties; their attitude is unchanged. The Chiefs and government find it almost impossible to put their plans into operation. They are resisting Bantu Authorities and Rehabilitation Schemes. The African Chiefs on the whole have a tradition of working with the A.N.C. from its inception. To continue on this has become more difficult in recent years, yet many of them are with the people. Some have in fact been deported as a result of their work but they do not complain.

53. There are some, however, who have become loyal agents of the government. They serve the government even better than the police. It is this group which has become desperate in its efforts to implement the government's plan and has become very cruel and brutal against the people. This distinction is necessary because some people condemn all Chiefs and some think all the Chiefs are with us.

54. The A.N.C. is as you all know illegal in some of the reserves; even in the Areas where it has not yet been banned the fact that meetings cannot be held without the consent of a Chief and the Native Commissioner places the organisation in a position of illegality. We are grateful for efforts made in various reserves, particularly in the Transvaal, Ciskei, Transkei and to some extent in Natal. We would like a greater effort now to mobilise the reserves. We need not have the people in the reserves joining A.N.C.; in view of many difficulties we should create a core in every reserve which will be useful in whatever action we may decide on. It would be better to create a peasant's organisation.

BANTU EDUCATION.

55. The struggle against Bantu Education is far from being over, although the boycott phase of it is now over.

56. Since its inception, this inferior type of education met with widespread and spontaneous protests; and in many areas the people called for a permanent boycott of Bantu Education Schools and their instruments—the Bantu Education School Committee and Boards. Quite notable withdrawals of children from school took place in places like Germiston, Benoni, Brakpan, Alexandra, Port Elizabeth, etc. Clearly, however, neither the A.N.C. nor the African Education Movement could provide alternative education. The Cultural Club Movement was founded with many difficulties and constant police intimidation.

57. The task which now faces the A.N.C. and the A.E.M. is one of counteracting effectively the poison of Bantu Education through the Cultural Clubs. These will cater for children particularly in places where there are no schools. We are determined to educate our children for a free society.

FINANCE.

58. It must be clear to all members from the account already given that financial commitments are beyond the capacity of the organisation. This places a challenge on every honest member of the organisation that he should pay according to the demands of the times. It is not too much to ask members to give at least a day's wages per annum in addition to other contributions. 2/6d. is ridiculously low for an organisation of the calibre of the A.N.C. With the growth of the organisation and the mass trials we will need more and more money.

PROBLEMS WITHIN THE A.N.C.

59. You will recall that during the period under review the A.N.C. was faced with serious disputes in the two most powerful A.N.C. provincial branches, the Cape and Transvaal. In the Transvaal, dispute arose out of the Provincial conference held in October 1957, the proceedings of which were challenged by certain branches. The dispute grew to such dimensions that the National had to take over the Administration of the Transvaal. A conference was held on the 1st and 2nd November . . . .

60. In the Cape some branches protested at the election of Mr. T. E. Tshunungwa by the Provincial Executive as Secretary on the grounds that prior to his arrest as a Provincial Secretary he abandoned the work of Congress without any explanation. An acting secretary had to be appointed. In this dispute two Committees came into being. The National Executive convened a conference on the 15th–16th August in Paarl to settle the dispute in the Cape Provincial Branches . . . .

61. Taking advantage of this situation, the entire reactionary force, the Nationalist Government, Africanists and the whole European Press and the so-called Bantu Press, all of which were using the Africanists to break and destroy our National organisation, launched an attack on us. We are happy to say that all those evil efforts were nipped in the bud. The invincible spirit of the people safeguarded the A.N.C. The enemy was once more beaten and the unity of the people once more restored.

62. In our last year's report we dealt with the policy of the A.N.C. as reflected in the three main policy documents outlined in the form of a memorandum in 1957, namely Africans' Claims, Programme of Action, and the Freedom Charter. This year we propose to deal with certain aspects of this policy in the light of an all-out propaganda campaign by the A.N.C. critics and the A.N.C. enemies and particularly because of the emergence of an Africanist organisation.

63. As a result of grievances and complaints from some branches of the A.N.C. against the handling of the affairs of the organisation, a daring attempt to subvert and disrupt the organisation was made by a small clique within the A.N.C. calling itself Africanist.

64. This group has been in existence although not openly since 1951 but completely disappeared during the Defiance Campaign and re-emerged in 1953. When the Freedom Charter was adopted by a special conference of the A.N.C. at the beginning of 1956 this group was routed and silenced until there was a dispute when they seized the opportunity of launching a malicious campaign of slander and subversion and disruption.

65. Whether the Africanists initiated the campaign on their own or they were instruments of other forces we cannot say. One thing is now clear. The government, the Africanists and other enemies of the A.N.C. including the hostile press joined hands and formed a united front against the Congress movement. They all claimed that the A.N.C. was preparing to establish a communist state on the basis of the Freedom Charter, that the A.N.C. was controlled and directed by the C.O.D., that the alliance of the Congress movement was detrimental to the true interest of the African

people. The Africanists then set themselves the task of breaking the special conference of the A.N.C. Transvaal, if necessary by force. When they realised that their efforts to break the Conference had failed because of the effective counter measures taken by the Organisation, they suddenly announced their secession. We welcome their departure from our organisation.

66. The methods used by the Africanists and other forces are precisely what all imperialists have used against the peoples' movements throughout the world. It may be correct to divide these elements into two, the one which believes that whenever Europeans are with the Africans they must be dominating. This is the group, be they black or white, which believes that the Africans cannot stand on their own. The other group has a clear objective, to divide the people and prevent the struggle from developing. The President-General on the authority of the Working Committee made an important statement on the 5th October at the Congress rally in regard to Africanists. We hope this statement will clear the position once and for all.

67. The fundamental points of the statement are:— That the A.N.C. is a democratic organisation whose sole interest is the achievement of its aim, and naturally any suggestion or criticism whose purpose is to improve the organisation and further the interest of Africans is not only welcomed but invited. The forums for the A.N.C. are open to all its members to make suggestions and to criticise the organisation and its leaders and to have these suggestions accepted or rejected. However, the A.N.C. is also an organisation with discipline. Once a member's point of view has been rejected by the majority he must abide by the decision until the matter is redebated. Alternatively if he cannot accept the decision of the majority, he must resign.

68. Since its inception, the A.N.C. accepted South Africa as a multi-racial Society in which all racial groups have the right to live in dignity and prosperity. In fact the A.N.C. was founded in order to unite the African tribes into a political force in order to demand full democratic rights within the multi-racial framework of our society. The Nationalism of the A.N.C. was one which was not exclusive and racialistic but broad and all embracing.

69. Early in its history of struggle the A.N.C. realised and accepted the fact that freedom was indivisible, and it was essential to work [with] all forces which were prepared to struggle for the same ideas. It is for this reason that the A.N.C. since 1912 joined forces with the coloured organisation "African People's Organisation". This policy of the A.N.C.

is contained in the "Africans' Claims" and was reaffirmed in the Freedom Charter. The Africans' Claims was adopted in 1945 [sic], and was based on the "Atlantic Charter". In both these documents there is no rejection of other racial groups. On the other hand, there is implicit in both documents a confirmation of the policy of racial co-operation.

70. What is the substance of the allegation that the A.N.C. is controlled by Indians, C.O.D. or Communists? This is obviously a malicious and dishonest form of propaganda which has no substance, in fact the main purpose of which is to discredit and divide Congress and its allies. It is well known to those who make these allegations that the A.N.C. leads the alliance and had worked with all organisations which do not oppose its policy, including Indians and Communists. The C.O.D. is a creation of the A.N.C. and the Indian Congress.

71. It will be remembered that the Bantu National Congress of Bhengu was sponsored by the Government precisely to spread anti-Indian and anti-progressive propaganda. The Bantu National Congress failed disgracefully because the people realised that Bhengu wanted to sell apartheid to them. The government hates and fears alliance, just as it hates and fears the Freedom Charter. The policy of the Congress was developed under the most fierce attack from the Government and its Agents.

72. The Africanists' Nationalism is nothing more than Dr. Verwoerd's policy of Development along their own lines. It is these renegades who have abandoned Congress policy of building a united force to struggle against the Government. Their policy is to wreck the organisation. There is now no longer any place for them within our organisation. They are a separate organisation hostile to the A.N.C.

TASKS OF THE YEAR.

73. During the period under review in terms of last year's resolutions, we were directed among other things to appoint a commission to deal with the problems of disunity and friction in the branches, to step up our propaganda machinery, to intensify the campaign against pass laws and their extension to the women, to campaign for a minimum wage of £1 a day, to campaign against the Group Areas Act, to produce a branch manual, to explore the possibility of launching a newspaper, to organise volunteers and convene a Conference to work for the defeat of the Nationalist Government and the creation of a strong united front. Some of these resolutions have been implemented; others have not. We have already dealt with the stay-at-home campaign. A commission of enquiry to deal with the friction in the branches has been appointed although it has not begun its work. The branch manual has been produced. We have already dealt with the

campaign against passes, Group Areas and £1 a day. The Conference of volunteers has not yet been called due to various problems, e.g. banning of meetings.

PROPAGANDA.

74. On the propaganda side the Committee has been appointed, but its work is far behind. It has not tackled the main problem of publishing a regular official bulletin and a newspaper.

It may be better that the Conference should itself appoint a special committee and give specific instructions of what precisely should be done.

ORGANISATION.

75. Our national organisation stands at the crossroads to-day. The Government's three-pronged attack on the African people and their organisations—the banning and deportation of leaders and active political workers, the prohibition of meetings of more than ten Africans [now rescinded], the strict and harsh control—the authorisation of the presence of every African in urban and proclaimed areas, and the demand and insistence on the African's very right to live being officially sanctioned, stamped and counter endorsed before the African could legally remain or move about in these areas—has created a very grave urgent political and organisational problem for the African National Congress.

76. Our aim should be to make the Congress a body that can survive any attack or on-slaught made upon it, no matter how severe, and to build the Congress into a true and undisputed spokesman for the Africans throughout the country. Nothing in this country has shown the importance of an efficient and powerful organisation more than the stay-at-home action during the election week.

77. We all admit that the potentiality of our organisation to mobilise the social forces is unlimited, but certain fundamental political organisational and administrative problems hamper our future progress and the growth of our movement. It will be readily appreciated that in the absence of a high political consciousness, a clear understanding and readiness to carry out duties, a sound co-ordination amongst members and organs of our organisation and generally efficient and smooth running organisation machinery, it is impossible to rally the people effectively for their historic task. It is therefore in the interest of our struggle that these problems should be discussed frankly and an honest and determined effort be made to solve them.

SUMMARY OF THE ACTIVITIES OF THE PROVINCES.

BRANCHES. (Youth League & Women's League).

78. *Transvaal.* In spite of the dispute in the Transvaal the political organisational work has not been relaxed as shown by the Provincial Conference. No less than 600 delegates, 200 of which were accredited delegates excluding 50 Africanists whose presence was merely to disrupt Conference, attended. Paid membership of the organisation exceeded that of the corresponding period 1952 when the Defiance Campaign was under way. Members came from all parts of the Province, others as far afield as the rural areas of Zeerust, Sekhukhuniland, Pietersburg and Bethal.

79. *Cape.* We must compliment the Cape because the Eastern Province has become a model of organisational efficiency. The Cape Province has also suffered a setback due to internal troubles. The new Executive however is now busy attempting to consolidate its position. In addition they are penetrating into the countryside. Branches have been established in the reserves, in Ciskei and Transkei.

80. *O.F.S.* The Province is still poorly organised; its machinery is not properly co-ordinated.

81. *Natal.* The busiest time for the Natal Province was during election week. Both Durban and Northern Natal Regions were very active. New branches have also been established.

82. *Women's League.* Everyone knows to-day that the African Women are in the front line in the struggle against passes. Their demonstrations in different parts of the country have resulted in a number of arrests; recently no less than 2,000 have been arrested and convicted. Sentences range from 3 weeks to 4 months with an alternative of a fine from £5-£50. We have been highly inspired with the courage and determination of our women folk. We should also point out, however, that the organisational machinery leaves much to be desired especially at the National Executive level. It is hoped that this conference will do something about this.

83. *Youth League.* It is encouraging to note that the Youth League is now becoming a mass organisation. It has a growing number of branches in the Transvaal. Its National machinery requires strengthening.

84. Friends, now that we have received [*sic*] the situation in the country and our organisation, the question which arises is what is to be done? The correct method in assessing the progress of an organization is the fulfillment of the tasks allocated. We should be in the state of readiness for the banning of the organisation. For more vicious onslaughts on our organisation. Therefore the following organisational tasks in addition to the political

tasks already dealt with should be undertaken.

(a) An immediate efficiency campaign on both administration and organisation be conducted by all branches. Members should endeavour to work according to stipulated time.

(b) Every member must be able to give a good account of any duty assigned to him.

(c) The tendency of giving inflated and exaggerated reports must be discontinued, as such a tendency leads to the taking of wrong decisions based on such reports.

RESPONSIBILITY.

85. All tasks of the African National Congress should be undertaken with the utmost responsibility, particularly by leading members.

No member should fail to fulfill his/her obligation if he or she has promised to carry out an undertaking.

Branches should never fail to give an account of their work to the Provincial Office.

All decisions of the African National Congress should be implemented without any delay, and reports should be furnished to the Provincial Office on how such decisions have been implemented. Branches should not be ashamed to register their failures on the implementation of any decision.

As a guide to the general membership, we suggest that all the leading members of the African National Congress throughout the country should be exemplary by undertaking to carry out these suggestions to the letter. It is considered that such an example will be a practical education to the general membership.

An education campaign on efficiency should be conducted among the members of the African National Congress and every lesson which has been taught must be put into practice to find out whether members are having any interest or enthusiasm in the campaign.

The best way to do it is to assign duties to some members and then check and recheck whether members so directed have carried out their undertakings with the strictest observance of time.

These suggestions will improve the efficiency of our organisation and will render members more competent and efficient in their style of work. One of the most important organisational tasks is to recruit new members. It is proposed that 120,000 new members be recruited by June 26th, 1959.

In conclusion, therefore, sons and daughters of Africa, we wish once again to make a solemn call to conference, learning and building from our experiences, to prepare with increased vigour for the tasks which face us in the coming year.

First and foremost our task is the building of unity within our ranks—MAXIMUM UNITY which is the only answer to increased repressions and threats against our organisation.

We must continually inspire people with their own achievements, the advancing march to freedom of the people of Africa, and their inevitable victory over Verwoerdism.

Let us go forward with confidence! Afrika! Mayibuye!

Document 32. "Freedom is the Apex." Address by Chief A. J. Lutuli at a public meeting for Whites organized by the South African Congress of Democrats, [n.d.]

Note: A tape recording of Lutuli's address before an audience of more than 300 people was reproduced "almost verbatim" in a printed pamphlet, *Chief A. Lutuli speaks to White South Africans: "Freedom is the Apex,"* issued by the S. A. Congress of Democrats, [n.d.].

Mr. Chairman, ladies and gentlemen, someone has said a man really has only one speech to make. He may clothe it in different words, but in essence it is the same speech. Those of us who are in the freedom struggle in this country have really only one gospel. We may possibly shade it in different ways, but it is a gospel of democracy and freedom.

If we are true to South Africa that must be our vision, a vision of S.A. as a fully democratic country. It cannot in honesty be claimed that she is yet really democratic, when only about a third of her people enjoy democratic rights, and the rest—notwithstanding the fact that they constitute the majority—are still subjected to Apartheid rule. I emphasise the words *are still*, because I do believe firmly that it is not a state that can be perpetuated. Apartheid rule is the antithesis of democracy. Apartheid—in theory and in practice—is an effort, to make Africans march back to tribalism.

A Deceitful Concept

Sometimes very nice and pretty phrases are used to justify this diversion from the democratic road. The one that comes to my mind is the suggestion that we Africans will: "Develop along our own lines." I do not know of any people who really have developed "along their own lines." My fellow white South Africans, enjoying what is called "Western civilisation," should be the first to agree that this civilisation is indebted to previous civilisations, from the East, from Greece, Rome and so on. For its heritage, Western civilisation is really indebted to very many sources, both ancient and modern.

There is really no possibility of anyone developing "along his own lines," as is often suggested. But in practice "developing along your own lines" turns out not to be development along your own lines at all, but development along the lines designed by the Government through the Native Affairs Department. Even in determining the laws that govern us and our development, there is no attempt to consult those who are affected. There is no contact between the governor and the governed at the present moment. "Developing along our own lines," has come to mean "Developing along *their* lines—the Government's lines."

The essence of development along your own lines, is that you must have the right to develop, and the right to determine how to develop. Its essence is freedom and—beyond freedom—self-determination. This is the vision we hold for our future and our development.

Freedom is the Apex

One might ask, "Is this vision of a democratic society in South Africa a realisable vision? Or is it merely a mirage?" I say, it *is* a realisable vision. For it is in the nature of man, to yearn and struggle for freedom. The germ of freedom is in every individual, in anyone who is a human being. In fact, the history of mankind is the history of man struggling and striving for freedom. Indeed, the very apex of human achievement is FREEDOM and *not* slavery. Every human being struggles to reach that apex.

It is sometimes suggested that people are "incited" to struggle for freedom. One wonders what that means. I admit that circumstances from time to time make it necessary to remind people of what lies at the apex. Naturally if I find a man in the mud, it is my duty to uplift him and remind him "You are not of the mud." If there be human beings who, for some reason or other, have forgotten their rights and wallow in the mud, it is the duty of all who see, to say to them, "Don't wallow in mud. Try to reach up to the apex." And the apex of human achievement and striving, as I have said, is freedom.

Let Us Share Responsibility

It is often said that the Non-European people merely strive for the good fruits of South African citizenship and not for its obligations. But that is not the aspiration of Black South Africa. We would like to share in the privileges and rights that go with democracy. But at the same time we are ready to carry all the obligations which flow from being part of a democratic country. I hasten to say that we do not approve of the state of affairs which obtains now, when on the basis of apartheid, it is said, "Where social services are directed to you or for you, *you* alone should bear the expense."

That we do not agree to. We feel that we should enjoy the rights which are enjoyed by all South Africans, and equally bear the obligations. But that is far different from saying to the poorest section of the community, "If you wish to enjoy any social services in South Africa, pay for it yourself." That policy at present being carried out in so far as non-Europeans—particularly Africans—are concerned, is a policy of denying us the privileges of freedom, while saddling us with more than our share of responsibility.

Emergent Africa

The yearning for freedom is not peculiar to South Africa. The whole of Africa is emerging into Freedom. We live in the midst of what has rightly been described as "Emergent Africa." Why should it be thought that Africans in this part of Southern Africa are different from Africans in Ghana? Africans in Ghana have received full democracy. In Nigeria they are about to receive full democracy. How can it be suggested that the Africans in the Union of South Africa will not yearn, like their brothers in the North, for freedom. The very fact that Africa is emerging to freedom should be a sign to all of us that our vision of democracy is coming and *will* be realized.

The African isn't the only one who has struggled for full participation in the South African democracy. Our people have been much impressed by the struggle of the Afrikaner in this country. He too struggled—in fact, in affairs less justified than ours, for he did enjoy a certain amount of freedom while we enjoy none. But he felt he did not enjoy it fully. It should be unnecessary to remind Afrikaner South Africans that nothing could stop their struggle until they got a full share in democracy for themselves. Should they not realize that this same truth applies now to the struggling Africans, who cannot be denied the privileges of democracy for ever?

We Are a Multi-Racial Community

I believe that our vision of democracy in South Africa will be realised, because there is a growing number of people who are coming to accept the fact that in South Africa we are a multi-racial community—whether we like it or not. I am not prepared to concern myself with such questions as "Where have you come from?" "Do you come from the North?" or "Did you come from Europe." It is not important. What is important for our situation is that we are all here. *That* we cannot change! We are all here, and no one desires to change it or should desire to change it. And since we *are* all here, we must seek a way whereby we can realise democracy, so that we can live in peace and harmony in this land of ours. More and more people are coming to accept that and to work for it.

Sometimes it would seem that the more apartheid is intensified, the more freedom lovers come together to oppose it. It is an encouraging feature, demonstrated by the fact that there exists today not only the Congress of Democrats under whose auspices you are meeting here, but also the Liberal Party, the Labour Party, the Black Sash, and many Church leaders who have seen and followed their duty to their fellow men.

Cherish Human Values

Man must participate in all the aspects of life; political, social and religious. A man is not whole if he is deprived of participating in some aspects of life; he will grow to be a lopsided man. It is not our aim to produce among Africans lopsided citizens of South Africa. It is my firm belief that more and more South Africans, regardless of colour, will come to see the justice of our cause, because it is not just *our* cause. It is a human cause and, I would say, a divine cause to try and build a climate in South Africa where human values will be respected.

We often hear the cry that if we extend democratic freedom to non-Whites we shall be surrendering our heritage. But I would like to suggest that you cannot preserve your heritage by isolating yourself, or by isolating other people; you can only preserve human values by propagating them and creating a climate where these values will flourish. Apartheid does not furnish that kind of climate; for the values which we cherish, can only develop to the full in a climate of peace and equality, where brotherhood is respected. In such a climate as that, these values will grow. We must deliberately propagate these values if we wish to maintain them. That is the only way of saving white civilization! Propagate it! Don't hoard it! For if you hoard it, it is going to shrivel with you. But if you propagate it, more people will develop these values, preserve them, and prevent their dying out. We are interested in the preservation of those values, for they are eternal values. Man throughout the ages, has striven for these values. Why should it be thought that we in South Africa, we blacks in South Africa, strive less?

World Opinion

Encouragement for those whose vision is a democratic South Africa, lies in the fact that today there is self-questioning within the apartheid camp. When people begin to question their own policies, there is some hope. A sinner who does not realise that he is a sinner, is not very far from damnation; the hope for man is greater when he begins to question. Now I say their questions may not amount to much, but certainly it is a hopeful sign that they now begin to question and wonder at the efficacy of apartheid. There is hope there, just as there is hope to be drawn from world opinion being in favour of democracy. (Applause). However badly our country fails to live up to democracy, world opinion is in favour of democracy. The whole world stands up and says "We stand for this cause." I don't think that we ourselves really believe that South Africa can remain isolated from the world. Otherwise we will find ourselves a colony of slaves, isolated and cut off from the rest of the world—slaves of our own making.

To me democracy is such a lovely thing, that one can hardly hope to keep it away from other people. Could anyone really successfully shield off beauty. We don't live in Parktown, but we appreciate the beauties of Parktown. We do. And as we move round Parktown from the townships we pause and admire the beauty. I do. I am not a Johannesburg man, but I pause to see the fine gardens, the beautiful houses and the surroundings. I stop and admire beauty. Can you everlastingly cut off a human being from beauty? And as you move about in some of these palatial places, and the scent of the flowers comes to you, can you really stop another from smelling that scent? (Laughter and applause). Can you ward others off? Can you really successfully do it? I suggest that democracy, being the fine thing it is, the apex of human achievement, cannot be successfully kept from the attainment of other men. I say not.

Yes there are difficulties on the road, and various blocks. But the biggest block is "apartheid," making it difficult for us to realise the vision glorious of a multi-racial democratic South Africa. But despite the blocks let us strive to develop this democracy.

A New Pattern of Democracy

It is often suggested, quite rightly, that democracy was developed in homogeneous communities—in Europe, possibly in Asia to an extent—in communities that were homogeneous in colour. Here in South Africa we are not a homogeneous community, not as far as race and colour are concerned nor possibly even in culture. It is suggested that people in homogeneous communities can very well speak of democracy being shared; but in a community like ours, diverse in very many respects, you can't hope to share democracy. But I personally believe that here in South Africa, with all our diversities of colour and race, we will show the world a new pattern for democracy. I think there is a challenge to us in South Africa to set a new example for the world. Let us not side-step that task. What is important, is that we can build a homogeneous South Africa on the basis not of colour but of human values. After all, we all admire our colour. I often say my black colour is proof of sunshine and is due to heat. (Laughter). I admire my black colour—I should. But in trying to build a new homogeneous democratic South Africa, colour and race should not come into the scene. It should not come into the scene in any part of the world; for men should be bound together by certain values which they cherish.

I may have more in common with you here than, possibly, with the less fortunate of my African brothers who are still in the Reserves, who have not had the privileges of civilization which I have had. I don't know whether you like that—I don't want to annoy you—but to me that is a pointer to the fact that we can build a new type of homogeneous society—new in South Africa and in any part of the world. The main thing is that man is my brother not by blood, but because we cherish the same values, stand for the same standards. (Applause). I believe personally that, notwithstanding the fact that our cultures are diverse, we come to live together and in the process of our coming together, I will come to admire certain aspects of your culture, others I will reject. But I think also you will find that there will be aspects of our culture which are good. And so can develop a true South African culture, built up of the best of all our cultures.

Our Guarantees

White people often ask us "What guarantee have we that you will not swamp us by your numbers?" I think that in a sense I have already replied to that by saying that some of us are not interested in numbers. I think that very stress on numbers is harmful. The criterion should rather be "Do we wish for democracy?" To this question Africans have already given an answer. What more proof do you want that Africans long for democracy, when in fact they are already making sacrifices for it. They are willing to preach and struggle for democracy to the extent that sometimes they become the guests of Her Majesty. (Laughter.) But I would like to take you further back. When they first came into contact with Europeans, our forebearers saw there some values which they liked.

Even in the wars between the English and my people I don't remember that missionaries, or even traders—excepting those who were found to be traitors—were ever molested. So I suggest that our people have given sufficient proof that they yearn for democracy; the question of numbers doesn't count, particularly *if we set them on the right road!* What the apartheid rulers have said does not lead people on the right road! If the Africans don't seem to be getting to democracy it is not their fault; go and blame apartheid! If you should feel you are in danger, it isn't because we seek to endanger you, but because we are not given the opportunity of developing fully along the democratic road.

How can you truly expect that democracy at its best can flourish in slums? How can you expect that democracy shall flourish in insecurity, when people do not have the wherewithal to live? Where Africans work in towns, it is admitted, that their wages are low. In Reserves from where they come, the holdings are so small that people can hardly make a civilized living. Now Prof. Tomlinson assures me that, having worked fairly hard in the reserve I can expect to get £66 per year from my holding. And he says "Now if you work your holdings scientifically I promise you £120, or £150." He promises me that. In seriousness can anybody raise a family, on this basis, at the civilized standards we should aspire to?—Can you raise a family on that basis?

Bantustan–a Negation of Democracy

Can you really develop a democratic people upon the lines of the so-called "Bantu Authorities"—where we will not participate in the ordinary machinery of Government, but will revert to a perverted form of tribalism? For "Bantu Authority" is the exact antithesis of democracy; it is a rule by some kind of council appointed even without consultation with the people, by the sole decision of the Chief and the N.A.D.—a Council in which the people have no say at all and which they can never change even if they wish to. Such a system cannot lead to democracy; it does not even respect Bantu custom. For while we may not have been democratic in your sense, yet in past times, our tribal authority was not autocratic. I dispute the theory that African chiefs were autocratic. As in all communities, you occasionally get a dictator, like my own Chaka who was undoubtedly a dictator but not typical even of the Zulu chiefs. I don't think that you would suggest that Napoleon was a sample of the best in Europe. Incidentally he and Chaka were contemporaries; it seems that it was an age when dictators were produced.

Go Forward in Faith

How can you breed a democratic people along such lines? This is a challenge to all of us who are here. I will not concern myself with your political views whether you are United Party, Congress of Democrats or Liberal. All I see here is white South Africa and black South Africa. I see people who are interested in the welfare of South Africa. And if you are interested in South Africa as a whole you should do your best to work for the realisation of this POSSIBLE vision. It *is* possible, this vision of a multi-racial democracy in South Africa. The difficulties may be great, but nothing has beaten man if he has striven. Man is striving to go to the moon. If he can do this, can anyone suggest that man cannot evolve a system in South Africa that will make our society a democratic, multi-racial group?

There is a challenge which you and I must meet. We cannot dodge it.

We often say that what we are doing, we do for posterity. It is a very dangerous claim to make because posterity may think quite differently from us; we may find posterity spitting on our grave. Let us not claim the authority of posterity for our failures to strike out on the road of democracy. I think it is Jan Hofmeyer who said "Having planted, go in faith." Don't be worrying about other things. Go in faith and believe in the sanity of posterity. There is in the Bible a verse which says that all those who are cowards, all those who grow apathetic because of the difficulties before them and run away from the struggle,—that they shall not be able to reach that Glorious place. It also says that the cowards will be together with all evil doers.

I cannot believe that all of us who are here will fail South Africa because we are cowards and apathetic. I believe we all will do our best—whatever the difficulties are—for the realisation of this glorious democratic South Africa we dream of.

APPLAUSE

Document 33. Report of the National Executive Committee of the ANC, Submitted to the Annual Conference, December 12–13, 1959

1. Once more as delegates of the African National Congress, we meet to review the situation both at home and abroad with a view of assessing the gains made by the Freedom fighters and the reverses suffered.

2. It is essential to take stock of the rapid changes in the world situation because we no longer live in isolation. Boundaries and oceans merely separate people physically but the changing political and economic situation has its impact effects beyond the narrow confines of a country.

3. As delegates charged with the duty of planning our struggle for the coming year it behooves us not to be superficial in examining the past year from which we will plan our forward march, but to study this report critically and to discuss it thoroughly, that those who have honoured us by sending us to this conference to be their eyes, ears and spokesmen can accept our decisions and resolutions with the confidence that they have received the serious and critical examination which they deserve.

4. The African National Congress is the premier national organisation and its Conference and decisions are of importance not only to the people of South Africa but to the world at large. A high standard of discussion on the important issues facing our organisation and carefully considered resolutions are therefore expected of us.

5. *THE INTERNATIONAL SCENE.* There are two significant features within the international scene in the year under review which bring fresh hope of a better life to the peoples of the world. The first is the further progress made by the Colonial peoples, particularly on our continent in the struggle to free themselves from oppression and exploitation. The second is the efforts of the big powers to ease international tension and thus avoid a devastating nuclear war.

6. *PROGRESS IN THE COLONIAL COUNTRIES.* During the past year there has been an unprecedented upsurge in Africa. Self-government has become the cry of the peoples throughout the length and breadth of the continent. That cry can no longer be resisted by the imperialists who are making a last desperate bid to withhold the legitimate rights of the African people.

7. This year has witnessed the growth and cementing of the solidarity of the African people in their struggle for independence, democratic rights and against imperialism. The historic Pan-African Conference which was held in Accra prior to our own Conference last year represents a milestone in the forward march of the people of Africa. It was an inspiration to the African people who have been strangled by the imperialists for hundreds of years under the worst oppression, exploitation and racial discrimination.

8. The Conference was attended by delegates from 62 organisations representing 200 million Africans and it adopted resolutions aimed at increasing unity and mutual assistance in the struggle and hastening the end of imperialism in Africa.

9. The Conference paid special attention to our situation in South Africa and resolved to commence a campaign to boycott South African goods.

10. It is with the deepest regret that we heard of the unfortunate death of Mr. George Padmore, one of the architects of this historic Conference, and adviser to the Prime Minister of Ghana, Dr. Kwame Nkrumah. His death is mourned by the whole of Africa.

11. Following in the wake of this historic Conference, which was a symbol of the united determination of all Africans to end colonialism and its oppression, there was a wave of activity in Africa.

12. *BELGIAN CONGO.* The first struggle was in the Belgian Congo, and it was ruthlessly suppressed by Belgian Authorities. Hundreds of Africans were killed and the people's leaders were arrested, including the delegates to the Accra Conference. Nevertheless, the revolt in the Congo resulted in swift and dramatic concessions in the granting of a limited democracy. Since then there has been continuous unrest in the Congo and a promise of further concessions. The Congo is still seething with revolt. There is no

alternative but to grant the people their legitimate demand for independence.

13. *THE FRENCH CAMEROONS*. Shortly after the demonstrations in the Belgian Congo in January there was an armed revolt in the French Cameroons. The 5 million people of the Cameroons whose country has been arbitrarily divided into two parts under British and French rule respectively demand a united and free Cameroon. Since 1955 the people of the Cameroons have been engaged in an armed struggle against the French imperialists. The leaders of the Union of Populations of the Cameroons have been exiled. The shocking atrocities committed by the French against the people of the Cameroons must be stopped forthwith and all foreign troops withdrawn. It is the task of the United Nations to see to it that the Government which receives Independence in January 1960 is the most representative Government comprising the people now in exile.

14. *NYASALAND*. With the return of Dr. Banda to Nyasaland the demands of the African people for secession from the Federation and independence grew in volume. This country is indisputably the Africans' because there are three million Africans and only 7,000 Europeans who are able to dominate the country because Nyasaland is part of the white-dominated Federation. In order to quell the struggle the Authorities of the Federation announced to the world that they had uncovered a plot hatched by the Congress to massacre Europeans and loyal Africans. A state of emergency was called in to terrorise the people, although the Devlin Commission discovered that there was no plot. The leaders are still detained. The Africans do not want the Federation for very obvious reasons and no amount of terrorism will make them accept it.

15. *RHODESIA*. A state of emergency was also declared in both Northern and Southern Rhodesia. The Congresses have here been banned and leaders detained without trial. The terror which was unleashed against the Africans confirms the view that the grant of independence to the Federation will result in untold misery and suffering for the African people. We demand the immediate lifting of the state of emergency and the release of the leaders and discussions with the people's leaders. During the year demonstrations and protests were organised against the state of emergency and demanding the release of the leaders.

16. *TANGANYIKA*. In Tanganyika the Tanganyika National Union which represents 9,000,000 people is pressing for independence by 1960. We would welcome the advent of an independent Tanganyika.

17. *UGANDA*. As a result of the trade boycott organised by the Uganda National Congress a state of emergency was declared in Uganda. A

National organisation was banned, and leaders arrested. Uganda has been deliberately kept backward by Britain through division and the maintenance of tribalism and feudalism. A law to prohibit all political boycotts has been introduced in Uganda. This is a repressive measure.

18. *KENYA*. There is some indication that the seven year old state of emergency will be lifted next year. This is long overdue and we deplore the fact that the lifting of the state of emergency will be accompanied by severe restrictions on the movement and political activities of the African people. Jomo Kenyatta has at least been released from prison but has been banished to some remote part of Kenya. Jomo must be freed completely.

19. *GUINEA*. Despite the threat by France to withdraw all economic aid for Guinea after she had decided to secede from the fraudulent French community, her development and progress under the courageous lead of Sekou Toure is an inspiration to all emergent African states.

20. *ALGERIA*. The war in Algeria which has now been going on for 6 years is one of the most savage acts by the French imperialists in Africa. The French Government has emerged as one of the most tyrannical imperialists in Africa today. The war in Algeria is wanton murder of Algerian patriots who are demanding nothing more than their land and rights. We call upon the French Government to recognise the right of the Algerian people to independence, withdraw troops and negotiate with the Algerian people's Government to bring an end to the six years war.

21. *ANGOLA AND MOZAMBIQUE*. The most ruthless, and stubborn imperialists today in Africa are Portuguese. It represents the spearhead of reaction and violence against the African people. It has a fascist head of Government and like France has a fraudulent scheme of pretending that African colonies are a part of Portugal and that it is prepared to assimilate Africans who have reached a certain standard of civilisation into their committees [communities?]. These devices are a cloak for the ruthless oppression and exploitation of the Africans. In Mozambique the Portuguese have a pass system similar to that in South Africa. A system of forced labour as barbaric as our own is imposed on the Africans. Political rights, including the right to associate are ruthlessly denied to the Africans. One author has described Mozambique as a "land of tombstones silence" for the Africans.

22. *INDEPENDENCE IN 1960*. We welcome the emergence of further independent states in Africa. In 1960 Nigeria, Togoland, Somaliland and the Cameroons will join the 9 independent states of Africa.

23. *CHINA AND INDIA*. Your Executive was concerned during the year with the border disputes between these two great and leading Asian

peoples. It addressed a letter to the Prime Ministers of both countries appealing to them to settle the matter amicably to maintain the solidarity of the Afro-Asian people.

24. *THE U.N.O.* Your Executive sent a memorandum to the present session of the United Nations. This memorandum is herein attached marked ANNEXURE "A". 67 nations including the U.S.A. voted against the racialist policies of the Union. Britain contended that the matter was a "domestic affair." South Africa resorted to its threadbare tactics of boycotting the discussions. We are happy to note that some nations are taking a positive stand against apartheid. South Africa has continued to defy the world opinion and the time has now come for the world to consider sanctions against her.

25. *WORLD PEACE.* This year the people of the world sighed with relief at the efforts of the big powers to ease international tension. The exchange of visits of the heads of Government of Britain, America, the U.S.S.R. and France have eased the tension. The proposed summit talks are urgent and we hope nothing will be done by any of the powers to halt this drift away from world war.

26. *FRANCE AND THE TESTING OF A-BOMB IN THE SAHARA.* A matter which has caused the people of the world grave concern has been the decision of the French Government to test an A-Bomb in the Sahara Desert. The French Government is apparently stubbornly determined to continue its test in the face of overwhelming opposition and protest by the people. Protests have been organised to the French Ambassador.

27. *SUPPLY OF ARMS TO SOUTH AFRICA.* We note with regret that the Nationalist Government has been able to import arms and ammunition and saracens for no other purpose but to use them against the people to suppress their legitimate struggle for human rights. The A.N.C. appeals to all democratic nations of the world not to supply arms to South Africa under these conditions.

28. *THE SITUATION AT HOME.* The political situation at home is characterised by two main features. On the one hand we have what appears to be the relentless march of the Nationalist Government to baasskap fascism, destroying every vestige of democratic right for the Africans and other Non-Europeans, and threatening all the people of South Africa with the spectre of a fascist republic. On the other hand we witness the growing resistance of the people both black and white, from different strata of society, from various groups, to the rising menace of Nationalist baasskap fascism which threatens to plunge all the people of South Africa into darkness.

29. *THE STUBBORN MARCH OF THE NATIONALISTS TO FASCISM.* The Nationalists appear to be deaf to the protests of the people and Governments of the world, and the overwhelming majority of the people of South Africa against their ruthless policy of Apartheid.

30. Instead of responding to the legitimate demands of the people for democratic rights the Nationalists have made further assaults on the rights of the people under the pretext that it was extending rights to them. The fraudulent Bantustan scheme which is merely Bantu Authorities "glorified" has been presented to the world as a scheme intended to extend 'self-government' to the Africans in their 'own areas' when in fact it is:

(a) the destruction of the last vestige of representation for the Africans in Parliament and other local bodies.

(b) the complete destruction of the very right of the African to vote.

(c) the use of the chiefs as administrative tools not only to see that their subjects obey the laws of the Bantu Administration Department, but also that they should destroy those whom De Wet Nel calls "wolves and jackals," clearly the opponents of apartheid.

31. The whole question of Bantustan is dealt with more fully in a document annexed hereto marked "B" from which it is clear that Bantustan is not merely a bluff but constitutes the most serious threat to the struggle for democratic rights and the unity of our people. It is the purpose of the Government to divide us into small hostile tribes and clans and to divert the attention of the people from the struggle for democratic rights.

The special paper referred to above was carefully prepared by Mr. GOVAN MBEKI, well known economist and authority on the problems of the reserves and rural areas.

THE A.N.C.'S ATTITUDE TOWARDS THE CHIEFS. The A.N.C. is not opposed to the chiefs as such. The Government is attempting to cause a conflict between the chiefs and the A.N.C. We must not fall into this trap and we warn chiefs not to allow themselves to be used as pawns against the A.N.C. Our struggle is primarily against the Government and those Africans including chiefs who support and pilot Government schemes.

32. *THE ASSAULT ON EDUCATION.* This year through the separate University Act the Government has succeeded in murdering Fort Hare and have passed an Act establishing Tribal Colleges and closing the doors of the Universities to the Non-European people. This is consistent with the policy of the Government in regard to 'Bantu Education'. The Minister Maree said that the trouble with Fort Hare was that it produced "black Englishmen". What he presumably wants to produce in his 'Bantu Colleges' are 'loyal Bantu' loyal to the scourge of apartheid.

33. Further amendments have been made to the Group Areas Act and the I.C. Act which vest autocratic powers in the Ministers of State.

34. *ASSAULT ON THE A.N.C.* In the Administrative field, numerous leaders including President-General, Chief A. J. Luthuli, the Deputy-President, the Secretary-General and Mr. Resha have been banned for five years and the President has been confined to Lower Tugela, Mr. Resha to Johannesburg for five years. Leaders of our allied organisations have also been banned and confined.

35. During the year members of Congress have been banished from their homes.

36. A further act of fascist repression has been the ban imposed on our own organisation in the Marico District in Rustenburg. Threats were freely made by Cabinet Ministers this year that the organisation would be banned throughout the country.

37. Saracens and arms have been imported and used for the purpose of intimidating opposition and protest. Recently, the Minister of Defence has announced a major reorganisation of the defence force for purposes of internal security. This is a step similar to that taken by Hitler in Nazi Germany when he used the storm troopers to crush his opponents into submission. This is an attempt by the Nationalist Government to intimidate and terrorise the growing opposition in the country and to entrench themselves through military force. These then are some of the signs of the stubborn march of the Nationalists towards fascism.

38. *THE NATIONALISTS ARE NOT INVINCIBLE.* However stubborn they might appear to be the Nationalists are not invincible. In fact they have reached the zenith of their strength and can be weakened and smashed, fearless [*sic*].

39. The sharp criticisms and doubts of the intellectuals particularly certain professors and members of SABRA, although it was not on fundamental issues, was some indication that all was not as well as might be thought within the Nationalist camp, and that even amongst Nationalists the thaw was setting in.

40. *THE UNITED PARTY.* It is sufficient to dispose of the United Party with a few words. Its so-called "white leadership" with justice policy demonstrates its political bankruptcy in a period when the world is aware that the issues in South Africa are straight-forward, either equality or apartheid oppression. There is no middle course.

41. The whole development in the world today poses a challenge to every individual, group or party to choose between the acceptance of the rights of man irrespective of colour or creed or reversal of the clock by maintaining

discrimination, oppression and exploitation. People might avoid making that choice for a time but sooner or later they are compelled to face the realities of the situation.

42. In South Africa the Nationalists have made their choice clear against any progress and for this reason they have a definite policy.

43. For a long time the United Party has bluffed the country and the world by pretending that they were opposed to the Nationalist Party's reactionary policies, at the same time in attempting to win votes from Nationalist Party supporters they have also been at pains to prove that they were the guardians of white supremacy and domination.

44. World development and the impact of the events within the country, which urge for democratic rights, are compelling the United Party to make its choice clear. In this context therefore the present split within the United Party is to be welcomed as consistent with world development.

45. *THE PROGRESSIVE PARTY.* We welcome the formation of the Progressive Party. Its rejection of racial discrimination and the colour bar in enunciating its policy is a significant development in South African politics. Although the A.N.C. does not necessarily approve of every aspect of the policy of the Progressives we welcome them in joining the ranks of those who are opposed to Nationalist apartheid.

46. The A.N.C. is irrevocably committed to a policy of universal suffrage as it is enunciated in the Freedom Charter. We hope that the Progressive Party will ultimately realize the necessity of adopting this essential franchise principle.

47. The development of the Progressive Party will be watched with keen interest by the A.N.C. particularly as it will constitute the real parliamentary opposition to the Nationalists and United Party racialist policies. We hope that it will not confine its activities to purely Parliamentary methods of struggle.

48. *THE ECONOMIC SITUATION.* The Nationalist Government is shamelessly devoting millions of pounds on implementing its ideological legislation when the economic condition of the people is deteriorating. Poverty, misery, unemployment, racial strife and friction are matters which the Government cares nothing for. In our report last year we stated that apartheid must necessarily aggravate the economic problems of our country. That has been confirmed by the low standard of living and growing unemployment. These conditions of the people have led to widespread unrest and disturbances throughout the country. Leading industrialists admit that this year was the most difficult one; but also because, as we pointed out last year in our report, because of the effects of recession and

the political uncertainties in our country which have frightened investors, the Government is at pains to convince the world that South Africa was safe for investors.

49. The Nationalists have demonstrated clearly that the purpose of apartheid is the economic strangulation of the African. In the economic and commercial field, as in all other fields, the Nationalists are determined to stop the progress of the Africans. Recently Mr. De Wet Nel has made it clear that African traders are going to be removed from their places of business because they constitute a threat to white businessmen.

50. *INCREASED TAXATION*. Despite the low wages paid to Africans against which we have protested from time to time the Government has since the beginning of the year increased taxation for African men and extended it to African women with effect from 1960. This will add considerably to the economic plight of the African people.

51. *THE GROWING UNITY AND RESISTANCE OF THE PEOPLE*. As a reaction to the violent onslaughts of the Nationalists upon the rights of the people there has been a growing determination amongst the people of South Africa, black and white, from within and outside the Congress Alliance to unite and resist the attacks of the Nationalists. The idea of a broad anti-Nationalist alliance of the organizations opposed to the Nationalists is becoming popular. It is such an alliance capable of using parliamentary and extra-parliamentary methods that can ultimately defeat the Nationalist Party.

52. During the year 14 organisations, including the Black Sash, Liberal Party, Labour Party and Congresses met under the Chairmanship of the Right Rev. Bishop Reeves of Johannesburg to discuss matters of common concern to fight against Nationalist tyranny. We wish to congratulate these organisations on their role in exposing the wickedness of Nationalist rule.

53. *THE ANTI-PASS STRUGGLE*. The Anti-Pass Council and Economic Boycott Committees were appointed in terms of Conference Resolutions.

54. The Council examined this resolution and noted that it declares that the struggle against the pass system is in fact a struggle against the very roots of the entire system of cheap labour, exploitation and oppression of the African people, against which there can be no short cut to victory. The proposals of the council were therefore based upon this fundamental fact. The Council made the following points inter alia:

(a) Some people thought that the only way of fighting against the pass laws is by destroying the passes. This in the view of the Planning

Council is not the only way of struggling against the pass system nor is it necessarily the most effective way.

(b) In the history of our struggle against the passes there are instances when the resentment of the Africans against the passes has been so high that they discarded them or burnt them, but sooner or later the passes have been re-imposed and disillusionment followed.

(c) It is not the document itself towards which we must exclusively direct our attention and devise a form of struggle but the role of the document in the whole structure of our country. In order to end the pass laws which are the root of our oppression we require, COURAGE, ENDURANCE AND DETERMINATION AND THE skilful use of the power is AVAILABLE TO US TO DEFEAT THE GOVERNMENT.

(d) The economic boycott in South Africa has unlimited potentialities. When our local purchasing power is combined with that of sympathetic organizations overseas we wield a devastating weapon.

55. In view of the Council the economic boycott weapon can be used effectively in our struggle against the pass laws. The boycott has the additional merit that it is not a defensive weapon. We are on the offensive and we are fighting on a battlefield chosen by ourselves, based on our own strength.

56. *RECOMMENDATIONS*. On the recommendation of the Council, the N.E.C. decided that the economic boycott of products of Nationalist-controlled institutions should be embarked upon as from 26th June, 1959.

57. *JUNE 26TH*. Apart from launching the economic boycott, the Council recommended that June 26th should be observed as a day of self-denial by the oppressed people and freedom fighters. This meant that in various areas Africans had to decide what form this self-denial would take. The following forms were suggested:

(a) No buying of any sort should take place on that day.

(b) Nobody should go to any place of entertainment, e.g. cinemas, and beer-halls.

The merit of such forms of self-denial were to test the DISCIPLINE, ENDURANCE AND DETERMINATION OF THE PEOPLE.

This plan was implemented with great success and drew in thousands of people throughout the country in rural and urban areas.

58. *ECONOMIC BOYCOTT*. The launching of a nation-wide economic boycott on the 26th June marked an important step in the use of this method of action. The international response was beyond all expectations.

59. The May Conference decided to use a potato boycott for a limited period as a demonstration and protest against the Transvaal potato farmers whose treatment of the African workers as revealed by a number of court cases shocked the world. The success of the boycott revealed the great power of this weapon. It was a resounding success to an extent that it was a difficult task to convince the people about the desirability of switching off from the potato boycott to the boycott of the Nationalist products. Clearly the calling off was unpopular and could not be understood by some of our members and the public. On the other hand, the N.E.C. was obliged to carry out what was decided by the special Conference as a boycott for a limited period and for a specific purpose. It was unwise to keep on postponing dates. A decision had to be taken in one way or another although the methods of calling off may not have been of the very best.

60. *THE BOYCOTT OF NATIONALIST PRODUCTS.* The Nationalists have been selected because they are the spearhead of oppression and exploitation, and they are a Government which is the most vicious in the history of our country. It is important to select your enemy and to deal him a telling blow.

61. It is important to understand that the economic boycott weapon will not be directed against the Nationalists only. It will be used at appropriate times against any institution which infringes upon the rights of the people.

62. The Economic Boycott Committee adopted a method of selecting articles such as cigarettes, coffee, tea, and fish. It was necessary to do this in order to avoid confusion and to intensify the campaign step by step. We have definitely not done sufficient to intensify the economic boycott. Wrong methods have been adopted by branches in prosecuting the economic boycott. It must be realised that our object is to avoid short-cuts in our campaign. It is not sufficient to go to shopkeepers and ask them not to stock the boycotted goods. We must persuade the consumers not to buy the goods by conducting house to house campaigns. It is essential that we should do this immediately.

63. *THE SECOND PHASE: The Anti-Pass Campaign 26th June, 1959–June, 1960.*
    Like the first phase of our campaign the second phase lays down that emphasis must be placed on efficiency, good organisation and painstaking attention to the immediate problems of the people, influx control, pass and beer raids, high rents, low wages and land and cattle restrictions. The key-note is once again UNITY of all sections of the population in a joint struggle to speak out their grievances.

64. Each province must immediately undertake the calling of "All-in Conferences" comprising the widest sections of people in every one of its regions, where pressing problems can be dealt with and actions taken. Conferences dealing with, for example, the rent question, beer and pass raids, must elect deputations to municipalities and Native Commissioners to put forward demands on behalf of the people. Arising out of these Conferences a multiplicity of deputations should follow, each deputation representing the interests of the people of various regions.

65. In the second phase, the problems of the people in the rural areas should be given special consideration. Each Region where issues such as Bantustan, cattle and land restrictions, wages and other problems, concerning those diverse strata will be taken up.

66. In order to hold successful rural people's conferences, each region should hold discussion with Congress members who are familiar with different rural areas to plan the regional conferences.

67. The next step in this phase is to spotlight December 10th, the international Day of Conscience when anti-segregationists and defenders of human rights the world over express their support for multi-racial democracy in South Africa.

68. Congress has a vital part to play in making this day of observance a great success. Each Congress must undertake to explain the meaning of this day to the section of the population it represents.

69. Each province should start now in planning a combined demonstration with as many organisations, churches etc., participating. December 10th, the day of Conscience in South Africa, must not only mean for us a successful demonstration, but it must result in an improvement in the relation between anti-Nationalist forces, and an increase in the number of organisations and individuals who support the cause of Human Rights.

70. From here onwards to the Africa Day celebrations, on April 15th, which we should make a historical event, and a demonstration of the massive support of the Congress movement, economic boycott and anti-pass campaign. Each area must organise thousands of supporters to attend public meetings on the day which should serve as a prelude to counter demonstrations during Union Festival Week.

71. Our fourth step is Provincial Workers' Conferences to be held early in 1960. The slogans for these Conferences should be 'delegates from every factory'. These workers' rallies to concentrate on encouraging the formation of Factory Committees and the election of deputations to demand £ 1 a day and recognition of African Unions.

72. From the Regional Conferences we should proceed to great anti-pass demonstrations in May, culminating in Nation-wide demonstrations against the official Union Day celebrations. The official Union Day celebrations shall be marked by counter-demonstrations by all democrats—mass meetings where the evils of the present constitution should be exposed.

73. The Congress Youth should be responsible for seeking the co-operation of all youth, sporting and cultural organisations, to support our counter-demonstrations.

The second phase of the campaign will culminate on June 26th, 1960 with great demonstrations throughout the country.

74. It will be realised from the plan that the main aspects of the programme are large counter-demonstrations against the 50th anniversary of the founding of the Union of South Africa, which legalised in all four provinces the right of Europeans to rule South Africa to the exclusion of non-whites. This plan and the organisational section of this report are the main issues which must receive the undivided attention of all the delegates.

75. The struggles against the passes have been carried out by the oppressed non-Europeans of this country at different times in different ways. We particularly would like to mention the civil disobedience by African women in 1913 and 1918, demonstrations of 1919, 1929 and 1930.

76. After many years of bitter struggle against the pass laws it has become necessary to choose a particular day historically linked with the anti-pass struggle, such day to be known as Anti-pass Day. The 31st March stands out as the most suitable date to commemmorate the anti-pass struggle for it was on that date in 1919 that the A.N.C. made a serious attempt to stage a systematic demonstration when thousands of passes were collected in Johannesburg and taken to the pass office.

77. *THE STRUGGLE OF THE PEOPLE IN NATAL.* There have been wide-spread people's demonstrations in Natal during the month of June and thereafter, in no less than 24 areas. The demonstrations have been largely by women and have led to a tremendous upsurge of political consciousness among the people of Natal. About 2,000 women have been arrested. In different areas the demonstrations took different forms, viz. protests to Bantu Commissioners and other authorities, meetings, dipping tank incidents, boycott of buses, picketing of beer-halls and driving men out of them, picketing potato sellers.

78. *WHAT ARE THE PEOPLE'S GRIEVANCES?* The issues which have been raised by the people have been: wages—the demand for £1 a day, and high cost of living, influx control, measures relating to the

betterment schemes and forced and free labour for Government schemes e.g. dipping, freedom to brew beer, removal either in urban or in rural areas, police raids and show of strength. It should be noted that except in the case of Durban and despite what Dr. Eiselen said there have been no clear formula of demands by the people. By and large the demonstrations in the cities have appeared to be directed against the beer-halls linked with an adequate wage and the demand for home-brewing.

79. Dr. Eiselen was sent down to "inquire on the spot". His conclusion was that the A.N.C. was directly responsible. He threatened communal punishment for these communities where property had been destroyed. In addition they would be compelled to disclose the so-called agitators. These disgusting proposals reveal the ruthlessness with which the Government wishes to suppress all protests. So far the actions of the police have been unable to stop the demonstrations.

Durban is the industrial heart of Natal. Around it, and much more closer than in the case of many other industrial centres are not only the urban locations, but also the reserves, from which Durban draws its labour force. The proximity of the reserves and migratory labour creates a much more closer link between urban and country.

80. Every week-end hundreds of workers go to the reserves. Whatever happens in Durban is transmitted more quickly to the reserves than in many other centres.

The lower wage structure in Durban has made the chronic crisis affect the people both in Durban and in surrounding reserves much more than in other areas.

The slower growth of industrial developments in the Durban-Pinetown area, the proximity of the reserves has produced acute unemployment problems, and it has made the hardships of influx control a more burning question.

81. Thus the poverty of the people in a period of economic crisis has driven the people to desperation and created a definite attitude.

82. *COMMENT*.

(a) Given a correct lead and more vigorous organisational activity even greater successes can be attained. It must be admitted, however, that a great deal of work had to be done in educating the people as to planned, disciplined activity.

(b) Nobody doubts that the activity of the people has in many areas been spontaneous. This is not something to be regretted. It should be looked upon as a challenge to the political movement to bring organisation to the people's struggle.

(c) Political struggles do not take place in the atmosphere of a carefully conducted experiment in a laboratory. They are very often untidy, tempestuous and destructive.

(d) Therefore the job of the organised political movement like Congress is to see the positive aspects of the people's upsurge to direct the struggle along the lines which will lead to greater strength and understanding and to prevent actions which are beyond the present stage. An All-in Conference was organised by Natal with great success.

83. *CHIEF LUTHULI AND THE GROWTH OF A MASS MOVE-MENT IN DURBAN.* The growth of Chief Luthuli's popularity throughout the country and the growth of a mass organisation in Durban have contributed towards sparking off the demonstrations. There is sufficient evidence that masses of people have come to identify Congress with resistance to persecution, and genuinely believe that what they do is consistent with both the spirit of the A.N.C. and its practice.

84. These then are the factors which may be summarised as the deteriorating conditions of the people and the growth of the organisation in Natal.

85. *TRADE UNIONS.* We congratulate SACTU for being accepted by the International Labour Organisation as the representatives of South African workers. The Union Government is now compelled to consult with SACTU whenever the question of sending a delegate arises. We are also pleased to note growing interest in the Non-European field of trade unions. SACTU's activities have inspired us. The response of Congress members has at last become significant. We particularly wish to mention Natal in this regard.

86. It is regrettable that A.N.C. members and branches have not realised the importance of working in trade unions. We have not paid sufficient attention to S.A.C.T.U.'s plan for the organisation of factory committees, nor to lectures which were circulated to the branches last year on Trade Unionism. It is only by studying these lectures that we can clearly understand the relations between the A.N.C. and Trade Unions.

87. One of the most important features in the development of organised workers in recent years is that various organisations and leading personalities among Europeans have not only taken interest but have also taken positive action.

88. *T.U.C., I.C.F.T.U. AND F.O.F.A.T.U.S.A.* It is to be regretted that at a time when progressive forces in the country are working for stronger organisation of African Trade Unions and for their improved

working conditions, there should emerge a splinter federation whose effect will be disunity of the people's movement versus the Nationalists and other reactionaries.

89. *MASS TRIALS*. The feature of mass trials is still our lot. Since October last year no less than 4,000 people have been arrested and convicted for political activities, to various terms of imprisonment including death.

90. Some of these cases are still coming before the Appeal Courts. Others have paid their fines and some are serving. The large number are those women who have been arrested for Anti-Pass demonstrations in the Transvaal and the women of Natal for influx control, dipping, higher wages, Bantu Authorities and against beer halls.

91. *SEKHUKHUNILAND*. Out of 306 people who have been arrested in Sekhukhuniland, 22 were sentenced to death, 4 have won their appeal. Among those facing the death sentence are 2 women.

92. *INCITEMENT TRIALS*. Other appeals coming before the Supreme Court are the incitement cases which arose out of the "Stay-at-home", April, 1958. The decision of the appeal Court will be of interest to the whole movement.

93. *TREASON TRIAL*. The Treason Trial continues. Here again we must make it absolutely clear as we have done before that the importance of this trial is that it is a trial of the entire liberatory movement. It is therefore dangerous to treat this case lightly because its outcome can have far-reaching effects in the whole struggle for equality and against racial domination. It is fortunate that we have the best defence in the land, yet our contribution towards the defence leaves much to be desired. Once more we wish to express our thanks to the Treason Trial Defense Fund Committee under the leadership of Bishop Reeves, and through this committee we wish to thank those committees which have consistently and tirelessly collected money in many parts of the world.

94. *BANS AND BANISHMENTS*. The Government's answer to the people's demands for rights is deporting and exiling their leaders. In addition to the scores of the people who have already been banished, the following were exiled during the year:

Messrs: Morolong, Baartman and Mrs. E. Mafeking from the Western Cape, Mr. C. Mnyandi from Durban and a number of people's leaders from Mabieskraal.

95. During the year a committee was established to attend to welfare of the banished. We are happy to report that great progress has been made by the committee.

96. The campaign against these bans and deportations has not been a success. It is probably due to the fact that people are beginning to accept these bans as mere routine. We would like to warn that these bans and deportations are endangering the existence of our organisation and must never be allowed to continue unchallenged.

96. [*sic*] *BANTU EDUCATION*. Our policy on Bantu Education as stated in our last Conference is further re-iterated, viz: that the boycott by withdrawal of children from Bantu Education schools is at present terminated but that the boycott of school boards and committees should be intensified. It has become clear from the workings of Bantu Education that these school committees have nothing to do with the transfer of control of education to African parents as is the case with the other communities. The functions of the school board and committees are merely that of acting as agents for Bantu Administration Department over the teacher and collecting money for the government. Once more we call upon the parents to withdraw from the schoolboard committee because there is not even an indirect benefit which the Africans derive from this existence. Another aspect of the Bantu Education Campaign decided last year was to re-organise the cultural clubs jointly with the A.E.M. and that the clubs should also cater for children who are attending Bantu Education schools. This has not been done.

97. *HIGHER EDUCATION ALSO TRANSFERRED TO B.A.D*. Another great setback in the sphere of African Education has been the passing of a law to enable the government to close mixed universities to Non-Europeans and to bury Fort Hare as a centre of high learning for Non-Europeans and to establish in its stead 'tribal' colleges.

98. For many years Fort Hare has been an inspiration to thousands of our youth. It has produced hundreds of our distinguished men of letters and science, the pride of the African nation in matters of high learning.

99. It is proper and fitting at this stage to congratulate the courageous stand taken by a large number of university professors, black and white, including the National Speaker of the African National Congress, Prof. Matthews, vice principal of Fort Hare. Men who would rather lose thousands of pounds and life-long careers than to serve under the dictatorship of the Nationalist arrogant politicians. We also congratulate our boys and girls who have demonstrated in no unmistaken terms their hatred of a system and their solidarity with those university leaders who took a firm stand.

100. It is regrettable, however, that we have to inform the Conference that during the year under review one resolution which has not been implemented by Congress organs was on Bantu Education. Even our Youth League, which has been charged from time to time with the main

task of combating the ill-effects of Bantu Education and promoting cultural activities among our youth, has been unable to do anything in this field. This Conference must devise means to remedy this situation.

101. *PROBLEMS OF ORGANISATION*. The subjects of organisation and allied problems have now become hardy annuals. All our Annual National Conferences since 1956 were called upon to debate them and to adopt some appropriate decisions. We are always harping at the same old theme. That this is so and that it should be so is quite understandable. It is an admission that conditions under which we live require organisation, and because there is real need for an efficient and influential organisation to direct the every day affairs and activities of our people. There can be no doubt or argument that at this critical period in our history when we are being ruthlessly uprooted, scattered about and gagged we really need such an organisation.

102. As a people's organisation our tasks are many and responsibilities are great. As stated elsewhere in this report, the Government is mercilessly harassing and playing havoc with our people. Yet while doing this the Government is at the same time doing its damndest to prevent the African people from raising their voices in a mighty protest against these injustices. As it is, Congress' very legal existence is threatened. Not only has the Government banned practically every senior leader of our organisation, banned our organisation in some parts of the country, prohibited in almost all proclaimed areas all public gatherings of a political nature, but it is also constantly making statements threatening to ban the whole organisation.

103. By "an Efficient and influential organisation" we do not only mean the recruitment of large numbers of people and their grouping into branches and committees, and calling them from time to time to take part in one or the other of our campaigns. We mean that in addition to those important and essential duties and functions all units and members, branches, branch committees, regional committees, provincial executive committees and individual members should be united in aim and purpose and should be fired with an indomitable spirit of determination to attain their objective. A sense of political awareness must permeate the whole membership, and the respective committees should plan the work properly, set targets and methodically supervise the general activities.

104. All secretaries, whether branch, regional or provincial must clearly understand that they are the trustees and lifeblood of the organisation and that as such great responsibilities rest on their shoulders. They must realise that the work of the organisation can be seriously interrupted by their not attending promptly to their duties, passing on directives or information received, supplying information required by higher organs or replying to correspondence. But members of committees, as co-trustees, are equally responsible for what happens in an area under their charge.

105. It is quite obvious from the foregoing that the Congress needs to be elevated to a high political, psychological and organisational plane. It has to be placed on a high degree of political alertness, discipline and organisational preparedness. And co-ordination between it and its auxiliary bodies must be improved and strengthened. It is also imperative that the Congress should have sufficient funds to enable it to carry out its political work efficiently and effectively. The creation of these desirable conditions is an urgent task facing every honest and sincere Congressman.

106. *RECRUITMENT OF NEW MEMBERS.* In order to be able to appreciate and properly tackle problems facing us, let us see what we said about them before and what we have achieved so far. The following resolution was passed at our 46th Annual National Conference held in Durban in December, 1958.

"This Conference having received and examined the political situation in the country, is convinced that the primary task of our organisation is to mobilise and rally the African people throughout the country, around the A.N.C. and build a powerful and efficient organisation capable of surviving any attack made upon it and lead the masses of the people in effective opposition to the Nationalist Government."

"Conference therefore directs all organs and members of the A.N.C. to commence with the efficiency campaign as outlined in the Executive Report forthwith."

"Conference further calls upon the Provinces, Regions and branches to fulfill the following membership target for the year 1959 by June 26th."

Cape	50,000
Transvaal	50,000
Natal	15,000
O.F.S.	5,000

107. We are convinced that a substantial increase in membership has been achieved by certain Provinces and Regions. With the exception of Natal, the main targets still remain as a challenge to all other organs of the A.N.C. One often hears accusations, by those who have failed to do their work, that "the National Executive does not do its work." The task of enrolling members into Congress is a job which has to be done locally. It is the responsibility of the Provincial, Regional and Branch Committees and their members.

108. Dark clouds are threatening our organisation. To avert these it is important and essential that we should enroll more new members so that

the Congress should enjoy mass support which is necessary for its defence against the onslaught of the reactionary Nationalist regime. Members must understand that the continued legal existence of the A.N.C. will largely depend on its own power, efficiency, discipline, ability and will to survive.

109. *NEED FOR POLITICAL EDUCATION.* The organisation will be strong when its members are enlightened on its policy and when they are sufficiently clear and convinced about the correctness of its aims and objects. To bring this about is one of our main tasks at present. We must have many members who are potential leaders, who can easily lead the struggle when the entire leadership is not there. It is therefore suggested that serious considerations be given to these proposals:—

(a) that as many members as possible be given political education and taught problems of organisation and administration. Lectures on administration are already available.

(b) that educational sub-committees be appointed in each Province to implement and supervise this decision, under the auspices of the National Propaganda Committee.

(c) that the National Executive Committee should prepare and supply the syllabus.

110. *NATAL PROVINCE.* Compared with previous years the Province has considerably improved its organisational machinery. There has been a great political upsurge and a rise of political consciousness among the African people in the Province, and an unprecedented influx of new members into the Congress and in trade unions. This has created new problems for our people there, problems of re-adjusting, absorbing and stabilising. Unless they are correctly tackled and solved these issues can be very harmful politically. We are confident that our Natal Provincial leadership will handle the situation properly and efficiently.

The province is divided into three main regions:—

(i) Durban region.
(ii) Northern region.
(iii) Midlands region.
(iv) Southern region.

There are also endeavours to bring about the whole of the rural areas under the orbit of the A.N.C. On this there is fertile ground for organisation because of the Bantu Authorities. Natal has not yet made a start in implementing the M. Plan.

111. *ORANGE FREE STATE.* Very little organisation and political work is being done in the O.F.S. The Province badly needs brave and public spirited political workers and organisers as well as propaganda material.

112. *TRANSVAAL PROVINCE*. In pursuance of the organisational plan the province has been divided into the following eleven regions.

1. Central and Western Region.
2. South Western Region.
3. West Rand.
4. Western Transvaal.
5. Eastern Transvaal.
6. East Rand.
7. Southern Transvaal.
8. South Eastern Transvaal.
9. Alexandra region.
10. Pretoria Region.
11. The Great North region.

113. It is, however, to be regretted that no proper organisational machinery has been set up in most of the areas through lack of properly trained personnel. Even in areas where there is a sufficient man-power our machinery has not yet been perfected through failure by our branches to implement the M. Plan whose importance cannot be over-emphasised.

114. We have every hope that efforts will be made to correct these organisational faults. Through the piece-meal ban imposed in certain rural areas, Congress has been deprived in the Transvaal of no less than 40 branches with an estimated membership of 6,000.

115. *CAPE PROVINCE*. To improve the organisational machinery an inspection Plan has been formulated and the whole Province has been divided into regions with a regional Inspectorate of three, under the Chairmanship of a Provincial Executive member.

This inspectorate plan has been set up on a zonal basis as follows:—

1. Western Cape.
2. Eastern Cape, including Midlands, Albany and East London.
3. Border: Stutterheim, Cathcart and Queenstown.
4. Transkei and Ciskei.
5. Kimberley district which has very little contact with the whole of the Cape.

116. This Province is implementing the M. Plan especially in the Eastern Cape.

117. To facilitate administration it is suggested that a Commission be appointed to examine the present provincial boundaries with a view to making recommendations for the definition of new boundaries to improve our organisation and administration.

118. *FUNDS*. Money is the lifeblood of all modern institutions, business undertakings and political organisations. Our organisation is no exception to this rule. It also needs money in order to function properly, and money has to be raised for the Congress. Without money for stamps, papers, printing, fares, telephones, rent, wages, etc., decisions of our Conference will be useless. It does no credit to delegates of Conference to ignore this very important question. Our responsibility will be shown by our attitude to this vital and fundamental issue.

119. Conference must devise ways and means of ensuring a steady flow of funds into the coffers of the Congress. The National Executive Committee must be provided with adequate funds. We must express our sincere thanks to some of our very good friends for the financial assistance they have given us during the year. It is not necessary nor is it advisable to mention their names here, yet without their contribution our task would be more difficult.

WHY FUNDS? Our organisation has now assumed a new character, that of a mass organisation run by part-time officials. This system was in order during the adolescent stage of the A.N.C., but in these troubled times our organisation needs dynamic leadership to cope with new development within the organisation. The next step is to introduce modern organisational methods. This means a movement run by TRAINED, POLITICALLY MATURE, FULL-TIME OFFICIALS who must be paid SALARIES. The idea that a huge organisation like ours, with all the duties and responsibilities that fall to it, can be run on a part-time basis, is ridiculous. The wonder is that so much is in fact done on that basis. But obviously this will never do for the present demands of the Congress organisation.

120. *THE M-PLAN*. This plan was conceived in 1952 immediately after the Defiance Campaign. It is an organisational plan designed to meet the situation of our time. Some of the Provinces have endeavoured to implement it, but others have not. There is no better organisational plan which has been evolved as yet. It is therefore essential that it should be implemented without further delay. During the year your executive issued a directive to the effect that it was compulsory for all Congress branches to implement this plan. Our aim is to get a proper organisational machinery which can withstand and defeat the savage onslaught of the enemy of the Non-Europeans in South Africa.

121. The Government is aware of the power of the A.N.C. and it will not take any of the activities of our organisation lying down. The Government has already demonstrated its hostility against our movement by banning in certain areas and also planting spies in our ranks.

121.[*sic*] *POLICY*. Two main lines of attack have recently been directed against the African National Congress. On the one hand, the Africanists and their supporters attack us for having formed an alliance with the other Congresses, which they say has robbed the A.N.C. of its effectiveness, handed leadership of the organisation over to others, and muffled the A.N.C.'s ability to voice the aspirations of the African people.

122. On the other hand, the A.N.C. is being attacked for being too "narrow", too exclusive in its membership. From several quarters, supposedly sympathetic to our struggle, we are being advised either to dissolve and merge with other organisations on a multi-racial basis, or to open our ranks and merely swallow these others. The existence of separate Congresses for different racial groups, we are told, is a tacit acceptance of racialism, and in conflict with our aim of a common society for all racial groups in a free South Africa.

123. It is necessary once and for all to get the record straight. Neither the A.N.C.—nor for that matter any of the other Congresses—were formed for or exist for the primary purpose of building a "multi-racial" or "non-racial" society. The A.N.C. was formed to unite and voice the views of Africans. That remains its primary purpose. Let those who will, call this "racialism". But most people who look at our achievements honestly and without malice will realise that the building of an all-Union organisation of Africans, built in the teeth of every obstacle that governments could muster against it, and the leading of that organisation to become a mighty power in the land is an achievement from which not only Africans but all democratic South Africans can draw pride and satisfaction.

124. It is true that one of our tasks has always been to fight for the political rights of our people. And in doing so, we have been farsighted enough—or, if you will sufficiently 'non-racial' in outlook—to join hands with other groups representing other oppressed peoples, organised workers and European opponents of the political colour bar, and to find together with them a common political programme. But that does not mean that the A.N.C. intends to abandon its functions as a national organisation of Africans, for those functions cannot be fulfilled by the alliance, nor does it presume to attempt to fulfill them.

125. *OPPRESSION OF A SPECIAL SORT.* Nobody can doubt that, however other groups may be oppressed, Africans are oppressed in a special way, by special laws which affect them in special ways. As a result the immediate grievances, aims and outlook of Africans, their daily needs and aspirations are not identical with those of other racial groups in South Africa, however identical their long-term aim of liberation might be. Is it possible to imagine, then, that Africans will not organise as a separate group with separate group interests as long as their position remains? If, for instance, the A.N.C. opened its doors to become a multi-racial

organisation, an all-in political party with a liberationist programme, would there not immediately be a need felt amongst Africans for a purely African organisation to put forward the views of Africans? Would that need not, in fact, be felt even by those who simultaneously supported the all-in body? And if it were not felt by them, would it not be felt by others? And if it were so, how could we of the Congress Alliance fail to support that organisation, to assist it and recognise it as the distinctive voice and spokesmen of the African people?

126. Let us put it this way. Everyone knows that the Chinese community in South Africa are subject to special discriminatory treatment. They are, in their own special way, an oppressed group. For years, as a community, they have tried to counter discriminatory treatment meted out to them by using the influence of their Consular representatives, by attempting to gain the ear of the authorities, by standing aloof from political action. What does the Congress movement, or any supporter of Congress today, say to the Chinese community? Surely we say to them, "Do not take injustice lying down! Organise as a community, unite as a community and fight for your rights!" Would we not have to give them the same advice whether or not there were a multi-racial organisation which fought generally for democratic rights for everyone? This is the precise point. Even if we "merged" the Congresses into one, we believe that we would be driven, willy-nilly again to build up special organisations of each section of the oppressed people, to unite them as communities, and to voice their special community views. If tomorrow, as a result of any step we take, there were no African National Congress, we would have to set out again, from the beginning, and build one.

127. *WHITE BATTERING RAM.* We know that a considerable part of the pressure for "one Congress" comes from European supporters of the democratic cause. It would be well for them too, to consider their special position in the country and the Congress Alliance. Their organisation, the Congress of Democrats, is not an organisation of an oppressed community, but rather an organisation of non-conformists from the ranks of the oppressor caste. To such people, whose courage in defying the conventional prejudices of white South Africa is for us all a source of pride, there may well appear to be something contradictory in their renunciation of the colour-bar side by side with their membership of separate organisations. But they too only have identical interests with the other members of the Congress Alliance when one speaks of long-term interests—of the common interest of all in liberation. But their immediate interests are surely not identical with ours. Their immediate interest, surely, is two-fold, first, that they act as the battering ram of the liberation

movement to break through the iron-hard cord of European colour prejudice and racialism, and second, that they establish by their deeds the right and justification for White South Africans to become part of the native people of a free South Africa, and not like the British in India or the Dutch in Indonesia—an alien community for whom there is no place in the years after liberation.

128. Even as it might be argued that, for C.O.D. to fill this role adequately, a multi-racial organisation would be the answer. Maybe so. But they do not enter the field of battle alone. Already we others are organised on community lines for the reasons we have stated. White South Africans cannot ignore this fact, or try to override it. They must fight with the weapons that come to hand. And for those who see that the road ahead must be followed alongside the liberation movements of the Non-White people, there is only one way, and that is the Congress way, the way of separate but allied fraternal organisations. No other way now meets the needs of the oppressed Non-White peoples, and because of the special position of the European supporters of liberation, they must admit themselves to these needs and not seek to "reform" the Congress movement to suit their special and unique position.

129. It is unfortunate that in a debate such as this, some people let their tongues run away with them. To suggest, for example, as one contributor does, that the South African Indian Congress, with its magnificent record of struggle in the course of uniting the Indian community, is some sort of "political ghetto" is offensive and ridiculous. To suggest, as does another contributor, that illegalisation of the Congresses is inevitable, is defeatist talk which can do no one any good, least of all the Congresses who have fought successfully over the years not by "organising for outlawed activity" as the correspondent suggests, but by organising against outlawing!

130. *THE HIGH WATER MARK*. But these are small matters. The large matter is this. Everywhere, among the proponents of an all-in multi-racial Congress we hear it said that our present state of existence smacks of "racialism" or gives rise to racial exclusiveness. This is a lie which must be nailed! On this let there be no doubts. The high-water mark of racial fraternity and co-operation in South Africa today is in the Congress Alliance. Let those who speak so glibly of "racialism" participate in the workings of this Alliance. Here they will find such an absence of racial feeling, such complete and easy acceptance of people of other racial groups as equals and as co-fighters as is not to be found anywhere in any South African group.

488

131. This is the plain fact. The Congress Alliance, formed of separate organisations, has raised a whole generation of South Africans of all races and colours in a new mould—in the mould of equality and brotherhood, in the mould which alone of all South African patterns can claim, 'Here there is no racialism.'

132. Let those whose theories about Congress lead them to conclude that we are fostering or pandering to racialism think deeply on this fact. There is something wrong with a theory that leads to a conclusion which is the exact reverse of truth and of reality. We know that most of those who so theorise are sincere and well-meaning supporters of our cause. It is therefore appropriate that they should seriously and soberly reconsider the theories which lead them so wide off the mark. If they do so, we have no doubt that they will come to accept as we of the Congresses accept today, that our course is vindicated not alone by theory but more—by practice. We feel sure that they will come to understand that the Congress movement stands where it does today because its organisational structure has fitted exactly the requirements of the special South African conditions in which we work. And they will come to understand too, that it is only in this way that we will finally, together, build the free South Africa, and so liberate us all from the shackles of oppression and from the pattern of separate organisation which oppression imposes upon us.

133. *PAN AFRICANIST CONGRESS.* A new organisation was established this year which styles itself the Pan Africanist Congress. The Africanists have shrouded their policy in obscure phrases, but they have made one thing clear, that they are opposed to the policy of the A.N.C.

134. The establishment of the organisation is a direct result of their disagreement with the policy of the A.N.C. in the main respects. Firstly, the adoption of the Freedom Charter which states that South Africa belongs to all who live in it and that all national groups shall have equal rights, secondly, the policy of the A.N.C. which accepts co-operation with other racial groups in the country.

The Africanists have deliberately omitted the formulations of a militant programme against Baasskap because their primary objective is not a struggle against the Government, but to sow confusion amongst the Africans in an attempt to weaken and undermine the African National Congress. They openly state that they will take no part in campaigns such as the anti-pass campaigns, because they claim to be fighting for a complete change of the political system, as if that does not demand taking up issues which vitally affect the masses of the African people whom they claim to be representing.

135. The only reason for this is to avoid any militant struggle. In this way they will remain a small group whose danger lies only in confusing the people and undermining the A.N.C. and may be used by reactionary forces opposed to the liberatory movement. The A.N.C. itself will be more united and stronger without them and will continue to be the true mouthpiece of the oppressed people of South Africa.

136. *DISCIPLINE, CLIQUES AND FACTIONS.* Our last Annual Conference took important steps in consolidating the Unity of our members and the various organs of the A.N.C. This is an essential pre-requisite for the success of any campaign and our struggle against the Nationalists.

137. The Africanists who were a source of nuisance and discord in our organisation have been routed and exposed, but there is no cause for complacency. It would be a mistake to dismiss the activities of the Africanists both inside and outside our organisation with contempt. On the other hand, whilst continuing to expose the Africanists in our midst and to the masses of our people, we should not commit the error of diverting our energies from the real and important enemies of the people, the Nationalists.

138. Not only do the Africanists threaten to corrode our unity but there is amongst us a tendency which, unless curbed and corrected, might hamper our organisation and weaken our campaigns. It should be said at once that at the present moment the tendency which is referred to exists amongst some loyal Congress men and women.

140.[*sic*] This tendency is that of creating cliques and factions. How does this tendency manifest itself? It manifests itself in meetings and discussions by the refusal of some people to discuss any matter objectively and rather to side and support friends or associates irrespective of the correctness of the view taken by those friends.

141. This clearly is a loyalty to individuals and groups rather than to the organisation. Cliquism also manifests itself by a tendency to oppose proposals made not on the merits but because they are made by a particular person. This loyalty to groups rather than to the organisation is the cause of unnecessary disputes and dissensions which sap the energies of our organisation. It has the effect of diverting the attention to an internal struggle within our organisation instead of unifying ourselves for the struggle against the Nationalists.

142. Cliquism also manifests itself by a tendency to recruit members into the organisation not primarily to support the policy of the organisation but to support certain individuals.

143. If we are to strengthen the organisation to face the vicious assaults by the Nationalists, then we must eliminate and rectify these tendencies. The problem is particularly urgent in our present circumstances.

144. It is the task of every member of Congress to make sure that he does not belong to a clique. It is also our task to try and assist those who manifest these tendencies by persuasion, discussion and political education that such tendencies weaken the organisation and endanger our cause. There must be a halt to this state of affairs. We cannot afford disputes and secret unofficial committees. If persuasion and discussion fail, disciplinary action should be adopted. However, although it is proper by discussion to expose these tendencies, it is equally dangerous to divert our attention from the main programme of our organisation and to concentrate on a campaign against cliques.

145. Our energies must always be directed to the fulfilment of our programme. Our task is to build unity. Our task is to strengthen our organisation and inspire the masses of the people. Our task is to sharpen the struggle against the passes.

146. Another tendency which is harmful to our organisation is that of attempting to undermine the authority of higher organs by conducting campaigns against members belonging to a particular committee or the committee as such. We should realise that by attempting to discredit higher committees or persons in higher committees the effect is to undermine the authority and effectiveness of the organisation. The proper place to take the National Executive to task is at the National Conference. The tendency of some members of imputing motives to directives coming from the National Executive or provincial executive and branch executive is harmful and must be stopped. Under these extraordinary and abnormal conditions it is the duty of every member to follow and carry out instructions implicitly. Congress demands it.

147. *PROPAGANDA.* Our propaganda machinery improved considerably during the last twelve months. We did not only issue pamphlets and statements on the various issues affecting our people, but a very important step was taken by the Congress when it published a printed newspaper for the first time since the *Abantu-Batho*, the A.N.C. newspaper ceased publication about 30 years ago. [*A.N.C. Bulletin*, a four-page paper printed in English, Sesutu, and Zulu and selling for four pence, appeared at an ANC conference in Johannesburg in May 1959. Robert Resha edited the first issue. *Contact*, June 27, 1959.]

148. The absence of a newspaper has always seriously hampered our propaganda work. It is absolutely essential that an organisation of our size should have its own newspaper to keep contact with the masses of the people and to mould their ideas.

141.[sic] The continuation of this important media of education and propaganda depends on how enthusiastically it is ordered, sold, read and discussed by members of Congress. Every member of Congress should become an agent of the bulletin and must report the money of the sales faithfully. It would be tragic and indeed treacherous if we should cease publishing merely because Congress members do not carry out their duties.

142. We should also welcome the independent printed newspaper "ISIZWE" which is published in Xhosa. The remarks above apply to it too.

143. *THE PROVINCIAL REPORTS AND AUXILIARY BODIES.* The picture in regard to the organisational position of the provinces has been drawn from the reports of the National Organising Secretary, Mr. T. Nkobi. During the year he visited all the provinces but could not cover every region and all the branches. The provinces have been unable to furnish the Head Office with regular monthly reports in regard to their political and organisational activities.

This also applies to both Women and Youth Leagues. This issue must be settled once and for all at this Conference by a clear and unambiguous resolution.

144. All the provinces, with the exception of the O.F.S., have been very active, particularly Natal, which became the centre of our political activities and increased its membership by more than ten times. Tickets sent to Natal and reported to have been used exceed the quota of Natal by several thousands.

145. The Transvaal improved its position in regard to membership but fell much below its quota. Its political activities in the urban areas have been improved, but declined in the rural areas largely due to the banning of the organisation and other factors too. The Cape Province has improved and in fact leads other provinces in regard to its organisational machinery and has also increased its activities in the rural areas. No improvement in regard to membership and political activities in the urban areas. This province is too wide and far apart. Mafeking, for instance, is more of the Transvaal than the Cape Province. O.F.S. has virtually collapsed as a province politically and organisationally. It does not appear to be logical that our organisational machinery should follow strictly the Governmental demarcations of the provinces.

146. *WOMEN'S LEAGUE.* In the last few years women are in the fore-front of the struggle but their organisational position is not in keeping with the political developments. For the first time, however, their National Conference was of a high standard both in regard to the standard of political discussion and the number of delegates who attended. Women's League

must now pay special attention to the creation of Women's League branches.

147. *YOUTH LEAGUE.* The Youth League has not yet become a mass movement. It has not yet attracted the youth of the country. This is largely due to the fact that its leadership is not organising the youth on the basis of an attractive programme. The Youth League has been directed from time to time to deal with cultural aspects of our life and many other issues which largely affect the life of our youth such as Bantu Education. The Youth League National Conference held during the year under review, though well attended, did not manage to direct its attention objectively to the problems of the Youth. Issues of personal character seem to have dominated the minds of the delegates.

148. *CONCLUSION.*

In conclusion, we have now placed before you, Sons and Daughters of Africa, the situation in our country and the world. We have painted a picture which shows that there are two forces in our country which are irreconcilably opposed to one another. On the one hand, you have the Nationalist party with its most reactionary policies carrying on its apartheid policy with determination. At its head is Dr. H. F. Verwoerd, uncompromising leader of the Nationalists whose policies are hated and condemned by the majority, at home and abroad. On the other hand, you have the African National Congress and other democratic organisations, led by Chief A. J. Luthuli, whose policies and ability to lead are admired by all the progressives at home and abroad. On his side he has the majority of the people and the democratic world. He has courage and conviction; history is on his side and time is in his favour.

149. It is important in concluding this report to re-state some of the important points raised by the report. They are:— Anti-Pass Campaign, Economic boycott, Bantustan, the Union celebration and counterdemonstration, political and organisational problems of the A.N.C. From this Conference it is expected that wise decisions will be clearly stated in the form of resolutions to meet the challenge of the Nationalists, to remedy our political weaknesses, to improve our style of work and organisational problems.

150. Sons and Daughters of Africa, let us take confidence from the events in the world, in Africa and in our own country which irrefutably confirm that our cause must triumph.

MAYIBUYE I-AFRIKA!

D. NOKWE
Secretary-General

THE ALL AFRICAN CONVENTION

Document 34. Presidential Address by W. M. Tsotsi, AAC, December 14–16, 1958 [Extracts]

It is once more my pleasant duty to address the delegates and visitors to the Annual Conference of the All African Convention, 1958. When at our last Conference in December, 1956, I suggested that we might not be able to meet in a conference again, some people might have thought that I was a pessimist. The failure of the All African Convention to hold its Annual Conference last year, owing to Herrenvolk interference, must indicate to us that we shall not always be able to meet as we like. There is no reason to hope that the virtual ban on meetings imposed by the ruling class on the majority section of the population in the rural areas, will not eventually be extended to the organisation which is representative of that section. The awareness of this fact must surely impress on us the urgent necessity of using the vital opportunity afforded us by this Conference as profitably as we can, bearing in mind that we might be prohibited from meeting in future. We must never forget that the whole African, indeed the whole Non-European population of this country looks to this Conference of the A.A.C. for leadership and guidance in the period of crisis immediately ahead of us. I would appeal to all of the delegates here to conduct themselves in the deliberations at this Conference with the grave seriousness and restraint consistent with the dignified status of the All African Convention.

The two years which have passed since our last Conference have seen the rapid implementation of the recommendations of the Tomlinson Report, that blue-print for the preservation of the so-called "Christian Capitalist Civilization" for the Herrenvolk, and the prevention of the development and extension of a free modern capitalist economy among the Non-Europeans by placing them in a Procrustean bed of tribal backwardness. In order to fill up the yawning gap which is thus being created in the country's economy, the ruling class has embarked on a form of state Capitalism for Non-Europeans only. With brutal callousness and deception the rulers give as a practical justification of their policy the reason that the Europeans will not willingly concede the political rights which an educationally and economically advancing Non-European population would rightfully demand, with consequent danger of conflicts between the two groups.

The Herrenvolk states that the poverty of the African people, the irregularity of their employment, their lack of technical knowledge, capital, organizing skill and initiative in business are "Attributable to their cultural background and are susceptible to change", but instead of encouraging this change the ruling class seeks to entrench the very tribal culture background on which it blames the backwardness of the people. Instead the Government through the South African Native Trust is by far the largest owner of Non-European occupied land; through its labour bureaux the largest recruiter and controller of Non-European labour and one of its largest employers. Very soon, through its projected Development Corporation, the Government will be the largest financier of African enterprises. This Development Corporation will be a huge concern "for promoting capital formation through commercial institutions." It will establish a "Bantu Commercial Bank," a "Bantu Savings and Credit Bank", a "Bantu Insurance Company", a "Bantu Building Society", etc. All this under the shameful pretence of a new economic trusteeship which asserts that "the Bantu must be guided to construct their own economy in their own soil, in their own milieu and out of their own spirit and energy and to move forward along the path of their own civilization according to the tempo of their own ability to develop."

The *deus ex machina* which has been set up to convert the African section of the Non-Europeans into a valuable asset in the Verwoerd & Co. Development Corporation (Pty) Ltd. is the Bantu Authorities. It will be one of the functions of these Authorities to crush the rising African professional and business class which demands a share in the economic power based on capitalist democratic rights, and to create a new African intellectual and business man who will submit to "traditional Bantu Principles" in all his professional and commercial dealings. In other words a Quisling type of African teacher and trader will be mass-produced through the Bantuised Schools which will be strictly controlled by the Government through its Native Commissioners, policemen, intellectuals, policemen-chiefs and Headmen etc. The stage has been set for a vital clash between a Herrenvolk-tribalist bureaucracy, on the one hand, and representatives and organisations of the people, on the other. We will see presently that while the bureaucracy is rapidly consolidating its forces and has even fired the first shots, the people's organisations are wavering and even breaking into pieces. The ruling class relies on its economic development programme, which holds out attractive plums to the quisling type of intellectuals and aspiring bourgeoisie, to entrench disunity in the liberatory movement and so weaken the demand for full equality. Those so-called progressives who stress the fight for economic welfare of the non-whites at the expense [of] the fight for the franchise are playing right into the hands of the Herrenvolk-tribal bureaucracy. . . .

We must realise that all the landlessness, poverty and homelessness of the African people, which I have described above, has been possible because of the exclusion of the Non-Europeans from the Government of the country. Because of their lack of political rights, because of their non-citizen status, the majority section of the population has been outlawed and foredoomed to a life of perpetual servitude. It is for this reason that the fight for full equality occupies the central position in the 10-Point Programme of the N.E.U.M. . . .

This warning apparently fell on deaf ears and the present unpleasant, unhealthy situation of division and strife within our organisations has developed. The position cannot be allowed to continue as at present and a quick solution has to be found if the health of our organisations is to be restored. As it will be the duty of this Conference to contribute to the resolution of our present difficulties, I have deemed it wise to give a broad analysis of the political differences as I see them.

First of all, I wish to state that the division has arisen as the result of the fact that certain individuals and groups within the movement are dissatisfied with the 10-Point Programme of the N.E.U.M. They consider that this programme is very inadequate for the solution of our political and social problems in South Africa. What creates confusion is that these opponents of the 10-Point Programme, instead of condemning the programme outright, pretend that their views are consistent with it. To denounce the 10-Point Programme would put them beyond the pale of the N.E.U.M. and render them without a political home.

The tendency to revise the 10-Point Programme has been called Jaffeism after its chief embodiment [Hosea Jaffe]. Since this term tends to upset certain members of the cult and evokes a defensive emotionalism, which obscures clear thinking, I shall not use it here. Rather will I describe the tendency as revisionism. In order to underline the fundamental implications of this tendency I shall quote extensively from a remarkable pamphlet written by a spiritual member of the group who is an avowed enemy of the N.E.U.M. There is this added advantage in quoting from this publication, namely that it is written under a pen name. The identity of the author is therefore presumably unknown to all of us and there is less danger of the cry of "Informer" being raised by those who are richly endowed with a persecution complex. I refer to the roneoed pamphlet "It is time to Awake!" by R. Mettler, which purports to be criticism of I.B. Tabata's *The Awakening of a People,* a book that is recognised by us in the Unity Movement as correctly setting out our political ideas.

R. Mettler makes no bones about attacking the 10-Point Programme from many angles. Basically his criticism is that *"The existing programme of the N.E.U.M. expresses the aspirations of the African Middle Class."* He criticises the resolution on the programme passed at the 1943 N.E.U.M. Conference to the effect that all our disabilities, economic, educational, social, cultural, flow from the lack of political rights, and that our struggle is therefore chiefly political. R. Mettler asserts that this attempt to separate political subjugation from economic exploitation "runs throughout the documents of this movement and leads eventually to the false positions they take up in all situations. Surely our lack of political rights flows from our separation from the ownership of the means of production," he profoundly concludes. . . .

The whole basis of the attack on the 10-Point Programme is the denial of the reality of colour oppression in South Africa and consequently the denial of the necessity for a National liberatory movement. On the contrary, the National problem is viewed as simply a class problem thinly covered over with a colour wash designed to conceal its identity. The expressed aim of the N.E.U.M. is to liquidate the National oppression of the non-Europeans in South Africa, that is, "the removal of all the disabilities and restrictions based on grounds of race and colour," and the "acquisition by the non-Europeans of all those rights which are at present enjoyed by the European population." . . .

We have to appreciate the danger to the movement of giving the revisionists a free hand to propagate their views from our platforms and our organs. It is not merely a question of creating division and strife within our organisations, bad enough though that is. Much more serious is the betrayal of the organisation to the Herrenvolk fascists. To give the 10-Point Programme a leftist interpretation, no matter how cockeyed, is to bring the whole movement within the definition of statutory communism and to run the risk of it being declared an unlawful organisation within the meaning of the Suppression of Communism Act. It is difficult to resist the inference that this is a consummation which many of the revisionists would devoutly wish as offering an easy method of escape from the hazardous tasks which presently devolve on them as members of the liberatory movement.

The lessons of the Treason Trials do not appear to have been sufficiently learnt by some of us. It is well known in liberatory movement circles that the majority of the persons who are members of the organisations involved in the Treason Trials are simple workers or peasants to whom the idea of mock elections could never have appeared subversive. Yet a few of these people have to stand their trial on a charge of High Treason precisely because a false coloration of leftism was imparted to their organisation by a few politically advanced petit-bourgeois intellectuals. All of us know that the tribalists of the A.N.C. and the merchants of the S.A.I.C. are incapable of demanding the "liquidation of capitalism, equal distribution of wealth, common ownership of the means of production, land, mines and factories," and yet the record would appear to indicate that this was part of the programme of these organisations. This sort of thing inevitably happens when a few so-called "leftist" theoreticians seize control and leadership of the people's organizations and proceed to impose on them ideas which are inconsistent with the aims and objects of the organisations and are in advance of the standard of political consciousness reached by the generality of the membership. The result is that in times of crisis the progressive facade breaks down and the political fraud is exposed. Then begins the splitting up of the organisations into the respective political groupings of its membership from the extreme right to the extreme left.

It was in order to avoid such an eventuality that the N.E.U.M. adopted a minimum programme and a federal structure. . . . The tragedy of the situation is that the internal differences should arise at a time when the need for the unity of the oppressed is greater than ever. At this very moment when the rest of Africa is beginning to awake and to cast away the imperialism and colonialism which has held it in thrall for centuries, when the cry for independence and self-determination is ringing with ever-growing insistence throughout the length and breadth of the "dark continent." At this time, moreover, when in our own country the most down-trodden of all, the African peasants and workers, are beginning to show fight. Just at the moment, I say, when the influence of its leadership should be felt throughout the continent of Africa, the N.E.U.M. must be rent asunder by divisions inspired by a few ambitious people in and around its leadership. This is a situation which we must try to remedy at all costs. If at this conference we cannot achieve a unity of ideas, we must achieve at least a clear demarcation of differences.

Those whose politics consist of stereotyped slogans and clichés will no doubt raise their eyebrows when I say it is our duty to guide and not to condemn categorically the emergent African nationalism. We have to recognise that, in so far as it is genuinely anti-imperialism and anti-colonialism, African nationalism is a progressive political force. . . . we have to implant in the minds of the poor peasants and workers who constitute the majority, the desire for an effective say in the control and direction of the destinies of their countries which can only come about as the result of the extension of full political equality to all. Political history has shown no other method of ending economic exploitation except through political control by the majority section of the population who, in a capitalist society, are inevitably the workers and the poor peasants. Once the importance of political rights has been driven home to the common man, he will take the necessary steps to achieve these rights, and, armed with this new power he will proceed to put an end to exploitive relationships in society.

These are some of the theoretical implications of the 10-Point Programme which this conference has to clarify for the benefit of those members of the movement who are genuinely seeking political enlightment. For those who have deliberately set themselves the task of wrecking the movement from within, more drastic action will have to be considered.

In conclusion let me express the hope that theoretical discussions, important though they are, will not take up too much of the Conference's time. The more vital questions affecting the practical struggles of the people against political emasculation and economic ruin, must take precedence. The large delegation of peasants present at this conference must not be allowed to go away feeling that their attendance has not been worth the trouble and expense which it has entailed. Let us therefore settle down to the business of this conference, namely to build up a movement which will be resilient and powerful enough to withstand and finally overcome Herrenvolk oppression, and so change this beautiful land of ours from a prison camp to a free society where all may live with dignity and justice.

THE FORMATION OF THE PAN AFRICANIST CONGRESS, 1957–1959

Document 35. "Forward to 1958!" Editorial by the Editor, in *The Africanist*, **December 1957**

Within a month's time we shall have passed another milestone on the long and tedious journey to freedom. Others, too, will have passed a milestone. But they will be travelling on the treacherous and slippery road to doom. In both cases there applies the law of inevitability. But the goals are different and so is the spirit of the travellers. The forces of "Tokoloho ka nako ea rona" are marching on, buoyant and confident, not *looking* at their hill, but *climbing* it: On the other hand, the forces of retrogression, stagnation and "man's inhumanity to man" are administering the last desperate kicks of a dying horse. Their doom is sealed; and they [know] it. The dawn of the glory of freedom is breaking, when man shall establish control over *things* and not over other *men*: And we know it. And thus we move into 1958.

The passing year has witnessed historic events, chief among which have been the women's militant struggle against "Passes for Women" and the militant disciplined struggle of our nurses against nursing apartheid. There have been the long-drawn-out Treason Trials and the magnificent June 26th "Stay at Home" observance. There has been the glorious Bus Boycott side by side with the abortive "Economic Boycott of Cigarettes and Tobacco." We have witnessed during 1957 a desire for unity and solidarity among the masses and a tendency towards crippling and contemptuous bureaucracy on the part of our leaders. It is a known fact that the Bus boycott was sabotaged by some unnamed individual "higher-up", acting under certain influences. It is equally well known that quite a number of branches in the Transvaal heard about the planned Economic Boycott after the police and the manufacturers had been informed about it by "New Age" and "The Star" and "Die Transvaler" etc. In fact, 1957 has been a year of

"Directives" and "Counter-Directives" from a variety of sources. But the struggle continues.

It continues, because the African masses today owe loyalty to the movement for liberation, to the concept of a disciplined, principled struggle for freedom, rather than to a particular individual or to a particular organisation. The point we are making is that, if the people today follow the ANC, it is not because of a sentimental attachment to the name or the organisation, but because they believe it to be the embodiment of their aspirations. So long as it gives the correct lead, they will follow it. But the more it deviates, the more it concentrates on opportunistic, vaporous *activity* as distinct from planned, programmatic *ACTION*, the faster the disillusioned masses detach themselves from it and sink into the mire of despair and apathy until a new Moses appears with a gospel ringing the correct chord.

The struggle in South Africa hinges on the twin problems of land and status. And our immediate battle is for *"STATUS,"* political, economic, social etc. And 1958 must be a STATUS YEAR. And having discovered that in liberatory struggles, it is the accumulation of small victories which builds up the confidence of the masses and imbues them with the sense of the inevitability of victory, we propose, for 1958, a campaign against the appelations by which the Herenvolk are pleased to know us. Next year, we are going to put a stop to the terms "Boys" and "Girls", which are so ungrammatically used by white South Africa. As from next year, these terms are going to be used in their strict and correct dictionary meaning. So say we. We will no longer have "Jack", "George", "Nancy", "Jane", etc. as handy labels to be attached to any black man or woman by any white man or white women, white boy or white girl. And we will start where we pay our hard-earned money for service—be it in a private shop or in a government office.

The best would be to start with the shops. We shall here demand that we be treated as customers and ADDRESSED AS SUCH! If the white boys and girls behind the city counters feel that that is too great a demand, they will either leave the shop or we shall make it a shop "FOR EUROPEANS ONLY". In short, we WILL DECLARE A TOTAL BOYCOTT on that shop, and the BOYCOTT will not be lifted UNTIL THAT SHOP CLOSES DOWN! We will stand no nonsense next year. This treatment will be meted out to ANY and EVERY shopkeeper in whose shop or business our people are treated as a nuisance rather than as welcome and desired customers. Whether the shopkeeper be black or white, coloured or Indian or Chinese etc. is immaterial. We demand OUR STATUS as customers.

We shall elaborate on this campaign in subsequent issues of the "AFRICANIST". But right now, we send out to our readers, the Christmas and New Year wishes of "STATUS AND LAND".

There is a song they sing in the deserted villages of Africa. It goes:
Noma sikhona, noma sesifile
Bakusala besho, bethi sasikhona!
(While we live, and even after we are gone,
They will remain saying, WE ONCE WERE!)
That, MA-AFRIKA, is the meaning of our struggle!

MAYIBUYE!!

Document 36. "The Nature of the Struggle Today." Article by Potlako K. Leballo, in *The Africanist*, December 1957

There is as yet no common agreement between the Africanists and the present leadership of Congress together with its allies on the nature of the struggle. To the Africanists the struggle is both nationalist and democratic, in that it involves the restoration of the land to its rightful owners—the Africans—which fact immediately divides the combatants into the conquered and the conqueror, the invaded and the invader, the dispossessed and the dispossessor. That is a national struggle. It has nothing to do with numbers and laws. It is a fact of history. And both sides are each held together by a common history and are, in the struggle, carrying out the task imposed by history. That task is, for the whites, the maintenance and retention of the spoils passed on to them by their forefathers and, for the African, the overthrow of the foreign yoke and the reclamation of "the land of our fathers." At the same time, our struggle is for democracy, if we understand democracy to mean the implementation of the wishes of the majority of the inhabitants of a country, as expressed in the laws of the country. A democratic struggle is essentially then, a recognition of *NUMBERS*, a National struggle is a struggle for the recognition of *heritage*. The Africans are in the fortunate position of being, not only the rightful owners of the land but also the majority of the population. Our struggle, therefore, is democratic, involving as it does, the dispossessed majority against the privileged minority.

The ANC leadership and its allies are preoccupied with the latter aspect of the struggle—the democratic, to the total exclusion, nay even the open renunciation and denunciation of the Nationalistic. And from that difference in our conception of the struggle, stem the differences in tactics and interpretation of events.

The forces involved in the Struggle:

Because we differ from the leadership in our conception of the nature of the struggle, we differ in our assessment of the forces for and against us. The Congress leadership, because it interprets the struggle as one for democracy and therefore a political struggle, designed to remove legal restrictions, recognises the foe as the present Nationalist government and accepts and treats everybody opposed to the Nationalist government whatever his motives and beliefs, as an ally. The congress leadership, therefore, if we are to judge by its actions and utterances, recognises the Nationalist government as the rightful government of the country whose policies, however, it is not in agreement with. The leadership, therefore, conceives of Congress as an Opposition party, with an alternative policy to which the people of South Africa are to be persuaded to subscribe. The difference between the United Party and Congress (as conceived by the leadership) lies in the policies they advocate and in their composition. The United Party is an All-White party, standing for white leadership and supremacy while Congress, in so far as its policies, under the present leadership, are determined by all the Congress, is multi-racial and stands for a democratic franchise. But both the United Party and the Congress leadership accept the Nats as the rightful government of the country whose policies, however, are disastrous to the country. And both believe that the essential thing to do is to oust the Nats. Both believe that the way to do so is by appealing to the people of South Africa for support for their policies. That is why a certain "African leader" in an issue of "Liberation," could state that "we (i.e. Congress) should water down our demands in order that we should muster the broadest support against the Nats."

Congress, according to the present leadership, is a political party aspiring to Parliament though, as yet, having no representative in Parliament. That is why it is so difficult to effect a boycott of the white Native representatives in Parliament, in spite of the unambiguous statement of the Nation-Building Programme of 1949. It is believed by our leaders that the number of Whites subscribing to the Kliptown Charter will increase so that one day a White party committed to the Kliptown Charter will form the government and implement the hopes and wishes expressed in that document!

But the AFRICANISTS who are committed to the overthrow of white domination, club together all who stand for the maintenance of the status quo and can find no common ground with the United & Labour Parties. The AFRICANISTS are aware, too, that when danger threatens the interests of the rulers, they modify their policies in order to gain support of the oppressed. That is what happened during the dark days of the last war. But as soon as the danger is past, the rulers return to their old policies with more ruthlessness in order to crush any awakened hopes. The Nationalist government has trodden on the corns of many groups and many people are prepared to go a very long way to get rid of this government. But that does not mean that they subscribe to a thoroughly democratic constitution. Many, in fact, hate the Nats, because they are threatening the status quo. We are familiar with the diversionary role of the Liberals. And

502

both Mrs. Ballinger's Liberal Party and Beyleveld's C.O.D. fulfill that role.

Current Events

I do not intend to list the numerous oppressive laws manufactured by the Nats, or revised by them. What is essential is to note their trend and the reaction of the people to them. The Bantu Education Act, the Native Laws Amendment Act, the Universities and Nurses Apartheid Bills, etc., have one thing in common. They are all part of a desperate attempt to delay the Nemesis of white domination. They all aim at creating a feeling of insecurity among the oppressed and thus making them a docile labour force which accepts resignedly its inferior status. In fact the aim is to make the oppressed BELIEVE that they are incapable of equalling, let alone surpassing, the white man in any field. We must learn that we can't do without the white man. We must believe that modern 20th century technology, which is the distinctive feature of so-called western civilisation, is, like everything good in S.A., "For Europeans only—Slegs vir Blankes."

Take the Passes for women. As [Harry] Bloom so ably illustrates in his book "Episode", when dealing with the "Permit", every African woman, in the eyes of the white conqueror, is a potential prostitute, an undesirable element—not a woman, mind you, or a mother. No. An *element*! That is why, therefore, there should be nothing wrong in subjecting her to indignity and humiliation. She is not a woman, just as her husband is not a man. If the dog, the man, carries a dog-collar in the form of a reference book, why not the bitch? Anthropologists all agree that a culture progresses only through contact. Prof. Childe goes further and states that a culture cannot remain static. It either progresses or retrogresses. And lack of contact leads to retrogression. And Eiselen, the Anthropologist, produces Bantu Education and ethnic grouping and Tribal Colleges TO STOP CONTACT on the side of the African, while maintaining it on the European side.

Reaction of the People.

But the people are not taking this lying down. The most important development in South Africa today is the militant resistance of the women to the extension of Passes to them.

The opposition is sporadic but brave. It is a little disorganised but courageous. Women in the rural areas and in Nationalist strongholds have defied Verwoerd and his henchmen. We praise the women for their stand and Congress for organising that stand with her limited means. But there is a danger which we Africanists foresee. And it is that we come to regard our duty and role as opposing Verwoerd's laws. The Nats. are carrying out their programme and if we are going to do nothing but oppose, we will never get anywhere, for every year will bring forth, as every year has brought forth, new oppressive laws, on top of the ones we are opposing. Thus while we are fighting Bantu Education, Passes for Women come along. While we are organising against that, Universities and Nurses Apartheid come along. Our sacred duty is to carry out OUR PROGRAMME, irrespective of what Verwoerd is doing. Let us take the offensive and pursue the Nation-Building Programme of 1949, relentlessly and honestly. And white domination will collapse. Whenever any item of that Programme has been implemented, no matter how emasculated, it has drawn overwhelming and enthusiastic support from the masses and has sent the conquerer shaking in his boots. I am thinking particularly of the Defiance Campaign, the One Day Stoppage of Work, the Economic and Bus Boycotts. If these had been honestly and relentlessly pursued in the spirit of true African Nationalism, we would be discussing PRODUCTION today and not oppression.

POLITICAL FAITH FOR AFRICAN FREEDOM

The salvation of the African people as a nation lies in the ideal of African Nationalism, a dynamic and most powerful philosophy with tremendous force for the overthrow of foreign domination in Africa. The late Lembede emerged with his thesis on Africanism. He gave us the direction as probably no other man could have done, and in doing so, saved us as a nation. We must have faith and devotion to duty with courage and a determination to defend our cherished ideals that Africa is for the Africans, that the Cause of Africa must triumph, that we must remember Africa first, that African nationhood must be achieved irrespective of whatever odds are facing us, and that our right to determine the destiny of our Fatherland is an inherent one. The dawn of the day must come when fascist foreign rule shall have collapsed into a rubble.

The Freedom Charter is a political bluff. It promises a little wonderful heaven if not Utopia around the corner. The question is: How to get there? The answer is: There must be immediate implementation of the Programme of Action of 1949 and the principles laid down therein, item by item, for the achievement of the aims of the envisaged little heaven or the very proposed Utopia round the corner. It is utterly useless to go around shouting empty slogans such as "The people shall govern", "The people shall share", without practical steps towards that government. We are merely being made tools and stooges of interested parties that are anxious to maintain the status quo.

Africa wills to be a nation, both for her own sake and that of humanity. Our Programme of African Nationalism must be implemented fully to the free and full development of our faculties and powers of our intellect and our aspirations. African National Congress has made a catastrophic blunder by accepting foreign leadership by the whites. How can we have leaders who are also led? If this white leadership is denied, why was one Joe Slovo of the Congress of Democrats allowed to become Chairman of the A.N.C. Commission of Enquiry in 1954, into disputes involving A.N.C. policies? He presided over this A.N.C. Commission as Chairman and passed sentences of expulsion against certain members of the A.N.C. including a member of the A.N.C. National Executive, from Congress.

What Constitutional powers did Mr. Slovo have in the A.N.C.? He being a white man and a non-member of the A.N.C., why was he given such powers by Mandela's regime at the time? These are powers vested only in the constitutional authority of the National Conference of the A.N.C. Why did Luthuli fail to intervene in the matter? Is this not leadership by whites?

Afrika desires the progressive improvement of her sons and daughters. She reveres genius and virtue, not hypocrisy and brute force. She desires instructors not masters; the worship of truth and not falsehood and in order that a self-confident African people must exist it is necessary that they should, through action and self-sacrifice attain political consciousness and consciousness of their destiny. This must be achieved by the Africans for the Africans. It is possible that the battles of Blood River, Keiskamahoek and Thaba-Bosiu will be fought again, this time under the banner of African Nationalism; here, history must be repeated, if our African revolutionary struggle must be victorious. In this struggle for African Freedom, there can be no compromise or apology, nor collaboration, nor servitude. Here, we fight it out and to the finish. We either go under or exist as a nation. We are convinced that the struggle is between the conquerors and the vanquished and there can be no compromise nor surrender on our part, nor can we agree to go 50's with the oppressor in Afrika.

It is time that we do not cringe on our knees before the enemies of African national independence, lest we be crushed by the weight of our own cowardice. There is no bravery possible for fearful people. We either perish or survive as an African nation. Our task can never be accomplished through insincerities to our principles nor by false doctrines of expediency; but only through persistent efforts; and self-sacrifice; by ceaseless preaching of our dynamic ideas of a new Afrika. We must destroy the so-called foreign experts in African Affairs in Afrika; the foreign rule; foreign traffickers, the place-hunters and the empty slogan-mongers from the East and West. We reject inexorably and outright the petty intruders, the would-be diplomats, West and Eastern functionaries who infiltrate into our ranks to whisper "friendliness" for the sake of white domination as preached by Strydom-DeVilliers Graaff axis and other non-African organisations.

We are putting forward to the African people with forcefulness and courage the postulates on African Nationalism, for the deliverance of our Fatherland from white fascism and win our independence from foreign rule. Together, let us seek the most active and effective method of struggle against the menace of foreign domination in Afrika. This is our urgent immediate task.

Afrika is our Fatherland by decree of Providence and Divine right. We rise to give a pledge that Afrika must be freed. Therefore, let us turn to the graves of our African martyrs, Moshoeshoe, Sekukuni, Makana, Tshaka and Dingani and pray for inspiration from them and from those who died for us in the Cause.

In conclusion, we must honour the memory of African revolutionary martyrs who have fallen beneath foreign tyranny; honour the tears of African mothers for their sons in prisons, in slavery, dead and in exile. We can no longer bear evil, injustice, usurpation and foreign arbitrary rule. If we ever betray the whole or part of our principles of African Nationalism, the Gods will destroy us.

i — AFRIKA

Document 37. Letter "giving notice" of Africanist disassociation from the ANC (Transvaal), signed by S. T. Ngendane, Secretary, to Mr. Speaker of the ANC (Transvaal) Conference, November 2, 1958

Mr. Speaker, Sir,

We have consistently advocated African Nationalism and whenever we have taken the political platform, we have fearlessly expounded African Nationalism.

In 1949, we got the African people to accept the nation-building Programme of that year. We have consistently and honestly stuck to that Programme.

In 1955, the Kliptown Charter was adopted which, according to us, is in irreconcilable conflict with the 1949 Programme, seeing that it claims that the land no longer belongs to the African people, but is auctioned for sale to *all* who live in this country.

In numerous Conferences of the A.N.C. we have made it clear that we are committed to the overthrow of White domination and the restoration of the land to its rightful owners.

In the Transvaal Provincial Conference held in the Communal Hall on Saturday 1st November, 1958, we again put across our case peacefully and logically.

It has, however, come to our notice that armed thugs have been brought in great numbers, at the invitation of the present Transvaal A.N.C. leadership for the specific purpose of murdering certain Africanists who are regarded as the leading persons in the movement.

Ours, Mr. Speaker, is a political battle aimed against the oppressor. We are not a para-military clique, engaged in the murder of fellow Africans.

For the above reasons, we therefore wish to notify this Conference that:
1. We will not be a party to any decisions taken at this Conference.
2. We have come to the parting of the ways. And we are here and now giving notice that we are disassociating ourselves from the A.N.C. as it is constituted at present in the Transvaal.

We are launching out openly, on our own, as the custodians of the A.N.C. policy as it was formulated in 1912 and pursued up to the time of the Congress Alliances.

Signed S. T. NGENDANE
(Secretary)

Document 38. "Future of the Africanist Movement." Questions and Answers by R. M. Sobukwe, in *The Africanist*, January 1959

Q. *Who are the Africanists?*

A. A simple answer would be that they are the members of the Africanist Movement. But, if one wishes to go deeper into the question, one would say that they are those Africans who believe that African Nationalism is the only liberatory outlook that can bind together the African masses by providing them with a loyalty higher than that of the tribe and thus mould them into a militant disciplined fighting force.

Q. *How long has your movement been in existence?*

A. The germ of the Movement was there even before the advent of the European. When Moshoeshoe brought together the scattered remnants of various African tribes and moulded them into a patriotic Sotho tribe, he was engaged in nation-building. Similarly Chaka's wars whereby he sought to establish a single authority in place of the many tribal authorities of Natal, were, we say, steps in the direction of nation-building. In the Cape the House of Gcaleka was recognised as the Paramount authority. There is no doubt that the pressure of social and economic conditions would in time have given rise to the Union of these territories.

As a political *organisation*, however, we trace our origin to 1912—the year the A.N.C. was born—with 1944 the year our Movement was given that purposiveness which helps to give clear direction and power to a mass struggle. It is in that year that *Lembede* and those in his immediate circle demanded from the A.N.C.:

1. A clear outlook: African Nationalism and Africanism.
2. A basic policy outlining our fundamental postulates with respect to our social intentions, especially in the ultimate future.
3. A Programme.

The first two demands, Lembede himself met, while the third was met in 1949 when the Africanists (known as the Congress Youth League) provided the A.N.C. with the popular Nation-Building Programme of 1949.

Q. *What are your differences with the A.N.C.*

A. First of all we differ radically in our conception of the struggle. We firmly hold that we are oppressed as a subject nation—the African nation. To us, therefore, the struggle is a national struggle. Those of the A.N.C. who are its active policy-makers, maintain, in the face of all the hard facts of the S.A. situation, that ours is a class struggle. We are, according to them, oppressed as WORKERS, both white and black. But it is significant that they make *no attempt* whatsoever to organise white workers. Their white allies are all of them bourgeoise!

Secondly we differ in our attitude to "co-operation" with other national groups. Perhaps it might be better to say we differ in our understanding of the term "co-operation." We believe that co-operation is possible *only between equals*. There can be no co-operation between oppressor and oppressed, dominating and dominated. That is collaboration, *not* co-operation. And we cannot collaborate in our own oppression! The A.N.C. leadership, on the other hand, would seem to regard collaboration and co-operation as synonymous. They seem to believe that all that is required for people to be "equals" is that they should declare that they *are* equals, and lo! the trick is done.

At the present moment the A.N.C. leadership regards anybody and everybody who is against the Nationalist government (for whatever reasons) as allies.

This latter attitude is the result of a mentality that continues to speak of South Africa as though it were an island, completely cut off from the continent and, therefore, able to fashion its own policies and programmes, unrelated to and unaffected by those of the other African States. We, on the other hand, have always been acutely aware of the fact that ours is a particular front in a battle raging across the continent. We claim Afrika for the Africans; the A.N.C. claims South Africa for all. To the A.N.C. leadership the present Nationalist government is the properly elected government of South Africa whose policies, however, it does not approve of. And the A.N.C.'s main struggle is to get the Nats out of power. The fact that the Nats are a logical product of past South African history and that what they stand for is approved and supported by the overwhelming majority of whites in the country has apparently escaped the notice of A.N.C. leadership.

We, however, stand for *the complete overthrow of white domination.* That means that the S.A. Act of 1909—that fossilised relic of the whiteman's exclusive privileges and prejudices—must be scrapped.

Q. *What is your answer to the accusation that you are anti-white?*

A. Our reply has been officially given in a statement apearing in the Golden City Post of Sunday 7th November, 1958 signed by Mr. P. K. Leballo (Chairman) and Mr. S. T. Ngendane (Secretary). On the material level we just cannot see any possibility of co-operation. To say that we are prepared to accept anybody who subscribes to our Programme is but to state a condition that one knows cannot be fulfilled. From past history, not only of this country but of other countries as well, we know that a group in a privileged position never voluntarily relinquishes that position. If some members of the goup appear to be sympathetic to the demands of the less-privileged, it is only in so far as those demands do not threaten the privileges of the favoured group. If they (the privileged) offer assistance, it is for the purpose of "directing" and "controlling" the struggle of the underprivileged and making sure that it does not become "dangerous."

Q. *But are you anti-white or not?*

A. What is meant by anti-whiteism? Is it not merely an emotional term without a precise signification? Let me put it this way: In every struggle, whether national or class, the masses do not fight an abstraction. They do not hate oppression or capitalism. They concretise these and hate the oppressor, be he the Governor-General or a colonial power, the landlord or the factory-owner, or, in South Africa, the white man. But they hate these groups because they *associate them with their oppression*! Remove the association and you remove the hatred. In South Africa then, once white domination has been overthrown and the white man is no longer "white-man boss" but is an individual member of society, there will be no reason to hate him and he will not be hated even by the masses.

We are not anti-white, therefore. We do not hate the European because he is white! We hate him because he is an oppressor. And it is plain dishonesty to say I hate the sjambok and not the one who wields it.

Q. *Do you regard all whites as oppressors?*

A. We regard them all as shareholders in the S.A. Oppressors Company (Pty.) Ltd. There are whites, of course, who are intellectually converted to our cause, but because of their position materially, they cannot fully identify themselves with the struggle of the African people. They want safeguards and check-points all along the way, with the result that the struggle of the people is blunted, stultified and crushed.

Q. *Do you include white leftists in your indictment?*

A. There are NONE! And there have never been any in South Africa—white or black. All we have had are quacks. In fact, like Christianity, Communism in South Africa has been extremely unfortunate in its choice of representatives.

Q. *Do you think the Africanist Movement will last?*

A. Not only will it last, it will flourish. History is already vindicating our stand as far as the continent is concerned. We are in step with the continent. And the reason is that we correctly interpret the aspirations of the African people. We are not exaggerating when we say that the demand for membership is more than we can cope with.

Q. *Why can't you cope with the demand?*

A. Because we lack funds. You see we do not want a blind following. We want an intelligent, informed and politically educated membership. We, therefore, require a full-time information service, full-time organisers and above all, well-run offices. We don't want undisciplined branches mushrooming all over the country. And to maintain the necessary contact, discipline and co-ordination, we need funds.

Q. *Do you think the African people will tolerate a splinter movement at this stage?*

A. The African people want freedom and they are extremely anxious to find themselves as a Nation. They are aware of the futility of the post-1949 struggles of the A.N.C. with more and more emphasis on spectacular activity as distinct from principled programmatic action. That is why they have welcomed our emergence.

Q. *What is your attitude to the A.N.C.*

A. We say, "Let the best man win." If the A.N.C. launches campaigns which we believe are for the good of our people, we will support them wholeheartedly. But we are not going to get ourselves involved in muddled, clumsy, senseless activity. We have the 1949 Programme to implement, and as it unfolds and its dynamism is revealed, the A.N.C. will cease to exist. Perhaps the Congress alliance may eke out a precarious existence for some time. But there will be only one organisation for the African people—and that will be the Africanist Movement.

510

Q. *Have you decided on a Name yet?*

A. No—not on a national level. Such matters as a name, policy, the Constitution, etc., will be finalised at the National Convention which we hope to hold in April. From then onwards we shall operate on a National level. And from then onwards we will sweep the country.

Documents 39a-39e. Inaugural Convention of the PAC, April 4–6, 1959

Document 39a. "Opening Address" by R. M. Sobukwe

Mr. Speaker, Sir, Sons and Daughters of Afrika!

Mr. Speaker has already informed you that we had hoped that this inaugural Convention of the Africanists would be opened by Dr. Kamuzu Hastings Banda, failing which, by Mr. Kenneth Kaunda of the Zambia African National Congress in Northern Rhodesia. Both have been unable to attend our convention, for both are now, in the language of the colonialists, "detained" in some concentration camps because they dared to demand the right of self-determination for the indigenous African people of Nyasaland and Northern Rhodesia. The honourable task of opening this conference has, therefore, fallen to me, an Africanist, and I wish to thank the Central Committee for the honour. I am particularly grateful for the opportunity this offers me to treat briefly of certain issues relevant to our struggle which, though adequately treated in the documents that will be considered by this Convention, require to be presented to such a gathering.

I hope, then, Mr. Speaker, in the course of my address, to answer broadly questions pertaining to our stand in contemporary international politics, our relation to the states of Afrika, both independent and dependent, our attitude to the entire nationalist movement in Afrika, our stand on the question of Race in general and the so-called racial question in South Africa. Finally, I hope to outline briefly our ultimate objectives.

INTERNATIONAL SCENE:

We are living today, Sons and Daughters of the Soil, fighters in the cause of African freedom, we are living today in an era that is pregnant with untold possibilities for both good and evil. In the course of the past two years we have seen man breaking assunder, with dramatic suddenness, the chains that have bound his mind, solving problems which for ages it has been regarded as sacrilege even to attempt to solve. The tremendous, epoch-making scientific achievements in the exploration of space, with man-made satellites orbiting the earth, the new and interesting discoveries made in the Geophysical Year, the production of rust-resistant strains of wheat in the field of agriculture, the amazing discoveries in the fields of medicine, chemistry and physics—all these, mean that man is well on the way to establishing absolute control over that environment.

However, in spite of all these rapid advances in the material and physical world, man appears to be either unwilling or unable to solve the problem of social relations between man and man. Because of this failure on the part of man, we see the world split today into two large hostile blocks, the so-called Capitalist and Socialist blocks represented by the U.S.A. and the Soviet Union respectively. These two blocks are engaged in terrible competition, use tough language and tactics, employ brinkmanship stunts which have the whole world heading for a nervous breakdown. They each are armed with terrible weapons of destruction and continue to spend millions of pounds in the production of more and more of these weapons. In spite of all the diplomatic talk of co-existence, these blocks each behave as though they did not believe that co-existence was possible.

AFRIKA'S POSITION.

The question then arises, where does Afrika fit into this picture and where, particularly, do we African nationalists, we Africanists in South Afrika, fit in?

There is no doubt that with the liquidation of Western imperialism and colonialism in Asia, the Capitalist market has shrunk considerably. As a result, Afrika has become the happy-hunting ground of adventuristic capital. There is again a scramble for Afrika and both the Soviet Union and the United States of America are trying to win the loyalty of the African States. Afrika is being wooed with more ardour than she has ever been. There is a lot of flirting going on, of course, some Africans [are] flirting with the Soviet camp, and others with the American camp. In some cases the courtship has reached a stage where the parties are going out together; and they probably hold hands in the dark but nowhere has it yet reached a stage where the parties can kiss in public without blushing.

This wooing occurs at a time when the whole continent of Afrika is in labour, suffering the pangs of a new birth and everybody is looking anxiously and expectantly towards Afrika to see, as our people so aptly put it *ukuthi iyozala nkomoni* (what creature will come forth). We are being wooed internationally at a time when in South Africa the naked forces of savage Herrenvolkism are running riot; when a determined effort is being made to annihilate the African people through systematic starvation; at a time when brutal attempts are being made to retard, dwarf and stunt the mental development of a whole people through organised "miseducation"; at a time when thousands of our people roam the streets in search of work and are being told by the foreign ruler to go back to a "home" which he has assigned them, whether that means the break up of their families or not; at a time when the distinctive badge of slavery and humiliation, the "dom pass" is being extended from the African male dog to the African female bitch. It is at this time, when fascist tyranny has reached its zenith in South Afrika, that Afrika's loyalty is being competed for. And the question is, what is our answer?

Our answer, Mr. Speaker and children of the Soil, has been given by the African leaders of the continent. Dr. Kwame Nkrumah has repeatedly stated that in international affairs, Afrika wishes to pursue a policy of positive neutrality, allying herself to neither of the existing blocs but, in the words of Dr. Nnandi Azikiwe of Nigeria, remaining "independent in all things but neutral in none that affect the destiny of Afrika". Mr. Tom Mboya of Kenya has expressed himself more forthrightly, declaring that it is not the intention of African states to change one master (western imperialism) for another (Soviet hegemony).

We endorse the views of the African leaders on this point. But we must point out that we are not blind to the fact that the countries—which pursue a policy of planned state economy—have outstripped, in industrial development, those that follow the path of private enterprise. Today, China is industrially far ahead of India. Unfortunately, however, this rapid industrial development has been accompanied in all cases by a rigid totalitarianism notwithstanding Mao Tse Tung's "Hundred Flowers" announcement.* Africanists reject totalitarianism in any form and accept political democracy as understood in the west. We also reject the economic exploitation of the many for the benefit of a few. We accept as policy the equitable distribution of wealth aiming, as far as I am concerned, to equality of income which to me is the only basis on which the slogan of "equal opportunities" can be founded.

Borrowing then the best from the East and the best from the West we nonetheless retain and maintain our distinctive personality and refuse to be the satraps or stooges of either power block.

RELATION TO STATES IN AFRIKA:

Our relation to the States in Afrika may be stated precisely and briefly by quoting from George Padmore's book, 'Pan Africanism or Communism'.

---

*According to Peter 'Molotsi, this sentence reflected the bias about China that was evident in the South African press at the time. After the experience of direct dealings with the Chinese, who have given support to the PAC since 1961, PAC leaders abroad revised their judgment. The sentence was deleted when the address was reprinted in March 1965 in *The Basic Documents of the Pan Africanist Congress of South Africa*, issued by Secretary, Publicity and Information, Pan Africanist Congress of S.A. (Lusaka, Zambia).

Discussing the future of Afrika, Padmore observes that "there is a growing feeling among politically conscious Africans throughout the continent that their destiny is one, that what happens in one part of Afrika to Africans must affect Africans living in other parts".

We honour Ghana as the first independent state in modern Afrika which, under the courageous nationalist leadership of Dr. Nkrumah and the Convention People's Party, has actively interested itself in the liberation of the whole continent from White domination, and has held out the vision of a democratic United States of Afrika. We regard it as the sacred duty of every African state to strive ceaselessly and energetically for the creation of a United States of Afrika, stretching from Cape to Cairo, Morocco to Madagascar.

The days of small, independent countries are gone. Today we have, on the one hand, great powerful countries of the world; America and Russia cover huge tracts of land territorially and number hundreds of millions in population. On the other hand the small weak independent countries of Europe are beginning to realise that for their own survival they have to form military and economic federations, hence NATO and the European market.

Beside the sense of a common historical fate that we share with the other countries of Afrika, it is imperative, for purely practical reasons that the whole of Afrika be united into a single unit, centrally controlled. Only in that way can we solve the immense problems that face the continent.

NATIONAL MOVEMENTS IN AFRIKA:

It is for the reasons stated above that we admire, bless and identify ourselves with the entire nationalist movements in Afrika. They are the core, the basic units, the individual cells of that large organism envisaged, namely, the United States of Afrika; a union of free, sovereign independent democratic states of Afrika.

For the lasting peace of Afrika and the solution of the economic, social and political problems of the continent, there needs must be a democratic principle. This means that White supremacy, under whatever guise it manifests itself, must be destroyed. And that is what the nationalists on the continent are setting out to do. They all are agreed that the African majority must rule. In the African context, it is the overwhelming African majority that will mould and shape the content of democracy. Allow me to quote Dr. Dubois, the father of Pan Africanism: "Most men in the world", writes Dubois, "are coloured. A belief in humanity means a belief in coloured men. The future of the world will, in all reasonable possibility, be what coloured men make it". As for the world, so for Afrika. The future of Africa will be what Africans make it.

THE RACE QUESTION:

And now for the thorny questions of race. I do not wish to give a lengthy and learned dissertation on Race. Suffice it to say that even those scientists who do recognise the existence of separate races, have to admit that there are border line cases which will not fit into any of the three Races of mankind.

All scientists agree that all men can trace their ancestry back to the first Homo Sapiens, that man is distinguished from other mammals and also from earlier types of man by the nature of his intelligence. The structure of the body of man provides evidence to prove the biological unity of the human species. All scientists agree that there is no "race" that is superior to another, and there is no "race" that is inferior to others.

The Africanists take the view that there is only one race to which we all belong, and that is the human race. In our vocabulary therefore, the word 'race' as applied to man, has no plural form. We do, however, admit the existence of observable physical differences between various groups of people, but these differences are the result of a number of factors, chief among which has been geographical isolation.

In Afrika the myth of race has been propounded and propagated by the imperialists and colonialists from Europe, in order to facilitate and justify their inhuman exploitation of the indigenous people of the land. It is from this myth of race with its attendant claims of cultural superiority that the doctrine of white supremacy stems. Thus it is that an ex-engine driver can think of himself as fully qualified to be the head of the government of an African state, but refuse to believe that a highly educated black doctor, more familiar with Western culture than the White premier is, cannot even run a municipal council. I do not wish to belabour this point. Time is precious. Let me close discussion of this topic by declaring, on behalf of the Africanists, that with UNESCO we hold that "every man is his brother's keeper. For every man is a piece of the continent, a part of the main, because he is involved in mankind".

IN SOUTH AFRIKA:

In South Africa we recognise the existence of national groups which are the result of geographical origin within a certain area as well as a shared historical experience of these groups. The Europeans are a foreign minority group which has exclusive control of political, economic, social and military power. It is the dominant group. It is the exploiting group, responsible for the pernicious doctrine of White Supremacy which has resulted in the humiliation and degradation of the indigenous African people. It is this group which has dispossessed the African people of their land and with arrogant conceit has set itself up as the "guardians", the "trustees" of the Africans. It is this group which conceives of the African people as a child nation, composed of Boys and Girls, ranging in age from 120 years to one day. It is this group which, after 300 years, can still state with brazen effrontery that the Native, the Bantu, the Kaffir is still backward and savage etc. But they still want to remain "guardians", "trustees", and what have you, of the African people. In short, it is this group which has mismanaged affairs in South Africa just as their kith and kin are mismanaging affairs in Europe. It is from this group that the most rabid race baiters and agitators come. It is members of this group who, whenever they meet in their Parliament, say things which agitate the hearts of millions of peace-loving Africans. This is the group which turns out thousands of experts on that new South African Science—the Native mind.

Then there is the Indian foreign minority group. This group came to this country not as imperialists or colonialists, but as indentured labourers. In the South African set-up of today, this group is an oppressed minority. But there are some members of this group, the merchant class in particular, who have become tainted with the virus of cultural supremacy and national arrogance. This class identifies itself by and large with the oppressor but, significantly, this is the group which provides the political leadership of the Indian people in South Africa. And all that the politics of this class have meant up to now is preservation and defence of the sectional interests of the Indian merchant class. The down-trodden, poor "stinking coolies" of Natal who, alone, as a result of the pressure of material conditions, can identify themselves with the indigenous African majority in the struggle to overthrow White supremacy, have not yet produced their leadership. We hope they will do so soon.

The Africans constitute the indigenous group and form the majority of the population. They are the most ruthlessly exploited and are subjected to humiliation, degradation and insult.

Now it is our contention that true democracy can be established in South Africa and on the continent as a whole, only when White supremacy has been destroyed. And the illiterate and semi-literate African masses constitute the key and centre and content of any struggle for true democracy in South Africa. And the African people can be organised only under the banner of African nationalism in an All-African Organisation where they will by themselves formulate policies and programmes and decide on the methods of struggle without interference from either so-called left-wing or right-wing groups of the minorities who arrogantly appropriate to themselves the right to plan and think for the Africans.

We wish to emphasise that the freedom of the African means the freedom of all in South Africa, the European included, because only the African can guarantee the establishment of a genuine democracy in which all men will

516

be citizens of a common state and will live and be governed as individuals and not as distinctive sectional groups.

OUR ULTIMATE GOALS:

In conclusion, I wish to state that the Africanists do not at all subscribe to the fashionable doctrine of South African exceptionalism. Our contention is that South Africa is an integral part of the indivisible whole that is Afrika. She cannot solve her problems in isolation from and with utter disregard of the rest of the continent.

It is precisely for that reason that we reject both apartheid and so-called multi-racialism as solutions of our socio-economic problems. Apart from the number of reasons and arguments that can be advanced against apartheid, we take our stand on the principle that Afrika is one and desires to be one and nobody, I repeat, nobody has the right to balkanise our land.

Against multi-racialism we have this objection, that the history of South Africa has fostered group prejudices and antagonisms, and if we have to maintain the same group exclusiveness, parading under the term of multi-racialism, we shall be transporting to the new Afrika these very antagonisms and conflicts. Further, multi-racialism is in fact a pandering to European bigotry and arrogance. It is a method of safeguarding white interests, implying as it does, proportional representation irrespective of population figures. In that sense it is a complete negation of democracy. To us the term "multi-racialism" implies that there are such basic insuperable differences between the various national groups here that the best course is to keep them permanently distinctive in a kind of democratic apartheid. That to us is racialism multiplied, which probably is what the term truly connotes.

We aim, politically, at government of the Africans by the Africans, for the Africans, with everybody who owes his only loyalty to Afrika and who is prepared to accept the democratic rule of an African majority being regarded as an African. We guarantee no minority rights, because we think in terms of individuals, not groups.

Economically we aim at the rapid extension of industrial development in order to alleviate pressure on the land, which is what progress means in terms of modern society. We stand committed to a policy guaranteeing the most equitable distribution of wealth.

Socially we aim at the full development of the human personality and a ruthless uprooting and outlawing of all forms or manifestations of the racial myth. To sum it up we stand for an Africanist Socialist Democracy.

Here is a tree rooted in African soil, nourished with waters from the rivers of Afrika. Come and sit under its shade and become, with us, the leaves of the same branch and the branches of the same tree.

Sons and Daughters of Afrika, I declare this inaugural convention of the Africanists open!   IZWE LETHU!!

Document 39b. "Manifesto of the Africanist Movement"

Note: This document was reprinted by the PAC in 1965 in the publication noted in the footnote to document 39a. The headings and boldface type were added in 1965 and did not appear in the original document. Some 1965 changes in wording are shown in brackets.

A. A chain of reaction.

The significant portion of our social milieu begins with the expansion of the markets founded by the rising commercial capital of Wesern Europe at the turn of the fifteenth century. Succeeding years witnessed the "discovery" of new lands by the Europeans, the Papal award of the whole of Africa to the Portuguese, increased European slave raids on Africa that denuded Africa of Africans and led to the establishment in the Americas of the greatest mass chattel slavery that the world had ever known. Africa had been successfully robbed of Africans. It was this chattel slavery that contributed substantially to the initiation of the European industrial revolution which in turn resulted in the unleashing of the forces of reaction which culminated in the rape of Africa at the close of the last century.

B. Land robbery and political subjugation.

Early European settlement of Africa, especially of its southern tip, was a direct result of the rise of European commercial capital. Wave upon wave of European settlers came to Africa and their penetration of the interior involved the loss of sovereignty by the indigenous peoples and the alienation of more and more portions of their land. With the rise of the industrial capital of Europe and its increased search for raw materials and more markets, the partition of Africa went apace and the doctrine of "effective occupation" was enunciated, a theory calculated to "sugar coat" the bitter pills of land robbery and political subjugation. More and more settlers came into the country until today there are 5,000,000 Europeans who up to the dawn of African liberation had constituted themselves a ruling class over the 250,000,000 indigenous peoples. Africans had been successfully robbed of Africa.

C. Established by the sword.

The advent of European imperialism and colonialism to Africa brought in its wake the phenomenon of white domination, whether visible or

exploitation and social degradation of the indigenous African masses.
Throughout this historical epoch, the age of white domination, whenever
the spokesmen or representatives of white domination have sprouted a
conscience, they have referred to the phenomenon as the "spread of
Western civilisation" or "the extension of Christian trusteeship". The
undisguised truth is that White domination has grounded down the status of
man and stunted THE NORMAL GROWTH OF THE HUMAN PERSON-
ALITY ON A SCALE UNPRECEDENTED IN HUMAN HISTORY. White
domination was established by the sword and is maintained by the sword.

D. Expulsion of imperialist exploiters.

Significant events of the twentieth century especially of the latter part of
it, have constituted a massive challenge to Herrenvolkism, a particular
manifestation of imperialism and colonism. Already European exploiters
and oppressors have been dramatically expelled from such countries as
Indonesia, India, China, Burma, Malaya, Vietnam, etc. These are today
being systematically routed and forcibly caused to retreat in confusion.
The post-war world has witnessed the expulsion of the European
imperialist exploiters and oppressors from large tracts of Africa and the
emergence of no less than nine sovereign and independent African states.
We are indeed witnessing a *gotterdamerung*—a twilight of the gods, the
twin gods of white domination.

E. Decolonisation and independence.

Elsewhere in Africa the progressive forces of African nationalism
continue to be locked in mortal combat with the reactionary forces of
Herrenvolkism. By the end of next year the peoples of Togoland,
Somaliland, the Cameroons and Nigeria will have achieved freedom. The
French policy of 'association' is also being rejected in favour of decolonisa-
tion and independence.

F. The liquidation of the forces of oppression.

To the chagrin of the imperialists the government of Free Algeria is a
reality. Tanganyika, Kenya and Uganda are on the verge of obtaining their
freedom from British imperialism. Contrary to their traditional policy the
Belgian imperialists have been forced to accede, at least in principle, to the
African people's demand for the recognition of their independence in the
Congo. The policy of partnership pursued in the Central African
Federation has been exposed for what it is: the greatest political fraud of
our times.

Even in those massive concentration camps, Angola and Mozambique, the African people have begun to reject the *Status quo* in favour of their own freedom. **The liquidation of the forces of oppression is a process that not even nuclear power can halt.**

G. *Right to shape own destiny.*

The days of European domination of Africa are numbered. Even in South Africa the writing is glaringly on the wall for those of our European rulers who can see and decipher it. For exactly three-hundred and seven years today, the African people have been criminally oppressed, ruthlessly exploited and inhumanly degraded. They have in the past, as they do now, declared themselves for freedom. They reject white domination in any shape or form. They are unflinchingly determined to wrest the control of their country from alien hands. They are determined to exercise the most fundamental of human rights, **the inalienable right of indigenous people to determine and shape their own destiny.** To the African people there can be no room in any way or in any part of Africa for any non-indigenous peoples who deny to the indigenous populations their fundamental right to control their own material and spiritual interests effectively. South Africa, which is an integral part of the continent, is the inalienable heritage of the African people and its effective control is their undoubted and unquestionable birthright.

H. *No longer with the ranks of the liberation Movement.*

Following the 'capture' of a portion of the black leadership of South Africa by a section of the leadership of the white ruling class, the masses of our people are in extreme danger of being deceived into losing sight of the objectives of our struggle. This captured black leadership claims to be fighting for freedom when in truth it is fighting to perpetuate the tutelage of the African people. It is tooth and nail against the Africans gaining the effective control of their own country. It is fighting for the maintenance of the *status quo*. It is fighting for the "constitutional guarantees" or "national rights" for our alien nationals.

It has completely abandoned the objective of freedom. It has joined the ranks of the reactionary forces. It is no longer within the ranks of the liberation movement.

I. *White domination without frills and trappings.*

These "leaders" consider South Africa and its wealth to belong to all who live in it, the alien dispossessors and the indigenous dispossessed, the alien robbers and their indigenous victims. They regard as equals the foreign master and his indigenous slave, the white exploiter and the African exploited, the foreign oppressor and the indigenous oppressed. They regard as brothers the subject Africans and their European overlords. They are too incredibly naive and too fantastically unrealistic to see that the interests of the subject peoples who are criminally oppressed, ruthlessly exploited and inhumanly degraded, are in sharp conflict and in pointed contradiction with those of the white ruling class. Citizen Toussaint once remarked that: "Whenever anybody, be he white or mulatto, wants a dirty job done, he always gets the Negro to do it." The charterist leadership, true to type, is doing the oppressor's dirty job, namely, seeing to it that the African is deprived for all time of his inherent right to control his country effectively; of seeing to it that whatever new social order is established in this country, the essentials of white domination are retained, even though its frills and trappings may be ripped off. This attitude has been labelled MULTI-RACIALISM by their white masters. They have even boldly suggested that being a multi-racialist is a virtue!

J. One race: The human race.

The African people are very much proud of their race—the human race. They recognise no inescapable fundamental differences among members of even the three main branches of that race: the Caucasoids, Mongoloids and Afrinoids.

They do not subscribe to the theory that there are inherent mental, emotional and psychological differences among the members of the different branches of the human species. They hold the granting of "rights" on the basis of ethnological origin to be the entrenching of racial arrogance and the continued maintenance of contempt for human worth and a disregard for human dignity.

They regard the differences that exist among various groups or subgroups of man to be mainly acquired, and they regard these differences to have been acquired in and through the individual. The African people recognize the influence of common environmental factors in the acquisition of group characters. They do not, and will not tolerate any division of their country for purposes that are calculated to foster racial arrogance, and the continued contempt for the worth of the human personality, and the disregard for human dignity. The African people are full aware that suggestions of apartheid, whether total or partial, of segregation social or political, of Christian trusteeship, white leadership with justice, of partnership etc., are all intended merely as a cloak for their continued oppression, exploitation and degradation. **They deny the foreigners any right to balkanise or pakistanise their country.** To any such schemes, programmes or policies, the African people cannot be a party. The African people are neither racists nor racialists, and they unreservedly condemn all forms of racialism, including multi-racialism. They do not nurse any crude hatred for the European peoples but they do cherish a deep-seated detestation for the Herrenvolk system.

K. Monolithic Giant – Union of African States.

The African people of South Africa recognise themselves as part of one African nation, stretching from Cape to Cairo, Madagascar to Morocco, and pledge themselves to strive and work ceaselessly to find organisational expression for this nation in a merger of free independent African states; a United States of Africa, which will serve as an effective bulwark against the forces of imperialism, colonialism, herrenvolkism and tribalism, and as a sure and lasting foundation for an Africanistic socialist democracy. The African people regard the development of such a nation as essential for the preservation of their sovereignty, of their vital material and spiritual interests and for the creation of conditions under which they will be enabled to make their lasting contribution to human advancement in a free Afrika.

The African people will not tolerate the existence of the other national groups within the confines of one nation. For the healthy growth and development of the African nation it is imperative that all individuals must owe their first, and only, loyalty to the African nation, and not to their ethnic or national groups. The African people regard the influence of material conditions in the development of a nation as being of greater significance than mere ethnic origin. Within the social environment of the African nation there will be room for all individuals who identify themselves materially, intellectually and spiritually with the African nation.

In South Africa the social force which upholds the material, intellectual and spiritual interests of the oppressed peoples is African nationalism, and the social force which upholds the material, intellectual and spiritual interests of the oppressor is Herrenvolkism. These antithetical forces shall find their final reconciliation only [or "everlasting"] in the synthesis of Africanism, in which the contradictory aspects shall have vanished and only the unifying factors which betray no instability shall remain. **Africanism is a social force that upholds the material, intellectual and spiritual interests of the individual.** In this way Africanism is the only logical and practical solution for the social question in Africa.

L. Social relations.

The basic question confronting the African people is identical with that which has faced mankind from the beginning of time itself: the problem of man's relation to his fellowman. It is the question of how man shall live with his fellowman in fellowship; in harmony and in peace. Man moves and has his being in a social environment. In the absence of social life the social question would fall away. Man's relation to his fellowman is determined by his primary needs. The social question, whose structural foundations are to be found in economic determinism, arises within the framework of social relations.

Man is, therefore, a social being and not an economic ANIMAL. To live in harmony with his fellowman, man must recognise THE primacy of the material and spiritual interests of his fellowman, AND must eliminate the tendency on his part to uphold his own interests at the expense of those of his fellowmen. It is only within such a set-up that the human personality can be developed and that respect for it can be developed.

M. Our historic tasks.

The historic tasks of the African liberation movement are clearly the product of Africa's history, of the forces and factors which have made it what it is. To attain complete freedom in Africa, the historic tasks of the movement are:

To forge, foster and consolidate the bonds of African nationhood on a Pan-African basis.

To implement effectively the fundamental principle that the dominion or sovereignty over and the dominion or ownership in the whole territory of the continent vest exclusively and inalienably in the indigenous peoples.

To create and maintain a United States of Africa that will serve and provide a concrete institutional form for the African nation.

To establish an Africanistic socialist democratic social order, recognising the primacy of the vital material, intellectual and spiritual interests of the individual.

A liberation movement must find concrete expression in organisational form and substance in order that it may achieve its historic tasks. The highest organisational form and structure in which the African liberation movement has found concrete expression in South Africa is the NATIONAL AFRICANIST CONGRESS and the various facets of its historic role are:

To create an organisational machinery for the galvanising of the oppressed, exploited and degraded African masses into an irresistible social force bent upon the destruction of all factors and forces that have reduced the stature of man and retarded his growth; and also bent upon the creation of conditions favourable for the restoration of man's worth and dignity and for the development of the African personality.

To establish for the liberation movement a training ground for the production of a determined, dedicated and disciplined collective leadership that will serve, not only as the symbol of national unity on a Pan-African basis, but also as the repository, guardian and custodian of the ideas, principles and methods of the movement, as well as of the policies and programmes of the organisation.

To provide an administrative machinery for the direction, guidance and control of the national liberation movement in its grand march towards the inevitable goal of complete freedom.

N. Africanism – A third social force.

Africanism is Pan-Africanistic in scope, purpose and direction. It is a social force that constitutes the third social force in the world. It serves the material, intellectual and spiritual interests of Africa, and does not in any way serve the interests of either the Eastern or the Western powers. It is continental in scope, covering the entire continent, from Cape to Cairo and from Madagascar to Morocco. It is a social force functioning through the media of African social conditions, and operates to liberate Africa and to create a socialist social order, original in conception, Africanistic in orientation, and creative in content. [It is a social force functioning through the media of African social conditions, and operating to liberate Africa and to create a social order original in conception, Africanistic in orientation, socialistic in content, democratic in form and creative in purpose.] Pan-Africanism became a concrete reality when African nationalists from all over the continent met at Accra. The All-Africa Peoples' Conference, held in Accra in December 1958, laid a promising organisational foundation for African nationalism on a Pan-African basis.

O. Final triumph

In its dialectical march towards the final synthesis of Africanism, African nationalism is destined to create the conditions favourable for the development of the African personality.

The final triumph of the liberation movement under the direction of the N.A.C. is assured. The movement must triumph because in their march to freedom the African people have history on their side. **The militant progressive forces of African nationalism are bound to crush the reactionary forces of white domination.** The movement must triumph because the N.A.C. alone has a message for the oppressed, that their salvation lies in manifest determination to unite as a nation and to struggle for the noble ends of freedom and self-determination. The movement must triumph because, having been purified in the crucible of oppression, the African people can demonstrate to the world genuine democracy in action, a democracy founded upon the ruins of the material and spiritual conflicts

524

and contradictions of the existing social order, a democracy in which man shall at long last find his true self, and a democracy in which the human personality shall blossom to the full.

Document 39c. Constitution

1. *NAME*

The name of the organisation shall be the Pan Africanist Congress, hereinafter referred to as the P.A.C.

2. *AIMS AND OBJECTS:*

(a) To unite and rally the African people into one national front on the basis of African nationalism.

(b) To fight for the overthrow of White domination, and for the implementation and maintenance of the right of self-determination for the African people.

(c) To work and strive for the establishment and maintenance of an Africanist socialist democracy recognising the primacy of the material and spiritual interests of the human personality.

(d) To promote the educational, cultural and economic advancement of the African people.

(e) To propagate and promote the concept of the Federation of Southern Africa, and Pan Africanism by promoting unity among peoples of Africa.

3. *MEMBERSHIP:*

(a) Any African who is of the age of 16 years or above and accepts the principles, programmes and discipline of the P.A.C. shall be eligible for membership, provided that:

(i) He/She is not a member of any political organisation whose policy is inconsistent with that of the P.A.C.

(ii) The National Executive Committee shall from time to time determine whether a certain organisation's policy is inconsistent with the cause of the P.A.C.

(iii) In doubtful cases applications shall be forwarded by the Local Executive Committee to the National Executive Committee, together with the reasons for doubt, before the application is accepted or rejected. Then and only then shall the NEC issue such applicant, upon payment of the enrolment fee, a membership card after which the applicant shall be regarded as a member of the P.A.C.

(b) Application for membership shall be normally made on duly prescribed forms which shall be completed by the applicant and forwarded for consideration by the National Executive Committee.

(c) Each individual member of the P.A.C. shall pay a subscription fee of 2/6 per annum.

(d) On enrolment each member shall be supplied with a membership card.

4. *FINANCE:*

(a) The general funds of the P.A.C. shall be derived from proceeds of functions (parties, dances, football matches, etc.), voluntary subscriptions, levies, appeals, donations, bequests, sales of P.A.C. literature, badges, subscription fees of individual members and other sources approved by the P.A.C.

(b) It shall be competent for the National Executive Committee to finance projects and to request the members to make contributions to such projects should general funds be inadequate.

(c) Funds contributed by members for any specific purpose shall not be alienated for any other purpose save by the resolution of the N.E.C.

(d) The National Executive Committee shall establish, manage and administer a National Reserve Fund, and at the end of the financial year the N.E.C. may vote a sum to be determined for this purpose.

(e) The N.E.C. shall at the end of each year prepare estimates of Revenue and Expenditure for the ensuing year, such estimates shall be submitted to the Annual Conference for consideration.

(f) The financial year of the P.A.C. shall begin on the 1st day of November to the 31st day of October the following year.

(g) All N.E.C. accounts other than recurring expenditure such as rent, salaries, petty cash, shall be submitted to the N.E.C. for approval prior to payment; and an amount not exceeding £10 shall be granted from time to time as petty cash.

(h) All national funds shall be deposited in a bank, and applications for withdrawal must be signed by the Treasurer-General and either the National Secretary or the President.

(i) Subscription fees shall be equally distributed between the three organs of the P.A.C. namely the Branch, the Region and the National organs. Also provision for the keeping of monies shall apply mutatis mutandis between the three organs of the P.A.C. unless otherwise indicated.

(j) The N.E.C. shall at the end of the financial year cause the Treasurer-General to prepare and submit audited accounts to the National Conference.

5. *THE NATIONAL FLAG.*

The official colours of the P.A.C. shall be green, black and gold. The P.A.C. flag shall be green field with a black map of Africa and a gold star in the north-west of Africa. Green shall represent the youth and vitality of the continent. Black shall represent the colour of its people, and gold shall represent the wealth actual and potential.

6. *THE ANNUAL AND SPECIAL NATIONAL CONFERENCE*

(a) The National Conference of the P.A.C. shall be the supreme organ of the organisation and shall lay down the broad basic policy and programme of the P.A.C. and its decisions shall be binding on all members and all organs of the Pan Africanist Congress.

(b) The annual National Conference shall be held at such time and place as may be decided upon by previous Conference or, in the absence of such a decision, by the National Executive Committee.

(c) The functions, duties and powers of the National Conference shall be supervisory, deliberative, administrative and determinative.

(d) A special National Conference may be called by the N.E.C. in cases of emergencies.

(e) Upon receipt of a requisition signed by one-third of the number of branches represented at the previous Conference, a special Conference shall be called by the N.E.C. in connection with the subject matter of the requisition within six weeks of the receipt of such requisition by the National Secretary or President.

(f) The Annual Conference shall consider reports and audited accounts presented by the N.E.C.

(g) Branches which are in full compliance with their fees shall be entitled to be represented at a General Conference by one delegate for every 15 members, provided that no single Branch shall be represented by more than 10 delegates.

(h) Any Branch of the P.A.C. which is in arrears with its subscription fees/levies shall have no right to participate in any General Conference.

(i) At least six weeks before the date for the holding of an Annual Conference the N.E.C. shall frame and circulate an agenda to all branches of the P.A.C. To secure inclusion in the agenda of items from the Region or Branches, these must be forwarded to the National Secretary at least 8 weeks before the date of the Conference. Delegates to the Conference shall be entitled to move amendments at Annual and Special Conferences to any resolutions or proposals, or to any proposed alteration to the Constitution that may appear on any agenda paper of such Conference.

(j) Only P.A.C. organs such as Branches, and not individual members, shall send resolutions for determination at the Annual or Special National Conference.

7. COMPOSITION OF THE ANNUAL NATIONAL CONFERENCE:

The National Conference shall be constituted as follows:

(a) Delegates from Branches elected subject to Section 6 (g) above.

(b) All members of the National Executive Committee and members of the National Working Committee shall be ex-officio delegates to the National Conference.

8. QUALIFICATION FOR DELEGATES TO NATIONAL CONFERENCE:

(a) All delegates to the National Conference must be bona fide members of the organs of the P.A.C.

(b) No person shall be a delegate for more than one organ of the P.A.C.

(c) No person who is in arrears with his subscription fee shall be eligible as a delegate to the National Conference.

(d) Every delegate must, as an individual, accept the Constitution, programme, principles and policies of the P.A.C. and conform to them.

9. COMPOSITION OF THE NATIONAL EXECUTIVE COMMITTEE:

(a) The N.E.C. shall consist of the following:—

(i) The President, the National Secretary, the Treasurer-General, Deputy Presidents from the Regions existing, the Secretariat consisting of the Secretaries for: Pan African Affairs, Foreign Affairs, Publicity and Information, Labour, Education, Culture, Economic Affairs, and the National Organiser and three other members.

(ii) The N.E.C. shall hold office for three years. After the Regional elections the National Secretary shall summon the National Executive Committee, including the Chairmen of Regions who ipso facto become Deputy Presidents, for the election of a Senior Deputy President from among the number of Deputy Presidents. This senior Deputy President shall hold office, until the expiry [*sic*] of the NEC period of office, irrespective of subsequent Regional Election results.

(iii) The members of the N.E.C. shall not hold office in either the Regional or Branch Executive Committees.

10. THE NATIONAL WORKING COMMITTEE:

The National Working Committee shall be the main suborgan of the National Executive Committee, and shall consist of:

(a) The President and

(b) Four other members elected by the N.E.C. from among themselves.

11. DUTIES AND FUNCTIONS OF THE NATIONAL WORKING COMMITTEE:

(a) The N.W.C. shall see to it that the decisions of the Conferences and those of the N.E.C. are duly executed and its policies are duly implemented.

(b) It shall supervise the administrative machinery of the organisation on national, regional and local levels, and shall take such measures as it deems fit to enforce the decisions and programme of the Pan Africanist Congress.

(c) The members of the N.W.C. shall normally reside in an area situated within a radius of 50 miles from headquarters to be indicated from time to time.

(d) The N.W.C. shall meet in a plenary session at least once in a month or, if emergency arises, from day to day to review the major trends, formulate tactics and modify strategy for the guidance of the N.E.C. and assume full powers for safe-guarding the basic programme of the P.A.C.

12. COMPOSITION OF THE REGIONAL CONFERENCE:

(a) The Regional Conference shall consist of representatives from each local branch as indicated in section 6. (g) above.

(b) The Regional Conference shall elect the Regional Executive Committee, composed of the following:—

(i) Chairman and Vice-Chairman.

(ii) Secretary and Assistant Secretary,

(iii) Treasurer, and

(iv) Four other Committee members.

All the above-mentioned shall be elected every two years.

13. *DUTIES AND FUNCTIONS OF THE REGIONAL EXECU-TIVE COMMITTEE:*

(a) To organise local Branches within the Region, and to co-ordinate their activities.

(b) To carry out the programme and policy of the P.A.C., and the instructions and directives received from the National Executive Committee.

(c) To make recommendations to the N.E.C. on matters affecting the welfare of the organisation within their region.

(d) To implement the decisions of the Regional Conference, provided that such decisions are not in conflict with the programme and policy of the P.A.C.

(e) To submit the annual statements and reports to the Regional Conference and to the N.E.C.

(f) To help manage, control and guide the work of the P.A.C. in Educational and Cultural organisations in their Region under the General supervision of the National Executive Committee.

(g) To undertake all such activities as may further the work of the P.A.C. in the Region concerned.

(h) The N.E.C. shall at the end of the financial year cause the Treasurer to prepare and submit audited accounts to the Regional Conference.

14. *REGIONAL FUNDS:*

The National Executive Committee shall determine the manner whereby any funds of the Region shall be kept.

15. *LOCAL BRANCHES:*

(a) The local Branch shall be the basic unit of the organisation of the P.A.C. Each shall be governed by a Branch Executive Committee, which shall consist of:—

(i) Chairman and Vice-Chairman,

(ii) Secretary and Assistant Secretary,

(iii) Treasurer, and

(iv) Four other members.

    (b) The Branch Executive Committee shall be elected at the Branch Annual Meeting.

    (c) There shall be a Branch meeting at least once a fortnight.

    (d) Fifteen members shall constitute a branch.

16. DUTIES AND FUNCTIONS OF THE BRANCH EXECUTIVE COMMITTEE

    (a) To carry on organisational and propaganda work among the masses in order to acquaint them with the standpoint of the P.A.C.

    (b) To keep in close contact with the masses, and to report periodically their experiences to the Regional Committee.

    (c) To study the educational and cultural life of the people in their area.

    (d) To foster the spirit of initiative among the masses by taking a leading part in organising them to solve their problems.

    (e) To recruit new members and to collect the P.A.C. membership dues.

    (f) To forward the list of members to the Regional Executive Committee and to report any act of indiscipline and other dishonour and disputes.

    (g) To discipline any member of the Branch as provided for in the Disciplinary Code.

    (h) To foster political and general education amongst P.A.C. members, especially the youth.

    (i) The Branch Executive Committee shall prepare and submit a financial statement to the Annual Members' Meeting which shall have been endorsed as correct by the Regional Committee.

17. AMENDMENTS:

    (a) This Constitution, or any part thereof, may be amended, rescinded, altered or added thereto by a two-thirds majority of members present and voting at an annual National Conference.

    (b) Proposals regarding any amendment of the Constitution must be sent to the National Secretary at least two months before the Conference at which they are to be considered, and circulated in writing to the Branches at least one month before the conference.

    (c) Two-fifths of the members shall constitute a quorum at any meeting.

Document 39d. "Disciplinary Code"

1. *NAME:*

The name of the organisation shall be the Pan Africanist Congress.

2. *MOTTO:*

S.S.S.   Service, Sacrifice and Suffering.

3. *AIMS:*

a.   African Nationalism [shall] be the basis of our political philosophy for an African Socialist Democratic State.

b.   To maintain ourselves and the movement as vanguard in the struggle for African liberation, with courage and determination.

c.   To wage the struggle in this country for national independence under the banner of the Programme of Action of 1949 adopted in Bloemfontein.

d.   Africanism shall be the ideal for an Africanist Socialist Democracy.

e.   To secure and maintain the complete unity of the movement.

f.   To maintain complete purity of the P.A.C. as the only organisation of the African people struggling for their national liberation in [South] Africa.

g.   To work with other nationalist democratic movements in Africa, with a view to the overthrow of imperialism, colonialism, racialism, tribalism and all forms of national and racial oppression of the African people.

4. *DISCIPLINE:*

i.   There shall be a Disciplinary Tribunal of Justice consisting of three or more members appointed by the National Executive Committee.

ii.   Its decision shall be reported to the National Executive Committee for ratification or otherwise.

iii.   Until appeal comes before the Annual National Conference the decision of the National Executive Committee shall be effective and binding.

5. *SANCTIONS AND PENALTIES.*

a.   The Disciplinary Tribunal of Justice shall enforce all the provisions of this Code in their entirety.

b.   Sanctions and penalties shall include fines, ostracism, isolation, suspension and outright expulsion for a long or short period, or for good.

6. *EXPRESSION OF IDEAS:*

i.   Statements relating to policy, programme of principles and tactical line of the P.A.C. should not be lightly uttered.

ii.   All public utterances or statements must reflect the policy and programme of principles of the P.A.C.

iii. Policy statements in the Press or Radio must be made by the National Executive Committee or the PRESIDENT, or the National Secretary.

iv.   Irresponsible statements made by anybody shall not be countenanced.

7. *RESPONSIBILITY.*

a.   Members must develop a high sense of responsibility and discipline with respect to all matters relating to the Pan Africanist Congress.

b.   They should refrain from tale-bearing, back-biting, gossiping, rumour-mongering and spreading lies and distortions of truth.

c.   Their utterances must reflect the ideas, philosophy, policy and programme of the P.A.C. The ideas of Africa for the Africans, Africans for Humanity and Humanity for God must be understood and appreciated.

8. *SPREADING IDEAS:*

i.   Members must spread the ideas of the P.A.C. through the Press, Radio and platforms fearlessly.

ii.   It is the duty of members to circulate ideas contained in official dogger's bills, circulars, lecturettes, journals, written addresses, etc.

iii. It should be the duty of each and every member to strive to convert people to the ideas of the P.A.C. and into the Movement itself.

iv.   Members must spread the ideas of our cause in the streets, in house to house campaigns, in the trains, in the restaurants, at State functions, cinemas, on the sport fields, at railway platforms, in social gatherings, tea parties, dance parties, in church, in school and at orations by the grave-side.

9. *ACQUISITION OF KNOWLEDGE:*

a. It shall be the duty of each member of the P.A.C. to improve, increase and develop his or her knowledge of the affairs of mankind in general, and of the continent in which we live in particular.

b. Members must read books and newspapers, for it is an offence to the P.A.C. to be ignorant of current events.

c. Members should make it their duty to read and to hold discussions. Lectures should be arranged to educate the rank and file and the less literate members.

d. The more theoretically advanced members should conduct classes for the less advanced.

e. A library of pamphlets, newspaper clippings, extracts from books, lecturettes, etc., should be compiled in order to improve and develop and build the ideas of the members around the central philosophy of African nationalism.

10. *PERSONAL HABITS:*

i. Members of the P.A.C. should develop healthy and sound personal habits.

ii. Members should maintain an exemplary standard of cleanliness.

iii. Members should deport themselves with honour, dignity and proper decorum in the sight of the movement and the nation.

iv. They should be punctual for their appointments, especially for meetings, discussion or other duties relating to the Pan Africanist Congress.

v. They should be tireless in day-to-day work in the interest of the P.A.C. and the nation.

vi. They should develop and demonstrate honesty, frankness and courtesy towards one another.

vii. They should develop and show a true respect for African womanhood and demonstrate in practice the theory of sex equality with respect to men and women of the Pan Africanist Congress.

viii. They should strive to be principled in their approach to the main problems of life and the world.

xi. They should develop a true love for the African people, the Fatherland, in particular, and for all mankind in general.

11. RELATION WITH OTHER MOVEMENTS:

a.   Africanists should be armed with theory to such an extent that they can meet other Movements or groups on a basis of equality, but must not promote the ideas of other Movements or Parties.

b.   Members of the P.A..C. should be keen to study different ideologies, especially the philosophy of African nationalism in order to equip themselves fully.

c.   Members should deport themselves with poise and calmness and dignity in the presence of other movements or Groups, in debating chambers or elsewhere.

d.   They should not display immaturity or pettiness, or apologeticness or ill-conceived inferiority.

e.   Their poise should be natural, dynamic and human but ruthless where necessary.

f.   Vanquish the other man with arguments, and not with a knuckle duster.

12. MEETINGS:

i.   There should be punctual attendance at meetings which should be made known in good time to all members concerned.

ii.   Meetings should be short, precise and to the point.

iii.   The Chairman of the meeting must be respected.

iv.   He must conduct the meeting in a proper procedure and with fairness to the members.

v.   His rulings must be respected by all members of P.A.C.

vi.   Clear decisions, with no equivocations, must be taken, and these should be practicable, and within the scope of the Pan Africanist Congress.

vii.   Meetings of the P.A.C. must be business-like and serious-minded. The Chairman must know his job well, and must have studied methods of conducting meetings.

viii.   Members must be open, frank, objective, brief and business-like in their approach to discussions. There should be no waste of time, redundancy or irrelevant bickerings.

13. DISCUSSION-DECISION.

a.   Decisions affecting the P.A.C. should be arrived at after the issue has been properly discussed by a quorum.

b. In the course of a discussion each and every member is free to air his views and to agree or disagree with all or any member of the movement, including the leader.

c. No man or woman will of necessity enjoy a privileged position entitling his or her views to greater weight than those of others merely because they are expressed by so-and-so. All views should have equal chance of acceptance. The weight of views should depend on relevance and substance, and not on who puts them forth.

d. All discussions shall be on a democratic basis. Every man or woman is entitled to a hearing, and each and all are subject to criticism.

e. Once a decision has been properly taken after a democratic and objective discussion of the subject matter, then it becomes binding on all. In the execution of such a decision no divergencies must be allowed. The leader of the movement has to issue directives which must be obeyed and carried out.

f. At that stage the leader exercises almost dictatorial powers which he wields with impunity, so long as he acts within the letter and spirit of the democratic decision and the Code.

14. *DEMOCRATIC CENTRALISM:*

a. This means that the power of directing the Pan Africanist Congress is centralised in the National Executive Committee which acts through the President who wields unquestioned power as long as he acts within the grounds laid by the decisions of the organisation which must have been democratically arrived at. It means a centralisation of directive and executive power takes place, so as to ensure the most effective implementation of a decision. If P.A.C. wants to forge ahead it must adopt and carry out this principle with firmness and thoroughness.

b. The President shall have emergency powers, which he may delegate, to suspend the entire constitution of the Pan Africanist Congress so as to ensure that the movement emerges intact through a crisis. At that time he directs the Movement by decree, and is answerable for his actions to the National conference.

15. *FACTIONALISM.*

i. Factionalism is the enemy of solidarity and unity of action.

ii. To destroy it at its roots, maximum self-criticism should be encouraged within the movement. A movement that adopts democratic centralism in its approach to its organisational problems will know how to deal with the virus of factionalism.

iii.   Where the normal processes of free discussion fail to curb factional tendencies, then firm iron discipline should come into play, and factional elements, no matter how important, should be chopped off without ceremony.

16. OATH OF ALLEGIANCE:

On my life, honour and fortunes I solemnly pledge and swear that I shall always live up to the aims and aspirations of the Pan Africanist Congress, and shall never, under any circumstances, divulge any secrets, or plans of the organisation, nor betray an Africanist; and that if I dare to divulge any secrets or plans of the Pan Africanist Congress, or betray a member of the cause, or use the influence of the P.A.C. for my own personal interest or advertisement, I do so at my own risk and peril. I will irrevocably obey and act upon the orders, commands, instructions and directions of the National Executive Committee of the Pan Africanist Congress. I will always serve, sacrifice, and suffer anything for the cause for which the P.A.C. stands, and will at all times be ready to go on any mission that I may be called upon to perform. I will make it my duty to foster the cause for which the P.A.C. stands, in any organisation that I may become a member of. I accept the leadership of the Pan Africanist Congress.

17. PUBLICATIONS:

The organisation shall publish its own literature whenever deemed desirable and directed.

18. OUR NATIONAL HEROES' DAY:

a.   The A.M. Lembede Anniversary held on the 31st July annually should be treated and regarded as African Heroes' Day, which all members of the Pan Africanist Congress should observe and rededicate themselves to the cause of Pan Africanism and the goal of United States of Africa.

b.   The Lembede Scholarship Fund should be firmly established so that the right youth of the country should be helped to obtain higher learning.

19. AMENDMENTS to this Code shall be made by a two-thirds majority of members present at an Annual National Conference, provided that notice has been given in accordance with provisions of the Constitution with regard to amendments.

Document 39e. "The Pan Africanist Oath of Allegiance"

(1) On my Life, Honour and Fortunes, I solemnly pledge and swear that I shall always live up to the aims and aspirations of the Pan Africanist Congress and shall never, under any circumstances, divulge any secrets nor betray an Africanist, and that if I dare to divulge any secrets, plans and movements of the P.A.C. or betray any member or the cause, or use the influence of the Pan Africanist Congress for my interests or advertisement, I do so at my own peril.

(2) I will irrevocably obey and act upon the orders, commands, instructions and directions of the N.E.C. of the Pan Africanist Congress.

(3) I will always serve, sacrifice and suffer anything for the cause for which the P.A.C. stands, and will at all times be ready to go on any mission that I may be called upon to perform.

(4) I will make it my aim and duty to foster the cause for which P.A.C. stands in any organisation that I may become a member.

(5) I accept the leadership of the Pan Africanist Congress. Should I fail to honour this Oath, I will accept death as Punishment.

Document 40. " 'Africanism' under the Microscope." Article by Joe Matthews, in *Liberation*, July 1959

The Pan-Africanist Congress which met during the Easter weekend in Johannesburg is reported to have devoted much time to the discussion of policy. Unfortunately the Conference was held largely behind closed doors. The public was not able to judge the attitudes of the Africanists first hand.

Nevertheless it is known that the conference considered two statements of policy. These were the opening speech by Mr. R. M. Sobukwe, elected President of the Pan-Africanists, and also a Manifesto presented by Mr. P. Raboroko.

The manifesto is couched in terms so tortuous as to be almost incomprehensible. The opening speech by Mr. Sobukwe contains certain propositions which cannot be left unchallenged.

After a few introductory remarks Mr. Sobukwe paid tribute to the scientific achievements that were fast establishing man's control over nature but remarked on the unwillingness or inability of man to solve the social relations between man and man. It is this failure, according to Mr. Sobukwe, which has resulted in the existence in the world of the capitalist and socialist sectors of the world. This facile explanation of the origins of capitalism and socialism is designed to conceal rather than clarify the realities of the present world situation.

538

Every schoolboy knows that there was a time when the economic system of production known as capitalism held sway throughout the whole world. By 1913 the capitalist system, after replacing feudalism, had established itself as the dominant mode of production. In that year capitalism was in that phase of development in which the supremacy of monopolies and finance-capital had established itself; in which the export of capital had acquired a great importance; in which the division of the world among the big international trusts had begun; in which the partition of all territories of the earth amongst the great capitalist powers had been completed. That is the phase scientifically referred to as Imperialism. It is precisely imperialism which reduced the whole of Africa into a colonial hunting-ground of capitalist exploitation. It is then that the problem of African freedom from imperialism and colonialism arose. Africa was divided amongst six or seven imperialist powers and that still represents the basic problem of the African continent today. No African patriot can forget this and divert the attention of his people away from this reality. There was no Soviet Union in 1913 and the whole of Africa was suffering under the iron heel of the imperialists.

In 1917 one-sixth of the earth broke away from the imperialist system and the first state controlled by the have-nots came into existence in the Soviet Union.

Today more than one-third of mankind are no longer under imperialism and are building their countries anew on the basis of a completely planned economy in which the profit motive has no part.

It does not help for Mr. Sobukwe to pretend that Africa is somehow exempt from the inevitable historical processes that are at work in the rest of the world. Mr. Sobukwe says that Africa is being wooed now by the two opposed systems or blocs. He says there is a new scramble for Africa. He employs other picturesque expressions. But he avoids saying categorically that Africa suffers today and has suffered for generations from the ravages of the Imperialist powers, Britain, United States, Belgium, Portugal, France etc. In Kenya, Algeria, and elsewhere foreign troops are attempting to halt the march to freedom of the African people. These same powers prevented Banda from accepting the invitation of the Africanists to open their conference. There is not one single private of the Red Army on African soil.

Borrowing terminology from the armoury of the capitalist press Mr. Sobukwe gives the impression that the Soviet Union is somehow trying to gain control of Africa. Knowing that there is not a tittle of evidence to substantiate this he confined himself to vague generalities.

Mr. Sobukwe is at least generous enough to acknowledge the superiority of the socialist economy over the capitalist. He has no choice. The most bitter enemies of socialism cannot deny this any longer. But he then goes on to deplore what he calls "totalitarianism" which he alleges exists in the socialist countries. In the name of the Africanists he makes a choice in favour of "political democracy as understood in the West." Mr. Sobukwe knows nothing of the socialist countries except what he hears from the capitalists. But at least he should have experienced "Western Democracy."

Can any African forget what Western democracy has meant to us? Has it not meant colonial slavery? Is Western Democracy to us not the suppression of liberty in Angola, Algeria, Nyasaland, Rhodesia and elsewhere? Has this western democracy not meant racial discrimination in the United States and South Africa? Mr. Sobukwe must not be surprised if he finds little enthusiasm amongst the African people for Western democracy. To us it means national oppression and exploitation.

For Mr. Sobukwe to say that Africa will borrow the best from the East and West is merely begging the question. He is inviting the Africans to ride astride two horses going in opposite directions. The whole world is marching to socialism and the only argument is on how to carry out the re-organisation of society on the basis of socialism.

The speech deals to some extent with National movements in Africa. It is a pity that Mr. Sobukwe does not describe what a national movement is and how it differs from a political party. If he had done this he would have been compelled to acknowledge that a national Movement unites all the people of an oppressed national group which has lost or is in danger of losing its independence. The National movement brings together the oppressed nationality as a whole no matter to what class they belong as long as they are prepared to fight for national freedom. In the interest of the struggle for national freedom the people sink their political, religious and other differences in the interests of the struggle. It is fatal for such a movement to start witch-hunts of "communists" or "Charterists." Those who engage in these witch-hunts can only be regarded as disrupters of the national movement in the interests of the ruling class which they assist objectively. As long as the African people have not achieved national freedom they will reject attempts to divide them on the basis of ideology. That is why splinter groups have been decisively rejected by the people for the past forty years. The African National Congress which is their mouthpiece remains their primary organisation for that reason.

Mr. Sobukwe deals in his speech with the question of the Indian people. His ideas of the political trends among the Indian people belong to a past era—thirty five years ago. According to him the merchant class among the Indian people provide the leadership of the Indians. He claims that the merchant class identifies itself with the oppressors in South Africa. I am certain that the Indian merchant class which is faced with ruin under the Group Areas Act would be pleased if the ruling class in South Africa showed some appreciation of the identification which it is alleged to exhibit towards the oppressors. That, however, is by the way. What must be contested is Mr. Sobukwe's claim that the merchant class constitutes the leadership of the Indian people. Has Mr. Sobukwe never heard of the struggle whereby the representatives of the merchant class were thrown out of the leadership of the Indian Congress in 1945? Does he not know the history of the Dadoo-Naicker leadership which took over the Indian Congress in the name of the masses? It is well-known that the merchants then formed their own organisation—the South African Indian Organisation. They broke away from the South African Indian Congress on the grounds that it was under the control of "leftists" and "communists." They complained of the Indian Congress policy of cooperation with other groups including the Africans. The Indian merchants demanded the formation of an all-Indian organisation where the Indian people will be by themselves without interference. Has Mr. Sobukwe heard these aims before? Is not the language of the Indian merchants very similar to his own?

No, Mr. Sobukwe, the correct thing to do is to study Indian history and learn a little of the struggle of the Indian national group against oppression in South Africa. The majority of the Indian people follow the lead of the Indian Congress which wholeheartedly supports the policy of the African National Congress.

In dealing with the ultimate goals of the Africanists Mr. Sobukwe remarked that the Africanists "do not all subscribe to the fashionable doctrine of South African Exceptionalism." This would be admirable if it were true. He, in common with other Africanists for instance, seems to deny that the Africans in South Africa suffer class oppression. They affirm that the Africans only suffer national oppression. There is no class struggle in South Africa, say the Africanists. This is the worst example of South African exceptionalism. The fact is that the African people suffer double oppression—national and class oppression. National or caste oppression means that all Africans whatever their class position suffer certain disabilities as such. But of course there are other disabilities that they suffer in common with workers of all races as part of the working class. In Ghana they have freed themselves from national oppression. But the class oppression still remains. In a certain historical situation the class struggle may be blurred by the national struggle but to forget it is treason to the masses of the people. Perhaps that is why the long opening speech by Mr. Sobukwe contains not one word of interest to the long suffering masses of our people—the farm labourers, peasants and urban workers.

Finally Mr. Sobukwe proposed a new definition of an African and affirmed the refusal of the Africanists to guarantee the rights of minorities. He was prepared to accept as an African everybody who owes loyalty to Africa and who accepted the democratic rule of an African majority. There is much in that definition which would be of great interest to students of logic. As far as we are concerned Africans will remain Africans no matter what definitions are adopted. The real point of importance is the fact that the Africanist policy is to refuse guarantee of rights to minority groups. According to Mr. Sobukwe only individual rights are recognised in the Africanist conception of democracy. Very generous indeed to at least recognise the rights of individuals!

But the whole point is that in countries where the population is not homogeneous, where there are a number of national groups, it becomes necessary to go further than merely to recognise the right of each individual citizen of the state. It becomes essential to create conditions under which those who do not belong to the numerically superior national groups are able to develop their languages, culture and customs without let or hindrance.

The Pan-Africanist Congress adopted as its policy the Declaration of Human Rights of the United Nations. They ought to remember that this Declaration was adopted after a world war caused by groups which refused to respect minority rights. The Nazis practised oppression of the Jewish minority by the majority. It is the "democratic German majority" which oppressed the Jews. True enough each individual Jew had equal rights theoretically in the state in common with other individuals. But no rights as a minority group.

The guarantee of full rights to minority groups is fundamental in any truly democratic society.

And it must be emphasised that this has nothing to do with the preservation of the privileged position of dominant minority groups exercised at the expense of the majority. In various parts of Africa, notably in Kenya, white minorities are demanding guarantees of their present privileged position even after the achievement of power by the Africans. Quite obviously this cannot be mistaken for the guarantee of the democratic rights of minorities. But the aims of the African people can clearly not be to replace the present set-up with one in which minorities are suppressed.

The African National Congress throughout the whole of its history has always been most careful about the safeguarding of the rights of minorities. Despite the sufferings inflicted upon the African people by non-African minorities, our national organisation has never allowed bitterness and desperation to dictate its policies on this question. The Africanists must take a look at what is happening to the English in South Africa and the manner in which their rights are fast disappearing. It is almost becoming a crime to speak English. Yet the English have equal rights with the Afrikaners as individuals! The Africans do not want to repeat the mistakes of Afrikaner Nationalism.

The question still remains as to the plan of the Africanists for the people NOW. The African people are under attack now more than ever. The issues that face them must be taken up with courage no matter what the odds are against which they are pitted. The people want a clear lead. They want "positive action" to use the popular expression of genuine African Nationalists throughout Africa.

On these matters Mr. Sobukwe gives us not a clue. Or is it perhaps that the risks of challenging the Nationalist government are too great? Every second African is a master of oratory and rhetoric. We do not need these any more. Even more important than what we will do when we are free is the immediate question of what we are prepared to do now. On that basis the people will judge any political group which desires to lead them. Visions, no matter how vividly portrayed, can never take the place of present-day realities.

Document 41. "The State of the Nation." Address by R. M. Sobukwe, on "National Heroes' Day," August 2, 1959

Mr. Speaker Sir, Sons and Daughters of Afrika. Just over three months ago, on the 6th April, we met in the Communal Hall in Orlando, Johannesburg, to launch the ship of freedom—the Pan-Africanist Congress. On that historic day the African people declared total war against white domination, not only in South Africa but throughout the continent. On that day there entered into the maelstrom of South African politics an organisation dedicated to the cause of African emancipation and independence; an organisation committed to the overthrow of white supremacy and the establishment of an Africanist Socialist Democracy.

Oppressed versus Oppressor.

It is just over three months that the Pan Africanist Congress has been born, but within that short space of time she has successfully pinpointed the basic assumptions in our struggle, namely that:—

1. The illiterate and semi-literate masses of the African people are the key to, the core and cornerstone of the struggle for democracy in this country.

2. African nationalism is the only liberatory creed that can weld these masses who are members of heterogeneous tribes into a solid, disciplined and united fighting force; provide them with loyalty higher than that of the tribe and give formal expression to their desire to be a nation.

3. The struggle in South Africa is part of the greater struggle throughout the continent for the restoration to the African people of the effective control of their land. The ultimate goal of our struggle, therefore, is the formation of a United States of Afrika.

These pronouncements have struck a responsive chord in the hearts of the Sons and Daughters of the land, and awakened the imagination of the youth of our land while giving hope to the aged who for years have lived in the trough of despair. Indeed, the aged can now truly say:

"Lord now lettest Thou thy servant
depart in peace, according to Thy will:
For mine eyes have seen Thy salvation."

The issues are clear-cut. The Pan-Africanist Congress has done away with equivocation and clever talk. The decks are cleared, and in the arena of South African politics there are today only two adversaries: the oppressor and the oppressed; the master and the slave. We are on the eve of a continental showdown between the forces of evil and the forces of righteousness; the champions of oppression and the champions of freedom. Realising this, the oppressor is panic-stricken and is making feverish preparations for a last-ditch stand in defence of white supremacy. On the other hand, the forces of freedom are gathering strength from day to day, disciplining, nerving and steeling themselves for the imminent struggle.

Afrika for Africans.

Once again, as in 1949, the African people are waiting expectantly and eagerly the emergence of a bold and courageous programme from the Pan Africanist Congress, an organisation that has its roots among the masses, and whose leadership comes from their loins. Not only has the Pan Africanist Congress succeeded in raising the eyes of our people above the dust of immediate conflict to the genuine democracy that lies beyond the stormy sea of struggle, but it has imparted a meaning and a purpose to their struggle. The African people, therefore, are awake! They are waiting, waiting eagerly and expectantly, waiting for the call, the call to battle, to battle for the reconquest of the continent of Afrika which for over 300 years has been the prostitute of the philanderers and rakes of western capitalism. IZWE LETHU I AFRIKA (Africa must come back)—that is the cry ringing throughout the continent. Afrika for the Africans. (A democratic rule of an African majority.) IZWE LETHU I AFRIKA! Those are the words that spell the doom of white supremacy in Afrika.

Position in the Continent.

Throughout the continent of Afrika the struggle is being relentlessly waged against the historical anachronisms of imperialism, colonialism and white supremacy. Precious African blood is flowing in Algeria, where the Sons and Daughters of Afrika, under the courageous leadership of Ferhat

Abbas of the government of Free Algeria are paying the supreme sacrifice for the recovery of the destroyed shrines.

Greater and greater efforts are being made by the independent countries of Afrika to mould, shape and assert the African personality, and to lay the foundations for a United States of Afrika. Just recently the heads of the States of Ghana, Guinea and Liberia met in conference to discuss methods of furthering the cause of Pan Africanism.

In Tanganyika, Nyerere is fighting for the revision of the multi-racial constitution imposed on the African people by imperialist Britain, and is pressing for the practical application of a non-racial democratic principle of "one man one vote". In Uganda, as our Bulletin stated, "British imperialism is locked in mortal combat with African nationalism." In Central Afrika tension is going high, and there is clear evidence that in the struggle between Kazamu Banda and Roy Welensky, Banda will emerge triumphant. In fact, the signs are that not only Nyasaland but also Northern Rhodesia as well, will secede from the unholy federation of Welensky and Lennox-Boyd.

South Africa.

Throughout Afrika, then, the forces of white supremacy are in retreat before the irresistible march of African nationalism. This is the era of African emancipation. Afrika holds the stage today. For the first time, positive action is being taken by the world against the inhuman policies of South Africa's white settler foreign minority governments. And the countries that have taken the lead in this world-wide boycott of South African goods are the countries of Afrika and those governed by people of African descent. And in South Africa, what is the position? Well you all know, that there has been talk from certain quarters of "hitting the nationalists in the stomach." We would have used the word "belly", but responsible, moderate leaders, you see, do not use such ugly words. There was such talk then, and lists were prepared. But immediately one so-called "nationalist concern" made certain sectional trade-Union concessions, it was no longer a nationalist controlled firm, and its products were no longer nationalist products. The old meaningless stunts are still being used by certain quarters. But there is a boycott of beerhalls launched by the courageous women of Durban—a movement originating from the masses and controlled by them. Nobody doubts its success. The evidence is there for all to see. If their "friends" do not interfere with the Durban women they will undoubtedly achieve their goal—acquiring for the African in Durban the status of human beings. There is also the potato boycott which, while commanding the active support of all persons because of the atrocities perpetrated by white farmers against African convict labourers, has unfortunately been handled by the quarters aforementioned. The result has been that these quarters which fear the militancy of the African people more than they loathe oppression, are hoping and praying that the boycott will fizzle out before they are compelled to call it off.

What of the Pan Africanist Congress?

We are met here today to commemorate our national Heroes' Day. We are, today, going down the corridor of time and renewing acquaintance with the heroes of Afrika's past—those men and women who nourished the tree of African freedom and independence with their blood; those great Sons and Daughters of Afrika who died in order that we may be free in the land of our birth. We are met here, today, to rededicate our lives to the cause of Afrika, to establish contact, beyond the grave, with the great African Heroes and to assure them that their struggle was not in vain. We are met here, Sons and Daughters of our beloved land, to drink from the fountain of African achievement, to remember the men and women who begot us, to remind ourselves of where we come from and to restate our goals. We are here to draw inspiration from the heroes of Thaba Bosiu, Isandlwana, Sandile's kop, Keiskama Hoek, Blood River and numerous other battlefields where our forefathers fell before the bullets of the foreign invader. We are here to draw inspiration from the Sons and Daughters of Afrika who gave their all to the cause and were physically broken in the struggle. We are met here, Sons and Daughters of Afrika, to take a trowel in our right hand and a shield and sword in our left, to commence the tremendous task of rebuilding the walls of Afrika.

We are gathered here, today, to reiterate our resolve to declare total war against the demi-god of white supremacy. We are here to serve an ultimatum on the forces of oppression. We are here to say Afrika must be free. We are here to make an appeal to African intellectuals and business men, African urban and rural proletariat, to join forces in a determined, ruthless, relentless and total war against white supremacy. We say to waverers and fence-sitters, choose now, tomorrow may be too late. Choose now, because very soon we shall be saying, with biblical simplicity, that He who is not with us is against us.

PAN AFRICANIST CONGRESS Programme.

The decks are cleared. The battle must be joined. Therefore, Sons and Daughters of the soil, in the name of the National Working Committee of the Pan Africanist Congress, I announce the STATUS CAMPAIGN—a campaign which once launched will not be called off until our goal is achieved. This is an unfolding and expanding campaign, involving the political, economic and social status of the African. It is all-embracing and multi-frontal, but is itself part of our unfolding and expanding dynamic nation-building Programme. Details of the campaign have already been circulated to all regions, with specific instructions that Branches be encouraged to discuss the campaign freely and frankly. I shall, therefore, not outline the campaign here, but shall deal instead with the objectives of this campaign.

Mental Revolution.

We have stated in the past, in all our documents, that whatever campaign is launched by any liberatory movement worth the name, must at all times be related to the ultimate objectives and must assist in building the fighting capacity of the masses.

Now for over three hundred years, the white, foreign, ruling minority has used its power to inculcate in the African a feeling of inferiority. This group has educated the African to accept the status quo of white supremacy and Black inferiority as normal.

It is our task to exorcise this slave mentality, and to impart to the African masses that sense of self-reliance which will make them prefer self-government to the good government preferred by the A.N.C.'s leader. It must clearly be understood that we are not begging the foreign minorities to treat our people courteously. We are calling on our people to assert their personality. We are not hoping for a change of heart on the part of the christian oppressor. We are reminding our people that they are men and women, with children of their own and homes of their own, and that just as much as they resent being called "kwedini" or "mfana" or "moshemane" by us—which is what "boy" means—they must equally resent such terms of address by the foreigner. We are reminding our people that acceptance of any indignity, any insult, any humiliation is acceptance of inferiority. They must first think of themselves as men and women before they can demand to be treated as such. The campaign will free the mind of the African and once the mind is free, the body will soon be free. Once white supremacy has become mentally untenable to our people, it will become physically untenable too, and will go. I am absolutely certain that once the STATUS CAMPAIGN is launched, the masses will themselves come forward with suggestions for the extension of the area of assault—and once that happens, the twilight of white supremacy and the dawn of African independence in this part of the continent, will have set in.

Soft Campaign:

Certain quarters have accused us of being concerned more with our status, with being addressed as "Sirs" and "Mesdames" than with the economic plight of the African people. Our reply is that such accusations can come only from those who think of the African as an economic animal—a thing to be fed—and not as a human being. It is only those who have been herrenvolkenised by their herrenvolk environment, people who have no idea whatsoever of the African personality, who can expect us to be lick-spittles in order to get more crumbs from the oppressor. Others again, have said that we have chosen a soft campaign, without any risks, because we fear to challenge apartheid totally. Let it be clear that we are not fighting just apartheid. We are fighting the whole concept of white supremacy. And we are fully aware of the nature and size of our task. And we will not shirk it. Right from the beginning of the campaign, the leaders will be in front. They will picket the concerns that are to be boycotted. And they will do so under our slogan of "no bail, no defence, no fine." And that slogan will not be changed until we land on the shores of freedom and independence.

Clarion call:

We therefore call first of all on the members of the Pan-Africanist Congress who are the hard core, the advance guard that must lead the struggle and on the African people in general. All of them, without exception, must wait for the call. They will be kept informed of every step we take. And when the call comes, we expect them to respond like a disciplined people. There is plenty of suffering ahead. There is plenty of suffering ahead. [*sic*] The oppressor will not take this lying down. But we are ready. We will not go back. Come what may. This campaign will be maintained, unfolded and expanded until Masiza's question is answered: "Koda kube nini Nkosi Zonke izizwe zisinyasha pantsi kweenyawo?" (Until when, oh Lord, will all nations trample us under foot)—until we can answer "no more". We will go on, Sons and Daughters of Afrika, until in every shanty, in every bunk in the compounds, in every hut in the deserted villages, in every valley and on every hill top, the cry of African freedom and independence is heard. We will continue until we walk the streets of our land as free men and free women, our heads held high. We will go on until the day dawns when every person who is in Afrika will be African and a man's colour will be as irrelevant as is the shape of his ears. We will go on, steadfastly, relentlessly and determinedly until the cry of "Afrika for the Africans, the Africans for humanity and humanity for God" becomes a

548

reality; until government of the Africans by the Africans for the Africans is a fait accompli.

We will not look back. We will not deviate, and as the heat of oppression mounts we shall become purer and purer, learning new lessons, and leaving all the dross of racialism and similar evils behind to emerge as a people mentally and physically disciplined, appreciative of the fact that:

There is only one man in the world,
And his name is All men.
There is only one woman in the world,
And her name is All women.

Sons and Daughters of Afrika, we are today on the threshold of a historic era. We are about to witness momentous events. We are blazing a new trail, and we invite you to be, with us creators of history. Join us in the march of freedom. March with us to independence. To independence now. Tomorrow the United States of Afrika.

IZWE LETHU!!

Document 42. Report of the National Executive Committee of the PAC, Submitted to the Annual Conference, December 19–20, 1959

Sons and Daughters of Afrika!

The Pan Africanist Congress was successfully launched as the liberation movement of the African people at a Convention held at the Communal Hall, Orlando, Johannesburg, from the 4th to the 6th of April, 1959. Ever since then your Congress has been able to forge ahead in its determined effort to realise our noble aspirations in our life time, namely,

To unite and rally the African people into one national front on the basis of African nationalism, and to fight for the implementation of the right of self determination for the African people.

It is our pleasant duty to bid you all welcome to this first National Conference of the Pan Africanist Congress. The fact that you are able to be here is proof positive of your consuming desire to strive for the cause of African independence and unity.

Since our historic and memorable inaugural Convention, a number of developments have taken place in our country which may be astonishing to individuals who are unfamiliar with the contradictions of White minority rule.

Throughout the year the imperialist Press has carried on a campaign of sustained vilification against us. But because of the determined work of our members, the work of your Congress has thus far been a resounding success. It is true that "since no Press built us up, no Press can destroy us."

The story of those confusionist "leaders" who would be too pleased to see us fall down is [too] well known to merit serious attention here. It may be mentioned, however, that some of them have grave misgivings about their ill-conceived attitude towards African nationalism. It is common knowledge that the emergence of the Pan Africanist Congress has resulted in endless spate of convulsions in the bosom of the Charterists.

In the oppressor's camp there has been unbounded fear. More recently there has been talk of "possible showdown with subversive elements." No stretch of imagination is required to see deeper into the irresponsible and stupid pronouncements of Erasmus. We are persuaded to regard the reorganisation of the White army as a compliment to our readiness to challenge the reactionary forces.

You have come together here with one aim in view—to take positive steps to crush, once and for all, White colonialism and imperialism in our Fatherland. We are fully aware of the difficulties and pitfalls that will be placed before us in our forward march. But we are on the march, and there is no turning back; there is no side-stepping, and no obstacles can stand up against us. We are vigilant and determined.

ORGANISATION:

The task of organising effectively was an up-hill one. As a young body, perhaps not well versed in the effective means of fund-raising, we have had to manage under great financial strain. Credit must go to the National Organiser who fulfilled his task of organising even at personal expense. Branches and Regions have been established throughout the country. Masses of people in the rural areas have been organised and brought nearer to the light of the Pan Africanist Congress. Progress in membership has been noticeably steady in the latter half of the period under review, as compared to the first four months of our existence. There are one-hundred and fifty-three (153) Branches with a total membership of thirty-one thousand and thirty-five (31,035). This falls far below our target of a hundred thousand (100,000) members. Despite that we are undaunted. The march goes on.

REGIONS: Your Congress has established five Regions:

WITWATERSRAND. This Region has not functioned well. There has been strained relationship between the Regional Executive Committee and Branches. Consequently the National Working Committee has suspended the former from office pending a special Regional Conference to be held as soon as convenient to thrash out matters in dispute. In the meantime administration of this Region is in the hands of the National Working Committee.

CAPE BORDER. Despite initial set-backs, good progress in this Region is now on record. The East London and Stutterheim Branches have done outstanding work in organising many people into the Pan Africanist Congress. Mention must be made of Queenstown where sterling work has been done by African women.

NATAL. Determined hard work has been carried out by this Region. However, much scope of work remains open.

O.F.S. This Region is composed of eight (8) Branches. It must be stated that the membership potentiality of this Region has hardly been tapped. Owing to meagre funds organisers from National Headquarters have not been able to visit this Region during the year.

WESTERN CAPE. This Region has to be congratulated for the very good work done. Mention must be made of its stream-lined office routine work, second to none amongst the Regions.

By and large, organisational work by the Regions has been [done] fairly well during the year. There is, however, one disturbing point that merits serious attention immediately. With the exception of the Western Cape Region, the rest have not followed strictly the instructions of National Headquarters with regard to the regular submitting of Regional Reports and financial statements.

It must be emphasised that the work of your Congress is great, and as such proper records have to be kept up to date. Regional Reports and finance records must be forwarded to National Headquarters with precise regularity. Most of our work could not be undertaken owing to lack of successful financial drives.

BRANCHES:

Branch level activity has been most encouraging. Again it must be pointed out that it is the task of the Regional Secretaries to submit regular reports to the National Secretary about the state of the Branches. Branches and Regions were provided with Statistical Forms to be used in their reports. Very few of these have been returned duly completed. With the exception of the Border Region and Queenstown and the W. Cape Region.

FINANCE:

As the National Treasurer's Report indicates, the question of finance has been the cause of great handicap. The attention of Branches and Regions is drawn to our regulations with regard to members' monthly levies. It is disturbing to note that the matter of levies has not been properly handled by the Branches and Regions throughout the year. You are urged to devise efficient means of raising funds in order to write off the deficit occurring in the financial accounts of the year.

PAID OFFICIALS:

In order to have effective and efficient organisational machinery, it is necessary that the National Organiser and National Secretary be paid officials of the Congress. Funds have to be voted, and made available, so that these officials may be kept in our permanent employment for the cause of Afrika.

"THE AFRICANIST":

This monthly journal is produced under very great difficulties because of insufficiency of funds, and also because some Branches do not report back monies in respect of the sale of it by them. Plans are afoot to have it printed so that mass distribution of it can be possible. Branches must know that failure to report monies due is not only dishonesty but also calculated systematic sabotage. Unless arrears are paid in, no copies shall be sent to defaulting Branches.

"PAC BULLETIN":

Some time back the Secretariat announced the launching of the fortnightly news-sheet, to be known as the "P.A.C. BULLETIN." The first and only issue of this bulletin was published in September. Owing to lack of enthusiastic team work within the Secretariat no subsequent issues have been released. We will not tolerate any laxity from any source, and are determined to enforce discipline within our ranks whatever the consequences.

FLAGS AND BADGES:

Monies have been received from certain Branches and Regions as deposits on our Flags and badges. Another difficulty of insufficient funds crops up here too. Most Branches have been slow to respond to the call for orders. However, an order for the mass production of these has been made with the manufacturers, and a further report in this matter shall be made in due course. These should have been available had all the Branches sent in their monies in time.

SECRETARIAT:

Keen progress is being made by the Secretariat. The Secretary for Pan African Affairs has established on a sound basis a firm link between your Congress and other nationalist movements in Afrika. The Secretary for Foreign Affairs has kept us informed about world trends. Against odds, the Publicity and Information Secretary has struggled to put across our message to the world through the Press. Because of the need to defend our ideological stand, the Secretary for Education was instructed to work jointly with the Secretary for Publicity and Information. Labour Secretary is to be congratulated for the magnificent work of his department in organising and founding a country-wide African workers' organisation. A vigilant eye has been kept on all matters that affect us by the Secretary for Economic Affairs. Cultural Affairs Secretary has been in the vanguard of our progress in the Western Cape.

STATUS CAMPAIGN:

Copies of the proposed Status Campaign were sent out to Regional Secretaries for distribution to the Branches, with specific instruction to discuss thoroughly this proposed campaign. Most Regions did nothing about this, and the matter has been left over to this Conference.

BOYCOTT OF S.A. GOODS:

In pursuance of a decision of the All African People's Conference, we have supported and encouraged the boycott of all South African Goods by countries abroad. A Press Statement to this effect was released earlier in the year. It is our opinion that the crippling of the monopolistic South African White economy shall have the effect of bringing back some sense to Verwoerd's government of minority rule.

TROUBLED AFRIKA:

Your Executive has interested itself in developments throughout colonial Africa.

CENTRAL AFRICAN FEDERATION. The early part of this year has witnessed some unrest in the Central African Federation. Dr. Hastings Banda, who courageously led his people against Welensky's oppressive government, continues to be detained in jail by the White man. Your

Congress has on several occasions expressed solidarity with the arrested leaders of Nyasaland, and demanded their immediate release from wrongful imprisonment.

BELGIAN CONGO. The Congo has been the scene of mass butchery of African inhabitants by the White settlers. Your Executive is of the firm opinion that there can be no peace in the Congo until Africans have been freed from the oppressive Belgian Colonial System. King Baudouin must leave the Congo, and, as in the rest of the continent, imperialists must quit Africa.

ALGERIA. Algeria continues to be the scene of ferocious fighting for freedom. The Algerians are demanding the return of their land to its rightful owners. The war of Algerian independence is being bitterly fought. It is a war of torture and treachery, of ambush and sabotage. We salute the Africans of Algeria who have consistently maintained their right "to take what is theirs by force if necessary."

Throughout colonial Africa the minority settlers continue to inflict severities and atrocities on innocent men, women and children. A redeeming feature in this whole sordid business of unjust foreign rule is the declared realisation of all African nationalists that peace and prosperity on the continent is bound up with the complete and unconditional liberation of the African people.

The outside world has to be reminded again that Africa is for the Africans, and is not an extension of Europe or any other continent; that true democracy can be established on the continent as a whole only when White supremacy has been destroyed; that it is our aim to bring about a government of the Africans by the Africans for the Africans, with everybody who owes his only loyalty to Afrika and who is prepared to accept the democratic rule of an African majority being regarded as an African. We aim at the establishment of an Africanist socialist democracy.

EMERGENT AFRIKA:

Effective contact has been kept up by your Congress with the new emergent states of Africa.

GHANA. The office of the Bureau of African Affairs, Accra, has shown great interest in the progress of the Pan Africanist Congress, and has kept us in regular supply of literature and information relevant to the noble cause of African freedom.

REPUBLIC OF GUINEA. Guinea, under the able leadership of Mr. Sekou Toure, has also been kept informed about our progress here. Your Executive is full of admiration for the increasing importance which this young African state is assuming in the international field.

554

AFRICAN LABOUR TALKS. A month ago there was held in Accra an All-African Trade Unions' Conference. Your Congress was invited to send two delegates to this meeting, but because of technical difficulties it was not possible to do so. An appropriate message was, however, forwarded to the Conference.

BASUTOLAND:

We are meeting on the eve of the first elections to be conducted under the new Constitution of Representative Government for Basutoland. While we are fully aware of its crippling limitations, we welcome the gains made by the people of Basutoland under this Constitution. The Basuto Congress Party is to be wished well in the forthcoming elections. Unto it we say: Fight your way through to a full and free Responsible Government for Basutoland, the only effective guarantee of independence for your people.

TRIBUTES:

African nationalist movements throughout the continent experienced the unfortunate loss of noble Son of Afrika, George Padmore, who was adviser on African Affairs to the Premier of Ghana. The late George Padmore was a courageous Son of Afrika who did much to promote the concept of Pan Africanism and the idea of a United States of Africa. Your Executive feels deeply his loss, and a message of condolence was sent to his principal, the Hon. Dr. Kwame Nkrumah. Your National Executive Committee decided to include the name of the late George Padmore in the list of our national heroes, and that due honour be paid to his name in all our coming commemorations of our National Heroes' Day.

We mourn the death recently of noble Son of Afrika Moses Loso, a courageous young Africanist who was chairman of the Orlando East Branch No. 2. Branches in the Witwatersrand Region have paid tribute to his memory.

OUR DESERT:

Your Congress is alarmed by the insistence of the French government to carry out their nuclear tests in the Sahara in furtherance of their predatory and genocidal ambitions. We have on several occasions protested to express our disapproval of the French to explode bombs in a part of our continent. Your Executive suggested Paris as the best suitable venue for such tests.

AT HOME:

In South Africa the year has witnessed the White man's continued determination to complete and worsen his plunder and rape of our country. The government's policy has reached the stage of maximum inhumanity.

De Wet Nel has shown almost lunatic feats in his endeavours to promote the so-called Bantustan schemes. Our stand has been that no man has any right to balkanise or 'pakistanise' any part of our continent. Cyprian Bhekuzulu, Botha Sigcau and others of the same type shall remain exposed as enemies of the people.

Fort Hare University College, the only seat of higher learning for Africans, has fallen victim to the pipe-dreams of Verwoerd's Bantu Education. Henceforth this College shall be under the thumb of Maree. The reorganisation of the staff and the recent appointments of new teachers there have only served to confirm our fears about the future of higher learning in this country. A bunch of backveld lecturers has been raked to fill up the posts vacated by the arbitrary dismissals of worthy instructors. Your Congress pledges itself to re-educate the youth of Afrika who, through no fault of theirs, are forced to gulp in poisonous Bantu Education.

Natal has been the scene of courageous fighting by African women against the unbearable contradictions of White minority rule. We salute the women of Natal for their determined stand against unjust foreign domination.

South West Africans have recently been invaded by the armed troops of Erasmus. We are alarmed at the naked brutality of force arrogantly displayed against the Windhoek Africans who were rightly resisting further inroads into their meagre rights.

Those are but some of the highlights of the year. Nothing has been said about the millions of souls forced to suffer by the unjust system which is the oppressive link in the vortex of the imperialist chain.

Sons and Daughters of Afrika! You are called upon to accept the challenge of oppression. You are called upon to formulate and forge ahead with a dynamic programme destined to crush, once and for all, white domination. The torch that was lit by the emergence of your Congress is blazing across this country. From now on events will take a rapid turn, and there will be no turning back. As never before, your Executive shall continue to be vigilant, and shall give greater strength to the Sons and Daughters of Afrika who look to the Pan Africanist Congress for vitality and sustenance in their fight for African freedom. Izwe lethu i Afrika!

19:12:1959.

Issued by the
National Executive Committee,
Pan Africanist Congress.

Signed:
Potlako K. Leballo

THE EVE OF SHARPEVILLE AND AFTERWARDS,
MARCH–APRIL 1960

**Document 43. "Passes Must Go Now . . . No Bail: No Defence: No Fine!!!"
Flyer issued by the National Executive Committee, PAC [following December
19–20, 1959]**

PASSES MUST GO NOW . . .
NO BAIL:
NO DEFENCE:
NO FINE!!!

Sons and Daughters of Afrika,

The national conference of the PAN AFRICANIST CONGRESS, held on the 19th and 20th December, 1959, decided that the President should call on the African nation to take DECISIVE POSITIVE ACTION against the PASS LAWS. The President, Mr. Mangaliso R. Sobukwe, shall make that call very soon.

Therefore Remember this Message!

1. Save food, save money now.
2. Send in your cash donations to the National Secretary, Pan Africanist Congress, P.O. Box 1610, Johannesburg. This money will assist the dependants of the nation.
3. Remember your leaders. The call to action shall come from them *only*. Do not be deceived by others.
4. Be on the alert. Know what we are fighting for, so that should anyone fall in the struggle you should know what he was fighting for.
5. There is no need for bloodshed. What is needed is UNITY and SACRIFICE. In 1960 we take our first step, in 1963 our last, towards freedom and independence.

FORWARD THEN — TO POSITIVE ACTION NOW.

———— o ————

Issued by the National Executive,
Pan Africanist Congress,
P.O. Box 1610,
JOHANNESBURG.
PASSES ARE HATEFUL
PASSES ARE HUMILIATING
PASSES ARE
DEGRADING.

OUR CAMPAIGN
IS FOR REAL
INDEPENDENCE

Document 44. Notes taken by African police constable at PAC meeting, Langa, Cape Town, February 14, 1960

Note: Reproduced from original typescript of notes on speeches delivered in Xhosa and translated into English: "Note taken by B/D/Const. L. Jubase at the Pan Africanist Congress meeting, Bunga Square, Langa, on 14/2/1960 from 1 p.m. to 4:30 p.m."

Gasson Ndlovu (chairman): Sons and daughters of Africa. This meeting is called by a new organisation called the Pan Africanist Congress. Here we have got strangers. Our president from Johannesburg. His secretary from Durban. One from external affairs, Mr. Ngendane. Sons and daughters of Africa, when I was taught playing sticks, I was told that if your opponent looks round, then it is your chance. Now it is our chance to [get] the Dutch people. Recently they were tackled by Mr. Macmillan. Now I want to talk to all the Africans about oppression. I will show you our president, Mr. Sobukwe, Mr. [S. T.] Ngendane, Mr. [A. B.] Ngcobo, and Mr. Leballo. I will call Mr. Mlokoti, my first speaker.

C. Mlokoti: Mr. Chairman, sons and daughters of this country, I thank you very much for welcoming our leaders of the Pan Africanist Congress, the organisation of the proper Africans. This organisation is for Africans. It is a new organisation. It was only formed on the 6th April last year. There were many days, but we appointed the 6th of April because the Dutch came here on the 6th of April in 1652.

The parliament in this country is only for the white people. It has got nothing to do with us. There had been white people who had been going around with us. They were calling themselves liberals and some, democrats. We do not want to be united with our enemies. Those white people go into one gate with Dr. Verwoerd. If you come with multiracialism, you will never face your enemy. Here now you are called Bantus, so that you should not claim any rights in this country. Here in Africa there is the Indian Congress. How can you go to India and then form an "African" National Congress? In India because [sic] you can find yourself under the Indian Government. There is no more room for Europeans in Africa. We want the Africans to rule because they are the majority. We want African Nationalism. We do not hate the white people. The Europeans are sitting alone in Parliament making all the laws to oppress you day and night. Do they like you? In that way? We have come to preach to you to leave all the organisations where you are led by Europeans, who call you good boys because you sell *New Age* for them.

A. Matrose: Africans, I will not be very long because everything has been said. We will not keep on repeating what has been said in the previous meetings. Mr. Mlokoti has explained everything about the organisation. I am very sorry to tell you that there are some of our people who believe that nothing is better unless it is brought about by a white man. These people will be slaves for good. You are Africans. You are not Bantus. We do not know anything like Bantus. I am very sorry for those people who are misled by white people to go and protest at the Native Affairs and other places. Please do not put women in front because you overpower them. Please do not be misled by white people. You are the second gold mine of the white people. Choose your way now. We are the only people who have the right to manage the affairs of Africa. Since the white people came to this country, people were no longer happy. Then oppression started. We want young people in this organisation. We have no work rights in this country. We have not even got wives, because when you come back from work you find her in the police station where you have got to pay four pounds.

S. T. Ngendane: Sons and daughters of Africa, the oppressed people. In the ancient days an organisation like this could not be controlled by such young people, but it has happened because of oppression. You can find this world is divided in two parts, North and East. You fight communism in the East. There is Britain, Europe, and France, which are now free, and they got everything which they got from Africa. Most of the people say India is for Indians, Russia is for Russians, but when it comes to Africa, it is said to be for everybody black and white. You know when a thief comes and steals your sheep and when you fight him and he overpowers you, can you share that flock of sheep with him? Now that is impossible. If you go to a cat and you ask it how he can live, it will tell you that it lives on mice.

We are socially degraded. If you walk in this country, you have got to show your permit. What we should try is dignity. If you go to Zululand, the Zulus are very proud of their country. Why should we not be proud of our country? You should be proud of being an African. This word Bantu means everybody. We are not non-Europeans. We are not Natives. We are Africans. We are economically exploited. We do not get enough money. We are oppressed because we are workers. If you work with a white man, you only get two pounds a week although you do the same work. You see some white people who work at the railways who cannot even read, but they have the right to vote in Parliament. Now the Pan Africanist Congress says we should get the same wages.

We never told the white people to go and make oppressive laws at Parliament, but all the laws are made without our consultation. Africa is a very rich country. It has got gold and other riches, but we do not enjoy any of those things. Now the Africans say it is enough, we have . . . [?] and many bad things have been done to us. Some Africans believe that nothing can be done by Africans alone, without a white man. We claim every square inch in Africa, from Cape to Cairo. We want to manage or mismanage every square inch in this continent. The Pan Africanist Congress says if you find some water in your house, you should first close the tap. This year we are going to [sic] and I am sure they are going to be abolished. We are calling you to freedom. Let us be united, and let us hope that we will never carry passes. We want Africans to be known as people. One Coloured teacher went to Ghana as a spy. We have the last hope. Nobody will liberate us. You must not be deceived. A call has been made to you to be united.

P. K. Leballo: On the African continent, we claim every square inch from Cape to Cairo. We do not retreat from the struggle. We are dedicated. For the first time in the history of this country, the nationalist government has been warned to leave the government [. . . ?]. You are called by the Pan Africanists. We will never share our country with the oppressors. The Pan Africanists are determined to sweep away the dogs of the oppressors. We call upon our forefathers, Tshaka, Makana, Dingaan, Moshesh, give us power to sweep away this oppression. Multiracialism will [be] exploited. We are now moving to the freedom of Africans. We shall not retreat. No compromising. Whether you are a teacher, a policeman, or a nurse, come to the Pan Africanist Congress. Nothing can be in our way. If we believe in freedom, let us forget about other organizations.

R. M. Sobukwe: We have come here to Cape Town to find out from you if it does not affect you, to work for low wages. It is something to you to leave your wives behind. One speaker said that it is useless trying to throw water outside. The best thing is to close the tap. When we try to work on passes, then comes out Bantu education. What should we do? We have got our own programme and the nationalists have got their own program and we will meet on the way. What we are standing for is equality. If one man is getting £ 450, why should the other get £ 6 a month? In the new Africa we are facing, no child will be educated by his father's money but will be educated by the state. In the new Africa we are going to, there will be no Indians, no Europeans, but we will all be Africans. There will be no special privileges for any class of people

We are against the Freedom Charter because it has false passages. It mentioned equality. How can a slave owner be equal with a slave? In Russia, Russians are governing; in Europe, Europeans are governing; but when it comes to Africa, Africans do not rule. It is stated that the majority should rule. Here in Africa, we are the majority, so we should rule. As we are now going to take a step about passes, we should first know what is what. After the last war, the Nationalists wanted to have their own organizations and have their own banks. Then later on they introduced Bantustans where they know very well that [they] would [build] their own factories and no Jews will have any say in those factories which will be built in the boundaries of the Bantustans, and the people who will work there will be those who are in the reserves. They introduce passes because they want to know your original home.

In 1963 we will stand for African independence. I will tell you when and how we are going to fight the passes. You will be informed three days before the action is taken. You must be ready. What we ask you to do is to

560

save food and money. I will appoint the day, and that day all the men will leave their passes behind and will go the nearest police station and then we will say, the dead bodies through these *dom* passes [?]. Your jails are full of people through these *dom* passes. All the money will be used by women and children, and all the men will be in jail. Since there was that trouble in Durban, the Dutch people are itching for a chance to shoot. We demand a minimum wage of £ 8.3 a week. Nonworkers will be chased away by the municipality.

We say when every person is arrested, no bail no fine should be paid. If your employer wants to pay your fine, you must first get instructions from your leaders. We must not let ourselves be provoked. Let the police and the government use violence. We say, save food and money. Tell your wives in time. I will give out circulars three days before the action is taken. Whenever the police give a command to disperse, it is impossible for a big gathering like this to disperse within three minutes. If you are arrested, you should tell them that the law under which I am charged is made by the white people alone and the accused are the Africans alone, and I am not prepared to plead. That is what you must say in court.

W. Phusa: I thank Mr. Chairman for giving me this chance. Today the people have seen our God, Mr. Sobukwe. What I like to say to the people is that they should give respect. More especially when we sing "Nkosi Sikelel' I-Afrika", you must please take off your hats.

E. Magwentshu, A. Matrose, C. Mlokoti, L. T. Mgweba, A. Gahvrone, B. Siboto, W. Phuza, K. Noboza, M. Sixishe, J. Sakati, S. Mfazwe, D. Phajane, P. Sikina, C. Makhohliso, W. Ntwana, Mrs. Seaduabana, Mrs. Gila, W. Dungelo, L. Masimini, P. Bomali, G. Ndlovu, all PAC members.

Document 45. "The Pan Africanist Congress Has a Message for the Down Trodden Black Masses of Afrika." Flyer issued by the PAC, [n.d.]

THE
PAN   AFRICANIST   CONGRESS
(A M A F R I K A   P O Q O)

HAS A MESSAGE FOR THE DOWN TRODDEN BLACK MASSES OF AFRIKA.

WE OF THE P.A.C. SAY:

(a) Africa must be free by 1960, from Cape to Cairo; Madagascar to Morocco.

(b) Africa for the Africans, Africans for Humanity, Humanity for God.

(c) Under the banner of African Nationalism we say that once we launch, (it does not matter what campaign) *there is no bail, there is no defence, there is no fine.*

(d) We are one with Dr. K. Banda, the great Jomo Kenyatta, Tom Mboya and Dr. Kwame Nkrumah, "the architect of the United States of Africa."

(e) Down with imperialism, colonialism and domination! Forward then to independence!! To independence *NOW*!!! Tomorrow the United States of Afrika!!!! Izwe Lethu, i-Afrika!!

Issued by the PAN AFRICANIST CONGRESS

1960! 1960!! 1960!!!

1960, The year of *DESTINY!*
1960, The year of *POSITIVE ACTION!*
1960, The year of *SERVICE, SACRIFICE, and SUFFERING* for the cause of Afrika, the heritage of our forefathers!
1960, The year of *DECISIONS!*
1960, The year of *African Independence and self-determination!*

Keep informed about 1960's *POSITIVE ACTION* against the *PASS LAWS.*
We are proud of a dynamic, relentless, determined and fearless leadership of the Pan Africanist Congress.

I z w e   L e t h u   i - A F R I K A .

Likhutshwa yi Pan Africanist Congress

THE PAN AFRICANIST CONGRESS IS ON THE VERGE OF LAUNCHING A UNION-WIDE POSITIVE DECISIVE CAM-PAIGN AGAINST THE PASS LAWS. YOU ARE SERIOUSLY AFFECTED BY THE ADMINISTRATION OF THESE FASCIST LAWS OF A WHITE FOREIGN MINORITY PSEUDO-GOVERNMENT IN OUR FATHERLAND. THESE LAWS MUST BE BROUGHT TO A COMPLETE STANDSTILL. THEY MUST BE BLOWN TO OBLIVION THIS YEAR, *NOW AND FOR EVER.* ARE YOU WITH THE DOWN TRODDEN BLACK MASSES OR ARE YOU WITH THE ENEMY? YOU MUST MAKE UP YOUR MIND *NOW.* TOMORROW MAY BE TOO LATE.

I Z W E   L E T H U   i - A F R I K A !

Likhutshwa yi PAN AFRICANIST CONGRESS

562

Document 46. "One Central Government in Africa." Article, by R. M. Sobukwe, March 1960

Note: The article reproduced here is from a typewritten manuscript dated March 1960. A slightly altered version was printed in *Drum*, November 1959 (East Africa, December 1959), pages 48–49.

Nobody disputes our contention that Africa will be free from foreign rule. What *is* disputed by many, particularly the white ruling minority, is that she will be free either "within our lifetime" or by 1963, or even 1973 or 1984. However, the African nationalist movements which met at the All-African Peoples' Conference in Accra in 1958 put down 1963 as the target date for African freedom.

If, however, by this date there are still parts of Africa that are under foreign rule, they certainly, they said, by 1973, every part of Africa must be free. Even though I live in South Africa, I have no doubt that this prophecy will be fulfilled. But the question is: AFTER FREEDOM THEN WHAT?

The ready answer of white ruling minorities is: chaos and a reversion to barbarism and savagery. The ready answer of all Pan-Africanists, and this includes all genuine African nationalist organisations on the continent, is: the creation of a United States of Africa and the advent of a new era . . . [*sic*] an era of freedom, creative production and abundance.

To many Africans the United States of Africa symbolises the fulfilment of an emotional urge for formal African unity. What its nature and structure will be—and its role and tasks—have not been determined. But before I give an outline of the United States of Africa we envisage, I will list some of the obstacles we are bound to come across. Let us assume that by 1973, every part of the continent will be free from foreign domination. In some parts the change-over will have been comparatively peacefully achieved. In others, there will have been bitter fighting, which will leave in its wake a legacy of destruction and hate. In such countries the first ten or fifteen years will be years of re-adjustment and feverish reconstructions. There will be plenty of work to do, and the capital for that work will be forth-coming from both East and West—because there can be no greater guarantee against both political and economic instability than the final recognition of the supremacy of African interests in Africa.

By then, the older states will have passed through the first two of the four stages defined by Dr. Nkrumah, at the All-African Peoples' Conference as:

The attainment of freedom and independence;
The consolidation of that freedom and independence;
The creation of unity and community between the free African independent states; and
The economic and social reconstruction of Africa.

These States will probably act as Big Brother to the younger States, but of course we will have recalcitrants. I am certain that some of the leaders of the African States who are "great"—either because the press has made them so or because they are one-eyed dwarfs in a land of blind dwarfs—will advance a number of excuses to put off complete unification of the African continent for fear of losing their "greatness". Others, while paying lip-service to the concept of Pan-Africanism, will probably demand autonomy for each State with the object of remaining in the public eye. Fortunately, all African nationalist leaders on the continent are Pan-Africanists, and are not likely to allow personal ambition to hamper the cause for which they have laboured and suffered so long in their countries throughout Africa.

On the structure of the United States of Africa, there appears to be no clear agreement yet among African nationalists. At the Accra Conference, Dr. Nkrumah stressed the necessity for such a communion of our own to give expression to the African personality. The conference adopted the late George Padmore's outline of an initial federation of states on a regional basis, finally merging into a federal United States of Africa.

The Pan Africanist Congress, though it has adopted the same outline, is not enamoured of federations because they entail compromise, sometimes on vital issues. Federations tend to kill effective unity, because inherent in them is the idea of "trial for a period" and the threat of ultimate secession by one State or another. So it is a unitary constitution that the Pan Africanist Congress envisages for the United States of Africa, with all power vested in a central government, freely elected by the whole continent on the basis of universal adult suffrage. In such a set-up, only continental-wide political parties committed to a continental programme cutting across sectional ties and interests, whether of a tribal or of a religious nature, are possible.

This will in turn promote the idea of African unity, and the concept of a free and independent African personality. The potential wealth of Africa in minerals, oil, hydro-electric power and so on, is immense. By cutting out waste, through systematic planning, a central government can bring about the most rapid development of every part of the State. By the end of the century the standard of living of the masses of the people will undoubtedly have risen dramatically under an African Socialist Government. Subsistence farming will have disappeared and a huge internal market will absorb a very large percentage of the industrial and agricultural products of the continent.

All nationalist movements on the continent aim at wiping out racialism, imperialism and colonialism in all their manifestations. In a United States of Africa there will be no "racial groups" and I am certain that with freedom of movement from Cape to Cairo, Morocco to Madagascar, the concentration of so-called minority groups will disappear.

Document 47. "Calling the Nation! No Bail! No Defence! No Fine!!!" Flyer announcing the launching of the anti-pass campaign on March 21, issued by R. M. Sobukwe, [n.d.]

C A L L I N G   T H E   N A T I O N !
NO BAIL!   NO DEFENCE!!   NO FINE!!!

This is the CALL the African people have been waiting for! It has come! On Monday the 21st March 1960, we launch our POSITIVE, DECISIVE CAMPAIGN against the PASS LAWS in this country.

(A) *OUR DEMANDS:*

1. We demand that the PASS LAWS BE TOTALLY ABOLISHED.

2. We demand a MINIMUM WAGE, established by Government legislation, of £35 per month, or £8.3.4 per week, which must be paid throughout the country.

3. We demand a guarantee that NO WORKER shall be dismissed as a result of this campaign.

4. We demand that the leaders will not be victims of the GOVERN-MENT or of the LOCAL AUTHORITIES as a result of the African people's positive action.

(B) These are my ORDERS, and if we must win, these ORDERS MUST BE FAITHFULLY CARRIED OUT:—
In every city, town and village, the men must leave their passes at home on Monday the 21st March 1960.

(C) Under the local leadership of the Pan Africanist Congress, the men will move to the chosen Police Station and there surrender themselves. The Leader will tell the Police: *"We all do not have passes. We will not carry passes again; millions of our people are arrested under the PASS LAWS, so you had better arrest us all, NOW.*

(D) If you are stopped by the Police on the way, and they demand Passes, surrender there and then for arrest. If ONE man is arrested for not having a PASS, you ALL stop there and then, and tell the Police you do not have passes either. Demand that they arrest you all.

(E) All men will go to jail under the slogan "NO BAIL, NO DEFENCE, NO FINE". The women will be assigned their historic role, but in the first phase of the struggle they must see to it that ALL MEN GO TO JAIL.

(F) *PERIOD OR DURATION OF CAMPAIGN:*
Nobody will call this Campaign off, except the National President, who will do so at the public meetings of the people. DO NOT ALLOW YOURSELVES TO BE DECEIVED BY NEWSPAPERS, CIR-CULAR LETTERS, or GOVERNMENT OFFICIALS.

So long as the Campaign is on, NOBODY WILL GO TO WORK.
Let us stick together, the people and the leaders. It is now time for
SERVICE, SACRIFICE AND SUFFERING. That is the spirit in
which we go into action!
FREEDOM FROM PASS LAWS, SLAVE WAGES, ETC. ETC.
ETC.!!
GOD SAVE AFRIKA AND HER PEOPLES.

> Issued by the National President,
> PAN AFRICANIST CONGRESS,
> (Mangaliso R. Sobukwe).

Document 48. Letter announcing the launching of the anti-pass campaign, from R. M. Sobukwe to Major-General Rademeyer, Commissioner of Police, March 16, 1960

> PAN AFRICANIST CONGRESS
> OFFICE OF THE PRESIDENT,
> P.O. BOX 1610,
> JOHANNESBURG.
> 16th March, 1960.

Major-General Rademeyer,
Commissioner of Police,
South African Police Headquarters,
CAPE TOWN.

Sir,

My organisation, the Pan Africanist Congress, will be starting a sustained, disciplined, non-violent campaign against the Pass Laws on Monday the 21st March, 1960. I have given strict instructions, not only to members of my organisation but also to the African people in general, that they should not allow themselves to be provoked into violent action by anyone. In a Press Statement I am releasing soon, I repeat that appeal and make one to the Police too.

I am now writing to you to ask you to instruct the Police to refrain from actions that may lead to violence. It is unfortunately true that many white policemen, brought up in the racist hothouse of South Africa, regard themselves as champions of white supremacy and not as law officers. In the African they see an enemy, a threat, not to "law and order" but to their privileges as whites.

I, therefore, appeal to you to instruct your men not to give impossible commands to my people. The usual mumbling by a police officer of an order requiring the people to disperse within three minutes, and almost immediately ordering a baton charge, deceives nobody and shows the

566

police up as sadistic bullies. I sincerely hope that such actions will not occur this time. If the police are interested in maintaining "law and order", they will have no difficulty at all. We will surrender ourselves to the police for arrest. If told to disperse, we will. But we cannot be expected to run helter-skelter because a trigger-happy, African-hating young white police officer has given thousands or even hundreds of people three minutes within which to remove their bodies from his immediate environment.

Hoping you will co-operate to try and make this a most peaceful and disciplined campaign,

I remain,

Yours Faithfully,

Mangaliso R. Sobukwe.
President,
PAN AFRICANIST
CONGRESS.

Document 49. "Press Release: Call for Positive Action," announcing the launching of the anti-pass campaign, [n.d.]

PRESS RELEASE:

CALL FOR POSITIVE ACTION.

In accordance with a resolution adopted at our National Conference, held in Orlando on the 19th and 20th December, 1959, I have called on the African people to go with us into Positive Action against the Pass Laws. We launch our campaign on Monday, the 21st of March, 1960, and circulars to that effect are already in the streets.

Meaning of campaign: I need not list the arguments against the Pass Laws. Their effects are well known. All the evidence of broken homes, tsotsism and gangsterism, the regimentation, oppression and degradation of the African, together with straight-jacketing of industry leads to one conclusion, that the Pass Laws must go. We cannot remain foreigners in our own land.

I have appealed to the African people to make sure that this campaign is conducted in a spirit of absolute non-violence, and I am quite certain that they will heed my call. I now wish to direct the same call to the police. If the intention of the police is to "maintain law and order," I say, you can best do so by eschewing violence. Let the saracens have a holiday. The African people do not need to be controlled. They can control themselves. Please do not give my people impossible orders, such as "disperse within three minutes." Any such order we shall regard as merely an excuse for baton-charging and shooting the people. If the African people are asked to disperse, they will do so orderly and quietly. They have instructions from me to do so. But we will not run away! If the other side so desires, we will provide them with an opportunity to demonstrate to the world how brutal they can be. We are ready to die for our cause; we are not yet ready to kill for it.

Finally, I wish to offer all those non-African individuals and groups who have expressed themselves as bitterly opposed to the Pass Laws, an opportunity to participate in this noble campaign which is aimed at obtaining for the African people those things that the whole civilised world accepts unquestioningly as the right of every individual. Here is an opportunity for you to help create history. Be involved in this historic task, the noblest cause to which man can dedicate himself—the breaking asunder of the chains that bind your fellowmen.

Remember: "Every man's death diminishes me. For I am involved in mankind."

Mangaliso R. Sobukwe.
PRESIDENT —
PAN AFRICANIST CONGRESS.

Johannesburg.
Date

Document 50. "Launching Address" [quoting text of R. M. Sobukwe's final instructions] by Philip Kgosana, March 20, 1960

Note: The full text appeared in *Contact*, April 16, 1960.

Sons and daughters of the soil, on Monday, 21st March, 1960, we launch our Positive Decisive Action against the Pass Laws. Exactly 7 a.m. we launch. Oh, yes, we launch—there is no doubt about it (ALL OVER.)

We have reached the cross roads—we have crossed our historical Rubicon—Izwe Lethu!

The choice before us:

At this stage of our struggle we have a choice before us. Are we still prepared to be half-human beings in our fatherland or are we prepared to be citizens—men and women in a democratic non-racial South Africa? How long shall we be called Bantu, Native, Non-European, Non-White, or black, stinking Kaffir in our fatherland? When shall we be called Sir, Mr., Mrs., Miss, Ladies and Gentlemen? How long shall we stay in the squalors of Windermere or the Sahara Desert of Nyanga West? How long shall we rot physically, spiritually and morally—*ema Plangeni*? How long shall we starve amidst plenty in our fatherland? How long shall we be a rightless, voteless and voiceless eleven million in our fatherland?

On what meat doth this our oppressive White Man Boss feed that he has grown so great? Sons and daughters of Africa—there is a choice before us. We are either slaves or free men—that's all.

What we are fighting for:

Our overall fight is against imperialism, colonialism and domination. I want to be properly understood here. Let the world take note, that we are not fighting Dr. Verwoerd, simply because he is Dr. Verwoerd; we are not fighting against the Nationalist Party or the United Party. We are not fighting against Europeans or Indians or Chinese. In short we are fighting against nobody. Our energies and forces are directed against a set-up, against a conception and a myth. This myth—others call it racial superiority, others call it herrenvolkism, others white leadership with justice, or white supremacy. We are fighting against the Calvinistic doctrine that a certain Nation was specially chosen by God to lead, guide and protect other nations.

That is our fight

We are not a horde of stupid barbaric things which will fight against a white man simply because he is white. No sensible person can do that.

AN ASSAULT

In order to destroy this myth of race superiority, the Pan-Africanist Congress has drawn up an unfolding programme—which starts to-morrow and ends up in 1963 with the realization of the United States of Africa. We start with the Pass Laws, then the next thing and the next, etc.—up to 1963.

THE PASS LAWS

We have decided to secure the total abolition of the Pass Laws. This means that not only the *dom* pass must go, but also the Labour Bureaux and influx control regulations must go with it. The question is how best we can achieve that.

The P.A.C. has made it clear that the first essential is a mental divorce from the Pass Laws. Our people have been so conditioned to the *dom* pass that they have been known to buy it for £ 15 or risk death in an attempt to salvage it from a burning building. In fact an African does not feel that he is himself if he does not feel the weight of the *dom* pass in his pocket. What is necessary, then, is for every African to make up his mind that from to-morrow he will never carry the *dom* pass.

THE CONDUCT OF THE CAMPAIGN

I wish here to quote the final instructions of the President of the Pan-Africanist Congress. Mr. Mangaliso Robert Sobukwe:

To All Regions and Branches of P.A.C.:

Sons and Daughters of the Soil, Remember Africa!

Very soon, now, we shall be launching. The step we are taking is historical, pregnant with untold possibilities. We must, therefore, appreciate our role. We must appreciate our responsibility. The African people have entrusted their whole future to us. And we have sworn that we are leading them not to death, but to life abundant.

My instructions, therefore, are that our people must be taught NOW and CONTINUOUSLY THAT IN THIS CAMPAIGN we are going to observe ABSOLUTE NON-VIOLENCE.

There are those in our own ranks who will be speaking irresponsibly of bloodshed and violence. They must be firmly told what our stand is.

Results of violence: Let us consider, for a moment, what violence will achieve. I say quite POSITIVELY, without fear of contradiction, that the only people who will benefit from violence are the government and the police. Immediately violence breaks out we will be taken up with it and give vent to our pent-up emotions and feel that by throwing a stone at a Saracen or burning a particular building we are small revolutionaries engaged in revolutionary warfare. But after a few days, when we have buried our dead and made moving grave-side speeches and our emotions have settled again, the police will round up a few people and the rest will go back to the Passes, having forgotten what our goal had been initially. Incidentally, in the process we shall have alienated the masses who will feel that we have made cannon fodder of them, for no significant purpose except for spectacular newspaper headlines.

This is not a game. We are not gambling. We are taking our first step in the march to African independence and the United States of Africa. And we are not leading corpses to the new Africa. We are leading the vital, breathing and dynamic youth of our land. We are leading that youth, NOT TO DEATH, BUT TO LIFE ABUNDANT. Let us get that clear.

The government, knowing that they stand to gain by an outbreak of violence, may most probably stoop down to the level of employing certain

African renegades, political [sic] or by throwing a stone at the police from a distance. Our Task Force will, therefore, have to move on either side of every batch and to make sure they deal with saboteurs. Anybody who agitates for violence or starts violence, whether he belongs to P.A.C. or not, we will regard as a paid agent of the government. Let the masses know that NOW.

The principal aim of our campaign is to get ourselves arrested, get our women remaining at home. This means that nobody will be going to work. Industry will come to a stand-still and the government will be forced to accept our terms. And once we score that victory, there will be nothing else we will not be able to tackle. But we must know quite clearly, NOW, that our struggle is an unfolding one, one campaign leading on to another in a NEVER-ENDING STREAM–until independence is won.

This is not a game. The white rulers are going to be extremely ruthless. But we must meet their hysterical brutality with calm, iron determination. We are fighting for the noblest cause on earth, the liberation of mankind. They are fighting to retrench an outworn, anachronistic vile system of oppression. WE represent progress. They represent decadence. We represent the fresh fragrance of flowers in bloom; they represent the rancid smell of decaying vegetation. We have the whole continent on our side. We have history on our side. WE WILL WIN!

The government will be ruthless. They will probably try to cut us off from one another, censor the Press, use their propaganda machinery to malign the leaders, mislead the people and spread falsehood about the compaign. Let nobody depend on either the Press or Radio. I, myself, MANGALISO SOBUKWE, [or] one of the P.A.C. leaders, acting on my behalf, will call off the struggle, after our demands have been fully met.

FORWARD THEN, TO INDEPENDENCE NOW,
TOMORROW THE UNITED STATES OF AFRICA!

Yours for emergent Africa, Mangaliso R. Sobukwe, President, Pan-Africanist Congress.

* * *

What we are not going to do:

We are not going to burn or damage any part of the Pass Book in any manner. We are not going to fight or attempt to fight, insult or attempt to insult, provoke or attempt to provoke the police in their lawful duties. We are not going to throw stones at the police or do anything that is going to obstruct the police. Any person who does all these things shall be dealt with by the police of course and we, as an organisation, shall further deal with him. Nobody is carrying money, knives or any dangerous weapon with himself to-morrow.

People are not going to join this struggle with evil personal interests in it. Nobody is going to burn any building, office, school or any property of the government. Nobody is going to cut wires or make attempts to cut the railway lines. Nobody is going to burn any bus or threaten anybody.

If anybody does all these things and the police begin to shoot, any person who will die or receive injuries shall be demanded on the head of the mischief maker. The Gods of Africa shall pass judgment on such a person.

The same applies to the police. We do not want to be provoked in any manner. We do not want to be given impossible instructions such as—disperse in three minutes—or some such mumbled orders. If the police officer wants us to disperse, we shall disperse. Our leaders will always be on the spot to tell us what to do. We do not want to be tossed about. If you baton charge us we shall not run away but we will not fight back. We shall leave you to the judgment of the eyes of the world and to the great Gods of Africa.

In short—we know what we are doing and we know how to do it:

My Prediction!

My prediction is that these police will not arrest us tomorrow. What they are going to do is to arrest the leadership—the so-called agitators or inciters.

The people will be told to disperse and go to work. In that case, the President's order is that you peacefully disperse, without making any noise or interjections. You go home, sit in your houses and paint the house or dig the garden or even play drafts.

NOBODY GOES TO WORK

You know our demands:

Abolition of Pass Laws, minimum salary of £35 and no victimization of leaders or the people.

Sabotage:

Be careful of *New Age, City Post* and possibly the *Argus*. Let us close our ears to what the newspapers say and continue with our dynamic programme. We shall win.

We said that "those who are not with us are with the enemy"—at least Mr. Nokwe told us where he stands in yesterday's "City Late." You know what is happening to the Hon. Adv. Duma Nokwe. Yes, it is the work of the good white man—umlungu osithandayo. Perhaps Duma Nokwe is not carrying a pass—we do not know.

Who is to blame:

Whether the struggle fails or succeeds, somebody is to blame for to-morrow's country-wide uprising. Strictly speaking, the campaign is not of our own choice. The hardened stubbornness of the oppressor-group has

572

driven us to a point of desperation. Whether the oppressor likes it or not the Pass Laws must go to-morrow. The myth of white supremacy must be blown to oblivion by the avalanche force of African Nationalism which sweeps the entire continent.

I request the Senior Police Officer in charge to phone Dr. Verwoerd after this meeting and tell him that, *"Hey, Okaffele baphambene ngoku!"* (Hey, the kaffirs have gone mad!)

Fellow Africans, the hour for service, sacrifice, and suffering has come. Let us march in unison to the United States of Africa. Let us march to a new and independent Africa with courage and determination. Let us unite and fight relentlessly for a noble cause.

Forward to Independence!

Forward!!!!!!

Document 51. "A Statement by the Emergency Committee of the African National Congress." Statement, April 1, 1960

The attempt to ban the African National Congress, which for half a century has been the voice of the voteless African majority in this country, is a desperate act of folly, committed by a Parliament which does not contain a single African.

We do not recognise the validity of this law, and we shall not submit to it. The African National Congress will carry on in its own name to give leadership and organisation to our people until freedom has been won and every trace of the scourge of racial discrimination has been banished from our country.

An Emergency Committee of the African National Congress has been established which will continue until our elected leaders have been released and our organisation restored to legality.

It is impossible for the Nationalist Government or anyone else to halt the onward march of freedom in Africa. Equality and freedom, and an equal share of all in the government, must come to South Africa, as it has come or is rapidly coming to every other part of this great continent.

The question before South Africa is not whether the cause of freedom and justice for the African people will win, but how it will be brought about.

Ever since its inception in 1912, the African National Congress has sought the path of peaceful negotiation and non-violent struggle. As responsible and patriotic South Africans, we have rejected the counsels of revenge, racial hatred and violence, and sought the co-operation of like-minded democratic South Africans of all races.

The violence which exists, and has always existed in this country comes not from our people but from the police and the evil laws which they are employed to enforce—laws like the pass laws which can only be maintained by never-ending brutality and terror.

But we wish to make it very clear that we have chosen the path of non-violent struggle not out of weakness and cowardice but because we are confident of the victory of our cause, and do not wish to see the country dragged through bloody upheavals which may leave a legacy of bitterness for generations to come. For this reason, we have always been, and are even now, when the Government has committed shocking outrages against our people and our leaders, prepared to meet others and discuss peaceful solutions.

However, it is now clear to all that no peace or order can be restored to South Africa while the maniac Verwoerd clique remains in the government. Every day that the Government remains in office can only serve to deepen and intensify the crisis, and to make more certain of continued disturbances and upheavals. The first essential towards resolving the crisis is that the Verwoerd administration must make way for one less completely unacceptable to the people, of all races, for a Government which sets out to take the path, rejected by Verwoerd, of conciliation, concessions and negotiation.

We cannot and never shall compromise on our fundamental demands, as set forth in the Freedom Charter, for the full and unqualified rights of all our people as equal citizens of our country. We do not ask for more than that; but we shall never be satisfied with anything less.

However, in order to resolve the present grave crisis, which is sweeping the country towards a terrible blood bath in which all will suffer, we submit the following urgent proposals:—

1. THE SO-CALLED STATE OF EMERGENCY WHICH IS NOTHING BUT A NAKED POLICE DICTATORSHIP MUST BE ENDED. OUR LEADERS MUST BE RELEASED, FREEDOM OF SPEECH AND ORGANISATION ESTABLISHED.

2. PASS LAWS MUST BE ABOLISHED.

3. WAGES MUST BE RAISED TO A MINIMUM OF AT LEAST £1 A DAY.

4. THE NAZI LAWS OF THE PAST DECADE, INCLUDING THE PUBLIC SAFETY ACT, SUPPRESSION OF COMMUNISM ACT, GROUP AREAS ACT, AND OTHER SIMILAR ACTS MUST BE REPEALED.

5. A NEW NATIONAL CONVENTION, REPRESENTING ALL PEOPLE ON A FULLY DEMOCRATIC BASIS, MUST BE CALLED TO LAY THE FOUNDATIONS OF A NEW UNION, A NON-RACIAL DEMOCRACY, BELONGING TO ALL SOUTH AFRICANS, AND IN LINE WITH THE UNITED NATIONS CHARTER AND THE VIEWS OF ALL ENLIGHTENED PEOPLE EVERYWHERE IN THE WORLD.

574

We call upon all our people, and upon all South Africans—Black and White, to rally around these demands and to struggle against the dictatorship of Nazi Verwoerd with all their courage, self-sacrifice and determination.

We call upon all the peoples and Governments of the whole world to help us in this noble struggle, a part of the aspirations of all humanity for peace and brotherhood.

We call upon the United Nations to quarantine the racialist Verwoerd Government by imposing full economic sanctions against the Union of South Africa.

Issued by: The Emergency Committee of the African National Congress

1st April, 1960

Document 52. "Congress Fights On . . . Release the Detainees!!!" Statement in *African National Congress Voice: An Occasional Bulletin*, No. 1, April 1960

CONGRESS FIGHTS ON

The African National Congress refuses to submit to the ban imposed on it by the Parliament of the Union of South Africa. We shall carry on our fight of the past half century for the rights and freedom of the African people. We shall continue our struggle for which we pledged ourselves to all the democratic demands of the Freedom Charter. We shall continue to work Underground until the unjust and immoral ban suppressing the A.N.C. has been repealed.

This bulletin, "Congress Voice," will be issued from time to time. Read it. Study it. Pass it on. But do not be caught with it, or tell anyone where you got it.

RELEASE THE DETAINEES!!!

All over South Africa, in big towns and small, hundreds of men and women are being held in prison under the Fascist Emergency Regulations. No charges have been made against them. They have not been allowed a hearing. In many cases they have been brutally treated and even assaulted, as was the case with the beloved and respected PRESIDENT-GENERAL OF THE A.N.C., Chief A. J. LUTHULI, an elderly man.

Even the names of these men and women, African, Coloured, Indian, European, are not allowed to be published. A thick blanket of silence is hung over their identity and their treatment.

Here for the first time, CONGRESS VOICE PIERCES THE BLANKET of silence and tells THE TRUTH ABOUT THE DETAINEES.

WHO ARE THEY?

We would like to give you a full list of their names—it is a roll of honour. The list at the end of this article is full as possible. Study the names. You will find all sorts of people there.

You will find the names of Thirty at present accused of High Treason. For more than three years they have been spending their lives in Court on the ridiculous frame-up of a charge brought by the Government. They include Adv. DUMA NOKWE, Secretary-general of the A.N.C., L. MASINA, the Secretary, and L. LEVY, the President, of the Congress of Trade Unions, and many other famous non-white leaders—all of whom have long been immobilized and ruined by the trial.

You will find in every town, leaders of the African National Congress, the Pan-African Congress, the S.A. Indian Congress, the Congress of Democrats, trade unionists, Liberals and other outspoken opponents of Apartheid.

But you will also find people who have taken no part in any sort of politics for ten and even fifteen years, whose names happen to appear on some sort of list or other once drawn up by our "Gestapo"—the Special Branch—and are now locked up without rhyme or reason, out of blind panic or sheer spite. You will find husbands and wives arrested in the small hours of the early morning, often leaving behind them small children to fend for themselves. Breadwinners, workers, professional men and women, businessmen—torn away from their work and their families—without a shred of justification.

AND THE CONDITIONS?

Not a word about the grim conditions of the political prisoners has been allowed to creep into the newspapers. But it is known that Dr. Verwoerd used the sinister expression "Special treatment" in Parliament to describe what would be meted out to the so-called "agitators." Don't forget—these people

> have not been charged with any crime. No evidence
> exists against them. They are innocent in terms of
> every sound legal and moral principle.
>
> Yet the facts are that their conditions are not
> better but *worse* than those of ordinary waiting-trial
> prisoners.

If even Chief Lutuli was assaulted, you can imagine what has been done by the coarse warders to less universally-known detainees, especially among the non-whites.

The prisoners complain of being put into a cell "normally used for hardened criminals" where they live *"under stress and discomfort."* They are crowded together *"under the most unhygienic and uncomfortable conditions."*

They are not allowed to have cooked food, fresh fruit and vegetables, etc., sent in by relatives and friends. The only additions to the uneatable prison foods—for which they have to pay *"abnormal prices"* to the jail authorities. [*sic*] In other words, the prices have to be padded with bribes and tips—a degrading system.

They are given dirty, unhygienic utensils to eat from, Indians are deprived of their staple foods—rice, ghee, and meat slaughtered according to Islamic rites.

Nowhere in the civilized world are political prisoners subject to such barbaric treatment.

END THIS ABOMINATION!

Sauer, as acting leader of the Government, says there will be a "new deal" for Africans.

Let them start by setting free these hundreds of men and women whose only "crime"—if they have indeed done anything at all—is that they opposed the laws, which he himself said were nothing but a "worry" to the Africans; that they asked for higher wages—and he admits wages are too low; that they demand a "new deal" for our people.

While South Africa holds hundreds of political opponents of the Government without charges or hearing, how can the Government pretend to the outside world that it is really democratic, or concerned with anything else but hanging on to baasskap and oppression at all costs?

Every true son and daughter of Africa will struggle to the bitter end to win the release of our leaders, and of every person of whatever race detained for whatever reason, under the Emergency Regulations. There can be no talk of a "return to normality" until these men and women are set free.

577

PEOPLE DETAINED UNDER EMERGENCY REGULATIONS:
1st List

(Further lists will be published in future issues)

JOHANNESBURG (Some in Pretoria jail)

Mr. F. Adam, Mr. Bob Asmal, Mrs. Y. Barenblatt, Miss M. Balfour, Mr. G. Beck, Mr. I. Bhana, Mr. F. Boshielo, Mr. L. Bernstein, Mrs. H. Bernstein, Mr. H. Berman, Mrs. M. Berman, Mr. L. Baker, Ex-Senator Basner, Mr. E. Brown, Mr. Y. Cachalia, Maulvi Cachalia, Mrs. G. Cohn, Mr. R. Cousins, Dr. P. Cohen, Miss B. DuToit, Mrs. M. Fischer, Mr. R. Fleet, Mr. H. Friedlander, Mrs. T. Gelb, Mr. H. Goole, Mr. V. Goldberg, Mr. J. Gaetsiwe, Miss F. Goldblatt, Mr. I. Heyman, Mrs. A. Heyman, Mrs. R. Hodgson, Mrs. V. Hashe, Mr. W. Hepner, Mr. P. Huyser, Miss S. Horwitz, Mr. J. Isacowitz, Mr. A. Jassat, Mr. L. Joffe, Mrs. H. Joseph, Mr. Paul Joseph, Mr. W. Kalk, Mrs. M. Kalk, Miss B. Kaplan, Miss W. Kramer, Mr. A. Kathrada, Mr. A. Kunene, Dr. A. Kazi, Mr. J. Lang, Mr. L. Levy, Mr. I. Levitan, Mr. S. Lollan, Mr. L. Massina, Mr. A. Mahlangu, Mr. N. Mandela, Mrs. B. Mashaba, Mr. P. Molaoa, Mrs. M. Moodly, Mr. L. Morrison, Mr. K. Maboee, Mr. I. Moumakoe, Mrs. D. Moloi, Miss E. Mkolonyana, Mr. A. Mohlela, Mr. E. Motsoaledi, Mr. P. Masisi, Miss E. Matobi, Mr. J. Motsabi, Mr. M. Moosajee, Mr. B. Moliwa, Mrs. M. Moodley, Mr. S. Motibeti, Mr. C. Mhana, Mr. B. Molewe, Mr. M. Moola, Mr. J. Madeira, Mr. J. B. Marks, Mr. M. Muller, Mrs. S. Muller, Mr. Molefe, Mr. S. Nathie, Mrs. L. Ngoyi, Mr. T. Nkobi, Adv. P. P. D. Nokwe, Mr. P. Nthithe, Mr. P. Nene, Mr. J. Ndlandla, Mr. J. Nkadimeng, Mr. Nkosi, Miss J. Palmer, Mr. C. Patel, Mr. H. Pillay, Dr. R. Press, Mr. G. Pahad, Mr. M. Rammitloa, Mr. Ramagadi, Mrs. D. Rachmann, Mr. A. Sibeko, Adv. J. Slovo, Mr. G. Spiri, Maulvi Salooje, Mr. B. Saloojee, Mr. V. Syvret, Mrs. R. Schlachter, Mr. W. Sisulu, Mr. M. Thandray, Mr. S. Theko, Mr. E. Weinberg, Mrs. V. Weinberg, Mr. E. Wentzel, Mr. H. Wolpe, Mr. I. Wolfson, Mr. S. Essackjee, Mr. M. Vania.

CAPE TOWN

Mrs. J. Bernadt, Mr. B. Bunting, Mrs. S. Bunting, Mr. J. Barnett, Mr. H. Bloom, Mrs. S. Carneson, Mr. I. Checkanowski, Miss A. Dawood, Mr. B. Desai, Mr. Dongana, Miss N. Dick, Mr. Ebrahim, Mr. Esitang, Mrs. Z. Gool, Mr. B. Gosschalk, Mr. G. Goldman, Mr. D. Goldberg, Mr. H. Gila, Mr. Huna, Mr. T. Hartley, Mr. N. Jibiliza, Mr. Kalipa, Mr. Kgosana, Mrs. K. La Grange, Mr. A. La Guma, Mr. J. La Guma, Mr. H. Lawrence, Mr. Lafele, Mr. M. Langa. Mr. Malindi, Mr. Mgugunyeka,

Mr. Malambela, Mr. Mamfanya, Mr. W. Msamame, Mr. Msusa, Mr. Mtatase, Mr. J. Mtini, Mr. Mpololo, Mr. K. Moodley, Mr. C. Malokoti, Mr. Mase, Mr. J. Ngwavela, Mr. T. Ngwenya, Mr. O. Mpheta, Mr. Phutego, Mrs. C. Rosier, Miss A. Reitstein, Mr. Sikepu, Mrs. A. Sihlangu, Mr. Stuurman, Mr. Sidinile, Mr. R. September, Mr. Storm, Mr. J. Schedrin, Mr. Tsomo, Mr. Talbot, Mr. A. Thorne, Mr. J. Tarshish, Mr. Yeki.

PORT ELIZABETH

Mr. Attwell, Mrs. Attwell, Mrs. F. Baard, Mr. A. Every, Mr. A. Latti, Mr. G. Mbeki, Mr. T. Mqota, Mr. R. Mhlaba, Mr. V. Mini, Mr. N. Ntshinga, Mr. T. Tshume, Mr. P. Vogel.

DURBAN

Mr. C. Amra, Mr. R. Bux, Mr. W. Cele, Mr. A. Docrat, Mr. J. Francis, Mr. J. Govender, Mr. Gookul, Dr. M. Hathorn, Mr. M. Isaacs, Mr. E. Kunene, Mr. E. Moola, Mr. T. C. Mehta, Mr. M. P. Naicker, Mr. M. D. Naidoo, Mr. R. D. Naidoo, Mr. S. Naicker, Mrs. D. Nyembe, Mr. B. Peters, Mr. R. G. Pillay, Mr. M. Pillay, Mr. S. V. Reddy, Mr. L. Rumsander, Mr. J. N. Singh, Mr. G. Singh, Mr. E. Shanley, Mr. D. Seedat, Mr. Veeranna.

PRETORIA

Mr. J. Brink, Chief A. J. Luthuli, Dr. C. Lang, Mr. T. Maimela, Mr. S. Maimela, Rev. Mark Nye, Miss Hannah Stanton, Mr. Nana Sita, Mr. Soobhoo, Dr. P. Tsele, Mr. Sigamoney (Sandy).

MARITZBURG

Mr. P. Brown, Dr. Chetty, Mr. T. Gwala, Dr. Motala, Dr. Meidner, Mr. D. March, Dr. Omar.

LADYSMITH

Mr. F. Bhengu, Mr. R. Coventry, Mr. E. Magdi, Dr. Sader.

ALICE

Prof. Z. K. Matthews.

CRADOCK

Canon Calata.

TRANSVAAL Country

Mr. D. Kajee (Schweizer Reinecke), Mr. G. Patel (Klerksdorp), Mr. M. Rasool (Kinross).

EAST LONDON

Over one thousand Africans have been arrested in repeated police and army raids in East London. Similar raids have taken place at Cape Town, Port Elizabeth, and other towns.

WATCH "CONGRESS VOICE" for later news.

DOES THE ANC ADVOCATE VIOLENCE?
TREASON TRIAL TESTIMONY, MARCH–OCTOBER 1960

Document 53. Testimony by Dr. Wilson Z. Conco, Chief A. J. Lutuli, Nelson R. Mandela, Robert Resha, Gert Sibande, M. B. Yengwa, Professor Z. K. Matthews [Extracts]

MR. TRENGOVE [of the prosecution]: Would you regard the Liberal Party as a party which agrees and supports the methods adopted by the Congress movement to achieve their objects?
DR. CONCO: Yes, the Liberal Party, may I just explain this, my lords, the Liberal Party agrees with us to this extent that it also recognises the universal franchise, not according to colour but for all the citizens in the country, they agree with them there; that racial discrimination must go, we agree with them there; that South Africa must have a Government who should represent all the people, there we more or less agree. And so are the Progressives and all the other groups which agree with our main object I would regard as the "forces of freedom" with us.

I won't ask you about the Progressives at this stage, does the Liberal Party agree with the methods adopted by the Congress movement in their liberatory struggle, apart from your objects, your methods, do they agree with that?— They might not agree as to methods, but with the objectives they do agree, with our main objective. I think there is some difference as far as methods. I must concede that.

Dr. Conco, aren't the methods by which the movement wants to achieve their object, aren't the methods really vital?— The methods are vital, my lord. May I make this explanation [about] the difference between the Liberal Party methods and the African National Congress. We believe in bringing about—that is attaining our objectives through extra-parliamentary methods. That is by demonstrations, defiance, disobedience and non-cooperation with the Government, and by that we will draw the attention of the white electorate to the real suffering of our people, as we did in the defiance campaign. The Liberal Party believes in fighting in parliament, in other words, having members elected and fighting for rights in the parliament, but we have no vote, my lord, and we could never influence parliament, I mean direct influence through the electorate.

RUMPFF J. [Mr. Justice]: Do you still want a change through Parliament?— We still want a change through Parliament, my lord, but indirectly by drawing the attention of the voters to our sufferings because some of the white people don't know how much non-Europeans suffer, and as I have already indicated, in our Defiance Campaign a lot of white people came to our support, not only here but in the world over—we got a lot of support from Britain, and some groups in America supported us. I'm just pointing out the difference in methods, my lord, but we agree on the objective.

MR. TRENGOVE: Do I understand you correctly that you believe that ultimately you want to influence Parliament to give you your rights?— Yes.

Is that your attitude?— Yes, we want to influence the electorate which is really who Parliament is responsible to. Parliament is responsible to the electorate.

In other words, you want to achieve your object ultimately through the ballot box?— Yes, that is our intention.

That's your intention, I see.

RUMPFF J: What is the object of the A.N.C. in regard to Parliament? Is it that Parliament should give the non-Europeans equal rights?— I didn't follow the question properly, my lord.

Is that the object, that through the electorate being influenced by your action and conduct they would vote people into Parliament who would give the non-Europeans full equal rights?— Yes, my lord.

Under the present Constitution?— Under the present Constitution of Parliament.

MR. TRENGOVE: And by endeavouring to influence the Electorate in this way you say that it is the A.N.C. policy to obtain relief for their various grievances by a process of reforms?— I don't follow that.

Do you want to influence the electorate and thereby Parliament by a gradual process of reform, to give you your rights?— Yes.

And to do away with your grievances and disabilities?— Yes.

Is that the A.N.C. policy, Dr. Conco?— That's the A.N.C. policy.

I want you to think about that again, doctor, because I will be dealing with that again very fully at a later stage. Is it the A.N.C. policy to achieve their object by a gradual process of reforms through Parliament?— Yes.

Dr. Conco, these words [in Nelson Mandela's address, Document 2] you say you don't understand them although they are expressly underlined—"the day of reckoning between the forces of freedom and those of reaction is not very far off"; what does "The day of reckoning" mean in ordinary English language?— I suppose it refers to the day when these objectives will be realised.

Why then "The day of reckoning"?— It's really the use of the expression, I don't know.

That's just the point, doesn't the day of reckoning contain some punitive element?— Not with me.

Not with you?— When I read from the above statement I don't get that meaning—apart from the fact that the day will come when these things will come true.

Is not very far off?— Yes.

Now, in 1954 did the African National Congress in 1954—1953—when this was written, believe that these reforms that they wanted through Parliament, a gradual process of reforms, that they would be getting in the near future?—Yes; in fact we believed that in 1954 and we still believe it now, that it's coming. It won't be long.

. . . .

MR. TRENGOVE: Dr. Conco, do I understand you correctly, that the A.N.C. pinned its faith on the inherent qualities of the ruling class, that decency and generosity—if pressure were brought to bear, that they would submit to that pressure rather than resist it?—

DR. CONCO: Yes, we appealed to

No, I don't want to know what you appealed to. Do you believe?— We believe that.

That whatever attitude the ruling classes held, that you would be able by your pressure to effect a change of heart?— Yes. We believe that very strongly.

Doctor, if you believe there could be such a change of heart, why did you resort to pressure and coercion; why didn't you rather try and persuade and negotiate with the ruling classes?— We've used all those methods; we had before the 1949 Programme—we approached the Prime Minister, we have approached the Minister of Native Affairs, we have approached all the departments of State. We have used those methods for years. I remember for instance in 1913, in the history of the National African Congress when the Land Act was passed, then all was done by the African National Congress to try and persuade the Government not to pass that Act; it affected Africans considerably. Those methods have been used. We still use the methods of persuasion, my lords. We still appeal to all sections, progressive sections of the white population in South Africa; we don't stop there.

So, doctor, what you were actually doing was that you were going to hold a pistol to the head of the ruling class; you're like a man who says 'I'm non-violent, I want to take your money', and then you hold a pistol to his head and say 'You've got an option now, either give me the money or resist'. Isn't that what your attitude was, isn't that the extent to which you were non-violent?— I don't know that example—I don't follow it very well.

Now, doctor, I put it to you that the official attitude of the African National Congress, to which you subscribe, was that the ruling class would not submit in spite of the coercion and pressure which was brought to bear upon them; that it's a characteristic in the Capitalist, Imperialist semi-Colonial Fascist State, that the ruling classes do not submit to pressure, and that they try to suppress or exterminate that pressure by violence and force; that that was the attitude of the A.N.C. as to the ruling class?— No, we didn't hold that attitude. Just to take for instance the Defiance Campaign: during the Defiance Campaign in 1952 there was hardly a white section which sympathised with the objects of the African National Congress, but after 1952 we got a terrific interest of a lot of progressive groups amongst the whites; thus we got the support of the Liberal Party and we had organisations like the C.O.D. available, and from 1952 up to now progressive opinion in the Church and other intellectuals have thought very seriously about the situation in South Africa and we now have a group like the Progressives—I'm just giving an example to confirm that we believe in this.

. . . .

MR. TRENGOVE: The African National Congress was working for the overthrow of the ruling classes?

A. J. LUTHULI: My Lords, the African National Congress was not working for the overthrow of the ruling classes. It was working for being

given an opportunity to participate in the government of the country.
Would it be incorrect that to say that the African National Congress was
working for the overthrow of the ruling classes?— My Lord, if it means that
the A.N.C. was working to just get rid of the ruling class which is White and
then take over a Black government, that would be incorrect.

We will come to that. The African National Congress was aiming at the
seizure of power in this country? Is that correct?— That is not correct, My
Lord. Again one must say that in the light of what I have said, it could only
mean having an opportunity to participate inasmuch as now we are not
participating in the government, but I would not interpret it to mean—in
fact it has never been the purpose of the African National Congress in the
light of its activities to say that it wants to seize power in the sense of
throwing out the White Government and replacing it by a Black
Government.

. . . .

MR. TRENGOVE: You held out the view that the White electorate had
certain inherent qualities of goodness and if you applied a little pressure,
those good qualities would result in the White man granting you your
claims?

A. J. LUTHULI: Some.

Wouldn't it have to be the majority?— I think, My Lords, I did indicate
in my evidence in chief that there are degrees and degrees of response, to
the struggle.

I am talking of the ultimate response. Utimately?— Ultimately, My
Lord, I repeat this that we hope that we will have brought pressure on the
electorate so that the majority of the electorate come to see the justice of
our claims and demands.

. . . .

MR. TRENGOVE: Now as a result of the pressure which you were
going to bring to bear on them, what would happen, why would the pressure
make the White man change his mind?

A. J. LUTHULI: My Lords, I don't know that I can satisfactorily
answer without going back to what I said in my evidence in chief, namely
this, that I indicated there and I indicate now that you would have some of
the Whites through sheer moral persuasion seeing the justice of our cause.
You might have others, My Lord, who through ignorance might not have
known the conditions under which we live, and maybe through prejudice,
but who when they see us struggling would begin to think and think on
this—think on our demands. There would still be yet another group which

would only come to concede, in fact maybe reluctantly, to our demands because of the fact that you are now affecting the man's interests.

· ·

MR. TRENGOVE: This change of mind or change of heart on behalf—on the part of the white electorate, either on the grounds of moral principles or out of self-interest, you say that it was all along the purpose of the African National Congress to effect that change of heart or change of mind, call it what you will?

A. J. LUTHULI: That is so.

You expect the white man to undergo this change of heart:— I do, My Lord.

And I take it you expected it only if you applied what one might call sufficient pressure?— That is so, My Lord.

Now what do you mean by applying pressure?— I mean, My Lord, applying pressure along lines clearly laid out in our Programme of Action.

We know what is contained therein. By the means set out in the Programme of Action you wanted to apply this pressure?— That is so, My Lord.

So it was not going to be a question of persuasion, it had to be pressure or coercion or intimidation of the White public, is that correct?— I don't know about the question of coercion or intimidation. All I am saying, My Lords, is this, that you would apply pressure. I don't know that you would be intimidating. You are merely applying pressure so that the man comes to consider otherwise. I don't know that you would call it intimidating. He thinks, and then he says, in the circumstances I think rather than jeopardise my interests I think I should concede.

So he wouldn't willingly concede?— I wouldn't say he would willingly concede. He would—the pressure would eventually get him to. He wouldn't be a man who starts off willingly.

· ·

MR. TRENGOVE: Incendiarism, is that a type of pressure that you think one could bring to bear on the public or the government to change its policies.

A. J. LUTHULI: No, My Lord.

What about burning of passes?— My Lords, I don't know that I would—well, it depends upon interpretation, but the question of burning a pass to me, if I may elaborate, is an entirely different proposition. I come to a position where I feel that in this country, South Africa ought to be free, I ought not to carry a pass. I come to the position when I feel that in order to demonstrate that, I must subject myself to whatever the law might do to me, and I just throw away my pass. That is all there is to it. In fact I am exerting pressure on no one, I am merely saying now as evidence of the fact that I hate a pass, I get rid of it.

Anything you hate you can set alight to?— I wouldn't say that, some things I would set alight to. I wouldn't say everything.

You said on Friday that you were against the burning of passes by individuals?— Yes.

If it took place on a mass scale then it would be different?— I did.

Do you still adhere to that view?— I do.

Did you on occasion commend in the past commend the burning of passes where it took place in isolated instances?— I didn't.

Leaving out what happened over the weekend, prior to that, had there been burning of passes by Africans?— There had been in past years and even in recent years, there have been instances where Africans have burnt passes.

You say that doesn't carry your approval?— It doesn't carry my approval, for reasons that I think I gave.

. . . .

MR. TRENGOVE: On the question of burning of passes, do you know if that type of certificate was issued by the African National Congress to women who burnt passes? That bears your signature at the bottom?

A. J. LUTHULI: That is so, My Lord.

And also the signature of Nokwe?— That is so.

And what does it say?— "African National Congress. Award of Merit. This award is conferred upon Johanna Moketeli in the name of the oppressed people of South Africa for outstanding service given in a spirit of selflessness and courage in resisting oppression on the occasion of the Anti-Pass Campaign, 1958 pass burning. By this service the day of liberation from oppression has been brought closer. Signed A. J. Luthuli, President-General. Nokwe,—D. Nokwe, Secretary-General."

Have you any comment to make?— I have no comment to make, save this My Lord, that quite frankly I had forgotten about the recent demonstration by women, when I said I don't recall in recent years—but I recall this.

What do you mean recent? 1958?— Yes, recent.

So that you did approve of the burning of passes in isolated areas in previous years?— My Lord, I don't know that I would take the situation here as having been an isolated case. If the questioner knows the situation—at the time women throughout the country were agitating greatly and we supported them, as African National Congress, against passes. Now some of the women in that struggle voluntarily, without any instructions from us, burnt their passes, and I wouldn't take that really as an isolated instance as an individual or a group burning a pass. Mind you, I think I must make it quite clear that insofar as the principle is concerned I am not against it. It was merely a question of saying well, if you do burn a pass, it must be furthering the struggle, and I would interpret this as having been help in furthering the struggle, insofar as the pass in concerned.

. . . .

MR. TRENGOVE: Assuming that the White people said that they were not prepared to grant a full franchise immediately, what would the attitude of the African National Congress have been at this time, 1952 to 1956?

A. J. LUTHULI: My Lords, all I can say to that is this, that as I have already indicated, the African National Congress had not discussed compromises, and I would not be truthful if I were to say now the African National Congress would do this, because I would not know. I might have my own views, but I cannot say the African National Congress would do this, because we had not come to the position of discussing compromises as we had not reached that stage at all. That is all that I can say, My Lords.

Now the position is this, and you know it very well, that the African National Congress—that this very question was considered by the African National Congress and its attitude was no compromise with the oppressor and no achievement of freedom by gradualistic reforms. You wanted full freedom immediately or nothing else?— My Lords, it is possible that there would be statements and maybe many statements by African National Congress leaders and documents, to that effect. But one must realise My Lords, the stage at which we are in the struggle. In other words, you must tell the people exactly where you stand and what you want. I do not think, My Lords, any leader can say to his people at the time of making the demands, I want this, but I'll take this.

BY MR. JUSTICE KENNEDY:

Why not, Mr. Luthuli?— I think you want to make your case very clear to your followers and to the world.

Did you not consider saying while we demand or desire full rights, we are prepared to negotiate in regard thereto and compromise about this?— No, My Lord. We—with respect, My Lords, we would say generally I think that in a situation such as ours of a struggle, you make your demand as strongly as you can, and wait to react to proposals. My Lords, I must say this that we have as an organisation, the A.N.C., made overtures to the Goverment, not on demands but to sit down and discuss. We have made those overtures ourselves, My Lord.

. . . .

MR. TRENGOVE: Now, you did not regard the white oppressor as being fair and reasonable; you regarded the white oppressor as being vicious and brutal?

A. J. LUTHULI: A section.

The ruling section; the majority?— The majority, yes.

. . . .

MR. TRENGOVE: Yes; and you also propagated the view—the African National Congress—that the white majority would resist pressure to the point of drowning the whole country in blood?

A. J. LUTHULI: I wouldn't say the African National Congress said so. You might hear individuals saying so, I won't deny that, but I don't think it was ever said by the African National Congress—never.

. . . .

MR. TRENGOVE: Mr. Luthuli, let's just examine the replies that you've been giving in the last quarter of an hour in the light of what is stated in this document, "No Easy Walk to Freedom" [by Mandela, Document 2]. . . . Then at the bottom of page 4 the writer states, "The cumulative effect of all these measures is to prop up and perpetuate the artificial and decaying policy of the white man. The attitude of the Government to us is that 'Let's beat them down with guns and batons and trample them underneath our feet'. 'We must be ready to drown the whole country in blood, if only there is the slightest chance of preserving white supremacy'." Now, Mr. Luthuli, that was the attitude of the African National Congress towards the reaction of the White majority in this country, if pressure is applied?

A. J. LUTHULI: My lords, that would be the view of the writer, but not of the African National Congress. I have already said so. I have already stated the view of the African National Congress. Its aim is not to try and force the Government to shed blood; it hoped the Government would see reason before that but if the Government doesn't see reason and goes on—I have already said the oppressed people will carry on their struggle, within the framework of the policy of the Organisation.

. . . .

MR. TRENGOVE: Do you regard the publication of this type of statement as dangerous?

A. J. LUTHULI: I would say that I could wish my colleagues had been a little more careful. I'd leave it on that basis.

Why, Mr. Luthuli?— The use of words and statements are liable to give a wrong point of view, a wrong interpretation of Congress view.

Yes, but what is wrong with this type of statement; what harm can it do?— I've already indicated, my lords, that this last particular statement as given me might have the interpretation that the Government would go on shedding blood and never coming to the point which I've already tried to tell this Court, that one always expects, even before the Government starts shooting—it might negotiate. Some other Government might do so. It depends upon the Government. But it's not our aim to say "I must force this Government to a position where it starts shooting", far from it.

. . . .

MR. TRENGOVE: Mr. Luthuli, I would now ask you to listen to a tape recording of a speech made by Resha on the 22nd November, 1956. The speech was made at 37 West Street, which was the offices of the African National Congress, is that correct, those were the offices?

A. J. LUTHULI: That is correct.

And Mr. Luthuli, it was a secret meeting, at which only certain delegates who presented their credentials were allowed to be present. . . .

TAPE RECORDING OF RESHA'S SPEECH PLAYED TO WITNESS [saying, "if you are a true volunteer and you are called upon to be violent, you must be absolutely violent, you must murder! Murder! That is all."]

Mr. Luthuli, you have listened to what the Crown alleges to be the voice of Resha who was really the Supreme Commander of the 50,000 top brigade of volunteers. Now would you just—you heard this speech?—I have, My Lords.

Do you agree that it is a subversive speech?— It is a speech inciting people to violent action?— My Lords, I will not say subversive because I don't know the legal meaning, but it is a violent speech, it is a very violent speech.

Did you hear the reaction of the people to whom he was speaking?— Yes, I heard.

And what was that reaction?— They applauded.

[The prosecution stated that E. P. Moretsele, chairman of the Transvaal ANC, presided at the meeting and that Duma Nokwe and Leslie Masina were among those present.]

. . . .

MR. TRENGOVE: Now do you know why these people tolerate this violent speech and applauded it?

A. J. LUTHULI: No, My Lords, I wouldn't know.

Is it entirely inconsistent with your alleged policy of non-violence?— In parts it is, yes.

Now Mr. Luthuli, did any of the members of the National Executive or anybody ever take any steps about this speech?— My Lords, I wouldn't know to what extent the Executive—the National Executive became aware of the speech. I wouldn't know. I was not aware of it, I don't know how many were aware of it, other than those who were there at the meeting, I wouldn't know.

Now having listened to the speech, are you shocked to hear that a speech of this nature was made?— There are some parts that shock me. There are some parts what one might call a fighting speech, but there are some parts that I absolutely don't like at all.

. . . .

MR. TRENGOVE: You see, Mr. Luthuli, if the Volunteer-in-Chief makes that type of speech, who is in a better position to know what the duties are of a volunteer than the Volunteer-in-Chief?

A. J. LUTHULI: Oh no, that doesn't follow. If I may make an illustration, My Lords, I don't know about army technique and things like that, but surely if a General were to do something that is not right, I don't think it can be said that because the General, therefore in fact the whole policy must now be aligned to what that particular general who is wrong, does. I wouldn't accept that proposition.

I am not asking you to approve of what he did. I want to know who was in a better position than Resha to know what the duties of a Volunteer are? Was there any person in a better position than Resha?— No, there wouldn't be any person in a better position than Resha to know the duties, that is true, that is quite true.

And I put it to you Mr. Luthuli that Resha made this speech and he gave those instructions to the Volunteers because that was exactly what Volunteers were expected to do? And you know that?— I don't. I don't. Because Resha would be expected to lead the Volunteers along the policy of Congress. Now if Resha as a general departs, he departs as Resha. It has nothing to do with the policy of the African National Congress, definitely.

And judging by the reaction of the people whom he addressed, do you think they thought he was departing from policy?— My Lords, it is difficult to say about the whole meeting, a group of people. No doubt it was a time when feelings were very high, and their applauding actuated by the feeling in the circumstances might be interpreted as approving. On the other hand, My Lord, insofar as the meeting applauding it would not necessarily be to say they are applauding the violent aspects. My Lord, I wouldn't really go as far as that. As I have already indicated, I don't approve, it would be contrary to Congress policy, and if they were applauding that part, then they are wrong. But on the other hand, My Lords, I think I am right in saying it was a time when the feelings of the people were high and therefore they could have been—applauding, actuated by the emotions of the times, not necessarily saying we are foregoing Congress policy. I am talking now of the crowd as a whole, My Lord.

. . . .

MR. TRENGOVE: Now Mr. Luthuli, do I understand you correctly that you say that the only explanation you can give for the speech that Resha made was that he was deviating from policy because he was inciting or making a violent speech?

A. J. LUTHULI: That is correct, My Lord.

And you can't suggest any reason why in those circumstances he should have done it?— My Lords, I wouldn't be able to say why in those circumstances he did it, and I don't like to advance excuses at all. I have said in general it was a tense moment, but I should think that even in a tense moment a responsible person should be able to hold himself.

. . . .

MR. TRENGOVE: . . . . I just want you to explain one or two matters which you already dealt with but which I am still unable to follow. The first one was that the people shall govern. According to that the attitude of the African National Congress was that everybody should have the vote, irrespective of sex, irrespective of colour?

A. J. LUTHULI: That is correct.

And there was to be no—apart from perhaps a qualification as to age, there was to be no other qualification?— That is correct, My Lord.

So that every person would be entitled to participate in parliamentary elections?— That is correct.

Now that was a claim on which the African National Congress was not prepared to compromise in any way?— That is correct, My Lord.

So that if there were any negotiation at any stage, that had to be conceded as fundamental?— I wouldn't go as far as that, My Lord, because when you come to negotiation, My Lords, there are several factors to consider, and I could not here from the witness box anticipate and say now this might happen. But let me illustrate a possibility, just a possibility, to indicate how difficult it would be in a witness box to say it would be this, a thing that has not been discussed. Supposing the government of the country came along and said look, we now accept in principle your demand for universal adult franchise, we accept it. But, we cannot implement that next year. We will have to consider certain factors because the country has been run after all on this basis, we will have to consider. Now my Lords, I take it that negotiators there would have to sit down or rather go and report back to other leaders, and the leaders would consider in the light of what the government says, so that I cannot say My Lords that—what will take place, but it is definitely a clear goal that we are striking for, uncompromisingly. On the other hand, supposing the government had to say now well, we have called you here, we want to improve wages and things like that.

We are just dealing with the vote?— Yes, but I am just giving an illustration, you touched on negotiation. And then they were to say well, insofar as the vote is concerned now we don't feel we can. I think the negotiators would simply say right away oh no, so far as that is concerned, we think that is a fundamental issue. Thank you for whatever you may do in the economic field, we are not throwing that away, but insofar as this is concerned,—so you see, one really can't anticipate and say what will happen at negotiation.

. . . .

MR. TRENGOVE: Mr. Luthuli, negotiation was never contemplated, and you know that?

A.J. LUTHULI: It has been all along anticipated. My Lord, even at this moment, we would be very, very happy if the government would take up the attitude of saying, come let us discuss. We would be extremely happy, in fact even to discuss, even if at the end of the discussions we didn't agree.

Mr. Luthuli, it is sheer hypocricy to make a statement like that and you know it. That was never your attitude?— You may be allowed in Court, I don't know what your rights are, but to call one a hypocrite, really it does hurt. And I will defend myself, My Lords, although if I recall at the time when I was being led by Counsel, reference was made to the fact that I wrote as President-General of the African National Congress a letter in 1957 with—to the Prime Minister, pleading exactly for what I am saying here now, and for me to be called a hypocrite, publicly be called a hypocrite, well Counsel has the right to say so, but it does hurt one.

. . . .

MR. TRENGOVE: Mr. Luthuli, I want to put it to you that you and the whole Congress movement, you accepted the position that the Freedom Charter was a revolutionary document, and that it couldn't be put into effect without breaking up the whole political and economic setup of the present South Africa, that is correct, is it not?

A. J. LUTHULI: I think that is generally correct.

And that one would have, once the demands are put into effect, one would have a state which differs radically and fundamentally from the present state?— My Lords, I think in some respects. I think that if you read the whole of the Freedom Charter, My Lords, you will find that the demands made in the Freedom Charter [are] as such demands really, My Lord, that you get in any bill of rights. For an example, I think that if you were to make comparisons with the Freedom Charter, you will find that.

I am not asking you to compare it with anything else. I am asking you to compare it with the present political and economic structure of the Union?— I am saying that in some respects there are radical changes, in others they wouldn't be so radical.

Mr. Luthuli, I also want to put it to you that you never expected that the White oppressor would ever accept your demands and concede your demands?— My Lords, I wouldn't be in Congress if I didn't expect that White South Africa would some day reconsider. That is my honest belief, and one has grounds for it. I think I have already indicated them, but I firmly believe that White South Africa will one day reconsider. When, My Lords, I cannot say.

But you were not prepared to wait for that one day. You were telling the people now, not next year or any other year, now. Your—leading members of your organisations said within a matter of five years. You weren't going to wait for the White electorate to change their minds and you know that, Mr. Luthuli?— I think that the Prosecuter in my view, My Lords, is really putting a wrong construction into a phrase or motto intended to gear people's determination.

. . . .

MR. HOEXTER [of the prosecution]: [Quotes from an anonymous lecture]. . . .

N. R. MANDELA: . . . . The statement that such radical changes cannot be expected by small concessions to the idea of race equality, that I agree with. I think it's a fair statement, as I have indicated. If the Government of the State says, "We have three representatives for you in the House of Assembly, we now want you to have nine, ten or twenty"—I would not accept that, because it is not what I desire. I want the vote to be extended to me; I don't want anybody to represent me. To that extent, if the writer meant that—and I believe that is what he means—then I agree with him wholeheartedly. You cannot create the State we visualise by concessions, by European representation in Parliament. You will create that State if the vote is extended to all sections of the population.

That we understand, Mr. Mandela. Now what I want to put to you is this: do you think that your Peoples Democracy could be achieved by a process of gradual reforms? Suppose, as a result of pressure, the ruling class were to agree next month to a qualified franchise for the Africans, an educational test perhaps—not a stringent one—and next year, as a result of further pressure, a more important concession is made—a further concession is made in 1962, and so on over a period of ten or twenty years—do you think that the Peoples Democracy could be achieved in that fashion?— Well, this is how I approach the question. I must explain at the outset that the Congress, as far as I know, has never sat down to discuss the question. . . . We demand universal adult franchise and we are prepared to exert economic pressure to attain our demands, and we will launch defiance campaigns, stay at homes, either singly or together, while the Government should say, "Gentlemen, we cannot have this state of affairs, laws being defied, and this whole situation created by stay at homes. Let's talk. In my own view I would say Yes, let us talk and the Government would say, "We think that the Europeans at present are not ready for a type of government where there might be domination by non-Europeans. We think we should give you 60 seats. The African population to elect 60 Africans to represent them in Parliament. We will leave the matter over for five years and we will review it at the end of five years." In my view, that would be a victory, my lords; we would have taken a significant step towards the attainment of universal adult suffrage for Africans, and we would then for the five years say, we will suspend civil disobedience; we won't have any stay at homes, and we will then devote the intervening period for the purpose of educating the country, the Europeans to see that these changes can be brought about and that it would bring about better racial understanding, better racial harmony in the country. I'd say we should accept it, but, of course, I would not abandon the demands for the extension of the universal franchise to all Africans. That's how I see it, my lords. Then at the end of the five year period we will have discussions and if the Government says, "We will give you again 40 more seats," I might say that that is quite sufficient, let's accept it, and still demand that the franchise should be extended, but for the agreed period we should suspend civil disobedience, no stay at homes. In that way we would eventually be able to get everything that we want; we shall have our Peoples Democracy, my lords. That is the view I hold—whether that is Congress' view I don't know, but that is my view.

. . . .

KENNEDY J: Mr. Mandela, assuming you were wrong in your beliefs, do you visualise any future action on behalf of the Government, by the Government?

N. R. MANDELA: Well, my lord—

Because I think the evidence suggests that you could not expect the Government to soften in its views. Have you any future plans in that event?— No, my lord. I don't think that the Congress has ever believed that its policy of pressure would ultimately fail. The Congress, of course, does not expect that one single push to coerce the Government to change its policy will succeed; the Congress expects that over a period, as a result of a repetition of these pressures, together with world opinion, that the Government notwithstanding its attitude of ruling Africans with an iron hand, that notwithstanding that, the methods which we are using will bring about a realisation of our aspirations.

MR. HOEXTER: Mr. Mandela, whether or not there would be success ultimately, one thing is clear, is it not, and that is that the African National Congress held the view, and propagated the view, that in resisting pressure by the Congress Movement the ruling class, the Government, would not hesitate to retaliate—would not hesitate to use violence and armed force against the Congress movement?— Yes; the Congress was of that view, my lords. We did expect force to be used, as far as the Government is concerned, but as far as we are concerned we took the precautions to ensure that that violence will not come from our side.

BEKKER J: What were those precautions?— Well, my lord, for example in 1952 when we lodged the Defiance Campaign, and secondly, my lord, you will notice that we frequently use 'stay at home' not 'strike' in the ordinary sense. Now, my lord, in a strike what is usually done is to withdraw workers from a particular industry and then have pickets to prevent the people from working in those industries which are boycotted. But the Congress theory [was] that to have pickets might attract police violence. We deliberately decided to use 'stay at home' where people are asked to remain in their houses.

· ·

MR. HOEXTER: As far as you know, has the onward march of the liberatory movement continued to manifest itself?

N. R. MANDELA: Yes, it has. Congress has become much more powerful and much more strong to-day.

And in your opinion is the possibility of this violence to which you refer therefore heightened—increased?— Oh, yes; we feel that the Government will not hesitate to massacre hundreds of Africans in order to intimidate them not to oppose its reactionary policy.

· ·

BEKKER, J [Mr. Justice]: Now, the difference which I want to discuss with you, if it is a difference, between the countries you mentioned and South Africa, is it not perhaps in this, what would you—what would the reaction of White supremacy be if it was made to realise that the demands of the Congress alliance would result in its supremacy being terminated once and for all?

N. R. MANDELA: Well, that has been a problem all along, My Lord.

That may be, but what do you think the reaction of White supremacy would be to that claim?— Well, for all I know they may be hostile to that type of thing. But already political organisations are arising in this country which themselves are striving for the extension of the franchise to the African people.

. . . .

BEKKER, J: Well, the question is now whether you can ever achieve that by the methods you are using?

N. R. MANDELA: No, but My Lord this is what I am coming to, that already since we applied these new methods of political action, this policy of exerting pressure, we have attained—we have achieved? [*sic*], we have won ground. Political parties have now emerged which themselves put forward the demand of extending the franchise to the non-European people.

Unqualified franchise? One man, one vote?— No, no, My Lord, it is qualified.

I would like to discuss this with you?— If Your Lordship could give me time? Now, it is true that these parties, both the Liberal Party as well as the Progressive Party are thinking in terms of some qualified franchise. But, if Your Lordship bears in mind the fact that when we initiated this policy, there was no political parties—none in the Union which thought along these lines, then Your Lordship will realise the revolution that has taken place in European parties in this country today. You are now having an organised body of the opinion, quite apart from the Congress of Democrats, who themselves are a force, quite apart from them, you are having an organised body of opinion amongst Whites who put forward the view that some limited form of franchise should be extended to Africans.

I don't think we are quite on the same—let me put it this way, wavelength. During the indictment period, did or did not—I think you said it was accepted by the Congress alliance that White supremacy would be hostile to this claim, one man one vote?— Yes, it is hostile, except to qualify of course that even during that period parties had already emerged which were putting forward this view, and therefore it was reasonable for us to believe that in spite of the hostility which we still encounter from the majority of the Whites, already our policy was succeeding.

What I also have in mind was this. The likelihood of achieving your aim really depends on what you claim. Is that fair enough?— Yes and no, My Lord.

If you claim the impossible, you cannot expect the impossible—I am not referring to the vote, I am referring to it as a basis on which we can proceed. If you ask me to do what is impossible for me to do?— Perhaps if Your

Lordship becomes practical, if you relate it to the question of franchise—

I am coming to that. I want to know whether the Congress alliance discussed or considered whether the—whether White supremacy in South Africa would without a show of arms surrender that which if surrendered would mean its end?— No, My Lord. The Congress has considered the question from the point of view firstly of its experience. The Whites being eager to retain political power exclusively for themselves—

That was considered?— That was considered. It was also considered that through this policy of exerting pressure we will force the Whites by using our numbers, our numerical preponderance, in forcing them to grant us what we demand, even against their will. We considered that, and we felt that that was possible.

How would you use your numerical numbers to force White supremacy to give what you want?— For example by staying at home and not going to work, using our economic power for the purpose of attaining our demands. Now My Lord, we were not looking—we were not hoping that these demands were going to be realised during the period of the indictment, no. We had in mind that in the foreseeable future it will be possible for us to achieve these demands, and we worked on the basis that Europeans themselves in spite of the wall of prejudice and hostility which we encountered, that they can never remain indifferent indefinitely to our demands, because we are hitting them in the stomach with our policy of economic pressure. It is a method which is well organised. The Europeans dare not look at it with indifference. They would have to respond to it and indeed, My Lord, they are responding to it.

. . . .

MR. FISCHER [of the defense]: Now Mr. Resha I want you to say something about the African National Congress policy with regard to violence. Do you know what that policy is?

R. RESHA: The African National Congress has no policy in regard to violence. The policy is absolutely non-violent.

Has there ever been any question about that?— There has never been a question about that policy at all.

And you accepted that policy?— I have accepted and preached that policy.

Have you ever taken a hand in preventing violence?— I have stopped and prevented violence.

Have you ever taken part in any violent action?— I have never taken part in any violent action whatsoever.

Now I want to ask you whether you have ever departed from this policy in any of your speeches?— I think I have.

Can you explain to the Court why you have departed from it if you have?— My Lords, when I think, of the brutal methods used by the government in imposing its inhuman policy on my people, I sometimes have grave doubts about the policy of non-violence. Sometimes it seems to me that if the government is prepared to use this force and violence in stifling every endeavour by my people to improve their lot and to attain some political rights, then sometimes I feel we too have the right to use this violence at times.

You would like to use the violence at times? If you sit down and ponder about what the policy should be, what is your conclusion?— When I sit down calmly, and consider the African National Congress policy, I realise that the only wise policy is the policy of non-violence.

But your other feeling, was that expressed in some speeches?— I think it is expressed in some of my speeches, but not frequently.

. . . .

MR. FISCHER: Now I want to turn to some of your speeches—you know by heart probably now the end of the much debated speech in which you suggested that if a volunteer were ordered to murder he should "murder, murder"?

R. RESHA: I think I know that speech by now [given by Resha on November 22, 1956, when he spoke as Transvaal volunteer-in-chief at a meeting called by the Transvaal executive committee and secretly tape recorded by the police].

Can you reconcile that with African National policy?— The example I used in that speech cannot be reconciled with the policy of the African National Congress.

. . . .

MR. FISCHER: Now I would like you to turn over the page, and have a look at a reference to madness at the foot of 8153, about two thirds of the way down the page, you say, "The second thing in a volunteer is to be vigilant, he must be sensitive towards anything that is happening to the African people." And then you say, "The third qualification of a volunteer is madness. You can never be a volunteer unless you are mad." What do you mean by that?

R. RESHA: I think I go further to show what I mean, "because if you are a gentleman, or if you are a lady, you can never get into the train and speak about Congress, you can never get into the bus and speak about Congress, only mad people and only volunteers can do that, because they are mad." What I was trying to put across was that Congress members must, wherever they are, preach the gospel of the African National Congress,· even if people think they are mad, because when you stand in the morning on a street corner and speak about freedom, passersby think you are mad, there must be something wrong with you. If you get into a train and say to the people, the time has come for us to work for a defiance campaign, people think you are mad and I was making that illustration here.

And you must do it even if people think you are mad?— That was my point.

Now I want to ask you whether there were any consequences of your speaking in this fashion about "murder, murder". Did anyone approach you about this?— I think a day after this meeting I was approached by Mr. Sisulu, the then Secretary-General of the African National Congress.

Was he at that time Secretary-General?— He was not, he was banned from participating in the affairs of the African National Congress, and he said to me that he had met Mr. Nokwe who was rather unhappy about my speech where I spoke about murder, and he wanted to know from me what was this all about. I then explained—my explanation to Mr. Sisulu was that it is likely that Mr. Nokwe misunderstood me, I did speak about murder, but that was an example when I was dealing with the discipline of volunteers.

Was it ever raised anywhere else at an Executive meeting or anything of that kind?— It was never raised in any Executive meeting, because there was no executive meeting between that day and the time of our arrest.

When were you arrested?— About fourteen days after that, on the 5th of December, 1956.

. . . .

MR. TRENGOVE: . . . At one stage you believed in violence as a means of achieving one's ends?

R. RESHA: I said in my evidence that it is the normal outlook of the youth at a given age to think that violence can solve their difficulties.

And I think you said—I am speaking subject to correction—I think you said that you shared that view at a certain stage?— I did.

Did you ever change your mind?— As I grew up I began to think much broader.

Did you ever at any stage decide for yourself that violence was a method that had to be discarded as a means of achieving your political ends?— I have thought that way and I was convinced. . . .

Now when did you become convinced of that?— I cannot put the date and time, but as I say, as I grew up and became experienced, took part in political activities, I was convinced that violence is not the method for one to achieve his political aspirations.

I just want to try and get a little closer to the date when you decided that or realised that. How long ago was that?— Well, on a question like that, I would say since I joined the African National Congress.

As far back as 1944?— That is right.

I am going to suggest that you never abandoned that idea and that you believe in violence as a means of achieving your political ends?— My Lord, that is not correct.

Dealing with the African National Congress Youth League, one of the aims of the A.N.C.Y.L. was to serve as a spearhead and shock brigade of the liberatory movement?— The Youth League had no different aims from those of the African National Congress, its mother body.

. . . .

MR. TRENGOVE: Now, how did you visualize the struggling masses of Africa were going to free themselves without the assistance of the white people?

R. RESHA: By struggling for their freedom.

Against whom would they struggle, against the white people?— Against the Government.

Against the white people?— Against the Government.

But now the white people constitute—?— Constitute the government of this country.

Oh, when you say the Government you mean the white people?— I do not mean the same.

Well, you are going to get your freedom, or you may get your freedom, you say here, without the assistance of the white people?— With or without.

. . . .

MR. TRENGOVE: Now the only way to get their freedom would be to persuade the white electorate to bring pressure to bear on the Government?

R. RESHA: The African people can themselves persuade the Government to give in. The pressure does not only come through the electorate.

So that you distinguish here between the white people and the white government?— That is so.

And how were you going to get the white government which had behind it the support of the white people—how were you going to bring them to their knees?— My Lords, in this country we have the government and its forces; we have thousands of Europeans who do not support the policy of the present Government, but do nothing else—they say "Well, we don't accept that policy but that's about all we can say"—so that those people, quite apart from the fact that they say they do not support the policy, they do nothing. They render no assistance, to the African people to change this government.

Mr. Resha, how many people do the Government consist of?— I don't understand that question.

You say you've got to bring the Government to its knees; how many people would be standing alone against your liberatory movement in the end?— I have not counted the number.

Surely, Mr. Resha, you realise that on this passage as it is put here, that the Government at the time when you take power without the assistance of the white people—that the Government would still have the support, the active support of a large number of the white population. That's what your message implies?— What my message implies?

When you say "The struggling masses will free themselves without the assistance of the white people"?— Free themselves or take power, Mr. Trengove?

Well, Mr. Resha, I'll leave the choice to you?— No, No; freeing is different from taking power.

Alright, I'll accept that. When you free youselves, you do it without the assistance of the white people?— That is so.

At that stage you know that the Government would still be able to call upon a large mass of white people to assist them in suppressing your struggle?—In the same way we would be in a position, having attained freedom, to call upon a large number of Europeans to assist us in forming a government that will be for the people of South Africa.

. . . .

R. RESHA: . . . . anyone in this country, a multi-racial country, who opposes Congress—and that person being an African—who opposes Congress in establishing a multi-racial society—in this multi-racial country—is therefore a traitor in the cause for which we stand.

MR. TRENGOVE: Such a person mustn't only be treated with contempt and suspicion but must be regarded as a traitor and an enemy of the people?— In the sense that he supports the present Government in its policy of preaching racial antagonism, in a multi-racial country. That person is not only a traitor, but an enemy of the people who seek freedom and harmony in this country.

And I take it that at an appropriate time the enemies, traitors, would have to be dealt with?— By whom?

By the people when once they have achieved freedom?— That I leave to the people.

You wouldn't have anything against it?— Against?

Against?— Against what?

A trial of traitors?— The people are struggling for freedom, and once they have achieved freedom their work will be to reconstruct South Africa into a happy country for all who live in it.

And then those that were traitors and enemies of the people before freedom would have to be dealt with?— That was your suggestion, Mr. Trengove.

It wasn't A.N.C. suggestion?— It never was.

. . . .

MR. TRENGOVE: Would the position then be, Mr. Resha, that in the present type of State as we have it, where a minority group, the white people, have the Government in their hands, that there is an inherent danger of that government being overthrown by the masses who do not enjoy those privileges?

R. RESHA: That is so.

And I take it that that danger is enhanced and increases as the masses are organised in a positive struggle for liberation?— That is so.

So that whatever the inherent dangers were in the present situation, your activities had the effect of increasing the stability, the danger to the stability and safety and security of the State?— That is so.

And the more successful your struggle became, the greater that danger became?— That is so.

Now, Mr. Resha, in that sense the Defiance Campaign in itself in 1952, particularly if it had been developed to its final stage, would have been dangerous to the safety and security of the State?— That is so.

And I take it, Mr. Resha, that that factor, that ever present factor of the inherent instability of the State was something which you sought to convey to the masses in raising the political consciousness of the people?— That is so.

. . . .

MR. TRENGOVE: Now Mr. Resha, when did the African National Congress realise for the first time that the Government was determined to force through this [Western Areas] scheme at the cost, need be, of violence and bloodshed, regardless of any consequences?

R. RESHA: My Lord, I am in difficulty in giving a date and time as to when Congress realised that, save to say that the possibility of the Government using force and violence was always there; we have known this Government through its years of rule [since 1948], and no less than 300 Africans have been killed by the police in that time, and whenever they decide to do anything force and violence is one of their main features.

Would it be correct to say that as early as the middle of 1954 you already realised that the Government was determined to force this scheme through regardless of the consequences, even if it required violence and bloodshed?— I said it is correct to say by that time we did—because that is about the period when the Government decided to embark on a legalised robbery of the rights of the African people, in the Western Areas, by bringing into being the Native Re-Settlement Act.

. . . .

MR. TRENGOVE: . . . . Did your organisation hold the view, as early as June, 1954, that the Government was about to provoke a racial clash in the Western Areas?
R. RESHA: It has always been the main feature of this Government to provoke racial clashes. It's one of its policies, main policies.

. . . .

Now, Mr. Resha, this racial clash that the Government was accused of wanting to provoke, that racial clash—would it be a violent clash?— The Government is always keen on a violent clash; as I have already mentioned no less than 300 of our people have been killed—and there is the situation of Sharpeville where innocent people were murdered coldbloodedly by this Government.

. . . .

Now, Mr. Resha, did the fact that the Government was prepared to resort to violence and bloodshed in forcing through this scheme—did that in any way deter the African National Congress and its allies from their objective, of making the Western Areas the Waterloo of apartheid?— Not at all. But the Congress and its allies did everything to avoid a bloodbath; and fortunately it succeeded.

Now, Mr. Resha, I want to put it to you that notwithstanding your accusation that the Government wanted to create a blood bath and force through this scheme by violence against the wishes of the people in the Western Areas, that one of the objects of your campaign was to force the Government to do just that; one of the objects was that you wanted to force the Government to remove the people by intimidation and force?— My Lords, that is absolutely incorrect and most unfounded.

You wanted to provoke the Government into using as much force as possible and resorting to what you call intimidation of the people?— We never wanted to provoke the Government at all. What we did want was to get rid of the Government, but insofar as the Western Areas was concerned our aim was to defeat the Government from removing the people of the Western Areas. That was our express aim.

. . . .

MR. TRENGOVE: I'm asking you a simple question, Mr. Resha; did you want to compel the Government to use intimidation against the people?

R. RESHA: I said yes long ago.

Now, Mr. Resha, here you have a Government that is only too willing to use force and intimidation—you want them to use force and intimidation against the people in the Western Areas?— What we want to do is to struggle for our rights, and no amount of force or intimidation on the part of the Government is going to deter us from striving for our rights in the land of our birth.

I want to put it to you, Mr. Resha, that you knew full well that the situation which you were creating in the Western Areas was such that it was the spark which started off the conflagration in this country?— I knew full well what? That what the Government did was intended to start a conflagration in the Western Areas—that was the intention of the, Government.

Now why would the Government want to start a conflagration?— Because it wanted to remove people by force, to rob them of their rights, and because it is natural that no person in this world wants to be robbed of his rights; as a result, no one takes it lightly. And the Government says, "If you don't do what we tell you we are going to use force."

But the Government were prepared to remove the people without bloodshed and violence?— The Government was never prepared to do that—sending 2,000 police, armed; do you call that a preparation to remove people without bloodshed?

But you regard that as a victory, that you compelled the Government to do that?— We regarded it as a victory, that they went away with their guns without shooting one person—because of our perfect organisation on that day. That is what we call a victory, on our side.

. . . .

MR. TRENGOVE: Mr. Resha, you have as justification for the steps that your Congress took in regard to the Western Areas campaign—you have from time to time referred to the alleged viciousness and brutality of the Government; you went as far back as the strike in 1946. Is that correct?

R. RESHA: That is so.

Now, Mr. Resha, I want to put it to you that you know that in all these campaigns that have been organised as far back as the 1946 Mineworkers Strike, that if it had not been for the restraint and tact of the police you would have succeeded long ago in involving the whole country in bloodshed?— My Lords, It has never been the policy of the African National Congress to involve this country in bloodshed. What the African National Congress has done, to the benefit of South Africa, and I think many right thinking people owe that to Congress, is that we have avoided bloodshed right through all these instances you have quoted.

Mr. Resha, do you know that in connection with the Mineworkers Strike the then Minister of Justice in a statement reported in the paper praised the restraint and tact of the police in dealing with that situation, Minister Lawrence. Do you know that?— Do I know that he said so, after people were injured? That was the restraint used by the police—that they injured innocent people.

. . . .

MR. TRENGOVE: And I want to put it to you, Mr. Resha, that what the Minister of Justice said about the attitude of the police and their actions in 1946, applied equally to the May Day Strike of 1951, Stay at Home, the Stay at Home on the 26th June, 1950, to the Defiance Campaign, and to the campaign in the Western Areas?

R. RESHA: You mean the same Minister made the same statement?

No; I said the actions of the police, the restraint with which they conducted themselves, and the actions they took to protect the public, that same type of statement would apply to every campaign up to the Western Areas campaign where you came in contact with the police?—My lords, it would appear that the Crown and the Minister of Justice look at the brutal assaults of the people and the murdering of people as restraint, something to commend the police for.

That is not how we look at it. If the Minister of Justice and the Crown are happy that the police baton charge defenceless and harmless workers and that that is a very good thing—then that is their outlook. So far as we are concerned we condemn it. If the Minister of Justice and the Crown view the killing of 18 people on the 1st May, 1951, as a commendable thing, and that the police acted with restraint, then we differ. If the Minister of Justice says that in sending 2,000 police to the Western Areas, fully armed, to go and look for arms which were never seen by any policeman, to intimidate and frighten the people of the Western Areas—if that is acting with restraint, then, of course, we are at variance with the Minister of Justice and the Crown. We regard it as being a very vicious thing indeed to baton charge people because they want their conditions of work to be improved. We regard it as being very bad indeed to kill 18 innocent people without one policeman having been charged for the loss of life. But if the Government thinks the police acted with restraint in killing 18 out of so many millions of Africans and that this was a good thing, then of course we differ, my lords.

Mr. Resha, you and your organisation have over the years subjected the police in having to carry out their very difficult task of maintaining law and order—you have subjected them to jibes and taunts and insults because you want these actions to take place?—My lord, throughout the years that have been referred to, there is not a single case of violence where a Congress member has ever been charged. The difficulties that are placed before the police have been put there by the Government which is making the police to implement laws which the people of South Africa are opposed to. That is the difficulty which is facing the police, and the Government, of course, can safely hide behind the machine guns of the police as if they are not responsible.

Mr. Resha, your statement that not a single member of Congress has been charged is exactly the point that I want to make, because in the Western Areas you embarked on a vicious and ruthless campaign in which you were using grievances of masses of people, and provoking action from both the Government and those people to suit your purposes?— My lord, there is no evidence before this Court, and anywhere else, to show that we have ever embarked upon such action. The evidence before this Court is clear and simple, that our methods of struggle were clearly and completely non-violent, and we succeeded in demonstrating in a practical way what we mean by non-violence. That is why, my lords, the charges that are placed against me by the powers that be failed even before we could go before the Magistrate. It is a clear demonstration. Insofar as the Western Areas is concerned, throughout that campaign I make bold to say—and which I am very happy about—that not one Congressite was arrested for any action involving rioting, in spite of the fact that people were killed by the police during these raids—in spite of the fact that the police broke down doors and entered peoples' houses—all that is, of course, commended by the Minister and the Crown.

. . . .

MR. TRENGOVE: Mr. Resha, why did you give this example of discipline, that if people are told to be violent they must murder, murder?

R. RESHA: I gave this example, my lords, merely to illustrate the importance of discipline.

According to the tape recording which was played in Court when you got to that point there was applause from your audience?— According to the tape recording when I finished speaking there was applause. . . .

Yes, the sentence is, "When you are disciplined and you are told by your organisation not to be violent you must not be violent; if you are a true volunteer and you are called upon to be violent, you must be absolutely violent, you must murder! Murder! That is all" and then the applause?— That is so.

Now apparently the people at that Conference thought this was a very good example of discipline?— I think so, insofar as it was an example of discipline.

And I put it to you, Mr. Resha, that they applauded you because that is exactly the discipline that you want?— That is completely unfounded and that is not the discipline which I want.

And that is why the people applauded?— I do not know why the people applauded, but that was not the discipline I wanted; I was merely giving an example.

No non-violent organisation would applaud a statement like that?— Congress happens to be known throughout the land [sic] and breadth of the world, to be a non-violent organisation; no one in this world has ever challenged that, and these people applauded.

And that was what Mr. Nokwe was afraid about, if the true nature of Congress was brought to the surface people might change their views?—If the true nature of Congress policy is likely to be misinterpreted by this example, Mr. Nokwe was worried.

. . . .

MR. TRENGOVE: Mr. Resha, I just want to put it to you that you were deliberately striving for a position where there would be a bloody conflict between the Government, trying to maintain its position, and the masses, trying to get the demands of the Freedom Charter?

R. RESHA: Your wishes have nothing to do with the policy of the African National Congress; the policy of the African National Congress is clear in all the documents you have been going through; you haven't found one document to support your school of thought, however you might wish it. What we want to bring about in this country is happiness for everybody, and we have chosen methods of struggle which have indicated clearly what our aims were, and we have succeeded in those methods hitherto. That is why to-day you have political organisations in this country which did not exist before the Defiance Campaign, like the Congress of Democrats, like the South African Liberal Party, like the Progressive Party. Political organisations which believe that in order to make it possible for all to live happily in this country, the policy should be changed, and that we should all share. These political organisations consisting of politicians and thinking men—all of them, including the Nationalist Government—have agreed that our policy is one of non-violence. We have never been accused in this country—and I think the man has still to be born—who wants bloodshed in this country.

Mr. Resha, your statement that numerous white political groups have arisen as a result of your campaigns, I want to put it to you that the main reason for these white political groups to have arisen is because the Communist Party was banned in 1950 and its former members had to find a new political home, or homes?— My lords, I don't know if Mr. Dadoo was a member of the Communist Party, I do not know if Mr. Alan Paton was a member of the former Communist Party, and in fact it is incorrect to say that the Congress of Democrats is there because the Communist Party was banned. These statements are most unfounded. One wonders where you get them from.

. . . .

MR. HOEXTER: You say that you believe that he who lives by the sword will die by the sword?

G. SIBANDE: That is so.

And you believe that in this country today the government lives by the sword?— Yes.

And you think it will die by the sword?— No, I do not say that.

What do you say?— I say if we want to take the government over by the sword, that government will also be taken away from us by the sword. When I say the government, I do not mean the government itself, I mean the government has given its police the right to use the sword.

And you say that in fact they use the sword to maintain power?— Yes.

Don't you believe then that they will lose power by the sword?— No, by peace, not by another sword.

So this will be an exception to the rule?— It is only a bad government, the government of the sword.

. . . .

MR. HOEXTER: The position is, is it not, that you believe that before freedom was achieved, there might well be the shedding of blood in this country?

G. SIBANDE: I just said it now, I do not believe in any freedom that will be attained by shedding of blood, because I even gave the example that what is brought by the sword will lose by the sword.

I am not suggesting for a moment that you are advocating bloodshed, I am asking— I am putting to you that you believed that as a result of the liberatory struggle, blood would be shed in this country, whether it is a good thing or a bad thing?— I believe that it can be got without the shedding of blood.

But you expected blood?— Yes, by expecting the shedding of blood, I know that that is one of the obstacles that we have got to meet.

And that would be one of the obstacles, that people would be killed?— There are many things that I can cite here that we have been killed by the police on many occasions.

You see, you said earlier this morning that the government knows only one method of keeping the people quiet and that is by killing them?— Yes, when I said that, that is what the Minister of Justice himself has said.

And that is why there are so many references in your speeches to the shedding of blood. You warn your followers that they must be prepared to shed blood?— Yes, and I know that when they are on the road to freedom, then they must expect many things.

Why must they expect killing?— My Lord, when the police find a group of people, the way that they know to separate those people is to shoot them. I remember on one occasion they entered a meeting at the Trades Hall, and when they came in they were ready, (Witness is indicating), that they should shoot the people at any time. It was then our duty to make the people sit down and not to heed what the police had in their hands.

But on that occasion there was no shooting?— Quite so, yes, but it is not an easy thing when you enter the door you are already pointing a gun at a person.

. . . .

MR. HOEXTER: What would happen when once the people have united?

G. SIBANDE: It would then come to a point where the Government will go to the people, and then that Government shall be the government of the people, having been chosen by the people. As the old people were used by the people, "Elke een vir homself en God vir ons almal", "Elke een vir homself en die Government vir almal", and the government would be a government for all the people.

Mr. Sibande, are you able to converse in Afrikaans?— No, my lords, I am not.

How many years of your life have you spent in either the Bethal or the Ermelo District?— I was born there and I grew up there.

Most of your life?— Most of my life.

Can you understand Afrikaans?— Yes; that's the language I've spoken almost all my life.

Now you say you didn't think that freedom would be achieved in a short time?— Yes, that's what I say.

. . . .

MR. HOEXTER: Now, Mr. Sibande, you wanted freedom in the shortest possible time, I take it?

G. SIBANDE: I personally, even if it said that we'll get it tomorrow, I wouldn't run away from that.

Yes, you wanted it in the shortest possible time?— Yes.

And you accepted as a leader of the National African Congress that it would not be achieved by speeches but that it would require action?— I believe in that but in this way: there is an expression in my language that says "A child who does not cry dies strapped to its mother's back".

And you supported all the campaigns which the African National Congress organised as part of the struggle for freedom?— Yes.

And you did so in order to achieve freedom as soon as possible?— Yes.

Did you think that the Defiance Campaign was dangerous to the country, to the safety of the country?— No, I never thought that.

By what methods, as you saw it, would freedom be achieved in this country?— By the actions of the people. The people wanted freedom; that is how freedom will be achieved in this country.

Now you did not believe that freedom would come as a result of a voluntary change of heart of the people who govern?— My lord, that is what I mean; because of the change of heart of the people, it will mean that all the hearts of the people of Africa will change. White and non-white. Then the people will force the government to change.

Yes; and how will they force the government?— By making a noise with the Government; for example, if the people say "We want that table", they will make a noise with the Government about that table, then some other people who are far away will hear of this noise and they will also talk to the Government about this thing that the people want. Then the very people in this country will not permit that the noise will go on for a long time, and they will say to the Government, "Government, you come to the people".

During the period of the Indictment, did you notice whether the attitude of the Government towards the oppressed people was hardening or becoming more sympathetic?— My lords, if the Government's heart was hard, I remember what the Bible says about Pharaoh. God knew that the Israelites had to get out of Egypt, but he hardened the heart of Pharaoh. What I see is that during this time we have got a lot of white friends who sympathise with us. Therefore I see that our work is going forward. Furthermore, the Government is also a human being, he must change.

Did you think that the attitude of the ruling class would become still harder or that it would soften?— My lord, personally I thought that the Government would soften.

Is that why you told your followers that there might be blood in the river?— No, that is not so—that is not so, my lords.

Why then did you tell them that there might be blood in the river that they would have to cross?— My lords, I have already said that when I make a speech I always give an illustration, and nobody can deny the fact that the road to freedom has never been an easy one. We know that on the road to freedom there are many things that we have got to face and meet. When I quoted the river I meant the difficulties that one had to expect on the road to freedom. Today, my lords, as I'm answering you I have no place where to stay; I can die anywhere. That is the same blood that I was talking about.

. . . .

MR. TRENGOVE: Mr. Yengwa, you knew, you personally held the view that before freedom was achieved, blood would have to flow in this country?

M. B. YENGWA: I don't know just where you get that information from. In fact I would like to know from you where you get that information, that I personally knew that blood would flow before freedom is won in this country. I think it's a very, very serious allegation and I'd like you to support it before I reply to it.

Did you hold that view, or didn't you?— I know, my lords, that I have to reply, but I think it's a very serious allegation, and I would like you to say how you get that information.

KENNEDY J: I think you should reply to the question?— I'm replying, my lord; there was nothing like that, and I know that there is no substance at all in that allegation; no substance whatsoever.

. . . .

MR. TRENGOVE: Mr. Yengwa, you said yesterday that the Christian influence in the African National Congress was stronger than the Marxist influence. Is that correct?

M. B. YENGWA: Yes, that is my view.

You had people appointed specially as preachers in your organisation?— Chaplains, yes.

Now, could you mention one or two of them?— I could mention the Rev. Calata; I'd mention the Rev. Sikakane.

Do you know Rev. Skomolo?— Yes, I've heard of him, but I don't remember him very well.

And Gawe?— Oh, yes, I know the Rev. Gawe.

Mr. Yengwa, I want to put it to you that when you say your policy is non-violent, what do you mean—do you mean that you are going to give the white people a chance of choosing either a bloody revolution, or to submit to your demands, and if they were not prepared to submit to your demands the other alternative facing them would be a bloody revolution?— I just don't know, my lord, how you arrive at that, but as far as I'm concerned I've told you the policy of the African National Congress, and we have no dual policies, violence and non-violence. Our policy is non-violent.

. . . .

MR. TRENGOVE: Now, I have here in front of me a document, A. 83, which it is alleged was found in possession of the African National Congress, Johannesburg, and it's the report, Agenda Book of the 21st Conference of the South African Indian Congress, and at page 2 it says: It's a message from J. J. Skomolo, Senior Chaplain of the African National

Congress, O.F.S. And it says this:". . . we are sure of our freedom in the not distant future, but how is it to come? By bloody revolution, or by a radical change in the minds of those who oppose it? It is for them to choose. It will be wiser for them to choose the way India got free. Then Africa will be a happy home for us all."?

M. B. YENGWA: I think this is an excellent message.

You agree with that?— I think it's an excellent message, a very good message, my lords.

You say that that would be consistent with the African National Congress view?— Yes; I want to explain this: that the reference to a bloody revolution as far as I can interpret it there, does not mean that it is the African National Congress that would indulge in a bloody revolution. The point is that we cannot exclude a bloody revolution in South Africa, but it would never be the African National Congress that would embark on a bloody revolution.

. . . .

MR. TRENGOVE: How much land held by Europeans at the moment would have to be expropriated or confiscated in terms of that clause [of the Freedom Charter]?

M. B. YENGWA: Now you're using the word 'expropriated' or 'confiscated.' I don't think either of them—I don't think here there is a question of any particular portion, or a particular percentage of the land—it's merely a question of seeing that the land is equitably distributed. The mechanics of distribution would have to be worked out in the future; I don't think it is dealt with here.

What did the African National Congress have in mind; how are you going to get hold of the large portion of the 87% of the land in order to distribute it equally?— Well, to get hold of it is a matter of an arrangement with the people in the country. I think any man—I don't think it matters who it is—there will be a stage where I think the people of South Africa will realise that this inequality is wrong; they'll find a way, as a group—as a multi-racial nation—as a common nation they'll find a way of distributing this land. It isn't a question of just Africans alone just grabbing the land; it's a question of agreeing between themselves and saying "Look, this is no good; 87% of the land belongs to about only 25% of the people".

Mr. Yengwa, before people agree to this they'll want to know what they're going to lose. Now what did the—?—You mean in terms of money?

In terms of land?— In terms of money, in terms of land?

How much land would have to be transferred to the non-white people. Surely that was considered by the African National Congress?— My lords, this is a question which involves a lot of other things; it involves goodwill, it involves a change of heart of the people, it is not only a question of shillings and pence. People are prepared to lose a lot in terms of shillings and pence for other greater things in life, and I think that is the way I personally look at it; that if it's a question of saving South Africa, it's a question of making South Africa a better place for all of us—then we have to appeal to the higher motives and higher values in the human being. And I think even the white man will ultimately have to see it this way, that it isn't just a question of his shillings and pence, it's a question of sacrifice for the common good, for the greater good.

You would expect a change of heart on behalf of the Europeans?— A change of mind more than a change of heart. A change of mind, a change of mental attitude towards the whole problem of South Africa.

Why not a change of heart, Mr. Yengwa?— Well, because I'm perhaps putting it in a way where only sentimentality only takes place; it is much more; I mean it's a real problem; it's not just a question of sentiment. For instance, I think the question of race prejudice is a question of heart, of sentiment only; there are other real issues involved which I think will have to be taken into account by the people who have to live together.

. . . .

MR. TRENGOVE: Would the races in any way be limited as to the amount of land they can hold?

M. B. YENGWA: The what?

The races in the country?— The races?

Yes?— No, there is no question of the races.

The Europeans—?—The point is, my lord, we are looking at the whole problem from a different angle because we are now racially orientated; we are looking at how much the African is going to get, how much the European is going to get. But in my own view that must die out as soon as we don't think in terms of Bantu, Englishman, Afrikaner—but think of South Africans, a common people with a common patriotism. That is how I look at it, so that actually the problems you are posing now apply now but they will never apply in a new society. They will have no place in a new society. In fact I look at the other man as a brother.

Mr. Yengwa, I want to put it to you that these details and these matters and these implications were never considered by the African National Congress, as to how they were going to limit it, and what compensation they would have to pay, and all that kind of thing. They never thought of that?— My lord, the question of thinking about those details is a matter in fact which I think would have been wrong to think of at that particular time, because those are the details that must actually be worked out at a particular time when conditions are different; you don't have to work out details of something like this, because this is merely an ideal of what you think a future society should be.

I want to put it to you, Mr. Yengwa, that they didn't think of it because they never intended to negotiate; they intended to overthrow the ruling class and to seize power and to confiscate the land, the mines, the banks, the monopoly industries in a new society?— I say, my lord, there is no basis for that; that conclusion has no basis at all on the paper we see here. There is no basis for arriving at the conclusion that you've arrived at, my lord.

You wanted to destroy the old society; you wanted to destroy the capitalist structure of the society?— No, my lord, I don't agree with these assumptions that you are making now, of destroying the old society, destroying capitalist society. I don't agree with that. I don't know where you get that.

. . . .

MR. TRENGOVE: Mr. Yengwa, apart from "Das Kapital" and "The Communist Manifesto", have you read any other works on Communism?

M. B. YENGWA: No, my lord.

No other works?— No, my lord.

And what did you mean when you said in your evidence you don't understand the Communist theory of revolution?— Well, I meant, my lord, that I have not read any particular— I've not read about the theory of revolution; I cannot tell you exactly the salient points, and the salient features of the Communist theory of revolution.

. . . .

MR. TRENGOVE: Mr. Yengwa, you know very well that the Communists throughout the world are there to overthrow existing social conditions in non-Communist countries by force, by violence. You know that?

M. B. YENGWA: Well, my lords, I do not know; I don't know the whole history of Communism; I am not able to say that I know.

And I want to put it to you that the Communists in the Liberatory Movement in South Africa were working in that direction, and with that in mind?— That was not what I knew and that is not what they told us. As far as I knew they supported the Congress policy and that was all that was required of them in the Congress Movement.

You said yesterday that the Communists never opposed or criticised the non-violent policy of the African National Congress?—No, they never did.

I put it to you that they didn't because the African National Congress hasn't got a non-violent policy?—My lords, I've been repeating over and over again, and I want again to repeat that the A.N.C. policy is non-violent, and I have not been able to find anything at all from what the Prosecutor has said or shewn me, to show in support of his allegation,

'Here is the evidence to show that what you say is wrong'. He is only alleging and putting it to me, one hundred and one times, that the A.N.C. policy was violent, but without a shred of evidence to support his allegation, my lords.

Mr. Yengwa, I want to put it to you that the methods that you people consistently and systematically advocated in order to achieve your freedom, are completely in line with Communist policy; and is exactly what the Communists want?— I don't know, my lords, what the Communists want, but I do know what the African National Congress want.

RUMPFF J: Isn't this argument, Mr. Trengove?

MR. TRENGOVE: Mr. Yengwa, I want to put it to you that throughout the period of the Indictment, all your propaganda and all your campaigns, were directed at preparing the masses for the overthrow of the State by indoctrinating them with Communist propaganda?— I deny that, my lord, most emphatically.

And I also put it to you that your activities throughout this period were intended to be a softening up process against the State?— What do you mean softening up process?

A process to cause the disintegration and the break-down of the State, so that you could take over by violence, when the time was ripe?— That is ridiculous, my lords.

And I put it to you that apart from that your purpose—your campaigns served a purpose which enabled you to test the mood of the masses to find out whether they were ripe to move from one stage to another?— My lords, that is not correct at all, it is totally wrong.

. . . .

MR. TRENGOVE: Is South Africa a Capitalist State?

M.B. YENGWA: As far as I'm concerned it has aspects of Capitalism, and it has aspects, too, of Socialism.

I want to know the African National Congress view?— The African National Congress view I think is the view that I'm giving you now.

Did they regard South Africa as a Capitalist State?— Both Capitalist and in some ways Socialist.

Did they regard South Africa as imperialist?— Yes, they do regard South Africa as having aspects of Imperialism.

Did they regard South Africa as Fascist?— They do regard South Africa as being Fascist.

Why?— Because the Government has very large powers over the lives of the people; in that way they regard South Africa as Fascist.

. . . .

MR. TRENGOVE: Now, how does the oppressor in an Imperialist State react when people fight for their freedom?

M. B. YENGWA: Well, my lords, he reacts like all human beings react in certain situations. I don't think there could be any particular plan. One may find certain features in a country, and entirely different features in another country. You'll find for instance that England now is giving freedom to countries like Ghana and Nigeria and India, and one cannot really say this is a pattern; there is no particular pattern; it depends on a particular government, and the policies it adopts later. There is no particular pattern.

Is that your view, or the view of the A.N.C.?— I think it's a factual view; the A.N.C. people are not wedded to any particular dogma; they are realists and they would see the situation as I see it.

I put it to you, Mr. Yengwa, that either you don't know the A.N.C. view or you are misrepresenting the A.N.C. view?— I know the A.N.C. view.

The A.N.C. view is that the Imperalist oppressor lives by force and terror?— I know the A.N.C. view, my lord, and that is the view I am expressing.

. . . .

MR. TRENGOVE: Mr. Yengwa, you didn't attack China for her intervention in Korea?

M. B. YENGWA: No, my lords.

Because she was a Communist country?— My lords, I don't just know why one must not do things because they are Communists. There are many things one does not do in the world, and it doesn't mean that one does not do those things because they are Communist—it is I think a very, very wrong deduction to make, and to say that everything a man does he does because it's done by Communists, or because Communism is there—I think we are independent people and we act independently, and we've got our own ideas; we are not commissioned by Communists, my lords.

Mr. Yengwa, the African National Congress held the view that throughout the world there was a struggle between the oppressor and the oppressed?— My lords, that is a correct view. The oppressor and the oppressed will always have a struggle; there will always be a struggle between the oppressor and the oppressed. It is a correct view, you will never find the oppressed merely sitting down and making no effort to liberate themselves.

And you held the view that the oppressor group was led by the United States of America?— My lords, there is a view which we held, that America being a leading Western power, by allowing itself to support the South African Government, was in fact making it difficult for us to get our liberation. It was a view which we held and there is a very good basis for it.

You regarded America as the leader of the oppressor group?— We regarded America as the leader of the Western Powers, and South Africa being part of the Western Powers, America was the leader of the oppressor group in South Africa.

Mr. Yengwa, did the African National Congress hold the view that the American Imperialism wanted to plunge the world into a blood bath?— My lords, that was not the view that was held by all the African National Congress members, and I do not think it was the view of the National African Congress as such.

Did the African National Congress hold the view that the American Imperialists were guilty of warmongering tactics?— Now, my lords, the word 'warmongering'—there is a word which perhaps would need to be described. Let me put it in my own way because I don't want to be in any difficulty about what you mean by warmongering. The fact that America was establishing bases in Africa and other countries created the view amongst the African National Congress people that America was actually precipitating a war, and that view was expressed; it might have been expressed in different words by different people—some people might have used the word blood bath and so forth—but the very fact that America was establishing bases in Africa and other countries made us believe that such a programme on the part of America would easily lead to, or precipitate a third World War.

Mr. Yengwa, I want to put it to you that what you objected to was that these War bases might be used against the Soviet Union?— My lords, that is not at all the point. We felt that Africa might become the battleground of the world, and that is what we were against.

Did the African National Congress Youth League ever condemn the attempts of America to establish war bases in Africa, as being preparation for a war against the Soviet Union?— I don't know.

You don't know?— No.

Would you agree with that attitude?— What is the type of attitude now?

That you condemned the United States for establishing war bases?— Yes, the African National Congress did, my lord.

Against the Soviet Union?— Yes, my lords, it is obviously against the Soviet Union; there is no doubt about it.

Do you know if the Soviet Union has war bases outside the Soviet Union?— No, my lords, I don't know.

Do you know whether it has any military pacts with any Government?— I know it has military pacts with some other governments.

With which governments?— Poland for instance, it has a military pact with Poland.

Have you condemned them for that?— My lords, these pacts and bases are not in Africa. The point is America has bases in Africa, and we did not want Africa to become the battleground of the world.

The North Atlantic Treaty Organisation, and the South East Asia Treaty Organisation were condemned by the African National Congress?— Yes, my lords, they are all part of the American Defence Scheme.

Throughout the world?— They are part of the American Defence Scheme throughout the world.

Mr. Yengwa, you held the view that you were fighting not only for the peace of South Africa, or for the peace of Africa, but for the peace of the whole world?— It is true, as I think anybody who wants peace, must fight for the peace of the whole world.

The Russian Military Pacts with Poland, doesn't that constitute a danger to world peace?— Well, my lords, it does; but it was not a matter which really we should have in my opinion exercised our minds on.

The de-militarisation of Germany, does that constitute a threat to South Africa?— The de-militarisation of Germany?

The re-militarisation of Western Germany?— Yes, my lord, I think any threat of war is in the long run a threat to peace in the world. I don't think you can have one part of the world preparing for war and thinking that you are quite safe; I think any part of the world that is preparing to wage war against any other part of the world would immediately engage the whole world in a world conflict.

Was the African National Congress against the re-militarisation of Germany?— I should think so, my lords; it should have been, as it was against the re-militarisation of any country.

Why was it not against the military pact between Poland and Russia?— My lords, as I say, the African National Congress would have been against the re-militarisation of any country in the world; whether it be Russia, whether it be Poland, whether it be Germany, whether it be the United Kingdom.

Then can you tell me why it was not against the military pact between Poland and Russia?— I don't think there is anywhere where you can find that the African National Congress stated it was in favour of the re-militarisation of Poland and Russia.

I'm not asking you that?— It amounts to that; if one is silent you cannot say he is therefore in favour, because that is the implication of your question.

I want to know why you didn't condemn it?— Yes, my lords, there are so many things I didn't do, and I had no particular reason for not doing them; I just didn't do them.

The African National Congress?—Yes, the African National Congress—there are many things that the African National Congress never did, and it just didn't do them because they just never had to do them at the time. But it doesn't mean that it was in favour of such things.

I'll tell you why it didn't do them; it was because as long as the Soviet Bloc and the Soviet Satellites prepared themselves for a war, it suited the

African National Congress; that's why you didn't condemn them?— That is ridiculous, my lords, absolutely ridiculous.

. . . .

MR. TRENGOVE: Which of those two blocks was leading the struggle for peace and freedom in the world?

M. B. YENGWA: My lords, what I do know is that Russia for instance has always consistently supported the struggle of the people of this country; it has never at any time failed to support us; it has always expressed itself as supporting the struggle of the Colonial peoples, and I think I've said before that to our mind and from what we saw, America was reluctant to state that they, and England too, have to some extent come out in support of our struggle in this very country. And it was natural that as far as we were concerned Russia was committed to supporting our liberatory struggle in this particular country. But that did not in any way mean that we supported the Russian—

That's not what I asked you, Mr. Yengwa?— I thought I should explain to you so that it should be clear in your mind what our position is.

. . . .

MR. KENTRIDGE [of the defense]*:* You yourself said in the passage which we referred to, that this government was relentless. Now bearing that in mind, would you explain how it was that you could be optimistic about your chances of succeeding aginst it?

Z. K. MATTHEWS: Well, our optimism was based upon the fact that this is not the only government that has been relentless in the history of political struggle. Other governments have been equally relentless and determined to—not to give in, to demands made by their subjects.

And they have subsequently done so.

What sort of countries or governments are you thinking about?— I would say an example like India for example. I can recall being in the United Kingdom and hearing Churchill speaking against the possibility of the Indians getting their independence, but it happened in his lifetime.

Did you expect a spontaneous change of heart from the government or from the White citizens of this country?— No government ever acts spontaneously in as far as I know, governments usually act as a result of pressure, either from the people who have put them into power, but usually as a result of pressure. They don't just go handing out gifts to people because they happen to be around. Governments don't act like that.

What about the White people generally in this country? Did you think that they would have a spontaneous change of heart in their attitude towards Africans?— No, we didn't expect that.

What did you think would happen?— We felt that we had to adopt forms of action that would influence them, that would make them aware of what was going on. Possibly even affect their own self interests, their pockets.

Do you think that type of pressure on White people in this country will work?— I think it will work. As far as I know they are human, the White people in this country too.

Have you had any evidence or suggestion, professor, that these methods of yours have had any effect on White people?— Yes, I think so. I think that it would be true to say that there are more White groups today who are conscious of the existence of the problems and who are working a change and changed outlook towards us. I could mention not only groups such as the Congress of Democrats and the Liberal Party, the Progressive Party, but even in circles such as Sabra, which is a pro-apartheid organisation, even in that organisation you find that there is a move,—things in South Africa are not as they ought to be and something ought to be done about it.

Have you seen any evidence that economic pressure brings about any result? In this country?— Yes, economic pressure brings about results, individual strikes here and there.

Do you think the business community in this country is at all sensitive to economic boycotts?— I think they are. I think the business community is particularly sensitive.

. . . .

MR. JUSTICE BEKKER: There is something I would like to debate with you here, professor. In your view, if the franchise were given to everybody over eighteen years, would that mean the end of what is called White supremacy in this country?

Z. K. MATTHEWS: Yes, I think it would. White supremacy as such.

Did—I would like to know what the approach of the African mind was to the possible reaction on the part of White supremacy on this demand? In other words, did the people think well, our demand involves something which will bring an end to White supremacy in this country. Was the question considered, what would the reaction be of White supremacy to this demand?— Yes, I mean what we would say to that is this, we did not expect as I say that White supremacy would readily concede these points.

This opens the real point of debate. Would it, if that was the demand, would pressure, in the mind of the Africans, would pressure suffice? Economic pressure?— Yes, certainly, we think it would suffice. We think that even the White supremacy is not impervious to political pressure and economic pressure. The thing is that up to now it hasn't been used to a sufficiently—on a sufficiently wide scale, and sustained over a sufficiently long period. In other words, we feel that as the A.N.C., we are still a weak body, but if that we were stronger than we are now, even the White supremacists would talk.

The power you command, as you said yesterday, over labour. That would be enough to bring White supremacy to its knees?— It is not a question of to its knees, but it is a matter of negotiation, of talking—I mean the suggestion that you bring people to their knees is that we have the idea of wanting to dominate them and becoming the top dog. That is not the idea of the A.N.C.

Did the A.N.C. consider how the White man would regard that claim? In the sense, well, if the A.N.C. demands that, they want to dominate?— No. our case is that to the extent that we in the A.N.C. stand for a policy of full citizenship rights for all, we are not out for domination.

Might not the White man say well, once that happens it is finished, the A.N.C. will dominate?— No, we have got experience of this kind of thing in other organisations. For example, take Church organisations. We have got plenty of churches in this country in which the Africans have a dominant vote in the Church as compared with the White members of the Church, but they haven't abused that vote and tried to dominate that particular Church.

That is, from the point of view of the A.N.C., I am rather trying to find out did the A.N.C. consider whether the White man, rightly or wrongly, that doesn't matter, whether the White man [may] not say well, once everybody has got the vote in this country, the inevitable will happen, the Black man will rule the country and the Black man will dominate?— We would say that was a mistaken view. It wouldn't be a case of one group ruling the country, that is not what we envisage.

You say it might be a mistaken view?— But it would be a view held, yes.

On the part of the White man?— Yes.

And how would that White man holding that view—how would he react to this claim? Was that considered?— That I can't say. I can't speak for him as to how he would react. He might react—

Anyway, it is your view, but the matter I suppose wasn't considered in this light?— No, it wasn't considered in that light.

. . . .

MR. KENTRIDGE: Did you not think that it was advisable to restrain the expressions of individual opinions?

Z. K. MATTHEWS: No, we didn't think it was advisable to impose a kind of censorship either of thought or of writing on our members.

Did you ever observe that sometimes in these journals the mode of expression was emotional?— Yes.

Did you disapprove of that?— No, I didn't disapprove. I understood it. I can understand people writing under the conditions in which Africans do write, with feelings of resentment and a sense of humiliation, people writing from that point of view are sometimes apt to be emotional in writing, and one understands that.

What about the young men in the Youth League, would that apply to them?— Yes. They would not be peculiar as far as youth are concerned. Youth in any group express themselves strongly and vigorously as compared with their fathers.

When they use political expressions let us say in Youth League Journals, do you think they were always carefully formulated?— No, I don't think so. That is now how political writers or political speakers work. They don't write as if they were writing academic theses. They let themselves go in their speeches.

Do you think that it is a proper approach to subject a polemical political article to a close linguistic analysis?— No, I don't think it is a proper approach at all. It is not a statute, you don't interpret a political speech the way you might interpret a statute, for example looking at every word and trying to find out what the meaning is of that word. You get the general sense.

. . . .

MR. KENTRIDGE: Now bearing in mind your knowledge and experience of the A.N.C. and of general African public work and political work in this country and your knowledge of the African people, do you think it is possible that—as a practical matter for an organisation like the A.N.C. to preach to the public a policy of non-violence, while it really wants to pursue a policy of violence?

Z. K. MATTHEWS: As I said already, that it seems to me that to adopt an attitude like that would be futile, because if you had a secret policy of violence, you would have at some time to tell your followers, amongst whom you have been preaching non-violence over a long period of time, you would have to reveal to them this secret policy, and my own impression would be that they would regard you as somebody who had deceived them all along and your following would fall away.

. . . .

MR. KENTRIDGE: Professor Matthews, I want to put to you to an allegation made by the Crown in this case and ask you whether you agree with it or not. Now in the Crown's opening address the following statement of fact is made. 'The Crown will ask the Court to infer from certain evidence, for example happenings at a beerhall, Johannesburg, that the bulk of the country's non-European population is likely to respond more quickly, more irresponsibly and more violently to illegal agitation than would be the case with a group whose general standard of civilisation was higher.' Now assume that this reference to the beerhall is a reference to a riot by Africans which took place at a Municipal beerhall in Johannesburg and naturally we may assume that there have been other riots in South

Africa at various times—what do you say to this proposition that the bulk of the country's non-European population is likely to respond more quickly, more irresponsibly and more violently to illegal agitation than would be the case with a group whose general standard of civilisation was higher?— Well, I should say definitely that I don't agree with that. I don't know of any scientific basis upon which that conclusion is based. I think it's grossly unfair to generalise about the bulk of the Bantu population on the basis of incidents such as you refer to there, the beerhall incident or similar incidents. I think Social Scientists who have worked with the Bantu, who have done actual field work with them, will disagree with that conclusion.

What about this reference to a comparison with a group whose general standard of civilisation was higher?— Well, in the first place I'm a little skeptical about the use of this word civilisation being higher; I don't know in what sense the word 'higher' is used in connection with civilisation there, but my own impression would be that even the so-called more highly civilised groups, subject to the same conditions to which the Bantu are subject in this country, would I think react more violently than they do.

More violently?— I think they would react more violently; I think the Bantu are a very patient people, a very law-abiding people. You will remember that General Smuts himself at one time referred to them as having the patience of an ass because of their very slow reaction to the conditions to which they are subjected.

Now this phrase 'illegal agitation'—let's assume that that means agitation directed at breaches of the law, do you consider that Africans in this country are prone to react violently to that type of agitation, if we can keep the word agitation?— In fact I dispute this contention about illegal agitation, because speaking for the African National Congress my own view is that the agitation of the African National Congress is not illegal; it is agitation, but it's not actually illegal. Now if you say agitation to break laws—if that is what you mean by 'illegal agitation' even there I would say that the Bantu would not readily do that sort of thing.

Assume then that emotional speeches are made to an African audience, do you think that such an audience is particularly likely to react in a violent way?— I think that what you would find—that possibly the reaction of an audience to such emotional speeches would be to approve of them, to clap and to applaud them, but not to react in a violent manner. I would suggest respectfully that what really does happen in a case like that is that you get an emotional release on the part of the people who are listening, to a sense of frustration which they have.

Yes. Does this mean that Africans do not resent the conditions under which they live in this country?— No, definitely not; they do resent them very much indeed.

And what form would such resentment take, if given expression?— Well, there is a whole host of possible reactions to resentment, but the burden of our work in the African National Congress has been to canalise the possible reactions and to see that they are confined to what we consider to be non-violent methods.

Do you think that the African people in this country are capable of understanding and responding to a call for non-violent methods?— I think they were—yes, I think very definitely that they were; yet at the same time, of course, we repeatedly stressed this because in the circumstances of this country, the temptation to do otherwise must be strong.

Now, in the same Opening Address it is alleged 'The Crown will contend that by the time of the arrests in this case the accused had deliberately created an explosive situation'—the time of arrests, of course, was December, 1956; now what do you say to the proposition that an explosive situation has been created in this country?— Well, I don't know what the writer means by an explosive situation. I would understand by explosive situation that explosive in the sociological sense, in that the relative rights and privileges of the people in this country—the Constitution of the country is such that it contains within it the seeds of dissension between the various sections of the population. I understand explosive in that sense, but that is not a situation which has been created by the African National Congress.

In your opinion, in the sense in which you have explained the word, did an explosive situation exist in this country?— In that sense it does so exist, yes.

Only in 1956?— No, it existed I should say since the State was created, in 1910.

MR. KENTRIDGE: Professor, a number of witnesses called by the Defence have said that the African National Congress was not an anti-white organisation but was in favour of multi-racialism. I want to ask you whether in the speeches which you heard in the Preparatory Examination you noticed some expressions indicative of hostility towards white people?

Z. K. MATTHEWS: I think in a few speeches, yes, that one could say they did border on that, but the main trend of A.N.C. speeches and activities is not anti-white. I say that most emphatically.

Let's just concentrate on those speeches which struck you at the Preparatory Examination as being suggestive of hostility towards white persons, apparently made on A.N.C. platforms. How would you account for the fact that there were such expressions?— Well, I think it must be remembered that many of the people who do speak on A.N.C. platforms speak with a great sense of frustration and resentment, and sometimes even bitterness about the conditions under which they live, and I am not surprised that occasionally you find speeches which go beyond, slightly, the official policy of the A.N.C.

Does the A.N.C. try and overcome that feeling of hostility towards white people which might exist in some of its members?— Yes, we do; yes, we stress that too in our meetings, that we are not fighting the white people as such, but that we are concerned with fighting against a system of which we do not approve, and to which we are subject.

And do you think that the A.N.C. during the period we are dealing with—that its activities or policies had any effect in the matter of the attitude of Africans towards white people?— Certainly amongst our members, yes. Our members have in the main stuck to the policy of cooperation with other groups and with the white people—people who have not been satisfied with this policy have cleared out of the A.N.C.

. . . .

Z. K. MATTHEWS: . . . surely we are not working for the year two thousand or three thousand. We are trying, as we say, to get freedom within our lifetime. We would like to enjoy it a bit.

MR. HOEXTER: I appreciate the aspirations, professor, but what I want to put to you is this, the opening sentence of this paragraph doesn't pose the question, should we strive to get our freedom quickly or slowly. It really poses a more fundamental question. It says, can such a radical sweeping change be made little by little, by one reform after another. Now what I would like to put to you at the outset is that in point of fact it should not be impossible for your ideal state to be achieved by a long, a protracted process of small, of gradual reforms. What do you say to that?

It should not—I say one can envisage such a process of gradual—?— Certainly, a small, slow process extending over centuries.

Or fifty years?— Yes.

. . . .

Z. K. MATTHEWS: . . . when one reads speeches like this, one must try and put oneself in the place of the people who were faced with this removal, and think of the feelings under which they were speaking, and you don't expect them to use, you know, the sort of polite speech, carefully calculated words which you would find in a Board of Directors meeting.

MR. HOEXTER: Perhaps not, professor, but don't you find it—I am referring to the portion I read you on page 7414, you have a recurrence of this strange notion, a notion which is strange to you, that the allegation that the government intended to turn the area into a blood bath for its own political ends is made?— I don't know that it is peculiar to the African National Congress for political opponents to attribute motives to one another which perhaps they cannot establish.

Motives of a planned massacre?— Yes,—not necessarily of a planned massacre, but motives.

Well, what does this mean, "intends to turn the area into a blood bath for its own political ends?" Doesn't that connote bloodshed on a large scale, deliberately engineered?— It could connote that, yes. If you are reading

625

the thing literally, it could connote that. What I am suggesting is that we mustn't read these speeches so literally as all that.

Did the A.N.C. want the people to believe that these were the motives of the government?— I don't know, I wouldn't say that they wanted the people to believe that. What they wanted to do was to rouse the resistance of the people and the determination of the people not to move. A political speaker would use expressions of this kind—

To induce what impression on his audience?— To strengthen the determination of his audience not to move, and to abide by the policy which he is trying to put forward. I think so.

To prepare them for the possibility of bloodshed?— One couldn't exclude the possibility of people getting hurt in the process.

This seems to be—so far from being excluded, this seems to be stressed as a very distinct possibility?— That may be so, but as I say, one mustn't interpret these speeches in the close word for word interpretation which you are applying to it.

Not the same interpretation one would apply—?— I can imagine, supposing this sort of thing was done with any group of Europeans in this country, I am quite certain their language would be stronger than this, they would take up arms. They wouldn't just say there is a possibility of us having to suffer in the process. They wouldn't tolerate it.

Now you have explained to us how you consider a speech of this type should be interpreted. Do you think a document setting forth policy should be interpreted—be scrutinized more closely, and that more importance should be attached to the words in a document?— Not a political document. Political documents—

Are worthless?— They should not be interpreted in that sense, political documents of any party.

What do you mean by political documents?— Documents written by politicians, that is what I mean by political documents. Not by a political scientist, but by a politician.

How would you classify executive reports, national executive reports of an organisation like the African National Congress?— I would say they are documents produced by people who are active in political organisations. They don't meet there as a Board of Directors. They meet there as people who are out—who feel it is their duty to express the feelings of their followers and often do so very strongly.

And you feel that people in that position may make reckless statements with impunity?— Sometimes they make statements like that, but at the same time I feel that in interpreting those statements, one must look at the background and the motivation behind the whole thing. You mustn't just look at them from the—as I say literal translation of the words.

Well, some of the statements I read to you this morning in official documents of the A.N.C., in those political documents, did they appear to you to be reckless statements?— I would say that some of them are overstatements, yes.

My question to you is—?— Not reckless. I would say they are overstatements of the situation. There is frequently—as I say, one must remember the state of mind of the people who are writing.

I want to put to you that that state of mind as we see it in this speech and in the documents we considered this morning, is a state of mind of recklessness?— I don't agree with that. A person who is right—a person who is writing with a feeling of indignation, may make statements which he wouldn't make if he was faced with a much calmer situation than that, and I wouldn't necessarily say that he was reckless.

Note: Extracts are taken from the following pages of the *Treason Trial Record:* *Conco:* 11,089–093; 11,180–11,182; *Lutuli:* 11,893–11,894; 11,939–11,942; 11,947–11,950; 13,087–13,088; 13,178–13,181; 13,655–13,656; 13,658–13,660; 13,662; 13,742–13,743; 13,745; 13,758–13,759; *Mandela:* 15,893–15,895; 15,959–15,960; 15,977; 16,118–16,122; *Resha:* 16,571–16,573; 16,579–16,580; 16,831; 16,883–16,884; 16,887–16,890; 16,892–16,893; 16,967–16,968; 16,970–16,971; 16,973–16,974; 16,977–16,978; 17,039–17,044; 17,063–17,064; 17,149–17,150; *Sibande:* 17,390; 17,393–17,394; 17,459–17,462; *Yengwa:* 17,635; 17,638–17,640; 17,648–17,652; 17,662; 17,664–17,666; 17,668–17,671; 17,680–17,684; 17,686; *Matthews:* 17,953–17,958; 17,972–17,973; 17,979; 18,016–18,019; 18,021–18,022; 18,140; 18,169–18,172.

RENEWED AND ABORTIVE "ALL-IN" EFFORTS, DECEMBER 1960–MAY 1961

Document 54. Resolutions, Adopted by the Consultative Conference of African Leaders, and Cables, Sent by the Conference to the United Nations and to Oliver Tambo, December 16–17, 1960

1. This Conference agrees on the urgent need for African Unity and pledges itself to work for it on the basis of the following broad principles:—

   (a) The removal of the scourge of apartheid from every phase of national life;

   (b) The immediate establishment of a non-racial democracy;

   (c) The effective use of non-violent pressures against apartheid.

2. This Conference of African Leaders from all walks of life having carefully examined the grave problems of our country places on record that:—

   (a) It is convinced that the absence of fundamental rights and in particular the right to have a say in the affairs of our country is the basic cause of suffering, strife, racial tension and conflict in our country;

(b) It is its considered view that the situation is further aggravated by the efforts of the Government to muzzle the political expression of the African people by banning of the African National Congress and the Pan Africanist Congress;

(c) There is no doubt that the imposition of a new constitution for a Nationalist Republic with contemptuous disregard for the views of the African people is a climax in this deteriorating process.

(d) This conference notes with concern that the developments in South Africa are diametrically opposed to those in the rest of Africa— WHEREFORE Conference warns that the situation in our country has created an atmosphere charged with the possibility of an eruption unless all sections of the people of our country halt this development. To this end the African Leaders here assembled consider that the African people are the most vital and potent force to direct changes in our country and that therefore their

UNITY IS ESSENTIAL.

In view whereof this conference resolves that because the African people were denied participation in the Republican Referendum they do not accept its result. This conference, therefore, calls upon the African people to attend an all-in conference representative of African People in the urban and rural areas whose purpose will be to:—

(i) demand the calling of a National Convention representing all the people of South Africa wherein the fundamental rights of the people will be considered;

(ii) consolidate the UNITY of the African People.

3. That to achieve the above ends a Continuation Committee be appointed which will make arrangements for an all-in African conference which must be held by not later than the end of FEBRUARY, 1961.

4. (a) This conference is alarmed by the use of military units in Pondoland and demands that the Government withdraw them forthwith, and stop the butcherings and Pass persecutions so that an atmosphere can be created for action to be taken to redress the just grievances of the people whose existence was admitted by a Government commission recently.

(b) This conference hails the struggle of the Pondo people who have by their courage and determination exposed the hypocrisy which suggested that the Bantu Authorities are acceptable to the African people both in the urban and rural areas.

(c) This conference calls upon the African people and democrats in the other racial groups to regard the Pondo People's resistance to Bantu Authorities as an integral part of the fight against apartheid.

5. That this conference appeals to the U.N.O. to send a Commission of Observers to Pondoland and to use its good offices to curb the alarming

628

military operations against unarmed people which constitutes a threat to peace in South Africa.

6. This conference of African Leaders welcomes the resolution of the Security Council of the U.N.O. and in particular the visit of the Secretary General, Mr. Dag Hammersjold, but urges that in order to have a true view of the situation in the country he should meet African Leaders.

7. This conference wishes to place on record that the raid carried on by the Police on this legitimate conference of African Leaders and the arbitrary arrest of some delegates demonstrates clearly the extent to which freedom of expression is being denied to Africans.

8. Conference demands the immediate lifting of the ban on the A.N.C. and P.A.C., the national organisations of the people.

CABLES

The Secretary-General,
The United Nations Organisation,
NEW YORK.

CONFERENCE OF AFRICAN LEADERS WELCOMES SECURITY COUNCIL RESOLUTION ON SOUTH AFRICA AND PROPOSED VISIT OF SECRETARY-GENERAL. FIRMLY URGE GET TRUE PICTURE OF SOUTH AFRICA BY MEETING AFRICAN LEADERS.

PONDOLAND SITUATION ALARMING. MILITARY OPERATIONS AGAINST UNARMED AFRICANS. RECOMMEND U.N.O. SEND COMMISSION OF OBSERVERS.

SUPPORT DEMAND SOUTH WEST AFRICAN PEOPLE FOR INDEPENDENCE. NATIONALIST GOVERNMENT NO MORAL NOR LEGAL RIGHT TO RULE.

W. B. NGAKANE
JOHANNESBURG.

MR. O. TAMBO,
NEW YORK.

AFRICAN LEADERS APPRECIATE WORK THE UNITED FRONT. CABLEGRAM SENT SECRETARY-GENERAL CONGRATULATING SECURITY COUNCIL RESOLUTION AND WELCOMING VISIT TO SOUTH AFRICA OF SECRETARY-GENERAL BUT URGE HE MEETS AFRICAN LEADERS. CONDEMN MILITARY OPERATIONS IN PONDOLAND. DEMAND

COMMISSION OF OBSERVERS. SUPPORT DEMAND OF SOUTH WEST AFRICAN PEOPLE FOR NATIONAL INDE-PENDENCE. NATIONALIST GOVERNMENT NO MORAL OR LEGAL RIGHT TO RULE.

Document 55. "The African Leaders Call to the African People of South Africa." Leaflet announcing the All-in African Conference of March 25-26, 1961, issued by the Continuation Committee of African Leaders, [n.d.]

The African Leaders Call To The African People Of South Africa

WORKERS, SPORTSMEN, CHURCHMEN, PROFESSIONAL MEN, MUSICIANS,

STUDENTS, PEASANTS, HOUSEWIVES

PREPARE FOR THE

All-In African Conference

TO BE HELD IN THE

City Hall

PIETERMARITZBURG, NATAL

ON

SATURDAY and SUNDAY

25th and 26th MARCH, 1961

630

AFRICANS, COUNTRYMEN, FELLOW-WORKERS, PREPARE FOR THE ALL-IN AFRICAN CONFERENCE FOR THE BUILDING OF OUR UNITY TO STOP VERWOERD AND HIS FASCIST REPUBLIC.

- The majority of the 3,000,000 white voters have elected to declare South Africa a Republic.
- The 3,000,000-strong white electorate has chosen to declare South Africa a Republic, with UTTER DISREGARD FOR THE VIEWS OF OUR 12,000,000 PEOPLE.
- They have given Verwoerd the green light to his Herrenvolk Republic.
- By this action they have endorsed and justified the oppression of our people under pass laws and all other vicious discriminatory laws of this Nationalist government.
- They have mandated the reactionary Broederbond politicians to be the dictators in our country.

ONE MAN—ONE VOTE

- Africans, countrymen, fellow-workers, let us unite against a BAASSKAP Republic; let us unite in our demand for a new DEMOCRATIC constitution (One Man—One Vote).
- As sons and daughters of this country, let us give a massive NO to Verwoerd's Republic.
- As workers and oppressed people, and as victims of Apartheid policy, let us unite against fascism in our country.
- Let us speak with one voice for all the eleven million Africans and say "NO" to white domination. Let us say: "Thus far and no farther."
- Let us tell them of our anger and hatred for Bantu Authorities, which has caused strife, division and death in Sekhukhuniland, Zeerust, and now Pondoland.
- Let us tell them to end all Pass Laws.
- Let us tell them we want no taxation without representation.
- Let us tell them of ONE UNIVERSAL EDUCATION for all and let us say NO to Bantu Education.
- Let us tell them of the millions of landless people who can no longer endure this form of strangulation and starvation.

LET US GET TOGETHER IN THE ALL-IN AFRICAN CONFERENCE AS CHURCHMEN, SPORTSMEN, PROFESSIONAL MEN,

MUSICIANS, WORKERS AND PEASANTS AND AS MEN FROM ALL WALKS OF LIFE.

LET US DEMAND THE CALLING OF A NATIONAL CONVENTION TO DRAW UP A NEW CONSTITUTION FOR THE PEOPLE OF SOUTH AFRICA.

- Let us now prepare as organisations, associations, clubs and different societies to send delegates to this Conference of the African people. Let us form our delegates' committees now. Call great meetings and elect our delegates. Collect money for fares and board and lodging now.

- Let us tell the white Rulers of South Africa that there is one and only one peaceful solution to the problems in our country: the immediate holding of a national convention for a democratic South Africa.

- Let us tell them that our patience is exhausted and time is running out fast.

- Let us warn all people that the atmosphere is explosive and we will live ever on the edge of a volcano unless all sections of the people of our country call a halt to the Nationalists.

- No constitutional changes without our consent!

- Let us unite and stop Verwoerd's Fascist Republic. No Bantu Authorities.

- Lift the ban of the African National Congress and the Pan African Congress.

COMPLETE THIS FORM

My organisation is interested in the Conference. Please supply further information.

Name of Organisation ....

Address ....

....

....

Issued by the Continuation Committee of African Leaders,
208 Macosa House, 17 Commissioner Street, Johannesburg.

632

Document 56. Resolutions of the All-in African Conference in Pietermaritzburg, March 25-26, 1961

A grave situation confronts the people of South Africa. The Nationalist Government after holding a fraudulent referendum among only one-fifth of the population, has decided to proclaim a white Republic on May 31st, and the all white Parliament is presently discussing a Constitution. It is clear that to the great disadvantage of the majority of our people such a Republic will continue even more intensively the policies of racial oppression, political persecution and exploitation and the terrorisation of the non-white people which have already earned South Africa the righteous condemnation of the entire world.

In this situation it is imperative that all the African people of this country, irrespective of their political, religious or other affiliations, should unite to speak and act with a single voice.

For this purpose, we have gathered here at this solemn All-In Conference, and on behalf of the entire African nation and with a due sense of the historic responsibility which rests on us . . .

1. WE DECLARE that no Constitution or form of Government decided without the participation of the African people who form an absolute majority of the population can enjoy moral validity or merit support either within South Africa or beyond its borders.

2. WE DEMAND that a *National Convention* of elected representatives of all adult men and women on an equal basis irrespective of race, colour, creed or other limitation, be called by the Union Government not later than May 31st, 1961; that the Convention shall have sovereign powers to determine, in any way the majority of the representatives decide, a new non-racial democratic Constitution for South Africa.

3. WE RESOLVE that should the minority Government ignore this demand of the representatives of the united will of the African people—

   (a) We undertake to stage country-wide demonstrations on the eve of the proclamation of the Republic in protest against this undemocratic act.

   (b) We call on all Africans not to co-operate or collaborate in any way with the proposed South African Republic or any other form of Government which rests on force to perpetuate the tyranny of a minority, and to organise and unite in town and country to carry out constant actions to oppose oppression and win freedom.

   (c) We call on the Indian and Coloured communities and all democratic Europeans to join forces with us in opposition to a regime which is bringing disaster to South Africa and to win a society in which all can enjoy freedom and security.

(d) We call on democratic people the world over to refrain from any co-operation or dealings with the South African government, to impose economic and other sanctions against this country and to isolate in every possible way the minority Government whose continued disregard of all human rights and freedoms constitutes a threat to world peace.

4. WE FURTHER DECIDE that in order to implement the above decisions, Conference—

(a) Elects a National Action Council;

(b) Instructs all delegates to return to their respective areas and form local Action Committees.

Document 57. "An Appeal to Students and Scholars." Flyer issued by the All-in African National Action Council, signed by Nelson R. Mandela, Secretary, [n.d.]

ALL-IN AFRICAN NATIONAL ACTION COUNCIL

MACOSA HOUSE, JOHANNESBURG

AN APPEAL TO STUDENTS AND SCHOLARS

Dear Friends,

I am writing this letter on the instructions of the All-In African National Action Council which was established in terms of a resolution passed by the All-In African Conference held at Pietermaritzburg on the 25th and 26th March, 1961. This conference was attended by 1,500 delegates from town and country representing 145 political, religious, social, sporting and cultural organisations. Its aim was to consolidate unity amongst Africans and to consider the decision of the Government to proclaim a Republic on May 31st this year. It was the opinion of Conference that the Government was not entitled to take such a decision without first seeking the views and obtaining the express consent of the African people. Delegates felt that under the proposed Republic, the racial policies of the Government would be intensified resulting in a further determination [sic] in the living conditions of our people. In its main resolution Conference called upon the government to convene a national convention, before May 31st this year, of all South Africans, to draw up a new democratic constitution. If the Government failed to call the convention before the above mentioned date countrywide demonstrations would be held on the eve of the Republic to compel the Government to do so. The resolution went further to call on the African, Coloured and Indian communities as well as European democrats not to co-operate with the proposed Republic or with any government based on force. Finally an appeal was made to democratic individuals the world over and to foreign governments not to have any dealings with the proposed Republic and to apply sanctions against it.

This conference has been acclaimed throughout the country as an important landmark in the struggle of the African people to achieve unity amongst themselves. Its challenging resolution is a stirring call to an action which promises to be one of the most massive and stunning blows ever delivered by the African people against white supremacy.

In its efforts to enslave the African people the Government has given particular attention to the question of education. The control of African education has been taken away from the Provincial Administrations and missionaries and is now vested in the Bantu Affairs Department so that it should conform with State policy. Instead of a free and progressive education calculated to prepare him for his responsibilities as a fully fledged citizen, the African is indoctrinated with a tribal and inferior type of education intended to keep him in a position of perpetual subservience to the whites. The matric results last year strikingly illustrated the disastrous effects of Bantu Education and show that even more tragic consequences will follow if the Nationalists are not kicked out of power. We call upon the entire South African nation to close ranks and to make a supreme effort to halt the Nationalists and to win freedom. In this situation all students have an important role to play and we appeal to you to:

1. Participate in full in the forthcoming demonstrations.

2. Refuse to participate in the forthcoming Republican celebrations and in all ceremonies connected with them.

3. To popularise the Maritzburg resolution amongst other students, the youth in factories, farms and in the streets, to your parents and relatives and to all people in your neighbourhood.

If you take these measures you will have made an important contribution to the historic mission of transforming our country from a white-dominated one to a free and prosperous nation.

N. R. MANDELA,
Secretary,
All-In African National Action Council

Document 58. Letter calling on the United Party to support a national convention, from Nelson R. Mandela to Sir de Villiers Graaff, May 23, 1961

23rd May, 1961.

Sir De Villiers Graaff,
Leader of the Opposition,
House of Assembly,
CAPE TOWN.

Sir,

In one week's time, the Verwoerd Government intends to inaugurate its Republic. It is unnecessary to state that this intention has never been endorsed by the non-White majority of this country. The decision has been taken by little over half of the White community; it is opposed by every articulate group amongst the African, Coloured and Indian communities, who constitute the majority of this country.

The Government's intentions to proceed, under these circumstances, has created conditions bordering on crisis. We have been excluded from the Commonwealth, and condemned 95 to 1 at the United Nations. Our trade is being boycotted, and foreign capital is being withdrawn. The country is becoming an armed camp, the Government preparing for civil war with increasingly heavy police and military apparatus, the non-White population for a general strike and long-term non-co-operation with the Government.

None of us can draw any satisfaction from this developing crisis. We, on our part, in the name of the African people—a majority of South Africans—and on the authority given us by 1,400 elected African representatives at the Pietermaritzburg Conference of March 25th and 26th, have put forward serious proposals for a way out of the crisis. We have called on the Government to convene an elected National Convention of representatives of all races without delay, and to charge that Convention with the task of drawing up a new Constitution for this country which would be acceptable to all racial groups.

We can see no workable alternative to this proposal, except that the Nationalist Government proceeds to enforce a minority decision on all of us, with the certain consequence of still deeper crisis, and a continuing period of strife and disaster ahead. Stated bluntly, the alternatives appear to be these: talk it out, or shoot it out. Outside of the Nationalist Party, most of the important and influential bodies of public opinion have clearly decided to talk it out. The South African Indian Congress, the only substantial Indian community organisation, has welcomed and endorsed the call for a National Convention. So, too, have the Coloured people, through the Coloured Convention movement which has the backing of the main bodies of Coloured opinion. A substantial European body of opinion, represented by both the Progressive and the Liberal Parties, has endorsed our call. Support for a National Convention has come also from the bulk of the English language press, from several national church organisations, and from many others.

But where, Sir, does the United Party stand? We have yet to hear from this most important organisation— the main organisation in fact of anti-Nationalist opinion amongst the European community. Or from you, its leader. If the country's leading statesmen fail to lead at this moment, then the worst is inevitable. It is time for you, Sir, and your Party, to speak out. Are you for a democratic and peaceable solution of our problems? Are you, therefore, *for* a National Convention? We in South Africa, and the world outside, expect an answer. Silence at this time enables Dr. Verwoerd to lead us onwards towards the brink of disaster.

We realise that aspects of our proposal raise complicated problems. What shall be the basis of representation at the Convention? How shall the representatives be elected? But these are not the issues now at stake. The issue *now* is a simple one. Are all groups to be consulted before a constitutional change is made? Or only the White minority? A decision on this matter cannot be delayed. Once that decision is taken, then all other matters, of how, when and where, can be discussed, and agreement on them can be reached. On our part the door to such discussion has always been open. We have approached you and your Party before, and suggested that matters of difference be discussed. To date we have had no reply. Nevertheless we still hold the door open. But the need *now* is not for debate about differences of detail, but for clarity of principle and purpose. For a National Convention of all races? Or against?

It is still not too late to turn the tide against the Nationalist-created crisis. A call for a National Convention from you now could well be the turning point in our country's history. It would unite the overwhelming majority of our people, White, Coloured, Indian and African, for a single purpose— round-table talks for a new constitution. It would isolate the Nationalist Government, and reveal for all time that it is a minority Government, clinging tenaciously to power against the popular will, driving recklessly onward to a disaster for itself and us. Your call for a National Convention now would add such strength to the already powerful call for it that the Government would be chary of ignoring it further.

And if they nevertheless ignore the call for the Convention, the inter-racial unity thus cemented by your call would lay the basis for the replacement of this Government of national disaster by one more acceptable to the people, one prepared to follow the democratic path of consulting all the people in order to resolve the crisis.

We urge you strongly to speak out now. It is ten days to May 31st.

Yours faithfully,

(signed) Nelson Mandela.

NELSON MANDELA.
ALL-IN AFRICAN NATIONAL ACTION COUNCIL.

Document 59. "Police Agents at Work . . . STAY AT HOME May 29 30 31."
Flyer issued by the ANC, [n.d.]

POLICE AGENTS AT WORK

The Police are using former members of the banned P.A.C. to break the demonstrations on the 29th, 30th and 31st May, 1961. These same people were used in exactly the same way to break up the three-day strike in April, 1958.

Masquerading as "African Nationalists" these fellows have issued a leaflet describing the forthcoming demonstrations as irresponsible.

Some members of the Continuation Committee, which organised the historic All-In African Conference at Pietermaritzburg, were arrested and are presently facing a criminal charge of taking part in the activities of a banned organisation. The leaflet issued by the so-called African Nationalists says that the demonstrations are planned by former leaders of the banned A.N.C. the very evidence the Police are looking for and need to secure a conviction.

At present the Police are making extensive investigations to discover the members of the National Action Committee. The other day, the Minister of Justice threatened to imprison all those who are planning the demonstrations. The purpose of these investigations and the Minister's threatened action was to kill the demonstrations before the campaign gathered momentum. Yet the leaflet issued by the so-called African Nationalists calls upon the National Action Council to walk straight into a Police trap by disclosing the names of its members. Come gentlemen, what is your true role in South Africa? Have you now ceased to be serious politicians genuinely interested in the liberation of the African people? Have you now become detectives whose duty is to know and track down people regarded by the Police as dangerous to white supremacy? Why do you want leaders to emerge and members of the National Action Council announced? Surely, only Police agents could advocate such a step. Even the name of Robert Sobukwe is dragged in by these people to help the Police to undermine the struggle of the African people to rid themselves of the cancer of white supremacy and the hardships imposed upon them by the Nationalist Government.

This is downright treachery. This pamphlet is the work of traitors and Police informers. It is a tragedy that people who until last year took part in the struggle of the African people should be now so disheartened and broken down, so scared of militant mass action that their only reaction to the historic resolution of Pietermaritzburg is to panick, desert their own people and side with the Police.

Do not listen to those who speak for and who serve the interests of your enemy—the Government. In the name of the entire African Nation, we call upon all our people in town and contry to rise in their millions and rally to the historic call of the Pietermaritzburg Conference. WE CALL UPON YOU TO STAND FIRM AS A ROCK AND BE UNITED AND NOT PERMIT DISRUPTERS TO DIVIDE YOU AT THE MOST CRITICAL TIME IN THE HISTORY OF THIS COUNTRY.

STAY AT HOME
May 29 30 31
Issued by African National Congress

Document 60. "Stay at Home" [on May 29-31]. Flyer issued by the National Action Council, [n.d.]

Stay at Home

PEOPLE OF SOUTH AFRICA!
THE PROTESTS GOES ON
ARRESTS CANNOT STOP US

We have made our demands known to the Government. We want a National Convention to make a constitution for a democratic South Africa.

VOTES TO ALL
DECENT WAGES FOR ALL
END PASS LAWS
END MINORITY WHITE DOMINATION

VERWOERD REPLIES NO!

He mobilises the army, starts police raids, arrests our leaders and arrests thousands for passes and taxes, bans our meetings. He tries to frighten the country with wild tales of violence.

OUR ANSWER TO VERWOERD

We are not going to be frightened by Verwoerd. WE STAND FIRM BY OUR DECISION TO STAY AT HOME ON MONDAY, TUESDAY AND WEDNESDAY.
No one who loves freedom should go to work on those three days.

LET US STAND TOGETHER, UNITED AND DISCIPLINED. DO NOT BE INTIMIDATED BY POLICE AGENTS AND PROVOCATEURS.

DOWN WITH VERWOERDS MINORITY REPUBLIC
FORWARD TO FREEDOM IN OUR LIFETIME

A W U P A T H W A

Issued by National Action Council

Document 61. "Poqo. Poqo. Poqo." [opposing the stay-at-home on May 29-31]. Flyer issued by the PAC, [n.d.]

POQO. POQO. POQO.

As you know, in the past the CONGRESS ALLIANCE have always started something and whenever their peak was reached ALL THEIR LEADERS RAN AWAY AND LEFT YOU, THE PEOPLE, behind to take the punishment.
What happened to Congress Alliance leaders with Emergency? Where are they now? They have already started to run. Find out and make certain for yourselves before following their instruction.
We, THE P.A.C., have, as you know, broken away from the Congress Alliance because their leaders are such COWARDS. Where are our leaders? Where is SOBUKWE our Chief?— In gaol with his followers!
WE, THE P.A.C., say: DO NOT FOLLOW CONGRESS ALLIANCE. THE P.A.C. DO NOT SUPPORT CONGRESS ALLIANCE with their present move to a National Convention.
We do not want our people to become RUSSIAN slaves as the CONGRESS ALLIANCE do.

We will watch you over the next few weeks. If you support the CONGRESS ALLIANCE for a Multi-Racial National Convention, then you are against the P.A.C.

We know what to do with our enemies.

ALL P.A.C. SUPPORTERS MUST GO TO WORK and not support the ALLIANCE.

NO STAY AT HOME ON 29-30 and 31 MAY. SUPPORT US. POQO—WE STAND ALONE!!!

Issued by: **THE PAN AFRICANIST CONGRESS.**

Document 62. "Clarion Call to African Nationalists." Article in *Mafube (The Dawn of Freedom)*, No. 1, issued by "African Nationalists", [written by A.P. Mda], May 1961

Sons and daughters of Africa—this is an historic hour. Behind us lies the glorious trail of the mighty Positive Action. Behind us lies the historic road from Sharpeville. You will recall the heroic deeds of the African Nationalists on Monday, 21st March, 1960, and onwards. You will recall the positive action which shook South Africa to its foundations and rocked the world.

You will recall the path which Mangaliso Sobukwe and his noble band trod—the path that led them to gaol! It is the path of Liberation—the road that leads to Freedom, to Independence and to the United States of Africa!! A new chapter has been opened in South African history, and you are the makers of that history!!

The call that has gone out from the Maritzburg Conference and from the Council of Action is a call to the African people to stage anti-Republican demonstrations on the eve of the declaration of the Boer Republic.

African Nationalists are hereby put on their guard. They must realise here and now that the immediate objective of these multi-racialists amounts to a misdirection of the African people. The African people are merely being asked to demonstrate against the Boer Republic. They are merely being asked to demonstrate in demand for a multi-racial convention.

The goal of struggle which Sobukwe set for South Africa and the entire Continent is being side-stepped. The people are being studiously turned from the goal of Freedom and Independence Now! They are being turned from the goal of an Africanist Socialist Democracy!! They are being turned from the goal of a United States of Africa!!

The multi-racialist approach is negative in that it is a mere protest. It is not imbued with the spirit of disciplined positive action nor does it derive motive force from the mighty power of African Nationalism.

The task of African Nationalists is not to abandon the people to the multi-racialists but to put the true issues before the African people, to clarify their real objectives, and to point out the right direction of our struggle on the basis of the Liberatory Programme of African Nationalism.

The urgent, historic task of African Nationalists during the present critical phase is to hold before the people the mighty vision of an Africa free and independent among the nations of the world.

Sons and Daughters of Africa! From the vagueness and confusion of multi-racialist charterism, must be created the clarity and positiveness of the Programme of National Emancipation. In place of the vacillation and loud-mouthed badinage of multi-racialism, must be raised the standard of the Positive Action of African Nationalism.

The people must be prepared, seasoned and ideologically conditioned for the final call which Sobukwe will make to cross the sea of struggle and reach the shore of freedom. In other words, the people must be rallied behind the national banner. They must be rallied under the mighty slogans which blazoned Sobukwe's road to prison.

The struggle is on, Sons and Daughters of Africa. The road to 1963 is before us. There can be no turning back, and there will be no turning back.

We must use this period (before and after the negative protest of May 31) as a preparation ground for an Africanist Socialist Democracy. We must do so by making even clearer our goals as against those of the misguided multi-racialists. We must give them a new and powerful impetus along the road to 1963!!

The oppressors are at bay! No power on earth can stem the tide of African Nationalism which is sweeping the African Continent like a Hurricane.

FORWARD THEN TO FREEDOM! TO FREEDOM NOW!! TO-MORROW THE UNITED STATES OF AFRICA!!!!

PART THREE

The Turn to Violence
Since May 31, 1961

TOWARD UMKONTO WE SIZWE

The Turn to Violence

African political leaders faced the future under the new South African republic with little hope that nonviolent pressures could bring about radical change. Hope for liberal if not radical change had existed for more than a hundred years, long before the formation of the ANC in 1912. During the nineteenth century, the leadership of courageous African chiefs who led their tribes in bloody but futile resistance to encroaching white rule had gradually given way to a new and accommodating African leadership. Even before adoption of the Cape Colony's nonracial franchise in the mid-nineteenth century, missionary schools and Western religion had begun to generate hope among a very small number of Africans that their claim to a share in political power would rest on "merit and not race." (The words are from the dedication to this volume.) For more than three decades before the Act of Union of 1910 and for half a century afterwards, literate and aspiring Africans in company with tribal chiefs acted nonviolently within the political system to express their opposition to reactionary trends and to appeal to the dominant whites. By 1949 political rhetoric had become more militant, and the ANC adopted a program that envisaged civil disobedience. During the Union's half-century, hopes were buoyed from time to time by signs of optimism among white liberals that a change in the direction of policy was possible, and African morale was sustained by occasional evidence of African unity and strength. But under the Union, and especially after 1948, the direction of official policy had been away from, rather than toward, the liberal aim of a nonracial common society. How confident Africans were during these years, especially during the repressive 1950s, that whites could be persuaded to change the direction of policy is difficult to know. It is equally difficult to ascertain the depth of the commitment Africans felt to nonviolence or the level of private expectations that violence was unavoidable.

At the time their organizations were banned, both ANC and PAC leaders had behind them a long African tradition of public commitment to nonviolence, as well as a record of action by leaders to curb and condemn disorder and rioting.[1] Although PAC speakers were wont to suggest that unlike the ANC they envisaged the use of violence, Sobukwe also appealed for "absolute nonviolence" before Sharpeville. An Indian sociologist has suggested that, contrary to white stereotypes, African political leaders, "given to the cult of suffering and . . . depending on Messianic statements," were tempermentally nonviolent; African history since 1910 suggests that "far from being wild and violent, Africans [in contrast to whites] are singularly unaggressive."[2] In any event, avoiding physical confrontation with the well-armed and ruthless South African police was a matter of immediate and practical common sense.

Yet among Africans who felt robbed of their land or cruelly harassed, there had always been angry talk of driving the white man into the sea. The atmosphere of violence surrounded Africans in the crowded townships where they themselves were victimized by *tsotsis,* African gangsters, and threatened by physical assault. In the usually placid rural areas, as well as in the towns, there was also a sporadic history of angry and spontaneous demonstrations and rioting in protest against unpopular policies. By the 1950s, many African leaders were becoming disillusioned with appeals to white authority and tactics of passive resistance. At the time of the Defiance Campaign in 1952 an influential Africanist pondered: did not reliance on such tactics impede the development of popular realization that the South African system was inherently violent and could be destroyed only by revolutionary violence? He half-hoped that the campaign would be repressed by violence because such action, by illuminating the real nature of the regime, would provoke mass retaliation and accelerate the struggle. It is unlikely, however, that such dark hopes were shared by the planners of the Defiance Campaign.

During the years preceding Sharpeville, popular talk of violence against whites seemed to be spreading, especially among young Africans. Popular impatience with ineffectual political action and the danger of all-out retaliation by the government in the wake of violent eruptions posed problems for leaders of both the ANC and PAC. They recognized the importance of political organization and discipline but felt pressed, even though ill-prepared, to undertake militant campaigns.

During the emergency following Sharpeville, African leaders had long hours in detention to discuss both the apparent unavoidability and the feasibility of violent methods. In describing the popular mood of May 1961, Nelson Mandela, speaking from the dock three years later, said: "It may not be easy for this Court to understand, but it is a fact that for a long time the people had been talking of violence—of the day when they would fight the White man and win back their country. . . ." (Document 75). ANC leaders had "always prevailed upon them to avoid violence," Mandela said, but from the beginning of 1961 criticism of nonviolence had grown among loyal members of the ANC. They were developing "disturbing ideas of terrorism," he said, and toward the end of May he learned that small groups that had come into existence in urban areas were spontaneously planning to implement these ideas, perhaps against Africans as well as whites.[3]

At the beginning of June 1961, "after a long and anxious assessment," Mandela and "some colleagues" abandoned the ANC's policy of nonviolence. They could not escape the conclusion, he said in his 1964 courtroom speech, that "fifty years of non-violence had brought the African people nothing but more and more repressive legislation." By 1961, he said, "all channels of peaceful protest had been barred to us." The government had deliberately created (in the words of Mandela's 1962 speech from the dock—Document 68) "the atmosphere for civil war and revolution." In anticipation of the peaceful stay-at-home demonstration at the end of May, it had "set the scene for violence by relying exclusively on violence with which to answer our people and their demands." "Only two choices" were left, he said in 1964, "submit or fight."

Mandela's rationale for violent methods of struggle, as he presented it in 1964, linked these methods coherently to the ANC's tradition of nonviolence, its desire for nonracial harmony, and Mandela's apparent hope that whites could still be persuaded to change their policies by means short of revolutionary overthrow. Four forms of violence were recognized: sabotage, guerrilla warfare, terrorism, and open revolution. Sabotage was adopted, and, assuming careful and rational control, no further decision on tactics was to be made until that method had been tested exhaustively. The decision to limit the use of violence arose, said Mandela, from the alarm he and others felt that whites and blacks were drifting toward civil war. Referring to the conflict between the British and the Boer republics, he said, "It has taken more than fifty years for the scars of the South African War to disappear. How much longer would it take to eradicate the scars of inter-racial civil war . . . ?" Because racial bitterness was to be kept to a minimum, rather than exploited, strict instructions were given that sabotage should not injure or kill people. Equally important was the hope that economic pressure could influence whites to act rationally: sabotage of the economic infrastructure would "scare away capital" and "in the long run be a heavy drain on the economic life of the country, thus compelling the voters of the country to reconsider their position."

How seriously these hopes were held is as speculative as the question asked earlier regarding hope that nonviolence could be persuasive. Whether or not whites could be manipulated by affecting their economic interests was uncertain. What complicated this question was the fact that sabotage was to be undertaken for other motives as well. Not only the country's economic nerves but also government buildings and other symbols of apartheid were to be hit, said Mandela, in order to inspire the people, provide an outlet for advocates of violence, and demonstrate (in effect) that the leaders were ahead of their followers. Furthermore, foreign sympathy and pressure on the South African government were expected "if mass action were successfully organized, and mass reprisals taken."

With this uncertain but hopeful rationale, the decision was made "to embark on violent forms of political struggle" and to form a "small, closely-knit organization" to undertake sabotage. Though the decision coincided with the formation of the Republic, Umkonto We Sizwe (meaning Spear of the Nation in Zulu, sometimes referred to as MK) was not formed until November 1961, according to Mandela. Unlike the ANC, in practice, it was open to persons of all races.

In flyers distributed on December 16, 1961, when its sabotage began, Umkonto described itself as "an independent body" that had placed itself "under the overall political guidance" of "the national liberation [or Congress] movement," although the main organizations in that movement "have consistently followed a policy of non-violence" (Document 66).

Undoubtedly the decision to form Umkonto was made by persons who were members of both the ANC and the Communist Party, although Mandela suggested in his 1964 speech that the Communist Party had extended support shortly after Umkonto was founded. But this mention of formal support by the Party seems academic in the light of the intimate de facto cooperation that existed among individuals before the Umkonto decision: cooperation between African nationalists like Mandela and Sisulu and white, Indian, and African Communists like Joe Slovo, Ahmed Kathrada, Kotane, and Marks.

That Mandela formed Umkonto on behalf of the ANC is an elementary and hardly surprising fact, say ANC leaders who are now in exile. In testifying on the role of the ANC, Mandela said in his 1964 courtroom speech that "a full meeting" of the National Executive Committee in June 1961 "carefully considered" his position and decided that the ANC could not engage in violence but would, in Mandela's words, "depart from its 50-year-old policy of non-violence to this extent": it would not discipline members who did so.[4] Later in the year, according to Mandela, the ANC again departed somewhat from its policy of nonviolence when it agreed that ANC offices in Africa should cooperate with Mandela when he traveled in 1961 to make arrangements for military training in case a decision was made later to move from sabotage to guerrilla warfare.

Thus, it could be argued that in June 1961 the ANC, although still recognizing that political action was essential, in fact abandoned its reliance on nonviolence and agreed to the formation of a military wing. But just how the ANC, traditionally open but at that time decimated, dangerously harassed, and still attempting to regroup, reached these decisions cannot be tidily explained. The picture is clouded not only by the fact that the national conference, the main policy-making organ, could not meet, but also by the fact that it had never adopted an alternative structure designed for such conditions. The president-general had the extraordinary emergency powers given to him in December 1952, but in 1959 a subcommittee was still considering plans for reorganization. Its proposal for a more centralized structure, eliminating provincial divisions, relying on regions and branches, and decreasing the size of the National Executive Committee from twenty-five to seven was put into effect by the working committee and the president-general, after the banning.[5]

No description of structure, however, can convey the informal, ad hoc nature of meetings and consultations within South Africa by leaders who met together when they could. In commenting on this period, Oliver Tambo has described the fluidity of collective decision-making by a national secretariat apparently composed of whatever leaders were available, and the impossibility of expecting a national executive committee to function formally in conditions of struggle. At the same time that an executive was being reconstructed outside South Africa, decisions of leaders who were able to come together as a working committee within South Africa were considered to be decisions of the National Executive Committee, once they were confirmed by the president-general.

Lutuli and Violence

All major policies, according to Tambo, were referred for approval to—and sometimes were disapproved of by—Lutuli, who was consulted in Groutville in Natal, where he was confined. But the chronic difficulty other leaders had keeping in close contact with Lutuli increased, and suspicions among critics of the left wing that Lutuli was being deliberately bypassed and kept only as a facade grew during 1961. There is little doubt that Lutuli knew of the drift toward sabotage. Nevertheless, he was not prepared either to insist on the expulsion of ANC members who were planning sabotage or to resign from the ANC in June because of its toleration of limited violence. Deeply troubled during this period by signs that violence would erupt, he was urged by African Liberals, Jordan Ngubane and H. J. Bhengu, to oppose the end-of-May stay-at-home. According to Ngubane, Lutuli was disposed to intervene in order to speak out against violence and asked for advice; but "perhaps unconsciously," thought Ngubane, he was beginning to question the efficacy of nonviolence.[6]

Just how Lutuli's mind worked during these days is uncertain. When he publicly burned his pass after Sharpeville in a form of symbolic sabotage, it was evident that his own impatience had been growing. He had consistently resisted any efforts that would damage the unity of the ANC. Perhaps he thought that by continuing in office he might still be influential in upholding standards of rationality for African political activity. The task of building African morale and of political education perennially needed the work of all hands. He might also be able to appeal to people of goodwill of all races at home before it was too late and he could call for pressures on South Africa from sympathizers abroad. In any event, he could hardly prevent determined men from proceeding with their own plans. In mid-1961 preparations for sabotage were still incomplete. If Mandela and others were determined also to avoid injury to human life, perhaps he could help deter the emergence of terrorism.[7] Even if Lutuli had broken with younger leaders on the question of violence, he could no longer influence the rank and file after mid-1962, because, under legislation passed that year, his words could no longer be publicly quoted.

Undoubtedly other members and supporters of the ANC opposed embarking on the path of violence, or were reluctant to do so, against such an overwhelmingly forceful regime. Leaders had to try to disseminate to a scattered following a political line that would appear legitimate as ANC policy and at the same time demanded of ANC followers secrecy, political activity, abstention from uncontrolled violence, and—in due course—an understanding of Umkonto while they were totally cut off from it. The difficulties of embarking on violence were recognized within the Communist Party, too, where there was also some opposition to this course of action. One account of joint meetings between members of the ANC and the Communist Party, attended at one stage by Lutuli, holds that one of the strongest voices in opposition to the use of violence because of its ineffectiveness in South Africa was that of Rowley Arenstein, a Durban lawyer who was a veteran Communist.[8]

Because it was important to protect persons who had been members of the ANC before it was banned from incurring additional jeopardy, ANC and Umkonto leaders avoided any public identification of the ANC as the sponsor of Umkonto. A particular effort was made to shield Lutuli, not only because of the wide usefulness of his reputation but also because of the need to protect him personally.[9] Not until early 1963, after the ANC had held its first post-Sharpeville conference (in Bechuanaland), did a statement distributed abroad and ascribed to the ANC's National Executive Committee link the ANC with Umkonto, describing it as "the military wing of our struggle" (Document 69).[10] Leaflets issued later by the ANC described Umkonto as the "Army of the Liberation Movement" (Document 70).

Lutuli's hopes for restraint and nonviolence had obviously withered long since. But unhappy as he might be about the dangerous pass to which African patriots had come, he could understand the depths of their frustration. He did not comment publicly on the men of Umkonto until after they (including Mandela) had been sentenced to life imprisonment in June 1964. Still president-general, Lutuli issued a bitter statement, which could not be published in South Africa, describing them as "brave just men" whom "no one can blame . . . for seeking justice by the use of violent methods; nor could they be blamed if they tried to create an organized force to ultimately establish peace and racial harmony . . . . They represent the highest in morality and ethics in the South African political struggle. . . ." Nevertheless, perhaps thinking only of pronouncements of the ANC's national conference within South Africa, he maintained that "the African National Congress never abandoned its method of a militant, nonviolent struggle, and of creating in the process a spirit of militancy in the people" (Document 77).

Political Action and Consultation

Whatever go-ahead signals may have been given in mid-1961 to a small and conspiratorial group to plan sabotage, there was no question of transforming a mass political movement with a fluctuating membership like the ANC's into an instrument of violence. Even underground, the ANC had important nonviolent functions to perform—engaging in political propaganda and promoting above-ground campaigns—once it was able to regroup and reorganize in accordance with the M-Plan. In 1961, and to a lesser extent in 1962, there were still limited opportunities for some individuals and organizations to promote protest and for publications like *New Age* and *Contact* to publicize these activities. Mandela himself, in a speech in Addis Ababa in January 1962, declared, "Certainly, the days of civil disobedience, of strikes, and mass demonstrations are not over and we will resort to them over and over again."[11]

In June 1961, with the announcement of Umkonto's formation still more than six months away, the ANC's line was that of the "all-in" conference of March 1961: non-cooperation with the Republic coupled with a demand that the government call a "sovereign" national convention. On the commemorative day of June 26, Mandela, as secretary of the All-in African National Council set up by the conference, issued a press statement containing the familiar rhetoric of struggle and declaring: "Non-collaboration is a dynamic weapon." By refusing to cooperate in the functioning of apartheid, by withdrawing labor, and by calling for international sanctions, the people would "make government impossible" (Document 63). Mandela reaffirmed the demand for a sovereign convention but now expressed no expectation that it would be called by the government.[12]

Non-collaboration was the central tenet of the NEUM and the AAC. In a newsletter issued shortly after June 1961, a faction of the AAC once again attacked the Congress Alliance and reasserted the AAC's claim to the boycott tactic (Document 64). The newsletter avoided any recognition that the situation in South Africa had changed markedly and restated the necessity "to work politically" under conditions of "chronic" emergency. Equally vague was the assessment by I. B. Tabata early in 1962 when he addressed the newly formed African People's Democratic Union of Southern Africa (APDUSA), which was intended to be an individual-membership body affiliated with the AAC and the NEUM. ". . . only through the efforts of the toiling masses," he said, "is it possible to put an end to this crisis" (Document 67).[13]

Meanwhile in the ANC, a dramatic note was being struck by Mandela. Cut off from his professional life and from his wife and children, he continued to be the spokesman for the National Action Council while living as a political outlaw. Until his arrest in August 1962 he was to be an elusive figure, dubbed "the Black Pimpernel." He traveled about the country in disguise, issued statements to the English-language press, held private meetings with whites as well as Africans, and was interviewed for BBC television.

Both private and public multiracial meetings were held from time to time during the latter part of 1961, a continuation of past efforts at contact and consultation. One remarkable change, however, was the final abandonment of initiatives by the South African Bureau of Racial Affairs to consult privately with Africans. SABRA's independent leadership was purged in September 1961 by conformist supporters of the government.[14] But Afrikaans-speaking intellectuals participated in private meetings organized by others. For example, they were among some fifty persons who met on July 1 at the Johannesburg home of the chairman of the Standard Bank and the *Rand Daily Mail* and other newspapers. Among those present were eleven Africans (including members of the banned ANC, with M. B. Yengwa representing Lutuli, but no one from the PAC), the South African Indian Congress, businessmen, church leaders, and representatives of the Liberal and Progressive parties. No member of the Congress of Democrats was invited. The meeting agreed that further interracial consultations should be held soon.[15]

Prominent liberal-minded and left-wing whites (sometimes including Progressives) also joined unbanned Africans, Indians, and Coloureds in addressing public meetings in Johannesburg, Cape Town, Durban, and Port Elizabeth from time to time during the remainder of the year, often focusing their demands on the need for a nonracial national conference or convention. Young Afrikaner Nationalists heckled speakers at meetings held on the traditional meeting ground of the Johannesburg City Hall steps and sometimes physically attacked them. In a more deliberative setting in Port Elizabeth late in October, a multiracial meeting that included Progressives endorsed the call for a national convention and called on churches to hold dedication services on December 16.[16] Although appeals for multiracial consultation were made in urgent tones, the fact that the time was not ripe for a "sovereign" convention, as Professor Matthews reminded a Cape Town meeting, was clearly understood by political realists.[17]

Coloureds and Unity with Africans

Calling for a national convention—a respectable form of propaganda—had become an anachronism in the latter part of 1961. The call was made either too late or too soon, a description that was also true of a Coloured "convention" movement which gathered momentum in the same period. The movement attracted a wide range of "respectables" who had been politically inactive and reached out to make common cause with Africans at a time when opportunities for free political association and action were rapidly disappearing.[18] Although the movement's momentum could not be maintained in the face of governmental intimidation and the trend of events, what has come to be known as the Malmesbury Convention of July 8–10, 1961, seemed of special importance at the time as a breakthrough, a sign that a wide spectrum of Coloured leaders was gradually shifting from passivity and suspicion or fear of Africans to political alignment with them.[19] The Malmesbury Convention has variously been described as the most representative gathering of Coloureds since 1939, since the heyday of the African People's Organization, or in South Africa's history.

The movement had two broad, successive aims: first, to organize a South African Coloured National Convention so that Coloureds could speak with one voice and, second, to become part of a South African National Convention that would prepare a new constitution for all South Africans, thus eliminating the category of "Coloured" and the need for a separate voice. The initiative for the movement came largely from leaders among the some 10,000 Coloured teachers—the Coloured elite because there were few other Coloured professionals—and, in particular, the Teachers' Educational and Professional Association. As government servants, teachers were in a precarious position and generally avoided taking formal positions.

The general secretary of the convention was Joseph Daniels, a member of the Liberal Party and business manager of *Contact*. The small South African Coloured People's Congress, affiliated with the Congress alliance, participated actively but not in a dominant role. Anti-CAD and NEUM, on the left, and George Golding's Coloured People's National Union, on the right, remained hostile and apart, but the usually passive Federal Council of Coloureds in Natal, and representatives of a variety of groups, including trade unions and the British Commonwealth Ex-Servicemen's League, did take part. Especially strong support came from a small group of Coloureds in the eastern Cape, where Africans were politically more advanced and tended to have closer political relations with Coloureds than they did in the western Cape.

One of the Coloured leaders was a young teacher in Port Elizabeth, Dennis Brutus, an eloquent and energetic promoter of a sports boycott campaign that was to attain international significance. While belonging to the NEUM, he had also met regularly with Africans and had arranged for Sisulu to meet with Coloured leaders. He and others from Port Elizabeth were en route to Cape Town to attend the scheduled opening of the Coloured conference on the evening of July 7, 1961, when they heard that the government, acting under the Suppression of Communism Act, had banned the holding of the meeting there or in nearby districts. Brutus worried about the problem of persuading the sponsors to set an early alternative date. They came, he knew, "from the section of 'respectable' Coloureds: professional people mostly, who had none of the experience of bannings, raids and general political persecution familiar to those long in the political struggle."[20]

The Coloured leaders had acted speedily and secretly, however, and on July 8 managed to bring together about 150 of some 300 delegates for an open-air meeting in the area of Malmesbury, about thirty miles from Cape Town. An Afrikaans-speaking farmer, contrary to the expectation of the government, had offered his farm as a venue. Committees met on the following day, and on the third day the delegates convened in a packing shed on another farm. Their resolutions, calling for an abolition of the color bar and repudiating governmental bodies like the Union Council for Coloured Affairs, were nearly completed when the security police broke in to observe and take notes.

The enthusiasm and sense of unity among the delegates were never recaptured in any later national meeting. A continuation committee existed for some years.[21] "Report-back" meetings were held, and a "preliminary report" of the "South African National Convention" was distributed. "Coloured" had been dropped from the name of the convention thereby causing some confusion. Brutus, among others, was subsequently banned, he on the eve of a multiracial "Eastern Cape Regional Consultation on a National Convention" held in Port Elizabeth on October 21, 1961.

Earlier that month, Coloured voters had gone to the polls for the second time on a separate roll to elect four whites to the House of Assembly. Members of Golding's group, who cooperated with the Union Council, and the Kleurlingvolksbond, a pro-government rural group, took part in the campaign; but only 4,740 voters (the previous low had been 14,451 in 1958) went to the polls—a showing for which the Malmesbury Convention could take some credit.

Liberals and Violence

While the Coloured Convention was meeting, the Liberal Party was holding its national congress in Durban on July 7–10, 1961. The Liberals had undergone an extraordinary transformation, becoming more radical, making remarkable strides in identifying themselves with blacks, advocating the building of a nonracial and extraparliamentary opposition, and inviting the application of foreign pressures on the South African government.[22] By 1960 the party had come out strongly for a policy of speedy implementation of one-man one-vote. At the time of Sharpeville, leading Cape Town Liberals had rushed with exhilaration into the fray in order to support Africans; and during the emergency that followed, a number of Liberals were detained for the first time. The banning of the ANC and the PAC then created a political vacuum among Africans which the Liberals moved vigorously to fill. At the time of the July 1961 Congress, total membership in the Liberal Party had increased to some 4,000 to 5,000 (from about 2,000 in 1958); probably a majority of these members, like the majority of the delegates at the congress, were now black.[23]

Meanwhile, from 1960, and especially after 1962, when white Liberals involved themselves in the Transkei, the government's showcase for separate development, the government steadily applied to the Liberal Party the techniques of intimidation, harassment, and repression that African movements had long suffered, until the party was scarcely able to function. Buffeted and vilified by the government, some white Liberals resigned or drifted away, and others joined the Progressive Party. As one white Liberal observed, whites who got involved in radical groups became "outcasts in their own community," whereas radical blacks who were persecuted by the government were acclaimed by their community as heroes and martyrs.[24] The Liberal Party was to survive nearly seven years of the Republic. Rather than go "all white" when new legislation prohibited racially mixed political parties in 1968, it dissolved itself.

What was not known to Liberal Party leaders in mid-1961 was that a few of its younger and more radical white members, including some university lecturers and professional men, had become so frustrated that they were abandoning the party's policy of nonviolence.[25] Seeking perhaps to match the revolutionary zeal of Communists, they hoped to demonstrate their solidarity with blacks by organizing a body like Umkonto (whose existence was still not known), that is, open to all races and committed to sabotage against property.[26] It was to be called the National Liberation Committee (NLC), which later became the African Resistance Movement (ARM). Only a few of its members were Africans. Whites who belonged to the Liberal Party retained their Liberal membership as a cover.

In mid-September 1961, discussing reports that blacks in South Africa were talking about shifting to sabotage and violence, the London *Observer* wrote, "Superficially, the situation in South Africa is quiet. It is the quietness, though, that comes when one period of struggle has ended and another has not yet begun."[27] A few weeks later, as the white political campaign for the general election of October 18 was nearing its end, NLC saboteurs cut the thick steel legs of a pylon carrying power lines in the northern suburbs of Johannesburg, disrupted telephone service, and burned an office of the Department of Bantu Administration and Development.[28] Anonymous warning calls were made to newspapers, and in Britain the press reported that unnamed South African political exiles in London had announced the formation of the National Liberation Committee.

General Election of October 18, 1961

The beginning of sabotage heated the atmosphere of crisis already stoked both by Afrikaner Nationalist politicians and by their left-wing opponents. In facing the general election, Nationalists had a new opportunity to call for white unity; and the left wing, another occasion for proclaiming the futility of seeking change through electoral and parliamentary activity. White political attitudes had been hardening since Sharpeville; the campaign and the election were to indicate that threats of black self-assertion had a tendency to polarize white public opinion, moving the vast majority of whites rightward, more securely into the Nationalist "laager." During the campaign, the tough, authoritarian John Vorster, who had become minister of justice in August, promised drastic action against "agitators" and—typically assuming that blacks acted only at the manipulation of whites—particularly white "agitators." *New Age*, sharing the universal expectation that the Nationalists would be returned to power, declared that the Nationalist victory would "prepare the ground for the all-out struggle between the forces of freedom and tyranny."[29] M. D. C. de Wet Nel, minister of Bantu administration and development, echoed this sentiment when he told a gathering of youthful supporters that electoral victory was to be regarded as "a mobilization order for the struggle that lies ahead. We will die, each and every one of us, rather than give up our nationhood."[30]

In explaining his decision to hold the election earlier than 1963, the year it was due, Dr. Verwoerd alluded to Sobukwe's promise of African freedom in that year.[31] The timing of the election had more obvious explanations, however; for example, it coincided with violence in the Congo and compelled the eleven Progressive members of Parliament to stand before they could consolidate their support. Fundamentally, however, Verwoerd sought to consolidate his own support for the next five years, the crucial period for Afrikaner Nationalist policy and, as he saw it, for whites throughout the world. If whites succumbed to the black masses, he truly believed, civilization would disappear because "civilization is made by the builders, not the imitators."[32]

On election day, the Nationalists won their greatest electoral victory since coming to power in 1948. They increased both their parliamentary and popular strength, winning for the first time in a general election a clear majority—53.5 percent—of the estimated popular vote (estimated because some seats were uncontested). Ten of the eleven Progressives were defeated. By winning three additional seats, the Nationalists were now only two votes short (105 of 160 seats) of two-thirds control of the House of Assembly (including within the opposition the four whites elected by Coloureds). The Nationalists not only enlarged their support among Afrikaners and won even more impressively among Afrikaans-speaking youth (eighteen-year-olds were voting for the first time in a general election), but also, through their appeals for white unity, appeared to have held on to the English-speaking voters who had voted for a republic in the 1960 referendum.

Anxious not to split the anti-Nationalist vote, the Progressives put up candidates only in safe opposition districts. Their solicitude was not reciprocated in the attitudes of the United Party, whose center of gravity was now farther to the right. The Progressives, said the United Party's conservative leader in Natal, proposed to give the blacks a weapon more powerful than the gun: "the vote to kick the white man out of South Africa."[33] In addition to electing the personally popular Helen Suzman in an affluent Johannesburg district, Progressives nearly won several other seats. In sixteen urban English-speaking districts, they won some 56,000 votes to 83,000 for the United Party. Their total vote was 69,042. But despite strong financial and press support, their strength was essentially only that of the liberal wing of the United Party. The London *Times* estimated that Progressives possibly numbered 150,000 in a total electorate of 1,800,000, or well under 10 percent.[34] Lutuli, still responsive to strains of liberal optimism, commented that the support won by the Progressives was an encouraging sign.[35] Privately, however, Progressives were deeply discouraged by the trend of events.

Political trends continued in favor of the Nationalists over the next five years. In 1966, they won their fifth general election in a row, increasing their popular majority to an estimated 60 percent of the total vote, including uncontested districts, and winning about three-fourths of all the seats in the House of Assembly.

Lutuli and the Nobel Peace Prize

The harsh reality of the Nationalists' entrenched political power was briefly overshadowed five days after the 1961 election by the announcement in Oslo, Norway that Lutuli had won the Nobel Peace Prize. "In the fight against racial discrimination," the prize committee said, "Lutuli has always advocated nonviolent methods."[36] The award was a tribute to Lutuli and the historical record of the ANC. Inasmuch as ANC representatives abroad and anti-apartheid groups had lobbied for the prize, however, it was also a propaganda coup. There was some substance, therefore, to furious charges by government spokesmen and the Afrikaans press that the award was "part of the international offensive" against South Africa.[37]

Confronted with Lutuli's request for a passport to travel to Oslo, the government obviously decided that it would be less damaging to grant his request than to refuse it. Ten-day passports were issued to him and his wife. Lutuli's travel through Durban to the Johannesburg airport was a triumphal procession. Photographs showed him tired but defiant, holding up a clenched fist rather than the thumbs-up salute as he shouted "Amandla [power]!" to cheering crowds.[38] Mass rallies were organized in his honor, some scheduled for December 10, the day of the prize ceremony and international Human Rights Day. Meanwhile, some critics of Lutuli's ties to whites charged that he had sold out to the Americans and British, who allegedly were the donors (an incorrect assertion) of the approximately $48,000 for the prize and also supported the South African government.[39]

Lutuli made the most of his trip. He spoke on British television, and at a press conference in Oslo he called for international sanctions and "outside pressure" that "might make the [South African] electorate take stock of the situation and act accordingly." He also read aloud a message of congratulations from President John F. Kennedy.[40] On December 11, at a dinner in his honor, Lutuli delivered the climactic speech of his career (Document 65). He reaffirmed his belief in nonracial democracy and nonviolence. Yet, speaking as a representative of the African continent, he recognized the legitimacy of armed struggle. "Our goal," he said, "is a united Africa in which the standards of life and liberty are constantly expanding. . . . This goal, pursued by millions of our people [throughout the continent] with revolutionary zeal, by means of books, representations, demonstrations and in some places armed force provoked by the adamancy of white rule, carries the only real promise of peace in Africa."

Lutuli returned to his home on the eve of December 16, a South African holiday of importance to Afrikaners. December 16 was the day of the Covenant, formerly Dingaan's Day, when Afrikaners commemorated the defeat of the Zulus at Blood River in 1838. It was also approximately the time of year when the ANC had traditionally held its national conference. Once again Lutuli was confined to his village, though he was still free to receive visitors and issue statements to the press and (in absentia) at public meetings.

Sabotage: December 16, 1961

In the meantime, while Mandela was out of sight and Tambo abroad, important leaders like Sisulu, Nokwe, and Govan Mbeki had been leading a precarious semi-public life, attempting to complement the work of Mandela. All three used *New Age* to explain the tactics of non-cooperation, to express optimism that South Africa would become increasingly isolated internationally, and to warn darkly of battles ahead.[41] The effect of such pronouncements on popular morale is difficult to estimate; in any event, if Africans were deliberately refusing to cooperate with governmental bodies, their actions were not conspicuous. Undoubtedly, the desire for dramatic and symbolic gestures was growing, but only a small number of committed activists were ready to translate their sentiments into deeds.

On the Day of the Covenant, African saboteurs exploded a series of small home-made bombs at symbolic targets. Electric power stations and government offices in Port Elizabeth and Johannesburg were struck with explosions, which killed one saboteur and blew off the arm of another (a member of the Dube advisory board). Similar bomb attempts were unsuccessful in Durban.[42] Flyers announced the existence of Umkonto as a nonracial and independent body, albeit one that looked to "the national liberation movement" for political guidance (Document 66). The flyers also pointed out that Umkonto was unconnected in any way with the National Liberation Committee. Although Umkonto's manifesto noted that its methods were a break with the past, a carry-over of attitudes was still evident: hope was expressed that it was still possible to bring "the government and its supporters to their senses" and achieve "liberation without bloodshed."

The explosions marked not only the beginning of a new phase of struggle by the ANC and its allies but also a counter-offensive by the government that was to reduce the extraparliamentary opposition to near-ruins within the next two years. Embarkation on a path of violence had been the outcome of disillusionment with the ineffectiveness of nonviolent tactics. Violent tactics, at least in the short run, were to prove equally unproductive.

TOWARD RIVONIA

The Regime Becomes Stronger, 1961–1963

On July 11, 1963, the police raided a secluded, twenty-eight–acre farm in the white suburb of Rivonia about ten miles north of Johannesburg: the underground headquarters of Umkonto We Sizwe. There they captured leaders of the Umkonto "National High Command" and voluminous evidence of plans for sabotage and revolution. The smashing of the headquarters and the mopping-up operations that followed marked "the death knell of amateurism," as one exiled leader put it when he heard the news. The raid was, indeed, catastrophic. Not only did it decapitate the major underground movement within South Africa but it also cut off the leaders outside, who had to add to their diplomatic and propagandistic functions the responsibility of planning for armed struggle. Such plans were now largely theoretical preparations for the indefinite future, for the virtual destruction of the underground in 1963 was due not only to the amateurism of the saboteurs but also to the growing professionalism of the police. The Rivonia raid was not a lucky break but the culmination of a systematic build-up of counter-insurgency measures. Furthermore, during the nineteen months between Umkonto's appearance and Rivonia, the government did much more than uproot most of the underground; it also demoralized and routed the radical opposition.

More than repressive techniques, however, underlay the growing strength of the regime. During 1961–1963 it went far to solidify the white camp and set South Africa on a course that during the next decade was to produce an economically and militarily powerful police state, which was also skillful enough to win some black collaboration at home and some propaganda success abroad. Lutuli in his Nobel Prize address had described South Africa as "a museum piece in our time . . . a relic of an age which everywhere else is dead or dying." Although he was correct in foreseeing that South Africa would continue to be the target of opprobrium—"the skunk of the world" in the words of *Die Burger*[43]—he did not envisage the creation of "an increasingly streamlined and expanding system of sophisticated dominance."[44]

Lutuli and other African leaders were also over-optimistic in their appeals for application of world-wide pressures and sanctions. Although a two-thirds vote recommending economic and diplomatic sanctions was finally achieved in the General Assembly of the United Nations on November 6, 1962, it was not supported by the major Western states. The Kennedy administration's spokesmen in the UN expressed abhorrence of apartheid and, in affirming that persuasion could still change the policy of the South African government, gave expression to a liberal optimism that was virtually dead within South Africa itself. The policy of the United States toward South Africa was subject essentially to the same indictment that it directed at the policy of black African states toward South Africa: its policy was one of rhetorical gesture. White self-confidence in South Africa had been bolstered by the inflow of American business investment into the republic, the setting up of an American deep-space tracking station near Johannesburg, and the conviction among whites, encouraged by many American officials, that fundamentally anticommunism was more important than antiracism in determining what side the United States was on. For Britain, South Africa's major trading partner, trade and defense considerations also outweighed concern for a more equitable social order.

In formulating domestic policies and priorities, Dr. Verwoerd was keenly aware that social and political control was not enough and that outlets were needed for the emotions that produced African nationalism. He recognized the government's need of policies that would show the world that apartheid was fair to all groups, even idealistic in its ultimate aims, rather than an ugly manifestation of prejudice and self-interest. The ideal of "separate development," through the so-called Bantustan program of developing rural tribal reserves as "homelands" for the major African groups, had long been deeply rooted in Nationalist thought and plans. Responding to the domestic and external pressures of 1961, the government decided to accelerate the Bantustan timetable, in particular, the political development of the Transkei reserve in the eastern Cape. Probably one motive was to provide a prototype for separate development in Southwest Africa, where South Africa had international obligations that were then at issue before the International Court of Justice.

On January 23, 1962, Dr. Verwoerd made what he called a "dramatic" announcement: "the Government will . . . grant the Transkei self-government."[45] African leaders of the Transkeian Territorial Authority, who for tactical reasons had taken at face value the implications of the government's policy and demanded self-government, worked with government officials during the remainder of 1962 in preparing a draft constitution. In May 1963, the Transkei Constitution Bill became law, and in December the Transkei, which had long possessed a representative organ, became a semi-autonomous territory with limited powers of self-government. Despite a state of emergency which had existed in the Transkei since 1960, under which meetings were restricted and leading white and African members of the Liberal Party were banned, an election had been held in November. Transkeians who lived outside as well as inside the territory voted for a legislative assembly of 45 elected members, who were outnumbered, however, by 64 appointed chiefs. The franchise for the election set a significant precedent: universal adult suffrage, one man (or woman), one vote. By a margin of more than 3 to 1, the voters elected members who opposed the Bantustan policy.

African nationalists usually condemned Transkeian developments as fraudulent, although they sometimes suggested in the 1950s, and again in 1962–1963, that Bantustan institutions might be exploited politically and that popular movements might arise in the reserves that could link up with the organized protests of urban workers. In any event, a major argument for using the Bantustans as a political platform from which to deal with both urban and rural grievances was the fact that political opportunities elsewhere were severely constricted. As new vehicles for pressure and for the building of African self-confidence, the "homelands" were potential embarrassments to the government; but they served also, on the whole, to provide effective arguments for supporters of apartheid at home and sympathizers abroad and to blur the image of an uncompromising African opposition.

Somewhat similar moves to win Coloured and Indian support for the government were underway, although neither group had a historic "homeland" within South Africa, and culturally Coloureds were indistinguishable from whites (particularly from Afrikaners). Dr. Verwoerd envisaged the Union Council for Coloured Affairs, established in 1959 with fifteen appointed and twelved elected members, developing into a limited Coloured Parliament within ten years. In the case of Indians, a major shift in government policy occurred in 1961. The Nationalist approach, endorsed by many English-speaking whites, had been to treat Indians as unassimilable persons who should be repatriated if possible. But in September 1961 the government established a Department of Indian Affairs because, according to the new minister, it "realized that the Indians are a permanent part of the population of this country." The government intended to follow a "pattern," he told Parliament in May 1962, that would be "more or less the same as that envisaged in respect of the Coloureds." Eventually, he said, he would guide Indians to a "measure of self-government."[46]

Opponents of the boycott strategy had always pointed out that the government could find collaborators to man its separate institutions in an unthreatening way. This assertion proved to be true among Coloureds and Indians as well as Africans. Initially, the conciliatory South African Indian Organization (SAIO), which had been formed by conservative businessmen, opposed the new department. The SAIO also cooperated with the Indian Congress in jointly condemning racially separate higher education. Nevertheless, accustomed to exclusion from political power, believing that protest was futile, and anxious to protect its business position, the SAIO was receptive to negotiation. In retaliation, the office of A. S. Kajee, a leading member of the SAIO and the only Natal Indian to attend the induction of the president in Pretoria in 1961, was damaged by a bomb in December 1962.

In addition to political positions in the Bantustans, the government also offered jobs or cash to Africans who performed useful roles in the coercive apparatus of the state, which expanded enormously after 1961. The government had no difficulty in recruiting informers, and the popular presumption that spies were everywhere infected the atmosphere of political talk. Reliance on African police also grew. Duma Nokwe regretfully pointed out in November 1961 that the proportion of Africans, Coloureds, and Indians in the police force had grown from one-third in 1933 to 40 percent in 1948 and 51 percent (12,829) in 1958.[47] This trend was a source of pride to the government, which pointed out that unlike preceding governments, it was giving higher responsibilities to African police "in their own areas." It was also attempting to indoctrinate them against "Communists" and "agitators."

But reliance on Africans was only a small part of defense against such enemies. Police and defense budgets expanded greatly. The Special Branch, in particular, was substantially enlarged, and some of its officers visited Algeria to observe French techniques of counter-insurgency. Programs were developed for the training and mobilization of white reservists. Communication systems were modernized. And attention was given to improving South African self-sufficiency in arms and strategic supplies.

The Sabotage Act, 1962

While engaged in these long-range measures, the government was moving toward the implementation of a series of carefully tailored policies that would effectively nullify what it considered specific threats to security. Of paramount importance was the avoidance of a declaration of another national emergency, with its devastating impact on the appearance of "normalcy." Existing legislation provided all the authority needed for emergencies. What was needed now was non-emergency legislation that enabled the government more effectively than in the past to immobilize key individuals and to silence them. With characteristic legal propriety, the government drafted detailed legislation. Its rationale was set forth simply in a Nationalist newspaper, *Sondagblad,* on October 22, 1961, shortly after the first sabotage and the election. John Vorster, the new minister of justice, had promised drastic action, it said. Accordingly, the cabinet was discussing legislation

to limit the freedom of speech and movement of 'agitators.' As has happened in the past, it can be done by confining a person to a certain area, or town, or even to his house. The form of house arrest which was used during the war was that a person was allowed only to go to his work, but in the evenings and at weekends he had to stay at home. Although the legislation is aimed at all 'agitators,' it is intended primarily for *Whites*. They are the most dangerous and the State knows who they are.[48]

The so-called Sabotage Act of June 27, 1962, meant that henceforth radicals could speak out in South Africa only at the sufferance of the minister of justice.[49] Passage of the bill through Parliament evoked public protest by whites that was reminiscent of the constitutional crisis of the early 1950s. The bill, which consisted mainly of amendments to existing legislation, introduced no new principles, but it furthered the trend toward greater ministerial discretion not subject to challenge in the courts and increasingly severe punishments for widely defined offenses. The bill, said the International Commission of Jurists, "reduces the liberty of the citizen to a degree not surpassed by the most extreme dictatorships of the Left or the Right."[50]

The conservative United Party, criticizing the erosion of the rule of law, opposed the bill in Parliament. Some upper-class white women, members of the Black Sash organization, once again joined dignified demonstrations in the streets, as they had a decade earlier. In Durban, for example, Mrs. Janie Malherbe, an Afrikaans-speaking Progressive and wife of the rector of the University of Natal, carried a placard alongside Alan Paton, president of the Liberal Party, and Dr. G. M. Naicker, president of the South African Indian Congress.[51] Some 6,000 to 8,000 whites walked in a silent procession through downtown Johannesburg. Other marches (when not locally banned), mass meetings, and silent vigils took place in major cities and at English-speaking universities. But protesters were almost numbed by repeated failure. Only a year later—after continued sabotage and, more important, the indiscriminate killing of a few whites—there was relatively little public protest, and almost none from the United Party, against new legislation (discussed below) that signaled the virtual end of habeas corpus.

A few days before the commemorative date of June 26, 1962, Lutuli in the pages of *New Age* called on nonwhites to "draw inspiration from the great battles of Tshaka and Moshesh, of Gandhi and Hintsa" and on democratic whites to "unite with all anti-Nationalist forces."[52] Lutuli's exhortation was to be his last public statement within South Africa, because the new act prohibited the reproduction of any statement made anywhere at any time (including any time in the past) by a person who was banned from attending gatherings. An individual could also be prohibited from communicating with other banned persons or receiving visitors. On July 30, 1962, 102 persons (52 whites, 35 Africans, 9 Coloureds, and 6 Indians) were listed as having been banned from gatherings; more than 50 more were added during the next eight months.[53] Lutuli was in effect exiled within South Africa; Oliver Tambo, who was abroad, could not be quoted either. The list also included the fervently anti-Communist Patrick Duncan.

The act required new newspapers to deposit up to the equivalent of $28,000, which would be forfeited if the newspaper was later banned. After six months had elapsed, possession as well as dissemination of a banned publication became an offense. On November 30, 1962, the influential *New Age*, though it had been a useful source of information to the government, was finally banned. According to its editor at the time, it had a circulation of about 20,000, about 90 percent of it among non-whites.[54] Undoubtedly each copy was seen by several persons. The publishers had taken the precaution to register another name before the deposit requirement went into effect; therefore, *New Age* reappeared the following week as *Spark*. Three months later, *Fighting Talk* was banned. No ban was placed on *Spark,* but, crippled by a series of bans on members of its staff, it announced in its issue of March 28, 1963, that it could appear no longer.

One of the most distinctive features of the Sabotage Act was its provision for the form of detention predicted during the preceding year: house arrest. The minister of justice was empowered to take steps ranging from a warning to cease "communistic agitation" (the words of the minister during the parliamentary debate) to house arrest for various periods of time per day up to twenty-four hours.[55] The first dozen house arrest orders were directed mainly at whites who had been members of the Communist Party but also included Helen Joseph and Walter Sisulu. Mrs. Joseph, a leader of the Federation of South African Women, had recently visited Africans banished to remote areas of the Republic. Other persons were threatened by a magistrate with house arrest if they did not cease their political activity. These and other new restrictions made life for political activists scarcely bearable, especially for persons who had been involved with publications, and many (but not Helen Joseph) soon requested and were granted one-way exit permits to leave South Africa. Whatever damage they might do abroad, the government was satisfied that it would be less threatening than their influence on Africans at home.

Restrictions on the leaders of the organizations allied with the ANC—the Congress of Democrats, the Indian and Coloured congresses, the Congress of Trade Unions, and the Federation of South African Women—and surveillance and harassment of these organizations were so extensive that there seemed to be little advantage to the government in banning the organizations themselves. Nevertheless, the Congress of Democrats was outlawed on September 14, 1962, thus becoming the first organization other than the Communist Party to be outlawed under the Suppression of Communism Act. A week earlier, the minister acted under a provision of the Sabotage Act empowering him to close certain places to public meetings. He prohibited for one year "any public gathering" except divine services on the Johannesburg City Hall steps, a traditional ground for the airing of dissent and one often used by the Liberal Party and the COD.

The most severe feature of the new act, as its popular name implied, related to the criminal offense of "sabotage." The act made it possible, the minister admitted, for minor offenses to be treated as capital crimes.[56] Because the act was "worded widely," he said, and sabotage carried a minimum penalty of five years in prison and a maximum penalty of death, prosecution could begin only if personally certified by the Attorney

666

General. A large number of acts constituted sabotage if they were proved to be wrongful and willful and fell into certain broad categories, for example, endangering public health or safety or law and order. Once the prosecution proved the foregoing, the burden fell upon the accused to prove the absence of political motivation. He would be acquitted if he proved that his offense was neither intended nor likely to produce any one of ten general consequences, for example, encouraging the achievement of "any political aim, including the bringing about of any social or economic change in the Republic." Trespass and the illegal possession of weapons or explosives also constituted sabotage unless this burden of proof was discharged.

Mandela: Abroad and on Trial, 1962

While the sabotage bill was pending, Mandela was on a six-month tour to meet leaders of African states, with a side trip to London, where he met Hugh Gaitskell and Jo Grimond, leaders of the British opposition parties. The attention he received and the impression he made contributed to the world-wide interest that the later Rivonia trial was to attract. Mandela had left South Africa secretly on January 11, 1962, to speak as a representative of the ANC (not Umkonto) at the conference of the Pan-African Freedom Movements for East and Central (and later, Southern) Africa in Addis Ababa.[57] Mandela's long-range timetable was suggested during the Rivonia trial in his description of this period. He began to study the literature of war and revolution, took a course in military training in Algeria, and discussed arrangements for South African recruits to receive such training and for matriculated students to enter institutions of higher education. When he returned, he said, some of his colleagues expressed doubts that the time was ripe for military training, because "it would be a long time before the possibilities of sabotage were exhausted." The decision was made, however, to go ahead with plans for military training because "it would take many years to build up a sufficient nucleus of trained soldiers to start a guerrilla campaign" in the event that this proved to be necessary.

On July 20, 1962, Mandela returned to South Africa, and on August 5 he was arrested in Natal, while disguised as a chauffeur and traveling with a white friend. Rumors circulated afterwards that Communists had betrayed Mandela. The rationale of the rumors was that leaders of African states had stressed the importance of African rather than non-African leadership in the struggle and that Mandela had forcefully expressed his agreement with this view in underground meetings in Johannesburg and Durban. Mandela at his trial dismissed these rumors as "sensational inventions of unscrupulous journalists" (Document 68). ANC leaders in exile have often expressed concern about the necessity to make clearly evident the "hegemony" (as one has expressed it) of Africans in the liberation movement. On the other hand, the will to believe that Mandela was reverting to an Africanist position at the time of his arrest has left some residue of sympathy for him among members of the PAC.

Mandela was not identified as an Umkonto leader ("Commander-in-Chief," according to later publicity of the ANC in exile) until 1964, when he was brought to trial in the famous Rivonia case. In 1962 he was charged with two counts: first, inciting workers in essential occupations to act illegally by staying away from work, and second, leaving the country without a valid permit. The presiding judge described him as "the brains behind the entire organization" of the three-day stay-at-home in May 1961 and sentenced him to a total of five years in prison on both charges. His trial was preceded by enthusiastic pro-Mandela rallies in various centers. In order to prevent other rallies, the government prohibited "any gathering related to Mandela in any place in the Republic of South Africa" for two days at the beginning of his trial. On October 20, all gatherings held to protest the arrest or trial of anyone for any offense were banned until April 30, 1963.[58]

During the five days in October 1962 when Mandela appeared in court and conducted his defense, and again while he was being sentenced on November 7, his dramatic conduct added to his almost legendary, possibly charismatic, reputation. Front-page press coverage described the tribal dress worn by Mandela and his wife, Mandela's clenched fist and shouts of "*Amandla!* [power!]" (which were roared back by the crowd) when he entered and left, and the excited scenes of singing and dancing Africans outside the courtroom. The tribal dress, in particular, excited comment: was Mandela now focusing his appeal on Africans rather than all races?

In an hour-long address before the court, Mandela denied that the white legal system could give a Black man justice. Like Sobukwe in 1960, he refused for this reason to enter a formal plea, and a plea of not guilty was entered on his behalf. In a later address before sentencing, Mandela did not allude to sabotage but referred to his mission underground as that of carrying out the decisions of the All-in Conference of 1961. He warned, however, that government violence would breed counter-violence—"the only language which this Government shows, by its own behaviour, that it understands" (Document 68).

Although Mandela was on the list of persons whose statements could not be published, the minister had said that reporting of judicial proceedings was permissible "as long as it is not abused by creating a forum for such persons." Apparently inhibited by this qualification, the *Star*'s lengthy report of the trial quoted only a few sentences from Mandela's address. *New Age,* however, a few weeks before it was banned, quoted him in a front-page headline: "White Court Cannot Dispense Justice."

668

Tactics and Dangers

While Mandela was abroad, the tensions and suspicions between the ANC and the PAC that had hobbled the functioning of the South African United Front during 1961 deepened until they were recognized to be beyond repair. Splits among PAC exiles on the question of participating in a multiracial front snarled the situation further. Late in January 1962, ANC and PAC representatives in Dar es Salaam announced that the front was dissolved, a fact confirmed at a meeting of representatives of the ANC, PAC, SAIC, and SWANU in London on March 13, 1962.[59]

During Mandela's trial, at the end of October 1962, the ANC held a conference in Lobatsi, Bechuanaland, its first since 1959. ANC leaders came both from within and without South Africa.[60] Referring to the conference, a newsletter "issued by the National Executive of the A.N.C." early in 1963 declared in capital letters: "OUR EMPHASIS STILL REMAINS MASS POLITICAL ACTION. . . . Political agitation is the only way of creating the atmosphere in which military action can most effectively operate" (Document 69). The newsletter appealed for African unity and an anti-government united front, but there was a bitter new tone as well: "an eye for an eye, a tooth for a tooth." And for the first time (so far as is known) in a statement purported to be by the National Executive Committee, the ANC was clearly linked with Umkonto, "the military wing of our struggle." The most immediate concern expressed by the newsletter, however, was the emergence since the Lobatsi conference of a new phenomenon on the South African scene that was as disturbing to the ANC as it was, for different reasons, to whites: "adventurous and futile acts of terrorism."

By limiting violence to the technical efforts of a small group, the leaders of the ANC and Umkonto made no allowance for any mass participation by way of crude forms of sabotage like arson or vandalism, not to mention bloodier actions.[61] They failed to weigh adequately the pent-up passions and frustrations of young Africans whose impatience for direct action against whites could not be satisfied by Mandela's timetable or his proposed new methods of non-cooperation plus careful sabotage.

ANC leaders were well aware, however, of the dangers to the liberation movement of undisciplined mass action (Documents 69 and 70). Easily placed under surveillance and penetrable by police spies and informers, large groups might make spontaneous moves against whites that would invite a police crackdown and mass reprisals on a scale that could provide a calamitous setback to plans for graduated pressures and calculated confrontation. Some PAC leaders in exile in Ghana and England also recognized the danger of "a premature move which will enable it [the government] to pounce and shatter the whole structure [of the liberatory forces] for years to come" (Document 71).[62] These fears proved valid in

1963 as a consequence of actions by Poqo and the PAC leadership in Basutoland.

Poqo and the PAC

The word "poqo," meaning "independent" or "standing alone" in Xhosa, was the Xhosa vernacular equivalent of "PAC" and was used in this sense both before and after the PAC was banned.[63] Organizationally, Poqo was an offshoot of the PAC, a spontaneous grass-roots movement in western Cape Province and in the Transkei, consisting of groups relatively isolated from each other with only the most tenuous links to the remnants of PAC leadership in South Africa or in Maseru. Most members were in their late teens or early twenties, more urbanized than migrant, with some years of formal education, and often unemployed.[64] Poqo had no hierarchical structure, no identifiable mass leaders, and no public statement of aims or ideology other than a reputation of generalized support for Sobukwe and the PAC and an "all-out" determination to smash white rule. What was qualitatively new in the attitudes of its members was the intensity of their desperation, their targeting of African collaborators as well as informers for death, and their readiness to kill whites indiscriminately. Unlike Umkonto, Poqo was genuinely a terrorist movement.

Although Poqo was geographically localized, the press took to labeling any manifestation of PAC activity or violence not attributed to other groups in the Transvaal, the Orange Free State, or Natal as "Poqo." An official commission concluded in 1963 that Poqo and PAC were the same. PAC leaders in exile, on the other hand, alternated between claiming Poqo as their own and denying responsibility for its acts (or dismissing it as semantic confusion). Unlike the PAC, which had been strong in the Cape Town area before 1960 but had placed little emphasis on recruiting formal members, Poqo attempted wide recruitment of dues-paying members. Beginning in 1962 much intimidation and petty corruption accompanied the collection of dues of two shillings and sixpence (35¢).

Poqo was named in many cases of assault and in some cases of murder of Africans and Coloureds in the western Cape and pro-government chiefs and headmen in the Transkei during 1962–1963. Twice in late 1962, at large open meetings it was decided that Chief Kaiser Matanzima, who was cooperating with the government, should be killed and groups of Africans traveled by train from Cape Town to their home areas in the Transkei to carry out the mandate. The police were, of course, notified by informers and arrested the would-be assassins. But two events, in particular, ignited latent white fears of a Kenya-type Mau-Mau movement in South Africa and a "night of the long knives": the killing of two whites and near-fatal attacks on three others in Paarl near Cape Town during the night of

November 21–22, 1962, and the hacking to death of five whites (including a woman and two young girls) sleeping at a roadside camp near the Bashee River Bridge in the Transkei on February 5, 1963.

In Paarl, tensions had been aggravated by autocratic and corrupt administration and unusually bad living conditions. The attack there was an example of impetuous and open action by a large group having no carefully worked-out plan. Several hundred Africans armed with crude weapons marched on the central police station, apparently to rescue some prisoners; when fired upon, they spread out into town, set fires and broke windows, attacked two houses, and killed a young women and her male defender who had run into the street. The Bashee River Bridge murders had no discernible explanation other than terrorism.

These events were followed by mass arrests, trials, and the formation of a governmental commission of inquiry which warned of the continuing danger of terrorism. By mid-1963, after threats by the PAC in Maseru, described below, thousands of suspected Poqo and PAC members were in detention or on trial. Their experiences at this time, their first political experiences in most cases, heightened the political consciousness of an embittered new generation of African youth.[65]

Deprived of its top leadership, the PAC had rapidly disintegrated after Sharpeville as an organization within South Africa. In August 1962, however, Potlako Leballo arrived in Maseru, Basutoland, and began to rebuild the movement by asserting his leadership as PAC national secretary and acting president.[66] His two-year prison sentence had expired in May 1962, and he had been banished to a remote area of Natal; but having been born in Basutoland, he was allowed to return there. Traveling on a British passport, he then visited the United Nations and capitals in Europe and Africa. Afro-Asian states assured him of aid if Black South Africans showed their readiness to launch revolutionary action on their own. Back in Maseru in December 1962, shortly after the Paarl riot, Leballo attempted on the eve of the PAC's proclaimed year of liberation, to step up preparations for a "launching," using couriers and cryptic letters to communicate with PAC groups in urban centers in the Republic. These groups were to collect weapons and at an undisclosed time plan attacks on strategic sites and individual whites, including national leaders, some of whom Leballo apparently hoped to have kidnapped.

In a call to African youth published in *Contact* on February 7, 1963, after the Bashee River killings, Leballo declared that in 1963 the PAC would cross its "historical Rubicon." Privately, Leballo described the Paarl and Bashee River killings as premature actions by groups that had "jumped the gun." But PAC's motto, he also told visitors, was "kill or be killed." During the early months of 1963 he sent telegrams and circulars to South Africa; some were discovered by the police and their recipients arrested. On March 21, a ten-page mimeographed newsletter issued in Maseru said that African nationalism was "now poised" for a "knock-out blow" and warned of "self-defence and vengeance" against women and children beyond the age of infancy who were part of the hostile white population.[67] On the same day, an interim report on the Paarl riot was tabled in Parliament, a report warning that Poqo and PAC were the same and that they posed a serious threat.

Leballo called a press conference on March 24, ostensibly to comment on the report.[68] Unable to control an urge to boast about his grandiose plans for "revolution"—or perhaps thinking that the PAC could benefit from an intensification of paranoia among whites—he announced that a violent "launching" throughout South Africa was imminent. The PAC, he said, was the same as Poqo and had a membership of 155,000, divided into 1,000 cells, poised to deliver the "blow" when he gave the word.[69]

A few days later, one of Leballo's secretaries was apprehended after crossing into South Africa carrying a large number of letters to be sent to PAC contacts. On April 1, the (British) Basutoland police (and South African plainclothesmen, if PAC witnesses are believed) raided the PAC's office in Maseru on the ground that illegal possession of arms was suspected. The press reported that membership lists containing 10,000 to 15,000 names were found. Several men were detained, but Leballo escaped into the Basutoland interior. Despite British and South African denials of collusion, it was widely assumed that these lists were turned over to South Africa because new arrests and detentions of PAC adherents in the Republic began almost immediately.

Leballo's plan was for nationwide "trouble" on April 7–8, 1963, Dr. Verwoerd said later, the weekend immediately following April 6, Van Riebeeck Day, and the fourth anniversary of the founding of the PAC.[70] Later, Leballo and his presidential council sought to maintain that no date had been set and that the situation was still unfolding.

Leballo's press conference signaled the beginning of a debacle for the PAC. Mass raids and arrests in South Africa, especially after passage of the "90-Day Act" on May 1, 1963, were a blow from which the PAC could not recover. Leballo himself was almost completely discredited as a leader except within a small circle of his personal colleagues. Sobukwe's three-year prison term was to have expired on May 3, but under the so-called "Sobukwe clause" of the May 1 legislation, he was held in continued detention, though with special privileges.[71] By June 5, 1963 the total number of alleged Poqo members arrested was 3,246.[72]

Climax: July 11, 1963

News of Poqo alarmed whites in general more than reports of sabotage, although even during 1963 Poqo and Umkonto caused little disturbance in the even tenor of life for white South Africa. The government, however, tended to take Umkonto more seriously. Although Vorster, typically unable to recognize the reality of black leadership, claimed that both the ANC and the PAC were "White-led and White inspired," the ANC, he said, was "*par excellence* the organization which has many more White brains at its disposal, not only overseas, but here as well."[73] By the time of the Rivonia raid, some 200 acts of sabotage had been committed.[74] This estimate includes minor acts. How many were the work of the ARM is not known. An ANC leaflet of May 1963 (Document 70) said that Umkonto had struck more than 70 times.

By early June 1963, 126 persons had been convicted under the Sabotage Act, the lightest sentence being eight years, and 511 were awaiting trial.[75] Sabotage was becoming more skillful and damaging, but during the period before Rivonia, only a few persons were injured and their injuries were slight. At Rivonia, 106 maps were found, listing among other targets: "police stations, post offices, bantu administration offices, both state and municipal, the homes of bantu policemen and bantu administrators, electric power stations and lines, pylons, railway lines and signal boxes, as well as telephone lines and cables."[76]

On May 1, 1963, legislation was enacted to "break the back" of Umkonto and Poqo, as Vorster later put it.[77] The General Law Amendment Act, or "90-Day Act," which virtually abrogated habeas corpus, was a landmark in the transformation of South Africa into a police state. It empowered any commissioned police officer to detain a person without warrant on certain broadly political grounds of suspicion, and to hold him for interrogation for repeated periods of ninety days. The police no longer needed to charge such a person before a court or to provide access to a lawyer or to accord him the privilege of protecting himself against self-incrimination. He could be held completely incommunicado. The United Party supported the bill, and only Helen Suzman, the Progressive Party's lone M.P., voted against it.

During the months before enactment of the 90-day law, Walter Sisulu and other leaders of the ANC discussed the problems of channeling popular impatience into nonviolent mass protest. Their thinking took a familiar form, as Sisulu indicated in court a year later. Speaking of the unrest in the western Cape over the proposed removal of Africans from that area, he said:

They [the Africans] were seething and planning acts of violence. My understanding was that the position was very desperate indeed. I heard that they were contemplating marching into town and breaking into shops. [Govan] Mbeki was sent down to deal with the situation and later, to appease the Africans, a plan was worked out. The plan was for an anti-pass campaign which would culminate in a national strike, and the burning of passes. We had in mind that by June we would be ready for a national strike. But this did not materialize. The 90-day clause had meanwhile been introduced, and this and other legislation created very great difficulties. The idea was put into the background. It was to have been the major ANC campaign of 1963.[78]

Sisulu, Mbeki, and Nokwe had been vainly attempting to function above ground. In 1963 Nokwe left the country secretly. Sisulu, the subject of repeated charges and brief periods of detention, was finally convicted in March 1963 and sentenced to six years in prison for engaging in incitement in May 1961 and furthering the aims of the ANC. In mid-April, while out on £ 3,000 bail and under twenty-four-hour house arrest, he disappeared into the underground.[79] On June 26, he commemorated the day by reading over a clandestine radio transmitter a message to "sons and daughters of Africa" that was both desperate and determined (Document 72).

The climax came on July 11 in a large cottage on the Rivonia farm purchased by the Communist Party. Sisulu was meeting with five others: Govan Mbeki, a journalist and former teacher with college degrees in arts and economics, who had been a key ANC figure in the eastern Cape for years; Raymond Mhlaba, who was over sixty and like Mbeki, an ANC veteran in Port Elizabeth; Ahmed Kathrada, who was in his mid-thirties and had been a full-time activist in the Transvaal Indian Congress for many years; Lionel Bernstein, an architect, a founder of the Congress of Democrats, and at one time an editor of *Fighting Talk*; and Bob Hepple, a young lawyer. When the security police burst into the room, the group was looking at a six-page memorandum, "Operation Mayibuye" (Document 73).[80] This document, generated within Umkonto and up for discussion, outlined a plan for guerrilla war and revolution.

TOWARD ROBBEN ISLAND

The Rivonia Trial

The Rivonia raid of July 11, 1963, was followed by an anti-climax: a trial in which Nelson Mandela, who was brought out of prison to become one of the accused, Walter Sisulu, Govan Mbeki, and others admitted that they were guilty of sabotage and preparation for guerrilla war. They denied, however, that a decision had been made to begin guerrilla activity.[81] For eleven months after the raid, the underlying question in the trial was whether or not they would be hanged, which would have transformed them, as heroes of the African opposition, into martyrs.

Mandela, Sisulu, and Mbeki, the most prominent leaders of the ANC (other than Lutuli) who were still inside the country, were members of the

National High Command of Umkonto. Hundreds of documents and other evidence of subversion were found at Rivonia and at two other sites, both used as hide-outs and one used as an arsenal. Many of the documents were in the handwriting of the accused, including a diary of Mandela. For him and the others, the trial was an opportunity to set the record straight and a platform from which to reach a worldwide audience as well as their own followers within South Africa. The trial was similarly an opportunity for the government to win support, especially (it thought) because white and Indian Communists were among the accused and alleged co-conspirators. Anti-apartheid groups succeeded in focusing unprecedented international attention on the trial and in generating pressures to end it or at least to save the defendants from the death penalty. On June 11, 1964, Judge Quartus de Wet found Mandela, Sisulu, Mbeki, and others guilty, and on June 12, 1964, he sentenced them to prison for life.

For nearly ninety days, the men arrested in the Rivonia cottage had been interrogated and detained in solitary confinement. Among others detained under the 90-day law who became defendants in the trial were Dennis Goldberg, a Cape Town engineer and leader of the Congress of Democrats who had been in the main Rivonia house at the time of the raid; Elias Motsoaledi and Andrew Mlangeni, minor figures in Umkonto who had been arrested some weeks earlier; Arthur Goldreich, the tenant at Rivonia, an industrial designer who had learned guerrilla tactics in Israel; Harold Wolpe, a lawyer involved in handling the Communist Party's money for purchase of the Rivonia property; and James Kantor, who was not involved in Umkonto or in politics but was a legal colleague and brother-in-law of Wolpe. Kantor was discharged at the end of the prosecution's case.

Meanwhile, Goldreich, Wolpe, and two Indian detainees, Moosa Moolla and A. Jassat, bribed a young guard and escaped from jail on August 11, eventually making their way to Swaziland and then to Tanzania. Probably the most dramatic escape in South African history, their exit from the country infuriated the prosecutors and police who considered Goldreich to be "the arch-conspirator."[82]

The far-reaching effects of the 90-day law were only partly evident after the Rivonia raid. Both high officials and the press spoke vividly of the culpability of the men under detention. Because technically they were not yet charged with an offense, the tradition of no public comment on a pending case could be ignored. What could not be known fully with regard to this and other pending cases was the treatment of persons who were being held incommunicado. During the ten months after May 11, 1963, 682 persons were detained, 61 of them for more than 90 days.[83] Some complained of assault, electric shock, and suffocation within plastic bags.

White prisoners were apparently not tortured, although some white members of ARM were beaten up; solitary confinement for long periods, however, was described by critics as a form of mental torture. Mandela himself was treated by his jailers with some respect and restraint, but Mlangeni, complaining that he had been tortured with electric shocks, displayed burns and scars after his detention. Motsoaledi complained of assault. More subtle were the psychological consequences of solitary confinement and relentless questioning. These practices posed a problem for the judge regarding the reliability of prosecution witnesses in the Rivonia trial, some of whom were Africans sympathetic to Umkonto who had been persuaded to testify for the state.[84]

Lawyers were unable to see the accused until two days before indictment on October 9. Leading the defense team was Bram Fischer, the distinguished lawyer, Afrikaner, and veteran Communist (at that time, secretly a member of the underground party). Two days later, after appeals abroad by Oliver Tambo, the United Nations General Assembly voted 106 to 1, with only South Africa in opposition, in criticism of South African political trials; but the United States, Britain, France, and Australia abstained on the operative paragraph, which called for an end to "the arbitrary trial now in progress."[85] At the end of October, Hepple was able to leave the dock because he had agreed to testify for the prosecution; later he managed to flee the country. After dismissal of the first indictment as inadequate, the trial finally got under way on December 3 with an expanded indictment. Each of the ten accused pleaded not guilty, all of them except Kantor in words similar to those of Mandela: "My lord, it is not I, but the Government that should be in the dock today. I plead not guilty."[86]

In addition to the ten defendants, the indictment listed twenty-four alleged co-conspirators, including Tambo, Nokwe, Resha, Kotane, Marks, Dr. Arthur Letele, and Tennyson Makiwane. Surprisingly, Lutuli's name was not listed. One defense attorney thought the exclusion was designed to drive a wedge between Lutuli and the accused. The prosecutor, however, repeatedly brought Lutuli into the case as an accomplice, and it was the accused who firmly refused to say anything that might incriminate him. Also listed as co-conspirators were the Communist Party, the ANC (which the prosecutor claimed was "completely dominated" by the Communist Party), and Umkonto.

The offenses alleged were: (1) recruiting persons for training in the preparation and use of explosives and in guerrilla warfare for the purpose of violent revolution and committing acts of sabotage, (2) conspiring to commit the aforementioned acts and to aid foreign military units when they invaded the Republic, (3) acting in these ways to further the objects of communism, and (4) soliciting and receiving money for these purposes from sympathizers in Algeria, Ethiopia, Liberia, Nigeria, Tunisia, and elsewhere. "Production requirements" for munitions for a six-month period were sufficient, the prosecutor said in his opening address, to blow up a city the size of Joahnnesburg.

The chief prosecutor was Dr. Percy Yutar, deputy attorney-general of the Transvaal, a Jew whose intense emotional involvement in the case was said to be due, in part, to his animus toward Jews who were Communists. He also shared the prevailing assumption of other white South Africans that "the rank and file of the Bantu in this country" were ". . . faithful and loyal."[87] In his opening address, he said:

> The planned purpose . . . was to bring about in the Republic of South Africa chaos, disorder and turmoil, which would be aggravated, according to their plan, by the operation of thousands of trained guerrilla warfare units deployed throughout the country at various vantage points. These would be joined in the various areas by local inhabitants, as well as specially selected men posted to such areas. Their combined operations were planned to lead to confusion, violent insurrection and rebellion, followed at the appropriate juncture by an armed invasion of the country by military units of foreign powers. In the midst of the resulting chaos, turmoil and disorder it was planned by the accused to set up a Provisional Revolutionary Government to take over the administration and control of this country.

He concluded (perhaps confusing the ANC with the PAC) by alleging that the accused and their organizations "had so planned their campaign that the present year—1963—was to be the year of their liberation from the so-called yoke of the white man's domination." In his final speech, Yutar declared for the first time that "the day of the mass uprising in connection with the launching of guerrilla warfare was to have been the 26th May 1963."[88] Choice of this date, six weeks before the Rivonia raid and a time when Umkonto possessed only an air rifle with which Mandela had once tried target practice, mystified the accused and their lawyers.

Yutar's summary of "the planned purpose" was a summary of "Operation Mayibuye," the draft memorandum found at Rivonia, which was, for Yutar, "the corner-stone of the State case." Whether or not this plan for guerrilla war and foreign intervention had been accepted was, in the minds of the defense, the crucial question affecting sentences. Sisulu testified that the plan had been prepared by a group that included Arthur Goldreich. Some members of the National High Command favored it very strongly, he said; others (himself included) opposed it very strongly; and many were undecided and wanted further discussion. Preparations for the eventuality of guerrilla warfare were made, he said, but no decision to launch it was taken. The judge agreed. (Bram Fischer is reputed to have killed the plan. In his own trial later, he described Operation Mayibuye as "an entirely unrealistic brainchild of some youthful and adventurous imagination. . . . If ever there was a plan which a Marxist could not approve in the then prevailing circumstances, this was such a one . . . . if any part of it at all could be put into operation, it could achieve nothing but disaster.")[89]

Yutar described the Rivonia trial as "a classical case of high treason par excellence."[90] The accused were not charged under the common law of high treason, however, but under the Sabotage Act, which also carried the death penalty. Prosecution for treason would have required a preparatory examination, useful to the defense, with two witnesses to every overt act, and proof beyond a reasonable doubt. Dr. Yutar, privately recalling the abortive Treason Trial of 1956–1961, chose to proceed under the Sabotage Act, which shifted much of the onus of proof from the prosecution to the defense.[91] In his final judgment, the judge agreed that the case was essentially one of high treason; but, perhaps ironically, he found in the fact that treason had not been charged a basis for deciding not to impose the death penalty—"the only leniency" he could show. Afterwards, Sir de Villiers Graaff, leader of the United Party, said that his "only regret" with the verdict was that Mandela and others had not been charged with high treason, because then "the world would have understood the outcome of this case very much better than it does at this moment."[92]

In a manner similar to that adopted by the defense in the Treason Trial, which sought to dismiss all expressions of violent intent as outside ANC policy, the defense in the Rivonia trial argued that even acts by Umkonto members could not be ascribed to the accused if the members had violated instructions against endangering human life. Although witnesses for the prosecution testified to such instructions, Yutar talked of murder and attempted murder. The defense reacted with outrage because no specific allegations were made. The judge agreed that other organizations as well as Umkonto were committing sabotage, sometimes on the same targets, and that only a small proportion of the 193 acts of sabotage (none of which had resulted in loss of life) had been proved to be the responsibility of Umkonto.

Potentially more important was the judge's agreement that the ANC and Umkonto were two separate though overlapping organizations, despite a governmental proclamation during the trial that the ANC was the same as Umkonto. The distinction between the two organizations was important for every ANC member who might be charged in the future, because the maximum penalty for membership in an unlawful organization was ten years in prison, whereas the penalty for sabotage could be death.

These gratifying gains hardly compensated, however, for the shattering effect on all the accused (except Kantor) of the detailed testimony of "Mr. X," who was Bruno Mtolo, the most active saboteur in Natal. He was the leading witness among 173 witnesses for the prosecution. Mtolo, a member both of the ANC and of the Communist Party, had become disaffected with Umkonto, claiming that its leaders pursued selfish interests and disregarded the welfare of their followers. The judge considered him a reliable witness, and the defense, an extraordinarily impressive witness of phenomenal memory and very quick mind. The defense also insisted, however, that his testimony was a distorted mixture of fact and fiction, and Mandela expressed to his lawyers anger at Mtolo's smearing of the ANC and Umkonto as Communist.[93]

Most distressing, however, was Mtolo's readiness to "go out of his way to implicate people who were not even suspected by the police . . . [and his volunteering of] an enormous amount of information."[94] After his release, an Afrikaans publisher brought out an autobiography in which Mtolo suggested that "there must be some higher reason" for the presence of whites and other races in South Africa and concluded with an appeal to Lutuli as the leader of "the Zulu nation" to draft a new ANC policy "acceptable to the people but also to the white Government."[95]

Mandela in the Dock

To sympathizers with the African opposition, there was the sharpest contrast between Mtolo, the traitor, and Mandela, the hero. Mtolo had never been the victim of banning orders; his only experience of prison was for theft; politically he had proved to be an opportunist. On the other hand, Mandela's stature as a steadfast African nationalist who had suffered repeated restrictions had been growing. Although deliberate efforts had been made to exalt his reputation, it is not surprising that a man of his ability, character, and flair for leadership should by 1964 have surpassed the rusticated Lutuli as the pre-eminent ANC leader. In his personal relations, the respect and affection of those who knew him was extraordinary. During the trial, his dignified bearing and unyielding attitude enhanced his reputation. He was also a physically impressive man, over six feet tall, at that time in his middle forties. Characteristically, on his first entrance into the courtroom, he faced the packed nonwhite gallery and raised his clenched fist, mouthing the word "*Amandla* [power]"; many Africans in the audience replied "*Ngawethu!* [to the people!]." African attendance at the trial, initially high, soon dwindled. The Special Branch took the name and address of every spectator, and a police photographer took pictures as they left.[96]

When opening the defense case on April 20, 1964, however, Mandela spoke without apparent emotion. Slowly and quietly, he read a statement from the dock, as he had in 1962 (Document 75). The accused had agreed that instead of taking the witness stand, where his position could be expressed only in piecemeal fashion, Mandela should provide a

framework for the testimony to follow and at the same time use the dock
to present to the widest possible audience a coherent and enduring
rationale for the actions of Umkonto and the ANC. With assistance from
colleagues and counsel, he prepared the speech, fully conscious of its
historic importance.

Mandela concluded with the following words:

> During my lifetime I have dedicated myself to this struggle of the
> African people. I have fought against White domination, and I have
> fought against Black domination. I have cherished the ideal of a
> democratic and free society in which all persons live together in
> harmony and with equal opportunities. It is an ideal which I hope to
> live for and to achieve. But if needs be, it is an ideal for which I am
> prepared to die.

". . . for perhaps thirty seconds," one of his lawyers has written, "there
was silence. One could hear people on the public benches release their
breath with a deep sigh as the moment of tension passed. Some women in
the gallery burst into tears. We sat like that for perhaps a minute before the
tension ebbed."[97]

Mandela had been in prison almost the entire period since passage of the
Sabotage Act and Dr. Yutar might well have expected him to take the stand
to seek exoneration on the ground that his culpability was minimal. But
Mandela affirmed that he was a leader both of the ANC and of Umkonto,
and in effect (despite his plea), guilty on all counts. He fully expected the
death sentence to be handed down, inasmuch as twenty-year sentences had
already been meted out for relatively minor offenses. Along with others, he
had planned what he would say on that occasion.[98] Outside, clandestine
flyers were circulated during the trial, warning in lurid terms about the
consequences of imposing the death penalty. An ANC flyer at the beginning of the trial had said, with a new and, for the ANC, uncharacteris-
tic, emphasis on the whiteness of the enemy, "If these leaders die in
Vorster's hands—you, White man, and all your family, stand in mortal
danger" (Document 74). Following Dr. Yutar's opening speech, another
flyer warned that if the accused were made scapegoats, they would "only
become imperishable symbols of our resistance" (Document 76).

In presenting a case that would appeal to the widest public, Mandela had
to deal with the question of the role and influence of the Communist Party.
Although the government's understanding of who was a Communist was
notoriously unsophisticated, the fact was that among the accused there
were three Africans (Mbeki, Mhlaba, and Motsoaledi), one white
(Bernstein), and an Indian (Kathrada) who were or had been members of
the Communist Party. The government's misperceptions had been on
display earlier during the debate on the 90-day bill, April 24, 1963, when

Vorster attempted to provide what he evidently thought was a sophisticated review of the "long history" of African politics.[99] "Many of the files I am working with today," he said, "date from the 'twenties." J.B. Marks (who had indeed been a member both of the Communist Party and of the ANC) had become secretary-general of the ANC in 1936, he declared (an assertion that was untrue); and "from that moment Communism took over the ANC hand over hand and made it its tool" (an assertion equally untrue).[100]

In court, Mandela denied that the ANC had ever been a Communist organization; its "ideological creed," he said, was "African Nationalism." In setting forth distinctions between the policies of the two organizations, he referred to the Freedom Charter, for example, which Vorster saw as "nothing else but the communistic blueprint for Southern Africa." Yet the Freedom Charter, as Mandela accurately observed, was "by no means a blueprint for a socialist State."

Speaking more personally, Mandela explained "why experienced African politicians so readily accept Communists as their friends. . . . for many decades Communists were the only political group in South Africa who were prepared to treat Africans as human beings and their equals; who were prepared to eat with us; talk with us, live with us and work with us." He welcomed the Communist Party's assistance; nevertheless, he had never personally joined it. He was, he said, "an African patriot," a socialist who had been influenced by Marxist thought, but not a Marxist. Furthermore, unlike the Communists, he admired Western parliamentary systems and, in particular, had "great respect" for British and American political and judicial institutions.[101] Sisulu, who was under cross-examination for some six days, also denied that he was a Communist and presented a similar description of the relationship between the ANC and the Communist Party.[102]

The intimacy of relations between non-Communist African nationalists and Communists, in South Africa and in exile, made it difficult for many anti-Communist observers to recognize that African nationalists could hold their own. This was especially true for white analysts who assumed that in any such collaboration Communists—particularly white Communists—would dominate.[103] Sisulu would say to friends: cannot these people see that *we* might be using the Communists? Communists did, nonetheless, have an importance that was vastly disproportionate to their numbers, which was not surprising, given their ability and dedication and the philosophical certitude that underpinned their sense of inevitable victory.

Expert students of Communist political behavior might suggest that Sisulu and Mandela were clandestine Communists whose denials both of party membership and of adherence to party doctrine were calculated to preserve for the ANC a respectable facade among non-Communist and anti-Communist sympathizers. Such a supposition was as difficult to prove as to disprove. Although they may have sought to appeal to the widest possible spectrum of opinion, the judgment of many who knew Mandela and Sisulu well was a simple one: they were pre-eminently independent-minded African patriots. Among the exiles, the judgment was notably true for Tambo. Despite the ANC's growing reliance on aid from Communist countries, the position of such men was strengthened by the fact that African Communists like Kotane and Marks were to an important extent also nationalists.

International Pressures

The day of Mandela's speech was also a notable occasion at the United Nations. A special group of experts on South Africa issued a report that was part utopian and part realistic. The appointment of this group had been one event in the series of international appeals and warnings made in reaction to the tightening of controls and police crackdowns within the Republic. Many of the appeals were directed at South Africa's major trading partners, especially Britain and the United States. A year after the two-thirds vote in the General Assembly calling for sanctions, Scandinavian initiative led to the unanimous passage by the Security Council on December 4, 1963, of a resolution to appoint a small group of experts "to examine methods of resolving the present situation in South Africa through full, peaceful and orderly application of human rights and fundamental freedoms to all inhabitants of the territory as a whole . . . ."[104]

The secretary-general appointed Mrs. Gunnar Myrdal, a Swedish diplomat, to chair the group and other diplomats from Britain, Morocco, Ghana, and Yugoslavia as members. South Africa refused entry to the group, which proceeded nevertheless to hear recommendations from South African exiles, among others. On April 20, 1964, the group (except for the Yugoslav, who had resigned because of the others' relative moderation) issued its report, ahead of schedule because it believed that South Africa was rapidly approaching the point of "explosion." It proposed a "course of reason and justice . . . the only way and the last chance to avoid . . . a vast tragedy."[105]

The group resuscitated the idea of a national convention and suggested that with UN help such a convention might lead to a constituent assembly, a detailed constitution, and the election of a representative parliament. Lutuli, Mandela, and Sobukwe were praised as nonracialists and men of "outstanding political responsibility." Not only they but also "all representative leaders" should be able to participate freely in planning the convention. Therefore, the report described as essential "an amnesty for all opponents to apartheid, whether they are under trial or in prison or under restriction or in exile.''[106]

This stunning unreality, which *Die Burger* felt confirmed "the cynical statement that there are no greater fools upon earth than a collection of experts," was balanced by the report's recognition of South Africa's "wave of economic prosperity," the sharp increase in white immigration, and the dramatic increase in British and American investment.[107] Pending a final reply from the South African government, the group proposed an expert examination of the economic and strategic aspects of sanctions and emphasized the crucial importance of American and British cooperation. An ultimatum was then proposed: if South Africa did not reply satisfactorily by a date to be set by the Security Council, the Council should impose sanctions.

The ulterior motive of the proposal for more expert study may have been a realistic one: to involve the United States and Britain in movement toward mandatory sanctions. If so, the effort was partly successful; both governments participated in the expert committee that was subsequently established. But U.S. policy toward South Africa continued to be ambivalent. The United States was hardly disposed to embark on an uncertain course, unsupported by American public opinion, against a currently stable and profitable system. By the end of 1965, the drive for sanctions had evaporated.

The Trial Ends: June 12, 1964

As the Rivonia trial neared its end, the world-wide campaign of protests and appeals for clemency was stepped up. Its culmination came on June 9 with action by the United Nations Security Council two days before the judge rendered his decision. The Council, with four abstentions, urged the South African government to end the trial, to grant amnesty to the defendants and to all others who were imprisoned or restricted "for opposing apartheid," and to renounce the execution of persons already sentenced to death "for acts resulting from" such opposition.[108] The U.S. representative, who abstained along with the representatives of Britain, France, and Brazil, emphasized that Washington shared the Council's concern (American diplomats had, indeed, expressed such feelings privately to South African officials), but was opposed to interference with a trial in progress.

Foreign reporters, photographers, and diplomats gathered in Pretoria on June 11, when the judge rendered his decision, and on June 12, when he announced sentences. There was no surprise in the fact that Mandela, Sisulu, Mbeki, Motsoaledi, Mlangeni, and Goldberg were found guilty on all four counts. The defense had hoped that Mhlaba, Kathrada, and Bernstein might escape conviction because of the skimpiness of evidence that they were parties to the conspiracy, although undoubtedly they could be prosecuted on other charges. But Mhlaba too was found guilty on all counts, and Kathrada, on one charge of conspiracy. Bernstein, however, was found not guilty. He was rearrested, released on bail, and placed under house arrest. Later he fled the country.

In pursuing their main aim, to save the accused from death, the defense called upon Harry Hanson, an eloquent lawyer who had not taken part in the trial, to argue in mitigation. He compared the African struggle for rights to the earlier and somewhat comparable Afrikaner struggle and cited South African precedents for temperate sentencing, even in cases of treason. One witness was called: Alan Paton, national president of the Liberal Party, who was a devout Christian and opponent of violence. Paton agreed that Communists held high positions in the ANC but denied that the ANC was dominated by the Communist Party. He praised the sincerity of Mandela, Sisula, and Mbeki, their lack of desire for vengeance, and asked "for clemency because of the future of this country."[109]   Hanson and Paton were making political appeals in a trial of politically inspired offenses. Dr. Yutar also responded politically. He conceded that questioning a witness in mitigation was unusual, "but I do so in order to unmask this gentleman," he said of Paton. "His only purpose is to make political capital."[110]

Justice de Wet sentenced all defendants found guilty to life imprisonment. "Most of the world," said the *New York Times,* "regards the convicted men as . . . the George Washingtons and Benjamin Franklins of South Africa, not criminals deserving punishment."[111] There was a great gap between this perception and the more cynical and limited perception of de Wet. "I am by no means convinced," he said, "that the motives of the accused were as altruistic as they wish the court to believe. People who organize a revolution usually take over the government, and personal ambition cannot be excluded as a motive."[112]

The accused waved to the audience as they descended below the dock. Outside, as on the preceding day, large numbers of police, some with dogs, stood ready to control the crowds and avoid any embarrassing incidents or disorder. Among some 2,000 people present there were only a few hundred Africans who showed their emotions. They responded to news of the verdict with shouts of *Amandla Ngawethu!* and the clenched fist and upright thumb of the ANC. Some unfurled banners—"We Are Proud of Our Leaders"—which the police seized. Many sang the African anthem. On the preceding day, the singing of *Nkosi Sikelel' I-Afrika* had been led by Mrs. Albertina Sisulu, resplendent in a Xhosa robe and headdress. When Mandela and the others were finally driven away, the crowd again shouted and saluted as the convicted men thrust their fists through the bars and shouted back: *"Amandla!"* On the same day, all except Goldberg, the one white, were flown to Robben Island, the maximum security prison some seven miles from the shores of Cape Town.

The ending of the Rivonia trial did not appear to stir white public opinion. The press praised the police, the prosecutor, and the judge, and evidence of effective security contributed to growing white complacency and support for the government. Within a week of the sentencing, four incidents of sabotage were reported, probably the work of the mainly white African Resistance Movement. Within a month or so, the police had smashed this idealistic and heroic but ineffectual group. Most devastating, however, was the political blow to Alan Paton and the Liberal Party when it was discovered that Liberals were among the members of ARM. On July 24 whites reacted with horror to the news that a bomb had exploded in the white section of the Johannesburg railroad station, killing one old woman and injuring some two dozen others. John Harris, a Liberal who had joined ARM but had broken its basic rule against injuring human beings, was found guilty of the bombing. He became the first white man among some 45 persons hanged for politically inspired acts of violence since 1960.

Such violence was a last flickering of protest. White South Africa, confident that it faced no dangerous challenge from the United States or other Western states, was facing a period in which white strength was to be consolidated rather than undermined and white initiatives to enlist black collaboration and compliance were to be accelerated. Meanwhile, Lutuli's bitter verdict on Rivonia stood (Document 77): sentencing "brave just men . . . to be shut away for long years in the brutal and degrading prisons of South Africa . . . will leave a vacuum in leadership," he said. "With them will be interred this country's hopes for racial co-operation."

EPILOGUE: 1974

A new political generation has been coming of age in South Africa during the past decade, one that hears little of the long history of African protest and challenge. For ten years Nelson Mandela, now fifty-six years old, Walter Sisulu, sixty-two, and Govan Mbeki, sixty-four, have been removed from the scene, serving their life sentences in the bleak surroundings of Robben Island. Robert Sobukwe, confined to Kimberley and under close surveillance, cannot be quoted or attend gatherings. Albert Lutuli, too, had become a "non-person," in this sense before his death in 1967. Oliver Tambo is in exile, leading the ANC as acting president from Zambia, Tanzania, and London. Within the splintered ranks of the PAC abroad, Potlako Leballo runs an office in Dar es Salaam and endures. Inside the Republic, the pall of police surveillance and the prevalence of informers inhibit discussion of past political movements that have been described for more than a decade in white South African parlance as "terrorist." More and more, the leaders of the earlier years become shadowy figures.

Young Africans, Coloureds, and Indians in 1974 are at the beginning of what may be a second quarter-century of Afrikaner Nationalist rule, or perhaps rule by a coalition that reflects the determination of whites to maintain their domination. Yet the familiar contradictions of South Africa—not only of the quarter-century since 1948 but also of the half-century preceding it—are unresolved. Economic reliance on African labor and the potential power of that labor force become greater, while official policy ensures that it continues to be a labor force without rights or security. The white regime attempts to win acceptance abroad as a government dedicated to self-determination and equal opportunity, while it dictates policies that forcibly uproot hundreds of thousands of Africans and which ignore the political aspirations of millions of urban Africans. The regime recognizes the vital importance of African co-operation on the one hand, and on the other steadily maintains and tightens police state control over African political expression.

Meanwhile, the economy is buoyant; the price of gold has soared; police and military strength is overwhelming; Western business and Western states are supportive. Also an atmosphere of change prevails which disarms many critics. There are changes in official policy, for example, allowing some multiracial (that is, "multinational") sport and formal relations with cooperative African, Coloured, and Indian leaders. Progressive-minded whites are renewing multiracial consultation and discussing constitutional changes, such as federation, that would improve relations with Africans; and in 1974 there was an unexpected increase of Progressive Party strength from one to seven members in Parliament. Business has demonstrated some responsiveness to pressures at home and abroad for higher wages and better conditions for Africans. These pressures have included strikes by tens of thousands of African workers (acting without visible leadership and without presentation of political demands). The fading of Portuguese domination in Mozambique and the precariousness of white rule in Rhodesia contribute to the growing sense that white South Africa must accommodate itself to pressures for change.

Some opponents of white domination—both South Africans and outsiders who reject violence—see in these developments the beginnings of fundamental, not merely superficial, change. Others who agree that fundamental change is occurring fear that the pace of change is fatally slow. But the changes of nearly a decade and a half since the trauma of 1960 may also be seen as changes that bolster and make more palatable the continuation of white rule. Africans have no ground for expecting a radical change in the direction of policy or a political breakthrough that would give them a share of power in the Cape Town Parliament.

Discovering the opinions of ordinary Africans is extraordinarily difficult for whites. One astute black foreigner who visited South Africa in 1974 found among Africans in widely diverse circumstances a mood of "rage at their impotence."[1] An able and articulate group of African "homeland" leaders has arisen within the system and achieved national and international prominence during the past decade, seeking whatever scraps of power they can find. They regard violence as unrealistic and self-defeating and use the platform of governmental institutions to criticize official policies and to appeal for advancement for their people. Chief Kaiser Matanzima, believing that the goal of a united South Africa in which whites accept Africans as political equals is impossible, has asked for sovereign independence for the Transkei within five years. Thus he has broken ranks with other homeland leaders, who believe that leverage depends on a unified front. Chief ministers Cedric Phatudi of Lebowa and Hudson Ntsanwisi of Gazankulu, on the other hand, regard separate development as doomed to failure and believe in cooperative development between black and white in an undivided and nonracial South Africa.[2] Agreeing with them is Chief Gatsha Buthelezi of KwaZulu, the homeland leader who has appealed most dramatically to mass African audiences. His roots are deep in the mainstream of African political thinking and tactics, and in appeals to whites, he continues to invoke Christian and liberal values. But on the twenty-fifth anniversary of the Nationalist Party's rule, he wrote, "I do not feel less of a 'kaffir' in 1973 than I did in 1948."[3]

Rejecting cooperation with whites in the gradual shaping of a broad multiracial South Africanism, another group of African leaders has articulated a new philosophy of "black consciousness." African university students have joined with Indian and Coloured students—all identifying themselves as "black"—to form the South African Students' Organization (SASO). Some of the Africans had been caught up as high school boys in the police raids of the early and mid-1960s. Their roots are in the Africanist strain of nationalist thinking that appears to be displacing the mainstream out of which Buthelezi comes. "Black consciousness" is also manifested in a "black theology" movement and in such organizations as the Black People's Convention (BPC).

In working out their own political philosophies, SASO leaders have found inspiration in the writings of black thinkers both in Africa and elsewhere. Many past African leaders, they believe, subtly accommodated themselves to white domination. SASO repudiates white liberals for attempting the impossible task of identifying themselves with black experience and aspirations. By continued association with these paternalistic mentors, they say, blacks risk political emasculation. The SASO leaders call for a reinterpretation of South Africa's black history, emphasizing not the moderate and patient efforts undertaken during the years of Union, but the culture of "pre-Van Riebeeck days" and, in the words of Steve Biko, their leading spokesman, "the heroes that formed the core of resistance to the White invaders . . . [and] the successful nation-building attempts by people like Shaka, Moshoeshoe and Hintsa."[4]

Responding to the new currents that helped to produce the black consciousness movement, the ANC in exile has adopted a heightened emphasis on the primacy of African "national consciousness" in the liberation struggle.[5] Meeting, coincidentally, a short time before the inauguration of SASO, the ANC held a conference at Morogoro, Tanzania in April 1969, probably its most important conference in twenty years. It saw as its enemy a growing "all-White solidarity"—from which a small number of revolutionary whites were excepted—and therefore a "confrontation on the lines of colour—at least in the early stages of the conflict." The first priority was "the maximum mobilisation of the African people as a dispossessed and racially oppressed nation . . . . It involves a stimulation and a deepening of national confidence, national pride and national assertiveness." At the same time, unity with Coloureds and Indians was seen as essential since they share "a common fate with their African brothers." Responding also to the perennial criticism that non-Africans dominated the Congress Alliance, the conference abandoned the multiracial structure as obsolete and welcomed members of other oppressed groups and white revolutionaries to become "fully integrated [within the ANC] on the basis of individual equality." The National Executive Committee, however, responsible to Africans "at home," was to be composed of Africans only.[6]

The analysis of African politics in South Africa is distorted if one exaggerates the distinction between major and secondary strands of thought and underemphasizes the degree of national unity that has existed. ". . . the founders of the ANC in South Africa from its very inception," the ANC's National Executive Committee stated at Morogoro, "were deeply conscious of the fact that the unity of the African oppressed and plundered people was of paramount and vital importance."[7] Thus, leaders often thought of as lacking in militancy are regarded by African nationalists today as great patriots for their contribution to the African cause in the circumstances of their times, for example, the Rev. James Calata, who was selfless in his efforts to pull the ANC together in the 1930s, or Professor Z. K. Matthews, who was sometimes criticized for excessive caution but was described by Nelson Mandela in a letter from prison as possessing "something of ruthless steel."[8] Although the history of African politics since 1912 has been marked by divergence and splits on tactics and strategy, by temperamentally different approaches and personal rivalries, African leaders have agreed fundamentally in their opposition to white divide-and-rule policies and in the importance they have ascribed to the building of African unity. They have also shown a striking capacity to come together at times of crisis.

Today the exiled leaders are committed to international boycott and armed struggle; the homeland leaders, to cooperation and pressure within the system and to the welcoming of Western investment in South Africa; and the SASO leaders, to the fundamental task at home of psychological and cultural conditioning for freedom. Some SASO leaders have already been banned, and the outspokenness of homeland leaders brings them close to the edge of white tolerance. The pre-1964 leaders who remain within the Republic are in limbo. Undoubtedly there are also leaders underground and potential leaders who are not publicly known. In existing circumstances, the coming together of reformers, radicals, and revolutionaries is impossible, as is the convening of the often-proposed widely representative multiracial convention. But the calling of such a convention continues to be urged. Inspired by the interest in proposals for federation or confederation, a leading English-speaking editor writes: "Let there be a national Indaba on this subject . . .—a huge national convention of all people of all parties and all races who are interested in the broad concept."[9]

Many of these contradictory strands of hope and challenge come together in the person of Chief Gatsha Buthelezi. As an African nationalist, described twenty years ago by Joe Matthews as "one of the most loyal sons of this soil," he has called for "black solidarity" in addressing crowds of some 15,000 persons in Soweto, Johannesburg, and has heard roars of "amandla [power]" in response.[10] In a review of the history of African politics, Buthelezi has traced "the good faith and goodwill we have shown over generations to White South Africans" and described "the disillusionment now so evident among young blacks . . . [as] a natural result of White intransigence."[11] Buthelezi too calls for dialogue between white South Africa and black South Africa, "which might yet avert violent confrontation" if the black leadership that the government now accepts is joined by "black political leaders of the past." What is needed, therefore, he says, if there is to be "real dialogue," is the release of Nelson Mandela and others from Robben Island, the lifting of the ban on Robert Sobukwe, and the granting of immunity to Oliver Tambo. ". . . while they might appear to be so-called 'subversive elements' to Whites, [they] are in fact heroes to blacks." Not mentioned, one may add, are the new "black" leaders and leaders still unknown.

Is real dialogue a fantasy? It may come too late, following "a confrontation . . . whose aftermath," in Buthelezi's words, "is too terrible to imagine." But surely at some time real dialogue must come. In the meantime, Africans within South Africa continue to reaffirm their quest for freedom and equality. Speaking at a memorial service for Albert Lutuli on July 23, 1972, Buthelezi concluded with "Nkosi Sikelel' I-Afrika [Lord Bless Africa]" and added a familiar slogan—introduced by Lembede, used by Sobukwe in 1949, by Moroka and Sisulu in announcing the Defiance

Campaign, by Lutuli in his first presidential address, and by the prosecution as a crucial phrase in the Treason Trial—"Freedom in Our Lifetime."[12]

Postscript

On June 16, 1976, while this volume was in press, some 10,000 African students, most of them teen-agers, massed in Soweto, the sprawling black township southwest of Johannesburg, against the government-imposed policy of using Afrikaans as one medium of instruction. Unlike the PAC's peaceful rallies that preceded the Sharpeville shootings in 1960, this demonstration was not led by the elected leaders of a political organization, but black power salutes identified the crowd as part of an emerging, politically-minded "black consciousness" generation. After police gunfire killed a thirteen-year-old African student, demonstrations and rioting erupted and spread over several days, reaching Pretoria, Durban, and the segregated African Universities of the North and Zululand. At least 174 Africans and two whites were killed and 1,139 Africans wounded, many more than at Sharpeville. And though African *tsotsis* were involved in the burning of official buildings and the widespread looting, the rioting revealed among school-going Africans a mix of rage against whites, exultation, and near suicidal bravado.

The police arrested more than a thousand Africans, who could be detained indefinitely without charge As in 1960 the white opposition called for consultation and change. Govern. ¬ent officials did consult with Africans, mainly members of officially-sponsored bodies, who had warned earlier of pent-up emotions, and on July 5 the government backed down on the compulsory use of Afrikaans in teaching. However, deep bitterness toward persuasive discrimination remains. Moreover, consultation was limited, excluding not only banned leaders such as Robert Sobukwe of the PAC and also those on Robben Island like Nelson Mandela, but younger leaders of the "black consciousness" movement, some of whom were on trial on charges similar to those in the historic Treason Trial.

The end of white domination in South Africa is not yet here—it may be very long in coming; but pressures for change—either radical change or change that effectively prolongs white political power—are mounting. Since 1974, Portuguese control has come to an end in Mozambique and Angola; black rule in Rhodesia and the withdrawal of South Africa from Namibia are now in sight; and the United States, the Soviet Union, and other world powers are deepening their involvement in southern Africa. The South African government is intensifying its Draconian restraints while pursuing a long-run policy designed to eliminate formally all Africans as citizens of the republic of South Africa. On October 26, 1976, its

690

internationally touted plan is to extend political independence to the Xhosa "homeland" of the Transkei. This unprecedented step will partition South Africa and add to the imponderables—the opportunities and obfuscations—that affect the liberation struggle. Will urban insecurity and tensions, for example, decline if urban Xhosa become Transkeian citizens—or stateless persons? Black leaders differ regarding Transkeian independence, as they have differed on other questions of tactics in the past, but fundamentally they continue to share the same goal: equality and universal suffrage in one South Africa.

July 6, 1976

NOTES

1. See Fatima Meer, "African Nationalism—Some Inhibiting Factors," in Heribert Adam (ed.), *South Africa: Sociological Perspectives* (London: Oxford University Press, 1971), p. 144.

2. Meer, "African Nationalism," pp. 144–145, 150.

3. The references to the beginning of 1961 and the end of May do not appear in Document 75 but in a draft of Mandela's final speech.

4. The source is Document 75 except for the reference to the meeting of the National Executive Committee in June 1961, which appears in an early draft of this document.

5. Conversation with Tambo, Nov. 6, 1973.

6. Ngubane, unpublished manuscript. According to Ngubane, Mandela had visited Lutuli at his home to ask him to leave South Africa for Swaziland before the end of May, but Lutuli had refused. Ngubane and Bhengu interpreted Mandela's request as a Communist effort to get rid of Lutuli because of his commitment to nonviolence and to build up Mandela's status as the leader.

7. Lutuli's frame of mind may be suggested by a comment made by M. B. Yengwa, a close associate, at a meeting in Port Elizabeth on October 21, 1961. "By banning our leaders who support non-violence," he said, "the government robs them of control of the direction of resistance. We do not want violence but our leaders who can prevent it, are in gaol." *Contact*, Nov. 2, 1961.

8. Conversation with Fatima Meer, 1964. See also Edward Feit, *Urban Revolt in South Africa, 1960–1964: A Case Study* (Evanston: Northwestern University Press, 1971), pp. 267–268.

9. In private discussions at the time, the position of Lutuli was compared with that of Archbishop Makarios, who while in exile was disassociated by his followers from the activities of the National Organization of Cypriot Fighters (E.O.K.A.).

10. Vorster referred to this statement as one contained in a monthly publication issued by the ANC's Cairo office and dated April 1963. *House of Assembly Debates*, June 12, 1963, cols. 7768–7769.

11. Address in Addis Ababa, Jan. 1962, reprinted in South African Studies 4, *Nelson Mandela Speaks: Speeches, statements and articles by Nelson Mandela* (London: The Publicity and Information Bureau, African National Congress—South Africa, n.d.), p. 50.

12. On the same day a similar statement in the form of a letter was sent to Dr. Verwoerd, who did not acknowledge it. His secretary described it as "an accumulation of threats." The letter appears in the record of Mandela's 1962 trial and, along with Mandela's cross-examination of Verwoerd's private secretary, is reprinted in a pamphlet, *We Accuse: The Trial of Nelson Mandela* (London: The African National Congress (S.A.), n.d.), pp. 12–13.

13. The AAC newsletter did not discuss violent methods, apparently considering them "stunts" in the absence of adequate political preparation based on its own 10-Point Programme. Some members apparently became impatient, however, because two years later the police arrested ten Coloureds and Africans who were reported to be NEUM members, some of them trained in Peking; they were charged with organizing the Yui Chui Chan Club to engage in sabotage. Muriel Horrell. *A Survey of Race Relations in South Africa, 1963* (Johannesburg: South African Institute of Race Relations, 1964), pp. 21 and 60.

Document 64, *The Voice . . .* , was signed in Cape Town by C. M. Kobus, an African who had split from Tabata (see above, p.   , footnote   ). Tabata, in the March 1961 leaflet cited below, accused "renegades" of "cloaking themselves in the mantle of the Convention and stealing the name of its well-known publication, 'The Voice,' using that famous organ to stab the Convention in the back."

APDUSA was formed in January 1961 at a conference called by the NEUM executive. *The Birth of the African People's Democratic Union of Southern Africa (APDUSA)*, a four-page printed leaflet issued by the Central Executive of AP-DUSA (L. Mqotsi, General Secretary), March 1961.

Tabata was the first president of APDUSA. Document 67 is his presidential address at the first national conference in Cape Town. Horrell's survey of 1963, p. 21, reported that "practically nothing is known" about APDUSA. In mid-1963, Tabata and four other Africans were reported to have left South Africa for Dar es Salaam. In September 1963, six Coloureds and Indians said to be APDUSA members were detained in Pietermaritzburg for distributing pamphlets. Horrell, *A Survey of Race Relations, 1963*.

14. Muriel Horrell, *A Survey of Race Relations in South Africa, 1961* (Johannesburg: South African Institute of Race Relations, 1962), pp. 79–80. See J. F. Holleman, *Sabra 1961: The Great Purge* (Durban: Institute for Social Research, University of Natal, 1961).

15. *Contact*, July 13, 1961; *New Age*, July 6, 1961.

16. *Contact*, Nov. 2, 1961; *New Age*, Nov. 2, 1961.

17. *New Age*, Oct. 19, 1961.

18. The discussion of the Coloured convention movement is based on the following sources: conversations with Albie Sachs (June 8, 1963), D. van der Ross, Victor Benjamin, and George Golding (1964), Sonny Leon (Oct. 1972), and Dennis Brutus (Nov. 1973); *Why a "Coloured" National Convention*, printed pamphlet published by the Planning Committee of the South African Coloured National Convention, June 1961; South African Coloured National Convention, Claremont Civic Centre, 7th, 8th, 9th, 10th July 1961 (printed program); South African National Convention, Preliminary Report (mimeographed), (Cape Town: National Continuation Committee, Aug. 19, 1961); Dr. R. E. van der Ross, "The Coloured 'Convention' Movement," *The Forum*, May 1961, pp. 9–10; Brian Bunting, "Towards a Climax," *Africa South in Exile*, July–Sept. 1961, pp. 56–66; D. A. B. [Dennis Brutus], "In a Cape Packing Shed," *Fighting Talk*, Aug. 1961, p. 14; "Resolutions of the Malmesbury Convention," *Fighting Talk*, Aug. 1961, pp. 15–16; and "Die Kleurling in sy plek" (the article is in English), *Forum*, Oct. 1961, pp. 16–18. Descriptions of the July 8–10 meetings appear in *Contact*, July 13, 1961, and *New Age*, July 13, 1961. A booklet containing the proceedings at the Convention was planned but, as far as is known, was not published.

19. *Why a "Coloured" National Convention*, cited above, said, ". . . (let's not deny it!) many Coloured people who don't want to change, fear that they will be swamped by other groups." Dr. Richard van der Ross, some of whose critics

accused him of favoring a bill of rights because he feared Africans, wrote before the Convention, "Contact must first be established, for it is an undeniable if regrettable fact that for the most part Coloured groups have had no effective contact with African groups. But, the Coloured people feel it necessary, when they enter into a more organic political relationship with Africans, to be so organised that they will at once demand respect, and be able to make a real contribution to the effort, rather than be mere fellow-travellers and hangers-on" (p. 10).

20. *Fighting Talk*, Aug. 1961, p. 14

21. The National Continuation Committee consisted of the following members (all had been members of the Cape Town Planning Committee except five members representing other areas): D. van der Ross (national chairman), Dr. Richard E. van der Ross (national vice-chairman), Joseph C. A. Daniels (national honorary secretary), Dennis A. Brutus (Eastern Cape), E. Bydell (Natal), H. J. Carelse, N. Daniels, Barney Desai, E. F. Doman, M. A. Gierdien, Bishop the Rt. Rev. Dr. Francis Gow, the Rev. R. Joorst, N. S. H. Kearns, Sonny Leon (Griqualand West), Stanley Lollan (Transvaal), Cardiff Marney, Councillor H. E. Parker, D. B. Smith, Sr., and L. Stone (Western Cape).

22. Janet Robertson, *Liberalism in South Africa: 1948–1963* (Oxford: Clarendon Press, 1971).

23. *Ibid.*, p. 217.

24. Violaine Junod, quoted in Robertson, *Liberalism in South Africa*, p. 222.

25. "The NLC . . . included socialists, disaffected members of the Liberal Party and of the Congress of Democrats, some Trotskyites, and some persons not known to have been previously involved in politics. A large proportion of the group was white, including a number of demolition experts . . . it was hostile to cooperation with Communists." John A. Marcum and Allard K. Lowenstein in John A. Davis and James K. Baker (eds.), *Southern Africa in Transition* (New York: Praeger, 1966), p. 265. No source is given for the description of the NLC's membership.

26. The writer has heard stories that some persons planned violence, in particular, the blowing up of Parliament while the cabinet was inside in order to create the kind of chaos that would compel the United Nations to send forces from Katanga to South Africa.

27. Special Correspondent, "Road to Violence in South Africa," *The Observer*, Sept. 17, 1961.

28. *New York Times*, Oct. 14, 1961.

29. *New Age*, Oct. 19, 1961.

30. *The Times* (London), Oct. 20, 1961.

31. *Ibid.*, Oct. 17, 1961.

32. *Ibid.*, Oct. 21, 1961.

33. Douglas Mitchell, quoted in Alex Hepple, *South Africa: A Political and Economic History* (London: Pall Mall Press, 1966), p. 167.

34. *The Times* (London), Oct. 20, 1961.

35. *The Economist*, Oct. 28, 1961.

36. *New York Times*, Oct. 24, 1961.

37. Translation from *Dagbreek en Sondagnuus*, Oct. 29, 1961. In commenting on the award, the first Nobel Prize to be received by a South African resident, J. de Klerk, the minister of the interior, said (as paraphrased by the press) that "South Africa set great store by the real achievements of their non-whites"; but he deplored "the debasement" of the award and its use for propaganda purposes. *The Times* (London), Nov. 4, 1961.

38. *New Age*, Dec. 14, 1961.

39. In conversation in June 1963, an independent African academic, who will not be named, claimed that Lutuli's acceptance of the prize had severely damaged

his reputation among Africans. Professor Matthews denounced such talk at a rally in Port Elizabeth, reported in *New Age*, Dec. 14, 1961.

40. *Christian Science Monitor*, Dec. 9, 1961. Kennedy's message read: "I have been moved by the award to you of the 1960 Nobel Peace Prize [the award was for 1960; at the same time the 1961 Nobel Peace Prize was awarded posthumously to Dag Hammarskjöld], and I join with many others from all parts of the world in extending sincere congratulations to you. This high recognition of your past and continuing efforts in the cause of justice and the advancement through peaceful means of the brotherhood of man is applauded by free men everywhere. Please accept my best wishes for your continued health and well-being."

41. See Govan Mbeki in *New Age*, Aug. 3, 1961; a series of three articles by Duma Nokwe, *New Age*, Nov. 9, 23, and 30, 1961; and Walter Sisulu, *New Age*, Dec. 28, 1961.

42. *New Age*, Dec. 21, 1961.

43. Quoted by Vernon McKay, *Africa in World Politics* (New York: Harper & Row, 1963), p. 85.

44. Heribert Adam, *Modernizing Racial Domination: South Africa's Political Dynamics* (Berkeley: University of California Press, 1971), p. 15.

45. Gwendolen M. Carter, Thomas Karis, and Newell M. Stultz, *South Africa's Transkei: The Politics of Domestic Colonialism* (Evanston: Northwestern University Press, 1967), p. 12.

46. *House of Assembly Debates*, May 17, 1962, cols. 5814–5821.

47. *New Age*, Nov. 23, 1961.

48. Quoted in translation in *Contact*, Nov. 2, 1961.

49. Discussion of the Sabotage Act and of Mandela's 1962 trial is taken largely from Thomas Karis, "South Africa," in G. M. Carter (ed.), *Five African States: Responses to Diversity* (Ithaca, N.Y.: Cornell University Press, 1963), pp. 544–545, 549–553.

50. Quoted in United Nations Security Council, *Report by the Secretary-General in Pursuance of the Resolution Adopted by the Security Council . . . on 4 December 1963* (S/5471) (Report of group of experts), S/5658, 20 April 1964, p. 14.

51. A picture appears in *New Age*, May 24, 1962.

52. *Ibid.*, June 21, 1962.

53. Muriel Horrell, *A Survey of Race Relations in South Africa, 1962* (Johannesburg: South African Institute of Race Relations, 1963), p. 46.

54. *The Star* (Johannesburg), Nov. 30, 1962.

55. See especially *House of Assembly Debates*, May 21–23, 1962, cols. 6058–6092, 6108–6115.

56. *Ibid.*, May 21, 1962, cols. 6075–6076.

57. The text of his speech is in South African Studies 4, *Nelson Mandela Speaks*, cited above.

58. The text of the two orders is in *The Star* (Johannesburg), Oct. 13 and 20, 1962.

59. See *Contact*, Oct. 5 and 19, Nov. 2, 1961, and *New Age*, Feb. 1, March 22, and an article by Dr. Y. M. Dadoo on March 29, 1962.

60. *New Age*, Nov. 1, 1962, reported that 50 to 60 delegates attended. Among those from abroad were Oliver Tambo, deputy president-general, Tennyson Makiwane, M. M. Piliso, Moses Mabhida, and (from Basutoland) Joe Matthews. Delegates from within South Africa, said *New Age*, came from "every corner" of the country.

A condition for permission to hold the conference was that the British police should be able to attend. Joel G. Joffe and M. Koff, *The Rivonia Trial* (available on microfilm from Cooperative Africana Microform Project of the Center for Research Libraries).

61. Ben Turok, a leader of the Congress of Democrats who was convicted on charges of sabotage in 1963, wrote ten years later: "Although it seems that the masses supported and even welcomed the resort to force, they could find no way of joining in and expressing their support. . . . Instead of using highly technical gadgetry, the movement might have begun with the simplest methods. . . . It has often been said that the very deep involvement of the Vietnamese peasants was due to the simplicity of the weaponry in the earliest days and it would seem that the parallel is appropriate." Ben Turok, "South Africa: The Search for a Strategy," *The Socialist Register 1973*, p. 361.

62. Only one issue of *Black Star* was published (in London). Conversation with 'Molotsi.

63. In *Black Star*, May 1963, from which Document 71 is taken, a note states that "poqo" is an old word "used in everyday speech by the Xhosa-speaking people to describe anything that is clear, pure, independent or autonomous." Africans used it in describing, for example, Dr. Malan's "purified" Nationalist Party and Selope Thema's group.

The discussion of Poqo is based largely on conversations with Archie Mafeje, June 29–30, 1963, and Peter Hjul, June 28, 1963, and notes by Gerhart.

64. Poqo members were not mainly migrants to the western Cape from the Transkei, as is sometimes suggested, although conditions were ripe for agitation among migrants. These conditions included the stringent application of pass laws in the western Cape, insecurity attendant on the long-range policy of removing Africans from that area, low wages, and the concentration of thousands of Africans without their families in "bachelor" barracks. Many Poqo activists were townsmen, the frequently unemployed sons of working-class or middle-class families that had lived in the western Cape since the mid-1920s. A smaller, semi-urbanized group were "flashy young men," who lived in flats and lodgings and often had a standard six (eighth-grade) education; they aspired to be townsmen. Apart from both groups was a much smaller number of educated middle-class or so-called "excuse me" persons.

Sometimes finding it difficult to recruit among the migrants, who lived in barracks, the activists (often called *tsotsis*, or gangsters, by the migrants) began to intimidate and even terrorize the countrymen. The latter complained to the police and organized to protect themselves. Such complaints added to the government's justification for anti-Poqo measures. Conversation with Mafeje. See also Monica Wilson and Archie Mafeje, *Langa: A Study of Social Groups in an African Township* (Cape Town: Oxford University Press, 1963).

65. Steve Biko, a key figure in the Black consciousness movement of the early 1970s, was expelled from Lovedale in 1963 at the age of seventeen at the time his older brother, also a student, was jailed for nine months as a suspected Poqo activist. Unpublished manuscript by Gerhart.

66. This paragraph is taken from notes by Gerhart.

67. "The Pan Africanist Congress Newsletter, Volume 2, Number 2, 21st March 1963."

68. This paragraph is taken largely from notes by Gerhart.

69. *The Star* (Johannesburg), March 25, 1963; *Contact*, April 5, 1963.

70. *House of Assembly Debates*, April 22, 1963, col. 4462.

71. Sobukwe was released in May 1969 and placed under twelve-hour house arrest in Kimberley. Leballo's apparent determination to launch his "revolution" prior to the expected release of Sobukwe in May 1963 has led some who know him to claim that Leballo meant thereby to pre-empt the leadership of the PAC, either by committing Sobukwe to a *fait accompli* or by insuring that Sobukwe would not be released. Notes by Gerhart.

72. *House of Assembly Debates*, June 12, 1963, col. 7771. By this date, 124 Poqo members had been convicted of murder, 77 were being tried for murder, and others were charged with attempted murder.

73. *Ibid.*, June 12, 1963, cols. 7764 and 7772.

74. Feit, *Urban Revolt*, pp. 325–349, lists 193 acts of sabotage that resulted in some damage before the Rivonia raid.

75. *House of Assembly Debates*, June 12, 1963, col. 7771.

76. Opening Address, "The State against Nelson Mandela and Nine Others" (typescript, n.d.), p. 10. The editors are indebted to Dr. Yutar for copies of this document and the indictment.
Sisulu testified that ANC policy was not to destroy railway lines. He added that he had been told by Umkonto members that the damaging of signal boxes would not cause accidents. *The Star* (Johannesburg), April 22, 1964.

77. *House of Assembly Debates*, June 10, 1964, cols. 7634–7636.

78. *The Star* (Johannesburg), April 21, 1964.

79. "Walter Sisulu, South Africa's Underground Leader," *African Revolution*, June 1963, pp. 126–130.

80. H. H. W. de Villiers, *Rivonia: Operation Mayibuye* (Johannesburg: Afrikaans Pers-Boekhandel, 1964), p. 4. An exiled ANC leader has said that after the plan had been rejected, copies were not destroyed that should have been. During the discussion that was interrupted by the raid, someone wanted to consult a copy, and a copy was found. It was shoved up the chimney during the raid but later discovered by the police.

81. In the following discussion of the Rivonia trial, the writer is generally indebted to Joel G. Joffe, solicitor for the defense, for the use of the valuable book-length manuscript, *The Rivonia Trial*, written by him and M. Koff. It is available on microfilm from the Cooperative Africana Microform Project of the Center for Research Libraries. See also James Kantor, *A Healthy Grave* (London: Hamish Hamilton, 1967); de Villiers, *Rivonia*; Lauritz Strydom: *Rivonia: Master Af!* (Johannesburg: Voortrekkerpers, 1964); Bruno Mtolo, *Umkonto we Sizwe: The Road to the Left* (Durban: Drakensberg Press Limited, 1966); and Mary Benson, "The Rivonia Trial in South Africa," *Motive*, Nov. 1964, pp. 10–14. Feit, *Urban Revolt*, has used the record of the trial as one of his sources.

82. de Villiers, *Rivonia*, p. 16.

83. See *Tyranny 90*, a printed pamphlet published in May 1964 by the "90-day" Protest Committee. This committee was headed by J. Hamilton Russell, a United Party member of Parliament who resigned his seat after the party failed to oppose the 90-day law, and A. van de Sandt Centlivres, the retired chief justice. The pamphlet refers to "full Parliamentary discussions of documented allegations, taken from Court records, of physical torture, including electric shock treatments, of 90-day detainees by the police." See also *House of Assembly Debates*, Jan. 22, 1964, cols. 138–147, Feb. 6, 1964, cols. 882–888, and United Nations Office of Public Information, *Apartheid and the Treatment of Prisoners in South Africa: Statements and Affidavits* (New York, 1967).

84. ". . . the prisoner becomes more malleable mentally and receptive to suggestion," according to Kurt Danziger, professor of psychology at the University of Cape Town. ". . . in his impaired and befuddled state, he may be unable to tell what is 'actually true' from what 'might be' or 'should be' true." Quoted in *Tyranny 90*, p. 11. Only one witness for the prosecution testified in court that he had been assaulted. He said later that he did not want to pursue the matter. Kantor, *A Healthy Grave*, pp. 167–168, and *Apartheid and the Treatment of Prisoners in South Africa*, cited above, p. 98.

85. *International Conciliation*, Nov. 1964, p. 105.

86. Kantor, *A Healthy Grave*, p. 164.

87. Joffe and Koff, *The Rivonia Trial* (microfilm).

88. *Ibid.* Several months before the Rivonia raid, Vorster quoted Sobukwe as saying that the last step "towards freedom and independence" would be taken in

696

1963 and added that the ANC had set the same date. *House of Assembly Debates*, April 24, 1963, col. 4644.

89. Statement by Abram Fischer at his trial, March 28, 1966, in *Apartheid and the Treatment of Prisoners in South Africa*, cited above, p. 41.

90. de Villiers, *Rivonia*, p. 28.

91. See de Villiers, *Rivonia*, pp. 28–29, for a conversation between Dr. Yutar and the author, a retired judge.

92. *House of Assembly Debates*, June 15, 1964, col. 8186.

93. Joffe and Koff, *The Rivonia Trial* (microfilm).

94. Kantor, *A Healthy Grave*, p. 173.

95. Mtolo, *Umkonto we Sizwe*, pp. 178 and 191–195.

96. Kantor, *A Healthy Grave*, p. 171. De Villiers, in his pro-government book, *Rivonia*, p. 33, simply says that on most days the public benches were not fully occupied.

97. Joffe and Koff, *The Rivonia Trial* (microfilm).

98. *Ibid.*; Kantor, *A Healthy Grave*, pp. 208–209.

99. *House of Assembly Debates*, April 24, 1963, cols. 4638–4644.

100. Colonel Buys, the Special Branch expert on communism, in a conversation on February 18, 1964, recognized that the ANC Youth League was African nationalist at first; he maintained that it became Communist in 1950. Colonel H. J. van den Bergh, head of the Special Branch, in a conversation on February 10, 1964, referred to the membership of Communists on the ANC's National Executive Committee in 1934 and in 1947 and concluded that effective Communist control of the ANC dated back to 1947 or 1950–52. He believed that through his "American colleague" he had convinced the U.S. State Department that the ANC was Communist-controlled.

Professor Feit believes that "by the mid-fifties the Communists had become the preponderant influence within the ANC . . . . all real decision-making powers were in the hands of Communists." *Urban Revolt*, p. 291. In his often-cited study, Feit is concerned that "many men and women of good will seem reluctant to believe the extent of Communist influence on the African opposition in South Africa" (p. 29). His analysis of the elusive questions of "influence" and "control" is subtle but, in the judgment of the editors, neither clear nor substantiated.

101. Colonel Buys has stated that Mandela was a Communist, a fact that Buys said became evident when Mandela became a member of the South African Peace Council and spoke on its behalf in 1948–49. Mandela was sent on his African tour, Buys believed, because he could make a good show of being an African nationalist.

Colonel van den Bergh called particular attention to one of the documents introduced in the trial: headed "How To Be a Good Communist," the document was in Mandela's handwriting. The editors were given this and other documents by Colonel van den Bergh.

Vernon Berrange of the defense team, in a conversation on February 18, 1964, said that Mandela had been embarrassed by his lack of knowledge of Marxist theory during the Treason Trial. In studying, it was his habit to copy material; thus, words would not be overwritten or crossed out. Mandela in his Rivonia speech described three lectures introduced in the trial and in his handwriting as "not my original work" but an effort to demonstrate to "an old friend" (presumably Kotane), who had been trying to get him to join the Communist Party, that lectures could be rewritten so as to avoid "obtuse" language and "the usual Communistic cliches and jargon."

102. Feit's judgment that "Sisulu was not only a Party member but in its highest councils" is based solely on trial evidence by Bartholomew Hlapane, an African Communist who testified for the state and listed Sisulu among those present at a Communist Party conference (not a meeting of the Central Committee) in late 1962. *Urban Revolt*, p. 292.

Bram Fischer, who was acting chairman of the Central Committee before his arrest in July 1964, said at his trial that meetings of the Central Committee "were occasionally attended by non-members—persons we wished to consult and who could be trusted because of their long record of service to the liberation movement in South Africa." Fischer in *Apartheid and the Treatment of Prisoners in South Africa*, cited above, p. 36.

Feit suggests that Mandela was a Communist but presents no evidence to support the suggestion. See *Urban Revolt*, pp. 263–264 and 278–279.

103. For example, Feit, *Urban Revolt*.

104. Quoted in *Report by the Secretary-General in Pursuance of the Resolution Adopted by the Security Council at its 1078th Meeting on 4 December 1963 (S/5471)*, S/5658, April 20, 1964, which contains the report of the group of experts.

105. *Ibid.*, p. 43.

106. *Ibid.*, pp. 18–20, 42. The Progressive Party's Molteno Commission in 1962 addressed itself to the problem of the conditions that should precede the calling of a national convention. Before such a convention met, in accordance with an act of Parliament, "legislation restricting in any way freedom of political organization of any non-White community . . . should . . . be repealed and freedom of organization restored to all." *Final Report of the Commission set up by the Progressive Party to make recommendations on a Revised Constitution for South Africa extending Franchise Rights to all civilized subjects of the Republic*, Molteno Report, II, Aug. 1962, p. 73.

107. The quotation from *Die Burger* is in *The Times* (London), April 23, 1964. Among others who reacted was Dr. Jan Steytler, leader of the Progressive Party, who condemned any outside effort to impose change (*The Guardian* [Manchester], April 22, 1964). Only the Liberal Party publicly welcomed the report's call for a national convention.

108. *New York Times*, June 10, 1964.

109. *The Star* (Johannesburg), June 12, 1964.

110. *Ibid.*

111. June 14, 1964.

112. Joffe and Koff, *The Rivonia Trial* (microfilm).

NOTES TO EPILOGUE

1. Conversation with E. R. Braithwaite, former ambassador from Guyana to the United Nations, Feb. 1974. See his *Honorary White* (New York: McGraw Hill Book Co., 1975).

2. *Comment & Opinion: A Weekly Survey of the South African Press and Radio* (Pretoria: Department of Information), Sept. 6, 1974, pp. 17–19.

3. *The Times* (London), May 26, 1973.

4. Steve Biko, "White Racism and Black Consciousness," in Hendrik W. van der Merwe and David Welsh (eds.), *Student Perspectives on South Africa* (Cape Town: David Phillip, 1972), p. 200.

5. See *Mayibuye (Special Conference Issue), Bulletin of the ANC, South Africa*, May 1969; *Sechaba, The Official Organ of the African National Congress, South Africa*, July 1969; and Sheridan Johns, "Obstacles to Guerrilla Warfare—a South African Case Study," *The Journal of Modern African Studies*, 11, 2 (1973), pp. 267–303. The quotations in this paragraph are from *Sechaba*, pp. 17, 21–22.

6. Constitutionally, the ANC was already open to non-African members, but in practice (according to Tennyson Makiwane) only one non-African had been invited to join: Mrs. Mary-Louise Hooper, an American who had served as a volunteer assistant to Lutuli.

The conference elected a new National Executive Committee, reduced from twenty-three members to nine. Elected to this committee were Oliver Tambo, acting president-general; Alfred Nzo, secretary-general; J. B. Marks, chairman of the National Executive Committee; Moses Kotane, treasurer-general; Joseph Matthews, Moses Mabhida, T. T. Nkobi, W. Mokgomane, and Mziwandile Piliso. The conference also established a Revolutionary Council, subordinated to the National Executive Committee, that was to include Indians, whites, and Coloureds. Dr. Y. M. Dadoo became its vice-chairman. *Mayibuye*, May 1969, p. 11; *Sechaba*, July 1969, p. 2; and conversation with Thami Mhlambiso, 1974.

7. "Political Report of the National Executive Committee to Consultative Conference of the ANC—Morogoro—April, 1969," typewritten, p. 19. Other extracts from this report appear in *Sechaba*, July 1969.

8. "Unlike many highly qualified intellectuals, Z. K. had no left-wing prejudices and worked in harmony with lovers of freedom from all schools of thought. There are some people inside and outside the movement who were critical of his cautious attitude. But I am not so sure now whether they were not [CENSOR] I believe there is something of ruthless steel in a man who, in spite of being holder of a lucrative and secure post [CENSOR] If we accept these facts as we must, then the question whether Z. K. was liberal, conservative or agitator becomes a purely terminological one, one which we must leave to academicians." Nelson Mandela to Mrs. Frieda Matthews, Oct. 1, 1970.

9. Allistair Sparks, now editor of the *Sunday Express* (Johannesburg), writing in the *Rand Daily Mail*, May 12, 1973.

10. Joe Matthews to "Dear Son of Africa [T. E. Tshunungwa], Nov. 9, 1954. *The Star* (air mail edition), Nov. 3, 1973, and *Rand Daily Mail*, April 1, 1974.

11. *Rand Daily Mail*, Oct. 1, 1973.

12. "Chief Albert John Mvumbi Luthuli—A Servant of His People. An Address by the Hon. Umntwana Mangosuthu G. Buthelezi: Chief Executive Councillor of KwaZulu Legislative Assembly on the Occasion of the Unveiling of the Tombstone Erected in Memory of the Deceased Leader of the African People: 23rd July, 1972" (mimeographed).

Documents

Document 63. Press statement, released by Nelson R. Mandela, Honorary Secretary of the All-in African National Council, June 26, 1961

The magnificent response to the call of the National Action Council for a three-day strike and the wonderful work done by our organizers and field workers throughout the country proves once again that no power on earth can stop an oppressed people, determined to win their freedom. In the face of unprecedented intimidation by the Government and employers and of blatant falsehoods and distortions by the press, immediately before and during the strike, the freedom loving people of South Africa gave massive and solid support to the historic and challenging resolution of the Maritzburg Conference. Factory and office workers, businessmen in town and country, students in university colleges, in primary and secondary schools, inspired by genuine patriotism and threatened with loss of employment, cancellation of business licenses and the ruin of school careers, rose to the occasion and recorded in emphatic tones their opposition to a White Republic forcibly imposed on us by a minority. In the light of the formidable array of hostile forces that stood against us, and the difficult and dangerous conditions under which we worked, the results were most inspiring. I am confident that if we work harder and more systematically, the Nationalist Government will not survive for long. No organization in the world could have withstood and survived the full scale and massive bombardment directed against us by the Government during the last month.

In the history of our country no political campaign has ever merited the serious attention and respect which the Nationalist Government gave us. When a Government seeks to suppress a peaceful demonstration of an unarmed people by mobilizing the entire resources of the State, military and otherwise, it concedes powerful mass support for such a demonstration. Could there be any other evidence to prove that we have become a power to be reckoned with and the strongest opposition to the Government? Who can deny the plain fact that ever since the end of last month the issue that dominated South African politics was not the Republican celebrations, but our plans for a general strike?

Today is 26th June, a day known throughout the length and breadth of our country as Freedom Day. On this memorable day, nine years ago, eight thousand five hundred of our dedicated freedom fighters struck a mighty blow against the repressive colour policies of the Government. Their matchless courage won them the praise and affection of millions of people here and abroad. Since then we have had many stirring campaigns on this date and it has been observed by hundreds of thousands of our people, as a day of dedication. It is fit and proper that on this historic day I should speak to you and announce fresh plans for the opening of the second phase in the fight against the Verwoerd republic, and for a National Convention.

You will remember that the Maritzburg Resolutions warned that if the Government did not call a National Convention before the end of May, 1961, Africans, Coloureds, Indians and European democrats would be asked not to collaborate with the Republic or any Government based on force. On several occasions since then the National Action Council explained that the last strike marked the beginning of a relentless mass struggle for the defeat of the Nationalist Government, and for a sovereign multi-racial convention. We stressed that the strike would be followed by other forms of mass pressure to force the race maniacs who govern our beloved country to make way for a democratic government of the people, by the people and for the people. A full scale and countrywide campaign of non-co-operation with the Government will be launched immediately. The precise form of the contemplated action, its scope and dimensions and duration will be announced to you at the appropriate time.

At the present moment it is sufficient to say that we plan to make government impossible. Those who are voteless cannot be expected to continue paying taxes to a Government which is not responsible to them. People who live in poverty and starvation cannot be expected to pay exorbitant house rents to the Government and local authorities. We furnish the sinews of agriculture and industry. We produce the work of the gold mines, the diamonds and the coal, of the farms and industry, in return for miserable wages. Why should we continue enriching those who steal the products of our sweat and blood? Those who exploit us and refuse us the right to organise trade unions? Those who side with the Government when we stage peaceful demonstrations to assert our claims and aspirations? How can Africans serve on School Boards and Committees which are part of Bantu Education, a sinister scheme of the Nationalist Government to deprive the African people of real education in return for tribal education? Can Africans be expected to be content with serving on Advisory Boards and Bantu Authorities when the demand all over the Continent of Africa is for national independence and self government? Is it not an affront to the African people that the Government should now seek to extend Bantu Authorities to the cities, when people in the rural areas have refused to accept the same system and fought against it tooth and nail? Which African does not burn with indignation when thousands of our people are sent to gaol every month under the cruel pass laws? Why should we continue carrying these badges of slavery? Non-collaboration is a dynamic weapon. We must refuse. We must use it to send this Government to the grave. It must be used vigorously and without delay. The entire resources of the Black people must be mobilized to withdraw all co-operation with the Nationalist Government. Various forms of industrial and economic action will be employed to undermine the already tottering economy of the country. We will call upon the international bodies to expel South Africa and upon nations of the world to sever economic and diplomatic relations with the country.

I am informed that a warrant for my arrest has been issued, and that the police are looking for me. The National Action Council has given full and serious consideration to this question, and has sought the advice of many trusted friends and bodies and they have advised me not to surrender myself. I have accepted this advice, and will not give myself up to a Government I do not recognize. Any serious politician will realize that under present day conditions in this country, to seek for cheap martyrdom by handing myself to the police is naive and criminal. We have an important programme before us and it is important to carry it out very seriously and without delay.

I have chosen this latter course which is more difficult and which entails more risk and hardship than sitting in gaol. I have had to separate myself from my dear wife and children, from my mother and sisters to live as an outlaw in my own land. I have had to close my business, to abandon my profession, and live in poverty and misery, as many of my people are doing. I will continue to act as the spokesman of the National Action Council during the phase that is unfolding and in the tough struggles that lie ahead. I shall fight the Government side by side with you, inch by inch, and mile by mile, until victory is won. What are you going to do? Will you come along with us, or are you going to co-operate with the Government in its efforts to suppress the claims and aspirations of your own people? Or are you going to remain silent and neutral in a matter of life and death to my people, to our people? For my own part I have made my choice. I will not leave South Africa, nor will I surrender. Only through hardship, sacrifice and militant action can freedom be won. The struggle is my life. I will continue fighting for freedom until the end of my days.

Note: Printed in *We Accuse: The Trial of Nelson Mandela,* booklet published by the African National Congress (S.A.), London [n.d.], pages 14-16.

702

Document 64. *The Voice of the All-African Convention Vigilance Committee.*
Newsletter, July 1961

This is the first issue of "The Voice" since the rulers of this country replaced the Non-Whites' Union yoke with a Republican yoke. In this issue we intend to deal with the twin questions: (i) What sort of South Africa do we wish to build? and (ii) How do we propose to reach that goal? In other words, what is *OUR AIM,* and what are *OUR METHODS* of struggle?

As everybody knows, this is not the first time that we of the All-African Convention are asking these questions. We asked them in the days when the AAC was young. We asked them at the time when the issues of dummy representation in the N.R.C., Parliament, Provincial Council, Bungas and Advisory Boards, and the issue of solving the problem of land-hunger were knee-haltered by bad leadership and clouded by illusions about "lesser evils." We asked them, in a fresh and bold way, when the AAC, after years on the wrong path, turned to the *New Road of NON-COLLABORATION.* That was in the years 1943-44 when we combined with the Anti-CAD to form the Non-European Unity Movement on the basis of the 10-Point Programme: in the years when we tried to bring the S.A. Indian Congress into the NEUM on the basis of that Programme, but could not persuade it to accept the principle of the full franchise; in the years when the ANC, not only left the AAC, but tried to bury it so as to enable the ANC leadership to work dummy representation. Today, we of the AAC ask these questions as comrades of the Anti-CAD in the Unity Movement. And our special reason for asking them now is that there is a special need at the present time to remind people inside and outside the AAC of the *BASIC POLITICAL PRINCIPLES* of our Movement.

The first question: Official "Herrenvolk" policy aims at bringing about a state of affairs in which, at the top, there will be what it calls the "two white nations" consisting of what it calls the "two white races." These two "nations" or "races" will rest on a base made up of "Bantustans," "Kleurlingstan" and "Indistan" said to consist of "Bantu," "Coloured" and "Indian" "races". "A policy of good neighbourliness" through white and non-white puppets and parrots is supposed to preserve forever this top-bottom or master-servant relationship.

Our AAC and NEUM policy is completely opposed to this. We recognize only *ONE RACE,* and that is the *HUMAN RACE.* We stand for the building of *ONE* nation in South Africa, in which *ALL* people—no matter what real or imaginary physical, cultural, religious, etc., variations they may represent—are equal citizens *BECAUSE THEY ARE ALL MEMBERS OF THE ONE HUMAN RACE.*

This is the standpoint of the AAC and the Anti-CAD. This policy stands opposed to the policy of multi-racialism put forward by various sections of the ruling classes, who carve the population up into many "races". It also stands opposed to the policy of multi-nationalism put forward by the Congress Alliance, which carves the population up into many "nations". Likewise it rejects the poisonous rubbish of majority races or nations and minority races or nations. What it stands for is a S. Africa in which there are no artificial "race" or political categories such as "white", "non-white", "Bantu", "African", "Coloured", "Indian", but only *CITIZENS* and, on the other hand, those who are insane or incurably criminal.

In a world and on a Continent where things are moving at breathless speed, it is only too easy for people to accept less than minimum democratic rights. Again and again, nowadays, we see cases in so-called "independent" Africa where the leadership, in exchange for political office or formal independence or other bribes, forfeits basic principles as far as the mass are concerned, e.g., freedom from economic exploitation, actual and not mere legal equality. They replace direct imperialist domination by indirect imperialism. And nothing basically changes as far as the majority of poor, hungry, homeless, landless, rightless people are concerned. A look at Basutoland or N. Rhodesia or Tanganyika or Egypt or Ghana or Nigeria or Bechuanaland, etc. will show the truth of this. What *WE* are struggling for is full democratic rights for *ALL*. And the 10-Point Programme is our *MINIMUM FOR ALL*. Nothing less will satisfy.

The second question: The Political goal can never be separated from the political ways in which that goal is to be reached. The aims of the struggle are inseparable from the methods of struggle.

The truth of this we can check from our political experience and history. Sections of the Non-White oppressed which are always looking for exemptions or special treatment for their group are usually the sections from which collaborators or potential collaborators and agents are drawn. First, in the old days, when there was a "Cape Native" and "Cape Coloured" vote to sell to this or that political party, the methods of struggle consisted of lobbying, petitions, deputations, round-table talks, back-door deals and protesting against a Bill, but accepting and working it when it became an Act. It was thought that these methods would eventually bring about a "change of heart". Meanwhile, the so-called "lesser evil" was to be accepted and worked—collaboration in their own oppression. Second, nowadays, there are the quislings or collaborators who are working the "Bantu Authorities", the Advisory Boards, the Union Council of Coloured Affairs, the "Bantu" school boards and committees. They all pretend that they are "fighting from within." But, in fact, all they are doing is to see what they can get for themselves and the groups or sections they represent. This was the game played by the "Bantuised" Bunga at its last meeting in Umtata. This is the game played by all the hangers-on of the B.A.D. and C.A.D. when trying to get bus licences, trading and business rights, liquor licences etc.

But the basic lesson that the aims of the struggle cannot be separated from the methods of struggle applies not only to the political activities of collaborators past or present. It applies equally to all those who work or claim to work inside the liberatory movement. We of the AAC, as part of the Unity Movement, want to win the demands of the 10-Point Programme as our *MINIMUM* goal. We want it for *ALL,* without "civilization" tests or other discriminatory qualifications. Our methods seek to reach and organize the mass of the people that these are their fundamental rights and that their own, independent and organized strength must win those rights. Our methods are rooted in non-collaboration and the political use of the boycott as a major weapon of struggle. Which means that we have to enlighten a whole people politically, to teach them how to use their strength and not to waste it on dramatic stunts or half-baked schemes based on the hope that the rulers will notice them, will become sorry or scared and will throw a bone to quieten the excited dog. We have to harness and co-ordinate their organized talents and numbers and will be federating them into local committees in every village or town or district or city. These local federated units must work together on the basis of the 10-Point Programme, and as part of the larger federation, which is the AAC, which in turn is in the federation of the NEUM.

Our policy is based upon a whole people in movement to bring about a democracy for a whole people. That is why we have this organizational machinery for getting a whole people into unified and independent political activity on the basis of their day to day struggles ALL DIRECTED TOWARDS *THE* GOAL. That is why we are against episodes and stunts which are no more than shows or exhibitions. We say that all oppression and exploitation come from the same soil. Thus all the hundreds upon hundreds of different workings and applications of oppression and exploitation must be opposed and struggled against as part of the same thing coming from the same soil. If we were soldiers in an army, we would put it this way: we would say that each battle is an important battle and must be fought; but each battle is part of a whole war; and so each battle must be fought on the basis of the general strategy; if we started to look upon each battle as an end in itself, as the be-all-and-end-all, then we would waste our soldiers, resources.

We of the AAC and the Anti-CAD as part of the NEUM therefore say: we have to move, to mobilise all the organizations of the people to tackle all their local problems on the basis of our Programme and as part of our Movement. Whether it is a Vigilance or a Civic or a Workers' or Peasants' or Teachers' Association—all must be looked upon as units or squadrons or divisions of the same liberatory movement or army.

This is the task that must be tackled *NOW* with energy and determination. It is absolutely useless to sleep for most of the year or to pretend to work during the year or to claim credit for the struggles of people driven to revolt by sheer desperation, and then to call a Xmas Conference to puff up everyone. It is even more useless to call recklessly upon people to stay at home for 3 days or 7 days in the hope of thus bringing "Herrenvolkism" tumbling into the dust. It is suicidal to call for a political strike without political preparation and a *programme based on the needs and desires of the mass.* What is needed now is a serious and sustained effort to teach and organise the people in a struggle which will continue to be conducted against a desperate "Herrenvolk" State living in a chronic "state of emergency". The whole country must learn how to work politically under these conditions. Any policy or method of struggle which does not understand this is doomed to chronic frustration and failure.

Issued by: The Vigilance Committee of the All-African Convention. Secretary, C. M. Kobus, P.O. Box 3915, Cape Town. July, 1961.

Document 65. Nobel Peace Prize Address by Chief A. J. Lutuli, December 11, 1961

In years gone by, some of the greatest men of our century have stood here to receive this Award, men whose names and deeds have enriched the pages of human history, men whom future generations will regard as having shaped the world of our time. No one could be left unmoved to be plucked from the village of Groutville, a name many of you have never heard before and which does not even feature on many maps—to be plucked from banishment in a rural backwater, to be lifted out of the narrow confines of South Africa's internal politics and be placed here in the shadow of these great figures. It is a great honour to me to stand on this rostrum where many of the great men of our times have stood before.

The Nobel Peace Award that has brought me here has for me a threefold significance. On the one hand it is a tribute to my humble contribution to efforts by democrats on both sides of the colour line to find a peaceful solution to the race problem. This contribution is not in any way unique. I did not initiate the struggle to extend the area of human freedom in South Africa; other African patriots—devoted men—did so before me. I also, as a Christian and patriot, could not look on while systematic attempts were made, almost in every department of life, to debase the God-factor in Man or to set a limit beyond which the human being in his black form might not strive to serve his Creator to the best of his ability. To remain neutral in a situation where the laws of the land virtually criticised God for having created men of colour was the sort of thing I could not, as a Christian, tolerate.

On the other hand the Award is a democratic declaration of solidarity with those who fight to widen the area of liberty in my part of the world. As such, it is the sort of gesture which gives me and millions who think as I do, tremendous encouragement. There are still people in the world today who regard South Africa's race problem as a simple clash between black and white. Our government has carefully projected this image of the problem before the eyes of the world. This has had two effects. It has confused the real issues at stake in the race crisis. It has given some form of force to the government's contention that the race problem is a domestic matter for South Africa. This, in turn, has tended to narrow down the area over which our case could be better understood in the world.

From yet another angle, it is a welcome recognition of the role played by the African people during the last fifty years to establish, peacefully, a society in which merit and not race, would fix the position of the individual in the life of the nation.

This Award could not be for me alone, nor for just South Africa, but for Africa as a whole. Africa presently is most deeply torn with strife and most bitterly stricken with racial conflict. How strange, then, it is that a man of Africa should be here to receive an Award given for service to the cause of peace and brotherhood between men. There has been little peace in Africa in our time. From the northernmost end of our continent, where war has raged for seven years, to the centre and to the south there are battles being fought out, some with arms, some without. In my own country, in the year 1960 for which this Award is given, there was a state of emergency for many months. At Sharpeville, a small village, in a single afternoon 69 people were shot dead and 180 wounded by small arms fire; and in parts like the Transkei, a state of emergency is still continuing. Ours is a continent in revolution against oppression. And peace and revolution make uneasy bedfellows. There can be no peace until the forces of oppression are overthrown.

Our continent has been carved up by the great powers; alien governments have been forced upon the African people by military conquest and by economic domination; strivings of nationhood and national dignity have been beaten down by force; traditional economies and ancient customs have been disrupted, and human skills and energy have been harnessed for the advantage of our conquerors. In these times there has been no peace; there could be no brotherhood between men.

By now, the revolutionary stirrings of our continent are setting the past aside. Our people everywhere from north to south of the continent are reclaiming their land, their right to participate in government, their dignity as men, their nationhood. Thus, in the turmoil of revolution, the basis for peace and brotherhood in Africa is being restored by the resurrection of national sovereignty and independence, of equality and the dignity of man.

It should not be difficult for you here in Europe to appreciate this. Your continent passed through a longer series of revolutionary upheavals, in which your age of feudal backwardness gave way to the new age of industrialisation, true nationhood, democracy and rising living standards—the golden age for which men have striven for generations. Your age of revolution, stretching across all the years from the 18th Century to our own, encompassed some of the bloodiest civil wars in all history. By comparison, the African revolution has swept across three quarters of the continent in less than a decade; its final completion is within sight of our own generation. Again, by comparison with Europe, our African revolution—to our credit— is proving to be orderly, quick and comparatively bloodless.

This fact of the relative peacefulness of our African revolution is attested to by other observers of eminence. Professor C. W. de Kiewiet, President of the Rochester University, U.S.A., in a Hoernle Memorial Lecture for 1960, has this to say: "There has, it is true, been almost no serious violence in the achievement of political self-rule. In that sense there is no revolution in Africa—only reform."

Professor D. V. Cowen, then Professor of Comparative Law at the University of Cape Town, South Africa, in a Hoernle Memorial Lecture for 1961, throws light on the nature of our struggle in the following words: "They (the Whites in South Africa) are, again, fortunate in the very high moral calibre of the non-White inhabitants of South Africa, who compare favorably with any on the whole continent." Let this never be forgotten by those who so eagerly point a finger of scorn at Africa.

Perhaps by your standards, our surge to revolutionary reforms is late. If it is so—if we are late in joining the modern age of social enlightenment, late in gaining self-rule, independence and democracy, it is because in the past the pace has not been set by us. Europe set the pattern for the 19th and 20th Century development of Africa. Only now is our continent coming into its own and recapturing its own fate from foreign rule.

Though I speak of Africa as a single entity, it is divided in many ways—by race, language, history and custom; by political, economic and ethnic frontiers. But in truth, despite these multiple divisions, Africa has a single common purpose and a single goal—the achievement of its own independence. All Africa, both lands which have won their political victories, but have still to overcome the legacy of economic backwardness, and lands like my own whose political battles have still to be waged to their conclusion—all Africa has this single aim; our goal is a united Africa in which the standards of life and liberty are constantly expanding; in which the ancient legacy of illiteracy and disease is swept aside, in which the dignity of man is rescued from beneath the heels of colonialism which have trampled it. This goal, pursued by millions of our people with revolutionary zeal, by means of books, representations, demonstrations, and in some places armed force provoked by the adamancy of white rule, carries the only real promise of peace in Africa. Whatever means have been used, the efforts have gone to end alien rule and race oppression.

There is a paradox in the fact that Africa qualifies for such an Award in its age of turmoil and revolution. How great is the paradox and how much greater the honour that an Award in support of peace and the brotherhood of man should come to one who is a citizen of a country where the brotherhood of man is an illegal doctrine, outlawed, banned, censured, proscribed and prohibited; where to work, talk or campaign for the realization in fact and deed of the brotherhood of man is hazardous, punished with banishment, or confinement without trial, or imprisonment; where effective democratic channels to peaceful settlement of the race problem have never existed these 300 years; and where white minority power rests on the most heavily armed and equipped military machine in Africa. This is South Africa.

Even here, where white rule seems determined not to change its mind for the better, the spirit of Africa's militant struggle for liberty, equality and independence asserts itself. I, together with thousands of my countrymen, have in the course of the struggle for these ideals, been harassed, and imprisoned, but we are not deterred in our quest for a new age in which we shall live in peace and in brotherhood.

It is not necessary for me to speak at length about South Africa; its social system, its politics, its economics and its laws have forced themselves on the attention of the world. It is a museum piece in our time, a hangover from the dark past of mankind, a relic of an age which everywhere else is dead or dying. Here the cult of race superiority and of white supremacy is worshipped like a god. Few white people escape corruption and many of their children learn to believe that white men are unquestionably superior, efficient, clever, industrious and capable; that black men are, equally unquestionably, inferior, slothful, stupid, evil and clumsy. On the basis of the mythology that "the lowest amongst them is higher than the highest amongst us," it is claimed that white men build everything that is worthwhile in the country; its cities, its industries, its mines and its agriculture, and that they alone are thus fitted and entitled as of right to own and control these things, whilst black men are only temporary sojourners in these cities, fitted only for menial labour, and unfit to share political power. The Prime Minister of South Africa, Dr. Verwoerd, then Minister of Bantu Affairs, when explaining his government's policy on African education had this to say: "There is no place for him (the African) in the European community above the level of certain forms of labour."

There is little new in this mythology. Every part of Africa which has been subject to white conquest has, at one time or another, and in one guise or another, suffered from it, even in its virulent form of the slavery that obtained in Africa up to the 19th Century.

The mitigating feature in the gloom of those far-off days was the shaft of light sunk by Christian missions, a shaft of light to which we owe our initial enlightenment. With successive governments of the time doing little or nothing to ameliorate the harrowing suffering of the black man at the hands of slavedrivers, men like Dr. David Livingstone and Dr. John Philip and other illustrious men of God stood for social justice in the face of overwhelming odds. It is worth noting that the names I have referred to are still anathema to some South Africans. Hence the ghost of slavery lingers on to this day in the form of forced labour that goes on in what are called farm prisons. But the tradition of Livingstone and Philip lives on, perpetuated by a few of their line. It is fair to say that even in present day conditions, Christian missions have been in the vanguard of initiating social services provided for us. Our progress in this field has been in spite of, and not mainly because of the government. In this the Church in South Africa—though belatedly—seems to be awakening to a broader mission of the Church, in its ministry among us. It is beginning to take seriously the words of its Founder who said "I came that they might have life and have it more abundantly."

This is a call to the Church in South Africa to help in the all-round development of MAN in the present, and not only in the hereafter. In this regard, the people of South Africa, especially those who claim to be Christians, would be well advised to take heed of the Conference decisions of the World Council of Churches held at Cottesloe, Johannesburg, in 1960, which gave a clear lead on the mission of the Church in our day. It left no room for doubt about the relevancy of the Christian message in the present issues that confront mankind. I note with gratitude this broader outlook of the World Council of Churches. It has a great meaning and significance for us in Africa.

There is nothing new in South Africa's *apartheid* ideas, but South Africa is unique in this: the ideas not only survive in our modern age, but are stubbornly defended, extended and bolstered up by legislation at the time when in the major part of the world they are now largely historical and are either being shamefacedly hidden behind concealing formulations, or are being steadily scrapped. These ideas survive in South Africa because those who sponsor them profit from them. They provide moral whitewash for the conditions which exist in the country: for the fact that the country is ruled exclusively by a white government elected by an exclusively white electorate which is a privileged minority; for the fact that 87 per cent of the land and all the best agricultural land within reach of town, market and railways is reserved for white ownership and occupation and now through the recent Group Areas legislation non-Whites are losing more land to white greed; for the fact that all skilled and highly-paid jobs are for whites only; for the fact that all universities of any academic merit are an exclusive preserve of whites; for the fact that the education of every white child costs about £64 p.a. whilst that of an African child costs about £9 p.a. and that of an Indian child or Coloured child costs about £20 p.a.; for the fact that white education is universal and compulsory up to the age of 16, whilst education for the non-white children is scarce and inadequate, and for the fact that almost one million Africans a year are arrested and gaoled or fined for breaches of innumerable pass and permit laws which do not apply to whites.

I could carry on in this strain, and talk on every facet of South African life from the cradle to the grave. But these facts today are becoming known to all the world. A fierce spotlight of world attention has been thrown on them. Try as our government and its apologists will, with honeyed words about "separate development" and eventual "independence" in so-called "Bantu homelands," nothing can conceal the reality of South African conditions.

I, as a Christian, have always felt that there is one thing above all about "*apartheid*" or "separate development" that is unforgivable. It seems utterly indifferent to the suffering of individual persons, who lose their land, their homes, their jobs, in the pursuit of what is surely the most terrible dream in the world. This terrible dream is not held on to by a crackpot group on the fringe of society, or by Ku-Klux Klansmen, of whom we have a sprinkling. It is the deliberate policy of a government, supported actively by a large part of the white population, and tolerated passively by an overwhelming white majority, but now fortunately rejected by an encouraging white minority who have thrown their lot with non-whites who are overwhelmingly opposed to so-called separate development.

Thus it is that the golden age of Africa's independence is also the dark age of South Africa's decline and retrogression, brought about by men who, when revolutionary changes that entrenched fundamental human rights were taking place in Europe, were closed in on the tip of South Africa—and so missed the wind of progressive change.

In the wake of that decline and retrogression, bitterness between men grows to alarming heights; the economy declines as confidence ebbs away; unemployment rises; government becomes increasingly dictatorial and intolerant of constitutional and legal procedures, increasingly violent and suppressive; there is a constant drive for more policemen, more soldiers, more armaments, banishments without trial and penal whippings. All the trappings of medieval backwardness and cruelty come to the fore. Education is being reduced to an instrument of subtle indoctrination. Slanted and biased reporting in the organs of public information, a creeping censorship, book-banning and black-listing—all these spread their shadows over the land. This is South Africa today, in the age of Africa's greatness.

But beneath the surface there is a spirit of defiance. The people of South Africa have never been a docile lot, least of all the African people. We have a long tradition of struggle for our national rights, reaching back to the very beginnings of white settlement and conquest 300 years ago.

Our history is one of opposition to domination, of protest and refusal to submit to tyranny. Consider some of our great names; the great warrior and nation-builder Shaka, who welded tribes together into the Zulu nation from which I spring; Moshoeshoe, the statesman and nation-builder who fathered the Basuto nation and placed Basutoland beyond the reach of the claws of the South African whites; Hintsa of the Xhosas who chose death rather than surrender his territory to white invaders. All these and other royal names, as well as other great chieftains, resisted manfully white intrusion.

Consider also the sturdiness of the stock that nurtured the foregoing great names. I refer to our forebears, who in the trekking from the north to the southernmost tip of Africa centuries ago braved rivers that are perennially swollen; hacked their way through treacherous jungle and forest; survived the plagues of the then untamed lethal diseases of a multifarious nature that abounded in Equatorial Africa and wrested themselves from the gaping mouths of the beasts of prey. They endured it all. They settled in these parts of Africa to build a future worth while for us their offspring.

Whilst the social and political conditions have changed and the problems we face are different, we too, their progeny, find ourselves facing a situation where we have to struggle for our very survival as human beings. Although methods of struggle may differ from time to time, the universal human strivings for liberty remain unchanged. We, in our situation, have chosen the path of non-violence of our own volition. Along this path we have organised many heroic campaigns. All the strength of progressive leadership in South Africa, all my life and strength, has been given to the pursuance of this method, in an attempt to avert disaster in the interests of South Africa, and [they] have bravely paid the penalties for it.

It may well be that South Africa's social system is a monument to racialism and race oppression, but its people are the living testimony to the unconquerable spirit of mankind. Down the years, against seemingly overwhelming odds, they have sought the goal of fuller life and liberty, striving with incredible determination and fortitude for the right to live as men—free men.

In this, our country is not unique. Your recent and inspiring history, when the Axis Powers over-ran most European States, is testimony of this unconquerable spirit of mankind. People of Europe formed Resistance Movements that finally helped to break the power of the combination of Nazism and Fascism with their creed of race arrogance and herrenvolk mentality.

Every people have, at one time or another in their history, been plunged into such struggle. But generally the passing of time has seen the barriers to freedom going down, one by one. Not so in South Africa. Here the barriers do not go down. Each step we take forward, every achievement we chalk up, is cancelled out by the raising of new and higher barriers to our advance. The colour bars do not get weaker; they get stronger. The bitterness of the struggle mounts as liberty comes step by step closer to the freedom fighter's grasp. All too often, the protests and demonstrations of our people have been beaten back by force; but they have never been silenced.

Through all this cruel treatment in the name of law and order, our people, with a few exceptions, have remained non-violent. If today this peace Award is given to South Africa through a black man, it is not because we in South Africa have won our fight for peace and human brotherhood. Far from it. Perhaps we stand farther from victory than any other people in Africa. But nothing which we have suffered at the hands of the government has turned us from our chosen path of disciplined resistance. It is for this, I believe, that this Award is given.

How easy it would have been in South Africa for the natural feelings of resentment at white domination to have been turned into feelings of hatred and a desire for revenge against the white community. Here, where every day in every aspect of life, every non-white comes up against the ubiquitous sign "Europeans Only," and the equally ubiquitous policeman to enforce it—here it could well be expected that a racialism equal to that of their oppressors would flourish to counter the white arrogance towards blacks. That it has not done so is no accident. It is because, deliberately and advisedly, African leadership for the past 50 years, with the inspiration of the African National Congress which I had the honour to lead for the last decade or so until it was banned, had set itself steadfastly against racial vaingloriousness.

We knew that in so doing we passed up opportunities for easy demogogic appeal to the natural passions of a people denied freedom and liberty; we discarded the chance of an easy and expedient emotional appeal. Our vision has always been that of a non-racial democratic South Africa which upholds the rights of all who live in our country to remain there as full citizens with equal rights and responsibilities with all others. For the consummation of this ideal we have laboured unflinchingly. We shall continue to labour unflinchingly.

It is this vision which prompted the African National Congress to invite members of other racial groups who believe with us in the brotherhood of man and in the freedom of all people to join with us in establishing a non-racial democratic South Africa. Thus the African National Congress in its day brought about the Congress Alliance and welcomed the emergence of the Liberal Party and the Progressive Party, who to an encouraging measure support these ideals.

The true patriots of South Africa, for whom I speak, will be satisfied with nothing less than the fullest democratic rights. In government we will not be satisfied with anything less than direct individual adult suffrage and the right to stand for and be elected to all organs of government. In economic matters we will be satisfied with nothing less than equality of opportunity in every sphere, and the enjoyment by all of those heritages which form the resources of the country which up to now have been appropriated on a racial "whites only" basis. In culture we will be satisfied with nothing less than the opening of all doors of learning to non-segregatory institutions on the sole criterion of ability. In the social sphere we will be satisfied with nothing less than the abolition of all racial bars.

We do not demand these things for people of African descent alone. We demand them for all South Africans, white and black. On these principles we are uncompromising. To compromise would be an expediency that is most treacherous to democracy, for in the turn of events the sweets of economic, political and social privileges that are a monopoly of only one section of a community turn sour even in the mouths of those who eat them. Thus *apartheid* in practice is proving to be a monster created by Frankenstein. That is the tragedy of the South African scene.

Many spurious slogans have been invented in our country in an effort to redeem uneasy race relations—"trusteeship," "separate development," "race federation" and elsewhere "partnership." These are efforts to side-track us from the democratic road, mean delaying tactics that fool no one but the unwary. No euphemistic naming will ever hide their hideous nature. We reject these policies because they do not measure up to the best mankind has striven for throughout the ages; they do great offence to man's sublime aspirations that have remained true in a sea of flux and change down the ages, aspirations of which the United Nations Declaration of Human Rights is a culmination. This is what we stand for. This is what we fight for.

In their fight for lasting values, there are many things that have sustained the spirit of the freedom-loving people of South Africa and those in the yet unredeemed parts of Africa where the white man claims resolutely proprietary rights over democracy—a universal heritage. High amongst them—the things that have sustained us, stand the magnificent support of the progressive people and governments throughout the world, amongst whom number the people and government of the country of which I am today guest; our brothers in Africa; especially in the Independent African States; organizations who share the outlook we embrace in countries scattered right across the face of the globe; the United Nations Organization jointly and some of its member-nations singly. In their defence of peace in the world through actively upholding the equality of man, all these groups have reinforced our undying faith in the unassailable rightness and justness of our cause.

To all of them I say: Alone we would have been weak. Our heartfelt appreciation of your acts of support of us, we cannot adequately express, nor can we ever forget; now or in the future when victory is behind us, and South Africa's freedom rests in the hands of all her people.

We South Africans, however, equally understand that much as others might do for us, our freedom cannot come to us as a gift from abroad. Our freedom we must make ourselves. All honest freedom-loving people have dedicated themselves to that task. What we need is the courage that rises with danger.

Whatever may be the future of our freedom efforts, our cause is the cause of the liberation of people who are denied freedom. Only on this basis can the peace of Africa and the world be firmly founded. Our cause is the cause of equality between nations and people. Only thus can the brotherhood of man be firmly established. It is encouraging and elating to remind you that despite her humiliation and torment at the hands of white rule, the spirit of Africa in quest for freedom has been, generally, for peaceful means to the utmost.

If I have dwelt at length on my country's race problem, it is not as though other countries on our continent do not labour under these problems, but because it is here in the Republic of South Africa that the race problem is most acute. Perhaps in no other country on the continent is white supremacy asserted with greater vigour and determination and a sense of righteousness. This places the opponents of *apartheid* in the front rank of those who fight white domination.

In bringing my address to a close, let me invite Africa to cast her eyes beyond the past and to some extent the present with their woes and tribulations, trials and failures, and some successes, and see herself an emerging continent, bursting to freedom through the shell of centuries of serfdom. This is Africa's age—the dawn of her fulfilment, yes, the moment when she must grapple with destiny to reach the summits of sublimity saying—ours was a fight for noble values and worthy ends, and not for lands and the enslavement of man.

Africa is a vital subject matter in the world of today, a focal point of world interest and concern. Could it not be that history has delayed her rebirth for a purpose? The situation confronts her with inescapable challenges, but more importantly with opportunities for service to herself and mankind. She evades the challenges and neglects the opportunities to her shame, if not her doom. How she sees her destiny is a more vital and rewarding quest than bemoaning her past with its humiliations and sufferings.

The address could do no more than pose some questions and leave it to the African leaders and peoples to provide satisfying answers and responses by their concern for higher values and by their noble actions that could be

> ". . . footprints on the sands of time;
> "Footprints, that perhaps another,
> Sailing o'er life's solemn main,
> A forlorn and shipwrecked brother,
> Seeing shall take heart again."

Still licking the scars of past wrongs perpetrated on her, could she not be magnanimous and practise no revenge? Her hand of friendship scornfully rejected, her pleas for justice and fair-play spurned, should she not nonetheless seek to turn enmity to amity? Though robbed of her lands, her independence and opportunities—this, oddly enough, often in the name of civilization and even Christianity—should she not see her destiny as being that of making a distinctive contribution to human progress and human relationships with a peculiar new African flavour enriched by the diversity of cultures she enjoys, thus building on the summits of present human achievement an edifice that would be one of the finest tributes to the genius of man?

She should see this hour of her fulfillment as a challenge to her to labour on until she is purged of racial domination, and as an opportunity of reassuring the world that her national aspiration lies, not in overthrowing white domination to replace it by a black caste, but in building a non-racial democracy that shall be a monumental brotherhood, a "brotherly community" with none discriminated against on grounds of race or colour.

What of the many pressing and complex political, economic and cultural problems attendant upon the early years of a newly-independent State? These, and others which are the legacy of colonial days, will tax to the limit the statesmanship, ingenuity, altruism and steadfastness of African leadership and its unbending avowal to democratic tenets in statecraft. To us all, free or not free, the call of the hour is to redeem the name and honour of Mother Africa.

In a strife-torn world, tottering on the brink of complete destruction by man-made nuclear weapons, a free and independent Africa is in the making, in answer to the injunction and challenge of history: "Arise and shine for thy light is come." Acting in concert with other nations, she is man's last hope for a mediator between the East and West, and is qualified to demand of the great powers to "turn the swords into plough-shares" because two-thirds of mankind is hungry and illiterate; to engage human energy, human skill and human talent in the service of peace, for the alternative is unthinkable—war, destruction and desolation; and to build a world community which will stand as a lasting monument to the millions of men and women, to such devoted and distinguished world citizens and fighters for peace as the late Dag Hammarskjold, who have given their lives that we may live in happiness and peace.

Africa's qualification for this noble task is incontestable, for her own fight has never been and is not now a fight for conquest of land, for accumulation of wealth or domination of peoples, but for the recognition and preservation of the rights of man and the establishment of a truly free world for a free people.

Note: The text above is almost identical with the text in publication No. 22/69, December 10, 1969, of the Unit on Apartheid of the United Nations: *Chief Albert J. Luthuli: Statements and Addresses*, pages 12–21. Virtually the same text appeared in *New Age*, December 14, 1961. Extracts were published in the *New York Times* and *The Times* (London) on December 12, 1961.

Document 66. *"Umkonto We Sizwe"* (Spear of the Nation). Flyer "issued by command of *Umkonto We Sizwe"* and appearing on December 16, 1961

Units of Umkonto We Sizwe today carried out planned attacks against Government installations, particularly those connected with the policy of apartheid and race discrimination.

Umkonto We Sizwe is a new, independent body, formed by Africans. It includes in its ranks South Africans of all races. It is not connected in any way with a so-called "Committee for National Liberation" whose existence has been announced in the press. Umkonto We Sizwe will carry on the struggle for freedom and democracy by new methods, which are necessary to complement the actions of the established national liberation organizations. Umkonto We Sizwe fully supports the national liberation movement, and our members, jointly and individually, place themselves under the overall political guidance of that movement.

It is, however, well known that the main national liberation organizations in this country have consistently followed a policy of non-violence. They have conducted themselves peaceably at all times, regardless of Government attacks and persecutions upon them, and despite all Government-inspired attempts to provoke them to violence. They have done so because the people prefer peaceful methods of change to achieve their aspirations without the suffering and bitterness of civil war. But the people's patience is not endless.

The time comes in the life of any nation when there remain only two choices: submit or fight. That time has now come to South Africa. We shall not submit and we have no choice but to hit back by all means within our power in defence of our people, our future and our freedom.

The Government has interpreted the peacefulness of the movement as weakness; the people's non-violent policies have been taken as a green light for Government violence. Refusal to resort to force has been interpreted by the Government as an invitation to use armed force against the people without any fear of reprisals. The methods of Umkonto We Sizwe mark a break with that past.

We are striking out along a new road for the liberation of the people of this country. The Government policy of force, repression and violence will no longer be met with nonviolent resistance only! The choice is not ours; it has been made by the Nationalist Government which has rejected every peaceable demand by the people for rights and freedom and answered every such demand with force and yet more force! Twice in the past 18 months, virtual martial law has been imposed in order to beat down peaceful, non-violent strike action of the people in support of their rights. It is now preparing its forces—enlarging and rearming its armed forces and drawing white civilian population into commandos and pistol clubs—for full-scale military actions against the people. The Nationalist Government has chosen the course of force and massacre, now, deliberately, as it did at Sharpeville.

Umkonto We Size will be at the front line of the people's defence. It will be the fighting arm of the people against the Government and its policies of race oppression. It will be the striking force of the people for liberty, for rights and for their final liberation! Let the Government, its supporters who put it into power, and those whose passive toleration of reaction keeps it in power, take note of where the Nationalist Government is leading the country!

We of Umkonto We Sizwe have always sought—as the liberation movement has sought—to achieve liberation, without bloodshed and civil clash. We do so still. We hope—even at this late hour—that our first actions will awaken everyone to a realization of the disastrous situation to which the Nationalist policy is leading. We hope that we will bring the Government and its supporters to their senses before it is too late, so that both Government and its policies can be changed before matters reach the desperate stage of civil war. We believe our actions to be a blow against the Nationalist preparations for civil war and military rule.

In these actions, we are working in the best interests of all the people of this country—black, brown and white—whose future happiness and well-being cannot be attained without the overthrow of the Nationalist Government, the abolition of white supremacy and the winning of liberty, democracy and full national rights and equality for all the people of this country.

We appeal for the support and encouragement of all those South Africans who seek the happiness and freedom of the people of this country.

Afrika Mayibuye!

Issued by command of Umkonto We Sizwe.

Note: Printed in *The Times* (London), December 28, 1961.

Document 67. Presidential Address by I. B. Tabata, African People's Democratic Union of Southern Africa, April 1962 [Extracts]

This is the first National Conference of the African People's Democratic Union of Southern Africa, which was founded at the beginning of last year. The name itself is aptly chosen. Anyone approaching the organisation sees writ large on its banners the central theme of its programme. The organisation stands firstly for democracy for all those who accept this country as their home and therefore regard themselves as Africans. Every human being who lives in this country and contributes to its welfare is a citizen and is therefore entitled to an equal say in the Government and management of the affairs of the country. In short, he is entitled to full democratic rights.

Clause (c) of the Constitution states one of the aims of this organisation as follows: "To struggle for the liquidation of national oppression of the oppressed people in Southern Africa, that is, the removal of all disabilities and restrictions based on grounds of race and colour and acquisition by the whole nation of those democratic rights enjoyed at present by only a small section of the population, namely the white people."

The programme "shall be the Ten Point Programme of the Non-European Unity Movement as laid down by the founding Conference of the N.E.U.M. in December, 1943."

This, then, puts A.P.D.U.S.A. fairly and squarely within the fold of the N.E.U.M. As a child of the Unity Movement it inherits the policy of non-collaboration with the oppressor, and the boycott as a weapon of struggle. It inherits also the traditions of the Unity Movement, its intransigence in matters of policy, its unflagging devotion to principles. It treasures the experiences of the Unity Movement accumulated over the years of hard struggle. In the coming battles A.P.D.U.S.A. will draw from the arsenal of ideas of the parent body, but, like all children who grow up under the tutelage of their parents, A.P.D.U.S.A. must expect and prepare itself for situations that have not been met before by the parent body. For this reason APDUSANS must steep themselves in the fundamental ideas and the guiding principles of the Unity Movement; for only thus will it be able to face up to the new situation.

From the start I would like to warn Conference that this address may seem rather sweeping in scope and not coming down to the day to day problems that face the people. This is deliberate. We have recently held a Conference of the Unity Movement in which all the burning questions of the day were dealt with. I have been made to understand that the papers read at the Conference are going to be published, if not separately, at least in the minutes. Since A.P.D.U.S.A. was part of that conference and will receive its share of the minutes, I deem it not only unnecessary but wasteful to cover the same ground. In addition to this, the address has attempted to avoid forestalling the papers that will be read in this Conference. In view of these considerations I have decided to limit myself to directing the thoughts of Conference towards certain aspects of our political life in the country. The central theme of this address is chosen to bring home to the membership the importance, the vital importance, of those classes who are generally accorded a lowly status in society, the toiling masses who carry society on their backs. Clause (c) of our Constitution, under "programme and policy", states:

"The democratic demands and aspirations of the oppressed workers and peasants shall be paramount in the orientation of A.P.D.U.S.A. in both its short term and its long term objectives." This is the first time to my knowledge that such a clause has been included in the Constitution of any organisations in the Unity Movement. This alone marks a development in the outlook of the Movement and in a way also reflects the time we are living in. If this address should succeed in illuminating the full meaning of this clause, I shall be satisfied.

A.P.D.U.S.A. is born during a time of crisis. If it is to survive it will have to learn not only to adapt itself to the present conditions but to develop such foresight as to be able to anticipate events and adjust itself accordingly. This presupposes a knowledge of the various forces at work and therefore of the environment in which it has to live. Social crises are not accidental phenomena. They follow certain laws that govern the development of men as social beings. They are part and parcel of the evolutionary process of mankind.

. . . .

If APDUSANS take their work seriously, they will have to realise that politics is a full-time job. It is not enough to go around organising the people, though this in itself is very important; but they themselves have to find time to study. Politics is a science and those who do not understand this are lost; for they are unable to know what is involved in the events taking place before their eyes. Science gives us conceptual tools to predict the future and it is this ability to predict that will enable us to survive. In a time of social ferment many organisations spring up, society becomes prolific in producing its political offsprings, but then the mortality rate also rises steeply. Many of them die out and only those that are furnished with the proper means of adaptability survive. In other words, only those organisations that arm themselves with the correct theory are able to live on and assist in guiding the struggle of the people towards a higher plane. We are at this moment living through that state of ferment.

Where capitalism is faced with an acute crisis it tends to move towards a totalitarian dictatorship: But a totalitarian régime of the fascist type is a condition of an unstable régime. By its very essence it can only be temporal and transitional. Naked dictatorship is a symptom of a severe social crisis. Society cannot exist permanently under a state of crisis. A totalitarian state is capable of suppressing social contradictions during a certain period, but it is incapable of perpetuating itself. A ruling class, like a wounded lion, becomes more vicious as it feels itself drawing near to its extinction. The more vicious it becomes, the more monstrous its laws against the oppressed, all the more insecure it must feel. The very condition of an acute social crisis means that the forces operating in society can no longer be accommodated within it. It is time to change the old social relationships. Only that class that is called upon to do so, by virtue of its historical role, can help to solve such a crisis. In this country it is the toiling masses, who are in the main the Non-European oppressed, those millions of workers and peasants toiling on the land, in the mines and in the factories, who are destined to lead this country out of the crisis and create a more rational social order. It is they who create the civilization and lay the basis for a cultural development. They, by virtue of their contribution, should be accorded their rightful place of dignity and worth in society. They should participate in the governing of the country for which they have done and continue to do so much. Without their labour all this magnificence, all this spectacular development, this wealth and progress would have been impossible.

. . . .

The point we are making is that labour and labour alone, whether it be manual, intellectual or technical, is the creator of wealth and civilization. Only those who are actively engaged in the complex of production, administration and research are necessary to human progress. The rest are drones and parasites that feed on society.

We are now in a position to see by looking into the past what labour has done for mankind. Let us now turn our attention to our own country, the Union of South Africa. It was mainly the labour of the Non-Whites that transformed the economy of the country in a short space of time from a pastoral agricultural economy to a mining economy, which in turn gave birth to an industrial economy. The curious thing in our country is that, while industrialism has taken root, the social relations insofar as the Non-Whites are concerned are those of a feudal economy. While the Non-Europeans have contributed a lion's share in creating wealth and civilization in this country, the herrenvolk have excluded them from enjoying the fruits of their own labour. Flying in the face of history, they are at this moment desperately trying to legislate into being a dead and long-buried tribalism or barbarism.

. . . .

In short, then, the manufacturing industry in this country is running at a loss insofar as external balance of trade is concerned. That is to say, it is unable to stand on its own feet. Yet, insofar as society internally is concerned, it is the manufacturing industry that provides the biggest national income, the bulk of which goes to the White section of the population, who constitute a minority in the country. It is from it that the extravagant salaries are paid to the Cabinet Ministers and Parliamentarians. It is from it that the luxurious buildings and other luxuries are paid for the whole army of functionaries and other hangers-on. It is this that pays for the amenities of Whites-only, grand holiday resorts for Whites-only, swimming pools, civic centres, entertainment and other luxuries for Whites-only. In short, it is out of this income that the Whites are afforded an artificially high standard of living, while the great majority, the Non-Whites, are languishing in poverty and are perishing from preventable diseases, because they earn less than a living wage.

. . . .

Long before Verwoerd came to South Africa, Imperialism had mapped out a political and social order that would maintain and perpetuate the existing economic structure. Every herrenvolk Government is charged with the duty of protecting the mining industry as the primary industry round which others revolve. All laws passed by every parliament of the herrenvolk had to bear this in mind. Goldmining consumes a terrific amount of unskilled labour; therefore Parliament had to see to it that the whole of the Non-White population, from which this labour is drawn, was kept mainly illiterate or semi-literate. This became the policy of every successive Government since Union.

. . . .

The point we are making is that without a radical alteration of the socio-economic set-up in this country, it is not possible for any herrenvolk Government to depart from the so-called traditional policy, whether it is called apartheid, segregation, multi-racialism or any other name. For it is not the names that politicians give to their policies that matter, nor is it the smooth oily tongues or vulgar formulations that decide the issue. It is the hard economic factors that dictate the policy and the programme of the Government in power. Those woolly-minded Non-European politicians who fail to grasp this fact will always remain abject sycophants of this or that section of the herrenvolk. Those simpletons who cry nostalgically for the return of the United Party days on the ground of the "lesser evil" reveal an abysmal ignorance of the forces at work. If the "lesser evil" of yesterday were in power today, under the pressure of the prevailing urgent problems, it would long ago have transformed itself into the "greater evil". That is why it is so ludicrous to see some Non-European intellectuals and politicians denouncing the Nationalist Party and in the same breath appealing to and even aligning themselves with the United Party and the ex-U.P. now organised as Progressive and Liberal Parties. It is tantamount to appealing to the old Nationalist Party of more peaceful days as against the present-day Verwoerdian Party, as though there were any intrinsic difference between the two.

. . . .

South Africa is divided into three main political camps. The two herrenvolk camps having the same aims, differ in their methods of achieving those aims. The third camp, i.e. the oppressed, is fundamentally opposed to the other two. The divisions amongst the local herrenvolk are sharpened by external events which flow from the larger war between capitalism and socialism. This war takes many forms. It sometimes breaks out into a shooting war limited in scope and at other times it shifts back to the "cold war" in its various aspects, economic, political, and with threats of nuclear warfare.

Both sides are preparing for an all-out war which will settle the dispute between the two systems. In these preparations each side is trying to win over as allies the so-called uncommitted countries, and this is of the very essence of the "cold war". The United Nations' Organisation as a public forum reflects the maneuverings of the two camps and affords the world an opportunity of gauging the varying fortunes in the battle for the so-called uncommitted countries. The West finds itself with certain definite disadvantages. All the emergent States still remember the centuries of oppression and humiliation to which they were subjected by Western Imperialism. To them colonialism is not yet dead. Every act on the part of the Western powers is watched with grave suspicion. The colonial and ex-colonial peoples have not forgotten the feel of the whiplash administered by those same people who today offer the hand of friendship. The Socialist East presses home its point of vantage. It accuses the West of hypocrisy. It argues that imperialism has not changed and cannot change its rapacious nature. If it can no longer afford to hold down its colonial policies by force, it will enslave its colonial people by economic means. It was imperialism in its hunt for super-profits that originally introduced the colour-bar and placed a stigma on all people of colour. It was imperialism that originated the theory of the inferiority of the Non-Whites. To this accusation the West has no reply. It is now trying its best to bury its past. It is in a hurry to establish new exploitive relations with the ex-colonies under the guise of this new so-called independence. In this way they seek to establish capitalist exploitive relations without the stigma of racism. In the battle to win over the Non-White nations throughout the world, imperialism is trying to forget its racist policies. It is in this respect that South Africa has become the polecat in the comity of Western Nations.

The South African Government under the leadership of the Broederbond, untrammelled by the wider considerations of the "cold war", has taken a granite stand on its racial policies. It upholds herrenvolkism as a noble ideal and defends it with a fanaticism of people engaged in holy war. This 18th century mentality is an embarrassment to imperialism. It would like a more enlightened section of the herrenvolk to take over the reins of government and bring South Africa into line with the rest of the Western policies. It is this intervention of imperialism that has sharpened the division between the two herrenvolk camps. The Progressive and the Liberal Parties, acting as agents of imperialism, are offering crumbs to a section of the oppressed

Non-White leadership in order to win them over to the camp of imperialism. That is why a number of intellectuals together with Non-White merchants are veering over to these parties. In so doing, they are renouncing the battle for liberation of the oppressed and throwing in their lot with imperialism in its fight for survival. It is not necessary here to explain that a replacement of one herrenvolk government by another would not make a tittle of difference to the sufferings of the workers and poor peasants. Neither the Progressive, nor the Liberal, nor any other herrenvolk Party can bring about a radical change as long as the present economic and social structures remain unchanged.

Verwoerd with his Broederbond sees the salvation of herrenvolkism in retribalisation of the Non-Whites, splitting them up into various ethnic groups and presenting each one with its own policeman-chief. These policemen-chiefs are going to be the front line of defence of herrenvolkism in this country; in the same way the intellectuals constitute the front line in the defence of imperialism. The rest of the oppressed must turn their backs on both sets of agents. APDUSANS recognise that neither imperialism nor South African herrenvolkism will ever assist them in the struggle for liberation. Only the oppressed people, together with those who have irrevocably cast in their lot with them, can solve their problems.

A.P.D.U.S.A. believes that in any society the people who create wealth and civilization, and are therefore responsible for the progress of mankind, are those who provide labour in its many forms. Here in South Africa the bulk of the people who create the wealth of the country are precisely those despised and neglected workers in the gold and coal mines; those workers on the sugar plantations, in the white farms and in the Reserves. We are not saying that the White worker does not make his contribution, but we are saying that it is the majority of the oppressed Non-Whites who contribute the lion's share to a civilization the fruits of which they are not permitted to enjoy. It is these nameless millions who have been reduced to a position of Calibans who carry the whole of South African society on their backs. In this sense all culture, science and technology, literature, music and drama, in short, all that goes by the name of Western Civilization in this country rests squarely on their backs.

This is the first lesson that every APDUSAN must learn. For it is only when we realise the supreme importance and worth of the toiling masses that we shall be able to adjust our attitudes properly towards them. Only then will the intellectuals in our midst rid themselves completely of any suggestion of condescension in their dealings with the masses. This is the sine qua non for the proper integration of the leadership with the oppressed masses. APDUSANS turn to the masses not with the idea of using them or their numbers but of identifying themselves with them, drawing strength and inspiration from them, while at the same time imparting to them that feeling of confidence, self-esteem and pride in their own achievements. Our belief is that those who create must decide what is to be done with what they have created. The producers of wealth in a society must be in the Government of the country. This is our attitude.

We have spent some time analysing the economic and social structure of the country in order to show how this determines the policies of every herrenvolk Government in power. The picture that emerges suggests a solution to our problems. It suggests an approach to the task of organisation. It reveals the weak spots in the armour of herrenvolkism, as well as our own sources of strength. As we are going to have a paper read at this Conference on "The Task of National Organisation", I shall not anticipate either the paper or the discussion under this head. I shall sum up this address with a few remarks on the Trade Union Question.

First of all we must examine those organs which are supposed to belong to the workers, namely, the trade unions. As things stand today, every officially recognised trade union has agreed to partition its members according to race. This alone renders them incapable of performing the function of true trade unions.

. . . .

It is obvious from this that, if the workers are to build effective organs for their protection, they can only do so outside the framework of "recognised" trade unions. The only legitimate recognition which must be the concern of the workers is not recognition by the Government but by the workers themselves. For a trade union is their own weapon. APDU-SANS, then, must go to the factories to discuss these matters. When the workers understand what a trade union should look like, they will build their own organs of defence and attack in the fight for their rights. In these organs they will have no colour bar.

Mr. Chairman, in conclusion I would like to say that if this address succeeds in directing the thoughts of Conference towards the necessity of finding a solution to the crisis that faces this country, and convinces the members that only through the efforts of the toiling masses is it possible to put an end to it, I would be satisfied. We believe that only that class which has a historical future can lead society out of the crisis. History has placed the destiny of our society in the hands of the toiling masses. If we are to succeed in our task of liberation, we must link ourselves dynamically and inseparably with the labouring classes, i.e. the workers and the peasantry. Without them we are nothing. With them we are everything, and nothing can stand in our way. No power on earth can hold us back in our march.

Note: The extracts above are reproduced from a printed pamphlet that appears to have been published in South Africa in 1962: *The African*

People's Democratic Union of Southern Africa (A.P.D.U.S.A.), Presidential Address, Delivered at Cape Town, April, 1962, by I. B. Tabata. Two slightly altered versions were published later: as a pamphlet printed in England in 1963 (*The African People's Democratic Union of Southern Africa (A.P.D.U.S.A.) (Affiliated to the All-African Convention and the N.E.U.M.), Presidential Address delivered at the First National Conference, April, 1962, in Cape Town, by I. B. Tabata*) and in a booklet published by the Alexander Defense Committee in New York City, November 1965 (*The Freedom Struggle in South Africa* by I. B. Tabata).

Document 68. Statements in Court, by Nelson Mandela, October 22 and November 7, 1962

Note: The text is taken from *I ACCUSE! SPEECHES TO COURT BY NELSON MANDELA*, a pamphlet printed on poor paper [n.d.]. Mandela's picture is on the cover and below it: "WHEN YOU HAVE FINISHED PLEASE PASS IT ON." The statements and excerpts from the trial record were reprinted later in the publication cited in the note to Document 63.

Your Worship, before I plead to the charge, there are one or two points I would like to raise.

CONDUCTS OWN DEFENCE.

Firstly, Your Worship will recall that this matter was postponed last Monday at my request until today, to enable Counsel to make the arrangements to be available here today. Although Counsel is now available, after consultation with him and my attorneys, I have elected to conduct my own defence. Some time during the progress of these proceedings, I hope to be able to indicate that this case is a trial of the aspirations of the African people, and because of that I thought it proper to conduct my own defence. Nevertheless, I have decided to retain the services of Counsel, who will be here throughout these proceedings, and I also would like my attorney to be available in the course of these proceedings as well, but subject to that I will conduct my own defence.

RECUSAL.

The second point I would like to raise is an application which is addressed to Your Worship. Now at the outset, I want to make it perfectly clear that the remarks I am going to make are not addressed to Your Worship in his personal capacity, nor are they intended to reflect upon the integrity of the Court. I hold Your Worship in high esteem and I do not for one single moment doubt your sense of fairness and justice. I must also mention that nothing I am going to raise in this application is intended to reflect against the Prosecutor in his personal capacity.

The point I wish to raise in my argument is based not on personal considerations, but on important questions that go beyond the scope of this present trial. I might also mention that in the course of this application I am frequently going to refer to the White man and the White people. I want at once to make it plain that I am no racialist, and I detest racialism, because I regard it as a barbaric thing, whether it comes from a Black man or from a White man. The terminology that I am going to employ will be compelled on me by the nature of the application I wish to make.

I want to apply for Your Worship's recusal from this case. I challenge the right of this Court to hear my case on two grounds.

I challenge it firstly because I fear that I will not be given a fair and proper trial. I challenge it in the second place because I consider myself neither legally nor morally bound to obey laws made by a Parliament in which I have no representation. In a political trial such as the present one which involves a clash of the aspirations of the African people and those of the Whites, the country's courts as presently constituted cannot be impartial and fair. In such cases Whites are interested parties. To have a White judicial officer presiding, however high his esteem, and however strong his sense of justice and fairness, is to make Whites judge their own case. It is improper and against the elementary principles of justice to entrust Whites with cases involving the denial by them of basic human rights to the African people. What sort of justice is this that enables the aggrieved to sit in judgement upon those whom they accused, a judiciary controlled entirely by Whites and enforcing laws enacted by a White Parliament in which we have no representation: laws, which in most cases are passed in the face of unanimous opposition from Africans.

BY THE COURT:

I am wondering whether I shouldn't interfere with you at this stage, Mr. Mandela. Aren't we going beyond the scope of the proceedings? After all is said and done, there is only one Court today and that is the White Man's Court. There is no other Court. What purpose does it serve you to make an application when there is only one Court, as you know yourself. What Court do you wish to be tried by?

BY THE ACCUSED:

Well, Your Worship, firstly I would like Your Worship to bear in mind that in a series of cases our Courts have laid it down that the right of a litigant to ask for a recusal of a judicial officer is an extremely important right, which must be given full protection by the Court, as long as that right is exercised honestly. Now I honestly have apprehensions, as I am going to demonstrate just now, that this unfair discrimination throughout my life has been responsible for very grave injustices, and I am going to contend that that race discrimination which outside this Court has been responsible for all my troubles, I fear in this Court is going to do me the same injustice. Now Your Worship may disagree with that, but Your Worship is perfectly entitled, in fact, obliged to listen to me, and because of that I feel that Your Worship—

BY THE COURT:

I would like to listen, but I would like you to give me the grounds for your application for me to recuse myself.

BY THE ACCUSED:

Well, these are the grounds, I am developing them, sir. If Your Worship will give me time—

BY THE COURT:

I don't wish you to go out of the scope of the proceedings.

BY THE ACCUSED:

—Of the scope of the application. I am within the scope of the application, because I am putting forward grounds which in my opinion are likely not to give me a fair and proper trial.

BY THE COURT:

Anyway, proceed.

BY THE ACCUSED:

As Your Worship pleases. I was developing the point that a judiciary controlled entirely by Whites and enforcing laws enacted by a White Parliament in which we have no representation, laws which in most cases are passed in the face of unanimous opposition from Africans, cannot be regarded as an impartial tribunal in a political trial where an African stands as an accused.

The Universal Declaration of Human Rights provides that all men are equal before the law, and are entitled without any discrimination to equal protection of the law. In May, 1951, Dr. D. F. Malan, then Prime Minister, told the Union Parliament that this provision of the Declaration applies in this country. Similar statements have been made on numerous occasions in the past by prominent Whites in this country, including Judges and Magistrates. But the real truth is that there is in fact no equality before the law whatsoever as far as our people are concerned, and statements to the contrary are definitely incorrect and misleading.

EQUALITY BEFORE THE LAW.

It is true that an African who is charged in a court of law enjoys on the surface the same rights and privileges as a White accused, insofar as the conduct of his trial is concerned. He is governed by the same rules of procedure and evidence as apply to a White accused. But it will be grossly inaccurate to conclude from this fact that an African consequently enjoys equality before the law. In its proper meaning equality before the law means the right to participate in the making of the laws by which one is governed. It means a constitution which guarantees democratic rights to all sections of the population, the right to approach the Court for protection or relief in the case of the violation of the rights guaranteed in the Constitution, and the right to take part in the administration of justice as Judges, Magistrates, Attorney-General, Prosecutors, law advisers and similar positions. In the absence of these safeguards the phrase "equal before the law" insofar as it is intended to apply to us, is meaningless and misleading.

All the rights and privileges to which I have referred are monopolised in this country exclusively by Whites, and we enjoy none of them. The White Man makes all the laws, he drags us before his courts and accuses us, and he sits in judgement over us. Now it is fit and proper to ask the question, Sir, what is this rigid colour bar in the administration of justice all about? Why is it that in this Courtroom I am facing a White Magistrate, confronted by a White Prosecutor, escorted by White Orderlies. Can anybody honestly and seriously suggest that in this type of atmosphere the scales of justice are evenly balanced? Why is it that no African in the history of this country has ever had the honour of being tried by his own kith and kin, by his own flesh and blood? I will tell Your Worship why: the real purpose of this rigid colour bar is to ensure that the justice dispensed by the courts should conform to the policy of the country, however much that policy might be in conflict with the norms of justice accepted in judiciaries throughout the civilised world.

"THE ATMOSPHERE OF WHITE DOMINATION"

I feel oppressed by the atmosphere of White domination that is around me in this Courtroom. Somehow this atmosphere recalls to mind the inhuman injustice caused to my people outside this Courtroom by the same White domination. It reminds me that I am voteless because there is a Parliament in this country that is White-controlled. I am without land because the White minority has taken the lion's share of my country, and I am forced to occupy poverty stricken reserves which are over populated and over stocked. We are ravished by starvation and disease because our country's worth—

BY THE COURT:

What has that got to do with the case, Mr. Mandela?

BY THE ACCUSED:

With the last point, Sir, it hangs together, if Your Worship will give me the chance to develop it.

BY THE COURT:

You have been developing for quite a while now, and I feel you are going beyond the scope of your application.

BY THE ACCUSED:

Your Worship, this to me is an extremely important ground which the Court must consider.

BY THE COURT:

I fully realise your position, Mr. Mandela, but you must confine yourself to the application and not go beyond it. I don't want to know about starvation. That in my view has got nothing to do with the case at the present moment.

BY THE ACCUSED:

Well, Your Worship has already raised the point that here in this country there is only a White Court. What is the purpose of all this? Now if I can demonstrate to Your Worship that outside this Courtroom race discrimination has been used in such a way as to deprive me of my rights, not to treat me fairly, certainly this is a relevant fact from which to infer that wherever race discrimination is practised, this will be the same result, and this is the only reason why I am using this point.

BY THE COURT:

I am afraid that I will have to interrupt you, and you will have to confine yourself to the reasons, the real reasons for asking me to recuse myself.

BY THE ACCUSED:

Your Worship, the next point which I want to make is this: I raise the question, how can I be expected to believe that this same racial discrimination which has been the cause of so much injustice and suffering right through the years should now operate here to give me a fair and open trial? Is there no danger that an African accused may regard the courts not as impartial tribunals, dispensing justice without fear or favour, but as instruments used by the White man to punish those amongst us who clamour for deliverance from the fiery furnace of White rule. I have grave fears that this system of justice may enable the guilty to drag the innocent before the courts. It enables the unjust to prosecute and demand vengeance against the just. It may tend to lower the standards of fairness and justice applied in the country's courts by White judicial officers to Black litigants. This is the first ground for this application: that I will not receive a fair and proper trial.

Now the second ground for this application is that I consider myself neither morally or legally bound to obey laws made by a Parliament in which I have no representation. That the will of the people is the basis of the authority of government is a principle universally acknowledged as sacred throughout the civilised world, and constitutes the basic foundation of freedom and justice. It is understandable why citizens who have the vote as well as the right of direct representation in the country's governing bodies should be morally and legally bound by the laws governing the country. It should be equally understandable why we as Africans should adopt the attitude that we are neither morally nor legally bound to obey laws which were not made with our consent, nor can we be expected to have confidence in courts that interpret and enforce such laws.

I am aware, Your Worship, that in many cases of this nature in the past South African courts have upheld the right of the African people to work for democratic changes. Some of our judicial officers have even openly critised the policy which refuses to acknowledge that all men are born free and equal, and fearlessly condemned the denial of opportunities to our people. But such exceptions, Your Worship, exist in spite, not because of the grotesque system of justice that has been built up in this country. These exceptions furnish yet another proof that even among the country's Whites there are honest men, whose sense of fairness and justice revolt against the cruelties perpetrated by their own White brothers to our people. The existence of genuine democratic values among some of the country's Whites in the judiciary, however slender they may be, is welcomed by me, but I have no illusions about the significance of this fact, healthy a sign as it may be. Such honest and upright men are few, and they have certainly not succeeded in convincing the vast majority of the rest of the White population that White supremacy leads to dangers and disasters.

"I HATE RACIAL DISCRIMINATION—"

Your Worship, I hate racial discrimination most intensely and in all its manifestations. I have fought it all along my life. I fight it now, and I will do so until the end of my days. I detest most intensely the set-up that surrounds me here. It makes me feel that I am a Black man in a White man's Court. This should not be. I should feel perfectly free and at ease with the assurance that I am being tried by a fellow South African who does not regard me as inferior, entitled to a special type of justice. This is not the type of atmosphere most conducive to feelings of security and confidence in the impartiality of the Court.

Now the Court might reply to this part of my argument by assuring me that it will try my case fairly and without fear or favour, that in deciding whether or not I am guilty of the offence charged by the State, the Court will not be influenced by the colour of my skin or by any improper motive. That might well be so. But such a reply will completely miss the whole point of my argument. As already indicated, my objection is not directed to Your Worship in his personal capacity, nor is it intended to reflect upon the integrity of the Court. My objection is based upon the fact that our courts as presently constituted create grave doubts in the mind of an African accused whether he will receive a fair and a proper trial. This doubt springs from objective facts relating to the practice of unfair discrimination against the Black man in the constitution of the country's courts. Such doubts cannot be allayed by mere verbal assurances from a presiding officer, however sincere such assurances may be. There is only one way, and one way only of allaying such doubts: By removing discrimination, particularly in judicial appointments. This is my first difficulty.

WHITE AND BLACK ETHICS.

I have yet another difficulty about similar assurances Your Worship might give. Broadly speaking Africans and Whites in this country have no common standard of fairness, morality and ethics, and it will be very difficult for me to determine what standard of fairness and justice Your Worship has in mind. In relationships with us, South African Whites regard as fair and just to pursue policies which have outraged the conscience of mankind, and of honest and upright men throughout the civilised world. They suppress our aspirations, bar our way to freedom and deny us opportunities in our moral and material progress, to secure ourselves from fear and want. All the good things of life are reserved for the White folk, and we Blacks are expected to be content to nourish our bodies with such pieces of food as drop from the tables of men with a White skin. This is the White man's standard of fairness and justice. Herein lies his conception of ethics. Whatever he himself may say in his defence, the White man's moral standards in this country must be judged by the extent to which he has condemned the vast majority of its citizens to serfdom and inferiority.

We, on the other hand, Your Worship, regard the struggle against colour discrimination and for the pursuit of freedom as the highest aspiration of all men. Through bitter experience we have learnt to regard the White man as a harsh and merciless type of human being, whose contempt for our rights and whose utter indifference to the promotion of our welfare makes his assurances to us absolutely meaningless and hypocritical.

I have the hope and the confidence that Your Worship will not treat this objection lightly, nor regard it as a frivolous one. I have decided to speak frankly and honestly, because the injustices I have referred to tend to undermine our confidence in the impartiality of our courts in cases of this nature, and they contain the seeds of an extremely dangerous situation for our country and people. I make no threats, Your Worship, when I say that unless these wrongs to which I have pointed are remedied without delay, we might well find that even plain talk before the country's courts is too timid a method to draw attention to our grievances.

Finally, I need only say that the courts have said that the possibility of bias and not actual bias is all that need be proved to ground an application of this nature. In this application I have merely referred to certain objective facts, from which I submit that the possibility be inferred that I will not receive a fair and proper trial.

BY THE COURT:

Mr. Prosecutor, have you anything to say?

BY THE PROSECUTOR:

Very briefly, Your Worship, I just wish to point out that there are certain legal grounds upon which an accused person is entitled to apply for the recusal of a judicial officer from the case in which he is to be tried. I submit that the Accused's application is not based on one of those principles, and I ask the Court to reject it.

BY THE COURT:

Your application is dismissed. Will you now plead to your charges?

BY THE ACCUSED:

I plead NOT GUILTY to both charges, to all the charges.

PLEA IN MITIGATION

I am charged with inciting people to commit an offence by way of protest against the law, a law in which neither I nor any of my people had any say in preparing. The law against which the protest was directed is the law which established the Republic in the Union of South Africa. I am also charged with leaving the country without a passport. This Court has found that I am guilty of incitement to commit an offence in opposition to this law as well as of leaving the country. But in weighing up the decision as to the sentence which is to be imposed for such an offence, the Court must take into account the question of responsibility, whether it is I who is responsible or whether, in fact, a large measure of the responsibility did not lie on the shoulders of the Government which promulgated that law, knowing that my people, as a whole who constitute the majority of the population of this country were opposed to that law, and knowing further that every legal means of demonstrating that opposition had been closed to them by prior legislation, and by Government administrative action.

PIETERMARITZBURG CONFERENCE

The starting point in the case against me is the holding of the Conference in Pietermaritzburg on March 25th and 26th last year (1961), known as the All-In African Conference, which was called by a Committee which had been established by leading people and spokesmen of the whole African population, to consider the situation which was being created by the promulgation of the Republic in this country, without consultation with us, and without our consent. That conference unanimously rejected the decision of the Government, acting only in the name of and with the agreement of the white minority of this country, to establish a Republic.

It is common knowledge that the Conference decided that, in place of the unilateral proclamation of a Republic by the white minority of South Africans only, it would demand in the name of the African people, the calling of a truly National Convention representative of all South Africans, irrespective of their colour, black and white, to sit amicably round a table, to debate a new constitution for South Africa, which was in essence what the Government was doing by the proclamation of a Republic, and furthermore, to press on behalf of the African people, that such new constitution should differ from the Constitution of the proposed South African Republic by guaranteeing democratic rights on a basis of full equality to all South Africans of adult age. The Conference had assembled, knowing full well that for a long period the present National Party Government of the Union of South Africa had refused to deal with, to discuss with, or to take into consideration, the views of the overwhelming majority of the population on this question. And, therefore, it was not enough for this Conference just to proclaim its aim, but it was also necessary for the Conference to find means of stating that aim strongly and powerfully, despite the Government's unwillingness to listen.

GENERAL STRIKE

Accordingly it was decided that should the Government fail to summon such a national convention before May 31st, 1961, all sections of the population would be called on to stage a general strike for a period of three days, both to mark our protest against the establishment of a republic, based completely on white domination over a non-white majority, and also, in a last attempt to persuade the government to heed our legitimate claims, thus to avoid a period of increasing bitterness and hostility and discord in South Africa.

At that conference an action council was elected and I became its secretary. It was my duty, as secretary of the committee to establish the machinery necessary for publicising the decision of this conference and for directing the campaign of propaganda, publicity and organisation which would flow from it. The court is aware of the fact that I am an attorney by profession, and no doubt the question will be asked why I, as an attorney who is bound, as part of my code of behaviour, to observe the laws of the country and to respect its customs and traditions, should willingly lend myself to a campaign whose ultimate aim was to bring about a strike against the proclaimed policy of the Government of this country.

In order that the court shall understand the frame of mind which leads me to action such as this, it is necessary for me to explain the background to my own political development and to try to make this court aware of the factors which influenced me in deciding to act as I did.

CHILDHOOD DAYS

Many years ago, when I was a boy brought up in my village in the Transkei, I listened to the elders of the tribe telling stories about the good old days, before the arrival of the white man. Then our people lived peacefully, under the democratic rule of their Kings and their 'amapakati', and moved freely and confidently up and down the country without let or hindrance. Then the country was our own, in name and right. We occupied the land, the forests, the rivers; we extracted the mineral wealth beneath the soil and all the riches of this beautiful country. We set up and operated our own Government, we controlled our own armies and we organised our own trade and commerce. The elders would tell tales of the wars fought by our ancestors in defense of the fatherland, as well as the acts of valour by generals and soldiers during those epic days. The names of Dingane and Bambata, among the Zulus, of Hintsa, Makana, Ndlambe of the Ama-Xhosa, of Sekhukhuni and others in the North, were mentioned as the pride and glory of the entire African nation.

DEMOCRACY IN AFRICAN SOCIETY

The structure and organisation of early African societies in this country fascinated me very much and greatly influenced the evolution of my political outlook. The land, then the main means of production, belonged to the whole tribe and there was no individual ownership whatsoever. There were no classes, no rich or poor and no exploitation of man by man. All men were free and equal and this was the foundation of government. Recognition of this general principle found expression in the constitution of the council, variously called *"Imbizo"* or *"Pitso"* or *"Kgotla"* which governs the affairs of the tribe. The council was so completely democratic that all members of the tribe could participate in its deliberations. Chief and subject, warrior and medicine man, all took part and endeavoured to influence its decisions. It was so weighty and influential a body that no step of any importance could ever be taken by the tribe without reference to it.

NO SLAVERY

There was much in such a society that was primitive and insecure and it certainly could never measure up to the demands of the present epoch. But in such a society are contained the seeds of revolutionary democracy in which none will be held in slavery or servitude, and in which poverty, want and insecurity shall be no more. This is the inspiration which, even today, inspires me and my colleagues in our political struggle.

AFRICAN NATIONAL CONGRESS

When I reached adult stature, I became a member of the African National Congress. That was in 1944 and I have followed its policy, supported it and believed in its aims and outlook for eighteen years. Its policy was one which appealed to my deepest inner convictions. It sought for the unity of all Africans, overriding tribal differences among them. It sought the acquisition of political power for the Africans in the land of their birth. The African National Congress further believed that all people, irrespective of the colour of their skins, all people whose home is South Africa and who believe in the principles of democracy and of equality of men, should be treated as Africans; that all South Africans are entitled to live a free life on the basis of fullest equality of the rights and opportunities in every field, of full democratic rights, with a direct say in the affairs of the Government.

THE FREEDOM CHARTER

These principles have been embedded in the Freedom Charter, which no one in this country will dare challenge for its place as the most democratic programme of political principles ever enunciated by any political party or organisation in this country. It was for me a matter of joy and pride to be a member of an organisation which has proclaimed so democratic a policy and which campaigned for it militantly and fearlessly. The principles enumerated in the Charter have not been those of African people alone, for whom the African National Congress has always been the spokesman. Those principles have been adopted as well by the S.A. Indian Congress and the Indian people and the S.A. Coloured People's Congress, and also by a farsighted, forward-looking section of the European population, whose organisation in days gone by was the South African Congress of Democrats. All these organisations, like the African National Congress, supported completely the demand for one man, one vote.

Right at the beginning of my career and experiences as an attorney I encountered difficulties imposed on me because of the colour of my skin, and further difficulty surrounding me because of my membership and support of the African National Congress. I discovered, for example, that unlike a white attorney, I could not occupy business premises in the city unless I first obtained ministerial consent in terms of the Urban Areas Act. I applied for that consent, but it was never granted. Although I subsequently obtained a permit, for a limited period, in terms of the Group Areas Act, that soon expired and the authorities refused to renew it. They insisted that my partner, Oliver Tambo, and I should leave the city and practice in an African location at the back of beyond, miles away from where clients could reach us during normal working hours. This was tantamount to asking us to abandon our legal practice, to give up the legal service of our people, for which we have spent many years training. No attorney worth his salt would agree easily to do so. For some years, therefore, we continued to occupy premises in the city, illegally. The threat of prosecution and ejection hung menacingly over us throughout this period. It was an act of defiance of the law. We were aware that it was, but nevertheless, that act had been forced on us against our wishes, and we could do no other than to choose between compliance with the law and compliance with our consciences.

IN THE COURTS

In the courts where we practised we were treated courteously by many officials but we were very often discriminated against by some and treated with resentment and hostility by others. We were constantly aware that no matter how well, how correctly, how adequately we pursued our career of law, we could not become prosecutors, or magistrates or judges. We became aware of the fact that as attorneys we often dealt with officials whose competence and attainments were no higher than ours, but whose superior position was maintained and protected by a white skin.

I regard it as a duty which I owed not just to my people, but also to my profession, to the practice of law and justice to all mankind, to cry out against this discrimination which is essentially unjust and opposed to the whole basis of the attitude towards justice which is part of the tradition of legal training in this country. I believed that in taking up a stand against this injustice I was upholding the dignity of what should be an honourable profession.

ACTION OF LAW SOCIETY

Nine years ago the Transvaal Law Society applied to the Supreme Court to have my name struck off the roll because of the part I had played in a campaign initiated by the African National Congress, a campaign for the defiance of unjust laws. During the campaign more than 8,000 of the most advanced and farseeing of my people, deliberately courted arrest and imprisonment by breaking specified laws, which we regarded then, as we still do now, as unjust and repressive. In the opinion of the Law Society, my activity in connection with that campaign did not conform to the standards of conduct expected from members, but on this occasion the Supreme Court held that I had been within my rights as an attorney, that there was nothing dishonourable in an attorney identifying with his people in their struggle for political rights, even if his activities should infringe upon the laws of the country; the Supreme Court rejected the application of the Law Society.

TREASON TRIAL

It would not be expected that with such a verdict in my favour I should discontinue my political activities. But Your Worship may well wonder why it is that I should find it necessary to persist with such conduct, which has not only brought me the difficulties I have referred to, but which has resulted in my spending some four years on a charge before the courts, of high treason, for which I was subsequently acquitted, and of many months in jail on no charge at all, merely on the basis of the Government's dislike of my views and of my activities during the whole period of the emergency of 1960.

MY CONSCIENCE

Your Worship, I would say that the whole life of any thinking African in this country drives continuously to a conflict between his conscience on the one hand and the law on the other. This is not a conflict peculiar to this country. The conflict arises for men of conscience, for men who think and who feel deeply in every country. Recently in Britain, a peer of the realm, Earl Russell, probably the most respected philosopher of the Western World, was sentenced, convicted for precisely the type of activities for which I stand before you today, for following his conscience in defiance of the law, as a protest against the nuclear weapons policy being followed by his own Government. For him, his duty to the public, his belief in the morality of the essential rightness of the cause for which he stood, rose superior to this high respect for the law. He could do no other than to oppose the law and to suffer the consequences for it. Nor can I. Nor can many Africans in this country. The law as it is applied, the law as it has been developed over a long period of history, and especially the law as it is written and designed by the Nationalist Government is a law which, in our view, *is immoral, unjust, and intolerable*. Our consciences dictate that we must protest against it, that we must oppose it and that we must attempt to alter it.

Always we have been conscious of our obligations as citizens to avoid breaches of the law, where such breaches can be avoided, to prevent clash between the authorities and our people, where such clash can be prevented, but nevertheless, we have been driven to speak up for what we believe is right, and work for it and bring about changes which will satisfy our human conscience.

Throughout its fifty years of existence the African National Congress, for instance, has done everything possible to bring its demands to the attention of successive South African Governments. It has sought at all times peaceful solutions for all the country's ills and problems. The history of the A.N.C. is filled with instances where deputations were sent to South African Governments either on specific issues or on the general political demands of our people. I do not wish to burden Your Worship by enunciating the occasions when such deputations were sent: all that I wish to indicate at this stage is that, in addition to the efforts made by former presidents of the A.N.C., when Mr. Strijdom became Prime Minister of this country, my leader, Chief A. J. Luthuli, then President of our organisation, made yet another effort to persuade this Government to consider and to heed our point of view. In his letter to the Prime Minister at the time. Chief Luthuli exhaustively reviewed the country's relations and its dangers, and expressed the view that a meeting between the Government and African leaders had become necessary and urgent.

GOVERNMENT REACTION

This statesmanlike and correct behaviour on the part of the leader of the majority of the South African population did not find an appropriate answer from the leader of the South African Government. The standard of behaviour of the South African Government towards my people and its aspirations have not always been what they should have been, and are not always the standards which are to be expected in serious high level dealings between civilised peoples. Chief Luthuli's letter was not even favoured with the courtesy of an acknowledgement from the Prime Minister's office.

LETTER TO VERWOERD

This experience was repeated after the Pietermaritzburg conference when I, as Secretary of the Action Council elected at that conference, addressed a letter to the Prime Minister, Dr. Verwoerd, informing him of the resolution which had been taken and calling on him to initiate steps for convening of such a national convention as we suggested before the date specified in the resolution. In a civilised country one would be outraged by the failure of the head of government even to acknowledge receipt of, or to consider such a reasonable request put to him by a broadly representative collection of important personalities and leaders of the most important community of the country, of the most numerous community of the country. Once again government standards in dealing with my people fell below what the civilised world would expect. No reply, no response whatsoever, was received to our letter, no indication was even given that it had received any consideration whatsoever. Here we, the African people, and especially we of the National Action Council, who had been entrusted with a tremendous responsibility of safeguarding the interests of the African people, we were faced with this conflict between the law and our conscience. In the face of the complete failure of the Government to heed, to consider, or even to respond to our seriously proposed objections and proposals for solution to our objections to the forthcoming Republic [sic], what were we to do? Were we to allow the law, which states that you shall not commit an offence by way of protest, to take its course and thus betray our conscience and our belief? Were we to uphold our conscience and our beliefs to strive for what we believe is right, not just for us, but for all the people who live in this country, both the present generation and for generations to come, and thus transgress against the law? This is the dilemma which faced us and in such a dilemma, men of honesty, men of purpose and men of public morality and of conscience can only have one answer. They must follow the dictates of their conscience irrespective of the consequences which might overtake them for it. We of the Action Council, and I particularly as Secretary, followed my conscience.

WOULD DO IT AGAIN

If I had my time over I would do the same again, so would any man who dares call himself a man. We went ahead with our campaign as instructed by the Conference and in accordance with its decisions.

The issue that sharply divided white South Africans during the referendum for a Republic did not interest us. It formed no part in our campaign. Continued association with the British Monarchy on the one hand, or the establishment of a Boer Republic on the other—this was the crucial issue in so far as the white population was concerned and as it was put to them in the referendum. We are neither monarchists nor admirers of a Voortrekker type of republic. We believe that we were inspired by aspirations more worthy than either of the groups who took part in the campaign on these. We were inspired by the idea of bringing into being a democratic republic where all South Africans will enjoy human rights without the slightest discrimination; where African and non-African would be able to live together in peace, sharing a common nationality and a common loyalty to this country, which is our homeland. For these reasons we were opposed to the type of Republic proposed by the National Party Government, just as we had been opposed previously to the constitutional basis of the Union of South Africa as a part of the British Empire. We were not prepared to accept, at a time when constitutional changes were being made, that these constitutional changes should not affect the real basis of a South African Constitution, white supremacy and white domination, the very basis which has brought South Africa and its constitution into contempt and disrepute throughout the world.

THE MAY 1961 CAMPAIGN

I wish now to deal with the campaign itself, with the character of the campaign and with the course of events which followed our decision. From the beginning our campaign was a campaign designed to call on people as a last extreme, if all else failed, if all discussions failed to materialise, if the Government showed no sign of taking any steps to attempt, either to talk with us or meet our demands peacefully, to strike, that is to stay away from work, and to bring economic pressure to bear. There was never any intention that our demonstrations at that stage, go further than that. In all our statements, both those which are before the Court and those which are not before the Court, we made it clear that the strike would be a peaceful protest, in which people were asked to remain in their homes. It was our intention that the demonstration should go through peacefully and peaceably, without clash and conflict, as such demonstrations do in every civilised country.

CIVIL WAR AND REVOLUTION

Nevertheless, around that campaign and our preparations for that campaign was created the atmosphere for civil war and revolution. I would say deliberately created. Deliberately created, not by us, Your Worship, but by the Government which set out, from the beginning of this campaign, not to treat with us, not to heed us, nor to talk to us, but rather to present us as wild, dangerous revolutionaries, intent on disorder and riot, incapable of being dealt with in any way save by mustering of overwhelming force against us and the implementation of every possible, forcible means, legal and illegal, to suppress us. The Government behaved in a way no civilised Government should dare behave when faced with a peaceful, disciplined, sensible and democratic expression of the views of its own population. It ordered the mobilisation of its armed forces to attempt to cow and terrorise our peaceful protest. It arrested people known to be active in African politics, and in support of African demands for democratic rights, passed special laws enabling them to hold without trial for twelve days instead of 48 hours that had been customary before, and held them, the majority of them, never to be charged before the courts, but to be released after the date of the strike had passed. If there was a danger during this period that violence would result from the situation in the country, then the possibility was of the Government's making. *They set the scene for violence by relying exclusively on violence with which to answer our people and their demands.* The counter measures which they took clearly reflected growing uneasiness on their part, which grew out of the knowledge that their policy did not enjoy the support of the majority of the people, while ours did. It was clear that the Government was attempting to combat the intensity of our campaign by a reign of terror. At the time the newspapers suggested the strike was a failure and it was said that we did not enjoy the support of the people. I deny that. I deny it and I will continue to deny it as long as this Government is not prepared to put to the test the question of the opinion of the African people by consulting them in a democratic way. In any event the evidence in this case has proved that it was a substantial success. Our campaign was an intensive campaign and met with tremendous and overwhelming response from the population. In the end, if a strike did not materialise on the scale on which it had been hoped it would, it is not because the people were not willing, but because the overwhelming strength, violence and force of the Government's attack against our campaign had for the time being achieved its aim of forcing us into submission against our wishes and against our conscience.

MASSACRE OF AFRICAN PEOPLE

I wish to return to the question of why people like me, knowing all this, knowing in advance that this Government is incapable of progressive democratic moves, so far as our people are concerned, that this Government is incapable of reacting towards us in any way other than by use of overwhelming brute force, why I, and people like me, nevertheless, decide to go ahead to do what we must. We have been conditioned to our attitudes by history which is not of our making. We have been conditioned by the history of White Government in this country to accept the fact that Africans, when they make their demands strongly and powerfully enough to have some chance of success, will be met by force and terror on the part of the Government. This is not something we have taught the African people, this is something the African people have learnt from their own bitter experience. We learnt it from each successive Government. We learnt it from the Government of General Smuts at the time of two massacres of our people: the 1921 massacre in Bulhoek when more than 100 men, women and children were killed and from the 1924 massacre, the Bondelswart massacre in South West Africa, in which some 200 Africans were killed. We have continued to learn it from every successive Government.

COUNTER VIOLENCE

Government violence can do only one thing and that is to breed counter violence. We have warned repeatedly that the Government, by resorting continually to violence will breed, in this country, counterviolence amongst the people, till ultimately, if there is no dawning of sanity on the part of the Government, ultimately the dispute between the Government and my people, will finish up by being settled in violence and force. Already there are indications in this country that people, my people, Africans are turning to deliberate acts of violence and of force against the Government, in order to persuade the Government, in the only language which this Government shows, by its own behaviour, that it understands.

FAILURE OF REPRESENTATION

Elsewhere in the world, a Court would say to me, "You should have made representations to the Government". This court, I am confident, will not say so. Representations have been made, by people who have gone before me, time and time again. Representations were made in this case by me; I do not want again to repeat the experience of those representations. The Court cannot expect a respect for the processes of representation and negotiation to grow amongst the African people; the Government shows every day, by its conduct, that it despises such processes and frowns upon them and will not indulge in them. Nor will the Court, I believe, say that, under the circumstances, my people are condemned forever to say nothing and to do nothing. If the Court says that, or believes it, I think it is mistaken and deceiving itself. Men are not capable of doing nothing, of saying nothing, of not reacting to injustice, of not protesting against oppression, of not striving for the good society and the good life in the ways they see it. Nor will they do so in this country.

UNCONVICTED CRIMINAL

Perhaps the Court will say that despite our human rights to protest, to object, to make ourselves heard, we should stay within the letter of the law. I would say, Sir, that it is the Government, its administration of the law, which brings the law into such contempt and disrepute that one is no longer concerned in this country, to stay within the letter of the law. I will illustrate this from my own experience. The Government has used the process of law to handicap me, in my personal life, in my career and in my political work in a way calculated, in my opinion, to bring a contempt for the law. In December, 1952, I was issued with an order by the Government, not as a result of a trial before a court and a conviction, but as a result of prejudice, or perhaps star chamber procedure behind closed doors in the halls of Government. In terms of that order I was confined to the Magisterial district of Johannesburg for six months and, at the same time, I was prohibited from attending gatherings for a similar period. That order expired in June, 1953 and three months thereafter, again without any hearing, without any attempt to hear my side of the case, without facing me with charges, or explanations, both bans were renewed for a further period of two years. To these bans a third was added: I was ordered by the Minister of Justice to resign altogether from the African National Congress and never again to become a member or to participate in its activities. Towards the end of 1955 I found myself free and able to move around once again, but not for long. In February, 1956, the bans were again renewed, administratively, again without hearing, this time for five years. Again, by order of the Government, in the name of the law, I found myself restricted and isolated from my fellow men, from people who think like me and believe like me. I found myself trailed by officers of the Security Branch of the Police force wherever I went. In short I found myself treated as a criminal, an unconvicted criminal. I was not allowed to pick my company, to frequent the company of men, to participate in their political activities, to join their organisations. I was not free from constant police surveillance. I was made, by the law, a criminal, not because of what I had done, but of what I stood for, because of what I thought, because of my conscience. Can it be any wonder to anybody that such conditions make a man an outlaw of society? Can it be wondered that such a man, having been outlawed by the Government, should be prepared to lead the life of an outlaw, as I have led for some months, according to the evidence before this Court?

SEPARATE FROM FAMILY

It has not been easy for me during the past period to separate myself from my wife and children, to say goodbye to the good old days when, at the end of a strenuous day at an office I could look forward to joining my family at the dinner-table, and instead to take up the life of a man hunted continuously by the police, living separated from those who are closest to me, in my own country, facing continually the hazards of detection and of arrest. This has been a life infinitely more difficult than serving a prison sentence. No man in his right senses would voluntarily choose such a life in preference to the one of normal, family, social life which exists in every civilised community.

LIVED AS AN OUTLAW

But there comes a time, as it came in my life, when a man is denied the right to live a normal life, when he can only live the life of an outlaw because the Government has so decreed to use the law to impose a state of outlawry upon him. I was driven to this situation, and I do not regret having taken the decisions that I did take. Other people will be driven in the same way in this country, by this very same force of police persecution and of administrative action by the Government, to follow my course, of that I am certain. The decision that I should continue to carry out the decisions of the Pietermaritzburg Conference, despite police persecution all the time, was not my decision alone. It was a decision reached by me, in consultation with those who were entrusted with the leadership of the campaign and its fulfilment. It was clear to us then, in the early periods of the campaign, when the Government was busy whipping up an atmosphere of hysteria as the prelude to violence, that the views of the African people would not be heard, would not find expression, unless attempts were made deliberately by those of us entrusted with the task of carrying through the strike call, to keep away from the illegal, unlawful attacks of the Special Branch, the unlawful detention of people for twelve days without trial, and unlawful and illegal intervention by the police and the Government forces in legitimate political activity of the population. I was, at the time of the Pietermaritzburg conference, free from bans for a short time, and a time which I had no reason to expect would prolong itself for very long. Had I remained in my normal surroundings, carrying on my normal life, I would have again been forced by Government action to a position of an outlaw. That I was not prepared to do while the commands of the Pietermaritzburg Conference to me remained unfulfilled. New situations require new tactics. The situation, which was not our making, which followed the Pietermaritzburg Conference, required the tactics which I adopted, I believe, correctly.

ONE OF A LARGE ARMY

A lot has been written since the Pietermaritzburg Conference, and even more since my arrest, much of which is flattering to my pride and dear to my heart, but much of which is mistaken and incorrect. It has been suggested that the advances, the articulateness of our people, the successes which they are achieving here and the recognition which they are winning both here and abroad are in some way the result of my work. I must place on record my belief that I have been only one in a large army of people, to all of whom the credit for any success or achievement is due. Advance and

744

progress is not the result of my work alone, but of the collective work of my colleagues and I, both here and abroad. I have been fortunate throughout my political life to work together with colleagues whose abilities and contributions to the cause of my people's freedom, have been greater and better than my own, people who have been loved and respected by the African population generally as a result of the dedicated way in which they have fought for freedom and for peace and justice in this country. It distresses me to read reports that my arrest has been instigated by some of my colleagues for some sinister purpose of their own. Nothing could be further from the truth. I dismiss these suggestions as the sensational inventions of unscrupulous journalists. People who stoop to such unscrupulous manoeuvres as the betrayal of their own comrades have no place in the good fight which I have fought for the freedom of the African people, which my colleagues continue to fight without me today. Not just I alone, but all of us are willing to pay the penalties which we may have to pay, which I may have to pay for having followed my conscience in pursuit of what I believe is right. So are we all. Many people in this country have paid the price before me, and many will pay the price after me.

"PENALTIES WILL NOT DETER ME"

I do not believe, Your Worship, that this Court, in inflicting penalties on me for the crimes for which I am convicted should be moved by the belief that penalties will deter men from the course that they believe is right. History shows that penalties do not deter men when their conscience is aroused, nor will they deter my people or the colleagues with whom I have worked before.

I am prepared to pay the penalty even though I know how bitter and desperate is the situation of an African in the prisons of this country. I have been in these prisons and I know how gross is the discrimination, even behind the prison walls, against Africans, how much worse is the condition of the treatment meted out to African prisoners than that accorded to whites. Nevertheless, these considerations do not sway me from the path that I have taken nor will they sway others like me. For to men, freedom in their own land is the pinnacle of their ambitions, from which nothing can turn men of conviction aside. More powerful than my fear of the dreadful conditions to which I might be subjected in prison is my hatred for the dreadful conditions to which my people are subjected outside prison throughout this country.

HATE RACIALISM

I hate the practice of race discrimination, and in doing so, in my hatred, I am sustained by the fact that the overwhelming majority of mankind hate it equally. I hate the systematic inculcation of children with colour prejudice, and I am sustained in that hatred by the fact that the overwhelming majority of mankind, here and abroad, are with me in that. I hate the racial arrogance which decrees that the good things of life shall be retained as the exclusive right of a minority of the population, and which reduces the majority of the population to a position of subservience and inferiority, and maintains them as voteless chattels to work where they are told and behave as they are told by the ruling minority, and I am sustained in that hatred by the fact that the overwhelming majority of mankind both in this country and abroad are with me.

NOTHING WILL CHANGE MY BELIEFS

Nothing that this Court can do will change in any way that hatred in me, which can only be removed by the removal of the injustice and the inhumanity which I have sought to remove from the political, social and economic life of this country.

"WHEN I AM RELEASED—"

Whatever sentence Your Worship sees fit to impose upon me for the crime for which I have been convicted before this Court, may it rest assured that when my sentence has been completed I will still be moved, as men are always moved, by their conscience; I will still be moved by my dislike of the race discrimination against my people when I come out from serving my sentence, to take up again, as best I can, the struggle for the removal of those injustices until they are finally abolished once and for all.

SECOND CHARGE

I now wish to deal with the Second Count.

When my colleagues and I received the invitation to attend the Conference of the Pan-African Freedom Movement for East and Central Africa, it was decided that I should leave the country and join our delegation to Addis Ababa, the capital of Ethiopia, where the Conference would be held. It was part of my mandate to tour Africa and make direct contact with African leaders on the Continent.

I did not apply for a passport because I knew very well that it would not be granted to me. After all the Nationalist Party Government, throughout the 14 years of its oppressive rule, had refused permission to leave the country to many African scholars, educationists, artists, sportsmen and clerics, and I wished to waste none of my time by applying for a passport.

The tour of the Continent made a forceful impression on me. For the first time in my life I was a free man; free from White oppression, from the idiocy of apartheid and racial arrogance, from police molestation, from humiliation and indignity. Wherever I went I was treated like a human being. I met Rashidi Kawawa, Prime Minister of Tanganyika, and Julius Nyerere. I was received by Emperor Haile Selassie, by General Abboud, the President of Sudan, by Habib Bourguiba, President of Tunisia, and by Modibo Keita of the Republic of Mali.

MET BEN BELLA

I met Leopold Senghor, I met Ben Bella, Prime Minister of Algeria, and Colonel Boumediene, the Commander-in-Chief of the Algerian Army of National Liberation. I saw the cream and flower of the Algerian youth who had fought French imperialism and whose valour had brought freedom and happiness to their country.

GAITSKELL AND GRIMOND

In London I was received by Hugh Gaitskell, leader of the Labour Party, and by Jo Grimond, leader of the Liberal Party, and other prominent Englishmen.

OBOTE

I met Prime Minister Obote of Uganda, distinguished African nationalists like Kenneth Kaunda, Oginga Odinga, Joshua Nkomo and many others. In all these countries we were showered with hospitality and assured of solid support for our cause.

SOUTH AFRICA WILL FAIL

In its efforts to keep the African people in a position of perpetual subordination, South Africa must and will fail. South Africa is out of step with the rest of the civilised world, as is shown by the resolution adopted last night by the General Assembly of the United Nations Organisation which decided to impose diplomatic and economic sanctions. In the African States I saw black and white mingling peacefully and happily in hotels, cinemas, trading in the same areas, using the same public transport and living in the same residential areas.

I had to return home to report to my colleagues and to share my impressions and experiences with them.

I have done my duty to my people and to South Africa. I have no doubt that posterity will pronounce that I was innocent and that the criminals that should have have been brought before this Court are the members of the Verwoerd Government.

Document 69. "The People Accept the Challenge of the Nationalists." Statement "issued by the National Executive of the A.N.C.," April 6, 1963

THE PEOPLE ACCEPT THE CHALLENGE
OF THE NATIONALISTS.

OUR POLITICAL LINE OF ACTION.

Our mass political line of action is inspired by our historic National Conference held at Lobatsi in November last year. The Conference was not significant only because it was fully representative of all the regions of the A.N.C. covering various strata of the African people, but also because of the militancy which characterised it, the impressive attendance of the youth on an unprecedented scale, and the fact that it was our first national conference since the banning of the A.N.C. in 1960.

It gave fullest attention to the strategy and tactics to be used in the new situation. Our New Year message expresses the spirit of the conference in general. This document therefore is not intended to give a profound and detailed analysis of the internal and external situation. It is a guide to our members of the political line of action to be followed during the present period in the year 1963. It is limited to this function particularly because of the grave conditions of illegality under which it is produced.

THE SPIRIT OF REVOLT.

The mass political action will demand that we arouse and raise to new heights the spirit of revolt among the people, against every aspect of white domination. In the situation of the present era, our fundamental aim in the liberatory movement is not just the repeal of individual laws, but the liquidation of the whole status quo. In other words, our object is the seizure of political power which is now the prerogative of the white minority. Our demands were clearly formulated by the All-In African Conference at Pietermaritzburg. Whatever political action we take must be seen in the light of these demands, viz. the Convocation of a constituent assembly.

The focal points of our struggle in this period are the pass laws and Bantu Authorities. The already insecure position of the Africans in the country under the pass laws is now aggravated by the notorious Urban Areas Act Amendment Bill. This Bill, when it becomes law, will complete the alienation process of their birth. The Amendment Bill, the pass laws and Bantu Authorities therefore become the central point of our struggle.

THE STRENGTH OF THE GOVERNMENT.

In our decision to launch a campaign against these measures and to work for seizure of political power by all means at our disposal, we have no illusions, we are aware that the Government is by no means weak. For years it has been consolidating its position of power. It has taken pains to accomplish its target of an army of 60,000 men. The Police Force is being increased, and is being perfected in its efficiency. Measures have been adopted to effect better co-ordination between the army and the police. Various semi-military organisations have been formed all over the country. These include Skiet Commandoes, Vigilance Associations, Police Reserves, Civil Guards, private armies of the Robby Leibrandt type, and women's Pistol Clubs. All these are in battle readiness, the country is in a state of siege. This militarisation of the country is cynically justified in the name of Law and Order by the rulers. It is clear to us that the fascists are equipping themselves with power in order to crush our resistance, perpetuate the oppression of the Africans, other Non-Whites and all democrats in South Africa.

The Government has equipped itself with enormous political power. It has passed a series of legislation culminating in two of the worst, the Suppression of Communism Act as amended, and the General Laws Amendment Act. With these they have banned political organisations of the people, jailed political leaders, gagged, exiled, banished and house-arrested them. Every conceivable restrictive order has been served on them. In their everyday lives they live in a state of outlawry, and are ever under the surveillance of the police. The crisis is deepening. It will continue to do so.

THE A.N.C. AND THE PEOPLE.

The people are even stronger. They are led by the most trusted and tried organisation, the A.N.C. It remains the one and only vanguard of the oppressed people in this country. The revolutionary mood of the people is growing. The hatred of the policies of this Government by the progressive world is also growing. Our external Mission has done magnificent work in exposing the immoral policies of the Nationalists abroad and in enlisting the sympathy of the democratic world. This is illustrated by the last resolution of the United Nations to impose sanctions on South Africa, by the decisions of the All-In African and PAFMECA conferences, and by the decisions of the Asian Conference. Internal and External situations favour us.

The African people are in the majority. Their common destiny and the unity it foments accord them greater power than that posed by this regime with all its modern weapons of destruction. The people's militancy and contempt for their ruling power assumes immense proportions. The most recent history of our struggle in town and country illustrates this fact.

METHODS OF STRUGGLE.

There are no short cuts in the political struggle. It is not a hit and a miss game. Our struggle today needs a leadership with the profound understanding of issues involved.

It is our duty as a political organisation to warn the masses of the people about certain adventurists who play just on the emotions of the people and take advantage of their desire for freedom, these people deliberately avoid an explanation of what the struggle entails, the people are told that by plunging the country into riots and terrorist acts, freedom will then be achieved and yet those methods can be very costly in life and time.

But it would be a mistake to regard the spontaneous actions of the people as inspired by opportunism of certain leaders. Some of these actions result from Government provocation, the people's patience becomes exhausted and the masses become desperate in the absence of a strong militant organisation. In these circumstances people are likely to resort more and more into senseless dangerous forms of action. If we embark on unplanned and misguided political actions, we are playing into the hands of the enemy. Sharpeville and Langa are still fresh in our memories, the Transkei and Paarl incidents still dominate our present-day politics. We know that in these acts are involved many honest and well-meaning elements of our oppressed people, whose hunger for freedom and desperation in their misery betray them into responding to these misguided calls. Our duty is to understand their motives, guide and direct their actions along the right course. Much as we admire the valour and militancy of the POQO rank and file, we cannot encourage them in their wrong acts, nor shall we refrain from condemning any activity of theirs that is calculated to discredit our struggle and bring ruin to our people.

It is elementary for any general, before going into battle, to analyse the forces for and against him, decide on the most effective and least dangerous course of attack because he wants to finish the battle as effectively in his favour and as rapidly as possible. Similarly in our fight against the Nationalists we must analyse the forces of the enemy and assess our own potential. Our target is simply the Nationalist Government, its supporters, fully fledged or half-hearted, and all the Government institutions of oppression. In other words we must destroy white supremacy wherever we see it. Any indiscriminate attack will strengthen rather than weaken our enemy, prolong rather than reduce the duration of our struggle, and can have disastrous effects for the whole political movement.

In the changed South African conditions of the struggle, we have the mass political wing of the struggle, spearheaded by the A.N.C. on the one hand, and the specialised military wing, represented by Umkhonto we Sizwe on the other. OUR EMPHASIS STILL REMAINS MASS POLITICAL ACTION. The political wing will ever remain the necessary and integral part of the fight. Political agitation is the only way of creating the atmosphere in which military action can most effectively operate. The political front gives sustenance to the military operations. The Umkhonto cannot survive in a sterile political climate. Our primary objective is the conquest of political power, in doing so African Unity is indispensable.

Umkhonto we Sizwe, as the military wing of our struggle is also guided by the same principle of acting only on the basis of scientific analysis of the objective conditions. It must continue this form of approach, not only during its elementary phase of sabotage, but also during the advanced stage of guerrilla warfare.

We once more appeal for unity of all African political organisations genuinely engaged in the struggle for freedom. Together with African

Unity, we advocate the policy of a united front of all anti-government African political organisations, organisations of the fellow oppressed Non-whites and all organisations of the progressive anti-Government elements.

In the light of this, we advise the Poqo groups against embarking on adventurous and futile acts of terrorism. Although the use of violence to obtain our political objectives has been sanctioned in South Africa, misguided violence or violence for its sake is undesirable and can be very costly to our people. Under extremely vicious conditions of oppression as we have in South Africa today, the temptation for people to lose their objectivity is strong. We may very well expect that there will be people in the not very far future, who will be spurred by their frustration and bitterness into perpetrating unnecessary and senseless acts of terrorism, ugly from every point of view. We strongly warn against such disastrous actions, they can have the gravest consequences for the movement.

THE TRANSKEI AND THE WESTERN CAPE ARE THE BATTLE FIELDS.

In their intensification of the pass laws, the implementation of the Bantu Authorities, the removal of Africans from the Western Cape and the introduction of the new bill, the Government have chosen the Western Cape and the Transkei as the battle fields in the fight between their forces of reaction and ours. We accept this challenge without regret.

Their arrogance and contempt for the people's rights have created an intolerable and provocative situation in the Western Cape and the Transkei. The people are hounded like animals in the Cape. Many are outlaws who habitate the mountain and the bush, with no means of earning a livelihood. Others are jailed and deported to destitution in the Transkei where if deemed undesirable they will be detained in jail for months without trial or be deported by some power-drunk quisling chief to a place of his own liking. Still more will be herded into concentration camps, stylishly called "work camps."

These courageous sons and daughters of Africa have resolved to fight for their inalienable right to freedom of movement and to sell their labour to whosoever they will. The people in the Western Cape have lost their patience. They can no longer put up with these evil schemes of the Government, the pass laws in all their variations.

The National Executive, having fully considered the implications of the removal of the Africans from the Western Cape, the full right of its effects on the lives of both old and young, and being convinced of the mood and militancy of the people, calls on the entire country to give its full support and solidarity with the people of the Western Cape, to take up the fight against the pass laws, the Amendment Bill, and Bantu Authorities. It has chosen the Western Cape and the Transkei as the front line in its onslaught on the Government. It has accepted the people's call for the elimination of the passes in whatever form that proves effective.

To do this, we must embark on an extensive and intensive agitational and educational propaganda in town and country, taking up people's issues however small they might appear. In the towns questions of low wages, high rents and the accompanying ejections from houses must be taken up. Other issues include Urban Bantu Councils, Bantu Education, the deportations of people's leaders, bannings of people, house arrests, banishments and other forms of police terror.

The country is equally important. The time has now come for us to adopt a new attitude towards rural areas by watching very closely the developments there and take up their grievances. Peasant committees of migrant workers in the cities and of people in the country-side must be formed promptly to co-ordinate activities. We must fight the culling down of stock, rehabilitation, landlessness, forced removals of people from their generations old homes, the permanent state of emergency in the Transkei, the tyranny people suffer under Verwoerdian chiefs like Matanzima and the mass starvation of the country dwellers while stacks of grain are hopelessly stored because they cannot be sold, at the time butter, milk and bananas prove useless to the farmers who have no markets for them, and are consequently dumped into the sea. The working conditions of teachers have also deteriorated since the advent of Bantu Education. They have lost their independence of thought, instead they are turned into robots who must do what Maree tells them. This scandal to the teaching profession must be taken up as well. No stone must be left unturned in the massive propaganda campaign. All these must be linked up with the central issue, the Urban Areas Act Amendment Bill, the Pass Laws and the Bantu Authorities.

NEW TACTICS IN THE CAMPAIGN.

We have said that in the new situation our attitude has changed. We say an eye for an eye, a tooth for a tooth. Similarly our campaign against the pass laws will not just assume the form of our former routine pass demonstrations and deputations to various officials in gigantic administrative bureaucracy. Neither shall we announce the date on which actions must be taken. If the Western Cape is ready for action, for example, they must go ahead. The other areas must double their pace so that action taken by one area must snow-ball all over the country.

Also important to note is the fact that passes for women are now compulsory. This means that the anti-pass campaign will be a joint struggle for both men and women. Our volunteers must be put on a war footing.

A PERMANENT CRISIS.

The burning of the passes requires a political crisis, and such a crisis must be built up. We must ensure that the unfolding struggle if it must succeed, must assume a permanent crisis. The people must resist oppression all the time, they must refuse to be governed in the manner the authorities choose to rule them. They must not remain on the defensive, but must take the initiative to attack without giving the rulers time to reflect. A successful campaign against the passes and Bantu Authorities will act as a landslide where the people will score victory, and nothing will stop them from seizing political power.

ORGANISATION.

In view of the hard and arduous struggle that lies ahead of us, we need to pause and assess our own strength and potential. There is no doubt that our organisational machinery does not measure up to the requirement of leading to victory such a trying struggle at the present moment. Even at the time we were operating legally we were not the desired political instrument. There can be no successful struggle without a powerful and efficient political machinery, consisting of the most dedicated, advanced and trusted elements. The building of such an organisation becomes our immediate task.

This necessitates a change in the character of our activities, in keeping with the changes in the national situation. First and foremost, we must call for a greater unity among our members—leaders and rank and file. We must halt vilification, mischief, gossip and factionalism. Our members must be absolutely reliable. They must be apt to any changes in the political environment and be able to make quick decisions and act on them meticulously and accurately.

The basis of our organisation is the M. Plan. By this we mean that in every region, area or street or wherever there are African people, if we do not have a seven men committee, we must at least have an adequate contact. We must guard against being mechanical and dogmatic in our implementation of the blueprint. We must adapt it to the peculiarities of our individual areas, in a manner that will ensure our effective control and influence over the African in every region.

YOUTH AND VOLUNTEERS.

An effective organisation will depend on two things, a strong core of youth and volunteers. The type of volunteers we have in mind are those of the defiance campaign, perhaps even of a higher quality but certainly not less.

In every war in every country, the youth has always been in the forefront. It is the cream of the fighting force. Any organisation whose programme does not appeal to the youth has very little chance of success. Similarly our volunteers can never be equal to the task if they consist only of older and senile men. They could only be effective if they are drawn mostly from the ranks of the youth.

The women equally take an important place in our liberatory movement. Their role is not important only because it accords them an opportunity to take their rightful place of equality with every one in society, but also because they are an indispensable section of our population in the fight for freedom. Attempts must be made for our ideas to infiltrate into every women's organisation, and the Federation of South African women must be strengthened, and the organisations affiliated to the latter, which do not yet support or sympathise with our ideas, must be infused with them.

WORKER'S POLITICAL CONSCIOUSNESS.

Also important in the forthcoming campaign and in all our struggles is the building of workers' organisations and trade unions, and the heightening of the political consciousness of the workers. We must champion their economic issues, high wages, trade union rights and better working conditions. We must inculcate in their minds the feeling of working class solidarity. Their awareness of their economic strength and their ability to demonstrate it are necessary for our major campaign.

ACCURATE REPORTS.

We have always stressed that our members must give accurate and honest reports about any situation. They must be direct, precise and to the point. We must try not to read our own desires and meanings into them. Reports, on which we base our assessments of the situation, can if incorrect, bring about the gravest consequences for the entire liberatory movement.

A grim period is unfolding, as our campaign unfolds and gains momentum the greater will be the torture and onslaught of the Nationalists. The Government will certainly be more ruthless than it has been, it already considers itself at war and is fighting a desperate battle. Every European citizen has been called to defend white supremacy. Whites have been called upon to sacrifice not only time and money but life itself.

It would be criminal on our part not to prepare the Africans throughout the country on a similar scale. No one can afford to be neutral in this situation. We can no longer afford a luxurious life. Every family in every part of the country must adjust itself and make up its mind about the role it must play. The times have changed, we must make only one call, WE DEMAND FREEDOM OR DEATH, there can be no middle course.

Document 70. "The A.N.C. Spearheads Revolution." Leaflet issued by the ANC, May 1963

The A.N.C. Spearheads Revolution Leballo? No!

The South African people are at war with Verwoerd. Twelve million people will be slaves no longer. For three hundred years the Whites have refused to hear our voice. The ways of peace have failed. Now we fight to be free. The Verwoerd government has made it impossible for us to win our birthright any other way.

The A.N.C. tells the people straight: the struggle that will free us is a long, hard job. Do not be deceived by men who talk big with no thought for tomorrow. Freedom is not just a matter of strong words. Neither is it simply brave men and heroic deeds. Impatience, which makes men lose their heads, will not bring freedom.

The White Supremacy state is powerful and has tried to prepare itself for revolution. It has money, it is well-organised, well-armed. Verwoerd and his henchmen will not be frightened out of power.

TO DESTROY VERWOERD WE MUST DESTROY THE IN-STRUMENTS OF WHITE POWER.

We will not win until we destroy the forces that make the White state powerful. We must break the instruments of oppression, take them over, and use them to smash White basskap.

WHAT ARE THE INSTRUMENTS OF WHITE POWER?

They are the army, the mines, the railways, the docks, the factories, the farms, the police, the whole administration.

HOW ARE [WE] TO SMASH THEM?

With planned, strategic violence. Already scared, the Whites are on the look-out. We must outwit them. We must hit them when they are not looking. We must strike where they do not expect it. We must hit them hardest where they are soft.

Organised Violence Will Smash Apartheid!

The Leballo way is useless

Young men, brave and impatient for freedom have joined PAC and POQO. The nation needs brave men! We are all impatient, thirsty for freedom. But impatience alone leads to recklessness, and recklessness can lose us the battle. The Leballo way is useless, worse than useless.

LEBALLO TALKS OF FREEDOM IN 1963

From Basutoland, Potlako Leballo challenges Vorster and says: "Our revolutionary council is discussing the time and manner in which positive action will be launched. It is imminent." Any sane man knows that the struggle will be longer than the eight months left this year. It took the Algerians seven years to get rid of the French. We will not smash Verwoerd in a day. Instead of organising, Leballo incites our bravest men to rush unarmed into the guns of Verwoerd as if freedom was a Christmas present.

LEBALLO TALKS TOO MUCH

Leballo has always been a boaster. He is confused: he says one thing today and denies it tomorrow. Now he has betrayed his people. Either Leballo genuinely believes there will be freedom in one action—in which case he is wrong, and other men will die for his mistakes, or else he knows the revolution will take time, but for some mysterious reason wants to deceive us.

THE P.A.C. LEADERS FIGHT AMONG THEMSELVES

There is no room in freedom organisations for ambitious men out for their own gain. The PAC leadership has shown it cannot work together. They expel a Philip Kgosane then a Madzunya. Next Leballo will expel Sobukwe. Can we trust these men? They talk the loudest, and think the least; they say one thing and mean another. Revolution is serious business. These men—vain, squabbling and confused—will waste our noblest soldiers as if they were toys.

PAC KNOWS NOTHING ABOUT WAR

A crowd of unarmed men on a midnight march to town cannot break the police, the army and all the oppression of Verwoerd. That was Paarl—a heroic effort born out of oppression, but badly conceived. It is no good to think in terms of impis, not of modern guerrilla war. PAC leaders like Leballo talk of revolution but do not work out how to make revolution. War needs careful plans. War is not a gesture of defiance. For a sum total of nine Whites killed—only one of them a policeman, and he killed by accident—hundreds of Poqos are in jail serving thousands of years imprisonment. For a wild boast Leballo has caused the round-up of unknown numbers of young fighters.

These ways achieve nothing politically. These ways squander men, make of the life and death struggle a game of prestige and big talk.

BRAVE MEN MUST KNOW HOW TO FIGHT

The leaders must have control over their soldiers. The soldiers must know what the leaders want. The freedom forces of South Africa must be coordinated—cell with cell, branch with branch, region with region—in revolution. There must be strong discipline—no actions going off half-cock.

NO MISUSE OF MANPOWER

It is a misuse of manpower to send out all men on every job, as if enough followers could make up for too little leadership. Freedom fighters must be trained. Ten men, well trained and organised, can often without fuss, do a job that 200 men, heroic but badly-led, would bungle.

DON'T MISTAKE THE REAL TARGET

Poqo is said to have killed five White road-builders in the Transkei recently. There are more effective ways of busting the White supremacy state. A few road-builders make no difference to the revolution. Instead, smashed railway lines, damaged pylons carrying electricity across the country, bombed-out petrol dumps cut Verwoerd off from his power, and leave him helpless. And these acts are only the beginning—

WHY MAKE ENEMIES OF OUR ALLIES?

The Leballos spurn men of other races. We say that just as Africans bear the brunt of oppression under the White state, so will the White state be broken by the main force of African people. But this is no reason we say, to reject comrades of other races whom we know are ready to fight with us, suffer, and if need be, die.

NO CRY OF DESPAIR!

The slogan POQO—'pure' is a panicky cry of blind leaders who thrust themselves away from others and for comfort in the dark, shout out they are alone. We have no need to worship isolation—the people are with us. We distrust despair, for it does not make good soldiers. Despair sent the men of Paarl, armed with nothing but their bravery, unorganised, untrained, and badly led, to meet the bullets of Verwoerd's police. Despair is dangerous. There is also no reason for it. We know we will win. The only question is how soon—and that depends on how we use our forces.

ABOVE ALL—SECURITY

Freedom fighters must keep their mouths shut. There is no room for those who give statements to the police. Young recruits who have a few drinks and start boasting are a danger. Arrested men who turn state witness betray the struggle. No abortive adventures. No police penetration of the freedom force!

Find a way—
But not the Leballo way
Umkhonto We Sizwe

—Army of the Liberation Movement—

* UMKHONTO IS FOR ACTIVISTS
We have struck against the White state more than 70 times (boldly yet methodically). We are trained and practised. We shall be more so.

* UMKHONTO IS ORGANISED
Our organisation is nation-wide. We can strike anywhere.

* UMKHONTO TRAINS THE YOUTH
We are ceaselessly, thoroughly, training an Army of Liberation.

* UMKHONTO HAS POWERFUL ALLIES
The African states and the democratic world are four-square behind us. We have allies among other races in South Africa.

* UMKHONTO HAS A PLANNED STRATEGY
Umkhonto can analyse the revolutionary situation. It knows how to use soldiers where they are most effective.

* UMKHONTO HAS LEADERSHIP
Our leaders are brave, intelligent men. They work together.

* UMKHONTO HAS NO NEED TO BOAST
The people are with us. We are for the people. Our words are deeds.

Three POQO men are due to hang. Hundreds are in jail, many for life. Who knows how many will be rounded up after the Leballo fiasco?

THESE ARE THE CASUALTIES IN THE FREEDOM STRUGGLE. WE QUARREL NOT WITH BRAVE MEN BUT WITH BAD LEADERSHIP. WE ATTACK PAC—LEBALLO POLICY NOT OUT OF PETTY RIVALRY BUT BECAUSE IT TAKES US BACK, NOT FORWARD ALONG THE FREE-DOM ROAD.

* Genuine freedom-fighters must find a way to fight together, in UNITY, in unbreakable strength.
* There is room in the freedom struggle for all brave men—and women

WE ARE PREPARED TO TALK UNITY TO WORK FOR UNITY; TO FIGHT UNITED WITH THE CORRECT POL-ICY AND THE CORRECT FIGHTING STRATEGY

WITH YOUR SUPPORT WE WILL WIN

Amandla Ngawethu!

Be Careful—But Let Others See This

Issued by: African National Congress

Note: "Amandla Ngawethu" is "Power to the People"

Document 71. "Editorial." [Anonymous] in *Black Star* [PAC], Vol. 1, No. 1, May 1963

The South African situation has now reached a critical point both for the government on one side and the liberatory forces on the other. The government is frantically trying for the head and the heart of the resistance movement. It wants to smoke out the leaders. It wants to panic them into a premature move which will enable it to pounce and shatter the whole structure for years to come. The provocations by the police, the show of force by the army, the frantic efforts to infiltrate the ranks of the resistance movement by means of paid informers, indicate that the government is desperate and cannot afford an indefinite war of nerves. On the other hand, time is on the side of the resistance movement. The government knows this and in an effort to force a show-down is using all its resources in police terror and fifth column infiltration.

The propaganda machinery of the government has tossed a bone in the ranks of the liberatory movement in the form of a Xhosa word *"POQO"*. Whilst the world is heatedly disputing as to who is poqo, what is poqo—let alone how poqo is poqo—the government is systematically roping in all its opponents. In February alone over 250 youths between the ages of sixteen and twenty-two have been sent to the new maximum security prison on the bleak Robben Island, off the coast of South Africa, Three people have been sentenced to death under the Sabotage Act. Acting on information supplied by the Basutoland police, 854 former members of the Pan Africanist Congress were arrested in one night alone.

The newspapers have been full of poqo the so-called terrorist organisation. In recent weeks a gruesome picture of a sinister organisation administering secret oaths and savage rites has been presented. A horrific image of bloodthirsty savage hordes intent on the blood of a white man has sent shivers down the spines of a reading public conditioned by propaganda to accepting everything without questioning.

It is important at this stage to get the picture clear. There is a reign of terror in South Africa. For years the government has been responsible for this. Authenticated data shows the ruthlessness with which the government is carrying out its programme to liquidate all opposition to its racist rule. All political organisations which provided disciplined political direction to their members have been suppressed. The leaders are all in jail or hunted from one underground cell to another—always just one jump ahead of the closing net. There has been a complete press black-out in the Transkei for the last three years. Jails are full of detainees who have never appeared before a court of law. Families are being uprooted, stock and produce maliciously destroyed by chiefs and their home guards to intimidate all opposition. Whole families have moved into the forests to seek refuge. Torture in the form of electric shock is now common practice. Large-scale reprisals against families of the detainees is now the order of the day. The Government is paying R50.00 for information leading to the arrest of so-called Poqo terrorists.

That white terror would in time beget black terror has been clear. While it is still a debatable point whether the present happenings in South Africa are manifestation of anti-whitism, there is no doubt that 99% of white South Africa has been and is anti-black. White South Africa is squarely to blame for whatever is happening today. Imagine a people despoiled, dispossessed of their land, without hope for the future, without recourse to law, a people kept under by a fascist government which is using all the power of the police force and the army to enforce its will on them. In such situations the people will administer their own form of justice. They will set up their own tribunals and, however crude these may be, they will dispense a people's justice which is often very rough. Throughout history, the people have visited their anger first against those of their kind who have betrayed them—the quislings, the informers, the political pimps. Already it is clear that a heavy price is being paid by those who would sell the struggle of the people for 50 pieces of silver—the current price paid by the South African Government.

The veil has been torn aside exposing a police-state reminiscent of Nazi-Germany. It is an old technique in all fascist states to find scape-goats to direct attention from the real issues. South Africa is applying this technique by a "poqo" scare, a monster of the government's own creation. Verwoerd has reached the end of the line—he has played out his best cards as the Resistance Movement mounts its offensive. It is clear that he and his kind are living on borrowed time.

Document 72. Broadcast, by W. M. Sisulu, on ANC Radio, June 26, 1963

Sons and Daughters of Africa:
   I speak to you from somewhere in South Africa.
   I have not left the country.
   I do not plan to leave.
   Many of our leaders of the African National Congress have gone underground. This is to keep the organisation in action; to preserve the

leadership; to keep the freedom fight going. Never has the country, and our people, needed leadership as they do now, in this hour of crisis.

Our house is on fire.

It is the duty of the people of our land—every man and every woman—to rally behind our leaders. There is no time to stand and watch. Thousands are in jail including our dynamic Nelson Mandela. Many are banished to remote parts of the country. Robben Island is a giant concentration camp for political prisoners. Men and women, including my wife, rot in cells under Vorster's vicious laws to imprison without trial. Men wait in the death cells to be hanged. Men die for freedom.

South Africa is in a permanent state of emergency. Any policeman may arrest any South African—and need not bring him to trial. People may be hanged for appealing to the United Nations to intervene. Under the Bantu Laws Amendment Bill, the pass laws will turn children into orphans, wives into widows, men into slaves. We must intensify the attack on the pass laws. We must fight against the removal of the Africans from the Western Cape. We must reject once and for all times, the Bantustan fraud. No act of Government must go unchallenged. The struggle must never waver. We the African National Congress will lead with new methods of struggle. The African people know that their unity is vital. Only by united action can we overthrow this Government. We call on all our people to unite and struggle. Workers and peasants; teachers and students; Ministers of Religion and all Churches. We call upon all our people, of whatever shade of opinion. We say:— The hour has come for us to stand together. This is the only way to freedom. Nothing short of unity will bring the people their freedom. We warn the Government that drastic laws will not stop our struggle for liberation. Throughout the ages men have sacrificed—they have given their lives for their ideals. And we are also determined to surrender our lives for our freedom.

In the face of violence, men struggling for freedom have had to meet violence with violence. How can it be otherwise in South Africa? Changes must come. Changes for the better, but not without sacrifice. Your sacrifice. My sacrifice.

We face tremendous odds. We know that. But our unity, our determination, our sacrifice, our organisation are our weapons. We must succeed! We will succeed!

Amandla!

Document 73. "Operation Mayibuye." Document found by the police at Rivonia, July 11, 1963

PART 1.

The white state has thrown overboard every pretence of rule by democratic process. Armed to the teeth it has presented the people with only one choice and that is its overthrow by force and violence. It can now truly be said that very little, if any, scope exists for the smashing of white supremacy other than by means of mass revolutionary action, the main content of which is armed resistance leading to victory by military means.

The political events which have occurred in the last few years have convinced the overwhelming majority of the people that no mass struggle which is not backed up by armed resistance and military offensive operations, can hope to make a real impact. This can be seen from the general mood of the people and their readiness to undertake even desperate and suicidal violent campaigns of the Leballo type. It can also be gauged by their reluctance to participate in orthodox political struggles in which they expose themselves to massive retaliation without a prospect of hitting back. We are confident that the masses will respond in overwhelming numbers to a lead which holds out a real possibility of successful armed struggle.

Thus two important ingredients of a revolutionary situation are present:—

a) A disillusionment with constitutional or semi-constitutional forms of struggle and a conviction that the road to victory is through force;
b) A militancy and a readiness to respond to a lead which holds out a real possibility of successful struggle.

In the light of the existence of these ingredients the prosecution of military struggle depends for its success on two further factors:—

A. The strength of the enemy. This must not be looked at statically but in the light of objective factors, which in a period of military struggle may well expose its brittleness and
B. The existence of a clear leadership with material resources at its disposal to spark off and sustain military operations.

The objective military conditions in which the movement finds itself makes the possibility of a general uprising leading to direct military struggle an unlikely one. Rather, as in Cuba, the general uprising must be sparked off by organised and well prepared guerrilla operations during the course of which the masses of the people will be drawn in and armed.

We have no illusions about the difficulties which face us in launching and successfully prosecuting guerrilla operations leading to military victory. Nor do we assume that such a struggle will be over swiftly. We have taken into account and carefully weighed numerous factors and we mention some of them:

a) We are faced with a powerfully armed modern state with tremendous industrial resources, which can, at least in the initial period, count on the support of three million whites. At the same time the State is isolated practically from the rest of the world, and if effective work is done, will have to rely in the main on its own resources. The very concentration of industry and power and the interdependence of the various localities operates as both an advantage and a disadvantage for the enemy. It operates as a disadvantage because effective guerrilla operations can within a relatively short period create far greater economic havoc and confusion than in a backward, decentralised country.

b) The people are unarmed and lack personnel who have been trained in all aspects of military operations. A proper organisation of the almost unlimited assistance which we can obtain from friendly Governments will counter-balance its disadvantage. In the long run a guerrilla struggle relies on the enemy for its source of supply. But in order to make this possible an initial effective arming of the first group of guerrilla bands is essential. It is also vital to place in the field persons trained in the art of war who will act as a nucleus of organisers and commanders of guerrilla operations.

c) The absence of friendly borders and long scale impregnable natural bases from which to operate are both disadvantages. But more important than these factors is the support of the people who in certain situations are better protection than mountains and forests. In the rural areas which become the main theatre of guerrilla operations in the initial phase, the overwhelming majority of the people will protect and safeguard the guerrillas and this fact will to some measure negative the disadvantages. In any event we must not underestimate the fact that there is terrain in many parts of South Africa, which although not classically impregnable is suitable for guerrilla type operations. Boer guerrillas with the support of their people operated in the plains of the Transvaal. Although conditions have changed there is still a lesson to be learnt from this.

Although we must prepare for a protracted war we must not lose sight of the fact that the political isolation of South Africa from the world community of nations and particularly the active hostility towards it from almost the whole of the African Continent and the Socialist world may result in such massive assistance in various forms, that the state structure will collapse far sooner than we can at the moment envisage. Direct military intervention in South West Africa, an effective economic and military boycott, even armed international action at some more advanced stage of the struggle are real possibilities which will play an important role. In no other territory where guerrilla operations have been undertaken has the international situation been such a vital factor operating against the enemy. We are not unaware that there are powerful external monopoly interests who will attempt to bolster up the white state. With effective work they can be isolated and neutralised. The events of the last few years have shown that the issue of racial discrimination cuts across world ideological conflict albeit that the West proceeds from opportunistic premises.

The following plan envisages a process which will place in the field, at a date fixed now, simultaneously in pre-selected areas armed and trained guerrilla bands who will find ready to join the local guerrilla bands with arms and equipment at their disposal. It will further coincide with a massive propaganda campaign both inside and outside South Africa and a general call for unprecedented mass struggle throughout the land, both violent and non-violent. In the initial period when for a short while the military adv. [sic] will be ours the plan envisages a massive onslaught on pre-selected targets which will create maximum havoc and confusion in the enemy camp and which will inject into the masses of the people and other friendly forces a feeling of confidence that here at least is an army of liberation equipped and capable of leading them to victory. In this period the cornerstone of guerrilla operations is "shamelessly attack the weak and shamelessly flee from the strong".

We are convinced that this plan is capable of fullfilment. But only if the whole apparatus of the movement both here and abroad is mobilised for its implementation and if every member now prepares to make unlimited sacrifice for the achievement of our goal. The time for small thinking is over because history leaves us no choice.

PART II.
AREAS.
1. Port Elizabeth—Mzimkulu.
2. Port Shepstone—Swaziland.
3. North Western Transvaal, bordering respectively Bechuanaland & Limpopo.
4. North Western Cape—South West.

PART III.
PLAN.
1. Simultaneous landing of 4 groups of 30 based on our present resources whether by ship or air—armed and properly equipped in such a way as to be self sufficient in every respect for at least a month.
2. At the initial stages it is proposed that the 30 are split up into platoons of 10 each to operate more or less within a contiguous area and linking their activities with pre-arranged local groups.
3. Simultaneously with the landing of the groups of 30 and thereafter, there should be a supply of arms and other war material to arm the local populations which become integrated with the guerrilla units.
4. On landing, a detailed plan of attack on pre-selected targets with a view to taking the enemy by surprise, creating the maximum impact on the populace, creating as much chaos and confusion for the enemy as possible.
5. Choice of suitable areas will be based on the nature of the terrain, with a view to establishing base areas from which our units can attack and to which they can retreat.

6. Before these operations take place political authority will have been set up in secrecy in a friendly territory with a view to supervising the struggle both in its internal and external aspects. It is visualised that this authority will in due course of time develop into a Provisional Revolutionary Government.

7. This Political Authority should trim its machinery so that simultaneously with the commencement of operations it will throw out massive propaganda to win world support for our struggle, more particularly:—

a) A complete enforcement of boycott,

b) Enlisting the support of the international trade union movement to refuse handling war materials and other goods intended for the South African Government,

c) Raising a storm at the United Nations which should be urged to intervene militarily in South West Africa.

d) Raising of large scale credits for the prosecution of the struggle,

e) Arranging for radio facilities for daily transmission to the world and to the people of South Africa.

f) If possible the Political Authority should arrange for the initial onslaught to bombard the country or certain areas with a flood of leaflets by plane announcing the commencement of our armed struggle as well as our aims, and calling upon the population to rise against the Government.

g) Stepping up transport plans, e.g. a weekly or bi weekly airlift of trainees outside the country in order to maintain a regular, if small flow of trained personnel.

h) In order to facilitate the implementation of the military aspect of the plan it is proposed the National High Command appoint personnel to be quartered at Dar under the auspices of the office there.

PART IV.

INTERNAL ORGANISATION.

In preparation for the commencement of operations when our external team lands, intensive as well as extensive work will have been done. For instance, guerrilla units will have been set up in the main areas mapped out in Part 1 above as well as in the other areas away from the immediate scene of operation.

Progressively sabotage activity throughout the country will be stepped up before these operations. Political pressure too, in the meanwhile will be stepped up in conjunction with the sabotage activity.

In furtherance of the general ideas set out above the plan for internal organisation is along the following pattern:—

1. Our target is that on arrival the external force should find at least 7,000 men in the four main areas ready to join the guerrilla army in the initial

onslaught. Those will be allocated as follows:—

   (a) Eastern Cape—Transkei   2,000
   (b) Natal—Zululand   2,000
   (c) North Western Transvaal   2,000
   (d) North-Western Cape   1,000

2. To realise our target in each of the main areas it is proposed that each of the four areas should have an overall command whose task it will be to divide its area into regions, which in turn will be allocated a figure in proportion to their relative importance.

3. The preparation for equipping the initial force envisaged in 1 above will take place in three stages, thus:

   (a) By importation of Military supply at two levels:
       (i) Build up of firearms, ammunition and explosives by maintaining a regular flow over a period of time.
       (ii) By landing additional [supplies] simultaneously with the arrival of our external force.
   (b) Acquisition and accumulation internally of firearms, ammunition and explosives at all levels of our organisation.
   (c) Collection and accumulation of other military such as food, medicines, communication equipment etc.

4. It is proposed that auxiliary guerrilla/sabotage units in the four main areas be set up before and after the commencement of operations. They may engage in activities that may serve to disperse the enemy forces, assist to maintain the fighting ability of the guerrillas as well as draw in the masses in support of the guerrillas.

5. It is proposed that in areas falling outside the four main guerrilla areas M.K. units should be set up to act in support of the activities in the guerrilla areas, and to harass the enemy.

6. In order to draw in the masses of the population the political wing should arouse the people to participate in the struggles that are designed to create an upheaval throughout the country.

PART V.

DETAILED PLAN OF IMPLEMENTATION.

In order to implement the plans set out above in Parts I to III we establish Departments which are to be charged with duties to study and submit detailed reports and plans in respect of each of their Departments with the following terms of reference:—

1. *Intelligence Department*
   This Committee will be required to study and report on the following:—
   (a) The exact extent of each area

(b) The portions of the country that are naturally suited for our operations and their location within each area.

(c) Points along the coast which would be suitable for landing of men and supplies and how these are going to be transferred from the point of landing to the area of operations.

(d) The situation of enemy forces in each area, thus:—
   (i) the military and the police as well as their strength
   (ii) military and police camps, and towns, and the distances between them,
   (iii) system of all forms of communication in the area,
   (iv) the location of trading stations and chiefs and headmen's kraals,
   (v) air fields and air strips in the areas.

(e) Selection of targets to be tackled in initial phase of guerrilla operations with a view to causing maximum damage to the enemy as well as preventing the quick deployment of re enforcements.

   In its study the Committee should bear in mind the following main targets:—
   (i) strategic road, railways and other communications
   (ii) power stations
   (iii) police, stations, camps and military forces
   (iv) irredeemable Government stooges.

(f) A study of climatic conditions in relation to seasons, as well as diseases common to the area.

(g) The population distribution in the areas as well as the main crops.

(h) Rivers and dams.

(i) And generally all other relevant matters

2. *External Planning Committee* which shall be charged with the following tasks:—

(a) Obtaining of arms, ammunition and explosives and other equipment

(b) In co-operation with our internal machinery, making arrangements for the despatch of items in 1 above into the country

(c) Obtaining of transport by land, sea and air for the landing of our task force and for the continued supply of military equipment.

3. *Political Authority*

We make a strong recommendation that the joint sponsoring organisations should immediately set about creating a political machinery for the direction of the revolutionary struggle as set out in Nos. 6, 7 and 8 of Part II and to set up a special committee to direct guerrilla political education.

4. *Transport Committee.*

This Committee is assigned the following duties:—

(a) The organisation of transport facilities for our trainees

(b) To organise transport for the re entry of our trainees

(c) To undertake any transport duties assigned to them from time to time.

5. *Logistics Department— Technical and Supply Committee*
   Its Functions are:—
   (a) To manufacture and build up a stock of arms, ammunition from internal sources.
   (b) To organise reception, distribution and storage of supplies from external sources.
   (c) To organise the training of personnel in the use of equipment referred to in (a) and (b) above.
   (d) Obtaining of all other relevant supplies necessary to prosecute an armed struggle, to wit, inter alia, medical supplies, clothing, food, etc., and the storage of these at strategic points.
   (e) Acquiring equipment to facilitate communications.
   (f) To undertake all duties and functions that fall under the Department of Logistics.

PART VI

MISCELLANEOUS

1. *Immediate Duties of the National High Command in Relation to the Guerrilla Areas:*
   (a) To map out regions in each area with a view to organising Regional and District Commands and N.K. [*sic*] units.
   (b) To achieve this we strongly recommend the employment of 10 full time organisers in each area.
   (c) The organisers shall be directly responsible to the National High Command.
   (d) The NHC is directed to recruit and arrange for the external training of at least 300 men in the next two months.

2. *Personal*
   (a) *Intelligence* Alex Secundus Otto
   (b) *External Planning Committee* Johnson, Thabo and Joseph together with a senior ANC rep. as well as co-opted personnel, seconded to us by friendly Govts.
   (c) *Transport Committee* Percy secundus Nbata.
   (d) *Logistics Dept.* Bri-bri secundus Frank

3. *Special Directives to Heads of Departments.*
   The Heads of Departments are required to submit not later than the 30th May, 1963, plans detailing:—
   (a) The structural organisation of their Department
   (b) The type and number of personnel they require to be allocated to them and their duties and functions.
   (c) The funds required for their work both for immediate and long term purposes.
   (d) Schedule of time required to enable them to fulfill given targets and what these are.

(e) Other matters relating to the efficient execution of the Departments'
Plans.

4. *Organisation of Areas. Organisors and Setting up of proper Machinery*
Rethau and James for this task.

Document 74. "The A.N.C. calls on you—SAVE THE LEADERS!" Two-page flyer issued by the ANC, October 1963

The A.N.C. calls on you—
SAVE THE LEADERS!

THE PEOPLE'S LEADERS ARE ON TRIAL! Their crime? They dared
to challenge White supremacy, apartheid and injustice. They were
determined to struggle for a free South Africa for all, regardless of skin
colour.

THE PEOPLES' LEADERS ARE IN DANGER! Vorster seeks to hang
some, to imprison others indefinitely. The whole of South Africa has
become a jail, with thousands imprisoned. Husbands and sons disappear;
many are beaten; some die. Others are brought to trial, in White courts,
with laws made by the all-White parliament, with White prosecutors and
judges. Our leaders are then accused of crimes like sabotage and treason.

*We say IT IS TREASON TO REMAIN SILENT IN THE FACE
OF INJUSTICE. We say OUR DEMANDS ARE REASONABLE,
CORRECT AND JUST. THIS IS RECOGNISED ALL OVER
THE WORLD.*

Today the whole world condemns South Africa, and every international
organisation from the United Nations downwards, tries to exclude South
African representatives of the apartheid system. Rejection of apartheid is
universal, yet when we seek to end apartheid, our organisations are made
illegal, our leaders are removed from us, our homes and families destroyed
by apartheid policies. Is it not right and natural to fight these things? And
when all other means are removed, should we not oppose force by force?

STAND BY THESE LEADERS! Vorster and Vewoerd seek to destroy
them and thus destroy us all. Only we can save them. We can save them by
demonstrations, strikes, mass action. Do not be afraid! The Government
may seem very strong. But they are not strong. They are alone, isolated and
despised by most South Africans and the whole of the rest of the world. If

we, the people, really start to move, to protest, to withdraw our labour, to refuse to move when evicted, to reject being herded into Bantustans, we can MAKE APARTHEID UNWORKABLE. It only exists because of US. We can bring the whole country to a standstill. ONLY SUCH MASS ACTION CAN SAVE MEN LIKE SISULU, MANDELA, KATH-RADA, MBEKI, BERNSTEIN and the OTHERS!

PROTECT THESE LEADERS! The Government say they have been able to destroy the underground movement with the Rivonia raid. The A.N.C. and its allies live on and fight on. Umkhonto continues to prepare for the fight and to strike at the Government. *LET US PROVE THE GOVERNMENT IS WRONG BY OUR MILITANT ACTION.*

SAVE THESE LEADERS! Vorster wants to terrify White South Africa, to exact his price. Whatever sentences are passed on these men will never bring our fight to an end. We still demand the right to govern ourselves, an end to pass laws and oppression and to racial discrimination. If we continue to fight for these things, we are fighting for ourselves and our children and the leaders who sacrificed themselves.

FREE THESE LEADERS! Let us show the world we are not terrorised, not passive, not indifferent, not idle. Let us raise a cry that will echo round the world—FREE THESE LEADERS! Among them are men and women of all races. We are proud of them all, Black, White, Indian and Coloured. We will be united to fight apartheid in every possible way to the very end.

The AFRICAN NATIONAL CONGRESS calls on you to organise now to save the Peoples' leaders–Smash Apartheid Tyranny– Free South Africa!

THE PEOPLE SHALL RULE!
AMANDLA NGAWETHU!

WHITE MAN—You are on trial . . .

The Government is putting the 'Rivonia' men on trial. Vorster claims he has caught the 'trouble-makers' . . . .
WHITE MAN—DOES THAT MAKE YOU FEEL SAFE?
   Vorster seeks the death sentence for some of them, imprisonment for the rest. . . .
WHITE MAN—WILL YOU SLEEP BETTER AT NIGHT?
   The prosecution will make your flesh creep with stories of 'hellish' military plots, sabotage, threats to the safety of the state. . . .
WHITE MAN—DO YOU KNOW WHAT THIS MEANS?

LET US TELL YOU WHAT IT MEANS. . . South Africa is in the first stage of civil war. Apartheid has brought that war. Over 3,000 men and women, mostly Africans, but including all races, are in jails for resisting apartheid. More will be tried. They come from all over South Africa. They are not criminals. Most of them are people of the highest integrity, intelligence and courage, gentle and compassionate, vitally concerned with problems of justice and freedom. In any normal society these people would be the rulers.

Our land is not normal. Violence is used every day against our people. They are violently uprooted by the tens of thousands and turned out of their homes. Families are violently divided, people are deprived of the right to decent wages, proper education, normal homes. Our organisations are violently suppressed, our leaders forcibly removed from us. We have been deprived of every legal, every legitimate means of protest.

When the Government wants to do something that conflicts with the rule of law, they pass a law to make it 'legal'. Then basest injustice becomes the law, and all those who oppose it become saboteurs. The Government prepares for open war against the people, training and arming every White man and woman, teaching schoolgirls to shoot, and schoolboys to fight the Black man, creating an atmosphere of fear and war.

. . . . ALL THIS IN THE NAME OF 'PRESERVING WHITE CIVILISATION'. All that is worthwhile in civilisation is being destroyed in South Africa. What are you trying to preserve?

WHITE MAN–THE WORLD IS AGAINST YOU! There is not an international gathering today, whether it is health, tourism, atomic energy or sport, where S. Africans are wanted. They are ostracised & despised everywhere. Even the United Nations itself adjourns in protest against the policies of White South Africa. You think the world doesn't understand our policies? They understand them too well. The principles on which apartheid is built were rejected when Hitler was defeated.

STOP AND THINK! Not only is apartheid opposed by the world—the majority of South Africans also oppose it. Do you really believe that Vorster and Verwoerd are the infallible leaders of all civilisation? That they are right and MOST of South Africa and the WHOLE of the rest of the world wrong? Do you really believe that by taking bitter reprisals against those who seek to end this tyranny, like the Rivonia people, that you are safeguarding your children's future?

If these leaders die in Vorster's hands—you, White man, and all your family, stand in mortal danger. We are pledged to fight for freedom to the very end. With this trial you will never destroy saboteurs—there are 13 million of us—but you will destroy yourself, your safety, your future. We swear to stand by them at all costs—and the costs will be YOURS!

It is not treason to seek to overthrow and destroy a govt. that does not rule in the interests of the majority. It is not treason to seek to end the dictatorship of Verwoerd and Vorster. But it IS treason to remain silent in the face of evil. The Rivonia people did no more than the people of America, Israel, France, Cuba—all those who have ever opposed wrong and fought for freedom.

Before it is too late—help save these leaders! Reject apartheid! Let your conscience speak!

Prove to the world, and to us Black people, that there is some honour and decency left among the White people.

WE WARN YOU–WE WILL NEVER GIVE IN. The longer this goes on, the more everyone will suffer.

WHITE MAN— *YOU* ARE ON TRIAL BEFORE THE EYES OF THE WORLD. What is there left for you to plead?

Issued by THE AFRICAN NATIONAL CONGRESS

Document 75. Statement during the Rivonia trial, by Nelson R. Mandela, April 20, 1964

I am the First Accused.

I hold a Bachelor's Degree in Arts and practised as an attorney in Johannesburg for a number of years in partnership with Oliver Tambo. I am a convicted prisoner serving five years for leaving the country without a permit and for inciting people to go on strike at the end of May, 1961.

At the outset, I want to say that the suggestion made by the State in its opening that the struggle in South Africa is under the influence of foreigners or communists is wholly incorrect. I have done whatever I did, both as an individual and as a leader of my people, because of my experience in South Africa and my own proudly-felt African background, and not because of what any outsider might have said.

In my youth in the Transkei I listened to the elders of my tribe telling stories of the old days. Amongst the tales they related to me were those of wars fought by our ancestors in defence of the fatherland. The names of Dingane and Bambata, Hintsa and Makana, Squngthi and Dalasile, Moshoeshoe and Sekhukhuni, were praised as the glory of the entire African nation. I hoped then that life might offer me the opportunity to serve my people and make my own humble contribution to their freedom struggle. This is what has motivated me in all that I have done in relation to the charges made against me in this case.

Having said this, I must deal immediately and at some length, with the question of violence. Some of the things so far told to the Court are true and some are untrue. I do not, however, deny that I planned sabotage. I did not plan it in a spirit of recklessness, nor because I have any love of violence. I planned it as a result of a calm and sober assessment of the political situation that had arisen after many years of tyranny, exploitation and oppression of my people by the Whites.

I admit immediately that I was one of the persons who helped to form Umkonto We Sizwe, and that I played a prominent role in its affairs until I was arrested in August, 1962.

In the statement which I am about to make I shall correct certain false impressions which have been created by State witnesses. Amongst other things, I will demonstrate that certain of the acts referred to in the evidence were not and could not have been committed by Umkonto. I will also deal with the relationship between the African National Congress and Umkonto, and with the part which I personally have played in the affairs of both organizations. I shall deal also with the part played by the Communist Party. In order to explain these matters properly I will have to explain what Umkonto set out to achieve; what methods it prescribed for the achievement of these objects, and why these methods were chosen. I will also have to explain how I became involved in the activities of these organizations.

I deny that Umkonto was responsible for a number of acts which clearly fell outside the policy of the organization, and which have been charged in the Indictment against us. I do not know what justification there was for these acts, but to demonstrate that they could not have been authorised by Umkonto, I want to refer briefly to the roots and policy of the organization.

I have already mentioned that I was one of the persons who helped to form Umkonto. I, and the others who started the organization, did so for two reasons. Firstly, we believed that as a result of Government policy, violence by the African people had become inevitable, and that unless responsible leadership was given to canalise and control the feelings of our people, there would be outbreaks of terrorism which would produce an intensity of bitterness and hostility between the various races of this country which is not produced even by war. Secondly, we felt that without violence there would be no way open to the African people to succeed in their struggle against the principle of White supremacy. All lawful modes of expressing opposition to this principle had been closed by legislation, and we were placed in a position in which we had either to accept a permanent state of inferiority, or to defy the Government. We chose to defy the law. We first broke the law in a way which avoided any recourse to violence; when this form was legislated against, and when the Government resorted to a show of force to crush opposition to its policies, only then did we decide to answer violence with violence.

But the violence which we chose to adopt was not terrorism. We who formed Umkonto were all members of the African National Congress, and had behind us the A.N.C. tradition of non-violence and negotiation as a means of solving political disputes. We believe that South Africa belonged to all the people who lived in it, and not to one group, be it Black or White. We did not want an inter-racial war, and tried to avoid it to the last minute. If the Court is in doubt about this, it will be seen that the whole history of our organization bears out what I have said, and what I will subsequently say, when I describe the tactics which Umkonto decided to adopt. I want, therefore, to say something about the African National Congress.

The African National Congress was formed in 1912 to defend the rights of the African people which had been seriously curtailed by the South Africa Act, and which were then being threatened by the Native Land Act. For thirty-seven years—that is until 1949—it adhered strictly to a constitutional struggle. It put forward demands and resolutions; it sent delegations to the Government in the belief that African grievances could be settled through peaceful discussion and that Africans could advance gradually to full political rights. But White Governments remained unmoved, and the rights of Africans became less instead of becoming greater. In the words of my leader, Chief Luthuli, who became President of the A.N.C. in 1952, and who was later awarded the Nobel Peace Prize:

"who will deny that thirty years of my life have been spent knocking in vain, patiently, moderately and modestly at a closed and barred door? What have been the fruits of moderation? The past thirty years have seen the greatest number of laws restricting our rights and progress, until today we have reached a stage where we have almost no rights at all".

Even after 1949, the A.N.C. remained determined to avoid violence. At this time, however, there was a change from the strictly constitutional means of protest which had been employed in the past. The change was embodied in a decision which was taken to protest against apartheid legislation by peaceful, but unlawful, demonstrations against certain laws. Pursuant to this policy the A.N.C. launched the Defiance Campaign, in which I was placed in charge of volunteers. This campaign was based on the principles of passive resistance. More than 8,500 people defied apartheid laws and went to gaol. Yet there was not a single instance of violence in the course of this campaign on the part of any defier. I, and nineteen colleagues were convicted for the role which we played in organizing the campaign, but our sentences were suspended mainly because the Judge found that discipline and nonviolence had been stressed throughout. This was the time when the volunteer section of the A.N.C. was established, and when the word 'Amadelakufa' was first used: this was the time when the volunteers were asked to take a pledge to uphold certain principles. Evidence dealing with volunteers and their pledges has been introduced into this case, but completely out of context. The volunteers were not, and are not, the soldiers of a Black Army pledged to fight a civil war against the Whites. They were, and are, the dedicated workers who are prepared to lead campaigns initiated by the A.N.C. to distribute leaflets; to organize strikes, or do whatever the particular campaign required. They are called volunteers because they volunteer to face the penalties of imprisonment and whipping which are now prescribed by the legislature for such acts.

During the Defiance Campaign, the Public Safety Act and the Criminal Law Amendment Act were passed. These Statutes provided harsher penalties for offences committed by way of protests against laws. Despite this, the protests continued and the A.N.C. adhered to its policy of non-violence. In 1956, one hundred and fifty-six leading members of the Congress Alliance, including myself, were arrested on a charge of High Treason and charged under the Suppression of Communism Act. The non-violent policy of the A.N.C. was put in issue by the State, but when the Court gave judgment some five years later, it found that the A.N.C. did not have a policy of violence. We were acquitted on all counts, which included a count that the A.N.C. sought to set up a Communist State in place of the existing regime. The Government has always sought to label all its opponents as communists. This allegation has been repeated in the present case, but as I will show, the A.N.C. is not, and never has been, a communist organization.

In 1960, there was the shooting at Sharpeville, which resulted in the proclamation of a State of Emergency and the declaration of the A.N.C. as an unlawful organization. My colleagues and I, after careful consideration, decided that we would not obey this decree. The African people were not part of the Government and did not make the laws by which they were governed. We believed in the words of the Universal Declaration of Human Rights, that "the will of the people shall be the basis of the authority of the Government", and for us to accept the banning was equivalent to accepting the silencing of the Africans for all time. The A.N.C. refused to dissolve, but instead went underground. We believed it was our duty to preserve this organization which had been built up with almost fifty years of unremitting toil. I have no doubt that no self-respecting White political organization would disband itself if declared illegal by a Government in which it had no say.

In some of the evidence the M. Plan has been completely misrepresented. It was nothing more than a method of organizing, planned in 1953, and put into operation with varying degrees of success thereafter. After April, 1960, new methods had to be devised, for instance, by relying on smaller Committees. The M. Plan was referred to in evidence at the Treason Trial, but it had nothing whatsoever to do with sabotage or Umkonto We Sizwe, and was never adopted by Umkonto. The confusion, particularly by certain witnesses from the Eastern Province, is, I think, due to the use of the phrase "High Command". This term was coined in Port Elizabeth during the Emergency, when most of the A.N.C. leaders were gaoled, and a Gaol Committee, set up to deal with complaints, was called the High Command. After the Emergency this phrase stuck and was used to describe certain of the A.N.C. Committees in that area. Thus we have had witnesses talking about the West Bank High Command and the Port Elizabeth High Command. These so-called "High Commands" came into existence before Umkonto was formed and were not concerned in any way with sabotage. In fact, as I will subsequently explain, Umkonto as an organization was, as far as possible, kept separate from the A.N.C. This explains why persons like Bennet Mashiyane and Reginald Ndube heard nothing about sabotage at the meetings they attended. But, as has been mentioned by Zizi Njikelane, the use of the phrase "High Command" caused some dissension in A.N.C. circles in the Eastern Province. I travelled there in 1961, because it was alleged that some of these so-called High Commands were using duress in order to enforce the new Plan. I did not find evidence of this, but nevertheless forbade it, and also insisted that the term "High Command" should not be used to describe any A.N.C. Committee. My visit and the discussions which took place have been described by Zizi Njikelane, and I admit his evidence in so far as it relates to me. Although it does not seem to have much relevance, I deny that I was taken to the meeting by the taxi driver John Tshingane, and I also deny that I went to the sea with him.

In 1960 the Government held a Referendum which led to the establishment of the Republic. Africans, who constituted approximately 70% of the population of South Africa, were not entitled to vote, and were not even consulted about the proposed constitutional change. All of us were apprehensive of our future under the proposed White Republic, and a resolution was taken to hold an All-In African Conference to call for a National Convention, and to organize mass demonstrations on the eve of the unwanted Republic, if the Government failed to call the Convention. The Conference was attended by Africans of various political persuasions. I was the Secretary of the Conference and undertook to be responsible for organizing the national stay-at-home which was subsequently called to coincide with the declaration of the Republic. As all strikes by Africans are illegal, the person organizing such a strike must avoid arrest. I was chosen to be this person, and consequently I had to leave my home and family and my practice and go into hiding to avoid arrest.

The stay-at-home, in accordance with A.N.C. policy, was to be a peaceful demonstration. Careful instructions were given to organizers and members to avoid any recourse to violence. The Government's answer was to introduce new and harsher laws, to mobilise its armed forces, and to send saracens, armed vehicles and soldiers into the townships in a massive show of force designed to intimidate the people. This was an indication that the Government had decided to rule by force alone, and this decision was a milestone on the road to Umkonto.

Some of this may appear irrelevant to this trial. In fact, I believe none of it is irrelevant because it will, I hope, enable the Court to appreciate the attitude eventually adopted by the various persons and bodies concerned in the National Liberation Movement. When I went to gaol in 1962, the dominant idea was that loss of life should be avoided. I now know that this was still so in 1963.

I must return to June, 1961. What were we, the leaders of our people to do? Were we to give in to the show of force and the implied threat against future action, or were we to fight it, and if so, how?

We had no doubt that we had to continue the fight. Anything else would have been abject surrender. Our problem was not whether to fight, but was how to continue the fight. We of the A.N.C. had always stood for a non-racial democracy, and we shrank from any action which might drive the races further apart than they already were. But the hard facts were that fifty years of non-violence had brought the African people nothing but more and more repressive legislation, and fewer and fewer rights. It may not be easy for this Court to understand, but it is a fact that for a long time the people had been talking of violence—of the day when they would fight the White man and win back their country, and we, the leaders of the A.N.C., had nevertheless always prevailed upon them to avoid violence and to pursue peaceful methods. When some of us discussed this in May and June of 1961, it could not be denied that our policy to achieve a non-racial state by non-violence had achieved nothing, and that our followers were beginning to lose confidence in this policy and were developing disturbing ideas of terrorism.

It must not be forgotten that by this time violence had, in fact, become a feature of the South African political scene. There had been violence in 1957 when the women of Zeerust were ordered to carry passes; there was violence in 1958 with the enforcement of cattle culling in Sekhukuniland; there was violence in 1959 when the people of Cato Manor protested against Pass raids; there was violence in 1960 when the Government attempted to impose Bantu Authorities in Pondoland. Thirty-nine Africans died in these disturbances. In 1961 there had been riots in Warmbaths, and all this time the Transkei had been a seething mass of unrest. Each disturbance pointed clearly to the inevitable growth among Africans of the belief that violence was the only way out—it showed that a Government which uses force to maintain its rule teaches the oppressed to use force to oppose it. Already small groups had arisen in the urban areas and were spontaneously making plans for violent forms of political struggle. There now arose a danger that these groups would adopt terrorism against Africans, as well as Whites, if not properly directed. Particularly disturbing was the type of violence engendered in places such as Zeerust, Sekhukhuniland and Pondoland amongst Africans. It was increasingly taking the form, not of struggle against the Government—though this is what prompted it—but of civil strife amongst themselves, conducted in such a way that it could not hope to achieve anything other than a loss of life and bitterness.

At the beginning of June, 1961, after a long and anxious assessment of the South African situation, I, and some colleagues, came to the conclusion that as violence in this country was inevitable, it would be unrealistic and wrong for African leaders to continue preaching peace and non-violence at a time when the Government met our peaceful demands with force.

This conclusion was not easily arrived at. It was only when all else had failed, when all channels of peaceful protest had been barred to us, that the decision was made to embark on violent forms of political struggle, and to form Umkonto We Sizwe. We did so not because we desired such a course, but solely because the Government had left us with no other choice. In the Manifesto of Umkonto published on the 16th December, 1961, which is Exhibit 'AD' [Document 66], we said:—

"The time comes in the life of any nation when there remain only two choices—submit or fight. That time has now come to South Africa. We shall not submit and we have no choice but to hit back by all means in our power in defence of our people, our future and our freedom".

This was our feeling in June of 1961 when we decided to press for a change in the policy of the National Liberation Movement. I can only say that I felt morally obliged to do what I did.

We who had taken this decision started to consult leaders of various organizations, including the A.N.C. I will not say whom we spoke to, or what they said, but I wish to deal with the role of the African National Congress in this phase of the struggle, and with the policy and objectives of Umkonto We Sizwe.

As far as the A.N.C. was concerned, it formed a clear view which can be summarized as follows:—

(a) It was a mass political organization with a political function to fulfil. Its members had joined on the express policy of non-violence.

(b) Because of all this, it could not and would not undertake violence. This must be stressed. One cannot turn such a body into the small closely-knit organization required for sabotage. Nor would this be politically correct, because it would result in members ceasing to carry out this essential activity: political propaganda and organization. Nor was it permissible to change the whole nature of the organization.

(c) On the other hand, in view of this situation I have described, the A.N.C. was prepared to depart from its 50-year-old policy of non-violence to this extent that it would no longer disapprove of properly controlled violence. Hence members who undertook such activity would not be subject to disciplinary action by the A.N.C.

I say "properly controlled violence" because I made it clear that if I formed the organization I would at all times subject it to the political guidance of the A.N.C. and would not undertake any different form of activity from that contemplated without the consent of the A.N.C. And I shall now tell the Court how that form of violence came to be determined.

As a result of this decision, Umkonto was formed in November, 1961. When we took this decision, and subsequently formulated our plans, the A.N.C. heritage of non-violence and racial harmony was very much with us. We felt that the country was drifting towards a civil war in which Blacks and Whites would fight each other. We viewed the situation with alarm. Civil war could mean the destruction of what the A.N.C. stood for; with civil war racial peace would be more difficult than ever to achieve. We already have examples in South African history of the results of war. It has taken more than fifty years for the scars of the South African War to disappear. How much longer would it take to eradicate the scars of inter-racial civil war, which could not be fought without a great loss of life on both sides?

The avoidance of civil war had dominated our thinking for many years, but when we decided to adopt violence as part of our policy, we realised that we might one day have to face the prospect of such a war. This had to be taken into account in formulating our plans. We required a plan which was flexible and which permitted us to act in accordance with the needs of the times; above all, the plan had to be one which recognised civil war as the last resort, and left the decision on this question to the future. We did not want to be committed to civil war, but we wanted to be ready if it became inevitable.

Four forms of violence are possible. There is sabotage, there is guerrilla warfare, there is terrorism and there is open revolution. We chose to adopt the first method and to exhaust it before taking any other decision.

In the light of our political background the choice was a logical one. Sabotage did not involve loss of life, and it offered the best hope for future race relations. Bitterness would be kept to a minimum and, if the policy bore fruit, democratic government could become a reality. This is what we felt at the time, and this is what we said in our Manifesto (Exhibit AD):—

"We of Umkonto We Sizwe have always sought to achieve liberation without bloodshed and civil clash. We hope, even at this late hour, that our first actions will awaken everyone to a realisation of the disastrous situation to which the Nationalist policy is leading. We hope that we will bring the Government and its supporters to their senses before it is too late, so that both the Government and its policies can be changed before matters reach the desperate stage of civil war".

The initial plan was based on a careful analysis of the political and economic situation of our country. We believed that South Africa depended to a large extent on foreign capital and foreign trade. We felt that planned destruction of power plants, and interference with rail and telephone communications would tend to scare away capital from the country, make it more difficult for goods from the industrial areas to reach the seaports on schedule, and would in the long run be a heavy drain on the economic life of the country, thus compelling the voters of the country to reconsider their position.

Attacks on the economic life lines of the country were to be linked with sabotage on Government buildings and other symbols of apartheid. These attacks would serve as a source of inspiration to our people. In addition, they would provide an outlet for those people who were urging the adoption of violent methods and would enable us to give concrete proof to our followers that we had adopted a stronger line and were fighting back against Government violence.

In addition, if mass action were successfully organized, and mass reprisals taken, we felt that sympathy for our cause would be roused in other countries, and that greater pressure would be brought to bear on the South African Government.

This then was the plan. Umkonto was to perform sabotage, and strict instructions were given to its members right from the start, that on no account were they to injure or kill people in planning or carrying out operations. These instructions have been referred to in the evidence of Mr. "X" and Mr. "Z".

The affairs of the Umkonto were controlled and directed by a National High Command, which had powers of co-option and which could, and did, appoint Regional Commands. The High Command was the body which determined tactics and targets and was in charge of training and finance. Under the High Command there were Regional Commands which were responsible for the direction of the local sabotage groups. Within the framework of the policy laid down by the National High Command, the Regional Commands had authority to select the targets to be attacked. They had no authority to go beyond the prescribed framework and thus had no authority to embark upon acts which endangered life, or which did not fit into the overall plan of sabotage. For instance, MK members were forbidden ever to go armed into operation. Incidentally, the terms High Command and Regional Command were an importation from the Jewish National underground organization Irgun Zvai Leumi, which operated in Israel between 1944 and 1948.

Umkonto had its first operation on the 16th December, 1961, when Government buildings in Johannesburg, Port Elizabeth and Durban were attacked. The selection of targets is proof of the policy to which I have referred. Had we intended to attack life we would have selected targets where people congregated and not empty buildings and power stations. The sabotage which was committed before the 16th December, 1961, was the work of isolated groups and had no connection whatever with Umkonto. In fact, some of these and a number of later acts were claimed by other organizations. (Put in newspaper cuttings.)

The Manifesto of Umkonto was issued on the day that operations commenced. The response to our actions and Manifesto among the White population was characteristically violent. The Government threatened to take strong action, and called upon its supporters to stand firm and to ignore the demands of the Africans. The Whites failed to respond by suggesting change; they responded to our call by suggesting the laager.

In contrast, the response of the Africans was one of encouragement. Suddenly there was hope again. Things were happening. People in the townships became eager for political news. A great deal of enthusiasm was generated by the initial successes, and people began to speculate on how soon freedom would be obtained.

But we in Umkonto weighed up the White response with anxiety. The lines were being drawn. The Whites and Blacks were moving into separate camps, and the prospects of avoiding a civil war were made less. The White newspapers carried reports that sabotage would be punished by death. If this was so how could we continue to keep Africans away from terrorism?

Already scores of Africans had died as a result of racial friction. In 1920 when the famous leader, Masabala, was held in Port Elizabeth gaol, twenty-four of a group of Africans who had gathered to demand his release, were killed by the police and White civilians. In 1921, more than one hundred Africans died in the Bulhoek affair. In 1924 over two hundred Africans were killed when the Administrator of South West Africa led a force against a group which had rebelled against the imposition of dog tax. On the 1st May, 1950, eighteen Africans died as a result of police shootings during the strike. On the 21st March, 1960, sixty-nine unarmed Africans died at Sharpeville.

How many more Sharpevilles would there be in the history of our country? And how many more Sharpevilles could the country stand without violence and terror becoming the order of the day? And what would happen to our people when that stage was reached? In the long run we felt certain we must succeed, but at what cost to ourselves and the rest of the country? And if this happened, how could Black and White ever live together again in peace and harmony? These were the problems that faced us, and these were our decisions.

Experience convinced us that rebellion would offer the Government limitless opportunities for the indiscriminate slaughter of our people. But it was precisely because the soil of South Africa is already drenched with the blood of innocent Africans that we felt it our duty to make preparations as a long-term undertaking to use force in order to defend ourselves against force. If war were inevitable, we wanted the fight to be conducted on terms most favourable to our people. The fight which held out prospects best for us and the least risk of life to both sides was guerrilla warfare. We decided, therefore, in our preparations for the future, to make provision for the possibility of guerrilla warfare.

All Whites undergo compulsory military training, but no such training was given to Africans. It was in our view essential to build up a nucleus of trained men who would be able to provide the leadership which would be required if guerrilla warfare started. We had to prepare for such a situation before it became too late to make proper preparations. It was also necessary to build up a nucleus of men trained in civil administration and other professions, so that Africans would be equipped to participate in the Government of this country as soon as they were allowed to do so.

At this stage it was decided that I should attend the Conference of the Pan-African Freedom Movement for Central, East and Southern Africa, which was to be held early in 1962 in Addis Ababa and, because of our need for preparation, it was also decided that, after the Conference, I would undertake a tour of the African States with a view to obtaining facilities for the training of soldiers, and that I would also solicit scholarships for the higher education of matriculated Africans. Training in both fields would be necessary, even if changes came about by peaceful means. Administrators would be necessary who would be willing and able to administer a non-racial State and so would men be necessary to control the army and police force of such a State.

It was on this note that I left South Africa to proceed to Addis Ababa as a delegate of the A.N.C. My tour was a success. Wherever I went I met sympathy for our cause and promises of help. All Africa was united against the stand of White South Africa, and even in London, I was received with great sympathy by political leaders, such as Mr. Gaitskell and Mr. Grimond. In Africa I was promised support by such men as Julius Nyerere, now President of Tanganyika; Mr. Kawawa, then Prime Minister of Tanganyika; Emperor Haile Selassie of Ethiopia; General Aboud, President of the Sudan; Habib Bourguiba, President of Tunisia; Ben Bella, now President of Algeria; Modiko Keita, President of Mali; Leophold Senghor, President of Senegal; Sekou Toure, President of Guinea; President Tubman of Liberia and Milton Obote, Prime Minister of Uganda. It was Ben Bella who invited me to visit Oujda, the Headquarters of the Algerian Army of National Liberation, the visit which is described in my diary, one of the Exhibits.

I started to make a study of the art of war and revolution and, whilst abroad, underwent a course in military training. If there was to be guerrilla warfare, I wanted to be able to stand and fight with my people and to share the hazards of war with them. Notes of lectures which I received in Algeria are contained in Exhibit 16, produced in evidence. Summaries of books on guerrilla warfare and military strategy have also been produced. I have already admitted that these documents are in my writing, and I acknowledge that I made these studies to equip myself for the role which I might have to play if the struggle drifted into guerrilla warfare. I approached this question as every African Nationalist should do. I was completely objective. The Court will see that I attempted to examine all types of authority on the subject—from the East and from the West, going back to the classic work of Clausewitz, and covering such a variety as Mao Tse Tung and Che Guevara on the one hand, and the writings on the Anglo-Boer War on the other. Of course, these notes are merely summaries of the books I read and do not contain my personal views.

I also made arrangements for our recruits to undergo military training. But here it was impossible to organise any scheme without the co-operation of the A.N.C. offices in Africa. I consequently obtained the permission of the A.N.C. in South Africa to do this. To this extent then there was a departure from the original decision of the A.N.C., but it applied outside South Africa only. The first batch of recruits actually arrived in Tanganyika when I was passing through that country on my way back to South Africa.

I returned to South Africa and reported to my colleagues on the results of my trip. On my return I found that there had been little alteration in the political scene save that the threat of a death penalty for sabotage had now become a fact. The attitude of my colleagues in Umkonto was much the same as it had been before I left. They were feeling their way cautiously and felt that it would be a long time before the possibilities of sabotage were exhausted. In fact, the view was expressed by some that the training of recruits was premature. This is recorded by me in the document, which is Exhibit R. 14. After a full discussion, however, it was decided to go ahead with the plans for military training because of the fact that it would take many years to build up a sufficient nucleus of trained soldiers to start a guerrilla campaign, and whatever happened the training would be of value.

I want to deal now with some of the evidence of "X" [Bruno Mtolo].

Immediately before my arrest in August, 1962, I met members of the Regional Command in Durban. This meeting has been referred to in "X"'s evidence. Much of his account is substantially correct, but much of it is slanted and is distorted and in some important respects it is untruthful. I want to deal with the evidence as briefly as possible:

(a) I did say that I had left the country early in the year to attend the Pafmecsa Conference, that the Conference was opened by the Emperor Haile Selassie, who attacked the racial policies of the South African Government and who pledged support to the African people in this country. I also informed them of the unanimous resolution condemning ill-treatment of the African people here, and promising support. I did tell them that the Emperor sent his warmest felicitations to Chief Luthuli.

(b) But I never told them of any comparison made between Ghanians and South African recruits, and could not have done so for very simple reasons. By the time I left Ethiopia the first South African recruits had not yet reached that country and Ghanian soldiers, as far as I am aware, receive training in the United Kingdom. This being the fact and my understanding, I could not possibly have thought of telling the Regional Command that the Emperor of Ethiopia thought our trainees after *two months* were better than the Ghanians after two years!

(c) These statements, therefore, are sheer invention, unless they were suggested to Mr. "X" by someone wishing to create a false picture.

(d) I did tell of financial support received in Ethiopia, and in other parts of Africa. I certainly did not tell him that certain African States had promised us 1% of their budgets. This suggestion of donating 1% never arose during my visit. It arose for the first time, as far as I am aware, at the Conference in May, 1963, by which time I had been in gaol for 10 months.

(e) Despite "X" 's alleged failure to remember this, I did speak of scholarships promised in Ethiopia. Such general education of persons who will one day be willing to take part in the efficient administration of a non-racial State has always, as I have pointed out, been an important aspect of our plans.

(f) I did tell them I had travelled through Africa and had been received by a number of heads of States, mentioning them all by name. I also told them of President Ben Bella's invitation to me to go to Oujda, where I met officers of the Algerian Army, including their Commander-in-Chief, Colonel Bommediene. I also said that the Algerians had promised assistance with training and arms. But I certainly did not say they must hide the fact that they were Communists, because I did not know whether they were Communists or not. What I did say was that no Communist should use his position in M.K. for communist propaganda, neither in South Africa nor beyond the borders, because unity of purpose was essential for achieving freedom. At this stage, I said that the exact form of a future society was unimportant. What we aimed at was the vote for all, and on this basis we could appeal to all social groups in South Africa and expect the maximum support from the African States. Mr. "X" denies this, but I could not have suggested any other than the true objective, nor could there have been any possible reason for hiding it.

(g) It was in this context that I discussed "New Age" and its criticisms of the Egyptian Government. In speaking of my visit to Egypt, I said that my visit coincided with that of Marshall Tito, and that I had not been able to wait until General Nasser was free to interview me. I said that the officials whom I had seen had expressed criticism of articles appearing in "New Age" which had dealt with General Nasser's attacks on communism, but that I had told them that "New Age" did not necessarily express the policy of our Movement, and that I would take up this complaint with "New Age", and try and use my influence to change their line, because it was not our duty to say in what manner any State should achieve its freedom.

(h) I told the Regional Committee that I had not visited Cuba, but that country's ambassadors in Egypt, Morocco and Ghana. I spoke of the warm affection with which I was received at these embassies and that we were offered all forms of assistance, including scholarships for our youth. In dealing with the question of White and Asian recruits, I did say that as Cuba was a multi-racial country, it would be logical to send such persons to this country as these recruits would fit in more easily there than with Black soldiers in African states.

(i) But I never discussed Eric Mtshali at the meeting, for the simple reason that I did not know him until I heard his name mentioned by [Bruno] Mtolo in this case.

On my return to Tanganyika, after touring the African Continent, I met about 30 South African young men, who were on their way to Ethiopia for training. I addressed them on discipline and good behaviour while abroad. Eric Mtshali may have been amongst these young men. But in any event, even if he was, this must have been before he visited any African State other than Tanganyika, and in Tanganyika, he would not have starved or been in difficulties since our office there would have looked after him. It would be absurd to suggest that the South African office in Dar-Es-Salaam would discriminate against him on the ground that he was a communist.

(j) Of course, I referred to Umkonto We Sizwe, but it cannot be true to say that they heard from me for the first time that this was the name or that it was "the military wing" of the A.N.C.—a phrase much used by the State in this trial. A proclamation had been issued by M.K. on the 16th December, 1961, announcing the existence of the body and its name had been known for seven months before the time of this meeting. And I had certainly never referred to it as a military wing of the A.N.C. I always regarded it as a separate organization, and endeavored to keep it as such.

(k) I did tell them that the activities of MK would go through two phases, namely, acts of sabotage and, possibly, guerrilla warfare, if that became necessary. I dealt with the problems relating to each phase. I stressed, just as he said, that the most important thing was to study our own history and our own situation. We must, of course, study the experiences of other countries also, and, in doing so, we must study, not only the cases where revolutions were victorious, but also cases where revolutions were defeated.

But I did not discuss the training of people in East Germany as testified to by Mtolo—nor do I have any recollection that anyone expressed any suspicions of M. P. Naicker.

(l) I did not produce any photograph in "Spark" or "New Age" as testified to by Mtolo—these photos were only published on the 21st February, 1963, after I was in gaol.

Whilst referring to Mr. "X" 's evidence, there is one other fact that I want to mention. Mr. "X" said that the sabotage which was committed on the 15th October, 1962, was in protest against my conviction, and that the decision to commit such sabotage had been taken between the date of conviction and the date of sentence. He also said that the sabotage was held over for a few days because it was thought that the police would be on their watch on the day that I was sentenced. All this must be untrue. I was convicted during November, 1962, and was sentenced on the same day to five years' imprisonment with hard labour. The sabotage in October, 1962, could, therefore, not have had anything to do with my conviction and sentence.

I wish to turn now to certain general allegations made in this case by the State. But before doing so, I wish to revert to certain occurrences said by witnesses to have happened in Port Elizabeth and East London. I am referring to the bombing of private houses of pro-Government persons during September, October and November, 1962. I do not know what justification there was for these acts, nor what provocation had been given. But if what I have said already is accepted, then it is clear that these acts had nothing to do with the carrying out of the policy of Umkonto.

One of the chief allegations in the Indictment is that the A.N.C. was a party to a general conspiracy to commit sabotage. I have already explained why this is incorrect but how, externally, there was a departure from the original principle laid down by the A.N.C. There has, of course, been overlapping of functions internally as well, because there is a difference between a resolution adopted in the atmosphere of a committee room and the concrete difficulties that arise in the field of practical activity. At a later stage the position was further affected by bannings and house arrests, and by persons leaving the country to take up political work abroad. This led to individuals having to do work in different capacities. But though this may have blurred the distinction between Umkonto and the A.N.C., it by no means abolished that distinction. Great care was taken to keep the activities of the two organizations in South Africa distinct. The A.N.C. remained a mass political body of Africans only carrying on the type of political work they had conducted prior to 1961. Umkonto remained a small organization recruiting its members from different races and organizations and trying to achieve its own particular object. The fact that members of Umkonto were recruited from the A.N.C., and the fact that persons served both organizations, like Solomon Mbanjwa, did not, in our view, change the nature of the A.N.C. or give it a policy of violence. This overlapping of officers, however, was more the exception than the rule. This is why persons such as Mr. "X" and Mr. "Z", who were on the Regional Command of their respective areas, did not participate in any of the A.N.C. Committees or activities, and why people such as Mr. Bennett Mashiyana and Mr. Reginald Ndubi did not hear of sabotage at their A.N.C. meetings.

Another of the allegations in the indictment is that Rivonia was the headquarters of Umkonto. This is not true of the time when I was there. I was told, of course, and knew that certain of the activities of the Communist Party were carried on there. But this is no reason (as I shall presently explain) why I should not use the place.

I came there in the following manner:—

(a) As already indicated, early in April, 1961, I went underground to organize the May general strike. My work entailed travelling throughout the country, living now in African townships, then in country villages and again in cities.

   During the second half of the year I started visiting the Parktown home of Arthur Goldreich, where I used to meet my family privately. Although I had no direct political association with him, I had known Arthur Goldreich socially since 1958.

(b) In October, Arthur Goldreich informed me that he was moving out of town and offered me a hiding place there. A few days thereafter, he arranged for Michael Harmel to take me to Rivonia. I naturally found Rivonia an ideal place for the man who lived the life of an outlaw. Up to that time I had been compelled to live indoors during the day time and could only venture out under cover of darkness. But at Liliesleaf I could live differently and work far more efficiently.

(c) For obvious reasons, I had to disguise myself and I assumed the fictitious name of David. In December Arthur Goldreich and his family also moved in. I stayed there until I went abroad on the 11th January, 1962. As already indicated, I returned in July, 1962, and was arrested in Natal on the 5th August.

(d) Up to the time of my arrest, Liliesleaf farm was the headquarters of neither the African National Congress nor the M.K. With the exception of myself, none of the officials or members of these bodies lived there, no meetings of the governing bodies were ever held there and no activities connected with them were either organized or directed from there. On numerous occasions during my stay at Liliesleaf farm I met both the Executive Committee of the A.N.C., as well as the N.H.C., but such meetings were held elsewhere and not on the farm.

(e) Whilst staying at Liliesleaf Farm, I frequently visited Arthur Goldreich in the main house and he also paid me visits in my room. We had numerous political discussions covering a variety of subjects. We discussed ideological and practical questions, the Congress Alliance, Umkonto and its activities generally and his experiences as a soldier in the Palmach, the military wing of the Haganah. Haganah was the political authority of the Jewish National Movement in Palestine.

(f) Because of what I had got to know of Goldreich, I recommended on my return to South Africa that he should be recruited to Umkonto. I do not know of my personal knowledge whether this was done.

Another of the allegations made by the State is that the aims and objects of the A.N.C. and the Communist Party are the same. I wish to deal with this and with my own political position, because I must assume that the State may try to argue from certain Exhibits that I tried to introduce Marxism into the A.N.C. The allegation as to the A.N.C. is false. This is an old allegation which was disproved at the Treason Trial and which has again reared its head. But since the allegation has been made again, I shall deal with it as well as with the relationship between the A.N.C. and the Communist Party and Umkonto and that Party.

The ideological creed of the A.N.C. is, and always has been, the creed of African Nationalism. It is not the concept of African Nationalism expressed in the cry, "Drive the White man into the sea". The African Nationalism for which the A.N.C. stands, is the concept of freedom and fulfilment for the African people in their own land. The most important political document ever adopted by the A.N.C. is the "Freedom Charter". It is by no means a blueprint for a socialist State. It calls for redistribution, but not nationalisation, of land; it provides for nationalisation of mines, Banks and monopoly industry, because big monopolies are owned by one race only, and without such nationalisation racial domination would be perpetuated despite the spread of political power. It would be a hollow gesture to repeal the Gold Law prohibitions against Africans when all gold mines are owned by European companies. In this respect the A.N.C.'s policy corresponds with the old policy of the present Nationalist Party which, for many years, had as part of its programme the nationalisation of the Gold Mines which, at that time, were controlled by foreign capital. Under the Freedom Charter nationalisation would take place in an economy based on private enterprise. The realisation of the Freedom Charter would open up fresh fields for a prosperous African population of all classes, including the middle class. The A.N.C. has never at any period of its history advocated a revolutionary change in the economic structure of the country, nor has it, to the best of my recollection, ever condemned capitalist society.

As far as the Communist Party is concerned, and if I understand its policy correctly, it stands for the establishment of a State based on the principles of Marxism. Although it is prepared to work for the Freedom Charter, as a short-term solution to the problems created by White supremacy, it regards the Freedom Charter as the beginning, and not the end of, its programme.

The A.N.C., unlike the Communist Party, admitted Africans only as members. Its chief goal was, and is, for the African people to win unity and full political rights. The Communist Party's main aim, on the other hand, was to remove the capitalists and to replace them with a working-class Government. The Communist Party sought to emphasize class distinctions whilst the A.N.C. seeks to harmonise them. This is a vital distinction.

It is true that there has often been close co-operation between the A.N.C. and the Communist Party. But co-operation is merely proof of a common goal—in this case the removal of White supremacy—and is not proof of a complete community of interests.

The history of the world is full of similar examples. Perhaps the most striking illustration is to be found in the co-operation between Great Britain, the United States of America and the Soviet Union in the fight against Hitler. Nobody but Hitler would have dared to suggest that such co-operation turned Churchill or Roosevelt into communists or communist tools, or that Britain and America were working to bring about a communist world.

Another instance of such co-operation is to be found precisely in Umkonto. Shortly after MK was constituted, I was informed by some of its members that the Communist Party would support Umkonto, and this then occurred. At a later stage the support was made openly.

I believe that Communists have always played an active role in the fight by colonial countries for their freedom, because the short-term objects of Communism would always correspond with the long-term objects of freedom movements. Thus Communists have played an important role in the freedom struggles fought in countries such as Malaya, Algeria and Indonesia, yet none of these States today are Communist countries. Similarly in the underground resistance movements which sprung up in Europe during the last World War, Communists played an important role. Even General Chiang Kai Chek, today one of the bitterest enemies of Communism, fought together with the Communists against the ruling class in the struggle which led to his assumption of power in China in the 1930's.

This pattern of co-operation between Communists and non-Communists has been repeated in the National Liberation Movement of South Africa. Prior to the banning of the Communist Party, joint campaigns involving the Communist Party and the Congress Movements were accepted practice. African Communists could, and did, become members of the A.N.C., and some served on the National, Provincial and local committees. Amongst those who served on the National Executive are Albert Nzula, a former

Secretary of the Communist Party, Moses Kotane, another former Secretary and J. B. Marks, a former member of the Central Committee.

I joined the A.N.C in 1944, and in my younger days I held the view that the policy of admitting Communists to the A.N.C., and the close co-operation which existed at times on specific issues between the A.N.C. and the Communist Party, would lead to a watering down of the concept of African nationalism. At that stage I was a member of the African National Congress Youth League, and was one of a group which moved for the expulsion of Communists from the A.N.C. This proposal was heavily defeated. Amongst those who voted against the proposal were some of the most conservative sections of African political opinion. They defended the policy on the ground that from its inception the A.N.C. was formed and built up, not as a political party with one school of political thought, but as a Parliament of the African people, accommodating people of various political convictions, all united by the common goal of national liberation. I was eventually won over to this point of view and have upheld it ever since.

It is perhaps difficult for White South Africans, with an ingrained prejudice against Communism, to understand why experienced African politicians so readily accept Communists as their friends. But to us the reason is obvious. Theoretical differences amongst those fighting against oppression is a luxury we cannot afford at this stage. What is more, for many decades Communists were the only political group in South Africa who were prepared to treat Africans as human beings and their equals; who were prepared to eat with us; talk with us, live with us and work with us. They were the only political group which was prepared to work with the Africans for the attainment of political rights and a stake in society. Because of this, there are many Africans who, today, tend to equate freedom with Communism. They are supported in this belief by a legislature which brands all exponents of democratic government and African freedom as Communists and bans many of them (who are not Communists) under the Suppression of Communism Act. Although I have never been a member of the Communist Party, I myself have been named under that pernicious Act because of the role I played in the Defiance Campaign. I have also been banned and imprisoned under that Act.

It is not only in internal politics that we count Communists as amongst those who support our cause. In the international field, Communist countries have always come to our aid. In the United Nations and other Councils of the world the Communist block has supported the Afro-Asian struggle against colonialism and often seems to be more sympathetic to our plight than some of the Western powers. Although there is a universal condemnation of apartheid, the Communist block speaks out against it with a louder voice than most of the White world. In these circumstances, it would take a brash young politician, such as I was in 1949, to proclaim that the Communists are our enemies.

I turn now to my own position. I have denied that I am a Communist, and I think that in the circumstances I am obliged to state exactly what my political beliefs are.

I have always regarded myself, in the first place, as an African patriot. After all, I was born in Umtata, forty-six years ago. My guardian was my cousin, who was the acting paramount chief of Tembuland, and I am related both to the present paramount chief of Tembuland, Sabata Dalinyebo, and to Kaizer Matanzima, the Chief Minister of the Transkei.

Today I am attracted by the idea of a classless society, an attraction which springs in part from Marxist reading and, in part, from my admiration of the structure and organization of early African societies in this country. The land, then the main means of production, belonged to the tribe. There were no rich or poor and there was no exploitation.

It is true, as I have already stated, that I have been influenced by Marxist thought. But this is also true of many of the leaders of the new independent States. Such widely different persons as Gandhi, Nehru, Nkrumah and Nasser all acknowlege this fact. We all accept the need for some form of Socialism to enable our people to catch up with the advanced countries of this world and to overcome their legacy of extreme poverty. But this does not mean we are Marxists.

Indeed, for my own part, I believe that it is open to debate whether the Communist Party has any specific role to play at this particular stage of our political struggle. The basic task at the present moment is the removal of race discrimination and the attainment of democratic rights on the basis of the Freedom Charter. Insofar as that Party furthers this task, I welcome its assistance. I realize that it is one of the means by which people of all races can be drawn into our struggle.

From my reading of Marxist literature and from conversations with Marxists, I have gained the impression that Communists regard the parliamentary system of the West as undemocratic and reactionary. But, on the contrary, I am an admirer of such a system.

The Magna Charta, the Petition of Rights and the Bill of Rights, are documents which are held in veneration by democrats throughout the world.

I have great respect for British political institutions, and for the country's system of justice. I regard the British Parliament as the most democratic institution in the world, and the independence and impartiality of its judiciary never fail to arouse my admiration.

The American Congress, that country's doctrine of separation of powers, as well as the independence of its judiciary, arouse in me similar sentiments.

I have been influenced in my thinking by both West and East. All this has led me to feel that in my search for a political formula, I should be absolutely impartial and objective. I should tie myself to no particular system of society other than of socialism. I must leave myself free to borrow the best from the West and from the East.

I wish now to deal with some of the Exhibits. Many of the Exhibits are in my handwriting. It has always been my custom to reduce to writing the material which I have been studying.

R.20, 21 and 22 are lectures drafted in my own hand but they are not my original work. They came to be written in the following circumstances:

(a) For several years an old friend with whom I worked very closely on A.N.C. matters and who occupied senior positions both in the A.N.C. and the Communist Party, had been trying to get me to join the Communist Party. I had had many debates with him on the role which the Communist Party can play at this stage of our struggle, and I advanced to him the same views in regard to my political beliefs which I have described earlier in my statement.

In order to convince me that I should join the Communist Party he, from time to time gave me Marxist literature to read, though I did not always find time to do this.

Each of us always stuck to our guns in our argument as to whether I should join the Communist Party. He maintained that on achieving freedom we would be unable to solve our problems of poverty and inequality without establishing a Communist State, and we would require trained Marxists to do this. I maintained my attitude that no ideological differences should be introduced until freedom had been achieved.

(b) I saw him on several occasions at Liliesleaf Farm, and on one of the last of these occasions he was busy writing with books around him. When I asked him what he was doing, he told me that he was busy writing lectures for use in the Communist Party, and suggested that I should read them. There were several lectures in draft form.

(c) After I had done so, I told him that they seemed far too complicated for the ordinary reader in that the language was obtuse and they were full of the usual Communistic cliches and jargon. If the Court will look at some of the standard works of Marxism, my point will be demonstrated. He said it was impossible to simplify the language without losing the effect of what the author was trying to stress. I disagreed with him and he then asked me to see whether I could redraft the lectures in the simplified form suggested by me.

(d) I agreed to help him and set to work in an endeavor to do this, but I never finished the task as I later became occupied with other practical work which was more important than trying to prove my point that Marxism could be expressed in more simplified terms than those habitually employed by Party members. I never again saw the unfinished manuscript until it was produced at the Trial.

(e) I wish to state that it is not my handwriting which appears on Exhibit R.23 which was obviously drafted by the person who prepared the lectures.

There are certain Exhibits which suggest that we received financial support from abroad, and I wish to deal with this question.

Our political struggle has always been financed from internal sources—from funds raised by our own people and by our own supporters. Whenever we had a special campaign or an important political case—for example the Treason Trial—we received financial assistance from sympathetic individuals and organizations in the Western countries. We had never felt it necessary to go beyond these sources.

But when in 1961 the M.K. was formed, and a new phase of struggle introduced, we realized that these events would make a heavy call on our slender resources, and that the scale of our activities would be hampered by the lack of funds. One of my instructions, as I went abroad in January, 1962, was to raise funds from the African States.

I must add that, whilst abroad, I had discussions with leaders of political movements in Africa and discovered that almost every single one of them, in areas which had still not attained independence, had received all forms of assistance from the socialist countries, as well as from the West, including that of financial support. I also discovered that some well-known African states, all of them non-Communists, and even anti-Communists, had received similar assistance.

On my return to the Republic, I made a strong recommendation to the A.N.C. that we should not confine ourselves to Africa and the Western countries, but that we should also send a mission to the socialist countries to raise the funds which we so urgently needed.

I have been told that after I was convicted such a mission was sent, but I am not prepared to name any countries to which it went, nor am I at liberty to disclose the names of the organizations and countries which gave us support or promised to do so.

As I understand the State case, and in particular the evicence of Mr. "X", the suggestion is that Umkonto was the inspiration of the Communist Party which sought by playing upon imaginary grievances to enrol the African people into an army which ostensibly was to fight for African freedom, but in reality was fighting for a Communist State. Nothing could be further from the truth. In fact the suggestion is preposterous. Umkonto was formed by Africans to further their struggle for freedom in their own land. Communists and others supported the movement, and we only wish that more sections of the community would join us.

Our fight is against real, and not imaginary, hardships, or to use the language of the State Prosecutor, "so-called hardships". Basically, we fight against two features which are the hallmarks of African life in South Africa and which are entrenched by legislation which we seek to have repealed. These features are poverty and lack of human dignity, and we do not need Communists or so-called "agitators" to teach us about these things.

South Africa is the richest country in Africa, and could be one of the richest countries in the world. But it is a land of extremes and remarkable contrasts. The Whites enjoy what may well be the highest standard of living in the world, whilst Africans live in poverty and misery. Forty per cent of the Africans live in hopelessly over-crowded and, in some cases, drought-stricken reserves, where soil erosion and the overworking of the soil, make it impossible for them to live properly off the land. Thirty per cent are labourers, labour tenants and squatters on White farms and work and live under conditions similar to those of the serfs of the Middle Ages. The other thirty per cent live in towns where they have developed economic and social habits which bring them closer in many respects to White standards. Yet most Africans, even in this group, are impoverished by low incomes and high cost of living.

The highest-paid and the most prosperous section of urban African life is in Johannesburg. Yet their actual position is desperate. The latest figures were given on the 25th March, 1964, by Mr. Carr, Manager of the Johannesburg Non-European Affairs Department. The poverty datum line for the average African family in Johannesburg (according to Mr. Carr's department) is R42.84 per month. He showed that the average monthly wage is R32.24 and that 46% of all African families in Johannesburg do not earn enough to keep them going.

Poverty goes hand in hand with malnutrition and disease. The incidence of malnutrition and deficiency diseases is very high amongst Africans. Tuberculosis, pellagra, kwashiorkor, gastro-enteritis and scurvy bring death and destruction of health. The incidence of infant mortality is one of the highest in the world. According to the Medical Officer of Health for Pretoria, tuberculosis kills forty people a day (almost all Africans), and in 1961 there were 58,491 new cases reported. These diseases not only destroy the vital organs of the body, but they result in retarded mental conditions and lack of initiative, and reduce powers of concentration. The secondary results of such conditions affect the whole community and the standard of work performed by African labourers.

The complaint of Africans, however, is not only that they are poor and the Whites are rich, but that the laws which are made by the Whites are designed to preserve this situation. There are two ways to break out of poverty. The first is by formal education, and the second is by the worker acquiring a greater skill at his work and thus higher wages. As far as Africans are concerned, both these avenues of advancement are deliberately curtailed by legislation.

The present Government has always sought to hamper Africans in their search for education. One of their early acts, after coming into power, was to stop subsidies for African school feeding. Many African children, who attended schools, depended on this supplement to their diet. This was a cruel act.

There is compulsory education for all White children at virtually no cost to their parents, be they rich or poor. Similar facilities are not provided for the African children, though there are some who receive such assistance. African children, however, generally have to pay more for their schooling than Whites. According to figures quoted by the South African Institute of Race Relations in its 1963 journal, approximately 40% of African children in the age group between 7 to 14, do not attend school. For those who do attend school, the standards are vastly different from those afforded to White children, In 1960/61 the per capita Government spending on African students at State-aided schools was estimated at R12.46. In the same years, the per capita spending on White children in the Cape Province (which are the only figures available to me) was R144.57. Although there are no figures available to me, it can be stated, without doubt, that the White children on whom R144.57 per head was being spent all came from wealthier homes than African children on whom R12.46 per head was being spent.

The quality of education is also different. According to the Bantu Education Journal, only 5,660 African children in the whole of South Africa passed their J.C. in 1962, and in that year only 362 passed matric. This is presumably consistent with the policy of Bantu education about which the present Prime Minister said, during the debate on the Bantu Education Bill in 1953:—

"When I have control of Native education I will reform it so that Natives will be taught from childhood to realise that equality with Europeans is not for them . . . People who believe in equality are not desirable teachers for Natives. When my Department controls Native education it will know for what class of higher education a Native is fitted, and whether he will have a chance in life to use his knowledge".

The other main obstacle to the economic advancement of the African is the industrial colour bar under which all the better jobs of industry are reserved for Whites only. Moreover, Africans who do obtain employment in the unskilled and semi-skilled occupations which are open to them, are not allowed to form Trade Unions which have recognition under the Industrial Conciliation Act. This means that strikes of African workers are illegal, and that they are denied the right of collective bargaining which is permitted to the better-paid White workers. The discrimination in the policy of successive South African Governments towards African workers is demonstrated by the so-called "civilised labour policy" under which sheltered unskilled Government jobs are found for those White workers who cannot make the grade in industry, at wages which far exceeded the earnings of the average African employee in industry.

The Government often answers its critics by saying that Africans in South Africa are economically better off than the inhabitants of the other countries in Africa. I do not know whether this statement is true and doubt whether any comparison can be made without having regard to the cost of living index in such countries. But even if it is true, as far as the African people are concerned it is irrelevant. Our complaint is not that we are poor by comparison with people in other countries, but that we are poor by comparison with the White people in our own country, and that we are prevented by legislation from altering this imbalance.

The lack of human dignity experienced by Africans is the direct result of the policy of White supremacy. White supremacy implies Black inferiority. Legislation designed to preserve White supremacy entrenches this notion. Menial tasks in South Africa are invariably performed by Africans. When anything has to be carried or cleaned the White man will look around for an African to do it for him, whether the African is employed by him or not. Because of this sort of attitude, Whites tend to regard Africans as a separate breed. They do not look upon them as people with families of their own; they do not realise that they have emotions—that they fall in love like White people do; that they want to be with their wives and children like White people want to be with theirs; that they want to earn enough money to support their families properly, to feed and clothe them and send them to school. And what "house-boy" or "garden-boy" or labourer can ever hope to do this?

Pass Laws, which to the Africans are among the most hated bits of legislation in South Africa, render any African liable to police surveillance at any time. I doubt whether there is a single African male in South Africa who has not at some stage had a brush with the police over his pass. Hundreds and thousands of Africans are thrown into gaol each year under pass laws. Even worse than this is the fact that pass laws keep husband and wife apart and lead to the breakdown of family life.

Poverty and the breakdown of family life have secondary effects. Children wander about the streets of the Townships because they have no schools to go to, or no money to enable them to go to school, or no parents at home to see that they go to school, because both parents (if there be two) have to work to keep the family alive. This leads to a breakdown in moral standards, to an alarming rise in illegitimacy and to growing violence which erupts, not only politically, but everywhere. Life in the townships is dangerous. There is not a day that goes by without somebody being stabbed or assaulted. And violence is carried out of the townships in the White living areas. People are afraid to walk alone in the streets after dark. Housebreakings and robberies are increasing, despite the fact that the death sentence can now be imposed for such offences. Death sentences cannot cure the festering sore.

Africans want to be paid a living wage. Africans want to perform work which they are capable of doing, and not work which the Government declares them to be capable of. Africans want to be allowed to live where they obtain work, and not be endorsed out of an area because they were not born there. Africans want to be allowed to own land in places where they work, and not to be obliged to live in rented houses which they can never call their own. Africans want to be part of the general population, and not confined to living in their own ghettos. African men want to have their wives and children to live with them where they work, and not be forced into an unnatural existence in men's hostels. African women want to be with their men folk and not be left permanently widowed in the reserves. Africans want to be allowed out after 11 o'clock at night and not to be confined to their rooms like little children. Africans want to be allowed to travel in their own country and to seek work where they want to and not where the Labour Bureau tells them to. Africans want a just share in the whole of South Africa; they want security and a stake in society.

Above all, we want equal political rights, because without them our disabilities will be permanent. I know this sounds revolutionary to the Whites in this country, because the majority of voters will be Africans. This makes the White man fear democracy.

But this fear cannot be allowed to stand in the way of the only solution which will guarantee racial harmony and freedom for all. It is not true that the enfranchisement of all will result in racial domination. Political division, based on colour, is entirely artificial and, when it disappears, so will the domination of one colour group by another. The A.N.C. has spent half a century fighting against racialism. When it triumphs it will not change that policy.

This then is what the A.N.C. is fighting. Their struggle is a truly national one. It is a struggle of the African people, inspired by their own suffering and their own experience. It is a struggle for the right to live.

During my lifetime I have dedicated myself to this struggle of the African people. I have fought against White domination, and I have fought against Black domination. I have cherished the ideal of a democratic and free society in which all persons live together in harmony and with equal opportunities. It is an ideal which I hope to live for and to achieve. But if needs be, it is an ideal for which I am prepared to die.

Note: This text, in mimeographed form, was made available to the editors by the Rivonia trial defense team. The Special Committee on Apartheid of the United Nations General Assembly reproduced the text on May 6, 1964 (A/AC.115/L.67) from a copy made available by Mary Benson.

Document 76. "The Message of Rivonia." Flyer [issued by the ANC], [n.d.]

"Thousands of hand-grenades, mines, time devices for bombs, chemicals—enough explosives to blow up Johannesburg." This, Dr. Yutar alleges, was what the Rivonia men planned to obtain, to be followed by guerrilla activity and military invasion . . . . .

Why? And how can such things happen in peaceful prosperous South Africa?

Why? Because 50 years of peaceful political campaigning—for which the A.N.C. leader, Chief Luthuli was awarded the Nobel Peace Prize—has achieved only indignities, assaults, imprisonment, banishment, banning orders, mass removals, house arrests and 90-day detentions. South Africa's rulers have answered the words and deeds of peace with acts of violence and war.

In 1958, Ben Schoeman stated: "Supremacy means that you have the political power in your hands and that you can be overthrown only by a revolution."

In 1958, after Eric Louw said at UNO that the South African Government would never permit the 'native races' to share in the control of the country, Mrs. Eleanor Roosevelt told him: "I have never heard anything quite so wicked, as to take from a people all hope, all possibility of ever peacefully acquiring some say in the government of their lives."

In 1960 the African National Congress and PAC were banned. Until then, the A.N.C. had always followed a non-violent policy—as testified beyond doubt by the police themselves in the 4½ year long Treason Trial.

When the rightful aspirations of people are forcibly suppressed, it is a declaration of war. South Africa is at war today. When the right to protest was taken from us it was inevitable that "we should rise up in the courage of our despair, against the authors of our agony." Only fools and cowards accept surrender, permanent inferiority and permanent oppression.

Read history—modern history. The Algerians spoke peace. The French offered them war; the Algerians answered with war—and won. You, the white South Africans offer only war. You know the answer.

The Government should be in the dock. "I am not guilty", Mandela said in Pretoria. "The Government is responsible for what has happened in this country," said Sisulu.

It is you, the white voters who put that Government into power and have maintained it since 1948. You voted for revolution in 1958—as Schoeman stated.

Violence and civil war will not be averted by the trial of the Rivonia men nor all those others accused of sabotage. These trials will only make the struggle more relentless. We will never surrender—we cannot. We are backed by all Africa—and the whole world. Nationalist oppression is hated and despised by the majority of people inside South Africa, and every-one outside. White supremacy is doomed.

Making scapegoats of the Rivonia men will not end this situation. They will only become imperishable symbols of our resistance, the resistance which cannot be destroyed. The Government, the rulers have brought revolution to our country. And in the end it is they who will be defeated.

This is the message of Rivonia. This is the message of history and nothing will change it.

WE WILL NEVER SURRENDER. WE WILL NEVER ACCEPT PERMANENT INFERIORITY.

DO NOT SUPPORT THE GOVERNMENT AND ITS POLICIES. THIS IS YOUR CHOICE.

Document 77. Statement following the Rivonia verdict, by Chief A. J. Lutuli, June 12, 1964

Sentences of life imprisonment have been pronounced on Nelson Mandela, Walter Sisulu, Ahmed Kathrada, Govan Mbeki, Dennis Goldberg, Raymond Mhlaba, Elias Motsoaledi and Andrew Mlangeni in the "Rivonia trial" in Pretoria.

Over the long years these leaders advocated a policy of racial co-operation, of goodwill, and of peaceful struggle that made the South African liberation movement one of the most ethical and responsible of our time. In the face of the most bitter racial persecution, they resolutely set themselves against racialism; in the face of continued provocation, they consistently chose the path of reason.

The African National Congress, with allied organizations representing all racial sections, sought every possible means of redress for intolerable conditions, and held consistently to a policy of using militant, non-violent means of struggle. Their common aim was to create a South Africa in which all South Africans would live and work together as fellow-citizens, enjoying equal rights without discrimination on grounds of race, colour or creed.

To this end, they used every accepted method: propaganda, public meetings and rallies, petitions, stay-at-home-strikes, appeals, boycotts. So carefully did they educate the people that in the four-year-long Treason Trial, one police witness after another voluntarily testified to this emphasis on non-violent methods of struggle in all aspects of their activities.

But finally all avenues of resistance were closed. The African National Congress and other organizations were made illegal; their leaders jailed, exiled or forced underground. The government sharpened its oppression of the peoples of South Africa, using its all-white Parliament as the vehicle for making repression legal, and utilizing every weapon of this highly industrialized and modern state to enforce that "legality". The stage was even reached where a white spokesman for the disenfranchised Africans was regarded by the Government as a traitor. In addition, sporadic acts of uncontrolled violence were increasing throughout the country. At first in one place, then in another, there were spontaneous eruptions against intolerable conditions; many of these acts increasingly assumed a racial character.

The African National Congress never abandoned its method of a militant, non-violent struggle, and of creating in the process a spirit of militancy in the people. However, in the face of the uncompromising white refusal to abandon a policy which denies the African and other oppressed South Africans their rightful heritage—freedom—no one can blame brave just men for seeking justice by the use of violent methods; nor could they be blamed if they tried to create an organized force in order to ultimately establish peace and racial harmony.

For this, they are sentenced to be shut away for long years in the brutal and degrading prisons of South Africa. With them will be interred this country's hopes for racial co-operation. They will leave a vacuum in leadership that may only be filled by bitter hate and racial strife.

They represent the highest in morality and ethics in the South African political struggle; this morality and ethics has been sentenced to an imprisonment it may never survive. Their policies are in accordance with the deepest international principles of brotherhood and humanity; without their leadership, brotherhood and humanity may be blasted out of existence in South Africa for long decades to come. They believe profoundly in justice and reason; when they are locked away, justice and reason will have departed from the South African scene.

This is an appeal to save these men, not merely as individuals, but for what they stand for. In the name of justice, of hope, of truth and of peace, I appeal to South Africa's strongest allies, Britain and America. In the name of what we have come to believe Britain and America stand for, I appeal to those two powerful countries to take decisive action for full-scale action for sanctions that would precipitate the end of the hateful system of *apartheid*.

I appeal to all governments throughout the world, to people everywhere, to organizations and institutions in every land and at every level, to act now to impose such sanctions on South Africa that will bring about the vital necessary change and avert what can become the greatest African tragedy of our times.

Note: Reproduced from United Nations, Unit on Apartheid publication No. 22/69, December 10, 1969, pages 34-35, which notes that the statement was issued by Lutuli on June 12, 1964 and read to the Security Council on the same day by the representative of Morocco.

Chronology

1953

Criminal Law Amendment Act

Public Safety Act

Bantu Education Act

Constitutional controversy over attempted removal of Coloured voters from the common roll; not resolved until 1956

Communists, after dissolving the Communist Party in 1950, reorganize underground

UN Commission on the Racial Situation in South Africa begins work

April 15: General election: the Nationalists increase their popular vote and parliamentary majority

May 8–9: Formation of the Liberal Party

June 28: Beginning of the campaign against Western Areas removal

August: Private meetings of prominent Afrikaners and English-speaking whites with African leaders

August 15: Professor Z. K. Matthews suggests a "Congress of the People"

August 21: Formation of the South African Peace Council

September 12: Formation of the South African Coloured People's Organization

October 10: Formation of the South African Congress of Democrats

December 7–10: Interracial church conference initiated by the Dutch Reformed Churches

1954

Government directs that municipalities house Africans in "ethnic groups"

March 21: ANC sponsors a planning conference for the Congress of the People

April: Formation of the Federation of South African Women

July 11: Sophiatown (Johannesburg) rally to protest removals from the Western Areas

July: Liberal Party accepts universal franchise as an ultimate aim

October: Tomlinson Commission submits report to the cabinet

November: Orlando ANC Youth League begins to issue *The Africanist*

December: J. G. Strijdom succeeds Dr. D. F. Malan as prime minister

1955

Enlargement of Senate gives government a two-thirds majority in a joint session of Parliament.

Government announces that Africans are to be removed eventually from the Western Cape

February 9: Government begins removal of Africans from Sophiatown (Johannesburg) to Meadowlands

March 5–6: Formation of the South African Congress of Trade Unions

April 1: Government transfers control of African education to the Department of Native Affairs; ANC planning boycott of Bantu education during this period

June 25–26: Congress of the People at Kliptown, near Johannesburg; adopts the Freedom Charter

July 31: Africanists sponsor "Lembede Memorial Service"

September 27: Nationwide police raid is largest yet

December: ANC conference re-elects Chief A. J. Lutuli to second three-year term

1956

Government begins systematically to issue passes to African women

February: Joint session validates the 1951 removal of Coloured voters from the common roll

March 31–April 1: Special ANC conference adopts the Freedom Charter

April 30: Minister of justice warns of arrests for treason

July: Afrikaner *volkskongres* meets to discuss the Tomlinson Commission report

August 9: Mass women's demonstration in Pretoria leaves petitions for prime minister

August: Successful ending of Evaton bus boycott after more than a year

October 4–6: Interdenominational African Ministers' Federation sponsors "all-in" conference to discuss the Tomlinson Commission report

December 5: Countrywide arrests for treason; proceedings that follow are not concluded until March 29, 1961

1957

Native Laws Amendment Act grants powers to forbid African-white contact

January 7: Johannesburg bus boycott begins; ends successfully after three months

February: SACTU conference calls for £1-a-day campaign; ANC (Cape) calls for similar campaign and economic boycott of some Afrikaner nationalist firms

May: Demonstrations, mainly by whites, against government's proposal to extend apartheid to higher education

June 26: Stay-at-home protest is widely observed

Disorder in Sekhukhuneland and Zeerust areas of northern Transvaal and eastern Pondoland in the Transkei

November: Pro-government South African Bureau of Racial Affairs resolves to consider sponsoring a multiracial conference (not held)

December 3–5: Multiracial conference at the University of the Witwatersrand, outgrowth of the October 1956 IDAMF "all-in" conference

December: ANC adopts new constitution providing for more centralized direction and local flexibility

1958

March 16: "National Workers' Conference" sponsored by SACTU and the Congress Alliance

March 17: Piecemeal banning of the ANC is underway as government declares it "an unlawful organization" in some rural areas

April 3: Coloureds vote for first time on separate roll for white representatives in Parliament

April 15: First Conference of Independent African States, in Accra; date commemorated in later years as African Freedom Day

April 16: General election: Nationalists gain further strength; ANC attempts "stay-at-home"

August 24: Prime Minister Strijdom dies; succeeded by Dr. Hendrik Verwoerd

October: United States for the first time supports anti-apartheid resolution in the United Nations instead of abstaining

November 2: Africanists break away from the ANC (Transvaal)

December: Africaans-speaking intellectuals of SABRA begin holding private meetings with African leaders

All-African People's Conference in Accra calls for economic sanctions against South Africa

ANC conference re-elects Lutuli to third three-year term

1959

Promotion of Bantu Self-Government Act; also provides for end of African representation by whites in Parliament (as of 1960)

Extension of University Education Act, extends apartheid to higher education

Formation of the business-financed South Africa Foundation

April 4–6: Formation of the Pan Africanist Congress

April: Lutuli received with acclaim at white public meetings in the Cape

May 30–31: ANC conference calls for potato boycott to protest treatment of African farm laborers; officially ends on August 31

June: Beginning of anti-pass demonstrations by African women in Natal

August 2: PAC's "National Heroes' Day"; Robert Sobukwe announces plans for "status campaign"

October: Formation of Federation of Free African Trade Unions of South Africa

November: Former United Party members of Parliament participate in formation of Progressive Party

December 10–11: Riots in Windhoek, South West Africa; 11 Africans killed

December 12–13: ANC annual conference resolves to launch anti-pass campaign on March 31, 1960

December 19–20: PAC holds its first annual conference; endorses its executive's plans for an anti-pass campaign

1960

February 3: British Prime Minister Harold Macmillan's "winds of change" speech in South African Parliament

March 16: Sobukwe advises Commissioner of Police that nonviolent anti-pass campaign will begin on March 21

March 21: Sharpeville: 67 Africans shot dead, 186 wounded

March 22: U.S. State Department rebukes South Africa

March 26: Lutuli burns his pass and urges Africans to follow his example

March 30: Government declares a state of emergency; detains nearly 2,000 political activists of all races

Mass column of about 30,000 Africans marches into center of Cape Town but withdraws peacefully; police then move to crush all manifestations of rebellion; later, leaders of the Liberal Party are detained and jailed for the first time

April 1: UN Security Council intervenes in the South African situation for the first time

April 8: Government announces banning of the ANC and the PAC

English-speaking white man attempts to assassinate Verwoerd

May 31: White South Africa celebrates the fiftieth anniversary of Union

June: ANC and PAC leaders in exile formally agree to cooperate in a South African United Front

August 31: End of the emergency

October 5: Majority of whites vote yes in referendum on becoming a republic

November: World Court case on South West Africa begins

November 30: Verwoerd's "granite wall" speech on Coloured policy

December 16–17: Consultative conference of Africans meets in Orlando (Johannesburg); calls for an "all-in" conference and sets up a continuation committee

1961

January: Dag Hammarskjold, UN secretary-general, visits South Africa

March 15: Verwoerd withdraws request that South Africa remain in the Commonwealth after becoming a republic

March 20: Arrest of all members of the continuation committee, including those who had resigned

March 25–26: ANC-dominated "All-in" African Conference in Pietermaritzburg, calls for national convention by May 31

March 29: After more than four years, Treason Trial accused are judged not guilty

April 17–19: Multiracial "Natal Convention" meets in Pietermaritzburg

May 19: Bans on most gatherings through June 26; large-scale raids and arrests late in May

May 29–31: Stay-at-home called for by the National Action Council of the All-in African Conference

May 31: South Africa becomes a republic

June: Mandela and others abandon the ANC's policy of nonviolence

July 8–10: Malmesbury Convention of Coloureds

August: John Vorster becomes minister of justice

September: SABRA's independent leadership is purged

November: Formation of *Umkonto We Sizwe*

October: Sabotage by the National Liberation Committee, which later becomes the African Resistance Movement (composed mainly of whites)

October 18: General election: Nationalists win their greatest victory

October 23: Lutuli awarded the Nobel Peace Prize and delivers address in Oslo, Norway on December 11

December 16: *Umkonto We Sizwe* begins sabotage and distributes manifesto

1962

January 11: Mandela leaves South Africa for a six-months tour of independent African states and England

January 23: Verwoerd announces that the Transkei will be granted modified self-government

March 13: Dissolution of South African United Front abroad is confirmed

April: Supreme Court upholds the appeal of members of the continuation committee, who had been found guilty of furthering ANC aims

June 27: Sabotage Act is enacted following public protests by whites

August 5: Mandela is arrested after having returned secretly to South Africa on July 20

September 14: Government outlaws the South African Congress of Democrats

October: ANC conference in Lobatsi, Bechuanaland, the first since 1959

November 6: UN General Assembly (by a two-thirds vote, with abstentions by the major Western states) recommends economic and diplomatic sanctions against South Africa

November 7: Mandela is sentenced to five years in prison

November 21–22: Violence by Africans in Paarl near Cape Town; killing of two whites; fanning of white fears of "Poqo"

November 30: Government bans *New Age,* which is succeeded by *Spark*

1963

February 5: Africans kill five whites near Bashee River bridge in the Transkei

March 24: Potlako Leballo, PAC acting president, announces in Maseru that violence is imminent in South Africa; PAC messengers are arrested shortly afterwards and South African police make mass arrests

March: Walter Sisulu is sentenced to six years in prison but goes underground while out on bail

March 28: *Spark* appears for the last time

May 1: "90-Day Act," a landmark in South Africa's movement toward becoming a police state.

July 11: Police raid the underground headquarters of *Umkonto We Sizwe* in Rivonia, Johannesburg

December 4: UN Security Council appoints a group of experts to examine methods of resolving the South African situation

December: The Transkei becomes a semi-autonomous territory with limited powers of self-government by an all-African, partially elected legislative assembly.

1964

April 20: Mandela addresses the court in the Rivonia trial

Report of UN group of experts on peaceful resolution of the situation in South Africa

June 9: UN Security Council resolution on the Rivonia trial

June 11: Judge finds Mandela, Sisulu, and others guilty and, on the following day, sentences them to life imprisonment

Bibliographical Note

This bibliographical note is intended as a guide for scholars and students interested in the larger body of original materials of African politics in South Africa and also for those beginning their study of South Africa. The footnotes in this volume provide a full listing of the documents, interviews, books, articles, newspapers, and unpublished manuscripts upon which the introductory essays are based. The student should also consult the bibliographical notes to Volumes 1, 2, and 4.

Nearly all of the documentary collection (including newspapers, letters, and manuscripts) on which the four volumes of *From Protest to Challenge* are based has been inventoried and microfilmed. Apart from sensitive material that will be withheld from circulation for various periods of time, these films will shortly be available for borrowing or purchase through libraries from the Cooperative Africana Microform Project (CAMP) of the Center for Research Libraries, 5721 Cottage Grove Ave., Chicago, Illinois 60637.

This collection, microfilmed in more than fifty reels, forms part of the substantial southern African holdings available from CAMP. Material at CAMP that is relevant to Volume 3 includes microfilms of the Treason Trial (the preparatory inquiry, the trial proper, and documents presented in evidence), later political trials, African and left-wing newspapers, the Dr. S. M. Molema papers, documents of the Congress of Democrats, and a wide variety of materials collected by Benjamin Pogrund, who has long been active in Johannesburg both as a journalist and as a scholar. Materials of political interest are also being made available through the American Theological Libraries Microfilm Project.

In order to enlarge CAMP's collection, particularly its political and ephemeral materials and oral data, an ad hoc steering committee of southern African specialists from a number of American universities, chaired by Gwendolen M. Carter, has organized the Southern African Research Archival Project (SARAP), aided by a small Ford Foundation grant. Its primary aim is to identify, through the services of a documentalist, southern African material held either by institutions or private individuals in the United States and Canada, to arrange for microfilming where possible, and to consider the feasibility of preparing a union catalogue. (The project is concerned mainly with South Africa and adjacent states including Angola and Mozambique, whose documentary materials have been collected at the University of California at Los Angeles.) SARAP also maintains liaison with many persons and institutions in Britain and in Africa with common interests in the collection and preservation of documentary resources.

Similar projects are under way in South Africa through the South African Institute of Race Relations, Box 97, Johannesburg, and in Great Britain through the University of London's Programme of Southern African Studies, and the Center for Southern African Studies at York University. Materials in Britain that are expected to become available or are now available either in original form or on microfilm include an unpublished autobiography of R. V. Selope Thema and the papers of Clements Kadalie, William Ballinger, Edward Roux, Mary Benson, Alex Hepple, and Albie Sachs. Material being microfilmed in South Africa and being made available through CAMP includes documents of the Industrial and Commercial Workers' Union, the papers of Dr. A. B. Xuma, and the records of the National Union of South African Students.

Books by Africans writing on South African politics are few. Of special interest for this volume are Albert Luthuli, *Let My People Go: An Autobiography* (London: Collins, and New York: McGraw-Hill, 1962; paperback edition, New York: World Publishing Co., 1970); Jordan K. Ngubane, *An African Explains Apartheid* (New York: Praeger, 1963); and Govan Mbeki, *South Africa: The Peasants' Revolt* (Harmondsworth, Middlesex, England: Penguin Books, 1966). See also Lewis Nkosi, *Home and Exile* (London: Longmans Green and Co., Ltd., 1965); Bloke Modisane, *Blame Me on History* (London: Thames and Hudson, 1963); and Naboth Mokgatle, *The Autobiography of an Unknown South African* (Berkeley: University of California Press, 1971). Alfred Hutchinson, an African accused in the Treason Trial, has written *Road to Ghana* (London: Victor Gollancz, Ltd., 1960).

A fascinating anthology of articles culled from a century of the *South African Outlook,* including articles by twenty-five Africans with photographs of twelve of them, has been edited by Francis Wilson and Dominique Perrot, *Outlook on a Century: South Africa 1870–1970* (Braamfontein, Transvaal: Lovedale Press, 1973). Three anthologies published in the early 1960s are Hildegarde Spottiswoode (ed.), *South Africa: The Road Ahead* (London: Bailey Bros. & Swinfen, Ltd., 1960), Marion Friedmann (ed.), *I Will Still Be Moved* (London: Arthur Barker, Ltd., 1963), and Ruth First (ed.), *No Easy Walk to Freedom: Articles, Speeches, and Trial Addresses of Nelson Mandela* (London: Heinemann, 1965). Some recent statements by Africans, Indians, and Coloureds who live in South Africa are included in N. J. Rhoodie (ed.), *South African Dialogue: Contrasts in South African Thinking on Basic Race Issues* (Johannesburg: McGraw-Hill Book Co., 1972).

First-hand accounts by white sympathizers and allies of the African opposition include the following: By religious figures: Father Trevor Huddleston, *Naught for Your Comfort* (London: Collins, 1956); Bishop Ambrose Reeves, *Shooting at Sharpeville: The Agony of South Africa* (London: Victor Gollancz, Ltd., 1960); Hannah Stanton, *Go Well, Stay Well: South Africa, August 1956 to May 1960* (London: Hodder & Stoughton, 1961); Rev. Arthur Blaxall, *Suspended Sentence* (London: Hodder & Stoughton, 1965); and the Rev. Charles Hooper, *Brief Authority* (London: Collins, 1960). On prison experiences, see Ruth First, *117 Days* (New York: Stein and Day, 1965); James Kantor, *A Healthy Grave* (London: Hamish Hamilton, 1967); Albie Sachs, *The Jail Diary of Albie Sachs* (London: Harvill Press, 1966); and *Stephanie on Trial* (London: Harvill Press, 1968); and Hugh Lewin, *Bandiet: Seven Years in a South African Prison* (London: Bailie & Jenkins, 1974). See also: Hilda Bernstein, *The World that Was Ours* (London: Heinemann, 1967); Helen Joseph, *If This Be Treason* (London: Andre Deutsch, 1963), and *Tomorrow's Sun: A Smuggled Journal from South Africa* (New York: John Day Co., 1966); Myrna Blumberg, *White Madam* (London: Victor Gollancz, Ltd., 1962); Lionel Forman and E. S. Sachs, *The South African Treason Trial* (London: John Calder, 1957); and Joel Carlson, *No Neutral Ground* (New York: Thomas Y. Crowell, 1973). For an account by a Canadian journalist who was in South Africa in early 1960, see Norman Phillips, *The Tragedy of Apartheid: A Journalist's Experiences in the South African Riots* (New York: David McKay, 1960). See also the autobiographical account by the English journalist, Tom Hopkinson, *In the Fiery Continent* (London: Victor Gollancz, Ltd., 1962).

Another group of books by South African whites deals more generally with the political scene or political developments and is of special interest because the authors were themselves politically involved: Margaret Ballinger, *From Union to Apartheid* (Folkestone: Bailey Bros. & Swinfen, Ltd., 1969); Alex Hepple, *South Africa: A Political and Economic History* (London: Pall Mall Press, 1966); John Cope, *South Africa* (New York: Frederick A. Praeger, 1965); Brian Bunting, *The Rise of the South African Reich* (Harmondsworth, Middlesex, England: Penguin Books, 1964); Alan Paton, *The Long View* (edited by Edward Callan) (London: Pall Mall Press, 1968); Patrick van Rensburg, *Guilty Land* (Harmondsworth, Middlesex, England: Penguin Books, 1962); Patrick Duncan, *South Africa's Rule of Violence* (London: Methuen & Co., Ltd., 1964); and Bishop Ambrose Reeves, *South Africa—Yesterday and Tomorrow: A Challenge to Christians* (London: Victor Gollancz, Ltd., 1962). Edward Roux's important *Time Longer than Rope: A History of the Black Man's Struggle for Freedom in South Africa* is brought briefly up to date in a second edition (Madison: University of Wisconsin Press, 1966).

For those beginning their study of South Africa, good introductions are

810

Leo Marquard, *The Peoples and Policies of South Africa* (4th ed., London: Oxford University Press, 1969) and Leonard M. Thompson, *Politics in the Republic of South Africa* (Boston: Little, Brown and Co., 1966). Comprehensive studies, which include extensive bibliographies, are Gwendolen M. Carter, *The Politics of Inequality: South Africa Since 1948* (New York: Praeger, 1958, 1959); Thomas Karis, "South Africa" in G. M. Carter (ed.), *Five African States: Responses to Diversity* (Ithaca, N.Y.: Cornell University Press, 1963); Pierre L. van den Berghe, *South Africa, A Study in Conflict* (Berkeley: University of California Press, 1967); Heribert Adam, *Modernizing Racial Domination: South Africa's Political Dynamics* (Berkeley: University of California Press, 1971); Heribert Adam (ed.), *South Africa: Sociological Perspectives* (London: Oxford University Press, 1971); and Christian P. Potholm and Richard Dale (eds.), *Southern Africa in Perspective: Essays in Regional Politics* (New York: The Free Press, 1972).

There is also a lengthy bibliography in Volume II, "South Africa, 1870–1966," of Monica Wilson and Leonard Thompson (eds.), *The Oxford History of South Africa* (London: Oxford University Press, 1971) and chapters on "The Growth of Towns" by David Welsh, "Afrikaner Nationalism" by René de Villiers, and "African Nationalism in South Africa, 1910–1964" by Leo Kuper.

On the African National Congress, the most vivid and sympathetic account is by Mary Benson, who has based much of her work on interviews and other original research: *The African Patriots: The Story of the African National Congress of South Africa* (London: Faber & Faber, 1963), redrafted as *South Africa: The Struggle for a Birthright* (Harmondsworth, Middlesex, England: Penguin Books, 1966 and New York: Funk & Wagnalls, 1969). A shorter history, with biographical chapters, is Anthony Sampson, *The Treason Cage: The Opposition on Trial in South Africa* (London: Heinemann, 1958). Peter Walshe's valuable historical study: *The Rise of African Nationalism in South Africa: The African National Congress, 1912–1952* (London: C. Hurst and Co., 1970; Berkeley: University of California Press, 1971), is supplemented by his booklet, *Black Nationalism in South Africa: A Short History* (Johannesburg: Ravan Press, 1973). More specialized studies are noted in the footnotes to this volume and the bibliographies cited above.

Index of Names

Index of Organizations

Note: This is a list of selected organizations. It omits a number of committees, councils, movements, foreign bodies and conferences, and it does not refer to the Chronology. In the case of documents of or relating to an organization, only the first page of the document is cited.

DATE DUE

28 Apr 77			

GAYLORD